MW00667392

THE NEW AMERICAN COMMENTARY

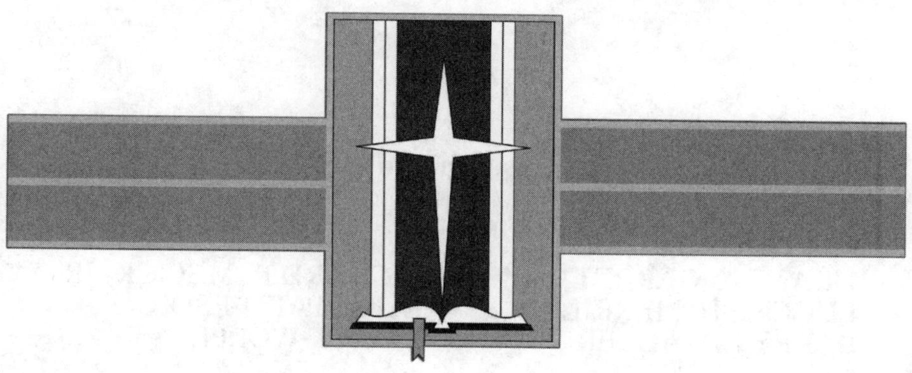

An Exegetical and Theological
Exposition of Holy Scripture

THE NEW AMERICAN COMMENTARY

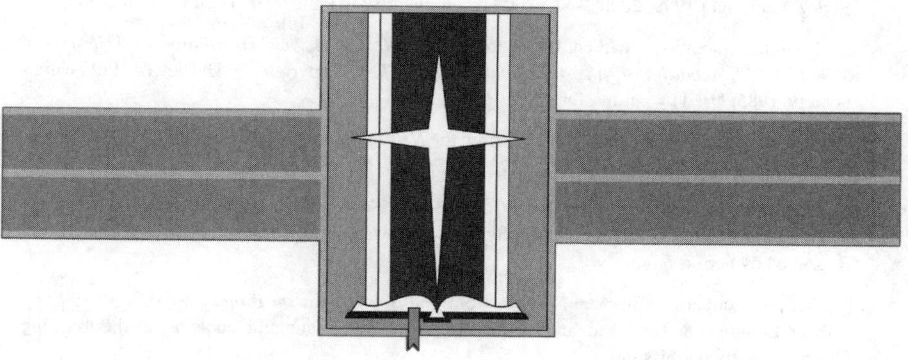

Volume
35

HEBREWS

David L. Allen

B&H PUBLISHING GROUP
Nashville, Tennessee

ISBN 978-0-8054-0135-6
Dewey Decimal Classification: 227.87
Subject Heading: BIBLE. O.T. Hebrews
Printed in the United States of America
'15 '14 '13 '12 '11 '10 • 8 7 6 5 4 3 2 1
LB

To

Sherri, my wife of 32 years and my best friend

my four children

Jeremy, Jared, Melody, Kali

my Daughter-in-law

Joelle

and my two precious grandchildren

Judah and Lydia

Editors' Preface

God's Word does not change. God's world, however, changes in every generation. These changes, in addition to new findings by scholars and a new variety of challenges to the gospel message, call for the church in each generation to interpret and apply God's Word for God's people. Thus, THE NEW AMERICAN COMMENTARY is introduced to bridge the twentieth and twenty-first centuries. This new series has been designed primarily to enable pastors, teachers, and students to read the Bible with clarity and proclaim it with power.

In one sense THE NEW AMERICAN COMMENTARY is not new, for it represents the continuation of a heritage rich in biblical and theological exposition. The title of this forty-volume set points to the continuity of this series with an important commentary project published at the end of the nineteenth century called AN AMERICAN COMMENTARY, edited by Alvah Hovey. The older series included, among other significant contributions, the outstanding volume on Matthew by John A. Broadus, from whom the publisher of the new series, Broadman Press, partly derives its name. The former series was authored and edited by scholars committed to the infallibility of Scripture, making it a solid foundation for the present project. In line with this heritage, all NAC authors affirm the divine inspiration, inerrancy, complete truthfulness, and full authority of the Bible. The perspective of the NAC is unapologetically confessional and rooted in the evangelical tradition.

Since a commentary is a fundamental tool for the expositor or teacher who seeks to interpret and apply Scripture in the church or classroom, the NAC focuses on communicating the theological structure and content of each biblical book. The writers seek to illuminate both the historical meaning and contemporary significance of Holy Scripture.

In its attempt to make a unique contribution to the Christian community, the NAC focuses on two concerns. First, the commentary emphasizes how each section of a book fits together so that the reader becomes aware of the theological unity of each book and of Scripture as a whole. The writers, however, remain aware of the Bible's inherently rich variety. Second, the NAC is produced with the conviction that the Bible primarily belongs to the church. We believe that scholarship and the academy provide an indispensable foundation for biblical understanding and the service of Christ, but the editors and authors of this series have attempted to communicate the findings of their research in a manner that will build up the whole body of Christ. Thus, the commentary concentrates on theological exegesis while providing practical, applicable exposition.

THE NEW AMERICAN COMMENTARY's theological focus enable the reader to see the parts as well as the whole of Scripture. The biblical books vary in content, context, literary type, and style. In addition to this rich variety, the editors and authors recognize that the doctrinal emphasis and use of the biblical books differs in various places, contexts, and cultures among God's people. These factors, as well as other concerns, have led the editors to give freedom to the writers to wrestle with the issues raised by the scholarly community surrounding each book and to determine the appropriate shape and length of the introductory materials. Moreover, each writer has developed the structure of the commentary in a way best suited for expounding the basic structure and the meaning of the biblical books for our day. Generally, discussions relating to contemporary scholarship and technical points of grammar and syntax appear in the footnotes and not in the text of the commentary. This format allows pastors and interested laypersons, scholars and teachers, and serious college and seminary students to profit from the commentary at various levels. This approach has been employed because we believe that all Christians have the privilege and responsibility to read and seek to understand the Bible for themselves.

Consistent with the desire to produce a readable, up-to-date commentary, the editors selected the New International Version as the standard translation for the commentary series. The selection was made primarily because of the NIV's faithfulness to the original languages and its beautiful and readable style. The authors, however, have been given the liberty to differ at places from the NIV as they develop their own translations from the Greek and Hebrew texts.

The NAC reflects the vision and leadership of those who provide oversight for Broadman Press, who in 1987 called for a new commentary series that would evidence a commitment to the inerrancy of Scripture and a faithfulness to the classic Christian tradition. While the commentary adopts an "American" name, it should be noted some writers represent countries outside the United States, giving the commentary an international perspective. The diverse group of writers includes scholars, teachers, and administrators from almost twenty different colleges and seminaries, as well as pastors, missionaries, and a layperson.

The editors and writers hope that THE NEW AMERICAN COMMENTARY will be helpful and instructive for pastors and teachers, scholars and students, for men and women in the churches who study and teach God's Word in various settings. We trust that for editors, authors, and readers alike, the commentary will be used to build up the church, encourage obedience, and bring renewal to God's people. Above all, we pray that the NAC will bring glory and honor to our Lord who has graciously redeemed us and faithfully revealed himself to us in his Holy Word.

SOLI DEO GLORIA
The Editors

Author's Preface

In the past 35 years, commentaries and monographs on the epistolary sphinx of the New Testament known as Hebrews have mushroomed. After languishing in the canonical attic for years, this treasure has been rediscovered of late, dusted off, and researched with new vigor, all to the benefit of the church. My own love affair with this epistle began in college and has continued unabated to the present time.

Several matters call for explanation regarding the approach taken in this commentary. The reader may be struck by the length and the breadth of the introduction. While it is a far cry from "comprehensive," it is somewhat more involved than most volumes in this series. This is made necessary by the plethora of theories concerning matters of authorship, date, recipients, and background. With respect to authorship, I have included more than the usual drive-by survey. Some contemporary scholars continue to advocate Pauline authorship, and their work must be addressed. Many who have dismissed Paul as a possible author have done so with a heavy hand, often with well-worn arguments. Although I think the Pauline theory is incorrect, it has a distinguished history and is not without internal support by comparing Hebrews to the Pauline Epistles. Likewise, Lukan authorship is often rejected as impossible based on borrowed and perhaps unexamined arguments—usually on the grounds that Luke was a Gentile. Such an approach neglects reflection on and interaction with what has been learned about Luke-Acts over the past 60 years, especially in three areas: (1) Luke was a consummate theologian; (2) he was an artful writer; and (3) he may have been Jewish, as many Lukan scholars now argue.[1]

Some will question the sparse references in the footnotes to parallels, comparisons, or possible allusions to Philo and Rabbinic Judaism. Three reasons explain why I have chosen not to footnote these comparisons extensively: (1) space constraints; (2) these are well documented in other commentaries;[2] and (3) Philonic influence on the author has been overblown in the past and criticized significantly since 1970. Where such references impact the interpretation of the epistle or shed significant light on its interpretation, they are cited in the footnotes. It should also be noted that first-century Judaism was not by any stretch of the imagination monolithic. There were various factions within

[1] See my *Lukan Authorship of Hebrews*, NACSBT (Nashville: B&H, 2010). The arguments I present there can only be briefly discussed in this commentary. For a survey of Lukan research from the middle of the twentieth century through 2005, see F. Bovon, *Luke the Theologian: Fifty-five Years of Research (1950-2005)*, 2nd ed. (Waco, TX: Baylor University Press, 2006).

[2] Westcott, Delitzsch, Spicq, Weiss, Grässer, F. F. Bruce, Attridge, Lane, Ellingworth and Koester are among those who have covered this ground thoroughly, so I refer the reader to their excellent commentaries cited in my select bibliography.

Judaism, all of which did not walk in lock-step in their treatment of the Old Testament. The Judaism from which Christianity sprang was Biblical Judaism. However, in the first century, Judaism was moving from a biblical base to a rabbinical base. Although our author exhibits knowledge of Second Temple Judaism—rabbinic, sectarian, or otherwise—he demonstrates less dependence on it and far more dependence upon Old Testament Judaism.

The New Testament documents indicate that Old Testament exegesis was the primary method of doing theology in the early church. This is no more clearly evidenced than with the author of Hebrews. For him, Psalm 110:1,4 serve as the "text" which he will, with the help of other Old Testament texts, expound theologically and apply to his hearers. From there the author identifies Jesus as Son, High Priest, and King. As Son, Jesus shares in the identity of God; as High Priest, he atones for sin; as Lord and King, Jesus reigns from the throne of God. The author of Hebrews was first and foremost an exegete and then a biblical theologian. His theology is predicated on his exegesis of Old Testament texts. He brings exegesis into the service of theology as an exegetical theologian, and he brings both into the service of preaching and thus into the service of the church as a preacher par excellence. He reads the Old Testament wearing Christological glasses just as Jesus instructed the disciples on the road to Emmaus to do in Luke 24.

Fairbairn once remarked, "He can be no theologian who is not first a philologian." Biblical theology must be the foundation for systematic theology, and exegesis the foundation of biblical theology. I have attempted to do the painstaking exegetical spade work before theological analysis of the epistle's constituent parts. Hebrews' tightly knit argument, the large number of words occurring only once in the Greek New Testament, and the sheer weight of exegetical data require a fair amount of exegesis which at times may seem tedious for the reader. I make every effort to tie all the exegetical data together at the conclusion of each section or the end of each chapter with a discussion of theological implications. Where there are several possible grammatical or syntactical construals of the text, I have generally listed at least most of the options and cited some of those who favor them. At the critical junctures within the epistle (e.g., Heb 1:1-4 and 6:4-6), I have attempted to sift the grammatical, syntactical, and semantic evidence and suggest a particular construal. At other points, I have merely listed the various options, and then presented the view I believe best fits the context.

The sermonic journey known as Hebrews contains what at first appear to be several hortatory digressions and diversions. Hebrews contains five so-called "warning passages." These passages are interwoven with the doctrinal sections very tightly. I do not view these hortatory sections as digressions, but as conveying the dominant semantic information with the doctrinal material functioning semantically as the grounds (support material). These hortatory sections are actually the goal of the argument: "on the basis of this . . . do this."

Hebrews is at heart a pastoral document where the author attempts to persuade his readers to a particular course of action.

I have attempted to pay close attention to conjunctions in the Greek text that link paragraphs and sections together since these are critical to the author's structure and argument. Information in the text that is "main line" versus that which is supportive or subordinate is signaled primarily by the use of conjunctions. The repetition of *echontes oun* (lit. "having, therefore") in 4:14 and 10:19, a construction found nowhere else in the epistle, signals the beginning of the second and third major discourse units in the epistle. I have understood the conjunction *gar* at the beginning of a paragraph as always indicating support material, just as it does at the sentence and clause level.

I have also attempted to identify and comment on the author's placement of words and phrases within clauses and sentences for semantic emphasis. This is especially important as a matter of authorial focus and reaps dividends not only in exegesis but also in preaching the epistle.

The reader will notice a disproportionate amount of space is devoted to the explanation of Heb 1:1-4 and Heb 6:1-6. The prologue is programmatic for the entire epistle, and a proper understanding of its puissant theology, purpose, and function is critical. Hebrews 6:1-6, if not the single most debated New Testament passage, certainly falls within the top five. It has proven to be an interpretative nightmare for everyone. It has simultaneously been the biblical headquarters from which flutters the banner of Arminianism and a thorn in the side of most Calvinists. We shall see that each tradition has something valuable to bring to the hermeneutical table of Heb 6:1-6, and each tradition has erred hermeneutically as well in my judgment.

The book of Hebrews is about Jesus the Son who became our High Priest and then became king when he sat upon the throne of God in fulfillment of Ps 110:1,4. This schema is presented in brilliant summary fashion in the prologue and then is developed in each of the three major divisions of the epistle (the Son in 1:5–4:13; the High Priest in 4:14–10:18; and the King in 10:19–13:21). Christology is intertwined with eschatology and applied pastorally to a congregation facing discouragement and spiritual drift due to persecution and failure to press on spiritually by means of obedience to the Word of God.

The value of Hebrews to the church cannot be overestimated. Its theological potency in revelation, christology, and eschatology contribute to the church's theological well-being in an age when doctrinal orthodoxy, especially in the areas of revelation and christology, is assailed. Hermeneutically, the use of the Old Testament by New Testament authors binds the two testaments together christologically in a way that the church today needs to rediscover. No New Testament writer has done this more masterfully than the author of Hebrews. Pastorally, this epistle teaches us that life's internal and external problems can only be met and solved by clear thinking about Christ and his finished work of atonement. Persecution is to be endured by Christians who are grounded in their understanding of the person and work of Christ. Spiritual progress to maturity is grounded in faithfulness to Jesus and in ongoing daily dependence on the living Christ as our intercessor. As T. Olbricht put it so well concerning Hebrews, "In depth Christological reflection is therefore the path to spiritual renewal . . . ."[3] Knowledge of the security of one's salvation and the certainty of our future eternal hope give hope daily amid the stress of internal problems and external persecution.

Hebrews is one of the most important books in the New Testament for its contribution to the nature, theology, and practice of preaching. It is itself a first-century sermon. As an exposition of Ps 110:1,4, it is a biblical, text-driven sermon. Its application to the church is drawn from its exposition of Old Testament texts. Hebrews is an example of doctrinal preaching as well in that its author teases out doctrinal insight from exegesis and application of Old Testament texts. It is also an example of pastoral preaching that addresses the needs of the local church by satisfying exposition, exhortation, and encouragement. The problem with much of contemporary preaching is its aversion to exposition in its focus on application. Application cannot be authoritative unless its foundation on Scripture is clearly laid. The author of Hebrews knew this only too well. We would be wise to pay heed to him and to his approach. He was not only a capable theologian but a creative preacher. His many uses of rhetorical features with the intent of turning the ear into an eye illustrate as much. For example, Heb 2:5-9 demonstrates the author's combination of exegesis and rhetoric in his treatment of Ps 8:7 and his verbal word play on *hupotassein*, "to subject." As Lane says, "Here is first-century exegesis in the service of preaching."[4]

My appeal to the preacher of Hebrews is this: preach this great book holistically, giving rightful place to the large semantic units in the text. Avoid an atomistic approach that tends to allow the chapters and verses as they appear in the English Bible to truncate the author's argument. We who preach should learn from this great expositor how to bring exegesis to bear on a text of Scripture and then apply its meaning to the church. In Hebrews we find all the ingredients necessary for solid expositional preaching: careful but creative exegesis, theological reflection and reasoning, a balance of exhortation and encouragement, pungent illustration of truth, and practical application—all creatively constructed into a masterful sermon that makes use of rhetorical techniques for maximum effect on the hearers.

---

[3] T. Olbricht, "Anticipating and Presenting the Case for Christ as High Priest in Hebrews," in *Rhetorical Argumentation in Biblical Texts: Essays from the Lund 2000 Conference*, ed. A. Eriksson, T. Olbricht, and W. Übelacker (Harrisburg, PA: Trinity Press International, 2002), 357.

[4] W. L. Lane, "Preaching and Exegesis in the First Century: Hebrews," in *Sharing Heaven's Music—the Heart of Christian Preaching: Essays in Honor of James Earl Massey*, ed. B. Callen (Nashville: Abingdon, 1995), 91.

When it comes to Hebrews and my response to it, F. W. Boreham, the great Australian Baptist pastor and wordsmith, said it best: "Other people may do as they will; but, for myself, I am going to rest all my insufficiency and inefficiency on His finished and perfect Saviourhood, leaving Him to complete my incompleteness in the world in which He reigns supreme."[5]

A work of this magnitude would never have seen the light of day were it not for so many to whom I owe a debt of immense gratitude. Ray Clendenen, with whom I share a love for linguistics and its impact on biblical studies, afforded me the opportunity to write this commentary. His careful editing hand coupled with his encouragement has been a rich blessing. Lynda McCallum, Administrative Assistant to the pastor at MacArthur Boulevard Baptist Church in Irving, Texas provided invaluable assistance during the research and early draft phases of this work through her remarkable organizational skills. Charles Savelle, Ph.D. student at Dallas Theological Seminary, edited the text and footnotes of early drafts of the first few chapters. Bryan Young, my student grader and assistant, also provided help during my days at The Criswell College. Upon my arrival as Dean of the School of Theology at Southwestern Baptist Theological Seminary, Jane Fiscus, administrative assistant to the Dean, was invaluable in innumerable ways, ministering to my research and writing needs with her inimitable sweet spirit and her incredible efficiency. Along the way, I have been blessed with graduate assistants Adam Hughes and Lewis Richerson, who assisted me in research and who are both now Ph.D. students in preaching at Southwestern Seminary. My former grader, Bobby McGraw, now in his second pastorate, has also devoted countless hours in editing, and for his labors I am truly grateful. Ted Williams, one of the seminary's finest and brightest M.Div. students, has assisted me beyond measure in copyediting. May the Lord reward him according to his labors. A remarkable Southern Baptist evangelist and also Ph.D. student in preaching at Southwestern Seminary, Vern Charette, has labored diligently to work through over 900 pages of manuscript and almost 3,400 footnotes with a fine-tooth comb to ensure accuracy. To you, sir, I owe more than I can say.

—David L. Allen
Southwestern Baptist Theological Seminary
Ft. Worth, Texas

---

[5] F. W. Boreham, *Cliffs of Opal* (London: Epworth, 1948), 31.

Abbreviations

Bible Books

Gen	Isa	Luke
Exod	Jer	John
Lev	Lam	Acts
Num	Ezek	Rom
Deut	Dan	1, 2 Cor
Josh	Hos	Gal
Judg	Joel	Eph
Ruth	Amos	Phil
1, 2 Sam	Obad	Col
1, 2 Kgs	Jonah	1, 2 Thess
1, 2 Chr	Mic	1, 2 Tim
Ezra	Nah	Titus
Neh	Hab	Phlm
Esth	Zeph	Heb
Job	Hag	Jas
Ps (pl. Pss)	Zech	1, 2 Pet
Prov	Mal	1, 2, 3 John
Eccl	Matt	Jude
Song	Mark	Rev

Commonly Used Sources

AB Anchor Bible
ABD *Anchor Bible Dictionary*, ed. D. N. Freedman. 6 vols.
ACCS Ancient Christian Commentary on Scripture, ed. T. C. Oden
ACNT Augsburg Commentary on the New Testament
AGJU Arbeiten zur Geschichte des antiken Judentums und des Urchristentums
AJBA *Australian Journal of Biblical Archeology*
AJT *American Journal of Theology*
AnBib Analecta biblica
ANF *Ante-Nicene Fathers*
ANRW *Aufstieg und Niedeergang der römischen Welt,* ed. H. Temporini and W. Haase
ApOTC Apollos Old Testament Commentary
AsTJ *Asbury Theological Journal*
AThR *Anglican Theological Review*
AUSS *Andrews University Seminary Studies*
BASOR *Bulletin of the American Schools of Oriental Research*

BBR Bulletin for Biblical Research

BDAG W. Bauer, F. W. Danker, W. F. Arndt, and F. W. Gingrich, *Greek-English Lexicon of the New Testament and Other Early Christian Literature,* 3rd ed.

BDF Blass, F., A. Debrunner, and R. W. Funk, *A Greek Grammar of the New Testament and Other Early Christian Literature*

BECNT Baker's Exegetical Commentary on the New Testament

BFCT Beiträge zur Förderung christlicher Theologie

BGBE Beiträge zur Geschichte der biblischen Exegese

BHT Beihefte zur historischen Theologie

Bib *Biblica*

BJRL *Bulletin of the John Rylands Library*

BNTC Black's New Testament Commentaries

BR *Biblical Research*

BSac *Bibliotheca Sacra*

BTB *Biblical Theology Bulletin*

BZ *Biblische Zeitschrift*

BzhTh Beiträge zur historischen Theologie

BZNW Beihefte zur ZNW

CBQ *Catholic Biblical Quarterly*

CBQMS Catholic Biblical Quarterly Monograph Series

CD K. Barth, *Church Dogmatics,* 5 vols., ed. G. W. Bromiley and T. F. Torrance

CGTSC Cambridge Greek Testament for Schools and Colleges

CivCatt *Civiltá cattolica*

CJT *Canadian Journal of Theology*

CNTC Calvin's New Testament Commentaries, trans. W. Johnson, ed. D. W. Torrance and T. F. Torrance

CNTOT *Commentary on the New Testament Use of the Old Testament,* ed. G. K. Beale and D. A. Carson

Cremer H. Cremer, *Biblico-Theological Lexicon of New Testament Greek,* 4th ed.

CRINT Compendia Rerum Iudaicarum ad Novum Testamentum

CTJ *Calvin Theological Journal*

CTSJ *Chafer Theological Seminary Journal*

CurBS *Currents in Research: Biblical Studies*

DLNT *Dictionary of the Later New Testament and Its Developments*, ed. R. P. Martin and P. H. Davids

DPL *Dictionary of Paul and His Letters,* ed. G. F. Hawthorne and R. P. Martin

DTIB *Dictionary for Theological Interpretation of the Bible*, ed., K. Vanhoozer

EBC *Expositor's Bible Commentary,* ed. F. E. Gaebelein, 12 vols.

EBib	*Etudes bibliques*
EdF	Erträge der Forschung
EDNT	*Expository Dictionary of the New Testament*, ed. H. Balz and G. Schneider, 3 vols.
EKKNT	Evangelisch-katholischer Kommentar zum Neuen Testament
EvJ	*Evangelical Journal*
EvQ	*Evangelical Quarterly*
EvRTh	*Evangelical Review of Theology*
ExpTim	*Expository Times*
FM	*Faith and Mission*
FN	*Filologia Neotestamentaria*
FRLANT	Forschungen zur Religion und Literature des Alten und Neuen Testaments
GAGNT	M. Zerwick and M. Grosvenor, *A Grammatical Analysis of the Greek New Testament,* 4th ed.
GGBB	D. B. Wallace, *Greek Grammar beyond the Basics*
GGNT	A. T. Robertson, *Greek Grammar of the New Testament*
GOTR	*The Greek Orthodox Theological Review*
GTJ	*Grace Theological Journal*
HALOT	*The Hebrew and Aramaic Lexicon of the Old Testament,* L. Koehler, W. Baumgartner, and J. J. Stamm, trans. and ed. M. E. J. Richardson
HCSB	Holman Christian Standard Bible
Her	Hermeneia
HeyJ	*Heythrop Journal*
HNT	Handbuch zum Neuen Testament
HTR	*Harvard Theological Review*
HUCA	*Hebrew Union College Annual*
IBC	Interpretation: A Bible Commentary for Teaching and Preaching
IDB	*Interpreter's Dictionary of the Bible*, ed. G. A. Buttrick, 4 vols.
Int	*Interpretation*
JBL	*Journal of Biblical Literature*
JETS	*Journal of the Evangelical Theological Society*
JNES	*Journal of Near Eastern Studies*
JOTT	*Journal of Translation and Textlinguistics*
JRH	*Journal of Religious History*
JSJSup	Supplements to the Journal for the Study of Judaism
JSNT	*Journal for the Study of the New Testament*
JSNTSup	Journal for the Study of the New Testament: Supplement Series
JTS	*Journal of Theological Studies*
KEK	Kritisch-exegetischer Kommentar über das Neue Testament
KNT	Kommentar zum Neuen Testament
LCC	Library of Christian Classics

L&N	*Greek-English Lexicon of the New Testament*, ed. J. P. Louw and E. A. Nida
LNTS	Library of New Testament Studies
LSJ	Liddell, H. G., R. Scott, H. S. Jones, *A Greek-English Lexicon.* 9th ed.
LW	*D. Martin Luthers Werke, Kritische Gesamtausgabe*. 65 vols. Weimar: Vergal Hermann Böhlaus Nachfolger. 1883–1966
MHT	*A Grammar of New Testament Greek*, by J. H. Moulton (vol. 1), W. F. Howard (vol. 2), and N. Turner (vols. 3–4)
MM	J. H. Moulton and G. Milligan, *The Vocabulary of the Greek Testament*
NA^{27}	*Novum Testamentum Graece.* Nestle-Aland. 27th ed.
NAC	New American Commentary
NACSBT	New American Commentary Studies in Bible and Theology
NASB	New American Standard Bible
Neot	*Neotestamentica*
NIBC	New International Biblical Commentary
NICNT	New International Commentary on the New Testament
NIDNTT	*New International Dictionary of New Testament Theology,* ed. C. Brown
NIDOTTE	*New International Dictionary of Old Testament Theology and Exegesis,* ed. W. A. VanGemeren
NIGTC	New International Greek Testament Commentary
NIV	New International Version
NIVAC	NIV Application Commentary
NJB	New Jerusalem Bible
NovT	*Novum Testamentum*
NovTSup	Novum Testamentum Supplements
NPNF	*Nicene and Post-Nicene Fathers*, ed. P. Schaff (Grand Rapids: Eerdmans, 1956). Series one ($NPNF^1$) or two ($NPNF^2$)
NRSV	New Revised Standard Version
NSBT	New Studies in Biblical Theology
NT	New Testament
NTAbh	Neutestamentliche Abhandlungen
NTC	New Testament Commentary
NTL	New Testament Library
NTS	*New Testament Studies*
OPTAT	*Occasional Papers in Translation and Textlinguistics*
OT	Old Testament
ÖTK	Ökumenischer Taschenbuch-Kommentar zum Neuen Testament
OTL	Old Testament Library
PNTC	Pillar New Testament Commentary
PRSt	*Perspectives in Religious Studies*

PSTJ	*Perkins (School of Theology) Journal*
RB	*Revue biblique*
REB	Revised English Bible
REC	Reformed Expository Commentary
ResQ	*Restoration Quarterly*
RevExp	*Review and Expositor*
RevistB	*Revista biblica*
RevQ	*Revue de Qumran*
RThom	*Revue thomiste*
RTP	*Revue de théologie ancienne et médiévale*
RTR	*Reformed Theological Review*
SBLDS	Society of Biblical Literature Dissertation Series
SBLSBS	SBL Sources for Biblical Study
SBLSCS	SBL Septuagint and Cognate Studies
SBLSP	*Society of Biblical Literature Seminar Papers*
SE	*Studia evangelica*
SJT	*Scottish Journal of Theology*
SL	*Studia liturgia*
SNT	Studien zum Neuen Testament
SNTSMS	Society for New Testament Studies Monograph Series
SP	Sacra pagina
Str-B	H. L. Strack and P. Billerbeck, *Kommentar zum Neuen Testament aus Talmud und Midrasch*, 6 vols.
SubBi	Subsidia Biblica
SwJT	*Southwestern Journal of Theology*
TBT	*The Bible Today*
TCGNT	*A Textual Commentary on the Greek New Testament*, ed. B. M. Metzger, 2nd ed.
TDNT	*Theological Dictionary of the New Testament,* ed. G. Kittel, et al., trans. G. W. Bromiley, 9 vols.
TDNTa	*Theological Dictionary of the New Testament,* ed. G. Kittel, et al., Abridged (one vol.) by G. W. Bromiley
TEV	Today's English Version
THKNT	Theologischer Handkommentar zum Neuen Testament
TJ	*Trinity Journal*
TJT	*Toronto Journal of Theology*
TLNT	C. Spicq, *Theological Lexicon of the New Testament*, trans. and ed. J. D. Ernest
TMSJ	*The Master's Seminary Journal*
TNT	*Translator's New Testament*
TNTC	Tyndale New Testament Commentaries
TR	Textus Receptus
TS	*Theological Studies*

TWOT	*Theological Wordbook of the Old Testament,* ed. R. L. Harris, G. L. Archer Jr., B. K. Waltke, 2 vols.
TynBul	*Tyndale Bulletin*
UBS[4]	*The Greek New Testament.* United Bible Societies, 4th ed.
WBC	Word Biblical Commentary
WBE	*Wycliffe Bible Encyclopedia*, ed. C. F. Pfeiffer, 2 vols.
WJA	*Writings of J. Arminius*, trans. J. Nichols and W. R. Bagnall (repr., Grand Rapids: Baker, 1977)
WMANT	Wissenschaftliche Monographien zum Alten und Neuen Testament
WP	A. T. Robertson, *Word Pictures in the New Testament,* 6 vols.
WTJ	*Westminster Theological Journal*
WUNT	Wissenschaftliche Untersuchungen zum Neuen Testament
ZAW	*Zeitschrift für die alttestamentliche Wissenschaft*
ZBK	Zürcher Bibelkommentare
ZNW	*Zeitschrift für die Neutestamentliche Wissenschaft und die Kunde der älteren Kirche*

OTHER ABBREVIATIONS

Cf.	confer, compare, see
Eng.	English
esp.	especially
fem.	feminine
Gk.	Greek
Hb.	Hebrew
lit.	literal(ly)
LXX	Septuagint
masc.	masculine
ms(s)	manuscript(s)
MT	Masoretic Text
pers.	person (1st, 2nd, or 3rd)
pl.	plural
sg.	singular
v(v).	verse(s)

Contents

Hebrews

INTRODUCTION OUTLINE

1. The Nature of the Book
2. Historical Circumstances
   (1) Authorship
      Historical Testimony
      The Argument for Paul
      The Argument for Barnabas
      The Argument for Apollos
      The Argument for Luke
   (2) Recipients
   (3) Location of the Recipients
   (4) Date of Hebrews
   (5) Conclusion: Summary Proposal of Authorship, Recipients, Destination, and Date
3. The Purpose of Hebrews
4. The Theology of Hebrews
5. The Use of the Old Testament in Hebrews
6. Hebrews and Textual Criticism
7. The Outline and Structure of Hebrews

INTRODUCTION

1. The Nature of the Book[1]

From the earliest days of Christian history, the epistle to the Hebrews has been shrouded in obscurity. It is the only truly anonymous letter in the New

[1] On this subject, H. Feld's extensive survey of Hebrews up to 1985 is unparalleled (*Der Hebräerbrief* [Darmstadt: Wissenschaftliche Buchgesellschaft, 1985] and "Der Hebräerbrief: Literarische Form, religionsgeschichtlicher Hintergrund, theologische Fragen," *ANRW* 2.25.4 (1987): 3522–601). C. Spicq's two volume commentary in French is still valuable for covering the field through the early 1950s (*l'Épître aux Hébreux,* in *Études Biblique*, ed. J. Gibalda [Paris: Librairie Lecoffre, 1952–53]). The best surveys in English include the introductory material in W. L. Lane, *Hebrews 1–8*, WBC (Dallas, TX: Word, 1991), xlvii–clvii; P. Ellingworth, *The Epistle to the Hebrews*, NIGTC (Grand Rapids: Eerdmans, 1993), 3–80; and C. R. Koester, *Hebrews*, AB (New

Testament. With regard to authorship, most modern scholars share the view expressed by Origen's dictum: "As to who wrote the epistle, truly only God knows."[2] Complicating the problem of authorship is the uncertainty regarding other background issues such as date, recipients, and place of writing. There is no clear and unequivocal internal evidence for any of these issues. Consequently, Hebrews is probably the most enigmatic book in the New Testament in terms of provenance.[3] The epistle's title "To the Hebrews" is generally viewed as not originally part of the letter's composition, but was an addition during the second century. Most think the title was deduced from the letter's content. In and of itself, the title is virtually no help in identifying the recipients of the epistle.[4]

Certainly much of the book's content is unique. It does not fit readily into the scheme of the Pauline, Johannine, or Petrine writings, yet it constitutes one of the most majestic presentations of Christology in the entire New Testament.[5] Its genre is mixed, sometimes being epistolary in nature, while at other times having a sermonic[6] character. Other terms used to describe its literary character are "essay," "treatise," "oration," "biblical exposition," and "exhortation."[7] The

---

York: Doubleday, 2001), 19–131, with Koester covering material through the end of the twentieth century. On the history of interpretation, cf. B. Demarest, *A History of the Interpretation of Hebrews 7:1–10 from the Reformation to the Present Day* (Tübingen: Mohr/Siebeck, 1976); R. Greer, *The Captain of Our Salvation: A Study in the Patristic Exegesis of Hebrews*, BGBE 15 (Tübingen: Mohr/Siebeck, 1973); and K. Hagen, *Hebrews Commenting from Erasmus to Bèza, 1516–1598* (Tübingen: Mohr/Siebeck, 1981); id., *A Theology of Testament in the Young Luther: The Lectures on Hebrews, Studies in Medieval and Reformation Thought* 12 (Leiden: E. J. Brill, 1974).

[2] Eusebius, *Ecclesiastical History*, 6.14.

[3] E. F. Scott's now famous description of Hebrews as "the riddle of the New Testament" is appropriate. See Scott, *The Epistle to the Hebrews: Its Doctrine and Significance* (Edinburgh: Clark, 1923), 1.

[4] See the discussion on the title in relationship to the epistle's canonicity in B. S. Childs, *The New Testament as Canon: An Introduction* (Philadelphia: Fortress, 1985), 413–15.

[5] B. Lindars ranked the author of Hebrews with Paul and John as one of the three great theologians of the NT (*The Theology of the Letter to the Hebrews* [Cambridge: Cambridge University Press, 1991], 1).

[6] An accessible treatment of the genre of Hebrews, showing both its sermonic and epistolary nature, can be found in A. Trotter, *Interpreting the Epistle to the Hebrews*, in Guides to New Testament Exegesis, ed. S. McKnight (Grand Rapids: Baker, 1997), 6:59–80. The earliest identification of Hebrews as a sermon is found in J. Berger, "Der Brief an die Hebräer, eine Homilie," in *Göttinger theologische Bibliothek* 3 (1797): 449–59. H. Thyen classified Hebrews as a homily in the Jewish-Hellenistic tradition of the type heard in Diaspora synagogues (*Der Stil der jüdisch-hellenistischen Homilie* FRLANT 47 [Göttingen: Vandenhoeck & Ruprecht, 1955], 17). For a helpful summary of Thyen's conclusions regarding the form of Hebrews, consult Lane, *Hebrews 1–8*, lxx–lxxi. On the sermonic nature of Hebrews, see H. Attridge, "Paraenesis in a Homily (λόγος παρακλήσεως): The Possible Location of, and Socialization in, the 'Epistle to the Hebrews,'" *Semeia* 50 (1990): 210–26.

[7] See B. Hunt ("The 'Epistle to the Hebrews': an Anti-Judaic Treatise?" *SE* 2 [1964], 2:408) for the suggestion that Hebrews may be a combination treatise and epistle. He envisioned that Paul may have taken a treatise by another author and sent it to one of his churches after adding the exhortations and greetings of chap. 13. This would account for its dual nature as well as the sup-

latter is especially appropriate because in 13:22 the author himself speaks of his work as a "word of exhortation." It is clear from the postscript in 13:22–25 that Hebrews is an epistle, yet it does not have the usual formulaic prescript. In fact, it begins like a sermon, reads like a sermon, but concludes like an epistle. The identical phrase "word of exhortation" occurs in Acts 13:15 where Paul and Barnabas were invited to speak in the synagogue in Pisidian Antioch. Lane rightly concluded that the phrase "appears to be an idiomatic, fixed expression for a sermon in Jewish-Hellenistic and early Christian circles."[8] It is now generally recognized that Hebrews is a written sermon. The frequent and well-placed imperatives and hortatory subjunctives coupled with the interweaving of exposition and exhortation support its sermonic nature.[9] From a linguistic perspective it is best to describe Hebrews as an example of hortatory discourse with large sections of embedded expository discourse.[10] Laansma described the epistle's exhortation as the "goal" and the exposition as the "means to the goal."[11] Lane rightly called the author a "gifted preacher" and noted,

> Hebrews is a sermon prepared to be read aloud to a group of auditors who will receive its message not primarily through reading and leisured reflection but orally. Reading the document aloud entails oral performance, providing oral clues to those who listen to the public reading of the sermon. . . . Hebrews was crafted to communicate its points as much aurally as logically. In point of fact, aural considerations, in the event of communication, often prove to be the decisive ones.[12]

---

posed change in style at chap. 13. However, F. Filson (*'Yesterday:' A Study of Hebrews in the Light of Chapter 13*, Studies in Biblical Theology 4 [London: SCM, 1967] has conclusively shown that chap. 13 is a part of the original document and was not added by a later writer. First John can be compared to Hebrews in that it has no epistolary beginning and it alternates between theological and parenetic (exhortatory) sections.

[8] Lane, *Hebrews 1–8*, lxx.

[9] R. Martin, *New Testament Foundations: A Guide for Christian Students* (Grand Rapids: Eerdmans, 1978), 2:348–49. rightly noted, against E. Dinkler ("The Letter to the Hebrews," in *IDB* 2:572), that the epistle could hardly be a collection of sermons brought together in a single treatise since its argument is so tightly woven.

[10] R. Longacre (*The Grammar of Discourse,* [New York: Plenum, 1983], 39) defined hortatory discourse as an attempt to convince or persuade hearers/readers to a certain course of action or to dissuade them from a course of conduct in which they have either already engaged in or are about to engage in. This is an accurate description of what takes place in Hebrews. See also L. L. Neeley, who has shown through discourse analysis that Hebrews is primarily hortatory discourse with embedded sections of expository discourse ("A Discourse Analysis of Hebrews." *OPTAT* 3–4 [1987]: 1–146.). See also G. Guthrie's *The Structure of Hebrews*: *A Text-Linguistic Analysis* (Grand Rapids: Baker, 1994) for an excellent analysis of several discourse features in the epistle. The most recent and thorough analysis of the discourse structure of Hebrews is C. Westfall, *A Discourse Analysis of the Letter to the Hebrews: The Relationship Between Form and Meaning*, LNTS 297 (London: T&T Clark, 2006).

[11] J. Laansma, "Book of Hebrews," *DTIB* 276–77.

[12] Lane, *Hebrews 1–8*, lxxv.

Lane's point is vital to grasp in the interpretation of the epistle. Much of the oral impact is lost in the translation from Greek to English. Lane's use of the word "crafted" is well chosen. The author is writing for the ear, not the eye. Logos and pathos blend in masterful ways to make Hebrews an extraordinary sermon.

Hebrews is unique in the New Testament in that it possesses no specific salutation but it does have a conclusion. Several suggestions have been offered to explain this. Some claim that the original introduction was lost accidentally. Yet this is not a likely solution since there are thousands of extant letters from the ancient world, many of which are autographs, and not one single autograph lacks the usual introduction. There is no record at all of the prescript alone becoming lost from any papyrus roll.[13] Some have suggested the prescript was omitted for canonical reasons. If Hebrews were written by someone other than an apostle, such as Barnabas or Apollos, supposedly this would hinder canonical acceptance. However, as Moffatt pointed out, if such had been the case some trace of the original would probably have survived.[14] Zahn and Riggenbach conjecture that the one who delivered the letter orally supplied the missing introduction.[15] Again, this is an unnecessary conjecture.

Others say that the introduction was deliberately omitted by the author. This is also very doubtful, for those who suggest that Paul omitted any reference to his name because he was the apostle to the Gentiles and was now writing a letter to Jewish Christians overlook that the letter itself makes it clear that the readers knew the author's identity.[16] Furthermore, an alteration of the introduction by adding the name of Paul (for purposes of achieving canonicity) would seem more likely than a total excision. The current consensus is that there never was a salutation or introduction. The beautifully balanced and classical sentence with which Hebrews begins has all the earmarks of the original introduction to the work.

Overbeck's elaborate scheme for seeing the ending of the epistle as a part of the later church's effort to legitimate the letter in the canonization process by means of an attribution of Pauline authorship is totally unnecessary.[17] Wrede argued that the author of Hebrews decided midstream in his letter to append a

---

[13] See A. Wikenhauser, *New Testament Introduction,* trans. J. Cunningham (New York: Herder & Herder, 1958), 346, 349, 359.

[14] J. Moffatt, *An Introduction to the Literature of the New Testament,* 3rd ed. (Edinburgh: T&T Clark, 1918), 429.

[15] T. Zahn, *Introduction to the New Testament*, (Minneapolis: Klock & Klock reprint, 1977), 2:312–15. Riggenbach, *Der Brief an die Hebräer*, 3rd ed., KNT 14 (Leipzig: Deichert, 1922), xviii–xix.

[16] Against E. Grässer, who argued that the author wanted to remain anonymous because he was a second generation Christian as implied in Heb 2:3 (*An die Hebräer, EKKNT* 17 [Zürich: Benzinger, 1990], 1:22).

[17] F. Overbeck, *Zur Geschichte des Kanons* (Chemnitz, 1880; reprinted Darmstadt, 1965), 30–70.

postscript in Pauline style in an attempt to make Hebrews appear to be a Pauline prison letter.[18] Wrede's theory is seldom affirmed today. Another minority view is that the postscript was not penned by the author, but was a later interpolation to provide grounds for the authority of the text. Rothschild argued that the postscript (Heb 13:20–25 in her view) "not only exhibits literary reliance on Paul's undisputed corpus, but also, as an aspect of this reliance, *appropriates Paul's identity as the author of Hebrews's own*."[19] Rothschild argued that the author of Hebrews composed the postscript as a deliberate forgery in Pauline style with the goal that Hebrews would be seen as Pauline and "published as part of an existing *corpus Paulinum*."[20] Amazingly, Rothschild argued that such identity falsification "is not only consistent with the personality behind Hebrews, but is its necessary correlative and that Hebrews' reception history attests the overwhelming success of this deception up until the Reformation."[21] E. J. Goodspeed likewise suggested that Hebrews may have been originally pseudonymously attributed to Paul rather than being anonymous.[22] But D. Guthrie countered that had the letter originally borne any ascription to Paul, "it is impossible to envisage any situation in which it would lose its ascription and still continue to be regarded with some favor. There are no parallels to this kind of thing among the pseudepigrapha."[23]

Neither can the theory of a Greek translation from a Hebrew or Aramaic original as suggested by Clement of Alexandria be sustained in light of the evidence. The many examples of Greek paranomasia (play on words, as in Heb 5:8) and other stylistic devices make it clear that Hebrews is not a translation of a Hebrew original. The same conclusion is reached after examining Hebrews' use of the LXX, since the Greek word *hupotassō* in Heb 2:8 does not occur in the Hebrew of Ps 8:6[7] that the author quoted, and yet the author's argument is built on this Greek word.

---

[18] W. Wrede, *Die literarische Rätsel des Hebräerbriefs* (Göttingen: Vandenhoeck & Ruprecht, 1906), 3–5

[19] C. Rothschild, *Hebrews as Pseudepigraphon: The History and Significance of the Pauline Attribution of Hebrews*, WUNT 235 (Tübingen: Mohr Siebeck, 2009), 4.

[20] Ibid.

[21] Ibid., 5.

[22] E. J. Goodspeed, *An Introduction to the New Testament* (Chicago: University Press, 1937), 257.

[23] D. Guthrie, *New Testament Introduction*, 4th ed. (Downers Grove: InterVarsity, 1990), 682.

The diverse proposals regarding the literary and conceptual background of Hebrews include Gnosticism,[24] Jewish mysticism,[25] Qumran,[26] Philonism,[27] and Christian tradition.[28] The overall rhetorical structure of Hebrews is likewise debated.[29] Koester is correct in his assessment that we cannot categorize Hebrews as either deliberative (exhortatory) or epideictic (praise or blame) examples of rhetoric since the two forms are so closely related and often occur in

---

[24] The Gnostic background was argued by Käsemann in 1939. E. Grässer, influenced by Käsemann's *Das Wandernde Gottesvolk*, viewed Hebrews 8 in terms of "cosmic dualism" (*Der Alte Bund im Neuen*, 109). See H. Koester, *History and Literature of Early Christianity*, vol. 2 of *Introduction to the New Testament*, 2nd ed. (Philadelphia: Fortress, 1982), 274, who also argued for a Gnostic background. G. Hughes strongly critiqued Grässer's approach (*Hebrews and Hermeneutics: The Epistle to the Hebrews as a New Testament Example of Biblical Interpretation*, SNTSMS 36 [Cambridge: Cambridge University Press, 1979], 137–42). See also L. D. Hurst's trenchant critique of Grässer and the Gnostic hypothesis in *The Epistle to the Hebrews: Its Background of Thought*, SNTSMS 65 (New York: Cambridge University Press, 1990), 70–75, where he even suggests that the "time may be ripe" to bring the discussion of a Gnostic background for Hebrews to a close (74). Hurst's critique remains unanswered.

[25] This was first proposed by H.–M. Schenke, "Erwägung zum Rätsel des Hebräerbriefes," in *Neues Testament und christliche Existenz, Festschrift H. Braun*, ed. H. D. Betz and L. Schrottroff (Tübingen: Mohr/Siebeck, 1972), 421–37, followed by R. Williamson, "The Background to the Epistle to the Hebrews," *ExpTim* 87 (1975–76): 232–37. It is generally rejected today; see Hurst, *Hebrews: Background and Thought*, 83–84.

[26] On the possible connection between Qumran and Hebrews, see C. Spicq, "*L'Épître* aux Hebreux, Apollos, Jean-Baptiste, les Hellenistes et Qumran," *RevQ* 1 (1959): 365–90; Y. Yadin, "The Dead Sea Scrolls and the Epistle to the Hebrews," in *Aspects of the Dead Sea Scrolls, ed. C. Rabin and Y. Yadin, Scripta Hierosolymitana* 4, 2nd ed. (Jerusalem: Magnes, 1965), 36–55; and J. Danielou, *The Dead Sea Scrolls and Primitive Christianity*, trans. S. Attanasio (Baltimore: Helicon, 1958). For an excellent discussion on the history of research on Hebrews and Qumran, see H. Attridge, "The Epistle to the Hebrews and the Scrolls," in *When Judaism and Christianity Began: Essays in Memory of Anthony J. Saldarini*, ed. A. J. Avery-Peck, D. Harrington, and J. Neusner, JSJSup 85 (Leiden/Boston: Brill, 2004), 315–42, and D. Guthrie, *Hebrews*, TNTC (Grand Rapids: Eerdmans, 1983), 40–41. Guthrie discussed five supposed connections between the Qumran community and Hebrews, and then concluded, "In view of all this there is justification for the view that the Qumran literature and cultic practices throw some light on the milieu to which the readers of this epistle belong, although it is questionable whether any direct contact can be made."

[27] According to C. Spicq, Grotius in the seventeenth century was the first to suggest the author of Hebrews had read Philo (*L'Épître aux Hebreux*, 1:39). More recently, L. T. Johnson reflected an open stance to the influence of Philo on the author of Hebrews, but he stopped short of saying the author had read Philo. His concluding comment sums up his position: "The Platonism of Hebrews is real—and critical to understanding its argument—but it is a Platonism that is stretched and reshaped by engagement with Scripture, and above all, by the experience of a historical human savior whose death and resurrection affected all human bodies and earthly existence as a whole" (L. T. Johnson, *Hebrews: A Commentary* [Louisville: WJK, 2006], 21).

[28] See Koester (*Hebrews*, 54–58) for similarities with the Synoptic Gospels, John, Paul, Peter, and Stephen.

[29] No consensus on the relationship of Hebrews to classical rhetorical categories exists. See A. T. Lincoln *Hebrews: A Guide* [Edinburgh: T&T Clark, 2006], 14–17) for an accessible survey of Hebrews and rhetoric. See also Koester, "The Epistle to the Hebrews in Recent Study," *CurBS* 2 (1994): 126; and D. Watson, "Rhetorical Criticism of Hebrews and the Catholic Epistles Since 1978," *CurBS* 5 (1997): 175–87.

the same speech.[30] What is not debated is the author's use of several rhetorical devices such as alliteration, assonance, *inclusio*, and a host of others.[31] Löhr analyzed the use of rhetorical terminology in Hebrews and concluded, "The phrases and expressions . . . can certainly be understood without any reference to the language of rhetoric. But taken together they might provoke—and indeed they did provoke for me—the impression that our author could have used them consciously, being well aware of their rhetorical background."[32] As Lane so aptly put it, "In Hebrews the voice of the writer is the voice of the speaker."[33] In light of the overall evidence, it seems moot to argue over whether Hebrews is an epistle or a sermon. It is both. The epistolary elements in Heb 13 "could well have been original and intentional, for the 'sermon' could well have been delivered (read aloud) as a 'letter.'"[34]

2. Historical Circumstances

(1) Authorship

Many have conjectured, some have conjured, but very few have been convinced in the search for the author of Hebrews. Most commentaries on Hebrews of recent vintage do not spend a great deal of time discussing matters of authorship and recipients. This is understandable in light of the multitude of theories available.[35] Three observations emerge. First, it is obvious there

[30] Deliberative rhetoric seeks to persuade people to follow a future course of action; epideictic rhetoric reinforces listener values through commendation and condemnation. See Koester, *Hebrews*, 82. Lane (*Hebrews 1–8*, lxxix) and D. DeSilva (*Perseverance in Gratitude: A Socio-Rhetorical Commentary on the Epistle to the Hebrews* [Grand Rapids: Eerdmans, 2000], 48, 57).

[31] C. Spicq provides an extensive list in *l'Épître aux Hébreux*, 1:351–78. See D. A. Black ("The Problem of the Literary Structure of Hebrews," *GTJ* 7 [1986]: 163–77) and A. T. Lincoln (*Hebrews: A Guide*, 19–21) for accessible listings in English. C. F. Evans (*The Theology of Rhetoric: The Epistle to the Hebrews* [London: Friends of Dr. Williams' Library, 1988], 3–19) is particularly helpful on the author of Hebrews' use of synkrisis (formal pairing of two persons for comparison or contrast). Evans took up interest in this specific rhetorical device in Hebrews upon reading G. Zuntz's comment (in his *The Text of the Epistles*) that it was the author's "excessive use" of synkrisis that caused him to regard Hebrews as originally a homily (*Theology*, 5).

[32] H. Löhr, "Reflections of Rhetorical Terminology in Hebrews," in *Hebrews: Contemporary Methods, New Insights*, ed. G. Gelardini (Leiden/Boston: Brill, 2005), 201.

[33] Lane, *Hebrews 1–8*, lxxvi.

[34] Johnson, *Hebrews*, 11.

[35] Helpful surveys and summaries of the various theories can be found in F. F. Bruce, "Recent Contributions to the Understanding of Hebrews," *ExpTim* 80 (1969): 260–64; id., *Acts*, rev. ed., NICNT (Grand Rapids: Eerdmans, 1998), 14–20; G. W. Buchanan, "The Present State of Scholarship on Hebrews," in *Judaism, Christianity and Other Greco-Roman Cults*, ed. J. Neusner (Leiden: Brill, 1975), 1:299–330; J. McCullough, "Some Recent Developments," 141–65; id., "Hebrews in Recent Scholarship": 66–86, 108–20); D. Guthrie, *New Testament Introduction*, 668–82; H. F. Weiss, *Der Brief an die Hebräer,* 61–78; Ellingworth, *Hebrews*, 3–21; Koester, *Hebrews*, 42–54. Koester's summary of authorship, recipients, destination and date would be very helpful for pastors.

have been numerous theories as to the authorship of the book. Second, the suggestions made by the patristic, Medieval, and Reformation scholars almost always involved persons who were well-known apostles or who were associated with the apostles in some close fashion such as Luke, Apollos, Barnabas, and Clement of Rome. Canonicity may have played a role in the theories of authorship among the church fathers,[36] but names suggested for possible authorship always involved those of the apostolic band. Third, not only is there no agreement as to authorship, but all other matters of background (such as provenance and recipients) have also been open to speculation from the church fathers until the present.

HISTORICAL TESTIMONY. The historical testimony[37] regarding the authorship of Hebrews begins with Clement of Rome's clear use of the epistle in his letter to the Corinthians (*1 Clement*). If Clement's epistle to the Corinthians can be successfully dated near the end of the first century, which is the traditional view, then the historical testimony concerning the authorship of Hebrews pre-dates the second century. Clement's silence as to the authorship of Hebrews may indicate that he himself did not consider Paul to be the author. Yet, as always, the argument from silence is weak and too much should not be made of it. Nor should much be made of the view that Clement of Rome could have been the author of Hebrews since chronological, not to mention stylistic, considerations would militate against it.[38] Since Hebrews was known early in Rome, as shown by Clement's use, how is one to explain the silence of the Roman church as to Clement's authorship if he were or could have been considered the author?

Pantaenus, head of the Alexandrian school of catechetes, ascribed Hebrews to the apostle Paul. But he observed that, contrary to Paul's custom in his other epistles, there is no salutation identifying him as the author. At the end of the second century, Clement of Alexandria, student of Pantaenus, was quoted by Eusebius as saying that Paul wrote Hebrews originally in Hebrew and that Luke translated it into Greek for a Hellenistic Jewish audience. Clement stated that it was this fact (Luke's translation) that accounted for the stylistic similarities between Hebrews and Luke-Acts. He conjectured that

---

[36] On the question of the canonicity of Hebrews, particularly as it relates to authorship, see J. H. Thayer, "Authorship and Canonicity of the Epistle to the Hebrews," *BSac* 24 (1867): 681–722; and Spicq, *l'Épître aux Hébreux*, 1:169–96.

[37] Helpful surveys include Lincoln, *Hebrews: A Guide*, 2–8; P. E. Hughes, *A Commentary on the Epistle to the Hebrews* (Grand Rapids: Eerdmans, 1977), 19–30; and Koester, *Hebrews*, 19–63. Koester, in addition to questions of authorship, provides the most comprehensive survey of the history of interpretation of the epistle.

[38] J. Conder (*A Literary History of the New Testament* [London: Seeley, Burnside, & Seeley, 1845], 443) argued that the difference between the canonical epistles and the earliest patristic writings warrants the conclusion that Hebrews could not have been written by Clement, Barnabas (assuming Barnabas is the author of the *Epistle of Barnabas*), or Polycarp.

Paul did not prefix his name to the epistle since the Jews were prejudiced and suspicious of him.[39]

The oldest extant text of Hebrews is found in p^{46} (c. AD 200) where it occurs immediately following Romans (most likely due to its length) in a fourteen-letter Pauline collection.[40] By the middle of the third century, Origen allowed for Pauline influence on the thoughts of the epistle, but he ascribed the style and actual writing to someone else.

> That the verbal style of the epistle entitled 'To the Hebrews', is not rude like the language of the apostle, who acknowledged himself rude in speech,' that is, in expression; but that its diction is purer Greek, any one who has the power to discern differences of phraseology will acknowledge. Moreover, that the thoughts of the epistle are admirable, and not inferior to the acknowledged apostolic writings, any one who carefully examines the apostolic text will admit . . . If I gave my opinion, I should say that the thoughts are those of the apostle, but the diction and phraseology are those of someone who remembered the apostolic teachings, and wrote them down at his leisure what had been said by his teacher. Therefore, if any church holds that this epistle is by Paul, let it be commended for this. . . . But who wrote the epistle, in truth, God knows. The statement of some who have gone before us is that Clement, bishop of the Romans, wrote the epistle, and of others that Luke, the author of the Gospel and the Acts, wrote it.[41]

Bleek interpreted Origen's remarks to mean "in its matter it is not inferior to the acknowledged apostolical writings, being in his opinion indebted for its argument to Paul, but for its style and finish to some disciple who jotted down his master's ideas, and then drew them out still further, and wove them together into a sort of commentary."[42]

That Paul used an amanuensis for most if not all of his letters and that this did not appreciably affect his style (with the exception of the Pastorals if their Pauline authorship is admitted)[43] argues against the hypothesis of Origen and others.

---

[39] Eusebius (*Ecclesiastical History* 6.14), quoting Clement of Alexandria's *Hypotyposes*.

[40] B. Metzger, *The Text of the New Testament* (New York and Oxford: Oxford University Press 1968), 37–38, 252. An accessible summary can be found in Lincoln, *Hebrews: A Guide*, 2–4. On the manuscript evidence for Hebrews, see W. Hatch, "The Position of Hebrews in the Canon of the New Testament," *HTR* 29 (1936): 133–51, who has one of the best discussions on the position of Hebrews in the NT canon. More recently on this issue, see D. Georgi, "Hebrews and the Heritage of Paul," in Gelardini, *Hebrews: Contemporary Methods, New Insights*, 240–44.

[41] Eusebius (*Ecclesiastical History* 6.25), quoting Origen.

[42] J. F. Bleek, *Introduction to the New Testament*, 2nd ed., trans. W. Urwick (Edinburgh: T&T Clark, 1869), 2:105.

[43] I consider all 13 epistles as genuinely Pauline.

Writers such as J. Hug, S. Davidson, and D. Black[44]—who argued that Origen's statement "as to who wrote the epistle" referred to the one who wrote it down for Paul, that is, who functioned as his amanuensis or translator—find themselves swimming upstream against the context and usage of the Greek *ho grapsas*. Both Hug and Black render the participle in Greek as "who wrote down" in an effort to maintain Pauline authorship, and they asserted that the context justifies such a translation. In fact, the opposite is the case. In the sentence immediately following, Origen refers to "Luke, who wrote (*ho grapsas*) the Gospel," meaning authorship and not "who wrote down" the Gospel as an amanuensis or translator.[45] The critique of this interpretation by Bleek and Thayer is difficult if not impossible to overcome.[46] Mitchell noted the many places in Eusebius's *Ecclesiastical History* where the Greek verb *graphō* ("to write") "refers both to authorship and to actual penning" and thus concluded "Black's distinction between author and amanuensis cannot be maintained in light of this evidence."[47]

Origen was the first to suggest the theory that the thoughts were from Paul but the composition was from someone else. In this way he sought to reconcile the two disparate views that came down to him, namely, some said Paul was the author and others that another Christian teacher wrote it. Thus, when Origen says that the tradition handed down to him included the possibility of Lukan authorship, it is clear that he means independent Lukan authorship—and not as a translator or an amanuensis or a collector of Paul's thoughts. When Origen says "but who wrote it, only God knows," he meant to indicate uncertainty as to which of Paul's disciples it was who developed his ideas and was thus the actual author.

The Alexandrian tradition regarding authorship continued to grow so that by the fourth century Paul was regarded as the author (either directly or indirectly) of the epistle. However, from the very beginning of this tradition, Hebrews was attributed to Paul usually in a tentative, indirect fashion.[48]

---

[44] See J. L. Hug, *Introduction to the New Testament,* trans. from the 3rd German ed. D. Fosdick (Andover: Gould & Newman, 1836), 590. S. Davidson (*An Introduction to the Study of the New Testament*, 2nd ed. [London: Longmans, Green, & Co., 1882], 1:190) also supports this view. Cf. D. A. Black, "On the Pauline Authorship of Hebrews (Part 2): The External Evidence Reconsidered," *FM* 16 (1999): 80–81.

[45] P. Maier's translation of Eusebius supports the traditional understanding of ὁ γραψας; see Maier, *Eusebius: The Church History, A New Translation with Commentary* (Grand Rapids: Kregel, 1999), 227.

[46] See Bleek, *Introduction*, 2:106; J. H. Thayer, "Authorship and Canonicity of the Epistle to the Hebrews," *BSac* 24 (1867): 707–8. B. Weiss (*A Manual of Introduction to the New Testament,* trans. A. J. K. Davidson [New York: Funk & Wagnalls, 1889], 2) stated emphatically "Origen himself has no doubt whatever that the epistle cannot possibly have proceeded from Paul on account of its language."

[47] A. C. Mitchell, *Hebrews*, SP (Collegeville: Liturgical, 2007), 3–4.

[48] S. Davidson (*An Introduction to the Study of the New Testament*, 216) noted, "If it be said that the very difficulties of style, phraseology, etc., presented by the epistle increase the force of

Turning to the Western Church, apparently no tradition regarding Pauline authorship existed. Rather, in the late second and early third centuries, Tertullian made reference to the epistle as having been written by Barnabas.[49] In the Roman Church, there was likewise no tradition of Pauline authorship until very late. Clement of Rome made the first reference to the epistle in his letters to the Corinthians, but he did not posit Pauline authorship. The Muratorian Canon (c. 170–210) referred to the 13 Letters of Paul but did not list Hebrews, thus giving evidence that the Roman church did not regard Paul as the author. The Shepherd of Hermas, Justin Martyr, Irenaeus, Gaius of Rome and Hippolytus all made use of Hebrews, but none ascribe its authorship to Paul. It was only toward the end of the fourth century that Pauline authorship began to be accepted in the Western Church and Hebrews gained a canonical position. What brought this about we do not know.[50]

In the fourth century Eusebius informed us that there were 14 well-known and undisputed Pauline Letters (including Hebrews), but he also pointed out that some did reject Hebrews as canonical on the grounds that the Roman church disputed its Pauline authorship.[51] Athanasius likewise included Hebrews among the Pauline Letters, placing it after the letters addressed to churches but before letters addressed to individuals. Hebrews is found in this position in Codexes Sinaiticus, Alexandrinus, and Vaticanus, all of which were produced in the fourth and fifth centuries.

Towards the close of the fourth century, Jerome tied together several strands of information that had come down to him. First, Hebrews was disputed as Pauline on stylistic grounds. Second, Tertullian considered Barnabas as the author. Third, others had suggested Luke or Clement of Rome as the author, or perhaps as an arranger of Paul's ideas, or even as the translator of Paul's Hebrew original into the polished Greek of the epistle. Fourth, Paul may have omitted his name since he was in disrepute with the readers.[52]

Jerome in the Latin Vulgate identified Hebrews as Pauline, as did Augustine, although both did so only tentatively.[53] Hebrews was firmly embedded in the list of canonical books by the time of the Synods of Hippo (AD 393) and Carthage (AD 397 and 419), where it was located at the end of the 13 Pauline

---

the external testimony, since nothing but a thoroughly authentic tradition could have maintained itself against these difficulties, we reply, that the difficulties changed the tradition by compelling the writers who followed it to resort to an *indirect* Pauline authorship. So far from enhancing, they weaken the strength of the external evidence by the hypothesis that the thoughts are Paul's, the composition and language another's."

[49] Tertullian, *On Modesty*, 20.

[50] See suggested causes in S. Davidson, *Introduction*, 1:194.

[51] Eusebius, *Ecclesiastical History* 3.3.5; 6.20.3. For a complete presentation of the patristic evidence on authorship, see F. Bleek, *Der Brief an die Hebräer* (Berlin: Dümmler, 1828), 1:81.

[52] Jerome, *Lives of Illustrious Men*, 5.

[53] Ibid.; *Epist.* 53.8; 129.3; Augustine, *On Christian Doctrine*, 2.8; *Civ.* 16.22. See the evidence for this presented by S. Davidson, *Introduction*, 1:223–26.

Letters—a fact which testifies to the uncertainty over Pauline authorship. This tradition prevailed throughout the Middle Ages. For example, Aquinas in the prologue to his commentary on Hebrews accepted Pauline authorship along with the theory of a Hebrew original that was then translated into Greek by Luke.[54]

With the dawn of the Reformation came a reversion to the skepticism of the patristic era concerning Pauline authorship. In the sixteenth century, Luther championed Apollos while Calvin preferred Luke or Clement of Rome. In the seventeenth century, H. Grotius suggested Lukan authorship of Hebrews and became the first to put forth linguistic evidence comparing Luke and Hebrews. In a very brief fashion Grotius showed similarities among just ten words and phrases.[55] The seventeenth, eighteenth, and nineteenth centuries witnessed a tug-of-war over Pauline authorship, but the twentieth century, even after W. Leonard's 1939 masterpiece in favor of Paul (see below), registered increasing skepticism regarding the Pauline theory and witnessed a flurry of theories regarding authorship. Oddly enough, the twentieth century dawned with the suggestion by Harnack[56] that Priscilla was the author, and in 1976 J. M. Ford proposed the last theory of the century, that Mary the mother of Jesus, assisted by Luke and John, wrote it.[57] These are the only two women who have been proposed as potential authors.

THE ARGUMENT FOR PAUL. A growing consensus against Pauline authorship developed in the twentieth century.[58] However, the patristic evidence for Paul, though inconclusive, should not be so easily dismissed as is often the case today. As shown above, of the three major traditions of authorship that circulated in the first four centuries, the Alexandrian tradition regarded Hebrews at least in some sense to be the work of Paul.

Although the majority of twentieth-century scholars rejected it, the Pauline authorship of Hebrews is most ably defended by the Catholic scholar William Leonard.[59] Roman Catholic scholars seem to be the largest single group who

---

[54] T. Aquinas, *Commentary on the Epistle to the Hebrews*, trans. C. Baer (South Bend: St. Augustine's Press, 2006), 7. See the Latin edition, *Super Epistolas Sancti Pauli Lectura: ad Hebraeos lectura,* 2.335–506, 8th rev. ed., ed. P. Raphael Cai (Rome: Marietti, 1953), 356.

[55] H. Grotius, *Annotationes in Epistolam ad Hebraeos*, in *Opera Omnia Theologica* (Amstelodamum: Apud Heredes Joannis Blaev), 2:1010.

[56] A. Harnack, "Probabilia über die Addresse und den Verfasser des Hebräerbriefs," *ZNW* 1 (1900): 16–41.

[57] J. M. Ford, "The Mother of Jesus and the Authorship of the Epistle to the Hebrews," *TBT* 82 (1976): 683–94. She actually suggested a tripartite authorship with Mary, John, and Luke. She had earlier suggested the author of Hebrews was a "Paulinist" who was responding to the activity of Apollos in Corinth ("The First Epistle to the Corinthians or the First Epistle to the Hebrews?" *CBQ* 28 [1966]: 402–16.)

[58] One exception is T. W. L. Davies (*Pauline Readjustments* [London: Williams & Norgate, 1927]), who argued that the entire epistle was written by Paul, addressed to the church at Corinth, and that it was actually the "previous letter" referred to in 1 Cor. 5:9.

[59] W. Leonard, *Authorship of the Epistle to the Hebrews* (Rome: Vatican Polyglot, 1939).

still support the Pauline hypothesis, although usually indirectly, and departure from the traditional position of the Roman Church has increased in recent years. Several articles have appeared recently, however, attempting to revive the Pauline hypothesis. Christos Sp. Voulgaris argued for it based on what he called "new evidence," namely, the connection between Heb 13:23, Phil 2:19–24, and Phlm 22.[60] His entire schema is plausible, but quite speculative. However, some plausibility can be given to the suggestion that Hebrews was written to Jerusalem after the death of James to quell uncertainty in the face of renewed persecution. On this dating, Hebrews would be placed only a few short years prior to the beginning of the Jewish War in AD 66.

E. Linnemann wrote a three-part article that appeared in 2000 and was translated into English in 2002. The strength of this article is its demonstration that commentators have often overstated the case against Paul.[61] Linnemann sought to bolster the Pauline case by the linguistic argument of lexical, stylistic, and literary comparison. Reviving the excellent work of C. Forster, she offered no new evidence as far as I can discern, but her article serves to highlight that Paul was not unaccustomed to using literary niceties and the lexical similarities that can be found between the Pauline Letters and Hebrews.[62] She raised once again the banner of C. Forster, M. Stuart, and W. Leonard by making a good case for Pauline authorship. Her article is divided into six sections: manuscript evidence, the testimony of the early church, style, vocabulary, particularities of Hebrews used against Paul, and the line of argument in Hebrews.

In evaluating the style of Hebrews, Linnemann criticized those who make "wholesale assertions" about Paul's inferior style. In fact, she subtitled a part of this section "Defamation" and castigates D. Guthrie, who "would presume to dress down the apostle Paul . . . as one would an ignorant grammar school pupil."[63] At this point, in spite of her strident language, I am in partial agreement with her. It appears to me that many times authors, especially modern authors, exaggerate the stylistic differences between Paul and Hebrews to the point of concluding the "impossibility" of Pauline authorship. Although the stylistic argument—perhaps the most devastating argument—against Paul is formidable, it does not render the view impossible, merely highly unlikely, as judicious scholars note.

---

[60] C. Sp. Voulgaris, "Hebrews: Paul's Fifth Epistle from Prison," *GOTR* (1999): 199–206.

[61] E. Linnemann, "Wiederaufnahme-Prozess in Sachen des Hebräerbriefes," in *Fundamentum* 2 (2000): 102–12 (Part 1), 52–65 (Part 2), and 88–110 (Part 3). It later appeared as "A Call for a Retrial in the Case of the Epistle to the Hebrews," trans. D. E. Lanier, *FM* 19/2 (2002): 19–59.

[62] Linnemann is often injudicious in her statements. For example, her statement, "up until the year AD 200, the Epistle to the Hebrews was generally considered to be a Pauline epistle," may come as a surprise to scholars. Who were those in the second century who considered it to be Pauline? The only name which can be produced is Pantaenus, whom Clement of Alexandria mentioned as saying Hebrews was written by Paul. This hardly justifies the use of "generally considered to be a Pauline epistle."

[63] Ibid., 27

It is here in the section on style that Linnemann's case is more substantial. She engaged H. Attridge point by point in the "Literary Characteristics of Hebrews: Language and Style" section of his commentary.[64] Linnemann succeeded in countering virtually all of Attridge's examples of Hebrews' "better Greek" with similar examples from the Pauline Letters, especially Romans. She considered 14 figures of speech ranging from alliteration to paronomasia and found Pauline examples for all of them. She admitted the range of vocabulary is higher in Hebrews than in the Pauline Letters of comparable length. But she concluded that none of the characteristics of elevated Greek in Hebrews is absent from the Pauline Epistles, and thus Attridge's claim of "better Greek" in Hebrews is invalid. However, merely showing that such literary characteristics are not absent in Paul should not be turned into evidence for Paul in light of other differences in style that she did not address. All things considered, her "retrial" in the case of the Pauline authorship of Hebrews ultimately results in a mistrial.

D. A. Black's two-part recent article is a helpful summary of the evidence presented by Leonard in his classic defense of Pauline authorship in 1939.[65] Black attempted to further the Pauline case by retracing the patristic evidence and showing that many during that era of the history of the church considered Pauline authorship possible. He misinterpreted Origen's *ho grapsas* by taking it to mean "served as Paul's amanuensis," and thus he concluded that Origen affirmed Pauline authorship. In the other half of the article, Black provided us with the most comprehensive linguistic and theological arguments for Paul since Leonard.

At this point the three main arguments for Pauline authorship need to be considered: (1) similar vocabulary, (2) some similar theology, and (3) the historical testimony from the church fathers. It is striking that not one commentator on the Book of Hebrews actually engages W. Leonard's arguments in favor of Pauline authorship. Leonard provided a considerable amount of evidence to support his claim, though many of his parallels were not unique to Paul and Hebrews and hence can have only limited value in questions of authorship identification. A critical reading of his evidence reveals that Leonard has made use of some evidence for similarity that could also be argued for other New Testament writers, especially Luke.

An overall evaluation of Leonard's arguments for the Pauline authorship of Hebrews leads to the following five conclusions. First, without a doubt this is the most comprehensive compilation of evidence for the Pauline hypothesis. When one couples the massive work of Leonard with those of M. Stuart and C. Forster in the eighteenth century, who devoted almost 800 pages between

[64] Ibid., 28–35; H. Attridge, *Hebrews*, 13–21.

[65] D. A. Black, "Who Wrote Hebrews: The Internal and External Evidence Reexamined," *FM* 18 (2001): 3–26. See footnote 55 above on Leonard's *Authorship of Hebrews*.

them to the defense of Pauline authorship,[66] it becomes clear to anyone open to the evidence that the Pauline hypothesis cannot be set aside with such ease as is often done in modern works. Paul's name must remain in the upper echelon of those who are possible candidates for authorship.

Second, Leonard gave too much weight to the testimony of the church fathers in favor of Pauline authorship.[67] Third, some of his evidence suffers from non-exclusivity—such as lexical, stylistic, or conceptual evidence—that is not wholly unique to the Pauline Letters and Hebrews but also occur in other New Testament writers. This does not mean that this evidence is totally inadmissible, only that it cannot be given as much weight as Leonard seemed to give it along with evidence that is found exclusively in Hebrews and one or more of the Pauline Letters.

Fourth, Leonard considered material from the Pauline speeches in Acts to be valid evidence for Pauline usage without emphasizing the Lukan composition of Acts as well as Luke's selectivity of speech material from Paul that fit his theological purpose. Thus, he used both the Pauline Epistles *and* Paul's speeches in Acts to compare to Hebrews. Although I consider the speeches in Acts to be genuine as to their reported speakers, due allowance must be made for the editing hand of Luke in their employment in the overall discourse of Acts. As a result, some of his evidence may just as easily apply to Luke as to Paul. Many New Testament scholars would consider Leonard's methodology here to be flawed.[68]

Fifth, Leonard's argument for Paul is often only an attempt to show that there is no essential contradiction between Paul and Hebrews. In the context of Leonard's overall discourse, conclusions drawn from a lack of conflict can only serve to strengthen the valid parallels that he did make, but they can never offer additional evidence in and of themselves in favor of his position. He tended to minimize the different conceptual emphases in the Pauline Letters and Hebrews to the point that they do not furnish evidence against the un-Pauline nature of its vocabulary, style, or content.

---

[66] M. Stuart, *A Commentary on the Epistle to the Hebrews*, 4th ed., rev. R. D. C. Robbins (Andover: Warren F. Draper, 1876), esp. 117–56; and C. Forster, *The Apostolical Authority of the Epistle to the Hebrews* (London: James Duncan, 1838). Stuart's work was the premier nineteenth century argument for Pauline authorship. Yet, as Conder noted, in Stuart's zeal to argue for Paul, he labored to prove, "in opposition to every critic ancient and modern, that Hebrews abounds in Hebraisms" (*The Literary History of the New Testament*, 448). But Stuart noted that the style of Luke is nearer Hebrews than the style of Barnabas (in the pseudo-epistle) to which Tertullian ascribes the authorship. Forster's work is the most complete tabulation of vocabulary similarities between Paul and Hebrews presented in chart form, including a harmony of the parallel passages in vocabulary, style, and content. E. Linnemann drew heavily on Forster's work for her recent articles cited above.

[67] This is also a problem with Black's suggestion of Paul in "Who Wrote Hebrews?"

[68] C. Forster (*Apostolical Authority*, 61–63) made the same mistake when he noted Paul's use of τιμωρέω in Acts 22:5; 26:11 compared with Heb 10:29. He saw this as evidence for Paul's authorship, but it can just as easily be evidence for Luke's authorship.

One final argument in favor of Pauline authorship was proposed by John Owen and has been put forth by many since.[69] Owen made note of the possible connection between Peter's statement in 2 Pet 3:15–16 and Hebrews: "Even as our beloved brother Paul also, according to the wisdom given unto him, wrote unto you; as also in all his epistles, speaking in them of these things; wherein are some things hard to be understood." Since Peter wrote to Jewish Christians of the dispersion, the question arises, Which Pauline epistle is in view here? Many have suggested that it is Hebrews. Peter's statement that some of Paul's writings are "hard to be understood" is said to parallel Heb 5:11.[70] F. F. Bruce countered this suggestion by pointing out that 2 Peter was not written specifically to Hebrew Christians and that the reference in 2 Pet 3:15 is, in his words, "surely to Rom 2:4."[71] It is doubtful to say the least that 2 Pet 3:15–16 applies to Hebrews at all.

In summary, the following problems provide the greatest evidence against the Pauline hypothesis. First, Paul's name does not appear in the prologue (or anywhere else) as is the custom with his 13 other epistles in the New Testament. In fact, in all of the 13 Letters of Paul his name is the first word in the text; yet in Hebrews Paul's name appears nowhere, even though the readers knew who the author was.

Second, Hebrews lacks the characteristic salutation that begins each of the Pauline Letters. After identifying himself, it was Paul's custom to state the location of the recipients of his letter, as in Rom 1:7, "to all in Rome." Then, typically a Pauline greeting would follow: "Grace and peace to you from God our Father and from the Lord Jesus Christ." But Hebrews lacks all three of these salutary characteristics that mark the Pauline Epistles.This has caused many scholars to deny Pauline authorship to Hebrews.

Third, from a stylistic perspective, Hebrews is certainly divergent in many ways from the 13 Letters of Paul. This fact has been noted from earliest times in the history of the church. As stated above, Clement of Alexandria, Origen, and Eusebius all mentioned the difference in style between the known writings of Paul and the epistle to the Hebrews. Godet wrote, "It is strange indeed that [Paul] should have written in polished Greek to the Hebrews, while all his life he had been writing to the Hellenes in a style abounding with rugged and barbarous Hebraisms."[72]

---

[69] J. Owen (*Hebrews*, 1:83–87) has the best discussion of this suggestion, but his conclusion is excessive: "I have insisted the longer upon this testimony, because, in my judgment, it is sufficient of itself to determine this controversy."

[70] C. Forster (*Apostolical Authority*, 38–39) thought 2 Pet 3:15–16 alluded to Heb. 5:11; 6:12; 9:26,28; 10:39. He concluded that Peter either unconsciously or consciously "imitated" Paul, and this proves that Peter had previously studied all the Pauline Letters, including Hebrews.

[71] F. F. Bruce, *The Epistle to the Hebrews*, NICNT (Grand Rapids: Eerdmans, 1964), xli.

[72] F. Godet, *A Commentary on the Gospel of Luke*, 4th ed., trans. E. W. Shalders and M. D. Cusin, 2 vols. in one (New York: Funk & Wagnalls, 1887), 320.

A certain similarity of style between chap. 13 and the writings of Paul has led some scholars to make the unlikely suggestion that Paul may have added this chapter to the letter.[73] Others have suggested that it is a fragment from an otherwise unknown Pauline epistle. However, chapter 13 gives no hint of having been added to Hebrews by Paul or anyone else. F. Filson has conclusively shown it to be an integral part of the text.[74]

It should be recognized, however, that stylistic comparisons by themselves are inconclusive. It can be demonstrated that an author may change his style deliberately to accommodate his subject matter. Furthermore, over the period of an author's life, his style may alter to such a degree that one could speak of an author's "early" writings and his "late" writings not only in terms of a change in thought patterns and content, but also in terms of style. Therefore, it would be overstating the case to base on stylistic comparisons a suggestion that Paul *could not* have written Hebrews.

But literary studies have shown that stylistic comparisons can establish a degree of probability regarding authorship. So, although I agree that the Pauline Epistles do betray certain stylistic features that tend to corroborate Pauline authorship of that corpus, the epistle to the Hebrews is stylistically so unlike Paul's Epistles that we can say that Paul probably did not write Hebrews.[75] F. D. V. Narborough stated, "I Peter is more Pauline than Hebrews, and yet no one would dream of assigning I Peter to St. Paul."[76] And DeSilva pointedly remarked, "To suggest that Paul was simply writing in a different style, as if preaching in a synagogue, is a desperate attempt to hold on to Pauline authorship."[77]

Fourth, Paul's theological focus is often different from the author of Hebrews.[78] As has been noted by many, there is a marked absence of characteristic Pauline thought, themes, and motifs. Delitzsch, in his two-volume commentary on Hebrews, stated, "It is, and must remain, surprising that as we dissect the Epistle we nowhere meet with those ideas which are, so to speak, the very arteries of Paul's spiritual system."[79]

---

[73] J. Conder, *Literary History,* 466.

[74] Filson, '*Yesterday*,' 15–16.

[75] R. Brown noted that the Greek style of Hebrews is "very different from Paul's" and that when parallels in phrasing and theology are cited, differences exist in most of them (*New Testament Introduction* [New York: Doubleday, 1997], 694).

[76] F. D. V. Narborough, *The Epistle to the Hebrews* (Oxford: Clarendon, 1930), 9.

[77] D. DeSilva, *Perseverance in Gratitude*, 24.

[78] For theological differences see Guthrie, *New Testament Introduction*, 672–73; B. F. Westcott, *The Epistle to the Hebrews* (Grand Rapids: Eerdmans, 1955 reprint), lxxvii–lxxviii; Moulton and Milligan, *The Vocabulary of the Greek New Testament* (Grand Rapids: Eerdmans, 1952), 24–26; and Lindars, *The Theology of the Letter to the Hebrews* (Cambridge: Cambridge University Press, 1991). This should not be interpreted to mean that Hebrews and Paul are "at odds" doctrinally. In fact, in their underlying concepts, they are similar in many areas.

[79] F. Delitzsch, *Commentary on the Epistle to the Hebrews* (trans. T. L. Kingsbury; Grand Rapids: Eerdmans, 1871, 1952 reprint), 2:412.

Paul and the author of Hebrews are not in conflict, but there is a different "feel" to Hebrews when compared to the Pauline Epistles.[80] For example, Paul's Letters never refer to Jesus as a priest, though he did use concepts from the law of Moses such as Passover, the mercy seat, and Jesus as an offering to God. Paul placed more emphasis on the method of Christ's sacrifice, whereas the author of Hebrews focused more on the result.[81] Some find it difficult to conceive of Paul writing Heb 2:17 because his theology of the cross eliminated the need for a high priest, the temple, and the Day of Atonement.[82] The way Paul thought about "the seed of Abraham" in his epistles and the approach taken by Hebrews and Luke in Luke-Acts are distinctly different.[83] D'Angelo noted Paul's stress on the discontinuity between the Mosaic covenant and the new covenant, whereas the author of Hebrews viewed the law as stressing more of the continuity between the two covenants.[84] Hauck pointed out that Paul never used the verb *hupomenein* ("persevere") for the sufferings of Christ as does the author of Hebrews.[85] Again, such examples should not be used to argue that Paul could not have written Hebrews, but that it is unlikely.

Fifth, the writer of Hebrews seemed to identify himself with second generation Christians, something that Paul would probably never have done: "How shall we escape if we ignore such a great salvation? This salvation, which was first announced by the Lord, was confirmed to us by those who heard him." (2:3). Elsewhere in his epistles Paul identified himself as an "apostle," the prerequisite of which was to have been an eyewitness of the resurrected Christ. In Acts 9, Luke recounts the experience of Paul on the road to Damascus when he met Jesus Christ and became a Christian. Paul referred later to this experience of salvation in the context of his apostleship when he said that he was "one born out of due time" (1 Cor 15:8, KJV). Nowhere in the 13 Letters does Paul ever refer to himself as the writer of Hebrews does in 2:3. Thus, it is unlikely that Paul would have written such a statement (see Gal 1:11–12).

---

[80] N. T. Wright's statement makes the point colorfully: "Entering the world of the letter to the Hebrews after a close study of Paul is a bit like listening to Monteverdi after listening to Bach" (*The New Testament and the People of God* [Minneapolis: Fortress, 1992], 409).

[81] J. E. Reynolds, "A Comparative Study of the Exodus Motif in the Epistle to the Hebrews" (Th.D. dissertation, Southwestern Baptist Theological Seminary, 1976), 207–8.

[82] See R. Anderson, "The Cross and Atonement from Luke to Hebrews," *EvQ* 71.2 (1999): 141.

[83] See the discussion in J. Chance, "The Seed of Abraham and the People of God: A Study of Two Pauls," *SBLSP* 32, ed. E. Lovering (Atlanta: Scholars Press, 1993), 384–411. Chance noted that in Luke-Acts, unlike Paul in Galatians and Romans, no character, including the narrator, refers to Gentiles as "children, seed, descendents, sons, daughters, or any other similar term of Abraham or any of the other ancestors of Israel. The seed of Abraham is the Jewish people. The gentiles are simply not in view" (p. 406). He later stated that Luke-Acts operates within a traditional Judaistic social context. Of course, Hebrews takes a similar approach as Luke-Acts here.

[84] M. R. D'Angelo, *Moses in the Letter to the Hebrews*, SBLDS 42 (Missoula, MT: Scholars Press, 1979), 256.

[85] F. Hauck, "ὑπομένω," *TDNT* 4:588.

Sixth, the unusual apology in Heb 13:22 ("Bear with my word of exhortation, for I have written you only a short letter") does not fit well with the length of the thirteen Pauline Letters. In fact, Hebrews is longer than eleven of the thirteen Pauline Epistles (only Romans and 1 Corinthians are longer) and more than twice as long as the average length of a Pauline epistle. Unless Paul had addressed other epistles of considerably greater length to this same readership, it does not seem likely that he would have written such a statement.

Seventh, Paul's treatment of the Old Testament differs from what we find in Hebrews. As an example, consider the quotation of Ps 8:6[7] in 1 Cor 15:27, Eph 1:22, and Heb 2:7. The Pauline quotations correspond with each other. Both have the same reading and the same comparison with that of the LXX. Both quote Ps 8:6b[7b], starting and ending at the same place. The author of Hebrews, however, showed three major differences here. First, he started the quotation much earlier (Ps 8:4[5]) but ends with the quotation in the same place. This longer version is probably an indication that he independently reworked Ps 8:6[7] from the early Christian tradition from which he received it.[86] Second, the reading of the section from Ps 8:6b[7b] in Heb 2:8 corresponds closely with the reading of the LXX against Paul's wording in 1 Cor. 15:27 and Eph 1:22. Third, Hebrews lacks the section from Ps 8:6a[7a] in the LXX, which is present in the MT.[87]

Another interesting example is Paul's quotation of Hab 2:4 in Rom 1:17 and Gal 3:11 as compared to the same quotation in Heb 10:37–38. In Romans and Galatians, Paul omitted the pronoun *mou* from the LXX text of the quotation ("The righteous one will live through *my* [God's] faith/faithfulness").[88] However, the textual tradition of Heb 10:37–38 is strongly in favor of the use of the pronoun by the author of Hebrews. In fact, Manson commended the author of Hebrews because he did not succumb to what he called the pressure of the Pauline textual tradition in quoting Hab 2:4.[89] In quoting the Old Testament, the author of Hebrews never used the formula "it is written," which is thoroughly, although not exclusively, Pauline.[90]

While there is some historical and internal evidence that Paul could have written Hebrews, the many examples of dissimilarity, coupled with the weak historical testimony to Pauline authorship, indicate that it is probable that Paul did not

86 D. Koch, *Die Schrift als Zeuge des Evangeliums: Untersuchungen zur Verwendung und zum Verständnis der Schrift bei Paulus*, BHT 69 (Tübingen: J. C. B. Mohr [Paul Siebeck], 1986), 245.

87 G. J. Steyn, "Some Observations about the Vorlage of Ps 8:5–7 in Heb 2:6–8," *Verbum Et Ecclesia* 24.2 (2003): 508–9.

88 See T. George, *Galatians*, NAC (Nashville: Broadman & Holman, 1994), 234.

89 T. W. Manson ("The Argument from Prophecy," *JTS* 46 [1945]: 135; R. Gheorghita, *The Role of the Septuagint in Hebrews* [Tübingen: Mohr/Siebeck, 2003]), 177 noted that UBS[4] gives the textual reading a "B" evaluation, upgraded from a "C" in the third edition.

90 See Bleek, *Introduction*, 2:101, on differences between Hebrews and Paul in the use of quote formulae.

write Hebrews.[91] New Testament scholarship has been reluctant to distance the epistle to the Hebrews completely from Pauline influence,[92] although it has also been reluctant to identify the epistle as Paul's. It would seem that the best solution to the evidence of the epistle itself would be to deny Pauline authorship, but to acknowledge that it is likely that the writer was considerably influenced by Paul or associated with the Pauline circle. Of the names suggested for the authorship of Hebrews by the early church fathers, they all possessed the distinction of having at one time or another been a part of the Pauline circle.[93]

B. Witherington, based on his comparison of Galatians with Hebrews, denied Pauline authorship, but suggested it is "likely" that the author of Hebrews reflects Pauline influence, particularly from Galatians, at key points in the argument. He considered it also likely that the author of Hebrews was a part of the larger Pauline circle.[94]

B. S. Childs noted the important indirect link between Paul and Hebrews that the early church recognized but misinterpreted when it sought to solve the issue historically. Because the writer was a co-worker with Timothy, Hebrews should not be assigned to a late stage in the development of the post-apostolic church. It "functions canonically as distinct and yet complementary to the Pauline corpus." He went on to note that historically, Manson may be right in his connection of the letter with Stephen, but canonically the letter's major function is in relation to the Pauline corpus.[95] This connection with Paul actually aids the arguments for Luke, Barnabas, and Apollos, since they all are a part of the Pauline circle. But, of course, none was so consistently associated with Paul as was Luke. Furthermore, the connection with Stephen would be further evidence for Luke. For Schnelle, the whole issue comes down to the relationship of Hebrews to the Pauline school, with two possibilities. Either the author belonged to the Pauline circle, or Hebrews was composed from the beginning as an anonymous writing with no intent of it being linked to Paul.[96]

---

[91] R. Brown (*An Introduction to the New Testament* [New York: Doubleday, 1997], 694) stated that the evidence against Paul having written Hebrews is "overwhelming."

[92] For example, H. Windisch (*Der Hebräerbrief*, 2nd ed., HNT 14, ed. H. Lietzmann [Tübingen: Mohr/Siebeck, 1931], 128–29) considered the author of Hebrews to be nearer to Pauline thought and themes than any other NT writer, but he rejected Pauline authorship.

[93] In recent years, discussion about whether the author belonged to the Pauline circle or not has continued. Primitive Christian tradition furnished Schröger with the basis for similarity between Paul and Hebrews ("Der Hebräerbrief—paulinisch?" in *Kontinuität und Einheit*, ed. P. G. Müller and W. Stenger [Freiburg/Basel/Vienna: Herder, 1981], 211–22). In the same year, A. Strobel (*Der Brief an die Hebräer*, 13th ed. [Göttingen: Vandenhoeck & Ruprecht, 1991]:13–14) suggested that the author might have belonged to the circle of people involved in the later Pauline missionary work. J. W. Thompson ("The Epistle to the Hebrews and the Pauline Legacy," *ResQ* 47.4 [2005]: 206) concluded that the relationship between Hebrews and the Pauline tradition was "minimal."

[94] B. Witherington III, "The Influence of Galatians on Hebrews," *NTS* 37 (1991): 146–52.

[95] B. S. Childs, *The New Testament as Canon: An Introduction* (London: SCM, 1984), 418.

[96] U. Schnelle, *History and Theology of the New Testament Writings*, trans. M. E. Boring (Minneapolis: Fortress, 1998), 380–81. Schnelle opted for the latter: "the author cannot be seen

We conclude that the best reading of the evidence suggests that Paul is not the author of Hebrews. As S. Davidson so cogently put it concerning Pauline authorship: "It is the diversity amid the similarity [with Paul's writings] which makes a different writer probable."[97] Delitzsch noted: "It breaths Paul's spirit, but it does not speak Paul's words."[98] It would seem that the present state of affairs on the subject of Pauline authorship can best be summed up by H. MacNeill and D. Guthrie. MacNeill wrote in the early twentieth century,

> In the course of this study numerous instances of contact with Pauline thought have appeared. But in every case the similarity has been somewhat superficial. The point of view and the method of presentation have been quite different. It would be exaggerating to say that the writer of this epistle was not influenced by Paul and his letters. But it is clear that this influence has been greatly exaggerated.[99]

Guthrie wrote in the latter half of the twentieth century,

> It should be noted that differences from Paul do not amount to disagreements with Paul. . . . Nor must it be supposed that these doctrinal differences necessarily exclude Pauline authorship. Yet, if they do not *require* its rejection, it must be admitted that they appear to suggest it.[100]

THE ARGUMENT FOR BARNABAS.[101] One name having the support of scholars ancient and modern is Barnabas. Tertullian presented this hypothesis and wrote in such a fashion as to imply that he had no doubts about it:

> For there is extant withal an Epistle to the Hebrews under the name of Barnabas—a man sufficiently accredited by God, as being one whom Paul has stationed next to himself in the uninterrupted observance of abstinence: Or else, I alone and Barnabas, have not we the power of working? And, of course, the Epistle of Barnabas is more generally

---

as a member of the Pauline school. It is rather the case that Hebrews represents an independent theology" (376).

[97] S. Davidson, *Introduction to the Study of the New Testament*, 1:215. He has an excellent presentation of the external (patristic) evidence for and against Pauline authorship (220–35).

[98] Delitzsch, *Hebrews*, 2:407.

[99] H. L. MacNeill, *The Christology of the Epistle to the Hebrews: Including Its Relation to the Developing Christology of the Primitive Church* (Chicago: University Press, 1914), 143.

[100] Guthrie, *New Testament Introduction*, 673.

[101] See G. Salmon, *Introduction to the New Testament*. 3rd ed. (London: John Murray, 1888), 446–48; E. Riggenbach, *Der Brief an die Hebräer*, KNT (Leipzig: A. Deichert, 1913), xl–xlii; G. Edmundson, *The Church in Rome in the First Century* (London: Longmans, Green, & Co., 1913); K. Bornhäuser, *Empfänger und Verfasser des Briefes an die Hebräer,* BFCT 35/3 (Gütersloh: Bertelsmann, 1932), 75–80. J. A. T. Robinson (*Redating the New Testament* [London: SCM, 1976], 217–20) believed Barnabas should be given serious consideration as the author. For arguments in favor of Barnabas, see P. E. Hughes, *Hebrews*, 28–29.

> received among the Churches than that apocryphal Shepherd of adulterers.[102]

Additional support for Barnabas is found in the fourth century *Tractatus Origenis* by Gregory of Elvira who wrote, "The most holy Barnabas says, 'Through him we offer to God the sacrifice of lips that acknowledge his name.'"[103] This is an allusion to Hebrews 13:15, so Gregory was attributing Hebrews to Barnabas. The fourth-century bishop of Brescia in northern Italy, Filaster, also mentioned Hebrews as having been written by Barnabas.[104] Jerome (c. 345–419) pointed out that Hebrews was received as Paul's, yet many considered it to be the work of Barnabas, Luke, or Clement.[105] The sixth-century Codex Claromantus lists "the Epistle of Barnabas" among the canonical books. The stichometric figures for this epistle are very close to Hebrews, and hence Westcott suggested that it is likely they are one and the same.[106]

While certainly not conclusive, there is patristic evidence to suggest Barnabas could be the author. This evidence is definitely identified with the Western (Latin) tradition, and it was in the West that the Pauline authorship met with its strongest denial.

Scholars offer several strands of evidence to support Barnabas as author, and these are the main ones. (1) He was a Levite of Cyprus (Acts 4:36) and hence his interest in the Old Testament ritual and sacrificial system (as is found in Hebrews) would be natural. (2) Barnabas was a member of the Pauline circle and would probably have contact with Timothy since Timothy came from the area evangelized by both Barnabas and Paul (see Acts 16:1).[107] (3) The Hellenistic outlook reflected in Hebrews is considered by some to suggest Barnabas as the author. When the Antiochene Hellenists were evangelized, it was Barnabas who was sent by the church at Jerusalem to coordinate this new thrust of the gospel (Acts 11:19–26). (4) Barnabas is called the "son of exhortation" (Acts 4:36), and the epistle to the Hebrews is called by its author a "word of exhortation" (Heb 13:22). (5) The Pauline flavor of the epistle could be accounted for on the supposition that Barnabas, as a traveling companion with Paul on his first missionary journey, would likely share the same outlook and conceptual framework as Paul. Thiersche argued that Hebrews was jointly authored by Paul and Barnabas with Barnabas as the primary author. Thus, Barnabas consented to the conclusion by Paul who in this way adopted the

---

[102] Tertullian, *On Modesty*, 20.

[103] Cited in Hughes, *Hebrews*, 25.

[104] Filaster, *Haeresibus,* 89.

[105] Jerome, *Lives of Illustrious Men*, 5.

[106] Westcott, *Hebrews*, xxviii–xxix. "Stichometry" is the term applied to the measurement of ancient texts into lines of fixed length.

[107] J. Owen (*Exposition of the Epistle to the Hebrews*, 1:70) questioned this evidence, noting Timothy was the companion of the writer and was unknown to Barnabas since he joined Paul after Paul and Barnabas separated.

whole document.[108] Based in part on the repeated use of "we" and "us" in the book, especially in 6:11 and 13:18, Dan Wallace has suggested Hebrews was co-authored by Barnabas and Apollos, with Barnabas as the main author and Apollos serving as his assistant.[109]

The high visibility of Barnabas in Acts coupled with his Levitical background makes him an obvious candidate for Hebrews, especially if it were written to the Jerusalem church. However, we have no extant writings of Barnabas to compare with Hebrews since the so-called *Epistle of Barnabas* is considered spurious. Bleek called Tertullian's view "an accidental oversight on Tertullian's part" arising from his confusion of Hebrews with the *Epistle of Barnabas*. Of course, this does not mean that it is impossible that Barnabas wrote it, merely that we have no way to do any comparative studies.

D. Guthrie,[110] following McNeile-Williams,[111] argued against Barnabas on the basis that if it had been known that he was the author, how is one to explain the rise of the Pauline hypothesis? The suggestion that Paul's name would have been appended to the epistle in order to gain canonicity is not, according to Guthrie, "conceivable."

Another argument against Barnabas may be the way in which the author of Hebrews has treated Levi and the tithe in Hebrews 7. The historical debates that existed in the first century between the priests and the Levites on this subject cannot be dealt with here,[112] but it is clear that a Levite would hardly have treated the subject in so priestly a fashion as appears to be the case with Hebrews.

Bargil Pixner has recently argued for Barnabas as the author with the recipients being Qumranian priests whom he identified with those converted to Christianity in Acts 6:7 ("a large number of priests became obedient to the faith").[113] Spicq and others championed this view of the recipients. Since Barnabas was a Levite, he would have reason and ability to write to such a group a letter like Hebrews.

---

[108] Thiersche, *Programme* issued at Marburg, 1847, *De Epistola ad Hebraeos*, cited in Bleek, *Introduction,* 2:112.

[109] D. Wallace, "Hebrews," *Biblical Studies Foundation* (http://www.bible.org/page.php?page_id=1360). Windisch (*Hebräerbrief,* 120) also posited a co-author for Hebrews.

[110] Guthrie, *New Testament Introduction,* 675.

[111] A. H. McNeile, *Introduction to the New Testament*, 2nd ed., rev. C. S. C. Williams (Oxford: Clarendon, 1953), 237.

[112] See W. Horbury, "The Aaronic Priesthood in the Epistle to the Hebrews," *JSNT* 19 (1983): 43–71.

[113] B. Pixner, "The Jerusalem Essenes, Barnabas and the Letter to the Hebrews," in *Qumranica Mogilanensia*, ed. Z. J. Kapera (Krakow: Enigma, 1992), 6:167–78. He noted that Qumran's opposition to the temple was directed against the Hasmonean high priests, whom they detested as illegitimate.

THE ARGUMENT FOR APOLLOS.[114] The popular theory that Apollos wrote Hebrews was first suggested by Luther.[115] None of the patristics opted for him, not even the Alexandrian school that claimed Apollos as its prime leader. I find it strange that his name would not be suggested as a possible author if the early church fathers had any reason to think that he could have written Hebrews. That he was not mentioned in connection with Hebrews weakens Luther's suggestion.

Those who argue for Apollos do so based on his description given by Luke in Acts and by Paul in the letter of 1 Corinthians. He was apparently a great orator and had "a thorough knowledge of the Scriptures" (Acts 18:24), two characteristics that appear to be true of the author of Hebrews. He was a member of the Pauline circle and was closely associated with Timothy (1 Cor 16:10–12) as was the author of Hebrews (Heb 13:23).

Apollos's connection with Alexandria would seem to explain the so-called Alexandrian coloring of the book. However, scholars have increasingly called this point into question. R. Williamson brought the most serious challenge against the alleged Platonism of the author of Hebrews, as well as the alleged influence of Philo.[116] He showed that the Old Testament Levitical cultus and typological milieu furnish a better explanation for the background of the thought of the author than Alexandrian influence.[117] He further catalogued a host of differences between Alexandrian thought and Hebrews. Consequently, what was once considered a strong argument in favor of Apollos has been severely weakened.

Two major problems, then, seem to preclude Apollos as having been the author. First, the lack of any support from early church tradition; and second,

---

[114] See F. Bleek, *Der Brief an die Hebräer erlautert durch Einleitung, Übersetzung und fortlaufenden Kommentar* (Berlin: Dümmler, 1828), 1:423–30; T. W. Manson, "The Problem of the Epistle to the Hebrews," *BJRL* 32 (1949): 1–17; C. Spicq, "l'Épître aux Hébreux," 365–90; Montefiore, *Hebrews*, 9–28; H. Attridge, *Hebrews*, 4 (n. 28); R. Nash, "The Notion of Mediator in Alexandrian Judaism and the Epistle to the Hebrews," *WTJ* 40 (1978): 89–115; G. Guthrie, "The Case for Apollos as the Author of Hebrews," *FM* 18 (2002): 41–56; L. T. Johnson, *Hebrews*, 41–44, and B. Witherington, *Letters and Homilies for Jewish Christians: A Socio-Rhetorical Commentary on Hebrews, James and Jude* (Downers Grove: InterVarsity, 2007), 22–24. Montefiore's argument that Hebrews was written by Apollos from Ephesus to the Corinthian church in AD 52 has been thoroughly critiqued in L. D. Hurst, "Apollos, Hebrews, and Corinth: Bishop Montefiore's Theory Examined," *SJT* 38 (1985): 505–13.

[115] See Koester (*Hebrews*, 35, n. 53) for detailed information on Luther's proposal. Koester noted that Luther's proposal actually first appeared in a sermon on Heb 1:1–4 which was published in 1522 (*Sermons* 7.167). See also Luther's *Commentary on Genesis* (1545). Luther attributed Hebrews to Apollos based on the supposed Alexandrian influence on the book. This has been shown to be vastly overrated in recent years, weakening the theory for Apollos significantly.

[116] See his *Philo and the Epistle to the Hebrews* (Leiden: Brill, 1970).

[117] Cf. W. Horbury, "The Aaronic Priesthood in the Epistle to the Hebrews," *JSNT* (1983): 43–71: "The author's closeness to Josephus rather than Philo on the issue of Levi and the tithe might suggest a 'marginal consideration' in favor of a Palestinian rather than an Alexandrian authorship" (68). The same could be said for the recipients as well.

the lack of any extant works of Apollos with which we may compare Hebrews.[118]

THE ARGUMENT FOR LUKE. As already mentioned, the patristic evidence suggests that Luke was in some way a candidate for the authorship of Hebrews. The reason for this appears to be the resemblance of style between Luke-Acts and Hebrews. The history of scholarship concerning Luke's possible involvement in the production of Hebrews reveals three hypotheses. First, Luke translated into Greek a Hebrew or Aramaic original written by Paul (Clement of Alexandria and others). Second, Luke was the co-author of Hebrews with Paul as the mind behind the epistle. Luke wrote down his thoughts, but there are varying views on how much freedom he possessed in the process (Hug,[119] Ebrard,[120] etc.). Third, Luke was the independent author of Hebrews (Delitzsch[121] and Eagar[122]).

Few, if any, modern scholars would argue that Hebrews is a Greek translation of a Hebrew or Aramaic original. The view that Luke could have helped Paul write Hebrews was popular in the nineteenth century, but it fell into disrepute in the twentieth century due to the increasing weight of the anti-Pauline hypothesis and the combination of two converging positions: (1) that Luke-Acts was written late in the first century and not necessarily by Luke the traveling companion of Paul; and (2) that Hebrews is likewise to be dated after-AD 70.[123]

---

118 Harnack's theory of Priscilla's authorship is intertwined with the role that Priscilla and Aquila played in Apollos's Christian instruction in Acts. See F. Schiele, "Harnack's 'Probabilia' Concerning the Address and the Author of the Epistle to the Hebrews," *AJT* 9.1 (1905): 290–308. Schiele attempted to further Harnack's hypothesis by arguing, as Harnack did, that the epistle was written to a Roman audience. See the excellent critique of Harnack's position in C. C. Torrey, "The Authorship and Character of the So-Called 'Epistle to the Hebrews," *JBL* 30 (1911): 137–56. R. Hoppin (*Priscilla: Author of the Epistle to the Hebrews* [New York: Exposition, 1969]) provided the most elaborate and best argument available for Priscilla as the author. Hoppin wrongly translated Heb 13:22 as "only to a slight extent have I given you orders" and interpreted the verse as Priscilla's apologetic from one who is hesitant to claim spiritual authority in the church (22). See her more recent attempt in "The Epistle to the Hebrews is Priscilla's Letter," *A Feminist Companion to the Catholic Epistles and Hebrews*, ed. A. J. Levine with M. Robbins, Feminist Companion to the New Testament and Early Christian Writings 8 (London: T&T Clark, 2004), 147–70. See the discussion on this issue by C. B. Kittredge, "Hebrews," in *Searching the Scriptures: A Feminist Commentary*, ed. E. S. Fiorenza (New York: Crossroad, 1994), 2:430–34. There is nothing beyond very limited circumstantial evidence to link Priscilla with Hebrews.

119 J. L. Hug, *Introduction to the New Testament*, trans. D. Fosdick from the 3rd German ed. (Andover: Gould & Newman, 1836).

120 J. H. A. Ebrard, *Exposition of the Epistle to the Hebrews*, trans. and rev. A. C. Kendrick, *Biblical Commentary on the New Testament*, ed. H. Olshausen (New York: Sheldon, Blakeman & Co., 1858), 615–23.

121 F. Delitzsch, *Hebrews*, 2:412–16.

122 A. R. Eagar, "The Authorship of the Epistle to the Hebrews," *Expositor* (6th series) 10 (1904): 74–80, 110–23.

123 Among the commentaries on Hebrews produced in the past few years, there is no evidence of any interest in investigating further the possibility of Lukan authorship of Hebrews. Ellingworth

Evidence of Heb 13:23–24 and the Pastorals. Hebrews 13:23–24 contains at least six clues concerning the background of the letter. First, the author and readers were associated with Timothy, since he is referred to as "our brother." Second, both the author and Timothy were away from the location of the readers and plan to travel to the readers' location shortly. Third, Timothy had apparently been imprisoned or at least detained in some form of custody and then released. Fourth, the author was apparently in the same locale as Timothy, but was himself apparently not imprisoned. Fifth, the recipients are exhorted to greet their leaders, implying a locale of considerable population with enough people to have a church with multiple leaders. It may be that this is evidence that the writer was not addressing an entire church, but rather a smaller group within the church. Sixth, whether writing from Italy, or away from Italy, the writer sent greetings from Italian Christians who are either—along with the writer—somewhere in Italy or Italian expatriates.

The groundwork is now laid for a historical reconstruction of the circumstances surrounding the writing of Hebrews. I propose that Luke wrote Hebrews from Rome after the death of Paul and before the destruction of Jerusalem in AD 70. Scriptural evidence for this thesis can be adduced upon a correlation of the statements made in the Pastoral Epistles with the text of Hebrews. While imprisoned in Rome, Paul penned 2 Timothy around AD 66 or 67, in which he hinted at his coming execution. Addressing Timothy, Paul said, "Do your best to come to me quickly" (2 Tim 4:9). Either before Timothy arrived or shortly thereafter, Paul was beheaded and then Timothy was probably imprisoned. Hebrews 13:23 says Timothy had been "set free," most naturally implying an imprisonment. The description of Timothy as "our brother" in this verse is reminiscent of Paul and links both Timothy and our author with the Pauline circle. In 2 Tim 4:11 Paul stated, "Only Luke is with me," thus placing Luke in Paul's company at or near the time of his death in Rome, probably AD 67 but no later than June 9 of AD 68, the date of Nero's suicide and the *terminus ad quem* for Paul's death.

Stylistic Evidence. An examination of the New Testament literature reveals that the writings of Luke and Hebrews alone approach the standard of Classical Greek style.[124] The similarity in vocabulary and style was noted as early as the second century. Hebrews shares 53 words that occur elsewhere in

---

was little impressed with the linguistic similarities noted by Spicq and others (*Hebrews*, 13–14). Attridge briefly mentioned the patristic statements regarding Luke as a possible translator of Paul's Hebrew original, but then he was inexplicably silent on the history of scholarship regarding independent Lukan authorship (*Hebrews*, xlix). Lane (*Hebrews 1–8*) devoted less than three pages to the issue of authorship.

[124] See N. Turner, *Style*, in J. H. Moulton, *A Grammar of New Testament Greek* (Edinburgh: T&T Clark, 1976), 4:106–13. S. Davidson (*An Introduction to the Study of the New Testament*, 209) noted: "We do not maintain that the language of Hebrews is free from Hebraisms, but that the diction is purer than Paul's. In respect to purity, it stands on a level with the latter half of the Acts."

the NT only in Luke-Acts, a significant number. In fact, two-thirds of the total vocabulary of Hebrews occur in Luke-Acts. C. P. M. Jones examined the lexical similarities between Luke-Acts and Hebrews and with balanced judgment explained their significance:

> But when all deductions have been made, the verbal correspondences are so numerous [between Luke-Acts and Hebrews] that a substantial area of common phraseology remains . . . which may well be indicative of a closer kinship in the presence of other corroborating factors.[125]

Westcott pointed out that "no impartial student can fail to be struck by the frequent use [in Hebrews] of words characteristic of St. Luke among writers of the New Testament."[126] He also wrote concerning the stylistic resemblance between the Lukan corpus and Hebrews,

> It has been already seen that the earliest scholars who speak of the Epistle notice its likeness in style to the writings of St. Luke; and when every allowance has been made for coincidences which consist in forms of expression which are found also in the LXX, or in other writers of the NT, or in late Greek generally, the likeness is unquestionably remarkable.[127]

Twenty-five years before Hobart's *Medical Language of Saint Luke* (1882),[128] Delitzsch, in an appendix at the conclusion of his two-volume commentary on Hebrews, suggested that the medical terminology found therein might serve as evidence for Lukan authorship. Believing Luke to have been the independent author, although having written at Paul's behest and having composed Hebrews from Pauline statements, Delitzsch argued that Luke's vocation as a physician harmonized well with the form of Hebrews in that the letter contains passages on anatomy (4:12), diet (5:12–14), and therapy (12:12–13).[129]

While it is true that in 1912 Cadbury challenged Hobart's evidence and conclusion,[130] not everyone accepted Cadbury's conclusion. A. T. Robertson argued that the weight of evidence was more in favor of Hobart.[131] Robertson's

---

[125] C. P. M. Jones, "The Epistle to the Hebrews and the Lucan Writings," in *Studies in the Gospels: Essays in Memory of R. H. Lightfoot*, ed. D. E. Nineham (Oxford: Basil Blackwell, 1955), 117–18. Compare this with the 56 words that are unique to Hebrews and the Pauline Letters.

[126] B. F. Westcott, *The Epistle to the Hebrews* (Grand Rapids: Eerdmans, 1955 reprint), xlviii.

[127] Ibid., lxxvi.

[128] W. K. Hobart, *The Medical Language of St. Luke: A Proof from Internal Evidence that "The Gospel According to St. Luke" and "The Acts of the Apostles" Were Written by the Same Person, and that the Writer Was a Medical Man* (Dublin: Hodges, Figgis, 1882; Grand Rapids: Baker, 1954 reprint).

[129] Delitzsch, *Hebrews,* 2:415.

[130] H. J. Cadbury, *The Style and Literary Method of Luke* (New York: Kraus reprint, 1969).

[131] A. T. Robertson, *Luke the Historian in Light of Research* (Edinburgh: T&T Clark, 1920), 12. For the entire discussion, see pp. 90–102.

critique of Cadbury has been left unanswered in much of the literature since his day. J. M. Creed, N. Geldenhuys, and W. Hendriksen have written commentaries on Luke's Gospel and agree with Robertson's assessment.[132] Likewise, C. Hemer has argued that Cadbury's critique of Hobart "does not amount to disproof of its essential contention."[133]

It has long been recognized that the style of the Pastoral Epistles has much in common with Luke-Acts. The probability that Luke was Paul's amanuensis for the Pastoral Epistles has been adjudged to be quite strong by a number of scholars.[134] The significance of this for the theory of Lukan authorship of Hebrews lies in the long-standing observation that, while Hebrews diverges significantly from the Pauline Epistles especially in matters of style, it nevertheless shares a certain similarity with them. W. H. Simcox made the observation that

> [Hebrews] has several words and phrases in common, not with St. Paul's writings generally, but with the isolated and peculiar group of the Pastoral Epistles. If this stood alone, it might at most serve so far to narrow speculation as to the authorship of our Ep., as to suggest that it is by a man whose intercourse with St. Paul had been chiefly towards the close of the latter's life.[135]

---

[132] J. M. Creed, *The Gospel According to St. Luke* (London: Macmillan, 1942), xix; N. Geldenhuys, *Commentary on the Gospel of Luke*, NICNT (Grand Rapids: Baker, 1951), 19–21; W. Hendriksen, *Exposition of the Gospel According to Luke,* NTC (Grand Rapids: Baker, 1978), 4–5.

[133] C. Hemer, *The Book of Acts in the Setting of Hellenistic History,* ed. C. Gempf (Tübingen: Mohr/Siebeck, 1989), 310–12.

[134] See C. F. D. Moule, "The Problem of the Pastoral Epistles: A Reappraisal," *BJRL* 47 (1965): 430–52; and R. Riesner, "Once More: Luke-Acts and the Pastoral Epistles," in *History and Exegesis: New Testament Essays in Honor of Dr. E. Earle Ellis for His 80th Birthday*, ed. S. Son (New York: T&T Clark, 2006), 239–58. On Paul's use of an amanuensis, see E. R. Richards, *The Secretary in the Letters of Paul* (Tübingen: Mohr/Siebeck, 1991); and M. Prior, *Paul the Letter Writer and the Second Letter to Timothy*, JSNTSup 23 (Sheffield: JSOT, 1989), 156. Richards argued cogently that Paul's references to others in the salutation and benediction of his letters was more than a literary nicety; instead, these references indicated that they had some subordinate role in the writing of the letter. This is supported by E. Ellis (*Prophecy and Hermeneutic in Early Christianity* [Grand Rapids: Baker, 1993]); C. K. Barrett (*A Commentary on the First Epistle to the Corinthians* [Peabody: Hendrickson, 1968]); and H. A. W. Meyer (*Critical and Exegetical Handbook to the Epistles to the Corinthians* [New York: Funk & Wagnalls, 1884], 154, n. 113, 114, 115). See the discussion in M. Prior (*Paul the Letter Writer and the Second Letter to Timothy* [Sheffield: JSOT, 1989], 45), who considered Timothy a co-author with Paul of 2 Corinthians, Philippians, Colossians, Philemon, and with Paul and Silas in 1 and 2 Thessalonians; thus his role in some of the Pauline Letters was "quite significant." Prior proposed the possibility that the differences between the Pastorals and the other Pauline Letters could be explained if Paul wrote the Pastoral Epistles alone with no secretarial assistance. A better possibility, which explains the similarity to Lukan style, is that Luke was the amanuensis, contributor, or possibly even a co-author with Paul.

[135] W. H. Simcox, *The Writers of the New Testament* (London: Hodder & Stoughton, 1902), 47.

Simcox noted that we are led a step further in this matter when we observe,

> [A] number of words and phrases are common to the Pastoral Epp. and Hebrews with St. John, or to Heb. and St. Luke only. Our first thought might be, that Origen was right—that St. Luke was the author of Heb. with or without suggestions from St. Paul, and that he may have been (in view of 2 Tim.iv.11 no one else could be) the amanuensis, or something more, of the Pastoral Epp.[136]

Although Simcox himself rejected Lukan authorship of Hebrews, he indicated that Luke's vocabulary has more in common with Hebrews than with any other canonical writer and that the Pastoral Epistles come next in degree of similarity.[137]

So according to stylistic evidence, the Pastoral Epistles are most like Luke-Acts and Hebrews in the New Testament. A possible correlation of this evidence would be to suggest that Luke is the independent author of Luke-Acts and Hebrews and that he was the amanuensis of the Pastorals as well.

A. R. Eagar suggested that the arguments used in favor of the Pauline hypothesis of the authorship of Hebrews are equally as strong in favor of Luke. Furthermore, the objections that make the Pauline hypothesis unlikely (such as anonymity and stylistic considerations) do not apply to the Lukan hypothesis. He concluded,

> [A]ll such arguments for the Pauline authorship of an Epistle as may also be applied to S. Luke become arguments for the Lucan authorship, since they are not affected, in his case, by the objections that make it impossible to apply them to S. Paul.[138]

He went on to argue that where Paul would be most likely influenced by Luke, he would demonstrate the strongest traces of Lukan peculiarities. Where Luke was not working with documents—or at least with documents that were not written in Greek—the individuality of his style would be most marked. From evidence in the New Testament, Eagar argued that Luke had some stylistic influence on Paul at the time of the writing of Colossians, 2 Corinthians,

---

[136] Ibid.

[137] Ibid., 52–53. See esp. his appendix (pp. 116–53) where he compares the vocabulary of Luke with the later Pauline and Catholic Letters as well as Hebrews. Cf. Feuillet, ("La doctrine des Epitres Pastorales et leursaffinites avec l'oeuvre lucanienne," *RThom* 78 [1978]: 163–74) who made this comparison and discussed it at length, concluding that the Pastorals were redacted by Luke. Also id., "Le dialogue avec le monde non-chretien dans les epitres pastorales et l'Épître aux Hebreux. Premiere partie: les epitres pastorales," *Esprit et Vie* 98 (1988): 125–28; and "Le dialogue avec le monde non-chretien dans les epitres pastorales et L'Épître aux Hebreux. Deuxieme partie: 'Épître aux Hebreux," *Esprit et Vie* 98 (1988): 152–59, where he continued the argument for Lukan redaction of the Pastorals as well as the similar Hellenistic background for the Pastorals and Hebrews.

[138] Eagar, "Authorship," 74–80, 110–23.

and the Pastorals due to their being together. He noted that in the sections of Luke-Acts where we might expect the individuality of Luke's style to be the strongest there is a large number of active verbals. Likewise, where Paul is said to have had Luke in his company at the time of writing, there is a higher percentage of active verbals in these Pauline Epistles. He concluded that the use of active verbals in the Pauline Letters "was probably due to the influence of S. Luke; and, as words of this class are more numerous in Hebrews than in any Pauline document, this deduction is obviously of some value in determining the authorship of our Epistle."[139]

There is a certain "academic" training that Luke evinces in his two-volume work. It is well recognized that the author of Hebrews likewise possessed an academic background. M. Hengel made this correlation at one point in discussing the way the Synoptic writers handled their quotations of Ps 110:1. He pointed out that neither Matthew nor Mark used the last line of Ps 110:1 but rather changed it under the influence of Ps 8:6[7] (Mark 12:36; Matt 22:44), and he then explained that only Luke corrects this change (Luke 20:42–43) as does the Byzantine text and the Old Latin version of Mark and Luke. He then remarked, "As with the author of Hebrews the higher—one could say also the 'academic' training of the author Luke—is evidenced in such philological-historical 'minutia.'"[140] Likewise, Trotter concluded that Hebrews "seems to have been written by someone trained in classical rhetoric and who used Greek with the ease of a native-born speaker and writer."[141] Krodel noted how Luke "never says everything at once, but expands and unfolds earlier themes as he moves step by step from one episode to another."[142] This is also the style of the author of Hebrews.

Lukan Influence on Paul. Traditionally scholars have focused on the influence of Paul upon Luke. Perhaps in light of the shift of opinion in recent years regarding Luke as an accomplished theologian in his own right (see further below), and if the theory of the Lukan authorship of Hebrews is correct, then the time has come for the consideration of some Lukan influence on Paul. In this vein D. Seccombe stated,

> Luke and Paul do appear to be at one in seeing a connection between the turning of the nation Israel to Christ and the Parousia. (Acts 3:19f; Rom 11:12,15) Reading Acts and Romans 11 side by side, one is struck by many suggestive similarities. The interesting thing is that Acts appears the more primitive, setting out the grist from which Paul has milled his extraordinary theology of the destiny of Jew and Gentile.[143]

139 Ibid., 78.

140 M. Hengel, *Studies in Early Christology* (Edinburgh: T&T Clark, 1995), 171–72.

141 A. Trotter, *Interpreting the Epistle to the Hebrews* (Grand Rapids: Baker, 1997), 184.

142 G. A. Krodel, *Acts* ACNT (Minneapolis: Augsburg, 1986), 281.

143 "The New People of God," in *Witness to the Gospel*, 370–71. This comment has implications for dating Acts and the Pauline Letters.

J. A. T. Robinson described the author of Hebrews by saying,

> The mantle of the Apostle [Paul] has in part fallen upon the writer himself. He can address his readers with a pastoral authority superior to that of their own leaders and with a conscience clear of local involvement (Heb. 13:17f.), and yet with no personal claim to apostolic aegis [i.e., authority]. There cannot have been too many of such men around.[144]

Luke was certainly one of the few men who could be accurately described by these words. Already the author of a Gospel and the only history of the Christian church from its inception through Paul's arrest in Rome (Acts), Luke was known and loved by the many churches to which he had traveled with Paul. Also, it is probably a safe assumption that the author was to some extent acquainted with the Pauline Epistles, given the lexical similarity noted above. Who more than Luke would have such knowledge of them?

Theory of Lukan Authorship. The above references can be converged into a theory of Lukan authorship of Hebrews in the following way. Luke was still in Rome at the time of Paul's death. Timothy arrived, was imprisoned, and sometime later was released. Both were known to the Christians at Antioch, the proposed destination for the epistle. Finally, Heb 13:24 says, "Those from Italy send you their greetings." This verse is more naturally understood to mean that the Christians now in Italy send greetings to a group living elsewhere. Although it is true that "those from Italy" could refer to Italian expatriates, it seems more natural to understand it otherwise. The phrase in Greek may be translated in any of three ways: "they who are in Italy," "they who are from Italy," or "they who are away from Italy." There is a similar use of the preposition *apo* in Acts 17:13. There we read "those who are from *(apo)* Thessalonica." The reference in context is to people living in Thessalonica. In light of this usage in Acts 17:13, we have good textual evidence for translating the Hebrews phrase as "those who are in Italy."[145]

R. Hoppin pointed out the problem that develops when we accept the translation "they who are away from Italy." Why should the author, in writing to Rome, send greetings only from expatriate Italian Christians, and not from all Christians in his company or in his city at the time of writing? One possible answer is that the reference is to Jewish Christians who were expelled from Rome under the Claudian persecution around AD 49 but who have regrouped in the location of the author. However, many Jews returned to Rome upon the death of Claudius in AD 54. It seems a bit odd for the author to bypass other

---

[144] Robinson, *Redating*, 219–20.

[145] A. Nairne, *The Epistle of Paul the Apostle to the Hebrews*, CGTSC (London: Cambridge University Press, 1922), 433. He translated 13:24 as "Those who are in Italy and send their greetings with mine from Italy."

Christians in his city and mention only this group if he were writing to Rome from a locale outside Italy.[146]

When one collates the material in Hebrews that has a bearing on authorship (i.e., style of writing, the theological depth, tightness, and intricacies of the argument) and the lexical, stylistic and theological similarities between Luke-Acts and Hebrews, it becomes apparent that someone like Luke must have been the author.

Over the past 30 years Lukan scholars worldwide, through the Society of Biblical Literature and other groups and individuals, have produced indisputable evidence that the author of Luke-Acts was an individual of remarkable literary and rhetorical skill. I have benefited greatly from their published results. Although it was true in the past that scholars often minimized the literary complexity of Luke-Acts,[147] the twenty-first century is witness to a new day where the author of Luke-Acts is universally viewed as a writer of immense ability and gifts. It is no longer possible to maintain that the author of Luke-Acts is somehow "inferior" or "incapable" of having written a work such as Hebrews.

Arguments against Lukan Authorship. Three major arguments have been lodged against the Lukan authorship of Hebrews. Perhaps the most significant has been the supposition that Luke was a Gentile by background while the author of Hebrews was obviously Jewish.[148] Actually, neither of these suppositions can be maintained with airtight certainty, although it does appear quite likely that the author of Hebrews was a Jew. In the nineteenth century, it was considered virtually certain that Luke was a Gentile, and this supposition became the reason many dismissed Luke as a possible author of Hebrews. For example, Henry Alford made this interesting admission with respect to Lukan authorship of Hebrews and the supposition of Luke's Gentile background:

> If we could explain away the inference apparently unavoidable from Col 4:14, Luke's authorship of Hebrews would seem to have some support from the epistle itself. Readers of this commentary will frequently be struck by the verbal and idiomatic coincidences with the style of Luke-Acts. The argument, as resting on them, has been continually taken up and pushed forward by Delitzsch, and comes on

---

[146] Hoppin, *Priscilla*, 103. The patristics uniformly interpreted 13:24 to place the author in Italy at the time of writing. Those who argue for Rome as the place of composition include H. Braun, *An die Hebräer,* HNT 14 (Tübingen: Mohr/Siebeck, 1984), 2; Bruce, *Hebrews*, 14; E. Grässer, "Der Hebräerbrief 1938–1963," 138–236; Strobel, *Der Brief an die Hebräer*, 13; and P. Vielhauer, *Geschichte der urchristlichen Literatur,* 2nd ed. (Berlin; New York: Walter de Gruyter, 1978), 251. See Attridge (*Hebrews*, 410, n. 79) for a list of places where the expression is used idiomatically to indicate place of origin rather than separation.

[147] C. Mount, *Pauline Christianity: Luke-Acts and the Legacy of Paul* (Leiden; Boston: Brill, 2002), 67.

[148] E.g., R. Gundry, *A Survey of the New Testament*, 4th ed. (Grand Rapids: Zondervan, 2003), 459: "Luke-Acts is Gentile in outlook; Hebrews very Jewish."

his reader frequently with a force which at the time it is not easy to withstand.[149]

But the notion that Luke was a Gentile is far from settled in Lukan studies today. At the beginning of the twentieth century, many were beginning to make mention of "the familiarity with Jewish affairs" that Luke "assumes on the part of his readers."[150] In recent years, the increasing awareness of the intensely Jewish aspects of Luke's writings has prompted a reevaluation of their theology and readership. The prevailing paradigm of Luke's supposed Gentile orientation began to be seriously challenged in the early 1970's by J. Jervell and E. Franklin, both of whom argued that the traditional understanding of Luke's background and purpose was in error.[151] Lukan scholars have probed this subject now for 40 years, so that both the books of Luke and Acts are now viewed by many against a Jewish background.[152]

---

[149] H. Alford, *Alford's Greek Testament: An Exegetical and Critical Commentary* (Grand Rapids: Guardian, 1976 reprint), 4:53. Alford refers to Paul's mention of "our dear friend Luke, the doctor" in Col 4:14 after seemingly identifying Aristarchus, Mark, and "Jesus, who is called Justus" as "the only Jews among my fellow workers for the kingdom of God" (NIV) in 4:10–11. Many scholars have noted it is not at all obvious from Col 4:10–14 that Luke was a Gentile. See esp. J. Wenham, "The Identification of Luke," *EvQ* 63 (1991), 3–44; and E. Earle Ellis, "'Those of the Circumcision' and the Early Christian Mission," *SE* 4 (1968): 390–99. The train of thought in Col 4:10–14 has been broken by the intervening two verses dedicated to Epaphras. Additionally, the use of the aorist tense "became" in v. 11 may very well refer to some specific critical situation in the past where the three men "of the circumcision" stood with Paul. Paul is surely not complaining that only three Jewish Christians labored with him. Finally, first century Judaism was not homogeneous; hence these three men mentioned may have been of a stricter Jewish mind-set over against more moderate Hellenistic Jews.

[150] E. D. Burton, "The Purpose and Plan of the Gospel of Luke," *Biblical World* 16 (1900): 258.

[151] See J. Jervell, *Luke and the People of God: A New Look at Luke-Acts* (Minneapolis: Augsburg, 1972; id., *The Unknown Paul: Essays on Luke-Acts and Early Christian History* (Minneapolis: Augsburg, 1984); id., *Theology of the Acts of the Apostles* (Cambridge: Cambridge University Press, 1996); cf. E. Franklin, *Christ the Lord: A Study in the Purpose and Theology of Luke-Acts* (London: S.P.C.K., 1975).

[152] For additional material dealing with the Jewishness of Luke-Acts not specifically discussed here, see G. Lohfink, *Die Sammlung Israels: Eine Untersuchung zur lukanischen Ekklesiologie* (Munich: Kosel, 1975); and J. C. O'Neill, *The Theology of Acts in Its Historical Setting* (London: S.P.C.K., 1961): 146–65. O'Neill specifically discussed Luke's debt to Hellenistic Judaism. The question of Luke's attitude toward the Jews has received intense scrutiny in recent years. E.g., see J. B. Tyson, ed., *Luke-Acts and the Jewish People: Eight Critical Perspectives* (Minneapolis: Augsburg, 1988), where eight scholars present their various views. Cf. J. B. Tyson, *Images of Judaism in Luke-Acts* (Columbia: University of South Carolina Press, 1992); and S. Mason, "Chief Priests, Sadducees, Pharisees and Sanhedrin in Acts," in *The Book of Acts in Its Palestinian Setting,* ed. R. Bauckham; vol. 4 of *The Book of Acts in Its First Century Setting,* ed. B. W. Winter (Grand Rapids/Carlisle, UK: Eerdmans/Paternoster, 1995), 115–178. J. Sanders (*The Jews in Luke-Acts* [Philadelphia: Fortress, 1987]) argued that Luke had a strongly anti-Jewish bias. A balanced presentation appears in Part III of *Literary Studies in Luke-Acts: Essays in Honor of Joseph B. Tyson*, ed. R. Thompson and T. Phillips; (Macon: Mercer University Press, 1998), where S. Heschel, R. Tannehill, R. Brawley, J. Sanders, T. Phillips, and R. Thompson all addressed this subject (pp. 235–344).

This is perhaps no more clearly demonstrated than in the conclusion R. Denova reached in her work on Luke-Acts. She agreed with others cited above that Luke's use of Hellenistic literary devices does not provide evidence that he was a Gentile. However, her reasons differ from those normally given and are based upon her narrative-critical reading of Luke-Acts. Her point is that the arguments used by Luke and the way in which they are applied in the construction of the text do not support the identification of Luke as a Gentile. Jewish arguments (both structure and content) are integrated into the narrative, but there is no integration of Gentile arguments, a fact that points away from the traditional understanding of Luke's recipients being non-Jewish. "When a particular interpretation from Scripture is offered as an argument, Luke anticipates a response by other Jews, not Gentiles."[153]

The point of view expressed by Luke in his two-volume work is consistently that of the Jewish Scriptures. Denova stated, "In my view, this type of argument strongly suggests that the ethnic background of the author of Luke-Acts is Jewish, and that he presented arguments that were of some importance to Jews."[154] Although Hengel accepted Luke's Gentile background, he could also assert that Luke had a knowledge of Judaism equal to or greater than other New Testament writers, including knowledge of the temple cultus, synagogues, customs and sects, and he reports them in an accurate way.[155] Schreckenberg likewise affirmed that "Luke shows a certain interest in, almost an inner connection with, the Jewish background to the New Testament events."[156]

The first volume of a new multi-volume series entitled *Luke the Interpreter of Israel* shows by its title how Luke's understanding of Judaism is now viewed among those concentrating on Lukan studies: *Jesus and the Heritage of Israel: Luke's Narrative Claim upon Israel's Legacy*. In this volume, 17 scholars present a "sea change" of opinion that Luke is the interpreter of Israel.

---

[153] R. Denova, *The Things Accomplished Among Us: Prophetic Tradition in the Structure of Luke-Acts* (Sheffield: Academic, 1997), 226.

[154] Ibid., 225. F. Bovon and C. Blomberg register their disagreement with the trend in Lukan studies that Luke stressed continuity over discontinuity with Judaism in Luke-Acts. F. Bovon attributed the shift of opinion to a post-holocaust desire not to offend Jews and a widespread disregard for the major studies in the 1960s and 1970s ("Studies in Luke-Acts: Retrospect and Prospect," *HTR* 85 [1992]: 175–96). Blomberg criticized studies holding this viewpoint, charging that "they lack consistent narrative-critical analysis" ("The Christian and the Law of Moses," in *Witness to the Gospel: The Theology of Acts*, ed. I. H. Marshall and D. Peterson [Grand Rapids: Eerdmans, 1998], 399). Blomberg seemed unaware of Denova's 1997 work, which is a first-class study of Luke-Acts from a narrative perspective. Finally, most of those suggesting a Jewish milieu for Luke-Acts are not unmindful of the discontinuity that Luke emphasizes as well.

[155] M. Hengel, *Acts and the History of Earliest Christianity*, trans. J. Bowden (London: SCM, 1979), 64 (trans. of *Zur urchristlichen Geschichtsschreibung* [Stuttgart: Calwer, 1979]).

[156] H. Schreckenberg and K. Schubert, *Jewish Historiography and Iconography in Early and Medieval Christianity* CRINT, Section 3, *Jewish Traditions in Early Christian Literature*, trans. P. Cathey; P. Tomson, exec. ed. (Maastricht/Minneapolis: Van Gorcum/Fortress, 1992), 2:47.

There is now an international consensus that Luke claimed Jesus as Israel's true heritage.[157]

R. Martin rightly noted the haste with which many concluded from Col 4:14 that Luke was a Gentile: "There is considerable evidence to argue the case that he was a Hellenistic Jew."[158] D. Pao's recent extensive study of Luke's use of Isaiah in Luke-Acts led him to conclude that "Luke is most likely a god-fearer if not himself a Jew."[159] A. C. Clarke, in reference to Plummer's comment about Luke's being the "versatile Gentile," supported strongly the opposite idea that Luke must have been a Jew if he is to be considered the author of Luke-Acts.

> I find this theory of the versatile Gentile very unconvincing. Greek was the literary language of the East and known to all Jews with any claim to culture. It is easy to see that a Jew when writing Greek would from time to time use native idioms and constructions. It is difficult to conceive the case of a Greek who became so saturated with Hebraic idioms as to use them when writing in his own tongue. If, therefore, the meaning of Col. iv. 10–14 is that *Loukas* was a Greek, it is hard to suppose that he wrote either of the works attributed to him.[160]

J. Jervell came to a similar conclusion:

> That Luke was able to write Greek in a good style does not show that he was a Gentile—many Jews did so. In spite of his ability to write decent Greek, he does so only seldom and sporadically. Most of his work he presents in what may be called biblical Greek, clearly influenced by the Septuagint, a Jewish book, written for Jews and not for Gentiles. Luke's stylistic home was the synagogue. He was a Jewish Christian.[161]

At the very least, Eric Franklin is right:

> Whether Luke was himself a Jew must remain an open question. At any rate, however, he must have been one who was influenced supremely

---

[157] D. P. Moessner, ed., *Jesus and the Heritage of Israel: Luke's Narrative Claim upon Israel's Legacy*; vol. 1 in *Luke the Interpreter of Israel*, ed. D. Moessner and D. Tiede (Harrisburg: Trinity Press International, 1999), see esp. 2–4, 49–51, 60, 66–67, 96–97, 168–70, 208, 217, 244–49, 322–24, 368.

[158] R. Martin, *Colossians: The Church's Lord and the Christian's Liberty* (Exeter: Paternoster, 1972), 146.

[159] D. Pao, *Acts and the Isaianic New Exodus* (Tübingen: Mohr/Siebeck, 2000), 25.

[160] A. C. Clarke, *Acts of the Apostles* (Oxford: Clarendon, 1933), 393.

[161] Jervell, *Theology of Acts*, 5. E. C. Selwyn (*St. Luke the Prophet* [London/NewYork: Macmillan, 1901], xxi) commented, "Luke was a Jew and there is no ground for the other supposition." Many argue, like M. Goulder (*Luke: A New Paradigm* [Sheffield: JSOT, 1994], 115), that the Semitisms in Luke 1–2 are not due to a Hebrew or Aramaic source but are in fact Luke's own Septuagintal style.

by the Jewish faith, one who loved our nation, who was moved by its law and captivated by its Scriptures, one who was led to see in Jesus a fulfillment of its hopes and a widening of its promises.[162]

There is a significant amount of evidence pointing to the Jewishness of Luke-Acts. If Luke were not Jewish, he produced a two-volume work that in terms of content, language, and emphasis betrays knowledge of and interest in matters Jewish. Given this, a major barrier against Lukan authorship of Hebrews is removed.

A second argument against Lukan authorship has been the notion that Luke has no high priestly Christology.[163] While it is true that none of the Gospel writers overtly portray Jesus as high priest, it can be demonstrated that Luke viewed him as such. This can be seen in the account of Jesus' ascension in Luke 24:50–51, where it is stated that Jesus lifted up his hands and blessed the disciples. While he was engaged in this act, he was "carried up into heaven." Talbert's words express the meaning of this act:

> This act of blessing is like that of the high priest, Simon, in *Sir* 50:19–20. With a priestly act the risen Jesus puts his disciples under the protection of God before he leaves them . . . Just as the gospel began with the ministry of the priest Zechariah, so it ends with Jesus acting as priest for his flock (cf. Heb 2:17; 3:1; 6:19–20).[164]

[162] E. Franklin, *Christ the Lord*, 79. Among others arguing for Luke's Jewish background (e.g., Reicke, Schlatter, Ellis, Wenham), see most recently G. Harvey, *The True Israel: Uses of the Names of Jew, Hebrew and Israel in Ancient Jewish and Early Christian Literature,* AGJU 35 (Leiden: Brill, 1996), 194.

[163] See Marshall, *Luke*, 909; R. Dillon, *From Eye-Witness to Ministers of the Word: Tradition and Composition in Luke 24*, AnBib 82 (Rome: Biblical Institute, 1978), 176. J. Nolland (*Luke 18:35–24:53*, WBC 35 [Dallas: Word, 1993], 1227–228); and D. Bock (*Luke 9:51–24:53,* BECNT [Grand Rapids: Baker, 1996], 1945) denied that Luke has any interest in a priestly Christology. But both Nolland and Bock pointed out that Luke's account of the ascension in 24:50–51 parallels *Sir*. 50:20–21.

[164] C. Talbert, *Reading Luke* (Macon, GA: Smyth & Helwys, 2002), 233. Calvin (*Hebrews*, 92), in reference to Luke 24:50 stated: "Without doubt He [Christ] borrowed the rite of raising His hand from the priests to show that He is the One through whom God the Father blesses us." Cf. Ellis, *Luke*, 279; Marshall, *Luke*, 908–9; and Hendriksen, *Exposition of the Gospel According to Luke,* 43. D. Sylva ("The Temple Curtain and Jesus' Death in the Gospel of Luke," *JBL* 105 [1986]: 239–50, esp. 247, n. 22) provides a list of those who claim that Jesus' lifting his hands to bless the disciples (Luke 24:50–53) is a priestly blessing: A. Schlatter, D. Daube, E. Ellis, E. J. Tinsley, W. Arndt, and W. Schmithals. Those who see it specifically as a high-priestly blessing include P. A. Van Stempvoort, "The Interpretation of the Ascension in Luke and Acts," *NTS* 5 (1957–58): 30–42; Marshall, *Luke*, 908–9; W. Grundmann, *Das Evangelium nach Lukas*, THKNT (Berlin: Evangelische, 1971), 3:453–54; R. J. Karris, "Luke 23:47 and the Lucan View of Jesus' Death," *JBL* 105 (1986): 65–74; and R. Meynet, "*La preghiera nel vangelo di Luca*," *CivCatt* (1998) III, 379–92. Meynet argued that this blessing was an act of adoption that constituted the disciples as Jesus' sons and heirs. A. Mekkattukunnel (*The Priestly Blessing of the Risen Christ: An Exegetico-Theological Analysis of Luke 24, 50–53*, *European University Studies* [Bern: Peter Lang, 2001], 171–230) and K. Kapic ("Receiving Christ's Priestly Benediction: A Biblical, Historical, and Theological Exploration of

Talbert cited texts from Hebrews that theologically describe this act and the resultant position of the ascended Lord in heaven. Of the four Gospel writers, only Luke recounts the ascension of Jesus. It is, in fact, the focal point of his two volumes. Douglas Farrow also saw in Luke's account of the ascension "weighty evidence" for a priestly Christology. "Are we not invited throughout (another uniquely Lukan story, about the boy Jesus in his Father's house, deserves mention here) to see in Jesus something of Samuel as well as David, and of the priestly as well as the kingly?"[165] Do we not see the same priestly and kingly roles combined in Hebrews? Mekkattukunnel has recently demonstrated that Luke's apparent disinterest in the priesthood of Jesus vanishes in the light of a closer reading of Luke.[166] Strelan provocatively entitled his recent volume *Luke the Priest*, in which he argued that Luke's demonstrable interest in matters related to the priesthood coupled with his authority to interpret the traditions of Israel indicated that Luke was himself a priest.[167] While this carries the evidence too far in my opinion, Strelan's volume illustrates the changing paradigm in Lukan studies.

The third major argument against Lukan authorship of Hebrews is the assumption that Luke had no theology of the cross.[168] Luke had his own way of highlighting the sacrificial aspect of Jesus' death. Mekkattukunnel made the point that "Luke omits not only Jesus' saying in Mark 10:45, but the whole Marcan pericope (Mark 10:35–45) in which it occurs. However, Luke takes up much of this Marcan material in the Last Supper context (cf. 22:24–27)."[169] He further noted that Luke sets Jesus' death in the Passover time frame, which points to the sacrificial character of his death (Luke 22:1,7,8,11,13,15; Exod 12:14,25,27).[170] Mekkattukunnel thus demonstrated Luke does have a theology of the cross.

Furthermore, as Carpinelli demonstrated, Jesus' words over the bread and cup at the Last Supper express the sacrificial nature of his death.[171] There is an allusion to Jer 31:31–34 and the "new covenant" in the Lukan account of

Luke 24:50–53," *WTJ* 67 [2005]: 247–60) have shown beyond a reasonable doubt that this act of Jesus is a priestly blessing.

165 D. Farrow, *Ascension and Ecclesia* (Grand Rapids: Eerdmans, 1995), 25.

166 Mekkattukunnel, *Priestly Blessing*, 176–77.

167 R. Strelan, *Luke the Priest: The Authority of the Author of the Third Gospel* (Aldershot, England/Burlington, VT: Ashgate, 2008), 113. D. Crump demonstrated Jesus' priestly self-understanding in his prayers. See his *Jesus the Intercessor: Prayer and Christology in Luke-Acts*, Biblical Studies Library (Grand Rapids: Baker, 1999).

168 H. Conzelmann, *Theology of Saint Luke* (New York: Harper & Brothers, 1960), 201.

169 Ibid., 177.

170 Ibid. "The emphatic way in which Luke presents Jesus as the 'firstborn' (2:7,23) reminds us of the Passover lamb which was the ranso[m] for the deliverance of the Israelites' first-born children."

171 F. G. Carpinelli, "'Do This as My Memorial' (Luke 22:19): Lucan Soteriology of Atonement," *CBQ* 61 (1999): 74–91.

the Last Supper, an allusion that is not found in the other Gospels but that is a major theme in Hebrews.[172]

Mekkattukunnel said Luke views Jesus' death on the cross as fulfilling and surpassing the Old Testament temple and priesthood. For Luke, Jesus is the supreme high priest and perfect mediator between God and humanity.[173] Carpinelli came to the same conclusion:

> As Jesus ascends, Luke depicts him giving Aaron's blessing as the high priest would after sacrifice on the Feast of Atonement. The sacrificial and expiatory interpretation of the cup connects with the Lucan running allusion to Sirach 50, where the glory and function of the high priest in the liturgy of the Day of Atonement are magnified . . . In Luke 22:14–23 and 24:50–53 Jesus is thus depicted functioning as a priest. The bread as memorial and the cup as the token of the covenant in Jesus' blood lay the narrative base for depicting the ascending Jesus completing the liturgy of the Day of Atonement. Jesus' giving the cup as new covenant in his blood and imparting Aaron's blessing bring narratively to full view Luke's image of Jesus' relation to the temple.[174]

Thus, the three arguments that have traditionally been used against Luke as the author of Hebrews lose their potency in the light of careful investigation of Luke-Acts. C. P. M. Jones' thesis that there is a "family likeness" in Christology and eschatology between Luke-Acts and Hebrews in comparison to the rest of the New Testament writers[175] was confirmed by John Drury, who noted with regard to them that "Luke and Hebrews are fundamentally at one."[176] Likewise, Goppelt placed his treatment of Luke and Hebrews in the same chapter because of the similarity he suggested exists between these works when compared to the rest of the New Testament. In every respect, Hebrews offers an interpretation of the gospel that is independent of Paul and John. Its interpretation was written for the community on a long journey, a community that was growing tired under the pressure of faith in the context of a hostile society. Goppelt also saw a "whole series of particulars" of agreement between Luke and Hebrews. He cited the "linguistic proximity" of the books, including "characteristic technical terms of community parlance," such as Christ as *archēgos*, church leaders as *hēgoumenoi,* and Jesus having been

---

[172] Jer 31:31–34 is a foundational OT passage for Hebrews 8–9.

[173] Mekkattukunnel, *Priestly Blessing*, 180–81.

[174] Carpinelli, 90.

[175] C. P. M. Jones, "The Epistle to the Hebrews and the Lucan Writings," in *Studies in the Gospels: Essays in Memory of R. H. Lightfoot*, ed. D. E. Nineham (Oxford, Basil Blackwell, 1955), 113–43.

[176] J. Drury, *Tradition and Design in Luke's Gospel: A Study in Early Christian Historiography* (Atlanta: John Knox, 1976), 21.

perfected (*teteleiōmenos*).[177] In addition, both Luke and Hebrews address a church situation "in a similar direction." The farewell address of Jesus (Luke 22) and the farewell address of Paul to the Ephesian elders (Acts 20) remind one of Hebrews 13:7–21. Goppelt's conclusion was that the above points of contact "suggest that the theology of Hebrews and that of Luke should be considered together."[178] In this way, Hebrews exhibits the greatest affinity with Luke-Acts in the New Testament.

When one considers the lexical, stylistic, and theological similarities between Luke-Acts and Hebrews coupled with the way in which a theory of Lukan authorship can be historically reconstructed from the texts themselves, there is impressive evidence that points to the Lukan authorship of Hebrews. No longer should it be said that "the points of connection between Luke and Hebrews are too slight to support a theory of common authorship."[179] At any rate, whoever the author was, he must be classed among the upper echelon of New Testament writers in terms of stylistic ability and theological prowess, as has been continually noted throughout church history.[180]

Many additional arguments can be marshaled in favor of Lukan authorship.[181] The combined evidence should evoke among New Testament scholars a closer look at Luke as the author of Hebrews.

(2) Recipients

The question of the recipients of Hebrews, like the other matters of provenance, has engendered considerable discussion.[182] The internal evidence of the epistle itself nowhere locates the readers, and thus the best that one can

---

[177] Goppelt, *Theology of the New Testament*, 2:265–66.

[178] Ibid., 266.

[179] D. A. Carson, D. J. Moo, and L. Morris, *An Introduction to the New Testament* (Grand Rapids: Zondervan, 1992), 396.

[180] E.g., Gheorghita, *Role of the Septuagint in Hebrews*, 2: "His knowledge and appropriation of the Scriptures as well as their crucial importance in the development of his theological argument are second to none among the NT writers. . . . It was the Greek text of the Jewish Scriptures that he used for his quotations with much more uniformity and precision than most of the other NT writers." Cf. Thiselton, "Hebrews," in *Eerdmans Commentary on the Bible*, ed. J. D. G. Dunn and J. W. Rogerson (Grand Rapids: Eerdmans, 2003), 1453: "Hebrews is the work of a theologian who is also a pastor and a fine expository preacher."

[181] See D. L. Allen, *The Lukan Authorship of Hebrews*, NACSBT (Nashville: B&H Academic, 2010).

[182] For a survey of the various theories, see Guthrie, *New Testament Introduction*, 682–701; Ellingworth, *Hebrews*, 21–29; and Koester, *Hebrews*, 64–79. For a summary of the major theories of the recipients and their circumstances, including the crisis and the response precipitated by it, see R. W. Johnson, *Going Outside the Camp: The Sociological Function of the Levitical Critique in the Epistle to the Hebrews*, JSNTSup 209 (Sheffield: University Press, 2001), 18–20. Cf. M. J. Marohl (*Faithfulness and the Purpose of Hebrews: A Social Identity Approach*, Princeton Theological Monograph Series, ed. K. C. Hanson and C. M. Collier [Eugene: Pickwick, 2008]), 8–25); K. Schenck (*Understanding the Book of Hebrews: The Story Behind the Sermon* [Louisville: WJK, 2003], 88–105); DeSilva, *Perseverance in Gratitude*, 2–20; and Koester, *Hebrews*, 64–79.

do is to sift the evidence and see where it leads. Three major views have been advocated as to ethnic background of the recipients. The traditional view is that the readers were Jewish Christians.[183] The superscription "To the Hebrews" prefixed to the epistle in the late second century is indicative of its contents. The Old Testament quotations—which focus on the tabernacle, the priesthood, the sacrificial system, Moses, Melchizedek, and Abraham (Heb 3; 7; 11)—indicate a Jewish audience. In the nineteenth century, a second view developed which argued that the recipients were Gentile Christians.[184] The argument of Hebrews can easily be applied to Gentiles, and in fact this has been done by most interpreters of the epistle. But as C. P. Anderson trenchantly pointed out, "The author himself does not do so, and such an extension requires considerable readjustment of his tightly woven logic and scriptural interpretation."[185] A third view suggests that the readers were a mixed congregation of Jewish and Gentile Christians.[186] The traditional view accounts for the evidence in the epistle itself.

Were the recipients Christians at large, similar to the readers of 1 and 2 Peter, or were they a definite congregation or a group within a specific congregation of Christians? The latter seems the better option based on the internal evidence of the epistle.[187] Three major theories regarding the location of the recipients have been suggested. The traditional view locates the recipients in or near Jerusalem. The title of the epistle combined with the theology of the tabernacle, the priesthood, and the sacrifices could be argued to point in this direction. The description of the persecution that the readers had endured likewise makes a Jerusalem destination possible. This view has been recently argued in a dissertation by Mosser.[188] He revisited the evidence for Jerusalem and noticed that this was the dominant view until the nineteenth century. He also marshaled strong evidence in favor of Jerusalem from Heb 13:13 where the author speaks of going "outside the camp." Mosser demonstrated that this

---

[183] Lane, *Hebrews 1–8*, lii–lv; Koester, *Hebrews*, 46–47; Lindars, *Theology of Hebrews*, 4; and Isaacs, *Sacred Space*, 67.

[184] J. Moffatt, *A Critical and Exegetical Commentary on the Epistle to the Hebrews*, ICC (Edinburg: T&T Clark, 1924), xxiv–xxvi), offered one of the best presentations of this theory in the twentieth century, which DeSilva (*Perseverance in Gratitude*, 2–7) did for the twenty-first century. This view has not garnered much support since the internal evidence of the epistle is so strongly against it.

[185] C. P. Anderson, "Who Are the Heirs of the New Age in the Epistle to the Hebrews?" in *Apocalyptic and the New Testament: Essays in Honor of J. Louis Martyn*, ed. J. Marcus and M. Soards, JSNTSup 24 (Sheffield: JSOT, 1989), 272.

[186] Ellingworth, *Hebrews*, 21–27; Trotter, *Interpreting Hebrews*, 28–31; DeSilva, *Perseverance in Gratitude*, 7; Schenck, *Understanding the Book of Hebrews*, 91–93.

[187] Childs, *The New Testament as Canon: An Introduction*, 242: "Most agree with Manson that there are enough concrete features within the letter to indicate a definite group rather than Christians at large."

[188] C. Mosser, "No Lasting City: Rome, Jerusalem and the Place of Hebrews in the History of Earliest 'Christianity,'" (Ph.D. dissertation, St. Mary's College, University of St. Andrews, 2004).

phrase always refers to Jerusalem or something within it during the Second Temple period. When the author of Hebrews calls on his readers to go "outside the camp," he is calling them to leave Jerusalem.[189]

A second possible destination is Rome. This view, probably the dominant one now, arose during the eighteenth century.[190] Lane has made a good case for a house church setting in Rome as the destination of the epistle.[191] R. Brown's defense of the Roman destination is given a substantive critique by M. Isaacs.[192] The Roman hypothesis has received its most trenchant critique recently from Mosser, who traced the rise of the Roman destination theory and then critically examined the evidence for it. His thorough analysis of the phrase "those from Italy send you their greetings" in Heb 13:24, a linchpin in the Roman argument, broke new ground. Mosser examined first-century manuscripts employing the preposition *apo* followed by a place name, as in Heb 13:24, and concluded "they consistently interpret the phrase to indicate the place *from which* the epistle was written."[193] An additional argument against the Roman hypothesis, not usually mentioned, is the reference to Timothy's release in Heb 13:23, which would not have been necessary if the epistle were written to Rome.[194] Of course, it could be argued that Timothy was imprisoned somewhere other than Rome, but given the information from the Pastoral Epistles, Rome is the most likely location of Timothy's imprisonment.

A third view posits Antioch in Syria as the destination of the epistle.[195] This view will be argued as viable in the discussion below. Some have attempted to show that the author wrote to a mixed audience of believers and unbelievers.[196] This theory is addressed throughout the commentary as I explain how the author addresses his audience. There are two ways this issue has been approached by those who advocate a mixed audience. F. F. Bruce and P. E. Hughes argued that the author addressed professing Christians without distinguishing in his writing whether some were actually unsaved, though that was probably the case. Thus, when the author of Hebrews used the term "brothers" in 3:12, he did not necessarily refer to one who was truly saved but to those who were

---

189 Ibid., 294–350.

190 Advocates include W. Manson, *The Epistle to the Hebrews* (London: Hodder & Stoughton, 1951), 162; R. Brown, *Antioch and Rome*, 142–51; F. F. Bruce, *Hebrews*, 13–14; S. J. Kistemaker, *Exposition of the Epistle to the Hebrews*, (Grand Rapids: Baker, 1984), 17–18; Ellingworth, *Hebrews*, 29; B. Weiss, *Der Hebräerbrief in zeitgeschichtlicher Beleuchtung*, (Leipzig: Hinrichs, 1910), 76; Salevao, *Legitimation in the Letter to the Hebrews*, 165–69.

191 Lane, *Hebrews 1–8*, lviii–lx.

192 Isaacs, *Sacred Space*, 31–37.

193 Mosser, "No Lasting City," 157.

194 This point was noted by J. M'Clintock and J. Strong, "Hebrews, Epistle to," in *Cyclopaedia of Biblical, Theological and Ecclesiastical Literature* (Grand Rapids: Baker, 1981 reprint), 4:147.

195 Advocates include Spicq, *l'Épître aux Hébreux*, 1:250–52.

196 P. E. Hughes, *Hebrews*, 18; J. MacArthur, *Hebrews* (Chicago: Moody, 1983), xi. The best recent case for a mixed audience is C. A. Thomas, *A Case for Mixed-Audience with Reference to the Warning Passages in the Book of Hebrews* (New York: Peter Lang, 2008).

in the church—presumably Christians but some not necessarily so.[197] In one sense, this approach would be affirmed by all as a truism in that there are probably those in each local church congregation who are not genuine believers. The issue is not, however, whether this is true, but whether the author assumes his audience to be composed of both believers and unbelievers. An extreme approach is taken by MacArthur who argued that the expository sections of the epistle were written to both groups, believers and unbelievers, but that the warning passages were addressed to unbelievers only.[198] MacArthur divided the recipients of Hebrews into three groups: (1) Jewish Christians, (2) Jewish non-believers who were intellectually convinced of Christianity's truthfulness, but remained unconverted, and (3) Jewish non-Christians who remained unconvinced of the truth of Christianity. This approach to the audience of Hebrews is not born out in the actual structure of the epistle, particularly in the author's use of pronouns and conjunctions. The commentary on Heb 6:4–8 addresses this issue in depth. Suffice it to say at this point that the mixed audience theory is theologically driven as an attempt to explain the rigorism of Hebrews.

Returning to the identity of the recipients, a promising solution to the question was first offered in 1923 by J. V. Brown when he suggested that the readers were a group of the former Jewish priests who had become Christians as mentioned in Acts 6:7. This theory was later argued by Spicq in his work on Hebrews.[199] With the exception of Spicq and P. E. Hughes, this suggestion has not been given the consideration that it deserves in New Testament circles.[200]

Brown not only argued for priests as the recipients of Hebrews, but he also attributed part of the writing to Luke as a collaborator with Paul. He suggested that Paul was the "chief framer, planner and compiler" of the epistle, but that

[197] Bruce, *Hebrews*, 66; Hughes, *Hebrews*, 146.

[198] MacArthur, *Hebrews*, x–xv. On p. xi he stated, "If, for example, as some have said, it was written exclusively to Christians, extreme problems arise in interpreting a number of passages which could hardly apply to believers. And because it so frequently addresses believers, it could not have been written primarily to unbelievers either. So it must have been written to include both." MacArthur's statement is based on his interpretation of the warning passages in Hebrews. The weakness of this suggestion in light of the evidence in the epistle itself is demonstrated in the course of this commentary.

[199] J. V. Brown, "The Authorship and Circumstances of Hebrews—Again!" *BSac* 80 (1923): 505–38; Spicq, *l'Épître aux Hébreux*, 1:226–31. See Bornhäuser, *Empfänger und Verfasser des Hebräerbriefes* (Gütersloh: Bertelsmann, 1932); M. E. Clarkson, "The Antecedents of the High Priest Theme in Hebrews," *AThR* 29 (1947): 89–95; and C. Sandegren, "The Addressees of the Epistle to the Hebrews." *EvQ* 27 (1955): 221–24.

[200] Hughes, *Hebrews*, 10–15. Lindars calls it a speculative reconstruction that "strains credulity" (*Theology of the Letter to the Hebrews,* 4). R. Brown and J. P. Meier's critique of Spicq's proposal is primarily based on Spicq's suggestion that the converted priests remained in Jerusalem (*Antioch and Rome: New Testament Cradles of Catholic Christianity* [New York: Paulist, 1983]: 143). The appeal to the LXX rather than Hebrew and the author's focus on the tabernacle rather than the temple as arguments against former priests being the recipients are not serious hurdles. D. Guthrie was more optimistic when he said that this must remain a conjecture, although a conjecture that deserves "careful consideration" (*New Testament Introduction*, 691).

Luke edited it.[201] As a result, Brown's theory concerning the authorship and recipients of Hebrews is the nearest to my own.

Brown was followed in his suggestion regarding the recipients as former Jewish priests by Bornhäuser in 1932, Clarkson in 1947, Ketter in 1950, Spicq in 1952, Braun and Sandegren in 1955, Rissi in 1987 and P. Grelot in 2003.[202] Spicq revised his theory in 1958–59 when he suggested that the priests had been influenced by the Qumranian community.[203] Spicq also followed Brown in noting a certain likeness between Hebrews and Stephen's speech in Acts 7. He saw portions of Hebrews as countering Qumranian speculations and concluded that Hebrews was written to Jewish priests who were Essene Christians. Within this group, he believed, were also former members of the Qumran community.

Both J. Danielou and Y. Yadin elaborated on this theory of Qumranian influence on the recipients of Hebrews in 1958. Danielou suggested that converted priests furnished the best explanation for the recipients of Hebrews. Believing John the Baptist to have been influenced by Essene tendencies, and accepting O. Cullmann's belief that Stephen's speech contains several points similar to the Essene manuscript called the Damascus Document, Danielou posited that the Hellenists of Acts 6 were actually converted Essenes.[204]

Yadin argued that Hebrews was written to a group of Jews who had originally belonged to the Qumranian sect and who upon their conversion to Christianity continued to maintain some of their previous views.[205] Hughes believed the recipients were former priests, but he found it unnecessary to postulate that they had formerly been at Qumran. The Qumran connection has been exaggerated, so all that needs to be said is that the readers, if they were former priests, may have been influenced by some of the views of this sect of Judaism. However, a careful reading of the epistle does not appear to indicate much influence.[206] Hughes called this view (that the recipients were former Jewish priests) the "best theory yet advanced to explain the occasion . . . of Hebrews."[207]

The suggestion that the recipients were former priests minus the Qumran connection has plenty of evidence to support it and merits its revival as one of

---

[201] J. V. Brown, "The Authorship," 533–36.

[202] P. Grelot (*lecture de l'épître aux Hébreux,* Lire la Bible 132 [Paris: Cerf, 2003], 190–91) argued that the recipients were converted Jewish priests who were now refugees in a city where nationalist Jews brought increasing pressure and hostility on them around AD 66. These priests lived on the margin of the church, which he located as most likely in Antioch.

[203] Spicq later altered his view ("*L'Épître* aux Hebreux," 365–90) to suggest the priests were members of Qumran.

[204] Danielou, *The Dead Sea Scrolls and Primitive Christianity*, 18–22.

[205] Yadin, "The Dead Sea Scrolls and the Epistle to the Hebrews," 36–55. Cf. H. Braun, *Qumran und das Neue Testament* I (Tübingen: Mohr/Siebeck 1966), 153.

[206] See the excellent discussion on the history of research on Hebrews and Qumran in P. E. Hughes, "The Epistle to the Hebrews," 351–53. Cf. Buchanan, "The Present State of Scholarship on Hebrews," *Christianity, Judaism and other Graeco-Roman Cults,* ed. J. Neusner (Leiden: Brill, 1975), 308–9.

[207] Hughes, *Hebrews*, 14.

the better possible solutions to the overall question. Given all the evidence, it seems to have greater explanatory power than any other theory. Josephus mentioned that there were some 20,000 priests, and according to Jeremias there were some 7,200 priests attached to the temple in Jerusalem alone.[208] Luke records in Acts 6:7 that a significant number of the priests became followers of Jesus. With the persecution recorded in Acts 8:1 raging in Jerusalem at the time of Stephen's martyrdom, some of these converted Jewish priests would no doubt have been forced out of Jerusalem along with other Christians. The question is, Where would they have gone? Luke did not tell us what became of these former priests mentioned in Acts 6:7, probably out of concern for their safety. If his volume had fallen into the wrong hands, it could have easily furnished a clue to their location. Perhaps this is why the recipients of Hebrews are never identified in the letter, though it is clear that the author knew their exact circumstances. That Jewish-Roman relations were strained to the point of war would be ample reason to protect former priests likely to be viewed by the Roman government as potential leaders in the Jewish cause.[209]

Assuming Acts to have been written around AD 63, the events narrated in Acts 6:7 would have begun approximately thirty years earlier. Where might those converted priests have gone? One of the most likely and one of the safest places would be Antioch in Syria.[210] There may have been a steady stream of converted Jewish priests leaving Jerusalem under persecution, and most likely some would flee to Antioch. In Acts 6:7 all three main verbs appear in the imperfect tense, emphasizing continuous action in past time: "So the word of God *spread*. The number of disciples in Jerusalem *increased* rapidly, and a large number of priests *became obedient* to the faith" (emphasis added). C. B. Williams translates this verse in the following way to bring out the force of the imperfects: "So God's message *continued to spread*, and the number of the disciples in Jerusalem *continued to grow* rapidly; a large number even of priests *continued to surrender* to the faith."[211] The Greek translated "large number"

[208] Jeremias, *Jerusalem in the Time of Jesus*, 198–207.

[209] This fact and the evidence that Hebrews was written to a group within a local church rather than to the whole church help explain the lack of a salutation and why the issue of authorship as well as recipients would become obscured in a relatively short time.

[210] Although I find it unlikely that exiled Jewish priests would relocate to Rome, R. Brown and J. P. Meier (*Antioch and Rome,* 154) suggested as much when they pointed out the possibility that in the Christian community in Rome there may have been "elements of that levitical heritage" referenced in Acts 6:7. Brown critiqued Spicq's theory on the supposition that the converted priests were located in Jerusalem. However, Spicq did not argue that the converted priests *remained* in Jerusalem, but rather were forced by persecution to relocate to some other place such as Caesarea, Antioch, or Ephesus (*L'Épître aux Hebreux*, 2:227). Brown was obviously more open to this theory if the priests are located somewhere other than Jerusalem, such as Rome. A Roman destination for Hebrews works just as well for the theory of Lukan authorship whether the recipients were former priests or not.

[211] C. B. Williams, *The New Testament: A Private Translation in the Language of the People* (Chicago: Moody, 1955); emphasis added.

makes it probable that several hundred and possibly even several thousand priests are referred to here. As Spicq pointed out, Hebrews addressed itself to priestly thoughts, attitudes, and viewpoints.[212]

One of the important themes of Hebrews, the high priesthood of Christ, is discussed in detail in the epistle. Would not such a theme be of great interest to former priests? On one occasion the readers were exhorted (in a figurative way) to continue their priestly duties: in Heb 10:19,22 the readers were told to "enter the Most Holy Place" with their "hearts sprinkled to cleanse [them] from a guilty conscience" and "having [their] bodies washed with pure water." Such priestly language would have been immediately understood and appreciated by former priests but would have been less so to the laity.

Apparently the recipients were not the entire church, but rather a section of the church as may be gleaned from Heb 5:12. Furthermore, they were addressed separately from their leaders as may be inferred from Heb 13:24. Downey pointed out in his exhaustive work on Antioch that it is very likely that several different groups of Christians existed in Antioch and that these probably met in different locations. One may presume that, at least on some occasions, the Jewish Christians and the Gentile Christians met separately. Some Christian Jews probably still observed the law in the matter of eating with Gentiles. A hint of this kind of thing is recorded in Gal 2:11–12 where Peter was willing to eat with Gentile Christians until a delegation from James and the Jerusalem church arrived in Antioch. Paul denounced Peter for separating himself from the Gentile Christians for fear of the Jerusalem delegation. Downey further suggested that the subsequent history of the Antiochene Christians made it probable that there were a number of different congregations and that they followed different lines of teaching and practice.[213]

Given this background and the statements in Hebrews itself, it is easy to conceive of former priests, now a part of the church at Antioch, who may have found reasons to stand aloof from the church.[214] Such an attitude could have

---

[212] Spicq, *L'Épître aux Hebreux*, 2:226.

[213] G. Downey, *A History of Antioch in Syria* (Princeton: University Press, 1961), 277. Cf. E. P. Sanders, *Judaism: Practice and Belief, 63 BCE–66 CE* (London: SCM; Philadelphia: Trinity Press International, 1992), 350–51; W. A. Meeks and R. L. Wilken, *Jews and Christians in Antioch in the First Four Centuries of the Common Era*, SBLSBS 13 (Missoula: Scholars Press, 1978); I. Levinskaya, *The Book of Acts in Its Diaspora Setting*; vol. 5 in *The Book of Acts in Its First Century Setting*, ed. B. W. Winter (Grand Rapids: Eerdmans, 1996), 127–35.

[214] Why the group addressed in Hebrews was failing to meet regularly with the church we are not told. We know that historically, in the two centuries preceding the Maccabean revolt, many of the priests, especially those of the upper echelon, became open to Hellenistic influences in an attempt to attain Hellenistic citizenship for themselves in Jerusalem. See the discussion in N. Walter, "Hellenistic Jews of the Diaspora at the Cradle of Primitive Christianity," in *The New Testament and Hellenistic Judaism*, ed. P. Borgen and S. Giversen (Peabody: Hendrickson, 1997), 41. By the time of the early church, the Sadducean high priestly families were much more hellenistically oriented than their Pharisee counterparts. If the recipients of Hebrews were former priests who had relocated to Antioch, perhaps there was some form of group conflict with others in the Antiochian

sparked the exhortation in 10:25: "Let us not give up meeting together." Lindars inferred from 13:17 that there was a rift between the leaders of the church and the group whom the author of Hebrews addressed. If the leaders had to give an account "sadly" (v. 17), "the implication is that the situation is extremely serious, and the leaders are at their wits end to know how to cope with it."[215] Following up on this last statement, Lindars suggested that the reason the author of Hebrews was involved in the first place is because he was himself a loved and respected member. It is possible that the author was a member of the congregation, but Lindars depends too heavily on chap. 13 for his supposition. He conjectured that the leaders had written to the author urging him to intervene. Since the author could not come in person, though he hoped to later, he responded with the letter of Hebrews. This accounts for its rhetorical character since the writer wanted to make the greatest impact. His intervention is the last resort. This aspect of Lindars's proposal is certainly possible.

Of those who have argued for former priests as the recipients of Hebrews, Spicq has presented the most effective case in his 1952–53 two-volume commentary. Spicq is often referenced by commentators as having argued for priests as the recipients of Hebrews, but interaction with his evidence is rare. An exception is Ellingworth who discussed six of Spicq's 12 arguments for priests and offers a brief rebuttal.[216] Given that Spicq's work was done over 50 years ago and that it has yet to be translated from the original French, it seems prudent to present his case again and include additional arguments that can be marshaled in favor of former priests being the recipients of Hebrews.[217]

Spicq began by noting that the depth of discussion in Hebrews demands all the more that the listener be interested in and able to understand it. He overstated the case when he said that "only the priests had enough intelligence" to comprehend the discussion, but his point that the letter addresses priestly concerns is true.[218] Spicq then proceeded to list 12 arguments in favor of his view. First, they were converted by the earliest disciples of the Lord (Heb 2:3). Second, they could have known the Roman Jews living in Jerusalem at the time of Pentecost who were converted (Acts 2:10) and who, after returning to Rome, would have added their greetings to those of the author of Hebrews (13:24).[219]

---

church. If the leadership of the Antioch church had become predominately Gentile, as is likely, this could be a plausible factor.

[215] B. Lindars, *Theology of Hebrews* (Cambridge: Cambridge University Press, 1991), 8.

[216] Ellingworth, *Hebrews*, 27.

[217] See Spicq (*L'Épître aux Hebreux*, 1:226–31) for his arguments.

[218] Ibid., 226. See J. H. Wray, *Rest as a Theological Metaphor in the Epistle to the Hebrews and the Gospel of Truth: Early Christian Homiletics of Rest*, SBLDS 166 (Atlanta: Scholars Press, 1998), 74: "I am convinced that the text of Hebrews implies a sophisticated and probably well-educated audience." See the comments by DeSilva, who noted that the stylish and difficult Greek combined with the extensive vocabulary of the epistle "suggests an audience capable of attending meaningfully to such language and syntax" (DeSilva, *Perseverance in Gratitude*, 8).

[219] Ibid., 227. Spicq did not believe the recipients were located in Rome.

Third, they were strengthened in the faith by the Holy Spirit through the work of Stephen (Heb 2:4; see Acts 6:8). Fourth, they should have been teachers (Heb 5:12), and this is commensurate with the teaching role that the priests had for the people as revealed in the Old Testament (Hag 2:11; Zech 7:8; Mal 2:7) as well as the New Testament.[220]

Fifth, the present tense *anistatai* ("arising," NIV "appears") in Heb 7:15 is reminiscent of Acts 20:17,18,28, and could have a hierarchical connotation. Such language would scarcely be applied to ordinary Christians, but would be consistent with priests having the authority required for giving counsel and making effective intervention. Sixth, the priests in Jerusalem had been used to the splendor of temple worship. Now, as Christians, they had lost their material and spiritual privileges as sons of Levi. They had been separated from the temple and had been forced to give up their ministry. They were reduced to the condition of ordinary people and persecuted as members of a hated sect. Discouraged (Heb 12:12–13; 13:5–6), they were tempted to return to Judaism (Heb 3:12–14; 6:4–6; 10:39). Thus, the writer of Hebrews attempted to transpose the material and visual aspect of temple worship into the domain of the conscience by highlighting the spiritual and inner nature of Christianity. Seventh, Jewish priests were permitted by Mosaic law to eat a portion of the sacrifice that had been offered. Now, as Christians separated from the temple worship, they no longer had that right. But they did have a superior privilege: spiritual participation in the sacrificed Christ, from which their former brother priests are excluded (Heb 13:10).

Eighth, Heb 10:18, as the conclusion of the doctrinal section Heb 7:1–10:18, affirms in absolute wording the elimination of the need for any sacrificial ritual. Ninth, because he was addressing priestly descendents of Levi, the author took "psychological precautions" and used doctrinal "circumlocutions" in order to denounce the foolishness of their attempted continuation of their priesthood. In an effort to show consideration for their feelings, the writer did not directly attack the priesthood in order to validate the priesthood of Jesus. Rather, he approached the matter from the priesthood of Melchizedek as a priestly order that preceded and superseded the Levitical order, and which in fact also typifies the priesthood of Christ. This is the gist of the argument in chap. 7.[221]

Tenth, the vivid description of Heb 6:6 and 10:29 is understood better against the backdrop of readers who had taken part in the death of Jesus. The Gospels make it clear that the priests and especially the chief priests were involved in masterminding the death of Jesus. The idea of "crucifying Jesus again" and putting him to open shame was used by the author to motivate these

[220] Ibid., 228. The priests played a significant role in Israel as intermediaries through whom God revealed his will in the form of *torah,* whose root idea means "to teach." It is used specially of the authoritative instruction given by the priests in Deut 17:9–11; 33:10, and many other places in the OT.

[221] Ibid., 230.

now converted priests to remain faithful to Jesus. Eleventh, the recipients of Hebrews had been victims of some persecution, including the loss of possessions (Heb 10:34). According to Spicq, they appear to be "rich" since they had enough to show generous hospitality (13:1–2), were tempted by greed (13:5–6), and were called upon to multiply their acts of kindness (13:16). Twelfth, the traditional title given to the book, "To the Hebrews," implies a body of men closely united, a homogeneous group. The recipients of Hebrews were a group of people in misfortune living together and sharing trials.

Childs's comment that the title construes the epistle as addressing the problem of the two covenants would certainly support Spicq's theory since this issue would be of paramount importance to former priests. Childs pointed out that Hebrews offers a programmatic statement of the theological relationship of the two covenants that receives its content not from the historical setting in the first century, but rather from Scripture. If the author were writing before AD 70, or even during the Jewish War (AD 66–70), the best way of proceeding would not be the historical approach but the Scriptural approach, which is exactly what the author of Hebrews did.[222]

Certainly each of these twelve arguments does not carry the same weight. Some are more circumstantial than others. But given the content and tone of Hebrews, one must admit that the theory of converted priests can account for a significant amount of the evidence from the text.[223] Scholer has shown how the author's use of temple language in Hebrews (*proserchesthai*, *eiserchesthai*, *teleioun*) is applied to the readers to characterize them as priests, including the incumbent obligation to function as priests in bringing sacrifices acceptable for worship (12:28; 13:15).[224]

(3) Location of the Recipients

The epistle nowhere specifically locates the recipients, hence suggestions are numerous. Early in church history and until the mid-eighteenth century, a Jerusalem or Palestinian destination held sway.[225] Its most recent proponent is Mosser, whose work is a formidable critique of the Roman destination and a

---

[222] Ibid., 231; Childs, *New Testament as Canon*, 415.

[223] Jerome indicated Philo was from a priestly family (*Lives of Illustrious Men*, 11). M. Barker ("Beyond the Veil of the Temple: The High Priestly Origins of the Apocalypses," *SJT* 51 [1998]: 6) conjectured that perhaps Philo's treatment of the creation stories, "the creation of the invisible world beyond the veil of the temple and then the visible world as its copy, is not an example of the Platonizing of Hellenistic Judaism but rather a glimpse of the priestly world even of his time." Likewise, perhaps the author's approach shares some similarity to Philo given his readership.

[224] J. M. Scholer, *Proleptic Priests: Priesthood in the Epistle to the Hebrews*, JSNTSup 49 (Sheffield: JSOT, 1991), 204–5.

[225] E.g., Chrysostom in his homilies on Hebrews suggested a Jerusalem destination. Examples of adherents to this view include Delitzsch, *Hebrews*, 1:21; Westcott, *Hebrews*, xxxix–xli; Spicq, *l'Épître aux Hébreux*, 1:247–250; Buchanan, *Hebrews*, 256–60; and Hughes, *Hebrews*, 15–19.

cogent argument for Jerusalem as the location of the recipients.[226] A. Nairne commented, "It is certain that the epistle would have been quite unsuited to the Church of Jerusalem as a whole,"[227] but this is a gross overstatement. The usual appeal that an author would not use Greek or quote exclusively from the LXX in addressing Palestinians can no longer be sustained in light of the evidence that perhaps as much as 20 percent of Jerusalem used Greek as their mother tongue, and the LXX was very much in use in Jerusalem in the first century AD.[228]

The nineteenth and twentieth centuries witnessed the development of the Roman destination for the epistle. First propounded by Wetstein in the mid-eighteenth century, the Roman destination is the majority view today.[229] Those who argue for a Roman destination depend heavily on Heb 13:24: "Those from Italy send you their greetings." This phrase is interpreted to mean that the readers were located somewhere in Italy and probably in Rome. However, the phrase can just as easily be interpreted to mean the epistle was written from Rome to some destination outside of Italy. Clement of Rome's citation of Hebrews in his epistle to the Corinthians is interpreted as evidence that the recipients were in Rome. The past trials the readers experienced (see Heb 10:32–34) are identified with the expulsion of Jewish Christians from Rome following the edict of Claudius in AD 49. Lane ably defends the theory that the recipients composed one of the house churches in Rome.[230]

Other destinations have been proposed, including Ephesus, Corinth, and western Asia Minor.[231] If the recipients of Hebrews were converted priests, then one logical suggestion that may also be supported with some biblical evidence—especially if the author of Hebrews is Luke—is Antioch in Syria. We know from Josephus that Jews were numerous in the city of Antioch, enjoying equal rights as citizens.[232] Furthermore, with a few exceptions, there was not the level of persecution of Jews in Antioch as in other cities.

Hebrews 6:10 says the recipients had ministered to the saints, so the Jerusalem offering given by the Antiochene church (Acts 11:27–30) may have been the referent of that verse. Of historical interest is Josephus's mention of the refusal by Antiochus to permit the observance of the Sabbath rest in Antioch

---

[226] Mosser, "No Lasting City," 275–321.

[227] A. Nairne, *Epistle to the Hebrews*, lvii.

[228] Cf. M. Hengel, *The "Hellenization" of Judea in the First Century after Christ*, trans. J. Bowden (London: SCM; Philadelphia: Trinity, 1989), 7–18.

[229] See Bruce, *Hebrews*, xxxi–xxxv; and Lane, *Hebrews 1–8*, lviii–lx.

[230] Lane, *Hebrews 1–8*, li–lx.

[231] For the latter, see J. Dunnill, *Covenant and Sacrifice in the Letter to the Hebrews*, SNTSMS 75 (Cambridge: Cambridge University Press, 1992), 23–24.

[232] Josephus, *Jewish War* 7.43. This was due to the proximity of Syria to Judea. On the relationship of Jews and Christians in Antioch from the first to the fourth centuries, see W. Meeks and R. L. Wilken, *Jews and Christians in Antioch in the First Four Centuries of the Common Era* (Missoula: Scholars Press, 1978), 13–36.

after about AD 67–69.[233] Hebrews 4:1–10 speaks of the Sabbath rest to come, a subject that would have appealed to Antiochene Jews at this time. Another interesting point is the statement in Heb 13:12–14 that "we have no continuing city, but we seek one to come." How appropriate this statement would have been to exiled Jewish priests living in Antioch, many of whom no doubt longed for Jerusalem and who needed to be reminded that the beloved city was not to be sought after.

The admonition of Heb 6:1–6 may have been given to counter pressure on those Jewish priests to return to Judaism and defend their nation against the eminent peril from the Romans. The crisis of the Jewish war, like a powerful vortex, drew in sectarians of all sorts to defend their homeland. Thus, even some from the Qumran community—which was a strict, isolationist sect—died at Masada while holding out against the Roman army. The same kind of pressure must have been brought to bear on many Jewish Christians. The possibility that some of their fellow countrymen would try to coerce them back into Judaism seems only natural under the circumstances of the times. We know from Josephus that violent attacks intensified on all those who refused to show solidarity with the Jewish resistance prior to the war.[234] These factors suggest Antioch as a possible location of the recipients of Hebrews.

If Luke is the author of Hebrews, evidence for Antioch increases since Luke is associated by both Scripture and tradition with Antioch in Syria. The Anti-Marcionite prologue to Luke's Gospel (dated around the years 160–180) states that Luke was a Syrian from Antioch. Eusebius in his *Ecclesiastical History* speaks of "Luke who was born at Antioch, by profession a physician." While the accuracy of these traditions cannot be established beyond question, it is reasonable to assume some factual basis for them in light of their early origin. Also of interest is that Antioch housed a medical school where Luke may have received his training as a physician.

Scripture itself provides some verification for these traditions in that Luke is very closely linked with Antioch. He has a more than passing interest in Antioch as can be observed from a consideration of statements found in his Gospel and Acts. For example, in Luke 4:25–27 Jesus reminded his hearers that there were some in Syria who were helped by the earliest of Israel's prophets. In Luke 6:17, Phoenicia is mentioned as the home of some who had come to hear Jesus preach the Sermon on the Plain. E. Franklin has shown that Luke-Acts "reflects what could well have been the life of the Antioch church. It may have arisen within that church. Luke-Acts could have been written to the Antiochene church. Its links with Paul's Letters could suggest a Roman provenance."[235] Lundbom, following J. Jeremias, noted that Luke 22:20 most

[233] Josephus, *Antiquities of the Jews,* 12.120.

[234] Josephus, *Jewish War*, 2.264–65.

[235] E. Franklin, *Luke: Interpreter of Paul, Critic of Matthew*, JSNTSup 92 (Sheffield: JSOT, 1994), 388.

likely depends on 1 Cor 11:25 where Paul's reference to tradition concerning the Lord's Supper perhaps reflects usage in the church at Antioch.[236]

M. Dods pointed out in reference to Antioch as the possible location of the recipients that "certainly they required some such exposition as is given in the Epistle, of the relation of Judaism to Christianity."[237] F. Rendall, among many others, has suggested Antioch as a likely destination for Hebrews:

> [T]here alone existed flourishing Christian Churches, founded by the earliest missionaries of the Gospel, animated with Jewish sympathies, full of interest in the Mosaic worship, and glorying in the name of Hebrews; who nevertheless spoke the Greek language, used the Greek version of the Scriptures and numbered amongst their members converts who had, like the author, combined the highest advantages of Greek culture with careful study of the Old Testament and especially of the sacrificial Law.[238]

Acts 11:26 speaks of the disciples being first called "Christians" at Antioch. This disparaging epithet was used by the pagans because it was in Antioch that members of the early Christian church first stood out from Judaism as a distinct sect.[239] Additionally, there is "no mention of hostility from synagogue authorities in Antioch."[240] W. R. Farmer argued that the decisive break between Jews and Christians in Antioch occurred as a result of the Jewish War (AD 66–70).[241] Even if Farmer's thesis can be sustained, Jewish influence on the Christian church in Antioch continued until the seventh century.[242] The statements made in Hebrews concerning the circumstances of the readers can be correlated with such a scenario.

Concerning the title that appears at the beginning of the book, "To the Hebrews," we know it was not a part of the original text but was a later addition. It is usually interpreted to mean that the copyists, either because of content or tradition, considered the epistle to have been addressed to Jewish Christians. That the term in early Christianity referred to "ritually strict Jewish believers . . . with a deep attachment to the ceremonial laws and to the Jerusalem temple"[243] certainly would fit the situation of converted priests. The title has

---

[236] J. R. Lundbom, *Jeremiah 21–36*, 475.

[237] M. Dods, "Epistle to the Hebrews," in *The Expositor's Greek Testament*, ed. W. R. Nicoll (Grand Rapids: Eerdmans, 1974), 4:223.

[238] F. Rendall, *The Epistle to the Hebrews* (London: Macmillan, 1888), 69. H. MacNeill (*Christology of the Epistle to the Hebrews*, 16) said that "there is nothing incongruous in supposing the church at Antioch to be the recipient of the letter." E. R. Perdelwitz viewed Hebrews as written to Rome and Antioch ("Das literarische Problem des Hebräerbriefes," *ZNW* [1910]: 59, 105).

[239] Haenchen, *Acts*, 312; Meeks and Wilken, *Jews and Christians in Antioch*, 16.

[240] Meeks and Wilken, *Jews and Christians in Antioch*, 18.

[241] W. R. Farmer, "Jesus and the Gospels," *PSTJ* 28.2 (1975): 31–36.

[242] Meeks and Wilken, *Jews and Christians in Antioch*, 18.

[243] Ellis, *Making of the New Testament Documents*, 288.

also often been viewed as indicating that the recipients were located in or near the land of Israel.[244]

Whether the author himself was a member of the church being addressed cannot be ascertained with any degree of certainty. Likewise, Lindars's supposition that the author was a member of the church, detained in another location, who had been asked by the church leadership to intervene in a difficult situation involving a smaller group within the larger church is pure speculation.[245] Nothing in the epistle allows one to draw such a conclusion with any reasonable amount of certainty.

(4) Date of Hebrews

Like everything else surrounding the background of this epistle, the date is also unclear. Neither the internal evidence of the text nor the external historical data provide enough information for a dogmatic commitment to any of the theories that have been propounded. Until recently, the *terminus ad quem* was said to be AD 96 since Hebrews is quoted by Clement of Rome in his epistle to the Corinthians, which is traditionally dated AD 96. However, both Clement's use of Hebrews as well as the traditional date for his epistle has been questioned. Attridge is probably correct in his assertion that the wording that appears in *1 Clement* is a "sure sign of dependence on Hebrews,"[246] but the traditional date for Clement's epistle is now considered suspect by many and cannot be used as a firm peg for the *terminus ad quem* for Hebrews.[247] Given the internal evidence of Hebrews itself coupled with the external historical data, it can be suggested that the date of Hebrews fits within a range of AD 60–100.[248]

There have been three major views relative to the dating of Hebrews: pre-AD 64, AD 67–69, or toward the end of the reign of Domitian, who died in AD 96. These views depend on five primary matters: (1) the supposed author (if

---

[244] Ellis (ibid., 288) believed it was addressed to "various congregations" of strict Jewish Christians in Palestine. In light of recent studies in Hellenistic/Diaspora Judaism and Palestinian Judaism, the case for a Palestinian destination is strengthened.

[245] Lindars, *Theology of Hebrews*, 8.

[246] Attridge, *Hebrews*, 7.

[247] See the discussion in Attridge, *Hebrews*, 6–9; Lane, *Hebrews 1–8*, lxii–lxvi; Lane, "Social Perspectives on Roman Christianity during the Formative Years from Nero to Nerva: Romans, Hebrews, 1 Clement," in *Judaism and Christianity in First-Century Rome,* ed. K. P. Donfried and P. Richardson (Grand Rapids: Eerdmans, 1998), 196–244; and Ellingworth, *Hebrews*, 29–33. The question of the dating of *1 Clement* was reopened by L. L. Welborn, "On the Date of First Clement," *BR* 24 (1984): 34–54.

[248] Attridge, *Hebrews,* 9. P. Eisenbaum ("Locating Hebrews Within the Literary Landscape of Christian Origins," in *Hebrews: Contemporary Method, New Insights*, 227–31) attempted to date Hebrews in the early second century AD based on three things: (1) her interpretation of Heb 2:3 as placing distance between Jesus and the current readers; (2) her suggestion that the author of Hebrews was aware of other early Christian writings, including one or more written Gospels; and (3) the supposed affinity of Hebrews to second-century writings. Her statement that "there is virtually no evidence tying Hebrews to the first century" (216) is certainly over the top.

Paul, then a date after AD 67 is impossible); (2) the location of the recipients; (3) the interpretation of the internal evidence; (4) the correlation of these with external historical data (e.g., if a Roman destination is assumed, was the persecution mentioned in the epistle during the reign of Nero or Domitian?); and (5) theological factors.[249]

A recent proposal of the post-AD 70 date by E. B. Aitken conjectures that the epistle was written in Rome during the aftermath of the temple's destruction and the Flavian triumph.[250] This proposal received salient critique by Mitchell, who nonetheless argued for a post-AD 70 date, relying heavily on the epistle's "christological tradition of the Roman churches as articulated in the Gospel of Mark."[251] D. Georgi sought to locate Hebrews during the reign of Domitian, "putting behind him [the author] the experience of Jewish and 'Christian' martyrdoms, at a time when the question of whether church and synagogue should separate was still undecided."[252] Those who favor a post-AD 70 date appeal to the supposed second-generation status of the readers and the absence of any reference to the temple, among other arguments.

The evidence for a pre-AD 70 date appears to me to be the stronger. Although all would be well advised to heed the sound counsel of Porter on the use and possible misuse of the present tense in reference to the temple cultus in Hebrews as an argument for a pre-AD 70 date,[253] the single most important argument for an earlier date for Hebrews is the deafening silence in reference to the fall of Jerusalem and the temple in AD 70. While related, the use of the present tense and the lack of any reference to the destruction of Jerusalem are two separate matters. Porter may be correct in his thorough analysis of the data regarding the use of the present tense. However, the issue of the author's silence regarding the destruction of Jerusalem and the temple is another (although related) matter. Those who would date Hebrews after AD 70 face the formidable task of explaining its silence on such a momentous event. How could the author, despite its immediacy, have failed to use the only absolutely

---

[249] There is no need to detail the various arguments since they are amply stated in the relevant literature. In addition to works listed previously in footnotes above, see Robinson (*Redating the New Testament*, 200–220) and Guthrie (*New Testament Introduction*, 701–5). P. Walker, "Jerusalem in Hebrews 13:9–14 and the Dating of the Epistle," *TynBul* 45 (1994): 39–71, is an incisive argument for the pre-AD 70 date. In that same year, S. Porter's article ("The Date of the Composition of Hebrews and Use of Present Tense-Form," *Crossing the Boundaries: Essays in Biblical Interpretation in Honour of Michael D. Goulder*, ed. S. Porter, P. Joyce, and D. Orton [Leiden: Brill, 1994], 295–313) is from a linguistic perspective on the use and misuse of the present tense in Hebrews and must be heeded by all who prefer a pre-AD 70 date.

[250] E. B. Aitken, "Portraying the Temple in Stone and Text: The Arch of Titus and the Epistle to the Hebrews," in Gelardini, *Hebrews: Contemporary Methods, New Insights*, 131–48.

[251] A. Mitchell, *Hebrews*, 8–11.

[252] Georgi, "Hebrews and the Heritage of Paul," 243.

[253] Porter, "The Date of the Composition of Hebrews," 295–313. Porter correctly noted the inappropriateness of equating time and tense as is common in older Greek grammars. Thus, the use of the present tense alone cannot be used for establishing the date of Hebrews.

irrefutable argument in his attempt to show the passing nature of the temple cultus and the Levitical system? Barton summarized the problem:

> If the temple at Jerusalem had been destroyed decades before, as the hypotheses under consideration suppose, the fact would have been well known, and the employment of language which implied that its cult was still going on would have made the Epistle ridiculous in the eyes of its first readers. To refuse to be guided by this, the most tangible and definite of all the clues which exist for determining the date of Hebrews, is to throw away the key to the problem and open the door to fruitless speculation and confusion.[254]

The reference in Hebrews to the continual offering of the Levitical sacrifices indicates the readers' inability to deal with the sin problem permanently. Then the author stated, "If it could, would they not have stopped being offered?" (Heb 10:2). Koester perceptively noted that the question expects the readers to agree with the author, which would have been difficult on their part at any point after AD 70 since the temple no longer existed. However, Koester rightly also noted that the lack of a specific reference to the temple in the epistle "makes this argument less than decisive."[255] Robinson is surely right when he pointed out that although the argument from silence proves nothing, it creates in the case of Hebrews a very strong presumption that places the burden of proof on those who argue for a post-AD 70 date.[256]

P. W. L. Walker furnished additional evidence for a pre-AD 70 date. He suggested that such a date is indicated not only by the author's reference to the temple, but by his treatment of the earthly Jerusalem and its significance. He argued that the key clue for dating the epistle is the issue of the Jerusalem temple. Was it still standing at the time Hebrews was written? The author's comments in 8:13; 10:37–39; 12:26–27; and 13:14 would seem to indicate so. Walker accepted the use of the present tense verbs at their face value and viewed this as evidence for a pre-AD 70 date, but his article is not a rehashing of the arguments based on the use of the present tense.[257]

---

[254] G. A. Barton, "The Date of the Epistle to the Hebrews," *JBL* 57 (1938): 200; cf. Robinson (*Redating*, 200–20) on this point.

[255] Koester, *Hebrews*, 53. On Heb 10:2 (along with Heb 8:4) as evidence for a pre-AD 70 date, see the points made by R. Gordon (*Hebrews*, 31–33). With reference to Heb 10:2 he noted, "The wording may at the least be considered injudicious if the verse was actually written at the time when the offering of sacrifices in Jerusalem *had* ceased" (32).

[256] Robinson, *Redating*, 205. See Witherington (*Letters and Homilies for Jewish Christians*, 27–28) who supports the pre-70 AD date due to the author's silence on the fall of Jerusalem: "With a writer as rhetorically astute as this author, the deafening silences are very telling about the date of writing."

[257] Walker, "Jerusalem in Hebrews 13:9–14 and the Dating of the Epistle," 40. Cf. his *Jesus and the Holy City: New Testament Perspectives on Jerusalem* (Grand Rapids: Eerdmans, 1996), 227–34. There are historical and literary parallels between Heb 13:14 and Luke 21:21, furnishing another link between Luke and Hebrews.

A. Nairne argued for a date shortly before AD 70. With the outbreak of the Jewish war, there may well have been a wave of patriotic nationalism that swept over Palestine and diaspora Judaism. This would have been a temptation to Christian Jews to revert to Judaism and the stability of the Jewish cultus.[258] Moule agreed with Nairne's assessment of the date and circumstances of the epistle:

> At such a time it is not only a fear of persecution and of being called traitors but also the human yearning for the ordered stability of an ancient system, with objective, tangible symbols, that will drive men back from the bold pioneering demanded by the Christian faith to the well-worn paths of the older way. It is to exactly such a temptation that the Epistle speaks, and it is thus, I think, that it becomes clearly intelligible.[259]

Nairne suggested that a date for Hebrews during the time of the Jewish war explains the language used in the epistle concerning the second coming of Christ. "Like the Gospel of S. Luke this Epistle found in those fearful days an interpretation of the 'coming.'"[260]

A further argument in favor of a date in the decade of the 60's can be adduced from the way Hebrews suggests that the tithe belongs to the priest (7:5). The argument that the tithe belonged to the priests and not to all the sons of Levi (Levites) was apparently hotly debated at this time. Josephus explained that the high-priestly families during the reign of Felix (c. AD 52–60) and Albinus (c. AD 62–64) abused this practice, thus raising the ire of the Levites since their claim to share in the tithes went unnoticed.[261] In AD 62 the Levites demanded recognition over against the priests in this matter as recorded by Josephus.[262] Horbury stated that the method of the author of Hebrews in discussing these matters places this book within the historical debates that occurred during the period of the First Jewish Revolt (AD 66–70) and thus furnishes another argument in favor of a date around AD 67.[263] In terms of the relationship of the church to Judaism, one must ask whether what we find in Hebrews suggests a time when the process of separation between the two had become all but complete or whether a time earlier in the process is best indicated. Hebrews is not a polemical attempt to legitimate the separation of Christianity from Judaism. Furthermore, it is clear that the separation certainly did not occur in the

[258] Nairne, *Epistle to the Hebrews*, lxxv–lxxvii.

[259] C. F. D. Moule, "Sanctuary and Sacrifice," *JTS*, N.S. (1950): 37.

[260] Nairne, *Epistle to the Hebrews*, 30. Grelot (*lecture de l'épître aux Hébreux*, 11, 103, 190–91) argued that the most probable date of writing was AD 67, written from Italy.

[261] *Antiquities of the Jews*, 20.181.

[262] Ibid., 20.216–18.

[263] W. Horbury, "The Aaronic Priesthood in the Epistle to the Hebrews," *JSNT* 19 (1983): 67–68.

first century.[264] The author of Hebrews was keenly interested in the relationship of Christianity to Judaism. In fact, the author was attempting to negotiate the thorny question of how Christianity was rooted in biblical Judaism, while being at the same time distinct from it. Anderson suggested that the "assumptions" concerning the people and the law in Hebrews locate it at an "early stage of the process" of disengagement.[265]

The evidence from the historical circumstances as well as the text itself support a date before the destruction of Jerusalem in AD 70, possibly around AD 67.[266] The reference to Luke in 2 Tim 4:11, the reference to "those from Italy" in Heb 13:24, and the combined references to Timothy both in 2 Timothy and Hebrews 13 can be easily and best explained by such a date.

The theory of Lukan authorship combined with a Roman provenance leads to the conclusion that the date that fits most of the internal and external data is around AD 67–68. As a member of the Pauline circle, it is highly unlikely that Luke could have written as late as the last decade of the first century. If the traditions surrounding his death are accurate, then he would have died around the middle of the decade of the eighties. I accept the traditional understanding of the scriptural evidence that indicates Luke was a member of the Pauline circle and one of Paul's traveling companions. Since Luke is mentioned in 2 Timothy near the time of Paul's death, it is reasonable to assume that he was there when Paul died. Pauline scholarship would not date Paul's death later than AD 67.

(5) Conclusion: Summary Proposal of Authorship, Recipients, Destination, and Date

Luke likely served as Paul's amanuensis for the Pastoral Epistles, which were written from Rome during Paul's second Roman imprisonment. Due to the nature of Paul's imprisonment, Luke was given greater latitude in the construction of the epistles, hence the stylistic similarities to Luke-Acts are explained. Luke remained in Rome after Paul's death where he wrote the epistle to the Hebrews around AD 67–68. Hebrews 13:24 is best interpreted as "those who are with me in Italy." This interpretation was the unanimous opinion of the patristics, even when Pauline authorship was denied.

The recipients of Hebrews were former priests who had converted to Christianity and had relocated to Syrian Antioch where they were a part of the church. Acts 6:7 informs us that "a great company of the priests became obedient to

---

[264] R. Hann ("Judaism and Jewish Christianity in Antioch: Charisma and Conflict in the First Century," *JRH* 14 [1987], 348) stated, "The relationship of Christianity to Judaism was an issue throughout the first century. Throughout the conflicts of the period, opposing groups accused each other of being excessively, or insufficiently, attached to the Jewish legal tradition."

[265] Anderson, "Who are the Heirs of the New Age in Hebrews?" 273.

[266] This date was also advocated by Spicq (*L'Épître aux Hebreux,* 1:257–61) and Robinson (*Dating*, 215) among many others. See Lindars (*Theology of Hebrews*, 19–21) who felt that a date later than AD 65–70 is not warranted by the evidence.

the faith." No more is said about them in Acts or the rest of the New Testament. Based on the audience profile of Hebrews, several reasons were given substantiating the claim that these former priests would fit the audience well. Their location in the Antiochene church is a reasonable conjecture given its importance in the early history of the church, Luke and Paul's connection with it, and what we know about it from Acts. That Antioch was a mixed congregation of Jews and Gentiles and that the city had a large and influential Jewish population could create the kind of social/theological matrix that Hebrews addresses.

3. The Purpose of Hebrews

Attempting to answer the question of the author's purpose in writing has produced several theories.[267] These generally revolve around doctrinal and pastoral motifs. Those who suppose a Gentile readership usually argue that the author's purpose was to assure them of the superiority of Christianity.[268] Related to this, many notice the repetition of the adverb "better," which occurs several times in the book and contrasts Jesus with some aspect of Judaism. This suggests that the purpose is to establish the superiority of the gospel to Judaism. This approach takes the purpose to be primarily doctrinal in nature. For example, R. Saucy, writing from a progressive dispensational perspective, suggested that the finality of Christ with respect to the transitory nature of the Levitical system is the key for the author.[269]

Historically, the most common purpose advocated suggests the author is attempting to dissuade his Jewish Christian readers from a relapse into Judaism brought on by increasing persecution and a desire for the stability of the old faith.[270] This basic view, with various modifications, was argued by Spicq, F. F. Bruce, Ellingworth, Dunnill, Lehne, and many others.[271] A theory that has also garnered support is W. Manson's thesis that has been adopted with certain qualifications by Lane, Lindars, and Hurst.[272] Manson found parallels

---

[267] These are summarized well by D. Guthrie (*Introduction,* 703–10), R. W. Johnson (*Going Outside the Camp*, 18–20), and M. J. Marohl (*Faithfulness and the Purpose of Hebrews*, 40–56).

[268] A. B. Bruce's *The Epistle to the Hebrews: The First Apology for Christianity* (Edinburgh, T&T Clark, 1899) is a classic defense of this position as illustrated by the title. Moffatt (*Hebrews*, xxiv–xxvi) argued for a Gentile audience as well; cf. Isaacs, *Sacred Space*, 23.

[269] R. Saucy, *The Case for Progressive Dispensationalism* (Grand Rapids: Zondervan, 1993), 56.

[270] This theory has lost considerable ground in recent years; see the critique by J. Dahms, "The First Readers of Hebrews," *JETS* 20 (1977): 365–75.

[271] For the specific nuances of this view laid out in chart form for easy access, including proposals as to the crisis facing the readers and the author's response, see R. W. Johnson, *Going Outside the Camp*, 18–19.

[272] W. Manson, *The Epistle to the Hebrews: An Historical and Theological* Reconsideration (London: Hodder & Stoughton, 1951). Cf. L. Hurst, *The Epistle to the Hebrews: Its Background and Thought;* and Lindars, *The Theology of the Letter to the Hebrews* (Cambridge: Cambridge University Press, 1991), 8–15. Lindars argued that the key text for identifying the crisis that

between the theology of Hebrews and Stephen's speech in Acts 7. He conjectured that the recipients were a minority within the church who were living too much on the Jewish side of their faith and neglecting the world mission of Christianity.[273] Jewett interpreted the epistle to be combating a Gnostic heresy.[274] Schmidt perceived the main problem of the readers to be "moral lethargy," which the writer challenged in his persistent warnings and exhortations to press on.[275]

W. C. van Unnik identified the purpose of Hebrews to be primarily pastoral, similar to that of Luke-Acts. He explored a number of parallels between the prologues of Luke-Acts and Heb 2:3–4 and concluded that the Hebrews passage furnishes the clue to understanding the Lukan purpose (at least for Acts):

> These words in the second half of this passage of the Epistle to the Hebrews may fittingly be used as a heading of Luke's second volume. I am firmly convinced that here we have found the scope of Acts, the angle under which we must see it to find the right perspective, or you may say: the hidden thread holding together the string of pearls.[276]

Hebrews 2:3–4 thus becomes an excellent explanation for the link between Luke's Gospel and Acts. Van Unnik concluded that it was certainly possible for the Lukan purpose to be similar to that of Hebrews: challenge believers to go on to maturity and not to waver in their faith.

Van Unnik's conclusions as to the similar notion of "witness" in Luke-Acts and Hebrews were confirmed by A. Trites who stated, "The idea of witness

---

precipitated the writing of Hebrews is 13:7–16: "The whole point at issue is a felt need on the part of the readers to resort to Jewish customs in order to come to terms with their sense of sin against God and need for atonement" (p. 10). The readers of Hebrews had lost confidence in the continuing efficacy of Christ's death to deal with their consciousness of sin. They had turned to the Jewish community, which made provision for ongoing sin through the sacrificial system, thus causing friction and division in the church. Lindars's reconstruction is unlikely, although it would fit the theory that the recipients were former Jewish priests quite well. But the book of Hebrews never draws a contrast between Jews and Gentiles.

[273] Manson, *Hebrews*, 24, 160. Thiselton's ("Hebrews," 1452) comment on Manson's view revealed the importance of Hebrews for many contemporary churches: "the crisis of the community, which may regularly apply today, is that the Christian group has lost its vision of the universal significance of Jesus Christ for world mission. In place of boldness, pilgrimage, and self-discipline, they have relapsed into a cozy, protective mind-set of 'maintenance' at the expense of mission. They have tamed and domesticated the gospel into a 'safe religion.'"

[274] Jewett conjectured the epistle was written by Epaphras and sent to the churches of the Lycus valley at about the same time as Colossians (*Letter to Pilgrims: A Commentary on the Epistle to the Hebrews* [New York: Pilgrim, 1981], 5–13). On the problem of Gnosticism and Hebrews, Jewett was preceded by F. D. V. Narborough, *The Epistle to the Hebrews* (Oxford: Clarendon, 1930), and T. W. Manson ("The Problem of the Epistle to the Hebrews," *BJRL* 32 [1949–50]: 1–17), who argued for Apollos as the author.

[275] T. E. Schmidt, "Moral Lethargy and the Epistle to the Hebrews," *WJT* 54.1 (1992): 167–73. This view fails to recognize the reality of persecution and suffering that the readers faced as well as failing to account for passages such as Heb 12:4–11.

[276] W. C. van Unnik, "'Book of Acts' the Confirmation of the Gospel," *NTS* 4 (1960): 49.

appears a number of times in the Epistle to the Hebrews, a fact suggested by the use of words drawn from the vocabulary of witness . . . and the idea of witness is very similar to that which is unfolded in greater detail in the Book of Acts."[277] He then added, "For the writer of Hebrews, as for Luke, the truth of one kind of testimony required confirmation by another, in this case, by the testimony of the scriptures."[278] After pointing out that Hebrews speaks of the Jewish law of evidence, signs and wonders functioning as confirmatory testimony, and the testimony of God himself through the Scriptures, Trites noted that "in all these ways it [Hebrews] deserves to be compared to the Book of Acts, where the same themes are developed and expanded."[279]

B. Lindars called attention to the structural emphasis of pastoral concern that is so prominent in vital sections of Hebrews where the writer sought to reassure the readers of the concern of Jesus their high priest. Such passages suggest, according to Lindars, that the readers were deeply troubled by their sense of sin.[280] This apparent self-consciousness of sin is a key factor in Lindar's assessment of the theology and purpose of Hebrews.[281] The key to the crisis, which precipitated the writing, can be found in 13:7–16. The author warned against "strange teachings" and unprofitable "foods" (v. 9). What is meant has to be deduced from the substance of the whole letter, and the contrast in v. 10 is helpful: "we have an altar from which those who minister at the tabernacle have no right to eat." Those who serve the tent are the Levitical priests, as described in chap. 9. This suggests that the strange teachings are the details of atonement sacrifice that were established there. If so, the whole point at issue is a felt need on the part of the readers to resort to Jewish customs in order to come to terms with their sense of sin against God and their need for atonement. Thus the central argument of the letter is precisely a compelling case for the complete and abiding efficacy of Jesus' death as an atoning sacrifice.[282]

The readers were neglecting meeting with the church (10:25) and were instead reverting to synagogue worship in order to feel the benefit of the sacrificial system. The reason for this was their own consciousness of sin (9:9,14; 10:2). Since atonement for sin was "constantly attended to in Jewish liturgy, their return to the Jewish community offered a practical way of coping with their need."[283] The purpose of Hebrews was to explain to the readers how Christ's sacrifice not only dealt with their past life but also their present and future sins. Reversion to the Jewish sacrificial system as a means of dealing

[277] A. Trites, *The New Testament Concept of Witness*, SNTSMS 31 (Cambridge: Cambridge University Press, 1977), 217.

[278] Ibid., 218.

[279] Ibid., 221.

[280] Lindars, *Theology*, 25.

[281] Ibid., 8–15.

[282] Ibid., 10.

[283] Ibid., 14.

with their present consciousness of sin was not the answer, according to the author of Hebrews.[284]

Lindars's theory founders on his suggestion that early Christian teaching did not make plain that post-baptismal sins are also covered by Christ's death. The preaching of Peter and Paul in Acts along with the Pauline Epistles would seem to contradict this aspect of Lindar's theory. If his assessment of the recipients' need is accurate, the problem must lie in their spiritual immaturity and thus their failure to receive spiritual truth (5:11–6:3), and not in the early church's lack of theological clarity regarding the application of the atonement to sin in the life of a Christian. Yet if the recipients were converted priests, it may have been the case that something like what Lindars suggests played a role as to the need of the recipients of Hebrews. If any group within the early church would have been in danger of what Lindars suggested, certainly converted priests would have to be at the top of the list. Lindars's suggestion has the advantage of merging the doctrinal heart of the epistle with the hortatory sections combined with the practical exhortations of chap. 13 into a unified whole.

Whatever the crisis facing the readers, it is clear that the author viewed them as Christians, most likely Jewish Christians, and he alternatively warned and encouraged them to press on to maturity in the faith. A determination of purpose must take into account that the epistle is primarily pastoral in nature and only secondarily doctrinal. The author uses exhortations and warnings, with the expositional portions of the epistle serving as the grounds for these exhortation and warnings. It is the hortatory sections of the epistle that should be considered most diagnostic of purpose.[285] Thus, the necessity of pressing on to maturity in the midst of difficulty (6:1–3) by means of drawing near, holding fast, and stirring one another up to love and good works (10:19–25) would appear to serve as a viable statement of purpose. Lane's assessment would appear to be correct:

> So using a number of effective pastoral strategies, he balanced instruction, exhortation, reminder, encouragement, and warning—alternating confrontation with affirmation—to stabilize the community and to move them beyond a lack of nerve to a fresh commitment to Christ and the gospel.[286]

4. The Theology of Hebrews

Space limitations prohibit a thorough discussion of the theology of Hebrews here. In this commentary, I address the theological implications in summary

[284] Ibid., 12–14.

[285] See the discussion on structure below.

[286] Lane, "Living a Life of Faith," 252. See his "Hebrews as Pastoral Response," in *Newell Lectureships*, ed. T. Dwyer (Anderson: Warner, 1996), 3:103–21.

fashion, usually at the end of each section treated. In addition to the many monographs that cover some aspect of the theology of the epistle, the critical commentaries and New Testament theologies provide a good overview of this subject.[287] It is now generally recognized that although Hebrews is a profound theological document from the first century, it is not a theological treatise per se.[288] Hebrews is a sermon with pastoral intent. Theology is employed in service to the church. Ultimately, for the author of Hebrews, truth is unto holiness.

A. Mitchell, a recent Catholic commentator on Hebrews, spoke to the issue of the Roman church's attempts from the Council of Trent to Vatican II to base the priesthood of bishops and priests on the eternal high priesthood of Christ. He judiciously called attention to the lack of references in the epistle to the eucharist or to any ministerial priesthood.[289]

On the issue of Hebrews and anti-Semitism or replacement theology,[290] only a brief word is necessary at this point. It has not been demonstrated that the author of Hebrews is guilty of anti-Semitism. There is no anti-Judaic polemic in the epistle. Hebrews does not address the issue of Jew/Gentile relationships. In fact, as Williamson correctly stated: "'Anti-Semitism' has no relevance whatsoever to the historical situation of Hebrews."[291] With respect to replacement theology or supersessionism, one will not find in Hebrews any notion that the Jewish people have been replaced by any other group, including the church. However, and this is crucial, it is clear there is a form of supersessionism in Hebrews. It is vital that this notion be defined properly. In Heb 8:13 the old covenant is superseded by the new. But this point is made by the author in his appeal to the Old Testament Scriptures themselves, namely Jer 31:31–33, which predicts this very thing. The author of Hebrews is arguing that Jesus has inaugurated the new covenant in fulfillment of Jeremiah's prophecy. This point is discussed at greater length in my comments on Heb 8:8–13.

---

[287] Especially helpful are G. Milligan, *The Theology of the Epistle to the Hebrews with a Critical Introduction* (Edinburgh: T&T Clark, 1899); D. Guthrie, *New Testament Theology*; B. Lindars, *Theology of Hebrews*; and B. Fanning, "A Theology of Hebrews," in *A Biblical Theology of the New Testament*, ed. R. Zuck (Chicago: Moody, 1994) 369–415. A. T. Lincoln (*Hebrews: Guide*, 82–106) provided a helpful summary. See I. H. Marshall, *New Testament Theology* (Downers Grove: InterVarsity, 2004), 605–27, 682–90. On the subject of eschatology in Hebrews, one must consult the seminal work of C. K. Barrett ("The Eschatology of the Epistle to the Hebrews," 363–93). The seminal work on the Christology of Hebrews is that of W. Loader, *Sohn und Hoherpriester: Eine traditionsgeschichtliche Untersuchung zur Christologie des Hebräerbriefes*, WMANT 53 (Neukirchen: Neukirchener Verlag, 1981).

[288] See L. Hurtado, *Lord Jesus Christ: Devotion to Jesus in Earliest Christianity* (Grand Rapids: Eerdmans, 2003), 498.

[289] A. Mitchell, *Hebrews*, 24–25.

[290] See the helpful summary of recent work on this subject in C. Williamson, "Anti-Judaism in Hebrews?" *Int* (July 2003): 266–79; cf. B. Horner, *Future Israel,* NACSBT (Nashville: B&H Academic, 2007).

[291] Williamson, "Anti-Judaism in Hebrews?" 276–77; cf. Mitchell, *Hebrews*, 25–28.

The clear teaching of Hebrews on this matter renders the following comment by Williamson inexplicable:

> Each covenant has its ongoing dilemmas with God's love and justice. But it is not as clear today as it was to the author of Hebrews that the new covenant is any less weak than the old in producing perfection or any more gracious in its attitude toward sinners. Nor does Hebrews make, finally, a convincing case that this new covenant, therefore, displaces the old, even if that displacement is limited only to cultic matters.[292]

5. The Use of the Old Testament in Hebrews

One of the most intriguing areas of research on Hebrews concerns the author's use of the Old Testament.[293] In addition to approximately 38 quotations in Hebrews, there are many allusions—perhaps as many as 55—and echoes of Old Testament passages.[294] There are 11 quotations from the Pentateuch and only one from the historical books. There is one quotation from Proverbs and seven from the prophetic books, with three from Jer 31:31–34. Most striking is that the author quotes from the Psalms 18 times.[295] A good case can be made for understanding Ps 110:1,4 as the key text that the author interpreted in the epistle. G. B. Caird's ground-breaking work identified four key Old Testament passages as the work's core quotations: Psalms 8; 95; 110; and Jeremiah 31.[296]

Another important point is the author's exclusive use of the LXX rather than the Hebrew text. This has often been used in the past to suggest that the author and/or his readers did not know Hebrew, that the recipients were Hellenistic Jews rather than Palestinian Jews, or that the author was writing to a Gentile

---

[292] Williamson, "Anti-Judaism in Hebrews?" 279. Such a comment illustrates a low view of biblical authority and a theological agenda driven by political correctness.

[293] Competent surveys of this subject with helpful bibliography include three works by G. Guthrie: "Old Testament in Hebrews," in *DLNT* 841–50; "Hebrews' Use of the Old Testament: Recent Trends in Research," *CurBS* 1.2 (2003): 271–94; and "Hebrews," *CNTOT* 919–95. The latter provides a brief and helpful analysis and commentary on each OT quotation in Hebrews, though it appeared too late to inform this commentary. Additional surveys of this subject can be found in A. T. Lincoln, *Guide*, 69–81; A. Trotter, *Interpreting Hebrews*, 190–202; K. Son, *Zion Symbolism in Hebrews: Hebrews 12:18–24 as a Hermeneutical Key to the Epistle*, Paternoster Biblical Monographs (Milton Keynes, UK: Paternoster, 2005), 3–9; L. T. Johnson, *Hebrews*, 21–25; along with his "The Scriptural World of Hebrews," *Int* 57 (2003): 237–50. Cf. the major commentaries such as Lane (*Hebrews 1–8*, cxii–cxxiv) and Ellingworth (*Hebrews*, 37–42) as well as my comments on 1:5–14.

[294] Scholars differ on the actual number of quotations. See R. Longenecker, *Biblical Exegesis in the Apostolic Period* (Grand Rapids: Eerdmans, 1975), 164–70; and Lane, *Hebrews 1–8*, cxvi.

[295] S. Kistemaker's *The Psalm Citations in the Epistle to the Hebrews* (Amsterdam: van Soerst, 1961) is an indispensable study on this topic.

[296] G. B. Caird, "The Exegetical Method of the Epistle to the Hebrews," *CJT* 5 (1959): 44–51.

audience. None of these conclusions is warranted by the author's exclusive use of the LXX. We now know that the LXX was used regularly even by Palestinian Jews in the first century. The intricate use and play on words from the Old Testament that the author used in his argument coupled with the sustained appeal to the Old Testament Scriptures and sacrificial system of the Old Testament make it highly unlikely that the recipients were non-Jews. Furthermore, it has been demonstrated that the author made use of rabbinical exegetical techniques found in the midrashim.[297]

The author's midrashic approach and his reverence for the Scripture can be seen in his treatment of Ps 110:4 in Heb 7:1–25. Throughout this passage he never refers to Jesus as "high priest" but always as "priest," even though he is speaking of the high priesthood of Jesus. Why does he do this? Most likely because the LXX text of Ps 110:4 says "You are a *priest*" rather than "You are a high priest." When he concludes his commentary on Ps 110:4, he returns to the title "high priest" for Jesus in Heb 7:25–28. In 7:26 the author returns to the first person plural that he had last used in 6:20. Outside 7:1–25, the author refers to Jesus as "priest" only once (10:21), and there he employs the adjective "great," which is a normal LXX expression designating the high priest.[298] Such careful following of the language of the LXX illustrates the author's reverence for written Scripture.

One of the distinctive features of the author's use of the Old Testament is the method of citation. Whereas Paul was fond of using "it is written," the author of Hebrews avoided this totally and instead used some form of the verb "to speak." In most cases it is God himself who is identified as the speaker through the psalmist or prophet. Four times quotations are attributed to Jesus and three times to the Holy Spirit. Four times the human authors are mentioned: Moses twice, David once, and the unusual "someone says" in Heb 2:6. In Heb 4:7, the unusual "God saying through David" is used. In addition, the author often used the present tense verb "to say" in quoting the Old Testament, illustrating for his readers and for us the living power of Scripture that is perennially applicable. Also, the author made no distinction whatsoever between the spoken and the written word of God. Words of human authors are understood by the author to be the very words of God—a view identical to Paul's in 2 Tim 3:16.[299] Only as the people of God hear the Word of God correctly from the Old Testament will

---

[297] For examples of rabbinic interpretive methodology in Hebrews, see Lane, *Hebrews 1–8*, cxix–cxxiv.

[298] J. Kurianal, *Jesus Our High Priest: Ps 110,4 as the Substructure of Heb 5,1–7,28* (European University Studies, Series XXIII, Theology, 693; Frankfurt am Main: Bern, 2000), 158.

[299] See D. Peterson, "God and Scripture in Hebrews," in *The Trustworthiness of God: Perspectives on the Nature of Scripture*, ed. P. Helm and C. Trueman (Grand Rapids: Eerdmans, 2002), 120–22. Peterson's survey of the entire epistle, which shows how the author of Hebrews sustains his appeal to the audience to listen to the voice of God from Scripture, is very helpful for gaining a concise understanding of the epistle as a whole. For a more detailed analysis of the author's hermeneutical method, see the ground-breaking work by G. Hughes, *Hebrews and Hermeneutics:*

they be able to press on to maturity and not drift away and draw back (2:1–4; 6:1–3; 10:22–25; 12:1–2).

For the author of Hebrews, the written Scripture is actually the very words of God spoken personally to the readers. Here propositional revelation is at one and the same time personal as well. This is illustrated in three places in Hebrews 10. In v. 30 the author introduced the quotation of Deut 32:35 with the words, "For we know him who said." Here the referent is God. In Heb 10:5 the author placed the words of Ps 40:6–8 on the lips of Jesus. Jeremiah 31:33 is quoted in Heb 10:15 with the citation formula, "The Holy Spirit also testifies to us." This not only illustrates the author's trinitarian understanding of divine inspiration when it comes to the Old Testament, but it also signifies the supremely authoritative character of these written Scriptures in that they are "spoken" by God, Christ, and the Holy Spirit. But even more than this, the author's use of Scripture in this chapter indicates his willingness to evoke the very authority of God for his own statements to his readers. Stanley wrote that in Heb 9:8 "our author goes beyond merely attributing the words of Scripture to the Holy Spirit, assigning to him at least part of the interpretive process as well. In other words, the Holy Spirit bears witness not only through the words of Scripture, but through the logical implications drawn from Scripture as well."[300]

Eisenbaum noticed a feature of the author's quotations of the Old Testament that is often missed: most of them are quotations of direct speech from the Old Testament rather than from narrative texts. The quotations contain "either the literal words of God (although often a character such as Moses is the actual speaker), the oracular utterances of the prophets, or the musings of the psalmist. Given the hermeneutical presuppositions of the time, we can safely assume that, for the author of Hebrews, these are all instances of divine utterance."[301] This provides evidence of the author's own understanding of Scripture as God's speech and of his interest in helping his readers to understand that Scripture is God speaking directly to them in their current situation.

In Heb 13:5–6 the author introduces a quotation from Deut 31:6 with the words "because God has said." He then introduces a quotation of Ps 118:6–7 with the words "So we say with confidence." This latter quotation is striking in that here the author does not refer to Scripture as being spoken by God, Christ, the Holy Spirit, any human author, or "Scripture says." Instead *both the author and readers* are the ones speaking Scripture, though not in the sense of

---

The Epistle to the Hebrews as an Example of Biblical Interpretation, SNTSMS 32 (Cambridge: Cambridge University Press, 1979).

[300] S. Stanley, "A New Covenant in Hebrews: The Use of Scripture in Hebrews 8–10," (Ph.D. dissertation, University of Sheffield, 1994), 218.

[301] P. Eisenbaum, *The Jewish Heroes of Christian History: Hebrews 11 in Literary Context*, SBLDS 156, ed. P. Perkins (Atlanta: Scholars Press, 1997), 92. Eisenbaum also noted that "the hermeneutical distinction that motivates our author to quote directly in one place, and to retell in another depends upon *whether or not he wants to render the biblical text as speech or as narrative*" (90).

its originating source. That the author can introduce a Scripture quotation in this way shows the normative claim on both author and readers that the Scriptures make in their current lives. Such usage also implies the author's desire to teach his readers that they are not in need of extra-biblical revelation to meet the trials and challenges of daily life; the written Scripture, which constitutes the very speech of God addressing them in the present time, is sufficient. In answer to the question "Does God still speak today?" our author would reply: "Yes indeed; he speaks in his written word, which is simultaneously the word of God, Jesus, and the Holy Spirit." The trajectory for understanding Scripture in this fashion was begun in the prologue when the author identified Jesus, the Logos, as God's "speech."

6. Hebrews and Textual Criticism

For the ministering Bible student who does not have the time to delve deeply into the various text critical issues in Hebrews, Trotter's table of the important textual variants is unsurpassed.[302] One should also consult B. Metzger's *A Textual Commentary on the Greek New Testament*,[303] in addition to the exegetical commentaries that deal with these matters in more detail. This commentary only deals with text-critical issues that significantly affect interpretation.

7. The Outline and Structure of Hebrews

In the same way that background questions for Hebrews have engendered diverse proposals, the outline and structure of the epistle are no different. Space considerations prohibit a thorough investigation of this subject. The best summary and evaluation of the various analyses of the structure of Hebrews are in C. Westfall's *Discourse Analysis of the Letter to the Hebrews* (previously cited).[304] Older commentators tended to organize Hebrews according to thematic content with little regard for the hortatory sections of the epistle. A traditional topical approach is to divide the epistle into two major sections: doctrinal (usually concluding at either 10:18 or 10:39) and practical (11:1–13:25).[305] A second approach, begun principally with the work of the Jesuit scholar A. Vanhoye, attempts to analyze the epistle more as an entire discourse

---

[302] Trotter, *Interpreting Hebrews*, 95–110. Also helpful is his listing of books on textual criticism to aid in the study of Hebrews (111–13).

[303] *TCGNT* 591–607.

[304] In addition to C. Westfall, see the surveys in Guthrie, *Structure*, 3–20; Lane, *Hebrews 1–8*, lxxxiv–xcviii; and Ellingworth, *Hebrews*, 50–58.

[305] See J. Brown, *Hebrews*, The Geneva Series of Commentaries, reprint edition (Edinburgh: Banner of Truth Trust, 1961), 10; F. F. Bruce, *Hebrews*, vii–x; and P. E. Hughes, *Hebrews*, 3–4. Part one of Hebrews is described by them as "doctrinal," "dogmatic" or "kerygmatic" while part two is labeled "practical," "parenetic," or "ethical."

using linguistic principles and discourse analysis.[306] He divided the epistle into five major sections arranged concentrically around the theme of Christ's priesthood. Nauck's tripartite division of Hebrews (1:1–4:13; 4:14–10:31; 10:32–13:17) has been very influential among scholars.[307] A third approach to the structure of the epistle follows the perspective of rhetorical criticism. Early practitioners include K. Nissilä and W. Übelacker.[308] Both suggested Hebrews is an example of deliberative or exhortatory rhetoric. Others take it as an example of epideictic or instructive rhetoric.[309]

Koester, for example, suggested the following outline, based on classical rhetorical categories:

- I. Exordium (1:1–2:4)
- II. Proposition (2:5–9)
- III. Arguments (2:10–12:27)
  - A. First Series (2:10–6:20)
    1. Argument: Jesus received glory through faithful suffering—a way that others are called to follow (2:10–5:10)
    2. Transitional Digression: Warning and Encouragement (5:11–6:20)
  - B. Second Series (7:1–10:39)
    1. Argument: Jesus' suffering is the sacrifice that enables others to approach God (7:1–10:25)
    2. Transitional Digression: Warning and Encouragement (10:26–39)

---

[306] See A. Vanhoye, *La structure littéraire de l'Épître aux Hébreux* (Paris: Desclée de Brouwer, 1976), which is his most comprehensive work on the subject. His *Structure and Message of the Epistle to the Hebrews* (Rome: Pontificio Instituto Biblico, 1989) is a more accessible treatment. Vanhoye analyzed the literary devices used in Hebrews and posited a chiastic framework for the epistle. See analyses by J. Swetnam ("Form and Content in Hebrews 7–13," *Bib* 55 [1974]: 333–48); Koester (*Hebrews*, 83); Westfall (*Discourse Analysis*, 8–11); and J. Bligh ("The Structure of Hebrews," *HeyJ* 5 [1964]: 170–77)—all of whom have highlighted the weaknesses of Vanhoye's approach. Bligh (*Chiastic Analysis of the Epistle to the Hebrews* [Heythrop: Athenaeum, 1966]) argued for the chiastic structure of Hebrews, as did L. Dussaut (*Synopse structurelle de l'Épître aux Hébreux: Approche d'analyse structurelle* (Paris: Desclée, 1981]), 3–163. Bligh ("The Structure of Hebrews," 176) wrongly concluded that the epistle is the work of two authors, one of whom sketched out the argument "perhaps in poor Greek," followed later by a stylist who rewrote it in good Greek. This supposedly explains the "anomaly" of the conceptual and verbal patterns in the epistle that do not mesh together well in Bligh's assessment.

[307] W. Nauck, "Zum Aufbau des Hebräerbriefes," in *Judentum, Urchristentum, Kirche: Festschrift for J. Jeremias*, ed. W. Eltester, BZNW 26 (Giessen: Töpelmann, 1960), 199–206.

[308] See K. Nissilä, *Das Hohepriestermotiv im Hebräerbrief: Eine exegetische Untersuchung* (Helsinki: Oy Liiton Kirjapaino, 1979); and W. Übelacker, *Der Hebräerbrief als Appell: Untersuchungen zu Exordium, Narratio und Postscriptum (Hebr 1–2 und 13,22–25)* (Stockholm: Almqvist & Wiksell, 1989).

[309] See T. H. Olbricht, "Hebrews as Amplification," in *Rhetoric and the New Testament*, ed. S. Porter and T. H. Olbricht, JSNTSup 90 (Sheffield: Academic, 1993), 375–87; and Koester, *Hebrews*, 80–96.

- C. Third Series (11:1–12:27)
  1. Argument: God's people persevere through suffering to glory by faith (11:1–12:24)
  2. Transitional Digression: Warning and Encouragement (12:25–27)
- IV. Peroration (12:28–13:21)
- V. Epistolary Postscript (13:22–25)[310]

In the latter half of the twentieth century, scholars began to take note of the significance of the hortatory sections of Hebrews in the overall structure (e.g., 2:1–4; 4:11,14–16; 10:19–25). O. Michel concluded that the most salient sections of Hebrews must be the hortatory passages.[311] This insight opened the door for a significant advance in the understanding of the structure of the epistle. Kümmel concurred and said the hortatory passages function as the goal and purpose of the entire discourse.[312] F. F. Bruce agreed with this assessment and argued that the climax of Hebrews is in 10:19–25: "The preceding argument leads up, stage by stage, to this exhortation, and what comes after reinforces it."[313] The text itself bears out this analysis, for in 13:22 the author speaks of his text as "a word of exhortation." The imperatives and hortatory subjunctives in the epistle should be ranked at the highest thematic level.

Building on these insights, L. L. Neeley, G. Guthrie, and C. Westfall have furthered the quest for the structure of Hebrews from the perspective of discourse analysis. One major study of the structure of Hebrews is L. L. Neeley's "A Discourse Analysis of Hebrews."[314] Neeley applied the discourse theory of her mentor Robert Longacre[315] to Hebrews. She utilized four major systems of information organization in discourse: (1) the combining of sentences into larger units—paragraphs and embedded discourses; (2) constituent structure—how discourse units function in the overall discourse; (3) distinction between backbone and support information; and (4) semantic organization.[316] Neeley concluded that the epistle comprises three major sections (1:1–4:13;

---

[310] Koester, *Hebrews*, 84–85. DeSilva proposed the major divisions to be 1:1–2:18; 3:1–4:13; 4:14–10:18; and 10:19–13:25 (*Perseverance in Gratitude*, 72–75).

[311] O. Michel, *Der Brief an die Hebräer*, KEK (Göttingen: Vandenhoeck & Ruprecht, 1975), 27.

[312] W. G. Kümmel, *Introduction to the New Testament*, trans. H. C. Kee (Nashville: Abingdon, 1975), 390.

[313] F. F. Bruce, "The Structure and Argument of Hebrews," *SwJT* 28 (1985): 6.

[314] Her thesis, "A Discourse Analysis of Hebrews" was originally done in 1976 and was published in *OPTAT* (1987): 1–146.

[315] For a summary treatment of Longacre's model, see D. Allen, "The Discourse Structure of Philemon: A Study in Textlinguistics," in *Scribes and Scripture: New Testament Essays in Honor of J. Harold Greenlee*, ed. D. Black (Winona Lake: Eisenbrauns, 1992), 77–96. See pp. 79–81 for a succinct overview of Longacre's theory.

[316] Neeley, "Discourse Analysis," 1. One of the strength's of Neeley's analysis is her careful attention to the conjunctions that link paragraphs and sections together.

4:14–10:18; 10:19–13:25) and that Hebrews is structured in an overall chiastic framework:[317]

A 1–4:13
  B 4:14–6:20
    C 7:1–28
    C′ 8:1–10:18
  B′ 10:19–10:39
A′ 11–13

She took the theme statements from the three major sections and produced the following macrostructure for Hebrews:

1:1–4:13	God has spoken to us in his Son
4:14–10:18	who as our high priest has offered a complete sacrifice for sins and by this obtained salvation for us.
10:19–13:21	Therefore let us draw near to God with a true heart in full assurance of faith in Jesus and the sufficiency of his finished sacrifice; let us hold fast the confession of the hope in him without wavering, and let us consider each other to stir up to love and good works.[318]

Building on Vanhoye and Neeley, G. Guthrie primarily analyzed discourse issues of cohesion, *inclusio*, and transition in Hebrews,[319] thus furthering our understanding of the overall structure of the book. His outline attempts to show semantic overlap that occurs between the alternating expository and hortatory genres in the epistle.[320] His chiastic framework of 3:1–12:2, however, is highly debatable.[321]

C. Westfall's analysis and outline, based on systemic-functional linguistics, is similar to Neeley's, especially in her decisions concerning major divisions.[322] Her work provides the most thorough analysis from a discourse perspective to date. She correctly noted the pivotal nature of the hortatory subjunctives at 4:14–16 and 10:22–25:

---

317 Neeley wrote, "A special feature of the lexico-semantic unity of Hebrews is a chiastic ordering of major semantic divisions in the discourse as a whole. These divisions, not corresponding exactly with the organization of Hebrews into embedded discourses on different levels of embedding, form another system of organization which is superimposed on the constituent structure and is also distinct from the backbone of the book" (ibid., 61–62).

318 Ibid., 61.

319 Guthrie, *Structure*, esp. 45–147; cf. id., *Hebrews,* NIVAC (Grand Rapids: Zondervan, 1998), 27–31, 39–40.

320 Ibid., 144.

321 Ibid., 136.

322 Westfall, *Discourse Analysis*, 297–301.

Most of the hortatory subjunctives provide a conclusion to the preceding unit and the point of departure for the subsequent unit. The author often marks the hortatory subjunctive unit as a conclusion with an inferential conjunction, but also expands the sentence with information and introduces the next unit, so that the hortatory subjunctive units look forward and backwards.[323]

The following outline attempts to incorporate the insights gleaned from Neeley, Guthrie, and Westfall, but it is closest to Neeley and Westfall.[324]

Prologue:	God has spoken with finality in Jesus the Son.	(1:1–4)
Division 1:	The superiority of the Son: his atonement impels us to hear and obey God's Word.	(1:5–4:13)
Section 1:	Because Jesus in his unique identity with God is superior to angels, and because he is our high priest who made atonement for our sins, we must listen to the truths about Christ and act on them.	(1:5–2:18)
Sub-Sec. 1:	The Son as God is superior to angels as revelation bearer.	(1:5–14)
Sub-Sec. 2:	Do not neglect the great truths about salvation.	(2:1–4)
Sub-Sec. 3:	Jesus accomplished atonement for us as our high priest.	(2:5–18)
Section 2:	Because the Son is faithful, we must be faithful and obey the word of God so we may enter into rest.	(3:1–4:13)
Sub-Sec. 1:	Jesus is superior to Moses.	(3:1–6)
Sub-Sec. 2:	Beware of unbelief that leads us away from Christ.	(3:7–19)
Sub-Sec. 3:	Strive through diligent obedience to enter God's Rest.	(4:1–13)
Division 2:	Christ's high priesthood and sacrifice ground our continued efforts to grow spiritually by pressing on to maturity, holding fast the confession, and drawing near to God's throne.	(4:14–10:18)
Section 1:	Since Jesus is our high priest, hold fast our confession and go on to spiritual maturity.	(4:14–6:20)
Sub-Sec. 1:	Since Jesus is our high priest, hold fast the confession and draw near to God.	(4:14–5:10)
Sub-Sec. 2:	Leave the elementary teachings about Christ and go on to maturity.	(5:11–6:8)
Sub-Sec. 3:	God's faithfulness to his promises to and through Christ provides strength to persevere.	(6:9–20)
Section 2:	Christ's priesthood is Melchizedekian, not Levitical.	(7:1–28)
Section 3:	The old covenant has been superseded by Jesus, who has inaugurated the new covenant by his death.	(8:1–10:18)
Sub-Sec. 1:	Jesus as high priest has obtained a heavenly ministry and inaugurated the new covenant.	(8:1–13)

[323] Ibid., 299.

[324] N. Miller, *The Epistle to the Hebrews: An Analytical and Exegetical Handbook* (Dallas: Summer Institute of Linguistics, 1988), is the work of a linguist based on the discourse analysis methods of J. Beekman, J. Callow, and M. Kopesec (*The Semantic Structure of Written Communication* [Dallas: Summer Institute of Linguistics, 1981]), and her outline of the epistle is found on pp. xvi–xviii. Miller's goal in this work is to provide "an extensive and in-depth resource book for translators and students" (vi). Her work is a valuable tool in examining the underlying semantic structure of Hebrews, especially at the lower levels of discourse meaning.

Sub-Sec. 2:	The limitations of the first covenant contrast with Christ's better covenant.	(9:1–14)
Sub-Sec. 3:	Christ is the mediator of the new covenant of salvation.	(9:15–28)
Sub-Sec. 4:	Jesus' sacrifice for sin was complete, final, and eternally effective.	(10:1–18)
Division 3:	Draw near, hold fast your confession, persevere by faith, and show love to one another.	(10:19–13:21)
Section 1:	Christians must draw near, endure, and love one another rather than sin willfully.	(10:19–39)
Sub-Sec. 1:	Draw near, hold fast, and love one another.	(10:19–25)
Sub-Sec. 2:	Do not continue sinning willfully.	(10:26–34)
Sub-Sec. 3:	Do not cast away your confidence	(10:35–39)
Section 2:	Christians must live by faith following the example of Old Testament saints.	(11:1–40)
Sub-Sec. 1:	Faith is necessary in the Christian life.	(11:1–2)
Sub-Sec. 2:	Faith sees God's promises from a distance.	(11:3–16)
Sub-Sec. 3:	Faith overcomes all adversity.	(11:17–40)
Section 3:	Live the Christian life with endurance; do not lose.	(12:1–29)
Sub-Sec. 1:	Christians must run the race with endurance.	(12:1–3)
Sub-Sec. 2:	Christians must endure God's discipline.	(12:4–13)
Sub-Sec. 3:	Christians must pursue peace and holiness.	(12:14–17)
Sub-Sec. 4:	Christians live not before terrifying Mt. Sinai but in Mt. Zion, city of the living God.	(12:18–24)
Sub-Sec. 5:	Obey and serve God with reverence and fear.	(12:25–29)
Section 4:	Show love in all things and obey church leaders.	(13:1–21)
Sub-Sec. 1:	Continue in love in all aspects of life.	(13:1–8)
Sub-Sec. 2:	Continue to offer daily sacrifice of praise.	(13:9–16)
Sub-Sec. 3:	Concluding exhortations and benediction	(13:17–21)
Conclusion and final greetings		(13:22–25)

Semantic analysis furnishes important evidence of the book's basic tripartite structure.[325] This will be presented at the appropriate place in the commentary. Following a well-crafted prologue (1:1–4), the first major section ends at 4:13. The second major section in the epistle (4:14–10:18) is concerned with Jesus's priestly office (4.14–7:28) and with his saving work (8:1–10:18). It also contains an extended warning (5:11–6:8) followed by encouragement (6:9–20). The third major section (10:19–13:21) is followed by a formal conclusion in 13:22–25. The three major discourse divisions each have their own function within the discourse. Though section two builds on section one by further developing thematic material introduced there, each of these two sections functions semantically

[325] See Nauck ("Hebräerbriefs," 203–4), which has been followed by many since. L. Neeley and C. Westfall's in-depth analysis of the discourse structure of Hebrews concluded that the text reveals a clear tripartite structure along the lines of those suggested by Nauck. K. Backhaus, whose literary analysis identified the same tripartite structure, assigned a single word to each section that summarizes how the author is pressing his readers to new spiritual insight: Hear (1:5–4:13), Interpret (4:14–10:18), Act (10:19–13:21). *Der neue Bund und das Werden der Kirche: Die Diatheke-Deutung des Hebräerbriefes im Rahmen der frühchristlichen Theologiegeschichte*, NTAbh 29 [Münster: Aschendorff Verlagsbuchhandlung, 1996], 63). G. Schunack followed the same tripartite structure (*Der Hebräerbrief*, ZBK [Zürich: Theologischer Verlag, 2002], 21, 60–61, 144–45).

to provide the grounds for the final section (10:19–13:21). This third section is actually the major hortatory section of the epistle. It begins with a hortatory paragraph (10:19–25) followed by both warning (10:26–31) and encouragement (10:32–39). This is followed by a lengthy expository section (chap. 11), but with a covert semantic message—"have faith." Hebrews 12:1 begins with the most pronounced conjunction in the epistle (*toigaroun,* "therefore") and introduces the major hortatory paragraph (12:1–3) that dominates the rest of the epistle. The remainder of chaps. 12 and 13 has numerous command forms (imperatives and hortatory subjunctives in Greek) identifying the majority of these paragraphs as hortatory in nature. This third section of the epistle (10:19–13:21) is best taken semantically as an example of an embedded hortatory discourse unit. It is preceded semantically by two embedded "grounds" units that furnish the basis of the final hortatory unit. Semantically, a hortatory passage has a higher prominence than its co-text that functions as ground or reason; hence, 10:19–13:21 is the most important information that the author wanted to convey. In the outline below, the word "EXHORTATION" is placed in all capitals and the two "grounds" sections are identified with lower case letters.[326] Embedded within each of these three major discourse units are other smaller units comprising paragraphs that semantically join to form these larger units.

I. Introduction/Prologue (1:1–4)
II. grounds[1] (1:5–4:13)
III. grounds[2] (4:14–10:18)
IV EXHORTATION (10:19–13:29)
V. Conclusion (13:22–25)

Once this overall structure is grasped, it becomes much easier to trace the argument of the epistle. For summaries of the argument of Hebrews that are rhetorically informed, Olbricht and DeSilva are helpful.[327]

OUTLINE OF HEBREWS

Prologue: God's Final Revelation in the Son (1:1–4)

[326] See Beekman, Callow, and Kopesec, *The Semantic Structure of Written Communication,* 106–7, on the grounds-EXHORTATION relationship. See the chart summary of the relations involving communication units on p. 112. The theory is overviewed on pp. 5–34 and detailed on pp. 35–140. B. Lindars ("The Rhetorical Structure of Hebrews," 384, 406) correctly noted, against Vanhoye, that the climax of the epistle's argument is in 10:19–12:29 because the purpose of the epistle is essentially practical.

[327] See T. Olbricht, "Anticipating and Presenting the Case for Christ as High Priest in Hebrews," in *Rhetorical Argumentation in Biblical Texts: Essays from the Lund 2000 Conference*, ed. A. Eriksson, T. Olbricht, and W. Übelacker (Harrisburg: Trinity Press International, 2002), 355–72; D. DeSilva, "The Invention and Argumentative Function of Priestly Discourse in the Epistle to the Hebrews," *BBR* 16 (2006): 295–323.

- I. The Superiority of the Son (1:5–4:13)
  - 1. Jesus' Identity and Work Demand Our Obedience (1:5–2:18)
    - (1) The Son's Superiority to Angels (1:5–14)
    - (2) Exhortation not to Neglect Salvation (2:1–4)
    - (3) Atonement Accomplished by Our High Priest (2:5–18)
  - 2. Faithful Obedience Necessary to Enter Rest (3:1–4:13)
    - (1) Jesus' Superiority to Moses (3:1–6)
    - (2) Beware of Unbelief (3:7–19)
    - (3) Exhortation to Enter God's Rest (4:1–13)
- II. Obligations of Jesus' Priestly Office and Saving Work (4:14–10:18)
  - 1. Perseverance and Maturity Grounded in Jesus' High Priesthood (4:14–6:20)
    - (1) Perseverance and Communion with God (4:14–5:10)
    - (2) Pressing on to Maturity (5:11–6:8)
    - (3) Persevering Strength Based on God's Faithfulness (6:9–20)
  - 2. Christ's Melchizedekian Priesthood (7:1–28)
  - 3. Jesus the Mediator of a New Covenant (8:1–10:18)
    - (1) Jesus' Inauguration of the New Covenant (8:1–13)
    - (2) Limitations of the First Covenant (9:1–14)
    - (3) Christ the Mediator of the New Covenant (9:15–28)
    - (4) Jesus' Effectual Sacrifice for Sin (10:1–18)
- III. Exhortation to Draw Near, Hold Fast, and Love One Another (10:19–13:21)
  - 1. Confidence to Persevere and Avoid Willful Sin (10:19–39)
    - (1) Spiritual Resources, Privileges, and Requirements (10:19–25)
    - (2) Dangers of Deliberate Sin (10:26–34)
    - (3) Need to Persevere (10:35–39)
  - 2. Conviction to Live by Faith (11:1–40)
    - (1) Necessity of Faith (11:1–2)
    - (2) Foresight of Faith (11:3–16)
    - (3) Accomplishments of Faith (11:17–40)
  - 3. Encouragement to Run with Endurance and Pursue Peace (12:1–29)
    - (1) Running with Endurance (12:1–3)
    - (2) Enduring Discipline (12:4–13)
    - (3) Pursuing Peace and Holiness (12:14–17)
    - (4) Arrival at Mount Zion (12:18–24)
    - (5) Dangers of Turning Away (12:25–29)
  - 4. Final Exhortations to Love and Humble Submission (13:1–21)
    - (1) Continuing in Love (13:1–8)
    - (2) Continuing Sacrifices of Praise (13:9–16)
    - (3) Continuing in Submission and Prayer (13:17–21)

Conclusion and Final Greetings (13:22–25)

PROLOGUE: GOD'S FINAL REVELATION IN THE SON (1:1–4)

The opening paragraph of Hebrews may be the stylistic apex of the entire Greek New Testament. With the possible exception of the prologue to Luke's Gospel, nothing quite like the lofty rhetorical and literary expression of Heb 1:1–4 occurs elsewhere in the New Testament.[1] The intricate structural organization of the clauses, phrases, and words that constitute the single four-verse sentence reveals the author's literary skill. The structural weight of the entire 72 words in Greek rests upon a single finite verb *elalēsen* and its subject *ho theos*: "God . . . has spoken." The author's use of rhetorical techniques such as alliteration, meter, rhythm, phonetic and semantic parallelism, syntactical/ semantic repetition, and chiasm are all evidenced in this sentence. Thiselton claims that these verses "provide one of the most arresting beginnings possible, combining elegance, alliteration, rhythm, rhetorical artistry, and unstoppable force with probably the most sophisticated and stylish Greek in the entire New Testament."[2]

The doctrinal sweep of these verses is breathtaking, making a major contribution to our understanding of the biblical doctrines of revelation, christology, soteriology, creation, and eschatology. The doctrine of revelation is reflected in vv. 1–2 in that God has spoken not only in the past but now definitively in one who is by nature a Son. It is the fundamental proposition of the author of Hebrews, as of all the biblical writers, that one cannot know God unless God makes himself known. This he has done supremely in Jesus. The majestic Christology places this paragraph alongside John 1:1–18, Phil 2:5–11 and Col 1:15–18 as one of the four key christological passages in the New Testament. Scarcely a major theological category is passed over in this panoramic paragraph. Virtually ever single word is pregnant with meaning.[3]

Consequently, due to the theological significance of the prologue, its programmatic function for the entire discourse,[4] and its structural and stylistic

---

[1] W. H. Attridge stated, "The rhetorical artistry of this exordium surpasses that of any other portion of the New Testament" (*The Epistle to the Hebrews*, Her [Philadelphia: Fortress, 1989], 36).

[2] A. C. Thiselton, "Communicative Action and Promise in Interdisciplinary, Biblical, and Theological Hermeneutics," in *The Promise of Hermeneutics*, ed. R. Lundin, et al. (Grand Rapids: Eerdmans, 1999), 146. Elsewhere he noted, "Much of the poverty of some preaching today derives from exclusive attention either to 'teaching,' 'exhortation,' or personal anecdote, in contrast to the richly multilayered, multilevel model of preaching, teaching, and praise seen here" ("Hebrews," in *Eerdmans Commentary on the Bible*, ed. J. D. G. Dunn and J. W. Rogerson [Grand Rapids: Eerdmans, 2003], 1454).

[3] Thiselton ("Hebrews," 1454) remarked, "These verses open a powerful sermon which is both expository (e.g., its use of Pss 2, 8, 95, 110) and intensely practical."

[4] G. Hughes recognized the significance of this verse for the entire epistle when he wrote that it is "the hermeneutical key to the whole theology of the two covenants" (*Hebrews and*

features that deserve careful explication, a disproportional amount of space is devoted to its treatment. An exegesis of the passage comes first, beginning with grammatical/syntactical structure and moving from there to consider matters of rhetorical and semantic structure. Finally, the theological implications of this classic passage are presented and used to critique contemporary theological trajectories, especially in the areas of revelation and Christology.

An analysis of the opening paragraph of Hebrews must include a discussion of several features: structure, theology, and its programmatic function for the rest of the epistle. Three aspects of structure are considered: grammatical/syntactical, rhetorical, and semantic.

Grammatical and Syntactic Structure of 1:1–4

Virtually all discussions of the grammatical and syntactical structure of the prologue point out that it has basically two segments.[5] The difference of opinion occurs over where to make the division between the two. Some understand the strategic placement of *huiō* in v. 2a to be the dividing line. For others, it is the relative pronoun *hos* at the beginning of v. 3—understanding it as dependent grammatically on *huiō* but introducing a series of relative and participial clauses with the Son as subject. Those who argue for the second view make a credible case.[6] But the first view is preferable that takes the instrumental *huiō* at the end of v. 2a to be the dividing line. Meier represents well those who take this approach, noting that the author has made *huiō* the "grammatical pivot" of the entire paragraph.[7] All subsequent relative and participial clauses modify it. Each of the constituent clause elements relates directly or indirectly to the main verb of the paragraph *elalēsen*. The relative *hos* at the beginning of v. 3 is dependent on *huiō* as are the two relative clauses that precede v. 3. D. J. Ebert argued for this approach from the proposed chiastic arrangement of the prologue.[8] Although he did not discuss the issue at hand, the central sections

---

Hermeneutics: The Epistle to the Hebrews as a New Testament Example of Biblical Interpretation, SNTSMS 36 [Cambridge: Cambridge University Press, 1979], 47).

[5] Attridge (*Hebrews*, 36) divided these verses into three segments with the third being v. 4. Most, however, see v. 4 as part of the second segment of the paragraph if they do not view it as beginning a new paragraph, as do F. Delitzsch, *Commentary on the Epistle to the Hebrews*, trans. T. L. Kingsbury [Edinburgh: T&T Clark, 1872; repr. Grand Rapids: Eerdmans, 1952], 1:39); P. E. Hughes, *A Commentary on the Epistle to the Hebrews* (Grand Rapids: Eerdmans, 1977), 50; and the TEV.

[6] See A. Vanhoye, *La structure littéraire de l'Épître aux Hébreux* (Paris: Desclée de Brouwer, 1976), 65–68, who is followed by W. L. Lane, *Hebrews 1–8*, WBC (Dallas: Word Books, 1991), 9; cf. C. R. Koester, *Hebrews*, AB (New York: Doubleday, 2001), 183; and Attridge, *Hebrews*, 36. On clauses beginning with ὅς that function as a new sentence, see E. A. Nida, et al., *Style and Discourse* (Roggebaai, Cape Town: Bible Society, 1983), 122.

[7] J. P. Meier, "Structure and Theology in Heb 1, 1–14," *Bib* 66 (1985): 172.

[8] See the discussion below and D. J. Ebert, "The Chiastic Structure of the Prologue to Hebrews," *TJ* (1992): 168.

of his chiasm begin with the first relative clause following *huiō*. If valid, this would further support the notion that *huiō* is the dividing point between the two segments of the paragraph.

Three additional arguments can be marshaled in favor of this view. First, there is a numerical symmetry that appears to exist between the prologue and the second paragraph (1:5–14). There are seven relative and participial clauses following *huiō* that serve to characterize the nature and work of the Son, and there is a catena of seven Old Testament quotations illustrating the Son's superiority to the angels in 1:5–14.[9] If this is by the author's design, and not coincidental, then most likely *huiō* is best seen as the line of demarcation between the two paragraph segments. Second, although *theos* remains the grammatical subject until the relative *hos* of v. 3, it is clear that from v. 3 onward the thematic focus has shifted to the Son. Third, the symmetrical elements of contrast between God's speech through the prophets and through the Son ("in the past"/"in these last days"; "to our forefathers"/"to us"; "through the prophets"/"by his Son") lend weight to viewing *huiō* as the end of the first segment and *hos* (v. 3) as introducing the first of several subordinate clauses, all of which modify *huiō*.

Everything through v. 2a, then, is dependent on the predication "God spoke." The subject *theos* and the main verb *elalēsen* form the load-bearing subject/predicate wall for the entire structure of 1:1–4.

1In the past God spoke to our forefathers through the prophets at many times and in various ways, 2but in these last days he has spoken to us by his Son, whom he appointed heir of all things, and through whom he made the universe. 3The Son is the radiance of God's glory and the exact representation of his being, sustaining all things by his powerful word. After he had provided purification for sins, he sat down at the right hand of the Majesty in heaven. 4So he became as much superior to the angels as the name he has inherited is superior to theirs.

1:1 The paragraph begins with two unusual and rhetorically balanced adverbs: *polumerōs,* "at many times," and *polutropōs*, "in various ways." The main issue to be resolved here is if they convey essentially the same semantic idea or if they are distinctive in meaning. From the perspective of lexical semantics, either view is viable. *Polumerōs* can denote something that occurs in many parts[10] and can be translated "in many portions" as in the NASB. Or it can have a temporal sense, denoting a number of related points of time,[11] and can be translated "at many times" as in the NIV. Third, it can be construed as indicating a number of different ways something may be done.[12] *Polutropōs*

[9] Meier presented a strong case for this numerical (and theological) symmetry in "Structure and Theology," 170–76.

[10] L&N 63.19.

[11] Ibid., 67.11.

[12] Ibid., 89.81.

denotes something that occurs in many kinds of ways and can be translated "in various ways" (NIV) or "in many ways" (NASB).[13]

If the author's focus is on the manner or mode alone, then these two terms can be viewed as essentially synonymous and the doubling is for rhetorical or stylistic effect.[14] If the temporal idea were intended, then the phrase would convey something like "at different times and in different ways" (HCSB). If the focus of *polumerōs* is on "part" or "portion," then the translation of the two adverbs would be something like "in many parts (portions) and in many ways (manners, modes)." The idea here, according to most commentators, is that each Old Testament prophet gave a part of the message, and these parts were given in different modes (dreams, visions, direct revelation).

Some view *polumerōs* as quantitative (in successive portions) and *polutropōs* as qualitative (in various forms).[15] *Polumerōs* can be interpreted as the multiplicity of successive acts, referring to different times (when) and people (through whom) God revealed. *Polutropōs*, then, expresses the multifaceted modality in which the speaking was accomplished. Here the focus is on the diversity of form and content of the revelation (visions, dreams, face to face [Num 12:8], intervention of angels, symbols).[16] Others suggest that the reference is not to the different methods of divine communication but to the nature of the revelation, that is, law, history, psalms, prophecy, object lessons, signs, and symbols. In Abraham he spoke in the form of promises; in Moses, law, history, and signs; in Isaiah, prophecy.[17] In other words, the focus is not on how he spoke to the prophets, but on how he spoke to the fathers *through* the prophets. The best approach combines both ideas of form and content since the text does not specify how the diversity of revelation is to be conceived and since a variety of examples of both form (e.g., visions) and content (e.g., law, prophecy) occur in the Old Testament.[18] Regardless of the mode used in

---

[13] Ibid., 58.29. L&N 89.82 supposedly gives an alternative nuance for this word, but the distinction is minimal (perhaps one emphasizing class or kind and the other emphasizing the relational idea of manner or mode).

[14] P. Ellingworth, *The Epistle to the Hebrews*, NIGTC (Grand Rapids: Eerdmans, 1993), 91. J. Moffatt, *A Critical and Exegetical Commentary on the Epistle to the Hebrews*, ICC (Edinburgh: T&T Clark, 1924; repr., Edinbugh: T&T Clark, 1963), 2, following Chrysostom, said the two adverbs form a hendiadys (rhetorical amplification of the same idea) for "variously."

[15] Delitzsch, *Hebrews*, 1:40. He said that the former refers to the truth of revelation and the second to modes of revelation.

[16] See G. Lünemann, *The Epistle to the Hebrews,* trans. from the 4th German edition by M. Evans, *Critical and Exegetical Handbook to the New Testament*, ed. H. A. W. Meyer (NY: Funk & Wagnalls, 1885), 390. D. A. DeSilva's translation is "in many pieces and in many ways" (*Perseverance in Gratitude: A Socio-Rhetorical Commentary on the Epistle to the Hebrews* [Grand Rapids: Eerdmans, 2000], 86), and this basic approach is taken by most commentators.

[17] See M. Vincent, *Word Studies in the New Testament* 4 (Grand Rapids: Eerdmans, 1946), 4:377.

[18] Attridge, *Hebrews,* 37; cf. B. F. Westcott, *The Epistle to the Hebrews* (London: Macmillan, 1892; repr., Grand Rapids: Eerdmans, 1955), 5.

the Old Testament, in every case the disclosures given by these modes were propositional in nature and verbal in form.[19]

It appears best not to see a temporal idea as the focus of *polumerōs* since the root meaning of the cognate adjective is "consisting of many parts."[20] However, the piecemeal nature of the revelation and the force of the two adverbs imply a temporal idea.

The semantic focus in these two words is distribution—the revelation came in parts at different times and in different ways. The contrast is between the multiplicity and diversity in form and content compared to the singularity and finality of revelation in the Son. The contrast does not involve contradiction since the same subject (God) governs both revelation in the prophets and in the Son. Rather, the idea is one of continuity amid contrast, as is the case with the first half of this paragraph and with the entire epistle. Together the adverbs express in an emphatic way the extent of the Old Testament revelation.[21]

The primary meaning of the temporal adverb *palai,* "in the past," is a point of time preceding another point of time (see "in these last days" in v. 2). Louw and Nida distinguish three uses of *palai*, noting that its use here focuses on an interval of considerable length between the two points.[22] The meaning is not that which is ancient as contrasted with the modern, nor is the primary focus "formerly" as contrasted with the present time,[23] although this is evident. Its meaning is further defined by the phrases "to our forefathers" and "through the prophets." The adverb is balanced by its counterpart "in these last days" in v. 2. Given the overall context, *palai* refers to the whole Old Testament period expressing when God spoke to the fathers.

The first activity of God mentioned by the author is locution. God speaks. The aorist participle *lalēsas* ("having spoken"; NIV, "spoke") modifies the finite aorist verb *elalēsen* ("has spoken") in v. 2. Many translators see the participle as semantically parallel to the finite verb: "God spoke to the fathers and/but

---

[19] As noted by J. I. Packer, *God Has Spoken* (Grand Rapids: Baker, 1988), 81.

[20] As in Attridge (*Hebrews,* 37) and DeSilva (*Perseverance in Gratitude,* 86).

[21] Lane, *Hebrews 1–8,* 10. G. von Rad, with reference to the "many and various ways" of Heb 1:1, wrongly used this statement to bolster his contention that the OT has no single, coherent theme, but rather is a series of "distinct and heterogeneous revelatory acts" (*Old Testament Theology*, trans. D. M. G. Stalker [New York: Harper & Row, 1962], 1:115).

[22] L&N 67.24; cf. the usage that implies completion of the previous point of time (67.22). Whether the usage in 1:1 implies a revelation given and *completed* in the past (as in Vincent, *Word Studies*, 4:378) is questionable. Actually, the context indicates that God's giving of revelation was not completed in the past since there was more to come in the last days in the Son. Furthermore, the adverb may express a temporal relationship to an event in the discourse, namely, God's speaking in the prophets *in the past* compared to his speaking in the Son *in these last days*, or it could be referring to the point of time long before the actual writing of the letter. L&N takes it in this latter sense (67.24).

[23] As in Delitzsch (*Hebrews*, 1:40). Ellingworth (*Hebrews*, 91) said that the context suggests the idea of "distant" time rather than merely "earlier," a comment commensurate with the sense of *palai* as "long ago."

he also spoke to us."[24] The participle carries a temporal idea ("after he spoke to the fathers . . . he spoke to us"), but this may not be the author's focus. It could be construed concessively: "*although* he spoke to the fathers . . . he spoke to us."[25] Since it is the same God who is speaking, the issue is not so much *when* he spoke (then versus now), nor that he spoke *to the fathers* and then *to us,* but that he spoke through *prophets* and now in one who is by his very nature a *Son.* Certainly the *when* and the *to whom* are paralleled, but the main focus would appear to be the relationship between the prophets and the Son: *prophētais* is both plural and definite, whereas *huiō* is singular and indefinite. It is further highlighted by the contrast between "in the past" and "in these last days" as well as by the use of the two adverbs signaling the piecemeal character of the revelation given to and by the prophets, as opposed to the unified and all encompassing revelation in the Son.[26]

The phrase *tois patrasin* ("to our forefathers") functions as the indirect object of *lalēsas.* Two primary questions need to be resolved here. Does the term refer only to the patriarchs of Israel or does it convey a more general meaning of "ancestor, forefather"? Second, does the article imply the possessive "our"? With regard to meaning, the more general meaning best comports with the lexical and contextual data. The word is commonly used in the New Testament to mean "ancestors."[27] Had the writer intended a more restrictive meaning, he had the option of using *patriarchai.*

Regarding the second question, it is sometimes inferred from the absence of *hēmōn* ("our") with *patrasin* that at least some of the recipients were Gentile Christians.[28] Four reasons render this unlikely. First, the article before the noun may function as a possessive[29] and is taken this way by many commentators and translators.[30] Second, the pronoun would have hindered the *p* alliteration in the verse (five words begin with *p*).[31] Additionally, Paul referred to "our forefathers" in 1 Cor 10:1 even though his audience was predominantly Gentiles. Third, Abraham is described in Rom 4:11 as "the father of all who believe," indicating an expansion in the New Testament of the usage of *patrasin* to describe spiritual ancestry.

God spoke to the Old Testament saints "through the prophets." The prophet in the Old Testament was one who proclaimed and interpreted divine

[24] See D. Guthrie, *Hebrews*, TNTC (Grand Rapids: Eerdmans, 1983), 61–63; P. Ellingworth and E. A. Nida, *Translator's Handbook on the Letter to the Hebrews* (London/New York: United Bible Societies, 1983), 4–5. The participle is translated this way in the NIV, NRSV, TEV, NJB.

[25] See the argument for this below.

[26] See the excellent discussion in Hughes (*Hebrews*, 36–37).

[27] BDAG 788.

[28] Westcott, *Hebrews,* 6; A. Vanhoye, *Le Christ est notre Prêtre* (Toulouse: Priere et Vie, 1969), 58; and Ellingworth, *Hebrews,* 92.

[29] *GGBB* 215–16.

[30] Moffatt, *Hebrews,* 3; Hughes, *Hebrews,* 25.

[31] As suggested by Attridge, *Hebrews,* 38.

revelation.[32] This phrase, *en tois prophētais*, is most likely an instrumental of means indicating God's speaking "through" or "by" the prophets.[33] Some interpreters take the phrase in a local/spatial sense: God's speaking "in" the prophets meant that God was dwelling in them and enabling them to speak his word.[34] The question here is one of focus and emphasis. Did the author intend to focus on the prophets as God's instruments of revelation, which they were, or was his focus on the fact of God's activity *in* them? Since both views are grammatically feasible and express a theological truth, is there any contextual or semantic clue that would tip the scales one way or the other?

The passage contrasts the prophets and the Son, and the nature of the contrast is between God's relationship to the prophets and to the Son. This is also expressed in the lack of the article with *huiō* in v. 2. The author was contrasting a prophet-kind of revelation with a Son-kind of revelation. This contrast lends itself more to the instrumental than the local/spatial idea. A second reason to consider *en* as instrumental is the corresponding semantic idea in 2:1–4: *di' angelōn* ("by angels") and *dia tou kuriou* ("by the Lord"). That 2:1–4 is closely connected to 1:1–4 is well established and the issue of relationship is again paramount.[35] Here, of course, the instrumental use of *dia* is clear.[36] Third, the two datives of indirect object "to our forefathers" and "to us," as the terminus of the action in the verb "spoke," place the focus on the instrumental use of *en*. Both prophets and Son are mediators of God's revelation of himself, with no direct object specified. This fits better the instrumental rather than the local use of the preposition. The focus is not on the content of the revelation, or on the way God spoke *to* the prophets, but on the nature and relationship of the mediators (prophets and Son) to God himself and on the way God spoke.

---

[32] See the classic by W. Beecher, *The Prophets and the Promise* (New York: Thomas Y. Crowell & Co., 1905; repr., Grand Rapids: Baker, 1975).

[33] F. F. Bruce, *The Epistle to the Hebrews*, NICNT (Grand Rapids: Eerdmans, 1964), 44; Lane, *Hebrews 1–8,* 11; Ellingworth, *Hebrews,* 92; Koester, *Hebrews,* 177; and most translations (cf. Heb 9:22).

[34] See H. Alford, "Prolegomena and Hebrews," *Alford's Greek Testament: An Exegetical and Critical Commentary*, 5th ed. (Boston: Lee & Shepard, 1878; repr., Grand Rapids: Guardian, 1976), 4:3. M. Dods made a good case, noting that "revelation now consisted not merely in what was said [προφήταις] but in what he was [υἱος]" ("Epistle to the Hebrews," in *The Expositor's Greek Testament*, ed. W. R. Nicoll [Grand Rapids: Eerdmans, 1974], 249); cf. Westcott, *Hebrews,* 6; G. Friedrich, "προφήτης," *TDNT* 6:832; R. C. H. Lenski, *The Interpretation of the Epistle to the Hebrews and of the Epistle of James* (Columbus, Ohio: Wartburg, 1946), 32; Robertson, *WP* 5:334; NASB. Lünemann explained that "God, in revealing Himself to the fathers by the prophets, was present in the latter, . . . in such wise that the prophets were only the outward organs of speech for the God who spoke in them" (*Epistle to the Hebrews,* 392). C. Moll (*The Epistle to the Hebrews*, in *Lange's Commentary on the Holy Scriptures,* trans. A. C. Kendrick [New York: Charles Scribner, 1868], 24) commented that ἐν seems to be used instrumentally only with things.

[35] On the close connection between 1:1–4 and 2:1–4, see T. Lewicki, *Weist nicht ab den Sprechenden!': Wort Gottes und paraklese im Hebräerbrief* (Paderborn/München: Ferdinand Schöningh, 2004), 48–61.

[36] Delitzsch (*Hebrews,* 1:42) noted that "the use here corresponds to the διά of Heb 2:3."

The phrase "through the prophets" also generates discussion on the referential extent of the meaning of "prophets." The reference is to Old Testament prophets, but many believe it includes Moses, Abraham (called "a prophet" in Gen 20:7), and even others in the Old Testament through whom God spoke.[37] Although the phrase can mean the Old Testament Scriptures, as perhaps it does in Luke 24:25, the translation "in the prophet's writings," which has occasionally been suggested, is probably not intended here.[38] The use that the author makes of the Old Testament in terms of his distribution of quotations from the Pentateuch, historical books, prophets, Psalms, and Proverbs indicates his regard for the entire Old Testament as a prophetic book.[39] The phrases "in the past," "to our forefathers," and "through the prophets" together serve to define temporally the reference to the Old Testament era, including at least the period from Abraham to Malachi and at most the entire Old Testament revelation.

1:2 The expression "in these last days" contrasts with "in the past" of v. 1 and is descriptive of the time when the readers of the epistle lived. The phrase "in these last days" *(ep' eschatou tōn hēmerōn)* is found in the Septuagint (with various inflections)[40] and translates a Hebrew temporal idiom for the future as distinct from the past.[41] The Jewish perspective of two ages—this age and the coming eschatological age—is well known. The rabbis debated in which age the Messiah would appear, finding Old Testament evidence both ways. It is probably best to link the two at the appearance of Jesus: the closing out of "this age" and the inauguration of "the coming age."[42] The phrase had come to have a technical eschatological significance in Jewish thought,[43] and this was incorporated into the New Testament. The author of Hebrews, like the other New Testament writers, viewed the life, death, resurrection, and exaltation of Jesus as the inauguration of "the last days." The present time in which the readers

---

[37] See Lünemann, *Hebrews*, 392; Westcott, *Hebrews,* 6; Moffatt, *Hebrews,* 3; and S. J. Kistemaker, *Exposition of the Epistle to the Hebrews*, (Grand Rapids: Baker, 1984), 26. Alford ("Hebrews," 3) considered the sense of the phrase to include those whose writings form the OT canon, and "all who were vehicles of the divine self-manifestation to the fathers."

[38] BDAG 891. Lünemann (*Hebrews*, 392) and Ellingworth (*Hebrews,* 92) argued against this meaning in 1:1, though Ellingworth conceded that this "is doubtless indirectly implied."

[39] G. B. Caird, "The Exegetical Method of the Epistle to the Hebrews," *CJT* 5 (1959), 47.

[40] Gen 49:1; Num 24:14; Deut 4:30; 8:16; Josh 24:27; Hos 3:5; Mic 4:1; Jer 23:20; 25:19; Ezek 37:24; 38:16; Dan 2:28,29,45; 10:14.

[41] Westcott, *Hebrews*, 6; Lane, *Hebrews 1–8,* 10. For the most comprehensive discussion of the Hebrew phrase בְּאַחֲרִית הַיָּמִים that stands behind the Greek ἐπ' ἐσχάτου τῶν ἡμερῶν, see W. Staerk, "*Der Gebrauch der Wendung* בְּאַחֲרִית הַיָּמִים *im AT Kanon,*" *ZAW* 11 (1891): 247–83. Lünemann (*Hebrews*, 393) correctly noted that τῶν ἡμερῶν τούτων should not be taken in apposition to ἐπ' ἐσχάτων with the meaning "at the period's close, which these days form." But Lenski (*Hebrews,* 31) interpreted the phrase in this way.

[42] Alford ("Hebrews," 3) said that the evidence makes this conclusion a "safe inference"; cf. Westcott (*Hebrews*, 6). In the 15 occurrences of the phrase in the LXX, the genitive plural ἐσχάτων is more common than ἐσχάτου (11 times and four times respectively), but with no appreciable difference in meaning.

[43] See G. W. Buchanan, "Eschatology and the 'End of Days,'" *JNES* 20 (1961): 188–93.

are living is "the last days" in contrast to the *palai* of v. 1. It is not only that the appearance of Jesus occurred during the last days, but that his appearance initiated the last days.[44]

The most salient verb in the paragraph, the load-bearing wall of the semantic structure, is the aorist *elalēsen* ("has spoken"). Everything in the exordium (Heb 1:1–4) ultimately revolves around this verb and around the proposition "God . . . has spoken to us by his Son." The subject "God" precedes the participle in v. 1 so that there is a significant amount of material between the subject and the verb. This particular verb occurs 16 times in Hebrews, 10 of which have God as the subject. Its synonym *legō* occurs 31 times, 16 with God as the subject; Christ is the subject three times and the Holy Spirit once. The semantic difference would appear to be that *laleō* focuses on the act of speaking rather than remaining silent, and *legō* focuses more on the content of what is said.[45] The term *logos* ("word") appears six times in Hebrews for divine revelation (2:2; 4:2,12; 5:13; 12:19; 13:7), and its synonym *rhēma* ("word" or "utterance") occurs four times (1:3; 6:5; 11:3; 12:19).[46] The significance of this usage of "speech" for divine revelation in Hebrews prompted Vos to write, "Revelation is the speech of God to man,"[47] and A. B. Davidson to remark, "Revelation when spoken is the 'word' of God."[48]

God's revelation in his Son is "to us." The first person plural is used frequently by the writer throughout Hebrews. Its use in 2:3 indicates that neither the author nor the readers had heard Jesus personally, and some infer from 2:3 that the writer and readers belonged to a second generation of believers.[49] At the very least, *hēmin* includes the author and recipients of the letter, and most commentators broaden its meaning to include the entire Christian community, including those who would hear the message in the future.[50]

It was marvelous enough that God should speak through the prophets, but now comes an extraordinary truth: God has spoken to us in one who is by his very character and nature a Son. The text could have read, "Now he has spoken to us through the apostles." The text does not move from multiple messengers

---

[44] Chrysostom eloquently expressed it this way: "[W]hen a long time had intervened, when we were on the edge of punishment, when the gifts had failed, when there was no expectation of deliverance, when we were expecting to have less than all—it was then that we were given more" (*On the Epistle to the Hebrews* 1.2 in E. M. Heen and P. D. W. Krey, eds. *Hebrews*, ACCS 10 [Downers Grove: InterVarsity, 2005], 7).

[45] See B. Klappert, "Word," *NIDNTT* 1106–17; *TDNTa* 509–14; R. T. C. Trench, *Synonyms of the New Testament* (London: Kegan Paul, Trench, Trubner & Co., 1890), 286–87.

[46] D. McLeod has an excellent discussion on the terminology of revelation in Hebrews ("The Theology of the Epistle to the Hebrews: Introduction, Prolegomena and Doctrinal Center" [Ph.D. dissertation, Dallas Theological Seminary, 1987], 163–78).

[47] G. Vos, *The Teaching of the Epistle to the Hebrews* (Grand Rapids: Eerdmans, 1956), 68.

[48] A. B. Davidson, *The Epistle to the Hebrews: with Introduction and Notes* (Edinburgh: T&T Clark, 1882), 101.

[49] Others think this is reading too much into the passage (see Ellingworth, *Hebrews*, 141).

[50] Ellingworth, *Hebrews*, 93; Alford, "Hebrews," 3.

in the past to multiple messengers in the present. As C. R. Koester noted, "Multiplicity gives way to the singularity of God's communication in the Son."[51] Whereas the prophets conveyed God's word in their speech (and writings), God spoke not only through Jesus' words, but also by his person and work. Jesus—in all he is, said, and did—reveals the Father. There is a higher category of revelation (Son versus prophets) because there is a higher category of relationship (Son to the Father over prophets to God).[52] In the New Testament there is no messenger and word-event formula as one finds in the Old Testament, such as "the word of the LORD came to Jeremiah" (e.g., Jer 28:12). On no occasion did Jesus say, "Thus says the Lord" or "The word of God came to me."

Amazingly, the author viewed the revelation of the Son as God's "speech" to us, and thus it is an appropriate metaphor for all that God does through Christ in the world and not just in reference to the words of Christ. Additionally, when Scripture speaks of the "word of the LORD" addressed to and through Old Testament prophets, the Son, as the second Person of the Trinity, is always involved as well. As the author made clear in Heb 11:3, it was God's speech that created the universe. Thus, the word that God now speaks through his Son is in no way discontinuous with God's word spoken through the prophets or even in creation. This indicates that the author of Hebrews considered speech to be an appropriate metaphor for divine revelation beyond that which is merely verbal.[53]

Several matters call for discussion. First, why would the author use *en huiō* (lit. "in Son") without the article? Greek grammar permits the article to be omitted in prepositional phrases and when referring to persons, especially in reference to unique persons and deity.[54] Although this may explain the omission,[55] the semantic context indicates that more important reasons apply. Most commentators conclude that the absence of the article focuses on the character and

---

[51] Koester, *Hebrews*, 185.

[52] O. Cullmann accurately reflected on the approach of the author of Hebrews: "He sees that Jesus' divine sonship rests on his mission, that it means imparting the divine revelation. He understands that this provides something in common with the OT prophets. Thus at the very beginning this book distinguishes Christ from the prophets as 'the Son.' The impressive thing about the confession of the 'Son of God' is the fact that the only Son who participated in creation and goes forth directly from the Father nevertheless participates as man, as the true High Priest, in human infirmity" (*Christology of the New Testament,* trans. S. C. Guthrie and C. A. M. Hall, rev. ed. [Philadelphia: Westminster, 1963], 305). Aquinas said that just as man clothes his thought in letters and sounds, "even so, God, wanting to manifest Himself to men, clothes with human flesh, in time, His Word conceived from all eternity" (in *Jo.*, c. 14, lect. 2).

[53] L. T. Johnson, *Hebrews: A Commentary,* NTL (Louisville: Westminster John Knox, 2006), 66, 70. T. Lewicki (*'Weist nicht ab den Sprechenden!'*, 141–44) traced the concept of God's "word" and "speech" throughout the hortatory sections of the epistle as well as other places, demonstrating the programmatic nature of the prologue for the entire discourse.

[54] See the discussion in BDF §254, 255.

[55] So Delitzsch, who thought υἱός here and in 7:28 should be regarded as a proper name (*Hebrews*, 1:42).

nature of the Son as compared to the prophets.[56] Furthermore, given the scope of the prologue, the lack of the article likely indicates that the revelation in the Son includes his incarnation, death, resurrection and second coming.[57]

Second, the lack of the article does not in any way imply that Jesus is just one of many "sons" that could have been chosen as agents of revelation. Such an idea is precluded by the meaning of "Son of God" in early Christian theology (see the discussion below) as well as by the context of Hebrews itself.

Third, the question arises as to how this phrase should be translated. It is almost impossible to render the meaning adequately in English. The translation "in a Son," reflecting the absence of the article, is often used but fails to reflect the qualitative meaning in Greek and leaves the ambiguous impression that Jesus is one son among many. Another issue is whether the possessive pronoun should be used: "in/by *his* son." This too detracts from the qualitative focus. There is no article or possessive pronoun in the text to convey possession and make the noun definite.[58] Additionally, the subsequent relative clauses serve to convey both ideas. But this leaves the awkward "in Son" as virtually the only alternative, and although it has the merit of not saying too much, it is grammatically incorrect for English, and with respect to the qualitative idea it says too little. To get the full intent of the Greek would require an unwieldy translation such as "in one who is by his very character and nature a Son."

Fourth, what is the meaning and use of "Son?" Without yet delving too deeply into the theological meaning of this term (see the theological discussion of the prologue below), we note several things briefly. First, a study of its usage in Hebrews reveals just how crucial this term is for the author and his theological development. It occurs without the article four times in Old Testament citations (1:5; 5:5; 12:5,6) and four times to stress the quality of the mediator (1:2; 3:6; 5:8; 7:28). With the article it occurs twice as an affirmation of divinity in relation to Christ's priesthood (4:14; 7:3) and twice in relation to apostates (6:6; 10:29).[59] Thus, 11 of its 12 uses occur in the first seven chapters. The use of the title "Son" without the article seven times in Hebrews is distinctive, as opposed to such expressions as "Son of God" or "Son of Man," which are more common. The author's connection of Ps 110:1 and Ps 8:7 to *huios* indicates

---

[56] See Alford, "Hebrews," 4; Lünemann, *Hebrews*, 393; Westcott, *Hebrews*, 7; Dods, "Hebrews," 249; Attridge, *Hebrews*, 39; and Lane, *Hebrews 1–8*, 11. Lane's comments sum up the position well: "The anarthrous ἐν υἱῷ is qualitative. The eternal, essential quality of Jesus' sonship qualified him to be the one through whom God uttered his final word. The antithesis in the two phrases of revelation lies in the distinction between the prophets who were men and the Son who enjoys a unique relationship to God."

[57] As noted by B. Demarest and G. Lewis, *Integrative Theology* (Grand Rapids: Zondervan, 1987), 1:108.

[58] On the absence of the article in this situation, see the discussion in Wallace, *GGBB* 245.

[59] C. Spicq, *l'Épître aux Hébreux, EBib* 1 (Paris: Librairie Lecoffre, 1952–53), 288. It occurs in 1:2,5 (twice),8; 3:6; 4:14; 5:5,8; 6:6; 7:3,28; 10:29.

that this title is definitive for the author, and its use in Heb 1:2 establishes the theme of the epistle.[60]

A crucial question that must be answered relative to the identification of Jesus as "Son" is the background of the term. Is the author's use informed by Hellenistic religious and/or philosophical thought, or is it derived more from Judaism? If the latter, is there any affinity to be found in the Qumran literature? Bultmann's thesis, that the term derived from Hellenistic paganism, need not detain us here since it has been shown to be incorrect. There is nothing in Hellenistic thought that even begins to compare with the concept of the Son of God as applied to Christ in the New Testament.[61] What about Old Testament Judaism? Three groups can be identified as being referred to as "sons of God" in the Old Testament: the people of God collectively, kings, and angelic beings.[62] Thus, although the term had a broad use in the Old Testament, it was never applied to a divine being. This appears to be the case with first-century Judaism, including the Qumran community, although Qumran evidence shows that Judaism was giving attention to the significance of God's fatherly relationship to the messiah his son as expressed in 2 Sam 7:14.[63] It is almost impossible to demonstrate a clear messianic expectation in terms of the use of the title "Son of God" in the Old Testament or in pre-Christian Judaism.

In the New Testament, the Christological concept of sonship as applied by Jesus to himself and by the apostolic writers to him indicates his full participation in deity.[64] This is certainly no less true for the writer of Hebrews. In fact, the "Son" concept dominates the Christology of Hebrews.[65] As has already been pointed out, the term *huios* is the hinge of the paragraph. It is what is said about the Son in the following clauses that makes it clear the term is an expression of deity. Although J. M. Robinson's remark, "The name of the

---

[60] M. Hengel, *Studies in Early Christology* (Edinburgh: T&T Clark, 1995), 169.

[61] See the discussion in Cullmann, *Christology of the New Testament*, 275–78.

[62] Ibid., 272–73.

[63] O. Michel and I. H. Marshall, "Son," *NIDNTT* 3:637. Fitzmyer drew attention to the possible significance of 4QpsDan A for Christology and especially for Luke 1:32–35. Cf. R. Longenecker, *The Christology of Early Jewish Christianity* (Naperville, IL: A. R. Allenson, 1970), 95.

[64] Cullmann, *Christology of the New Testament*, 305. See the bibliography on "Son of God" in Michel and Marshall, "Son," *NIDNTT* 3:665–66.

[65] In addition to Cullmann, *Christology,* see Westcott (*Hebrews,* 424–28) and G. Milligan's *Theology of the Epistle to the Hebrews* (Edinburgh: T&T Clark, 1899), 72–95. Both of the latter, although dated, offer a succinct and clear discussion of the meaning and use of "son" in the epistle; J. S. Lidgett, *Sonship and Salvation* (London: Epworth, 1921). Cf. J. D. G. Dunn, *Christology in the Making*, 2nd ed. (Grand Rapids: Eerdmans, 1996), 52–62; Michel and Marshall, "Son," in *NIDNTT* 3:634–68; F. Hahn, *Titles of Jesus in Christology*, trans. H. Knight and G. Ogg (New York: World Publishing, 1969). Lane (*Hebrews 1–8*, cxl) noted that in 1:1–4:14 the dominant Christological expression is the description of Jesus as "the humiliated and exalted Son." Attridge (*Hebrews,* 54–55) has a brief but helpful excursus on sonship in Hebrews, outlining the various suggestions offered to explain the apparent differences in the Christological focus, particularly with reference to Psalm 2.

Father is the Son,"[66] goes too far and obscures the distinct persons within the Trinity, it does get at the exclusive relationship between Jesus and God. It is this exclusive relationship the Son has with the Father that so qualifies Jesus to be the mediator of the knowledge of God and his salvation for humanity.[67] As such, "Son" expresses an intimacy, oneness, and solidarity of relationship with the Father; but it also emphasizes the humanity of Christ and his solidarity and oneness with his "brothers" whose humanity as Son he shares (2:10–18)—as the immediate context of chap. 2 and the entire thrust of the book reveal. The title "high priest" first occurs in 2:17,18 (though Christ's function as high priest is implied in 1:3), and in 4:14 the two terms "Son" and "high priest" are juxtaposed by the author and remain significantly so through chap. 7.

In this comparison between revelation through the prophets and revelation through the Son, the author identified what is common and what is distinctive in both revelations. That the same verb is used indicates historical continuity of both periods, and that "God" is the subject of both revelations likewise indicates continuity. The revelation in both periods is also substantially one and the same since it is God's Word being spoken. What is unique is the contrast between the prophets and the Son. In the New Testament, one never finds a messenger and word-event formula like one finds with the Old Testament prophets. Nowhere does Jesus ever say: "Thus says the Lord" or "The word of God came to me."

Hebrews 1:1–2 indicates that the author was thinking in spheres of both contrast and continuity. It is important to keep these two perspectives in balance. In light of the author's constant use of the Old Testament to validate his Christocentric interpretations, it is impossible to interpret the author here in the prologue as intimating the obsolescence of the Old Testament as revelation. In fact, as Lane correctly noted, God's final revelation in Christ can be understood only within the context of God's revelation to Israel in the Old Testament. The recipients of Hebrews would have understood that God's word spoken through the Son was an extension of Old Testament revelatory history.[68] Smillie explained that sometimes the comparisons in Hebrews that occur later in the epistle have caused interpreters to read back into the prologue "nuances of contrast that are not actually there in the text." He rightly concluded that if one magnifies contrast here, then one's interpretation of the rest of the epistle will be one of contrast. On the other hand, if there is some continuity

---

[66] J. M. Robinson, ed., *The Nag Hammadi Library in English*, 3rd ed. (San Francisco: Harper & Row, 1988), 49.

[67] Cf. Matt 11:25,26 and Luke 10:21,22: "No one knows who the Son is except the Father, or who the Father is except the Son and anyone to whom the Son chooses to reveal him." Here the Son is described as the mediator of revelation about the Father, and the implication is that the Son shares in the divine nature of the Father. But in Heb 1:2–3 it is explicitly stated that the Son is the full revelation of the Father because he shares in the divine nature of the Father.

[68] Lane, *Hebrews 1–8*, 11.

between God's revelation in the Old Testament and his revelation in the Son, then the trajectory of interpretation will be one of "deliberate development" from the Old Testament revelation to that of the Son.[69] This is not to minimize the contrast that the author develops, particularly in Heb 7:1–10:18. However, the contrast has more to do with the temporary nature of the Mosaic law and temple cultus versus the finality of Jesus and his atoning work rather than with inferiority of revelation.

Most interpreters of Hebrews have overemphasized discontinuity in Heb 1:1–2, with sweeping ramifications. The fountainhead of this is probably Chrysostom, who in his sermons on Hebrews stressed the contrast between God's revelation in the Old Testament and the New Testament. Calvin concluded from Heb 1:1 that the Old Testament was inferior to the New Testament and was thus in one sense imperfect.[70] He is not alone in this assessment. The result is often a lopsided supersessionism that does not adequately relate the two testaments. Linguistically, although both the participle *lalēsas* in v. 1 and the finite verb *elalēsen* in v. 2 are related chronologically, "the correspondence of verbal aspect here indicates affinity, not contrariety, between the modes by which God 'has spoken.'"[71] How could the author of Hebrews have made use of the Old Testament in his quotations and allusions as much as he did if he operated on the principle of discontinuity? Smillie, referencing Wider, showed that the contrasting of the pairs of terms in Heb 1:1–2 is implicit, but the author did not draw explicit antitheses from them.[72] Smillie noted that of the 11 comparative Greek words the author used throughout Hebrews, many of them in a contrastive fashion, not one is used in Heb 1:1–2. No adversative particles occur in these two verses.[73]

The view that the author's purpose in writing was to dissuade his readers from apostatizing to Judaism has colored the way this passage and the entire book are interpreted. This in turn leads to the conclusion that Hebrews is anti-Judaic, even anti-Semitic. The author did argue that the old covenant has been rendered obsolete by the new covenant in Jesus Christ, but he did so by showing that the Old Testament itself affirms this, so it is neither anti-Judaic nor anti-Semitic. The old covenant *revelation* is certainly not obsolete since the author uses it as the linchpin on which he builds his case. In fact, the author on

[69] G. Smillie, "Contrast or Continuity in Hebrews 1.1–2?" *NTS* 51 (2005): 559. Smillie concluded by saying: "Hebrews' opening words are a ringing declaration of continuity. . . . The rest of the treatise uses the very words spoken through those prophets to glorify that son" (560).

[70] J. Calvin, *The Epistle of Paul the Apostle to the Hebrews and the First and Second Epistles of Peter,* CNTC, trans. W. Johnson, ed. D. W. Torrance and T. F. Torrance (Grand Rapids: Eerdmans, 1963), 5–6.

[71] Smillie, "Contrast or Continuity," 547.

[72] Ibid., 548. See D. Wider, *Theozentrik und Bekenntnis: Untersuchungen zur Theologie des Redens Gottes im Hebräerbrief,* in BZNW 87 (Berlin: Walter de Gruyter, 1997), 12–22.

[73] Smillie, "Contrast or Continuity," 550–52. "It appears that many commentators proceed from an assumption of discontinuity, and then project it into these verses" (552).

occasion placed the old covenant revelation on the lips of Jesus. The very word of God in the Old Testament is proclaimed "in these last days" by Jesus the Son who is in continuity with the prophets of old, and the author of Hebrews makes constant use of the words of these prophets to glorify Jesus.[74]

In v. 2 the author moved to describe further the exalted status of the Son in several relative and participial clauses, each identifying the Son in his relationship to the Father, to creation, to the redemption of humanity, and to eschatological sovereignty. The cumulative effect is to show why God's revelation through the Son is the highest, fullest, and most complete he can give. While *theos* remains the grammatical subject until v. 3, the focus shifts to the Son with the introduction of the first relative clause *hon ethēken* ("whom he appointed"). The Greek text places a partial stop (semicolon in English) at the end of v. 2, probably to indicate that *theos* is functioning as the grammatical subject to that point. The two relative clauses following "Son" in v. 2 are grammatically dependent on *huiō*. The verbs in these clauses, *ethēken* ("he appointed") and *epoiēsen* ("made"), have "God" as their subject. The relative *hos* beginning v. 3 (translated "The Son" in the NIV) has as its antecedent *huiō* (dative, "son") in v. 2, but is in the nominative case to indicate its function as the subject of the main verb in the last clause of v. 3. Four participles modify the main verb *ekathisen* ("he sat down"). Three precede the main verb:[75] *hōn* ("The Son is"), *pherōn* ("sustaining"), and *poiēsamenos* ("After he had provided" in v. 3); one follows the main verb: *genomenos* ("So he became" in v. 4).

How many statements are made about the Son in the remainder of the paragraph? Depending on how the clauses are divided, answers can range from six to eight.[76] Since all of these options are grammatically and syntactically possible, the main thing to note is that, semantically, there are eight propositions further describing the Son in vv. 2b–4.

The first clause, "whom he appointed heir of all things," is striking in its scope. The Son has been appointed by God (understood as the subject of the action inherent in the noun) to inherit all things. The verbal nature of the noun

[74] Ibid., 560.

[75] I.e., they are "preposed," a linguistic term that means "occurring before the main verb"; "postposed" means "occurring after the main verb."

[76] The count would be six (so Dods, "Hebrews," 249) if we (1) consider the ἀπαύγασμα and χαρακτήρ statements in v. 3a as one, based on the single ὃς ὤν introducing them both, (2) count the main verb ἐκάθισεν as one, and (3) exclude the participle γενόμενος in v. 4 as stating collateral information since it is postposed to the main verb. If we distinguish the ἀπαύγασμα and χαρακτήρ phrases as representing two statements, the count would be seven (so Bruce, *Hebrews*, 46–50). Likewise, the count would be seven if we don't distinguish the compound clause of v. 3a, count the main verb ἐκάθισεν, and include the γενόμενος of v. 4 (so Meier, "Structure and Theology," 173). Seven is also the number of statements about the Son if we include the γενόμενος of v. 4 and exclude the main verb ἐκάθισεν—viewing it semantically as completing the main point of the paragraph (which it certainly does): "God spoke in a Son who is now exalted (seated) at God's right hand." Finally, if we distinguish two statements introduced by ὃς ὤν in v. 3a, count the main verb ἐκάθισεν, and include the γενόμενος of v. 4, we have eight statements about the Son.

"heir" is sometimes brought out in translations: "to posses at the end" (TEV), "to enter into possession of" (TNT), "everything will someday belong to the son" (CEV). God has promised everything to the Son as his inheritance. The content of the inheritance is said to be "all things."[77] In light of the context, it would seem that nothing material or spiritual is excluded from the inheritance. The entire created order is intended. The context also relates this inheritance to the full scope of the Son's redemptive work as well as his eternal status as Son. The inheritance is essentially God's eschatological rule over all things.[78]

The term *klēronomos* and its cognates are put to theological use by the author throughout the epistle.[79] What was promised to God's people and looked toward by them in the Old Testament has now been received by the Son. Paul referred to Christians as "heirs" with Christ (Rom 8:12–17; Gal 3:23–4:7), and the writer of Hebrews said that God has "appointed" Christ to be "heir of all things," the verb carrying the sense of installation in a position.

Exactly when the Son was appointed heir is a matter of debate.[80] Some see the Son as having always been heir because of his divine nature.[81] Others, including most of the church fathers and modern commentators, point to the time of Christ's incarnation and redemptive work.[82] This matter receives attention at great length in the section on the theology of 1:1–4.

There is a close link between Christology and cosmology in three of the four great Christological passages in the New Testament: John 1:1–18, Col 1:13–20 and Heb 1:1–4. The clause "through whom he made the universe" further identifies the Son in his preincarnate role as protological agent of creation. God is again the subject with the genitive relative *hou* having as its antecedent "Son."

---

[77] P. D. Dognin's attempt at translating the clause in the sense of God's appointing the Son as heir of the prophets and not of "all things" is misguided and lacks linguistic warrant ("Épître aux Hébreux traduction inédite du prologue (He 1,1-4)," *RB* 112.1 [2005]: 80–100).

[78] There is an allusion here to Ps 2:8 that is further developed in 1:5–14, where the royal son is assured that he will receive "the nations" as his "inheritance." Lane (*Hebrews 1–8*, 12)—in reference to Langkammer's observation concerning the literary similarity between Heb 1:2 and Gen 17:5 where Abraham is said to be "heir," receives a new name, and is "appointed," thus marking the inauguration of redemptive history—concluded that this similarity suggests that the author drew upon "the OT motif of the investiture of the heir in order to connect the beginning of redemptive history with its accomplishment in the Son." Cf. H. Langkammer, "'Den er zum Erben von allem *eingesetz* hat' [Hebr 1,2]" *BZ* 10 (1966): 273–80.

[79] See the discussions in Westcott (*Hebrews*, 167–69) and Ellingworth (*Hebrews*, 94–95): "In Hebrews as a whole, the use of κληρονομέω and cognates suggests that Christ has now received from God a possession which was only promised and looked forward to by people in OT times (κληρονόμος, 6:17; 11:7; κληρονομέω, 1:4,14; 6:12; 12:17; κληρονομία, 9:15; 11:8)."

[80] See the discussion in the older commentaries, particularly Lünemann (*Hebrews*, 393–95); Alford ("Hebrews," 5); and Milligan (*Theology*, 86–87). It is interesting how little is said of this debate in many of the newer commentaries. It is scarcely mentioned as an issue by Attridge, Lane, Ellingworth, or Koester.

[81] So Alford, "Hebrews," 5; Westcott, *Hebrews*, 7.

[82] So Delitzsch, *Hebrews*, 1:43–44; M. Bourke, "The Epistle to the Hebrews," in *Jerome Biblical Commentary* (Englewood Cliffs, NJ: Prentice-Hall, 1968), 2:383.

Regardless of one's view as to when Christ was made heir of all things, it is impossible not to see in the Son's agency in the creation of the universe a statement of his eternal preexistence. It is likely that the author implied the Son's deity in this statement as well, since the emphasis falls on the verb "made" and not on the preposition "through."[83] Verse 3 is a statement of the Son's deity.

One question surrounding this clause is the meaning of the direct object *tous aiōnas* ("the universe"). Twice in Hebrews the author speaks of *aiōnas* ("ages, universe") as the object of God's creation (1:2; 11:3). Four different interpretations have been suggested, though the first two are considered by the majority of scholars to be incorrect. First, some see here and in the epistle as a whole a Platonic/Philonic dualistic philosophy at work, which informs the author's understanding and use of this term. Second, those who see a Gnostic background for Hebrews[84] take the reference to mean "personified superhuman forces which control the various cosmic spheres and time spans."[85] It is generally considered to be a settled issue in the interpretation of the book that the author was neither dependent on a Platonic/Philonic philosophical background, nor was he or his readers influenced by Gnostic notions of aeons.

A third view identifies *aiōnas* here as the material universe. This is the translation in the NIV and many other versions. Understood this way, the term is here roughly synonymous with *kosmos*. The fourth view is really an expansion of the third view, and takes *aiōnas* to include not only the material universe but also the vast periods of time and all that transpires in them. To put it in contemporary scientific language, *aiōnas* includes the space-matter-time continuum that is the universe, the totality of all things existing in time and space.[86] It seems best to include both the temporal and spatial idea in the term. It occurs in

---

[83] As noted by J. A. Bengel, *New Testament Word Studies,* trans. C. T. Lewis and M. R. Vincent (Grand Rapids: Kregel, 1973), 2:576. L. S. Chafer (*Grace: The Glorious Theme*, 13th ed. [Grand Rapids: Zondervan, 1970], 145) translated Heb 1:2 "by whom he programmed the ages," which at the time he wrote would have seemed odd, but in light of today's computer technology it actually gets at the idea fairly well.

[84] E. Käsemann regarded the background of v. 3 to be what he called "Hellenistic aeon theology." He compared Hebrews to Philippians, noting that the latter relates the effects of Christ's obedience cosmically, whereas the former relates them to community. D. Guthrie critiqued Käsemann as giving insufficient attention to the Jewish background to Hebrews and to the point that the epistle can be understood apart from an appeal to a Gnostic background (*New Testament Theology*, rev. ed. [Downers Grove: InterVarsity, 1981], 362). The allusion to the OT prophets would "strongly suggest" a Jewish background.

[85] R. Jewett, *Letter to Pilgrims: A Commentary on the Epistle to the Hebrews* (New York: Pilgrim, 1981), 22.

[86] See Lenski, *Hebrews*, 35; Westcott, *Hebrews,* 8–9; Bruce, *Hebrews,* 4; Ellingworth, *Hebrews,* 96; H. Sasse, "αἰών, αἰώνιος" *TDNT* 1:197–209; Lünemann, *Hebrews*, 395. The latter suggested that the meaning is essentially equivalent to the preceding πάντων and the following πάντα of v. 3. Attridge (*Hebrews*, 41) noted that although both the temporal and spatial ideas are present, the focus is more on the spatial; cf. J. Héring (*The Epistle to the Hebrews,* trans. A. W. Heathcote and P. J. Allcock [London: Epworth, 1970], 3. F. J. Schierse (*Verheissung und Heilsvollendung: zur theologischen Grundfrage des Hebräerbriefes* [München: Karl Zink, 1955], 67–75) restricted

its temporal sense in 6:5 and 9:26, but the context here indicates that more than the temporal idea alone is intended. In both Jewish apocalyptic and rabbinic literature, the Hebrew terminology has both spatial and temporal connotations as well.[87] Concerning the use of *aiōnas* here, John of Damascus remarked, "This kind of age is to eternal things exactly what time is to temporal things."[88] Theodore of Mopsuestia said of this notion of Jesus as God's agent of creation, "The 'creator of the ages' means nothing different than 'everlasting, existing beyond every age, having his own limitless existence.'"[89] The NEB translators render the word *aiōnas* "all orders of existence" here, and "universe" in 11:3.

That Jesus should be considered the agent of creation by the author is very much in line with other New Testament writers, particularly Paul and John, who affirm the Son's role in identical fashion with the author of Hebrews (John 1:3,10; 1 Cor 8:6; Col 1:16). Thus, in the New Testament, creation is seen as the work of the Word (John 1:1–3), Christ (1 Cor 8:6; Col 1:16), and the Son (Heb 1:2). The Son is not simply the instrumental cause of all things. Rather, he is ascribed the status of Creator that he shares with the Father.[90] Given the location of this clause in the prologue, the author understood creation as an aspect of revelation as well as salvation. From the author's comment that "the universe was formed at God's command" (Heb 11:3), it is clear that the author conceived of creation as an intrinsically verbal event that reveals the God who spoke it into being.[91] As Hendrikus Berkhof put it, "We confess our belief in creation with an eye to Christ. From Him we learn the final purpose of creation . . . Creation is the preamble to salvation."[92]

These two clauses—"whom he appointed heir of all things" and "through whom he made the universe"—appear to be deliberately related by the author. There is a minor break that NA^{27} and UBS^{4} place at the end of v. 2. The two clauses have "God" as their subject, whereas the remainder of the clauses in vv. 3–4 do not. In addition, there is a shift in tense from v. 2 to v. 3: aorists in v. 2 but present participles in 3a. The meaning of the *kai* before *epoiēsen* is

---

aiōnas to the invisible world, but there are no grounds for doing this in light of general usage, and certainly not in light of the author's use in 11:3.

[87] Attridge, *Hebrews*, 41.

[88] John of Damascus, *Orthodox Faith* 2.1, in Heen and Krey, eds. *Hebrews*, 8.

[89] Theodore of Mopsuestia, *Fragments on the Epistle to the Hebrews* 1.2–3, in Heen and Krey, eds., *Hebrews*, 8.

[90] W. Pannenberg stated in reference to Heb 1:2 that "if from all eternity, and thus also in the creation of the world, the Father is not without the Son, the eternal Son is not merely the ontic basis of the existence of Jesus in his self-distinction from the Father as the one God; he is also the basis of the distinction and independent existence of all creaturely reality" (*Systematic Theology*, trans. G. W. Bromiley [Grand Rapids: Eerdmans, 1991–98], 1:23). "In the Son is the origin of all that differs from the Father" (p. 22). Hebrews 1:3 indicates that the Son "sustains" the universe that he has created and guides it to its final consummation.

[91] Johnson, *Hebrews*, 66.

[92] H. Berkhof, *Christian Faith: An Introduction to the Study of Faith*, trans. S. Woudstra (Grand Rapids: Eerdmans, 1979), 166, 168.

usually taken as "also." But the conjunction can, after a relative pronoun, have a sense of "precisely as such."[93] Some take *kai* as basing Christ's heirship on the fact of his mediation in creation. Ellingworth called this "tortuous."[94] The order is probably better explained by the author's use of chiasm that begins and ends with the idea of inheritance; hence, it appears before the protological statement. The position of the *kai* could indicate that creation preceded the appointment to heirship, otherwise the *kai* would have been clause initial.[95] Or the author may have located the time of the Son's appointment as heir in the eternal relationship with the Father and not as a result of his salvific work after the incarnation. Thus, the appointment clause precedes the creation clause. Lane, following D. W. B. Robinson, took the *kai* in an adversative sense: "whom he appointed heir and who yet is the one through whom he created the world."[96] Such a concessive use of *kai* is possible, and in light of the overall semantic structure of the prologue (see below) it seems likely.

The *kai* indicates a special relation between these clauses because God made his Son heir of all things; he "also" made the worlds as he did, namely, through (*dia*) the Son. It makes no difference whether the historical aorist is dated in eternity or time. From all eternity Christ was heir. The inheritance was "paid out" when his work on the cross was completed.[97] On this approach, the preincarnate Son was heir in eternity; he received the inheritance at his exaltation as the incarnate Son.[98] Since Jesus is the heir, God made (created) that which he would inherit through the Son's agency. The point is not our comprehension of the divine act of creation but our apprehension of the true nature of

---

[93] E. Grässer, *Text und Situation; gesammelte Aufsätze zum Neuen Testament* (Gütersloh: Mohn, 1973), 214; and Meier, "Structure and Theology," 178. Delitzsch, (*Hebrews*, 1:43) said that the καί here is "more than a mere expletive"; Dods ("Hebrews," 250) agreed: "The καί brings out the propriety of committing all things to the hand that brought them into being . . . He only can guide the universe to its fit end who at first, presumably with wisdom equal to His power, brought it into being."

[94] Ellingworth, *Hebrews*, 95; cf. H. Braun, *An die Hebräer*, HNT (Tübingen: Mohr, 1984), 22.

[95] A point made by H. L. MacNeill, *The Christology of the Epistle to the Hebrews* (Chicago: University Press, 1914), 56. He also noted that ἔθηκεν is not definitely modified, thus referring to a definite time in history when Christ was appointed heir.

[96] Lane, *Hebrews 1–8*, 12; D. W. B. Robinson, "The Literary Structure of Hebrews 1:1–4," *AJBA* (1972), 183–85. This could be more accurately labeled as an ascensive use of καί and translated as "also, even" or "indeed." Contrast is not the communication relation being expressed here. It would seem that the semantic category here is one of concession ("although")—contraexpectation ("yet")—"although he is the heir, yet he is also the creator." Lane correctly identified the meaning, but he mislabeled the καί as adversative.

[97] See Lenski's discussion of the significance of the καί (*Hebrews*, 34).

[98] Theodoret of Cyrus, *Interpretation of Hebrews* 1, in Heen and Krey, eds., *Hebrews*, 8: "In other words, Christ the Lord is heir of all things, not as God but as man: as God he is maker of all things, and the creator of all things is Lord of all by nature, whereas the heir is made master of what he was previously not lord." If the "all things" includes redeemed humanity, then there is a measure of truth in Theodoret's statement since only by the incarnation and the cross could salvation be purchased for them and since they thus become Christ's inheritance.

the Son.[99] Jesus is heir because of his relationship as Son with the Father. His heirship and his sonship all identify the Son as both divine and co-equal with the Father.

The Son's essential relationship to the Father is shown not to have begun in time but to have existed before all time. God is the creator; the Son is the mediator of creation. His exaltation after the crucifixion (as the incarnate Son) is the correlative of that which he possessed already before all time (as the preincarnate Son). The *kai* serves to point out this connection.[100] The *kai* connects the two clauses and indicates the second closely follows the first semantically. The semantic relationship is discussed in detail below. "The *kai* of the second clause accentuates the fact that what follows is in accord with that which precedes, not that which precedes is in accord with that which follows."[101]

In addition to the syntactical importance of *kai,* which tightly links the two clauses in more than simply a conjunctive way, the semantic idea of consummation (heir of all things) and creation (made the universe) go together. What is unusual is the order in which they appear: consummation first, then creation. We would have expected the order to be reversed. But the prologue ends in v. 4 with the Son having inherited a name superior to the angels, so an *inclusio* of "inheritance" brackets the statements made about the Son. The focus of the author throughout the epistle was not on the role of the Son in creation, but the Son's inheritance by virtue of his suffering and exaltation is given marked prominence. "Inheritance" is an important lexical item in the epistle, along with the concepts of enthronement and exaltation. In these four verses, after we are told that God has spoken in the Son, the statement is finished by the use of the semantic idea of the Son's being "seated" or "enthroned" at God's right hand. The sense of these first two clauses in the latter part of v. 2 is the Son as the alpha and omega, the first and the last, the one who creates and the one who consummates. The Son made it all and he inherits it all. But the order of these clauses and then the repetition of the root in *keklēronomēken* in v. 4 at the end of the paragraph indicates that the author's thought really moves from the eschatological to the protological and then back to the eschatological. The Son inherits all he has made.[102]

---

[99] A point well stated by Lenski (*Hebrews*, 35).

[100] Delitzsch, *Hebrews*, 1:43–44.

[101] Lünemann, *Hebrews*, 395. B. Weiss, (*Biblical Theology of the New Testament*, trans. J. E. Duguid [Edinburgh: T&T Clark, 1882], 2:188) connected the two clauses and noted that the Son's elevation to be heir of all things is accounted for by his being God's agent in creating the ages: "The propriety for effecting the creation of the world by Him, expressed by the καί, can have been but to furnish a reason for the latter fact, a reason from which the former idea was formed. He, who was made Lord over all, must have had *a priori* a relation to that all."

[102] "He would not, like some negligent trustees, let the estate go to rack and ruin and disintegration," as R. Ward so deftly commented on Christ's role as "heir" of all he created (*The Pattern of Our Salvation: A Study of New Testament Unity* [Waco: Word Books, 1978], 13).

The connection of these two clauses as descriptive of the Son, along with the author's profound statement that the Son is God's speech, perhaps indicates more than meets the eye. In Gen 1:3–31 creation is the result of God's speech. God created the universe by his word (Heb 11:3). C. R. Koester perceptively noted the author's point in the prologue is the consistency in God's speech from the time of the prophets to the Son. The way God spoke at the last days, in one who is the Son, corresponds to the way he spoke, not only through the Old Testament revelation (prophets), but also at the beginning of creation—through the Son he created the universe. The author connected God's word in the last days, not only with the Old Testament revelation but also with the very beginning of creation. Furthermore, the Old Testament as well as Jewish tradition provided the language necessary for making this connection by identifying God's creative word with his wisdom. Wisdom is personified as God's agent in creation (Prov 8:22–31; cf. *Wis* 7:22; 8:1; 9:1–2).[103]

Thus, both the critical importance of the order of these clauses as well as their immediate use after the introduction of the Son indicate their importance in the author's theology. The Son's exaltation has such a far reach that it extends back to his preincarnate eternal relationship with the Father, includes his role in creation at the beginning of time, and with the inclusion of v. 3 as the incarnate Son's soteriological role, culminates with the fulfillment of his appointment as heir with his exaltation at the right hand of God. Thus, the Son is the "eschatological culmination" of God's revelation begun in the Old Testament Scriptures.[104] That so much could be said in the confines of four verses is a testimony to the author's theological ability. God's protological, eschatological, and soteriological purposes, otherwise undisclosed, are now revealed in his Son.[105]

1:3 The first clause of v. 3 describes the Son's relation to the Father, demonstrating his qualifications to function as the mediator of revelation. The clause is introduced by the relative *hos*, which has as its antecedent *huiō* (v. 2). It is

---

[103] Koester, *Hebrews*, 185–86; but see Fee's critique (summarized below) of equating Jesus with wisdom.

[104] This is the phrase used by J. A. Dearman, "Theophany, Anthropomorphism, and the *Imago Dei*: Some Observations about the Incarnation in the Light of the Old Testament," in *The Incarnation: An Interdisciplinary Symposium on the Incarnation of the Son of God,* ed. S. T. Davis et al. (Oxford: University Press, 2002), 32. "The author of Hebrews characteristically views the various moments in the Christological drama from the vantage point of exaltation" (Meier, "Structure and Theology," 179). Cf. J. W. Thompson, "The Structure and Purpose of the Catena in Hebrews 1:5–13," in *The Beginnings of Christian Philosophy*, CBQMS (Washington, DC: Catholic Biblical Association, 1982), 128–40.

[105] As Cullmann noted, "Hebrews also does not distinguish between the Creator and the Redeemer. We have emphasized from the beginning that this later distinction is not a New Testament one. The distinction between the Father and the Son does not mean a distinction between creation and redemption, but between God in so far as one *can* theoretically speak of him also apart from his revelation, and God in so far as the New Testament *does* speak of him only as the one who reveals himself. This is just what Hebrews means also" (*Christology of the New Testament,* 311).

followed by the present participle *ōn* and has a compound predicate coordinated by *kai*. This present participle *ōn* is followed by another present participle, *pherōn* ("sustaining"), and both should be construed as concessive adverbial modifiers of *poiēsamenos*. The significance of these grammatical features is discussed below when considering the semantic structure of this paragraph. Simply stated, even though they are adverbial and not adjectival modifiers of *huiō*, they serve among the seven affirmations about the Son.

The Son is "the radiance of God's glory and the exact representation of his being." Each word pulsates with deity. A major interpretive issue is whether this first clause in v. 3 is to be taken metaphorically or metaphysically. The Greek word for "radiance" *(apaugasma)* occurs only here in the New Testament. It is used in the LXX of personified wisdom's relation to eternal light (*Wis* 7:2b). It appears in *1 Clement* 36:2 where Jesus is called the *apaugasma tēs megalōsunēs* (of God).[106] In *Wis* 7:26 preexistent wisdom is said to be "the reflection [*apaugasma*] of eternal light . . . and an image [*eikōn*] of his goodness." Likewise, in Philo the *logos* appears as both the "image" and "reflection" of God, and *apaugasma* is used of both the relation of the human spirit to the divine *logos* and of personified wisdom's relation to the world.[107] Some see as a background for *apaugasma* the Hellenistic-Jewish concept of *eikōn* ("image").[108] Yet in both *Wisdom* and Philo, wisdom and *logos* are impersonal and should not be seen as the background for New Testament christological statements. Although the New Testament writers, including the author of Hebrews, may have been aware of these uses (it is likely that the author of Hebrews was aware of them), they do not contain the robust theological content with which the New Testament authors invest these terms.[109] At most, one might say that the author of Hebrews intentionally used such terms as *apaugasma*, which occur in Philo and other writers, but he did so in a heightened theological sense by connecting them with the preexistent Christ in a manner

[106] Regarding G. Theissen's suggestion that the similar uses reflect an independent drawing upon a common liturgical tradition designating Jesus as high priest (*Untersuchung zum Hebräerbrief*, SNT 2 [Gütersloh: Mohn, 1969], 33–38), see the critique by G. L. Cockerill, "Heb 1:1–14, *1 Clem* 36:1–6 and the High Priest Title," *JBL* 97 [1978]: 437–40) or the summary of Cockerill's critique by Lane (*Hebrews 1–8*, 14).

[107] See BDAG 99, for these and additional extra-biblical references; cf. O. Hofius, *EDNT* 1:118; *TDNTa* 87.

[108] So Hofius, *EDNT* 1:118.

[109] So Cullmann (*Christology of the New Testament*, 127) who noted that the writer of Hebrews "goes well beyond anything said of the wisdom of God in the biblical (e.g., Prov 8:22–31) or extra-biblical writings (e.g., *Wis* 7:22; 9:2, 9), as we can see both from a closer examination of his use of terms and from the climax of his statement in verse 3b." K. Barth protested against applying Prov 8:22 to Christ in Heb 1:1–4. (*CD*, *The Doctrine of Creation*, 3:53). Yet it would appear that the main "current" of Christological development flowing through the first century was, as Cullmann noted, wisdom Christology. A. Nairne (*The Epistle of Priesthood* [Edinburgh: T&T Clark, 1913], 37) has succinctly expressed the difference between Philo and Hebrews: "Philo deals with allegories, the Epistle with symbols."

wholly unknown outside the biblical writings.[110] Although some suggest that this word alone does not indicate the preexistence of the Son, most affirm that such is at the very least implied. It is, in fact, affirmed when considered in the context of 1:1–4 and the rest of Hebrews.[111]

The principal lexical issue here is whether *apaugasma* should be taken in an active sense such as "effulgence, radiance," or in a passive one such as "reflection."[112] Since it is used in both senses in the extra-biblical literature, and since the word is a *hapax legomenon* in the New Testament, it is difficult to decide the issue on lexical grounds alone.[113] Contextually, either option is viable as well. Historically, the church fathers unanimously chose the active sense, but in more recent times scholars and translators have been divided on the issue.

In favor of the active sense is the patristic testimony and the emphasis on Christ's equality with God.[114] In favor of the passive sense is the sentence structure of 1:3, with *apaugasma* parallel to *charaktēr*, "exact representation," and both semantically synonymous.[115] Since *charaktēr* originally indicated the "stamp" or "impress" made upon an object, it can be interpreted in a passive sense: "Jesus bears the very stamp of God's nature." Correspondingly, *apaugasma* is then taken in the passive sense of "reflecting the glory of God."

An additional argument for the passive interpretation is the ending of the word itself. Had the *mos* ending been used, the active sense would be required, according to Lünemann. But since the ending is *ma*, indicating result, the passive is demanded. Lünemann translated the word as "reflected radiance," and

---

[110] Excellent discussions of this word may be found in Grässer, *Text und Situation,* 218–28; O. Michel, *Der Brief an die Hebräer*, KEK 13 (Göttingen, Vandenhoeck und Ruprecht, 1936), 97–98, esp. the lengthy footnote on the parallels in extrabiblical literature; H. F. Weiss, *Der Brief an die Hebräer*, KEK 13 (Göttingen: Vandenhoeck & Ruprecht, 1991), 145–46; and Lünemann (*Hebrews*, 396–97), who has one of the better arguments for the passive sense. For a discussion of the patristic exegesis of v. 3 see F. M. Young, "Christological Ideas in the Greek Commentaries on the Epistle to the Hebrews," *JTS* ns 20 (1969): 150–63.

[111] See the excellent discussion followed by bibliography in D. Capes, "Preexistence," *DLNT* 955–61; for his discussion of preexistence in Hebrews, see pp. 957–58.

[112] H. MacNeill identified three possible meanings: (1) a shining forth, referring to the process or action; (2) that which is radiated ("brightness"), referring to the result; and (3) a further result, "reflection." He pointed out that the latter two are the only likely meanings for the noun "since the word by its formation should denote result" (*Christology of Hebrews*, 57).

[113] The active or passive meaning in extra-biblical sources cannot be determined with certainty. The passive is preferred in Plutarch, while the active sense appears preferable for *Wisdom* and Philo, according to BDAG 99. See the discussion in Cremer 118–19.

[114] The NIV favors the active sense, which is supported by Delitzsch (*Hebrews*, 1:48–49), Westcott (*Hebrews*, 11), Robertson (*WP*, 5:336), F. F. Bruce (*Hebrews*, 48), and Hughes (*Hebrews*, 42). Hughes explained that the passive sense would essentially render the following statement "exact representation of his being" a tautology.

[115] So Hofius, *EDNT* 1:118.

noted that a threefold idea is contained in it: (1) independent existence, (2) descent or derivation, and (3) resemblance.[116]

Since both interpretive options are possible, and since both convey essentially the same idea (whether the Son is the radiance or the reflection of God's glory does not diminish his deity, preexistence, or Sonship), either interpretation can be considered valid.[117] Given the overall context coupled with the patristic testimony, perhaps the active sense has a slight edge. The moon does not give light in the same way the sun does. Either way, Hofius is surely right when he pointed out that the focus here is not as much on the mediation of revelation as it is on the character of the revealer himself. "Both christological predicates underscore the divine origin, divine nature, and divine omnipotence of the preexistent One."[118]

That which the Son radiates is the Fathers glory (*doxēs*), taking the genitive here as objective. "Glory" has as its primary Old Testament counterpart *kābōd*, although it translates no less than 25 Hebrew terms in the Septuagint. According to Ezekiel, heavenly beings, including angels, are endowed with glory.[119] During the intertestamental period, "glory" came to be applied to things associated with God, including the angels. This probably plays into the thought process of the author when in the next paragraph (Heb 1:5–14) he contrasts the Son with angels. Angels are called *doxai* in 2 Pet 2:10 and Jude 8.

Its New Testament use is shaped by the Old Testament, a point that liberates the term from any Hellenistic or Gnostic association. The word is sometimes used in the sense of "splendor" for persons other than God as in Jesus' reference to Solomon in Matt 6:29. When it is applied to God and Jesus, the primary sense is that of the divine nature in either its invisibility or its perceptible manifestation; glory is the divine "mode of being."[120] As in the Old Testament, where God's presence and outworking of his plan of salvation exhibited his glory, so in the New Testament God's work of salvation in and through the Son

---

[116] Lünemann, *Hebrews*, 397. Descent or derivation can only be inferred if the passive sense is accepted, whereas the other two are true regardless.

[117] According to L&N 14.48, it is impossible to determine whether the active or passive is intended here. If active, they suggest the translation "He shines with God's glory," or "God's glory shines through him." If taken in the passive sense of "reflection," the translation "God's glory shines back from him" captures the thought. L. T. Johnson (*Hebrews*, 69) pointed out that the distinction between "radiance" and "reflection" in the final analysis does not really matter "when we remember that with light, reflection becomes radiance, and radiance is what is reflected."

[118] Hofius, *EDNT* 1:118; MacNeill's discussion remains one of the best (see *Christology of Hebrews*, 55–63).

[119] See the discussion with examples in *NIDNTT* 2:45.

[120] *TDNTa* 179–80. For excellent discussions on "glory," see B. B. Warfield, *The Lord of Glory* (New York: American Tract Society, 1907); P. Lewis, *The Glory of Christ* (Chicago: Moody, 1997); H. Hegermann, "δόξα," *EDNT* 1:344–48; C. Spicq, "δόξα," *TLNT* 1:362–79; S. Aalen, "δόξα," *NIDNTT* 2:44–52; and N. Turner, *Christian Words* (Nashville : Thomas Nelson, 1981), 185–89. C. R. Koester identified ὑπόστασις as "parallel" to δόξα, probably meaning to suggest that it is parallel in a semantic sense. He claimed that "transcendent reality" is closest to the author's intended meaning, although syntactically this would seem to be closer to the descriptive genitive (*TDNTa* 1239).

reveals the glory of God. We see God's glory in Christ Jesus. Stephen "saw the glory of God, and Jesus standing" (Acts 7:55). If the *kai* ("and") is to be taken in an epexegetical sense, then the meaning would be Stephen "saw the glory of God, namely Jesus, standing at the right hand of God."[121]

W. Grudem suggested that when "glory" is used of the bright light that surrounds God's presence, it is not strictly an attribute of God since it is not God's character being described, but rather the "created light or brilliance that surrounds God as he manifests himself in his creation."[122] It should be noted that Grudem is assuming two things in this statement: (1) God's character is not in focus, and (2) the glory is "created light." One or both of these assumptions may be incorrect.

Jesus is the effulgence of God's glory because he shares the same divine nature as the Father, yet he is distinct from the Father in his person.[123] The Council of Nicaea said, regarding the relationship of the Son to the Father in reference to the Son's essential deity, that Jesus is "light from light."[124] The preincarnate Christ shared in the divine glory because he is "God of very God"; the incarnate Christ reveals the divine glory because he is the embodied revelation of God's essential glory. Furthermore, in this revelation, Jesus does not reveal something other than himself, nor does he reveal something other than God.

To the magnificent statement that "the Son is the radiance of God's glory," the author coordinated another thought: the Son is also "the exact representation of his being." This description of the Son parallels the previous statement in form: predicate nominative followed by the genitive prepositional phrase. "Exact representation" translates the Greek *charaktēr*, another *hapax*

---

[121] It is construed this way by R. Martin, *Carmen Christi: Philippians 2:5–11—in Recent Interpretation and in the Setting of Early Christian Worship*, rev. ed. (Grand Rapids: Eerdmans, 1983), 111; and Turner, *Christian Words*, 187.

[122] W. Grudem, *Systematic Theology: An Introduction to Biblical Doctrine* (Grand Rapids: Zondervan, 1994), 220–21.

[123] Theodore of Mopsuestia, *Commentary on John* 1.1.1, in Heen and Krey, eds., *Hebrews*, 11: "With great care he [the author] turns from a statement of their distinction to an indication of their perfect likeness."

[124] M. Schiffren ("Biblical Hypostases and the Concept of God," *SBLSP* [Atlanta: *Scholars Press*, 1997], 197) correctly saw the parallelism between "glory" and "substance" in the two clauses, but then she stumbled when she claimed that God's glory and God's actualized being are revealed in the world in contrast to God's essence or his unactualized (ultimate) being (ὑπόστασις). Thus, Jesus is removed a step further from God's essence since he is the "reflection" of God's glory. So according to Schiffren, Jesus is "two levels removed" from God's ultimate being. This is precisely the opposite of what the author of Hebrews is saying. The terms for "effulgence" and "exact representation" were chosen by the author to indicate that not an iota of essential difference can be said to divide the Father from the Son. "The only way God the Father's glory can shine in the person of the Son is if they are *homoousios* (identical in essence)" (C. Mosser and P. Owen, "Mormonism," in *To Everyone an Answer: A Case for the Christian World View: Essays in Honor of Norman L. Geisler*, ed. F. Beckwith, W. L. Craig and J. P. Moreland [Downers Grove: InterVarsity, 2004], 346.

legomenon, which means "impress, reproduction, representation." It referred originally to an engraved character or impress made by a die or seal, and it was commonly used for an impression on coins.[125] The word "is used from the time of Herodotus . . . of the distinguishing features, material or spiritual, borne by an object or person; of the traits by which we recognize it as being what it is."[126] The word connotes "a reproduction of each characteristic feature of the original."[127]

The predication is completed by the genitive *hupostaseōs autou* ("of his being"). The basic meaning of this word is "substantial nature, essence, actual being, reality."[128] It primarily connotes the essential nature of something, its "real being," or one who is "just like what he [God] really is."[129] The point is "what God is, the Son is: they share the same 'imprint of being.'"[130]

That both of these clauses are coordinated by *kai* and introduced by the present participle *ōn* ("being," translated "is" in the NIV) indicates that the author was speaking ontologically and eternally, not functionally, for in the latter case the sonship was by adoption rather than by nature.[131] The present tense of the participle *ōn,* with the lone exception of *pherōn*, "sustaining," is surrounded by verbs and verbals in the aorist or perfect tenses. This is not without significance theologically. "Amid this string of discrete past actions,

---

[125] BDAG 1077; cf. MM 683.

[126] Westcott, *Hebrews*, 12; cf. Alford, *Hebrews*, 7–8. These terms in v. 3a bring out emphatically the reasons why the Son is qualified to reveal the Father. Paul made use of another similar word, εἰκών, to denote Christ as the "image" of God in Col 1:15 and 2 Cor 4:4. Bruce (*Hebrews*, 48) noted that χαρακτήρ expresses this concept "even more emphatically" than εἰκών.

[127] Dods, "Hebrews," 252. Philo used this term some 51 times, including reference to the image of God in man, as it were, stamped by the *Logos*. For the references and appropriate cautions not to exaggerate the similarities between Philo and the author of Hebrews at this point, see Lane, (*Hebrews 1–8*, 13). Moffatt (*Hebrews*, 6) correctly stated regarding the relationship between Philo and Hebrews: "The unique relation of Christ to God is one of the unborrowed truths of Christianity, but it is stated here in borrowed terms."

[128] BDAG 1077. Cf. *TDNT* 3:421–31; H. W. Hollander, *EDNT* 3:406–7 (used "more or less philosophically of *reality* or *being*"); *TDNTa* 1237–39; G. Harder, *NIDNTT* 1:710–14; and R. E. Witt, "ΥΠΟΣΤΑΣΙΣ," *Amicitiae Corolla* 322, 325. This noun occurs only five times in the NT, three in Hebrews. For philosophical uses of ὑπόστασις in Philo and others, see Spicq, *TLNT* 3:421, n. 1.

[129] The latter phrase is how Louw and Nida express it (58.1); see Attridge's "fundamental reality" (*Hebrews*, 44).

[130] Johnson, *Hebrews*, 70.

[131] So Westcott, *Hebrews*, 425. He further stated that the two concepts of ἀπαύγασμα and χαρακτήρ are complementary: "In ἀπαύγασμα the thought of 'personality' finds no place . . . ; and in χαρακτήρ the thought of 'coessentiality' finds no place. The two words are related exactly as ὁμοούσιος and μονογενής, and like those must be combined to give the fullness of the Truth." This term and its use in Heb 1:3 would play an important role in the Christological controversies of the fourth century, even greater than John 1:1–18. See C. Gunton, *Yesterday and Today: A Study of Continuities in Christology* (Grand Rapids: Eerdmans, 1983), 65; for full discussion see F. M. Young, "Christological Ideas in the Greek Commentaries on the Epistle to the Hebrews," *JTS* 20 NS (1969): 150–63.

the present stative participle *ōn* stands out like a metaphysical diamond against the black crepe of narrative."[132] Within the Godhead, the persons of Jesus and God are distinct, but the divine nature is common to both. What God is in his substantial nature, the Son is as well. This fact makes it impossible to speak of the Father and Son in categories of "greater" and "lesser" as was sometimes the case with the Arians in the fourth century Christological debates.[133] Gregory of Nyssa chided those who spoke in such terms to learn from Heb 1:3 "not to measure things immeasurable."[134]

After describing the Son's relationship to God, the author informs us of the Son's relationship to all of creation. The Son sustains all things by his powerful word. The clause is introduced with the present active participle of *pherō* ("sustaining"). The basic meaning in this context is that of upholding, sustaining, and carrying to a proper goal. "All things" are sustained, a reference to the totality of the created universe. The means by which it is sustained is the Son's "word" *(rhēma)*, which is "powerful."

Like the previous clauses, several lexical, syntactical and semantic questions need to be answered. First, the meaning of *pherōn* in this context is debated. There are five possibilities: (1) "to bear up, to sustain"; (2) "to bear along" in the sense of "guide, rule"; (3) "to bear patiently, to endure"; (4) "to create" in the sense of bringing something into being; and (5) "to bear the sins of the world."[135]

Contextually, only the first two options are viable.[136] It is also possible that *pherō* could be interpreted contextually as "to cause to continue to exist,"[137] but this is unlikely for two reasons. First, the focus of the three clauses in v. 3 seems to be on a state of being, not that of continued existence. Second, the verbs *menō* and *diamenō* would be more appropriate if this were the intended meaning, since they encode notions of continuance in terms of existence. In Heb 1:11 the semantic concept of continued existence is conveyed by the use

---

[132] Meier, "Structure and Theology," 180. To this point the author's theological trajectory follows the path from exaltation to creation to preexistence.

[133] At Chalcedon in 451, the council concluded that Christ was "complete in Godhead and complete in manhood, truly God and truly man . . . two natures, without confusion, without change, without division, without separation." See E. E. Cairns, *Christianity Through the Centuries*, 3rd ed. (Grand Rapids: Zondervan, 1996), 136.

[134] Gregory of Nyssa, *On the Faith*, in Heen and Krey, eds., *Hebrews*, 12.

[135] Listed by Ellingworth, *Hebrews*, 100. There are actually 13 semantic categories for this word (L&N 2:256), and only two or three are contextually possible. For the meaning of φέρω, see L&N 13.35; K. Weiss, *TDNTa* 1252–53; *EDNT* 3:419. For its meaning and usage here, see esp. the discussion by Hughes (*Hebrews*, 45–46), who interacts with Westcott, Moffatt, Spicq, Erasmus, and Aquinas concerning the particular nuances of meaning in φέρειν.

[136] Option 5 is obviously inappropriate, and option 4 is unlikely since it would needlessly repeat the statement in 1:2 and would tax φέρω with an extremely rare usage.

[137] L&N 13.35.

of *diameneis* in reference to the Son's eternal existence as compared to the temporary and transitory nature of the universe's existence.[138]

The author's use of this concept of sustaining and maintaining the universe reflects Jewish usage in the Old Testament (Exodus) as well as rabbinic and Targumic literature.[139] Philo identified God himself as sustaining the world, while at other times ascribing this function to the *Logos*.[140] The *Shepherd of Hermas* contains a statement that, in light of its early dating (c. AD 90–140), is of some interest in comparison to Heb 1:3: "The name of the Son . . . carries the entire world."[141] All things considered, it is likely that both meanings one and two above, sustaining and guiding, are intended here.[142] The Son is sustaining the universe in a dynamic way; he is "carrying along" or guiding it towards its intended goal, rather than merely passively supporting creation as if it were a burden.

A second syntactical issue is of some significance in determining the relation of this participial clause to the previous two relative clauses ("whom he appointed heir" and "through whom he made the universe"). This clause is tightly linked to the previous two by the use of the particle *te*.[143] The Son's relation to God involves, by its very nature, his relation to the world. Even as he is in his relation to God, so he is in his relation to the world. Since he is God's agent in creation (1:2), and since he is also the radiance of the Father and the exact representation of his being, then logically he is also the one who sustains the universe.[144] The author stated the Son's role as agent in the creation of the universe in v. 2, and here he indicated the universe's continued sustaining and guidance by the Son. *Ta panta* is likely synonymous with *pantōn* in v. 2

[138] So L&N 13.89; but against Bruce (*Hebrews*, 49): "The creative utterance which called the universe into being requires as its complement that sustaining utterance by which it is maintained in being."

[139] Examples cited in *EDNT* 3:419.

[140] In *De somniis*, 1.241 and *Rer. Div. Her.* 7, God is the agent, and in *Mig. Abr.* 6 the *Logos* is the agent. The latter reference employs the meaning of guiding the universe on its course.

[141] *Similitudes* 9.14.5. Hermas was a former slave (emancipated at Rome), and contemporary of Clement of Rome. Given the possible Roman provenance or destination of Hebrews, one might conjecture that Hermas was aware of Heb 1:3. Delitzsch referred to this statement by Hermas as being "in allusion to" this clause in 1:3 (*Hebrews*, 1:52).

[142] So Westcott (*Hebrews*, 13) who gave examples of uses from the fathers and Philo, and Lenski (*Hebrews*, 38) who argued that both thoughts occur in 1:3c: "he bears all things so that his will and his purpose are fulfilled."

[143] For the grammatical use of τέ, see Robertson (*GGNT* 1178–79), who said that its use indicates "something additional, but in intimate relation with the preceding." N. Turner (MHT 3:339) likewise said that τέ joins words more closely than καί and it joins words or clauses that have a logical affinity. Such is the case in Heb 1:3.

[144] Westcott brought this out nicely: "We now pass from the thought of the absolute Being of the Son to His action in the finite creation under the conditions of time and space. The particle τέ indicates the new relation of the statement which it introduces. . . . [T]he providential action of the Son is a special manifestation of His Nature and is not described in a coordinate statement: what He does flows from what He is" (*Hebrews*, 13).

and refers to all there is in the universe. The article probably indicates that the universe is being viewed in its totality.[145]

The final phrase, "by his powerful word," is the personal pronoun with the genitive of quality,[146] a Hebraism (lit. "the word of his power") with the meaning "his powerful word." The phrase expresses the means by which the Son sustains the universe, and it further unifies the entire paragraph: God "spoke" in one who is a Son; the Son was the agent of creation that came into existence from the spoken word (Gen 1:1–3); now the Son sustains the universe through his own "word."[147] Paul made a similar statement in Col 1:17, which says that Christ "holds all things together."

The question arises as to why the author used *rhēma* here rather than *logos* for the concept of "word."[148] *Rhēma* is used four times in Hebrews (1:3; 6:5; 11:3; 12:19), two of which (1:3; 11:3) have to do with the act of creation. *Rhēma* has three semantic categories: word, statement, and event. The first two are sub-categories under the general semantic umbrella of communication. When *rhēma* is used in the first sense, it connotes a minimal unit of discourse, sometimes a single word. When it is used in the sense of "statement," it connotes something stated or said with primary focus on the content of the communication. In this sense, it is indistinguishable from *logos* in meaning, and employment of either noun would be a matter of stylistic preference. The third sense of "event" indicates a matter, thing or happening to which one may refer.[149] Of these three semantic categories, it would appear that *logos* is not used in the first sense of a minimal unit of discourse or a single word, but is a synonym of *rhēma* in the other two uses.

Rhēma is probably used here in this context for two primary reasons. First, it is used in Hebrews *exclusively* of God speaking, and the author has just identified the Son with the Father in the previous two clauses. Furthermore, the Son's speaking is the expression of his providential will and has the force of a command that the universe obeys. Second, *rhēma* is more expressive since the focus is not so much on the actual content of what is said but rather on the act of utterance, which is "powerful" to sustain the universe.[150]

---

[145] Westcott (*Hebrews*, 14) took the article to indicate all things in their unity. It would seem that the author of Hebrews has a penchant for expressing the totality of the universe in this way since in 2:8 he altered the LXX by adding the article before πάντα, and then again twice in v. 10 he used the articular construction.

[146] MHT 3:214.

[147] The antecedent of αὐτοῦ ("his") is υἱός ("Son"), not θεός ("God").

[148] See Delitzsch, *Hebrews*, 1:52–53; Ellingworth, *Hebrews*, 101.

[149] See L&N 33.9, 33.98, and 13.115 respectively.

[150] As Westcott (*Hebrews*, 14) put it: "As the world was called into being by an utterance (ῥῆμα) of God, so it is sustained by a like expression of the divine will." For evidence that the antecedent of αὐτοῦ ("his powerful word") is the Son and not the Father (as has been occasionally erroneously suggested), see Alford (*Hebrews*, 10).

Theologically, "upholding all things" indicates at least three truths. First, the Son is distinct from creation itself. He exists apart from it. He is not dependent upon it, but it is dependent on him. Second, this sustaining reflects a positive agency of moving creation to its designed goal. This is not a mere refraining from destruction. Third, it involves divine "concurrence" with secondary causes in that God is immanent in the operation of natural phenomena according to natural law, though not so as to preclude miracle.[151] With respect to the Son's sustaining of creation, Calvin said that God is no "idle" God.[152] As Thiselton stated, "Through Christ, God keeps the cosmos from falling into the abyss of non-being."[153]

The author turned his attention from the preincarnate Christ to what Christ accomplished in history on the cross as the incarnate Son. "After he provided purification for sins" translates an adverbial participial clause temporally modifying the finite verb *ekathisen* ("he sat down"). The act of enthronement occurred consequent to the act of purification. This particular clause is in many ways crucial for the author's argument. Here is the implicit reference to the high priestly work of Christ intimated through the cultic language of *katharismon*. The bulk of the expositional sections of Hebrews further expand on this theologically.

There is a textual issue here that merits brief discussion. Some manuscripts add *di' heautou* ("through himself"; cf. KJV) or *di' autou* ("through him") before *katharismon*. Zuntz made a case for the genuineness of the addition.[154] Yet the textual evidence is very weak, and the addition was probably made to clarify the meaning of the middle voice in *poiēsamenos*.[155] These two factors favor the originality of the text without the gloss.

The author's use of *katharismon* ("purification") introduces a theme developed extensively in the doctrinal sections of the epistle. The term is used for both physical as well as cultic cleansing in the New Testament. The term occurs 19 times in the LXX, with the focus on ritual purification (see Exod 29:36; Lev 15:13). It occurs in Exod 30:10 concerning the Day of Atonement ritual, and our author developed the connection between Christ and the Day of Atonement in Heb 8:1–10:18. The word is also used, as here, for cleansing

---

[151] These three truths were noted by J. L. Garrett, *Systematic Theology* (Grand Rapids: Eerdmans, 1990), 1:325.

[152] J. Calvin, *Institutes*, 1.16.4.

[153] A. C. Thiselton, "Hebrews," 1455.

[154] G. Zuntz, *The Text of the Epistles: A Disquisition upon the Corpus Paulinum* (London: Oxford, 1953), 43–45. Delitzsch (*Hebrews*, 1:54) also argued for it but admitted that the middle voice alone shows that the act of atonement "was done by Him, not through the instrumentality of any outward means, but by interposition and within the sphere of His own personality."

[155] So Lane, *Hebrews 1–8*, 5; cf. *TCGNT* 592. A. H. Trotter (*Interpreting the Epistle to the Hebrews*, in Guides to New Testament Exegesis, ed. S. McKnight [Grand Rapids: Baker, 1997], 98) agreed, noting that the middle voice already brings out the notion of Christ's sacrifice of himself (cf. 7:27) and needs no clarification.

of sin through the death of Christ. This noun occurs seven times in the New Testament (five in the Gospels, once in Hebrews, once in 2 Peter), but never in Matthew's Gospel or the Pauline Epistles.[156]

In the religious world of Greece and Rome, there were systems of ritual purification, but it is clear from the context of Hebrews that the author drew on the Old Testament sacrificial system as the milieu for his theological discussion of Christ's atonement. In the Old Testament sacrificial economy, sin defiled the person, and this necessitated a cleansing by the sprinkling of blood upon the altar from a sacrifice. The threefold result of the sacrificial offering was the objective removal of sin, the provision of forgiveness, and the cleansing of the sinner.[157] This is dealt with in detail by the author in Hebrews 9.

It is our "sins" (pl. *hamartiōn*) that are cleansed. Although Hebrews uses the plural (13) slightly more than the singular (10), there is no discernible difference of meaning.[158] *Katharismon* is the direct object of the participle *poiēsamenos. Hamartiōn* is an objective genitive[159] with an understood indirect object "for us": Jesus has cleansed us of sins.

Both Exod 30:10 and Lev 16:30 are instructive for understanding the author's concept of "cleansing" here and throughout Hebrews. Exodus 30:10 refers to the instructions that the Lord gave to Moses concerning the altar of incense on the Day of Atonement (Yom Kippur). The LXX rendering of this passage contains the Lord's instructions to Moses for Aaron to make atonement on the horns of this altar annually on Yom Kippur: "from the blood of purification [*katharismou*] he shall cleanse [*katharieí*] it." In Lev 16:30, the Lord told Moses that on the Day of Atonement, Aaron was to make an atonement for the people "to cleanse you from all your sins [*katharisai humas apo pasōn tōn hamartiōn humōn*], and you shall be cleansed [*katharisthēsesthe*]." It is a fundamental principle in the Old Testament that both sin and its resultant impurity in the life of the individual must be dealt with if the worshipper is to

156 See *TDNTa* 384. For bibliography on this word and the concept of "purification," see H. Thyen, *EDNT* 2:218. The verbal form occurs 17 times in the Gospels, three times in Acts, three times in Paul's Letters, four times in Hebrews (where it is always linked to Christ's death as a sacrifice), once in James, and twice in 1 John. Its infrequency in Paul as compared to Hebrews might have some bearing on the issue of Pauline authorship.

157 Cremer, 319, compared the use of καθαρισμὸν in Heb 1:3 with 2 Pet 1:9. He explained that the focus in 1:3 is on the objective removal of sin, while in 2 Pet 1:9 the word denotes the purification accomplished in the subject ("and has forgotten that he has been cleansed from his past sins").

158 See W. Grundmann, "ἁμαρτάνω," *TDNT* 1:313–16; and Ellingworth, *Hebrews*, 102.

159 The phrase "purification for sins" (καθαρισμὸν τῶν ἁμαρτιῶν) is syntactically unusual. Apollonius's Canon states that two syntactically joined nouns are either both articular or both anarthrous. Exceptions include 400 examples as reckoned by S. D. Hull, "Exceptions to Apollonius' Canon in the NT: A Grammatical Study," *TJ* 7 NS (1986): 3–16. Most of these exceptions are explainable by other criteria as noted by S. Porter, *Idioms of the Greek New Testament* (Sheffield: Academic Press, 1995), 112. This phrase appears to be one of about 30 exceptions not covered by the criteria above.

approach God.[160] Purification by sacrifice is necessary if one is to "draw near" to God as the author exhorted his readers to do several times in the epistle (7:19; 10:22).[161] At this point in Hebrews, the author has said that the Son has made purification for sins (implying his incarnation and high priestly role), but it remains for the author to explain later that the Son as high priest is also the one who became the sacrifice for sins.

Poiēsamenos is an adverbial temporal modifier of the finite verb *ekathisen* ("he sat down"), expressing temporal sequence. The NIV begins a new sentence with this participle and brings out the temporal sequence between the participle and the main verb of the next clause: "After he had provided purification for sins, he sat down." The participle is probably best translated "when he made" or "after he made" to bring out the temporal idea, but it has the secondary meaning of causation.[162] The seating could not take place until the cleansing was completed.

A number of linguistic and semantic factors converge in this participial clause to illustrate the special focus that the author placed on it. First, it is introduced without a connective in contrast to the previous clauses. This is one way the author could focus on the clause. Second, the author shifted from the present tense in the previous clauses to the aorist participle *(poiēsamenos)*. The emphasis on Christ's equality with God in v. 3a "has as its point of reference the statement in v. 3c regarding the atoning death: only the Son in the unity of his being and acting with God could bring about purification from sins through his death. Thus the work of redemption is inseparable from the person of the redeemer."[163]

This is a vital connection in this paragraph and throughout Hebrews. The atoning work of the Son is inextricably connected with the fact of his full deity as Son in relation to the Father. His high priestly work is predicated upon his sonship, hence the author's development of Christ's sonship before that of his high priesthood in the epistle (see discussion below). At crucial junctures, the author reiterates that it is the Son who is appointed high priest. It is helpful to compare 7:28 with 8:1, where the author began a new section and summarized his main point: "For the law appoints as high priests men who are weak; but the oath, which came after the law, appointed the Son, who has been made perfect forever" (7:28); "The point of what we are saying is this: we do have

---

[160] See the quote of Ebrard in Alford ("Hebrews," 10–11) on the OT background of καθαρισμόν.

[161] Whatever reference to the Wisdom tradition may have been in the mind of the author in the previous statements about Christ, Wisdom tradition cannot be the ground for this assertion by the author. Lane (*Hebrews 1–8*, 15), referring to F. Bovon, "Le Christ, la foi, et la sagesse dans l'Épître aux Hebreux," *RTP* 18 (1968): 143.

[162] *GGBB* 624.

[163] Hofius, *EDNT* 1:118.

such a high priest, who sat down at the right hand of the throne of the Majesty in heaven" (8:1).[164]

Third, the participle's direct object, *katharismon*, is first in the clause (fronted) and the participle is placed last.[165] This gives marked prominence to the concept of "purification of sins" in relation to the previous clauses. Fourth, the use of the middle voice in *poiēsamenos* serves to intensify the focus on the one who provides the purification in the sense that "he himself and no other" made purification for sins.[166] These four syntactical factors tend to give marked prominence to this clause, the equivalent of bold, italics, or underlining for emphasis. There is a fifth semantic factor that clinches the focus on this clause, but that discussion is below when the overall semantic structure of the communication relations in the prologue is considered. For now, suffice it to say that even though the three adverbial participial clauses of v. 3 all modify the main verb *ekathisen*, the focus of the author and the most dominant semantic information is conveyed by the final clause "after he provided purification for sins." This linguistic fact is born out in the epistle as the dominant theological sections explain in detail just how it is that God, through the Son who is the high priest, procured this "purification for sins."

The seventh and final clause in v. 3 describing the person and work of the Son is now introduced by the finite verb *ekathisen*. It is followed by a location orienter ("at the right hand") identifying where he sat down as well as the royal dignity that accompanies the enthronement.[167] The use of "majesty" stands as a circumlocution for the name of God, followed by another location, "in heaven" (lit. "on high").[168] The subject of this finite verb is actually the relative pronoun *hos* "who" (nominative case), that begins v. 3. All the intervening

---

[164] The last use of "Son" in the epistle occurs at 10:29 in the phrase "Son of God" where the author warned the readers of the severity of God's punishment for those who "trampled the Son of God under foot" and who "treated as an unholy thing the blood of the covenant that sanctified him."

[165] "Clause final" is a linguistic phenomenon that has gone unnoticed here by virtually every commentator. A notable exception is Meier ("Structure and Theology," 184), who stated that by shifting the participle to the end of the clause, it becomes rhetorically and theologically juxtaposed to the finite verb ἐκάθισεν.

[166] This classical use of the middle participle with καθαρισμόν expresses the same idea as the cognate verb. Cf. the footnote discussion in DeSilva (*Perseverance in Gratitude*, 90–91).

[167] Δεξιᾷ ("right") is an adjective modifying an omitted word ("hand"). This is an example of implied information in a discourse. When used in the singular and qualifying no other noun, δεξιᾷ refers to the right hand. It is pointless to debate whether ἐν δεξιᾷ denotes place or dignity since contextually it obviously means both.

[168] In 8:1 an almost identical statement is made: "who sat down at the right hand of the throne of the Majesty in heaven," where the actual word for heaven is used in the Greek text. Here the circumlocution "on high" signifies "heaven." Whether the phrase is syntactically connected with ἐκάθισεν (as in Moffatt and Lane) in a local/spatial sense ("heaven, heavenly sphere"), or with μεγαλωσύνης (as in Alford and Dods) in the sense that the majesty is "on high" and references supreme spiritual authority and rule, does not appreciably alter the meaning of the clause.

participial clauses function as adverbial modifiers of this finite verb *ekathisen*. The NIV begins a new sentence with v. 3 ("The Son is ...").

The aorist indicative of *kathizō* ("to sit down") indicates the specific act of enthronement that occurred after the completion of atonement and implies that the atonement was satisfactorily completed.[169] That the Son is seated "at the right hand of the Majesty in heaven" indicates royal supremacy. The reference is to the place of honor, authority, and power that the Son has taken,[170] and combines in this thought the resurrection and ascension, which temporally preceded the enthronement.[171]

Since God's throne is in heaven, the entire phrase "at the right hand of the majesty in heaven" actually subsumes both the spatial sense as well as that of supreme spiritual authority. For the Son to sit at the right hand is to share God's power without limitation, but there is implied subordination of the Son to the Father in that the Father gives this status to the Son.[172] This subordination is functional and not essential, as previous statements in the prologue make clear.

The crucial factor here is that it is the incarnate Son who is enthroned at the right hand of God. Though the incarnation is not specifically mentioned in 1:1–4, it is implied by the statement that the Son has made atonement for sins, which he did as the incarnate Son. Furthermore, it is the focus of attention in 2:14: "Since the children have flesh and blood, he too shared in their humanity so that by his death . . . " These final two clauses are syntactically and semantically connected, articulating the two major themes of Hebrews: high priestly sacrifice of the Son and kingly exaltation of the Son. This theme of Christ exalted to the right hand of God permeates the Christology of the epistle.

1:4 Most commentators see this verse as concluding the paragraph, with v. 5 beginning a new paragraph and section.[173] Some, however, begin the new section with v. 4.[174] Westfall rightly argued for the unity and cohesion of 1:1–4 on linguistic grounds.[175]

---

[169] See the use of the perfect κεκάθικεν in 12:2.

[170] The right hand is a metaphor for honor and power in both biblical and non-biblical Greek. The entire phrase highlights the supreme exaltation of the Son without compromising the Father's position in any way. See D. M. Hay, *Glory at the Right Hand: Psalm 110 in Early Christianity*, SBLMS 18 (Nashville: Abingdon, 1973), 91.

[171] The lack of reference to the resurrection should not be alarming since the author assumed it. He viewed the exaltation as including resurrection, ascension, and exaltation all in one sweep. See Hay, *Glory*, 43–45; Lane, *Hebrews 1–8*, 16.

[172] Ellingworth, *Hebrews*, 103.

[173] So Attridge, *Hebrews*, 36; Lane, *Hebrews 1–8*, 16–17; Ellingworth, *Hebrews*, 103; and Koester, *Hebrews*, 174.

[174] So Delitzsch, *Hebrews*, 1:39; P. E. Hughes, *Hebrews*, 50; Lenski, *Hebrews*, 42; and N. Miller, *The Epistle to the Hebrews: An Analytical and Exegetical Handbook* (Dallas: Summer Institute of Linguistics, 1988), 13.

[175] C. Westfall, *A Discourse Analysis of the Letter to the Hebrews: The Relationship Between Form and Meaning*, LNTS 297 (London: T&T Clark, 2006), 90–91.

Those who consider v. 4 as part of the preceding paragraph do so for syntactical and stylistic reasons. Syntactically, v. 4 is introduced by the adverbial causal participle *genomenos*, which modifies *ekathisen* and is preceded by the demonstrative pronoun of degree *tosoutō* and the comparative adjective *kreittōn*, "better," yielding (lit.) "so much better than." Stylistically, the prologue can be construed in a chiastic framework, with v. 4 rounding out the parallel to v. 1 and thus binding the unit together.[176]

Those who consider v. 4 to begin a new paragraph do so primarily on linguistic grounds.[177] They note that the comparison to angels is the main focus of the discussion in vv. 5–14. Some advocate a chiastic structure that takes in vv. 2b–3 and thus conclude that v. 4 best begins a new paragraph.[178]

Verse 4 is a transition verse between the two paragraphs, but it seems best to construe it syntactically with v. 3 and to see it as an example of a tail-head linkage between two paragraphs, which is when a lexical item at the end of one paragraph serves as an introduction to the theme of the next paragraph. This linguistic device is common in Hebrews.[179] In addition, the paragraph is framed by reference to the Son as a superior bearer of revelation in comparison to the prophets (v. 1) and to angels (v. 4). In the Old Testament, angels played a key role in mediating revelation, such as the giving of the law, a concept not unknown to the New Testament writers as well (Acts 7:38–39; Gal 3:19). While the connection is implicit in the prologue, it becomes explicit in 2:2. Lane correctly observed that the angels in v. 4 are the counterparts to the prophets in v. 1.[180]

Three propositions are encoded in the clause of v. 4: (1) the Son is superior to the angels; (2) the Son has inherited a name; and (3) the Son's name is superior to that of the angels. The thought runs as follows. Since the Son has

---

[176] As argued by D. W. B. Robinson ("Literary Structure of Hebrews 1:1–4," 185) and followed by Lane, *Hebrews 1–8*, 6–7. See the section on rhetorical structure below.

[177] So Lenski (*Hebrews*, 42): "We make a division at this point because of the thought, which makes a comparison with the angels, and not because of the construction, for this continues with another aorist participle."

[178] Hughes, *Hebrews*, 49.

[179] See A. Vanhoye's "hook words" in *Structure and Message of the Epistle to the Hebrews,* SubBi 12 (Rome: Pontifical Biblical Institute, 1989), 36–38.

[180] Lane (*Hebrews 1–8*, 17) stated, "This conception was shared by the writer and his readers (2:2). The description of the Jewish law as 'the message declared by angels' in 2:2 is determinative for the interpretation of the reference to the angels in v. 4 . . . . The shift from *the prophets* to *the angels* is deliberate, for it is the writer's intention to announce as the subject of his first major section (1:5–2:18) the superiority of the Son to the angels." Westfall (*Discourse Analysis*, 91) concurred. The suggestion that the comparison between Christ and the angels was prompted by the problem of angel worship or by an angelomorphic Christology is unnecessary since the context does not indicate that either of these were problems for the readers. See E. Grässer, "Zur Christologie des Hebräerbriefes," in *Neues Testament und christliche Existenz,* ed. H. D. Betz and L. Schottroff (Tübingen: Mohr, 1973), 89–91. Lane (*Hebrews 1–8*, 8–9, 17), Ellingworth (*Hebrews*, 103–4), and DeSilva (*Perseverance in Gratitude,* 92) concurred. F. Schröger (*Der Verfasser des Hebräerbriefes als Schriftausleger*, [Regensburg: Pustet, 1968], 75) listed those who argue that the author of Hebrews polemicizes against angel worship.

inherited a name because of his exaltation, and since his name is superior to that of the angels, then the Son is superior to the angels.

Verse 4 engenders several crucial questions. (1) How is the participle *genomenos* functioning in the clause? (2) What is the "name" that Christ inherits? (3) When did he inherit it? (4) What did the writer mean when he said that Christ "became as much superior than the angels as the name he has inherited is superior to theirs"? Does this statement imply that there was a time when he was not superior to them? We consider each one in order.

The participle is an adverbial modifier of the finite verb *ekathisen*. Some see it as expressing simultaneous action with the main verb in the sense of "he sat down and was shown to be superior to the angels."[181] Others take the participle to express the reason for the Son's exaltation at God's right hand in the sense that "he was seated at God's right hand because he became better than the angels."[182] Still others take it in a resultative sense: as a result of his purification of sins and enthronement, he became better than the angels.[183] The latter two options are often difficult to distinguish in some contexts, as here, but either reason or result seems to capture the author's meaning. Actually, it appears that *genomenos* introduces a reason clause for the result that is stated by *ekathisen,* "he sat down." It is both grammatically and semantically subordinate in that a participle modifying a main verb is syntactically subordinate to it. Semantically, in the communication relation of reason-result, the reason portion of the proposition is less semantically important than the result, which always receives the prominence.[184]

That v. 4 focuses on the "name" is clear from the emphatic position of *onoma* at the end of the sentence. The text of v. 4 does not identify the "name" that Christ inherited. Some have suggested his name given at birth, Jesus. Others, comparing this passage to Phil 2:5–11, have opted for "Lord."[185] Still others identify the "name" with the as yet unknown and inexpressible heavenly name mentioned in Rev 19:12.[186] M. Rissi suggested that the name is "at once three:

---

[181] Bruce, *Hebrews*, 50. Meier stated, "To translate γενόμενος as 'showing himself' or 'proving himself to be,' as some modern versions do, does not do justice to the thought here and avoids the contrast with ὢν in 1,3a" ("Structure and Theology," 185).

[182] Miller, *Hebrews*, 13.

[183] So Alford, "Hebrews," 13; Dods, "Hebrews," 253; and the NIV.

[184] J. Beekman, J. Callow, M. Kopesec, *The Semantic Structure of Written Communication* (Dallas: Summer Institute of Linguistics, 1981), 112–13.

[185] See L. T. Johnson (*Hebrews*, 73) who based his decision on the author's allusion to Ps 110:1, "the Lord says to my Lord."

[186] Delitzsch, *Hebrews*, 1:60. C. Gieschen, following W. Lueken, suggested 1 Enoch 69 as the conceptual background for the divine name as the "Word of Power" in Heb 1:3–4. He found evidence of an angelomorphic Christology in the prologue (*Angelomorphic Christology: Antecedents and Early Evidence*, AGJU [Leiden: Brill, 1998], 294–314). For a critique of the supposed angelomorphic Christology in Hebrews, see comments on 1:5–14.

Son, God and Lord."[187] Others have suggested that the name is not intended here to be specific, but refers rather to his being designated as Son in the sense that his position is superior to that of the angels.[188] These suggestions, while undoubtedly true, are not what the author has in mind. In this case, the context provides the answer. There can be little doubt that the name the author intended to convey is that of "Son." It is the name given in v. 2 in an emphatic way,[189] and it is the focus of the catena beginning in v. 5: "For to which of the angels did God ever say, 'You are my Son . . .'"[190]

The question of when did Christ inherit the name "Son" must be answered only after taking the immediate context into account as well as the broader context of the epistle and then the entire New Testament. This issue receives more in-depth discussion in the section below on the theology of the prologue, but at this point it seems one can say that Messianic sonship rests upon prior eternal sonship, but it is the former and not the latter that is primarily in view here.[191] What the Son was in himself before all time is now contrasted with what he has become (aorist *genomenos*) after his atoning work—seated at the right hand of God and exalted above angels.[192] It is likely that the author used the perfect *keklēronomēken* instead of the aorist because Christ did not first obtain this name at the time of his seating at the right hand; as the preexisting *Logos*, he had already obtained it.[193] The name "Son" belongs to Jesus by inheritance,

---

[187] M. Rissi, *Die Theologie des Hebräerbriefes*, WUNT 41 (Tübingen: Mohr/Siebeck, 1987), 52. Author's translation.

[188] So Moffatt, *Hebrews*, 8; and Kistemaker, *Hebrews*, 32.

[189] Attridge, *Hebrews*, 47.

[190] Based on the context, Meier commented that the attempt to avoid taking the name as "Son" is "an exercise in avoiding the obvious" ("Structure and Theology," 187). See K. Schenck, "Keeping His Appointment: Creation and Enthronement in Hebrews," *JSNT* 66 (1997): 93. Additionally, the two citations from Psalms in Heb 1:5 create an *inclusio* with the word "Son" (υἱός μου...εἰς υἱόν). On the other hand, R. Bauckham made this cogent point: "God's eschatological achievement of his purpose for this whole creation, his kingdom, begins with Jesus' enthronement. This is why he 'inherits' the divine name: it is in his rule from God's throne that the rule of the one God is to be acknowledged by all creation. God is to be known to all by his name when all creation recognize Jesus as the one who exercises God's rule. He is identified for them by the unique divine name. Many commentators, on the other hand, suppose the name here to be 'the Son', because it is as Son that Christ is distinguished from the angels in the following verses. But the Son is *the* one who inherits from his Father, not *what* he inherits. What he inherits should be something that belongs to his Father, not something uniquely the Son's, as the title Son is. The parallel with Phil. 2.9 suggests the much more intelligible idea that the one who sits on the divine throne is given the divine name, the tetragrammaton" (R. Bauckham, "Monotheism and Christology in Hebrews 1," in *Early Jewish and Christian Monotheism*, ed. L. Stuckenbruck and W. North, JSNTSup 263 [London: T&T Clark, 2004], 175).

[191] Dods, "Hebrews," 253.

[192] Delitzsch, *Hebrews*, 1:58–59.

[193] Lünemann, *Hebrews*, 400. The perfect tense "stands at the climax to the section (cf. v. 2) by drawing attention to the state of inheritance as the crowning glory of this act of enthronement" (S. E. Porter, *Verbal Aspect in the Greek of the New Testament, with Reference to Tense and Mood*, in Studies in Biblical Greek 1 [New York: Peter Lang, 1989], 263).

by virtue of the incarnation, and by virtue of the atonement he accomplished as the incarnate Son.[194] Also, the perfect tense stresses the present possession of the "name."

The fourth question, regarding the meaning of Christ's superiority to the angels, is answered by the context of Hebrews 1–2. The use of *diaphoros* (from the root meaning "different") intensifies the comparison and indicates a difference that marks Jesus as superior. Yet this does not imply that there was ever a time when the Son was lower than the angels in rank. This is established in the catena of quotations in vv. 5–14. After establishing the superiority of the Son (chap. 1), the author explained how it is that Jesus was made "for a little while" lower than the angels via the incarnation (chap. 2) for the purpose of the cross (2:9). The coming of the Son to earth to accomplish redemption was a descent from the heavenly to the earthly sphere, and since angels inhabit the heavenly sphere, the incarnation involved Jesus "becoming for a little while" lower than the angels. Jesus was superior to the angels from eternity by virtue of his deity, he temporarily became lower than the angels by leaving the heavenly sphere to come to earth to accomplish his salvific work, and as a result of the accomplishment of this work he has been exalted by God to the right hand of the throne in heaven where he has received the inheritance of the "name."[195]

The shift from v. 3 to v. 4 is from universal to particular since the following paragraph (1:5–14) gives v. 4 detailed development and furnishes the theme for 1:5–2:18.[196]

Rhetorical Structure of 1:1–4

Hebrews is noted for the variety of its rhetorical features that have often been discussed, especially since the mid-point of the last century.[197] The pro-

[194] So Westcott, *Hebrews*, 17; and Michel, *Hebräer*, 105.

[195] Moffatt, Windisch, and Michel suggested that the characterization of angels as "sons of God" in the OT is probably the background for the author's choice of the title "son" to describe Jesus. In fact, it would seem that the opposite is the case. The sonship of Jesus is prior to the high priestly work he performs and is the theological matrix from which the high priesthood of Christ is developed in the epistle. The angels are mentioned not so much because they were called "sons" of God, but that the Jews considered them mediators of the divine revelation. Moffatt, *Hebrews*, 10; Windisch, *Der Hebräerbrief*, HNT (Tübingen: Mohr [Siebeck], 1931), 15; and O. Michel, *Der Brief an die Hebräer*, KNT (Göttingen: Vandenhoeck & Ruprecht, 1966), 111.

[196] As pointed out by Lünemann (*Hebrews*, 390).

[197] See "Nature of the Book" in the introduction for a discussion of the many rhetorical devices used in Hebrews and for helpful bibliography on the subject, including Nida, *Style and Discourse*; Trotter, *Hebrews*, 164–77; and D. Watson, "Rhetorical Criticism of Hebrews and the Catholic Epistles Since 1978," *CurBS* 5 (1997): 175–207, which offers a good survey of this subject with respect to Hebrews through 1997 (see esp. pp. 181–87). An important study by W. G. Übelacker combines rhetorical analysis with discourse analysis to suggest that Hebrews is an example of deliberative rhetoric with the prologue functioning as the rhetorical *exordium* (*Der Hebräerbrief als Appell* [Lund: Almqvist & Wiksell, 1989]). D. A. DeSilva made use of Greco-Roman rhetorical handbooks coupled with Greek and Jewish speeches in an attempt to demonstrate that the author

logue itself is a rich source of rhetorical examples. Both Attridge and Lane provided examples of alliteration such as word order variation, repetition, parallelism.[198] The careful attention to literary structure that the author evinced in the prologue led Grässer to make a salient point that must not be missed. One must analyze the literary structure, not as something alongside exegesis, but *as* exegesis.[199]

It is likely that the prologue is chiastic. Robinson presented the case and was followed by Hughes, Lane, Ebert, and Ellingworth.[200] Ebert's proposal varied from previous suggestions in that the symmetrical pattern of the prologue has a central point that has no parallel in the paragraph and hence is highlighted by the author.

A The Son contrasted with the prophets (vv. 1–2a)
  B The Son as messianic heir (v. 2b)
    C The Son's creative work (v. 2c)
      D The Son's threefold mediatorial relationship with God (vv. 3a–b)
    C´ The Son's redemptive work (v. 3c)
  B´ The Son as messianic king (v. 3d)
A´ The Son contrasted with angels (v. 4)

Ebert offered impressive linguistic reasons to justify the above structure. First, each member on the one side of the two clauses (vv. 3a–3b—*ōn* and *pherōn*) mirrors a corresponding member on the other side (notice the A-B-C / C´-B´-A´ parallel). For example, the use of the finite verb *epoiēsen* in v. 2c corresponds to the participle *poiēsamenos* in v. 3c.[201] Second, the two clauses in vv. 3a–3b are closely linked grammatically by the use of *te*, as we noted above. Third, the subject of the four verbal ideas in vv. 1–2 is "God," whereas beginning with v. 3a the subject shifts to the "Son" and remains so through

used honor and shame language to promote the values of a minority culture audience (*Despising Shame: Honor Discourse and Community Maintenance in the Epistle to the Hebrews*, SBLDS, 152 [Atlanta: Scholars Press, 1995]); cf. his commentary on Hebrews. One of the better early treatments of the subject of rhetorical criticism and the NT is found in G. Kennedy, *New Testament Interpretation through Rhetorical Criticism* (Chapel Hill: University Press, 1984). For bibliography on rhetorical structure of Hebrews, see B. Witherington, *Letters and Homilies for Jewish Christians: A Socio-Rhetorical Commentary on Hebrews, James and Jude* (Downers Grove: InterVarsity, 2007), 93–96,

198 Attridge, *Hebrews*, 20–21; Lane, *Hebrews 1–8*, lxxv–lxxx. D. Black provided a helpful discussion of 12 rhetorical elements ("Hebrews 1:1–4: A Study in Discourse Analysis," *WTJ* [1985]: 181–92).

199 Grässer, *Text und Situation*, 183.

200 D. W. B. Robinson, "Literary Structure," 178–85; Hughes, *Hebrews*, 49; Lane, *Hebrews 1–8*, 6–7; D. Ebert, "The Chiastic Structure of the Prologue to Hebrews" *TJ* 13 (1992): 163–79; and Ellingworth, *Hebrews*, 95.

201 Yet the lexical parallels between κληρονόμον in v. 2 and κεκληρονόμηκεν in v. 4 do not occur in the corresponding parallel sections of Ebert's chiasm.

the end of the paragraph. As noted above, the "Son" at the end of v. 2 is the pivot of the paragraph. Fourth, the tense structure of the paragraph tends to highlight the central section in that the two center clauses are present tense participles flanked by aorists in vv. 1–2 and 3c–4. Fifth, the same theme occurs at the center and at the two extremes of the structure. At the center the Son is described as God's supreme self-expression based on his relationship to the Father and to creation. On the outer perimeters of the paragraph the Son, who is greater than the prophets and angels, is presented as the supreme revelation of God. Likewise, the use of "son" in v. 2a is paralleled by the reference to the "name" in v. 4, (which serves as another argument that the "name" inherited is that of "Son"). Finally, the two clauses in the center both begin and end with poetic euphony (*hos ōn* and *pherōn*; *tēs hupostaseōs autou* and *tēs dunameōs autou*).[202]

Ebert concluded that such a structure for the prologue serves to highlight the Son in a threefold way: as prophet, priest, and king. The emphasis at the center (D) and at both extremes (A/A´) speaks of the Son's role as God's final agent of revelation. "The main purpose of the threefold statement about the Son at the center is not to define his ontological relationship with the Father, though this is done implicitly. It is rather to stress the divine-revelatory capacity of the Son (D)."[203] The Son as king is emphasized in the B/B´—the son is messianic heir (v. 2b) and he is messianic king (v. 3d). The Son's priestly function is highlighted in the C/C´ statements: the Son's creative work (v. 2c) and his redemptive work (v. 3c). Ebert's proposal has merit and makes good sense of the overall structure.

Ellingworth's commentary appeared only one year after Ebert's article and hence does not register Ebert's contribution to the issue at hand. Ellingworth also suggested a chiastic arrangement for the prologue:

God has appointed Christ as heir.	enthronement
Through him he created the world	action in the universe
He reflects God's glory	relation to God
He bears God's stamp	relation to God
He upholds the universe	action in the universe
(When he had made purification,)	(reason for)
He sat down at God's right hand	enthronement[204]

Ellingworth offered no comment on his proposed structure, though it is similar to the previous chiasm. The parenthetical "when he had made purification" appears to receive little focus in this structure, yet as we noted above, there are

[202] Ebert, "Chiastic Structure," 168–70. The NIV reflects the cohesiveness of these central clauses by rendering them together as an independent sentence.

[203] Ibid., 177.

[204] Ellingworth, *Hebrews*, 95.

numerous linguistic reasons for suggesting that the author his given it marked prominence in the text.

L. T. Johnson understood Heb 1:3–4 to form "a chiastic expansion on v. 2b–c, rather than a true development: *a*. the Son inherits all things; *b*. the Son participates in creation; *c*. the Son makes purification for sins and sits at God's right hand; *b*´. the Son is the image of God and sustains all things; *a*´. the Son inherits a name greater than the angels."[205] He considers the middle term to be central both spatially and thematically. The focus is on God's treatment of the sin problem through the Son's saving work on the cross.

It seems clear that the author made use of the rhetorical device of chiasm to structure the prologue, even if different pairings of clauses and themes have been proposed. This device further tightens the pregnant propositions made about the Son as God's final revelation and highlights the prologue as programmatic for the remainder of the epistle.

Some have suggested that the prologue may use early Christian hymnic or confessional material. Evidence for and against this hypothesis is ably presented in recent commentaries and is not presented here.[206] It appears that the evidence does not favor the author's use of early Christian traditional material. The prologue has all the earmarks of the author's direct construction.[207]

Semantic Structure of 1:1–4

The prologue begins with two propositions:

Proposition 1	God spoke to the fathers by the prophets in the past
Proposition 2 (main)	God spoke to us in one who is a Son in these last days

These two propositions are related to one another in a contrastive way: not that God spoke then versus now or to the fathers versus to us, but that he spoke by prophets but now in one who is far superior to the prophets—a Son. The participle *lalēsas* adverbially modifies *elalēsen*; thus, the clause with the main verb is semantically dominant. This makes it unlikely that the two clauses should be interpreted as semantically equivalent as in "God spoke to the fathers and he spoke to us," or "God spoke to the fathers, but he spoke to us also." Perhaps a better approach would be to see a concession-CONTRAEXPECTATION meaning here: "although God spoke to the fathers by the prophets, yet now he has spoken to us in one who is a Son." The main contrastive idea is the means of God's communication—prophets versus Son. The surprise element is not

[205] Johnson, *Hebrews*, 68.

[206] See the discussions in Attridge, *Hebrews*, 41–48; Lane, *Hebrews 1–8*, 7–8; Ellingworth, *Hebrews*, 96–98; and Guthrie, *Structure of Hebrews*, 81.

[207] As argued convincingly by J. Frankowski, "Early Christian Hymns Recorded in the New Testament: A Reconsideration of the Question in the Light of Hebrews 1:3," *BZ* 27 (1982): 183–94.

that God should reveal himself; this was common in the Old Testament. The surprise element is that he should reveal himself through one who is by his character and nature a Son! This fact is what is contrary to our expectation.

The next two relative clauses appear to be related by simple coordination via *kai*. The conjunction *kai* has three primary grammatical categories: (1) additive, where it functions as a simple coordinating conjunction; (2) ascensive, where it functions in the sense of "also, even, or indeed"; and (3) adjunctive, which "introduces another thought into the discussion."[208] Young listed several semantic categories under the adjunctive use of *kai*, including concession (NKJV). Concession may be expressed semantically as a "concession-CONTRAEXPECTATION"[209] relation in which one of two propositions expresses a situation and the other expresses an unexpected result. An example is Col 1:21–22: "Although you were formerly alienated from God [concession], he has now reconciled you [CONTRAEXPECTATION]."

The two relative clauses in Heb 1:2 are coordinated by *kai*, but semantically much more appears to be communicated than merely the coordinated addition of adjectival clauses modifying "Son." Lane, like Robinson, identified the *kai* in v. 2 as "adversative" and translated *kai* as "yet." Lane and Robinson have the right idea but the wrong nomenclature. The *kai* in v. 2 is not a true adversative since the two clauses are not being contrasted, at least not in an adversative way. Such a reading would require a translation using the word "but" or some similar word to express a true adversative. It appears that Lane understood the semantic role between the two clauses to be that of concession. He later identified the three adverbial participles in v. 3 as concession.[210]

Normally, a concession-CONTRAEXPECTATION relationship appears in that order, with the CONTRAEXPECTATION proposition appearing last and receiving the semantic prominence. But it would appear that in Heb 1:2 the first relative clause functions as the contraexpectation while the second clause gives the concession. In other words, the Son has been appointed heir of all things, although he is the one who also created all things. One would normally expect these semantic concepts of inheritance and creation to be reversed: he created all things and he inherits all things. The author apparently placed the focus not only on the second clause that follows the *kai*, which would normally receive the marked prominence, but by fronting the contraexpectation in the order of the clauses, he was also able to cast it in the light of focused prominence. At the same time the author has balanced the contraexpectation clause in a chiasm

---

208 R. A. Young, *Intermediate New Testament Greek: A Linguistic and Exegetical Approach* (Nashville: B&H, 1994), 188.

209 See Beekman, et al., *Semantic Structure,* 104–6, for a description of this communication relation. CONTRAEXPECTATION is capitalized to illustrate the semantic weight and natural prominence that this part of the communication unit receives.

210 Lane (*Hebrews 1–8*, 5) is correct. His translation reads, "This Son, although the radiance . . . and although sustaining . . . yet made purification for sins and then sat down."

with the last clause of v. 3, which parallels its semantic content: "he sat down at the right hand of God." Being appointed heir of all things and being seated at the right hand of God comprise the A and A´ of the chiasm that is formed by the seven relative and participial clauses in vv. 2–3.[211]

Although the normal order for a concession-contraexpectation relation would place the contraexpectation last, the reverse order is possible. Young's example of Luke 18:7 actually presents this order. "And shall God not avenge his own elect" is the contraexpectation proposition that precedes the concession "though [*kai*] he bear long with them?" The prominent statement is the first proposition.[212] Thus, the two relative clauses in Heb 1:2 are related to one another in a CONTRAEXPECTATION-concession relationship. This semantically parallels the communication relationship of the first two clauses of vv. 1–2a.

The next three clauses of v. 3 are closely related syntactically and semantically as we have shown above. The first two are coordinated with each other by *kai* and the third is closely connected to the previous two by the addition of *te*. As indicated earlier, Lane offered a translation of these verses that understands their meaning to be that of concession-contraexpectation: "This Son, although the radiance . . . and although sustaining . . . yet made purification for sins."[213] Given the linguistic evidence that the author has placed semantic prominence on the clause "having made purification for sins," and given the contrast between the revelation through prophets and that which came in the Son, it does not seem unwarranted to suggest that a similar communication relation exists here as well.

We now turn to the final two clauses of v. 3, which for reasons discussed above are likewise closely linked together. The three previous clauses are related to the participle *poiēsamenos* as concession-CONTRAEXPECTATION. The *poiēsamenos* functions as the adverbial temporal modifier of *ekathisen* and expresses the idea of "after he made purification for sins, he sat down." The enthronement is expressed by the finite verb *ekathisen*, but its relation to the participle is such that the seating could only occur after the purification had been accomplished. We have already seen how the author has given marked prominence to the *poiēsamenos* clause. It is so closely related semantically that the two propositions, "he made purification for sins" and "he sat down at the right hand," must be understood together. The enthronement temporally is related to the atonement in that the former could only occur after the latter was completed, but in a theological sense the enthronement was dependent on the atonement. As heir of all things (v. 2), the Son is not actually exalted to the

[211] See discussion above in the section "Rhetorical Structure of 1:1–4." Lane's chiasm (ibid.) of the entire prologue is presented on pp. 6–7. A better case can be made for the chiastic arrangement consisting of the seven clauses that adjectivally modify the word "Son." See the chiasms proposed for the prologue above.

[212] Young, *Intermediate New Testament Greek,* 189.

[213] Lane, *Hebrews 1–8*, 4–5.

throne as heir until the atonement is completed. Even then, the consummation of his heirship will not be completed until the eschaton: "we do not see everything subject to him" (2:8); and 2:9 says, the Son is "now crowned with glory and honor because he suffered death." The close connection between the enthronement and the atonement here in 2:9 is further commentary on the virtually identical thought of 1:3.

These last two clauses receive marked prominence by their relationship to the previous clauses and by the enthronement being the termination of the Son's redemptive work, expressed by the finite verb *ekathisen*. These two concepts, atonement and exaltation, are the theological focus of the epistle.

It is clear that *genomenos* furnishes the reason for the result of exaltation in v. 3. It also follows (is postposed to) the main verb, whereas the previous three clauses precede it (preposed). Since result always receives the dominant stress in a reason-result relationship,[214] v. 4 expresses a subordinate idea via the adverbial participle. Verse 4 also rounds out the lexical parallelism and semantic chiasm of the entire paragraph. The perfect indicative *keklēronomēken* corresponds to the *klēronomon* of v. 2. The paragraph begins with the Son being appointed heir of all things and ends with him inheriting a name superior to the angels because of his completed work of atonement and subsequent exaltation.

The dominant communication role expressed in the prologue is that of concession-contraexpectation. Thus, one could understand the author to be conveying the following in a paraphrased fashion:

> Although God spoke through the prophets, his final revelation is his Son. This Son, although creator of all things, is also the designated heir of all things. This Son, although he is everything that God is in terms of essence and although he is the sustainer of the universe, yet, contrary to expectation, he and he alone made atonement for our sins, and thus was exalted to the right hand of God. He obtained this position of superiority over the angelic hosts by inheriting the name "Son," which is superior to the angels, who are merely God's created messengers. God spoke to us in one who is by his character and nature a Son. Although fully divine as Son, yet the Son is also the incarnate Savior who redeems through the sacrifice of himself for sins, and as a result is exalted to the position of supreme Sovereign over the universe. The Son, as supreme prophet, priest, and king, possesses all the credentials to be the final revelation, redeemer, and regent of the Father to us.

[214] Beekman, et al., *Semantic Structure*, 112.

The communication relation of concession-contraexpectation is not the same as pure contrast. The author expressed more continuity than contrast in Heb 1:1–2. This point is vital in the interpretation of the epistle.

THEOLOGICAL IMPLICATIONS. In light of the profound theological truths articulated in the prologue and its programmatic function for the entire discourse, an examination of the theological implications of this passage is expedient. Issues of revelation, Christology, protology,[215] soteriology, and eschatology are all found in this majestic paragraph.

1. Nature of Revelation. The central crisis of twentieth-century theology, which carried into the twenty-first century, is the nature of revelation. From its traditional theological formulation in orthodox theology, Carl Henry pointed out, it has of late "been stretched into everything and stripped into nothing."[216] Many now find the concept of a God who reveals himself to be archaic. In fact, twentieth-century theologians questioned two foundational tenets of theology: (1) can God speak? and (2) can we speak of God? Both are language issues. K. Barth's refusal to equate Scripture with the Word of God exerts immense influence in contemporary theology. Likewise, the dawn of the new millennium came with a Christological crisis, fueled by the departure from Christian Scripture as divine revelation. Hebrews 1:1–4 stands as a crucial corrective in these areas.

Theologians permitted God to act in history and then identified this action as revelatory. This was fine as far as it goes, but the problem is that it did not go far enough.[217] For the most part, theologians placed a gag order on God and would not permit him to speak verbally.[218] But God's action is not

---

[215] "Protology" has to do with the doctrine of creation.

[216] C. F. H. Henry, *God, Revelation and Authority* (Waco: Word Books, 1976), 2:7. J. Moltmann, (*Theology of Hope* [New York: Harper & Row, 1967], 52ff.) and Henry (2:157–66) traced the modern restatement of God's self revelation in the developments from Hegel to Hermann to Barth to Bultmann. An excellent study of the current issues surrounding the concept of revelation can be found in P. Avis, ed., *Divine Revelation*, ed. P. Avis (Grand Rapids: Eerdmans, 1997). Chapters 2 and 3, by G. Daly and P. Avis respectively, deal with revelation in Catholic and Protestant theology.

[217] So T. Long, *Hebrews*, in IBC (Louisville: John Knox, 1997), 7. Long stated that God's "speech" of revelation "is, of course, a metaphor." Long speaks of revelation as "an event," and God is a God who "speaks eventfully" (p. 8). Long identified 24 ways that God's metaphorical "speech" is made known, including political movements, a waterfall, and the "humdrum of committee meetings" (p. 9). The Bible is number 17 on his list. Long's Barthian understanding of revelation and his low view of biblical authority shows in his comment on the phrase "by the prophets" in Heb 1:1: "The phrase more likely refers not to the written texts of the Old Testament, but to the *people* described there whose human words and activity became the vehicle of divine speech and disclosure" (p. 10). The irony of this statement is evident when compared to the author of Hebrews' own understanding of the OT Scriptures as the very speech of God.

[218] So E. Brunner (*The Christian Doctrine of God: Dogmatics* [Philadelphia: Westminster, 1950], 1:23–27), who argued that the Scripture is not the very Word of God, but rather "indirect" revelation (a Kierkegaardian notion) mediated through human words. See the recent discussion of K. Barth's similar views on God's word in N. Wolterstorff, *Divine Discourse* (Cambridge:

speech-less any more than his speech is action-less. God's work and God's word are coherent.[219] According to Hebrews (as well as all Scripture), God is self-communicative. Because God speaks in Jesus and because Jesus is God's living Word, "we do not know God against his will or behind his back, as it were, but in accordance with the way in which he has elected to disclose himself and communicate his truth."[220]

Until the modern age, both Protestant and Catholic orthodoxy understood the Bible to be divine revelation in written form.[221] Various forms of higher criticism have, since the nineteenth century, brought about a state of affairs whereby most non-evangelical theologians no longer equate Scripture with divine revelation. This state of affairs also affects how theologians view God's revelation in Christ as expressed in Heb 1:1–2.

Since the author began by stating that God spoke "through the prophets," it is appropriate to ask about the nature of God's speech through the prophets. The concept of revelation in the Old Testament means nothing less than the self-disclosure of God who is both the subject and the object of revelation. Revelation is a personal encounter with the living God mediated through the Word of God.[222] The activity of God as a medium of his self-disclosure is so closely connected to the Word of God that they are sometimes inter-blended synonymously and simultaneously.[223] In Exodus 1–12 the word of God comes first, followed by the act of God. Thus, revelation is not contained in the deed only, but in the

---

Cambridge University Press, 1995), 63–74. Post-liberals like Frei, Lindbeck, and Hauerwas, as the heirs of Barthian neo-orthodoxy, continue this theological trajectory in post-liberalism.

[219] See the excellent discussion by J. Webster, "Hermeneutics in Modern Theology: Some Doctrinal Reflections," *SJT* 51 (1998), 3:307–41. The interdependency of God's revelation in Christ and in Scripture is ably presented by C. F. H. Henry in his six-volume magnum opus, *God, Revelation, and Authority*.

[220] T. F. Torrance, *Divine Meaning: Studies in Patristic Hermeneutics* (Edinburgh: T&T Clark, 1995), 5.

[221] This can be verified for Protestant theology in H. D. MacDonald, *Theories of Revelation: An Historical Study 1700–1960* (Grand Rapids: Baker, 1979), and in a comparison of Vatican Council I (1869–70) and Vatican Council II (1962–65) statements on divine revelation. With respect to Christ as the revelation of God, Vatican II's *Dei Verbum* affirmed that the essential content of revelation "is made clear to us in Christ, who is the Mediator and at the same time the fullness of all revelation" (*DV*, 2). *Dei Verbum* went through five drafts. Interestingly, the first draft affirmed the inerrancy of Scripture with this phrase: "absolute immunity of the entire sacred Scripture from error." The final draft, under liberal influence, excised these words, broadened the interpretation of inspiration, and accepted the presence of errors in the Bible. For discussions of revelation from a Catholic perspective as a result of Vatican II, see R. Latourelle, *Theology of Revelation* (Staten Island: Alba House, 1966); and A. Dulles, "Faith and Revelation," in *Systematic Theology: Roman Catholic Perspectives*, ed. F. S. Fiorenza and J. Galvin (Minneapolis: Fortress, 1991), 1:91–128.

[222] See G. S. S. Thomson, *The Old Testament View of Revelation* (Grand Rapids: Eerdmans, 1960); H. W. Robinson, *Inspiration and Revelation in the Old Testament* (New York: Oxford University Press, 1946).

[223] Ibid., 176.

words of God that accompany that deed.[224] In fact, the word is confirmed by the deed. Further, all the appearances of God in the Old Testament are speaking appearances.[225] The phrase "Word of Yahweh" virtually represents a technical term for the prophetic revelation of the Word in the Old Testament.[226]

This leads to the oft-debated question in modern theology as to the nature of God's revelation. When Heb 1:1 refers to God speaking in a Son, is this to be interpreted literally or metaphorically? To describe God as one who speaks must, according to many, be understood only in metaphorical terms.[227] But the Old Testament as well as Hebrews indicates that "God spoke" is not a metaphor for non-verbal communication. The verb is being used literally and means that God has communicated with us "by means of significant utterances: statements, questions, and commands, spoken either in His own person or His behalf by his own appointed messengers. The rest of the epistle [Hebrews] makes this plain."[228]

2. Revelation in the Old Testament. According to Heb 1:1, God spoke "at many times and in various ways" to the fathers by the prophets. Revelation in the Old Testament includes the media God used to express his word to Israel. Such media included verbal discourse, dreams, visions, signs, symbols, among

---

[224] In reference to this passage, J. R. Vannoy stated, "The words and deeds of God are joined together in a snug system of confirmatory revelation whereby God commits himself verbally to what he proposes to do, and then confirms that as a veracious word by doing precisely what he said he would do" ("Divine Revelation and History in the Old Testament," in *Interpretation and History*, ed. R. L. Harris, et al. [Singapore: Christian Life Publishers, 1986], 69).

[225] L. Köhler, *Old Testament Theology* (Philadelphia: Westminster, 1957), 130.

[226] So O. Grether (*Name und Wort Gottes im Alten Testament*, BZAW 64 [1934]: 63–77), and B. Klappert ("Word" in *NIDNTT* 3:1087); cf. J. I. McKenzie, "The Word of God in the Old Testament," *TS* 21 (1960): 183–206.

[227] "To speak of the word of God is to use the language of metaphor" (T. Fretheim, "Word of God," in *ABD* 6:961). Surprisingly, he then in the next paragraph explained God's speaking in the OT in very literally terms: "There is no word of God to human beings apart from the words and other symbols by which human beings communicate. There is thus no pure, unmediated word of God. But the finite is capable of the infinite; human words can bear the divine word. One cannot finally sort out the divine word from the human. However, they are bound up together in every reported word of God in the OT. But the word, nevertheless, is called the word of God." J. Ellul (*Humiliation of the Word*, trans. J. Hanks [Grand Rapids: Eerdmans, 1985], 48–51) likewise assured us that the words "God speaks" should be understood metaphorically, but then he proceeded not four pages later to say that the relationship between God and Adam "is a dialogue and word. It is language, and nothing else" (p. 51).

[228] Packer, *God Has Spoken,* 65. This is likewise affirmed by B. S. Childs (*Old Testament Theology in a Canonical Context* [Philadelphia: Fortress, 1986], 125), who explained that "Thus says the Lord" should be taken literally: "The role of the messenger was to communicate the exact letter of the message in the form of direct address (Gen. 32:4). Thus, in an analogous fashion the prophet functioned only as a vehicle of a message which he delivered unchanged from its source." Interestingly, Barth affirmed God's "speech" as literal, yet his unremitting conviction that the Bible is not the Word of God undercut his efforts (*CD* 1/1, 132–33). See the excellent discussion of Barth's notion of revelation as God's speech in T. Ward, *Word and Supplement* (Oxford: University Press, 2002), 106–30.

others.[229] Furthermore, the choice of vocabulary by Old Testament writers to express this revelation is both varied and precise.[230] With respect to the prophets, the revelatory word of the Lord always accompanied a vision or dream. Thus, revelation in visions is also verbal revelation.[231] Interestingly, Jeremiah reported no visions accompanying his reception of the Word of the Lord, yet it came to him with all the immediacy of an objective experience that he described in terms of a dialogue between himself and God.[232] In a similar vein, divine speech is never understood to be unambiguously divine since Samuel could mistake it for a human voice (1 Sam 3:1–10).[233]

When it comes to the Old Testament prophet, Wolff identified an essential distinguishing feature as the "supremacy of the word." It is always *the* Word, never *a* word of the Lord that the prophet declares.[234] It was the coming of the word of revelation—not the reception of the Spirit of revelation—that made a man a prophet of the Lord.[235] The most frequent of all the modes of communication used by God to disclose himself to humanity in the Bible is verbal discourse. The term "word" in the sense of divine revelation is the most common term for revelation in the Old Testament. The phrase "word of the Lord" occurs 394 times in the Old Testament.[236] The Lord's word was a medium of revelation throughout Old Testament history including the time of the patriarchs

---

[229] For a full listing and discussion of the modalities of revelation in the OT, see Beecher, *The Prophets and the Promise,* 115–32. Garrett provided a complete list without discussion (*Systematic Theology,* 1:94).

[230] According to Thomson, "They tell us that 'God was revealed' (*niglah*) at El-beth-el (Gen. 35:7). In Genesis 12:7 'God appeared' (*nirʾah*), literally 'was seen.' In Numbers 23:3,4,16, God 'met' (*niqrah*) Balaam, literally 'encountered.' In the Old Testament the Lord also 'became known' (*nodhaʾ*, Exod. 6:3), or 'made Himself known' (*hithwadha*, Num 12:6) and in order to 'instruct' or 'teach' men His intentions (*horah*, Isa. 2:3, 28:26). But it was especially, and very frequently, to 'speak his word' (*dibber*, or *ʾamar*, Jer. 1:4ff) that God made Himself known" (*Old Testament View of Revelation*, 10–11). Vriezen suggested that *torah* should be rendered "word of revelation" (*An Outline of Old Testament Theology*, rev. ed. [Oxford: Blackwell, 1970], 256).

[231] Thomson, *Old Testament View of Revelation*, 28. Cf. Köhler, *Old Testament Theology,* 5. B. S. Childs, *Old Testament Theology in a Canonical Context* (Philadelphia: Fortress, 1986), 41, stated, "Because God speaks, his primary medium is his word . . . . In the prophetic literature the vision is usually subordinated to the all-encompassing force of the word of God: 'Thus saith the Lord.'" Cf. W. Zimmerli: "The speech of the Old Testament is heard speech" ("Die Weisung des Alten Testamentes zum Geschäft der Sprache," *Das Problem der Sprache in Theologie und Kirche*, ed. W. Schneemelcher [Berlin: Töpelmann, 1959], 20).

[232] Thomson, *Old Testament View of Revelation*, 61.

[233] As noted by Fretheim, "Word of God," 961.

[234] H. W. Wolff, *Gesammelte Studien zum Alten Testament,* Theologische Bücherei 22 (München: Kaiser, 1964), 216.

[235] Thomson, *Old Testament View of Revelation,* 39. He went on to say that the coming of the word as revelation presupposes the presence of the Spirit as the source of prophetic inspiration: "Ezekiel's dynamic ministry was in the Spirit (2:2), and through the Spirit the revelatory Word came to him (2:1–3, 3:24, 11:4f). In Moses, too, the Spirit (cf. Num 11:17,25,29) and divine revelation through the Word are conjoined, and in the Messiah, upon whom the Spirit came to proclaim the Word (Isa. 61:1)."

[236] BDB 182.

(Gen 12:1–4; 15:1–7; 17:1–22; Deut 1:8), the Mosaic period (Exod 3:4–4:17), the united and divided kingdoms (2 Sam 7:4; 23:2; 1 Kgs 17:2–18:1; 22:19; 22:5–13,19; 2 Kgs 1:3; 3:11–27), and in the subsequent exilic and postexilic period (Jer 37:16–17).

Old Testament revelation was predominately verbal and auditory rather than visual. Habakkuk 2:2 says that when visions are given, God sometimes instructs that they must be converted into written text. Similarly, Rev 1:11 states that John is told to "write on a scroll what you see." The Old Testament prophets speak of God's actions as his "word." God was known to Israel in the Old Testament in and by his speaking. Throughout the Old Testament, God's revelation is identified with speaking and hearing, and with written text and the reading of written texts. Jesus made use of the spoken word exclusively according to the Gospel, and this may be invested with theological significance. In continuity with this biblical focus, the author of Hebrews gave priority to the importance of hearing the Word.[237]

3. Revelation as Verbal and Personal. So it is surprising that much of modern theology is unwilling to affirm that God's self-disclosure in the Old Testament was verbal. A prime example is E. Brunner's sub-conceptual doctrine of divine disclosure. He suggested that God only addresses us in transcendent personal confrontation. Brunner contrasted God's communication through Jesus with the "word of God" in prophets and apostles *a la* Heb 1:1–2. But from this, Brunner drew a false conclusion that is contradicted by the book of Hebrews and its use of Old Testament quotations. "Now the old is over and past, even the Old Covenant with all the forms of revelation proper to it. These are all severed from the new revelation."[238] This is exactly what Hebrews says has *not* happened! There is continuity between the prophets and Jesus, and the authority of the Old Testament Scripture abides as evidenced by the use of the present tense citation formulae throughout Hebrews. Brunner's erroneous trajectory continues when he said that there is still a relation between the revelation and the spoken word since the incarnation, but now the meaning of the phrase "word of God" has been drastically altered. "The spoken word is now no longer the revelation itself, or, to put it more exactly, it is no longer directly 'revelation,' but only indirectly." The spoken word is "an indirect revelation when it bears witness to

[237] See the important discussion of these matters in A. Wilder, *Early Christian Rhetoric: The Language of the Gospel* (London: SCM/Harper & Row, 1964), 18–21. Wilder argued the point that language is more fundamental then graphic representation except when "the latter is itself a transcript in some sense of the word of God" (p. 19). Wilder opined that orthodoxy exalted the written word and neglected the oral feature that "inheres in the very nature of the Word of God, that is, its nature as an event in personal relations; and the Word therefore, is not just a bearer of a certain content of meaning which can be isolated, but a happening which brings something to pass and moves towards what it has in view" (p. 24). Thankfully, orthodoxy has been in the process of remedying this oversight during the past forty years.

[238] Brunner, *Christian Doctrine of God*, 23.

the real revelation."[239] This theological sleight of hand by Brunner should be challenged. What are the grounds for this conclusion? He offered none.

Brunner elaborated further that man's "reaction" to revelation in Christ can no longer be simply described as "hearing." The relation has now become personal: "The fact that He Himself takes the place of the spoken word is precisely the category which distinguishes the Old Testament revelation—the revelation through the speech—from the New Testament revelation, the revelation in Christ."[240] In response to Brunner, when God spoke in the Old Testament, it was personal. Additionally, our relationship with the risen Lord is partly mediated by his written Word. Since the words of Scripture cannot be revelational in Brunner's view, he effectively nullified his insistence that God speaks, even in Jesus.[241] Modern theology desperately needs to heed the warning of Carnell: "Protestants must recover the Reformation balance between revelation as a disclosure of God's person and revelation as a disclosure of God's *will*. The first is mystical and inward; the second, objective and propositional. If we drive a wedge between personal and propositional revelation, we evacuate Christian theology of its normative elements."[242] The knowledge of God includes information from him and about him. The knowledge of God about which the gospel speaks is both relational and informational. Views of revelation since the Enlightenment have tended to disconnect information and relationship, as seen in Brunner's approach.[243] A. McGrath provided a balance in this area: "To assert that revelation involves information about God is not to deny that it can also involve the mediation of the presence of God, or the transformation of human experience."[244]

This idea of revelation as "indirect speech" is not a scriptural notion, but rather one based upon a faulty philosophical premise harking back to the Kantian bifurcation and perpetuated by Kierkegaard's notion of "indirect

---

[239] Ibid., 25.

[240] Ibid., 26–27.

[241] Speaking of Jesus, Brunner wrote, "His actual 'speech' belongs to the mystery of His Person . . . Certainly, as we have said, His whole teaching is saturated, illuminated by the fact of His Sonship, and the consciousness of His Sonship . . . But this does not provide us with any standard for the estimate of His historical self-testimony . . . For even this explicit testimony to Himself could never be anything other than something indirect, simply an indication, a suggestion, a hint. No 'historically verified word of Jesus' can be, as such, *the* revelation, the Gospel; no historically verified witness to Himself, no Messianic saying, as such, is the revelation of the mystery of His Person. As Jesus then (objectively) bears witness to Himself . . . so also His (historical) self-testimony is not the Gospel about Jesus Christ, but the prophetic indirect indication pointing towards His own Word" (*The Mediator*, 429).

[242] E. J. Carnell, *The Case for Biblical Christianity* (Grand Rapids: Eerdmans, 1969), 173.

[243] See the excellent discussion of this point in P. Jensen, *The Revelation of God*, Contours of Christian Theology (Leicester, InterVarsity, 2002), 90–92. Cf. D. Cairns, *A Gospel Without Myth?* (London: SCM, 1960), 213–18.

[244] A. McGrath, *Christian Theology: An Introduction* (Oxford: Blackwell, 1994), 155.

revelation."[245] K. Barth succumbed to this philosophical error and perpetuated it as a theological error in his refusal to equate Scripture with the very Word of God. Barth's threefold analogy of the Word of God (the Word of God preached in the church, written in Scripture, and revealed in Jesus Christ) is well known and is given considerable ink in his famous *Church Dogmatics*.[246] But his concept of the word of God as "indirect identity"[247] is the issue here. For Barth, revelation is first and foremost an event. The Scripture witnesses to this event of revelation in Christ. But here Barth ran into trouble with his trinitarian analogy of the Word of God. If the words of Jesus, as the "speech" of God, are truly the Word of God in human words (via the incarnation), then the words of Jesus in the Gospels do not "witness" to God's revelation, but are revelation. Furthermore, by virtue of a trinitarian understanding of revelation, the words of the Old Testament prophets and the apostles of the New Testament likewise are the Word of God. They certainly claim to be so, and Paul understood them this way since the Old Testament is "the very words of God" (Rom 3:2).

In Barth's threefold analogy of the Word of God, Jesus is one form of the *Logos*. But Barth missed the point that in Scripture, Jesus is revealed as *the Logos*, not merely one form of the *Logos*. It is at this point that T. Work's trenchant critique of Barth's understanding of revelation is appropriate for our purposes in considering the theological implications of Heb 1:1–4. Barth's trinitarian analogy for the Word of God cannot stand the strain he placed upon it. T. Work's probing questions reveal the problems for Barth. For example, if revelation is an event only,[248] why does Scripture cite Scripture? Why would Jesus himself bother to practice Scripture? How can it be that during Jesus'

---

[245] E. Kant taught that the epistemological structure that the human mind supplies exists in the form of categories for knowing. Since all human knowledge must be mediated by these categories, one cannot know anything that is not so mediated. As a result, a radical disjunction between the noumenal world and the phenomenal world was created. Since our knowledge is always perceptually modified by the categories of the mind, the real world is not only unknown but unknowable. This filtered down to theology by way of Kierkegaard and heavily influenced twentieth century theologians like Barth and Brunner. The words of Scripture could not be God's direct revelation to people. For an excellent critique of the notion that God does not speak in Scripture from the perspective of philosophical theology, see W. Alston, *Divine Nature and Human Language: Essays in Philosophical Theology* (Ithaca: Cornell University Press, 1989); and Wolterstorff, *Divine Discourse*, esp. 58–74, 130–70, for his critique of Barth, P. Ricoeur, and J. Derrida. For a critique of this notion from the standpoint of hermeneutics and trinitarian theology, see K. Vanhoozer, *Is There a Meaning in this Text?* (Grand Rapids: Zondervan, 1998); T. Work, *Living and Active: Scripture in the Economy of Salvation*, Sacra Doctrina (Grand Rapids: Eerdmans, 2002), 67–100; Ward, *Word and Supplement,* 106–130. For a critique of this notion homiletically, see D. L. Allen, "A Tale of Two Roads: Homiletics and Biblical Authority," *JETS* 43 (2000): 489–515.

[246] For two excellent resources evaluating Barth's theology of revelation, see R. Chia's *Revelation and Theology: The Knowledge of God in Balthasar and Barth* (Bern: Peter Lang, 1999); and T. Work, *Living and Active*.

[247] Barth, *CD*, 1.2 (p. 492).

[248] For a presentation and critique of revelation as event, see M. Erickson, *Christian Theology*, 2nd ed. (Grand Rapids: Baker, 1998), 207–12.

childhood, past revelation tutors present revelation (Luke 2:41–52)? Taking Barth's view of revelation as always an event, T. Work noted how Barth's notion of "indirectness of identity" between Scripture and the Word causes the Scripture to become revelation when it is so *used* by God (as an event). Barth's entire Trinitarian analogy of revelation is jeopardized when he failed to carry through the hypostatic union in the analogy. Barth replaced verbal union (Jesus and the words of Scripture) with verbal adoption (the words of Scripture are used by the *Logos* as "witness" to the Word), with a net loss for both Jesus as the Word and Scripture as the very words of the *Logos* as well. Barth took the position that human words were adopted and used by God as the Word of God since prophets and apostles, as human beings, cannot speak the Word of God.[249] Of course, one of Barth's motivations for his theology of revelation was his commendable desire to protect God's transcendence. But when this is done at the expense of a full-orbed doctrine of revelation that not only includes events but words, the effect actually questions God's power to reveal himself in a true and accurate way.[250]

T. F. Torrance succumbed to the Barthian error on Scripture as well. He attempted a linguistic justification for why Scripture is a "second-order" revelation by arguing that the incarnate Word (Jesus) is not ontologically identical with Scripture since Scripture is "contingent upon and controlled" by the first-order relation of hypostatic union in Christ himself. Torrance correlated his understanding of revelation with the realist view of language as sign and reality signified. Words fulfill their semantic function when one looks away from them to the realities they signify.[251] But Torrance, like Barth, failed to carry forth his analogy of the hypostatic union and instead replaced verbal union with verbal adoption. He assumed with no justification that human language is "utterly inadequate" to speak of God or convey divine truth. Somehow God "assumes, transforms and uses words so that they are made to indicate more than they can express beyond their natural capacity."[252]

Revelation is an event, and supremely so in the person and work of Jesus Christ. But Jensen correctly stated,

> [T]here is no need in limiting the event by declaring *a priori* that the giving of speech does not constitute an event. The mighty acts of God included mighty deeds of speech. Christianity is essentially promissory in nature, and the idea that we have in revelation the elusive speech-acts of God, intended though it is to preserve God's freedom, manages to compromise his faithfulness in speech . . . . Can we really

[249] See the entire discussion in T. Work, *Living and Active*, 78–84.

[250] See the excellent critique of Barth on this issue in Ward, *Word and Supplement*, 130–35.

[251] T. F. Torrance, *Reality and Evangelical Theology* (Philadelphia: Westminster, 1982), 94–96.

[252] Ibid., 108.

> arrive at the doctrine of the Trinity, given the "revelation as event" approach, or does it arise from the exact language of Scripture?[253]

Even the deeds of Jesus recorded in the Gospels are accessible to us only verbally. Jensen also argued that it is not possible to call the Bible a witness to revelation:

> When we obey his word, we obey him; when we trust his word, we trust him; when we preach his word, we preach him. He is not his word, and yet he is, for his word is the appointed place of our relationship. His word communicates his self to us: "If you remain in me and my words remain in you, . . . " (John 15:7).[254]

T. Work showed where the approach of Barth (and Torrance) faces difficulty once the point is conceded that the human words of Jesus are truly the Word of God in human words. First, Jesus often cited Scripture along with his own words. Second, his endorsement of the Old Testament is complete (Matt 4:4,7,10; 5:17–18). Its words are his words. Work wondered how the biblical passages Jesus did not quote could have been any more indirect or derivative forms of revelation than those he did quote. Finally, T. Work concluded that despite Jesus' uniqueness, his words are no more divine than those of the prophets and the apostles. "Verbal union is not hypostatic union in that language is not full personhood. Inlibration [i.e., putting thoughts into written words] is not incarnation because words are not flesh . . . This means that God's presence in the human words of apostles, prophets . . . is real presence, but not full personal presence."[255] God's revelation has one source: Jesus the divine Word and speech of God, as Heb 1:1–2 affirms. It is the incarnation, assumed in the prologue of Hebrews and affirmed in Hebrews 2 as well as throughout the epistle, which renders Barth's distinction between the Word of God and human words invalid.[256]

Hebrews 1:1–3 avoids two other errors Barth and his cadre espoused. First, if Scripture is equated with the Word of God, then there is the supposed danger in Barth's mind of this encroaching on the supremacy of Christ as presented in 1:1–4.[257] But as T. Ward rightly observed, to succumb to this move "places

[253] Jensen, *The Revelation of God*, 25–26.

[254] Ibid., 88.

[255] Work, *Living and Active,* 95. Full personal presence of the Godhead occurs only in the incarnation.

[256] Ibid., 84–88. Philosophical theologians like W. Alston (*Language and Human Nature*), Wolterstorff (*Divine Discourse*), and K. Vanhoozer (*Is There a Meaning in this Text?*) continue to show that language is entirely adequate for God's use in conveying information about himself to us. Linguistic theologians like R. Longacre have also made this point (*The Grammar of Discourse*, Topics in Language and Linguistics [New York: Plenum, 1983]).

[257] Barth, *CD* 1.1:111–12, 296. This concern dates back to the early church fathers, but it has not been a problem for orthodoxy when Christ and his word have been rightly related. Augustine wrote, "We are to love the things by which we are borne only for the sake of that towards which

Christian theology in danger of sawing off the branch on which it wishes to sit."[258] The author of Hebrews exhibited his reverence for Scripture in his method of quotation as well as the use of it he makes in his theological argument. But he saw no danger of a high view of Scripture—where the words of Scripture are the very words of God—encroaching on the supremacy of Christ as God's final revelation.[259] The author of Hebrews was able to hold in balance the twin truths of Christ as the Word of God and Scripture as the Word of God.

The second error is the notion that revelation is given only in Jesus. All else is, according to Barth, only witness to that revelation. Barth failed to take into account the continuity expressed in Heb 1:1–2 where it is God who speaks in both the Old Testament (and by implication from v. 3, in the apostles) as well as in Jesus Christ. Barth's student, W. Pannenberg, even went so far as to state that the Word of God "never has in the Bible the direct sense of the self-disclosure or self-revelation of God, not even in Heb. 1:1–2."[260] This is nothing short of dogmatic presupposition in the face of the clear teaching of Scripture. It is the consistent teaching of the New Testament, and especially Hebrews, that the revelation given outside Jesus (prophets and apostles) did not occur independently of Jesus as the *Logos*. Jesus stands in an inseparable and

---

we are borne" (*On Christian Doctrine,* in *NPNF* 2:1, chap. 35, paragraph 39. As T. Ward aptly put it, "The 'sufficiency of Scripture' is not a 'self-sufficiency of Scripture'" (*Word and Supplement,* 10).

[258] Ibid., 7.

[259] Cairns (*Gospel without Myth*, 213–18) addressed this issue masterfully. He drew a distinction between "knowledge of" (personal encounter) and "knowledge about," explaining that "knowledge of" cannot occur without an increase in "knowledge about" since most of what we know about people is derived from our own or other people's knowledge of them. Knowledge about someone in no way diminishes the "freedom of sovereignty of the person thus 'known about'" (p. 215). Through Christ, God desires that we should not only have knowledge "about" him [God], but also a knowledge "of" him. God can be known because he chooses to make himself known in Christ.

[260] Pannenberg, *Systematic Theology*, 1:240. Since Pannenberg was a student of Barth, his statement reflects the maxim that what one generation allows in moderation, the next may do in excess. Pannenberg's objections to what he called the "simple and naïve understanding of God's self-revelation as the Word of God" (p. 241) led him to opt for the "indirectness" of God's self-revelation. Why? Because in the Bible "the direct content of the reception of revelation is not God himself but ourselves and our world" (p. 244). His appeal to Exod 33:20, when Moses asked to see the glory of God and is told that he may see it from behind, that is, indirectly, illustrates his reasoning: "Only by the indirectness of his self-revelation is the majesty of God in the revelation of his deity preserved" (p. 244). Pannenberg completely ignores that God "spoke" to Moses directly and propositionally. And what of the giving of the law to Moses by God? Was not this "direct" self-revelation? Even evangelicals like D. Bloesch (*God the Almighty*, in *Christian Foundations* [Downers Grove: InterVarsity, 1995], 61) get carried away with this notion of "indirectness" in revelation: "Revelation, as Kierkegaard saw so clearly, is fundamentally indirect communication." This belief informs the acceptance by all post-liberals and even some evangelicals of the Barthian paradigm of revelation in the Bible as witness.

intimate relationship to the totality of God's disclosure by virtue of a trinitarian understanding of revelation.[261]

When the continuity factor in Heb 1:1–2 between God's revelation given by the prophets and given in Jesus is suppressed, or when the diversity factor is exaggerated, the result is a lopsided view of God's revelation in the Old Testament prophets that can ultimately lead to a denial that God spoke his word through them. In reference to Heb 1:1–2, Packer noted that the 66 books of the Bible are both the product and the proclamation of this revelatory process. Revelation is a divine activity that in form was verbal and cumulative.[262] It is clear that the author of Hebrews regarded all the Old Testament as not only revelation from God, but verbal revelation from God. His entire epistle is based on several crucial Old Testament passages of Scripture. Furthermore, his method of quoting the Old Testament with formulae such as "God says" and "the Holy Spirit says," combined with his frequent use of the present tense to introduce Old Testament citations, underscore this as well.

When the contrast in Heb 1:1–2 is overemphasized to the neglect of its continuity, the revelation in Christ is oftentimes viewed as "superior" to the revelation of the Old Testament prophets in the sense that the latter is merely "verbal" while the former is "personal." Yet for the author of Hebrews, in spite of the finality of God's revelation in the "Son," no qualitative distinction is made between these revelations in terms of their truth value or in terms of their verbal form. Not only did the author of Hebrews identify the former revelation in the prophets with the Old Testament Scriptures, but he also saw no difference of authenticity between the revelation in the prophets and in the Son.[263] The superiority of the Son to the prophets has to do with four issues: (1) his identity—he is the eternal Son and shares the Father's divine essence; (2) his role—he accomplished God's redemptive plan;[264] (3) his incarnation—he is

---

[261] This is developed with keen insight by Vanhoozer, *Is There a Meaning in This Text?*, 456–57; and Work, *Living and Active*, 33–123.

[262] Packer, *God Has Spoken*, 45. Furthermore, "the fact we must face is that if there is no verbal revelation, there is no revelation at all, not even in the life, death, and resurrection of Jesus of Nazareth" (p. 76). Also, "if there are no revealed truths, then the theological statements made by Jesus are not revealed truths; and what, in that case, are we to make of His solemn assertions, 'my teaching is not mine, but his that sent me'?" (p. 79).

[263] D. Peterson, "God and Scripture in Hebrews," in *The Trustworthiness of God: Perspectives on the Nature of Scripture*, ed. P. Helm and C. Trueman (Grand Rapids: Eerdmans, 2002), 123. C. F. H. Henry likewise affirmed this when he said the apostles saw no tension between the enfleshed *Logos* and the Scriptures. "On what foundations do these superlative statements about Christ in Heb 1:1–4 rest? Solely on God's scripturally revealed word. God has revealed himself in the past through the words of prophets, then by those very prophetic words the superiority of the Son is established. Scripture itself is the very speech of God" (*God, Revelation and Authority*, 4:52). Irenaeus expressed the same idea regarding Heb 1:1–2: "The mystery of God who uses the mouth and words of the prophets is the mystery of God beginning his apprenticeship as Word Incarnate among men" (*Against Heresies*, IV, 12, 4).

[264] C. Gunton stated, "While it is undoubtedly true that God identifies himself through the action of the Spirit to be the Father of our Lord Jesus Christ, the focus of that action . . . is the

God in human flesh, fitting him to accomplish his redemptive role;[265] and (4) his ultimacy—his appearance inaugurated the eschatological era ("in these last days"), and he is exalted at God's right hand. Although Jesus is the very "image" and "speech" of the Father, the author of Hebrews used the phrase "word of God" to denote the propositional revelation about him. How can one escape the conclusion that in Heb 2:3 and 12:25–29 (the first and last of the "warning passages") the essence of God's revelation is "verbal communication from God, conveyed through Christ and his apostles"?[266] In Heb 2:2–3, both the angel-mediated law and the Word in the Son require an identical demand for response. The only difference is in degree, not quality.[267]

4. Jesus as God's Unique Revelation. What is it about this revelation in the Son, according to Heb 1:1–2, that is contrasted with the revelation in the Old Testament, and for that matter the apostles as well, and that thus renders the revelation in the Son superior? The answer is, the Son's incarnation. As we saw above in our exegetical study of the passage, that which is contrasted is the "Son" kind of revelation with that of the prophets. What distinguishes the prophets from the Son? They spoke the word of God; the Son is the Word of God. The distinguishing feature is the incarnation that enabled the Son to make atonement for all, something the prophets and apostles could not do.[268]

Orthodox theology has always affirmed that it is the particularity of Jesus in the incarnation that is revelatory of God. This point is well made by Richard Bauckham, who stated that the revelation of God through Christ is both

---

salvation brought by Jesus of Nazareth. *The center is not divine self-identification but divine saving action*" (*A Brief Theology of Revelation* [Edinburgh: T&T Clark, 1995], 111).

[265] E. Brunner stated, "The existence of the God Man, as such, constitutes revelation and salvation. This is why He is called the Mediator, not primarily on account of His work, but because of what He is in Himself" (*The Mediator, A Study of the Central Doctrine of the Christian Faith* [Philadelphia, Westminster, 1947], 404). Brunner's connection of revelation and salvation is correct, but he appears to subsume the work of Christ into his person in an unhealthy way that implies what he is in himself is enough to make him Mediator. It was his work on the cross as the God-Man that makes Christ the Mediator. The author of Hebrews tied these two together (Christ's person and work) in the prologue.

[266] Packer, *God Has Spoken,* 72–73. Packer listed five faulty notions of revelation. (1) Revelation took the form of progress from faulty thoughts of God to more exact ones. (2) Revelation took place by divine deeds, not divine words. (3) Inspiration of statements does not guarantee their truth. (4) The scriptural record of revelation is not itself revelation. (5) Revelation is personal and not propositional (p. 62). All of these are refuted in terms of what Hebrews directly or indirectly affirms concerning revelation. In addition to Packer and standard evangelical systematic theologies, helpful treatments of revelation from an evangelical perspective include Jensen, *The Revelation of God;* and MacDonald, *Theories of Revelation* (both cited previously). The latter remains unsurpassed for dealing with the subject from a historical perspective.

[267] So Hughes, *Hebrews and Hermeneutics*, 8.

[268] Latourelle (*Theology of Revelation*, 365) expressed it well: "The incarnation offers a solution to the serious difficulty posed by revelation—that of an authentic communication of God's plan to the human mind. Jesus is co-naturalized both to human discourse and divine thought. The union of natures and the unity of person authorizes the transfer from the divine milieu, in all its inaccessibility, to the human milieu, and at the same time assures the fidelity of the transmission."

"continuous with the Old Testament . . . and novel in the radical form which this particularization takes, namely, the incarnation." He also said that Jesus' incarnation is for the purpose of being "savingly present."[269] There is, of course, a soteriological emphasis in the prologue of Hebrews: the Son "makes purification for sins" before he is enthroned at the right hand of God. As stated earlier, there are exegetical reasons why the author gave marked prominence to this clause. It is this work of atonement that furnishes the doctrinal theme of the epistle worked out in the motif of high priest, and it is the incarnation that, although only hinted at in the prologue, is developed in chap. 2 and beyond and forms the foundation of the Christology elaborated throughout.

Bauckham made the perceptive observation that in the New Testament, the Christological use of the term "reveal" is mostly eschatological with reference to the *parousia*. It is only in the eschaton, when God's salvific plan is fully realized, that the Son's kingdom reign over all things will be finally achieved. Thus, Bauckham preferred the term "definitive" to "finality" in speaking of Jesus as God's revelation.[270] It seems best when speaking of Jesus as God's revelation to understand the concept of finality in the sense of "ultimacy" and not that of "chronological lastness."[271] In speaking of the continuity of revelation from the Old Testament to Christ and the apostles, "cumulative" is superior to "progressive" in that the latter term is used by those in the history of religions school to indicate an evolutionary development theologically.[272] Others refer to Christ as "God's consummatory Word."[273] These understandings are supported by the prologue in conjunction with what is said of the Son in Hebrews 2. Although Christ is the heir of all things, he will inherit all things only after the incarnation and atonement, and only with total consummation in the eschaton. All things are not yet placed under his feet. Thus, with respect to Heb

[269] R. Bauckham, "Jesus the Revelation of God," in *Divine Revelation*, ed. P. Avis (Grand Rapids: Eerdmans, 1997), 192–93. He also delineated three theological views of Jesus as the revelation of God (pp. 175–81): (1) Jesus illustrates the moral character of God. Jesus is revelation in the sense that he illustrates to us what God is like. He is unique only in degree, not in kind. (2) In Jesus the possibility of the divine-human union is actualized as a revelation of its possibility for all people. (3) Jesus reveals the unique presence of God in his incarnation as expressed in traditional orthodoxy.

[270] Ibid., 195.

[271] As does Garrett, *Systematic Theology* 1:105. If revelation is cumulative and culminates in Christ and the NT canon, then we must privilege the revelation given in Christ and the NT apostles, as Hebrews affirms. But, although Christ is the cornerstone and capstone of revelation, the OT is not thereby superseded as God's revelation, even though the OT sacrificial system along with aspects of the law are superseded by the coming of Christ.

[272] Packer (*God Has Spoken*, 86) preferred the term "cumulative."

[273] Henry, *God, Revelation, and Authority,* 5:396. The title of B. F. Westcott's sermons on Hebrews was *Christus Consummator: Some Aspects of the Work and Person of Christ in Relation to Modern Thought* (London: Macmillan & Co., 1886). These sermons were preached in Westminster Abbey during his residence there from August 1885 to January 1886.

1:1–2, the Gospel narratives are the continuation as well as the climax of the Old Testament narratives.[274]

Another crucial aspect of the Son's revelation of the Father in Heb 1:1–2 is the statement that he is both the agent and sustainer of creation (1:2–3). If the Son is the mediator of creation, then he is not only the foundation for the knowledge of God; he is also the "basis of created rationality," the basis for the possibility of knowledge of any kind.[275] Also, by virtue of humanity's creation in the image of God, there is a moral kinship that renders it possible for humanity to receive God's revelation as well.[276]

The upshot of all this is that God's "speech" in Jesus the Son is "something that God says, something that God does, and something that God is."[277] Placing this in the order of Heb 1:1–4, God's revelation in Christ is something that God says (God has spoken through the prophets and in a Son), something that Jesus as God is (the radiance of his glory and exact representation of his being), and something that Jesus as God does (he created the universe and he made purification for sins). Thus, God's revelation in Christ is being, word, and event. It incorporates all the categories that theologians have fought over relative to the nature of revelation: is it personal, propositional, or eventful? It is in reality all three. The incarnation of the *Logos* makes it personal. The speech of the *Logos*, including prophets (Old Testament) and apostles (New Testament), makes it propositional. The atonement provided by the *Logos* makes it eventful—in

[274] Bauckham, "Jesus the Revelation of God," 191–92.

[275] This epistemological point is well made by Gunton (*A Brief Theology of Revelation*, 124). R. Gruenler, in his excellent critique of Kant, alluded to the epistemological significance of Heb 1:3: "What is lacking in modern liberal hermeneutics . . . is a biblically based philosophical realism that attests a reality beyond the human mind and which communicates itself to human observers through the network of discourse built into it by God who creates and sustains it by his word of power (Heb. 1:3)" (*Meaning and Understanding* [Grand Rapids: Zondervan, 1991], 2:67). Latourelle made the point well: "Revelation *by word* presupposes God's *language of creation.* It is not simply that they have been chosen by Christ that our human concepts and terms are adaptable to the expression of mystery: it is rather because they are essentially *not unrelated* to the Divine Person that Christ can make use of them. . . . The revelation of Christ presupposes the truth of analogy" (*Theology of Revelation,* 366–67). The created order possesses both a contingent reality and a contingent rationality. In the incarnation, Jesus shares fully in human existence and rationality "in order to be understandable and communicable . . . to all men" (Torrance, *Reality and Evangelical Theology*, 90–91).

[276] As Thomson said about God not being *wholly* other than man, "We are bound to postulate of God a moral personality akin to our own. If there were not such a kinship, divine revelation would be impossible. But if God and man have kinship at the moral level of personality, and if God has willed to reveal Himself to man, then the strong anthropomorphic language in the Old Testament's teaching about God, and the use of human categories to formulate its concept of God, become not merely legitimate but necessary" (*The Old Testament View of Revelation,* 15).

[277] Vanhoozer, *Is There a Meaning in This Text?*, 205. Ward accepted a speech-act view of language (*Word and Supplement,* 307): "It soon becomes clear that persons, actions, and words are tied inextricably together." This, of course, has immense repercussions for the issues of revelation and inspiration, and also provides another platform for the orthodox doctrine of the inerrancy of Scripture.

fact, the supreme event in history.[278] There is thus a unity and continuity in God's revelation. As Warfield said in reference to Heb 1:1–2: "In whatever diversity of forms, by means of whatever variety of modes, in whatever distinguishable stages it is given, it is ever the revelation of the One God, and it is ever the one consistently developing redemptive revelation of God."[279]

The prologue of Hebrews also has a lot to say about Christology.[280] Hebrews 1:1–4 is one of the four great Christological mountain peaks of the New Testament; the others are John 1:1–18; Phil 2:5–11; Col 1:13–20. Although Hebrews develops the theme of the high priesthood of Christ more than any New Testament book, its definitive Christological title is actually that of "Son," and its use in Heb 1:2 establishes the theme Christologically for the entire epistle. It is only after the identity of Jesus as the Son of God, exalted above the angels and Moses, has been established that the writer goes on to demonstrate how this position qualified Jesus to be the high priest. As Son he intercedes (4:14; 7:25; 9:24,28), and as Son he discharges his priestly functions (7:16; 9:14). The exposition of the high priestly work of Jesus is couched in the theological matrix of sonship.[281]

In the Gospels, the term "Son" is used to express Jesus' relationship to God as his Father (Matt 11:27; Luke 10:22). The Father himself addressed Jesus as his Son at the baptism and the transfiguration (Mark 1:11; 9:7), and the demons likewise addressed him as Son (Matt 4:3,6; Mark 3:11; 5:7).[282] Christ's preexistence is assumed in the New Testament passages that speak of God sending his Son (John 3:17; Rom 8:3; Gal 4:4). Although he did not use the term "Son"

---

[278] Vanhoozer suggested a trinitarian theology of communication. God, as a communicative agent, relates to humanity through words and the Word. His very being is self-communicative act that both constitutes and enacts a covenant of discourse: speaker (Father), Word (Son [and Scripture as Word of God, I would add]), and reception (Holy Spirit). Speech-act theory serves as a handmaiden to a trinitarian theology of communication. If the Father is the locutor (speaker), the Son is the preeminent illocution (utterance). The Holy Spirit is the condition and power of receiving God's message, and as God the perlocutor (intender), the Holy Spirit is the reason that his words do not return to him empty; see Vanhoozer, *Is There a Meaning in This Text?*, 456–57. Cf. Torrance (*Reality*, 89): "His words were done as well as spoken, and his deeds spoke as much as his words." Speech-act theory is put to good use by T. Ward in his outstanding *Word and Supplement*. This work seeks to recover the classical doctrine of Scripture against both post-liberal (Barthian) and revisionist theologians.

[279] B. B. Warfield, *Inspiration and Authority of the Bible* (Philadelphia: Presbyterian and Reformed, 1948), 96. Or, to gloss C. Gunton (*A Brief Theology of Revelation*, 125): "There are varieties of mediation ['at various times and in many ways'], but there is one Lord ['by His Son']."

[280] C. K. Barrett ("The Christology of Hebrews," in *Who do You Say That I Am?*, ed. M. A. Powell and D. Bauer [Louisville: Westminster John Knox, 1999], 110–127) provided a succinct overview of this crucial subject.

[281] So Hengel, *Studies in Early Christology*, 169; and H. R. Mackintosh, *The Doctrine of the Person of Jesus Christ*, 2nd ed. (Edinburgh: T&T Clark, 1913), 84. For a full discussion on Jesus as "Son of God" in the NT as well as Hebrews, see E. Schweitzer, "Son of God," *TDNT* 8.362–91; C. Brown, "Son," *NIDNTT* 3:665–66.

[282] See I. H. Marshall, "Divine Sonship of Jesus," *Int* 21 (1967): 87–103.

in Phil 2:5–11, Paul did not believe that Jesus surrendered his divine nature at the incarnation, since he regarded Jesus as God's Son during his life and death.[283] Fuller claimed that, in spite of its presence in the Synoptic Gospels, the title "Son of God" did not come into use until after the resurrection. In Rom 1:4 Paul used the Greek term *horizō* to state that at his resurrection/exaltation Jesus "was declared" to be the Son of God. This belief seems to have arisen through the application of Ps 2:7, which was already interpreted messianically at Qumran,[284] to the risen Jesus (Acts 13:33; cf. Heb 5:5).

Several matters call for discussion in this vein. First, in light of what is said about Jesus in the prologue of Hebrews, the question arises as to whether Hebrews expresses a *Logos* Christology. This is often debated,[285] yet the book itself indicates that the only reason for not viewing the Christology of Hebrews in this way is the absence of the word *logos*. The Alexandrian language used to describe the Son in Heb 1:3, whether or not borrowed from Philo, is certainly in many respects synonymous with *Logos*. Two of the titles in Philo are applied to Christ by the author of Hebrews later in the epistle: "firstborn" and "high priest." If Heb 4:12–13 are interpreted to refer to Christ as the *Logos* of God, then the case is even stronger. Given all the factors, it would seem that Hebrews can be closely related to John 1:1–18 as expressing a *Logos* Christology.[286] It should be noted, however, that the degree of personification of the *Logos* as Jesus in John 1 and derivatively in Heb 1:1–4 exceeds anything in Hellenistic Judaism.[287]

Second, the question of the relation of the prologue to wisdom Christology must be briefly explored. Commentators are quick to connect what is said of the Son as the one who made the universe (Heb 1:2) with personified wisdom

---

[283] See Martin, *Carmen Christi*, 194; cf. D. R. W. Wood and I. H. Marshall, "Son of God," in *The New Bible Dictionary*, 3rd ed. (1996); R. H. Fuller, "Son of God," *Harper's Bible Dictionary*, ed. P. Achtemeier (San Francisco: Harper & Row, 1985); Dunn, *Christology in the Making*, 12–64, 163–250; M. Hengel, *The Son of God* (Philadelphia: Fortress, 1976).

[284] Fuller ("Son of God," 978) stated, "It is a matter of dispute whether the term 'Son of God' was already current in pre-Christian Judaism as a messianic title as Mark 14:61 would seem to suggest. But in view of the discovery of Ps 2:7 in a messianic application in the Dead Sea Scrolls (4Q Flor. 10–14), it is probably safe to conclude that it was just coming into use in this context during the period of Christian origins."

[285] Hughes (*Hebrews and Hermeneutics*, 5–24) understood the author of Hebrews as identifying the *Logos* with the Son. M. Isaacs (*Sacred Space*, [Sheffield: JSOT, 1992], 198–99) disagreed. K. Schenck ("Keeping His Appointment: Creation and Enthronement in Hebrews" *JSNT* 66 [1997]: 112), is surely misleading in his assertion that in Heb 1:2, God spoke through the Son, but Christ is not equated with this Word.

[286] See P. A. Rainbow, "*Logos* Christology," *DLNT* 665–67.

[287] J. Neusner, "*Logos*," *Dictionary of Judaism in the Biblical Period* (1996) 2:388. Mackintosh (*Doctrine of the Person of Christ*, 86) summed it up well: "The Christ of Hebrews does replace the Philonic *Logos*, in which philosophy had, as it were, been dreaming of a Savior; but to state the one in terms of the other is impossible. With a sovereign freedom, the author of Hebrews argues that what philosophy has aspired to is given in Christ."

as God's intermediary in creation (Prov 8:22–36) and the wisdom tradition.[288] There are similarities. But Fee's caution that the New Testament writers did not identify personified wisdom with the preincarnate Christ is well taken.[289] Nowhere in the tradition, he says, is it explicitly stated that wisdom is God's agent in creation. Rather, wisdom is personified as present in another sense, a literary sense, as the attribute inherent in God by which he ordained all things. In fact, Prov 8:22–36 asserts only that wisdom was the first of God's creation, emphasizing her priority in time; thus, wisdom is pictured as present at creation, but not as the mediator of creation. The point of Prov 8:22–36 is to show in a literary way through personification that creation reflects God's wise design. Fee concluded that there is no verbal or even conceptual link between what is stated in the wisdom tradition and what the New Testament writers explicitly said.[290] The evidence indicates that the parallels between Hebrews and wisdom literature should not be used as proof of literary dependence, but neither should they rule out the possibility of allusion.[291]

Third, Heb 1:4 says that Jesus has inherited a name. Two questions arise: what is the name? and when did he inherit the name? The answer to the first question is given in the commentary above: the name must be "Son." The second question is not as easily answered. Did he inherit the name at creation (1:2), in his earthly life (5:8), or at his exaltation (1:4–5)? The text implies that Jesus inherited the name after the atonement and exaltation, or at least after the atonement and in conjunction with the exaltation. But this does not lead to an adoptionistic Christology.[292] According to the prologue, the name was not given to him in his preexistent state, but the inference that he was "Son" in his preexistent state seems unavoidable. This may be attested by the use of the perfect *keklēronomēken* instead of the aorist (v. 4) because Jesus did not first obtain the name at the time of exaltation, but had already obtained it as

[288] See DeSilva, *Perseverance in Gratitude*, 87.

[289] G. Fee, "St. Paul and the Incarnation: A Reassessment of the Data," in *The Incarnation: An Interdisciplinary Symposium on the Incarnation of the Son of God*, ed. S. Davis, et al. (Oxford: University Press, 2002), 62–92.

[290] Ibid., 76–78. J. Frankowski ("Early Christian Hymns Recorded in the New Testament: A Reconsideration of the question in Light of Heb 1, 3," *BZ* 27 [1983]: 183–94) pointed out that χαρακτήρ and ὑπόστασις occur in Philo with reference to the *Logos*, but not in Wisdom. Schenck ("Keeping His Appointment," 108) likewise stated that wisdom "cannot definitively be said to move beyond personification." Dunn (*Christology*, 170) was explicit regarding all Jewish intertestamental literature: "There is no clear indication that the Wisdom language of these writings has gone beyond vivid personification."

[291] R. Gheorghita, *The Role of the Septuagint in Hebrews*, WUNT (Tübingen: Mohr/Siebeck, 2003), 93–94.

[292] Felix, bishop of Urgella, Spain, held an adoptionistic Christology based on subordinationist language in Scripture that believers are "sons" of God by adoption and "brothers" of Christ. Thus, Felix taught that Christ was, on his human side, the Son of God by adoption. This was challenged by Alcuin and later condemned by the Synod of Frankfort in 794 (L. Berkhof, *History of Christian Doctrines* [Grand Rapids: Eerdmans, 1941], 112).

the preincarnate *Logos*.[293] The use of Ps 2:7 in the paragraph following the prologue furnishes additional contextual evidence that Jesus was the Son in his preincarnate state.[294] Additionally, if the author drew upon the wisdom tradition of Proverbs 8, then by analogy Christ's sonship existed not only prior to the incarnation but prior to creation.[295]

Both Rom 1:4 and Acts 13:33 seem to indicate that Paul (and Luke) regarded the resurrection as the time of his appointment to sonship.[296] Most view it as occurring at the exaltation following the resurrection. This seems apparent from Heb 1:3–4, which states that Christ "sat down at the right hand" of God and "became as much superior to the angels as the name he has inherited." The citation of Ps 2:7 in this context makes clear that the name is that of "Son."

A problem develops in Heb 5:8, which states that Christ was a "son" during his earthly life. But Schenck is correct that the context of 5:8 alludes to the appointment language of 1:5–6 in order to relate Christ's high priestly appointment to his enthronement as Son. There are, according to Schenck, three possible resolutions to the tension between 1:2 and 5:8 on sonship: (1) Christ was Son as a result of his exaltation; (2) the author used "Son" in two different senses: his eternal identity as Son and his incarnate role as Son in accomplishing redemption (and these are neither unrelated nor contradictory); (3) a real contradiction exists due to (a) the author's use of two different Christological traditions, or (b) the metaphorical nature of the language.[297] Thus, the author made a distinction between Christ's identity as Son (which he has been eter-

[293] So Lünemann, *Hebrews*, 400.

[294] As Calvin expressed it, "He who was the Son of God became the Son of man, not by confusion of substance, but by unity of person. For we maintain, that the divinity was so conjoined and united with the humanity, that the entire properties of each nature remain entire, and yet the two natures constitute only one Christ" (*Institutes*, II.14.1). Later Calvin argued, "Since angels as well as men were at first created on the condition that God should be the common Father of both; if it is true, as Paul says, that Christ always was the head, 'the first-born of every creature—that in all things he might have the pre-eminence,' (Col. 1:15,18), I think I may legitimately infer, that he existed as the Son of God before the creation of the world" (ibid., II.14.5). See Calvin's sustained argument that Jesus is "Son" in his preincarnate, eternal being (2.14.6–8).

[295] So Calvin (*Institutes*, II.14.8). It has been asserted that both NT authors as well as the early church fathers found references in the OT theophanies to the preincarnate Christ. See A. T. Hanson, *Jesus Christ in the Old Testament* (London: S.P.C.K., 1965), which mentions this concerning the NT authors; and A. Harnack, *History of Dogma* (New York: Dover, 1961), 3:30, which did so of the Fathers. A helpful discussion on this subject is J. A. Dearman, "Theophany, Anthropomorphism, and the *Imago Dei*," 31–46.

[296] Language use becomes very important here. In reference to Acts 13:33, Dunn said that the resurrection is the "day of his appointment to divine sonship, as the event by which he became God's Son" (*Christology in the Making*, 36). The former clause is defensible; the latter is problematic in the light of the NT as a whole. The latter could entail an adoptionistic Christology. Dunn was off the mark in asserting a concept of preexistent sonship in Heb 1:1–3 along the same lines that Philo ascribed to the *Logos* and that the Wisdom tradition ascribed to Wisdom (p. 208). Yet he concluded, "The special contribution of Hebrews is that it seems to be the first of the NT writings to have embraced the specific thought of a preexistent divine sonship" (p. 55).

[297] Schenck, "Keeping His Appointment," 95–96. Schenck opted for the second view.

nally) and his role as Son (which he accomplished by incarnation, atonement, resurrection, and exaltation).[298]

The author's explanation of the Son's redemptive work is in keeping with his understanding of the Son's eternal sonship. As Son, Christ discharges his priestly functions (7:16; 9:14), and as Son he intercedes (4:14; 7:25; 9:24,28). The author's fusion of the themes of "Son" and "high priest"—as well as their theological import—are evident in his careful placement of the two together in 4:14 and 7:28 (4:14 begins the second major division of the epistle, and 7:28 closes a major division). Both the eternality and perfection of the new covenant are guaranteed because Christ is the Son of God who is thus capable of being our effective high priest.

Yet there is a paradox in Hebrews regarding the Son's relation to the Father. The deity of Jesus is explicitly asserted in the prologue and elsewhere in the epistle. But the Son's dependence on the Father is also affirmed. In 1:2 the Father "appointed" the Son as heir; in 1:13 the Father exalts the Son; in 5:5 the Son is dependent on the Father for his calling as high priest; and in 13:20 the Father resurrected the Son. Mackintosh called this antinomy an indissociable [inseparable] duality for New Testament Christology.[299]

It is also apparent that the author viewed Christ's sonship against the Old Testament backdrop of the messianic Son of David who is exalted to eternal dominion.[300] The author's combination of Ps 2:7 with 110:1 (see Heb 1:5–14) and the critical importance of these two Old Testament citations and their development in the theological sections of the epistle reveal the author's placement of Christ's sonship against this background.

As Son, Jesus is infinitely superior to the angels (1:8), Moses (3:1–6; 10:29 by implication), and the Levitical priesthood (7:28). As Son, through the incarnation and atonement, he identified himself with us and wedded us to himself in such a way that we are "sons" because of what he accomplished. As the "source of eternal salvation" (5:9), he has been designated by God "high priest" forever, representing us to the Father eternally through his ongoing high priesthood. Hebrews 7:28 states that "the oath, which came after the law, appointed the Son, who has been made perfect forever." At the conclusion of the second major division of the epistle, the author returned to this dominant theme

[298] It is clear in Hebrews that the focus of sonship language centers on the exaltation of Christ. See Westcott, *Hebrews,* 21; and esp. D. Peterson, *Hebrews and Perfection*: *An Examination of the Concept of Perfection in the "Epistle to the Hebrews,"* in SNTSMS 47 (Cambridge: Cambridge University Press, 1982).

[299] Mackintosh, *Doctrine of the Person of Christ,* 84–85. For a survey of how the Fathers interpreted Christ's sonship, see W. Schneemelcher, "Meaning of υἱὸς θεοῦ in Early Church Christology," *TDNT* 8:395–96.

[300] The motif of divine sonship in the sense of appointment to office and also the assignment of dominion over all things is clear in Second Temple messianic Judaism (F. Hahn, *The Titles of Jesus in Christology*, 284). On Davidic sonship in Hebrews, see E. Grässer, "Der historische Jesus im Hb.," *ZNW* 56 (1965): 74–76.

of exaltation that began in 1:1–4: "But when this priest had offered for all time one sacrifice for sins, he sat down at the right hand of God" (10:12).

Christologically speaking, Hebrews affirms the importance of the ontological as well as the functional aspects of Christ's divine sonship. Soteriology is dependent upon Christology. Cullmann is thus incorrect to claim that "it is only meaningful to speak of the Son in view of God's revelatory action, not in view of his being."[301] This is an overstatement of the situation and underplays the importance of Heb 1:3. The author of Hebrews based function on ontology. Likewise, J. Dunn believed that the author of Hebrews had no concept of preexistence ontologically.[302] Not only is this assertion contradicted by what is stated in the prologue, but also by what is stated in the catena of seven Old Testament quotations that follow (Heb 1:5–13). There it becomes clear that the Son is the creator of all things and sits on the throne of God. Furthermore, God addressed the Son as both "God" and "Lord." The catena of quotations asserts the divine identity of Jesus the Son and hence his preexistence. It would be better to say, as did Henry, that throughout the New Testament, the title Son of God remains primarily a functional designation that emphasizes Jesus' obedience in the mission of divine revelation and redemption while also affirming his eternal Sonship.[303]

The author of Hebrews divided the career of Jesus into three different stages: preexistence, incarnation (earthly period—"days of his flesh"), and exaltation. A clear demarcation separates the first from the second, but the latter two overlap.[304] Thus the prologue and the thrust of the entire epistle declare that Jesus is the supreme revelation from God to man because he, as one who is by his character and nature God's Son, supremely combines in his person and work all three Old Testament categories of prophet, priest, and king. As the Son, he fulfills the prophets and serves as God's final word to man. As the Son, he functions as our priest, making the atoning sacrifice of himself for man. As the Son, he is the fulfillment of the Son of David messianic promises, the heir who reigns upon the throne eternally.[305] Henry summed it up well:

> The *preexistent* Christ was the revealing agent within the Godhead antecedently to creation; the *preincarnate* Christ was the revealing agent in the created universe, and also of the Old Testament redemptive disclosure; the *incarnate* Christ is the embodied revelation of God's essential glory and redemptive grace. All these functions, . . . the *risen and glorified* Christ gathers into one, as the *glorified* Christ he will be

[301] Cullmann, *Christology of the New Testament*, 293.

[302] Dunn, *Christology in the Making*, 52.

[303] Henry, *God, Revelation, and Authority*, 2:240.

[304] H. MacNeill, *The Christology of the Epistle to the Hebrews* (Chicago: University Press, 1914), 32.

[305] Christologically, this threefold focus on Christ as prophet, priest, and king is a major theme in the Reformers. See Calvin, *Institutes* 2.15.425–432.

the revealing agent in God's final judgment and consummation of all things.[306]

Finally, a number of doctrinal and philosophical errors are refuted by Heb 1:1–4. First, all theories that assert that the Son's preexistence is not personal, to quote Bernard Weiss, "go to wreck on 1:1–4."[307] Second, docetism[308] is excluded by the prologue. Third, naturalism, the view that nature constitutes the whole of reality, is rejected. Concomitantly, both pantheism and panentheism are excluded since the world is a contingent reality created by God and not the actual body of God, and because God is not somehow "in" the created order as some animating spirit. Fourth, postmodern deconstruction with its negative view of language and meaning is refuted in that God's choice of words to reveal himself attaches meaning and value to human language. Fifth, postmodern relativism and pluralism, with their epistemological claim that truth is perspectival and socially constructed, lead to the conclusion that all religions are equally valid and at the same time equally invalid as a means of discovering ultimate truth with a capital "T." Hebrews rejects such a notion by affirming the superiority of God's revelation in Christ over Judaism and all other religions. God has spoken his final word in Jesus. Sixth, the notion that God's revelation is not verbal, but only personal, is refuted.[309]

Christologically, the prologue affirms the unique preexistence of Christ, his incarnation as fully God and fully man. In essence, Jesus as the God-Man is the only one who could procure salvation through his blood atonement. Hebrews 1:1–4 refutes modalistic monarchianism, the heresy that identifies the Father, Son, and Spirit as successive revelations of the same person and denies that the Godhead consists of three Persons who have one essence or nature. The prologue also refutes dynamic monarchianism, which claims that Jesus achieved deity only after the resurrection. Finally, it refutes all attempts to establish Christology "from below," such as the infamous "Jesus Seminar," which interprets Jesus as merely an "example"—one who illustrated for man what God is like; or to see Jesus as the one who actualized a divine-human union and revealed this possibility to all people.

---

[306] Henry, *God, Revelation, and Authority*, 3:205–6.

[307] B. Weiss, *New Testament Theology*, 2:189.

[308] "Docetism" is the view that Jesus' human body only "seemed" or "appeared" to be truly human, but was in fact a phantom or spirit.

[309] Clearly by the author of Hebrews, but also by Barth (*CD* 1.1, 136–37): "The personalizing of the concept of the Word of God, which we cannot avoid when we remember that Jesus Christ is the Word of God, does not mean its deverbalizing." With the aid of speech-act theory, we can assert from Heb 1:1–4 that the concept of God as a God who speaks and acts is a fundamental theological conviction entailing the truth that to speak is not merely to state propositions or to refer to the world of reality; it is also fundamentally to perform actions. Language is a means by which persons, including God, act in relation to other people. Furthermore, the concept of God as a God who speaks also underlies the doctrine of the sufficiency and inerrancy of Scripture. See Ward, *Word and Supplement*, 13–16.

Lastly, the schism between Judaism and Christianity so often reflected in the New Testament documents rises from a conflict over the divine sonship of Jesus. This is the focal point of contention between Judaism and Christianity. Bauckham proposed that the Jewish monotheistic understanding of God in the period of the Second Temple involved God's identity (i.e., who God is) rather than in terms of the divine nature (i.e., what divinity is). Early Christianity, conscious of the Old Testament theological framework for the identity of God, understood Jesus to be included in the unique identity of the one God of Israel—a Christological monotheism, so to speak. Psalm 110:1, as used by the author of Hebrews and other New Testament writers, underscores this. Jesus has been a part of the Godhead eternally and thus, as distinguished from the creation, Jesus is the agent of God's creative activity. Thus, an adoptionist Christology that would lead to any form of ditheism is avoided. Bauckham also explained why Hebrews 1 is fundamental in illustrating the extent to which early Christology was an exegetical enterprise in the way the author skillfully wove together the catena of seven Old Testament quotations, using current methods of Jewish exegesis, which were then pressed into the service of Christological monotheism.[310] Like all the New Testament writers, the author of Hebrews operated from a Christology that identified Jesus in the "unique identity" of God. The argument, common in the "History of Religions School," that such a Christology could not have originated within the context of Judaism—and is rather the result of a transition in Christian theology from Jewish thought to Hellenistic philosophy in the second, third, and fourth centuries—is the opposite of the truth (as Bauckham noted). Greek philosophy, with its Platonic categories, actually made it more difficult to ascribe full deity to Jesus. "Nicene theology was essentially an attempt to resist the implications of Greek philosophical understandings of divinity and to re-appropriate in a new conceptual context the New Testament's inclusion of Jesus in the unique divine identity."[311]

The author of Hebrews, using the Old Testament, showed why the Old Testament itself points beyond Judaism to its ultimate fulfillment in Christ the Word incarnate. The recipients of Hebrews, likely Jewish Christians, would have benefited greatly from the theological sections that develop the theme of sonship and high priesthood and that serve as the grounds for the exhortations and warnings that convey the purpose of the epistle.

---

[310] Bauckham, "Monotheism and Christology in Hebrews 1," 167–68. Elsewhere, with respect to the use of Ps 110:1 by NT authors, including Hebrews, Bauckham wrote, "Early Christians used the text to say something about Jesus which Second Temple Jewish literature is not interested in saying about anyone: that he participates in the unique divine sovereignty over all things" (*God Crucified: Monotheism and Christology in the New Testament* [Grand Rapids: Eerdmans, 1998], 31).

[311] Bauckham, *God Crucified*, 78. First-century Judaism was not monolithic. Rabbinic traditions during the intertestamental period were as strong an influence on Jews of the first century as was the OT, and in some instances these traditions were antithetical to the OT. Jews of the first century accepted a mystery in the Godhead. The word *ʾeḥad* ("one") in Deut 6:4 describes a composite unity, not a magisterial plural.

I. The Superiority of the Son (1:5–4:13)
  1. Jesus' Identity and Work Demand Our Obedience (1:5–2:18)
    (1) The Son's Superiority to Angels (1:5–14)
    (2) Exhortation not to Neglect Salvation (2:1–4)
    (3) Atonement Accomplished by Our High Priest (2:5–18)
    Excursus: Hebrews 2:14 and the Extent of the Atonement in John Calvin and John Owen
  2. Faithful Obedience Necessary to Enter Rest (3:1–4:13)
    (1) Jesus' Superiority to Moses (3:1–6)
    (2) Beware of Unbelief (3:7–19)
    (3) Exhortation to Enter God's Rest (4:1–13)

II. THE SUPERIORITY OF THE SON (1:5–4:13)

If the prologue were not unique enough, the author's second paragraph is likewise full of surprises. Using a string of seven Old Testament quotations, the author supported his claim that Jesus, as Son, is superior to the angels. After the prologue, the author plunged into this series of Old Testament quotations designed to prove, albeit not in a formal way, his assertions about Christ's sonship and his superior status as God's revelation to humanity. The author quoted Ps 2:7; 2 Sam 7:14; Deut 32:43; Ps 104:4; 45:6–7; 102:25–27; 110:1 in this order.

Since the author used only the Septuagint (LXX) for his quotations, a word should be said about the role of the LXX in the book of Hebrews. The study of the LXX in relation to the New Testament has become a burgeoning field of research.[1] In recent times, the use of the LXX in the book of Hebrews has received more careful attention.[2] Detailed study reveals that oftentimes the *wording* of the LXX when compared to the Masoretic Text (MT) provides the author more ammunition to drive home his theological point. Certain features of the Greek text were more suitable for a messianic application than the corresponding Hebrew source, making it unlikely that these quotations were

[1] A helpful introductory work on the LXX is K. Jobes and M. Silva, *Invitation to the Septuagint* (Grand Rapids: Baker, 2000), which covers the waterfront in three broad areas: (1) history of the LXX; (2) LXX in biblical studies; and (3) the current state of LXX studies.

[2] For an excellent overview of this topic, see R. Gheorghita, *The Role of the Septuagint in Hebrews*, WUNT (Tübingen: Mohr/Siebeck, 2003), 7–25, who surveyed the field under the headings "textual approach," "exegetical-hermeneutical approach," and "rhetorical approach." Cf. G. Guthrie, "Old Testament in Hebrews," *DLNT* 841–50; id., "Hebrews' Use of the Old Testament: Recent Trends in Research," *CurBS* 1.2 (2003): 271–94; and his significant work in "Hebrews," *CNTOT*, 919–95.

randomly chosen. On the contrary, their presence and use in Hebrews displays careful thought by the author. Gheorghita summed up the matter well: "The interdependence between reading the OT in light of the Christ-event and interpreting the Christ-event in light of the OT is at the heart of understanding the Author's use of the OT."[3]

Several questions often arise about these seven Old Testament quotations. First, what is the origin of this catena of quotations, and how were they brought together in this form and order?[4] A few legitimate possibilities exist. (1) The author used a testimonia collection,[5] a compilation of biblical texts used by the early church primarily for apologetic and missionary purposes. (2) The author quoted these passages because they were consistently used in the order of worship of the early church.[6] (3) The author collated these passages for his own theological purpose.[7] It is certainly possible that some truth exists in all three of these suggestions, but option three would appear to be the most likely scenario.

---

[3] R. Gheorghita, *The Role of the Septuagint in Hebrews*, 25; see pp. 70–71.

[4] Two major studies on the quotations in Hebrews were done by S. Kistemaker, *The Psalm Citations in the Epistle to the Hebrews* (Amsterdam: G. van Soest, 1961); and F. Schröger, *Der Verfasser des Hebräerbriefes als Schriftausleger* (Regensburg: Verlag Friedrich Pustet, 1968). These have been supplemented by more recent work in articles and commentaries. Cf. A. H. Cadwallader, "The Correction of the Text of Hebrews Towards the LXX," *NovT* 34 (1992): 257–92.

[5] This position is ably defended in M. Albl, *"And Scripture Cannot Be Broken": The Form and Function of the Early Christian Testimonia Collections*, NovTSup 96 (Leiden: Brill, 1999), 201–11. *First Clement* 36:2–6 is a close parallel to Heb 1:5–13, and many scholars believe *1 Clement* is literarily dependent on Hebrews; e.g., P. Ellingworth, "Hebrews and 1 Clement: Literary Dependence or Common Tradition?" *BZ* 23 (1979): 264–65; and H. Attridge, *The Epistle to the Hebrews*, Her (Philadelphia: Fortress, 1989), 6–7. But Albl argued to the contrary, indicating that Clement has a different conception of Christ's high priesthood than Hebrews, and no clear pattern exists for *1 Clement*'s adaptations of the Hebrew's catena. W. L. Lane (*Hebrews 1–8*, WBC [Dallas: Word Books, 1991], 7) affirmed the possibility that the writer of Hebrews used a testimonia collection, but he concluded that the evidence shows Clement borrowed from Hebrews and that a comparison of the two cannot confirm use of a testimonia collection. Albl concluded that the question of Clement's dependence upon Hebrews must remain open (p. 204). If Albl's point that Clement did not explicitly link high priesthood with Christ's death is valid, it would furnish another argument against Clement of Rome as the author of Hebrews. P. Ellingworth (*The Epistle to the Hebrews*, NIGTC [Grand Rapids: Eerdmans, 1993], 109–10) offered five reasons to question the *testimonia* theory. R. Bauckham claimed that it goes beyond the evidence to suggest the catena in Heb 1:5–13 comes from a *testimonia* collection ("Monotheism and Christology in Hebrews 1," in *Early Jewish and Christian Monotheism*, ed. L. Stuckenbruck and W. North, JSNTSup 263 [London: T&T Clark, 2004], 170). Cf. H. Bateman, "Early Jewish Hermeneutics and Hebrews 1:5–13: The Impact of Early Jewish Exegesis on the Interpretation of a Significant New Testament Passage," in *American University Studies*, Series VII, Theology and Religion 193 (New York: Peter Lang, 1997), 149–206. Bateman compared Heb 1:5–13 to 4QFlorilegium and noticed numerous similarities.

[6] So M. Barth, "The Old Testament in Hebrews: An Essay in Biblical Hermeneutics," in *Current Issues in New Testament Interpretation*, ed. W. Klassen and G. Snyder (New York: Harper & Row, 1962), 73.

[7] A possibility suggested by R. Longenecker, *Biblical Exegesis in the Apostolic Period* (Grand Rapids: Eerdmans, 1975), 180.

Second, what Old Testament text did the author use.[8] It is clear that he seldom quoted from the MT but preferred the LXX. Sometimes, however, his quotations often do not agree with either of the two main manuscripts of the LXX—LXX^A or LXX^B. Sometimes his quotations agree with the MT, in whole or in part, against a LXX text. This phenomenon has created a conundrum for scholars. How is one to explain the author's variation from the LXX? Some conclude that the author sometimes used a Hebrew text.[9] Others believe he used exclusively some form of the LXX. Thomas took the position that LXX^A and LXX^B represent two traditions from a single translation, and the author of Hebrews used a text of this translation before it was subjected to extensive editing.[10] At least five different possibilities have been suggested for this phenomenon in Hebrews: (1) citation from memory; (2) intentional adaptation by the author; (3) errors of transcription in his manuscript; (4) a lost version of the Greek Old Testament was used; and (5) the use of liturgical sources.[11] It has long been recognized that New Testament authors are not bound to reproduce their sources verbatim. It seems clear from the overall evidence that the author of Hebrews has occasionally modified his sources, but only with the clear purpose of stylistic enhancement, theological clarification, or greater emphasis. None of these alterations change or adversely affect the contextual sense of the quotation.[12] There is strong evidence the author used an early LXX text.[13]

Bateman thoroughly analyzed the seven Old Testament quotations, comparing their appearance in the MT, the LXX, and Hebrews. He identified Ps 2:7; 2 Sam 7:14; and Ps 110:1 as "corresponding citations" in that they demonstrate a one-to-one correspondence in all three texts. He designated Ps 104:4; 45:6–7; and 102:25–27 as "conflicting citations" since they reflect differences in two areas: between the LXX and the Hebrew text, and between the LXX and Hebrews. Bateman concluded relative to these citations:

> The author reproduces the minor translational liberties in the Septuagint but adds his own interpretive changes—neither of which distort the conceptual sense of the Old Testament. Unlike the translator of the Septuagint, however, the author of Hebrews applies and thereby

[8] For a detailed discussion of this issue, see Bateman, "Early Jewish Hermeneutics."

[9] G. Howard, "Hebrews and the Old Testament Quotations," *NovT* 10 (1968): 215.

[10] K. Thomas, "The Old Testament Citations in Hebrews," *NTS* 11 (1964–65): 325.

[11] Ibid., 303. Thomas said there is no evidence the author knew of two different readings and chose between them. He concluded that the variations originated with the author himself (319–21).

[12] See the excellent discussion of this issue in Bateman, "Early Jewish Hermeneutics," 123–47; and D. Leschert, *Hermeneutical Foundations of Hebrews: A Study of the Validity of the Epistle's Interpretation of Some Core Citations from the Psalms* (Lewiston, NY: Edward Mellen, 1994), 243–56.

[13] Thomas, "Old Testament Citations," 324; Bateman, "Early Jewish Hermeneutics," 144.

> recontextualizes the conceptual sense of these Old Testament passages to describe the Son's superiority over angelic beings.[14]

In Heb 1:6b the author cited Deut 32:43, which Bateman listed as a "controversial citation" since it is one of two possible passages being cited (the other being Ps 96:7). Three options have been proposed to solve the problem of textual variation. (1) The citation could be a conflation of both suggested texts. (2) Due to the similarity of the text in Heb 1:6b, some have suggested the Hymn of Moses (Odes), which was appended to the Greek Psalter, as the author's source. (3) The most likely option (according to Bateman) is that the citation corresponds with Deut 32:43b of LXX^{A}, which may be based on an older reading, possibly 4QDeut 32:43.[15]

Third, were these Old Testament texts considered messianic in pre-Christian Judaism or in the Judaism of the first century? If not, how were they originally identified and used Christologically by the New Testament writers? There can be no doubt that pre-Christian or first-century Judaism viewed some of these texts messianically.[16] Also, given the widespread use of some of these texts by other New Testament authors, it is evident that an interpretive tradition had developed that utilized these texts messianically, and the author was dependent on that tradition in the church.[17] Psalm 8 was not considered messianic in Jewish apocalyptic or rabbinic writings, yet it was used with messianic import several times by the New Testament authors, either in quotation or allusion (Matt 21:16; Mark 12:36; 1 Cor 15:25–28; 1 Pet 3:22), including Heb 2:5–9. How did this come about? It is not likely that the New Testament authors began to interpret some Old Testament passages in a messianic sense simply "out of the blue." The root of this interpretation began with Jesus himself when, for example, in Mark 12:36 he referred to Ps 110:1 to point to himself as the Son of God in his teaching in the temple. Luke recorded twice that Jesus explained to the disciples from the Law, the Prophets, and the Writings (the complete Old Testament canon) the things concerning himself (Luke 24:27,44–45.) The author of Hebrews was an heir to this tradition.

Fourth, was the author engaged in a polemic against angel worship? This could easily be inferred from what is said about Jesus' superiority to the angels. But the key to answering this question lies in the content of the prologue and 1:5–14 as well as the surrounding contextual material. There are two strong reasons not to consider this passage as a polemic against angel worship. First, there is virtually no reference to angels after chap. 2. And second, the semantic

---

[14] Bateman, "Early Jewish Hermeneutics," 141.

[15] Ibid., 142–44.

[16] Kistemaker, *Psalm Citations in Hebrews*, 17, 24; D. M. Hay, *Glory at the Right Hand: Psalm 110 in Early Christianity* (Nashville: Abingdon, 1973), 21–33.

[17] Longenecker (*Biblical Exegesis*, 177) believed that the author was primarily dependent on the NT exegetical tradition. He pointed out that only in 4QFlorilegium are 2 Sam 7:14 and Ps 2:1–2 given possible messianic status.

focus of the prologue, which is programmatic for Hebrews, is the reality of God's revelation in his Son. Judaism viewed angels as playing a role in the giving of the law at Mt. Sinai.[18] It is the superiority of the revelation coming through the Son that led the author to contrast the Son with angels, not the concern that his readers were engaged in angel worship. There is no evidence that the readers practiced this. When 2:1–4 is taken into consideration, it is clear that the author's focus on angels is due to the issue of their participation as agents of God's Old Testament revelation.

But another issue looms large here. The author carefully presented in the prologue the full deity of the Son, and he again asserted this fact in vv. 5–14 when he chose a quotation in v. 8 where the Father addressed the Son as "God." There was no need to argue for the superiority of Jesus over the angels as that was not in question among early Jewish Christians. What was an issue—indeed, it was the watershed issue between Jews and Christians—was the deity of Christ and the Jewish attempt to deny it by claiming to preserve monotheism. Early Jewish Christians faced accepting the deity of Jesus while preserving historical monotheism. This was the heart of the author's theological purpose in the first two chapters. He wanted to affirm the deity of Christ while connecting him to God's overarching plan of redemption through Israel's Messiah—one who was no mere man or angel (agents used by God in giving revelation in the past), but who was himself God in human flesh. Hebrews 1:5–14 was not intended to show the superiority of Jesus to angels; that was never in question. It is intended to show his deity to a monotheistic Jewish-Christian audience; thus, the superiority of his revelation, as compared to any other mediators such as prophets or even angels, is affirmed.

Fifth, did the author of Hebrews present an angelomorphic Christology? Possibly in the first century AD but certainly in the immediately following centuries, there was talk of Jesus as appearing in angelic form, but this was *outside the New Testament*. And even outside the New Testament, Jesus was not generally understood to be an angel; rather he was called "Angel"—sometimes because people perceived him to be angelic in function, and occasionally people recognized him as having taken on angelic form temporarily.[19]

In favor of such a position is Gieschen, who presented the case that—while Hebrews distinguishes between Christ and the angels—one need not interpret this as precluding the presence of angelomorphic Christology. Gieschen found evidence of angelomorphic terminology and traditions in Hebrews' concept of the phrase "Word of Power" in the prologue (v. 3, NIV "powerful word"), the "firstborn" (1:5–14), the Son as "creator," "Glory," and "Enthroned Son" in the

---

[18] Stephen and Paul, both Jews, reflect this tradition in Acts 7:53 and Gal 3:19.

[19] P. Carrell, *Jesus and the Angels: Angelology and the Christology of the Apocalypse of John*, SNTSMS (Cambridge: Cambridge University Press, 1997), 98–111. Cf. L. T. Stuckenbruck, *Angel Veneration and Christology: A Study in Early Judaism and in the Christology of the Apocalypse of John*, WUNT (Tübingen: Mohr/Siebeck, 1995).

prologue, and Jesus as the "Apostle" (3:1–6). The author's focus on the high priesthood of Christ furnished the door through which he would bring Jewish traditions about angelomorphic high priests into the New Testament.[20]

The evidence simply does not support an angelomorphic Christology in Hebrews or anywhere else in the New Testament. As in the case with the supposed use of Philo by the author of Hebrews, similar vocabulary does not prove adherence or dependence on a tradition. Besides, if the readers were somehow influenced by an angelomorphic Christology, why did the author focus on Melchizedek (Hebrews 7), who was viewed by some in Judaism as a heavenly being? Furthermore, the angelomorphic traditions in rabbinic theology appear to have developed after the New Testament era anyway, and occasionally in some patristic writers.

A better and more productive approach to the question of how Jesus came to be worshipped as a divine being by early Jewish Christians who regarded themselves as monotheists is provided by Bauckham. The recipients of Hebrews were most likely Jewish Christians and thus fall within this category. Second Temple Jewish monotheism was not monolithic, and the New Testament authors ascribe to Jesus the characteristics that include him in the unique identity of the one God of Israel.[21] Furthermore, the use of Ps 110:1 in Hebrews as well as other places in the New Testament is foundational for Christology. Bauckham stated,

> [It is also] a major impediment in the way of attempts to see early Christology as the transference to Jesus of a Jewish model already well developed and well known in relation to various principal angels and exalted patriarchs. There is no convincing case of allusion to Psalm 110:1 (or to any other part of the Psalm) in Second Temple Jewish literature.[22]

The concern of early Christology as evidenced by the use of Ps 110:1 was to understand the identification of Jesus with God. Early and later Judaism provided little or no opportunity for such an equation, even with what is said about intermediary figures such as angels. Stuckenbruck argued that there is no hint in Judaism that a cultus was organized around angelic beings, and he further stated that the exalted position of angels in Judaism "did not directly

[20] C. Gieschen, *Angelomorphic Christology: Antecedents and Early Evidence*, AGJU (Leiden: Brill, 1998) 294–314. D. Hannah concluded that Hebrews 1–2 indirectly identifies a tradition existent during NT times that Jesus was identified with an angel—and he concluded that this was a tradition both the author and readers of the epistle rejected (*Michael and Christ: Michael Traditions and Angel Christology in Early Christianity*, WUNT [Tübingen: Mohr/Seibeck,1999], 109:137–39).

[21] R. Bauckham, "The Theme of God and the Worship of Jesus," in *The Jewish Roots of Christological Monotheism: Papers from the St. Andrews Conference on the Historical Origins of the Worship of Jesus*, JSJSup 63 (Boston: Brill, 1998), 60 (see esp. 43–69).

[22] Ibid., 62.

contribute to the *inception* of early Christian devotion to Christ alongside God."[23]

Sixth, how did the author's Christological interpretation of the Old Testament avoid the arbitrary imposition of Christian interpretive methodology without distorting its original meaning? By his use of the Old Testament, the author affirmed that his treatment was correct from the viewpoint of the Old Testament itself. This is a crucial aspect of the issue of the relationship between the Old and New Testaments.[24]

The step from God's revelation through prophets to his revelation in his Son involves something new from God's revelatory perspective, but not something so new that it was not already latent in the Old Testament. This is illustrated in Heb 1:5–14 in several ways, two of which include the application of Ps 102:24–27 in Heb 1:10 to Christ as creator of the universe,[25] and the use of Ps 110:1 in Heb 1:13 and three other times in the epistle as the foundational verse for the author's Christology.[26]

Similarly, Clements contended that the New Testament authors were not imposing a distorted, alien concept in their interpretation of the Old Testament prophets; rather, they were extending a method of interpretation already begun by the Old Testament prophets.[27] The author argued not only from Old

---

[23] L. T. Stuckenbruck, "'Angels' and 'God': Exploring the Limits of Early Jewish Monotheism," in *Early Jewish and Christian Monotheism*, ed. L. Stuckenbruck and W. North, JSNTSup 263 (London: T&T Clark, 2004), 68. Hannah (*Michael and Christ,* 137–39) acknowledged that Heb 1 does not engage in a polemic against angelomorphic Christology and thus was not an error that the readers had imbibed, but he believed "it *was* in the air" so the author of Hebrews gains credibility with his readers by indicating to them his opposition to such a Christology.

[24] The literature on this subject is immense. For a good review, see J. Charlesworth, "What Has the Old Testament to Do with the New?" in *The Old and New Testaments: Their Relationship and the "Intertestamental" Literature* (Valley Forge: Trinity Press International, 1993), 39–87; Cf. D. L. Baker, *Two Testaments, One Bible: A Study of the Theological Relationship between the Old and New Testaments*, 2nd ed. (Leicester: Apollos, 1991), 257–70.

[25] See G. Lindeskog, "The Theology of Creation in the Old and New Testaments," in *The Root of the Vine: Essays in Biblical Theology,* ed. A. Fridrichsen (New York: Philosophical Library, 1953), 17–19. Jesus is described in the words of Ps 102:24–27, which is addressed to God as creator of all. Lindeskog wrote that the revelation in the Son involves both something new and a "bold reinterpretation" of the OT. In fact, in light of such passages as Deut 6:4, where the Hebrew word *ʾeḥad,* "one," signifies composite unity, passages such as Prov 30:4–5 and Isa 48:12–16, which affirm a trinitarian perspective, indicate the NT revelation in the Son is not so bold a "reinterpretation" of the OT as Lindeskog and others might think. See J. Sailhamer, *Introduction to Old Testament Theology: A Canonical Approach* (Grand Rapids: Zondervan, 1995), 155; J. Borland, *Christ in the Old Testament* (Geanies House, Fearn, Ross-Shire, Great Britain: Mentor, 1999).

[26] See Newman, et al., *The Jewish Roots of Christological Monotheism*, 61–63.

[27] R. Clements, *Old Testament Theology* (London: John Knox, 1978), 131–54. B. S. Childs called Clement's approach here a "highly creative, illuminating attempt to break new ground" (*Old Testament Theology in a Canonical Context* [Philadelphia: Fortress, 1986], 129). C. F. D. Moule noted that the author of Hebrews engaged in a "lively defense" of the Christian use of the OT in the tradition of Stephen "by carrying the attack behind the enemy's lines: read your scriptures, Stephen is saying in effect, and you will find that it is the scriptures themselves that tell you to look beyond Moses and beyond the Temple" (*The Birth of the New Testament*, 2nd ed. [London:

Testament quotations, but also *to them*, according to Clements, because he recognized that readers may misinterpret so as to undermine the completeness and finality of Christianity. In Hebrews, the Old Testament is used to illumine Christian doctrines, and Christian doctrine to illumine the Old Testament. The author of Hebrews sought to show how the Old Testament should be interpreted in light of Jesus, God's final revelation. The author's use of the Old Testament reveals its value for Christians in knowing God's revelation. In fact, for Hebrews, God's Old Testament revelation is absolutely necessary for an understanding of the significance of his revelation through Jesus.[28]

Even though the author's interpretation of the Old Testament is not identical with traditional Jewish interpretation, there is a certain consistency in the way he handled the intended meaning of the Old Testament. It would appear that many first-century Jewish interpreters quoted from the Old Testament with respect to its original context, and the same appears to be true for New Testament authors as well.[29] The author of Hebrews did not distort the original textual meaning, yet he built his exegetical case in continuity with the Old Testament.[30] According to M. Barth, the interpretation of the Old Testament in Hebrews is threefold. (1) dialogical—a careful listening to God and listening in on the dialogue between God and man in Scripture; (2) Christological—the author's quest, not for facts and principles, but for Jesus in his fullness; and (3) homiletical—the communication of the superiority of the Son followed by recurring exhortation urging the readers to participate in the life and service of the church.[31]

The correct interpretation of this catena of quotations is heavily dependent on careful recognition of its structure. The number of quotations, seven, is significant and roughly corresponds to the seven propositions made about the Son in the prologue.[32]

1. Jesus' Identity and Work Demand Our Obedience (1:5–2:18)

[5]For to which of the angels did God ever say,

"You are my Son;
today I have become your Father"?

Adam & Charles Black, 1966], 75). Moule viewed Hebrews as representing "precisely" the kind of debate that the trial of Stephen indicates (76).

[28] These points are well made by R. Clements, "The Use of the Old Testament in Hebrews," *SWJT* 28 (1985): 36–45.

[29] D. I. Brewer, *Techniques and Assumptions in Jewish Exegesis before 70 CE* (Tübingen: Mohr, 1992), 167–69. The same is true for the NT authors according to G. K. Beale, "Did Jesus and His Followers Preach the Right Doctrine from the Wrong Texts? An Examination of the Presuppositions of Jesus' and the Apostles' Exegetical Method," *Themelios* 14 (1989): 90–91.

[30] See the excellent discussion in Leschert, *Hermeneutical Foundations of Hebrews*, esp. 243–56.

[31] Barth, "The Old Testament in Hebrews," 76–77.

[32] On the connection of 2:1–4 with the prologue, see T. Lewicki, '*Weist nicht ab den Sprechenden!': Wort Gottes und paraklese im Hebräerbrief* (Paderborn/München: Ferdinand Schöningh, 2004), 48–61.

Or again,

"I will be his Father,
and he will be my Son"?

6And again, when God brings his firstborn into the world, he says,

"Let all God's angels worship him."

7In speaking of the angels he says,

"He makes his angels winds,
his servants flames of fire."

8But about the Son he says,

"Your throne, O God, will last for ever and ever,
and righteousness will be the scepter of your kingdom.
9You have loved righteousness and hated wickedness;
therefore God, your God, has set you above your companions
by anointing you with the oil of joy."

10He also says,

"In the beginning, O Lord, you laid the foundations of the earth,
and the heavens are the work of your hands.
11They will perish, but you remain;
they will all wear out like a garment.
12You will roll them up like a robe;
like a garment they will be changed.
But you remain the same,
and your years will never end."

13To which of the angels did God ever say,

"Sit at my right hand
until I make your enemies
a footstool for your feet"?

14Are not all angels ministering spirits sent to serve those who will inherit salvation?

(1) The Son's Superiority to Angels (1:5–14)

1:5 Hebrews 1:5–14 is one paragraph that falls structurally into three subparagraphs: vv. 5–6, vv. 7–12, and vv. 13–14. These are marked in the text by the author's use of introductory quotation formula in vv. 5,7 and 13. Each of the three paragraphs has as its main point the contrast of the Son with angels.[33] The parallel rhetorical introduction of v. 5 and v. 13 is "to which of the angels

[33] Bateman noted the terms "Son" and "angels" serve as "literary linchpins" between the prologue and the exposition of 1:5–14 ("Early Jewish Hermeneutics," 216). Cf. D. Anderson, *The King-Priest of Psalm 110 in Hebrews* (New York: Peter Lang, 2001) on the use of Ps 110 in Heb 1:5–14 as well as the entire epistle. For his treatment of 1:5–14, see pp. 137–76.

did God ever say."[34] There is a semantic relationship between the first quotation (Ps 2:7) in v. 5 and the last quotation (Ps 110:1) in v. 13 since both Psalm 2 and Psalm 110 are coronation psalms. These quotations are parallel to the first and last statements about the Son in the prologue: "heir of all things" (1:2b), and "he sat down at the right hand" (1:3c).[35] The quotation formula used by the author in introducing these Old Testament quotations are informative: rather than the usual "it is written," the author used the verb "to say" in three different tenses—aorist (v. 5), present (vv. 6, 7), and perfect (v. 13). This is in keeping with the author's emphasis on the Scripture as divine speech and its present impact, though the actual words were spoken centuries earlier. As J. P. Meier well noted, the author can "insinuate" his theological program by the order he gave to the Old Testament quotations and in any introductory or concluding remarks he made. Meier found a "general correspondence" between the catena in 1:5–14 and what is said of the Son in 1:1–4.[36] The tail-head linkage of "angels" in 1:4 and 1:5 coupled with the subordinate connector *gar* indicates that the catena of quotations functions as the grounds for the statement in 1:4 and probably for the entire prologue.[37] Also, in Ps 2:7–8 the concept of "inheritance" is prominent as in Heb 1:2,4.

1:5–6 Both Ps 2:7 and 2 Sam 7:14 are quoted in Heb 1:5, and Deut 32:43 is quoted in Heb 1:6 following a lengthy quotation formula ("And again, when God brings his firstborn into the world, he says"). Several important facts should be noticed about the first two quotations. First, both quotations in v. 5 express virtually identical information, and the two form a lexical chiasm around "Son" and "Father":

> You are my *Son*,
> today I have become your *Father*
> I will be his *Father*,
> and he will be my *Son*.[38]

---

[34] Rhetorical questions are often used to signal some new aspect of the same subject. See J. Beekman and K. Callow, *Translating the Word of God* (Grand Rapids: Zondervan, 1974), 243. The rhetorical question in v. 5a is equivalent to an emphatic negative according to Ellingworth (*Hebrews*, 110).

[35] So J. P. Meier, "Structure and Theology in Heb 1,1–14," *Bib* 66 (1985): 168–89; and id., "Symmetry and Theology in the Old Testament Citations of Heb 1,5–14," *Bib* 66 (1985): 504–33. Cf. Lane, *Hebrews 1–8*, 22–23.

[36] Meier, "Symmetry and Theology," 504–5. See the discussion of 1:5–14 linked to 1:3 in D. Guthrie, *New Testament Theology* (Downers Grove: InterVarsity, 1981), 362–64.

[37] In traditional Greek grammar, γάρ is considered a coordinating conjunction. From a semantic standpoint, however, it usually introduces clauses, sentences, or paragraphs that present cause or reason for the previous clause, sentence, or paragraph, and for this reason it is always semantically subordinate. Friberg and Friberg always tag γάρ as a subordinate conjunction (D. Friberg and B. Friberg, *Analytical Greek New Testament* (Grand Rapids: Baker, 1981), 833–34. Explanatory γάρ or inferential γάρ likewise introduce semantic subordination.

[38] The chiasm is seen in the NIV translation, but the Greek text does not use the term "Father" in the quotation of Ps 2:7; rather, "Father" is semantically understood in the phrase "I have begot-

Second, they were considered messianic texts by the Qumran community,[39] the Jewish people,[40] as well as by the apostolic writers.[41] The manner of citation indicates that the author considered these texts to be messianic.

Third, the historical context of Ps 2:7 is a royal psalm about the Hebrew monarchy and reflects a kingly coronation liturgy in the Davidic dynasty.[42] But it is clear that neither Solomon nor any other king in the Davidic line completely fulfilled this Psalm. When it became apparent that none of the kings of the Davidic line was capable of fulfilling this prophecy due to their increasing moral and spiritual failure, postexilic and Second Temple Judaism transferred their fulfillment to the future Messiah who would arise from David's line. It is thus apparent that our author's application of Psalm 2 to Jesus as the Messiah is prefigured in the Jewish exegetical tradition.

Fourth, Ps 2:7 indicates that although angels collectively are referred to in the Old Testament as "sons" of God (as were kings and Israel as a nation) in both the MT and the LXX, this status was never conferred on any individual angel.[43] All of these points served the author well in his choice of Ps 2:7 as the lead quotation in the catena: Jesus is the promised Messiah who is now enthroned and fulfills the Davidic promise of a "seed" and a "Son," and he received the name "Son" directly from the Father, a name no angel ever received. Jesus is superior to the angels as God's final revelation.[44]

A major interpretive issue in 1:5 is the meaning of *sēmeron* ("today"). Five major views have been propounded. It could refer to (1) the "eternal generation" of the Son; (2) the incarnation, either with a specific focus on the birth of Jesus, or as indicative of his incarnation generally; (3) the baptism of Jesus; (4) the

ten you." See Lane, *Hebrews 1–8*, 25; and H. Bateman, "Two First-Century Messianic Uses of the OT: Heb 1:5–13 and 4QFlor 1.1–19," *JETS* 38 (1995): 24.

[39] 2 Sam 7:14 is cited in 4QFlor 1.10–11; Ps 2:1–2 is quoted in 4QFlor 1.18–19.

[40] S. Kistemaker (*Exposition of the Epistle to the Hebrews* [Grand Rapids: Baker, 1984], 36) noted that the use of this psalm in the synagogue reflected its messianic interpretation.

[41] Ps 2:1–2 is quoted in Acts 4:25–26; Ps 2:7 is quoted in Acts 13:33. Ps 2:7 is applied to Jesus at his baptism in Matt 3:16–17; Mark 1:10–11; and Luke 3:21–22; allusions occur in Rom 1:4; Rev 12:5; 19:15. Furthermore, 2 Sam 7:12 (the Davidic "seed") is interpreted messianically in John 7:42; Luke 1:32–33; and Acts 13:23. The so-called Western text of Luke 3:22, parallel to Mark 1:11, records the heavenly voice speaking the fuller wording of Ps 2:7: "You are my Son; today I have become your Father" as is quoted in Heb 1:5. For textual arguments pro and con, see D. Bock, *Luke 1:1–9:50*, BECNT 3a (Grand Rapids: Baker, 1994), 346–47. Paul's Pisidian sermon in Acts 13, specifically vv. 33–37, correlates Ps 2:7 with 2 Sam 7:14, as does Hebrews 1. Thus, that the early church attributed to these texts messianic significance.

[42] See P. Craigie, *Psalms 1–50*, WBC 19 (Waco: Word, 1983), 62–69. Many have suggested that the threefold division of this paragraph (vv. 5–6, vv. 7–12, vv. 13–14) corresponds to the three stages of a coronation liturgy, evidence for which may be found in the OT. See the discussion with bibliography in Ellingworth (*Hebrews*, 108–9).

[43] The use of τίνι gives the sense of "any individual angel," and ποτε signifies "on any occasion."

[44] Many of the themes of Psalms 2 occur elsewhere in Hebrews; e.g., see Ellingworth, *Hebrews,* 112–13.

resurrection; or (5) to the exaltation and enthronement of Christ.[45] Although there is a sense in which each of these interpretations is valid—Delitzsch noted the "elasticity" of the use of *sēmeron*[46]—the context of v. 4 points to Jesus' exaltation and enthronement as the best interpretation of "today." According to the prologue, and in light of the overall theology of Hebrews, Christ's exaltation presupposes his deity, incarnation and resurrection.

Since Psalm 2 is a royal coronation psalm, "become" in v. 5 applies to coming into the royal position of kingship, and the moment of this becoming was the exaltation and enthronement which followed the resurrection. Delitzsch stated that the ancient synagogue interpreted the "firstborn" of Ps 89:27 in this royal sense and regarded it as messianic.[47] The "eternal generation" of the Son[48] is not in view in these verses, and it was post-apostolic theological development during the second century that was regularly discussed in the Trinitarian controversies of the fourth and fifth centuries. To read such a concept into the New Testament would be anachronistic.

It would seem that the focus in Heb 1:5 is on the entrance and the permanence of the sonship of Christ as the fulfillment of the promised Davidic kingship.[49] Bateman was correct that Ps 2:7 and 2 Sam 7:14 are linked exegetically and conceptually in the Old Testament and in Second Temple Judaism, and that both texts are fulfilled in the sonship of Jesus.[50]

Hebrews 1:6 contains a number of exegetical questions that need resolution. First, what is the source of this quotation? Five options are possible: (1) Deut 32:43b; (2) Deut 32:43d; (3) Ps 97:7; (4) Odes 2:43b; and (5) 4QDeut 32:43b.

---

[45] See Attridge, *Hebrews*, 54–55, and Ellingworth, *Hebrews*, 113–14, for discussion and bibliography, respectively, on each view.

[46] F. Delitzsch, *Commentary on the Epistle to the Hebrews,* trans. T. L. Kingsbury (Edinburgh: T&T Clark, 1872; repr., Grand Rapids: Eerdmans, 1952), 1:65.

[47] Ibid., 64.

[48] The doctrine of "eternal generation" is found in Articles 21 and 22 of the Athanasian Creed: "The Father is made of none, neither created nor begotten. The Son is of the Father alone; not made nor created, but begotten." Theologians use the phrase "eternal generation" to explain the use of the "begetting" of Jesus in John 1:14,18; 3:16,18; 1 John 4:9. L. Berkhof (*Systematic Theology* [Grand Rapids: Eerdmans, 1979], 93) described the eternal generation as "of the personal subsistence rather than of the divine essence of the Son." Origin was the first to use the idea of "eternal generation," defining it in such a way as to subordinate the Son to the Father in respect to essence (L. Berkhof, *History of Christian Doctrine* [Grand Rapids: Baker, 1975], 83–84).

[49] The use of ποτε in 1:5 shifts from a past implicature signaled in v. 1 by πάλαι to a present implicature. See S. E. Porter, *Verbal Aspect in the Greek of the New Testament, with Reference to Tense and Mood*, in Studies in Biblical Greek 1 (New York: Peter Lang, 1989), 263.

[50] Bateman, "Early Jewish Hermeneutics," 218. Longenecker (*Biblical Exegesis*, 179) identified these two quotations in Heb 1:5 as exegetically linked by the *gezerah shawah* principle, which indicates that "they are applied in a corporate solidarity fashion to Jesus as the true King of Israel (Ps. 2:1–12) and David's greater Son (2 Sam 7:12–17)." Shalom Paul noted that 2 Sam 7:14 "is generally acknowledged to be an adoption formula, which serves to provide the legal basis for the grant of eternal dynasty to the Davidic line" ("Adoption Formulae: A Study of Cuneiform and Biblical Legal Clauses," *MAARAV* 2.2 [1979–80]: 178). He indicated that the same is true for Ps 2:7–8.

In the MT of Deut 32:43 the quoted line in Heb 1:6 is absent, but the LXX has an expanded reading not found in the MT. In the Hebrew text from Qumran (4QDeut 32:43), the line quoted in Heb 1:6 is present, and in the appendix to Psalms in the LXX, Ode 2:43b contains the identical version found in Heb 1:6.[51] The occurrence of these lines in 4QDeut suggests that a Hebrew source was known at Qumran.[52] Attempts to suggest that the shift from "sons" to "angels" in Heb 1:6 indicate influence from the LXX of Ps 97:7 fail to take the Odes version into account.[53] There are several options, which are listed here in ascending order of probability. (1) The changes were made by the author himself given the context of Hebrews 1. (2) The difference could be due to picking up "angels" from Deut 32:43d if the LXX version of Deuteronomy 32 was used.[54] (3) A version like the one in Ode 2, having liturgical connections, could have been the author's source.[55] (4) Probably the best option, given the evidence, is that the author quoted Deut 32:43b from a Greek text not now known and to which 4QDeut gives indirect support.[56]

One key issue is whether the translation of *Elohim* in 4QDeut 32:43b was originally "the angels of God" or "sons of God." Cockerill concluded that the limited LXX evidence tended to support "angels of God" as the original translation of *Elohim,* though this is not the usual translation for this word. The phrase "angels of God" in Heb 1:6 "is based on but omits the article of the original reading of Deut 32:43b LXX."[57] The significance of this translation is discussed below.

In v. 6 some think *palin* ("again") should construed with *eisagagē* as a temporal modifier with the meaning "he again brings . . . into," while others suggest that it modifies *legei* with the meaning "again he says," thus introducing another in a series of quotations (as in 1:5b). In favor of the former is its position in the clause: after *hotan de* but immediately before *eisagagē*. If it were to be construed with *legei,* its position would likely be *palin de*. *Palin* is used as a connective to introduce a quotation in other verses (2:13; 4:5;

---

[51] For an in depth discussion of this question, see G. Cockerill, "Hebrews 1:6: Source and Significance," *BBR* 9 (1999), 51–64; and G. J. Steyn, "A Quest for the *Vorlage* of the 'Song of Moses' (Deut 32) Quotations in Hebrews," *Neot* 34 (2000): 263–72. For a good summary discussion, see Ellingworth (*Hebrews*, 118–19).

[52] Jellicoe noted that here we have for the first time "Hebrew textual authority for an Old Testament quotation" by the Hebrews author (*The Septuagint and Modern Study* [Winona Lake, IN: Eisenbrauns, 1968], 277). See P. W. Skehan, "A Fragment of the Song of Moses (Deut 32) from Qumran," *BASOR* 136 (1954), 12–15.

[53] Steyn, "A Quest for the *Vorlage*," 267.

[54] See ibid., 268, for these first two options.

[55] So Kistemaker (*Psalm Citations in Hebrews*, 22–23).

[56] See Steyn ("A Quest for the *Vorlage*," 268), Cockerill ("Hebrews 1:6: Source and Significance," 60–64), and Ellingworth (*Hebrews*, 119), who represents those holding to the last possibility.

[57] Cockerill, "Hebrews 1:6: Source and Significance," 57–60. I assume Cockerill meant the article in the *Odes 2* version of Deut 32:43.

10:30). Following Heb 4:5, it occurs in the same context in v. 7 with its temporal meaning. Those who interpret it in this fashion generally interpret the verse to refer to the second coming of Christ. In favor of this is the term's use in Heb 1:5b to connect quotations. Its use with *de* in the sense of "on the other hand, in contrast" is not without parallels, and the sense is consistent with the scope of the passage.[58] Contextual usage and the probable meaning of "when God brings his firstborn into the world" as the time of the enthronement and exaltation of the Son seem to support taking *palin* as modifying the speech orienter *legei*.

A third exegetical issue to consider is the interpretation of *oikoumenē* ("world" in v. 6). There is significant debate about the difference between *oikoumenē* and *kosmos*, the more general and common word for "world" in the New Testament. Although *oikoumenē* usually refers to the inhabited human world, our author used this word in Heb 2:5, its only other occurrence in Hebrews, to designate the heavenly realm with a future connotation.[59] In 2:5, the phrase "the world to come" translates this noun and the participle of *mellō* ("coming"). F. F. Bruce explained that, as Heb 2:5 points out, "in the new age which his enthronement has inaugurated, it is to him, and not to angels, that the *oikoumenē* is made subject."[60] The focus in the prologue is on the enthronement of Christ and a key theme of Hebrews is Christ's entrance into the heavenly sanctuary and his enthronement. The reference to angels worshipping Christ would be fitting for Christ's return to glory and his enthronement at the right hand of the Father. If this perspective is correct, then it is difficult to apply the meaning *eisagagē . . . eis tēn oikoumenē* in 1:6 to the incarnation, birth, baptism, or second coming of Christ. The problem with taking Christ's entrance into the "inhabited world" as a reference to his birth is brought out when one considers what the author says in Heb 2:5–9. It was at the incarnation that Jesus became *lower* than the angels (see Ps 8:5). It was at his enthronement that the angels were subjected again to him.

Taking the entire epistle into consideration, Ellingworth suggested that the implied meaning of Heb 1:6a is "In the past, God brought his own people out of the desert into the inhabited land of Canaan. Now he has brought Christ out of death into the glory of the heavenly assembly."[61] K. Schenck captured the meaning in a way that fits the context: "The God who enthrones Christ as the royal Son leads him into the heavenly world, where he seats him at the right hand of

---

[58] So B. F. Westcott, *The Epistle to the Hebrews* (Grand Rapids: Eerdmans, 1977), 22. But F. F. Bruce (*The Epistle to the Hebrews*, NICNT revised [Grand Rapids: Eerdmans, 1990], 56) did not think the word order is as conclusive as Westcott maintained. He took πάλιν as a connector signaling another quotation.

[59] See the discussion in O. Michel, "οἰκουμένη," *TDNT* 5:157–59.

[60] Bruce, *Hebrews*, 58, esp. n. 78.

[61] Ellingworth, *Hebrews*, 118.

the throne of grace. As befits a cosmic king, God instructs the servant angels to bow in obeisance to the one who has now been exalted above them."[62]

The interpretation of the aorist subjunctive *eisagagē* ("brings . . . into") following the temporal conjunction *hotan* ("when") is challenging. The problem is that *hotan* has no clear connection in the verse, so the time reference is ambiguous. Cases have been made for Christ's preexistence, incarnation, birth, baptism, enthronement in heaven after the resurrection, and parousia (the Second Coming).[63] Both the grammatical and patristic evidence is divided on this issue. The key here again is context. When what is said about the Son in the prologue, namely, that he has been seated at the right hand of God following the completion of the atonement (Heb 1:4), is coupled with the context of Heb 2:5 ("It is not to angels that he has subjected the world to come"), the best interpretation is to take the time reference as the Son's enthronement and exaltation.[64]

The meaning of *prototokos* ("firstborn"), is likely parallel with Paul's use of this term in Col 1:15,18, where Christ is said to be "the firstborn over all creation" and "the firstborn from among the dead."[65] Given the overall context of Hebrews 1 and the context of the two immediately preceding quotations, *prototokos* most likely continues the Davidic-enthronement motif. Psalm 89:27 (88:28 LXX) may have been in the author's mind: "I will also appoint him my firstborn, the most exalted of the kings of the earth."[66] The word is an honorific title signifying priority in rank.

In summary, according to Heb 1:5–6 God declares three things to be true about the Son, that is, three reasons the Son is superior to the angels. First, the Son has been inaugurated as the Davidic king by the Father at the Son's exaltation (v. 5). Second, this new position is a permanent position or dynasty (v. 6a). Third, as a result of this exaltation, all the angels are called by God to worship the Son (v. 6b); thus, he has complete authority over them.[67]

The author's use of Heb 1:6 ("Let all God's angels worship him") reveals just how adept he was in exegetical and theological acumen. The text itself does not specify the object of worship, but since the author identifies the speaker as God, the object must be someone other than God the Father. Some, like

---

[62] See K. Schenck ("A Celebration of the Enthroned Son: the Catena of Hebrews 1," *JBL* 120 [2001]: 479), who suggested that both the immediate context and the "inner logic" of the catena indicate that it should be read against the backdrop of royal enthronement.

[63] See Vanhoye, *Situation du Christ* (Paris: Cerf, 1969), 152–56; Lane, *Hebrews 1–8*, 26–27; Meier, "Symmetry and Theology," 507–10; and Koester, *Hebrews*, AB (New York: Doubleday, 2001), 192, for discussion and bibliography. Bateman ("Early Jewish Hermeneutics," 222) argued for the baptism of Christ.

[64] See the excellent discussion by Meier ("Symmetry and Theology," 507–10).

[65] So H. Montefiore, *A Commentary on the Epistle to the Hebrews* (New York: Harper; London: Black, 1964), 46.

[66] So Vanhoye (*Situation*, 158), and Meier ("Symmetry and Theology," 510).

[67] See the excellent discussion in Bateman ("Early Jewish Hermeneutics," 218–24).

Attridge, think the author intended the text to refer to Christ because it has been taken out of context.[68] Bauckham rightly disputed this line of thinking. It was precisely because the author knew the context well enough to realize that in Deut 32:43, the speech of God begins in v. 39 and the antecedent of "him" in v. 43a had to be someone other than God the Father and yet someone to whom worship is due. God the Father thus commanded the angels to worship someone other than himself, and the author interpreted the reference to be the Son.[69]

1:7 A new sub-paragraph unit, 1:7–12, is marked off by the introductory statement of what God says about the angels—"In speaking of the angels he says" (v. 7)—and what God says about the Son—"But about the Son he says" (v. 8). The author contrasted what God says about angels (v. 7) with what he says about the Son (vv. 8–12). The *men . . . de* construction of vv. 7–8 binds these two verses together closely in a contrastive way. The sense is "on the one hand . . . but on the other hand." Virtually all translations fail to make this sense explicit and simply use "but" to begin v. 8.

In v. 7 the author begins giving further proof of the superiority of the Son to the angels by contrasting their status as servants, created beings, and changeable nature with the Son's sovereign, unchangeable, and eternal nature. The speaker continues to be God and the quotation is from Psalm 104, which is a nature psalm. In Heb 1:7 the word "angels" identifies them as a class of beings, and in Greek both lines contain a double accusative: "angels . . . winds," "servants . . . flames." This can be construed in two ways. Most commentators take the first accusative in each line ("angels" and "servants") as functioning as the object of the participle translated "makes," and the anarthrous nouns "winds" and "flames" serve as predicates with the verb "to be" implied. Ellingworth's argument that "winds" and "flames" are the objects with "angels" and "servants" functioning as the predicates on the basis that the LXX text could not be interpreted in this way was long ago answered by Delitzsch.[70]

There is a problem with the NIV's translation of Ps 104:4 where "messengers" is used instead of "angels." The note on Ps 104:4 in the NIV Study Bible implies these messengers are inanimate ("winds" and "flames of fire"), not heavenly angelic beings. The question concerns whether the psalmist is personifying "winds" and "flames" in reference to angelic beings, or whether the author intended to identify inanimate "winds" and "flames" as his messengers. The former interpretation better accounts for the LXX rendering of "angels." The note on Heb 1:7 in the NIV Study Bible ("The Septuagint . . . reflects the developing doctrine of angels during the period between the OT and the NT")

---

[68] Attridge, *Hebrews*, 57.

[69] Bauckham, "Monotheism and Christology in Hebrews 1," 179.

[70] Ellingworth, *Hebrews*, 120–21; F. Delitzsch, *Commentary on the Epistle to the Hebrews* (Edinburgh: T&T Clark, 1871), 1:73–74.

leaves one with the implication that the MT and the LXX are at odds at this point.

The author's intent in this quotation is debated, and there are three main views. (1) God may change the angels into wind and fire, a rabbinic concept. (2) The angels either act in or assume the form of wind and fire, in the sense of "*media* of manifestation," to use Delitzsch's phrase.[71] (3) The point of comparison between angels and these forces of nature is either in the sense of being changeable or swift and destructive. The main point, in light of what the text says in vv. 10–12, is the transitory and mutable nature of angels compared to the eternality of the Son. The superiority of the Son over the angels is grounded in "the unchanging Son's act of creating changeable angels"—understanding "making" in the sense of creating and the Son as the subject.[72] This is Bauckham's view, who suggested that the term *leitourgous* ("servants") should be understood in its cultic sense and that "angels" should be understood with the basic meaning of "those who are sent." He claimed that both of these aspects recur in v. 14 and connected "his servants" (v. 7) to the angels' worship of the Son in the previous quotation, the result being that the Son is understood as the subject of the quotation in v. 7.[73]

1:8–9 Verses 8–12 introduce two more quotations that further contrast the eternality of the Son with the angels, concluding with the statement "you remain the same and your years will never end" (v. 12b). The question must be raised as to whether v. 8 indicates that the Father is speaking "about" the Son or actually "to" the Son in Psalm 45. The words in Psalm 45 are not addressed directly to the Son, but the use of *legei* in v. 7, which is understood again here in v. 8, implies that God is directly addressing the Son. This further indicates the superiority of the Son in contrast with the angels since God speaks "about" them, but speaks directly "to" the Son.

Verses 8–9 quote Ps 45:6–7 (7–8) from the LXX (44:6–7). The historical setting of Psalm 45 cannot be pinpointed with precision, but general agreement exists that it originated during the monarchy and is a royal psalm commemorating the wedding of a king in the Davidic line.[74] There are two textual problems that must be addressed which impact our exegesis of these verses. The first has to do with the relation of v. 8 to Ps 45:7. The author made two changes in Heb 1:8b. He inserted a *kai* at the beginning of the second line so that the verse reads, "*and* righteousness will be," which in effect draws a distinction between the two halves of the quotation in 1:8. Second, he transposed the article

---

[71] Delitzsch, *Hebrews*, 1:74.

[72] As does Meier, "Symmetry and Theology," 512–13.

[73] Bauckham, "Monotheism and Christology in Hebrews 1," 179–80.

[74] Craigie, *Psalms 1–50*, 338. Leschert (*Hermeneutical Foundations of Hebrews*, 243–44) speculated that the psalmist hoped this earthly king might be one to fulfill the Davidic covenant; hence, its inclusion in the Psalter, at a time when the wedding it celebrated was long forgotten, can only be explained in terms of lingering messianic expectations.

hē from the second use of *rhabdos* ("scepter") to the first. Whereas the LXX reads "the scepter of your kingdom is a scepter of righteousness," Heb 1:8 says, "righteousness will be the scepter of your kingdom." From a semantic standpoint, there is no change of meaning; it appears to be done primarily for stylistic reasons to create a parallel between 1:8a and 1:8b. The second textual problem has to do with the last word in v. 8, whether the pronoun should be the third singular *autou* ("his") or the second singular *sou* ("your"). Arguments for each view are laid out by M. Harris and need not be discussed in detail here.[75] Most textual critics and commentators opt for the second person singular *sou*.

The major exegetical issue in vv. 8–9, entailing immense repercussions theologically, has to do with whether the noun *ho theos* in v. 8a should be taken as a nominative, in which case it may be either the subject ("God is your throne") or the predicate ("your throne is God"), or whether it should be taken as a vocative ("Your throne, O God").[76] As with the textual problem above, this issue is fraught with exegetical detail, all of which need not be rehearsed, so a summary of the major evidence is offered and then theological conclusions are drawn.

There are three main reasons for taking *ho theos* as nominative. First, although the phrase "God is your throne" does not occur in the Old Testament, similar concepts such as "God is my rock" are found. Second, the reading *rhabdos tēs basileias autou*[77] ("the scepter of his kingdom") in v. 8b comports much better with *ho theos* as a nominative. Third, the context focuses on contrasting the Son with the angels with respect to function more than essence or being. This sort of contrast makes it less appropriate to address the son as God than to make comment on the eternality of his reign, and the nominative fits this best.[78]

In contrast to those who prefer the nominative, four lines of evidence are adduced to support taking *ho theos* as a vocative. First, it is highly likely, though not without debate, that the LXX of Ps 44:7, from which the author of Hebrews was quoting, has *ho theos* as a vocative. Second, the word order likely favors a vocative rather than a second nominative in third position. Third, the New

[75] M. J. Harris, *Jesus as God: The New Testament Use of Theos in Reference to Jesus* (Grand Rapids: Baker, 1992), 210–12. Cf. *TCGNT* 662–63.

[76] In the ensuing discussion, I am heavily indebted to M. Harris's carefully reasoned discussion of this question in *Jesus as God*, 212–27. In addition, the most thorough examination of this issue and the use of Ps 45:6–7 in Hebrews 1 is Leschert (*Hermeneutical Foundations of Hebrews*, esp. pp. 23–78). JPS has "your divine throne"; REB has "God has enthroned you"; and NJB has "Your throne is from God."

[77] This variant was the accepted reading in the Nestle critical text of 1963. A second consideration of syntax involves πρὸς . . . λέγει in vv. 7,8. If the syntax of v. 8 mirrors v. 7, namely to "say about," then θεός is nominative. This mirroring sense is, though, more a result of syntax judgment than determinative of it.

[78] Each of these reasons is countered by Harris (*Jesus as God*, 213–14). It is difficult to understand why the author would make the statement "Your throne is God forever," or what he would have meant by saying that God is the throne on which the Son sits.

Testament uses *legei pros* overwhelmingly to mean "say to." The structural movement of Heb 1:8–13 underscores this sense in 1:8. Fourth, the overall context and flow of argument in 1:5–14 supports the vocative reading. The strong antithesis drawn between the son and the angels, including the point that the angels are potentially addressed *by* God, but the Son is addressed *as* God, suggest that the author has in mind the vocative use. Harris supported by extensive footnotes that the overwhelming majority of grammarians, commentators, translators and general studies on this issue take *theos* as a vocative.[79]

The statement "your throne, O God, will last for ever and ever" (v. 8) makes the point that if the personal rule of the Son is eternal then the Son as ruler is thus likewise eternal. The author addressed this eternal rule at strategic places using Ps 110:4 where the eternality of Melchizedek's order of priesthood is applied to Jesus (Heb 5:6; 6:20; 7:17). The deity of the Son is affirmed in the prologue as well as in the catena of quotations whether *theos* in v. 8 is taken as a vocative or not. But Bauckham's suggestion that the rarity of the use of the word *theos* for Christ in the New Testament is "not of great christological moment"[80] underplays the author's theological point because the use of *theos* underscores the point that even the Old Testament Scriptures themselves, apart from Christian influence, prepare the way for an acceptance of Jesus as the Son who is fully God.

The second half of v. 8 reads "and righteousness will be the scepter of your kingdom."[81] The Greek word for "righteousness" here is not the common term *dikaiōsunē*, but the synonym *euthutēs* that has the connotation of "straightness." The "scepter of righteousness" is probably a genitive of quality while the "scepter of your kingdom" is an objective genitive with the meaning of "rule over the kingdom." The point is that the Son's rule will be a just rule. The relationship between the two halves of this clause can be interpreted in one

[79] Ibid., 216–18. Among grammarians who take it this way is D. Wallace (*GGBB* 59), who identified the usage as "nominative for vocative" (otherwise called a "nominative of address"). He briefly discussed four reasons. (1) It is an overstatement to argue that the writer could have used the vocative, because this occurs in the NT only in Matt 27:46. (2) Since Hebrew lacks a vocative form, the LXX is reticent to use the vocative form. (3) The accentuation in the Hebrew of Ps 45:7 suggests a pause between "throne" and "God," and this indicates that Jewish tradition took "God" as direct address. (4) The sense of the μὲν . . . δὲ construction in vv. 7–8 is best brought out by this rendering.

[80] Bauckham, "Monotheism and Christology in Hebrews 1," 182–83. He understood the text's significance in that sitting on the divine throne "was the most powerful symbol Jewish monotheism had for the inclusion of a figure in the exercise of the unique divine sovereignty over all things." This fact is certainly true and no doubt was one reason the author chose this text.

[81] There are two textual variants here, one more significant than the other. Taking the lesser first, some manuscripts omit the definite article with the first ῥάβδος ("scepter") and add it before the second ῥάβδος. It would seem likely that the definite article should appear before the first ῥάβδος, but the meaning is not altered either way; the difference would be merely one of focus. The other variant involves a few manuscripts that have αὐτοῦ ("his") in place of σου ("your"). *TCGNT* (592–93) accepts the later as most likely. Ellingworth (*Hebrews*, 122–123) has a good discussion of the textual issues here.

of two ways. Most (including the NIV) take the first phrase to be the subject and the second to be the predicate: "and righteousness will be the scepter of your kingdom." Some take the first phrase as the predicate and the second as subject: "the scepter of your kingdom is a scepter of righteousness." Again, the meaning is not altered either way.

The quotation of the Psalm 45 continues in v. 9: "You have loved righteousness and hated wickedness; therefore God, your God, has set you above your companions by anointing you with the oil of joy." When applied to Christ, the question arises as to whether the first part of v. 9, loving righteousness and hating wickedness, is limited to the earthly life of Jesus (note the aorist tenses), or (more likely) to a timeless present with the sense of "you love righteousness and hate wickedness." A similar issue arises with the anointing. It could refer to his anointing at his baptism by John, symbolized by the Holy Spirit's descent on him (even though the Gospel writers did not use anointing terminology), or to Jesus' statement in Luke 4:18 where he quoted Isa 61:1 (cf. Acts 10:48). Interestingly, the expression "oil of gladness" is used in Isa 61:3 (although the LXX renders the Hb. *šemen śāśôn*, "oil of joy," with terms different from our author. It could also be a symbolic reference to his anointing by God as king (and priest) at his exaltation. Although any of these three is possible, it is likely that the reference is of a more general nature and thus symbolic of the Son's eternal supreme joy. The genitive construction "oil of gladness" can be taken appositionally, "the oil which is gladness," in which case the meaning would be the oil is a symbol of gladness. It could also be taken as qualitative where "gladness" would describe the joyous occasion of the anointing.

After wrestling with the meaning of the *ho theos* in v. 8, one is faced with the grammatical construction *ho theos ho theos sou* ("God, your God") in v. 9b. Primarily based on the parallel with the usage in v. 8, many take the first *theos* as vocative and the second as nominative and the subject of the verb: "because of this, O God [Jesus], your God [the Father] has anointed you."[82] But Harris argued that the first *ho theos* should be taken as a nominative and thus subject of the verb and the following *ho theos* should be taken in apposition to it. He suggested four reasons. First, the parallelism between Ps 45:3c and 45:8b suggests that the first *ho theos* in 45:8b is a nominative since the corresponding *ho theos* in v. 3c cannot be taken as a vocative. Second, since the author was not averse to adjusting the subject-predicate order in v. 8b to avoid ambiguity, Harris surmised that he might have done so here had he regarded the first *ho theos* as a vocative. Third, in all the double uses of *ho theos* followed by either *mou* ("my"), *hēmōn* ("our"), or *sou* ("your") in Psalms, the first *ho theos* is nominative according to Harris. But the vocative cannot be ruled out in Ps 21:2; 42:4; 62:2. Fourth, the reason that the author cites both vv. 7,8 of Psalm 45 is not to introduce a further comparison between the Son and angels "but primarily to

[82] See n. 59 in Harris (*Jesus as God*, 218) for references.

demonstrate that to address the exalted son as 'God' is to compromise neither the primacy of the Father nor the subordination of the Son. It is appropriate for the Son to address the Father as 'my God' as it is for the Father to address the Son as 'God.'"[83] Ellingworth made the point that if v. 9 stood alone, the first *ho theos* would naturally be understood as a nominative, but he, following Attridge, took it as a vocative in light of the parallelism with v. 8.[84] According to Cullmann, the main point in Heb 1:8–9 is that the author "unequivocally applies the title 'God' to Jesus."[85]

The final question to be addressed in this verse is the identity of the "companions" (*metochous*). They are often viewed as angels. But this is unlikely since the focus is on the superiority of the Son to angels, and all the other uses of this term in Hebrews refer to Christians (3:1,14; 6:4; 12:8). Better is the view that the companions are the "many sons" of 2:10, who in v. 11 are called the Son's "brothers" and who in 3:14 are referred to as "those who have come to share in Christ," which translates the same Greek word in 1:9. It is possible that both angels and Christians are in view. Whoever the companions are, the point is that the Son is anointed and they are not (*para* probably here conveys an exclusive rather than merely a comparative sense).[86]

What then is the theological significance of this vocative in 1:8? Within the entire context of 1:5–13 where the superiority of the Son to the angels is proven by numerous contrasts, it is not so much in these contrasts, stark though they be, that the Son is seen to be so incomparable with the angels. Rather, the chief point made by the author in these verses is the Son belongs to an altogether different category than the angels. He possesses the divine nature since he is addressed by God as God. No angel was ever given the title *theos* because no angel possesses the divine nature. Jesus, as eternal deity, exists on an entirely different plane than the angels who are created beings. It is the author's intent in quoting Psalm 45 to advocate the full deity of the Son as indicated by the use of the vocative *theos*.[87]

---

[83] Harris, *Jesus as God*, 220.

[84] Ellingworth, *Hebrews*, 124; Cf. Attridge, *Hebrews*, 59; O. Cullmann, *Christology of the New Testament*, trans. S. C. Guthrie and C. A. M. Hall, rev. ed. (Philadelphia: Westminster, 1963), 310.

[85] Cullmann, *Christology*, 310–11. The Greek text of this Psalm has nuances that could have contributed to the author's messianic interpretation/application of it to Christ, according to Gheorghita (*Role of the Septuagint*, 60).

[86] See BDAG 758: "When a comparison is made, one member of it may receive so little attention as to pass fr. consideration entirely, so that 'more than' becomes *instead of, rather than, to the exclusion of*." BDAG gives the translation: "he has anointed thee and not thy comrades." *GAGNT* 655, renders παρά "rather than" (cf. HCSB).

[87] As noted by Cullmann (*Christology*, 310) and against those who would claim that the writer had no intention of suggesting that Jesus is God or that the deity of the Son is not necessary to the author's point in Hebrews 1. See L. D. Hurst, "The Christology of Hebrews 1 and 2," in *The Glory of Christ in the New Testament* (Oxford: Clarendon Press, 1987), 159, on the importance of the theology of 1:8.

In the broader context of Hebrews 1–2, as well as the entire book, the attribution of deity to Jesus the Son in chap. 1 is balanced by the focus on his humanity in chap. 2. He is both fully God and fully man. As the Christological councils recognized, Jesus being both "God" and "Son" balances the Father's primacy and the Son's subordination in that the Son addresses the Father as "my God" and the Father addresses the Son as "God." While the Son is fully God, he is not only fully divine but also fully human by virtue of the incarnation. The author of Hebrews considered Jesus to be fully divine, asserting that Jesus possesses the divine nature (1:3), exists eternally (7:16; 9:14; 13:8), existed before the universe (1:10), existed before human history (1:2), existed before his incarnation (10:5), and existed before Melchizedek (7:3). He is the creator (1:10), sustainer (1:3), and heir of the universe (1:2). He is at one and the same time "God" (1:8), "Lord" (1:10), and "Son of God" (4:14). Likewise, Jesus is fully human (2:11), without sin (4:15), belonging to the tribe of Judah (7:14), and one who experienced the gamut of human emotions such as weeping (5:7), temptation (4:15), suffering (5:8), and death (2:9). This balanced Christology is crucial for a proper interpretation of Hebrews.

1:10–12 In vv. 10–12, the author introduced a sixth quotation, this one from Ps 102:25–27. The quotation affirms, in reference to the universe, the Son's activity in creation (v. 10) as well as his eschatological activity (vv. 11–12), with the focus on the latter. A conceptual *inclusio* of beginning and ending occurs with the use of "in the beginning" (v. 10a, an allusion to Gen 1:1) and "your years will never end" (v. 12d). The eternality of the Son has already been established in the prologue, which states that it was through the agency of the Son that the universe was created, and vv. 7–8 affirm his eternality also. Now this theme is developed in vv. 10–12.

Although Psalm 102 was originally addressed to God, the author of Hebrews quoted it as addressed to the Son by virtue of the introductory "He also says," which continues the introductory formula of v. 8. This quotation constitutes the third direct address of the Father to the Son. The Son has already been addressed by God as "God," and now the words of Psalm 102 are addressed to the Son who is called "Lord."[88] The quotation is from the LXX with a few alterations,[89] including the addition of *kurios* ("Lord"), the movement of *su* ("you") to the clause beginning for emphasis (it could be rendered, "In the beginning it was you who . . ."), and the addition of the phrase "like a garment" before "and you will be changed" (v. 12b). Whether the latter was a part of an alternative LXX text used by the author or was inserted by him for clarity is unknown. Where the LXX has "and like a robe you will change [*allassō*]

---

[88] The addition of κύριος ("Lord") may have been the reason for the author's choice of this psalm in the catena according to Gheorghita (*Role of the Septuagint,* 62). The use of κύριος as a title in Hebrews indicates the author's intent to identify Jesus with Yahweh in the OT (cf. 7:14; 8:8,10,11; 10:16; 13:6,20).

[89] See Lane (*Hebrews 1–8*, 30–31) for the list.

them" (Ps 101:27) in v. 12, our author has "like a robe you will roll them up [*helissō*]," which heightens the vivid imagery and illustrates the author's penchant for word play.[90]

The NIV does not reflect that *su* ("you") heads its clause in v. 10a (after *kai*, "and"). But it was important for the author theologically, who was stressing the Son's existence before all creation. Since he preexists all things, he can be the creator of all things. This quotation serves, by its very structure, the author's purpose of identifying Jesus as the Son who existed eternally before all things were created and whose eternality will extend beyond all created things.

"You laid the foundations" is an idiomatic expression for the act of creation (v. 10a). That the heavens are the work of God's "hands" is a metonymy referring to divine power. The phrase "work of your hands" (v. 10b) is placed first in the clause for emphasis just like "you" (v. 10a). All the focus is on the activity of the Son as Lord, who was God's agent in the creation of the universe. Contrast is intended in v. 11 where both the pronouns "they" and "you" are overtly expressed to signal emphasis. The antecedent of "they" includes both the "earth" and the "heavens" (v. 10).

The point of contrast in vv. 11=12 is the perishability of the universe against the eternality of the Son, hence the simile of the worn out, rolled up garment. The main point is the twice repeated "you remain" in reference to the Son. The first (v. 11) renders the Greek word *diameneis,* with the prefix *dia* and the present tense emphasizing permanent existence, namely, eternality. The second "remain" (v. 12) is simply the present indicative of the Greek verb *einai* ("to be") preceded by the emphatic use of the pronoun "you," which the NIV renders as "you remain the same." The contrast is underlined by the pronoun "you" with the meaning of "but you yourself (unlike the perishing universe) remain the same." There is probably little or no distinction to be seen in the use of *himation* ("garment") and *peribolaion* ("robe"). Both refer to an outer garment that "wears out," which here describes the universe (v. 11) and elsewhere (8:13), interestingly enough, the first covenant (cf. Isa 50:9; 51:6).

These two verses contain a clear example of both semantic and grammatical chiasm. There are seven propositions arranged in inverse order that can be seen in both the propositional content as well as the verb tenses:

They will perish	(future tense)
But you remain	(present tense)
They will all wear out like a garment	(future tense)
You will roll them up like a robe	(future tense)
Like a garment they will be changed	(future tense)
But you remain the same	(present tense)
And your years will never end	(future tense)

[90] See discussion in S. Motyer ("The Psalm Quotations of Hebrews 1: A Hermeneutic Free-Zone?" *TynBul* 50, no. 1 [1999]: 20), followed by Gheorghita (*Role of the Septuagint*, 61).

The point of the quotation is to stress the impermanence of creation as contrasted with the eternality of the Son. In reference to this quotation, Ellingworth stated that "future tenses refer to change, and present tenses to a permanent state."[91] The verb tenses in vv. 10–12 (present, aorist, and future) explicate the Son's eternality in contrast with the created universe's temporality. Verse 12 concludes that the Son "will remain the same" forever and that his "years will never end." This quotation serves, by its very structure, the author's purpose of identifying Jesus as the eternal Son.

One should not miss the possible foreshadowing in vv. 10–12 of things to come in the epistle. In Jewish thought, the inner sanctuary and outer courts of the temple served to symbolize heaven and earth. This symbolism does not work in reverse. If, as Gleason suggested, the original *sitz im leben* of Psalm 102 was a lament of the destruction of Solomon's temple, it is possible that this is a metaphorical reference to the temple. Even though earth and heaven [the temple] perish, the Lord is the same and his years have no end. These verses have their counterpart in 12:26–28 where once again the author appeals to Psalm 102, where he stated that what was once thought stable is now shaken. Gleason suggested that the author's intent here is to emphasize the stability of Jesus at a time when the Herodian temple was on the verge of being destroyed.[92]

This quotation also prepares the reader for what is brought out later in 7:3, where Jesus the Son is compared to Melchizedek as the eternal, abiding high priest who "remains forever." Finally, the transitoriness of the old covenant is a theme that the author steadily built to a climax at 8:10–13. God considers the old covenant to be "worn out" and he has already made the change to the new covenant through the blood of Jesus the Son. Psalm 102:25–27 provides the author with a text to be interpreted messianically, a text to establish the eternality of the Son in comparison to the universe, and by analogy, it provides a portent of what is to come later in the epistle with respect to the relationship of the old covenant to the new covenant—temporariness versus permanence.

1:13–14 The third and final sub-paragraph of Heb 1:5–14 contains the seventh quotation (v. 13) of the catena and a summary comment by the author in v. 14 that serves simultaneously as closure for this paragraph and as an introductory link to 2:1–4. The quotation formula "to which of the angels did God ever say" is overtly given because the addressee has shifted from the Son back to the author's audience, hence the parallel with the almost identical quotation formula of v. 5. The use of the perfect tense here rather than the aorist of v. 5 shifts the aspectual focus from punctiliar to durative. The exaltation took place in the past from the perspective of the author, but with an abiding effect—eternal enthronement. The use of *de* (v. 13) marks a contrast with what

[91] Ellingworth, *Hebrews,* 128.

[92] R. Gleason, "Angels and the Eschatology of Heb 1–2," *NTS* 49 (2003): 97.

has been said about the Son (vv. 8–12) with what is now said about angels. The question is rhetorical, and implies a negative response, but it also implies that God did say this to the Son.

In the New Testament, Ps 110:1 is uniformly interpreted as messianic and applied to Jesus.[93] It is used by Jesus in the Gospels to prove his messiahship (Matt 22:42–45). This messianic interpretation forms the background to its use in the preaching of the apostles in Acts and the epistles. The exaltation of Christ at the right hand of God is a New Testament concept consistently connected with Ps 110:1.[94] The specific function of the quotation is twofold. First, in relation to what has been said in the prologue and now in 1:5–12, and in light of its accepted messianic character by the early church, it powerfully confirms the supremacy of Christ by virtue of his exaltation. Second, in relation to the argument of 2:1–18, and especially the exposition of Psalm 8 in 2:5–9, Ps 110:1 fits the author's focus on the period from Christ's enthronement to his final triumph; the "until" of 1:13 anticipating the "yet at the present" of 2:8.[95] That the Son sits at the right hand of God implies kingship, enthronement, authority, supremacy, and superior dignity. No notion of a time limit to the Son's rule should be inferred from the phrase "until I make" since the Son's eternal rule has already been established in v. 8. The "footstool" metaphor of v. 13 could be translated "until I put you in control of your enemies" or "until I cause you to rule over your enemies."[96]

The author's rhetorical question in v. 14 serves as a summary statement of vv. 5–13 rather than v. 13 alone. This is supported by the lexical repetition of "ministering" and "spirits," both of which occurred in v. 7. The emphatic negative *ouchi* ("not") and the emphatic use of *pantes* ("all") give the rhetorical question even more punch. "Ministering" translates the Greek word *leitourgikos*, which, along with its cognates in Hebrews, is always used (with the exception of this chapter) in speaking either of Old Testament worship or the function of Christ's priesthood. That the angels are "sent" implies delegated authority, in contradistinction to the Son who, although sent by God to provide salvation, has supreme authority. God is the implied agent of the sending in

---

[93] In the NT, Ps 110:1 and 110:4 are used together only in Hebrews. Psalm 110:1 is directly quoted only once (Heb 1:13), and it is alluded to on five occasions (1:3; 8:1; 10:12–13; 12:2). Psalm 110:4 is quoted three times (5:6; 7:17,21) and alluded to three times (5:10; 6:20; 7:3). See Hay, *Glory at the Right Hand,* 37; W. Loader, "Christ at the Right Hand—Ps. CX in the New Testament," *NTS* 24 (1978): 199–217; id., *Sohn und Hoherpriester. Eine traditionsgeschichtliche Untersuchung zur Christologie des Hebräerbriefes,* WMANT 53 (Neukirchen-Vluyn: Neukirchener Verlag, 1981), esp. 15–29; Hengel, *Studies in Early Christology*, 119–225, id., "'Sit at My Right Hand!' The Enthronement of Christ at the Right Hand of God and Psalm 110"; and esp. Anderson, *The King-Priest of Psalm 110 in Hebrews*, 164–76.

[94] So F. Hahn, *Titles of Jesus in Christology* (London: Lutterworth, 1969), 287, followed by Hengel, *Studies in Early Christology*, 134.

[95] Ellingworth, *Hebrews*, 130–31.

[96] L&N 1:37.8.

v. 14. The Greek text uses the noun "service" preceded by the preposition *eis* denoting purpose (lit. "for service"). The event proposition contained in the noun "service" is accurately rendered by a verbal proposition in the NIV: "sent to serve."

"Those who will inherit salvation" are the beneficiaries of angelic ministry. They must be believers—the many sons being brought to glory (2:10). This verse illuminates the interplay of realized eschatology with its "already" and futuristic eschatology with its "not yet." The doctrinal sections of the epistle focus on the former, while the parenetic sections focus on the latter. Meier put it well: "What the Son-become-man already is on the basis of the past act of exaltation (*hon ethēken klēronomon, keklēronomēken*), the believing community is called to be at the end of its pilgrimage towards the heavenly city (*tous mellontas klēronomein*)."[97] "Those who will inherit salvation" are the believers who are destined to this inheritance.[98] The implication of the inheritance is that it is a prior arrangement for a yet future event that has been bequeathed to all believers by the Son. The Son has the power to give this inheritance to believers since he (according to v. 2) has been appointed heir of all things. All three of the last three words in the Greek text of 1:14 are major themes that are developed in the rest of the epistle: (1) *mellō*—used seven additional times primarily of the eschatological realities promised but not yet fully realized; (2) *klēronomein*—the believer's reception of a permanent possession; and (3) *sōtērian*—the final salvation that believers will inherit. Ellingworth paraphrased v. 14: "All these angels, as we have been showing from scripture, are subordinate to God and therefore to Christ as Son. They live to worship God in heaven, and serve him by being sent on earthly missions for the benefit of those to whom God is to give salvation."[99]

This catena of quotations serves as the grounds for what was stated about the Son in the prologue. By concluding the catena of quotations with Ps 110:1, the author referred back to v. 3 where he stated that the Son, after he made purification for sins, sat down at the right hand of God. Structurally, this functions as an *inclusio* and binds the chapter together. Westfall correctly stated that the author's choice of quotations "grammaticalizes an interpersonal intimacy or directness between God the Father and the son [*sic*] that sets the son [*sic*] apart in his ability to transmit God's message and his status as the ultimate messenger."[100]

The final two verses are also related to 2:1–4 through tail-head linkage since the "angels" and "salvation" are topics in these verses too. Verse 13 also

[97] Meier, "Symmetry and Theology," 520.

[98] Dods, "The Epistle to the Hebrews," in *The Expositors Greek Testament*, ed. R. Nicoll (London: Hodder & Stroughton, 1903; repr., Grand Rapids: Eerdmans, 1974), 4:257–58.

[99] Ellingworth, *Hebrews*, 133.

[100] C. Westfall, *A Discourse Analysis of the Letter to the Hebrews: The Relationship Between Form and Meaning*, LNTS 297 (London: T&T Clark, 2006), 93.

prepares the way for what is said in 2:5–9. Psalm 110 and Psalm 8 are connected elsewhere in the Gospels and in Paul. It is likely the same occurs here. God's salvation plan for his people is accomplished by and realized in the incarnate, crucified, resurrected, and exalted Son. The author could not have affirmed what he did in 2:5–9 without first having established that Christ is the fulfillment of Ps 110:1. Finally, the relationship of vv. 13–14 to the rest of the epistle can be seen in that—since the kingly imagery of Ps 110:1 is applied to Jesus—the priestly imagery of Ps 110:4 is applied to him as well. This will find its theological expression in Heb 5:1–10:18.

Rhetorically, according to Bateman, the author wove together the seven Old Testament quotations in the form of a "conceptual chiasm" to make a theological statement about the Son:

A The Son's Status as Davidic King (Ps 2:7; 2 Sam 7:14) (1:5)
B The Son's Status as God (Deut 32:43; Ps 104:4) (1:6,7)
C The Son's Status as Divine Davidic King (Ps 45:6,7) (1:8,9)
B´ The Son's Status as God (Ps 102:25–27) (10–12)
A´ The Son's Status as Davidic King (Ps 110:1) (1:13)

Bateman's conclusion is that "two Jewish concepts about a future Davidic king and God are merged hermeneutically and exegetically and thereby find fulfillment in one person, the Son."[101] The repetition of and placement of Ps 110:1 at the beginning (1:3 where it is an allusion) and the end of the catena as well as its use throughout Hebrews mark it as the key Old Testament passage for the author of Hebrews. The author considered Jesus to be the Son and Messiah who was promised to David, who inaugurated the Davidic kingdom by his exaltation to the right hand of the Father in heaven, and who thus began the fulfillment of the Davidic covenant.[102] The implication is that the Son's rule will have an earthly dimension that will be fulfilled, according to premillennialists, in a one thousand year earthly reign over all the nations and in an eternal, cosmic dimension where he reigns over all things.

In summary, Hebrews 1 affirms that God has no greater messenger than his Son for a world in desperate need of redemption, and Jesus as the Son is both the supreme revealer and the supreme revelation. Three titles are given to Jesus in chapter 1: Son, God, and Lord. The focus is on the "Son," with "God"

[101] Bateman, "Early Jewish Hermeneutics," 244; and his "Two First-Century Messianic Uses of the OT," 11–27, esp. 26–27. Bauckham likewise saw a chiastic pattern in these verses with the fourth quotation at the center. The first three quotations characterize the Son as Son. The fifth and sixth quotations characterize the Son as eternal. The first line of the fifth quotation, "Your throne, O God, is forever and ever," and the last line of the sixth quotation, "your years will never end," are semantically equivalent. The seventh quotation is a summary conclusion. The fourth quotation is central because it contrasts the angels with the Son, the theme of the first three quotations, and then contrasts the angels with the Son as eternal, which is the theme of the fifth and sixth quotations ("Monotheism and Christology in Hebrews 1," 177).

[102] So argued by Anderson, *The King-Priest of Psalm 110 in Hebrews*, 138–76.

indicating the writer's attribution of deity to the Son and "Lord" indicating his sovereignty. The Son is superior to the angels since he is "God" who receives worship, and "Lord" since he is the sovereign, changeless creator. By what is stated in vv. 3,8,9, the author not only proved the superiority of Jesus to the angels, he also affirmed that Jesus shares co-equally with the Father the divine nature while remaining distinct from him.[103] The use of "all" in v. 14 sums up the entire catena by placing Jesus in the position of God in relation to the angelic hosts in that he shares in the divine eternality and sovereignty, whereas the angels are mere created beings and servants. The final quotation, placing Jesus on the divine throne, attributes to him, according to Jewish understanding, divine identity.

While a number of issues remain unresolved in this catena of quotations, one thing seems crystal clear: the author's exegetical method of reading the Old Testament with Christocentric glasses appears squarely within the apostolic tradition as evidenced in the New Testament. He has also made use of accepted Jewish exegetical techniques coupled with an explication of Second Temple Jewish theology about God to illustrate both the divine nature of Jesus and how he can be worshipped as God in a monotheistic Jewish framework.

(2) Exhortation (2:1–4)

[1]We must pay more careful attention, therefore, to what we have heard, so that we do not drift away. [2]For if the message spoken by angels was binding, and every violation and disobedience received its just punishment, [3]how shall we escape if we ignore such a great salvation? This salvation, which was first announced by the Lord, was confirmed to us by those who heard him. [4]God also testified to it by signs, wonders and various miracles, and gifts of the Holy Spirit distributed according to his will.

Hebrews 2:1–18 is part of a larger section that begins with 1:5 and comprises two subsections: 1:5–14 and 2:1–18. This second subsection begins with a paragraph unit in 2:1–4 that links the two sections together. The use of *dia touto* ("therefore") signals a shift in topic followed by a warning of the danger of neglecting to listen to the things spoken by the Lord and "those who heard him"; it also signals a shift in genre from expository to hortatory.[104] The use of "we" and "us" indicates a shift to a more direct address to the readers. The two paragraphs in chap. 1 (vv. 1-4,5–14) function as the grounds or reason for the

[103] See the concluding remarks of Harris (*Jesus as God*, 227) in his discussion of 1:8–9.

[104] See L. L. Neeley for the discourse paragraph boundary markers that reveal the onset of a new paragraph in Heb 2:1–4: "Frequent shift between expository and hortatory genres is a pronounced characteristic of Hebrews. The distinctions between these two genres is indicated in the surface structure, especially by the verbal system. Hortatory genre is characterized by imperative verbs or subjunctives with imperative intent, and first and second person predominate. In expository genre, verbs are generally indicative, and third person has greater frequency" ("A Discourse Analysis of Hebrews," *OPTAT* 3–4 [1987]: 3–4, 6). Cf. G. Guthrie, *The Structure of Hebrews: A Text-Linguistic Analysis*, (Leiden: Brill, 1994), 63–64.

exhortation in 2:1–4, with the focus on the *person* of Christ; the following three paragraphs (vv. 5–9,10–13,14–18) function as the grounds or reason for 2:1–4 as well, with the focus on the *work* of Christ.[105] Furthermore, in 1:1–14, Jesus is superior to the angels as *Son*, while in 2:5–14 he is superior to the angels as *man* via the incarnation, atonement, and exaltation. Hebrews 2:1–4 is the only hortatory paragraph in the first two chapters.[106]

The analysis of 2:1–4 begins with its internal structure, both syntactically and semantically.[107] The syntactic structure may be displayed with a slightly more literal rendering.

Therefore [*dia touto*]
it is necessary [*dei*]
  to pay attention more carefully [*perissoterōs*]
    to what we have heard
  so that we do not drift away [*mēpote pararuōmen*].
²*For* [*gar*]
  if the message spoken by angels was binding,
  and [if] every violation and disobedience received its just punishment,
  ³[then] how shall we escape
    if we ignore such a great salvation?
      which [salvation]
        was first announced by the Lord,
        was confirmed to us by those who heard him.
          ⁴God also testifying to it [the salvation]
            by both signs,
            and wonders,
            and various miracles,
            and gifts of the Holy Spirit
              distributed according to his will.

At the very least, the adverb *perissoterōs* indicates the comparative idea of paying closer attention to something, although some think the comparative form expresses a superlative meaning: "we should give the very closest attention

[105] See Beekman, Callow, and Kopesec, *The Semantic Structure of Written Communication* (Dallas: Summer Institute of Linguistics, 1981), 106–7, for a discussion with illustrations of the semantic category of grounds in discourse.

[106] F. C. Synge's theory that the paragraph is an interpolation (*Hebrews and the Scriptures* [London: S.P.C.K., 1959], 44–45) is unsupported and has been well answered by W. Lane: "It is neither necessary nor plausible and is sufficiently refuted by literary and thematic considerations" (*Hebrews 1–8*, 36).

[107] For semantic structure, see N. Miller, *The Epistle to the Hebrews: An Analytical and Exegetical Handbook* (Dallas: Summer Institute of Linguistics, 1988), 31–38; and P. Cotterell and M. Turner *Linguistics and Biblical Interpretation* (Downers Grove: InterVarsity, 1989), 201–3, 217–23). For lexical and syntactical information see J. H. Greenlee, *Exegetical Summary of Hebrews* (Dallas: Summer Institute of Linguistics, 1998), 41–51.

to."[108] A negative purpose introduced by *mēpote* followed by the aorist subjunctive *pararuōmen* concludes v. 1: "so that we do not drift away." The verb "drift" here is usually taken to have an active meaning in spite of its passive form, but some take it with the meaning of "to be drifted past; to be carried away; to be flowed by." Verse 1 is one sentence in the Greek text and the main point of the paragraph, with vv. 2–4 (a second complete sentence in the Greek text) modifying it, as indicated by the *gar* ("for") in v. 2. The second sentence begins with two conditional clauses governed by a single *ei* ("if"). The consequence is found in vv. 3–4 expressed primarily by the rhetorical question, "how shall we escape?" This is followed by another condition expressed by the conditional participial clause, lit., "ignoring such a great salvation." The rest of the paragraph is a complex relative clause introduced by the pronoun *hētis*, "which," and describes this salvation. The participial (genitive absolute) construction beginning v. 4 serves to describe further the confirmation by affirming that God himself testified to the salvation message with signs, wonders, miracles, and gifts given by the Holy Spirit.

Syntactically, the two-sentence paragraph comprises a warning in v. 1 followed by two conditional statements. Semantically, the *gar* ("for") beginning vv. 2–4 marks the verses as the grounds or reason for the exhortation to pay careful attention to what has been heard. Within v. 1, the statement "we must pay more careful attention . . . to what we have heard" is actually a condition in the form of an exhortation followed by the consequence to be avoided: "so that we do not drift away." The reason given in vv. 2–4 is essentially, "We shall not escape [some form of punishment] if we ignore such a great salvation." The reason such foolishness is so perilous is that the law, given through the agency of angels under the old covenant, was binding and all disobedience was punished. Thus, no one can escape punishment if he disobeys the message of salvation given in the superior new covenant.[109]

Several points of similarity can be noted between Heb 1:1–4 and 2:1–4. The prologue states that God has spoken "to us" in the Son in these last days, while in 2:1–4 the message of salvation was confirmed "to us." In 1:1–4 God speaks in the Son, and in 2:1–4 the Son preaches the word of salvation while God validates the message. In 2:1–4 God formerly spoke "by angels" in the old covenant but now speaks by the Son in the new covenant. In 1:1–4 God formerly spoke by prophets, but now he speaks to us in the Son. In both paragraphs, the language of speaking and hearing predominates.[110] In both paragraphs there

---

[108] So J. A. Moffatt, *A Critical and Exegetical Commentary to the Hebrews,* ICC (Edinburgh: T&T Clark, 1924), 17; P. E. Hughes, *A Commentary on the Epistle to the Hebrews* (Grand Rapids: Eerdmans, 1977), 73; and Lane, *Hebrews 1–8*, 37.

[109] See the discussion in Miller (*Hebrews*, 31–38) and Cotterell and Turner (*Linguistics*, 217–23) on the semantic relationships within the paragraph.

[110] Two rhetorical features occur in both paragraphs: alliteration with the Greek letter π and the use of rhyming. Also notice the adverbs that begin 1:1 and the use of words ending in –σιν in 2:4.

is a sense of discontinuity, but this sense is likewise overshadowed in both paragraphs by the continuity between the old covenant people and the new covenant people, since God is the ultimate speaker in both covenants (and in both paragraphs). Both covenant communities governed by the Old and New Testaments were constituted by an act of divine revelation. Neither paragraph is in opposition to written Scripture since the reference to the prophets in 1:1–4 includes their writings and encompasses the entire written Old Testament as the speech of God. Lane correctly points out that "the message spoken by angels" (2:2) is semantically simply another way of expressing that God spoke his Word through the prophets (1:1).[111] Although the New Testament canon was incomplete at the time of the writing of Hebrews, the New Testament Scriptures are just as much the Word of God as the Old Testament since they were pre-authenticated by Jesus in John 16:13–15.

2:1 Hebrews 2 begins with the connector *dia touto* ("therefore"). The issue is determining how far back into chap. 1 it reaches. Ellingworth construed "therefore" to connect only to the final words of 1:14 with the meaning, "Because God intends to give us salvation as a permanent possession, we must be all the more attentive to what he and others have said about it."[112] "Therefore" could connect the entire paragraph in 1:5–14 to 2:1–4, or most likely, it includes the entire argument of Hebrews 1.

The hortatory nature of 2:1–4 is immediately obvious in v. 1: "We must pay more careful attention, therefore, to what we have heard, so that we do not drift away." The combination of *dei* ("must," lit. "it is necessary") with the comparative adverb *perissoterōs* ("more careful") followed by *prosechō* ("pay attention to") and *pararuōmen* ("drift away") arrests the attention of the reader with a strong warning. The use of *dei* indicates strong necessity. Whether a logical or moral necessity or both is difficult to decide, but the immediate and broader context of Hebrews favors both.

Prosechein is in this context most likely a technical nautical term meaning "to hold a ship toward port"[113] since the author used *pararrein* ("to drift"), another nautical term, in the same verse. The term also can be used in a general non-nautical sense, and some commentators prefer to so take it in this verse. But given the overall context and the similar metaphor in Heb 6:19 (an anchor that holds sure and steadfast), the nautical reference is likely. It has been suggested that *prosechein* indicates the fastening of the anchor to the seabed to

---

Picturesque vocabulary is found in 2:1–4. Lane probably overstated the contrast, claiming that the language of chap. 1 was "sanctioned by the LXX," whereas here we have "an idiomatic Hellenistic diction" (*Hebrews 1–8,* 35). Preferable is Ellingworth's view that this passage "combines rare or distinctive expressions with Septuagintal or traditional Christian language" (*Hebrews,* 134).

[111] Lane, *Hebrews 1–8*, 38.

[112] As noted by Ellingworth, *Hebrews*, 135.

[113] See LSJ 1512; but BDAG (880) does not mention this meaning.

keep the ship from drifting.[114] What better way for the author to picture for his readers a sense of drifting from the truth of what they had been taught than by the use of the metaphor of a drifting ship carried by currents beyond some fixed point. The author used a cognate *(katechein)* when he exhorted the readers to "hold on" or "hold firmly" (3:6,14; a third use is in 10:23, "hold unswervingly").

Ellingworth suggested that the author may have had in mind Moses' exhortation to the people in Deut 32:46, "Take to heart all of these words" (*prosechete tē kardia epi pantas tous logous toutous*) when he used the term *prosechein,* since he quoted Deut 32:43 in Heb 1:6.[115] This suggestion seems plausible given that the warning in 2:1–4 had to do with failure to obey the word of God and that Heb 3:7–4:11 uses the example of the exodus generation that did disobey God's word. Interestingly, the only other place where *prosechein* is followed by the strong negative *mēpote* ("so that . . . not") as here is in Luke 21:34, "Be careful, or your hearts will be weighed down." In v. 33 Jesus said that "Heaven and earth will pass away, but my words will never pass away."

The readers are exhorted to pay close attention "to what we have heard." As used in Hebrews (with the exception of 12:19), the phrase "to what we have heard" implies submissive acceptance of what is heard. The author makes prominent throughout the epistle the theme of salvation as that which is spoken by God and the prologue states God "has spoken" in his Son, Jesus. Contextually, "to what we have heard" refers to the message received from both Jesus and the early Christian witnesses.[116] The consequence of failing to pay attention to the word is that the readers will "drift away," where the word in Greek can mean "drift" or "slip away" as the lexicons indicate.[117] The context and that the verb is not followed by an object probably indicate that the author intended the meaning "drift away."

2:2 Verse 2 begins a comparison between the circumstances surrounding the giving of the law to Moses through angelic mediation on Mt. Sinai and the salvation brought by Christ (v. 3). The argument is *a fortiori* from law to gospel, a hermeneutical method described by the rabbis as *qal wahomer* (light and heavy). The belief that angels acted as intermediaries in the giving of the law to Moses may have originated in Deut 33:2 where the LXX reads "angels were with him at his right hand." Since the author just made reference to Ps 110:1 (see 1:13) where God told the Son, not angels, to sit at his right hand, the connection with Deut 33:2 is even more likely. Both Josephus

[114] So P. Teodorico, "Metafore nautiche in *Ebr.* 2, 1 e 6, 19," *RevistB* 6 (1958): 33–49. The term also occurs twice in Luke's writings (Acts 8:6,10) and once in Peter's (2 Pet 1:19), all meaning "to pay attention to a speaker."

[115] Ellingworth, *Hebrews,* 136.

[116] Ibid.

[117] See BDAG 770; and *TDOT* 7:478–79. In the LXX of Prov 3:21, παραρρεῖν is used to translate the Hebrew לוז + מֵעֵינֵי "to escape from someone's sight" (HALOT).

and the New Testament affirm this tradition of angelic mediation.[118] The use of "by" (NIV) to express agency here leaves unclear that it is God who gave the law through angelic mediation. It is preferable to render the preposition *dia* as "through" rather than "by," which implies God as the ultimate speaker. The use of "message," which translates *lalētheis logos* ("the message spoken"), instead of "law" is most likely due to the author's focus on God's speaking rather than on the actual content of what was spoken, namely, the law.

The message that came through angelic mediation is said to be *bebaios* ("binding"), which in the papyri is virtually a technical term implying legal security.[119] It occurs again in v. 3 and other crucial places in the epistle (3:14; 6:19; 9:17). It qualifies something as valid with the additional connotations of being trustworthy, dependable, reliable, unalterable, and securely established (here the result of having been spoken by God). A second conditional statement (with the conditional particle implied) occurs in v. 2b: "every violation and disobedience received its just punishment." "Violation" renders *parabasis* and refers to a "transgression" or "infringement" in the sense of overstepping. The reference is almost always to the Jewish law that is being transgressed (see Rom 2:23; Gal 3:19). "Disobedience" renders *parakoē*, which can be defined as "unwillingness to hear."[120] In the New Testament this word refers to a failure to listen and thus heed what God is saying (Matt 18:17; Mark 5:36) or to disobedience as a result of inattention (Rom 5:19; 2 Cor 10:6).[121] The first word emphasizes the *character* of sin as transgression; the second word emphasizes the *cause* of sin as inattention. Both nouns imply willful rejection that issues in disobedience. The punishment for such disobedience is "just" (*endikos*) based on what is right and appropriate. The only other use of this word is in Rom 3:8 where it is translated "deserved." *Misthapodosia* ("punishment") occurs only in Hebrews and in later ecclesiastical literature. It is used here in an ironic sense because the meaning of the term is normally reward in the sense of receiving payment, but here the "reward" is actually "punishment."[122] Westcott captured the meaning of the verse well: "The necessity of heedful care is grounded on the certainty of retribution."[123]

---

[118] Josephus, *Ant.* 15.5.3; Acts 7:38; Gal. 3:19. See J. G. McConville's argument for his translation of Deut 33:2b: "and with him myriads of holy ones, angels at his right hand" (*Deuteronomy,* ApOTC [Downers Grove: InterVarsity, 2002], 462, 465).

[119] G. A. Deissmann, *Bible Studies: Contributions Chiefly from Papyri and Inscriptions to the History of the Language, the Literature, and the Religion of Hellenistic Judaism and Primitive Christianity*, 2nd ed., trans. A. Grieve (Edinburgh: T&T Clark, 1903), 104–9; cf. MM 107–8.

[120] BDAG 766.

[121] See the discussion in M. Erickson, *Christian Theology* (Grand Rapids: Baker, 1984), 2:567.

[122] Koester, *Hebrews*, 206.

[123] Westcott, *Hebrews*, 37.

2:3 The rhetorical question beginning v. 3 ("how shall we escape?") expresses the consequence of "ignor[ing] such a great salvation."[124] *Pōs* ("how?") in rhetorical questions, especially after a conditional sentence, has the force of a strong negative: "we shall in no way escape."[125] The word *ameleō* ("ignore"), which can also be translated "neglect," occurs again in Heb 8:9 as part of a quotation of Jer 31:31–34: "because they did not remain faithful to my covenant, and I *turned away* from them, declares the Lord." Jesus used the term in a parable describing those who "paid no attention" to the invitation to the marriage supper (Matt 22:5). In the immediate context of Heb 2:1–4 and the broader context of Hebrews as a whole, the author applied the word to believers so that the thought is not that the readers might fail to listen to the message when first given, but rather to cherish and heed it after having first known it. What they must not ignore is "such a great salvation."[126] The noun *sōtēria* ("salvation") picks up the thought of 1:14 where the angels serve those who are the heirs of salvation. The word here, as there, indicates salvation in its entirety at its completion in the eschaton. Three tenses of salvation can be discerned in the New Testament: Christians have been saved, are being saved, and one day shall be saved. The later eschatological sense of full, final, and complete salvation in the sense of deliverance from all sin and punishment is in view here. The author of Hebrews characteristically sees salvation more from a futuristic perspective as that which God will ultimately confer on his people. Ellingworth correctly noted *sōtēria* is one of those nouns that has embedded within it two possible semantic aspects. It may mean the act or state of being saved (the predominant sense in the New Testament), or it could mean the message about salvation, which best fits the context and its use in Heb 6:9.[127]

Two important interpretive points need to be made here. First, the reasons for the neglect are not stated. One should refrain from speculation until the epistle itself sheds more light on this. Second, the text does not mention what one will not escape from, although some form of judgment or retribution is implied by the comparison in v. 2. If ignoring or neglecting this great salvation is interpreted to mean rejecting it, then final judgment is in view.[128] But the text does not say that salvation was rejected, and there is a difference in rejecting and neglecting. This impinges on the question of the spiritual identity of the readers, whether they were Christians or not—a topic taken up later.

Two characteristics of this great salvation are presented in the remainder of v. 3. First, it was first announced by the Lord and it was confirmed "to us" by

---

[124] The participial form can indicate the protasis of a conditional statement, as here, and is thus translated "if we ignore."

[125] Ellingworth, *Hebrews*, 139.

[126] The correlative adjective τηλικαύτης ("such a great") is used like a demonstrative pronoun. cf. S. Porter, *Idioms of the Greek New Testament* (Sheffield: Academic Press, 1995), 135.

[127] Ellingworth, *Hebrews*, 139.

[128] Dods, "Hebrews," 259.

those who heard him. What makes the neglect of this salvation such an egregious act is that its greatness is measured by who first gave it—none other than the Son, the Lord Jesus Christ. The first characteristic is presented in a fairly common Greek idiom that literally translated would read, "which having received a beginning to be spoken by the Lord," but "which was first announced by the Lord" (NIV) is correct. Lane pointed out how, in a comprehensive sense, Jesus' entire life and ministry, including his preaching, death, resurrection and exaltation, is said to be the beginning of the message of salvation.[129] This message was proclaimed "by" the Lord, where the preposition *dia* parallels its use in v. 2, "by angels." Just as the angels were agents, so Christ as the Son is God's agent, but as we have seen, he is more than just a mediator, he is God himself. The aorist participle *labousa* is treated by most translators like a finite verb expressing action preceding the following verb (as in the NIV). But Lane took the participle as indicating an action prior to the following verb: "First announced by God through the Lord himself, it was guaranteed to us."[130] It could also be a temporal adverbial participle: "After it was at the first spoken through the Lord, it was confirmed to us" (NASB). Westcott observed that *laleisthai* ("spoken") following the participle *labousa* calls attention to the author's present preaching and that it was based on the original preaching of Christ.[131]

Second, this salvation was "confirmed to us by those who heard him." The author continued the comparison of the giving of the law by using the verbal form of the same word translated "binding" (v. 2), which is rendered "confirmed" in v. 3. The referent "those who heard him" need not be limited to the apostles. By speaking of "hearers," the focus is on the message, not an office or position. The text does not specify who or what was heard with any overt object; hence, the object could be Jesus[132] or the message of salvation.[133] Neither does the text affirm the second generation status of the author and readers, although it would seem to indicate such is the case.[134] The concern in Heb 2:3–4 is to connect the message the listeners had received with Jesus himself.[135] Though others brought the message of salvation, the true mediator of the message is the Son himself, which is the whole point of the prologue and this paragraph.

2:4 The paragraph concludes here with the unusual compound participle *sunepimarturountos,* which never occurs in the LXX and is found only here

[129] Lane, *Hebrews 1–8,* 39.

[130] Ibid., 35.

[131] Westcott, *Hebrews,* 39.

[132] Lane, *Hebrews 1–8,* 39; Ellingworth, *Hebrews,* 141.

[133] Attridge, *Hebrews*, 67. Cf. the phrase here with Luke 1:2.

[134] Most commentators since the Reformation era have remarked on the unlikelihood that such a statement would have been made by the apostle Paul. This is one of the arguments against the Pauline authorship of the epistle.

[135] As Koester rightly noted (*Hebrews,* 311).

in the New Testament.[136] It is, according to Ellingworth, emphasized by its position, rarity, complexity, and length.[137] The meaning is "to bear witness at the same time together with," and in this context it means that God joins the witness of the early preachers to confirm the truth of their witness by performing attendant miracles concomitant with their preaching of the gospel. Four words are used to describe God's joint witness. *Sēmeiois* ("signs") indicates a miracle but with the focus not on the miracle but on the meaning of the miracle. *Terasin* ("wonders") indicates a miracle that cannot be explained by natural means and that generates astonishment. These first two nouns are joined by *te kai* ("both . . . and"), which serves to join the two words more closely and probably indicates that both words refer to the same kind of miracles. *Semeia kai terata* became a stock phrase for the exodus, which served to identify God's working among his people with miracles. The combination is found in the Synoptic Gospels, John, Paul, and most frequently in Acts (eight times in chaps. 1–15). *Dunamēsin* ("miracles") indicates a mighty deed, an act of power. Here the focus is that miracles are a demonstration of God's power. The word is qualified by the adjective "various" indicating variety and diversity.[138] *Merismois* ("gifts") indicates distribution of gifts. Koester noted that this word is used for distribution of various things, including an inheritance. It is possible that the author had in mind "a kind of preliminary apportionment of future inheritance" such as in Eph 1:14.[139]

The genitive *pneumatos hagiou* ("of the Holy Spirit") can be taken objectively, in which case it was God who gave the Holy Spirit and the translation would be "distributing the gifts of the Holy Spirit,"[140] or subjectively, in which case it is the Holy Spirit who distributes the gifts.[141] These four nouns are instrumental datives, indicating the means by which God added his witness. These gifts were given "according to his will," meaning God's will, and since the pronoun "his" is fronted before the noun "will," it is given emphasis by

[136] P. Healey and A. Healey stated that in a stretch of non-narrative discourse where a major participant is assumed throughout but not topicalized for an extended part of the discourse, the genitive circumstantial participle construction can be used to reintroduce the participant without emphasis. Such is the case in Heb 2:4 where God is the major participant in the entire epistle up to this point, but was last referenced in 1:13. This use of the genitive participial clause occurs again in 9:8a with the Holy Spirit as the subject, and in 11:4,40 with God as the subject. ("The 'Genitive Absolute' and other Circumstantial Participial Clauses in the New Testament," unpublished manuscript [Dallas: Summer Institute of Linguistics, 1979], 142).

[137] Ellingworth, *Hebrews,* 141. Lane translated the phrase "while God . . . plainly endorsed their witness" (*Hebrews 1–8*, 34).

[138] Hughes took the first three nouns together rather than as three different forms of miracles (*Hebrews,* 40).

[139] Koester, *Hebrews,* 207; referencing *P. Oxy.* #493.

[140] So H. Alford, "Prolegomena and Hebrews," in *Alford's Greek Testament: An Exegetical and Critical Commentary*, 5th ed. (Boston: Lee & Shepard, 1878; repr., Grand Rapids: Guardian, 1976), 4:31; and Dods, "Hebrews," 260.

[141] So Lane, *Hebrews 1–8,* 34.

the author. *Thelēsis* ("will") is used only here in the New Testament. As distinguished from *thelēma*, the definite expression of will, it describes the active exercise of will.[142] Although the phrase "according to his will" could modify "gifts" alone, it may modify all four nouns.

The drift from the word that the author warned about is all the more disastrous in light of the past reception of the word on the part of the readers. The superior authority of the gospel is shown in its original announcement by the Lord, in its confirmed truthfulness in the proclamation to the readers by those who heard the Lord, and in God's diverse supernatural attestation to its truth.

THEOLOGICAL IMPLICATIONS. Several theological issues come into play in this paragraph. First, it is obvious that the author placed a high priority on the preaching of the gospel. In fact, as indicated earlier, many see Hebrews as a written sermon. The linguistic dominance and prominence of verbs of speaking and hearing in the epistle illustrate this. Second, this is the first of five so-called "warning passages" in Hebrews. The author alternated between exposition and exhortation. Chapter 1 is expositional in nature, without a single hortatory verb, and furnishes the ground for the exhortation in 2:1–4. The pastoral concern of the author is seen primarily in these hortatory sections. Obedience to the word is necessary; neglect leads to some form of retribution, though just what that entails is not spelled out in this paragraph. Third, this paragraph indicates that the readers are Christians. The author included himself in the warning, for he spoke of the gospel being confirmed "to us" and used metaphors of drifting and neglect to indicate that the readers possessed the salvation of which he spoke. Fourth, since the Son is God, how can he be the mediator? The answer is because he is the incarnate Son. The mediation of the Son depends on his incarnation as well as his deity, a point that is made theologically in 2:5–18. "An angel is neither God nor man. The mediatorial qualification of the Son is infinitely superior to that of the angels, for, as both God and man, he is uniquely qualified to effect reconciliation between God and man."[143] The author of Hebrews agreed with Paul that there is "one mediator between God and men, the man Christ Jesus" (1 Tim 2:5).

A fifth theological issue has to do with the duration of the miraculous gifts in v. 4. Both Lane and Ellingworth sought to show from the use of the present tense participle (NIV "testified," lit. "testifying") in v. 4 that God continues to give confirmation up to the point of time of the writing of Hebrews; thus one is left to infer, by extension, that these miraculous gifts are in vogue today. Lane remarked that the present participle "implies that the corroborative evidence was not confined to the initial act of preaching, but continued to be displayed within the life of the community."[144] But this is problematic on two counts.

---

[142] Westcott, *Hebrews,* 40.

[143] Hughes, *Hebrews,* 78.

[144] Lane, *Hebrews 1–8,* 39. B. B. Warfield held to the cessationist view (*Miracles: Yesterday and Today* [Grand Rapids: Eerdmans, 1953], 6), and W. Grudem argued the non-cessationist view

First, the present participle cannot be made to carry the semantic weight of ongoing miracles up to the time of the writer, and certainly not up to the present time. Second, to suggest such actually misses the point of the passage. The confirming testimony of God via the miracles was given to those who heard the Lord, not to the author and his readers. If God was still giving the gifts of miracles referred to in v. 4 at the time of the author and his readers, the text does not say so. In fact, the text may reasonably be interpreted to mean just the opposite, or at the very least to imply just the opposite.[145] The use of *sun* ("with") in the compound participle that begins v. 4 indicates that God bore witness *with* someone "to us." He did not bear witness "with" us and "to" us at the same time. Those whom God bore witness with must be "those who heard" the Lord. It was they who were performers of the gifts; the author and his readers were not performers but observers. Some of the readers of the epistle no doubt had contact with first-generation believers and thus had witnessed such miracles. The implication of this would be that the sign gifts lasted only so long as the eyewitnesses—meaning apostles and perhaps others—who heard the Lord lived. In the New Testament, the work of Christ and the apostles was "confirmed" by "signs and wonders" (see Acts 2:22; 14:3; Rom 15:18–20; 2 Cor 12:12). Jesus is the "cornerstone" of the church, and the apostles and prophets are the "foundation" (Eph 2:20). Apostolic ministry and miraculous gifts are linked together, and the significance of the latter is tied to the foundational nature of the former with respect to the church.[146]

In addition, the use of the past tense (aorist in Greek) "confirmed" implies that the miraculous gifts did not continue. Wallace made the point well:

> If such gifts continued, the author missed a great opportunity to seal his argument against defection. He could have simply said: "How shall we escape if we neglect so great a salvation, which was . . . confirmed to us by those who heard *and is still confirmed* among us while God bears witness with signs."[147]

Wallace was careful not to overstate the case when he said that Heb 2:3–4 "involve[s] some solid inferences that the sign gifts had for the most part ceased."[148] Koester likewise took a judicious approach to this question:

(*Systematic Theology: An Introduction to Biblical Doctrine* [Grand Rapids: Zondervan, 1994], 367) as it relates to Heb 2:3–4. S. Ferguson offered an irenic presentation of the cessationist view that covers the NT waterfront very well (*The Holy Spirit*, in *Contours of Christian Theology*, ed. G. Bray [Downers Grove: InterVarsity, 1996], 221–39).

[145] The best and most balanced treatment of this issue in Heb 2:3–4 is by D. Wallace ("Hebrews 2:3–4 and the Sign Gifts," at http://www.bible.org, 1–3). I am indebted to his analysis in this section.

[146] In one sense, virtually all Christians are cessationists in that apostleship was a gift that ceased at or near the end of the first century AD.

[147] Wallace, "Hebrews 2:3–4 and the Sign Gifts," 3.

[148] Ibid.

> The author did not seek to replicate the earlier ecstatic experience, since the basis of faith was not the miracles, but the message that was confirmed by the miracles. It is not clear whether the author assumed that miracles were still being done in his own time or whether the time of miracles had ceased. The author emphasizes perseverance rather than hope for miracles.[149]

Thus, Heb 2:3–4 has some bearing on the debate about spiritual gifts today between cessationists and non-cessationists. If all the miraculous gifts of the Spirit were active at the time of the writing of this epistle, one would expect vv. 3–4 to be written differently. If all the miraculous gifts were active at the time of the writing of Hebrews because some of the eyewitnesses (apostles and others) were still alive, the text seems to imply that once the eyewitnesses died the miraculous gifts ceased.

Hebrews 2:3–4 contains a good summary statement of what one finds in the book of Acts regarding the preaching of the gospel and the presence of signs and wonders. This point was well developed by W. C. van Unnik who argued that Acts is the "confirmation" of the Gospel of Luke. He saw the overall purpose of Luke-Acts as presenting God's plan of salvation through Jesus and how that salvation was brought to those who did not see Jesus incarnate.[150] Van Unnik appealed to Heb 2:3–4 as being descriptive of what Luke has accomplished in writing his two-volume work. The meaning of Heb 2:3–4 is that there is a solid bridge between the saving activity of Jesus and those who have had no personal contact with him. It is in the confirmation of this salvation sanctioned by God through miraculous gifts that the solidity of this bridge can be seen.[151] Van Unnik's conclusions as to the similar notion of "witness" in Luke-Acts and Hebrews was supported by Trites who pointed out that "the idea of witness appears a number of times in the Epistle to the Hebrews, a fact suggested by the use of words drawn from the vocabulary of witness . . . and the idea of witness is very similar to that which is unfolded in greater detail in the Book of Acts."[152]

---

[149] Koester, *Hebrews,* 211.

[150] W. C. van Unnik, "The 'Book of Acts': the Confirmation of the Gospel," *NTS* (1960): 26–59 (see esp. pp. 49, 58).

[151] Ibid., 48. The following comparisons were made by van Unnik (pp. 89–90): (1) The phrase in Heb 2:3 (ἥτις, ἀρχὴν λαβοῦσα λαλεῖσθαι διὰ τοῦ κυρίου) is parallel to Acts 1:1 (περὶ πάντων, ὦ Θεόφιλε, ὧν ἤρξατο ὁ Ἰησοῦς ποιεῖν τε καὶ διδάσκειν. (2) Some elements that are motifs in Acts occur in Heb 2:3–4: salvation, the idea of "bearing witness," signs and wonders, and distributions of the Holy Spirit. (3) The activity of God described in Heb 2:3–4 recalls "speaking boldly for the Lord" in Acts 14:3: τῷ μαρτυροῦντι [ἐπὶ] τῷ λόγῳ τῆς χάριτος αὐτοῦ, διδόντι σημεῖα καὶ τέρατα γίνεσθαι διὰ τῶν χειρῶν αὐτῶν. (4) The συν- in the compound verb of Heb. 2:4 emphasizes that there are other witnesses too; van Unnik referred this to the preceding verb ἐβεβαιώθη. The believers described as "those who heard him" (v. 3) are witnesses, which corresponds to Acts 1:8, "and you will be my witnesses."

[152] A. Trites, *The New Testament Concept of Witness,* SNTSM 31 (Cambridge: Cambridge University Press, 1977), 217.

Luke made it clear in his Gospel as well as in Acts that the word and the preaching of the word take precedence over miracles.[153] The source of the apostles' power to preach and work miracles is the prophetic Spirit they received at Pentecost. Their mission, like that of Jesus, is presented in prophetic terms throughout Acts and is characterized above all as a mission to speak the word of God. Like the author of Hebrews, Luke understood the preaching of the early church as standing in direct continuity with the preaching of the prophets in the Old Testament and with the prophetic ministry of Jesus. The risen Jesus continues his prophetic preaching ministry through the apostles and missionaries.[154] One cannot fail to be struck by the number of times the phrase "signs and wonders" occurs in Acts, and that it invariably occurs in close proximity to specific formal references to the "word" (*logos* or *rhēma*) of God. O'Reilly[155] pointed out how Luke deliberately pairs references to "word" with the phrase "signs and wonders," and in three cases the *inclusio* forms an a-b-a structure with "signs and wonders" as the middle element sandwiched between references to the "word." The significance of this as a commentary on Heb 2:3–4 can be seen in O'Reilly's comment:

> Hence, although the word, the word of the Lord, and the word of God are found in many contexts where there is no mention of signs, the signs are never found except in the immediate context of the word. This first glance at the data reveals, therefore, that while the word in Acts has a quite independent status relative to the "signs and wonders," the latter do not have a similar standing in relation to the word. From the literary point of view they are dependent on the word. This suggests that there is also perhaps a theological dependence, something which in any case we would expect given Luke's close adherence to the Old Testament conception of "signs and wonders.[156]

Whether or not Heb 2:3–4 favors the cessationist view, one must at least concede that the author, like Luke, placed greater emphasis on the preaching of the Word and saw miracles in a secondary, confirmatory role for the early church. The passage's emphasis is that our adherence to Christ is mediated and normalized by our adherence to the witness and doctrine of the apostles.[157]

---

[153] Against H. Conzelmann (*Die Mitte der Zeit: Studien zur Theologie des Lukas*. 4th ed. [Tübingen: Mohr, 1977], 177–80), who was adequately refuted by R. Dillon (*From Eye-Witnesses to Ministers of the Word: Tradition and Composition in Luke 24,* AnBib 82 [Rome: Biblical Institute, 1978], 127–28). Cf. I. H. Marshall, *The Gospel of Luke* (Exeter: Paternoster, 1978), 198–210; and esp. L. O'Reilly, *Word and Sign in the Acts of the Apostles: A Study in Lukan Theology,* Analecta Gregoriana 243 (Rome: Editrice Pontificia Universita Gregoriana, 1987).

[154] O'Reilly, *Word and Sign in the Acts of the Apostles*, 43–44.

[155] Ibid., 191–92.

[156] Ibid., 192.

[157] So R. Latourelle, *Theology of Revelation* (Staten Island: Alba House, 1966), 374.

The author's references to "what we have heard" (2:1) and to "those who heard him" (2:3) recall the topic sentence of the first paragraph (1:2) and thus show that he intended for everything in 1:1–14 to highlight the profound importance for the readers to heed the message.[158] Since this "great salvation" is the message about the Son, since he himself is the mediator of the message, and since he himself is God in human flesh, the possible failure on the part of the readers to obey such a word motivated the author to write this pastoral letter of warning and encouragement.

(3) Atonement Accomplished by Our High Priest (2:5–18)

5It is not to angels that he has subjected the world to come, about which we are
speaking. 6But there is a place where someone has testified:

> **"What is man that you are mindful of him,**
> **the son of man that you care for him?**
> **7You made him a little lower than the angels;**
> **you crowned him with glory and honor**
> **8and put everything under his feet."**

In putting everything under him, God left nothing that is not subject to him. Yet at
present we do not see everything subject to him. 9But we see Jesus, who was made
a little lower than the angels, now crowned with glory and honor because he suf-
fered death, so that by the grace of God he might taste death for everyone.
10In bringing many sons to glory, it was fitting that God, for whom and through
whom everything exists, should make the author of their salvation perfect through
suffering. 11Both the one who makes men holy and those who are made holy are of
the same family. So Jesus is not ashamed to call them brothers. 12He says,

> **"I will declare your name to my brothers;**
> **in the presence of the congregation I will sing your praises."**

13And again,

> **"I will put my trust in him."**

And again he says,

> **"Here am I, and the children God has given me."**

14Since the children have flesh and blood, he too shared in their humanity so
that by his death he might destroy him who holds the power of death—that is, the
devil— 15and free those who all their lives were held in slavery by their fear of
death. 16For surely it is not angels he helps, but Abraham's descendants. 17For this
reason he had to be made like his brothers in every way, in order that he might
become a merciful and faithful high priest in service to God, and that he might
make atonement for the sins of the people. 18Because he himself suffered when he
was tempted, he is able to help those who are being tempted.

---

158 D. DeSilva, *Perseverance in Gratitude: A Socio-Rhetorical Commentary on the Epistle to the Hebrews* (Grand Rapids: Eerdmans, 2000), 104.

2:5–9 Hebrews 2:5–18 is comprised of two main paragraphs: vv. 5–9 and vv. 10–18. The latter is further comprised of two sub-paragraphs: vv. 10–13 and vv. 14–18. Koester (and others) attempted to discern the structure of Hebrews by using classical rhetorical categories. He saw 1:1–2:4 as an "Exordium" with 2:5–9 as the "Proposition," and 2:10 begins the "Argument" that ends at 12:27.[159] While the author no doubt was rhetorically literate, this schema is too artificial for the intricate structure of the epistle and fails to see the semantic and linguistic interconnectedness of 2:5–18.

The conjunction *gar* links the new unit begun at 2:5 with the preceding section.[160] It has been translated "now,"[161] "for,"[162] "because,"[163] and untranslated (NIV). The paragraph initial semantic function of *gar* is to introduce grounds for what has been said previously. Scholars vary as to just how far back the *gar* reaches. To some it introduces the grounds for the argument beginning with 2:2.[164] To others it introduces the second grounds for the exhortation in 2:1, the first being 2:2–4.[165] Hewitt took it as introducing the grounds for 1:14, meaning "angels are ministering spirits, since it is not to them that the coming world is subjected."[166] Still others linked the present discussion begun at 2:5 with the preceding discussion concerning the Son's supremacy back in chap. 1.[167]

The word "angels" is emphatic by forefronting "It is not to angels" to highlight the contrast that is coming later in the passage. The anarthrous use of the noun places the focus on angels regarding their nature: "not to such as be angels." This is an example of the rhetorical device litotes, a figure of speech that emphasizes a positive fact by negating the contrary. The aorist tense of *hupotassō* ("he has subjected") refers to the time when the subjection was made and indicates God's firm decision not to put angels in control of the future world.[168] God is the implied subject of the verb. The present active participle of *mellō* ("to come") is adjectival. The word is a periphrastic form for the future tense and is sometimes translated adjectivally as "future." *Oikoumenē* ("world") always refers in the New Testament to the inhabited

[159] Koester, *Hebrews*, 84–85, 219–20. Moffatt called 2:5–9 the "prelude" to vv. 10–18 (*Hebrews*, 20).

[160] See Neeley for the linguistic criteria in determining paragraph units in Hebrews ("Discourse Analysis," 18–19), and G. Guthrie for the linguistic reasons why 2:5 begins a new paragraph (*Structure*, 63–64). Attridge's extensive footnote on the use of γὰρ here and in Hebrews is helpful (*Hebrews*, 69–70).

[161] Lane, *Hebrews 1–8*, 42, 45; and NRSV.

[162] KJV and NASB.

[163] L&N 89.23.

[164] Alford, "Hebrews," 31.

[165] Miller, *Hebrews*, 39.

[166] T. Hewitt, *The Epistle to the Hebrews: An Introduction and Commentary* (London: Tyndale, 1960), 65.

[167] E.g., Bruce, *Hebrews*, 71; and Lane, *Hebrews 1–8*, 45. Although the γάρ in 2:5 grammatically connects with 2:1–4, the semantic connection probably does reach back into chap. 1.

[168] So Alford, "Hebrews," 31; and Ellingworth, *Hebrews*, 145–46.

world, specifically of humanity, and possess both temporal and spatial connotations. The phrase *tēn oikoumenēn tēn mellousan* ("the world to come") is common in rabbinic and apocalyptic Judaism.[169]

One key question surrounding *oikoumenēn* is whether it refers to a future earthly world, possibly the millennium, or the world of heaven. Given the immediate context and the tenor of the epistle as a whole, it would seem that, whatever it means, the "world to come" was inaugurated at Christ's enthronement (see Heb 1:6 where the same Greek word is used) and is consummated at Christ's second coming.[170] Lane linked *oikoumenē* to Heb 1:6 and to what he called "equivalent expressions" in 6:5 ("the coming age") and 13:14 ("the city that is to come"). These uses reflect "a class of statements in the Psalter [Ps 93:1; 96:10] that proclaim the establishment of the eschatological kingdom of God."[171] Lane gave the word an interpretive translation, "heavenly world," but such a translation cannot be fully justified by the meaning and usage of the word *oikoumenē* or by the context of the passage itself. The noun is commonly used to denote "the inhabited earth" and not "heaven" or some generic meaning like "future world," "future life," or "heavenly world." For example, in Luke 2:1, the NIV says "the entire Roman world"; Acts 11:28 has "the entire Roman world"; Acts 17:6 has "all over the world"; Acts 19:27 has "the world"; and Acts 24:5 has "all over the world." G. W. Buchanan took the meaning in Heb 2:5 in a literal and earthly sense for the Messianic age, "when the Romans would be subdued, and the Messiah would rule as king from his throne at Jerusalem."[172] This issue is discussed further below.

The phrase "about which we are speaking" indicates that the author's thought connected to 1:5–14 since *oikoumenē* occurs in 1:6. The present tense refers to present time for the author and the use of the first person plural refers only to the author.[173]

The verb "testified" in v. 6 initiates an Old Testament quote and is a compound verb with prefixed *dia* meaning "to assert solemnly" with the implication that the quotation is to be taken very seriously. A positive contrast to the preceding negative statement of v. 5 is signaled by the conjunction *de*. There is an implied ellipsis, "the situation is quite different, because . . . ."[174]

"There is a place where someone" should not be interpreted to mean the author did not know or remember the Old Testament passage quoted. Rather, by the use of these indefinite words in Greek, the author assumed his readers knew and would recognize the quotation. Since he regarded all of the Old Testament as the Word of God, the author did not identity of the human author of

---

[169] R. Gleason, "Angels and the Eschatology of Heb 1–2," 101.

[170] So Bruce, *Hebrews,* 71–72.

[171] Lane, *Hebrews 1–8,* 45–46.

[172] G. W. Buchanan, *To the Hebrews,* AB 36 (Garden City: Doubleday, 1972), 26.

[173] Ellingworth, *Hebrews*, 147.

[174] So Alford, "Hebrews," 33.

the quotation unless it suited his purpose to do so.[175] Some take the phrase as designed to produce a rhetorical effect,[176] which cannot be discounted in light of the author's penchant for rhetorical features.

The citation is from Ps 8:4–6[8:5–7].[177] The rhetorical question implies surprise that God would care for undeserving human beings and thus indicates that God values them.[178] The implied conclusion in 1:5 is that God put man, not angels, in control of the future world. The author quoted Psalm 8 as grounds for that conclusion. Semantically, there is something of a concession-contraexpectation relationship with the meaning "even though man is insignificant, yet you have made him so great."[179] The psalmist's use of "man" refers to humanity in this context. The singular sometimes is translated as plural to indicate it refers to mankind.[180] The term "mindful" conveys the idea of being concerned, which is further seen in the parallel term *episkeptomai* ("care") in the second line, which was a medical term in Greek for a visit from a doctor. Lenski translated it "to look in upon."[181]

Does the phrase "son of man"[182] echo Jesus' use of it in referring to himself? Two arguments are often made why the author likely did not intend Psalm

---

[175] P. G. Müller explained that the focus is not on the human author, but since the Word of God is a living word, the authority comes from the words themselves as spoken by God and not so much the human author who stands behind them ("Die Funktion der Psalmzitate im Hebräerbrief," *Freude an der Weisung des Herrn. Beiträge zur Theologie der Psalmen: Festgabe zum 70 Geburtstag von Heinrich Gross*, ed. E. Haag and F. Hossfeld [Stuttgart: Katholisches Bibelwerk, 1986], 238). Cf. Lane, *Hebrews 1–8*, 46.

[176] Dods, "Hebrews," 261–62; Alford, "Hebrews," 33.

[177] Whether Ps 8:6 is an example of pre-Pauline Christian tradition with respect to the Christological interpretation of the psalm, as is usually assumed, or whether its place in that tradition was due to Paul as suggested by D. Koch (*Die Schrift als Zeuge des Evangeliums. Untersuchungen zur Verwendung und zum Verständnis der Schrift bei Paulus*, BzhTh 69 [Tübingen: Mohr, 1986]), cannot be established with certainty. The quotation occurs in Matt 21:16 and twice in Paul as well as in Hebrews. Given the Matthean usage, and if Matthean priority in terms of the Synoptic Problem is correct, it is likely that the tradition antedates Pauline usage. Either way, the author of Hebrews made independent use of the quotation, as is shown by G. Steyn, "Some Observations about the Vorlage of Ps 8:5–7 in Heb 2:6–8," *Verbum Et Ecclesia* 24 (2003) 2:508. On the Psalm citations in Hebrews, see S. Kistemaker, *Psalm Citations in Hebrews*; and P. Müller, "Die Funktion der Psalmzitate im Hebräerbrief," 223–42. On the use of Psalm 8 in Heb 2:5–9, see W. Loader, *Sohn und Hoherpriester: Eine traditionsgeschichtliche Untersuchung zur Christologie des Hebräerbriefes*, WMANT (Neukirchen-Vluyn: Neukirchener, 1981), 53:29–38.

[178] Some take it as an exclamation (rather than question) of surprise; e.g., M. Luther said it should be translated "What a man he is!" (*Lectures on Titus, Philemon and Hebrews*, in *Luther's Works*, ed. J. Pelikan [St. Louis: Concordia, 1968], 29:128.

[179] As noted by Miller, *Hebrews,* 41.

[180] So NRSV, TEV; CEV has "humans."

[181] R. C. H. Lenski, *The Interpretation of the Epistle to the Hebrews and of the Epistle of James* (Columbus, OH: Wartburg, 1946), 73. BDAG (378) took the idea to mean God's visitation to bring salvation. The word is found otherwise primarily in Luke-Acts with the meaning of God's concern and help (Luke 1:54; 7:16; Acts 15:14).

[182] See G. W. Buchanan on "the son of man" in Heb 2:6 ("The Present State of Scholarship on Hebrews," in *Judaism, Christianity and Other Greco-Roman Cults*, ed. J. Neusner [Leiden: Brill,

8 as a direct messianic reference. First, the Jews did not normally interpret the psalm messianically.[183] Second, unlike most of its other uses in the New Testament, the phrase here has no definite articles (it usually has the definite article with each of the two nouns).[184] The latter reason is severely weakened by a few exceptions (John 5:27; Rev 1:13; 4:14) and by the LXX of Dan 7:13 (clearly messianic), where the article is also absent. Jesus himself cited Ps 8:2 in Matt 21:16 and applied it to himself. There is no other occurrence of this phrase in Hebrews. Psalm 8 may have been considered messianic, and the author may have seen a connection between the phrase "son of man" in v. 4 and Jesus' "Son of Man" sayings in the Gospels.[185] But the discussion is rendered academic by v. 9, where the psalm is connected with Christ in a messianic way—whether or not "son of man" is a Christological title. Further, the connection between Psalm 110 and Psalm 8 here (1:13; 2:6–8a) and elsewhere in Scripture indicates that the author understood both as messianic. Attridge discussed three possible interpretations of the "man" as related to Jesus that the author may have had in mind: a "Son of Man" Christology,[186] the "heavenly Adam" of Alexandrian Judaism,[187] and "Adamic Christology" as found in the New Testament.[188] The second option is excluded from possibility, but a blending of the other two seems likely to be what the author is doing, at least by v. 9.

1975], 1:319–21).

[183] So noted by Kistemaker, *Psalm Citations in Hebrews*, 29. See F. Maloney, who argued that pre-Christian Judaism saw the "son of man" concept in Psalm 8 messianically, as shown by the Targum's individualistic and messianic interpretation of the psalm. He believed that this prepared the way for the NT author's reading the psalm Christocentrically ("The Reinterpretation of Psalm VIII and the Son of Man Debate," *NTS* 27 [1981]: 656–72). Bruce stated that the expression "son of man" has had "for Christians a connotation beyond its etymological force, and it had this connotation for the writer of Hebrews" (*Hebrews*, 73).

[184] See Lane, *Hebrews 1–8,* 47; J. D. G. Dunn, *Unity and Diversity in the New Testament* (Philadelphia: Westminster, 1977), 35–40.

[185] The debate as to whether the "Son of Man" sayings in the Gospels are authentic or are creations of the early church community need not detain us here. There is ample evidence for their authenticity.

[186] So O. Michel, "Son of Man," *TDNT* 3:138; Spicq, *l'Épître aux Hebreux* (Paris: Librairie Lecoffre, 1952–53), 2:31; S. Kistemaker, *Hebrews*, 66; P. Giles, "The Son of Man in the Epistle to the Hebrews," *ExpTim* (1975): 328–32; Hughes, *Hebrews*, 85; Bruce, who saw a "tacit identification" of the Son of Man in Ps 8:4 with Dan 7:13 (*Hebrews*, 35); Cullmann, *Christology*, 188; and Lane, *Hebrews 1–8*, 47. Lane noted that the quotation may "be applied to Jesus without finding in the vocabulary an implied reference to the Son of Man christology of the Gospels" (47). Cullmann said that the author's interpretation of Psalm 8 "indicates that he apparently had quite precise information about the Son of Man doctrine" (*Christology*, 188), which is against J. Dunn, who suggested that the author had no such knowledge (*Christology in the Making*, 2nd ed. [Grand Rapids: Eerdmans, 1996], 91).

[187] As found in Philo, *Legum allegoriae* 1.31–32.

[188] Attridge, *Hebrews,* 73–75; see Rom 5:12–21; 1 Cor 15:21–22. For a biblically solid exposition of Adamic Christology in the context of Heb 2:6–9, cf. Dunn (*Christology in the Making*, 108–11); and B. Fanning, "A Theology of Hebrews," in *A Biblical Theology of the New Testament*, ed. R. Zuck (Chicago: Moody, 1994), 378.

A crucial question in v. 7 is the referent for "him": mankind or Jesus as the Son of Man? Most commentators have opted for the former and do not believe Jesus is in view until v. 9. Others have understood the psalm to refer directly to Christ.[189] Given the overall context, the quotation probably refers both to mankind and to Christ since the author considered Jesus to be the God-Man, the true restorer of humanity.[190]

The translation "mere mortals" (TNIV) instead of "man" (NIV) is problematic on three fronts. First, there is a possible connection with Jesus as the "Son of Man" and the new translation obscures this. Second, *anthrōpos* in Greek is in the singular (though it can be understood in some contexts to refer to humanity) and should be so translated in this context. Genesis 1:26–28 stands behind Psalm 8, as does the use of the Hebrew *ʾādām* ("man"), which is the term for Adam and Eve and all their descendents and thus unites the human race in solidarity with Adam as the head of the race. The collective use of *ʾādām* in Gen 1:26–28 binds their plurality into a unity that parallels the unity in plurality in the Godhead. Changing the singulars to plurals shifts the focus of Psalm 8 away from Adam as the representative head of the human race and obscures the notion of the unity of the race, a vital point in Heb 2:10–18. Third, to change the word or phrase to a more "gender neutral" expression, especially in light of the other two problems above, is simply an exercise in linguistic political correctness. Translating it this way excludes a legitimate interpretative possibility. Since one cannot know for certain it the author intended a connection between the LXX of Psalm 8 and Jesus' numerous references to himself as the "Son of man," the singular *anthrōpos* should not become a plural. This may be a case in Scripture of "studied ambiguity," where an author has allowed a certain linguistic wiggle room via his choice of language—thus inviting the readers to connect the dots for themselves.[191] Another problem with this translation is that even if it can be shown that "Son of Man" was not a messianic title in Psalm 8 (and it is likely that it is not), the Hebrew parallelism between "man" and "son of man" in the two lines (going from the generic to the specific) in-

---

[189] So J. Calvin, *The Epistle of Paul the Apostle to the Hebrews and the First and Second Epistles of Peter,* CNTC (Grand Rapids: Eerdmans, 1963), 22–23. Luther said that "in the proper sense, this verse can be understood only as referring to Jesus" (*Lectures on Titus, Philemon and Hebrews*, 125–26).

[190] Barth agreed with the author's exegesis of Psalm 8, which identifies "man" with Jesus and places this in the context of God's revelation of himself and his covenant with Israel: "'What is man?' gathers its point from the fact that this covenant has been made, that God has been mindful of man and visited him as this has taken place in Israel in this covenant, in the manifestation and revelation of the person of God. The Psalmist's astonishment is at the incomprehensible divine mercy which this action displays. Hence it is not a rhetorical, unanswered question. What is man? He is the being of whom God is so mindful, when He so visits, that He makes Himself his Covenant-partner" (*CD*, III, 2, 20). This, the author of Hebrews affirmed, God has done in Christ.

[191] DeSilva, *Perseverance in Gratitude*, 109.

vites the reader to narrow the focus from humanity in the first line to a specific member of humanity (male or female) in the second line.[192]

The quotation continues in v. 7, where "you" is understood to refer to God as the subject. The translation "a little lower" is the rendering of *brachu ti*, which can indicate either degree ("a little bit" or "somewhat"[193]) or time ("a little while" or "a short time"[194])—an ambiguity difficult to capture in English. Most commentators think the adverbial expression in the MT that the LXX renders as *brachu ti* is best taken in the qualitative sense. In the LXX, the temporal meaning appears most likely. The author of Hebrews built on this temporal sense in his exposition of Psalm 8 since his use of the adverbial particle *nun* ("now") in v. 8 requires a temporal meaning, according to Gheorghita.[195]

Jesus is the one who was "made . . . a little lower than the angels," (or better, HCSB: "made lower than the angels for a short time," i.e., while on earth).[196] M. Luther took the meaning of v. 7 to be: "Thou madest him to be forsaken and deserted by God or the angels, and not for a long time but for a little while, yes, less than a little while, that is, for a very short time, namely, for three days, because thou didst deliver Him over into the hands of sinners."[197]

The only significant deviation from the MT in the LXX of Ps 8:5[8:6] is the use of *angeloi* ("angels") for the Hebrew *Elohim*, which could be translated "God" or "angels." The Septuagint translators and the author of Hebrews understood *Elohim* to refer to angels.[198] The controversy is rendered moot when we recognize that the author gained little for his argument by substituting "angels" for "God," if "God" is the meaning of the original Hebrew. In actuality, the LXX rendering is less forceful to his argument since being a little lower than the angels is not like being a little lower than God. Whether he used "God" or "angels," his argument would still carry its point, for in either case he would prove the very lofty nature of man, which is the intent of the

---

[192] See the discussion on this issue in V. S. Poythress and W. A. Grudem, *The TNIV and the Gender-Neutral Bible Controversy* (Nashville: B&H, 2004), 58–60. The best detailed discussion is D. Leschert, "What is Man? Ps 8:4–6 and Heb 2:5–9 from Adam to Christ to Gender-Neutral Translations" (unpublished paper, Evangelical Theological Society, Nov. 16, 2001). Gender-neutral proponents should recognize that even though a phrase like "son of man" in Ps 8:4 refers to humanity collectively and thus women are included, to change the phrase to "humanity" obscures the verbal allusion to solidarity with Adam that the author intended, and it also obscures the allusion to Christ that the author made overtly in Heb 2:9.

[193] Alford, "Hebrews," 35–36; Dods, "Hebrews," 262; and the NIV. L&N translated it, "You caused him to be somewhat less" (78.43).

[194] So Moffatt, *Hebrews*, 22; Hughes, *Hebrews*, 85; Kistemaker, *Hebrews*, 64–65; Attridge, *Hebrews*, 69–70; Lane, *Hebrews 1–8*, 43; L&N 59.14; and most versions except KJV and NIV.

[195] Gheorghita, *Role of the Septuagint*, 106.

[196] DeSilva, *Perseverance in Gratitude*, 110.

[197] Luther, *Lectures on Titus, Philemon and Hebrews*, 127.

[198] See the discussions on this issue in Leschert (*Hermeneutical Foundations of Hebrews*, 87–91) and P. Craigie (*Psalms 1–50*, WBC 19 [Waco: Word, 1983], 108, with bibliography).

quotation.[199] The combination "glory and honor" emphasizes man's exalted position in creation.

The quotation concludes in v. 8a with the phrase "and put everything under his feet," meaning "to subordinate." Man has been put in control of all creation. The previous line in the LXX text is omitted by our author: "you have set him over the works of your hands."[200] DeSilva is probably correct when he noted that this omission points to the author's desire to elevate a Christological reading over a general anthropological one by focusing on the scope and completion of the subjection, and that the author has yet to specify the identity of the "him" in this quotation in order to sustain "the suspense or the ambiguity purposefully."[201]

The author began his comment on the quotation by the use of *gar*, which indicates the grounds for 2:5 and is an explanatory amplification and restatement of the quote. Some manuscripts omit *autō* ("him") in the phrase "In putting everything under him"[202] (2:8b). God is the understood subject of the infinitive translated "putting everything under." In subjecting everything to humanity, God has left nothing "unsubjected," that is, God left nothing that man could not be in control of. "Everything" is the translation of *ta panta*, where the definite article makes it all inclusive—all of creation. Nothing in the created order can claim exemption from humanity's authority.

The crucial issue here is identifying the antecedent of "him." The *autō* can refer to humanity, or to both humanity and Christ.[203] It seems best to take the latter view, in that while *autō* indicates the human race in context, Jesus as the Son of Man is the head of the human race and thus cannot be excluded from its scope.[204] Lane said that the unfulfilled condition causes us to see that the promise is not to mankind in general but to Jesus who fulfilled God's plan.[205] That may be a reasonable inference from the text, but it is not stated until v. 9. The author connected Christ as the representative man in v. 9 with the fulfillment of the Psalm 8 quotation. Again, the original context of Psalm 8 focuses on humanity, but the author read it through Christological lenses. Mason correctly identified the way the author of Hebrews has read Psalm 8: "The quota-

[199] F. Johnson, *The Quotations of the New Testament from the Old Considered in the Light of General Literature* (Philadelphia: American Baptist, 1895), 7–8.

[200] For a thorough discussion of this omission from a text-critical standpoint and from a theological standpoint, see Ellingworth (*Hebrews*, 148–49) and Steyn ("Observations about the *Vorlage*," 503–5). UBS[4] omits it with a "B" rating; only the KJV includes it.

[201] DeSilva, *Perseverance in Gratitude*, 109.

[202] UBS[4], 744, retains it with a "C" rating.

[203] See the detailed arguments for both positions in Ellingworth (*Hebrews,* 150–52).

[204] So Calvin, *Hebrews*, 23. Calvin took it to be a reference to Jesus. David's meaning was with reference to humanity. The author of Hebrews had no intention of changing this meaning, but focused attention on the suffering and death of Christ, "which was shown forth for a short time, and then the glory with which he is crowned for ever, and he does this more by alluding to the words than by expounding what David meant" (ibid.) Cf. Ellingworth, *Hebrews*, 151–52.

[205] Lane, *Hebrews 1–8*, 48.

tion is best interpreted as intentionally ambiguous: it is applied to Jesus but intended to evoke its original application to humanity in general in order to stress Jesus' solidarity with humanity."[206]

"Yet at present we do not see everything subject to him" brings into focus the contrast between the quote and the present reality both for the readers and for us. The author expected the promise to be fulfilled as he stated in 2:9. *Nun* ("yet") may be logical,[207] with the translation "but as it is," though it is better to take it as temporal: "now at the present time." What was evident to his readers the author admitted overtly.

The author interpreted Psalm 8 as applying to a future time, not to the present age as it most assuredly did for its pre-Christian readers. The underlying logic of his thought is that, since no Scripture can prove ultimately invalid, universal subjection will be true for the coming age, even though it is not yet an observable reality for this age.[208]

The use of *de* ("but") in v. 9 indicates strong contrast and that the statement in v. 8 is true in spite of the negative circumstance just mentioned. Although all things are not yet subject to Jesus, we do see him exalted—thus the subjection of all things to him must inevitably follow. The word order in Greek at the beginning of v. 9 is important (lit.): "but the one lowered a little in comparison to angels we see: Jesus."[209] The perfect participle translated "made lower" refers to Jesus' incarnation; he retains his humanity even in his glorified state. Again we are faced with the little phrase *brachu ti* ("a little"). Some take it as indicative of degree,[210] and others as a temporal reference.[211] It is in the emphatic position in the sentence, emphasizing the brevity of the time.[212]

"Jesus" is in apposition to "who was made a little lower than the angels." The use of the personal name points to his humanity and its location in the clause is emphatic by word order. The remainder of the verse is difficult to construe. The word order of the text reads, "because of the suffering of death with glory and honor crowned." The preposition *dia* ("because") is emphatic by forefronting and may indicate the reason for being crowned ("because he suffered death he was crowned with glory and honor")[213] or the purpose for being made lower

---

[206] E. Mason, *You are a Priest Forever: Second Temple Jewish Messianism and Priestly Christology of the Epistle to the Hebrews*, in Studies on the Texts of the Desert of Judah 74 (Leiden: Brill, 2008), 20. This is also the approach of Lane, *Hebrews 1–8*, 41–50.

[207] So Bruce, *Hebrews*, 75.

[208] DeSilva, *Perseverance in Gratitude*, 109.

[209] Greenlee, *Exegetical Summary*, 59.

[210] NIV; Dods, "Hebrews," 263–64.

[211] See Lane, *Hebrews 1–8*, 48. Ellingworth (*Hebrews*, 154) suggested that the author intended the meaning of βραχύ τι to be taken in a temporal sense in 2:8–9, even though its original context in the quotation was probably degree. See the discussion in Steyn ("Observations on the *Vorlage*," 507).

[212] Lane, *Hebrews 1–8*, 48.

[213] Ibid., 43, 49; Ellingworth, *Hebrews*, 155.

("he was made lower than the angels in order to suffer death").[214] Both are true. Had the incarnation never occurred, Jesus' death on the cross would have never occurred. The two phrases form the center of a chiastic structure.[215] "He suffered death" renders the verbal idea in the plural noun *pathēma* followed by the genitive *tou thanatou*. The genitive may be the object: he suffered (experienced) death; or it may be appositional: his suffering consisted in death. The perfect passive participle *estephanōmenon* ("crowned") is also fraught with difficulty in terms of what it is to be connected with. There are three possibilities: (1) the immediately preceding phrase, "because he suffered death he was crowned with glory and honor";[216] (2) the following clause, "he was crowned with glory and honor so that his death would be effective for everyone";[217] (3) as a parenthetical statement that completes the quotation from Psalm 8.[218] The time that Jesus was crowned with glory and honor could be during his earthly life, especially his baptism and transfiguration,[219] or when God exalted him to the right hand after the resurrection.[220] As previously stated, in 1:1–4 this most likely refers to Jesus' exaltation after his resurrection, since for the author glory is the sequel to the passion.

Verse 9 concludes with "so that by the grace of God he might taste death for everyone." Instead of "by the grace" some manuscripts read "apart from," but the best evidence supports the former reading.[221] Metzger thought *chariti* was originally in the text and that a scribe replaced it with *chōris*, thinking it was intended to be a correction of *chariti*.[222] Bruce concluded *chōris theou* was corrected by *chariti theou*, but that *chōris theou* was not part of the original text. He conjectured that it was introduced

> as a marginal gloss against Heb 2:8 . . . . The glossator intended 'apart from God' to qualify 'everything'—'everything, that is to say, apart from God himself . . . .' In due course the marginal gloss was introduced into the text at a point where the scribe thought it appropriate—in Heb 2:9. . . . [I]t seems more likely to me [against Metzger] that

[214] Moffatt, *Hebrews*, 28; Bruce, *Hebrews*, 76.

[215] So Hughes, *Hebrews*, 90; Lane, *Hebrews 1–8*, 49.

[216] Bruce, *Hebrews*, 76; Lane, *Hebrews 1–8*, 49; and most translations.

[217] Dods, "Hebrews," 263.

[218] Moffatt, *Hebrews*, 25.

[219] Dods, "Hebrews," 263.

[220] Lane, *Hebrews 1–8*, 43, 49.

[221] UBS[4] reads "grace" with an "A" rating. To A. von Harnack the variant was original (*Studien zur geschichte des Neuen Testaments und der alten kirche* [Berlin/Leipzig: W. de Gruyter & Company, 1931] 1:235ff.). G. Zuntz (*The Text of the Epistles: A Disquisition upon the Corpus Paulinum* [London: Oxford, 1953], 34), Elliott ("When Jesus was Apart from God: an Examination of Hebrews 2:9," *ExpTim* 83 [1972]: 11:339–41), D. Peterson (*Hebrews and Perfection: An Examination of the Concept of Perfection in the 'Epistle to the Hebrews,'* SNTSMS 47 [Cambridge: Cambridge University Press, 1982], 216), and Ellingworth (*Hebrews*, 155–57) read "apart from."

[222] *TCGNT* 594. Metzger, along with the UBS committee, gave χάριτι an "A" rating.

chariti theou was not originally in the text but was the emendation of a second scribe who could make no sense of *chōris theou* in the context.[223]

Hughes noted that some church fathers took this to mean that Jesus suffered in his humanity but not in his divinity, a view rejected by orthodox interpreters. Other church fathers took the meaning to be Christ died for all "except" for God, who needed no redemption.[224] Possibly the variant emerged in order to clarify this point. A third view takes the meaning to be "separated from" God. It is possible the reading fell into disfavor since it could be used to support a Gnostic interpretation. Ellingworth supported the variant with "some hesitation."[225] Hughes, after tracing the history of discussion on the variant, correctly concluded that the reading "apart from" should be rejected since the weight of the textual evidence is against it and the contextual evidence supports the reading *chariti theou*, "by the grace of God."[226]

"Tasting" death is an idiom meaning to experience death fully. It is an emphatic expression for dying. Both "the suffering of death" and "tasting death" occur in this verse and are parallel in meaning. The final clause is introduced by *hopōs* ("so that"), which has three possible meanings: (1) the purpose for being made lower,[227] "he was made lower than the angels in order that he might taste death"; (2) the purpose for being crowned;[228] and (3) the purpose for both.[229] The means by which Christ's work of salvation was accomplished is said to be "the grace of God." "For everyone" is emphatic by word order, stressing that Christ's death and subsequent triumph was for mankind's benefit. The word *pantos* ("everyone") can be either masculine, referring to human beings only,

---

[223] F. F. Bruce, "Textual Problems in the Epistle to the Hebrews," in *Scribes and Scripture: New Testament Essays in Honor of J. Harold Greenlee*, ed. D. A. Black (Winona Lake: Eisenbrauns, 1992), 28–29.

[224] Hughes, *Hebrews,* 94–97.

[225] Ellingworth, *Hebrews*, 156.

[226] Hughes, *Hebrews*, 97. Cf. V. Taylor, *The Text of the New Testament* (London: Macmillan and Co./New York: St. Martin's Press, 1961), 104–5. Further light on this variant is shed by S. P. Brock ("The Use of the Syriac Fathers," in *The Text of the New Testament in Contemporary Research: Essays on the Status Quaestionis*, ed. B. Ehrman and M. Holmes, in Studies and Documents 46 [Grand Rapids: Eerdmans, 1995], 230), who pointed out that Ephrem's *Commentary on the Pauline Epistles* is preserved only in Armenian, but it contains a quotation that helps to identify the original Peshitta reading of Heb 2:9b. The variant "apart from God" occurs regularly in Peshitta mss and editions belonging to the church of the East, but χάριτι θεοῦ occurs in most Greek witnesses, Peshitta mss, and the Syrian Orthodox tradition. The solitary quotation of the verse in Ephrem shows that he must have known the reading attested by the later Syrian Orthodox ms tradition. "Evidently, then, the reading 'apart from God' (already known to Narsai in the late 5th century) was introduced into the Peshitta tradition of the Church of the East under the influence of Theodore of Mopsuestia—the 'exegete' par excellence of that tradition" (ibid., 230).

[227] So Hughes, *Hebrews*, 90–91; and Lane, *Hebrews 1–8*, 43, 49.

[228] Dods, "Hebrews," 263; Alford, "Hebrews," 38–39.

[229] Westcott, *Hebrews*, 46; Bruce, *Hebrews*, 76.

or neuter, meaning "everything."[230] Although *huper,* "for," could be taken here in the sense of "on behalf of," it probably means "instead of" (cf. John 11:50, 2 Cor 5:15; Gal 3:13), indicating that the atonement was substitutionary in nature.[231] The preposition's object being "everyone" points to the universal nature of the atonement: Christ died for the sins of all people.[232]

Verse 9 is pivotal in the overall argument of 2:5–18. DeSilva said: "The reason for, and result of, the Son's incarnation and exaltation is that he might taste death on behalf of everyone by God's grace. This is the point that the author interjects into his interpretation of the psalm—it is not connected to anything in the psalm text itself—and that he went on to develop in 2:10–18."[233] The salvation inaugurated by Christ is accomplishing creation's original purpose. Jesus, as man, fulfills God's original intent for man in Genesis 1. As man, Jesus became subject to angelic administration temporarily. The author drew from Psalm 8 the implication of Jesus' identification with man as subordinate to angels in both his incarnation and his permanent exaltation over them.

Psalm 8 is used by other New Testament authors in a messianic way (Matt 21:16; 1 Cor 15:27; Eph 1:22) and by the author of Hebrews as well.[234] Only through the cross of Christ and what the Son of Man, Jesus, did for all men on that cross, can the hopes of a fallen creation be realized. Hughes explained:

> The application to Christ of what this psalm says about man is explained by the fact that the incarnate Son was the perfect, indeed the only perfect, man, and that the intention and achievement of his incarnation was precisely to restore to fallen man the dignity and the wholeness of his existence as he reintegrated in himself the grand design of creation. Psalm 8 relates to the whole of mankind, but it finds its true focus pre-eminently in him who is uniquely the Son of man and in whom alone the hurt of mankind is healed. Only in union with him can man become man as God meant and made him to be.[235]

2:10–18 Verse 10 begins a new sub-paragraph with *gar*, which can be interpreted as introducing the reason Jesus had to die[236] or as offering an

[230] Ellingworth took it in the latter sense (*Hebrews*, 157), while Hughes took it in the former sense. If taken in the latter sense, Hughes (*Hebrews*, 93–94) indicated that the meaning could be a wider collectivity involving the whole order of creation.

[231] See M. Erickson, *Christian Theology*, 2nd ed. (Grand Rapids: Baker, 1998), 2:814; Robertson, *GGNT* 630–31.

[232] Not everyone who accepts a universal atonement (e.g., some moderate Calvinists) interprets the "everyone" in 2:9 to refer to every single human being.

[233] DeSilva, *Perseverance in Gratitude*, 110.

[234] According to E. Ellis, Heb 2:6–9 establishes through midrashic techniques that Ps 8 is fulfilled ultimately in Jesus (*Prophecy and Hermeneutic in Early Christianity* [Grand Rapids: Baker, 1993], 162, 193).

[235] Hughes, *Hebrews,* 84.

[236] Dods, "Hebrews," 264; Hughes, *Hebrews*, 97–98.

explanation for the incarnation in v. 9.[237] It is difficult to choose between these two options and both may have been in the author's mind. The use of *eprepen* ("fitting") relates back to the phrase "by the grace of God" in the previous verse. Although there is no overt reference to "God" in this verse, it is clear that he is the understood subject who is further described as "for whom are all things and by whom are all things," meaning "who made everything and for whom everything was made." Aquinas said that this phrase describes God as both the efficient and final cause of the universe.[238] The *ta panta* ("all things") is reminiscent of 1:2 and refers to the sum total of all things in the universe.

The crux of v. 10 is the participle *agagonta* ("bringing").[239] Who is bringing many sons to glory, the Father or the Son? The participle could be connected with the contiguous articular noun *ton archēgon* since it agrees with it in case, gender, and number. If so, the Son would be the subject of the action. Another option is to connect the participle with the dative *autō* ("him").[240] The majority of interpreters connect the participle to God the Father, in spite of a clear antecedent, by seeing the participle as agreeing with the unexpressed subject of the aorist infinitive *teleiōsai*.[241]

The aorist tense of *agagonta* also presents difficulty to the interpreter. Does it imply a completed act such as "when he brought"? It is difficult to square this with Heb 11:40, which says that the Old Testament saints cannot be made perfect "apart from us." It could be construed as an ingressive aorist or as expressing "coincident action (*by bringing in*)."[242] Hughes explained it as a proleptic aorist, which views as a whole all the work of Christ and its attendant consequences.[243] The verbal aspect of the participle can be either timeless, viewing the action as a completed event simultaneous with that of the aorist infinitive *teleiōsai*, "to perfect," or future, anticipating the future completion of Christ's work.[244] Semantically, the participle may indicate a temporal circumstance referring to the time when God acted ("it was fitting for God to perfect Jesus through suffering when he brought"), but it more likely signals purpose ("in order to bring").[245]

"Many sons" refers to believers and contrasts with the one Son. "Many" is inclusive since it does not here convey the idea "many, but not all." The "many sons" are brought into "glory," an eschatological focus on the heavenly life, but

[237] Lane, *Hebrews 1–8*, 55; Ellingworth, *Hebrews*, 158.

[238] As noted by Hughes, *Hebrews,* 98.

[239] For a thorough discussion of the exegetical issues involved, see Hughes, *Hebrews,* 101–2.

[240] So Dods, "Hebrews," 265; and Bruce, *Hebrews*, 77.

[241] As in Acts 11:12; 15:22; 25:27. So Attridge, *Hebrews,* 82; and Lane, *Hebrews 1–8,* 55–56.

[242] Héring suggested the former (*The Epistle to the Hebrews*, trans. A. W. Heathcote and P. J. Allcock [London: Epworth, 1970], 18–19), while Turner held to the latter (*MHT* 3:80).

[243] Hughes, *Hebrews,* 102.

[244] Moffatt argued for the first sense (*Hebrews*, 31); Bruce (*Hebrews*, 77) and Ellingworth (*Hebrews*, 160) the second; and Hughes (*Hebrews*, 102) and Lane (*Hebrews 1–8*, 56) the third.

[245] So Bruce, *Hebrews*, 77; Lane, *Hebrews 1–8*, 55; and the NIV.

this epistle and the rest of the New Testament plainly indicate the heavenly life is partially shared by the "many sons" in this life.[246]

The unusual designation *archēgos* ("author") for Jesus in v. 10 occurs only three other times in the New Testament (12:2; Acts 3:15; 5:31) and is variously translated "originator," "initiator," "founder," "founding leader," "pioneer leader," "pioneer," "leader," "captain," "champion," and "author." The word has a broad semantic range in secular Greek, but the main idea seems to be that of a leader who stands at the head of a group and who opens the way for others to follow.[247] In Heb 2:10, the meaning appears to be twofold: that of an originator or initiator as well as leader or pioneer.[248] The objective genitive "of salvation" has the meaning "he provided their salvation."

The noun "suffering" is plural but is sometimes translated in the singular (NIV). It could include all of Christ's sufferings or just his death on the cross.[249] The latter meaning is likely in focus. In what sense was Jesus "perfected"? The author gives no hint that Jesus was in some way lacking morally or otherwise. Rather, the perfecting had to do with qualifying him to be the leader of salvation through human suffering, the focus being on his suffering on the cross that accomplished the atonement and salvation for the "many sons."[250] But Cullmann argued persuasively that Jesus' perfecting must include some sense of moral perfection. By this he did not mean that Jesus was lacking morally. By the word "moral" Cullmann meant that Jesus had to go through the stages of human life and his final sacrifice on the cross in order to fit him for the task of high priestly service to the church. Jesus' ability to be tempted and to suffer in his humanity indicates that the "idea of moral 'perfection' within the concept of τελειουν [*teleioun*] was not in the least offensive to the author."[251] Jesus' sinlessness is presented in Hebrews (e.g. 4:15) against the backdrop of his humanity and susceptibility to temptation, which is a part of the perfecting process that the author had in mind. This is what Cullmann meant by "moral" perfection as indicated by his comparison of Heb 5:8 with

---

[246] Alford, "Hebrews," 43.

[247] BDAG 112; L&N 36.6; 68.2; P. G. Müller, "ἀρχηγόν," *EDNT* 1:163–64. For a more extensive analysis of this term as used in the NT, see P. Müller's ΧΡΙΣΤΟΣ ARCHEGOS: *Der religionsgeschichtliche und theologische Hintergrund einer neutestamentlichen Christusprädikation*, EH 23, Theologie 28 (Bern: Lang, 1973). For general discussions of this word, cf. J. J. Scott, "*ARCHĒGOS* in the Salvation History of the Epistle to the Hebrews," *JETS* 29 (1986) 1:47–54; G. Johnston, "Christ as *ARCHEGOS*," *NTS* 27 (1981):381–85; D. Jones, "The Title 'Author of Life (Leader)' in the Acts of the Apostles," *SBLSP*, ed. E. H. Lovering Jr. (Atlanta: Scholars Press, 1994), 627–35; Bruce, *Hebrews*, 80; and Ellingworth, *Hebrews*, 160–61.

[248] Peterson, *Hebrews and Perfection*, 55–63; I. Wallis, *The Faith of Jesus in Early Christian Traditions*, SNTSMS 84 (Cambridge: Cambridge University Press, 1995), 148.

[249] Dods held to the former ("Hebrews," 265), and Ellingworth to the latter (*Hebrews*, 161).

[250] Dods, "Hebrews," 265; Bruce, *Hebrews*, 80–81.

[251] Cullmann, *Christology*, 93–94. But, to avoid the implication that there was something somehow morally lacking in the character of the Son, it would be better to speak of Christ's perfection as "functional" or something similar rather than "moral."

5:9. The use of the word "learned" in 5:8 sheds light on the use of "perfect" in 5:9. The two are seen as parallel: through suffering Jesus "learned" obedience and through suffering he was "made perfect." Additionally, the perfection of Christ includes an aspect of "fulfillment." Through the sufferings of Christ culminating in the cross, Jesus fulfilled everything needed to be the "author" of our salvation.[252]

The solidarity of Jesus with his people necessitated his suffering. By means of his sufferings and his being "made perfect," he would "perfect" his people. The term in Greek, *teleioō,* "make perfect," has different meanings. Delling interprets the term here in the sense of "to qualify."[253] BDAG lists two options for its meaning: (1) bring something to its goal/accomplishment; and (2) to "consecrate, initiate."[254] Mason is probably right when he suggested that the author of Hebrews seems to be playing on the verb's different meanings. Following the proposal by Attridge, he understands the meaning to be "a vocational process by which he is made complete or fit for his office."[255]

Thus, the question, Why did God become man? is answered: Jesus "must be able to suffer with men in order to suffer for them," as Cullmann expressed it.[256] Jesus, as our high priest who himself had suffered, provides help when we too are suffering.

Christ's humbling himself through the incarnation and then through his suffering and death on the cross brings him honor because he is the author of our salvation. There is, as Calvin said, no better ground for this plan of atonement "other than it thus pleased God." This is the reason for the circumlocution "for whom and through whom everything exists." This phrase could have been omitted, but the author's purpose was to remind us that what God himself decides must be deemed best, "whose will and glory is the proper end of all things."[257]

The conjunction *gar* (left untranslated in the NIV) connects v. 11 with the previous verse. Its function is to introduce either the grounds for bringing the many sons to glory in the previous verse, or the reason it was fitting for God to perfect the Son through suffering.[258] The two attributive participles are used

---

[252] P. Davids, *More Hard Sayings of the New Testament* (Downers Grove: InterVarsity, 1991), 89. See K. McCruden, "Christ's Perfection in Hebrews: Divine Beneficence as an Exegetical Key to Hebrews 2:10," *BR* 47 (2002): 40–62.

[253] *TDNT* 8:83.

[254] BDAG 996.

[255] E. Mason, *You are a Priest Forever: Second Temple Jewish Messianism and Priestly Christology of the Epistle to the Hebrews*, in Studies on the Texts of the Desert of Judah 74 (Leiden: Brill, 2008), 22. See Attridge, *Hebrews*, 86.

[256] Cullmann, *Christology,* 97.

[257] Calvin, *Hebrews,* 25.

[258] Moffatt held to the former sense (*Hebrews*, 32), while Dods ("Hebrews," 265) and Ellingworth (*Hebrews*, 163) held to the latter.

nominally in a timeless sense.[259] "Those who are made holy" are believers, the "many sons" of v. 10. But the question remains, who is "the one who makes men holy"? It is neither the Holy Spirit nor God the Father, but the Son. The verb *hagiazō* occurs twice in v. 11 ("make . . . holy" and "made holy"), and both here and throughout this epistle it describes the total experience of the Christian life from conversion to glorification (9:13; 10:10,14,29; 13:12). *Hagiazō* means to set apart to God by purification of sins. The combination of "make holy" and "to make perfect" here in 2:10–11 and in 10:14 makes the two terms overlap semantically.[260]

The concept of holiness in our epistle is both positional (10:10,29) and progressive (2:10; 10:14). The readers are told that the endurance of present discipline will result in the sharing of God's "holiness" (12:10) and therefore they are to "make every effort . . . to be holy" (12:14). DeSilva noted that when the author referred to Jesus as "the one who makes men holy," he applied to the Son a LXX designation for God as the one who "makes [the people] holy" (see Exod 31:13).[261]

Jesus ("the one who makes men holy") and believers ("those who are made holy") are *ex henos pantes* ("of the same family"; lit. "all from one"). The numeral *henos* can be either masculine or neuter in Greek, giving rise to alternative meanings. If masculine here, then the "one" may refer to God, Adam, or Abraham. If it refers to God, the focus is on a common spiritual origin. If the reference is to Adam, the focus is a common humanity. Abraham is mentioned in 2:16, but if he were intended here in v. 11, the author would likely have named him. Others opt for a neuter rendering since the context is about the incarnation.[262] This sense is seen in the NIV, "of the same family." Because of this solidarity between the Son and the "many sons," the author stated that "Jesus is not ashamed to call them brothers," which is an affirmation by negating the opposite—he is proud to call them brothers. Not only are all believers a "band of brothers," but they are also brothers of Christ. Hughes explained it well: "Our brotherhood with Christ rests not solely on the fact of his incarnation, but much more precisely on the redemption which that incarnation en-

---

[259] So Dods, "Hebrews," 265–66; and Moffatt, *Hebrews*, 32. Cf. R. Ward, who said: "I can understand this as a principle of grammar but doubt its applicability here. Surely the present tenses denote repetition, not repetition by 'resanctifying' anyone, but the repetition which takes place as men one after another put their faith in Christ—and are sprinkled with his blood. Thus the text means: 'He who keeps on sanctifying one man after another and they who are sanctified one after another . . . .' The means is Christ's sprinkled blood. This is brought out beautifully in the tense arrangements of 10:14, 'by one offering he has brought to the goal for ever those who one after another are sanctified'" (*The Pattern of Our Salvation: A Study of New Testament Unity* [Waco: Word Books, 1978], 68–69.

[260] Noted by Cullmann, *Christology*, 100.

[261] DeSilva, *Perseverance in Gratitude*, 115.

[262] E.g., Calvin, *Hebrews*, 26; and Bruce, *Hebrews*, 81.

abled him to accomplish at the cross."[263] In the Gospels, it is after the cross and resurrection that Jesus referred to his disciples as "my brothers" (Matt 28:10; John 20:17). The subject of the verb "ashamed" is Jesus and the present tense is timeless, implying Scripture's permanent witness to this truth.[264] Lane translated the verb as "blush" and suggested that the connection with v. 10 indicates that the occasion is the second coming of Christ when God will lead many sons to glory.[265]

Verses 12–13 contain three Old Testament quotations from two passages. Psalm 22:22 and Isa 8:13–17 offer proof that the Son has made the declaration in the previous verse. The key to understanding why the author chose these verses is to connect their use with the broader Old Testament context in which they originally occurred. The New Testament authors and the early church viewed Psalm 22 as messianic. Jesus quoted Ps 22:1[22:2] while on the cross, so the author in Heb 2:12 took the psalmist's words and made them Jesus' words. This is not problematic given his understanding of the divinity of Christ and the close connection between God and his written word.[266] In Ps 22:11[22:12] the psalmist cried out for "help" from his enemies. In v. 19[20], the psalmist called to the Lord, "you, O Lord . . . help me." The author of Hebrews echoed this theme of help in his exhortations to seek "help" from the Son (2:17–18; 4:16).

The New Testament authors viewed Isa 8:13–18 as messianic also (Luke 2:34; Rom 9:33; 1 Pet 2:8). Isaiah 8:17 fittingly describes Jesus' confidence in and dependence on the Father during his earthly ministry, thus illustrating his full manhood.[267] The third quotation is from Isa 8:18. The context of Isa 8:17–18 follows an oracle (8:11–15) that warns the prophet Isaiah to look to the Lord for "sanctuary" rather than the city of Jerusalem. R. Gleason may be

---

[263] Hughes, *Hebrews*, 106.

[264] So Ellingworth, *Hebrews*, 166.

[265] Lane, *Hebrews 1–8*, 59.

[266] Against Attridge. DeSilva stated that "the way in which the author puts OT words on Jesus' lips to make his point is striking, using the scriptural tests as a living 'witness' in the court, as it were. This has some important implications for his view of the Scriptures: since the final word was spoken through the Son, the earlier words can frequently find their 'true' meaning when spoken by him as well" (*Perseverance in Gratitude*, 115–16).

[267] Why should our author have assumed that this passage from Isa 8 was spoken by Christ? One possible answer is because the LXX of Isa 8 has the words "and he will say" inserted before v. 17, which gives the impression that a speaker other than the prophet is introduced. So G. Lünemann, *The Epistle to the Hebrews,* trans. from the 4th German edition M. Evans, *Critical and Exegetical Handbook to the New Testament*, ed. H. A. W. Meyer (New York: Funk & Wagnalls, 1885), 440. Moffatt, *Hebrews*, 33; and H. C. G. Moule, *Birth of the New Testament*, 3rd ed. (London: A. C. Black, 1981), 79–80. Moule concluded: "If this is the right explanation, here are two non-Christian Messianic intrusions in to the Greek Bible, requisitioned by our writer for his Christian purposes" (80).

correct that the author may have been thinking of the impending Roman invasion of Jerusalem (cf. Heb 13:14).[268]

The use of the present participle *legōn* to introduce the quotations is in apposition to the infinitive "to call" and functions as a restatement of the latter half of the previous verse: "that is, he says."[269] Two questions arise. First, who made this statement? Second, when did he make it? It seems clear that Jesus is the speaker, but the statement could have been made in his earthly ministry, in his exalted state, or at his second coming.[270] There is no record of such a statement in the Scriptures during Jesus' earthly ministry, though this does not rule out the possibility. Better is option two or three. The "congregation" refers to the church with the implication that Jesus is participating in the worship of God along with believers as evidence of his brotherhood with them.[271]

The meaning of the second Old Testament quotation, "I will put my trust in him" (v. 13) is problematic. The periphrastic future perfect *esomai pepoithōs* implies a state of trust: "I will be in a condition resulting from having trusted."[272] The *ego* ("I") is emphatic. Most commentators read this statement as Jesus' confession of trust in God, which shows his solidarity with human beings in utter dependence on God. DeSilva, in an interesting twist, suggested that the author would have the believer see himself as the object of Jesus' declared trust.[273]

The "Here am I" implies the Son's readiness to obey the Father. The previous quotation is now continued with "and again" functioning as an introductory phrase because the author is making a different point.[274] "The children" can be identified as belonging to (1) God,[275] (2) Christ,[276] or (3) Christ with God giving them to him, thus emphasizing that both Christ and his brothers have the same human nature.[277] One crucial point the author made in 2:10–13 is that Jesus as the "sole tether" connects the addresses to God's inheritance for them, which is further developed in 6:19–20.[278]

Verse 14 begins a subparagraph ending with v. 18. It begins with *oun* (left untranslated in the NIV) and introduces a conclusion from the preceding argument. *Epei* ("since") introduces the grounds for the conclusion that means,

---

[268] Gleason, "Angels and the Eschatology of Heb 1–2," 99.

[269] Greenlee noted that this point is not made by any of the commentators (*Exegetical Summary*, 69).

[270] Hughes opted for the first (*Hebrews*, 107–8), Bruce for the second (*Hebrews*, 82), and Lane for the third (*Hebrews 1–8*, 59).

[271] Dods, "Hebrews," 266.

[272] So translated by Greenlee, *Exegetical Summary*, 71.

[273] DeSilva, *Perseverance in Gratitude*, 116.

[274] Dods, "Hebrews," 266–67; Bruce, *Hebrews*, 83.

[275] So Dods, "Hebrews," 267; Ellingworth, *Hebrews*, 170.

[276] So Bruce, *Hebrews*, 84; and Lane, *Hebrews 1–8*, 60.

[277] Lenski, *Hebrews*, 88.

[278] DeSilva, *Perseverance in Gratitude*, 111.

"Since the children have a human nature, therefore Jesus took on human nature as well." The phrase (lit.) "have blood and flesh"[279] probably does not indicate any significance in the word order.[280] The use of the perfect tense of *kekoinōnēken* ("have"; lit. "share in common") implies an existing state of humanity, and since it is followed by the aorist of Christ's sharing in humanity as well, it further emphasizes not only the common humanity but the common state of humanity shared by Jesus and Christians.[281]

At this point, the author defined and described the necessity and the purpose of the incarnation. That Jesus "too shared in their humanity" is an emphatic statement of the doctrine of the incarnation, so explicitly stated "that no possible place is left for the unreal phantom Christ of the docetic heresy."[282] The aorist *meteschen* ("shared") indicates the time when Jesus took on human nature, which would have been at his virgin conception, culminating in his birth in Bethlehem. The *hina* ("that") clause introduces a purpose of the incarnation: "that by his death he might destroy him who holds the power of death—that is, the devil." The aorist *katargēsē* ("destroy"; lit. "render powerless") probably indicates that Christ's death on the cross was a single act that accomplished this purpose.[283] It was necessary for Jesus to assume human nature, for only by doing so could he truly be a substitute for the sins of humanity: the perfect God-man dying in the place of sinful people.[284] As the orthodox theologians argued against Apollinarius, what the Logos did not take to himself he could not redeem.

Since, as Luther said, "even the devil is God's devil," and since death came into the world because of Adam and Eve's sin, and since God was the one who decreed physical death as a consequence of sin, in what sense might it be said that Satan holds the power of death? It is because he was the instigator of sin through his temptation of the first couple in the garden. God, not Satan, holds the ultimate power of death, "but the power which he presently wields is also the power by which he is destroyed."[285]

---

[279] L&N (9.15) translates this as "human beings."

[280] Hughes, *Hebrews*, 110.

[281] Porter, *Verbal Aspect*, 251.

[282] Ibid., 110.

[283] So Ellingworth, *Hebrews*, 173.

[284] Calvin, *Institutes*, 2.12.4.

[285] Hughes, *Hebrews,* 112. O. Weber said: "We read that God has power over death in Ps. 90:3,7ff., Matt. 10:28, and often. The fact that according to Heb. 2:14 this is the power of the devil does not make him into a god of death, in that he had his power as a result of the effective No of God" (*Foundations of Dogmatics*, trans. and ed. D. Guder [Grand Rapids: Eerdmans, 1981], 1:624). The comment by Luther is appropriate: "by his wonderful wisdom he compels the devil to work through death nothing else than life, so that in this way, while he acts most of all against the work of God, he acts for the work of God and against his own work with his own deed" (*Lectures on Titus, Philemon and Hebrews,* 135). He further stated: "He who fears death or is unwilling to die is not a Christian to a sufficient degree" (137).

In v. 15 the articular present active infinitive of *zaō* is used as a noun ("life")[286] and can be interpreted in one of two ways: it could express (1) the second purpose of the incarnation;[287] or (2) the result of the preceding thought: "in order that he might destroy the devil and therefore set these people free."[288] The phrase "in fear" is the dative of cause meaning "because of fear," and the "fear of death" is an objective genitive meaning "they feared death." Christians fear death no longer because of the victory of Christ over death and the grave.[289] Paul expressed a parallel thought: "For since death came through a man, the resurrection of the dead comes also through a man. For as in Adam all die, so in Christ all will be made alive" (1 Cor 15:21–22). Paul's view of corporate solidarity is essentially the same as the author's in Heb 2:10–18.

Gregory of Nyssa said: "The Deity was hidden under the veil of our nature that so, as with ravenous fish, the hook of the Deity might be gulped down along with the bait of flesh."[290] This famous fishhook metaphor was first suggested by Cyprian,[291] who derived it from Job 41:1, "Can you pull in leviathan with a fishhook?" Leviathan later became symbolically identified with Satan. John of Damascus rejected the notion that the devil had received a ransom. He took "death" as the tyrant that swallowed up the body "as a bait is transfixed on the hook of divinity."[292] Although such metaphors are more helpful for illustrative purposes than they are theological truth, a Christus Victor (Christ is Victor) theme does run throughout the New Testament, beginning with Jesus' conflict with the devil and demons in his earthly ministry (Luke 10:18–20) and ending with the final destruction of Satan (Rev 20:10).

The ransom theory of the atonement claims that the death of Jesus somehow paid a ransom to the devil. But, as Oden rightly noted, this theory is contrary to Heb 2:14–15 where the author explicitly stated that the death of Christ was a triumph over the devil, not a ransom paid to him.[293]

In summary, Athanasius' comment on the incarnation of Christ is potent:

---

[286] This is the only such usage in the NT (Porter, *Verbal Aspect*, 369).

[287] Bruce, *Hebrews*, 86.

[288] Ellingworth, *Hebrews*, 174–75.

[289] Calvin's comment on the fear of death in Heb 2:15 is interesting in light of the warning passages in Hebrews: "As an overdose of fear comes from ignorance of the grace of Christ, so it is a sure sign of unfaithfulness" (*Hebrews,* 31). See the excellent section on the fear of death in ancient Greek and Latin authors in Moffatt (*Hebrews*, 35–36).

[290] Gregory of Nyssa, *The Great Catechism*, in *NPNF*^{2} vol. 5, *Select Writings and Letters of Gregory, Bishop of Nyssa*, trans. W. Moore and H. Wilson (London: Parker & Co., 1893; repr., Edinburgh: T&T Clark/Grand Rapids: Eerdmans, 1994), 494.

[291] Cyprian, *Expositio Symboli*, MPL 21, 354–55.

[292] John of Damascus, *Exposition of the Orthodox Faith*, in *NPNF*^{2} (Edinburgh: T&T Clark/Grand Rapids: Eerdmans, 1997), 72. See the excellent discussion of the ransom metaphor in patristic thought in T. Oden (*The Word of Life*, *Systematic Theology* [San Francisco: HarperCollins, 1992], 2:400–1).

[293] Oden, *Word of Life*, 399; cf. Col 2:13–15.

> The body then, as sharing the same nature with all, for it was a human body, though by an unparalleled miracle it was formed of a virgin only, yet being mortal, was to die also, conformably to its peers. But by virtue of the union of the Word with it, it was no longer subject to corruption according to its own nature, but by reason of the Word that was come to dwell in it was placed out of the reach of corruption. And so it was that two marvels came to pass at once, that the death of all was accomplished in the Lord's body, and that death and corruption were wholly done away by reason of the Word that was united with it. For there was need of death, and death must needs be suffered on behalf of all, that the debt owing from all might be paid. Whence, as I said before, the Word, since it was not possible for him to die, that he might offer it as his own in the stead of all, and as suffering, through his union with it, on behalf of all, "bring to nought him that had the power of death, that is, the devil; and might deliver them who through fear of death were all their lifetime subject to bondage."[294]

Verse 16 begins with *gar* and indicates the summary or conclusion of what has been said in 2:10–15. It also explains the reason for the incarnation in v. 14.[295] The use of the emphatic particle *dēpou* ("surely") indicates strong affirmation and assumes knowledge that the readers already have and that they are in agreement with the author's statement.[296] The verb *epilambanetai* ("he helps") literally means "to lay firm hold of" or "to appropriate." It is used of taking hold of a person in either a friendly or hostile sense. It occurs three times of taking hold of someone's hand, either literally or figuratively.[297] Paul used the term in the sense of taking hold of eternal life (1 Tim 6:12,19), and Luke used it of Jesus' enemies taking hold of his words to trap him (Luke 20:20,26). Context is the key to how the verb should be translated. From the early church until the time of the Reformers, this verb was interpreted to mean that the Son took on humanity via the incarnation. However, in the seventeenth century there was a departure from this interpretation to the more general sense of "coming to the aid of." Since then, many scholars have taken the verb that way.[298] But in the seventeenth century Turretin pointed out that in the more than 40 occurrences of *epilambanomai* in the LXX, it never has the metaphorical sense of aid.[299]

---

[294] Athanasius, "*On the Incarnation*," in *Christology of the Later Fathers*, LCC (Philadelphia: Westminster, 1954), 74.

[295] So Alford, "Hebrews," 51; and Bruce, *Hebrews*, 87.

[296] Moffatt, *Hebrews*, 36; Lane, *Hebrews 1–8*, 52, 63.

[297] BDAG 374.

[298] E.g., Alford, "Hebrews," 51–52; and Westcott, *Hebrews*, 54–55.

[299] F. Turretin, *Institutes of Elenctic Theology*, trans. G. Giger, ed. J. Dennison (New Jersey: P&R, 1994), 2:308; This has been noted by many since. See Hughes, *Hebrews*, 116. DeSilva (*Perseverance in Gratitude,* 120) commented: "'Laying hold' here speaks of Jesus' role as rescuer, deliverer, and protector of his client in the new exodus from the shakable realm and entrance into the

The absence of the definite article with "angels" and with "Abraham's descendants" (lit. "seed of Abraham") in Greek indicates they refer to a class.[300] The "seed of Abraham" may be either the Jewish race as a whole or both Jews and Gentiles.[301] Hughes took the first view, arguing that the author frames the incarnation within the perspective of the covenant with Christ the incarnate Son.[302] But the covenant perspective could still be in view if both Jews and Gentiles were intended. Lane's claim that the author's use of "seed of Abraham" is an allusion to Isa 41:8–10 is well founded given the linguistic and semantic parallels: *sperma Abraam, mē phobou, eboēthēsa*, and *antelabomēn.* (The author of Hebrews likely substituted the cognate *epilambanetai* for the latter term in light of Jer 31:32, where the exodus is described as God's taking Israel by the hand, *epilambanetai*, to lead them out of bondage.)[303] This is another example of the author's rich and deep understanding of the Old Testament and his Christocentric reading of the text.

It is grammatically possible to take "fear" in 2:15 as the subject of "helps" (lit. "takes hold of") in 2:16. In this case, the author would be employing brachylogy where the subject of a sentence is taken from a preceding noun in an oblique case without a referential pronoun to aid in the transition. If this is the case, a possible translation would be: "For it [the fear of death] clearly does not seize angels, but it does take hold of the seed of Abraham."[304] The use of the verb *epilambanomai* to characterize fear as "seizing" or "taking hold of" or even as "gripping" someone is completely within its normal semantic range. In a similar way, the Peshitta version takes "death" as the subject of *epilambanomai.*[305] The original readers may have thought: "How could Jesus, who died by crucifixion, be superior to angels who, by their very nature, do not even die?" The author argued that the incarnation enabled Jesus to die and thus destroy the one who held the power of death. The fear of death does not affect angels at all, but it certainly does human beings. On this interpretation, 2:16 brings into sharp focus the difference between angelic nature and human nature and serves to strengthen the author's argument as to why it was necessary for Jesus to have a mortal, human nature.[306] However, it is probably best to take "Jesus"

'rest' of God." This is an example of the patron-client, honor-shame grid through which DeSilva viewed the epistle. His analysis here seems strained at best.

300 E. g., Ellingworth, *Hebrews*, 177.

301 The former is supported by Alford ("Hebrews," 51) and the latter by Moffatt (*Hebrews*, 37) and Hughes (*Hebrews*, 119).

302 So Hughes, *Hebrews,* 119.

303 Lane, *Hebrews 1–8,* 63–64.

304 So argued by M. Gudorf, "Through a Classical Lens: Hebrews 2:16," *JBL* 119 (2000): 1:105–8.

305 A. Bonus noted that the reading is supported by 14 of the 20 Syriac manuscripts he inspected ("Heb. ii:16 in the Peshitta Syriac Version," *ExpTim* 33 [1921–22]: 234–36); cf. Metzger, *The Early Versions of the New Testament* (Oxford: Clarendon, 1977), 56. The meaning would be: "For not over angels has death authority, but over the seed of Abraham it has authority."

306 Gleason, "Angels and the Eschatology of Heb 1–2," 107.

as the subject of the verb *epilambanomai*, where the verb is being used in a positive sense of "help."

"For this reason" begins v. 17 and can be interpreted as a conclusion based on v. 16,[307] as introducing a summary of vv. 10–16,[308] or as a restatement of v. 14.[309] The phrase "in every way" is emphatic by word order and strengthens the verb "to be made like."[310] "Brothers" is resumed from v. 11, and the phrase "in every way," referring to the Son's incarnation, is well described by Hughes: "This likeness is nothing less than complete identification: assimilation, not simulation."[311] The *hina* ("in order that") clause may introduce one purpose for Christ's becoming a high priest, or the purpose for Christ's becoming united with humanity.[312] What was alluded to in 1:3 is here stated overtly, namely, that Jesus is the high priest who makes atonement for the people. This theme is developed throughout the remainder of the doctrinal sections of the epistle. The other key title for Jesus besides "Son" is "high priest" as evidenced by the repetition of this term (see 3:1; 4:14,15; 5:1,5). The role of the high priest is essentially representation, and "representation requires identification."[313] As high priest, Jesus is both "merciful" and "faithful" (the two are parallel) "in the things pertaining to God" (2:17).[314] This latter phrase can be connected with either "merciful and faithful" or just "faithful."[315] The adjective "faithful," while possibly referring to Jesus' earthly life, or to his earthly and heavenly ministry, is more likely a reference to his ongoing high priestly ministry.[316]

Such language may be taken from 1 Sam 2:35, where God promised that he would "raise up . . . a faithful priest . . . and firmly establish his house." Interestingly, in 3:1–6 the author combined the concept of the "house" and God as "the builder" coupled with the faithfulness of the Son compared with that of Moses.[317]

An important translation issue as well as a theological issue has to do with the correct rendering of the word *hilaskomai* ("make atonement") in v. 17,

---

[307] Dods, "Hebrews," 269; Hughes, *Hebrews*, 119.

[308] Lane, *Hebrews 1–8*, 64; Ellingworth, *Hebrews*, 179–80.

[309] Moffatt, *Hebrews*, 37.

[310] Ellingworth, *Hebrews*, 180.

[311] Hughes, *Hebrews,* 119.

[312] Dods supported the former ("Hebrews," 269), and Lane the latter (*Hebrews 1–8*, 64).

[313] Succinctly stated by Hughes, *Hebrews,* 120.

[314] Calvin took the phrase to mean "that he might be merciful, and therefore faithful" (*Hebrews,* 33). He viewed "the things pertaining to God" (translated by the NIV as "in service to God") as the things that have the purpose of reconciling men to God. The accusative of manner, otherwise known as adverbial accusative or the accusative of reference/respect, is the construction used in Greek: "with reference/respect to things pertaining to God."

[315] Alford supported the former view ("Hebrews," 54), and Dods the latter ("Hebrews," 269).

[316] So I. Wallis, *The Faith of Jesus Christ in Early Christian Traditions*, 148; he was preceded by Westcott, *Hebrews,* 57; Grässer, *Der Glaube Im Hebräerbrief*, Marburger Theologische Studien 2 (Marburg: N. G. Elwert Verlag, 1965), 21–22; and Hughes, *Hebrews*, 120.

[317] DeSilva, *Perseverance in Gratitude*, 120.

which is rendered either "expiate"[318] or "propitiate."[319] The literature on this subject is immense. L. Morris's magisterial study of this subject provides clear and irrefutable evidence that the term *hilaskomai*, although a complex term that includes in it the idea of expiation of sin, nevertheless conveys the concept of the averting of divine wrath and represents a "stubborn substratum of meaning from which all usages can be naturally explained."[320] Even though *hilaskomai* in 2:17 is transitive with "the sins of the people" as its object, the NIV marginal note offers an alternative reading "that he might turn aside God's wrath, taking away." Such a marginal reading as an option to the NIV's "make atonement" indicates that the translators recognized the word contains an element of averting wrath, hence the term "propitiation." Hill pointed out that the frequent references to divine wrath and its aversion in the contexts of the *hilaskomai* word group in the New Testament suggest that the idea of propitiation belongs to the terms.[321] The difference between "expiation" and "propitiation" is that "expiation" signifies the cancellation of sin whereas "propitiation" denotes the turning away of the wrath of God. Misconceptions about the doctrine of propitiation often occur when pagan ideas are read into the uses of the word in the Old and New Testaments—a problem chiefly responsible for the modern and mistaken attempts to give the verb the sense of expiate (see NEB, RSV).[322] Scripture consistently teaches that humanity's sin has incurred the wrath of God and that this wrath is only averted by the substitutionary atonement provided by Christ on the cross. Nor will it do to suggest that the term is used in the New Testament to explain that God is not angry with us because he has already been appeased. Turretin's comment on this is appropriate: "The blood of Christ was not shed to prove the remission of sin, but to obtain it."[323]

---

[318] Bruce (*Hebrews*, 78–79) and Ellingworth (*Hebrews*, 188–89) argued for "expiation" in this context.

[319] Hughes (*Hebrews*, 122) and Lane (*Hebrews 1–8*, 66) argued for "propitiation" in this context.

[320] L. Morris, *The Apostolic Preaching of the Cross* (Grand Rapids: Eerdmans, 1955), 155 (see esp. pp. 125–60). The classic argument that the term should be translated "expiation" is by C. H. Dodd ("ΙΛΑΣΚΕΣΘΑΙ, Its Cognates, Derivatives, and Synonyms, in the Septuagint," *JTS* 32 [1931]: 352–60), which also appeared in his *The Bible and the Greeks* (London: Hodder & Stoughton, 1935), 82–95. For an excellent discussion of the terms (including bibliography), see J. M. Gundry-Volf , "Expiation, Propitiation, Mercy Seat," *DPL* 279–84.

[321] Quoted by R. Ward, *Pattern of our Salvation*, 61.

[322] Hughes has a good discussion of the issue (*Hebrews,* 121–22). J. Stott stated, "If we are to develop a truly biblical doctrine of propitiation, it will be necessary to distinguish it from pagan ideas at three crucial points, relating to why a propitiation is necessary, who made it and what it was" (*The Cross of Christ* [Downers Grove: InterVarsity, 1986], 171–74. It is necessary because of God's wrath against sin; unlike the pagan contexts, it is God, not man, who takes the initiative to offer the sacrifice by his grace; and the sacrifice itself is none other than God in the person of his Son, Jesus. See the excellent excursus on this subject in D. Akin, *1,2,3 John*, in NAC 28 (Nashville: B&H, 2001), 253–65.

[323] Turretin, *Institutes*, 2:434. Universalism cannot be taught or inferred from Heb 2:10–18. K. Barth's concept of Jesus Christ being "the electing God" and "elected man"—which implies

Evangelical theology insists on taking *hilaskomai* in the sense of "propitiation" because that is the meaning of the word and that is the heart of the doctrine of the atonement.[324]

Verse 18 begins with *gar* (untranslated in the NIV), which gives the reason that Christ's becoming like his brothers enabled him to become a merciful and faithful high priest. F. W. Farrar took the *en hō* to mean "in that particular wherein," and thus translates "in that sphere wherein He suffered";[325] but it is better to take it in a causal sense, "*because* he was tempted" (as in the NIV). The *autos* is emphatic, "he himself." The perfect tense *peponthen* ("suffered") indicates that the cross resulted in Jesus' ever available compassion for his "brothers" in their time of need. The aorist participle *peirastheis* ("when he was tempted") can be construed in several ways. (1) It could indicate the means of the suffering: "he suffered by means of being tempted."[326] (2) It could indicate action parallel to the suffering: "he suffered and was tempted."[327] (3) It could be causal of the suffering: "he suffered because he was tempted."[328] (4) It could be temporal: "he suffered when he was tempted."[329] (5) Less likely is to view the participle as defining the area in which Jesus suffered: "he was tempted in what he suffered."[330] Options one and three seem to be the most likely.

The two phrases "was tempted" and "those who are being tempted" may have either a negative sense or a neutral sense.[331] Perhaps the best resolution is to see both as primarily indicating testing (neutral) but with temptation (negative) as an included secondary meaning.[332] The present tense followed

---

that all humanity shares in the election—is likewise excluded by these verses.

[324] E.g., Grudem, *Systematic Theology,* 575. C. K. Barrett stated: "It would be wrong to neglect the fact that expiation has, as it were, the effect of propitiation" (*The Epistle to the Romans,* BNCT, [New York: Harper, 1957], 78.) The verb ἱλάσκομαι includes both meanings of expiation and propitiation as Leon Morris has conclusively demonstrated (Morris, *Apostolic Preaching*, 155). P. K. Jewett, ("Propitiation," in *The Zondervan Pictorial Encyclopedia of the Bible*, ed. M. Tenney [Grand Rapids: Zondervan, 1975], 4:904–5) said: "If one reduces the language of Scripture from 'propitiation' to 'expiation' in all instances, he still must answer the question, 'Why should sins be expiated?' What would happen if no expiation were provided? Can one deny that, according to the teaching of Scripture, men will die in their sins?" A logical implication of the denial of propitiation is that God will ultimately forgive everyone, regardless of how one is related to Christ—an increasingly popular opinion, but one that is contrary to Scripture.

[325] F. W. Farrar, *The Early Days of Christianity* (London: Cassell, 1884), 200.

[326] E.g., Moffatt, *Hebrews*, 39; and Miller, *Hebrews*, 63.

[327] E.g., Bruce, *Hebrews*, 88.

[328] E.g., Dods, "Hebrews," 270.

[329] E.g., the NIV.

[330] So Alford, "Hebrews," 55.

[331] Moffatt (*Hebrews*, 39), Hughes (*Hebrews*, 123–24), and the NIV take both in the negative sense; Bruce (*Hebrews*, 88–89) and Lane (*Hebrews 1–8*, 66) took both in the neutral sense of testing.

[332] So Ellingworth, *Hebrews*, 191. Calvin took it in a neutral sense meaning "experience" or "testing" (*Hebrews*, 33).

by the aorist infinitive usually signals imperfective aspect,[333] which is what the Greek text has, *dunatai* ("he is able") followed by *boēthēsai* ("to help"). Thus, the author expressed Jesus' continuing ability to help believers. Grudem offered a helpful analogy about a woman obstetrician who wrote a textbook on childbirth. Then she became a mother herself and could sympathize much more fully with other pregnant women.[334]

The help that Jesus gives to the readers is important to the author. He used it here, at 4:16, and at 13:6 where he cited Ps 118:6–7, "The Lord is my helper, I will not be afraid. What can man do to me?" The word *boētheō* is used generally in the LXX to denote military assistance, and its cognates sometimes describe God's eschatological deliverance of Israel.[335] It is possible that when the author wrote Heb 2:17–18, he had Ps 79:9 on his mind: "Help us, O God our Savior, for the glory of your name; deliver us and forgive [show yourself propitious to] our sins for your name's sake." The parallel can be seen in the LXX since both passages contain the verbs *hilaskomai* and *boētheō*.[336]

The author strongly denied the Son's help for angels (2:16), which prepared the way for the promise of help from Jesus for believers (2:17–18). Gleason suggested that the author's exhortation to seek help from Jesus must be seen in light of the widespread reliance on angels for personal protection and national deliverance, a practice well attested within both Jewish and Christian literature during the Greco-Roman period.[337]

Looking at Heb 2:10–18 as a whole, the incarnation functions salvifically but also pastorally in the care of souls: since Jesus suffered, he is able to help all who suffer through temptation. "He suffered the risks and vulnerabilities of human existence, and because of this we can identify with the God who identifies with us."[338]

THEOLOGICAL IMPLICATIONS. This passage is one of the most important in the entire New Testament on the doctrine of the incarnation of Jesus. It is clear from the prologue that Christ as the Son is fully divine and is thus

---

[333] Porter, *Verbal Aspect*, 487.

[334] Grudem, *Systematic Theology*, 532.

[335] See the discussion in Gleason, "Angels and the Eschatology of Heb 1–2," 104–7.

[336] As suggested by Hughes, *Hebrews,* 124.

[337] Gleason, "Angels and the Eschatology of Heb 1–2," 105. He stated the "amulets from Palestine and Syria that illustrate the common use of the verb 'to help' to request assistance from angels. Similar inscriptions on Christian amulets from the Greco-Roman period indicate that the Jewish reliance upon angels eventually became widely accepted within the early Christian community. Examples include Christian amulets containing prayers to angels for protection, curses, good luck, and healing. Their inscriptions often list angelic names of power together with Jesus in order to add to their potency for the bearer. This highlights the relevance of the exaltation of Christ over the angels in the book of Hebrews. Rather than seek help from angels, the readers are encouraged to come to the exalted Son who 'has inherited a more excellent name than they' (Heb 1:4). For Jesus is 'the Lord their helper' (13:6) and therefore able to 'help' them (2:18) and provide 'help' in time of need (4:16)" (pp. 106–7).

[338] Oden, *Word of Life*, 123.

eternal, so 2:5–18 must be interpreted in this light. It is, therefore, a curious oddity that G. B. Caird, followed by L. D. Hurst, should make the argument that Hebrews 1–2 are not concerned with a preexistent figure who became a man, but rather with a man who is raised to an exalted status by God.[339] Caird believed that Psalm 8 in Heb 2:5–10 was the most important and the most misunderstood Old Testament passage in the epistle. Psalm 8 and the way the author used it in Heb 2:5–18 points to the destiny of mankind, which Caird believed was the overall theme of the epistle.[340] If the interpreter accepts what Caird and Hurst seem unwilling to accept—namely, the deity and thus the eternality of the Son as the focus of Hebrews 1—he is then prepared to benefit from the points they make about the focus of chap. 2 being on the exaltation of the *incarnate* Son following his suffering and death on the cross. Jesus thus fulfilled Psalm 8 by his atoning work, which enables redeemed humanity, the "many sons," also to be brought into the picture of the fulfillment of Psalm 8 in that they too will have supremacy over the angels in the eschaton. Hurst is certainly correct in saying that the point of Hebrews 1 is "to lead the readers of the epistle to the glory of mankind foretold in Psalm 8 and explored in chapter two."[341]

Given the statement in Heb 2:5 that it is not to angels that God has subjected the world to come, one is left to wonder what eschatological role the original readers could have mistakenly attributed to the angels.[342] Apparently it was thought by some that angels would "rule" in the coming age, and the author corrected this misconception by showing from Psalm 8 that such is not the case. The defeat of the enemies of God in that day will be at the hands of the Son who has been exalted by God after his incarnation, crucifixion, and resurrection.

Psalm 8 has as its background Gen 1:26–28, where both the dignity and the destiny of humanity is set forth. The author did not build his case directly on a messianic interpretation of Psalm 8, though it is clear that other the New Testament writers, like the author of Hebrews, connected the psalm with Christ. In Christ, the exalted status of humanity portrayed in Psalm 8 has been fulfilled.

---

[339] Caird, "Son by Appointment," in *The New Testament Age: Essays in Honor of Bo Reicke*, ed. W. C. Weinrich (Macon, GA: Mercer, 1984), 1:73–81; L. D. Hurst, *The Glory of Christ in the New Testament*, ed. L. D. Hurst and N. T. Wright, (Oxford: Clarendon Press, 1987), 151–64.

[340] Brawley analyzed the discourse structure of Hebrews using the analytic theories of Greimas and Courtes ("Discoursive Structure and the Unseen in Hebrews 2:8 and 11:1: A Neglected Aspect of the Context," *CBQ* 55 [1993]: 81–98). Like Caird, he considered 2:5–8 as introducing the theme that culminates in chap. 11, the rhetorical high point of the letter. His main thesis is that the theme of what is not seen (Heb 2:8) is a preparatory qualification "reducing the ambiguity of the meaning of faith in 11:1" (p. 85). Heb 11:1 "has to do with the reality of the ultimate subjection of all things to Christ, which is hoped for and not seen" (85).

[341] Hurst, *The Glory of Christ in the New Testament*, 163–64.

[342] A question well asked and answered by Gleason, "Angels and the Eschatology of Heb 1–2," 100.

The author typologically connected Psalm 8 with Christ,[343] understood (as in Paul) as the last Adam, the representative man, who achieves for humanity the dominion that had been lost due to Adam's sin.

Three propositions are given in v. 9 that are then further explained in 2:10–18. The Son's incarnation and coming to earth are expressed by "made a little lower than the angels." As the God-man, and according to God's will, Christ died for humanity, expressed by "so that by the grace of God he might taste death for everyone." As a result, he was exalted by God, expressed by "now crowned with glory and honor." The author's strategy here reveals him to be a deft interpreter and communicator. The noble position of humanity in Ps 8:5 became by paronomasia a reference to the incarnation of the Son. The glory and honor that man possessed in Ps 8:5 by his being created in the image of God (Gen 1:26–27) became a statement about the exaltation of Christ after the crucifixion. The reference to an individual man ("son of man") and then—by extension and Hebrew parallelism—humanity in Ps 8:4 became an oblique reference to Jesus as the "Son of Man."[344] None of this was lost on the original audience.

Hebrews 2:10–18 is a crucial passage on the incarnation that would play a major role in the Christological controversies of the fourth and fifth centuries. Hebrews 2:14 emphasizes the full humanity of Jesus and his solidarity with humanity. The verb tenses are critical for a correct understanding of the verse: the perfect tense *kekoinōnēken* points to humanity's constant state, while the aorist tense *meteschen* with ingressive force denotes Christ's entrance into a new, albeit permanent, state of incarnation.[345] The question is often discussed by commentators whether Heb 2:10–18 represents a Christology "from above" or "from below," that is, a preexistent Christology or a functional Christology. Dunn and Knox argued for a Christology from below and operated from a position that concluded if Jesus was fully human, he cannot be divine or preexistent.[346]

This is, of course, a non sequitur. The author of Hebrews established in chap. 1 that he operated from a preexistent Christology. The shift in focus in chap. 2 to a more functional Christology "from below" is solely for the purpose

[343] Longenecker, *Biblical Exegesis*, 171–74; L. Goppelt , *Theology of the New Testament*, ed. J. Roloff, trans. J. Alsup (Grand Rapids: Eerdmans, 1981), 2:244–46.

[344] See Fanning, "A Theology of Hebrews," 378–79.

[345] So most commentaries. Cf. B. Fanning on the aspectual differences between the perfect and aorist tenses (*Verbal Aspect in New Testament Greek*, Oxford Theological Monographs [Oxford: Clarendon Press, 1991], 136–40).

[346] Dunn, *Christology in the Making*, 98–128; J. Knox, *The Humanity and Divinity of Christ: A Study of Pattern in Christology* (Cambridge: Cambridge University Press, 1967), 61–70, 93–95. Dunn stated that any preexistent Christology in Hebrews "has to be set within the context of his indebtedness to Platonic idealism and interpreted with cross-reference to the way in which Philo treats the Logos" (p. 54), but this flounders on the evidence that the author of Hebrews was hardly indebted to either Platonic or Philonic thought.

of emphasizing the humanity of Christ and the necessity of the incarnation to the Son's atoning work on the cross.

In what way does the human nature of Jesus differ from all other people? It differs in that his human nature does not have a different human personality of its own, but rather subsists in the divine personality. This two nature-one person Christology does not destroy the true humanity of Jesus. Some have taught that in order to preserve Christ's real humanity, his human nature must have a separate personality all its own.

But such a claim actually makes the incarnation impossible since there can be no true incarnation so long as the man Christ is a separate, distinct person from the Son of God. Scripture nowhere describes the incarnation as the activity of the second member of the Godhead in a human person distinct from God, or as God causing someone to give perfect expression to his will. Hebrews 2:14 teaches that the person of the Son of God, in distinction from the Father and the Holy Spirit, took human nature into his person.

As a result of the incarnation, Jesus has two natures, but he is not two persons. This hypostatic union is the joining of two distinct natures in one person, without creating a "hybrid" third nature. Jesus is the "God-man"; he is not 50 percent God and 50 percent man. And Christ's divine nature must not be thought of in the same way that the Holy Spirit indwells believers. The human nature of Jesus is a real humanity without a sin nature. There is a perfect commingling[347] of the two natures in Jesus as a result of the incarnation. The two natures in Christ interpenetrate each other, yet both natures remain intact. There is no double personality or independent functioning of the two natures. The divine nature was not changed into the human nature nor was the human nature absorbed into the divine. Monophysitism, the early church Christological heresy that Jesus had only one nature, is an ultimate denial of the true humanity of Jesus and thus a denial of the incarnation. Nineteenth-century liberal kenotic Christology, which misinterpreted Phil 2:5–11 by teaching that the eternal Son of God abandoned his divine nature at the incarnation, must also be rejected.

To put the matter in theological terms, the human nature of Jesus does not have its own subsistence *(autupostatos)*, nor does it lack subsistence *(anupostatos)*; it has its own subsistence *(enupostatos)* in the one who is himself the second member of the Trinity, God the Son.[348] Finally, it should be noted that the incarnation is permanent in that the divine Word took upon himself humanity and remains after his resurrection and exaltation for all eternity the God-man.

[347] Some Reformed theologians, by denying the communion of natures, ended up directly contradicting Scripture. The debate between Lutheran and Reformed theologians on this issue is quite interesting. See O. Pieper, *Christian Dogmatics* (St. Louis: Concordia, 1951), 2:122, 152ff.

[348] See the discussion in Pieper, *Christian Dogmatics*, 80–81; B. Demarest and G. Lewis, *Integrative Theology* (Grand Rapids: Zondervan, 1987), 2:343; and J. L. Garrett, *Systematic Theology* (Grand Rapids: Eerdmans, 1990), 1:624–25.

"Unlike the avatars of the East, the incarnation was a permanent assumption of human nature by the second person of the Trinity. In the ascension of Christ, glorified humanity has attained the throne of the universe."[349]

The incarnation makes Jesus one of us, and thus we are called """ in Heb 2:11–13. This "band of brothers" motif prepares the way for 2:14. Psalm 8:5 says that God crowned humanity with "glory and honor," but Christ the incarnate Son brings "many sons to glory" (Heb 2:10). He is able to "sanctify" them because as one of them, his death atones for their sins. This leads to another theological point in this passage. It was God's plan all along that Jesus should, by his suffering and death, procure salvation for sinful humanity. This is evidenced by the phrase "by the grace of God" (v. 9) and by the statement that "it was fitting that God . . . should make the author of their salvation perfect through suffering" (v. 10).

Another theological point in this passage is the necessity of the death of Christ on the cross to make atonement for sinful humanity. The statements that "it was fitting that God should" and "he had to be made like his brothers . . . [to] make atonement for the sins of the people" (Heb 2:10,17) present Christ's death on the cross as absolutely essential to God's plan of salvation. Likewise, the cross was necessary for humanity to be restored to the place of "glory and honor" (v. 9) through Jesus the *archēgos* ("author") of salvation. As our *archēgos* Jesus leads us to "glory," which includes the fulfillment of humanity's position in Psalm 8 and Gen 1:26–27. Other passages speak explicitly of the necessity of the suffering of the incarnate Christ on the cross (Luke 24:26; Heb 2:10; 8:3; 9:22–23).

The perfecting of Christ through suffering should be carefully defined theologically. There is no hint in the text that Jesus was somehow morally imperfect. In fact, this epistle makes crystal clear in 4:15 that Jesus, though he was tempted in all points as a member of the human race, "yet [he] was without sin." This perfecting was for the purpose of qualifying or preparing Christ for his high priestly service. The *teleioō* word group is used in the LXX for the consecration of priests, and the use of this word in Hebrews to describe the perfection of Jesus always occurs in the context of his high priestly service (2:10; 5:9; 7:28).[350] Furthermore, the word conveys the thought of "mature," "full grown," "fully fitted for use." In his humanity Jesus experienced suffering and death, which allowed him to accomplish the atonement on the cross. Through the life experiences of suffering and death, he is a merciful high priest able to help us when we are tempted (2:18). His sufferings were the testing grounds,

---

[349] A. H. Strong, *Systematic Theology* (Valley Forge, PA: Judson, 1907), 698.

[350] See M. Silva, "Perfection and Eschatology in Hebrews," *WTJ* 39 (1976): 60–62. D. Peterson argued that the τελειόω word group in Hebrews doesn't carry the cultic sense, but the contextual use of the word group in Hebrews indicates otherwise (*Hebrews and Perfection: An Examination of the Concept of Perfection in the "Epistle to the Hebrews,"* SNTSMS [Cambridge: Cambridge University Press, 1982], 47:26–30).

as it were, in which he "learned obedience" (see Heb 5:8–9). We see through a glass darkly here, as Liddon well described: "Nor do the prerogatives of our Lord's Manhood destroy Its perfection and reality, although they do undoubtedly invest It with a robe of mystery, which Faith must acknowledge, but which she cannot hope to penetrate."[351]

There is nothing in Hebrews 2 that would support divine passability, the notion that God suffered on the cross. Theopassionism was condemned by the early church as a heresy, but it has become for many the new orthodoxy.[352] The incarnation of the Son and his suffering on the cross do not entail the concomitant notion that God suffered on the cross. The purpose of the incarnation was to equip Jesus to do as the God-Man what he could not do as God, namely, suffer and die. The focus of the author of Hebrews when it comes to the suffering of Christ is on redemption. As Peterson said: "The suffering of Christ in our writer's presentation is primarily regarded in its *redemptive* role, Christ achieving for others the salvation that they could not achieve for themselves (1:3; 2:9,14–15,17; 5:9; 9:12,14,15,26,28; 10:10,12,14,19–20; 12:24; 13:12)."[353]

Having come to the end of chap. 2, it is appropriate to look again at what the author has said about Christ's sonship. Several points seem clear at this stage in the epistle. Jesus did not become God's Son for the first time at his exaltation, and he was not given the name "Son" because of his exaltation.[354] In Heb 1:1–2:18 there are three stages of sonship, and each one is vitally connected to the other. First, according to the prologue, Jesus has always been the Son in his preexistent state. Second, there is a sense in which he became the Son in connection with his incarnation that enabled him to learn obedience through suffering (2:5–18). Third, upon completion of his suffering, he was exalted by God to a new stage of sonship (1:4–5).[355]

The connection of 2:5–18 with what was stated in 1:6 about the Son now comes into focus. Both Psalm 2 and 2 Samuel 7 contextually portray the eschatological dimension of the messianic rule. The future earthly dimension of Jesus' rule as Davidic King is pictured in Heb 1:6 where "firstborn" probably should be given the sense it carries in Ps 89:26–27, which is another passage

[351] H. P. Liddon, *The Divinity of Our Lord and Savior Jesus Christ: Eight Lectures Preached Before the University of Oxford in the Year 1866* (London: Rivingtons, 1884), 23. Liddon went on to note three things. (1) Christ's manhood is not unreal because it is impersonal, that is, because it does not possess a separate human personality other than that of the Divine Word. (2) Christ's manhood is not unreal because it is sinless, since the virgin birth accomplished both. (3) Christ's humanity is not impaired by his attributes of deity (23).

[352] E.g., J. Moltmann, *The Crucified God* (Minneapolis: Fortress, 1993); and R. Bauckham, *God Crucified: Monotheism and Christology in the New Testament* (Grand Rapids: Eerdmans, 1998).

[353] Peterson, *Hebrews and Perfection*, 175. Cf. K. DeYoung, "Divine Impassability and the Passion of Christ in the Book of Hebrews," *WTJ* 68 (2006): 48.

[354] Against Dunn, *Christology in the Making*, 1–56; and Caird, "Son by Appointment," 73–81.

[355] See the discussion on 1:2–5. For a helpful summary of "sonship" in Hebrews, see Fanning, "A Theology of Hebrews," 386.

picturing the Davidic ruler as God's son, even his "firstborn." The reference to bringing the Son into the *oikoumenē* ("the [inhabited] world"; 1:6) at first seems to refer to the incarnation, but in light of 2:5–9 the angelic worship is difficult to connect with that event since the incarnation was what actually made Jesus "lower" than the angels for a time. In Heb 1:6 angelic worship is directed toward the Son when he is brought into the *oikoumenē* as the royal firstborn. Westcott noted that the clause with *hotan* and the aorist subjunctive indisputably refers to a future occurrence.[356] Thus 2:5–9 clarifies the sense of 1:6 by picking up the contrast with angels with an added, "it is not to angels," and a back reference, "of which we are speaking" (2:5). In 2:6–9 "the world to come" (v. 5) is subjected to Jesus as Son of Man who perfectly fulfills Psalm 8. If *oikoumenē* is to be interpreted in a literal earthly sense, as seems likely, and given the author's point of the Son fulfilling the Davidic promises in the Old Testament passages he quoted (esp. Ps 110:1), then it is difficult not to see in this word a reference to the future earthly millennium.[357] The author of Hebrews has portrayed Jesus as the King who will fulfill the Davidic promise in two stages: the already/not yet.[358] Thus Jesus' Davidic kingship in Hebrews has two dimensions: a rule presently in effect, inaugurated yet invisible, and a visible rule on this earth that is yet to be consummated but is certain of fulfillment.[359]

Ever the pastor, the author took anthropology, Christology, and eschatology in Heb 2:5–18 and placed it in the service of the church. Humanity has not fulfilled her destiny as stated in Gen 1:26–27; but in Christ who became man and who made atonement for humanity's sin, humanity will do so in the eschaton. Meanwhile, the church must view the present suffering from the perspective of her union with Christ, whose union with our human nature and consequent suffering culminated in the cross and perfectly fitted him to be our merciful high priest who comes to our aid. Chrysostom, in his sermon on Heb 2:5–7, caught the pastoral heart of the author of Hebrews and reflected it in his effort to encourage his hearers: "If then all things must be made subject to Him, but have not yet been made subject, do not grieve, nor trouble thyself . . . .The King has not yet clearly conquered. Why then art thou troubled when suffering affliction?"[360]

---

356 Westcott, *Hebrews*, 22. Hughes disagreed (*Hebrews*, 58).

357 The meaning of οἰκουμένη as an earthly realm is defended by Buchanan (*Hebrews*, 17–18, 26–27, 64–65). Cf. Michel, *TDNT* 5:159; Fanning, "A Theology of Hebrews," 386; R. P. Lightner, *Evangelical Theology: A Survey and a Review* (Grand Rapids: Baker, 1986), 171. Premillennialists say that the realization of Christ's dominion in Heb 2:9 will occur in the future millennial kingdom.

358 So Barrett, "The Eschatology of the Epistle to the Hebrews," 364.

359 D. Bock, "The Reign of the Lord Christ," in *Dispensationalism, Israel and the Church: The Search for Definition*, ed. C. Blaising and D. Bock (Grand Rapids: Zondervan, 1992), 37–67.

360 Chrysostom, *The Homilies of St. John Chrysostom, Archbishop of Constantinople, on the Epistle to the Hebrews*, in *NPNF* 14, revised with Introduction and Notes, F. Gardiner (Edinburgh:

Before closing this chapter, a word needs to be said about how the author perceived the role of angels in relation to Christology. It is clear that Hebrews 1 focuses on the exaltation of Jesus above the angels, while in Hebrews 2 the focus shifts to his incarnation and death where he is temporarily made lower than the angels. In both chapters Jesus is emphatically distinguished from the angels: in Hebrews 1 he is not one of the angels, but a member of the Godhead; in Hebrews 2 he is human, and thus not one of the angels. As Heb 2:16 makes clear, Jesus had to be human in order to provide help to humans, not to angels. Bauckham is correct that the prominence of angels in these two chapters must take account of their relationship to the divine Son of God who is above them and the human Son of God who is, in his earthly life, below them. Thus it would seem that the author contrasted Jesus with the angels for additional reasons than simply to explain the Son's revelation as superior to that of the law of Moses as brought out in the hortatory paragraph of Heb 2:1–4.[361] Assuming that the purpose of Hebrews 1–2 is to set the stage for further theological reflection by clear identification of Jesus with God and humanity, then the author used angels as "indicators of ontological status" for Jesus in the Jewish monotheistic worldview. Unlike Jesus as Son, angels possess neither divine nor human nature, but rather serve those who are the heirs of salvation, as 1:14 makes clear. They serve the author's purpose of Christological definition.[362]

In the light of Hebrews 1–2, the seriousness of the warning in 2:1–4 is evident. Since God has spoken decisively in one who is a Son; since this Son is coequal with the Father, sharing in the divine nature in an exclusive sense; since the Son has condescended to become man in the incarnation in an inclusive sense, and has suffered death on our behalf as our substitute; since this Son and high priest has not only been raised from the dead but has been exalted by the Father and as the God-man is destined to rule over all things as Lord; since the Son is fully human in both roles now as Lord who reigns from heaven and as high priest who has atoned for sin; then we better pay close attention to all that God has done and is doing for us in this Son who is our Lord and our high priest. As the author put it: "how shall we escape if we ignore such a great salvation?" (2:3).

Excursus: Hebrews 2:14 and the Extent of the Atonement in John Calvin and John Owen

Hebrews 2:14 plays an important role in John Calvin's understanding of the incarnation and the extent of the atonement. Calvin explained in his *Institutes*

T&T Clark/Grand Rapids: Eerdmans, 1996), 383. He continued: "Again, he reminds them of the Cross, thereby effecting two things; both persuading them to bear all things nobly, looking to the Master . . . . Then he shows that the Cross is 'glory and honor,' as He Himself also always calls it, saying, 'That the Son of Man might be glorified . . . .' If then he calls the [sufferings] for His servants' sake 'glory,' much more shouldest thou the [sufferings] for the Lord" (ibid.).

[361] Bauckham, "Monotheism and Christology in Hebrews 1," 170–71.

[362] Ibid., 172–73.

that Christ united himself with humanity in the incarnation.[363] The incarnation was absolutely necessary for the death of Christ on the cross to be applicable to human beings. It is this shared humanity that made it possible for the work of Christ on the cross to be something accomplished on behalf of all humanity. From Calvin's *Institutes* as well as his sermons and other writings, K. Kennedy demonstrated that Calvin understood Christ's sharing in our human nature as the ground for a universal rather than a limited atonement.[364] For example, Calvin stated regarding Jesus' death on the cross that "he willed in full measure to appear before the judgment seat of God His Father in the name and in the person of all sinners."[365] Calvin made no distinction here between the elect and the non-elect. Kennedy said that "because it was his human flesh which he offered, a flesh which he shares with all of humanity, and which was offered in the *person* of all sinners, his death became a death for all of humanity."[366] Kennedy presented and discussed several other examples of Calvin's connecting Christ's humanity with our humanity as the basis for his work on the cross for all men.

Kennedy then proceeded to examine the Dortian rational for the concept of "limited atonement" in Calvinism. The logic is as follows: if Christ died for all, how is it that not all are ultimately saved? If Christ's death atoned for the sins of the world, then no further payment can be exacted from anyone. Logically, either all will be saved, or Christ did not die for all. How is it that Christ's death is not applicable to some people when Christ shared in all people's humanity? The typical Reformed answer is that Jesus' taking on a human nature shared by all is merely coincidental to the fact that the elect are human. Kennedy pointed out that this is the argument of John Owen, based on Heb 2:14, in his famous *The Death of Death in the Death of Christ*. Owen argued that it was only for the "children" (the elect) that Jesus took on human flesh.[367] Kennedy also indicated that Calvin in his *Institutes*, contrary to Owen, located the fulcrum separating the elect from the non-elect in one's faith and subsequent union with Christ.[368] For Calvin, Heb 2:14 is proof of Christ's partnership with us in our humanity. Calvin then mentioned a possible objection to his use of Heb 2:14: since we are all the same flesh with Christ, all will be saved. Kennedy made the salient point that here one would expect Calvin to counter this objection of universalism with an appeal to limited atonement as Owen did. Surprisingly, Calvin did not do so.

---

[363] Calvin, *Institutes*, 2.12.1.

[364] K. Kennedy, *Union with Christ and the Extent of the Atonement in Calvin*, in *Studies in Biblical Literature* 48, ed. H. Gossai (New York: Peter Lang, 2002). See esp. pp. 75–103.

[365] Calvin, *The Deity of Christ and Other Sermons*, trans. L. Nixon (Grand Rapids: Eerdmans, 1950), 52. In another sermon Calvin referred to Christ before Caiaphas and described Jesus as standing there "in the person of all cursed ones and all transgressors" (*Deity of Christ*, 95). Speaking of Luke's genealogy of Christ and of Luke going all the way back to Adam, Calvin remarked that this shows "that the salvation brought by Christ is common to the whole human race, inasmuch as Christ, the author of salvation, is descended from Adam, the common father of us all" (*Institutes* 2.13.3).

[366] Kennedy, *Union with Christ*, 83.

[367] J. Owen, *The Death of Death in the Death of Christ* (Edinburgh: Banner of Truth Trust, 1959), 63.

[368] Calvin, *Institutes*, 2.13.2.

Instead, Calvin argued that what separates the elect from the non-elect is that only believers obtain saving union with Christ. "In this passage, Calvin does not limit the atonement, he merely limits the actual application of salvation . . . . Calvin appeals to the believer's faith and union with Christ as being that which differentiates him from the non-believer."[369]

There are many other passages in Calvin's sermons and commentaries where he articulates universal atonement. One such place is Calvin's discussion of Heb 9:28, "Christ was sacrificed once to take away the sins of many people." Commenting on this passage, Calvin stated: "He says many meaning all . . . as in Rom 5:15. It is of course certain that not all enjoy the fruit of Christ's death . . ., but this happens because their unbelief hinders them."[370] There is not a single passage in the *Institutes* where Calvin discussed or even mentioned the notion of limited atonement. Many Calvinists and non-Calvinists alike have argued that Calvin himself never articulated limited atonement and that it was not until the Council of Dort that this doctrine became codified in Reformed theology.[371]

2. Faithful Obedience Necessary to Enter Rest (3:1–4:13)

[1]Therefore, holy brothers, who share in the heavenly calling, fix your thoughts on Jesus, the apostle and high priest whom we confess. [2]He was faithful to the one who appointed him, just as Moses was faithful in all God's house. [3]Jesus has been found worthy of greater honor than Moses, just as the builder of a house has greater honor than the house itself. [4]For every house is built by someone, but God is the builder of everything. [5]Moses was faithful as a servant in all God's house, testifying to what would be said in the future. [6]But Christ is faithful as a son over God's house. And we are his house, if we hold on to our courage and the hope of which we boast.

(1) Jesus' Superiority to Moses (3:1–6)

The structure of Hebrews includes three large discourse units: 1:1–4:13; 4:14–10:18; and 10:19–13:25. The first one (1:1–4:13) can be divided into two smaller discourse units: 1:1–2:18 and 3:1–4:13.[372] Whereas Heb 1:1–2:18 was

---

[369] Kennedy, *Union with Christ*, 89.

[370] Calvin, *Hebrews*, 93–94.

[371] E.g., N. Douty, *The Death of Christ: A Treatise which Considers the Question: "Did Christ Die only for the Elect?"* (Irving: Williams and Watrous, 1972); R. T. Kendall, *Calvin and English Calvinism to 1649* (Oxford: University Press, 1979); and C. Daniel, "Hyper-Calvinism and John Gill" (Ph.D. dissertation, University of Edinburgh, 1983). See esp. Daniel's 51-page appendix where he addressed the question "Did John Calvin Teach Limited Atonement?" After a careful survey of Calvin's writings, Daniel concluded that he did not. Cf. K. Kennedy, *Union with Christ*, 21–74. See also D. Allen, "The Atonement: Limited or Universal?" in *Whosoever Will: A Biblical-Theological Critique of Five-Point Calvinism,* ed. David L. Allen and Steve Lemke (Nashville: B&H Academic, 2010), 61–107.

[372] See W. Nauck, "Zum Aufbau des Hebräerbriefes," in *Judentum, Urchristentum, Kirche: Festschrift for J. Jeremias*, ed. W. Eltester, BZNW 26 (Giessen: Töpelmann, 1960), 199; Hughes, *Hebrews*, 3,125; and Bruce, *Hebrews*, 90. Ellingworth (*Hebrews,* 193) and Lane (*Hebrews 1–8,*

primarily expository in terms of genre (the exception being the paragraph in 2:1–4), the discourse genre of 3:1–4:13 is primarily hortatory. A number of imperatives and hortatory subjunctives characterize this section, along with the predominate use of first and second person verbs. The hortatory nature of Heb 3:1–6 is signaled by a change in topic, the use of direct address via the vocatives, the use of an imperative in 3:1, and an imperatival idea semantically encoded in the conditional clause of v. 6. The paragraph is unified by lexical cohesion with the repetition of "house," the comparison and contrast of Jesus and Moses, and the use of *inclusio* with the name "Jesus" in v. 1 and the "Christ" in v. 6.[373] The paragraph can be summarized in three points: (1) Moses was a servant; Jesus is the Son; (2) Moses was a part of the house; Jesus is over the house; and (3) Moses testified of what was coming; Jesus fulfilled the testimony.

Why did the author compare and contrast Jesus with Moses? A likely reason is that Moses held a distinctive place of honor in normative Judaism, Philo, and Sectarian Judaism, and this included the belief by some that Moses was superior to the angels.[374] Philo's writings indicate that by the first century AD Moses had come to be extolled not only as law-giver but also as high priest.[375] If the recipients were Jewish believers, as most scholars have concluded, then Moses' relationship to Jesus would have been a topic of interest. But there is little evidence that the author was refuting a "new Moses Christology," as he refuted a supposed "angelic Christology."[376] The author did not denigrate Moses in any way, but rather compared him favorably to Jesus in 3:1–2. Even when the contrast between the two is drawn in 3:3–6, nothing is said of Moses' failures as recorded in the Pentateuch, which would have been an easy mark for the author had he desired merely to show the superior faithfulness of Jesus over Moses.[377] There is apparently no apologetic or polemical purpose behind

---

68) erroneously extend the unit from 3:1 to 5:10. Westfall (*Discourse Analysis*, 127, 133, 142) erroneously extends the unit to 4:10, with 4:11–16 functioning as the "discourse peak and point of departure" for the next major discourse unit.

[373] For detailed analysis of the structure of the passage, see Westfall, *Discourse Analysis*, 111–27; A. Vanhoye, *Our Priest in God: The Doctrine of the Epistle to the Hebrews* (Rome: Biblical Institute Press, 1979), 86–92; P. Auffret, "Essai sur la structure littéraire et l'interprétation d'Hébreux 3, 1–6," *NTS* 26.3 (1980) 179–80, 380–96; M. R. D'Angelo, *Moses in the Letter to the Hebrews*, SBLDS 42 (Missoula, MT: Scholars Press, 1979), 65–199; Neeley, "Discourse Analysis of Hebrews," 6–8, 13, 32, 45–46, 80–81; and G. Guthrie, *Structure*, 65–66. Note the alliteration and assonance of the α in 3:1 as well as the proliferation of π in 3:1–6.

[374] See full discussion in M. D'Angelo, *Moses in the Letter to the Hebrews,* 95–149. Hence B. Scott, "Jesus' Superiority over Moses in Hebrews 3:1–6," *BSac* 155 (1998): 203, can say: "contrasting Jesus to Moses is a step beyond Heb. 1:5–13, not a step backward."

[375] Philo, *Vit. Mos.* 2.66–186; *Praem. Poen.* 52–55; *Gig.* 52–54. See M. Isaacs, "Hebrews," in *Early Christian Thought in Its Jewish Context*, ed. J. Barclay and J. Sweet (Cambridge: Cambridge University Press, 1996), 150.

[376] So E. L. Allen, "Jesus and Moses in the New Testament," *ExpTim* 67 (1955–56): 104–6.

[377] A point well made by B. Scott, "Jesus' Superiority over Moses," 209.

the metaphor of the "house" in 3:1–6; rather, the comparison with Moses introduces the following paraenesis in the latter half of v. 6 and the hortatory section to follow in 3:7–4:13.[378]

Basically, Heb 3:1–6 is something of a midrash on Num 12:7. In addition, two other Old Testament passages lurk in the foreground or at the very least in the background of the author's thought:

Num 12:7	"my servant Moses; he is faithful in all my house"
1 Sam 2:35	"I will raise up . . . a faithful priest . . . I will firmly establish his house
1 Chr 17:14	"I will set him over my house"

Lane, like Aalen and D'Angelo, commented on the connection between 1 Chr 17:14 and 17:13 since the latter was referenced by the author in Heb 1:5 and since the statement "faithful to the one who appointed him" in 3:2 reflects the double meaning in the LXX of the former.[379] As Koester noted, the interplay of these texts allows the language to be applied to three aspects of Jesus' identity: (1) Moses and Jesus (Num 12:7); (2) Son of God (connecting 2 Sam 7:14 and 1 Chr 17:13 with Heb 1:5) where the wording helps connect Jesus' role as Son with his faithfulness over God's "house"; and (3) priest (1 Sam. 2:35).[380] Lane thought the paragraph relies on the complex oracle concerning the royal priest in 1 Chr 17:14 and 1 Sam 2:35 coupled with Num 12:7 where the authority of Moses is related to the oracle. This "indicates that the theme of Jesus' priesthood is not held in abeyance in 3:1–4:14 but is taken up immediately following its announcement in 2:17–18."[381]

3:1 The inferential particle *hothen* ("therefore") indicates a conclusion drawn from the preceding thought and provides the reason for considering Jesus. Semantically, the word gives the grounds for the exhortation about to be made. It marks a summary conclusion and places semantic dominance on 3:1–6 in relation to the preceding section: Since Jesus is the apostle and high priest, consider him.[382] Some suggest that the term links not only the previous paragraph or section, but also takes in all that has been said in the first two chapters about the Son.[383] Koester said the term consistently appears in Hebrews in the

---

[378] E. Grässer, "Mose und Jesus. Zur Auslegung von Hebr 3:1–6," *ZNW* 75 (1984): 15; and Attridge, *Hebrews*, 111.

[379] Lane, *Hebrews 1–8,* 76; S. Aalen, "'Reign' and 'House' in the Kingdom of God in the Gospels," *NTS* 8 (1961–62), 215–40; see the discussion in D'Angelo, *Moses in the Letter to the Hebrews,* 71–92; F. F. Bruce, *Hebrews,* 93, and Gheorghita, *The Role of the Septuagint in Hebrews*, 111–12.

[380] Koester summarized and tied all this together nicely in his discussion (*Hebrews,* 243–44).

[381] Lane, *Hebrews 1–8*, 79.

[382] See the discussion in C. Westfall, "Moses and Hebrews 3:1–6: Approach or Avoidance?", *Christian-Jewish Relations Through the Centuries*, ed S. Porter and W. R. Pearson, in JSNTSup 192, Roehampton Papers 6 (Sheffield: Academic Press, 2000), 190.

[383] Delitzsch, *Hebrews* 1:153; Lane, *Hebrews 1–8,* 73.

middle of an argument rather than at the beginning of a new major section,[384] rightly suggesting that 3:1–4:13 should not be taken as beginning a new major discourse unit but rather connects with 1:1–2:18. The next major discourse unit begins at 4:14.

The author addresses "holy brothers." Bruce rendered this phrase "members of a holy brotherhood."[385] The author includes Christian women in the designation as well. That which is "holy" implies separation from the world by having been chosen and set apart by God. In apposition to "holy brothers" is a noun phrase the NIV translates as a relative clause: "who share in the heavenly calling." This second phrase is governed by the adjective *metochos*, used as a noun meaning "partner," "companion," "partaker," or "co-sharer." It can also be rendered as a participle to bring out the active idea inherent in the meaning of the word: "sharing in a heavenly calling."[386] The word is something of a technical term for believers who have responded to God's salvation call.[387] It was used at 1:9 in the quotation from Ps 45:7, and the verb form *metechō* was used at 2:14 for Christ's sharing in humanity's "flesh and blood."[388] It describes participation in some common blessing or privilege; the bond of union lies in that which is shared, and not in the persons themselves.[389]

The believers share in a "heavenly calling." The adjective *epouranios* ("heavenly") describes the nature of the calling; it has a heavenly source and a heavenly nature, so it comes from God.[390] The genitive noun *klēsis* ("calling") tells what believers partake of: they share a heavenly calling.[391] Whether the author's intent was to suggest the call was from heaven, to heaven,[392] or both is really a moot point since neither the text nor the context specifies the intended meaning and since both are true theologically. It is difficult to be too specific here, but the heavenly calling may be identified with the "great salvation" of 2:3 or the glorious destiny of man in 2:7–10. It is heavenly in origin in that it is from God, it is heavenly in quality, and it is heavenly in purpose in that it leads us to God.[393] This phrase ("share . . . calling") further describes the "holy brethren" and serves to remind the readers of their high calling and their responsibility to it. There is a back reference to 1:1; 2:3,11 as well.[394]

[384] So Koester, *Hebrews*, 224, 242. His reasoning for not beginning a new major section at 3:1 is sound.

[385] Bruce, *Hebrews*, 90.

[386] So BDAG 643; Lane, *Hebrews 1–8*, 74.

[387] Schmidt, "καλέω," *TDNT* 3:487–93. See also L&N 34.8.

[388] Westfall, in comparing the use of this word for Jesus in 2:14 who shares in our humanity, poignantly stated: "The identification of believers as partners (μέτοχοι) in the heavenly calling is the other side of the coin of 2:14" ("Moses and Hebrews 3:1–6," 193).

[389] So Westcott, *Hebrews*, 73.

[390] L&N 12.17, translate the adjective "from God" to indicate source.

[391] As noted by Greenlee, *Exegetical Summary*, 86.

[392] Lane said that the call from God is a call to enter his presence (*Hebrews 1–8*, 74).

[393] N. Miller, *Hebrews*, 65.

[394] Delitzsch, *Hebrews* 1:153.

The readers are exhorted to "fix [their] thoughts on Jesus," who is designated "apostle" and "high priest." The compound verb *katanoeō* means "consider attentively," where the *kata* prefix intensifies the verb. That which the readers are to consider about Jesus is his faithfulness as apostle and high priest.[395] The use of the term "apostle" indicates Jesus was sent by God with authority to speak for God and represent God to mankind.[396] Lane summarized three proposals on the source and significance of the Christological title "apostle."[397] First, the high priest was regarded by the rabbis as the representative (Aramaic *shaliach*) of God before the people on the Day of Atonement. The translation of *shaliach* would be *apostolos*.[398] A key problem with this is that the *shaliach/apostolos* terminology is not found in the Old Testament. Second, a variant reading of Exod 23:20 (LXX) in one of the Targums has "my apostle" instead of "angel"; it also occurs in two other places in Exodus. Third, Exod 3:10 (LXX) implies Moses was called and sent by God to Pharaoh, hence the use of the term in Heb 3:1.[399]

The interesting connection in Num 13:2 (LXX) between the noun *archēgos* ("leaders") and the verb *apostellō* ("send") may have been in the author's mind since he used the term *archēgos* earlier (2:10).[400] Contextually, it is possible that the author connected Jesus, God's chief "apostle" who was sent by God, with his apostles, as in 2:3.[401] More likely than this or any of the views above, the title connects contextually with the thought of 1:1–2:4, that Jesus is superior to the prophets (1:1) and to the angels (2:4). There are a number of words from a similar semantic domain as *apostolos* in 1:1–2:4 ("prophet" and "spoke" in 1:1,2; verbs of speech such as "say" or "speak" [four times in 1:5–13; twice in 2:1–4]; "angel" [8 times in 1:4–2:16], "sent" [1:14 of the activity of angels], and "declare" in 2:12 where Jesus is the implied subject;) which illustrate the programmatic nature of the prologue for the entire epistle where we are told that the Son is the ultimate messenger of God.[402] The Moses as prophet motif is found later in three places (8:6; 9:15; 12:24). Furthermore, other places in the New Testament cast Moses as a prophet, such as Acts 3:22–26; 7:30–39, both of which have Deut 18:15–19 behind them. The New Testament authors, especially Luke, considered miraculous signs in accordance with Deut 13:2–12

---

[395] Moffatt, *Hebrews,* 41; Lane, *Hebrews 1–8,* 74–75.

[396] See the survey of the use of this term in the LXX, NT, Philo, in Spicq, "ἀπόστολος" *TLNT* 1:186–94; and Ellingworth, *Hebrews,* 199–200. On the use of ἀποστέλλω, see K. Rengstorf, *TDNT* 1:408–13.

[397] Lane, *Hebrews 1–8,* 75–76.

[398] See Manson, *Hebrews: An Historical and Theological Reconsideration,* 53–54; Rengstorf, "ἀπόστολος," *TDNT* 1:408–13.

[399] P. R. Jones, "The Figure of Moses as a Heuristic Device for Understanding the Pastoral Intent of Hebrews," *RevExp* 76 (1979): 98.

[400] So Ellingworth, *Hebrews,* 200; Koester, *Hebrews,* 243.

[401] Delitzsch, *Hebrews,* 1:154.

[402] See Westfall, "Moses and Hebrews 3:1–6," 194–95.

to serve as authenticating miracles of a prophet. That miraculous signs are ascribed to Moses in both the Old Testament (Exod 4:1–9) and the New Testament (Acts 7:36), as well as Moses' prophetic status in Acts 7:30–39, confirms that the New Testament writers considered him one of the prophets.[403]

Second Temple Judaism applied the title "apostle" to Moses. Such a connection could be derived from Exod 3:10 where God "sends" Moses. The verb "sends" is used in both the MT and the LXX of Exod 3:10. Lierman suggested that Heb 3:1 appears to be "the earliest extant specific reference to the apostleship of Moses,"[404] although it should be noted that the author of Hebrews does not explicitly call Moses an apostle. The title "high priest" is coordinated to "apostle" by the conjunction *kai* ("and"), with the definite article governing both nouns showing both refer to Jesus. The term "high priest" was first introduced in 2:17 and indicates Jesus' work of atonement and his ongoing representation of redeemed humanity to God in heaven. Hebrews 2:5–18 serves as the grounds for the title in 3:1. The two titles identify the two functions that Jesus fulfills. He represents God to humanity as apostle and he represents humanity to God as high priest.[405] The two terms indicate Jesus is the final revelation of God who authorizes his word (apostle) and his work (high priest).[406] As apostle, Jesus was sent by the Father (John 17:18) and through him God acts (John 14:10). It is also possible, though less likely, that the combined titles are a hendiadys and thus express one thought: "a high priest sent (by God)."[407]

While one should not think that the author had in mind a Christology that nearly equates Jesus with Moses, Westcott thought it nevertheless seemed clear by implication that the author considered Moses as apostle and high priest due to the comparison in Heb 3:1–6.[408] Jesus is called the apostle and high priest "whom we confess" (lit. "of our confession," *homologia*). There is a certain ambiguity in the author's use of this word, resulting in several views on its referent: (1) the content of the faith one confesses,[409] (2) the act of confessing,[410] or (3) the person whom one confesses, namely Jesus.[411] If the author meant

---

[403] See the discussion in J. Lierman, *The New Testament Moses: Christian Perceptions of Moses and Israel in the Setting of Jewish Religion*, WUNT 173 (Tübingen: Mohr Siebeck, 2004), 50, 61–63.

[404] Ibid., 76. On the use of the concept of apostle for Moses in Second Temple Judaism, Samaritan and Rabbinic literature, see pp. 71–73.

[405] So suggested by Luther, *LW* 57, 3.137–38, and by many since, such as Bruce, *Hebrews,* 91.

[406] Rengstorf, *TDNT* 1:414–20.

[407] So Ellingworth, *Hebrews,* 200.

[408] Westcott, *Hebrews*, 74.

[409] Ibid.; Moffatt, *Hebrews,* 41; and Ellingworth, *Hebrews,* 199, who viewed it as a common Christian confession, but in the author's own distinctive language—Jesus as the high priest.

[410] Riggenbach, *Der Brief an die Hebräer*, 3rd ed., KNT 14 (Leipzig: Deichert, 1922), 69.

[411] This view takes the genitive as objective, as do Dods ("Hebrews," 272), Bruce (*Hebrews,* 91), and the NIV. Westcott said that this sense "falls short of the meaning" (*Hebrews,* 74). Hughes combined views one and three (*Hebrews,* 129).

option one, he left unstated what one confesses about Jesus.[412] The latter option is the most likely. The name "Jesus" is emphatic since the author placed it at the end of the clause. It also links this verse with the following one, thus marking the beginning of the author's argument about the superiority of Jesus over Moses.

There is a significant amount of semantic back reference to Hebrews 2 in 3:1. Jesus as "apostle" harks back to 1:1–2:4, especially 1:2 and 2:3. Jesus as "high priest" refers back to 1:3 and 2:5–18, especially 2:17. The readers were told to "fix [their] thought on" Jesus, and in the hortatory paragraph 2:1–4 they were exhorted to "pay more careful attention, therefore, to what we have heard." The use of the human name "Jesus" links to 2:9 where this name "Jesus" is first used and which is the lead in to 2:10–18 and the high priestly work of Christ. In 3:1, believers are "sharers" in the heavenly calling, reminiscent of 2:14 where it is said that Jesus shared in humanity and was crowned with glory and honor. The "holy brothers" of 3:1 are holy because of Jesus' suffering that sanctified them, and in 2:11a, they are "brothers" because the incarnate Son is not ashamed to call them brothers in 2:11b.

3:2 Verse 2 begins with the adjective "faithful," which describes Jesus and is emphatic by word order. "The one who appointed him" is an articular participle in Greek with God as the subject-agent of the action "appoint." The verb *poieō* takes its specific meaning from the context, and most commentators and translators take it here in the sense of "appoint," referring to Jesus' appointment by God as apostle and high priest.[413]

Jesus was faithful to God who appointed him "just as Moses was faithful in[414] all God's house." Here the author began a comparison between Jesus and Moses. Two key interpretive issues surface at this point: the meaning of "house" (also translated "household" or "family"); and determining the antecedent of

---

[412] Attridge pointed out that the term is used in Hebrews in a general sense of "that which we confess" (*Hebrews,* 108).

[413] A few take it in the sense of "create," referring to God's having "created" Jesus either in his generation as firstborn or in his incarnation. Against D'Angelo, *Moses in the Letter to the Hebrews*, it is highly doubtful there is any reference here to the eternal generation of the Son. This was a Christological discussion later among the early church fathers. Nor is this a reference to the incarnation, a view prominent among the church fathers who interpreted this verse, in reaction to the Arians, to mean that God created the human nature of Jesus. See Moffatt, *Hebrews,* 42; and Wallis, *Faith of Jesus Christ in Early Christian Traditions,* 148. See Ellingworth, *Hebrews*, 202, and further material in Hughes, *Hebrews*, 129–30, who has an excellent discussion of how the Arians used this verse countered by Athanasius, Chrysostom, and later Alcuin. Chrysostom asked, "What did he make him?" and gave the correct answer: "apostle and high priest," meaning he was "made" in the sense of "appointed." Hughes remarked: "This is a much more effective line of rejoinder to the Arian misinterpretation of this text, and it is surprising that, instead of pressing it, the fathers seem generally to have incommoded themselves by attempting to combat the Arian interpretation while adopting the Arian translation" (130).

[414] ἐν with a dative object indicates the place in which the faithfulness occurred.

the pronoun *autou* ("his") in the phrase "his house," since *autou* could refer to God, Christ, or Moses.

As to the meaning of "house" in this context, there are three possibilities.[415] First, it can refer to Christendom as the spiritual community of God (1 Tim 3:15; 1 Pet 2:5; 4:17).[416] This is closely related to the Pauline theme of the church as the temple of God (1 Cor 3:16; 6:19; 2 Cor 6:16; Eph 2:19–21). Second, it can mean "household" or "family." This usage is relatively uncommon in the New Testament (about 18 occurrences and only one in Heb at 11:7).[417] Third, it could be a priestly house, as Heb 10:21 indicates. The context of Num 12:7 points to a priestly interpretation of "house" where the tabernacle was the center of worship and priestly duties.[418]

Moses was called a priest explicitly only once in the Old Testament (Ps 99:6), and he was from the tribe of Levi (Exod 2:1–10). The Pentateuch affirms Moses' acting as the priest at both the inauguration of the nation and Aaron as priest (Exodus 19–20; 28–29). Moses' actions were often priestly even though Aaron and the Levites performed the priestly duties. For example, Moses sanctified Aaron and the tabernacle, served at the altar, and made atonement for the people (see Exod 29:1; 24:6; 32:30 respectively). And Moses, not Aaron, passed on the high priesthood to Eleazar on Mount Hor (Num 20:22–29).[419]

In Numbers 12 Aaron and Miriam challenged Moses' leadership. God's rebuke of Aaron and Miriam was against the backdrop of the tabernacle; in fact, God called the three of them into the tabernacle before he rebuked Aaron and Miriam, which included the words "my servant Moses; he is faithful in all my house" (v. 7). Moses' fidelity in constructing the tabernacle according to God's directions is an important theme in the Pentateuch. The author may have had the tabernacle in mind when he called Moses a "servant . . . testifying" (3:5) since the tabernacle is often called "the tent of testimony." Hodges, who championed this view of "house," concluded that the "house" over which the Son presides as priest is the functioning priestly and worshipping community today.[420] Whatever sense "house" may have had in Num 12:7, the author

---

[415] O. Michel, "*oikos*" in *TDNTa*, 674–75; BDAG 698–99; P. Weigandt, *EDNT* 2:500–3; J. Goetzmann, *NIDNTT*, 248–51. O. Michel took the "house" in Num 12:7 to be all Israel as the people of God or as God's "royal household" (*Der Brief an die Hebräer* 6th ed.; Meyer Kommentar 13, [Göttingen: Vandenhoeck & Ruprecht, 1966], 96).

[416] Goetzmann (*NIDNTT*, 249) and O. Michel ("*oikos,*" 675) listed Heb 3:2–6 with this meaning. This usage predominates in the Pauline and Petrine Letters.

[417] BDAG lists Heb 3:2–6 with this meaning (699).

[418] B. Levine pointed out that the Hb. בֵּיתִי ("my house") elsewhere "refers consistently to 'My Temple' . . . . This is the only time in Scripture that we find YHWH's heavenly household designated by the term *bayît*" (*Numbers 1–20*, in *AB* 4a [New York: Doubleday, 1993], 331).

[419] For a survey of the rabbinic literature on the subject of Moses as priest, see Lierman (*New Testament Moses*, 70). He noted that the only matter largely unresolved among the rabbis regarding Moses' priesthood was whether it lasted his whole lifetime or ended with the accession of Aaron.

[420] Z. Hodges, "Hebrews," *The Bible Knowledge Commentary*, ed. J. Walvoord and R. Zuck (Wheaton: Victor, 1989), 786. Goetzmann (*NIDNTT*, 249), speaking of Eph 2:19–22, said that the

indicated that the church as the people of God is in some sense "his house" (Heb 3:6b).[421]

The second interpretive issue has to do with the antecedent of *autou* ("his"), which modifies "house." Is the antecedent God, Christ, or Moses? Most commentators understand "house" to be God's, at least down to v. 5.[422] Some take it as Christ's house.[423] Others see it as Moses' house. The author probably left the antecedent ambiguous deliberately to exploit it before making it clear in v. 6.[424] It would seem best to see God as the antecedent here as the NIV brings out overtly: "just as Moses was faithful in all God's house." Some manuscripts omit *holō* ("all") before "house."[425]

The NIV translation of v. 2a renders the clause introduced by the present participle *onta* as a new sentence with the English past tense: "He was faithful to the one who appointed him." The clause further describes Jesus in one of three ways: (1) in an attributive sense;[426] (2) as a second accusative with the predicate *piston* ("faithful") describing the characteristic that they were to consider about Jesus—"consider Jesus, as being faithful";[427] or (3) as simply the predicate of an indirect statement—"consider that Jesus was faithful."[428] Semantically, the clause may serve to indicate grounds or reason: "regard him well since [because] he was faithful."[429] Some see in the present tense an implication of the Son's general character of faithfulness. Although grammatically the present tense often does not convey present meaning, in this case it would appear that it does.[430]

By a tactful move, the author placed Moses in the foreground as being also an example of fidelity with the phrase "as was Moses." The author never intended

---

semantic concepts behind "house of God" and "temple of God" intertwine.

[421] Goetzmann, *NIDNTT*, 249.

[422] So Lane, *Hebrews 1–8,* 77, with the meaning "God appointed Jesus in his [God's] house"; and Ellingworth, *Hebrews*, 201.

[423] E.g., A. T. Hanson, *Jesus Christ in the Old Testament* (London: S.P.C.K., 1965), 48–58.

[424] Attridge, *Hebrews,* 109.

[425] The variant is placed in brackets in the UBS^4 text and given a "C" rating (*TCGNT* 594–95). It is omitted by Hughes, who has a good discussion of the issue (*Hebrews,* 131). Cf. Ellingworth, *Hebrews,* 201; and Lane, *Hebrews 1–8*, 70–71.

[426] So Alford, "Hebrews," 58; Hughes, *Hebrews,* 129; and most translations.

[427] So Delitzsch, *Hebrews,* 1:155.

[428] So Moffatt, *Hebrews,* 41.

[429] So Miller, *Hebrews*, 67.

[430] Ellingworth did not think the participle ὄντα conveys present meaning (*Hebrews,* 202). But Alford argued the opposite case: "the present participle may always be contemporary with a previously expressed verb, of any tense, provided that verb be absolutely in construction with the participle . . . . But a present participle standing absolutely, or with a present verb, must retain its present force" ("Hebrews," 85). Wallis suggested that the present participle points to Jesus' present faithfulness in his role as priestly intercessor (*Faith of Jesus Christ in Early Christian Tradition,* 145–50). Koester thought it better to interpret the faithfulness contextually according to 2:17 and 3:7–19 to refer to Jesus' testing in contrast to the unfaithfulness of the exodus generation (*Hebrews,* 243). I see no reason why both cannot be true.

to offer a polemic against Moses or Judaism in any way here. The remaining verses develop, primarily by a comparison between Jesus and Moses, a "how much more" argument that shows the superiority of Jesus over Moses and thus the greater heed the readers should pay to the things spoken about Jesus.

3:3 Verse 3 is the beginning of a new sentence in Greek introduced by the subordinating conjunction *gar* (not translated in the NIV). The author continued the comparison begun in v. 2 by indicating the reason for carefully considering Jesus. Several translations take *gar* as indicating a contrast with the preceding verse with the sense that Jesus and Moses are similar, but Jesus is worthy of more honor. What contrast is indicated is not drawn from the conjunction but from the phrase "greater honor than Moses" occurring later in the verse. Westfall understood the conjunction to signal an explanation that could be glossed by the use of "except" as in: "Jesus was faithful [in his house] like Moses was [faithful] in his house, except this one [Jesus] is worthy of greater glory than Moses."[431]

The name "Jesus" is not in the Greek text, though it is supplied by the NIV. Rather, the demonstrative pronoun *houtos* ("this one") is used to refer to Jesus and is emphatic by word order. God is the understood agent behind the verb "worthy," and the perfect tense probably implies the permanence of the worthiness beginning with Jesus' exaltation.[432]

Jesus is worthy "of greater honor" than Moses, and *pleionos* may indicate "greater" in the sense of degree (NIV) or "more" in the sense of quantity (KJV; NASB). The former is most likely correct in that *para* with the accusative indicates a comparison implying greater degree, the basis of which is "honor." *Doxa*, which normally means "glory," can also have the sense of "honor" as it probably does here.

The author introduces his illustration of the builder of a house with the phrase *kath' hoson*, (lit.) "in accordance with as much as." The phrase can be taken in one of two ways: *comparison*, indicated by "as" or "just as" (NIV); or *degree*, indicated by "as much as" (NASB). Both make good sense in the context. The use of "builder" raises two questions: (1) does it refer to the one who built the house or to the one who founded the house(hold);[433] and (2) who is the builder? The answer to the first question depends on how one interprets "house" as noted above, but there is little difference in meaning either way. The builder could be Jesus. Both Héring and Ellingworth held this view and suggested that the reference is to Jesus prior to his incarnation.[434] But most

---

[431] Westfall, "Moses and Hebrews 3:1–6," 187.

[432] Ellingworth, *Hebrews*, 204.

[433] Hughes, *Hebrews*, 132. Lane (*Hebrews 1–8*, 77) and the NIV took it in the former sense, while Alford ("Hebrews," 60) and Moffatt (*Hebrews*, 42) took it in the latter sense.

[434] Héring explained that "Jesus has himself constructed a house, namely, the new covenant, whilst Moses was not even the architect of the old" (*Hebrews*, 25). Hughes likewise viewed Jesus as the builder of the house and suggested this was probably based on the messianic prophecy of

commentators consider God the builder in light of v. 4, and this appears to be the better interpretation.

3:4–6 Verse 4 is often erroneously taken as a parenthetical statement separating two comparative statements about Jesus (v. 3) and Moses (v. 5).[435] Others have correctly pointed out that this ignores the author's use of conjunctions and particles in the structural development of his argument.[436] The conjunction *gar*, not *kai*, introduces v. 4, grammatically subordinating the verse to the thought of v. 3 in order to clarify it semantically. The conjunction governs the next three verses since *kai* connects v. 4 to v. 5 (v. 5 begins a new sentence coordinated with the previous one). Thus, v. 4 is not parenthetical but marks a transition from "assertion to explanation."[437] Lane's analysis of the development of the author's thought is on target:

vv. 1–2	introduction of the comparison between Jesus and Moses
v. 3	assertion of Jesus' superiority to Moses
vv. 4–6	explanation for this assertion
v. 6b	relevance for the congregation[438]

The *kai* at the beginning of v. 5 coordinates the relationship between Jesus and Moses, and *men . . . de* coordinates them in 3:5–6: "And Moses was faithful on the one hand in his entire house as a servant in order to witness to what was to be said. On the other hand, Jesus is faithful over his house as a son."[439] The adversative conjunction *de* introducing the clause "but God is the builder of everything" (v. 4) indicates a contrast between the preceding individual statement and the following general statement. It also serves to safeguard against any misunderstanding that there may be many builders. In the Greek text, the articular participle *ho kataskeuasas* would be translated "the one who built," opening the question as to the subject of the clause. Most take the subject to

---

Zech 6:12–15 (*Hebrews,* 132). N. Miller attempted to show how the author clarified his meaning to avoid contradiction if Jesus is taken to be the builder of the house in v. 3: "Having given in verse 2 the grounds for the exhortation in verse 1 to consider Jesus as apostle and high priest, and having clarified that grounds with a comparison (v. 2) and a contrast (v. 3), the author feels it necessary to avoid any possible misapprehension or contradiction between identifying the household as God's in verse 2 and identifying Jesus as its preparer in verse 3. Jesus is the special preparer or founder (v. 4a), but He does it as the Son and under the universal foundership of God the Father (v. 4b). Thus v. 4 seems to serve, along with vv. 5,6, as an *illustration* for the purpose of *clarification.* When the Son and heir of the Father is seen as the founder, no contradiction exists" (*Hebrews,* 69).

[435] So Moffatt, *Hebrews,* 40–43; Spicq, *L'Épître aux Hebreux,* 2:66–68; Buchanan, *Hebrews,* 57–58; Hughes, *Hebrews,* 133; and Héring, *Hebrews,* 25.

[436] See esp. Vanhoye, *La structure littéraire de l'Épître aux Hébreux* (Paris: Desclée de Brouwer, 1976), 88–89; Auffret, "Essai sur la structure littéraire et l'interprétation d'Hébreux 3, 1–6," 380–96; Lane, *Hebrews 1–8,* 72–73; and Westfall, "Moses and Hebrews 3:1–6," 186–88.

[437] Lane, *Hebrews 1–8*, 72.

[438] Ibid., 72–73.

[439] So noted and translated by Westfall, "Moses and Hebrews 3:1–6," 188.

be *theos* ("God") and the predicate becomes "the one who built" (NIV). Others take the subject to be "the one who built" and the predicate is "God," thus referring to Christ's deity.[440] This rendering is unnatural, however, and was well critiqued long ago.[441]

In keeping with his tight-knit argument, the author introduced v. 5 with *kai*, which may be understood in one of three ways (listed in descending order of probability). (1) It could be an explicative, connecting a clause that explains and summarizes vv. 2–4, and thus translated "and so." In this vein, some see it introducing an additional reason for expecting to find Jesus to be faithful; others as a second proof of Jesus' superiority over Moses.[442] (2) It could be ascensive, sharpening the contrast being drawn, and thus translated "indeed." (3) It could be adding another reason for expecting to find fidelity in Christ and thus ascribing to him greater glory. Both Lane and Ellingworth take it as further clarifying and explaining the previous comment concerning the faithfulness and superiority of Jesus contrasted with Moses.[443]

Verse 5 contains the reference to Num 12:7, "Moses was faithful as a servant in all God's house." This is a repetition of what was stated in v. 2, but with the addition of "servant." The faithfulness of Moses entailed the carrying out of his responsibilities reliably.[444] The *hōs* ("as") is not comparative but shows the position where the faithfulness is demonstrated: faithfulness in his role as servant.[445] A *therapōn* ("servant") was an honored servant in an intimate relationship with the master, and the word carries the connotation of one who offered his service rather than being in forced servitude.[446] There are five words for *servant* in the New Testament, and this one is the most honorable since it indicates service performed with care and fidelity. In the New Testament, it is applied only to Moses. The *men . . . de* construction in vv. 5–6 shows that "servant" is contrasted with "Son." Moses, as it were, "managed" God's people as a servant, though he was also a part of God's people. Moses fulfilled this service, "testifying to what would be said in the future." This unusual clause is introduced by *eis* followed by the accusative *marturion* ("testimony"), indicating purpose, and connects to the entire preceding clause.

---

[440] See J. A. Bengel, "Hebrews," in *Bengel's New Testament Commentary*, trans. C. T. Lewis and M. R. Vincent (Grand Rapids: Kregel, 1981), 2:599–600; Lenski, *Hebrews,* 105–6.

[441] See Lünemann, *Hebrews,* 459.

[442] Dods ("Hebrews," 273) is an example of the former, and Moffatt (*Hebrews,* 43) the latter.

[443] Lane, *Hebrews 1–8*, 78; and Ellingworth, *Hebrews*, 206.

[444] Ellingworth, *Hebrews,* 207. Lane said it means both "appointed" and "faithful" due to the context (*Hebrews 1–8*, 78). On the question as to whether the adjective πιστόν in 3:2 and 3:5 should be translated "faithful" or "trustworthy," see the discussion in V. Rhee (*Faith in Hebrews: Analysis within the Context of Christology, Eschatology, and Ethics* [New York: Peter Lang, 2001], 95) and R. Gheorghita (*The Role of the Septuagint*, 116).

[445] Miller, *Hebrews*, 70.

[446] See LSJ 363.

The noun *marturion* ("testimony") is rendered as the verbal "testifying" in the NIV. The Greek is rounded out by the future passive articular genitive participle *tōn lalēthēsomenōn* ("to what would be said in the future"). The genitive participle is objective, expressing the contents of the noun with the meaning "the testimony consisted of the words later spoken." The interpretive issue here is, what does the participle refer to? The problem cannot be solved on grammatical grounds alone. The passive probably implies divine action, but it does not specify through what intermediary.[447] At least three possibilities present themselves. (1) It could refer to the gospel that Jesus would announce during his ministry with little or no reference to Moses.[448] (2) It could mean that Moses would testify to the gospel that Jesus later proclaimed.[449] (3) It could indicate what Moses would later say to the Israelites as God's prophet.[450] Option two seems the most likely, since the context concerns a contrast with Moses and Jesus.

Verse 6 continues the contrast begun in v. 5 with the other half of the *men . . . de* construction ("on the one hand . . . on the other hand") by stating that "Christ is faithful as a son" over the house. The contrast is between two pairs: "servant" and "son"; "in all God's house" and "over God's house." There is implied information that must be supplied in translation as a predicate to complete the thought in English. Four options are available: (1) "is faithful"[451]; (2) "was faithful"; (3) "is" (to be supplied following "but Christ")[452]; and (4) "was" (to be supplied following "son").[453] Ellingworth preferred the present tense since it is the tense most often implied in Greek and since the passage is about the believer's present relationship with Christ.[454]

The question again arises as to whose house it is. The NIV gives an interpretive translation: "but Christ is faithful as a son over God's house." This follows numerous commentators and translators. The KJV takes Christ as the owner of the house. Lane and Attridge accept the mainly Western textual variant reading "which" for "whose," primarily because it is the more difficult reading.[455] As

---

[447] So Ellingworth, *Hebrews,* 208. Porter said that this participle "cannot have an absolute future reference here since the things spoken of were already revealed at the time of narration (actual past reference), but does have relative reference to Moses, . . . A volitional pragmatic implicature makes sense of a context in which Moses was a witness of the things expected to be spoken by God" (*Verbal Aspect*, 418).

[448] This is the position taken by Delitzsch (*Hebrews,* 1:163) and Ellingworth (*Hebrews,* 208).

[449] Bruce, *Hebrews,* 78; Lane, *Hebrews 1–8,* 93; and Koester, *Hebrews,* 246.

[450] So Dods ("Hebrews," 273–74) and Héring (*Hebrews,* 26). Héring took the genitive participle as explanatory. See the discussion of the options in Miller (*Hebrews*, 72–73).

[451] So Alford, "Hebrews," 62–63; Lane, *Hebrews 1–8*, 71; and the NIV.

[452] So Hewitt, *Hebrews,* 79.

[453] So *The Epistle to the Hebrews*, in *Lange's Commentary on the Holy Scriptures,* trans. A. C. Kendrick (New York: Charles Scribner, 1868), 67.

[454] Ellingworth, *Hebrews,* 209.

[455] Lane, *Hebrews 1–8,* 71; Attridge, *Hebrews,* 104; Zuntz, *Text of the Epistles*, 92ff. UBS^4 reads "whose" with an "A" decision.

in Heb 1:2—where Christ's lordship over all the world is immediately followed by the statement that the he is the creator of all things over which he is Lord—so now Jesus as Son is Lord over the house (3:6) and yet it is he who was the builder of the house (3:3).[456] What does it mean for Jesus to be faithful as God's Son? Since the "house" includes the community of believers, and since Jesus was "faithful" in his appointment as high priest, then his faithfulness likely relates primarily to his continuing ministry as high priest. Furthermore, the faithfulness of Jesus in Heb 3:2,6 should be read within the broader context of the book regarding God's faithfulness to his promises (10:23; 11:11).[457]

The author concluded this paragraph with a direct address to his readers as in v. 1: "And we are his house, if we hold on to our courage and the hope of which we boast." "We" is emphatic and emphasizes the corporate nature of the people of God. Both the KJV and the NASB reflect the variant in some manuscripts that insert "firm to the end" after "we hold fast," but most agree that the words should be omitted.[458] The readers are exhorted through a mitigated command expressed as a conditional clause to "hold on" to their "courage." The Greek word *parrēsia* ("boldness"; lit. "all speech") can also mean "openness, confidence," though the NIV opts for "courage." The term occurs in strategic places in the author's argument (see 4:14; 10:19–21). The use of "boldness" here and throughout the epistle suggests a cultic setting. Jesus as our high priest has provided access to God for his children (4:14–16; 10:19–21).[459] Vorster concluded that the word in 3:6 and 10:35 "refers to the '*conviction*' of the readers that they have free entrance to God through Christ. It is a conviction the believer has before man and which he should keep and not throw away."[460] This would be all the more appropriate if the recipients were former Jewish priests.

Parrēsia is followed by the noun *kauchēma* ("boast"), which is also translated verbally in the NIV ("we boast"). It refers to the object of boasting. In the Greek text, both *parrēsia* and *kauchēma* are followed by the genitive *elpidos* ("hope"), which here refers either to what is hoped for or to the basis or reason for hope.[461] "Hope" can be related to "boast" as an objective genitive, in which case it explains what is being boasted about. This is the way many commentators take it, but it can be construed with both nouns.[462]

The conditional clause "if we hold on" means that holding fast shows who God's people are. There is simply not enough information in this verse, or in

---

[456] So noted by B. Weiss, *Biblical Theology of the New Testament*, trans. J. Duguid (Edinburgh: T&T Clark, 1883), 2:189.

[457] Wallis, *Faith of Jesus Christ in Early Christian Traditions,* 149–50.

[458] *TCGNT* (595) gives it a "B" decision.

[459] On the use of "boldness" see W. C. van Unnik, "The Christian's Freedom of Speech in the New Testament," *BJRL* 41 (1961–62): 484–86; and W. S. Vorster, "The Meaning of *parrēsia* in the Epistle to the Hebrews," *Neot* 5 (1971): 51–59. See also discussion on 4:16.

[460] W. S. Vorster, "Meaning of *parrēsia,*" 57.

[461] See L&N for the former meaning (25.61) and the latter (25.62).

[462] So Moffatt, *Hebrews,* 43–44; and Miller, *Hebrews*, 74.

the paragraph for that matter, to interpret these words to mean that failure to hold on would result in the loss of salvation. The author addressed the community as a whole ("*we* are his house") and did not speak in an individualistic fashion.

Westfall correctly noted that the relatively emphatic conclusion in 3:6b, which correlates the readers with the Israelites, serves as a main clause at the paragraph level in a more narrow sense than 3:1 since it specifies the point of the comparison.[463] This conditional clause, although grammatically subordinate, conveys semantically prominent information since it brings the paragraph full circle by direct address to the readers as in v. 1.[464]

V. Rhee suggested a chiastic arrangement for Heb 3:1–6:

A parallelism by use of the word "consider"	3:1
B the faithfulness of Jesus	3:2a
C description of Moses	3:2b
D parallelism with "house" and "build"	3:3
D´ parallelism with "house" and "build"	3:4
C´ description of Moses	3:5
B´ the faithfulness of Jesus	3:6a
A´ parallelism by use of the word "consider"	3:6b

In this proposed structure the center sections (D and D')

> show parallelism by the words *oikos* (house) and *kataskeuazō* (to build). Sections C and C´ complement each other in that both describe Moses: C´ is a further explanation of C. Sections B and B´ are parallel with each other in that both describe the faithfulness of Jesus: B´ is a further explanation of B. Sections A and A´ show parallelism by the word *katanoēsate* (consider) (3:1) and *kataschōmen* (hold firm) (3:6). Both terms express similar concepts.[465]

From the above discussion, we are in a position to address the subject of the main theme of Heb 3:1–6. It is almost universally acknowledged that the theme has to do with Jesus as superior to Moses, for this truth is clear from the text. However, Westfall argued that this approach reflects a misunderstanding about the passage:

---

463 Westfall, "Moses and Hebrews 3:1–6," 200. She took v. 6 as an "expository apposition" to v. 1 (partners) in the sense that the readers are partners with Christ in their heavenly calling, or by another name, they are his house (p. 192).

464 R. Longacre showed how often something grammatically subordinate in a discourse can contain information that is semantically prominent (*The Grammar of Discourse*, [New York: Plenum, 1983], 10–13).

465 V. Rhee, "The Christological Aspects of Faith in Hebrews 3:1–4:16," *FN* 25/26.13 (2000): 80–81.

> It takes the least prominent material in the passage, and moves it into a powerful thematic position. The consequent reading of the passage lacks coherence. The superiority of Jesus over Moses cannot account for all of the material in the passage and results in a tendency to explain parts of the passage such as vv. 2b and 4 as parentheses. Furthermore, the following co-text in 3.7–15 becomes a non sequitur. On the other hand, if the subheading read 'Partners of a Heavenly Calling', it would reflect the theme which the author chose, and would suggest a topic entity that can better account for the material in the passage.[466]

The comparison between Moses and Jesus in 3:2–6a is not developed further. In fact, Moses is not mentioned again until 7:14. Likewise the "house" metaphor is abandoned. But the author continued to refer to Jesus' apostleship and to the statement in the prologue that God has spoken in a Son in the following two chapters through the repetition of the refrain "Today . . . if you hear his voice" (3:7,15; 4:7) as well as the description of the word of God in 4:12–13 that forms an *inclusio* with 1:2. There is nothing mentioned of Jesus' identity as a high priest until this topic is resumed at the beginning of the second major section of the epistle in 4:14, and this topic will remain the focus through 10:18, the conclusion of the second major section of the epistle.[467] If Westfall's analysis is correct, the superiority of Jesus over Moses would be a secondary theme in the passage.

Westfall's analysis may be further supported by the fact that Heb 3:1–6 shifts the focus from Jesus to the readers, a focus which is developed in 3:7–4:13. Up to 3:1, there was only one hortatory paragraph (2:1–4). In 3:1–6 we have two imperatival ideas expressed; the present imperative in v. 1 and the surrogate imperative (the conditional clause) in v. 6b. The new paragraph beginning in v. 7 is an Old Testament quotation that begins with an imperative. This is followed by another imperative at the beginning of the next sub-paragraph in the section (v. 12). Verse 13 contains another imperative, which is followed by the surrogate imperative in the conditional clause "if we hold firmly" (v. 14b) and by the repetition of the command in the Old Testament quotation "Today . . . do not harden your hearts" (v. 15). The next paragraph begins with another imperative: "Therefore . . . let us be careful that none of you be found to have fallen short of it" (4:1). This is followed by the third repetition of the Old Testament quotation: "Today . . . do not harden your hearts" (4:7).

The last imperatival idea occurs in 4:11 as a hortatory subjunctive at the end of the unit 3:1–4:13. In addition to the imperatives and hortatory subjunctives, the use of the second and third person plural throughout 3:1–4:13 provides

---

[466] Westfall, "Moses and Hebrews 3:1–6," 201.

[467] Ibid., 199. Westfall pointed out that none of the statements about Moses is marked as a main clause and v. 1 is the only finite clause not linked specifically by a conjunction. She also said that Jesus as the high priest is taken up as a new topic in 4:14 ("Moses and Hebrews 3:1–6," 192).

semantic cohesion, showing that the author's focus was on the readers and that he wanted them to interact with the truth that Jesus is God's apostle, God's final word. The author's argument moves along the following trajectory: Since Jesus "shared" in human nature (2:14); since as sanctifier he is one with those whom he sanctifies (2:11) and thus is not ashamed to call the readers "brothers" (2:11); and since the readers are "holy brothers and "partakers" of the heavenly calling (3:1) and comprise "his house" (3:6), then failure to listen to him places one under the judgment of God like the exodus generation.

THEOLOGICAL IMPLICATIONS. There are at least three theological implications from Heb 3:1–6. First, it is apparent from the immediate and remote context that these verses are not intended to be polemical in any way. No specific error is attacked or refuted. The danger is not a misguided elevation of Moses; rather it is the refusal to hear and obey God who has spoken with finality through his Son, Jesus, as is evident from the only hortatory paragraph to appear in the epistle up to this point (2:1–4).

Second, Lane is correct to see in these verses a pastoral response to a confused and dispirited congregation.[468] The readers' need of faithful perseverance motivated the author to dwell both on the faithfulness of Moses but even more on that of Jesus. By comparing Jesus with the angels and Moses, "the author is able to impress upon the hearers that human beings have never enjoyed the help of a more able mediator . . . " (that is, Jesus is superior to the angels and Moses) " . . . nor ever been granted access to God more open and direct than that which the Son provides" (that is, God did speak to Moses face to face but Jesus is God in human flesh and he speaks to us).[469] F. W. Farrar stated:

> The angels had come in the name of God before Israel, and Moses had come in the name of Israel before God; the High Priest came in the name of God before Israel, wearing the name Jehovah on the golden *petalon* upon his forehead, and in the name of Israel before God, bearing the names of their tribes on the oracular gems upon his breast. Christ is above the angels . . . and is not only the messenger of God to men, but as High Priest is the propitiatory representative of men before God. The distinctive exaltation of Christ above Angels and above Moses as regards His mediatorial work, rests in His High-Priestly office.[470]

Moses is no doubt inferior to Christ, as the author made clear, but what is said about Moses here indicates he is superior to all the other prophets. Actually, Moses is the first of the prophets and the prototype of the prophet

[468] Lane, *Hebrews 1–8*, 80.

[469] DeSilva, *Perseverance in Gratitude*, 138.

[470] F. W. Farrar, *The Early Days of Christianity*, 200–1.

like Moses God promised to "raise up" in Deut 18:15.[471] Moses' calling as a servant was for a testimony (v. 5), which would foreshadow the fulfillment of the old covenant when Jesus came. Thus, H. O. Wiley added another point about the superiority of Christ over Moses: the fulfillment is greater than the witness.[472] Although not overtly stated, this is a clear implication of vv. 5–6a.

Third, there is a genuine continuity between Old Testament Israel and New Testament believers; there is one true people of God ("his house") throughout all the ages of human history.[473] Paul's parable of the olive tree in Rom 11:16–24 illustrates the relationship that exists between Israel and the church. The olive tree is a reference to Israel, but nowhere did Paul state that Israel as a whole has been set aside. Rather, he pointed out that "some of the branches have been broken off" (v. 17). These branches represent the unbelieving portion of Israel as the people of God. The wild olive represents the Gentile world, and Gentile Christians were grafted into the good olive tree. This is the continuity of the olive tree as the people of God, for Gentile Christians are grafted into the good olive tree and are not designated as a new tree. Thus there is continuity from the people of God in Old Testament times to the people of God in the New Testament age. That some branches were broken off does not imply that they all were. Paul told the Gentiles that they have no ground for boasting because they have not in fact displaced Israel; rather, they have been grafted onto Israel and are now members of the "people of God." The point of this parable is that the root of Israel is never uprooted to make way for a new "tree," for the original root continues to give nourishment to the people of God. As there is one tree, so there is one house since "God is the builder of everything" (Heb 3:4). Whether the antecedent of "house" in v. 6 is God or Christ, the point remains the same: there is continuity between God's people in the Old Testament and God's people in the New Testament, an important theme developed in Heb 1:1–2.

(2) Beware of Unbelief (3:7–19)

7So, as the Holy Spirit says:

"Today, if you hear his voice,
8 do not harden your hearts
as you did in the rebellion,
during the time of testing in the desert,
9where your fathers tested and tried me
and for forty years saw what I did.
10That is why I was angry with that generation,
and I said, 'Their hearts are always going astray,

---

[471] See Westcott, *Hebrews,* 77; Hughes, *Hebrews,* 135; and DeSilva, *Perseverance in Gratitude,* 136.

[472] H. O. Wiley, *The Epistle to the Hebrews* (Kansas City, MO: Beacon Hill, 1959), 104–5.

[473] Hughes, *Hebrews,* 132.

and they have not known my ways.'
[11]So I declared on oath in my anger,
'They shall never enter my rest.'"

[12]See to it, brothers, that none of you has a sinful, unbelieving heart that turns
away from the living God. [13]But encourage one another daily, as long as it is called
Today, so that none of you may be hardened by sin's deceitfulness. [14]We have come
to share in Christ if we hold firmly till the end the confidence we had at first. [15]As
has just been said:

"Today, if you hear his voice,
do not harden your hearts
as you did in the rebellion."

[16]Who were they who heard and rebelled? Were they not all those Moses led
out of Egypt? [17]And with whom was he angry for forty years? Was it not with
those who sinned, whose bodies fell in the desert? [18]And to whom did God swear
that they would never enter his rest if not to those who disobeyed? [19]So we see that
they were not able to enter, because of their unbelief.

Hebrews 3:7–19 is a literary unit with two major sections. The first section (Heb 3:7–11) is a quotation of Ps 95:7b–11, and the second section (Heb 3:12–19) is a commentary on Ps 95:7b–11. The two units are tightly framed, the first being demarcated as a quotation and the second using *inclusio* by the lexical repetition of *blepō* and *apistia* in v. 12 and v. 19.[474] Verse 12 contains an overt warning signaled by an imperative, and v. 19 contains a covert warning expressed semantically by the indicative mood that parallels the warning of v. 12. The quotation of Ps 95:8a with the overt imperative "do not harden your hearts" is positively answered in the second unit by v. 14: "We have come to share in Christ if we hold firmly till the end the confidence we had at first." The two warnings in 3:12 and 3:19 that bracket the unit serve as a linguistic and theological frame for the covert command to have faith, which is expressed semantically in a conditional clause in v. 14.

Hebrews 3:7 begins the second warning passage in the book, but where it ends is debated. It may end with v. 19, or it may extend to 4:13. Many interpret the warning passages as interrupting the flow of the author's argument, and hence these passages are often seen as digressions. This serious structural mistake is made by many older commentators. More recent ones have rightly understood them as integral to the argument of the epistle.[475]

[474] See Lane, *Hebrews 1–8,* 83.

[475] P. Grelot said that the warning passages interrupt the exposition (*Une lecture de l'épître aux Hébreux*, Lire la Bible 132 [Paris: Cerf, 2003], 20). Grelot took the second warning passage as a homily on Ps 95:2–11 and suggested that this pericope was originally an independent sermon text that had been preached in the church and was being reproduced by the author at this point in the epistle (34). This is difficult to sustain in light of the tight cohesion permeating the entire epistle.

What is the relationship of 3:7–19 to 3:1–6? The author introduced the quotation in v. 7 with *dio* ("so"), an emphatic marker of result.[476] This connector probably plays more than one role in the immediate context. It carries forward the thought of v. 6b and relates it to the admonition in v. 8, "do not harden your hearts." The *dio* clause indicates the consequence of the necessity of holding fast to be Christ's household: we are Christ's household if we hold fast.[477] It also probably reaches to the "See to it, brothers" in v. 12, which is the beginning of the next semantic unit.[478] The semantic relationship would then be grounds—exhortation, with the grounds being the quotation of Ps 95:7b–11 in Heb 3:7–11 and the exhortation being the imperative of v. 12. As an inferential conjunction, *dio* often marks the gathering up of the previous line of thought and connecting it to a new line of thought: "since it is only by maintaining boldly our confidence, therefore, see to it that none of you has an evil, unbelieving heart."[479]

The challenge is to determine how 3:7–19 is a result of 3:1–6, a relationship either ignored or inadequately explained.[480] Some commentators see an implied contrast between the faithfulness of Jesus and the unfaithfulness of the wilderness generation.[481] But since the comparison in 3:1–6 is between Moses and Jesus, it is unlikely that the original readers would have seen a contrast between Jesus and the wilderness generation. All the explicit contrasts in 3:7–4:11 are made between the exodus generation and the hearers, not the exodus generation and Jesus.[482] The co-text in Hebrews 1–2 was primarily linked to the description of Jesus in 3:1, and the following co-text in 3:7–19 is explicitly linked to the readers' identity as described in 3:1 and 3:6. There is no mention of Moses' house in 3:6. The parallel is broken but picked up again in 3:7–15. It would seem, then, that the main point of connection is that of the wilderness generation who were unfaithful and the original readers who were being exhorted not to follow suit.

There are several text-critical issues in these verses involving differences between the LXX and the author's Old Testament quotations in Hebrews.[483]

---

[476] L&N 89.47. On the use of διό in Hebrews, see Ellingworth, *Hebrews,* 217.

[477] Greenlee, *Exegetical Summary*, 98.

[478] It is a mistake to connect the διό with βλέπετε in v. 12 but at the same time consider the intervening quotation as parenthetical, as do Kistemaker (*Hebrews,* 85) and others. As T. Zahn remarked: "The stylistic ability of the writer forbids the hypothesis that the clause beginning with διό is not to be continued until ver. 12, so that all that is between would be a parenthesis" (*Introduction to the New Testament* [New York: Charles Scribner Sons, 1917; repr., Minneapolis: Klock & Klock, 1977], 2:337).

[479] Miller, *Hebrews*, 75. See Wallace, *GGBB* 673.

[480] As noted by Westfall, "Moses and Hebrews 3:1–6," 197.

[481] E.g., Ellingworth, *Hebrews,* 213.

[482] So Westfall, "Moses and Hebrews 3:1–6," 197.

[483] For a discussion of these, see Ellingworth, *Hebrews,* 218. A significant study on Heb 3:7–11 is R. Gheorghita, *The Role of the Septuagint in Hebrews*, 47. See also P. Enns, "The Interpretation of Psalm 95 in Hebrews 3.1–4.13," in *Early Christian Interpretation of the Scriptures of Israel,* ed. C. A. Evans and J. A. Sanders, JSNTSup 148 (Sheffield: Academic Press, 1997), 353.

The divergences between the Hebrew text and the LXX are few and minimal with three exceptions. The first one is that the proper nouns "Massah" and "Meribah" are not transliterated by the LXX translators. Instead, they are translated as *en tō parapikrasmō* ("in the rebellion") and *kata tēn hēmeran tou peirasmou* ("during the time of testing"). The change could indicate a shift of focus from spatial location in the Hebrew text to the spiritual failure of the people. These two descriptive phrases do characterize the sins of the people during the entire 40 years of wilderness wanderings.[484]

The second exception is the insertion by the author of *dio* in 3:10, which alters the punctuation so that the reference to 40 years becomes attached to the previous statement. In the MT and the LXX, the 40 years was the duration of God's wrath, but the author of Hebrews portrayed that 40 years as a time when the people witnessed God's work of grace and blessing. In 3:17, however, the author speaks of the 40 years as the time of God's anger ("with whom was he angry for forty years?"), making it more difficult to postulate that he deliberately altered the text, as is often suggested.[485] More likely, the author viewed Israel's time in the wilderness as a time of testing, with God's blessings and anger both being demonstrated.[486] P. Enns explained why the author cited Psalm 95 and its reference to the 40 years in two different ways within the confines of eight verses: "The reason he cites the Psalm differently is that in 3:17 he is talking about *Israel*, while in 3:10 he is talking about the *church*. In 3:17, the author is looking back to the original context of the Psalm, and so he cites it the way it was intended."[487]

The third deviation occurs in 3:10 with the substitution of *tautē* ("this") for *ekeinē* ("that") before the noun "generation." This deliberate change shows the author's desire to contextualize Psalm 95 for his audience and to sound a note of urgency for his readers.[488] In 3:16 the lexical cognate of "rebellion" coupled with the cognate of "testing" used in 2:18 and again in 4:15 unites these verses in a comparison of the exodus generation, the author's generation of readers, and Jesus' testing as well.The author did not engage in hermeneutical "cheating" in the adjustments he made to the text of Ps 95:7b–11 in Heb 3:7–11.[489]

---

[484] Koester, *Hebrews*, 264. Granted the LXX consistently renders מַסָּה as πειρασμὸς, "testing" (Exod 17:7; Deut 6:16; 9:22; Ps 95:8) or πεῖρα (Deut 33:8) and renders מְרִיבָה as λοιδόρησις / λοιδορία, "railing, abuse" (Exod 17:7; Num 20:24), ἀντιλογία, "dispute" (Num 20:13; 27:14; Deut 32:51; 33:8; Ps 80:8 [Eng 81:7]; 105:32 [Eng 106:32]), παραπικρασμός, "provokation, rebellion" (Ps 94:8 [Eng 95:8]), and only in Ezekiel (47:19; 48:28) by the interesting transliteration Μαριμωθ.

[485] J. Moffatt, *Hebrews*; 45, and many others.

[486] So Vanhoye, *La structure,* 92–94, and Leschert, *Hermeneutical Foundations of Hebrews*, 191.

[487] P. Enns, *Inspiration and Incarnation: Evangelicals and the Problem of the Old Testament* (Grand Rapids: Baker, 2005), 141–42.

[488] Spicq, *L'Épître aux Hebreux*, 2:74; Bruce, *Hebrews,* 95; Montefiore, *Hebrews,* 76.

[489] J. Laansma, "Hebrews' Use of the Old Testament: Reflections on Heb 3:7–4:13" (unpublished paper for the Evangelical Theological Society meeting, November 2001), 11.

Standing behind his use of Psalm 95 is the historical record in Numbers 14. The author saw continuity between both texts, and his adjustments are made with the needs of his audience in mind and in such a way that he did no violence to the meaning of the text. Thus the author's approach must be distinguished from that of midrashic allegory.[490]

3:7 The quotation of Ps 95:7b–11 is introduced here by the unusual statement, "as the Holy Spirit says," which occurs again only twice in the epistle (9:8; 10:15), though not in the identical fashion as here. This nomenclature indicates that the author viewed Scripture as the voice of the Holy Spirit, which gives added emphasis to the divine authority of the command.[491] More important than the human author is the divine author.

The significance of the present tense *legei* ("says") is debated.[492] The issue is whether the author intended the present tense to indicate that the Holy Spirit is speaking *now* to the hearers. It is difficult not to see such an intention on the part of the author given the choice of the quotation that focuses on "today" coupled with this citation formula. This phrase indicates three things: (1) the Holy Spirit speaks in Scripture; (2) the Holy Spirit spoke through Scripture to the author's original audience; and (3) the Holy Spirit speaks to God's people today through this text when they read these words.

Of further interest is why the author chose to quote Psalm 95 and not Numbers 14, which is the historical account of the events behind Psalm 95. The liturgical use of Psalm 95 as a preamble to synagogue services is well known in Judaism. Psalm 95 alludes to the occasion in Exod 17:1 where the people grumbled against God at Rephidim because of the lack of water. Moses struck the rock and water gushed forth. He named the place "Massah" ("testing) and "Meribah" ("embitterment"). The Greek terms in Heb 3:8 correspond to the LXX rendering of the Hebrew words "Massah" and "Meribah." Although the background of Psalm 95 is Numbers 14, it is the language of Psalm 95 that furnished the author with the themes that he developed through Heb 4:11.

The use of *sēmeron* ("today") is significant in several ways. Its use in Psalm 95 refers to the time of the psalmist, which was several hundred years after the

---

[490] Leschert, *Hermeneutical Foundations of Hebrews*, 193. According to T. Zahn, the author did not quote Ps 95:7–11 in 3:7–11 as a Scriptural proof, but rather put what he himself desires to say in the language of Psalm 95. This is indicated by the quote formula and the alteration of the quoted text. The formula "as the Holy Spirit says" is not used to indicate they are taken from Scripture but to soften the "harshness" of the sudden transition from his own words in Heb 3:9 to those of God (*Introduction to the New Testament*, 2:320–23).

[491] Delitzsch summed up well the author's view of Scripture: "Every word of Scripture is as such a word of the Holy Ghost; for Scripture in all its parts is *theopneustos* (2 Tim. 3:16)" (*Hebrews*, 1:168).

[492] Hughes (*Hebrews*, 141) and Lane (*Hebrews 1–8*, 85) supported the notion that the present tense of λέγει means the Holy Spirit is speaking now in the experience of the readers. What was spoken or written concerning the exodus generation, though spoken or written centuries earlier, has immediate relevance to the readers addressed by the author.

events of Numbers 14. Although the original readers of the book of Hebrews were several hundred more years removed from the writing of Psalm 95, the author intended for his readers to see the "today" as addressing them. "Today" is given emphasis by its word order in the clause, which serves to heighten the urgency of the warning.

Some suggest that the conditional particle *ean* ("if") carries the meaning of temporality and should be translated "*when* you hear his voice."[493] But most see the condition as indicating uncertainty about hearing God's voice: either about whether God will speak again, or about whether the intended hearers are willing to listen.[494]

Regarding the antecedent of "his voice," Hanson suggested that it is Christ's voice.[495] But it is more likely God's voice, and thus Heb 3:12 and 4:12 form bookends for an entire section of the epistle with reference to a warning about the danger of disobeying God.[496]

3:8 The words *mē sklērunēte* ("do not harden") form a subjunctive of prohibition. The warning is against hardening one's own "heart" through willful disobedience. The heart in both the Old Testament and the New Testament includes not merely the emotions of human nature, but the mind and the will as well. They were not to harden their heart as in the "rebellion." The use of "as" introduces a comparison to reinforce the preceding exhortation. The definite article "the" before "rebellion" points to the specific instance referred to in 3:9 when there was a lack of water. The phrase "in the rebellion" is something of a euphemism for the geographical location of Meribah.[497] The use of *kata* ("during") with the accusative case in Greek indicates time according to most commentators and virtually all translations (NIV—"during the time of testing"), although it is occasionally understood in a comparative sense with the meaning "according to the manner of."[498] The question of the relationship of the phrase "during the day" to the other phrases in the text is not easily answered. It may be subordinate to "rebellion," indicating the time of the rebellion.[499] It could refer to the incident at Massah.[500] Lane suggested that it refers to the day they refused to enter the Promised Land according to Numbers 14.[501] Finally, some take it as inclusive of the entire

---

[493] So Hewitt, *Hebrews*, 81.

[494] The former view is taken by Dods ("Hebrews," 275) and the latter by Bruce (*Hebrews*, 98–99).

[495] Hanson, *Jesus Christ in the Old Testament*, 60.

[496] Ellingworth, *Hebrews*, 219.

[497] So Alford, "Hebrews," 65; and Dods, "Hebrews," 275.

[498] As in Dods, "Hebrews," 275.

[499] So Alford, "Hebrews," 65; and Miller, *Hebrews*, 75.

[500] So Dods, "Hebrews," 275; and Hughes, *Hebrews*, 142.

[501] Lane, *Hebrews 1–8*, 85.

40 years of testing.[502] Likewise, "rebellion" and "time of testing" could refer to two separate incidents, but probably not.[503]

3:9 Verse 9 provides an interpretive comment on the preceding thought introduced by "where." The KJV translates it temporally as "when," but it is more likely to be taken as indicating place. The phrase "tested and tried me" is (lit.) "tried by testing." Lane translates "by testing" as "through their distrust."[504] The NIV renders Gk. "saw my works" as "saw what I did." The *kai* ("and") can introduce an added thought: "and in addition they saw" or, more likely, a concession: "although they saw." God's "works" may have a penal sense or a good sense.[505] Most take "my works" to be connected with "they saw," but Morris construed it with the entire preceding clause.[506] The "forty years" is linked with the preceding phrase and indicates the length of time they saw God's works. However, in the original Hebrew and the LXX, this phrase is related to the clause that follows, explicating God's wrath. This represents a subtle change by the author in the quotation to emphasize a theological point. There is also an abrupt change from "his voice" in v. 7 to "my works" in v. 9.

3:10–11 This change is illustrated in v. 10 by the use of *dio*, which introduces the result of their testing and clarifies that the "forty years" is to be taken with what precedes and not with what follows (as in the Hebrew and LXX). The author also substituted "this" for "that" before "generation," implying that his generation was included along with those of the Old Testament.[507] The use of "always" connotes the idea of continually or constantly going astray during the 40 years of wilderness wandering. The *kai* ("and") indicates the result of the preceding thought: "I became angry and so I said."[508] The last "and" in v. 10 is the translation of *de* in Greek and is translated "but" by Lane.[509] "They have not known my ways" means the wilderness generation willfully refused to do what God told them to do. There is a difference of opinion as to where the quotation introduced by "and I said" ends. Some take it as ending with "they did not know my ways," while others see it as ending with "heart" in the pre-

---

502 So Moffatt, *Hebrews*, 45.

503 Alford ("Hebrews," 65) and Hewitt (*Hebrews*, 81) took it in the former sense; Dods ("Hebrews," 275) and Hughes (*Hebrews*, 142) took it in the latter.

504 Lane, *Hebrews 1–8*, 81.

505 Alford ("Hebrews," 66) and Moffatt (*Hebrews*, 45–46) took it in the former sense; Lenski (*Hebrews*, 114) and Kistemaker (*Hebrews*, 92) took it in the latter. Dods, "Hebrews," 275, took it in both senses.

506 Morris, "Hebrews," in *Expositor's Bible Commentary*, 34. See Hughes (*Hebrews*, 143) and all translations which take "my works" to be construed with "they saw."

507 Zahn took the reference to "forty years" to be to the author's generation from AD 30–70 (*Introduction to the New Testament*, 320–21), as did Bleek (*Introduction to the New Testament*, 2nd ed., trans. W. Urwick [Edinburgh: T&T Clark, 1869], 2:436–40). Thus the reference is to unbelieving Israel. Zahn also deduced from this that the epistle was written after AD 70 (323).

508 Miller, *Hebrews*, 80.

509 Lane, *Hebrews 1–8*, 81.

ceding clause as shown by the insertion of "but they."[510] The phrase "and they did not know my ways" could be related to the preceding phrase and express a second charge against them, or it may be stating the same charge.[511] Koester pointed out that the "ways of God" have two aspects: the ways God prescribes for his people, and the ways God himself acts.[512]

The quotation concludes in v. 11 with "so," indicating result.[513] God "swore" means he "declared on oath," as the NIV correctly translates. The phrase "in my anger" denotes the reason he swore the oath. The NIV's "they shall never enter" is (lit.) "if they shall enter"; it is rendered "they shall not enter" in the KJV and "they shall certainly not enter" by Lane.[514] The oath is a conditional clause with the consequence "suppressed," implying a suppressed preceding thought such as "May God do so to me if . . . ."[515] According to Miller, when used by God, it may imply something like "I am not God if . . . ."[516]

There are "striking connections" between Psalm 95 and Isa 66:1, which has the only other occurrence of *katapausis* ("rest") in the LXX and which is quoted in Acts 7:49.[517] The concept of "rest" plays a significant role in the remainder of Hebrews 3, where it occurs in vv. 18,19 and throughout Heb 4:1–11. The exodus theme is the dominant motif in this entire section. Attridge noticed that this motif is either overplayed (as by Käsemann) or underplayed (as by Hofius).[518] The association of Gen 2:4 and Ps 95:11, although possible when working from the Hebrew text, is more likely to have arisen as a consequence of the author's use of a Greek text.[519]

3:12 The final paragraph of this chapter (3:12–19) comprises the author's application of the quotation to his readers. It is primarily hortatory in nature. The situation of the original readers (3:12–14) is compared to that of the wilderness generation (3:15–19). The question of how v. 12 is related to what precedes is not easy to answer. Some say it is connected to the *dio* of 3:7[520] and is parenthetical. Others begin a new sentence with v. 12 and see it as an application of the preceding comments.[521]

---

[510] Bruce (*Hebrews*, 95) and the NIV took it in the former sense; Lane (*Hebrews 1–8*, 81) in the latter.

[511] Hewitt (*Hebrews*, 82) and Miller (*Hebrews*, 81) took it in the former sense; Lenski (*Hebrews*, 114–15) in the latter.

[512] Koester, *Hebrews,* 256. He also has a good discussion of the meaning of God's "wrath" (p. 257).

[513] L&N 89.52.

[514] Lane, *Hebrews 1–8*, 81.

[515] So Alford, "Hebrews," 67; and Dods, "Hebrews," 276.

[516] Miller, *Hebrews*, 82.

[517] Ellingworth, *Hebrews,* 220.

[518] Attridge, *Hebrews,* 114, footnote 15.

[519] Gheorghita, *Role of the Septuagint*, 55.

[520] E.g., Alford, "Hebrews," 68; and Westcott, *Hebrews,* 83.

[521] So Moffatt, *Hebrews*, 46; and Lane, *Hebrews 1–8*, 86.

The imperative "see to it" introduces an urgent warning, implying "that there is urgent cause for apprehension founded on the actual state of the case."[522] But it should not be interpreted to suggest that the author thought the "evil unbelieving heart" already existed among the readers. As noted previously, the heart includes the entire human personality of mind, will, and emotions. The noun *apistia* ("unbelief") is translated by the NIV as a participle, "unbelieving." The genitive phrase "heart of unbelief" is, according to Delitzsch, a qualitative genitive "in the widest sense," not the genitive of cause or the genitive of consequence.[523] Westcott argued that "evil heart" should be seen closely together with "unbelieving," which characterizes the "evil heart."[524] Unbelief stands in contrast to "faithfulness," which was the glory of Moses and Christ (3:1–6). This "unbelief finds its practical issue in 'disobedience.'"[525] The importance of the heart for the author appears later in 8:10 and 10:10, where the Jeremiah quotation indicates that the new covenant includes a provision for a clean and established heart. In Heb 10:22, with language very similar to 3:12, the author exhorted his readers to draw near to God with a "true heart . . . having our hearts cleansed from an evil conscience." Finally, the author spoke of the heart being strengthened by grace (13:9), which contrasts with a hard heart due to sin's deceitfulness (3:13).

According to Delitzsch, the *apistia* is both the root and the fruit of *ponēra,* and we don't have to decide between the meaning of "unbelief" or "unfaithfulness": the word contains both meanings "which mutually involve each other."[526] *Mēpote* introduces a clause that can be interpreted as expressing the content of seeing: "see to it that there not be an evil unbelieving heart."[527] It can also be taken to indicate purpose: "Take care, brethren, [in order] that there not be" (NASB). *Mēpote* followed by the indicative implies urgent cause of apprehension founded on the actual state of the case and marks the reality and urgency of the danger.[528] The entire construction to this point may be Semitic, as noted by many.[529]

A key phrase in v. 12 that impinges on the interpretation of the warning passages in Hebrews 6 and 10 is *en tō apostēnai*, the aorist active infinitive of *aphistēmi* ("that turns away"). Lane agreed with the NIV and translated the phrase "that turns away," taking the infinitive in an epexegetical sense. The

---

522 Delitzsch, *Hebrews*, 1:173.

523 Ibid., 174. See BDF §165.

524 Westcott, *Hebrews,* 83.

525 Ibid. This phrase "evil, unbelieving heart" verbally resembles 4 Ezra 3:20–22; 4:30; 7:92.

526 Delitzsch, *Hebrews,* 1:174. Following Danker, DeSilva explained that in common Greek usage, the noun *pistis* ("faith") "refers both to the responsibility accepted by another to discharge some duty or provide some service and the trust placed in that person by the one who awaits the fulfillment of the obligation" (*Perseverance in Gratitude*, 144).

527 So Bruce, *Hebrews*, 99–100; Lane, *Hebrews 1–8*, 82; and the NIV.

528 Delitzsch, *Hebrews* 1:183; and Westcott, *Hebrews,* 83.

529 Bruce, *Hebrews,* 145. Stephen's similar statement, "turning back in their hearts to Egypt" (Acts 7:39), echoes Num 14.

word carries with it the notion of movement away from a point of reference—in this case, the living God. In Acts 15:38 it means "desert." There is little doubt that the author was thinking of Num 14:9 (LXX): *apo tou kuriou mē apostatai ginesthe*, where the very word in its nominal form is used. In Num 14:9 the basic meaning of the Hebrew word is "to rebel." The Greek noun can mean either "rebel" or "apostate," and context must determine which is intended. Both meanings appear to be equally legitimate in the present context. Gheorghita gave a "slight advantage" to the reading "do not become apostates."[530] On the other hand, Wevers translated it, "do not rebel against YHWH," noting that the LXX rendering best fits the Hebrew verb.[531]

The language and imagery of Hebrews 3 are paralleled in the other warning passages in the epistle with such verbs as *pararreō* ("*drift* away" in 2:1), *parapiptō* ("*fall* away" in 6:6), and *apostrephō* ("*turn* away" in 12:25). Gheorghita stated:

> In the NT the primary meanings of the verb ἀφίστημι [*aphistēmi*] are "to (physically) depart, to be separated from" (Lk. 2:37, 4:13, Acts 12:10, 15:38, 19:10) and "to (be) release(d)", or "to send away" (Lk. 13:27, Acts 3:38, 22:29, 2 Cor. 12:8). In addition to these frequent connotations, the verb ἀφίστημι and its cognate noun ἀποστῆναι [*apostēnai*] are occasionally employed by other NT writers with the same meaning as in Hebrews. Especially in the latter writings of the NT the verb is used with the specific meaning of "falling away from the faith / Lord" (Lk. 8:13) and it probably acquired the status of *terminus technicus* to describe the falling away from the faith (1 Tim. 4:1, 2 Tim. 2:3 [sic]).[532]

The semantic range of this verb in the NT is much less extensive than in the LXX, where no less than 40 different Hebrew verbs are employed.[533] The

---

530 Gheorghita, *The Role of the Septuagint,* 109. He stated that the case for "commit apostasy" as opposed to "rebel" is "strengthened by the Greek translation of Num 32:9 and Deut 1:28, two subsequent passages relating the particular event that took place during the encampment in Hazeroth (Num 12:16)" (110–11). He admitted that the case for the meaning "apostate" remains open to debate but concluded his discussion of this issue with the following: "Whether Num. 14:9 LXX μὴ ἀποστάται γίνεσθε ὑμεῖς should be read 'do not become rebels', identical with the Hebrew text, or 'do not become apostates', thus departing from the meaning of the Hebrew text, it is almost certain that the Author read it with the latter and not the former meaning. If the former rendering is correct, the meaning shift took place in the process of translation, if the latter, the meaning shift occurred as a result of translation. The Septuagint consequently supplied not only the lexical unit underlying the Author's allusion to Num 14, but also a particular theological perspective on that event in Israel's history" (111). I cannot see how Gheorghita could draw this conclusion given the evidence he himself presented.

531 J. Wevers, *Notes on the Greek Text of Numbers* (Atlanta: Scholars Press, 1998), 214.

532 Gheorghita, *Role of the Septuagint,* 108.

533 J. A. L. Lee contended that in the Pentateuch, the verb is used with a broad semantic range. He listed five different meanings: (1) "to cause to revolt"; (2) "stand back, aloof"; (3) "withdraw,

phrase in Num 14:9 (LXX) is *mē apostatai ginesthe*, which translates the Hebrew *ʾal-timrōdû* ("do not rebel"). The Hebrew verb *mārad* ("to revolt/rebel") and its cognate noun *mered* ("rebellion"; only in Josh 22:22)[534] are translated by the verb *aphistēmi* or its cognates more than a dozen times in the LXX. Our author used the verb *aphistēmi* only once in this passage and did not use it again in any of the other warning passages, which argues against understanding his meaning as "apostasy" in the traditional sense of that term.

The author warned his readers not to turn away from "the living God." The absence of the Greek articles in this phrase focuses on God's character and nature. Westcott translated it "from Him who is a living God" because of the anarthrous construction, and he explained that the phrase suggests "the certainty of retribution on unfaithfulness."[535] This phrase corresponds to "as I live" in Num 14:21,28. In 14:3–4 the wilderness generation was about to abandon God by faulting him for bringing them out of Egypt. According to Num 14:9, Joshua warned the people not to abandon God by disobeying his command to enter the promised rest. By analogy, the readers of Hebrews were in danger of doing the same thing, as chap. 4 makes clear. Rhetorically, the author connected the "living God" (3:12) with "the word of God is living" (4:12) to form a possible chiasm—God/living and living [word]/of God.

Lane and the NIV take the infinitive clause *en tō apostēnai* as a comment on the unbelieving heart as one "that turns away."[536] Ellingworth said it expresses the possible result of the unbelieving heart: "should fall away as a result of disbelief." His point that the danger the author fears for his readers "seems to have been a passive drift (2:1) away from faith rather than active revolt" tones down the harshness of the term and tends to interpret the infinitive in light of 2:1 rather than vice versa.[537] Hughes interpreted the phrase to mean "a heart that is evil because it is unbelieving." Following Aquinas, Hughes correctly explained that this is not a case of a heart that has not yet come to belief, but a heart that departs from belief.[538]

This falling away is not passive but deliberate disobedience. This is the antithesis of the spirit of those who draw near to God (see 10:22). Peter referred to those who have "left the straight way and wandered off" (2 Pet 2:15). He

---

depart" (from an activity or place); (4) "rebel, revolt"; and (5) "shrink, abstain" (*A Lexical Study of the Septuagint Version of the Pentateuch,* SBLSCS 14 (Chicago: Scholars Press, 1983) 35–38.

[534] *HALOT* 2:632.

[535] Westcott, *Hebrews,* 83. The phrase is common in the LXX and the NT and occurs several times in Hebrews (9:14; 10:31; 12:22).

[536] See Lane, *Hebrews 1–8*, 82; and the NIV.

[537] Ellingworth, *Hebrews,* 222. Attridge correctly stated that passive disbelief is not only what the author has in mind in light of his use of "disobedience" in the following verses (*Hebrews,* 116). Ellingworth is correct that the phrase "cannot be pressed to imply a return to paganism."

[538] Hughes, *Hebrews,* 145. Koester is correct when he noted: "The explanatory comment in 3:12b shows that the unbelieving heart is not primarily one that has never come to belief, but a heart that abandons the God it has known" (*Hebrews,* 258).

went on to say about them that "if they have escaped the corruption of the world by knowing our Lord and Savior Jesus Christ and are again entangled in it and overcome, they are worse off at the end than they were at the beginning" (2 Pet 2:20).[539] The author used *apostēnai* only this once in the entire book, which leads to a crucial question: If *apistia* and *apeithēs* are synonyms for *apostēnai*, then is apostasy in the usual theological sense what the author had in mind? It is highly unlikely that the theological sense of the term is what the author intended.

These verses contain an important aspect of the New Testament's use of the Old Testament. The author's reference to the failure of the exodus generation as a warning for his readers is an example of Paul's statement in 1 Cor 10:6–11 that Old Testament events are written as warnings for the church.

3:13 Verse 13 parallels v. 12 with another imperative, "encourage one another," but with a positive focus signaled by the adversative conjunction *alla* ("but") to balance out the warning. The contrast highlights the command. This encouragement probably includes within it an element of warning as well as reproof with the present tense implying ongoing encouragement.[540] Virtually the same statement is made again in Heb 10:25. The use of the pronoun "one another" is reciprocal rather than the reflexive ("encourage yourselves"). The inclusion of *hekastēn* with "day" adds emphasis to the statement and has both a temporal and distributive meaning. This statement and 10:25 may indicate that the readers met together daily.

Both here and throughout the epistle (4:1,11; 10:24–25; 12:15–16; 13:1–3), the author challenged the community of readers to devote themselves to watching out for each other. Collective responsibility was the order of the day for the author. The warnings were addressed to the entire community, but there is a double reference in vv. 12–13 to individual members. Ellingworth says this illustrates the author's conviction, expressly stated in 12:15, that it only takes one unbelieving member to corrupt the entire community.[541] If the individual is left alone, the author would have agreed with R. Robinson when he wrote, "Prone to wander, Lord I feel it; prone to leave the God I love."[542] The quotation in v. 8a uses the second person plural, and the author retained it in v. 12 and v. 13. Interestingly, beginning with v. 14 and continuing through the end of this entire section (4:13) and into the opening paragraph of the next major

---

[539] Cf. Luke 8:13; Jer 10:5–10. There is a similar use of this word in *Shepherd of Hermas* 2.3.2: "you are saved by not having fallen away [ἀποστῆναι] from the living God."

[540] On παρακαλέω, its meaning and usage, consult C. Bejerkelund's thorough study of the word as it is used in the Pauline Letters (*Parakalō: Form, Funktion und Sinn der parakalō-Sätze in den paulinischen Briefen* in Bibliotheca Theologica Norvegica 1 [Oslo: Universitetsforlaget, 1967]). A chiasm occurs in v. 13: "encourage" (παρακαλεῖτε) one another each "day" (ἡμέραν), as long as "Today" (Σήμερον) it is "called" (καλεῖται).

[541] Ellingworth, *Hebrews,* 221.

[542] From the hymn "Come Thy Fount of Every Blessing," by R. Robinson, a Baptist pastor in Cambridge in the eighteenth century.

section (4:14–16), all the exhortations are "we" forms. Ellingworth correctly observed that the change is not merely stylistic but integral to the argument as developed in Hebrews 4.[543]

The clause "as long as it is called Today" means that encouragement is to continue as long as "Today" lasts. The context does not specify this length of time, but it is to be understood as more than a single day from the context and especially from Heb 4:7. It could refer to the second coming of Christ;[544] it could be taken in a more generic sense as referring to the time while there is still opportunity to hear God speaking. Whatever the exact meaning, a sense of urgency is indicated since it is obvious that "Today" will not last indefinitely. The Greek definite article precedes the word "Today," which signals one of three things: (1) the word "Today" itself;[545] (2) specifying the today as "this today"; and (3) as a reference to the entire quotation introduced by "Today."[546] The differences between these three options are negligible for interpretation.

The *hina* ("so that") clause expresses the purpose for the mutual encouragement. The position of the phrase "of you" is emphatic. The aorist passive subjunctive of *sklēruno* ("may be hardened") has the passive voice of permission, "to let oneself be hardened." The passive voice may have the force of the middle voice, "they hardened themselves." Hughes took the subjunctive as indicating that the hardening had not yet occurred.[547] The phrase "deceitfulness of sin" personifies sin as a power. Most take the genitive here as subjective; it is sin that deceives.[548]

There is a certain lack of specificity among the terms the author used in these verses. Theologically it is reading too much into the words "sinful, unbelieving heart that turns away from the living God" to interpret it in the sense of apostasy as do many interpreters, for the context does not define what the author intended. Taking the Greek term *apostēnai* as it is used here and burdening it with the theological baggage of apostasy is premature. No doubt, many commentators, aware of what comes in Hebrews 6 and 10, are willing to label the term with the meaning of apostasy and interpret it either in an Arminian sense as the loss of salvation, or in a more Calvinistic sense (e.g., John Owen),

---

[543] Ellingworth, *Hebrews,* 221.

[544] So argued by Ellingworth, *Hebrews,* 224, and others.

[545] So Alford, "Hebrews," 80; Ellingworth, *Hebrews*, 251.

[546] So Kistemaker, *Hebrews*, 110.

[547] Hughes made this point because of the author's use of the aorist subjunctive and not the present subjunctive (*Hebrews,* 148).

[548] Ellingworth said it is probably objective, but by the translation he gave, "sin deceives" (*Hebrews*, 225), he apparently meant to say "subjective." Other options are qualitative—"sinful deception"; epexegetical—"deception, which is sin"; and ablative (genitive) of source, as Alford took it ("Hebrews," 69). The concept of sin expressed in Numbers 14 involves distrust towards God's promises and failure to obey God by trusting those promises. This is a key point for the author of Hebrews. His notion of "sin" throughout the epistle is connected to disbelief and disobedience, as in Heb 11:24–26.

as describing one who was never truly converted in the first place. It should not be overlooked that the word *apostēnai* does not occur in either Hebrews 6 or 10. One wonders why it would not be used there if the author had apostasy in mind since the warnings in those two chapters are more severe than the warning in chap. 3. It is entirely possible that the author did not think about apostasy in the traditional theological sense of the term. Rather, he probably used the word to describe disobedience that incurs God's judgment in line with what happened in Numbers 14. In Num 14:20 the text explicitly says that God had "forgiven" the people in accordance with Moses' intercessory prayer. Does this mean that the exodus generation had committed final apostasy against God? Apparently not, since God provided for them and protected them for the next 38 years during their desert experience. In fact, nowhere in Numbers 14 did Moses explicitly mention the irrevocability of the loss of the wilderness generation.[549] What the people lost was the opportunity to enter the Promised Land, not their covenant status as the people of God. Based on what the author said in Heb 3:12–13, one may infer that apostasy is in view. But it must be admitted that this is an inference since it is not stated directly in the text, and it is not at all certain that such is implied in the text. It is better to interpret it broadly as distrust, disobedience, or disloyalty, and not attempt to define the exact scope of the warning.[550]

3:14 Introduced by *gar* (untranslated in the NIV), this verse provides the grounds for the warning of 3:12. It may refer back to 3:6, repeating the warning found there, which is the subject of the command in 3:13.[551] "We have come to share" translates the perfect tense of *ginomai* ("to become") with the noun *metochos* ("partner"). The perfect tense possibly intimates a relationship begun in the past that continues in the present, but it definitely indicates the aspect of a "timeless conclusion."[552]

The two nouns in the construction *metochoi tou Christou* ("partakers of Christ") can be construed in more than one way. It may indicate having a personal interest in Christ,[553] but this seems too generic for the context. Many take the phrase to mean that believers are partners with Christ, reflecting the root meaning of the Greek word *metochos.*[554] Others interpret the genitive

---

[549] Duly noted by DeSilva, *Perseverance in Gratitude*, 146.

[550] A caution wisely given by Ellingworth, *Hebrews,* 221–22.

[551] So Dods, "Hebrews," 276–77.

[552] Porter, *Verbal Aspect*, 269.

[553] Moffatt, *Hebrews*, 47.

[554] So Dods, "Hebrews," 277; and Lane, *Hebrews 1–8*, 87. See NRSV and the NET Bible for the translation "partners." Bateman took the phrase "we have become partners with Christ" to imply "that the community takes part in activities and experiences with King Jesus. The added presence of βεβαίος with μέτοχος would appear to emphasize an associate 'partnership' with Christ in a legal sense, one that is similar to a business relationship" ("Introducing the Warning Passages in Hebrews: A Contextual Orientation," in *Four Views on the Warning Passages in Hebrews*, ed. H. W. Bateman [Grand Rapids: Kregel, 2007], 49).

Christou as an objective genitive, meaning that Christ is the object of partaking in the sense of "we participate in Christ."[555] A combination of the latter two interpretations gets nearest the mark.

Eanper introduces a conditional clause, and "if" is a bit weak for this compound particle. A better rendering would be "if indeed."[556] The word is stronger than the usual conditional particles *ei* and *ean*. Ellingworth treated the condition as an open one, implying the possibility of not fulfilling the condition.[557] However, speaking in reference to the conditional statements in Heb 3:6 and 3:14, Fanning stated:

> Careful attention to the wording shows that these lines do not cite what *will* be true if they hold on, but what is *already* true of them, and which is to be evidenced by their endurance through temptation. The writer asserted that their continuance in faith will demonstrate that they *are* (present tense in Gk.) members of God's household, not that it will make it so in the future. Holding on to their confidence will reveal the reality they already *have* come to share (perfect tense) in Christ, not what they will share . . . . The warnings about falling away and exhortations to endure are designed to make this point.[558]

The verb *katechō* ("hold") conveys the idea of maintaining or possessing. That which the readers are told to "hold" is the "confidence we had at first," which refers to the readers initial faith in Christ. The word *hupostasis* ("confidence") can also mean "trust," "assurance," or "steadfastness." Up to and including the time of the Reformation, the word was usually taken here in a philosophical/theological sense as in Heb 1:3. But since the nineteenth century it is understood here as "firm confidence," a meaning that builds etymologically from the root of the word as that which "stands under something" as a foundation.[559] This is followed by the adjective *bebaios* ("firmly"). The believer is to hold firmly "till the end," which the author did not explain. It could refer to the end of a person's life, the end of the age, the return of Christ, or as Lane took it, entrance into God's final rest, linking this statement with "rest" in v. 18.[560] The almost identical phrase in Greek occurs in Heb 6:11, where the readers are encouraged "to show this same diligence to the very end, in order to make your hope sure."

3:15 The crucial issue in v. 15 is what should be grammatically connected to *en tō legesthai* ("As has just been said"), the preceding or the following.

---

[555] So Alford, "Hebrews," 70; Attridge, *Hebrews*, 117–18; and the NIV.

[556] As in BDAG 268; and L&N 89.68. Delitzsch stated: "The ἐάνπερ . . . implies that the first proposition holds true in all its extent, provided only that the second be added" (*Hebrews* 1:179).

[557] Ellingworth, *Hebrews*, 227.

[558] B. Fanning, "A Theology of Hebrews," 410.

[559] See Delitzsch, *Hebrews*, 1:178–79.

[560] Lane, *Hebrews 1–8*, 88.

Both are possible and commentators seem about evenly divided on the issue. If it is taken with the preceding clause, it gives the reason for what is stated. Lane (against Hofius) views it as a summary of 3:12–14.[561] If it is taken with what follows, it is the condition whose consequence is expressed in the next verse (as in the NIV).[562]

3:16 The theme of "rebellion" continues in v. 16, which probably refers to the rebellion at Kadesh in Numbers 14.[563] The conjunction *gar* is construed by some as a weak transition, but it indicates the reason that the wilderness generation was excluded, a reason that, as Greenlee pointed out, is implicit in the answer to the rhetorical question, "Who were they who heard and rebelled?" The point is that they should not harden their hearts because those who did so at Kadesh were excluded from God's Canaan rest.[564] The aorist participle *akousantes* (lit. "having heard") can be interpreted syntactically in one of three ways: (1) temporally, expressing the thought that when or after they had heard, they rebelled;[565] (2) concessively, "although they heard, they rebelled";[566] or (3) as parallel in thought to "rebel": "they heard and they rebelled" (as in the NIV).

The author answers his rhetorical question with another one: "Were they not . . . ?" The rebels God was angry with were "those Moses led out." Moses was the intermediate agent; God was the actual leader. This question is connected to the first by the adversative connecting particle *alla* ("but"; untranslated in the NIV), which has three possible semantic functions. First, it could negate the uncertainty implied in the preceding question, with the sense that the question was not necessary since all who came out of Egypt (over 20 years of age) did not enter.[567] Second, it could negate the response that it was only some who did not enter.[568] Third, it could be seen as a rhetorical confirmation in the sense of "really, indeed."[569]

3:17 In v. 17 the focus shifts from the people who rebelled to God who was angry with them over their rebellion. Miller viewed the semantic function

---

[561] Ibid. See O. Hofius, *Katapausis*: *Die Vorstellung vom endzeitlichen Ruheort im Hebräerbrief,* WUNT 11 (Tübingen, Mohr, 1970), 133–37.

[562] So Koester: "since the quotation reintroduces the terms 'hearing' and 'rebelling' that are taken up in 3:16 and because γάρ was often used to link questions to what preceded" (*Hebrews*, 261).

[563] The question of whether the first word in the text should be τινές ("some") or τίνες ("who?") is ably discussed by Ellingworth (*Hebrews*, 229–30) and need not detain us here. The former held sway up until the mid-eighteenth century, but the vast majority of modern commentators favor the latter reading.

[564] So Alford, "Hebrews," 71. The point about implicature was made by Greenlee (*Exegetical Summary,* 116).

[565] Alford, "Hebrews," 71; and Dods, "Hebrews," 277.

[566] So Ellingworth, *Hebrews,* 231, and Lane, *Hebrews 1–8*, 82.

[567] Alford, "Hebrews," 72.

[568] Dods, "Hebrews," 278; and Moffatt, *Hebrews*, 48.

[569] So Lane, *Hebrews 1–8,* 81; and the NASB.

of this clause as continuing the reason for the exhortation in 3:15. Again, the question of v. 17a is answered with another rhetorical question in v. 17b. God was angry with "those who sinned, whose bodies fell in the desert." A further relative phrase descriptively states "whose bodies fell in the desert." The Greek term *kōla* is too strong a word to be rendered by the innocuous "bodies." "Corpses" or "carcasses" would be more apt. This relative phrase may imply something along the lines of sudden death, but it surely links their sin with their death in the wilderness. Though expressed in the surface structure as a negative, "was it not with those," the proposition encoded is clear: "it was with those who sinned" that God was angry.

3:18 Verse 18 begins with *de*, which is rightly translated "and." It continues the grounds for the exhortation of 3:15. The key word in this verse is the aorist active participle of *apeitheō* ("those who disobeyed"). The focus of this word is not so much unbelief as it is disobedience.[570] The implied subject of the future infinitive translated "that they would never enter" is those who rebelled against whom God's oath is declared.[571] The future infinitive *eiseleusesthai* ("enter") expresses timelessness in that it is not connected to any external temporal reference and refers to an impossible state of affairs.[572]

3:19 Verse 19 is the conclusion of the preceding argument begun in v. 12 and is introduced by *kai* ("so"): "So we see that they were not able to enter, because of their unbelief." The noun *apistia* ("unbelief") is emphatic by word order since it is placed last in the clause. The use of the present tense in v. 19 after a series of aorists in vv. 16–18 is stylistically effective.[573] In v. 18 the author chose the verb *apeitheō* ("disobey"), but in v. 19 he used the noun *apistia* ("unbelief"). The latter word occurs in v. 12, thus forming an *inclusio*. The Greek text supplies *apeithountes* without a direct correspondent to the Hebrew text. Gheorghita offers three possible explanations. First, the LXX translators may have had a different source than the MT. Second, perhaps the translators paraphrased rather than translating directly. Third, the prepositional noun *mēʾaḥărê* in Num 14:43 "was read as a derivative of the Hebrew root *mrḥ*, usually translated by the verb ἀπειθεῖν [*apeithein*]".[574] The author chose the word to describe most accurately the sin of the desert generation from a theological perspective.

---

[570] See Alford, "Hebrews," 72–73; and Dods, "Hebrews," 278.

[571] In 3:18 the phrase εἰ μὴ τοῖς ἀπειθήσασιν appears to come from Num 14:23, although it is not identical to the Septuagint. The phrase in 3:11 is an exact quote from the Septuagint in Ps 95:11, which duplicates the Hebrew. Robertson explained that the conditional as a negative oath is "an imitation of the Hebrew idiom, though not un-Greek in itself" (*GGNT* 1024). Both phrases express the same semantic content that makes a simple negative statement: in 3:11 the conditional with the future indicative is used, whereas in 3:18 a simple negation with the future infinitive occurs. There is no difference in meaning.

[572] Porter, *Verbal Aspect*, 419.

[573] Lane, *Hebrews 1–8*, 84.

[574] Gheorghita, *Role of the Septuagint*, 81.

The author does not repeat the strong word *apostēnai* ("fall away") that he used in v. 12. The focus is on unbelief that resulted in disobedience. It is anachronistic to read later theological concepts of apostasy into this passage, as it is not clear at all that the theological sense of "apostasy" was used prior to the Christian era.[575]

THEOLOGICAL IMPLICATIONS. Verses 7–19 call for serious theological reflection. The influence of Numbers 14 is so pervasive in Heb 3:7–19 that it must be studied carefully.[576] Even though the people corporately sinned against God at Kadesh, Num 14:20 explicitly says that, because of the intercession of Moses, God forgave the people of their sin and still treated them as his covenant people. Yet because of their disobedience they paid a high price: they were not permitted to enter the promised rest in Canaan.

A key point in the interpretation of Heb 3:7–19 is the meaning of the conditional clause in 3:6 and 3:14. It is clear that in the main clauses in these verses the author addressed his readers corporately and assumed they were believers. To be part of Jesus' "house" and "sharers" with him implies that they were Christians. Reference to the congregation corporately is followed by a conditional qualification that essentially says "point A is true if point B is true." "We have become partakers of Christ in the past if we hold firmly to our confession in the future" is the sense the author intended, leaving the readers to draw the conclusion that future perseverance indicates past salvation, and lack of future perseverance indicates one was not truly saved in the past. The verse does not say: "If we do not hold on to our confidence, then although you were once saved, nevertheless now you lose your salvation." That is actually just the opposite of what the verse says. The clear implication is well stated by Guthrie: "perseverance does not gain salvation, but demonstrates the reality that true salvation indeed has been inaugurated."[577] Failure to hold on to one's confidence does not cause one to lose salvation; it indicates that one was not truly saved in the first place.[578]

A second theological point in this passage is that putting God to the test is an evidence of unbelief and disobedience on the part of God's people. Hughes explained:

> In their obduracy they failed culpably to learn the great lesson of God's unfailing faithfulness, with the result that he was *provoked* by

[575] So noted by G. Dorival, *Les Nombres,* in *La Bible d'Alexandrie (LXX)* (Paris: Editions du Cerf, 1995), 4:318.

[576] See esp. Hofius, *Katapausis*, 11–131. He presented a complete list of parallels between Num 14 and Heb 3:12–19 (pp. 117–53). Cf. Laansma, *"I Will Give You Rest:" The Rest Motif in the New Testament with Special Reference to Mt 11 and Heb 3–4*, in WUNT 2/98 (Tübingen: Mohr Siebeck, 1997), 260, 262–64, 273. For full bibliography, see the commentary on 4:1–13.

[577] G. Guthrie, *Hebrews*, 136; cf. Gundry-Volf, *Paul and Perseverance: Staying in and Falling Away* (Louisville: John Knox, 1991), 9–47.

[578] See also W. Grudem's discussion on Heb 3:14 (*Systematic Theology*, 793).

> the repeated manifestations of their mutinous temper ("They *always* go astray in their hearts") to punish them by causing them to forfeit the blessing of entry in the *rest* that lay ahead for the people of God.[579]

What happened at Kadesh became the symbol of Israel's disobedience, and the author of Hebrews took over that theme as a warning to his generation.

A third theological issue has to do with whether the sin of so-called apostasy was a real possibility or not. Whichever interpretation is taken, whether the basic meaning is "to rebel" or "to apostatize," the language indicates a real danger and not merely some "virtual" falling away that in reality cannot occur.

(3) Exhortation to Enter God's Rest (4:1–13)

1Therefore, since the promise of entering his rest still stands, let us be careful that none of you be found to have fallen short of it. 2For we also have had the gospel preached to us, just as they did; but the message they heard was of no value to them, because those who heard did not combine it with faith. 3Now we who have believed enter that rest, just as God has said,

> **"So I declared on oath in my anger,**
> **'They shall never enter my rest.'"**

And yet his work has been finished since the creation of the world. 4For somewhere he has spoken about the seventh day in these words: "And on the seventh day God rested from all his work." 5And again in the passage above he says, "They shall never enter my rest."

6It still remains that some will enter that rest, and those who formerly had the gospel preached to them did not go in, because of their disobedience. 7Therefore God again set a certain day, calling it Today, when a long time later he spoke through David, as was said before:

> **"Today, if you hear his voice,**
> **do not harden your hearts."**

8For if Joshua had given them rest, God would not have spoken later about another day. 9There remains, then, a Sabbath-rest for the people of God; 10for anyone who enters God's rest also rests from his own work, just as God did from his. 11Let us, therefore, make every effort to enter that rest, so that no one will fall by following their example of disobedience.

12For the word of God is living and active. Sharper than any double-edged sword, it penetrates even to dividing soul and spirit, joints and marrow; it judges the thoughts and attitudes of the heart. 13Nothing in all creation is hidden from God's sight. Everything is uncovered and laid bare before the eyes of him to whom we must give account.

---

[579] Hughes, *Hebrews,* 143.

Hebrews 4:1–13 continues the thought of the previous chapter. The author uses a threefold lexical *inclusio* which serves to give coherence to 3:12–4:13: *apistia* ("unbelief") occurs in 3:12,19; *eiselthein . . . katapausin* ("entering rest") occurs in 4:1,5; and *apeitheia* ("disobedience") in 4:6,11. Words in the semantic domain of faith (3:12,19; 4:2,3) and obedience (3:18; 4:6,11) serve to tie the sections together as well. The quotation of Ps 95:7–11 also provides cohesion since it is used in 3:12–19 as a warning based on history and in 4:1–11 as a word of promise and encouragement, with the intent of garnering an obedient response from the readers. From a rhetorical standpoint, Wills sees a threefold pattern connecting 3:7–4:11:[580]

3:7–18	Exempla
3:19	Conclusion
4:1	Exhortation
4:2	Transition
4:3–8	Exempla
4:9–10	Conclusion
4:11	Exhortation

Wray suggested that Heb 3:1–6 provides a thesis statement about the faithfulness of Jesus, and Heb 3:7–4:13 serves as an "extended proof/sermon illustration of faithfulness 'from the opposite.'"[581] She further noted that Hebrews 11 provides "extensive examples of faithfulness from a positive perspective, yet with the same conclusion as Heb 3:7–4:13, i.e., 'all of these died without having received the promise.'"[582]

There is a clear shift to the topic of "rest," marking 4:1 as the beginning of a new section. Where it ends is the topic of debate. Some carry it all the way to v. 16. Lane concluded the section with v. 14.[583] The NIV and most commentators conclude the section with v. 13. Ellingworth concluded it with v. 11 and Bruce with v. 10.[584] From a discourse perspective, 4:14 is probably the beginning of a new unit since it is parallel with 10:19, which also begins a new unit. Both units begin with *oun echontes* ("therefore having"). A clear *inclusio* occurs in vv. 1 and 11 with the repetition of the hortatory subjunctives "let us fear" and "let us make every effort" and the semantic concept of "entering the rest." The unit is given cohesion by the repetition of the semantic concept of

[580] L. Wills, "The Form of the Sermon in Hellenistic Judaism and Early Christianity," *HTR* 77 (1984): 277–99.

[581] J. H. Wray, *Rest as a Theological Metaphor in the Epistle to the Hebrews and the Gospel of Truth: Early Christian Homiletics of Rest*, SBLDS 166 (Atlanta: Scholars Press, 1998), 53–54.

[582] Ibid., 54. She pointed out that if the author intended his hearers to make the connection between Heb 4:1 and Heb 11–12, the connection is only implicit and not explicit, since "rest" is never mentioned after 4:11. She is correct that the connection is implicit, but incorrect in her assertion that the author does not take this theme up after 4:11 (see discussion below).

[583] Lane, *Hebrews 1–8*, 97.

[584] Ellingworth, *Hebrews,* 258; Bruce, *Hebrews,* 103.

"entering the rest" in vv. 1,3a,3b,5,6,10,11. The unit is further subdivided by two paragraphs: vv. 1–5 and vv. 6–11, both formed by *inclusios*: the concept of "entering rest" in v. 1 and v. 5, and the concept of "not entering because of disobedience" in vv. 6,11. In both of these sub-paragraphs, part of Ps 95:7–11 is quoted.[585]

Building on Heb 3:6–19, the focus in 4:1–11 is the need for perseverance, while the development of the "rest" motif in 4:3–10 is semantically subordinated to it.[586] Hebrews 4:1–2 functions as a transition and summary of 3:7–19 and 4:3–13.[587]

4:1 Verse 1 is introduced by *oun*, indicating a conclusion based on the preceding verse.[588] The events of the exodus generation are now applied to the readers' present situation. The verb translated "to be careful" is emphatic by word order. The NIV's translation is too weak for the seriousness which the verb itself, as well as the context, evokes.[589] Lane translates it "let us begin to fear."[590] By the use of *mēpote*, ("lest," but untranslated in the NIV) the author indicates a sense of possibility. Though the Greek present participle translated "still stands" is passive, it is translated in an active sense by the NIV, with the meaning that the promise is still being offered.[591] The present tense indicates time concurrent with the main verb. It is better to take the participle as temporal rather than causal. The promise is not the "rest" but rather entrance into it.[592] The key term in Heb 4:1–11 is *katapausis* ("rest"). It is sometimes given an interpretive translation that represents the theological perspective of the author. For example, both Hughes and Lane translate it as "heavenly rest." Given the ambiguity of the term in this context, it is much better to utilize the translation "rest."[593]

The author's use of *dokē* ("seems," left untranslated in the NIV) used with an impersonal subject indicates that this word tactfully softens the force of

[585] Vanhoye, *La structure*, 96–99; Lane, *Hebrews 1–8*, 95–96.

[586] Laansma, "I Will Give You Rest," 260, 273.

[587] G. Guthrie, *Hebrews*, 149.

[588] Ibid. "These two verses, therefore, serve as a transition and summarize the content of both 3:7–19 and 4:3–13. . . . Further, 4:1–2 exhorts the hearers to take action on the basis of the author's discussion."

[589] Balz and Schneider, *EDNT* 3:429.

[590] Taking the verb in an ingressive sense. Lane, *Hebrews 1–8*, 92. Lane stated this verb "implies that the attitude toward the word of God in Scripture within the community has not been acceptable" (*Hebrews 1–8*, 97). This plural hortatory subjunctive exhorts the readers to do something without necessarily including the author in the command (Porter, *Idioms of the Greek New Testament*, 58).

[591] L&N 13.92; BDAG 520–21. Ellingworth (*Hebrews*, 239) suggested the Greek verb can be used in the sense of "bequeath," a common usage in the papyri.

[592] Laansma, *"'I Will Give you Rest',"* 285. See also Miller, *Hebrews*, 99.

[593] On the history of the interpretation of κατάπαυσις, "rest," including bibliography, see the excursus in Attridge (*Hebrews*, 126–28). For more detailed critical study, consult O. Hofius, *Katapausis*; J. Laansma, *"'I will Give You Rest'"*; and Wray, *Rest as a Theological Metaphor*, 53–54. The theological implications of this term are developed at the end of this section on 4:1–13.

the following infinitive "to be found" to avoid any specific statement that any of the readers have or will miss out on the promise.[594] Westcott takes it in just the opposite sense of intensification, while Delitzsch and Laansma combine both senses.[595] Others take the verb to be used in a forensic sense of "be judged to be."[596] Koester noted the verb "can also refer to a person's own thoughts . . . and this seems appropriate here since the warnings have to do with attending to one's thoughts (3:12,13; 4:1), which are exposed to God (4:12–13)."[597]

The Greek perfect infinitive "fall short" is translated by Lane as "to be excluded."[598] Another possible meaning, gleaned from the papyri, is the notion of "coming too late," a translation adopted in the Jerusalem Bible.[599] The perfect tense indicates the sense of an abiding state existing at the time expressed in the verb "be found." Guthrie, following Hughes, noted the perfect infinitive suggests one who is not a Christian in that he has never entered the rest of God.[600] This is contextually problematic since the author describes his readers as believers and is warning them, as believers, of an impending danger.

The first question that comes to mind is what exactly are the readers to fear? Four possibilities are offered: (1) that the "rest" was promised to Israel, who has missed it by becoming Christians;[601] (2) that they have missed the opportunity;[602] (3) disobedience: "let us be fearful of disobeying"; or (4) failing to enter the rest.[603] The context seems to favor the last view.

Another issue concerns the relationship of the participle translated "still stands" to the noun "rest." Three possibilities exist: (1) temporal, "while it is still standing"; (2) reason, "since it . . . still stands," as in the NIV; or (3) concessive, "although." There is little difference in meaning between the first two. The concessive view seems unlikely.

What exactly does the author have in mind when he warns of the possibility of falling short? Lenski wrongly took it to mean that one who is Jewish has lost God's rest by becoming a Christian. Dods likewise missed the meaning when he interpreted it to mean that one thinks he was born too late and thus has missed the promise.[604] Many take it to refer to the time of the final judgment

---

[594] Alford, "Hebrews," 74; followed by Ellingworth, *Hebrews,* 239.

[595] Westcott, *Hebrews*, 93; Delitzsch, *Hebrews*, 1.186; Laansma, *"'I Will Give You Rest,'"* 285.

[596] So Moffatt, *Hebrews,* 50; Attridge, *Hebrews,* 124.

[597] Koester, *Hebrews,* 269.

[598] Lane, *Hebrews 1–8,* 92; BDAG 1043–44; cf. L&N 13.21; 65.51.

[599] MM 661.

[600] G. Guthrie, *Hebrews,* 150; Hughes, *Hebrews*, 158.

[601] Lenski, *Hebrews,* 126–27.

[602] Dods, "Hebrews," 278.

[603] Alford, "Hebrews," 74; Hughes, *Hebrews,* 156; Lane, *Hebrews 1–8,* 97.

[604] Lenski, *Hebrews,* 126; Dods, "Hebrews," 278–79.

when one will miss the eternal rest of heaven.[605] None of these options seems likely.

The concept of promise is prominent in Hebrews. The author speaks about promises made to Abraham (6:12–17; 11:9–17). Believers are heirs to God's promises which are ultimately fulfilled in Jesus (8:6; 10:23,36; 11:39–40). The promise of the land and "rest" which the rebellious exodus generation forfeited according to Numbers 14 was renewed for their children in Num 14:31. The author skillfully uses Psalm 95 to show that the promised rest is still available to his readers as well. Ellingworth helpfully pointed out several "general statements" which can be made about the use of "promise" in Hebrews: (1) the act of promise and the content of the promise are closely related; (2) Hebrews refers exclusively to God's promises; (3) no difference in meaning exists between singular and plural forms of "promise"; (4) no distinction in meaning is discernible with and without the article; (5) Old and new covenant are somehow connected because of the promises made to the fathers and to believers in the New Testament; (6) a variety of verbs are used to connote having or receiving the promises.[606]

Lane noted the debate in early second-century Judaism about whether God's oath of Numbers 14 and Psalm 95 implied exclusion of the people eschatologically in the day of final redemption, and he suggested the possibility that the readers were familiar with this through previous association with the Hellenistic Jewish synagogue.[607] His suggestion, however, is merely speculative.

4:2 Verse 2 begins with *kai gar*, "for we also," which places emphasis on the connection with the preceding thought. The point is not to contrast the exodus generation with the present readers. The *kai gar* serves to connote two things: (1) it states the promised rest is still available to the readers; and (2) it indicates the supporting reason for the exhortation in 4:1 to be careful.[608]

"The message they heard" does not refer to "the gospel," but to the promise of rest. This genitive phrase in Greek has been understood in three different ways: (1) as a qualitative (descriptive) genitive—"the heard word";[609] (2) as an expression of the recipient and the event—"the message they heard";[610] and (3) in apposition to "word"—"the word, that is, the message."[611] This message is said to be "of no value," that is, of no profit or benefit.

The periphrastic perfect indicative *esmen euēngelismenoi,* ("we also have had the gospel preached to us,") focuses on the lasting effects of the readers hearing the message, while the aorist of v. 6 ("had the gospel preached") refers

[605] Alford, "Hebrews," 74; Hughes, *Hebrews,* 156; Bruce, *Hebrews,* 105.

[606] Ellingworth, *Hebrews,* 238–39.

[607] Lane, *Hebrews 1–8*, 98.

[608] Ibid., 96.

[609] Moffatt, *Hebrews*, 50; Lane, *Hebrews 1–8*, 93.

[610] Bruce, *Hebrews* 103; and NIV.

[611] Alford, "Hebrews," 74–75.

to the wilderness generation's hearing. Ellingworth noted the close relationship between *euangelizomai* and *epangelia* here and in Acts 13:32, both of which occur in a context where *euangelizomai* may refer to acts as well as words.[612] The phrase "just as they did" is emphatic and links one generation of God's people (Old Testament Israel) with another (New Testament Christians).

There is a textual issue regarding the participle translated "combine."Is it masculine accusative plural or masculine nominative singular? UBS[4] reads accusative plural with a "B" decision. The nominative singular is read by Hughes, Bruce, and the NIV. If the singular is correct, the reference would be to the "word" combining with faith in the listeners. If the plural is correct, the reference would be to people of the exodus generation joined with the readers of the epistle.[613]

The passive participle is translated in the active voice in the NIV, "combine [it with faith]." If the nominative singular is the correct reading for the participle, then the dative *tē pistei*, "with faith," is instrumental. The participle indicates the reason why the word did not profit the people: the word was not combined with faith in the hearers.[614] "Those who heard" is ambiguous with respect to their identity. Does it mean Joshua and Caleb or current believers? Most likely the meaning is current believers.[615] Something similar to this is expressed in Heb 11:40, where Old Testament saints are not "perfected" apart from their Christian counterparts. Koester thinks the ambiguity serves the author's argument in stressing the similarities between his readers and the exodus generation.[616] "Those who heard" carries the connotation of paying attention to by obeying.[617] Grässer rightly stated that faith is the proper response to a promise. It is in this sense that those who believe have entered God's rest in a proleptic sense.[618] Hebrews 4:2 harks back to 2:3–4. What was the message

---

[612] Ellingworth, *Hebrews,* 240–41. On εὐαγγελίζω, see TLNT 2.82–92; Friedrich, "εὐαγγελιζομαι," *TDNT* 2:707–37.

[613] See discussion in F. F. Bruce, "Textual Problems in the Epistle to the Hebrews," *Scribes and Scripture*, 29–30; Ellingworth, *Hebrews,* 242; and Koester, *Hebrews,* 270. V. Taylor noted this verse illustrates the influence of exegesis on textual decisions (*The Text of the New Testament: A Short Introduction* [London: Macmillan and Co., 1961], 105). Another textual issue between the readings τοῖς ἀκούσασιν and τῶν ἀκουσάντων is generally decided in favor of the former reading.

[614] Greenlee, *Exegetical Summary*, 126–27.

[615] Attridge (*Hebrews,* 126) took the reference to be to the readers of the epistle. He noted this is a bold statement and was the cause of the "plethora of variants in the textual tradition."

[616] Koester, *Hebrews,* 270.

[617] L&N 36.14.

[618] Grässer, *Glaube*, 13–17. So also A. Lincoln, "Sabbath, Rest, and Eschatology in the New Testament," in *From Sabbath to Lord's Day* (Grand Rapids: Zondervan, 1982), 191, followed by Lane, *Hebrews 1–8,* 99. Grässer's notion that Hebrews reflects the despair in the church at the delay of the parousia is criticized by G. Hughes (*Hebrews and Hermeneutics: The Epistle to the Hebrews as an Example of Biblical Interpretation*, in SNTSMS 32 [Cambridge: Cambridge University Press, 1979], 137–42), who said neither this nor his dating of the epistle late in the first

which the Exodus generation heard? It was the announcement of Caleb and Joshua concerning the land.[619]

4:3 Verse 3 is introduced by *gar* and can indicate the grounds for the preceding statement, or according to Moffatt, the grounds for the statement in 4:1.[620] The NIV translates it as "now" to show transition to the next point. The participle translated "we who have believed" identifies the subject of the verb "enter," with the aorist tense specifying the preceding act of faith as that which enables entrance into the "rest." The verb "enter" is emphatic by word order since it is first in the sentence. The significance of the present tense verb "enter" is the key interpretive issue in this verse. Is the rest to be entered into something available in this life or is it future when one arrives in heaven? It can be understood to imply their entrance into rest is certain at some point in the future, probably heaven.[621] More likely, however, it indicates that they were in the process of entering the rest.[622] It may be that the concept of rest in this passage connotes both a future expectation and a present reality.[623] Miller took the present tense as iterative, "with each believer, in consequence of his faith, entering in."[624] According to Guthrie, no specific statement is given as to when or where the rest is entered.[625]

This statement is followed by "just as," which introduces the grounds for the preceding thought and shows that this quotation corresponds to the preceding quotation in Heb 3:11. The quotation is introduced by the perfect verb *eirēken* ("has said"), and most consider "God" as the subject (as in the NIV).[626] The quotation begins with "as," which may introduce a comparison with what follows or a consequence of what precedes.[627] The phrase "they shall never enter" accurately renders the Greek idiom, which (lit.) reads "if they shall enter," indicating strong negation.

The author rounds out the statement in v. 3 with the clause "and yet his work has been finished since the creation of the world." This is a concessive clause making the point that the "rest" was certainly available to be entered, and although God's works were completed and the rest available, yet they did not enter into it. The expectation was that they should have entered. The NIV uses

---

century can avoid the criticism of circularity, since the theology of Hebrews with respect to faith is based on the late first century date, and vice versa. See Attridge, *Hebrews,* 311–14.

[619] Lane, *Hebrews 1–8*, 98.

[620] Moffatt, *Hebrews*, 51.

[621] Lünemann, *Hebrews,* 481; Ellingworth, *Hebrews,* 246; and Koester, *Hebrews,* 271. Robertson ("Hebrews," *WP* 5:36) called this usage here an emphatic futuristic present.

[622] Dods, "Hebrews," 279; Attridge, *Hebrews,* 126; and Lane, *Hebrews 1–8,* 99.

[623] Lane, *Hebrews 1–8*, 99.

[624] Miller, *Hebrews,* 106.

[625] Guthrie, *Hebrews*, 151.

[626] Ellingworth (*Hebrews,* 247) argued that "Scripture" should be the subject, noting that grammatically it is simpler to make "Scripture" the subject of all the quote formula in vv. 3–5.

[627] Bruce (*Hebrews*, 104) took it in the former sense, while Lane (*Hebrews 1–8,* 92–93) and the NIV take it in the latter sense.

"creation" to render the Greek "foundation of the world," which is preceded by the preposition "from" and gives a temporal orientation as to when the "work" was finished.[628]

4:4 Verse 4 introduces the grounds for the conclusion of v. 3. In a way reminiscent of Heb 2:6, the author's quotation formula is indefinite but not uncertain as to the location of the quotation as the passage was well known. Again, most take the subject of the verb "he has spoken" to be God,[629] but Bruce argued that the subject should be "scripture" since the quotation from Genesis is narrative in terms of discourse genre and not direct address by God. "Day" is supplied in virtually all translations as the Greek reads (lit.) "concerning (about) the seventh."[630] The quotation is taken from Genesis 2:2 and affirms God rested after he finished his work of creation.[631]

4:5 Verse 5 begins, literally, "and in this again." "This" can refer to the same subject matter being discussed in a second quotation,[632] or it may refer to the present passage quoted in Heb 4:3.[633] The difference is negligible. However, with reference to the meaning of "again," four options can be noted. Ellingworth took it to mean the author is making a second point.[634] Lünemann interpreted it to mean the author is repeating a quotation in the sense of "in the same passage again."[635] Morris took it to mean the warning is being repeated in another passage.[636] Alford understood it in the sense of "on the other hand," meaning the following passage quoted in v. 5 explains the preceding one in v. 4.[637] Miller suggested that the purpose of this quote is not to show that the "rest" was not entered into, that is, it is not drawing a contrast between the "rest" and the exodus generation's relation to that rest, but rather its purpose is to continue the identification of the "rest" back then with the "rest" available now. Following Dods, she pointed out the emphasis in v. 5 is on "my." This verse reinforces what was stated in Heb 4:3.[638]

4:6 The *epei oun* which begins v. 6 (lit. "since therefore") is not reproduced in the NIV, where *epei* is left untranslated and *oun* is translated "therefore" but

---

[628] Ellingworth, *Hebrews,* 247. Laansma ("*'I Will Give You Rest,'*" 280) gave three cogent reasons the "works" mentioned in 4:3 does not include the *katapausis*. Whether there should be a comma, semicolon, or period at the end of v. 3 is discussed by Ellingworth (245).

[629] So F. Schröger, *Der Verfasser des Hebräerbriefes als Schriftausleger* (Biblische Untersuchungen 4; Regensburg: Pustet, 1968), 109; Lane, *Hebrews 1–8,* 100.

[630] Bruce, *Hebrews,* 104.

[631] Lane (*Hebrews 1–8,* 100) noted Psalm 95 followed by Gen 2:1–3 was recited in the synagogue liturgy for the beginning of the Sabbath. Koester (*Hebrews*, 278) thinks this is difficult to verify given the limited available evidence.

[632] So Dods, "Hebrews," 279; and Lane, *Hebrews 1–8,* 92, who translated "in this context."

[633] So Bruce, *Hebrews,* 104.

[634] Ellingworth, *Hebrews,* 249.

[635] Lünemann, *Hebrews,* 279.

[636] Morris, "Hebrews," in *Expositor's Bible Commentary*, 41.

[637] Alford, "Hebrews," 79.

[638] Miller, *Hebrews,* 110–11.

placed at the beginning of v. 7. This is not altogether problematic since v. 7 is actually the conclusion which is introduced by the *oun* in v. 6. *Epei* connects v. 6 closely with v. 5 as introducing the conclusion to the preceding argument and/or implication of it. Ellingworth said it introduces two conditions: the continued availability of God's rest, and the failure of the exodus generation to enter it.[639] Verses 6-7 make the point that some will enter, although others formerly did not enter. "Disobedience" is the reason those in the wilderness generation did not enter the "rest." The statement in v. 6 harks back to what was stated in 4:1 and forward to the summary statement that is made in 4:9.

4:7 In v. 7, the author now made clear from the Old Testament quotation of Psalm 95, that his readers have opportunity to enter God's rest "today." Psalm 95, taken in connection with the quotation of Gen 2:2, indicates that the rest is still available up to the time of the author's day. This is brought out by the statement, "when a long time later he spoke through David." The promise of rest was still available in the time of David, hundreds of years after the exodus generation's failure to enter the rest.

The phrase "through David" is interpreted in one of two ways. Either God spoke by David as his instrument, or the reference is to the book of Psalms which is attributed to David even though he is not the actual author of all of the Psalms.[640] The "today" in the quotation should be connected with the prohibition against hardening the heart rather than with the "hearing." The phrase "as was said before" refers to the writer's own previous use of the quotation. The use of "again" could be construed with "said," but it is perhaps better to take it as modifying the verb "set." The repetition of "today" in both the quotation formula and the quotation indicates the prominence of the availability of God's rest. The contrast here is not between Israel and the church, but between the wilderness generation and the author's generation.[641] The final period of salvation history has been inaugurated by the appearance of Jesus (1:1–2). During this present time, entrance into "rest" remains a possibility.[642]

Wray noted a chiasm in 4:2–7 that highlights the author's focus on the theme begun in the prologue that God has spoken.[643]

---

[639] Ellingworth, *Hebrews,* 250.

[640] W. Goudge (*A Commentary on the Whole Epistle to the Hebrews*, in *Nichol's Series of Commentaries* [Edinburgh: J. Nichol, 1866; repr., Grand Rapids: Kregel, 1980], 309–10) wrongly concluded from the mention of David in reference to the quotation of Psalm 95 that David was the author of the entire book of Psalms. He entertained and answered (to his satisfaction but not to ours) the major objections. For example, with regard to Psalm 137, which describes the Babylonian captivity, he argued David was the author "by a prophetical spirit," that "he might foresee what would fall out, and answerably pen psalms fit thereunto."

[641] As rightly noted by Ellingworth, *Hebrews,* 251.

[642] Hofius, *Katapausis*, 56–57; Lane, *Hebrews 1–8,* 101.

[643] Wray, *Rest as a Theological Metaphor*, 74.

A the good news came to us just as it did to them (4:2)
B but the word they heard did them no good because they were not united in faith with those who have heard
C the faithful enter into the rest (4:3)
D They shall not enter into my rest
E the work was finished from the foundation of the world
F For [God] has spoken . . . (4:4)
E´ God rested on the seventh day from all his works
D´ They shall not enter into my rest (4:5)
C´ It remains for some to enter into it (4:6)
B´ those who formerly received the good news did not enter because of disobedience
A´ saying through David so long afterward,
as was said previously (4:7)

"Good news" (*euangelizomai*) occurs in Hebrews only in 4:2 and 4:6. The author links this concept with that of "promise" in 4:1 such that 4:6 provides a restatement of 3:19–4:1 according to Wray:

So we see that they were
A unable to enter because of unfaithfulness (3:19)
Therefore, let us fear, lest,
B while the *promise*
C to enter the rest remains . . . (4:1)
C´ Since therefore it remains for some to enter into it
And those who formerly
B´ received the *good news*
A´ did not enter because of disobedience (4:6)[644]

The phrase *di' apistian* ("because of unfaithfulness") in 3:19 is also parallel with *di' apeitheian* ("because of disobedience") in 4:6. Thus, the good news is defined by the "promise" to enter in Heb 4:1.

4:8 Verse 8 is connected to the previous verse by *gar* which introduces a contrary to fact condition and serves as the grounds for the preceding argument. The sense is "If Joshua had given rest . . . [which he didn't], God would not have spoken . . . [which he did]." The semantic relationship expressed by the conditional is perhaps best construed as giving the grounds and then drawing an inference: if Joshua had given them rest (ground), God would not have spoken about another day (inference).[645]

[644] Ibid., 76.

[645] So noted by Porter, *Verbal Aspect*, 319. The Greek imperfect with ἄν marks the inference drawn.

According to many, the author intends no parallel between Joshua and Jesus by the use of *Iēsous*, which can be rendered both "Jesus" and "Joshua." Others believe there is some connection or play on words intended by the author in the sense that the reference is primarily to Joshua, but secondarily to Jesus.[646] Given the author's penchant for wordplay, together with his many quotations and allusions to Deuteronomy,[647] the latter option is best. For the author of Hebrews, like Deuteronomy, it is clear that Joshua is never the ultimate agent of the anticipated rest for the people of God. Allen has perceptively noted that Joshua's name in Greek is never the subject of the verb *katapauō* in the LXX of Deuteronomy. "When the verb is used transitively, specifically in relation to the gift of the land, the subject is always *kurios*, and there is no human mediator. Hebrews' proposition that Joshua 'never rested' Israel (Heb 4:8) is entirely correct, for that task was never assigned to him; it remained a divine prerogative (Deut 3:20; Josh 1:13; 22:4; 23:1)."[648]

The Greek text does not make explicit the one who "would not have spoken." It would seem the speaker is God, with the imperfect tense indicating repeated speaking. Hewitt understood the speaker to be the Holy Spirit.[649] "Later" is (lit.) "after these things," which probably means after the entrance into Canaan.

4:9 The conjunction *ara*, "then," beginning v. 9 is better translated "consequently" by Lane. Miller translated it "we may safely infer, then," to bring out the inferential aspect of the conjunction.[650] Just how far back it reaches is difficult to decide.

The author now leaves the term *katapausis* and inserts *sabbatismos*, translated here usually as "Sabbath rest." Many believe the author of Hebrews coined the term *sabbatismos* since it occurs nowhere in Greek literature prior to Hebrews and this is its only occurrence in the New Testament.[651] Others point out two facts that mitigate against this: the noun occurs in the writing of Plutarch

---

[646] Hèring, *Hebrews,* 31; Attridge, *Hebrews,* 130.

[647] D. M. Allen (*Deuteronomy and Exhortation in Hebrews: A Study in Narrative Re-presentation*, WUNT 238 [Mohr Siebeck, 2008], 108–9) noted Hebrews quotes from Deuteronomy six times, alludes to it six more times, and additionally exhibits five "echoes" and three narrative allusions. The majority of these derive from Moses' speech in Deuteronomy 29–32. "The song of Moses is of particular significance, yielding at least 8 specific references but also offering a profitable faithfulness/faithlessness paradigm for Hebrews to exploit within its paraenesis." Allen went on to conclude that the argument of Hebrews mirrors Deuteronomy: "Such acute similarities cannot be dismissed as superficial, but rather demonstrate further ways in which not just Deuteronomy's text and themes, but also its very rhetoric and position, are replayed within the NC context of Hebrews" (198).

[648] Ibid., 108.

[649] Hewitt, *Hebrews,* 88.

[650] Miller, *Hebrews,* 117.

[651] Spicq, *L'Épître aux Hebreux* 2:83; Moffatt, *Hebrews*, 53; M. Isaacs, *Sacred Space: An Approach to the Theology of the Epistle to the Hebrews* (Sheffield: JSOT, 1992), 84.

and several times in Christian literature after and independent of Hebrews.[652] Lane took it as "Sabbath celebration," giving a more precise description of the promised rest.[653] Ellingworth said the main distinction between *sabbatismos* and *katapausis* "appears to be that they denote respectively temporal and spatial aspects of the same reality."[654] Some have suggested that *katapausis* and *sabbatismos* are semantically equivalent.[655] Hofius concluded that *sabbatismos* refers to an eternal Sabbath celebration of believers in the eschaton, where the priestly people of God praise God around his throne.[656]

Wray offered a critique of this equation, arguing that while this may be logically deduced from what we know of the sparse use of this term in Plutarch and Justin Martyr, we have no clear statement within the text of Hebrews itself or the rest of the New Testament as to its intended meaning. She notes that two clues within the text itself identify the author's use of *sabbatismos*. First, the parallel between Heb 4:6, *apoleipetai tinas eiselthein eis autēn,*" where the antecedent of *autēn* is God's rest in 4:5, and Heb 4:9, *apoleipetai sabbatismos tō laō tou theou,* makes it clear that the author equates *sabbatismos* with God's "rest." Second, it is clear that v. 10 serves to provide a further explanation/ amplification of v. 9.[657]

However, *contra* Wray and Attridge (who takes the same position), *katapausis* is not redefined as a *sabbatismos*, but both are certainly related.[658] Bateman rightly called the equation of the two terms "an erroneous assumption" and accepted Laansma's interpretation of *sabbatismos*.[659] However, Bateman's agreement with DeSilva that there is no allusion to an earthly millennial kingdom in Hebrews can be challenged. It would be better to say that there is no *overt* reference to an earthly millennial kingdom in Hebrews. As we have seen in Hebrews 1–2, it is possible there is an allusion to such a millennial kingdom. In reference to DeSilva's comment, Bateman is correct to point out that though he agreed with DeSilva, this is not to say there is no earthly millennial kingdom to come in the future.[660]

Guthrie suggested the author may have had a specific Sabbath rest in mind, which he drew from Lev 16:29–31; 23:26–28,32. In these passages the Sabbath

---

[652] Hofius, *Katapausis*, 103–6; Attridge, *Hebrews,* 131; Laansma, *"'I Will Give You Rest,'"* 276.

[653] Lane, *Hebrews 1–8,* 101. From a premillennial perspective, it is possible this distinct term describes the future aspect of the rest as including but not limited to the millennium, while κατάπαυσιν emphasizes the present aspect of the rest.

[654] Ellingworth, *Hebrews,* 255.

[655] BDAG 909.

[656] Hofius, *Katapausis*, 110.

[657] Wray, *Rest as a Theological Metaphor*, 82–83. Cf. Hofius, *Katapausis*, 106; Lane, *Hebrews 1–8*, 101.

[658] Laansma, *"'I Will Give You Rest,'"* 275.

[659] Bateman, "Introducing the Warning Passages in Hebrews," 53.

[660] Ibid.

command to "do no work" is associated with the high-priestly offering on the Day of Atonement, a theme the author takes up vigorously in 8:1–10:18. The immediate statement in 4:14 about the high priesthood of Jesus supports this connection. Thus, according to Guthrie, "the Sabbath that remains for God's people is a new covenant Day of Atonement Sabbath in which they are cleansed from their sins."[661]

The concept of "rest" is mentioned no more in Hebrews, but the concept of "entering" is common: Heb 6:19–20; 9:12,24–25; 10:19–20. Jesus has entered into heaven itself so that we may have confidence to enter *now* according to 10:19–25. This is crucial to the understanding of the epistle and the meaning of "rest." The "rest" for the believer is surely an eschatological rest, but that is not the focus nor the meaning in Hebrews. Whatever the rest is, it is available now and not only in the future when believers get to heaven.

4:10 Verse 10 begins with *gar* indicating the grounds for referring to God's rest as a Sabbath rest in the previous verse. "Anyone who enters" indicates action at the same time as the main verb "he has rested."[662] It could refer to believers entering the rest in this life.[663] Some argue that the time of entering is not in focus, that finishing one's works allows a complete appropriation of God's rest.[664] Lane viewed the aorist tense in *katapausen* as proleptic: "what is enunciated as a consequence of the condition . . . is expressed as if it had already come to pass, the condition being regarded as fulfilled."[665] Porter took the aorist to be a timeless aorist, where the author appears to be expressing a "definitional tautology," and translates "for one who enters into his rest, indeed he himself rests from his work."[666]

What is the antecedent of "his" preceding "rest"? There are two possibilities: (1) God[667] and (2) "Jesus."[668] The vast majority of commentators and translators rightly choose the former. The phrase "ceased from his works" is taken by some to indicate eschatological rest in heaven,[669] a definite possibility. It is better not to make this inference since the works are not defined or described. If this is what the writer meant, he did not explicitly say so. The final two words in the verse, "from his," refer to God's works rather than believers since the preceding *autou* "his" before "works" refers to believers.[670]

---

[661] Guthrie, *Hebrews*, 154–55.

[662] Ellingworth, *Hebrews,* 255–56.

[663] Morris, "Hebrews," 43; Miller, *Hebrews,* 120.

[664] Miller, *Hebrews,* 121.

[665] Lane, *Hebrews 1–8*, 94.

[666] Porter, *Verbal Aspect*, 237.

[667] Dods, "Hebrews," 280; Hughes, *Hebrews,* 161; Lane, *Hebrews 1–8,* 102, and most translations.

[668] Alford, "Hebrews," 81–82.

[669] Bruce, *Hebrews,* 109–10; Hughes, *Hebrews,* 161; Moffatt, *Hebrews,* 53; Lane, *Hebrews 1–8,*102.

[670] Alford, "Hebrews," 82; Ellingworth, *Hebrews*, 256.

4:11 Some begin a new discourse unit here.[671] More accurately, the UBS[4] text takes v. 11 to conclude the paragraph begun in 4:1. "Therefore" introduces a conclusion by way of exhortation. *Spoudazō* is translated "let us make every effort." The idea is "to push on with something zealously."[672] It is likely an ingressive aorist, with the sense of "let us become zealous."[673] The author included himself with the readers. The purpose for the effort is to enter the rest.

The aorist active subjunctive of *piptō*, "to fall," is translated "to perish" by Lane, with Zerwick and Grosvenor.[674] Ellingworth took it to mean "destruction," as in 3:17 (cf. Num 14:29; 1 Cor 10:10; and *parapiptō* of Heb 6:6). It is emphatic by word order.[675] Some take this "falling" as everlasting destruction. Some think the writer has in mind the Israelites whose bodies fell in the wilderness.[676] Contextually, this seems unavoidable. As we have already seen, the exodus generation that died in the wilderness is nowhere in the Pentateuch or in Hebrews said to have perished eternally.

The *hina* clause, "so that," can be taken as negative purpose of the preceding exhortation, or as negative result. The former is illustrated by Miller: "if you don't push on to enter, you will fall." The latter is illustrated by Lane: "otherwise, one of you might perish."[677] The phrase "by following their example of disobedience" can be taken in one of four ways: (1) it is taken by the NIV as meaning in imitation of Israel's unbelief; (2) by means of the same kind of disobedience as Israel's disobedience;[678] (3) to fall into so as to be in the same kind of unbelief as Israel;[679] (4) to perish in the same manner because of unbelief.[680] The latter two options are the least likely. Of the former two options, the difference between them is negligible, but perhaps a slight edge should be given to option (1) since the author used the word "example." Semantically this clause is an illustration by comparison. Vanhoye made the interesting observation that the author always uses plurals in speaking of Christians' access to God (4:3,11a; 6:19; 10:19,22; 12:1; 13:13), and singulars when speaking of the possibility of falling away (3:12; 4:1b,11b; 10:29; 12:15).[681]

Looking at 4:1–11 as a whole, there are five possible meanings of the concept of "rest". (1) God's creation rest (Gen 2:2). (2) Israel's Canaan rest (Joshua; Psalm 95). (3) The Christian's spiritual rest (victory through obedience).

---

[671] Bruce, *Hebrews*, 111.

[672] Harder, "σπουδάζω," *TDNT* 7:559.

[673] Lane, *Hebrews 1–8*, 94.

[674] Ibid.; GAGNT 661.

[675] Ellingworth *Hebrews*, 259.

[676] Kistemaker, *Hebrews*, 113. Wray (*Rest as a Theological Metaphor*, 86–87) made this connection between 3:17 and 4:11 as well.

[677] Miller, *Hebrews*, 122; Lane, *Hebrews 1–8*, 93–94.

[678] So Bruce, *Hebrews*, 111; Ellingworth, *Hebrews*, 258–59.

[679] So Alford, "Hebrews," 82; Moffatt, *Hebrews*, 54.

[680] So Dods, "Hebrews," 281; Miller, *Hebrews*, 122.

[681] Vanhoye, *Hebrews*, 100.

(4) Millennium rest (Heb 4:9). Hebrews 4:9 is in the future tense but since it is unlikely the reference is to heaven, it could be a reference to the millennium. The unfaithful Christian will suffer loss at the judgment seat of Christ. He will not rule with Christ during the millennium: Mark 10:24–31; 2 Cor 5:10; 2 Tim 2:11–13; Rev 2:25–27. This ties in with 6:4–6 and pressing on to maturity. Fruitfulness or barrenness will be revealed at the judgment seat (Heb 6:7–8. John 15:6; 1 Cor 3:9–15; 2 Cor 5:10–11). (5) Heavenly rest. It is clear that even within the context of these 11 verses, several of the above meanings can be discerned. No doubt (1) and (2) are used. It is likely that (3) is also used. Some premillennialists see a reference to (4) in light of Heb 2:5, while many interpreters view the concept of "rest" in a primarily futuristic way as in (5).[682] Options 1 and 2 do not apply to the readers of the epistle or to Christians today. The difficulty is choosing between the final three options. The context of vv. 1–11 makes it difficult to choose between a strictly present or a strictly eschatological meaning. Choosing one over the other leaves something unexplained in the verses. The best approach is to see a reference to both. Such a dualism is not unknown in the New Testament. It is reflective of the "already/ not yet" tension that pervades the sayings of Jesus in the Gospels as well as what we find in Paul's Letters. I have treated this issue more thoroughly below when discussing the theological implications of this passage.

4:12–13 The entire section is concluded in vv. 12-13. Wray wrongly read the structure of verb plus *oun* as indicating a new section, but this does not begin until v. 14. Hebrews 4:12–13 can still be read as an amplification of the warning in 4:11.[683] Verse 12 begins a new paragraph according to the UBS[4] Greek text and the NIV. The use of *gar*, "for," serves to indicate the reason for seeking to enter God's rest: nothing escapes God's notice and he will judge unbelief.

Many have suggested a hymnic background/structure for these verses,[684] but the smooth transition coupled with the use of *logos* ("word") indicates the author's own composition. The phrase *ho logos tou theou*, "the word of God," is found in Hebrews only here and in 13:7 and can have two interpretations. The majority of the church fathers and medieval theologians saw it as referring to Jesus the Son.[685] Since the Reformation, the phrase has usually been interpreted as the written Word of God. In this latter interpretation, the genitive is subjective and the reference includes both Old and New Testaments. Lane

[682] A helpful bibliography for 3:7–4:11 can be found in Käsemann, *The Wandering People of God: An Investigation of the Letter to the Hebrews*, trans. R. Harrisville and I. Sanders (Minneapolis: Augsburg, 1984), 1–66; and Wray, *Rest as a Theological Metaphor*, 175–93.

[683] Wray, *Rest as a Theological Metaphor,* 86; γάρ indicates the conclusion of 4:11 and in a sense the conclusion of 4:1–11.

[684] H. Braun, *An Die Hebräer,* HNT 14 (Tübingen: Mohr Siebeck, 1984), 117; Michel, *Hebräer*, 197; Nauck, "Zum Aufbau des Hebräerbriefes," 205.

[685] So Athanasius in his *Orations Against the Arians*, 2.21, 72; and Chrysostom, *NPNF* 14:398.

noted "the word of God" must have specific reference to the text of Scripture extensively cited in 3:7–4:11, especially Ps 95:7–11.[686] While this specific text is certainly included, it would seem that the phrase cannot be restricted to this, but given the immediate and broader context of the entire epistle, must include God's spoken or written word, including his word expressed through Jesus. Dunn believed that the identification of the "word of God" as the gospel was so firmly established in Apostolic Christianity that the equation of Christ with the Word "does not seem to have occurred" to the author. For him, the word of preaching is personified and identified with Christ because the gospel is the life, death, and resurrection of Christ. Dunn compared the Lukan concept of "the word" as representing the gospel and not a hypostatization of Christ. He surveyed the power of the word preached in several Pauline texts and concluded that Heb 4:12 is in this same pattern. For him, there is "no inherent logic" in the New Testament author's own understanding of their experience or in the language they used to describe it "which made it necessary for them to push the concept of the word beyond that of the (impersonal) power of God to that of a hypostatization or divine being."[687] This perspective is difficult if not impossible to square with the Prologue of John's Gospel where Jesus is described as the "Word" of God.

The best argument for interpreting *logos* in 4:12–13 as Jesus the Word in a Johannine sense is made by Swetnam.[688] The evidence is actually quite strong. First, it was virtually the only view during the time of the church fathers and the Middle Ages, with Chrysostom being the sole dissenter during the time of the fathers. While tradition cannot be the *sine qua non* of interpretation, such unanimity is certainly significant. Second, the immediately preceding and following contexts support this interpretation. Although there are parallels within the New Testament to the sword imagery, such as John 12:48, the immediate context makes this interpretation more difficult ("oddly exaggerated" is Swetnam's phrase). In Heb 4:2 the good news is called the "word of hearing" (NIV "the message they heard"), and it seems contextually odd for the author to use *logos* in a threatening tone. There is also the difficulty of seeing two meanings of *logos* ("word" and "account") within the confines of two verses. Hebrews 4:14, connected by *oun*, closely links "since we have a great high priest." with the preceding *logos* (though it is true the *oun* could be reaching back to the total section of 4:1–13).

---

[686] Lane, *Hebrews 1–8,* 102–3.

[687] Dunn, *Christology in the Making*, 233.

[688] J. Swetnam, "Jesus as *Logos* in Hebrews 4, 12–13," *Bib* 62 (1981): 214–24. For the material in the next three paragraphs of the text, I am indebted to Swetnam's analysis. Twenty years later, Swetnam maintained and summarized his position in "The Context of the Crux at Hebrews 5, 7–8," *FN* XIV (2001), 103–7. This interpretation was revived in the twentieth century by R. Harris, *Testimonies* II (Cambridge: [s.n.], 1920), 52–57.

Third, from a lexical perspective, it makes more sense to translate *machaira* as "knife" rather than "sword," given what is stated in the remainder of v. 12.[689] Also, the use of *gar* which introduces v. 12 may refer back to the main clause of the preceding sentence and not the purpose clause to which it is immediately joined (as is the case in all other such constructions in Hebrews). The point of the author would be this: although the exodus generation failed to enter rest, Christians will succeed because of the work of Jesus, the Logos, in their lives. The use of *zōn* ("living") to qualify "word" implies personality. Nowhere else in Hebrews is this word used to describe non-personal life, but it is used four times of God, twice of Jesus, and five times of human life.[690] The introductory *kai* in v. 13 is best seen in an adversative sense where the author changed the subject from Jesus in v. 12 to God in v. 13. Verse 12 is taken in a positive way, while v. 13 is the negative counterpart. In Heb 4:12, Jesus as the Word is the "agent of interior change in man." In 4:13 he appears as an intercessor with God, so Swetnam translated:

> "And yet no creature is hidden before him, but all things are bare and exposed before his eyes, with whom on our behalf is the Word. . . . The Word is "with" God to act as one who pleads with God in favor of Christians who sin. This is why 4,14 follows logically from 4,13 with no break in the thought when it speaks of the 'high priest' . . . and why 4,15–16 speaks about the sympathy of the high priest and the importance of turning to him for mercy."[691]

A final argument in favor of taking the "word" in 4:12 to refer to Jesus is the connection of these verses with the prologue, Heb 1:1–2 to form an *inclusio*. It is likely that 4:14 is the beginning of a new major section of the epistle. The author began in the prologue with the statement "God spoke" in one who is a Son; now he concludes this section with a reference to God's "Word," the Son, in Heb 4:13.

G. Smillie has recently taken up the case that *logos* at the end of v. 13 corresponds to the first use of *logos* in v. 12. He noted that both uses are articular in form and bracket Heb 4:12–13. The usual interpretation of the final phrase in v. 13 is "as an idiom from the language of the business world: 'to whom we must give account.'" To attribute such diverse meaning of the same word in the short confines of two verses is

---

[689] This meaning is given by Michaelis, "μάχαιρα," *TDNT* 4:524–27. The Greek term μάχαιρα was so used in Josh 5:2–9 of the knives used for circumcision. The reference to Joshua in 4:8 aids in the comparison as well.

[690] Swetnam, "Jesus as *Logos*," 216.

[691] Ibid., 221–22. Swetnam said the translation "on our behalf is the Word" is the best idiomatic way to render in English the Greek construction ἡμῖν ὁ λόγος.

> uncharacteristic of a writer who demonstrates the literary sensibilities of our author that he would, . . . bring the pericope to a close using *ho logos* as the very last word in a figurative expression with a meaning having little to do with the principle theme of the discourse.[692]

How are we then to translate this final clause? Part of the answer depends upon the syntax of *hēmin*, whether it is an indirect object, "concerning whom is the word to us," or a dative of means, "to whom is the word by us." Smillie rejected the former as too contrived and redundant, but thinks the latter has promise, "indicating some sort of reciprocal responsibility towards God on the part of those addressed by his word."[693]

Smillie examined all the places in the New Testament where *logos* is used in the sense of "to render account" with the following conclusions: (1) *logos* is linked with some form of the verb *didōmi* "to give" when this meaning is intended; (2) *logos* is anarthrous (with one exception) in this idiom; and (3) *logos* always appears in the accusative case. In light of this, he found it difficult to see the meaning in Heb 4:13 as "render account" since no form of the verb *didōmi* (or any other verb) is present, *logos* is articular, and it is in the nominative and not the accusative case.[694]

If, as Smillie suggested, the author was engaging in word play in the double use of *ho logos*, then perhaps a colloquial rendering such as "towards whom the word is [now] up to us" contributes towards capturing the author's meaning as well as his means of verbalizing that meaning.[695] Hughes offered a similar translation: "He to whom the Word has been given shall be required to give a word in return."[696] Finally, Smillie mentioned how this interpretation of the phrase harmonizes well with Heb 4:14 where we read: "let us hold firmly to the faith we profess (*homologias*, NIV "faith we profess)." "Confession" is cognate with "word" in Greek, and both "are invitations to affirm or profess the word the readers have heard."[697]

---

692 G. Smillie, "The Other ΛΟΓΟΣ at the end of Heb. 4:13," *NovT* 47.1 (2005): 19.

693 Ibid., 20. Swetnam ("Jesus as *Logos*," 222) translated it "with whom on our behalf is the Word." Spicq (*L'Épître aux Hebreux*, 91) translated it "the Word, to whom we must render our Word." Others, such as M. Barth ("The Old Testament in Hebrews," in *Current Issues in New Testament Interpretation,* ed. W. Klassen and G. Snyder [New York: Harper & Row, 1962], 63), find less word play, but take the meaning to be "of whom we speak." Grässer offered the following translation: "Vor dem wir uns zu verantworten haben," which could be rendered "to whom we now have a responsibility to give an answer" (*An die Hebräer* EKKNT 17 [Zurich: Benziger, 1990], 1:239).

694 Smillie, "The Other ΛΟΓΟΣ," 22.

695 Ibid., 24.

696 G. Hughes, *Hebrews and Hermeneutics*, 11.

697 Smillie, "The Other ΛΟΓΟΣ," 25: "At the end of v. 13, the author says in effect, 'Now it is our turn to return the word to him,' then, in v. 14, he urges the readers to hold fast onto this word they profess."

Those who interpret *pros hon hēmin ho logos* as "to whom we must give an account," rely on the similar uses found elsewhere in Scripture such as in Luke 16:2 and Heb 13:17. This interpretation is likewise grammatically feasible and harmonizes well with the entire section of 3:7–4:11 and the conclusion of 4:12–13.

In summary, Swetnam found the interpretation of *logos* as Scripture in Heb 4:12–13 exegetically difficult for four reasons. First, the terminology is inconsistent: the change from *logos* as "word" in v. 12 to *logos* as "account" in v. 13 is "bizarre." Second, the imagery is inconsistent. The shift from the penetrating power of the word in v. 12 to that of a sacrifice or wrestling hold in v. 13 is problematic. Third, the description of a "sword" for the image of sacrifice or wrestling hold is inconsistent. Fourth, the language is inconsistent. If *logos* refers to Scripture in Heb 4:12–13, it is difficult to account for the connector *oun* "therefore" in v. 14, since there the high priest theme is brought back into play, but there is no reference to this theme in 4:12–13. Both Attridge and Ellingworth interpreted the conjunction in v. 14 to be resumptive of the thought which has been interrupted since 3:7. Swetnam noted there is no explanation for why the author would do this if this is what he has done.[698]

But Swetnam veered into less secure territory when he connected the *machaira* in v. 12 with the double-edged knife of circumcision used by Joshua in Josh 5:2 and then took it to refer to the knife of sacrifice used by Abraham in Genesis 22. This "two-edged" knife alludes to the two functions of circumcision (v. 12) and sacrifice (v. 13). That v. 13 should be so interpreted is, according to Swetnam, confirmed by the use of *pros ton theon* "before God" in v. 13 connected with Jesus' high priestly role in v. 14 and his intercessory role in v. 16.[699] For Swetnam, Heb 4:12 sums up 3:7–4:11, "which discusses the spiritualized promise of land, i.e., God's rest, and prepares the way for the following part, about Christ's priesthood." The author was implicitly indicating "why entrance into the spiritualized land of God's rest is possible: Jesus, who is equal to God, is able to effect the spiritual circumcision of the heart needed for such an entrance."[700]

Returning to the rest of v. 12, the theme of "living" here ascribed to the Word of God and first introduced in 3:12 occurs six more times in Hebrews (7:8,25; 9:14; 10:20,31; 12:22). The forefronting of "living" at the beginning of the clause is emphatic by word order. By the use of "living and active," the author denoted that the Word possesses the power to effect its own utterance.[701] It possesses an energizing power that renders it always effective in accomplishing its purpose. One is reminded of Isa 55:10–11, where the word will not return void but will accomplish God's purpose. In addition, the word

[698] J. Swetnam, "Context of the Crux," 103–4.

[699] Ibid., 105–6. Although possible, this interpretation seems rather farfetched.

[700] Ibid., 107.

[701] Lane, *Hebrews 1–8*, 103.

of God is emphatically compared to a "double-edged" sword in its power to penetrate the depths of the human soul.

The term here translated "sword," *machaira*, sometimes has the technical meaning of a surgeon's knife or the knife used by the priests to slaughter and carve sacrificial animals. Michaelis argued that the context forbids the translation of "sword" and instead the image drawn is that of a knife used by a priest or butcher, or possibly a surgeon. The priestly usage may be in view in Luke 22:38. Surgeon's knives were sometimes two edged while ordinary knives were not usually so.[702] How fitting would be such imagery if it came from the pen of Luke the physician? If the translation of *machaire* is the "knife" used by the priest to slay the sacrificial animal, then the thought of the passage has greater coherence.

How are we to interpret the division of soul and spirit and the joints and marrow? Ellingworth summarized the four possible meanings.[703] First, the reference could be to a tripartite division of soul, spirit, and body along the lines of 1 Thess 5:23. Second, the division could be between soul and body on the one hand, and between joints and marrow on the other. Third, the division is between each of the four mentioned entities. Fourth, the meaning could be along the lines of "within soul, within spirit," and "between joints and marrow." Spicq inferred from the similarity of this passage to what is said in Philo of the Logos dividing human faculties as proof of Philo's influence on Hebrews. But as is generally agreed, Williamson has shown that such is not the case.[704]

Another interpretive issue has to do with whether "joints and marrow" are to be understood literally or figuratively. Most likely a metaphorical sense is intended where the sword or knife of Scripture pierces deep within our bones to probe, even dividing the marrow within.[705]

The meaning of "laid bare" has been debated since early times. Two views are most likely. It may picture a wrestler using a choke hold on his opponent's neck,[706] or the neck of the sacrificial animal laid bare for the knife.[707] Given the overall context, the first option seems more likely. The word connotes the picture of total exposure and utter defenselessness. If the "word" of God in 4:13 refers not to Jesus but to the spoken/written word, then the use of "eyes

---

[702] Michaelis, "μάχαιρα," *TDNT*a, 573. Both "sharper than" and "two edged" are built on the same Greek root τομός from τέμνω, "to cut." God's speech or word is compared to a sharp sword in Isa 49:2 and Rev 1:16; 19:15,21.

[703] Ellingworth, *Hebrews,* 263. A good discussion of biblical psychology is F. Delitzsch, *A System of Biblical Psychology*, 2nd ed., trans. R. E. Wallis (Grand Rapids: Baker, 1966). His discussion of Heb 4:12 can be found on pp. 109–19.

[704] C. Spicq, *L'Épître aux Hebreux* 1:50–53; Williamson, *Philo and the Epistle to the Hebrews* (Leiden: Brill, 1970), 386–409.

[705] Grudem, *Systematic Theology*, 479; Ellingworth, *Hebrews,* 363.

[706] Grässer, *an die Hebräer*, 1:238–39; Lane, *Hebrews 1–8,* 94.

[707] Attridge, *Hebrews,* 136. See BDAG 1014.

of him" would be a personification of the word.[708] It is probably better to see a shift from the spoken/written word of 4:12 to God or Jesus in 4:13. Lane noted the correlation with this passage and what was stated in Num 14:43–45 where the exodus generation fell by the sword when they tried to enter Canaan in disobedience to God's word. The readers are threatened by the sword of the word of God, exposing their thoughts and rendering them defenseless before God.[709]

THEOLOGICAL IMPLICATIONS. We are now in a position to consider the theological implications of Hebrews 4:1–13. It seems prudent to note at the outset that the focus on "rest" serves to emphasize the author's contention, initiated in the prologue, that there is continuity between the people of God under the old covenant and under the new covenant. He consistently explained the new covenant in the light of the old covenant. The use of Psalm 95 and the focus on "Today" indicates God, who spoke to the fathers by the prophets, is still speaking today.

A few still champion some form of Käsemann's thesis that the author of Hebrews drew the motif of *katapausis* from antecedents in Philo rather than from the Old Testament, which led to its entry into Christian Gnosticism. For Käsemann, the author of Hebrews used Psalm 95 merely in an attempt "to anchor in Scripture a speculation already in existence."[710] However, the majority of scholars tend to agree with Hofius who convincingly argued that the concept of "rest" is found in Jewish thought and is specifically the point of Psalm 95. Although most English commentators like Lane, Ellingworth, and Laansma agreed with Hofius's critique of Käsemann's thesis, they were not necessarily in agreement with Hofius's thesis that the "rest" in Hebrews 3–4 refers to God's resting place in the heavenly temple where Jesus has already entered as a forerunner and where believers will enter and share in an eternal Sabbath celebration around the throne of God.[711]

Two of the most recent studies on the concept of "rest" in Heb 3:7–4:11 are by Wray and Laansma.[712] Laansma, in an evaluation of Wray's *Rest as a Theological Metaphor*, correctly chided her for suggesting that the author of Psalm 95 made a "hermeneutical leap" by shifting God's promise in Num 14:22–23 from the land to "rest." This is neither a leap nor one performed by

[708] So Grässer, *An Die Hebräer* 1:239–40.

[709] Lane, *Hebrews 1–8,* 102–3; followed by Koester, *Hebrews,* 280.

[710] Käsemann, *Wandering People of God*, 74. For a summary of the debate between Käsemann and Hofius, including the mediating positions, see J. Laansma, *"'I Will Give You Rest,'"* 10–13. For a survey of the discussion beginning with Käsemann until Hofius, see Hofius, *Katapausis*, 5–16 and more recently H. Feld, *Der Hebräerbrief*, EdF 228 (Darmstadt: Wissenschaftliche Buchgesellschaft, 1985), 42–48.

[711] O. Hofius, *Katapausis;* J. Laansma, *"'I Will Give You Rest,'"* 117–22; 316. Lane (*Hebrews 1–8*, 102) basically affirms Hofius's thesis.

[712] Wray, *Rest as a Theological Metaphor*; Laansma, *"'I Will Give You Rest.'"*

the psalmist. The psalmist wrote from within an established tradition which characterized the land as "rest."[713]

He also disagreed with Wray's conclusion against Hofius, who argued that the term *sabbatismos* is neither identical in meaning nor interchangeable with *katapausis*. Hofius took the meaning to be "the eternal sabbath celebration of salvation, i.e., the perfected community's before God's throne."[714] On the contrary, Wray took *sabbatismos* as being equivalent to God's rest.[715] But Hofius's evidence is solid and makes good sense in the context of Hebrews, especially when read in the light of Heb 12:22–24.

Hofius argued extensively that "rest" in Ps 95:11 means "resting place" and that *katapausis* in its spatial usage is a technical term for the temple in the LXX.[716] Laansma, however, concluded from Ps 95:11 and from the use of *katapausis* in the LXX that it is not tenable to identify in a simple fashion God's "rest" with the temple. He did note "that this noun is used in such a way throughout the LXX that a reader of the Greek would doubtless have a tendency to associate it closely with the temple."[717]

Laansma and Wray also differed over the spatial nature of the concept of *katapausis*. Wray took it in a non-spatial sense while Laansma considered *katapausis* to mean "resting place".[718] Finally, whereas Wray thought the "rest" motif is dropped after 4:11, Laansma believed that this theme is deeply embedded in the imagery used throughout Hebrews. Wray's study is, according to Laansma, "methodologically flawed" in that she attempts "to work over a *theological theme* in terms of a specific *vocabulary*."[719] In spite of this, however, Wray's work is helpful, particularly in its rhetorical analysis of the pericope.

According to Heb 3:7–4:11, God both promised and provided a rest for the people of Israel in the exodus generation. Those who disbelieved and disobeyed did not enter God's Canaan rest. Joshua, Caleb, and the younger generation that believed did enter Canaan rest according to Exod 33:14; Deut 3:20; 5:32–33; and Josh 23:1. But the promise was not exhausted at this time. Psalm 95 indicates the rest was still available some four centuries after its initial promise and provision, implying that "rest" means more than just entrance into the land of Canaan. Such an enlargement of the scope of the original promise was what occurred when Abraham originally received the promise of land and posterity, but the promise was not exhausted in his descendents. It was expanded to

---

[713] Laansma, "Hebrews' Use of the Old Testament," 27.

[714] Hofius, *EDNT* 3:219; *Katapausis,* 102–15.

[715] Wray, *Rest as a Theological Metaphor*, 91.

[716] Hofius, *Katapausis*, 49.

[717] Laansma, "*'I Will Give You Rest,'*" 59, 99–101, 314–16. This fact has implications for the possible priestly readership as suggested in the introduction.

[718] Wray, *Rest as a Theological Metaphor*, 146; Laansma, "*'I Will Give You Rest,'*" 276–83.

[719] Laansma, "Hebrews Use of the Old Testament," 30.

include all believers in Christ as Gal 3:16,22,29 make clear.[720] Whatever the "rest" is in Hebrews, it is distinguished from the land as well as the Sabbath.

The promised land is not equivalent to the promised rest for our author. Moses is twice presented as a model of faithful service to God in Heb 3:2–5 and Heb 11:23–28, yet he along with the wilderness generation failed to enter the promised land before he died. On the other hand, Joshua is identified in Heb 4:8 with the people who failed to enter the rest, though he himself did enter the land and led in the conquering of Canaan. Joshua's name is absent from the Hall of Faith in Hebrews 11, although there is mention of the fall of the walls of Jericho, which of course occurred under Joshua's leadership.[721]

In Heb 4:8, we are justified in interpreting the "rest" messianically. When Joshua led the people into Canaan, God gave the people "rest." Yet that was not the final extent of the rest which God had in mind, hence the statement in Psalm 95 and our author's argument which he builds upon this fact. Contrary to Bruce and many others who take the same approach to Heb 4:9, the "rest" is not only what believers enjoy in heaven. That will indeed be "rest," but that is not what the author is suggesting here. Hofius has proven there is a clear eschatological dimension to this metaphor of "rest."[722] But this is not the whole story. The author's goal is to inspire faithfulness in the Christian community today. Hebrews 4:9 is attempting to stir believers on to serve the Lord faithfully while still on the earth.[723] "In Heb 3:3 and 3:14, the relationship of the faithful to Christ is described, not as a possession, but as participation, a participation which must be maintained."[724] Miller is correct when she said: "It is not the non-fulfillment of the promise that is the point but its non-fulfillment *where unbelief prevails*, and that the promise is not exhausted by past appropriations or non-appropriations."[725]

To make the Old Testament concept of "rest" in the land of Canaan symbolic of heaven alone[726] is problematic for both Calvinists and Arminians on a number of fronts. First, that the exodus generation was barred from entry because of their disobedience is contradictory to the doctrine of the eternal

---

720 Miller, *Hebrews,* 116.

721 See the discussion in Wray, *Rest as a Theological Metaphor,* 81.

722 Hofius, *Katapausis,* 106–10. Wray, *Rest as a Theological Metaphor,* 92, correctly noted: "As careful as the author is to explicate fully the psalm text and to warn against the loss of ENTERING INTO THE REST, the phrase is used rhetorically in the service of the encouragement to faithfulness . . . " but then incorrectly concluded the sentence with: " . . . and not as an eschatological doctrine."

723 So Hewitt, *Hebrews,* 92; and Wray, *Rest as a Theological Metaphor,* 80. See the overview of positions in Attridge, *Hebrews*, 127–28.

724 A salient point made by Wray, *Rest as a Theological Metaphor,* 91.

725 Miller, *Hebrews,* 113.

726 Many have equated entrance into the land of Canaan with entrance into heaven: Pink, *An Exposition of Hebrews* (Grand Rapids: Baker, 1968), 196; A. B. Davidson, *The Epistle to the Hebrews* (Edinburgh: T&T Clark, 1959), 91–92; P. Fairbairn, *Typology of Scripture* (Philadelphia: Daniels & Smith, 1952; repr., New York: Funk and Wagnalls, 1900), 2:3–4.

security of the believer. Second, the exodus generation had to work to obtain the inheritance in Canaan, which does not square with the doctrine of justification by faith alone. Third, out of the entire exodus generation, only two men who were over 40 years of age entered the promised rest, Joshua and Caleb. Are we to assume that all of those who died in the wilderness were not a part of God's covenant people, Israel, and thus were eternally lost? Moses himself did not enter the Promised Land because of his own disobedience. Surely no one would think to suggest that he was therefore eternally lost.[727]

Carter made the interesting point that the notion that rest is only referring to heaven may be "a carryover from certain aspects of Roman Catholic theology, according to which there is not and cannot be any certainty of salvation in the present life."[728] Since the author's purpose was to bolster commitment and perseverance in the lives of his hearers, it would seem better to see the "entrance" into the "rest" as being in some sense a present reality for believers.

Thus, it seems best, given all the evidence, to understand the "rest" to have a threefold dimension: the present time, a state entered at death, and that which is experienced by the believer at the eschaton. The already/not yet eschatology of the author makes this interpretation likely.[729] It is difficult to limit the rest to a location or specific point in time. Genesis 2:2 as used by the author indicates God's rest is open ended. The "rest" must be seen as a present reality and not only as a reality at death or in the eschaton. Guthrie raised a salient question: how could the readers seem to have fallen short of the rest *now* if it lies entirely in the future?[730] In that case, all Christians would be "short" of it. Barrett's conclusion perhaps stated it best: "The 'rest,' precisely because it is God's, is both present and future; people enter it, and must strive to enter it. This is paradoxical, but it is a paradox that Hebrews shares with all primitive eschatology."[731]

The typological parallel is not between the earthly land as "rest" in the past and the heavenly land as "rest" in the future. Rather, the true typology which the author focused on is that between the two communities, his own and the exodus generation, both of which were confronted by the same word of God.[732] The "rest" described here is not a "sedating" of human life, a spiritual

---

[727] See A. Nairne, *The Epistle of Paul the Apostle to the Hebrews*, CGTSC (Cambridge: Cambridge University Press, 1984), 67; J. Dillow, *The Reign of the Servant Kings* (Hayesville, NC: Schoettle, 1992), 56.

[728] C. Carter, "Hebrews," in *The Wesleyan Bible Commentary* (Grand Rapids: Eerdmans, 1969), 6:65.

[729] So taken by Attridge, *Hebrews,* 128; D. Leschert, *Hermeneutical Foundations of Hebrews*, 168–70; G. E. Ladd, *Theology of the New Testament*, ed. D. Hagner, rev. ed. (Grand Rapids: Eerdmans, 1993), 622; and others.

[730] Guthrie, *Hebrews*,

[731] Barrett, "The Eschatology of the Epistle to the Hebrews," 372.

[732] Ellingworth, *Hebrews*, 97–98; Laansma, "'*I Will Give You Rest*,'" 275.

"retirement," an invitation to quietism, a period of idleness, or immobility as a life style.[733]

Is *katapausis* a place or a state? Those who take it as a place include Käsemann, Hofius, Weiss, Grässer, and Ellingworth.[734] Attridge and Lane took it as a state, but Attridge said it might be a place.[735] *Sabbatismos* is not so much a locale, but a Sabbath celebration. Laansma concluded "The *katapausis* is construed as a locale as God's own resting place, where he celebrates his own Sabbath. . . . The salvation thereby described comes to them also as a promise, the promise that they will enter into God's resting place."[736]

Is *katapausis*, "rest," present or future? Those who take it as a present realization point to the present tense of *eiserchomai* in Heb 4:3 and the eschatological outlook of "already/not yet" throughout the epistle.[737] Laansma summarized the points made by those who take it primarily in a futuristic sense, although allowing for the present as well. His arguments include the following: (1) the imagery of Psalm 95 suggests a *corporate* entrance into the rest, implying a future entrance; (2) the *katapausis* comes to us as a promise, which suggests future hope; (3) the demand to "strive" to enter the rest appears to place the reader before rather than in the act of entering; (4) if the rest is present, the "works" of Heb 4:10 would seem to be interpreted as something along the lines of "self-justifying works" or "dead works," but this is unlikely since Christians are not in the present at rest from their works; (5) the exhortation as a whole is related to the Parousia contextually in 3:14.[738] However, in light of Heb 6:4–6 and 12:22–24, Laansma was uncomfortable restricting the meaning to an eschatological rest: "It does seem strange that elsewhere in the epistle he would think in such vivid terms of a present participation in the heavenly world, but think of entrance into the same place *qua katapausis* as only an eschatological-future event."[739] Laansma summed up his discussion on the nature of *katapausis*:

---

[733] J. M. Lochman, *The Faith We Confess*, trans. D. Lewis (Philadelphia: Fortress, 1984), 254–55.

[734] Käsemann, *Wandering People of God,* 68; Hofius, *Katapausis*, 109–10, Weiss, *Biblical Theology*, 268ff.; Grässer, *An die Hebräer*, 1:209–220; Ellingworth, *Hebrews,* 235.

[735] Attridge, *Hebrews,* 97. Lane (*Hebrews 1–8,* 98,102) leaned towards taking it as a state as well.

[736] Laansma, "*'I Will Give You Rest',*" 334.

[737] Westcott, *Hebrews,* 95; D. Hagner, *Hebrews,* NIBC (Peabody, MA: Hendrickson Publishers, 1990), 49; Attridge, *Hebrews,* 126.

[738] Laansma, "*'I Will Give You Rest,'*" 306–7.

[739] Ibid., 310. F. Johnson (*Quotations of the New Testament from the Old* [Philadelphia: American Baptist Publication Society, 1896], 370) noted concerning the "rest" in Hebrews 4 that it is "a universal spiritual experience of those who believe, that it is past, present, and future; past, in the experience of all in every age who have believed; present, in the experience of all who now believe, whether they are on earth on in heaven; and future, as all the blessed spiritual experiences of Christians in this life are foregleams of 'the glory to be revealed.'"

> The common use of the word *katapausis* for a 'resting place,' its present usage and context, and the strong testimony in Jewish literature for an other worldly or future resting *place* cumulatively tilt the balance of probability in favor of taking it straightforwardly here as 'resting place.[740]

The local meaning is probably the best interpretation of the "rest" throughout the entire passage. The connection between *katapausis* and *sabbatismos* is that God's *resting place* is where he enjoys his ongoing *Sabbath celebration.* "It is *in* this place that the people of God will ultimately rest from their works . . . and thus join in the *sabbatismos* (4,9–10)."[741] Only on the seventh day, when we enter God's eschatological *sabbatismos*, will we be, as Augustine said, "ourselves."[742]

Scripture speaks, according to Turretin, of a threefold "sabbath:" (1) a temporal sabbath which included a weekly day, an annual time ever seventh year when the land was to remain uncultivated, and the year of Jubilee which was the forty-ninth year; (2) a spiritual Sabbath, which included cessation from sinful works during their lives; and (3) a heavenly sabbath where we rest eternally with God. Related to this "sabbath" rest, Scripture also speaks of a threefold "rest" in Heb 4:1–11: (1) God's creation rest; (2) Israel's Canaan rest; and (3) a Christian's spiritual and eternal rest, which Turretin apparently takes to include two aspects: the spiritual rest Christians can enjoy now in this life, and eternal rest in heaven. Turretin noted the "rest" in Hebrews 4 cannot refer to creation rest or Canaan rest as these have already passed away. The phrase in v. 3, "although the works were finished since the creation of the world," eliminates creation rest and the statement in 4:8 that Joshua did not lead the people into "rest" obviates Israel's Canaan rest as the meaning. This leaves only one alternative, the conclusion of 4:9, that there remains a rest available which is different from both God's creation rest and Israel's Canaan rest.[743] It may be that the author chose to use the unusual word *sabbatismos* in 4:9 to indicate that the rest which he intends is not the same as creation rest or Israel's Canaan rest.

Is it conceivable that the "rest" of Heb 4:10 may have reference to a millennial fulfillment? Although the majority of commentators do not think so, several have made this case.[744] Buchanan's analysis of this section, particularly Heb 4:8–11, challenges the assumptions made by many about the

---

740 Laansma, "'*I Will Give You Rest,*'" 281.

741 Ibid., 283.

742 In reference to Augustine's famous quote, "Our hearts are restless till they find rest in Thee" (*NPNF* 1:45).

743 F. Turretin, *Institutes of Elenctic Theology*, ed. J. Dennison, trans. G. Giger (Philadelphia: P&R, 1994), 2:78–81.

744 See Buchanan, *Hebrews*, 61–79; Delitzsch, *Hebrews* 1:197ff.; G. H. Lang, *Hebrews,*77–78; and W. C. Kaiser Jr., *The Uses of the Old Testament in the New* (Chicago: Moody, 1985), 168–74. They argue for a millennial reference, as does J. Dillow, *Reign of the Servant Kings*.

spiritual nature of the rest. He criticized those who make the assumption that God's promise of rest is a purely spiritual and a purely eschatological matter. For example, Buchanan noted F. F. Bruce rejected a millennial interpretation of the rest on the grounds that such is an importation of a concept alien to Hebrews, then went on to chide Bruce for importing his own alien concept, namely, a spiritualizing of the rest.[745] Likewise, Dillow has made the case for understanding the "rest" in Heb 4:9 to be a reference to a future millennial reign of Christ on the earth: "The writer is evidently setting before his Christian readers the hope of an inheritance in the land of Canaan which was made to Israel."[746] He continued:

> As Christian believers they will have an inheritance in the land of Canaan in the consummation of the present kingdom if they make every effort to finish their course. . . . That we should make "every effort" to do this proves that entrance into heaven is not meant. Otherwise a salvation by works is taught![747]

Dillow drew the conclusion that the content of the inheritance spoken of in Hebrews 3–4 is the millennial land of Canaan. The inheritance-rest is participation with Christ in his millennial reign. "Consistent with its usage throughout the New Testament, the inheritance (rest) must be earned . . . Not all Christians will make that effort or will make equal effort, and those distinctions will be acknowledged by Christ . . . during the millennial kingdom."[748]

The theme of "promise" in Heb 3:7–4:13, which is identified specifically as "entering into rest," reappears in chaps. 11–12. Here it is identified as the promise of a "heavenly city." It is not clear whether the author made or intended his readers to make the connection between the concept of "rest" and the "heavenly city." There is nothing overt in the text which makes this connection.[749] It is, however, possible that the author had such a connection in mind.

The rest is related to the redemptive work of Christ. When believers cease from their works, they enter rest. The crucial question then is what are these works? It would seem from the immediate context as well as that of the entire book that these "works" are "works of consecration, the faith and obedience required to establish and maintain covenant relationship with God."[750] This rest is not a ceasing from works of self-righteousness, or from works understood as the requirements of Judaism. Neither is in view in our passage. Spiritual rest is

---

[745] Buchanan, *Hebrews,* 72; Bruce, *Hebrews,* 107.

[746] Dillow, *Reign of the Servant Kings*, 108.

[747] Ibid.

[748] Ibid., 109.

[749] So Wray, *Rest as a Theological Metaphor,* 91, 93. Comparing Heb 4:2 with 11:39–40 and 12:22–24, she said: "The temporal focus of 'today' shifts to a spatial focus. The promise of entering the "rest" . . . has experienced metamorphosis into the author's true concern, the promise of entering into the heavenly city." Note the similarities in 12:22–24 to 3:7–4:13.

[750] Miller, *Hebrews,* 120.

ongoing maturity and perseverance, a community ethic, made possible by faith and obedience. The failure to reach the "rest" in Heb 4:1 is the consequence of the warning given in 3:12.

We may also conclude, based on 3:1–4:13, that the concept of faith for the author of Hebrews includes Jesus as the object of faith in a soteriological sense, and not merely an ethical category of steadfastness based on Jesus' faithfulness as some of suggested.[751] Jesus is both the object of faith in a soteriological sense as well as the model of faith in a practical sense. This is demonstrated well by V. Rhee from the meaning of *homologia* ("confession") in Heb 3:1, which includes both the apostleship and high priesthood of Jesus; the meaning of "our courage and the hope of which we boast" in Heb 3:6, where the object of our hope is the high priesthood of Jesus; and the references to God's word in 3:7–4:13. Disobeying God's voice (the word of God) is equivalent to failing to receive the message of salvation; the exhortation to "take heed" to God's word simply means to believe the message of salvation in Jesus.[752]

Another theological issue, which is actually hermeneutical in nature, is how much the author's treatment of Old Testament Scripture in Heb 3:7–4:13 resembles rabbinic midrash. Leschert examined this issue thoroughly and has drawn a number of conclusions. The author's view of the inspiration of Scripture and his application of it to his readers' situation is similar to Jewish midrash. Yet he did not find hidden meanings in Scripture or wrest a text from its context, as is evident from his careful exegetical use of Psalm 95 in the light of Numbers 14. The author's use of the midrashic technique *gezerah shawah*,[753] in joining Ps 95:11 with Gen 2:2, has long been noted by commentators. It is also possible that the technique *Dabar ha-lamed me-inyano* was used, where the meaning is established by its context.[754] Leschert concluded that when it comes to midrashic style, there is nothing "intrinsically illegitimate" and "we have not detected any use of midrashic methodology or presuppositions in this section of Hebrews which distorts the meaning of the OT."[755]

Eschatologically, Heb 3:7–4:11 is in line with other New Testament authors who consistently take the perspective that the coming age somehow has already begun with the advent of Christ, and thus the two, in a sense, overlap. Sometimes this view of the two ages is presented in linear and historical terms (horizontally) and sometimes in more spatial terms such as heaven and earth (vertically). For the author of Hebrews, the last days began with the first coming of

[751] The case is well argued by V. Rhee, "The Christological Aspects of Faith," 75–88, against Grässer, *Glaube*, 63–66, and Attridge, *Hebrews*, 311–14. For a more detailed presentation, consult V. Rhee, *Faith in Hebrews*.

[752] Rhee, "The Christological Aspects of Faith," 76–83, 88.

[753] An exegetical technique whereby a term in one verse is interpreted according to its use in another.

[754] Leschert, *Hermeneutical Foundations of Hebrews*, 188–90.

[755] Ibid., 197.

Jesus (Heb 1:1–2) and culminate in the second coming (9:23–28). As Laansma well noted, the author of Hebrews placed more of the emphasis on the "vertical" perspective, especially in chaps. 8–12.[756] Why does the author do this? Laansma speculated this is his rhetorical strategy for dealing with the problem of the present sufferings of the church in light of the new covenant salvation which is going to effect ultimate deliverance from such sufferings. All present appearances to the contrary, this new covenant salvation, about which the Scriptures spoke, is the only salvation there ever has been and that will ever be.[757]

In light of the available evidence, it seems best to conclude that the author of Hebrews is not dependent upon Philo, Gnosticism, or Jewish apocalyptic for his theology of rest in Hebrews 3–4. He was "a serious student of the OT who is drawing out of the text what he believes to be embedded in it."[758] Hebrews 3:7–4:11 presents a distinctly Christian interpretation of the Old Testament.

Another theological implication of these verses has to do with progressive creationism. The inclusion of Gen 2:2 in Heb 4:4 paves the way for the argument that the creative days of Gen 1 are not to be understood as literal 24-hour days, but rather as successive epochs of perhaps millions of years. Since God's rest is equated with the seventh day of creation, and his rest extends from the completion of creation until now, then this seventh day is, according to progressive creationists, obviously not a 24-hour day. If the seventh day was not literally 24 hours in length, then neither are the other six.[759]

But there are problems with this reasoning. When one considers the grammar of Gen 2:2 in the LXX and what is stated in Heb 4:4, the most that can be said is that God rested on the seventh day. Nothing is said as to whether this rest in some way continues to the present time, nor is there any indication as to how long the rest lasted if it is not still somehow in progress. All that can be said for sure is that God rested from his creative work in the past. If the aorist tense is ingressive, as is likely, the focus is on the inception of the rest, not on the duration of it or whether it corresponds to the seventh day. There are no exegetical grounds for suggesting that the seventh day of creation is still in effect.[760]

In drawing the discussion to a close, the author of Hebrews clearly thought the first generation of Jewish Christians found themselves in a parallel situation with their exodus generation counterparts. Forty years of wilderness wandering was the lot of the exodus generation prior to entrance into the land. From the crucifixion of Jesus until the destruction of Jerusalem and the temple by the Romans was also a period of forty years. Both groups lived in what might

[756] J. Laansma, "Hebrews' Use of the Old Testament," 8.

[757] Ibid., 9.

[758] Laansma, "*'I Will Give You Rest,'*" 356.

[759] E.g., H. Ross, *Creation and Time* (Colorado Springs: NavPress, 1994), 49.

[760] This argument is articulated in A. Kulikovsky, *Creation Ex Nihilo Technical Journal* 13.2 (1999): 61–62.

be called the "formative" years of a new movement of God in their midst. Whereas the exodus generation benefited from the leadership of Moses and Joshua, now the new people of God have a leader who is far superior, namely Jesus. To fail to respond to him in faith would have disastrous consequences as in the wilderness failure of the exodus generation. If Hebrews was written during the turbulent times of the Jewish War (AD 66–70), and specifically toward the end of that period, it is not unlikely that the author reflected upon the watershed event of the exodus generation at Kadesh Barnea and used it typologically or analogically with his present generation of Jewish Christians. The "today" which the author takes up from Psalm 95 is invested with ultimate significance.

Structurally, Heb 4:13 concludes the first major section of the epistle, which is bracketed (i.e., an *inclusio*) by God speaking in a Son in the prologue and speaking in his Word in 4:12–13. Theologically, v. 13 indicates something else as well. Christ's high priesthood, which plays such a key role in the epistle, actually develops out of the revelation of Jesus as "Son." He is able to be "high priest" because he is first a "Son."[761]

From an overall discourse perspective, we can now see how the author has very carefully made the case that Jesus is exalted above angels and Moses because of his high-priestly office and mediatorial work. If we remember that the entire discourse unit of 1:5–4:13 is bisected into two sections with the second section beginning in 3:1, we are able to discern a parallel structure developed by the author between these two sections. Christ is superior to the angels in Heb 1:5–14, and he is superior to Moses in 3:1–6. The exhortation in 2:1–4 is paralleled by the exhortation in 3:7–19. In 2:5–18, Jesus raised humanity beyond the status of angels, and in 4:1–13 he did what Moses and Joshua failed to do: bring his people into true "rest." He is our high priest who helps us in Heb 2:17–18, and he is again the same in Heb 4:14–16.[762]

---

[761] So noted by T. Häring, "Über einige Grundgedankedes Hebräerbriefes," *Monatsschrift für Pastoraltheologie*, 17 (1921): 261–62.

[762] This parallel structure was noted by J. H. A. Ebrard, *Exposition of the Epistle to the Hebrews*, trans. and rev. A. C. Kendrick, *Biblical Commentary on the New Testament*, ed. H. Olshausen (New York: Sheldon, Blakeman & Co., 1858), 1:166–67.

DIVISION OUTLINE

II. Obligations of Jesus' Priestly Office and Saving Work (4:14–10:18)
  1. Perseverance and Maturity Grounded in Jesus' High Priesthood (4:14–6:20)
    (1) Perseverance and Communion with God (4:14–5:10)
    (2) Pressing on to Maturity (5:11–6:8)
    (3) Persevering Strength Based on God's Faithfulness (6:9–20)
  2. Christ's Melchizedekian Priesthood (7:1–28)
  3. Jesus the Mediator of a New Covenant (8:1–10:18)
    (1) Jesus' Inauguration of the New Covenant (8:1–13)
    (2) Limitations of the First Covenant (9:1–14)
    (3) Christ the Mediator of the New Covenant (9:15–28)
    (4) Jesus' Effectual Sacrifice for Sin (10:1–18)

II. OBLIGATIONS OF JESUS' PRIESTLY OFFICE AND SAVING WORK (4:14–10:18)

1. Perseverance and Maturity Grounded in Jesus' High Priesthood (4:14–6:20)

(1) Perseverance and Communion with God (4:14–5:10)

**14Therefore, since we have a great high priest who has gone through the heav-
ens, Jesus the Son of God, let us hold firmly to the faith we profess. 15For we do not
have a high priest who is unable to sympathize with our weaknesses, but we have
one who has been tempted in every way, just as we are—yet was without sin.
16Let us then approach the throne of grace with confidence, so that we may
receive mercy and find grace to help us in our time of need.**

**1Every high priest is selected from among men and is appointed to represent
them in matters related to God, to offer gifts and sacrifices for sins. 2He is able to
deal gently with those who are ignorant and are going astray, since he himself is
subject to weakness. 3This is why he has to offer sacrifices for his own sins, as well
as for the sins of the people.**

**4No one takes this honor upon himself; he must be called by God, just as Aaron
was. 5So Christ also did not take upon himself the glory of becoming a high priest.
But God said to him,**

> **"You are my Son;**
> **today I have become your Father."**

[6]And he says in another place,

> **"You are a priest forever,**
> **in the order of Melchizedek."**

[7]During the days of Jesus' life on earth, he offered up prayers and petitions with loud cries and tears to the one who could save him from death, and he was heard because of his reverent submission. [8]Although he was a son, he learned obedience from what he suffered [9]and, once made perfect, he became the source of eternal salvation for all who obey him [10]and was designated by God to be high priest in the order of Melchizedek.

From a discourse perspective, Heb 4:14–10:18 forms the second of three major discourse units in the epistle. The phrase *echontes oun*, "having therefore," in 4:14 and 10:19 signals the onset of a new discourse section. Following the hortatory paragraph of 4:14–16, one can divide 5:1–10:18 into two sections: 5:1–7:28 and 8:1–10:18. The section covering 5:1–7:28 is marked by the bracketing (an *inclusio)* of 5:1–3 and 7:27–28. Both sections include the following common features: high priest, appoint, to offer, sacrifice from sins, weakness, for the sins of the people.[1] That Heb 4:14–16 begins a new major section in the epistle is confirmed by the relative absence of concepts that are also found in 3:7–4:13.[2] There is a back reference to 3:1–6 with the repetition of four words: "high priest," "confession," "Jesus" and "Son." The lexical density of these words throughout Hebrews is striking: "high priest" (11), "confession" (5), "Jesus" (13), and "Son" (15). This passage introduces the theological discourse of Heb 5:1–10 on Christ as the high priest. There is a chiastic structure formed by the lexical and semantic repetition of "confession" in 3:1, "confidence" in 3:6, "confidence" in 3:14, and "the faith we profess" in 4:14. The section begins in 3:1 with the admonition to "fix your thoughts on Jesus . . . whom we confess," and the new section in 4:14 begins with the similar exhortation to "hold firmly to the confession [NIV "the faith we profess"]."[3]

---

[1] G. Guthrie, *The Structure of Hebrews: A Text-Linguistic Analysis*, (Leiden: Brill, 1994), 83; and his *Hebrews*, NIVAC (Grand Rapids: Zondervan, 1998), 186; J. Kurianal, *Jesus Our High Priest: Ps 110, 4 as the Substructure of Heb 5,1–7,28,* European University Studies, Series XXIII, Theology, 693 (Frankfurt am Main: Bern, 2000), 235–61.

[2] Lane wrongly begins a new major discourse unit with 4:15 on the basis that, apart from 4:14, which is hortatory in nature, 4:15–5:10 is expository. He infers a transition indicated by repetition with slight variation of the concept of "having a high priest," and this "apparent redundancy marks a shift . . . from exhortation to exposition," thus introducing a new unit (*Hebrews 1–8*, WBC [Dallas: Word Books, 1991], 111). H. Montefiore, *A Commentary on the Epistle to the Hebrews* (New York: Harper; London: Black, 1964), 90, likewise begins a new section with v. 15. C. Westfall, *A Discourse Analysis of the Letter to the Hebrews: The Relationship Between Form and Meaning*, in LNTS 297 (London: T&T Clark, 2005), 142, takes Heb 4:11–16 as the point of departure for the second major discourse unit of Hebrews.

[3] See A. Vanhoye, *La structure littéraire de l'Épître aux Hébreux* (Paris: Desclée de Brouwer, 1976), 54; W. Schenck, "Hebräerbrief 4.14–16. Textlinguistik als Kommentierungsprinzip," *NTS* 26 (1979–80): 242–52; G. Guthrie, *Structure*, 78.

4:14–16 Hebrews 4:14 should have been a new chapter division in the Bible since it begins a major discourse section of the epistle and since Hebrews 5:1 is introduced by the subordinating conjunction *gar* "for." Verse 14 begins with *oun*, which introduces an exhortation based on the immediately preceding paragraph, or it resumes the topic of the high priesthood of Jesus in 2:17 or 3:1 after an interruption. Spicq and Ellingworth take the latter position and identify the interruption as 3:7–4:13.[4] The causal present participle *echontes* conveys the meaning "since we have" and serves as grounds for the two exhortations which follow in 4:14–16. Lünemann connected it with the participial phrase "having a great high priest" (NIV "since we have a great high priest ") as indicating a conclusion to the preceding section.[5]

Given the context of the previous chapters, Jesus is a "great" high priest for a number of reasons. He is highly exalted; superior to Moses, Aaron and the Levitical priests; and designated as Son of God. The translation "gone through" renders a perfect participle functioning attributively and indicating a state resulting from a previous action: Jesus is now permanently in God's presence having passed through the heavens via the ascension.[6] The phrase "Jesus the Son of God" is in apposition to "a great high priest" and is given emphasis by the author by being placed at the end of the clause. The two titles, "Jesus" and "Son" may reflect Christ's dual nature: human and divine. It is difficult to decide whether the reference here to "Jesus" harks back to Heb 4:8 where there is an implied contrast with "Joshua."[7]

On the grounds of the high priesthood and sonship of Jesus the readers are exhorted to hold fast continually (present tense) the confession. One's grip is to be firm and steadfast, as the verb *krateō* indicates. This exhortation will be repeated at 6:18 and 10:23. "The confession" (*tēs homologias,* NIV "the faith we confess"),[8] includes the divine sonship, the unique oneness of Jesus with the Father, as a means of imparting divine revelation (Heb 1:1–2). It also includes a high priestly Christology which is combined with that sonship throughout Hebrews. These two themes are interwoven here, again in 5:8 where although

---

[4] P. Ellingworth, *The Epistle to the Hebrews*, NIGTC (Grand Rapids: Eerdmans, 1993), 266; Spicq, *l'Épître aux Hebreux* (Paris: Librairie Lecoffre, 1952–53), 2:91. The term "interruption" is too strong given the way the author of Hebrews weaves his units together.

[5] G. Lünemann, *The Epistle to the Hebrews,* trans. from the 4th German ed., trans. M. Evans, *Critical and Exegetical Handbook to the New Testament*, ed. H. A. W. Meyer (New York: Funk & Wagnalls, 1885), 491–92. The present tense signals a continuing state of priesthood (J. H. Greenlee, *Exegetical Summary of Hebrews* [Dallas: Summer Institute of Linguistics, 1998], 150).

[6] Greenlee, *Exegetical Summary,* 150.

[7] Alford thinks there is such a connection ("Prolegomena and Hebrews," in *Alford's Greek Testament: An Exegetical and Critical Commentary*, 5th ed. [Boston: Lee & Shepard, 1878; repr., Grand Rapids: Guardian, 1976], 4:88), but Ellingworth, *Hebrews,* 267, denies it.

[8] For the meaning of ὁμολογίας, see Heb 3:1.

Jesus is a Son, yet he learned obedience, and again in Heb 7:3 when Christ is compared to Melchizedek.[9]

The *gar* of v. 15 subordinates it to v. 14, and semantically indicates the grounds for holding fast the confession.[10] Lane noted it counteracts the inference that the exalted state of Jesus would somehow hinder his ability to identify with human weakness.[11] This verse is structured in a negative-positive way with two balanced participial phrases separated by *de*, "but." Two concepts deserve attention in the first phrase: the infinitive of *sumpatheō*, "to sympathize with," and the noun *astheneia* "weakness." The former is a compound verb, (lit.) "to suffer with," and connotes sympathy on the part of Jesus derived from the reality of his incarnation. *Sumpatheō* appears to include sympathy based on common experience, always includes the element of active help, and should not be limited to the psychological notion of "feeling."[12] The latter ("weakness") occurs again in 5:2; 7:28; and 11:34. The word is variously taken to mean moral weakness, intellectual and moral weakness, and physical, moral, or spiritual weakness.[13] The word denotes "objective ineffectiveness rather than merely feelings of inadequacy."[14] The context would indicate that the weaknesses are the sources of the temptation in that they render one susceptible to temptation and sin. The use of the double negative in Greek serves to make the point in a forceful manner.

The second participial clause of 4:15 is introduced by the adversative *de* and provides the positive side to the contrast. The perfect passive participle of *peirazō* ("to be tempted/tested") confirms that the past temptations of Christ have abiding sympathetic results for us who are tempted. Context determines whether the word means "to tempt" or "to test." The final phrase, "without sin," indicates that the meaning of the participle must include temptation and not merely testing. Two prepositional phrases using *kata* ("in accordance with, in conformity to") with an accusative object are rendered "in every way, just as we are." The noun in the first phrase is *panta*, "everything," and in the second phrase it is *homoiotēta*, "likeness." Lane translated, "in quite the same way as we are."[15] The point here is that Jesus' likeness to us via the incarnation means

---

[9] See the discussion in O. Cullmann, *Christology of the New Testament,* trans. S. C. Guthrie and C. A. M. Hall, rev. ed. (Philadelphia: Westminster, 1963), 304–5.

[10] M. Dods, "The Epistle to the Hebrews," in *The Expositors Greek Testament*, ed. R. Nicoll (London: Hodder & Stroughton, 1903; repr., Grand Rapids: Eerdmans, 1974), 4:283; N. Miller, *The Epistle to the Hebrews: An Analytical and Exegetical Handbook* (Dallas: Summer Institute of Linguistics, 1988), 131.

[11] Lane, *Hebrews 1–8,* 107.

[12] Ibid., 114.

[13] So Dods, "Hebrews," 284; Ellingworth, *Hebrews,* 268; and Alford, "Hebrews," 89, respectively.

[14] A. Thiselton, "Hebrews" in *Eerdmans Commentary on the Bible*, ed. J. Dunn and J. Roberson (Grand Rapids: Eerdmans, 2003), 1461.

[15] Lane, *Hebrews 1–8,* 107.

he was tempted in the same way that all humanity is tempted, but with this difference: he never sinned.[16]

Oun should be translated "therefore" or "consequently" in v. 16 rather than the weak "then" of the NIV since it functions as the conclusion of vv. 14–15 and gives the grounds for the exhortation "let us come."[17] The use of the present tense hortatory subjunctive *proserchomai*, "let us come," is used several times in the epistle and is always used by the author in a cultic sense of approaching God in worship and priestly service.[18] The use of the present tense indicates the readers are exhorted to come as often as needed; when they come it is to be "with confidence" or "with boldness," or as Lane translated, "with a bold frankness."[19] The phrase "throne of grace" can be taken as a qualitative genitive, "a throne characterized by grace," or as a genitive (ablative) of source, "the throne from which grace comes." In characteristic Hebrew metonymic fashion, the throne substitutes for God who sits on the throne. Miller takes the sense of the passage to be: "(Since Jesus is now our high priest,) let us confidently approach the throne of God, for He is willing to act graciously toward us. In this way we may ask that God will show mercy to us and act graciously to send help to us just when we need it most."[20] Bruce viewed the author's reference to "throne of grace" as the antitype to the mercy seat in the earthly tabernacle/temple.[21] Whether the author intended a reference to the Day of Atonement ritual where the priest approached the mercy seat with the

---

[16] Some take the final phrase "without sin" in the sense of "apart from sin" and conclude that the sinless nature of Jesus precluded any response to the temptation to sin. Such a reading is "linguistically forced" according to Ellingworth (*Hebrews,* 269). Cf. Lane, *Hebrews 1–8,* 108. The genitive phrase can be written as an event proposition for clarity: "he did not sin." The phrase encodes semantically the notion of contra-expectation: "although he was tempted, yet he did not sin" (Miller, *Hebrews,* 131). Other places in the NT that affirm the sinlessness of Jesus include John 8:46; 2 Cor 5:21; 1 Pet 2:22; and 1 John 3:5.

[17] See L&N 89.50.

[18] J. Schneider, "προσέρχομαι," *TDNTa,* 262. "Cultic" denotes language having to do with the worship, ritual, and function of the tabernacle/temple.

[19] Lane, *Hebrews 1–8,* 107. Schlier, "παρρησία," *TDNT* 5.872ff., identified three shades of meaning for παρρησία in Greek political usage: (1) a citizen's right to full expression in the assembly; (2) openness to truth; and (3) courage to speak openly, candor. The latter meaning fits the context of Heb 4:16. Cf. W. S. Vorster, "The Meaning of *PARRESIA* in the Epistle to the Hebrews," *Neot* 5 (1971): 57.

[20] Miller, *Hebrews,* 134. B. Demarest and G. Lewis (*Integrative Theology* [Grand Rapids: Zondervan, 1987], 2:360) contrasted the way God is approached in Christianity versus the way he is approached in other religions: "Those who by faith identify with Christ need not approach God through countless intermediaries or dead 'spiritual masters' in the next life (as Theosophists and others do). Christians need not wait for countless rebirths in order to evolve morally and spiritually to the level at which they can approach the ultimate Reality directly (as Hindus, Buddhists, and others do). In our approach to God we are not limited to having a high priest enter the Holy of Holies once a year as our representative (as in Judaism). We need not convey our heartfelt concerns to human priests or to Jesus' mother, Mary [as in Catholicism]."

[21] F. F. Bruce, *The Epistle to the Hebrews*, NICNT revised (Grand Rapids: Eerdmans, 1990), 116.

sacrificial blood is unclear, but the Day of Atonement was a once-a-year event, whereas here we are told to approach continually.

The purpose for coming to the throne of grace is that we might receive "mercy" and find "grace for timely help" (NIV, "grace to help us in our time of need"). The two phrases "receive mercy" and "find grace" are chiastically arranged in the Greek text, which probably indicates the two phrases overlap in meaning.[22] When there is a difference perceived, it is usually along the lines of mercy in forgiveness of sins and grace to needed assistance in some trial or temptation.[23] The Greek phrase "for timely help" can be construed with "finding grace,"[24] or as is more likely, with both "mercy" and "grace."[25] The Greek noun *boētheia* "help," preceded by the adjective translated "timely," is rendered verbally in the NIV as "to help us in our time of need."[26]

THEOLOGICAL IMPLICATIONS. The most significant theological issue in this paragraph has to do with the meaning of v. 15, particularly the second half of the verse. The debate over whether Jesus could or could not have sinned, the peccability/impeccability debate, has as its *crux interpretum* this verse.[27] Several points should be kept in mind. First, the New Testament writers, including the author of Hebrews, affirm Christ's complete sinlessness in his incarnation. Second, the term "peccability" does not presuppose a sin nature in Christ since virtually all who affirm "peccability" would disavow such. Third, the issue cannot be resolved by appeal to Heb 4:15 alone. Fourth, the Scriptures affirm Christ's full identification with fallen humanity with the single exception stated here in v. 15: he was without sin. Fifth, the Scriptures also affirm that the temptations and testings which Jesus faced were in fact real.[28] The temptation narratives of the Gospels confirm this: Matt 4:1–11; Mark 1:12–13; Luke 4:1–13.

---

[22] So Alford, "Hebrews," 90; and Ellingworth, *Hebrews,* 270.

[23] E.g., B. F. Westcott, *The Epistle to the Hebrews* (Grand Rapids: Eerdmans, 1977), 110; Dods, "Hebrews," 284.

[24] So P. E. Hughes, *A Commentary on the Epistle to the Hebrews* (Grand Rapids: Eerdmans, 1977), 174; and Lane, *Hebrews 1–8,* 107.

[25] So Alford, "Hebrews," 90; and Ellingworth, *Hebrews,* 270.

[26] "A man is merciful when he takes to heart the need of another. Jesus Christ has once and for all taken our need to heart. . . . But although he did it once and for all [on the cross], He did not do it once only. Risen from the dead, He lives and takes it to heart with undiminished severity. This is His passion today" (K. Barth, *CD*, IV/3, 396).

[27] H. Thielicke (*The Evangelical Faith*, ed. and trans. G. Bromiley [Grand Rapids: Eerdmans, 1974], 2:376) called this issue "perhaps the ultimate problem of Christology." Cf. M. Shuster, "The Temptation, Sinlessness and Sympathy of Jesus: Another Look at the Dilemma of Hebrews 4:15," in *Perspectives on Christology: Essays in Honor of Paul K. Jewett*, ed. M. Shuster and R. Muller (Grand Rapids: Zondervan, 1991) 211–30; K. Barth, CD, IV/1: 257ff., VI/1, 258–60. Barth's thoughts on this verse are worth pondering by the theologian and the homiletician.

[28] See W. Grudem, *Systematic Theology: An Introduction to Biblical Doctrine* (Grand Rapids: Zondervan, 1994), 537–38. Cullmann (*Christology*, 95), took the phrase in 4:15 "tempted in every way as we are" to refer both to the form of the temptations as well as to the content, and comments that this verse, which goes beyond what we read in the Synoptics about the temptation of Jesus, "is

The issue of the temptation of Jesus involves one in a host of difficult questions. As divine, Jesus possessed the moral attribute of holiness. He has no sin nature. Since according to Jas 1:13, "God cannot be tempted by evil," the question arises how could Jesus then be tempted at all? Is temptation even possible if sin on the part of Jesus is impossible? "In logical terms, is not temptation without sin a contradiction in terms, an antinomy?"[29] Hebrews 4:15 asserts the genuineness of Jesus' temptations. Furthermore, the text does not say either way whether Christ could or could not sin. What of the doctrine of God's impassibility? Hebrews 4:15 seems to indicate that in some way the Triune Godhead was affected by the incarnation in that Jesus as the God-man "experienced firsthand the full nature of evil,"[30] particularly in his death on the cross.

The debate about Heb 4:15 involves those who believe that Jesus Christ was "able not to sin" (the peccability position) and those who believe he was "not able to sin" (the impeccability position). The former believe Christ could have sinned, but of course he did not. The latter believe he was unable to sin. The major arguments for the peccability position generally revolve around three issues: (1) Christ's humanity, (2) Christ's temptability, which implies the ability to sin;[31] and (3) Christ's free will, which implies peccability. The major arguments for the impeccability position include: (1) Christ's deity, (2) God's decreed plan of redemption, which cannot fail, hence Christ could not have sinned; and (3) Christ's divine attributes, including immutability, omnipotence ,and omniscience.[32]

Exegetical considerations alone cannot settle this issue from Heb 4:15, or for that matter, from any New Testament passage which speaks directly or indirectly to the issue. One must weigh all of the texts and reason to a theological conclusion. If one is to come to some reasonable conclusion on the subject, a careful definition of terms is mandatory. What do we mean by "able" to sin or

perhaps the boldest assertion of the completely human character of Jesus in the New Testament." Furthermore, there is no trace of a docetic Christology in these verses: "Jesus was really a man, not just God disguised as a man" (p. 96).

[29] Thielicke, *Evangelical Faith,* 377. Thielicke put the matter well: "Temptation is a problem because it presupposes susceptibility to it. On this side, then, we view Jesus as open to temptation. We construe his humanity so unconditionally and uncompromisingly that only his solidarity with us is seen and not his difference from us. On the other hand, we could choose not to go so far. But then we deprive him of the central core of susceptibility to temptation and consequently of his humanity" (378–79).

[30] M. Erickson, *The Word Became Flesh* (Grand Rapids: Baker, 1991), 607.

[31] So P. Davids, *More Hard Sayings of the New Testament* (Downers Grove: InterVarsity, 1991), 93: "Could he have sinned? Scripture never enters into such philosophical speculation. But it certainly implies that there was virtue in not sinning and that the test was real, which seems to imply the possibility of failing."

[32] These positions are helpfully summarized by M. Canham, "*Potuit Non Peccare* or *Non Potuit Peccare*: Evangelicals, Hermeneutics, and the Impeccability Debate," *TMSJ* 11/1 (2000): 94–96.Canham, along with Shuster, "Temptation, Sinlessness, and Sympathy of Jesus," 197–209, has one of the best overall analyses of the issue I have seen, though his solution is less than satisfying.

not to sin? This question is related to another: what was the nature of Christ's humanity? Is it identical to Adam's humanity prior to the Fall, fallen humanity, or glorified humanity in the eschaton? Adam was certainly "able not to sin" and yet he did sin. Glorified humanity will be without the ability to sin. Hence, Adam before the fall was peccable, but after his entrance into heaven and reception of a glorified body, he will be impeccable. If one defines Christ's human nature as identical to that of Adam before the Fall, then peccability becomes a live option. On the other hand, if one defines Christ's human nature as identical to glorified humanity, then impeccability follows. K. Barth said Christ took "the nature of man as he comes from the fall," yet he does not mean by this that Jesus possessed a sin nature nor that he was not sinless, for he also says: "In His likeness He was also unlike in that He did not yield to temptation."[33] In another place Barth put it this way: "In becoming the same as we are, the Son of God is the same in quite a different way from us; in other words, in our human being what we do is omitted, and what we omit is done."[34]

Of course, one should ask, what does it mean to sin? If sin is narrowly defined to exclude evil inclinations and include only "willfully entertaining or acting upon those inclinations" by deliberate disobedience, then Jesus could have been tempted "by every sort of fleshly desire, proud ambition, and rebellious impulse . . . without ever actually sinning." But as M. Shuster cogently noted: "The desire to sin is sin."[35]

Another crucial issue is the definition of *peirazō*, whether it should be translated as "test" or "tempt" in Heb 4:15, Jas 1:13, and Matt 4:1. It can mean either, depending on the context. Complicating the question further, the author of Hebrews had available to him a synonym, *dokimazō*, which always means "testing." Those who advocate peccability interpret the word to mean "temptation," while those who argue for impeccability sometimes restrict the meaning to "testing" based on Jas 1:13–15, albeit a testing that includes the meaning of temptation defined as outward solicitation to do evil, not as an inward propensity. The author says Jesus was tempted "in every way" as we are. This exact phrase in Greek was used by the author in 2:17: Christ had to be made like his brothers "in every way." The author takes great pains to stress that Jesus is identified with the humanity of his people.

Likewise, how we define the phrase "without sin" in Heb 4:15 impinges on the issue. Is the meaning "without resulting in sin" or "without having a sin nature?" Both sides affirm both truths, but impeccability advocates choose the latter and conclude since Jesus had no sin nature, he could not have sinned.

---

[33] Barth, *CD* IV/1: 258–60. Cf. *CD* I/3:153: "[T]here must be no weakening or obscuring of the saving truth that the nature which God assumed in Christ is identical with our nature as we see it in the light of the Fall." Likewise Westcott (*Hebrews*, 108) noted: "Christ assumed humanity under the conditions of life belonging to man fallen, though not with sinful promptings from within."

[34] Barth, *CD* I/3: 155.

[35] Shuster, "Temptations, Sinlessness, and Sympathy of Jesus," 199.

Exegetically, since "without sin" follows immediately the perfect participle *pepeirasmenon*, it is likely that the meaning of "without sin" is "without resulting in sin" and the meaning of *pepeirasmenon* is "tempted," and includes trials, rather than "tried" that excludes temptation.[36] However, it is possible to understand the author as focusing on a distinction in the process of temptation rather than focusing on the result of temptation.

D. Bloesch noted how crucial it is to distinguish between internal and external temptation in relation to the impeccability debate.[37] Peccabilists argue that Jesus was incapable of internal temptation since he had no sin nature, but like Adam in his pre-fall state, he was capable of succumbing to external temptation. Impeccabilists argue that the deity of Jesus makes it impossible for him to sin, even as the incarnate God-man.[38]

In arguing the peccability position, M. Erickson, following T. Morris, distinguished between the epistemic possibility of sin and the logical possibility: "On such grounds, it was really possible for Jesus to decide to sin, but the divine nature precluded his actually doing so. As long as his divine nature did not preclude his thinking that he could perform the sin, there was genuine temptation. . . . He chose not to sin, thus never encountering the fact that he could not have sinned."[39] Erickson also suggested another possible approach to the issue: that of distinguishing between the possibility of what *could* occur and the likelihood of what *would* occur. If one takes the position that it is unlikely that Jesus would sin, it could be argued that in this case there are conditions under which Jesus could have sinned, but it was certain those conditions would not all be fulfilled. On this approach, according to Erickson, Jesus could have decided to sin, but it was certain that he would not.[40]

Calvin rightly used Heb 4:15 to refute those, like Abelard, who argued that the suffering of Christ in the garden of Gethsemane was only pretense ("theatrical demonstration" according to Abelard) in light of his deity. "These detractors are, moreover, deceived in this one point: they do not recognize in Christ a weakness pure and free of all vice and stain because he held himself within the

[36] Canham, "*Potuit Non Peccare* or *Non Potuit Peccare*," 105–7. Ellingworth, (*Hebrews*, 268–69), argued for "tempted" against H. Attridge (*The Epistle to the Hebrews*, Her [Philadelphia: Fortress, 1989], 140). On "temptation," see W. R. Baker, "Temptation," *DLNT* 1166–70.

[37] D. Bloesch, *Essentials of Evangelical Theology* (San Francisco: Harper & Row, 1978), 1:96, 115.

[38] H. P. Liddon, *The Divinity of Our Lord and Savior Jesus Christ: Eight Lectures Preached Before the University of Oxford in the Year 1866* (London: Rivingtons, 1884), 524–25: "Our Lord's Manhood, then, by the unique conditions of its existence, was believed to be wholly exempt from any propensity to, or capacity of, sinful self–will. . . . Thus to any direct temptation to evil He was simply inaccessible. . . . It is clear that Holy Scripture denies the existence, not merely of any sinful thinking or acting, but of any ultimate roots and sources of sin, of any propensities or inclinations, however latent and rudimentary, towards sin, in the Incarnate Christ."

[39] Erickson, *The Word Became Flesh*, 562; T. Morris, *The Logic of God Incarnate* (Ithaca, NY: Cornell University Press, 1986), 65.

[40] Erickson, *The Word Became Flesh*, 562–63.

bounds of obedience."[41] With respect to their extent and genuineness, T. Oden noted that the temptations of Jesus were "real appeals to his real freedom. His resistance was a real act of freedom in saying no on behalf of a larger yes to his vocation."[42] Luther said we should not think of Christ as an "unfeeling block." As man, Christ was subject to every temptation.[43] Luther, in a sermon on Psalm 8, created an unnecessary bifurcation in the hypostatic union of Christ when he averred that Christ's deity, as it were, lifted the drawbridge, withdrew its power, and left the humanity to fight for itself.[44] Augustine, along with other fathers, compared the temptation of Jesus to the testing of metal. Gold may be tested; if it is gold, it will emerge as genuine gold every time. Analogously, Jesus may be severely tempted and tested, but it is impossible that he should fail the test.[45]

A. B. Edersheim and M. Canham argued that both peccability and impeccability must be affirmed as true and that what we have here is a theological antinomy. Canham resolved the issue by asking the question:

> "Is Jesus Christ God or man?" He is of course both, and thus affirming both positions is necessary to capture the whole truth of the situation. . . . the only truly satisfying answer to the question of whether Christ ontologically could or could not sin is that he was both peccable and impeccable in His incarnation, and that in his *kenosis* the exercise of His human attribute of peccability apparently limited (in some sense) the exercise of His divine attribute of impeccability.[46]

This position is adequately refuted by Lewis and Demarest, though Canham considers their arguments "weak."[47]

---

[41] J. Calvin, *Institutes of Christian Religion*, trans. F. Battles (Grand Rapids: Eerdmans, 1995), 1:518. The incarnation subjected Jesus to humanity with its frailty, trials, pressures, and influences of the world of evil, which confirmed the genuineness of his temptations but did not necessitate his sinlessness.

[42] T. Oden, *The Word of Life* in *Systematic Theology* (San Francisco: Harper Collins, 1992), 2:244. Demarest and Lewis, *Integrative Theology*, 2:335, surmise based on Heb 4:15 that Jesus must have been tempted sexually.

[43] M. Luther, in Psalms, *LW* 5:387.

[44] Luther, *LW* 45:239.

[45] Augustine, *NPNF* 8:45. Cf. J. Calvin, *The Epistle of Paul the Apostle to the Hebrews and the First and Second Epistles of Peter*, CNTC (Grand Rapids: Eerdmans, 1963), 55–56. Jesus experienced temptation to the fullest intensity precisely because he is sinless. Westcott's oft-quoted statement is on target: "Only one who has not yielded to sin can know the fullest degree of the strength of temptation—for he who sins yields to temptation before it has reached the greatest possible force. . . . He who falls yields before the last strain" (*Hebrews*, 60).

[46] Canham, "*Potuit Non Peccare* or *Non Potuit Peccare*," 114. Cf. A. B. Bruce, *The Humiliation of Christ* (New York: A. C. Armstrong & Son, 1892), 269; and A. Edersheim, *The Life and Times of Jesus the Messiah* (Grand Rapids: Eerdmans, 1942), 1:298–99.

[47] Canham, "*Potuit Non Peccare* or *Non Potuit Peccare*," 114; Demarest and Lewis, *Integrative Theology*, 2:346. Canham appreciated the strength of the impeccabilist position, but when he remarked: "Therefore, the very fact that Jesus was God demands the retention of a belief in His full

A number of odd and awkward positions have been taken on this issue. H. Berkhof, appealing to the resurrection, seems to take an impeccability position but then stated: "He [Jesus] had no idea of his sinlessness on which he, encouraged by it, could fall back."[48] H. Montefiore noted the ambiguity of the phrase "without sin" and posited it could mean something like "except for those sins which result from previous sins."[49] F. Schleiermacher affirmed the sinlessness of Jesus but denied the reality of the temptations.[50] Niebuhr affirmed the reality of the temptations but denied the sinlessness of Jesus.[51] H. Johnson and J. Knox believed Jesus assumed a human nature which had been affected by the fall.[52] R. Williamson suggested that Jesus participated in the actual experience of sinning.[53] Similarly, B. Lindars rightly noted the New Testament does not argue for the sinlessness of Jesus based on his divine nature, but then wrongly asserted that we need not "suppose that he never did anything wrong throughout his human life. The point is that he was without sin in any respects which would have disqualified him for his God-given task of reconciling humanity with God."[54] Others, following the lead of Hegel, see in Heb 4:15 an example of "degree" or "docetic Christology," according to which Jesus is achieving a quality of perfection and illustrating the inherent divinity of mankind. Such a "Christology from below" actually achieves, according to Gunton, the exact opposite of what it sets out to accomplish. "By putting all their eggs in the basket of an immanentist understanding of Jesus, exponents lift him far outside of our human

---

though not exclusive impeccability" (p. 110), one wonders just what "full though not exclusive" means.

[48] H. Berkhof, *Christian Faith: An Introduction to the Study of the Faith*, trans. S. Woudstra (Grand Rapids: Eerdmans, 1979), 297. This is also the position of P. T. Forsyth, *The Person and Place of Jesus Christ* (Philadelphia: Westminster, 1910), 302–3.

[49] Montefiore, *Hebrews*, 91.

[50] F. Schleiermacher, *The Christian Faith* (Edinburgh: T&T Clark, 1928), 414–15. For him, Jesus' temptations were conflicts between desire and non-desire. See the refutation of this in Thielicke, *Evangelical Faith*, 2:377–79; and W. Pannenberg, *Systematic Theology*, trans. G. W. Bromiley (Grand Rapids: Eerdmans, 1991–1998), 306. Pannenberg noted that Jesus' sinlessness has been his distinguishing attribute since Irenaeus and Tertullian: "The idea of redemption as a transferring of the Redeemer's own state to believers was possible, of course, only because Schleiermacher substituted the thesis of a prototypical perfection of God–consciousness for the doctrine of Christ's deity (93.2). Whereas the Christology of the early church found the uniqueness of Jesus in his deity, Schleiermacher saw it as a purely human uniqueness, i.e., as the constant power of his God–consciousness." (p. 307). Cf. W. Pannenberg, *Jesus: God and Man* (London: SCM, 1968), 354.

[51] R. Niebuhr, *The Nature and Destiny of Man* (New York: Scribner, 1941), 2:73.

[52] H. Johnson, *The Humanity of the Saviour* (London: Epworth, 1962), 116; J. Knox, *The Humanity and Divinity of Jesus* (Cambridge: Cambridge University Press, 1967), 49.

[53] R. Williamson, "Hebrews 4:15 and the Sinlessness of Jesus," *ExpTim* 86 (1974): 4. See the trenchant critique of Williamson in D. Peterson (*Hebrews and Perfection: An Examination of the Concept of Perfection in the 'Epistle to the Hebrews,'* SNTSMS [Cambridge: Cambridge University Press, 1982], 188–90).

[54] B. Lindars, *The Theology of the Letter to the Hebrews* (Cambridge: Cambridge University Press, 1991), 63.

sphere, and necessarily so, for they must either do this or abandon Christology altogether." Citing Heb 4:15, Gunton noted that the author of Hebrews did not use a "logical ladder from the human to the divine," therefore "a Christology from below whose *only* resource is some kind of transcendental anthropology seems logically bound either to do that [take the human Jesus out of our sphere] or to concede the content of traditional Christology."[55]

In conclusion, it is clear that whether Jesus could or could not have sinned, the fact is he did not sin according to Heb 4:15. The preponderance of evidence seems to tilt the scales in favor of the impeccability position. God is unchanging, thus if Jesus as the Word, the Second Person of the Trinity, was impeccable before the incarnation, should he not be so as the incarnate God-man? How could he be peccable unless one comes dangerously close to dividing the hypostatic union of the two natures, which it seems that many peccabilists do? In the incarnation, Jesus' humanity was an addition to his deity, but it did not ontologically change his divine nature. As Grudem said: "Jesus' human nature never existed apart from union with his divine nature. . . . Both his human nature and his divine nature existed united in one person."[56] It is difficult to avoid the conclusion that if Jesus had sinned, such would have involved both his human and divine natures. This leads to the logical conclusion that God himself would have sinned, which is impossible due to his nature and attributes revealed in Scripture. Grudem summed it all up: "Therefore, if we are asking if it was *actually* possible for Jesus to have sinned, it seems that we must conclude that it was not possible. The union of his human and divine natures in one person prevented it."[57]

Jesus was capable of being tested and of being tempted, though he possessed no sin nature. The sinlessness of Jesus becomes a way for the author of Hebrews to manifest the deity of Jesus visibly in his humanity. "In this sinlessness we see Him, as it were, transfigured."[58] But does such a position negate the reality of the temptations or his ability genuinely to sympathize with us in our temptations? It does not. Jesus faced the temptation of the possibility of avoiding the suffering of the cross, but to do so would have meant disobedience to his Father, something to which our Lord never succumbed, not only during his Gethsemane and Calvary agony, but during all "the days of his flesh" as well. "[S]uffering temptation and temptation produced by suffering is not in itself sin, nor does it require that sin have a prior foothold."[59] It would seem that the

[55] C. Gunton, *Yesterday and Today: A Study of Continuities in Christology* (Grand Rapids: Eerdmans, 1983), 17. Thielicke (*Evangelical Faith*, 368) offered the same critique of Schleiermacher and others who "see in Christ the ideal or prototype of humanity, as though there were fulfilled in him that which is only broken and corrupted by sin in us," but from a different angle. Cf. Pannenberg, *Systematic Theology*, 2:307.

[56] Grudem, *Systematic Theology*, 538–39.

[57] Ibid., 539.

[58] A. Nairne, *The Epistle of Priesthood* (Edinburgh: T&T Clark, 1913), 123.

[59] Shuster, "Temptation, Sinlessness, and Sympathy of Jesus," 206.

incarnation, as a permanent uniting of the two natures into one person, guaranteed his solidarity with us for all time (Heb 2:10–1), and made it impossible for Jesus to avoid the cross without disobeying the Father and hence committing sin. Thus, it is the point of our author to affirm Christ's sympathy with us in our trials and temptations not only by virtue of his solidarity with us as our high priest, but also by his difference from us, namely, his sinlessness.[60]

This issue plunges one into the depths of theological and philosophical thought which no one can plumb adequately. We see through a glass darkly. The words of H. Thielicke seem appropriate: "When the theological supply outruns the demand of faith, theology becomes speculation. This principle applies in exemplary fashion to the temptation of Jesus."[61] This verse's inclusion between two prominent hortatory verses, followed by the author's exposition of the high priesthood of Christ, especially Heb 5:7–8, serves the author's purpose of strengthening and comforting his readers amid their trials and temptations. Hebrews indicates that the readers were in danger of disobedience and this may very well have been related to the issue of impending suffering which the community was in danger of recoiling from.

5:1–10 Hebrews 5:1–10 forms a unit whose theme, the high priesthood of Jesus, was first introduced back in 2:17. The unit is divided into two sections: 5:1–4 and 5:5–10.[62] Many have discerned a chiastic structure in this section.[63] The following is given by G. Guthrie and is based on Lane:[64]

A The old office of high priest (v. 1)
    B The sacrifice offered by the high priest (v. 1)
        C The weakness of the high priest (vv. 2–3)
            D The appointment of the high priest (v. 4)
            D´ The appointment of Christ, the new priest (vv. 5–6)

[60] Shuster noted: "Thus, exactly because Jesus truly suffered and was tempted . . . he is able to sympathize with us in our weaknesses and temptations . . . he neither condemns nor excuses us. His sympathy, which gives both comfort and strength, depends precisely upon his both being, and not being, a human being like us" (ibid., 208). Heb 4:15 illuminates the point of the statement in Heb 5:2 that the high priest must be able "to deal gently" with sinners.

[61] Thielicke, *Evangelical Faith*, 2:382. With regard to the relationship of Jesus' susceptibility to temptation and his sinlessness, Thielicke wisely concluded we cannot know the "how." It cannot be investigated. Jesus is not trapped in solidarity with us. "Love and power are at work for us here, the love which meets us in solidarity and the power which brings us to our goal." If we go behind the result "yet without sin" to the "how," "we slip into hopeless speculation about the natures" (382).

[62] F. Laub, *Bekenntnis und Auslegung: die paränetische Funktion der Christologie im Hebräerbrief* (Regensburg: F. Pustet, 1980), 113–19, wrongly began the new section at 5:3.

[63] Cf. Westcott, *Hebrews,* 121; Vanhoye, *La structure*, 107–13; Peterson, *Hebrews and Perfection*, 81; Attridge, *Hebrews,* 138; Lane, *Hebrews 1–8*, 111; Lindars, *Theology of Hebrews,* 61; Ellingworth, *Hebrews,* 271; and G. Guthrie, *Hebrews,* 192.

[64] G. Guthrie, *Hebrews,* 192; Lane, *Hebrews 1–8*, 111.

C´ The suffering of the new priest (vv. 7–8)
B´ The sacrificial provision of the new priest (v. 9)
A´ The new office of high priest (v. 10)

At the very least, a clear chiasm occurs in the arrangement of two key points which the author makes in this section. There are two general qualifications which every high priest must meet: (1) ability to sympathize with those whom he represents, and (2) appointment to the office by God. These are given in this order in vv. 1–4 and then are applied to Jesus in inverse order in vv. 5–10.

Thematically, 5:1 is the continuation of the author's thought from 2:10–18. Hebrews 5:1 is connected to the immediately preceding section by the subordinating conjunction *gar*, which serves to introduce the grounds for the exhortation of 4:16. Grammatically, it belongs with vv. 1–3, but logically governs vv. 1–10, not so much in an explanatory but rather demonstrative fashion in that what one finds thematically in 4:15–16 is further demonstrated to be true in 5:1–10.[65] The notion of mercy mentioned in 4:15 becomes the main point of 5:1–4. Hebrews 5:5–10 identifies Jesus with suffering humanity, and his own submission to suffering qualifies him for the priestly office in 5:9–10. "These emphases reinforce the statement in 4:15 and give it specific content."[66] Additionally, Heb 5:1–10 "shifts attention to the new topic of high priesthood, anchors the topic as applied to Christ in divine decree, and reflects on it eloquently in light of both Psalms material and Gospel narrative."[67]

5:1 Hebrews 5:1 as a unit is introduced by *gar* which is not made explicit in the NIV text: "[for] Every high priest is selected from among men." The language of the verse is "deliberately general and comprehensive."[68] In the Greek text, the prepositional phrase "from among men," signifying source, is emphatic by word order since it occurs prior to the present passive participle "is selected." This participle may be construed as descriptive of the high priest;[69] as indicating a reason for appointing the high priest in the sense "every high priest, since he is chosen from among men, is appointed;[70] or as parallel with the following verb "appointed."[71] The high priest is "appointed," present passive, on behalf of men, rendered by the NIV as "appointed to represent them." The two uses of the passive voice are important here, pointing out that no man may appoint himself to this position, but the decision and action are God's alone. The phrase in Greek "in the things pertaining to God" is rendered by the

[65] See F. Delitzsch, *Commentary on the Epistle to the Hebrews,* trans. T. L. Kingsbury (Edinburgh: T&T Clark, 1872; repr. Grand Rapids: Eerdmans, 1952), 1:225–26.

[66] Lane, *Hebrews 1–8,* 111.

[67] G. Guthrie, *Hebrews,* 193.

[68] Hagner, *Hebrews,* NIBC (Peabody, MA.: Hendrickson Publishers, 1990), 60.

[69] Lane, *Hebrews 1–8*, 116.

[70] Alford, "Hebrews," 91; Dods, "Hebrews," 285.

[71] Ellingworth, *Hebrews*, 272; and the NIV.

NIV as "to represent them in matters related to God."[72] The verse concludes with a purpose clause "to offer gifts and sacrifices for sins." *Prospherein* occurs 19 times in Hebrews, but not in Paul. The word has its source in the sacrificial vocabulary of the LXX.[73] The author both carefully connects and distinguishes between two classes of offerings when he refers to "both gifts and sacrifices" using the *te . . . kai* construction.[74]

Lünemann takes the *hina* clause in apposition to the previous clause: "he is appointed in matters related to God, namely to offer."[75] How are we to construe the relationship of the "gifts" and "sacrifices?" Commentators are divided. Some consider the two terms as essentially synonymous,[76] while others view them as distinct: "gifts" refers to offerings not involving shed blood, and "sacrifices" means all offerings involving the death of an animal.[77] Bruce was probably correct that "gifts" is a more comprehensive term normally including sacrifices "but not coextensive with them." The terms are used together here of "offerings."[78] The final phrase "for sins" probably refers to both gifts and sacrifices since the two nouns are connected by the Greek particle *te*.[79]

The office and function of the priest differs from that of the prophet. Whereas the prophet speaks on behalf of God to men, the priest functions to bring men to God. This necessitates a close identification of the priest with the people whom he represents. Thus, in 4:14–5:10, the focus is on the humanity of Christ. That the present participle, translated "appointed from among men," rather than the aorist participle, is used here further highlights this necessity. This was first addressed by the author in Heb 2:10–18. Hebrews 2:11 points out the identification of Jesus with his people in terms of point of origin. By virtue of the incarnation, Jesus is enabled to enter into a physical unity with humanity, thus preparing him for the high priestly role. Finally, in Heb 2:17, he "had to be made like his brothers in every way," qualifying Jesus to be our high priest, a theme which is picked up again in 4:14–5:10.[80]

5:2 The key word in v. 2 is the very first word in the Greek text, *metriopathein*, fronted for focused prominence and translated in the NIV as "to deal

[72] This is an adverbial accusative of reference: "appointed with reference to the things relating to God."

[73] Lane, *Hebrews 1–8,* 108; K. Weiss, "προσφέρω," *TDNT* 9:65–68.

[74] Lane, *Hebrews 1–8,* 108

[75] Lünemann, *Hebrews,* 503–4.

[76] Alford, "Hebrews," 91; J. A. Moffatt, *A Critical and Exegetical Commentary to the Hebrews,* ICC (Edinburgh: T&T Clark, 1924), 61–62; Ellingworth, *Hebrews*, 273–74.

[77] Lünemann, *Hebrews*, 503; Lane, *Hebrews 1–8*, 116.

[78] Bruce, *Hebrews,* 119. The combination occurs again in Heb 8:3 and 9:9.

[79] Miller (*Hebrews,* 137) took the particle as referring only to "sacrifices," while Lünemann (*Hebrews,* 503) and Dods ("Hebrews," 285) connected it with the whole clause beginning with "to offer."

[80] Whether there would have been a priesthood for Jesus without an Adamic fall and plan of redemption, Westcott (*Hebrews*, 137–410) argued affirmatively; but G. Vos (*The Teaching of the Epistle to the Hebrews* [Nutley, NJ: P&R, 1974], 98–100) argued the opposite.

gently."[81] The word essentially denotes a happy medium between two extremes and is translated as "curb his emotions" by Koester.[82] A priest would need to avoid personal feelings of impatience or disgust with the sinner while interceding with God on the sinner's behalf. Since the high priest, as a man himself, could err in two extremes, irritation and indulgence, a balance between the law and love, between Stoic indifference and exasperated anger, is needed. The present tense signifies a timeless, general truth.[83]

The participle "being able" (NIV "he is able") has been interpreted in various ways. Some take it as indicating the reason the high priest is able to make the offerings and sacrifices.[84] Miller took it as giving the grounds for the conclusion that Christ is a valid high priest.[85] Many translations and commentaries take it as signifying an additional comment concerning high priests.[86] Some see it as a further describing the high priest.[87]

The two participles translated "those who are ignorant and going astray" are milder than the word "sin," and express the feeling of one who is himself a sinner towards others who, like himself, also sin. Both refer to the same persons as the single definite article linking the two indicates.[88] Bruce and others took the phrase as a hendiadys with the meaning "those who go astray through their ignorance."[89] The present tense is iterative. The Old Testament distinguishes between unintentional sins and sins committed "with a high hand" (Lev 4:2–12; 5:15; Num 15:22–31). The latter category of sins could not be atoned for by the priest on normal days of the year, but Delitzsch carefully showed from the Old Testament itself that not even every "high handed" sin was beyond atonement, especially on the Day of Atonement.[90] The grounds or reason for the high priest's sympathy is indicated by "since." The high priest's "weakness" here includes moral weakness which makes him susceptible to sin. Biblical examples of such "weakness" begin with Aaron in Exod 32, who participated in the construction of the golden calf, thus leading the nation into

---

[81] This word is a *hapax legomenon* in all of Biblical Greek. On the meaning of this word, consult E. K. Simpson, "The Vocabulary of the Epistle to the Hebrews," *EvQ* 18 (1946): 36ff.; W. Michaelis, "μετριοπαθέω," *TDNT* 5.938; and Bruce, *Hebrews*, 120. See C. R. Koester, *Hebrews*, AB (New York: Doubleday, 2001), 286; and Ellingworth, *Hebrews*, 275, for examples in secular literature and Philo.

[82] Koester, *Hebrews*, 281.

[83] Ellingworth, *Hebrews*, 275.

[84] Alford, "Hebrews," 91.

[85] Miller, *Hebrews*, 137.

[86] Greenlee (*Exegetical Summary,* 160), noted that none of the commentators discuss the point specifically.

[87] Alford, "Hebrews," 91; Dods, "Hebrews," 286.

[88] Lane, *Hebrews 1–8*, 107, 108; Moffatt, *Hebrews*, 62; Bruce, *Hebrews*, 120.

[89] Bruce, *Hebrews*, 120. Lane (*Hebrews 1–8*, 107) translated "those who sin through ignorance."

[90] See the discussion in Delitzsch, *Hebrews*, 2:229–31.

their first experience with idolatry, and Joshua the son of Jehozadak was also unfit for office (Zech 3:3–9).

5:3 The untranslated *kai* in v. 3 probably does not introduce a completely new point,[91] but rather is the logical consequence of what was stated in the end of v. 2: because the high priest himself has inherent weakness and is prone to sin, he must offer a sin offering for himself.[92] The phrase "for his own sins" is emphatic by word order in that it precedes the infinitive "to offer." There is an implied object, a sin offering, which follows the infinitive "to offer." Verse 3 serves to amplify the reason given in v. 2: because of his own weakness, the high priest must offer sacrifices for his own sins. The triple use of the preposition *peri* ("for") in this verse focuses prominence on the purpose of the offering (Gk. "for the people for himself for sins"), whereas "to offer" expresses the means. BDAG noted that when the preposition *peri* is used with *hamartia*, the preposition has the sense of "to take away" or "to atone for" (see 1 Pet 3:18; Heb 10:18).[93]

The specific directions given by God for the Day of Atonement in Lev 16:6–17 include the high priest presenting a sin offering for himself as well as for the people.

5:4 The "honor" in v. 4 refers to the honor of filling the office of high priest. Lane noted that Josephus used the term "honor" to refer to the office of high priest and hence he translated the term "office."[94] This verse is connected with v. 1 and introduces a second qualification for the high priest. The intervening two verses are subordinate to v. 1. The NIV phrase "upon himself" occurs first in Greek for emphasis. The participle translated "be called" can be temporal,[95] or an attributive modifier ("he who is called"),[96] or expressing a specific requirement, as the NIV ("he must be called"). Koester perceptively noted the paragraph 5:1–4 is framed by "take": "one does not 'take' the honor of priesthood (Heb 5:4), one is 'taken' for the office by God (5:1)."[97] Ellingworth took the final *kai* as ascensive with the meaning "especially."[98]

Verse 4 states the second qualification for the high priest, he must not be self-appointed but God-appointed. The priesthood is a divine vocation, not merely a human institution. The office of high priest began with Aaron himself being appointed by God (Exodus 28 and Leviticus 8). Even those like Samuel (1 Sam 7:3–17) who were not of Aaronic descent served in the high priestly capacity by direct call from God. Historically, one can see the violation of this

---

[91] Against Ellingworth, *Hebrews*, 277.

[92] Lünemann, *Hebrews*, 504.

[93] BDAG 798.

[94] Lane, *Hebrews 1–8*, 107–8; Josephus, *Antiquities*, trans. H. S. Thackeray (Cambridge: Harvard University Press, 1930), 3:188–89.

[95] Alford, "Hebrews," 93; Dods, "Hebrews," 287; Moffatt, *Hebrews*, 63.

[96] Bruce, *Hebrews,* 118.

[97] Koester, *Hebrews*, 287.

[98] Ellingworth, *Hebrews*, 280.

principle prior to and during the Hasmonean period, under Herod the Great in the later part of the first century BC, under Roman governors as well as members of the Herodian family up to the fall of Jerusalem in AD 70.[99] However, Jesus himself, especially in John's Gospel, constantly makes reference to the Father "who sent him."[100]

5:5 Verse 5 begins the second section of the overall paragraph with *houtōs*, translated "so" by the NIV, but with the meaning "thus" or "in this way."[101] This conjunction has been interpreted in at least three ways: (1) as indicating the conclusion of the superiority of Christ's priesthood;[102] (2) as introducing the comparison of Christ to Aaron in 5:4;[103] and (3) as semantically connecting the section of the epistle up to this point, which focused upon Christ's sonship with the section that will follow in chap. 7–10 emphasizing Christ's priesthood. Ellingworth calls these verses a "major pivot" in the epistle's structure.[104]

Lane makes much of the title "Christ" here rather than the human name "Jesus" as indicating Christ's position as Messiah and implying his appointment to the high priesthood by God.[105] Ellingworth does not think the author ever used "Christ" in the epistle as a messianic title.[106]

The NIV renders the verb *edoxasen* by the phrase "take [upon himself] the glory," but Louw and Nida see the verb as continuing the concept of "honor" in the previous verse, which seems better in the context.[107] The infinitive that the NIV translates "of becoming" may be explaining (epexegetical) "glorified."[108] Lane wrote that it "defines more closely the content of the action denoted in the previous verb [*edoxasen*]."[109] Alternatively, it could express either purpose,[110] or result—he did not glorify himself resulting in his becoming a high priest.[111] The quotation is introduced by a participial phrase with a main verb left unexpressed. This verb could be an understood "glorified him";[112] it could be an implied "appointed him," as in several translations, including the NRSV; or it

---

[99] Josephus, *Jewish War*, trans. G. Williamson, rev. M. Smallwood (Harmondsworth, Middlesex: England/New York: Penguin, 1981), 4:155–57.

[100] John 8:42; 9:4; 11:42; 12:44,45,49; 14:24; which overtly reference Christ being "sent" by the Father, not to mention the many other places in this Gospel that are semantic equivalents.

[101] L&N 61.9.

[102] Miller, *Hebrews,* 142.

[103] Lane, *Hebrews 1–8,* 117.

[104] Ellingworth, *Hebrews,* 281. Ellingworth is certainly correct as to the focused emphasis on the two major sections, and that this section reflects a major pivot, but it is doubtful if this connector οὕτως can carry this much semantic freight.

[105] *Hebrews 1–8,* 118.

[106] Ellingworth, *Hebrews*, 281.

[107] L&N 87.8.

[108] Moffatt, *Hebrews*, 63.

[109] Lane, *Hebrews 1–8,* 108.

[110] Lünemann, *Hebrews*, 506.

[111] Alford, "Hebrews," 93.

[112] Dods, "Hebrews," 287; Hughes, *Hebrews*, 179–80.

could be translated "said" in lieu of a main verb, as does the NIV: "but God said to him."

In Heb 5:5–10, the author makes the key point that the high priesthood of Jesus is fundamentally distinct from the Levitical priests. The author returned to Ps 2:7, which played a crucial role in the argument of Heb 1:5–13, establishing the supremacy of the Son. On the interpretation of this Psalm quotation, see discussion above on Heb 1:5. The author's choice of this quotation may have been its focus on appointment to royal power and not that of ancestry or parentage.[113] There it was determined that the meaning of "today I have begotten you" refers to the Father's installation or inauguration of the Son at his enthronement following the crucifixion and resurrection.

5:6 The quotation of Ps 110:4 in v. 6 is startling. This verse is not used by any other New Testament author, yet our author makes more references to Ps 110:4 than any other Old Testament text. It is quoted three times and alluded to eight times. It is the key Old Testament text for the author's high priestly Christology. One thing, however, seems clear from the two quotations that are juxtaposed in these verses: the author is demonstrating that God who declared Jesus as "Son" also has appointed him as high priest. This is actually not so much a new thing since this connection was implied in the prologue, but here for the first time it is made explicit.[114] Lane is correct when he notes, "The general similarity of 5:5–10 and 1:3–13 is sufficient to imply that the writer understood Jesus to have been acclaimed as divine Son and priest concurrently at his ascension."[115] Delitzsch argued persuasively that the close connection of Ps 2:7 with Ps 110:4 here, coupled with the use of the title *ho Christos*, "Messiah," which in Hebrew is not a priestly title but a kingly one, is meant to indicate the writer as saying: "He who made not Himself a King, but was anointed to that dignity by God [Ps 2:7], in the same way took not to Himself the *doxa* High Priest, but solemnly received it from God too [Ps 110:4]."[116]

The use of "order" has been interpreted in two ways. Some see it as referring to rank,[117] but this is unlikely since there was no succession of Melchizedek's priesthood. Others take it as referring to similarity.[118]

The high priestly office received its authority by appointment from God (Exod 28:1; Lev 8:1; Num. 16:5). The duties of the high priest are found in

---

[113] Lane, *Hebrews 1–8,* 118.

[114] See D. M. Hay, *Glory at the Right Hand: Psalm 110 in Early Christianity* (Nashville: Abingdon, 1973), 114–15; S. Kistemaker, *The Psalm Citations in the Epistle to the Hebrews* (Amsterdam: G. van Soest, 1961), 116–24; Attridge, *Hebrews,* 145–47; M. C. Parsons, "Son and High Priest: A Study in the Christology of Hebrews," *EvQ* 60 (1988) 195–215; Lane, *Hebrews 1–8,* 118; Ellingworth, *Hebrews,* 282; and Guthrie, *Hebrews*, 189.

[115] Lane, *Hebrews 1–8,* 118.

[116] Delitzsch, *Hebrews*, 1:235.

[117] Alford, "Hebrews," 94; Dods, "Hebrews," 288; and Moffatt, *Hebrews*, 64.

[118] BDAG 989; L&N 1:588; Delitzsch, *Hebrews*, 1:237, who links it with the parallel statement in 7:15; Lane, *Hebrews 1–8*, 107, 109; and Ellingworth, *Hebrews*, 283.

Exodus 29 and Leviticus 1–6,16. His most significant work occurred once a year on the Day of Atonement as outlined in Lev 16:1–25. On that day, the high priest was required to offer a special sacrifice for his and his household's own sins before he offered the sacrifice for the people (Lev 16:11). Jesus' high priesthood is "forever" in the sense that it is permanently effective by virtue of his deity and hence his eternality.

5:7 The most difficult passage exegetically and theologically in this section is Heb 5:7–8.[119] The NIV translation "life on earth" accurately renders the sense of the (lit.) "in the days of his flesh." The two nouns, "prayers" and "petitions," are essentially synonymous, although the second word is stronger than the first; the combination adds urgency to the pleading.[120] Likewise, the two nouns translated "cries" and "tears' indicate an anguished pleading with a loud noise that may be inarticulate.[121]

The participle translated "offered up" may include the concept of sacrifice. Interestingly, all the major translations render it as the main verb, except the KJV/NKJV, which translates it temporally ("after he had offered up"). Miller interpreted the participle concessively ("although he offered up").[122] The author does not make explicit what Jesus prayed for. We are only told he prayed "to the one who could save him from death" with the outcome that "he was heard." The latter expression is regularly found in Scripture with the implication that one's prayer is granted.[123] This would seem to rule out the view that Jesus' prayer was to avoid or be protected from physical death on the cross (cf. John 12:27).[124] One more clue to Jesus' prayer is the phrase that appears to give the reason "he was heard," that is, *apo tēs eulabeias*. The preposition *apo* is probably causal,[125] but the noun *eulabeias* can mean either "reverence" before God (NIV "reverent submission") or "fear,"[126] implying that fear of death may have motivated Jesus' prayer and been what he was

---

119 Besides the commentaries, cf. J. Swetnam, "The Crux at Hebrews 5,7–8," *BSac* 81 (2000): 347–61; id., "The Context of the Crux at Hebrews 5,7–8," *FN* 14 (2001): 101–20, esp. 112–20; C. Estrada, *Hebreos 5, 7–8: Estudio historico–exegetico*, AnBib 113 (Roma: Editrice Pontificio Istituto Biblico, 1990); and W. Loader, *Sohn und Hoherpriester. Eine traditionsgeschichtliche Untersuchung zur Christologie des Hebräerbriefes,* WMANT 53 (Neukirchen-Vluyn: Neukirchener Verlag, 1981),81–141.

120 Lünemann, *Hebrews,* 509; Dods, "Hebrews," 288.

121 Ellingworth, *Hebrews*, 289.

122 Miller, *Hebrews*, 145. She takes ἔμαθεν in 5:8 as the main verb.

123 See 1 Kgs 8:30,45,49; 9:3; 2 Kgs 19:20; 20:5; 2 Chr 7:14; 33:13; Neh 1:6,11; Job 22:27; Ps 6:9; 39:12; 54:2; Isa 38:5; Jer 7:16; 29:12; Matt 6:7; Luke 1:13; Acts 10:31.

124 According to K. Barth (*CD* IV/1, 270), "[T]his is not a kind of return of willingness to obey, which was finally forced upon Jesus and fulfilled by Him in the last hour; it is rather a readiness for the act of obedience which He had never compromised in His prayer."

125 That ἀπό introduces the reason Jesus was heard is the view of the NIV; Westcott, *Hebrews*, 127; Bruce, *Hebrews,* 128–29; Attridge, *Hebrews*, 151; Lane, *Hebrews 1–8*, 107, 109; Ellingworth, *Hebrews*, 290–91; and Koester, *Hebrews*, 289.

126 Hagner (*Hebrews*, 64–65) provided a succinct survey of the views.

delivered from.[127] This latter view founders on the meaning and usage of *eulabeia* here and elsewhere.[128] The noun occurs again in Heb 12:28 where it connotes "godly fear" in the sense of reverence. The *eulabeia* word group is used only by Luke and the author of Hebrews and is always used by Luke in the sense of "reverence."[129] Consequently, Jesus may have simply prayed for God's will to be done. Swetnam concluded that Jesus prayed to die so he could bring salvation to others.[130] Another view is that Jesus prayed for deliverance from premature death in the garden of Gethsemane, which would prevent his death on the cross.[131] Most consider that his prayer involved deliverance from death in some way, perhaps through the resurrection.[132]

It would be wrong, however, to say that Jesus' prayer could not have been motivated by fear. But what Jesus feared, or more accurately, dreaded, was not the torturous death on the cross, but that he would have laid upon him the sins of the whole world. "God made him who had no sin to be sin for us." (2 Cor 5:21). Jesus would face the judgment of God on our behalf; this knowledge,

---

[127] This was the view of Calvin, *Hebrews*, 65; J. Héring, *The Epistle to the Hebrews*, trans. A. W. Heathcote and P. J. Allcock (London: Epworth, 1970), 40; G. W. Buchanan, *To the Hebrews*, AB 36 (Garden City: Doubleday, 1972), 98; Cullmann, *Christology*, 96. Cullmann, *Christology*, 96, noted, "The whole context forces upon one the sense of ordinary human fear as the meaning of εὐλαβείας. This is just what the temptation is. The ἀσθένεια of Jesus shows itself precisely in the fact that he was afraid, that he had the ordinary human fear of death!" Bultmann critiqued the view that God's "hearing" of Jesus' prayer could only mean that he was delivered from death (Bultmann, "εὐλαβής," *TDNT* 2:753). Luther proffered the oddly incorrect view that God heard Jesus' prayer because of his reverence for Jesus (Luther, *Lectures on Titus, Philemon, and Hebrews*, *LW*, ed. J. Pelikan [St. Louis: Concordia Publishing House: 1968], 29:177–78). Harnack's conjecture that a negative particle originally appeared before "heard" and was inadvertently lost is without any manuscript evidence.

[128] See esp. the excellent study by C. Estrada, *Hebreos 5, 7–8*, 220–35.

[129] Luke 2:25; Acts. 2:5; 8:2; 22:12; Heb 5:7; 11:7; 12:28. This is one example of how one's view of authorship may impinge on interpretation. If Luke was the author of Hebrews, the usage of this word in Hebrews could be more confidently compared to its use in Luke-Acts. Delitzsch (*Hebrews*, 1:246) thought Luke was the author of Hebrews. Cf. T. Lescow "Jesus in Gethsemane bei Lukas und im Hebräerbrief" *ZNW* 58 (1967):215–39.

[130] J. Swetnam, *Jesus and Isaac: A Study of the Epistle to the Hebrews in the Light of the Aqedah*, AnBib 94 (Rome: Pontifical Biblical Institute, 1981), 182–84.

[131] This is argued by T. Hewitt, *The Epistle to the Hebrews: An Introduction and Commentary* (London: Tyndale, 1960), 99–100, who bases too much on the preposition ἐκ.

[132] Ellingworth, *Hebrews*, 288. Cf. Aquinas, *Commentary on the Epistle to the Hebrews* 14 (South Bend: St. Augustine's, 2006), Book 14, Section 300), 257; Alford, "Hebrews," 95; Dods, "Hebrews," 288–89; Hughes, *Hebrews*, 183, Moffatt, *Hebrews*, 66; Bruce, *Hebrews*, 127–29. The resurrection view is found in Attridge, *Hebrews*, 150; Ellingworth, *Hebrews*, 184; Koester, *Hebrews*, 288; Lünemann, *Hebrews*, 510, and many others. Referring to Purdy's argument that the verse simply cannot be explained since Jesus' prayer did not result in his deliverance from the cross, Thiselton, "Hebrews," 1462, remarked: "But it is unnecessary to make such heavy weather of it."

more than anything else, brought such an anguished cry that dark Gethsemane night.[133]

5:8 The conjunction *kaiper* ("although") modifies the participle translated "he was" (lit. "being") and semantically encodes concession: "although being Son, he learned obedience."[134] The present participle "being" may refer to Jesus' state at the time of the main verb "learned," but as Greenlee noted, none of the commentators mention this.[135] At the very least it refers to the eternal nature of Jesus as Son, as has already been established in the epistle. The anarthrous use of "Son" may, as in the prologue, focus on the quality and nature of his sonship, although without the article the noun is definite in its reference to Christ alone. Being such, Jesus was still not given exemption from suffering. Although there is no article accompanying "Son," the articular use of *hupakoēn*, "obedience," signifies the act or habit of obedience.[136]

To say that Jesus "learned obedience" in v. 8 means that Jesus learned by experience in that he practiced obedience.[137] Cullmann noted that this statement, "he learned obedience," is "the most important confirmation of Hebrews' conception of Jesus' full humanity," in that it presupposes human development along the lines of Luke 2:52.[138] This "learning" culminated in his obedience to death on the cross (cf. Phil 2:5–11).

"He learned obedience from what he suffered" includes all of his suffering throughout his life, but has specific focus on the night of agony in Gethsemane and the agony on the cross climaxing in his death.[139] Lane takes it as referring to his death.[140] There is an implied antecedent of the pronoun "which" that is the understood object of the preposition: "from what he suffered."[141] The common play on the words "learned" and "suffered" in classical Greek is well documented.[142]

These verses, along with the rest of the epistle, indicate that the author of Hebrews is less interested in *how* Jesus became a man than he is in Jesus *being* man, since this is the key to the high priestly office. As Cullmann said,

---

[133] Elizabeth C. Clephane expressed it poetically in the classic hymn, "The Ninety and Nine": "But none of the ransomed ever knew how deep were the waters crossed, nor how dark was the night the Lord passed through, ere he found his sheep that was lost."

[134] So Lünemann, *Hebrews*, 511; Alford, "Hebrews," 97–98; Dods, "Hebrews," 289; Ellingworth, *Hebrews*, 187; and Lane, *Hebrews 1–8*, 107, 110.

[135] Greenlee, *Exegetical Summary,* 171.

[136] Delitzsch, *Hebrews*, 1:239. G. Vos, *Hebrews*, 104, called this the "generic" article and noted the articular use signified "Christ learned what obedience meant in its inner essence."

[137] Koester, *Hebrews*, 290.

[138] Cullmann, *Christology*, 97.

[139] So Delitzsch, *Hebrews,* 1:242–44; Alford, "Hebrews," 98; Bruce, *Hebrews*, 131; and Ellingworth, *Hebrews*, 292.

[140] Lane, *Hebrews 1–8,* 121.

[141] Lünemann, *Hebrews,* 511–12.

[142] Koester, *Hebrews*, 290.

Jesus "must be able to suffer with men in order to suffer for them."[143] The juxtaposition of Ps 110:4 with Ps 2:7 is significant. Psalm 2:7 occurs three times in the New Testament, twice in Hebrews and in Acts 13:33. The reference in Acts as well as in Heb 1:5 refers to the resurrection, and thus there is no reason not to see the same contextual meaning here. Jesus became a priest after the order of Melchizedek at his resurrection and exaltation. Swetnam teases all this out by noting that resurrection is possible for Jesus only because of the incarnation and his death on the cross. Christ's "testing" parallel's that of Abraham in Genesis 22, and this interpretation is further supported by the author's comments in Heb 11:17. The use of "he offered" in Heb 5:7 refers, according to Swetnam, to his words on the cross in citing Psalm 22. Even though he was a Son, his offer of sacrifice was accepted by God in that he was "heard," and this is an implied contrast with what happened in Genesis 22 as alluded to in Heb 11:17–19.[144] Christ is then "made perfect," appropriately for his divine nature, at his resurrection according to Heb 5:9. Jesus is no longer subject to death.[145]

One of the major interpretative issues surrounding these two verses is the debated background. Five possible sources underlying Heb 5:7–8 have been suggested: (a) the "Paideia" tradition; (b) the Psalms; (c) a Hellenistic-Jewish prayer tradition; (d) an early Christian Christ-hymn; and (e) the Gethsemane pericopes in the Gospels. Paideia tradition finds its strongest support in the word play in v. 8 of *emathen* and *epathen*, a common feature in classical Greek as well as in Hellenistic Judaism and Philo. The play on words conveys the idea "suffering leads to instruction."[146] Although there are some parallels between

---

[143] Cullmann, *Christology,* 97.

[144] See Swetnam, *Jesus and Isaac,* 46; Swetnam, "Context of the Crux," 114.

[145] Swetnam, "Context of the Crux," 113, 116. "Consequently, at Heb 4,13, given the relevance of Ps 22 at Heb 5,7–8, there would seem to be no reason for not thinking that the author of Hebrews had Christ's active offering of Himself in mind precisely as fulfillment of the sacrifice of Isaac by Abraham presented in Heb 11:17–19" (115). So far so good, but this reasoning assumes that Heb 5:7–8 has as its source specifically Psalm 22, which is possible, but tenuous. Also, at this point, Swetnam's Catholic theology suddenly intervenes when he avers that Jesus continues to exercise his sacrificial ministry through the Christian's partaking of the Eucharist which is the meaning of Heb 4:16, "let us draw near," namely, to the table of the Lord and "obey" Jesus whose command is "Do this in remembrance of me" (pp. 116–18). As God promised Abraham a "seed," so in Hebrews "this progeny is brought to a spiritualized, Christianized fulfillment transcending the promise of physical progeny as the original promise in Gen 22 is usually understood" (p. 120). This progeny, like Melchizedek, is without beginning and without end. "Eucharist generates God's People," (118). Swetnam's allegorical eisegesis is apparent here.

[146] See L. K. Dey, *The Intermediary World and Patterns of Perfection in Philo and Hebrews,* SBLDS 25 (Missoula, MT, 1975), 222ff. The phrase ἔμαθεν ἀφ᾽ ὧν ἔπαθεν is analyzed by J.Coste, "Notion Grecque et Notion Biblique de la 'Souffrance Éducatrice,' (á propos d'Hebreux 5:8)," *Recherches de Science Religieuse* 43 (1955): 496, who concluded that the Christology of Hebrews as a whole will not allow us to interpret this expression in terms of the profane notion of "educative correction." He noted that a first-century educated Greek might have misinterpreted Heb 5:8 as meaning Jesus at first failed to recognize the need to obey his God but afterward learned to submit, thus becoming an example to others.

what is said of Jesus and the paideia tradition, the differences are clear. Jesus' suffering and death has atoning value, whereas the tradition in Hellenistic Judaism did not ascribe such to any Jewish martyrs. All that can be claimed is that there are certain affinities with the paideia tradition in Heb 5:7–8.

Others have suggested one or more of the Psalms (LXX) as standing behind Heb 5:7–8. Again, this is a plausible suggestion, but direct dependence on any single psalm has not been proven and it would seem cannot be proved.[147] A third possible source suggested as lying behind Heb 5:7–8 is Hellenistic-Jewish prayer tradition, where a righteous man, such as Abraham or Moses, prays.[148] A fourth possible source behind Heb 5:7–8 is a primitive Christ-hymn,[149] but this has not found widespread support.[150] The most likely source behind Heb 5:7–8 is the Gethsemane tradition of the Gospels, especially Luke's Gospel. While it should be noted there are no direct linguistic parallels, there are clear conceptual parallels which indicate the author was drawing on this tradition at this point.[151]

5:9 Verse 9 continues the complicated syntax of the passage. The aorist participle translated "made perfect" is related to the main verb "he became" as a prior temporal event: he was first made perfect and then he became. Both the death and resurrection/exaltation of Christ are viewed as one single event preceding his becoming the source of salvation.[152] Miller takes it as encoding means: "by means of his being perfected, he became the source."[153] Peterson views v. 9 as giving the reason for the Son having to learn obedience through suffering.[154]

We are told that Jesus "learned obedience from what he suffered and, once made perfect, he became the source of eternal salvation." The importance of "perfection" language in Hebrews is evidenced by the number of times the author uses this word for Jesus, as well as in other related contexts. It occurs, for example, in 2:10; 5:9; and 7:28 of Jesus; and in 7:19; 9:9; 10:1,14; 11:40; 12:2,23 in various verbal forms. It occurs adjectivally or nominally in 5:11–14 and 6:1. The word is used "frequently in cultic contexts (pagan and Jewish) to express 'cleanness' or 'wholeness.'"[155] The verbal form broadly signifies bringing something to completion, its proper end or goal. As used in Hebrews,

---

147 A. Strobel, "Die Psalmengrundlage der Gethsemane–Parallele Hbr 5,7ff., *ZNW* 45 (1954): 252–66. See the discussion in Peterson, *Hebrews and Perfection*, 87, 235.

148 Dey, *Patterns of Perfection,* 224ff.

149 G. Schille, "Erwägungen zur Hohepriesterlehre des Hebräerbriefes," *ZNW* 46 no. 1–2, (1955): 81–109.

150 R. Deichgraber, *Gotteshynrius und Christushymnus in der frühen Christenheit* (Göttingen: Vandenhoeck & Ruprecht, 1967), 174, 175, denies any hymnic background based on the clear prose character of the verses and the impossibility of arranging the prose line by line.

151 So Hughes, *Hebrews,* 182, who says it is "beyond doubt"; Bruce, *Hebrews*, 127. See also K. Barth, *CD*, IV/1, 260, who thinks it "obviously" refers to Gethsemane; Cullmann, *Christology,* 96; and Peterson, *Hebrews and Perfection*, 86–88.

152 Ellingworth, *Hebrews,* 294.

153 Miller, *Hebrews*, 151.

154 Peterson, *Hebrews and Perfection*, 93.

155 D. DeSilva, *Perseverance in Gratitude: A Socio-Rhetorical Commentary on the Epistle*

it does not connote any ethical or moral advance in reference to Jesus or to believers.[156] "The *telei–* words in Hebrews, then, share in common the sense of bringing something to, or having something arrive at, its appointed end (whether that end be naturally, divinely, or ritually appointed)."[157]

Several views have been expressed as to the meaning of Jesus having been "once made perfect":[158] (1) he was brought to the goal of learning and suffering through his death;[159] (2) he suffered in completing the atonement on the cross;[160] (3) he completed the qualifications for his high priesthood though his sufferings;[161] (4) by his obedience, death, resurrection and glorification, Jesus completed the qualifications for becoming high priest;[162] (5) it refers to his resurrection and glorification;[163] (6) it refers to Jesus' moral development that made it possible for him to offer a perfect sacrifice;[164] (7) it means not that Jesus was "made perfect" but that he was "sanctified."[165]

The linguistic basis for a cultic reading of *teleiōtheis* is marginal, but it is difficult to conceive, in the light of the epistle as a whole, that this was not a part of the author's thinking. This verb is probably best taken in the broader sense of vocational qualification and personal completion, in a non-moral sense of course, which includes within its semantic orbit the notion of consecration.[166] In both Heb 2:10 and 5:9, the perfecting of Christ is connected to his sufferings. According to Heb 2:14–18, Christ's sufferings functioned in some sense as the means by which Jesus is qualified to be high priest. According to Heb 5:8,9, Jesus learned obedience from what he suffered, resulting in his being

---

to the Hebrews (Grand Rapids: Eerdmans, 2000), 195. In Exodus 29, as well as several places in Leviticus, the term means to "consecrate" or "ordain" to the priesthood.

[156] G. Delling, "τελειόω," *TDNT* 8:77.

[157] DeSilva, *Perseverance in Gratitude,* 196.

[158] On the history of the interpretation of "perfection" in Hebrews, in addition to Peterson, *Hebrews and Perfection*, 1–20, cf. J. M. Scholer, *Proleptic Priests: Priesthood in the Epistle to the Hebrews*, JSNTSup 49 (Sheffield: JSOT Press, 1991): 185–200. Other works on the theological meaning of "perfection," in addition to Peterson and Scholer, include P. J. DuPlessis, *ΤΕΛΕΙΟΣ: The Idea of Perfection in the New Testament* (Kampen: J. H. Kok, 1959); Delling, "τελειόω," *TDNT* 8:49–87; and the excursus in DeSilva, *Perseverance in Gratitude*, 194–205, which is an accessible summary of the issues. The theological implications of "perfection" are discussed below.

[159] Hughes, *Hebrews*, 187.

[160] Lane, *Hebrews 1–8*, 122.

[161] Dods, "Hebrews," 289–90; Lane, *Hebrews 1–8*, 122.

[162] Hewitt, *Hebrews*, 98; Bruce, *Hebrews*, 132.

[163] Alford, "Hebrews," 98.

[164] Moffatt, *Hebrews*, 67.

[165] Calvin, *Hebrews*, 66.

[166] DuPlessis, *ΤΕΛΕΙΟΣ*, 215; Peterson, *Hebrews and Perfection*, 97. B. Lindars, *Theology of Hebrews*, 45, rightly noted the word carries no sense of "moral perfection" since there is no suggestion in Heb 4:15 or elsewhere "that Jesus was previously imperfect morally."

made "perfect." He was, by the process of suffering and death, prepared for the office of high priest.[167]

Of further interest is that outside of Hebrews, the only place in the New Testament where Jesus is described by *teleioō* is in Luke 13:32. Here the sense of "perfection" is identical to that which is found in Hebrews, namely, the attainment of heavenly perfection through suffering and death.[168] Although Peterson does not think that *teleioō* as it is used in Luke and Hebrews carries with it the cultic significance which it obviously has in certain LXX passages,[169] Ellis believes that *teleioō* in Luke 13:32 points to the goal of Christ's consecration and enthronement into the messianic office based on the Old Testament cultic background of the term.[170] Peterson's view, that the assumption of *teleioō* as having cultic significance for the author of Hebrews is invalid because it could not be expected that his readers would understand the connection,[171] would itself be invalid if the readership consisted of former priests as I have argued.

Peterson acknowledges that the cultic application of *teleioō* for "initiation" or "consecration" of a priest occurred "well into the Christian era" but he does not define what this phrase means in terms of length of time after the events of Christ's death and resurrection. He argues that based on the LXX usage of *teleioō* alone it cannot be suggested that in Hebrews the term carries the sense of "priestly consecration."[172]

Swetnam has noted the link between Luke's theological concept of the "testing" of Jesus (e.g., Luke 22:28) and the posture of the writer of Hebrews with respect to the same concept.[173] Hebrews 2:18 and 4:15 place an emphasis on Jesus' testing through suffering and his resultant perfection. On the concept of the testing and perfection of Christ, Luke and Hebrews are in close agreement. Luke emphasizes Jesus' faithfulness to God via temptations and his acceptance of death as God's will.[174]

---

[167] Attridge, *Hebrews*, 86–87; Scholer, *Proleptic Priests*, 187–88. Some, like DeSilva (*Perseverance in Gratitude*, 198–99) understand the passage to be "fully comprehensible" if the notion of perfection is taken in the general sense of being brought to the final goal.

[168] Peterson, *Hebrews and Perfection*, 33–45.

[169] Ibid., 28–30.

[170] E. E. Ellis, *The Gospel of Luke*, The New Century Bible Commentary (Grand Rapids: Eerdmans, 1974; repr., London: Oliphants, 1977), 189.

[171] Peterson, *Hebrews and Perfection*, 29.

[172] Ibid., 47. If Luke was Jewish and the author of Hebrews as I have contended, J. D. Derrett's point may be strengthened that the Lukan use of the verb form τελειοῦμαι in Luke 13:32 is continually mistranslated and that behind this word stands the Hebrew original *šlm* which can mean in effect "I shall die" might be strengthened. The saying in Luke 13:32 is viewed by Derrett as a punning epigram which arose in an environment of Hebrew speakers. Derrett believed Deut 16:16–17:7 stands behind Luke 13:31–35. (J. D. Derrett, "The Lucan Christ and Jerusalem: τελειοῦμαι [Luke 13:32]," ZNW 75 [1984]: 36–37).

[173] Swetnam, *Jesus and Isaac*, 175.

[174] See J. Neyrey, *The Passion According to Luke: A Redaction Study of Luke's Soteriology* (New York: Paulist, 1985), 179–81.

The concept of Jesus as the ruler over Israel in the latter days, in fulfillment of the Davidic prophecies in 2 Sam 7:14, and the Christological designation of Jesus as the Son in Ps 2:7, is prominent in Heb 1:5–13 and 5:5, and is found as well in many places throughout Luke's writings (e.g., Luke 1:32,33; Acts 2:30; and 13:33).[175] Although Luke never directly quotes 2 Sam 7:14, it is found to be the key Old Testament passage, along with Ps 2:7, undergirding his infancy narratives (Luke 1 and 2), Peter's sermon at Pentecost (Acts 2) and Paul's speech in the synagogue in Pisidian Antioch (Acts 13).[176] There is a conceptual allusion to 2 Sam 7:14 which stands behind the Christological discussions of much of Luke-Acts and Hebrews, yet with the exception of a non-Christological allusion in 2 Cor 6:18 (where it is applied to Christians instead of Christ) this passage is nowhere quoted or alluded to in the rest of the New Testament. Likewise, Ps 2:7 is quoted only by Luke and Hebrews in the entire New Testament (Acts 13:33; Heb 1:5; 5:5).

Not only is Ps 2:7 quoted only in Acts and Hebrews, but it is used similarly in both books. For example, in the context of Heb 1:5 where the significance of Christ's enthronement is thematic, the *sēmeron gegennēka* of Ps 2:7 is a reference to the manifestation of Christ's sonship at the inauguration of his seating at the right hand of God by means of his resurrection and ascension. This is paralleled in Acts 13:33 where Paul applies Ps 2:7 to the resurrection of Christ.[177] The motif of Jesus as the Davidic ruler in fulfillment of 2 Sam 7:14 and Ps 2:7 holds greater significance for Luke and Hebrews than any other New Testament writer.

The description in Heb 5:7 of Jesus praying in the garden on the eve of his crucifixion is virtually identical to the same account in Luke 22:44. Hebrews 5:7 describes Jesus as praying with "loud cries and tears." All three Synoptic Gospels mention the prayer in the garden of Gethsemane, but only Luke

---

[175] R. Brawley traces Luke's view of Christ's fulfillment of the Davidic and Abrahamic covenants in Luke 1–4. He shows how Luke resolves the ambivalence between the two covenants when Zechariah echoes Gabriel's allusion to the Davidic covenant to Mary by speaking of a horn of salvation in the house of God's servant David (Luke 1:69). This salvation is then grounded in God's fidelity to a promise to Abraham in Luke 1:72–73. "The Davidic covenant is a particular way God's promise to Abraham comes to fulfillment." ("The Blessing of All the Families of the Earth: Jesus and Covenant Traditions in Luke-Acts," in *SBLSP* 33, ed. E. Lovering [Atlanta: Scholars Press, 1994], 252–68 [esp. p. 256]). Luke was not creating a new thing with this correlation; Abrahamic and Davidic covenant traditions were already united in some of Israel's traditions according to R. Clements, *Abraham and David: Genesis XV and its Meaning for Israelite Tradition* (Naperville, IL: Alec Allenson, 1967), 47–60, 81–82. The author of Hebrews shares the same theological perspective as Luke regarding Christ's fulfillment of the Davidic and Abrahamic covenants.

[176] See D. Bock, *Proclamation from Prophecy and Pattern*, JSNTSup 12, ed. D. Hill (Sheffield: JSOT Press, 1987), 60–89, 240–49; R. F. O'Toole, "Acts 2:30 and the Davidic Covenant of Pentecost," *JBL* 102 (1983): 245–58; D. Goldsmith "Acts 13:33–37: A Pesher on II Samuel 7." *JBL* 87 (1968): 321–24; and Bruce "To the Hebrews or to the Essenes?" *NTS* 9 (1962–63): 217–32. Both O'Toole and Goldsmith suggest that Acts 13:32–37 may be a pesher on 2 Sam 7:12–16.

[177] Peterson, *Hebrews and Perfection*, 85.

describes Jesus as "being in anguish, . . . and his sweat was like drops of blood falling to the ground" (Luke 22:44).[178] In addition, only Luke records the visit of the strengthening angel, which is an example of the purpose of angels as recorded in Heb 1:14. Luke is the gospel writer known for his interest in and emphasis on the humanity of Christ, and Hebrews, more than any other New Testament epistle, emphasizes the humanity of Christ and his ability as our great high priest to identify with those who are his. Also, it is only in Heb 5:8 and Luke 2:52 that we have a statement in Scripture regarding Jesus' inner human development. Along this line, Barnabas Lindars speaks of the creative theology of the author of Hebrews, noting that the author's metaphorical use of the priesthood concept for Jesus is derived from the model of the Gethsemane tradition.[179]

W. R. Paton suggested that the Greek word *agōnia* was often used to describe the kind of agony that a runner experienced in an athletic contest just prior to the start of the race, and that this meaning best fits Luke 22:44.[180] He has since been followed in this suggestion by Neyrey[181] and Brown.[182] Brown further pointed out that in 4 Maccabees the martyr Eleazar is compared to a noble athlete, and in 2 Macc 3:16–17 the high priest experiences *agōnia* of soul that leads to bodily trembling.[183]

The parallel to Heb 5:7–10; and 6:20 where Jesus is said to be the forerunner and also to 12:1–2 where the same Greek word *agōnia* occurs is unmistakable. In Heb 12:1, the race is said to be "marked out for us." This same participle is used again in 12:2 in reference to the "joy" that was "set before him." The implication is that God "set" it before Jesus, and thus in v. 1 he set the race before us. The Lukan description of Jesus in the garden of Gethsemane can be paralleled to these passages in Hebrews in a remarkable way.

---

[178] For a detailed discussion of the similarities between the Gethsemane prayer and Heb 5:7–8, consult Lescow "Jesus in Gethsemane," 215–39, and his "A L'evocation de l'agonie de Gethsemani dans L'Épître aux Hebreux (5, 7–8)," *Esprit et Vie* 86 (1976): 49–53. See also the bibliography in Brown, *The Death of the Messiah: From Gethsemane to the Grave, A Commentary on the Passion Narratives in the Four Gospel* (New York: Doubleday, 1994), 1:111–16.

[179] Lindars, *Theology of Hebrews*, 126.

[180] W. R. Paton, "ΑΓΩΝΙΑ (Agony)," *Classical Review* 27 (1913): 194. See also discussions on the meaning of this term in W. Grundmann, *Das Evangelium nach Lukas* (Berlin: Evangelische Verlagsanstalt, 1971), 412; Lescow, "Jesus in Gethsemane," 223; J. W. Holleran, *The Synoptic Gethsemane* (Rome: Gregorian University Press, 1973), 97–99; E. Stauffer, "ἀγών," *TDNT* 1:135–40; and V. C. Pfitzner, *Paul and the Agon Motif* (Leiden: Brill, 1967).

[181] Neyrey, "The Absence of Jesus' Emotion—The Lucan Redaction of Lk 22, 39–46," *Bib* 61 (1980): 153–71; cf. his *The Passion According to Luke*, in Theological Inquiries: Studies in Contemporary Biblical and Theological Problems, gen. ed. L. Boadt (New York: Paulist, 1985), 58–62.

[182] Brown, *The Death of the Messiah*, 1:189–90.

[183] Ibid. D. L. Allen, *The Lukan Authorship of Hebrews* (Nashville: B&H Academic, 2010), which establishes the relationship between Luke-Acts and the Maccabean writings.

Returning to the last clause of v. 9, commentators are divided over how to construe the clause "he became the source of eternal salvation." It could express the result of Jesus' sufferings that brought about his perfection.[184] Greenlee expresses the sense, "he suffered and was perfected; as a result he became the source of salvation."[185] Miller takes it as expressing the result of "he learned" with the meaning, "he learned obedience and as a result he became."[186] Bruce takes it as expressing the result of Jesus having been perfected: "that as a result of having been perfected, he became."[187] The key point here is Christ's obedience is the basis for our obedience.

The participle *prosagoreutheis* in v. 10 is translated as a finite verb in the NIV text. The word can mean "appointed" or "conferring a title." It would seem the time is commensurate with the resurrection and ascension, although Hughes noted it occurred both from eternity as well as following his resurrection and exaltation.[188]

5:10 Here is the author's paraphrase of the quotation from Ps 110:4. The author uses "high priest" rather than "priest" in the free rendering of Ps 110:4, probably indicating the two terms are not used indiscriminately. Vos explained the change by context: the reference is a prelude to the subsequent argument where Christ is contrasted both with Melchizedek and Aaron. When compared to Aaron explicitly or implicitly, the author uses "high priest" for Christ. When Christ is compared to the Levitical priests, he is called "priest." Hebrews 9:6–7 indicates the two terms are not used indiscriminately.[189]

THEOLOGICAL IMPLICATIONS. Several theological implications may be derived from these 10 verses. First, Jesus is superior to the Levitical priests for the following reasons: (1) he is without sin (2:17–18; 4:15); (2) he did not need to offer sacrifices for his own sins (5:3); (3) he offered himself as the perfect sacrifice (5:7–8); (4) his death on the cross was a sacrifice offered once for all (9:13–14,25–26); (5) he mediates an eternal covenant superior to the Sinai Covenant (8:1–2; 9:15).[190] These latter two await explicit treatment in Hebrews 8–9.

Hebrews 4:14–5:10 continues the emphasis on the uniqueness of Christ's sonship and the reality of his humanity. Here the focus shifts specifically to the temptations experienced by Jesus, along with his suffering, illustrating the pastoral nature of the epistle. These sufferings and temptations which Jesus faced as man during his earthly life were the means by which he obeyed the will of God. The necessity of his exemplary obedience also included the necessity that

---

[184] Dods, "Hebrews," 290; Lane, *Hebrews 1–8*, 122.
[185] Greenlee, *Exegetical Summary*, 173.
[186] Miller, *Hebrews,* 151.
[187] Bruce, *Hebrews,* 132.
[188] Hughes, *Hebrews,* 188.
[189] G. Vos, *Hebrews*, 94.
[190] P. Redditt, "Leviticus, Book of," *DTIB* 449.

such obedience be rendered *as man*, including obedience even unto death on the cross (Phil 2:5–11). Jesus' obedience in his suffering and death on the cross effected the sacrificial aspect of his priestly ministry and also enabled him to apply its benefits as a sympathetic high priest.[191] Whereas the passage began with a negative focus on Christ resisting temptation (4:15), it concludes with a positive focus on Christ's obedience (5:7–10). The connection of sonship and priestly ministry was tacitly made by the author in Heb 1:3. There, under the umbrella of sonship, Christ's priestly ministry stands in an intermediate position between that of prophet ("sustaining all things by his powerful word") and king ("he sat down at the right hand of the Majesty in heaven").[192] Hebrews 4:14–5:10 makes it clear that the author of Hebrews thinks of Christ's priesthood both in terms of appointment and function. The Levitical priesthood, composed of fallible men, is not God's final word; Jesus, both Son and high priest forever, is (Heb 1:1–4).

Jesus, as our high priest, is totally sufficient to meet every need, spiritual or material, of every Christian at any time. As the man of sorrows, wholly familiar with suffering according to Isa 53:3 and Heb 4:15, he is able to help when we are tempted, tried, suffering, abandoned, betrayed, bereaved, and even when we enter the valley of the shadow of death.

Another theological question engendered by Heb 4:14–5:10 is when did Jesus actually become high priest? The answer to this question has occupied commentators in no small measure. The answer turns on the correlation of three issues: the purposes of the incarnation, the nature and function of his priesthood, and the meaning of his perfection. We have seen, both from Heb 2:10–18 and 4:14–5:10, just how important the fact of the incarnation is for our author and his theology. Protestants as well as Catholics have often neglected the theological significance of the incarnation as a result of Enlightenment attacks on the deity of Christ. These attacks often forced them into a defensive posture. Consequently, but for the most part inadvertently, a subtle docetic tendency often slipped into Christology, such that theologians sometimes neglect the full implications of the incarnation, and theologically speaking, one aspect of the incarnation is the high priestly vocation and ministry of Jesus. During the era of the church fathers with its battles over the deity of Christ, the nature and significance of Christ's humanity, and hence his high priesthood, recessed into the background. The development of Mariolatry met a need in the life of the church that should have been met by a full-orbed orthodox understanding

---

[191] Peterson, *Hebrews and Perfection*, 95. "His incarnate experience and development as a man is presented in 2:5–18 and 4:14–5:10 particularly as a vital preparation and qualification for his redemptive role. . . . to give primary emphasis to the perfecting of Christ as *man*, rather than as Savior, is to obscure the real focus of our writer in favor of a subsidiary theme" (p. 101).

[192] G. Vos, *Hebrews*, 105.

of the high priestly ministry of Christ.[193] Failure to take the full humanity of Christ into consideration, as well as his full deity, is a Pandora's box of doctrinal error within the church.

In answering the question as to when Jesus became high priest, the important juxtaposition of the two quotations, Ps 2:7 and Ps 110:4, makes the point that Jesus entered his high priestly office at his resurrection/ascension/exaltation. The notion, common among Roman Catholic commentators,[194] that Jesus' priesthood was inaugurated or consecrated at the incarnation is based on the assumption that the perfection of Christ's priesthood lay in the union of the two natures in one person. But as crucial as the incarnation is for the author's theology and argument, Hebrews makes it clear that the central essence of the priest's mediatorial role is his atoning work, which is the means of mediation between God and man.[195]

This is further supported by what is said of Christ's "perfection" in Heb 5:1–10. With respect to the meaning of "perfection" in terms of Christ's being qualified to be high priest, Peterson concluded that the perfection should be understood vocationally. "[T]hose who interpret this qualification in strictly official terms, either as a consecration through death or transfer to the heavenly sphere, fail to give adequate expression to our writer's total perspective."[196]

> Any view that recoils from the concept of development and proving, with respect to the incarnate Christ, is saying less than our writer says. On the other hand, to interpret the perfecting of Christ essentially in terms of his moral development or his "realization of the perfect man" is to put the emphasis where our writer does not put it. The focus is on his redemptive death and the heavenly exaltation that makes the eternity of his priesthood and sacrifice. His human experience is presented as a preparation for his once-for-all act of atonement and the extension of this work into eternity (7:25).[197]

We thus conclude that Jesus entered into the high priestly office upon completion of the atonement made by his death on the cross and his resurrection/ascension/exaltation to the right hand of God.

---

[193] These points are well made by R. Letham, *The Work of Christ*, in Contours of Christian Theology, ed. G. Bray (Downers Grove: InterVarsity, 1993), 118–19.

[194] E.g. Spicq, *L'Épître aux Hebreux* 2:193; A. Cody, *Heavenly Sanctuary and Liturgy in the Epistle to the Hebrews* (Meinrad, IN: Grail Publications, 1960), 96–102.

[195] Peterson, *Hebrews and Perfection*, 82, 103, 110ff., and his excellent appendix, "When Did Jesus 'Become' High Priest?" on pp. 191–95. Although one must admit there is no explicit answer to the question given in Hebrews, Heb 5:1–10 and 7:1–10:18 indicate the high priestly ministry of Jesus is prepared for by the incarnation, but is consummated by his death on the cross followed by his resurrection/ascension/exaltation.

[196] Peterson, *Hebrews and Perfection,* 103.

[197] Ibid. After a lengthy hortatory section including warning and encouragement in Heb 5:11–6:20, the author resumes his doctrinal analysis of the high priesthood of Jesus in Heb 7.

Cardinal John Henry Newman, in a great sermon on Heb 5:7–8, wisely warned us of the danger, and captures the same passion with which the author of Hebrews himself warns us, namely, when we merely speak first of Jesus as God, then as man "we seem to change the Nature without preserving the Person . . . speaking of His human nature and His Divine nature so separately as not to feel or understand that God is man and man is God."[198] Newman noted that many of those who wind up denying the deity of Jesus

> begin by being Sabellians, that they go on to be Nestorians, and that they tend to be Ebionites and to deny Christ's divinity altogether. . . . Meanwhile the religious world little thinks whither its opinions are leading; and will not discover that it is adoring a mere abstract name or a vague creation of the mind for the Ever-living Son, till the defection of its members from the faith startle it, and teach it that the so-called religion of the heart, without orthodoxy of doctrine, is but the warmth of a corpse, real for a time, but sure to fail.[199]

A more trenchant and timely warning could not be imagined.

(2) Pressing on to Maturity (5:11–6:8)

[11]We have much to say about this, but it is hard to explain because you are slow to learn. [12]In fact, though by this time you ought to be teachers, you need someone to teach you the elementary truths of God's word all over again. You need milk, not solid food! [13]Anyone who lives on milk, being still an infant, is not acquainted with the teaching about righteousness. [14]But solid food is for the mature, who by constant use have trained themselves to distinguish good from evil.

[1]Therefore let us leave the elementary teachings about Christ and go on to maturity, not laying again the foundation of repentance from acts that lead to death, and of faith in God, [2]instruction about baptisms, the laying on of hands, the resurrection of the dead, and eternal judgment. [3]And God permitting, we will do so.

[4]It is impossible for those who have once been enlightened, who have tasted the heavenly gift, who have shared in the Holy Spirit, [5]who have tasted the goodness of the word of God and the powers of the coming age, [6]if they fall away, to be brought back to repentance, because to their loss they are crucifying the Son of God all over again and subjecting him to public disgrace.

[7]Land that drinks in the rain often falling on it and that produces a crop useful to those for whom it is farmed receives the blessing of God. [8]But land that produces thorns and thistles is worthless and is in danger of being cursed. In the end it will be burned.

Semantically, the section beginning with Heb 5:11 shifts to hortatory discourse from the previous expository section (5:1–10) and extends to Heb 6:20.

---

[198] M. Davies, ed., *Newman Against the Liberals: 25 Classic Sermons by John Henry Newman* (New Rochelle, NY: Arlington House Publishers, 1978), 233–34.

[199] Ibid., 234.

Hebrews 5:10 concludes with a reference to Melchizedek[200] and 6:20 ends with the identical reference. Neeley noted that 6:20 is marked by "formalized closure": "He has become a high priest forever, in the order of Melchizedek."[201] Thus, 5:11–6:20 is a complete discourse unit. This unit can be subdivided into two primary sections, 5:11–6:12 and 6:13–20. There is considerable disagreement as to whether the break should be made after 6:8 or after 6:12. In favor of the former, often overlooked by commentators, is the use of the vocative in Heb 6:9. The vocative case occurs five times in Hebrews: 3:1,12; 6:9; 10:19; 13:22. Hebrews 6:9 resumes the backbone of the discourse after a strong warning and may perform "the added semantic function of reassuring the readers of the author's love [note the only use of *agapētoi* in the epistle] and confidence in them."[202] Semantically, paragraph breaks are often signaled by a return to the backbone of the discourse. This shift is often signaled by the use of verbs expressing the attitude of the author, as in Heb 6:9: "we are confident of better things in your case." In favor of making the break after v. 12 is the lexical *inclusio* formed by *nōthroi* followed by *ginomai* occurring at 5:11 and 6:12.[203] Additionally, the genre of 5:11–6:12 is hortatory and 6:13–20 is expository. At the very least, 6:9–12 is a sub-paragraph semantic unit, whose onset is marked by the vocative within a larger paragraph unit that may be construed as covering 5:11–6:12. The entire section, Heb 5:11–6:20, can be further subdivided into paragraphs: 5:11–14; 6:1–8,9–12,13–20. Some take 5:11–6:3 as a unit.[204]

The tendency to regard Heb 5:11–6:20 as a "digression" that "interrupts" the exposition of Heb 5:1–10 and 7:1–10:18 is unwarranted given the ability of the author to interweave exhortation and exposition in this epistle.[205] This section begins the third warning passage of the epistle. Hebrews 5:11–14 explains why the author does not proceed with his doctrinal treatment of Christ's high priesthood. The author chides the readers for their lack of maturity. Although they have been Christians long enough that they should themselves be teachers, yet they have regressed to the point that they are in need of being taught again the elementary principles of basic doctrine.

---

200 Discussion of Melchizedek is delayed until chap. 7. On Jewish and Christian speculation about Melchizedek, see the lengthy footnote with bibliography in Bruce, *Hebrews*, 134, and the footnotes here on Hebrews 7.

201 L. L. Neeley, "A Discourse Analysis of Hebrews," *OPTAT* 3–4 (1987): 13.

202 Ibid. Others who make the break at 6:8 include Spicq, *L'Épître aux Hebreux*, 2:141; and O. Michel, *Der Brief an die Hebräer* 6th ed., Meyer Kommentar 13 (Göttingen: Vandenhoeck & Ruprecht, 1966), 230.

203 Vanhoye, *La structure*, 110, 115–20; Attridge, *Hebrews,* 156; Lane, *Hebrews 1–8*, 134; and G. Guthrie, *Structure*, 83.

204 Attridge, *Hebrews*, 156.

205 Lane is correct when he noted: "It is preferable to regard the unit as a preliminary exhortation, which provides an appropriate preamble to the central exposition that follows in 7:1–10:18" (*Hebrews 1–8*, 34).

In the paragraph 5:11–14, vv. 12 and 13 each introduces a new sentence beginning with *gar*, thus denoting subordination to v. 11. Verse 14 begins with *de* and is given a hyperordinating tag by Friberg and Friberg, signaling that it introduces a coordinate clause of greater semantic weight than the preceding clause.[206]

The passage raises the crucial question as to the nature of the readers' immaturity. Are they spiritually immature because they have never gone on to maturity, or are they immature because they have regressed because of disobedience? Furthermore, is the immaturity ethical, doctrinal, or something else? Lane questioned the reconstruction that says the readers had never been exposed to deeper theology on the grounds of what the author has already written to this point. The developed Christology does not indicate immature believers in that sense. In addition, there is no attempt by the author to review the basics. Some have concluded that the author is engaging in irony, "calculated to shame them and to recall them to the stance of conviction and boldness consonant with their experience."[207] While it is ironic that these believers ought by now, from the author's perspective, to be teachers, the irony is in the reality of their immaturity rather than in the author's rhetorical technique.

5:11 Verse 11 begins with the preposition *peri* followed by the relative genitive pronoun *hou*, and (lit.) means "about this." The key question is whether the antecedent of this pronoun is neuter or masculine. If it is taken as neuter, it can have a general topical reference with the meaning of "about this subject," which contextually is the high priesthood of Jesus. If it is masculine, the reference would be either to " or Christ.[208] There is little practical difference between the two.[209] The authorial plural *hēmin* refers only to the author. The author has "much to say" that is "hard to explain," two expressions that are common in classical Greek. The phrase "hard to explain" may refer to the author, the readers, or the subject matter. Most take it in the first sense, but Bruce takes it as referring to the readers,[210] and Lane takes it as referring to the

[206] D. Friberg and B. Friberg, *Analytical Greek New Testament* (Grand Rapids: Baker, 1981), 668.

[207] Lane, *Hebrews 1–8*, 135; also Attridge, *Hebrews*, 157; Michel, *Hebräer*, 230; and Loader, *Sohn*, 85.

[208] Those who take it in the former sense include Spicq, *L'Épître aux Hebreux*, 2:140; Moffatt, *Hebrews*, 69; Hughes, *Hebrews*, 189; Attridge, *Hebrews*, 156; Lane, *Hebrews 1–8*, 136; and the NIV. Those who take it in the latter sense referring to Melchizedek include Alford, "Hebrews," 99; Dods, "Hebrews," 290; Bruce, *Hebrews*, 133; and Ellingworth, *Hebrews*, 299, who takes it as referring "on syntactical grounds" to Melchizedek, but "Christ" is implied due to the "later development of the argument."

[209] Ellingworth and Nida, *A Handbook on the Letter to the Hebrews* (London: UBS, 1983), 102–3, think it is better to make the translation specific and avoid vague phrases such as "about this" or "about him." They take the antecedent as masculine and suggest the meaning could be expressed as "about Christ being a high priest like Melchizedek."

[210] Bruce, *Hebrews*, 133. So also Koester, *Hebrews*, 300, based on the following causal clause.

subject matter, basing his decision on the use of the word in Hellenistic writers.[211] The reason for the difficulty in explanation is expressed in the causal clause "because[212] you are slow to learn," the NIV rendering for the (lit.) "you have become dull in hearing." The perfect tense "you have become" indicates the readers were previously in better spiritual condition, but now are in a state of dullness. There is no indication that the readers must remain in such a state. This word, *nōthroi*, translated "slow," occurs only here and in Heb 6:12 in the New Testament, and connotes lethargy and mental dullness.[213] The Greek *akoais*, (lit.) "hearing," is a dative of respect rendered "to learn,"[214] and probably contrasts the readers' state with what has just been said about Jesus in Heb 5:7–10, where both concepts of "hearing" and "obedience" occur. The readers have not "been making the sort of theological effort that the Christological reflection of his [the author's] work represents."[215] The teaching that the author will give in Heb 7:1–10:18 is not difficult in and of itself, but the author finds it hard to present in such a way that the readers will understand because of their dullness.

5:12 Verse 12 provides an explanation (*gar*) as to why the author considers the readers to be "slow to learn." Semantically it introduces a contrast between what the readers are and what they should be. Because they have been Christians long enough, they should by now be able to teach others. But in fact, they need to be taught. The participle *opheilontes*, translated "though . . . you ought," is concessive,[216] and the word conveys the notion of duty.[217] It was commonly believed that mature people should be able to teach the less mature. "Teachers" as used here probably does not denote the office of teaching, as the word is sometimes used in the New Testament. The meaning here is that mature believers have the capacity to teach, even if they are not filling the office of teacher.[218] The participle modifies the subject of the verb *echete*, "you have."

[211] Lane, *Hebrews 1–8*, 136. Ellingworth, *Hebrews*, 300, accepts this interpretation as well, but thinks a sharp distinction should not be drawn between the three views, since the meaning may imply "teaching difficult in itself, and therefore doubly difficult for you to understand in your present state."

[212] P. Andriessen and A. Lenglet propose that ἐπεί should be translated "otherwise" ("Quelques passages difficiles de L'Épître aux Hebreux [H5,7.11; 10,20; 12,2]," *Bib* 51 [1970]: 207–20.) This, however, is sufficiently answered by Peterson, "The Situation of the 'Hebrews' (5:11–6:12)," *RTR* 35 (1976): 14–21. A good summary of the issue is found in Lane, *Hebrews 1–8*, 130–31.

[213] H. Preisker, "νωθρός," *TDNT* 4:1126; *TLNT* 2:552–54. The usage in Heb 6:12 does not refer to the readers "becoming more lazy than you are" but rather means "don't go on being lazy."

[214] Dods, "Hebrews," 291, suggested the word connotes "intelligent hearing."

[215] Attridge, *Hebrews*, 158. Moffatt translates, "The fault lies with you, not with the subject" (*Hebrews*, 69). Bruce, *Hebrews*, 134, takes the meaning to be something along the lines of "it is not easy for me to put it in a way that you will understand," because their minds are sluggish.

[216] Bruce, *Hebrews*, 133, takes it as temporal, "When you ought."

[217] See BDAG 743.

[218] Bruce, *Hebrews*, 135. See 1 Thess 1:8 for a similar semantic and syntactic construction. The noun "teachers" could be verbalized to make clear the point, as does Moffatt in his translation: "by this time you should be teaching other people" (*Hebrews*, 69).

The object of this verb is the noun "need." The "need" is further defined by the present infinitive "to teach," semantically implying a process.[219] The subject of the infinitive "to teach" is the indefinite pronoun translated "someone." The object of the infinitive is "you." This reads (lit.) "need you have [for] someone to teach you again." The indefinite pronoun "someone" functions as the subject of the infinitive "to teach."[220]

The instruction they need is said to be "the elementary truths of God's word." This noun, *stoicheion*, connotes "elementary concept," "basic or fundamental principle," and can be used of the letters of the alphabet.[221] It is followed by the descriptive genitive translated "elementary."[222] This is followed by the compound genitive phrase (lit.) "of the oracles of God," translated "of God's word." This phrase is commonly used to refer to the Old Testament as divine revelation, but context makes it likely the author employs it here to include the content of the Christian message in Heb 6:1, without confining the meaning strictly to such.[223] The final genitive *tou theou*, "from God," likely indicates the source of the "oracles" or "words."

The final phrase of v. 12 is introduced by *kai* in the Greek text, but is rendered as a new sentence: "You need milk, not solid food."[224] "Milk" refers to basic instruction in the faith, and is further defined in Heb 6:1–2. "Solid food" refers to the more advanced truths, particularly the high priesthood of Christ and all that it entails. A parallel is often drawn with 1 Cor 3:1–4, but it is

---

[219] Ellingworth, *Hebrews*, 303. Greenlee, *Exegetical Summary*, 178: "The infinitive tells what the need is . . . a need to teach you."

[220] Some manuscripts have τινὰ, "someone," while others read τίνα, "which," or τινα with no accent, which can have either meaning. UBS[4] reads τινὰ with a "C" decision. This reading fits the context best. If it is read as "which," it functions as the subject of the clause it introduces: "teach you what the rudiments are" (Greenlee, *An Exegetical Summary*, 179). The pronoun has occasionally been taken as interrogative. Alford, "Hebrews," 101, and Lünemann, *Hebrews*, 516, suggested that the use of the indefinite pronoun implies reproachfully the notion that "anyone" could teach them.

[221] BDAG 946. Cf. L&N 58.19; G. Delling, "στοιχεῖον," *TDNT* 7.670–87.

[222] One could take the genitive "elementary" as modifying "truths," as does Bruce, *Hebrews*, 133, in his translation "the preliminary ABC." It would seem highly unlikely that τῆς ἀρχῆς could refer to the time when the oracles began to be taught, as Dods, "Hebrews," 291. The author's semantic repetition in the use of στοιχεῖα and ἀρχῆς serves to emphasize the point.

[223] So Attridge, *Hebrews*, 159; Ellingworth, *Hebrews*, 304; and Hughes, *Hebrews*, 190; against Westcott, *Hebrews*, 133, who restricts the meaning to the OT as Scripture. Koester, *Hebrews*, 301, remarked: "The basic elements of God's oracles (Heb 5:12) and the basic word of Christ (6:1) are not identical, but neither can be taken without the other."

[224] The Greek uses a complicated periphrastic construction: the perfect of γίνομαι, "you have become," is followed by the present participle ἔχοντες, "having," with its object, "need." "The author of Hebrews uses the Perfect γεγόνατε to describe the state of his readers, in which they are seen as in progress requiring milk, not solid food, since they have been lazy" (Porter, *Verbal Aspect*, 491). He further explains, "γίνομαι appears to be the aspectually marked lexical equivalent of the lexically vague εἰμί, and thus its vague meaning is suitable to any number of contexts, while still contributing an aspectual semantic component." Porter translates the latter part of Heb 5:12: "and you are [become] in a state of having a need for milk, [and] not of solid meat."

doubtful if any literary or historical relationship exists, as these were common metaphors in the Hellenistic period as well as in the apostolic era (1 Pet 2:2).

5:13 A new subordinate sentence (*gar*) begins here that functions as the reason for the latter part of v. 12 (note the repetition of "milk").[225] Anyone who can understand only the basic elements of Christian doctrine "lives on milk" and is inexperienced or unacquainted with the "teaching about righteousness." The word translated "not acquainted" connotes lack of skill or experience.[226] That which the readers lack skill in is the "teaching about righteousness," which probably refers to the ethical dimensions of Scripture, taking "righteousness" here not in the forensic sense of "justification" but in the ethical sense of matters of right and wrong.[227] The final clause introduced by *gar* functions as a reason for the immediately preceding statement and is translated "being still an infant." Although a subordinate clause, it receives semantic emphasis by being placed at the end of v. 13. The word "infant" here refers to a child who has not been weaned.

5:14 Verse 14 is the second half of the sentence begun in v. 13 and introduces a contrast "but" (*de*) which, as noted above, semantically conveys greater weight than the preceding clause. The noun *teleios*, "mature," is fronted in the Greek text for emphasis. The author draws a sharp contrast between an "infant" and one who is "mature."[228] It is difficult to capture the feel of the Greek word order and syntax in an English translation.[229] The NIV is particularly

---

[225] So Lünemann, *Hebrews*, 517; Dods, "Hebrews," 292; Ellingworth, *Hebrews*, 305. Alford, "Hebrews," 102, views the γὰρ as introducing a reason for vv. 11–12. Verses 13–14 expand on the notions of "milk" and "solid food," but in reverse order.

[226] See BDAG 100; L&N 28.15.

[227] So Ellingworth, *Hebrews*, 306. The noun δικαιοσύνη has been understood in one of three ways: (1) physiologically or psychologically, with reference to an inability to speak or comprehend correctly; (2) in an ethical sense as in Num 14:23 LXX; and (3) in the sense of teachings foundational to Christianity or more specifically in context to teaching about Melchizedek. The entire genitive phrase λόγου δικαιοσύνης may be grammatically construed in a number of ways: (1) adjectivally, in the sense of right teaching; (2) as a genitive of content, "the teaching whose content is righteousness"; (3) as an objective genitive, "teaching about righteousness." The NIV takes it as an objective genitive. Surprisingly, Lane, *Hebrews 1–8*, 138, appeals to a second century "technical" use of the phrase by Polycarp: "Polycarp's use of the motifs of endurance to the end and of imitation in a context referring to known martyrs as those who had obeyed 'the word of righteousness' is suggestive for the interpretation of Hebrews. . . . If this is the proper linguistic context for interpreting verse 13, it suggests that what was involved in the regression of the community was a failure in moral character rather than in keen theological insight." The problem with Lane's interpretation is that it is anachronistic in its appeal to the second century.

[228] Koester, *Hebrews*, 303, pointed out the Philonic use of the word "for those who had completed the course of education and were qualified to be teachers." Ellingworth, *Hebrews*, 308, stated this is the only place in Hebrews where the word applies to people. Τελείων is a rare predicate genitive of possession.

[229] The latter part of the verse reads in Greek: τῶν διὰ τὴν ἕξιν τὰ αἰσθητήρια γεγυμνασμένα ἐχόντων πρὸς διάκρισιν καλοῦ τε καὶ κακοῦ. The genitive article τῶν governs the participle ἐχόντων. This participle is in apposition with τελείων at the beginning of the verse. There is quite a bit of intervening material between the article and noun ἐχόντων: (1) There is an adjectival

weak in its translation of the latter half of v. 14. It does not make explicit the noun *aisthētērion*, meaning "sense," "faculty," or "capacity to understand." The word is difficult to define, but it would seem to include intellectual, moral, and spiritual capacity, perception, or sense.[230] This capacity is said to be "trained," where the Greek participle can be either middle or passive voice. The NIV takes it as a middle voice and translates "trained themselves." This training is accomplished by "constant use" *hexis*, where the word in Greek primarily means a state resulting from training, not the process of training.[231] Ellingworth suggested that the noun indicates a state, not a process, and when used with the participle "have trained themselves" points to "the process of exercising which results in a particular [*hexis*]."[232] The prepositional phrase "to distinguish" is the translation of *pros* with the noun meaning "ability to judge" or "ability to decide,"[233] and includes intellectual as well as moral discernment, thus good and bad doctrines as well as moral discrimination. It is rightly rendered verbally rather than nominally by virtually all translations. The use of "good and evil" probably alludes to Num 14:23 (LXX), given the significance of Numbers 14 for Hebrews 3–4, where the children are said not to know "good or evil" because of their lack of maturity.

Ellingworth and Nida paraphrase the meaning of vv. 13–14 as: "Anyone who lives on milk is a baby who does not know by experience what is right. But mature people, on the other hand, can take solid food, because they have learned by practice and training to be sensitive to the difference between good and evil."[234]

In summary, Heb 5:11–14 gives three indicators for the immaturity of the readers. First, their inability to teach others; second, they need "milk" and not

---

participle γεγυμνασμένα in the predicate position. This participle is in agreement with (2) αἰσθητήρια, which functions as the direct object of ἐχόντων. This is preceded by (3) διὰ with its accusative object ἕξιν, which can indicate means (NIV) or reason (KJV; NASB). The final prepositional phrase following the participle ἐχόντων is introduced with πρὸς with its accusative object διάκρισιν, which can be taken as purpose, result, or content. A lit. rendering would be something like "but solid food is for the mature, namely, those who have the senses trained by/because of constant use for the purpose/with the result of/to distinguish(ing) both good and evil."

[230] On this word, consult L&N 32.28; BDAG 29; and G. Delling, "αἰσθητήριον," *TDNT* 1:188. Ellingworth and Nida, *Handbook*, 106, point out that αἰσθητήριον "involves physical or mental fitness, for example, in Sirach 30.14, where it means that a person is 'in good condition.' The rare word which RSV translates 'faculties' does not refer only to intellectual powers; in the Septuagint of Jeremiah 4:19 it includes emotional awareness."

[231] So J. A. L. Lee, "Hebrews 5:14 and '*hexis*': a History of Misunderstanding," *NovT* 39 (1997): 151–76. See Koester's translation, *Hebrews*, 303, "who, because of this state." The word is unique in the NT, but common in philosophical Greek. See Attridge, *Hebrews*, 161, for examples.

[232] Ellingworth, *Hebrews*, 309. "The perfect indicates a continuous process, and, together with ἐχόντων, suggests that γεγυμνασμένα is to be understood with verbal force (Bleek) rather than as a predicate adjective (Moffatt); but the difference in meaning is slight."

[233] Whether πρὸς is taken as indicating purpose, result, or content (so virtually all translations, including the NIV), makes little difference in terms of overall meaning.

[234] Ellingworth and Nida, *Handbook*, 105.

solid food; third, they are spiritually untrained in distinguishing good from evil. The crucial thing to note here is that this paragraph is dealing with an issue of sanctification, not salvation. This contextual clue is crucial for a correct interpretation of Heb 6:1–8.

We now turn our attention to what may be the most difficult passage to interpret in the entire epistle: Heb 6:1–8. Several considerations are important to keep in mind. First, contextually, Heb 6:1–8 connects closely with Heb 5:11–14. This must not be lost sight of in the exegesis of the passage. Second, Heb 6:1–8 must be taken together as a semantic unit.[235] Hebrews 6:9 marks a new paragraph with the use of the vocative *agapētoi* and the conjunction *de*. Third, there are three sub-paragraphs that make up Heb 6:1–8: vv. 1–3,4–6, and vv. 7–8. The first sub-paragraph is introduced with the conjunction *dio*, "therefore," and this governs the entire eight verses, serving to connect them closely with Heb 5:11–14.[236] Verses 4–6 are introduced with the subordinating conjunction *gar*, which is left untranslated in the NIV. Verses 7–8 likewise begin with *gar* and are subordinate to the previous sub-paragraph. Fourth, the theme of these verses, as stated in v. 1, is the exhortation "let us go on to maturity." This continues the spiritual immaturity/maturity theme begun in Heb 5:11–14.

6:1–2 Hebrews 6:1–2 is one sentence in the Greek text with the imperatival notion "let us press on to maturity" flanked on each side by two participles (lit.): "leaving the elementary teachings" and "not laying again a foundation." Both participles denote action concomitant with that of the main verb "let us go on to maturity." Some translations, such as the NIV, and commentators interpret the participle "having left" as a finite verb parallel to "let us move on." To "leave" connotes the idea of to leaving something behind in order to pass on to something else. That which is left is the "elementary teachings" about Christ.[237] The meaning here is not that of abandoning the basic teachings of Christianity, but rather the necessity of recognizing the foundational character of these teachings and thus the impropriety of going over the same ground. The readers are exhorted to move on to another level, a level commensurate

[235] NA[27], UBS[4], and Friberg and Friberg all see Heb 6:1–8 as a paragraph unit.

[236] Friberg and Friberg, *Analytical Greek New Testament*, 668–69, give διὸ in 6:1 and δὲ in 6:9 a hyperordinating tag that signals that it introduces semantic information that is not merely coordinate with the preceding paragraph, but more prominent than the preceding paragraph. In 6:1, διό introduces a conclusion: the readers should press on from a state of immaturity to that of maturity.

[237] The Greek could connote the idea of "omit" or "pass over." The genitive is objective, expressing the content of the teaching: "about Christ." The case for the subjective genitive is made by J. C. Adams, "Exegesis of Hebrews vi.1f.," *NTS* 13 (1967): 378–85, where he translates, "let us leave on one side Christ's original teaching and let us advance towards maturity." What they are to leave behind is a "preoccupation with the content of Christ's own teaching" (383). According to Adams, the nature of the apostasy spoken of in 6:6 is that the readers "have accepted the message of Jesus, but not his person and work" (384). Such a meaning cannot be sustained contextually.

with those who are mature, a level of "fuller appreciation and application of that teaching."[238] The clause "not laying again the foundation" is the negative expression of the positive concepts "leaving" and "pressing on." The goal is "maturity"[239] and pressing on is the means by which the goal is reached. The verb *pherōmetha* indicates swift and energetic movement.[240] The verb may be construed in the middle voice in the sense of "to bring oneself forward," but most likely it should be taken as passive, suggesting God as the one who moves the readers along to the desired goal.[241] Christians are dependent upon God and his grace to enable them to press forward to maturity.

Lane adequately refuted the notion that the six items mentioned in Heb 6:1–2 are not necessarily distinctly Christian by noting that each of these six is related to the high priestly Christology that will be developed in Hebrews 7–10.[242] Both context and the history of interpretation of this passage confirm that Heb 6:1–2 refers to Christian teaching.[243]

The noun "foundation" governs a list of six nouns in the genitive case in 6:1b–2. The author wants his readers to move beyond a foundation "of repentance . . . of faith . . . [of] instruction (about baptisms) . . . [of] the laying on (of hands) . . . [of] the resurrection (of the dead), . . . [of] judgment." They may be understood as three groups of two: repentance and faith, baptismal instruction and laying on of hands, and resurrection and eternal judgment. The noun *didachēs,* "instruction," however, has a textual variant: the same noun but in the accusative case (*didachēn*). If the variant is original, then "instruction" is in apposition to "foundation," which consists of repentance and faith. The other four items make up the content of that instructional foundation. The genitive case has the majority of witnesses, but a number of scholars take it in the accusative

---

[238] Lane, *Hebrews 1–8*, 139.

[239] Some, like Ellingworth, *Hebrews*, 312, take "maturity" to refer to mature teachings that are the means whereby the readers come to maturity. More likely, the reference is to the maturity of believers, as the NIV.

[240] Bruce, *Hebrews*, 137. Lane, *Hebrews 1–8*, 140, stated: "In this context spiritual maturity implies receptivity and responsiveness to the received tradition (5:14), an earnest concern for the full realization of hope (6:11), unwavering faith and steadfast endurance (6:12)."

[241] R. C. H. Lenski, *The Interpretation of the Epistle to the Hebrews and of the Epistle of James* (Columbus, OH: Wartburg, 1946), 175, takes it as middle. Lane, *Hebrews 1–8*, 140, and Ellingworth, *Hebrews*, 312, both take it as passive. The first person plural also implies the author includes himself along with the readers, against Hewitt, *Hebrews*, 103–4, who by implication, takes it as referring to the readers alone, and S. T. Bloomfield, *The Greek Testament*, 14th ed. (Philadelphia: J. B. Lippincott & Company, 1869), 2:421, who, following many commentators before him, takes it as referring to the author alone, in the sense of "I want to move on in my teaching."

[242] Lane, *Hebrews 1–8*, 140. For the opposing viewpoint, consult Adams, "Exegesis of Hebrews," 378–85. Ellingworth's statement in *Hebrews*, 313, "The list contains nothing distinctively Christian, and of course nothing exclusively Jewish" is correct. That the six items listed in Heb 6:1–2 are all consistent with Judaism has been affirmed by Michel, *Hebräer*, 145; and Nairne, *Epistle of Priesthood*, 15.

[243] R. C. Sauer, "A Critical and Exegetical Reexamination of Hebrews 5:11–6:8" (Ph.D. diss., University of Manchester, 1981), 176–78, provides one of the best arguments for this point.

case.[244] All things considered, it seems best to categorize the statements into three groups of pairs arranged perhaps temporally with the first pair focusing on the past, the second pair focusing on the present, and the third pair focusing on the future.

What does the author mean by "acts that lead to death" (lit. "dead works")? The phrase is used elsewhere only in Heb 9:14. Hughes viewed the phrase as "theological shorthand" for the "state of unregenerate man and his activities."[245] These dead works are, according to F. F. Bruce, "probably not the works of the law, not even the sacrificial ceremonies prescribed by the cultic law. . . . They are works which issue in death because they are evil."[246] It is unlikely that "acts that lead to death" refers to "idolatry" since the readers were probably not Gentile converts. The noun "repentance" conveys the verbal idea of "turning from," involving a complete internal change of mind, heart and will that results in an external change of actions. The positive counterpart to repentance is "faith in God" and is closely joined with the preceding phrase by the author. The two phrases are "inseparably complementary"[247] and are used by the author to indicate Christian conversion.

Another issue concerning *didachēs* is whether it is to be rendered "teaching" or "doctrine." The former can be taken to indicate the activity of teaching, while the latter would focus more on the doctrine concerning such things as baptisms.[248] The latter appears most likely. A third issue concerns the content and extent of the *didachēs*. Is the content only the "baptisms," both "baptisms" and the "laying on of hands," or the remainder of the verse including all four statements. Virtually all commentators and translators see the word as governing the rest of v. 2.

The meaning of the next two phrases is debated. The puzzling use of the plural *baptismōn*, "baptisms," may indicate Jewish ritual ablutions, or refer to

---

[244] Moffatt, *Hebrews*, 74–75; Bruce, *Hebrews*, 137–39; and Lane, *Hebrews 1–8*, 132, 140, are examples of those who interpret the structure in this way, based on the two different Greek words translated "and," one of which indicates a closer connection than the other. This is, however, a tenuous syntactical point on which to base the structure. See the discussions in Hughes, *Hebrews*, 196; and Ellingworth, *Hebrews*, 313–14. F. F. Bruce, "Textual Problems in the Epistle to the Hebrews," in *Scribes and Scripture: New Testament Essays in Honor of J. Harold Greenlee*, ed. D. A. Black (Winona Lake: Eisenbrauns, 1992), 30–31, has the best short discussion of the matter. "It is difficult to see why διδαχῆς should have been changed to διδαχήν, while the accusative might easily have been changed to the genitive under the influence of the series of adjacent genitives." UBS[4] gives the genitive singular an "A" decision, which indicates the committee felt the reading was certain.

[245] Hughes, *Hebrews*, 197.

[246] Bruce, *Hebrews*, 139–40. DeSilva, *Perseverance in Gratitude*, 307, stated concerning these dead works that they "are most assuredly not the cultic regulations of the OT."

[247] Hughes, *Hebrews*, 198. Calvin's view that "faith" should be equated with the summary of Christian doctrine found in the "Articles of Faith" needs no refutation (Calvin, *Hebrews*, 72).

[248] See Greenlee, *Exegetical Summary*, 189, for the various commentators and translations on both sides of the question.

differences between Jewish and Christian baptism.[249] It is possible that the use of the plural here may refer simply to multiple events of people being baptized. If this is the author's meaning, one could use the singular "baptism" in translation, since the phrase "instruction about baptism" implies several people being baptized. More likely is that the plural signifies purification ceremonies of a Jewish sort that probably would have been employed by Jewish Christians as well, then the meaning conveyed would be along the lines of "rituals for purifying people."[250]

The early church fathers tended to interpret this passage as a reference to Christian baptism.[251] Modern commentators usually see a broader reference, inclusive of Christian baptism, but also referencing other washings. Westcott argued the meaning was to new Christians who were taught the difference between Christian baptism and ritual washings.[252] More recently, Cross attempted to make the case that the author may have had in mind a metaphorical "baptism of blood," namely, martyrdom. Noting that there is clear evidence for a connection between baptism and martyrdom in the writings of Tertullian, Hippolytus, and Chrysostom, he thought it possible that such a notion might be traceable back to the words of Jesus in Mark 10:38–39 and Luke 12:50, where the metaphorical use of "baptism" applies to Christ's suffering and death on the cross. Building on an article by Jeanes,[253] he argued for "a continuous tradition of speaking about martyrdom in terms of the baptism of blood which originated in the early ministry of Jesus."[254] He admitted his case is inconclusive, but considered it possible that "baptisms" in Heb 6:2 may have included such a metaphorical reference to martyrdom.[255]

The phrase "laying on of hands" most likely refers to the symbolic New Testament rite, following immediately upon baptism, symbolizing the imparta-

---

[249] The former viewpoint is taken by several commentators, including Dods ("Hebrews," 294), Hughes (*Hebrews*, 201–2), and Bruce (*Hebrews*, 141–42). The latter position is argued by Ellingworth (*Hebrews*, 315–16) and Lane (*Hebrews 1–8*, 132). It is highly unlikely that the reference is to the distinction between Christian baptism and that of John the Baptist as suggested by Montefiore. Cf. A. Cross, "The Meaning of 'Baptisms' in Hebrews 6:2," in *Dimensions of Baptism: Biblical and Theological Studies*, ed. S. Porter and A. Cross, JSNTSup 234 (Sheffield: Sheffield Academic Press, 2002), 163–86.

[250] As noted by Ellingworth and Nida, *Handbook*, 111; cf. Lenski, *Hebrews*, 177.

[251] For example, Tertullian interpreted the plural to be a reference to triple immersion; Augustine took it to refer to baptisms of water, blood and desire; and Athanasius oddly takes the plural to refer to repeated heretical baptisms (see Attridge, *Hebrews*, 164; Ellingworth, *Hebrews*, 315; and A. Cross, "The Meaning of 'Baptisms," 163).

[252] Westcott, *Hebrews*, 147; followed by A. Cross, "Meaning of 'Baptisms,'" 165.

[253] G. Jeanes, "Baptism Portrayed as Martyrdom in the Early Church," *SL* 23.2 (1993):158–76.

[254] A. Cross, "Meaning of 'Baptisms,'" 170.

[255] Ibid., 186. There is no direct link that can be made, so it would be anachronistic in my view to see such a connection in Heb 6:2.

tion of the Holy Spirit. It is unlikely the phrase extends its meaning to include other matters such as blessing, healing, or ordination.[256]

"Resurrection" here most likely entails a general resurrection of all people, righteous and unrighteous, since it is followed by "eternal judgment."[257] It is impossible to determine whether "eternal judgment" is being used in a neutral sense or if it connotes the condemnation of the unrighteous. The word "judgment" may focus more on the process of judging or to the actual verdict rendered, with the latter meaning being the most likely.[258]

6:3 Verse 3 is an enigmatic statement, often overlooked or given an anemic treatment by commentators.[259] What does the writer mean by "God permitting, we will do so"? The first issue one must address is the antecedent of "this." Four options exist: it may refer (1) to going on to maturity,[260] (2) to the more advanced teaching,[261] (3) it may refer to the author's giving mature teaching enabling the readers to go on to maturity,[262] or (4) not only to pressing on to maturity, but to both attendant circumstances expressed by the participles, "leaving behind the elementary teachings" and "not laying again the foundation." The first and fourth options are contextually most likely. When the author employs "we," he is most likely indicating what he and his readers intend to do rather than stating what he intends to do, namely, press on to more mature, advanced teaching. Since the two attendant circumstances are semantically connected to the main verb "let us press on," they are pulled into its orbit and constitute the antecedent reference to "this" in v. 3.[263] The force of the Greek and the connection of v. 3 to v. 1 can be seen if we consider v. 2 a parenthesis for the moment

---

[256] The "Six-Principle Baptists," a small group in England and America, got their name from the stress they placed on adherence to these six basics of the faith in Heb 6:1–2, especially their focus on the laying on of hands. The seventeenth-century English Baptist John Griffith was an early leader of the Six-Principle Baptists. See his *God's Oracle & Christ's Doctrine, Or, The Six Principles of Christian Religion* (London: R. Moon, 1665), 139. The laying on of hands is a rite generally observed by Baptists during ordination to the ministry or deaconate. Six-Principle Baptists practice the laying on of hands after baptism as a prerequisite to church membership. They developed out of the General Baptists of England and have always been Arminian in theology. The significance of Hebrews 6 for Griffith and the Six-Principle Baptists can also be seen in Griffith's *A Treatise Touching Falling from Grace* (London: Hen. Hills, 1653), where many of the arguments Griffith makes in favor of the possibility of believers losing their salvation come from Hebrews 6. See R. Knight, *History of the General or Six Principle Baptists in Europe and America* (Providence, RI: Smith and Parmenter, 1827; repr., New York: Arno, 1980); and L. McBeth, *The Baptist Heritage* (Nashville: Broadman and Holman, 1987), 139, 149, 226, 703.

[257] So Ellingworth, *Hebrews*, 316.

[258] See also the notion of "judgment" in Heb 9:14 and 10:27.

[259] For example, Moffatt, *Hebrews*, 76, said the statement was added by the author as a "pious comment." See the survey summary of treatment in Greenlee, *Exegetical Summary*, 191.

[260] See Ellingworth, *Hebrews,* 317.

[261] See Moffatt, *Hebrews,* 76.

[262] See Bruce, *Hebrews,* 143–44.

[263] T. Nichols, "Reverse Engineered Outlining: A Method for Epistolary Exegesis," *CTSJ* 7 (2001): 34–38; Wallace, *GGBB* 334–35.

and thus translate: "Let us be carried on into perfection, and this we will do, God granting us mercy that we may be so enabled."[264] As Ellingworth and Nida pointed out, it is essential to treat vv. 1–3 as a unit for translation purposes and to show that v. 3 refers to pressing forward to maturity.[265]

The question of whether God will "permit" this is crucial to our understanding of Heb 6:4–6. This statement harks back to what was said in Hebrews 3–4 and the reference to the exodus generation's disobedience in the wilderness and subsequent consequence of God's judgment: namely, they were not "permitted" to enter Canaan. Because the writer has in mind what he had written in Hebrews 3–4, he makes the statement "God permitting, we will do so." This is followed by the subordinating conjunction *gar*, "for," in v. 4. The sense is: we will press on to maturity if God permits, for we know about those (the wilderness generation) whom God did not permit to press on and enter the Promised Land.

6:4–6 Hebrews 6:4–6 is considered by many to be the most difficult interpretative passage in all the book of Hebrews, and some would say in the entire New Testament. Because so much of the interpretation of the warning passages as well as the entire epistle hinges on this paragraph, considerable attention to its exegetical, historical and theological aspects is mandated.[266] Most attempts at analyzing this passage fall into the trap of putting theology before exegesis. While it is impossible to come to this or any text with a hermeneutical *tabula rasa*, it is at least incumbent on each interpreter to suspend, as far as is possible, presuppositions concerning the various theological positions centered around this text. Since biblical theology must precede systematic theology, a thorough linguistic, exegetical, and historical examination of this passage is in order.[267] Only then will we be in a position to theologize. Therefore, our approach is to: (1) examine the overall structure; (2) determine the syntax of the individual participial clauses; (3) determine the meaning of the four participial clauses in vv. 4–5 and the meaning of the two participial clauses following the infinitive in v. 6; (4) determine the spiritual condition of those described by the four participial clauses in vv. 4,5; (5) determine the meaning of *parapesontas* in v. 6; (6) determine what is meant by "impossible to be brought back to repentance";

[264] As translated by R. T. Kendall, *Once Saved, Always Saved* (Chicago: Moody, 1985), 221. See also TEV, which repeats the statement "Let us go forward" from v. 1.

[265] Ellingworth and Nida, *Handbook*, 108.

[266] It is surprising that Lane (*Hebrews 1–8*) devotes only two pages to a discussion of Heb 6:4–6. Attridge (*Hebrews*) devotes five and a half pages, half of which are footnotes. Ellingworth (*Hebrews*) devotes only eight pages to Heb 6:4–6 out of his 736 pages of introduction and commentary.

[267] A. T. Robertson, the great Greek grammarian, was fond of quoting A. M. Fairbairn's dictum: "he can be no theologian who is not first a philologian." Or to put it more colorfully, in the words of N. Söderblom, cited by D. A. Carson in *Exegetical Fallacies*, 2nd ed. (Grand Rapids: Baker, 1996), 27, "Philology is the eye of the needle through which every theological camel must enter the heaven of theology."

(7) determine if this text is related to the Kadesh-Barnea episode, as was the case in Hebrews 3–4, or has other Old Testament echoes or allusions; (8) survey the patristic, Reformation, and modern interpretations of this passage; and (9) synthesize this data into an interpretive theological framework.

Hebrews 6:4–6 is the *crux interpretum* of Heb 5:11–6:8, and really for the entire book. This sub-paragraph is closely connected to the previous paragraph (6:1–3) by the use of *gar*, a subordinating conjunction translated "for." Just how this conjunction is functioning to connect vv. 4–6 with vv. 1–3 is a matter of dispute. Five possibilities may be distinguished. First, some see it as indicating the grounds for "not laying again the foundation" in 6:1.[268] Second, it may indicate the grounds for the imperatival idea in 6:1, "let us press on to maturity."[269] Third, Moffatt takes it as expressing the grounds for the statement "we will do so" in v. 3.[270] Fourth, it may indicate the grounds for 6:1–3 as a whole.[271] Fifth, it perhaps indicates the grounds for the statement "God permitting."[272]

Since the phrase "not laying again the foundation" is not semantically the most dominant information in the preceding paragraph, the first option is unlikely. Semantically, the hortatory subjunctive "let us press on to maturity" is focal in the preceding paragraph, therefore option two is certainly possible. Since v. 3 begins a new sentence coordinated with the previous sentence by *kai*, "and," Moffatt's suggestion is also possible. The fourth option is likewise possible in that the author could be subordinating vv. 4–6 to vv. 1–3 as a unit. The fifth option connects vv. 4–6 with the conditional clause that occurs at the end of the sentence in v. 3 as explaining the reason why those who "fall away" cannot be renewed to repentance, namely, because God will not permit it. Options two, four and five would seem to fit best, with the weight of probability given to option four or five. Two semantic reasons may be offered in support. First, the author has a penchant in both of these paragraphs to group larger units together: the three pairs of phrases in vv. 1–2 and the five participial phrases in vv. 4–6. Second, *gar* can connect not only two sentences, but also two paragraphs. Such appears to be the case here, especially since vv. 4–6 are actually a single sentence in the Greek text. These verses are related to vv. 7–8 by another *gar*, which functions to introduce a supportive illustration. The theme of this section that begins in 5:11 is the necessity of pressing on to maturity as believers.

The Greek syntactical structure of 6:4–6 is difficult to untangle in an English translation. The three verses make up one sentence in Greek. The subject of the sentence actually does not appear in the text until v. 6 with the infinitive

[268] So Dods, "Hebrews," 296; Ellingworth, *Hebrews*, 318.
[269] So Lünemann, *Hebrews*, 532; Lane, *Hebrews 1–8*, 141.
[270] Moffatt, *Hebrews*, 76.
[271] So Alford, "Hebrews," 108; Dods, "Hebrews," 296.
[272] So Miller, *Hebrews*, 168.

translated "to be brought back." This is followed by the prepositional phrase "to repentance" and preceded by the adverb *palin,* "again." This entire phrase functions as the subject of the sentence. The predicate is an understood linking verb translated "is" followed by the predicate nominative "impossible," which is the first word in v. 4 of the Greek text. The main clause of the entire three-verse sentence thus reads: "It is impossible . . . to be brought back to repentance." The question then is who is being referred to; who is it impossible to renew to repentance? Asked in another way, what is the direct object of the infinitive *anakainizein,* "to renew, restore" (NIV "to be brought back" translates an active infinitive as if it were passive)? The direct object is actually five substantival participles in vv. 4–6a grouped together by the accusative plural article *tous*, which is translated "those who." The sense is "it is impossible to renew again to repentance those who . . ." and then five substantival participles describe and define the people to whom the author refers. They are said to be those who (1) "have once been enlightened," (2) "who have tasted the heavenly gift," (3) "who have shared in the Holy Spirit," (4) "who have tasted the goodness of the word of God and the powers of the coming age," (5) and "who have fallen away." Thus, to this point, it states, "It is impossible to renew again to repentance those who have been once enlightened, who have tasted the heavenly gift . . . and who have fallen away." In v. 6, the infinitive phrase translated "to be brought back to repentance" is followed by two adverbial participial phrases translated "because they are recrucifying the Son of God and subjecting him to public disgrace." These two participles define the cause or reason for the impossibility of repentance.[273]

The first major exegetical question has to do with the nature of the five participles in vv. 4–6: are they to be construed as adjectival (substantival) or adverbial? The first four participles are easily identified as substantival participles since they are governed by the article *tous* in v. 4.[274] Grammatically, an articular participle rules out the adverbial (circumstantial) usage. The key question has to do with the fifth participle in the list, *parapesontas*, translated "falling away": is it substantival or adverbial? Many construe this participle to be adverbial because of its distance from the article and its negative connotation whereas the other four participles express positive notions. It is sometimes given a conditional translation as in the NIV: "if they fall away"; a temporal translation as in the NRSV and the NASB: "then have fallen away"; or a simple adverbial rendering: "falling away." Von Kamecke's analysis of participle usage patterns in Hebrews revealed "the writer displays a certain fondness for using substantival participles (many of which are addressed to, or about,

---

[273] Moffatt, *Hebrews,* 79. The two participles "crucifying" and "disregarding" give the reasons that repentance is impossible.

[274] Ibid., connects it with only the first four participles.

his audience),[275] often employing them in other warning and exhortation passages."[276] Furthermore, the structure of one article governing two or more participles is not limited in Hebrews to 6:4–6. Thus, as Von Kamecke noted, Heb 6:4–6 "does not stand out as a grammatical oddity."[277]

Although the adverbial usage is certainly possible in this context, it seems much better, on grammatical and semantic grounds, to interpret *parapesontas* as a substantival participle parallel to the previous four participles.[278] There are three key clues that point in this direction. First, the use of the article in v. 4 at the very least governs the first four participles. Consistency would seem to indicate that it likewise governs the final participle in the group. All five participles are in the accusative case, masculine in gender, and plural in number. All five function as the direct objects of the infinitive "to renew again." These factors would tend to indicate that the fifth participle would function grammatically as the previous four.

The second clue is the use of the conjunctions *te . . . kai . . . kai . . . kai* linking the five participles. These are often overlooked by those who assign an adverbial meaning to the fifth participle "falling away." This use of parallel conjunctions serves to bind these participles together as a unit.[279] Versions like the NIV, which opt for an adverbial translation of *parapesontas,* typically ignore the last *kai* in the list at the beginning of v. 6.[280] Von Kamecke, concurring with Michael Palmer, pointed out that one does not find adjectival and adverbial participles conjoined in the same grouping in the New Testament, and concluded with respect to Hebrews, "the writer never pairs an adjectival participle with an adverbial participle, or vice versa."[281]

The third semantic clue that these participles are substantival is their bracketing within an infinitival clause. This discourse feature appears to be used by the author to "package" the five participles into a single unit. These three

---

[275] F. Von Kamecke, "Implications for the Rendering of *Παραπεσοντας* in Hebrews 6:4–6," (Ph.D. diss., Trinity Evangelical Divinity School, Deerfield, IL, 2004), 147–49, lists 15 examples.

[276] Von Kamecke, "Implications," 147–49, lists eight examples.

[277] Ibid., 155.

[278] The most thorough study of this question to date is Von Kamecke's recent dissertation, "Implications," which has the most detailed linguistic argument for the substantival use of all five of the participles in Heb 6:4–6. See also the important article on this subject by J. Sproule, "*Παραπεσόντας* in Hebrews 6:6," *GTJ* 2, no. 2 (1981): 327–32. Sproule surveyed several Greek grammarians on this specific participle and summarized the results: "none of the correspondents were aware of any instance of an articular adjectival participle occurring in the NT with a 'conditional' meaning." Cf. E. Grässer, *An die Hebräer* EKKNT 17 (Zurich: Benziger, 1990), 1:354; Wallace, *GGBB* 633; Attridge, *Hebrews*, 167; and L. Sabourin, "Crucifying Afresh for One's Repentance (Heb 6:4–6)." *BTB* 6 (1976): 264–71, as examples of those who affirm the substantival usage.

[279] Wallace (*GGBB* 633) pointed out that this usage of the conjunctions "*approximates* a Granville Sharp plural construction."

[280] In the newer TNIV, the adverbial rendering is abandoned for the substantival rendering.

[281] Von Kamecke, "Implications," 162, following M. Palmer, *Levels of Constituent Structures in New Testament Greek, Studies in Biblical Greek* 1 (New York: Peter Lang, 1995), 48.

factors strongly suggest that *parapesontas* should be interpreted, like the previous four participles, as substantival and be given the translation "who have fallen away."[282] The significance of this for interpretation is twofold. First, the five participles identify and describe one group of people.[283] Second, since the participle is not adverbial, it cannot be given a conditional or temporal translation. Whether the group described in 6:4–6a should be identified with genuine believers or not is a question that awaits examination of the meaning of each participial phrase in vv. 4–5 and the interpretation of *parapesontas* in v. 6.

We now turn to an examination of the meaning of each individual participial clause. "Those who have once been enlightened" most likely refers to the initial illumination that results from a response to the preaching of the gospel or early Christian teaching.[284] The same word occurs in Heb 10:32 with reference to the readers' initial response to the gospel. That the word was used in the second century AD and beyond as a reference to baptism has little significance here as the word was not so used in the New Testament.[285] The question of the meaning and extent of *hapax,* "once," must be addressed. As to meaning, it implies a once for all act that cannot be repeated.[286] As to extent, Ellingworth connects it only with "being enlightened," while Lane, and many before him, argue that it modifies all four participles in vv. 4–5.[287]

---

[282] The attributive participle in Greek coupled with its complements often semantically functions in the same way as a relative clause. The same is true in English as well. Such constructions are semantically equivalent in that they are simply different ways of saying the same thing. See MHT 3:152; C. F. D. Moule, *The Idiom Book of New Testament Greek* (Cambridge: Cambridge University Press, 1953), 164; and R. W. Funk, *A Beginning-Intermediate Grammar of Hellenistic Greek*, 2nd ed. (Atlanta: Scholars Press, 1977), 523–24, 600–601. Funk stated that the attributive participle and object are "perhaps best rendered into English by a relative clause" (600). The author of Hebrews makes considerable use of substantival participles. Von Kamecke ("Implications," 165) concluded that the adverbial usage in Heb 6:6 cannot be ruled out, "but there is no compelling reason to construe it as adverbial. In fact, structural clues in the passage lead one to surmise that it is articular. If it is articular, it must be adjectival, and, since it is not modifying any other noun, it is substantival."

[283] Robertson, *GGNT* 777, 785–89. The pattern of conjoining adjectival participles by the use of καί is prevalent in Hebrews (2:9; 5:2; 6:7; 7:1; 8:13; 10:29). Additionally, examples where the author sandwiches material between the article and participle as in 6:4–6 can be seen in 5:14; 6:12; and 7:5.

[284] See Attridge, *Hebrews*, 169, who calls the phrase "a common image for the reception of a salvific message," with accompanying examples from the OT and NT. Koester lists many references to light imagery in both Scripture and extra-biblical literature where movement from sin to God, ignorance to knowledge, and death to life are concerned (Koester, *Hebrews,* 313–14).

[285] Hughes, *Hebrews*, 208, provides a good survey of this usage from the second century onwards.

[286] So Alford, "Hebrews," 108; Moffatt, *Hebrews*, 78; and Lane, *Hebrews 1–8*, 141. Against this notion, see W. Grudem, "Perseverance of the Saints: A Case Study from Hebrews 6:4–6 and Other Warning Passages in Hebrews," in *The Grace of God, the Bondage of the Will*, ed. T. Schreiner and B. Ware (Grand Rapids: Baker, 1995), 1:133–81.

[287] Ellingworth, *Hebrews*, 319; Lane, *Hebrews 1–8*, 141.

The "heavenly gift" is a euphemism for salvation,[288] which the readers have "tasted." The Greek word for "tasted" is the same here and in v. 5 and is used metaphorically indicating "to eat or drink," thus experiencing something fully, not merely a superficial participation in something. There is no connotation in the word itself of tasting but not swallowing.[289] This can be seen from the usage in Heb 2:9 where Jesus "tasted" death for everyone, meaning he experienced the full force of physical death. This metaphorical rather than literal usage also precludes a reference here to the Lord's Supper, although Ellingworth thinks the meaning cannot be entirely excluded.[290] The third participial phrase describes those "who have shared in the Holy Spirit." The NIV translation renders the noun *metochous*, "partakers, sharers" with the verbal idea "shared." The author used this word previously in 3:1 and 3:14 to describe the close relationship that his readers share in the heavenly calling and in Christ. To become a "partaker" of the Holy Spirit indicates primarily "participation in" and denotes a close association with the Holy Spirit, implying reception of the Holy Spirit into one's life. It is very unlikely the phrase refers to the reception of spiritual gifts of the Holy Spirit, as Hughes suggested.[291]

The fourth phrase, found in v. 5, combines "the goodness of the word of God" and "the powers of the coming age" with the participle "tasting" (NIV "have tasted"), the same Greek word in the previous verse.[292] The use of the Greek particle *te,* "and," also serves to connect closely these two phrases.[293] Some connect "good" with both "word" and "powers,"[294] but the majority of commentators and virtually all translations rightly connect it only with "word." The adjective can be attributive: "the good word," or used in the predicate position: "the goodness of the word,"[295] as in the NIV. God is the source of this word, whose content includes the full revelation of God spoken and written.

---

[288] Attridge, *Hebrews*, 170, said that the descriptor "heavenly" denotes its source and goal. H. Hohenstein, "A Study of Hebrews 6:4–8," *Concordia Theological Monthly* 27 (June 1956): 439, identified the "heavenly gift" as the giving of the Holy Spirit in Acts, where several times "gift" appears with the giving of the Spirit (Acts 2:38; 8:20; 10:45; 11:17).

[289] Against Grudem, "Perseverance of the Saints," 145–47. "Taste" is used to describe total participation in salvation in 1 Pet 2:3. F. W. Farrar, *The Epistle to the Hebrews* (Cambridge: Cambridge University Press, 1883), 82, candidly exposed Calvin's misguided attempt to twist the meaning of this term: "'those who had as it were *tasted with their outward lips* the grace of God, and been irradiated *with some sparks* of His light.' This is not to explain Scripture, but to explain it away in favour of some preconceived doctrine. It is clear from 1 Peter ii: 3 that such a view is not tenable."

[290] Ellingworth, *Hebrews*, 320. See P. Teodorico, "Metafore nautiche in *Ebr* 2,1 e 6, 19," *RevistB* 6 (1958): 33–49, who attempts to develop this meaning.

[291] Hughes, *Hebrews*, 210.

[292] The shift from genitive to accusative with γεύομαι in vv. 4,5 is "subtle and suggestive" according to MHT 1:66, and "hardly accidental" according to *GGNT* 507, but neither elaborates further.

[293] Grässer, *An die Hebräer*, 1:352.

[294] Dods, "Hebrews," 297.

[295] Moule, *Idiom Book*, 36: "the direct object of the verb is virtually a substantival clause."

The reference may be to the gospel as God's revelation.[296] The second half of the clause speaks of the powers of the coming age, which has been interpreted generally in one of two ways. First, Jewish theology conceived of two ages: this age and the age of the Messiah. The New Testament authors, following Jesus' teaching, understood the new age as having dawned with Christ's first coming, and yet there is an eschatological sense awaiting final fulfillment in the eschaton. The powers of this "coming age" may be viewed in this sense. Alternatively, the author may have been thinking of the new age as beginning with Christ's second coming. Either way, the powers of the coming age are experienced now, although they await ultimate experience in the eschaton. These powers may include the miraculous events marking the early history of the church as described in Heb 2:4. Here as in Heb 1:1–3; 2:1–4; 3:7–19; 4:12–13 and in chap. 12, "word" and "power" are conjoined by the author.[297]

It is pertinent at this point to ask what is the spiritual nature and condition of those described in vv. 4–5. Later I discuss the participle translated "fall away" (lit. "falling away") in v. 6, but for now, it is a better course of action to seek to determine the spiritual nature of those referred to without recourse to v. 6. The obvious implication is that these four phrases describe someone who is a believer. It is difficult to imagine the author using such terminology to describe apparent or pseudo-believers, much less those who profess salvation, but who do not actually, in his mind, possess it. Appeal is often made to the fact that the author shifts from the first person in Heb 6:1–3 to the third person in Heb 6:4–6 to support the contention that those described here are merely professors or false believers. This is taken to indicate that the author is no longer thinking of his readers, but is referring to a group who, in the final analysis, are not genuine believers.[298] This linguistic observation, coupled with the negative statement in v. 6 that they have "fallen away," leads numerous interpreters to view the group as those who are not genuine believers. However, Gromacki correctly pointed out that there are no third-person pronouns in the Greek text of this passage, "but they serve as the translation for the articular participle (*tous phōtisthentas*, [lit.] 'the ones having been enlightened'). This switch indicates that the author wanted to present the warning in an impersonal, objective fashion rather than in a direct appeal as used before (2:3; 3:8,12)."[299]

The ablest defender of this approach in recent times is W. Grudem, who argued the terms alone are inconclusive as to whether the people referred to were genuinely converted, because "they speak of events that are experienced both

[296] See H. F. Weiss, *Der Brief an die Hebräer*, KEK 13 (Göttingen: Vandenhoeck & Ruprecht, 1991), 344–45; and Ellingworth, *Hebrews*, 321. The author's use of ῥῆμα and not λόγος carries no significance here since they can be used synonymously (see Attridge, *Hebrews*, 170).

[297] See comments on Heb 2:1–4.

[298] So Hewitt, *Hebrews*, 106.

[299] R. Gromacki, *Stand Bold in Grace: An Exposition of Hebrews* (Grand Rapids: Baker, 1984), 107.

by genuine Christians and by some people who participate in the fellowship of a church but are never really saved."[300] Grudem correctly recognized that until the mention of what he calls "apostasy" in v. 6, "there is nothing negative in the description: the terms all indicate positive events that are generally experienced by people who become Christians."[301] He argued that in spite of what is said about them in Heb 6:4–5, the group described possessed none of the signs of saving faith. This, he thinks, is made clear by what the author says in 7–12. Grudem does not think there is evidence to say that these were "false believers." His position is that their outward affiliation with the church meant that one could not tell their status "until they fell away."[302]

Grudem analyzes each of the descriptive phrases in Heb 6:4–5 to show them, individually and together, to be inconclusive as to whether they indicate genuine salvation. He acknowledges that "enlightened" is used sometimes in the New Testament in a manner that could speak of conversion, but he points out that at other times it has only the literal meaning of giving light or the metaphorical usage of learning in general. The word is used in Heb 10:32, but Grudem argues this does not prove the word means "heard and believed the gospel." Yet virtually every commentator notes that Heb 10:32 indicates the author was addressing his readers as believers. Grudem thinks that the Greek word *phōtizō* is not a technical term for believing the gospel. This is not in dispute. What is affirmed is that the word is on occasion used metaphorically in contexts in the New Testament that describe the conversion experience, and such is the case in Heb 6:4 and 10:32. Grudem recognizes McKnight's criticism of Nicole's article where Nicole takes a possible meaning for "enlightened" as something other than genuine conversion and then extrapolates that meaning in Heb 6:4. He accuses McKnight of the same thing when McKnight asserts that "enlightened" signified genuine conversion, but then he does not show why the word cannot mean merely "heard and understood the gospel." Grudem appears to miss the point that McKnight and many others make concerning the meaning of "enlightened" in context: the word is used metaphorically to describe a genuine believer. Grudem's appeal to the lexical definition

---

[300] Grudem, "Perseverance of the Saints," 139, 152.

[301] Ibid., 139. This statement violates Grudem's stated principle at the beginning of the article that one should not put theology before exegesis since he assumes that v. 6 refers to apostasy before he has done any exegetical work to make that determination. R. Nicole, whose argument on this subject Grudem is developing, likewise concedes that these statements otherwise apply to Christians, yet he attempts to show that none of them individually nor all jointly necessarily apply to Christians ("Some Comments on Hebrews 6:4–6 and the Doctrine of the Perseverance of God with the Saints," in *Current Issues in Biblical and Patristic Interpretation* [Grand Rapids: Eerdmans, 1975], 360). His evidence that the six statements need not refer to saved people is found on pp. 360–61.

[302] Ibid., 140. Grudem seems to argue that since these terms "might" or "could" mean something other than their clear and obvious meaning in Heb 6:4–6, then they must, contextually, mean that.

of *phōtizō,* for which no meaning of "be converted" is listed, is vitiated by his own statement three pages later that "Greek lexicons do not generally define words with reference to unique meanings in each New Testament author."[303] Context contributes to the meaning of a given word, and the overall context of Heb 6:4–5, even including v. 6, points to a meaning of genuine belief.

Grudem then attempts to show that "tasting" does not mean "fully experienced." He appeals to Josephus' *Jewish War* (2.158) where the Essenes are said to attract those who "have once tasted" their philosophy. Since Josephus means that they had not made the philosophy their own, one cannot claim in Heb 6:4 that the word means the people referenced there had a genuine saving experience. In fact, Grudem claims the people did have "a genuine experience of the heavenly gift and the word of God and the powers of the age to come," but, as he says, this is simply not the point. "The question is whether they had a *saving* experience of these things."[304] Grudem acknowledged that those who "tasted the heavenly gift" had some experience of the power of the Holy Spirit, but such experiences "do not themselves indicate salvation."[305]

Turning to the statement "partakers of the Holy Spirit," Grudem acknowledges that the word *metochos* as used in Heb 3:14 refers to a saving experience, but then argues that the word can mean a "loose association." He argues that regeneration is not the only way people "partake" of the Holy Spirit, and thus we cannot assume that is the sense intended in Heb 6:5. The phrase could simply mean they were partakers of some of the benefits that the Holy Spirit gives.[306]

In this fashion, Grudem whittles every phrase in Heb 6:4–5 to the point that he argues they cannot be used definitively to refer to genuine salvation. He does acknowledge based on the terms alone that a reasonable argument for genuine believers can be made. But he then concludes that the terms can be used "to describe either Christians or non-Christians," and thus "our decision must be that *the terms by themselves are inconclusive*."[307] Grudem goes on to argue against a reference to genuine believers based on the context of Heb 6:7–12.

Besides prematurely determining that the falling away in v. 6 refers to "apostasy" before he does any exegetical spadework, Grudem draws other disconcerting conclusions when he comments in reference to the group described in Heb 6:4–5, "They have probably had answers to prayer in their own lives and felt the power of the Holy Spirit at work, perhaps even using some spiritual gifts."[308] Here we have unsaved people receiving answers to their prayers, ex-

---

303 Grudem, "Perseverance of the Saints," 145.

304 Ibid., 146.

305 Ibid.

306 Ibid., 148.

307 Ibid., 152. Grudem has been rightly criticized (R. Gleason, "The Old Testament Background of the Warning in Hebrews 6:4–8," *Bib* 155, no. 617, [1998]: 63) for giving precedence to other NT authors over that of the author of the epistle and his own usage of terms.

308 Grudem, "Perseverance of the Saints," 153.

periencing the work of the Holy Spirit (other than regeneration of course), and possibly using spiritual gifts. Exactly how or where this is affirmed anywhere else in the New Testament, Grudem does not say. Precisely how an unsaved person can possess a spiritual gift is a mystery left unexplained. Grudem's treatment of Heb 6:4–6 illustrates the tendentious nature of much of the Calvinistic exegesis of this passage.

The sheer force of the descriptive phrases militates against such an interpretation. How can it be conceivable that such descriptive phrases as enlightenment, experience of the heavenly gift of salvation, full sharing in the Holy Spirit, sharing in the Word of God and the powers of the coming age, do not have believers as their referent? Each of these statements finds their counterparts scattered throughout the New Testament, and when used in the same context as here, they refer to those who are genuine believers. Grudem's affirmation that the group's outward affiliation with the church made it impossible to determine their status until they "fell away" is a fact not in dispute. No matter one's theological position on this passage, all would affirm such a statement. Unsaved people can and do participate in the church; the wheat and the tares grow together. At issue is whether unsaved people can be so described *by an author who thinks or knows them to be unsaved.* The issue of determining their status is not the point *for the author*. By the descriptive language he chooses, he indicates their status as believers. Had the author wanted to convey their status as unbelievers, he could have done so. There is no direct statement that those described in Heb 6:4–6 were unbelievers. If the author is referring to unsaved people, this is the only place in the New Testament where such language can be said to be used in this fashion.

There is a growing consensus crossing the Calvinist/Arminian divide that the language of Heb 6:4–6 describes genuine believers.[309] David Armistead stated, "if one follows the standard exegetical methodology of looking first at the pericope itself, honesty demands that Heb 6:4–8 speaks of a true Christian."[310] The general approach of those who suggest the reference in Heb 6:4–6 is to apparent believers is to point out these descriptive terms "normally refer to Christians" but "might" or "could" mean something other than their clear and

[309] A point made and supported by evidence in Von Kamecke's "Implications," 91. The view that Christians are in view in Heb 6:4–6 is at least as old as *The Shepherd of Hermas* and was not seriously challenged until Calvin. M. Erickson, a moderate Calvinist, concluded: "The vividness of the description, and particularly the statement 'who have shared in the Holy Spirit,' argues forcefully against denying that the people in view are (at least for a time) regenerate" (Erickson, *Christian Theology*, 2nd ed. [Grand Rapids: Baker, 1998], 1004). R. Peterson, "Apostasy," *Presbyterion* 19.1 (1993): 21, "These verses seem to describe believers; the burden of proof lies with someone claiming they do not." A. Mugridge, "Warnings in the Epistle to the Hebrews," *RTR* 46, no. 3 (1987): 77, stated in reference to those described in Heb 6:4–6: "it becomes clear that the author is describing genuine believers."

[310] D. Armistead, "The 'Believer' Who Falls Away: Heb 6:4–8 and the Perseverance of the Saints," *Stulos Theological Journal* 4.2 (1996): 144.

obvious meaning. What is it that drives them to this conclusion? From a Calvinistic perspective, it is the interpretation of falling away as apostasy. Since, by definition, Calvinists correctly affirm the New Testament doctrine of the eternal security of believers, whatever "fall away" means in Heb 6:6, it cannot mean apostasy that results in loss of salvation. Since Calvinists usually argue for apostasy in Heb 6:6, they are forced theologically into a corner as to the spiritual condition of those described in Heb 6:4–5: they must be unsaved.

Taken together, these descriptive clauses in Heb 6:4–6 appear to describe genuine believers.[311] Delitzsch asks: "[H]ow can we doubt for a moment that it is the truly regenerate whom he is here describing?"[312] Both Heb 2:1–4 and 3:7–4:13 are lengthy expressions of concern the author has for his readers, yet it is clear in both of these passages that he affirms his readers as believers. Furthermore, the immediate context beginning with 5:11–14 likewise refers to the readers as genuine believers, although spiritually immature believers. There is no evidence the author ever addresses anyone in the epistle other than those whom he considers to be believers whom he alternatively instructs, warns, and encourages. Hebrews 10:35 makes it explicit the audience is composed of genuine Christians.

History of Interpretation of Hebrews 6:4–6. At this point, it is important to survey the history of interpretation of this passage including the spiritual condition of those described in Heb 6:4–6.[313] On the nature of the danger threatening the community, there have been four main proposals: (1) post-baptismal sins, (2) sins requiring extreme discipline, (3) high-handed apostasy, and 4) the unpardonable sin or the "sin unto death."[314]

The ante-Nicene fathers were concerned with two things in relation to this passage: the rigorist debate and the rebaptism debate. These two issues sometimes intertwined. As far as the fathers were concerned, it is clear they unanimously interpreted the passage as referring to Christians.[315] Tertullian's statement: "People are not Christians unless they persevere to the end"[316] is not an affirmation that one can lose salvation, but merely affirms those who persevere is an indication they are genuine believers. The post-Nicene fathers generally follow this lead, but there are exceptions. It would appear the earliest interpretation of Heb 6:4–6 as describing unbelievers is in Basil and Gregory

[311] G. Borchert, *Assurance and Warning* (Nashville: Broadman, 1987), 172, gives six arguments that the reference is to believers.

[312] Delitzsch, *Hebrews*, 1:287.

[313] Koester, *Hebrews*, 19–63, covers some of this material in his general survey of the history of interpretation of the entire epistle. The best specific survey of the history of interpretation of Heb 6:4–6 is Von Kamecke, "Implications," 18–114. Cf. Thomas, *Case for Mixed-Audience*, 25–96.

[314] Thomas, *Case for Mixed-Audience*, 140.

[315] See *Shepherd of Hermas*, Commandment 4.3; Tertullian, *On Modesty*, 20 (*ANF* 4.97); and Clement of Alexandria, *Stromateis* ii.13, who in speaking on Heb 10:26, said God grants to those who are "in faith," meaning Christians, "a second repentance," if they fall into sin. See the discussion in Koester, *Hebrews*, 23–24.

[316] Tertullian, *On Prescription Against Heretics*, 3 (*ANF* 3.244).

of Nyssa.[317] Theognostus of Alexandria affirmed the rigorist position when he said in reference to Heb 6:4, "for those who have tasted of the heavenly gift, and been made perfect, there remains no plea or prayer for pardon."[318] Steve Harmon correctly pointed out the main issue for the fathers was the question of whether it was possible for those who had fallen into sin after baptism to repent and be forgiven. If they repent, must they be rebaptized? Hebrews 6:4–6 was the key passage from the middle of the third century AD onward in the controversy over post-baptismal sin.[319] Chrysostom asserted of Hebrews 6 that repentance is possible, but rebaptism is not, basing this on the statement that it is "impossible" because they would be "crucifying afresh" Jesus by reentering the baptismal waters since the believer can be crucified and buried with Christ only once in baptism.[320] Ambrose understood Heb 6:4–6 to be a reference to baptism.[321] Jerome argued the possibility of a Christian sinning after baptism because if this were not possible, it would not be possible for the writer of Hebrews to speak of falling away in 6:6.[322] Theodoret of Cyrus stated unequivocally: "It is out of the question, he is saying, for those who have approached all-holy baptism, shared in the grace of the divine Spirit and received the type of eternal goods to make their approach again and be granted another baptism."[323] John of Damascus likewise took Heb 6:4–6 to indicate no rebaptism was permitted.[324]

Without commenting on the validity of the fathers' interpretation of Heb 6:4–6, two things appear to be clear. First, as Harmon stated in summarizing the early church fathers' view of Heb 6:4–6: "The passage is not so much about the loss of salvation or the impossibility of forgiveness after straying from the faith as it is about the impossibility of doing again that which Christ has already done by virtue of the believer's union with Christ's crucifixion and resurrection in baptism."[325] The church fathers who speak about this subject in direct reference to Heb 6:4–6 make it clear they believe the passage describes believers.[326] This is a significant point in the quest to determine the spiritual nature of those discussed in Heb 6:4–6.

---

[317] Basil, *On the Holy Spirit*, 24.56 (*NPNF*[2] 8:36); Gregory of Nyssa, *On Virginity*, 22 (*NPNF*[2] 5:367), quoting Heb 6:8 "whose end is to be burned," refers to the unsaved.

[318] Theognostos of Alexandria, *From His Seven Books of Hypotheses or Outlines*, 3 (*ANF* 6:156).

[319] S. Harmon, "Hebrews in Patristic Study," *RevExp* 102 (2005), 225. Cf. E. M. Heen and P. D. W. Krey, eds., *Hebrews*, ACCS 10 (Downers Grove: InterVarsity, 2005), 83. For an excellent discussion of how the church fathers treated this question, see Hughes, *Hebrews*, 212–19.

[320] Chrysostom, *Homilies on Hebrews*, 9.

[321] Ambrose, *Concerning Repentance*, 2.2.7–8 (*NPNF*[2] 10:345–46).

[322] Jerome, *Against Jovinius*, 2.3 (*NPNF*[2] 6:389).

[323] Theodoret of Cyrus, *Interpretation of Hebrews* 6, in Heen and Krey, eds., *Hebrews*, 84.

[324] John of Damascus, *Exposition of the Orthodox Faith*, 9 (*NPNF*[2] 9:77).

[325] S. Harmon, "Hebrews in Patristic Study," 227. Von Kamecke concurred, "Implications," 30. In modern times, this viewpoint of Heb 6:4–6 has been advocated by P. E. Hughes, "Hebrews 6:4–6 and the Peril of Apostasy," *WTJ* 35 (1972–73): 151–53.

[326] Von Kamecke, "Implications," 31.

In the 16th century, the Catholic Council of Trent (1545–63) concluded that salvation could be lost by one of two means: unbelief or mortal sin. Calvin took the position in his *Institutes* that those in Heb 6:6 were unsaved, a position he reiterated in his Hebrews commentary.[327] He taught that those in Heb 6:4–6 were recipients of God's grace in ways short of regeneration, yet even their apostasy is predestined.[328] He posited a twofold "falling away": one general, in the sense that every sin in the life of a believer is a "falling away": and the other particular, which is apostasy understood as a renunciation of Christ. This latter apostasy is, according to Calvin, the sin of blasphemy against the Holy Spirit. Calvin answered the question of why the author, in addressing believers, should speak about apostasy: "[T]he danger was pointed out by him in time, that they might be on their guard." In answer to the question how those who have "made such progress afterwards fall away?" Calvin prefaced his answer by affirming God calls none effectually but the elect, the elect are beyond the danger of falling away, and only the elect are regenerated. He then stated:

> But I cannot admit that all this is any reason why he should not grant the reprobate some taste of his grace, why he should not irradiate their minds with some sparks of his light, why he should not give them some perception of his goodness, and in some sort engrave his word on their hearts. . . . There is therefore some knowledge even in the reprobate, which afterwards vanishes away, either because it did not strike roots sufficiently deep, or because it withers, being choked up.[329]

Calvin thus identified those in Heb 6:4–6 as unbelievers, but who had strong Christian influence and involvement within the church.[330] Farrar realized Calvin was "far too good a scholar" to defend the erroneous conditional translation

[327] *Institutes,* 3.3.21. Calvin, *Hebrews*, 75: "If any one asks why the Apostle makes mention here of such apostasy while he is addressing believers, who were far off from a perfidy so heinous; to this I answer, that the danger was pointed out by him in time, that they might be on their guard. And this ought to be observed; for when we turn aside from the right way, we not only excuse to others our vices, but we also impose on ourselves. Satan stealthily creeps in on us, and by degrees allures us by clandestine arts, so that when we go astray we know not that we are going astray. Thus gradually we slide, until at length we rush headlong into ruin. We may observe this daily in many. Therefore the Apostle does not without reason forewarn all the disciples of Christ to beware in time; for a continued torpor commonly ends in lethargy, which is followed by alienation of mind."

[328] Calvin, *Hebrews*, 75–76. B. Fanning critiques Calvin's speculation at this point, noting there is nothing in Heb 6:4–5 to suggest a description of "an inward, genuine, but preliminary, work of God that he subsequently abandons because they are nonelect" (Fanning, "Classical Reformed Response," in *Four Views on the Warning Passages in Hebrews*, ed. H. Bateman [Grand Rapids: Kregel, 2007], 137).

[329] Ibid.,138.

[330] Calvin, *Institutes*, 1:555. This position has been argued recently by Thomas, *Case for Mixed-Audience*, 143.

"if they fall away," but he also correctly noted Calvin's view of Heb 6:6 that those who "fall away" are unregenerate in the sense of being false converts or half converts is "untenable."[331]

In the seventeenth century, William Gouge suggested that Heb 6:4–6 referred to apostates who themselves professed the characteristics in Heb 6:4–5, and it was from this state of their profession that they fell into apostasy.[332] Shortly afterward, John Owen made a distinction between inward, genuine repentance and outward, false repentance. He viewed the group described in Heb 6:4–6 in the latter category. Since Owen, the vast majority of reformed commentators have argued the common theme that Heb 6:4–6 describes only apparent believers who are, in fact, not Christians.[333]

Some of the early seventeenth century General Baptists in England such as Thomas Helwys and John Smyth taught the possibility of apostasy on the part of believers, but later in the same century their creeds make no reference to apostasy.[334] In the United States in the eighteenth and nineteenth centuries, Freewill Baptists and General Baptists believed in the possibility of apostasy. However, the majority of Baptists have affirmed the doctrine of perseverance, as can be gleaned from any review of their confessions of faith.[335]

The Spiritual Condition of Those Who "Fall Away." We are now prepared to turn our attention to the question of the spiritual condition of those described in Heb 6:4–6. The position that the group described in Heb 6:4–6 are believers traces back to the earliest church fathers as we have seen. Luther also took this position, as did Arminius.[336] John Wesley was clear on the matter: "Must not every unprejudiced person see, the expressions here used are so strong and clear, that they cannot, without gross and palpable wrestling, be understood of any but true believers?"[337] He further commented: "On this authority, I believe a saint may fall away; that one who is holy or righteous in

---

[331] F. W. Farrar, *Hebrews*, 107.

[332] W. Gouge, *A Learned and Very Useful Commentary on the Whole Epistle to the Hebrews* (London: Joshua Kirton, 1665), 401.

[333] E.g., R. Nicole, "Some Comments," and Wayne Grudem, "Perseverance of the Saints." This article by Grudem is probably the most extensive argument for this position (see esp. pp. 139–50). He provides a helpful listing of those who argue Heb 6:4–6 refers to those unsaved (p. 139, footnote 13). Others arguing this viewpoint include Carson, "Reflections on Christian Assurance," *WTJ* 54 (1992): 19. R. Peterson, "Apostasy," 22–23, argues for a mixed audience based on 6:7–8; J. MacArthur, *Hebrews* (Chicago: Moody, 1983), xii–xiii, likewise argues for a mixed audience; and D. Mathewson, "Reading Hebrews 6:4–6 in Light of the Old Testament," *WTJ* 61.2 (1999): 209–25.

[334] J. L. Garrett, *Systematic Theology* (Grand Rapids: Eerdmans, 1990), 2:424.

[335] See the survey in ibid., 425–26.

[336] Luther, *LW* 29:182; J. Arminius, *A Letter on the Sin Against the Holy Spirit*, in *WJA* 2:511–38. Arminius takes Heb 6:6 to be an example of blasphemy against the Holy Spirit as did Calvin (*WJA* 2:512–13).

[337] J. Wesley, "Predestination Calmly Considered," in *The Complete Works of John Wesley* (Peabody, MA: Hendrickson, 1984), 10:248.

the judgment of God himself may nevertheless so fall from God as to perish everlastingly."[338] The majority of contemporary commentators, even including some Calvinists, affirm that the group described in Heb 6:4–6 are believers.[339] Among Calvinists who see Heb 6:4–6 as referring to believers is Yeager, who chides those who desire to reduce the language to a description of something less than genuine conversion because it places them at odds with other doctrines in the Calvinist system. Yeager wrote: "This yields the conclusion that a sinner who was almost saved, but who resisted the call of the Holy Spirit will never again be able to repent. It seems not to occur to these people that this view proves more than they wish it to prove, in that it denies 'effectual call' and 'irresistible grace' and the statement of Phil. 1:6."[340]

If Heb 6:4–6 refers to mere professors who do not genuinely share in salvation, several questions come to mind. Why would such mere professors be warned of apostasy? One cannot apostatize from something never possessed in the first place. Another problem with this approach is why would the author exhort non-Christians to press on to maturity as he does in Heb 6:1? The obvious thing to do would be for the author to exhort those whom he considered unconverted to be converted.[341] Sauer's response to this problem is inadequate: "warning them of apostasy and pressing upon them the need to persevere, and urging them to examine themselves to see whether or not they are in the faith, is the writers way of tactfully exhorting them to faith should any be unconverted."[342] However, the author does not urge his readers to examine themselves to see whether or not they are saved; rather, he assumes

---

[338] Ibid., 340.

[339] E.g., Ellingworth, *Hebrews*, 46; W. Lane, *Hebrews: A Call to Commitment* (Vancouver, BC: Regents College Publishing, 2004), 90; G. Cockerill, *Hebrews: A Bible Commentary in the Wesleyan Tradition* (Indianapolis, IN: Wesleyan Publishing House, 1999), 137; S. McKnight, "The Warning Passages of Hebrews: A Formal Analysis and Theological Conclusions," *TJ* 13 NS (1992): 24–25; I. H. Marshall, *Kept by the Power of God* (Minneapolis: Bethany Fellowship, 1969), 142; F. Matera, "Moral Exhortation: The Relation between Moral Exhortation and Doctrinal Exposition in the Letter to the Hebrews," *TJT* 10.2 (1994):181; M. Eaton, *No Condemnation: A New Theology of Assurance* (Downers Grove: InterVarsity, 1995), 215; T. K. Oberholtzer, "The Warning Passages in Hebrews—Part 3: The Thorn-infested Ground in Hebrews 6:4–12," *BSac* 145 (1988): 319; Gleason, "The Old Testament Background," 66, 91; Hewitt, *Hebrews*, 108; W. Manson, *Hebrews: An Historical and Theological Reconsideration* (London: Hodder & Stoughton, 1951), 63–64; M. Emmrich, "Hebrews 6:4–6—Again! (A Pneumatological Inquiry)," *WTJ* 65 (2003): 83–95; and Borchert, *Assurance and Warning*, 172. W. Sailer, "Hebrews Six: An Irony or a Continuing Embarrassment," *EvJ* 3 (1985): 79–88, examines the thesis of R. F. White, who argued the warning is ironic in nature because the readers are warned to avoid something they cannot actually experience. A. Snyman, "Hebrews 6:4–6: From a Semiotic Discourse Perspective," in *Discourse Analysis and the New Testament* (Sheffield: Sheffield Academic Press, 1999), 365–66, takes a similar approach, viewing the impossibility of repentance as an instance of hyperbole.

[340] R. Yeager, *The Renaissance New Testament* (Gretna, LA: Pelican, 1985), 16:202. Yeager himself takes the Loss of Rewards view on the passage.

[341] So Barnes, *Notes, Explanatory and Practical, on the Epistle to the Hebrews* (New York: Harper & Brothers Publishers, 1861), 131.

[342] Sauer, "Critical and Exegetical Reexamination," 270.

throughout the epistle that they are saved. As to "tactfully exhorting them to faith," the writer displays his willingness to speak with candor and force in the many strong exhortations and warnings found in the epistle. Alford asks, how is it any more difficult to renew to repentance those spoken of in Heb 6:4–6 than any other unsaved church member or unbeliever?[343] All things considered, based on the terms used as well as the immediate and remote context, it seems best to interpret the passage as referring to genuine believers.

From this we turn to an examination of the meaning of the participle *parapesontas* in v. 6 translated "fall away" (lit. "falling away"). It is connected to the previous participles by *kai*, which can be taken in an adversative sense, "and yet," with the sense of "despite all the previous blessings they received, yet they fell away."[344] The word occurs only here in the New Testament and thus merits careful study of its cognates within Hebrews, the New Testament, as well as occurrences and usage outside the New Testament. Liddell and Scott assign the following meanings to *parapiptō* in Classical Greek: "to fall beside . . . to fall in one's way." When followed by the genitive of the object from which one had fallen, they assign the meaning "to fall aside" or "away from."[345] Hebrews 6:6 does not contain any genitive of the object such as "Christ" or "the faith" defining that from which they fell away.[346] The major Greek lexicon defines *parapiptō* as "to fall beside, go astray, miss, fall away, commit apostasy."[347] Bauder defines it as "to fall beside, befall, go astray, err."[348] Michaelis added the senses of "to be led past, to go astray, to be mistaken."[349] Louw and Nida give the meaning "to abandon a former relationship or association, or to dissociate . . . to fall away, to forsake, to turn away." They consider *ekpiptō* (Gal 5:4), *apostrephomai* (Heb 12:25), and *aphistēmi* (Heb 3:12) to be in the same semantic domain.[350] Balz and Schneider list the meanings as "miss, fall away, fall," and state, "Hebrews has in mind here a fundamental and conscious rejection of the Church."[351]

There are eight occurrences of *parapiptō* in the LXX: once in Esther, five times in Ezekiel, and two in the Apocrypha: Wisdom 6:9 and 12:2.[352] From the fifth century to the third century BC, there are 106 occurrences of *parapiptō* in

---

343 Alford, "Hebrews," 113.

344 BDF 227; cf. Sauer, "A Critical and Exegetical Reexamination," 233.

345 LSJ 601.

346 NT examples where the genitive of the object occurs with terms cognate or synonymous with παραπίπτω include Gal 5:4; 1 Tim 4:1; Heb 3:12; 2 Pet 3:17; and Rev 2:5. See discussion in H. Harless, "Fallen Away or Fallen Down? The Meaning of Hebrews 6:1–9," *CTSJ* 9.1 (2003): 11.

347 BDAG 770; cf. MM 488–89.

348 W. Bauder, *NIDNTT* 1:608.

349 W. Michaelis, "παραπίπτω," *TDNT* 6:170.

350 L&N 449.

351 *EDNT* 3:33.

352 E. Hatch and H. A. Redpath, *A Concordance to the Septuagint and the Other Greek Versions of the Old Testament*, (Grand Rapids: Baker, 1984), 2:1063.

extra-biblical Greek. Thirty-five of these occur in medical, zoological, astronomical and geometric contexts. Of the remaining uses, 26.8% mean "to occur or befall"; 8.5% mean "a chance or unexpected occurrence;" 18.3% mean "opportunity" (with *kairos*); 16.9% mean "to fall beside or alongside" and "to fall or fall in"; 11.3% mean "to gain entrance"; 9.9% mean "to miss or fail"; 4.2% mean "to make a mistake"; 2.8% mean "to transgress"; and 1.3% mean "to be lost" (in reference to small quantities of grain).[353]

From the Koine Greek period, roughly second century BC through the first century AD, there are 57 instances of *parapiptō*, one third with the meaning "to fall beside or alongside; to fall or fall in; to fall upon." Clement of Rome used it twice in the sense of "to sin," and Plutarch used it in this sense once. Another third of the total usages have the meaning "to occur, to occur by chance," and "opportunity." The sense of "to be lost" occurs once.[354] Moulton and Milligan list examples of usage including the meaning of "to fall into," the breaking of contractual terms, and something being lost.[355] In the New Testament, the nominal form *paraptōma* always denotes "sin" but never "apostasy."[356]

Parapiptō is used in the general sense of "to sin" five times in Ezekiel (14:13; 15:8; 18:24; 20:27; 22:4). With the exception of Ezek 22:4, *parapiptō* is the equivalent for the Hebrew *maʿal*, which means "to act unfaithfully." In fact, *parapiptō* is used in Ezek 14:13 and 18:24 in conjunction with the most common Hebrew verb meaning "to sin," *ḥāṭāʾ*. In none of these examples does *parapiptō* indicate apostasy it defined as a complete turning away from God.[357]

From this evidence it seems clear that linguistically there is little if any support for the meaning of apostasy. The word was not used in this sense in Classical Greek, the LXX, or Koine Greek. Given these facts concerning the usage of *parapiptō*, one must wonder why a few lexicographers and many commentators feel compelled to translate or interpret the participle in Heb 6:6 as meaning "apostasy?"[358] There are two possible answers to this question, both of

---

353 I am indebted to the excellent unpublished work on this subject by H. Harless using the *The Thesaurus Linguae Graecae* and the Duke Databank of Documentary Papyri.

354 Ibid.

355 MM 488–89.

356 W. Michaelis, "παράπτωμα," *TDNT* 6:171–72.

357 Hohenstein, "A Study of Hebrews 6:4–8," 537, correctly stated that the verb παραπίπτω does not have the technical meaning of "apostasy." However, he thought that the context necessitated interpreting the word as meaning "apostasy." Bruce, *Hebrews*, 147–48, likewise argued the reference to "apostasy" is not drawn from the root meaning of the word but rather its context. Gleason, "The Old Testament Background," 81, pointed out the verb itself does not mean "apostasy."

358 E.g., W. Bauder, *NIDNTT* 1:610–11, who assigns the figurative sense to πίπτω and its cognates, peculiar to the NT, of "to lose salvation, and so, to go to eternal destruction," a sense he says is found "in the Gospels, Paul, Heb, and Rev." While he mentions Heb 3:17 and 4:11 as referring to apostasy, strangely there is no reference at all to Heb 6:6. Likewise, Ellingworth, *Hebrews*, 322, believes that it is not the word παραπεσόντας itself but the context of Heb 6:6 that

which likely coalesce in the thinking of many. They are giving a theological interpretation to the word based more on an interpretation of the surrounding context of Hebrews 6 and less on lexicography. The reasoning is simple. It is impossible to renew those described in Heb 6:4–6 to repentance because "they are crucifying the Son of God all over again and subjecting him to public disgrace." Therefore, one could logically infer that the author means to express a falling away from Christ or the gospel that is so serious as to preclude any possibility of repentance and reclamation. In traditional theological language, this would be apostasy. The second answer is that they are operating from a preconceived theological notion of the meaning of the word in Heb 6:6. This preconception is evidenced on the Arminian side as the belief that one can be truly saved and yet through apostasy lose that salvation. On the Calvinist side, the preconception is that one who is truly saved cannot lose their salvation; therefore, this must be referring to an apostasy that only apparent believers can commit.

Take, for example, the defense of the Arminian position on Heb 6:6 by Scot McKnight and the defense of the Calvinistic position by Nicole and Grudem. McKnight correctly identifies the group described in 6:4–5 as believers. He studied the five warning passages together and the immediate context of 6:6 and concluded, based on the severity of the language, that apostasy must be in view. He assumed the meaning of *parapiptō* as "apostasy" before he ever treated the word itself. In fact, a weakness of his article is that he never actually examined the word itself and its usage outside the New Testament with the exception of calling attention to its uses in the LXX. In a similar fashion, Nicole and Grudem concluded that the context of the entire book as well as the immediate context of Heb 6:6 indicate *parapiptō* means "apostasy" of those who were never genuine believers in the first place. Grudem refers to their sin as "apostasy," then says that to translate the verb by "to commit apostasy" is "a bit too specific" for the Greek word. He references the translations in the NASB and the NIV, which translate, correctly I might add, with the words "fall away." He then, surprisingly, makes this statement: "the context does indicate that the falling away is so serious it could be rightly called 'apostasy.'"[359] Such a conclusion is unwarranted given the linguistic evidence. Grudem and Nicole likewise fail to do a word study of *parapiptō* to support their contention.

Based on the aforementioned evidence, if *parapiptō* means to apostatize in the conventional theological understanding of that word, *it is the singular*

"virtually requires a reference to apostasy here." He takes the participle παραπεσόντας, not as conditional, but as concessive by implication. Likewise, I. Salevao, *Legitimation*, 287, concludes that the term is justifiably taken to mean "apostasy" because of "the use of the word in the LXX, the nature and tenor of the warning passages in Hebrews, and the metaphors associated with the warning passages."

[359] Grudem, "Perseverance of the Saints," 153. Nicole, "Some Comments," 362–63, says the sin of the apostates is blasphemy and examples Judas.

exception of the known uses of the word. In the LXX, *parapiptō* is used to translate several different Hebrew words, the most frequent of which is *maʿal.* The most common usage is that of "transgressing" against the Lord, though never in the sense of irremediable apostasy. A good example is Ezek 20:27, where the LXX uses *parepeson* (from *parapiptō*) in the sense of "transgress" against the Lord by profaning the Sabbath and by idolatry.

The meaning of *parapiptō* must be considered against the background of the use earlier in the book of the cognate form *piptō,* meaning "to fall." In Heb 4:11, the author warned of the necessity to be diligent to enter the rest, lest anyone "fall" (*piptō*). Semantically there is a connection between 6:6 and 4:11 with 3:12, where the author speaks of someone who "turns away from the living God." In 3:12 the verb is *apostēnai,* but the usage indicates the two verbs are conceptually related.[360] The same Hebrew word, *maʿal,* often translated in the LXX by *parapiptō*, is translated with *aphistēmi* (*apostēnai*) in 2 Chr 26:18, where the sin is not apostasy. The verb *parapiptō* appears interchangeable with *apostēnai* in 2 Chr 26:18; 28:19; 29:6; and 30:7.[361] The upshot of all this is the conclusion that *parapiptō* is not the most appropriate word to express a complete renunciation of Christ. Its use in Heb 6:6 does not describe a fall that is a denial of Christ.

The opinion is often argued that Hebrews addressed a mixed audience of believers and non-believers based on the alternating warnings and encouragements where the warnings are addressed to the unsaved who are part of the church, without the author knowing exactly who they are, and the encouragements addressed to the believers.

We have already seen how difficult this is to sustain in the light of the epistle itself. If the meaning of Heb 6:4–6 were intended by the author to address unsaved people, then two things seem absent from the picture: a clear tone of uncertainty with respect to their spiritual condition, and clear statements of their need of genuine conversion. Instead of either of these, what we find are clear statements from the author encouraging the readers in what God has already done for them in securing their salvation (3:6,14; 5:9; 4:16; 6:18; 7:25; 9:12,15; 10:14,19,23,35). The traditional theory of the purpose of Hebrews, the relapse theory, has come under scrutiny in more recent years and has been increasingly questioned as an accurate reflection of the author's purpose. The approach to the purpose of Hebrews taken in this work likewise rejects the relapse theory (see the Introduction). If the problem of the readers was not a rejection of Christ and an attempted return to Judaism, then the appeal to such in defining Heb 6:6 as apostasy is problematic.[362] For example, Sauer makes the following comment:

---

[360] Lane, *Hebrews 1–8*, 142.

[361] Hohenstein, "A Study of Hebrews 6:4–8," 537.

[362] See Delitzsch, *Hebrews* 1.288, as an example of one who accepts the relapse theory as informing the definition of apostasy given to παραπεσόντας in Heb 6:6.

> Their sin is a clearly resolved moral and intellectual denunciation of a previously held profession of faith. Therefore, while *parapesontas* only alludes to a relapse back into Judaism, it is a direct reference to an intentional falling away from, and a willful rejection of, the previously known and professed truth of the gospel which had been so clearly disclosed and so abundantly verified for them.[363]

However, as we have seen, there is nothing in the word itself nor in the immediate or remote context that warrants such a conclusion.

We are now prepared to move to the next phase of our investigation, namely, the meaning of "It is impossible . . . to be brought back to repentance, because to their loss they are crucifying the Son of God all over again and subjecting him to public disgrace." As we have seen, the Greek text sandwiches a considerable amount of material between the statement "it is impossible" in v. 4 and the phrase "to be brought back to repentance" in v. 6. The use of *adunaton,* "impossible" is probably emphatic by word order, being placed first in the sentence. The subject of the infinitive "to renew" is unstated, raising the question, "impossible for whom?" Some interpret the sense here to mean it is impossible for men to renew them to repentance, but not for God to do so.[364] Most, however, take this as a reference to actual impossibility, and this is supported by the other three occurrences of *adunaton*, in Hebrews, which are unambiguous in their meaning of absolute impossibility (6:18; 10:4; 11:6).[365] Contextually, it is impossible to renew them because God himself won't permit it (v. 3). The word "again" in Greek is added for emphasis.[366]

The object of "renew" is "repentance." If, as many argue, the group described in Heb 6:4–6 are not genuine believers, how is it possible for them to be "renewed" to repentance? They would never have repented the first time.[367] If they cannot be "renewed" to repentance, implicit in the use of "renew" is the fact of previous repentance. If they had repented (6:1), then they are genuine believers; and if genuine believers, then they cannot be mere professors. Nicole attempted to blunt the force of this problem by suggesting, as did William Gouge and John Owen, that what is in view here is outward repentance, and

[363] Sauer, "Critical and Exegetical Reexamination," 237.

[364] So Bruce, *Hebrews*, 144.

[365] The adjective ἀδύνατον always appears passively in Hebrews with the meaning "impossible." See O. Betz, "might," *NIDNTT* 2:606.

[366] Moffatt, *Hebrews*, 79.

[367] The significance of the Greek πάλιν supports this interpretation. Examples of those who take the initial repentance in Heb 6:6 as false repentance include A. W. Pink, *An Exposition of Hebrews* (Grand Rapids: Baker, 1968), 294; and Hughes, *Hebrews*, 207. Nicole is candid enough to admit that such a view is not "entirely free of difficulty" ("Some Comments," 361). Calvinist interpreters generally take the repentance here to be spurious because the doctrinal system calls for repentance to be the result of regeneration; e.g., R. Dabney, *Lectures in Systematic Theology* (Austin: Shepperson & Graves, 1871; repr., Grand Rapids: Zondervan, 1972), 655.

not inward repentance, which is the genuine fruit of regeneration.[368] One could also query if repentance initially was spurious, why would it be desirable to renew anyone to that kind of repentance? It will likewise not do to argue that the repentance was real but ineffective because it was not accompanied by faith.[369] In fact, according to Heb 6:1, the author mentions repentance and faith as the first two fundamentals of Christian doctrine, and the clear implication is that he viewed these as being true of his readers, including the group described in Heb 6:4–6. Repentance is often associated with believers, not just unbelievers (2 Cor 7:10; 12:21; 2 Tim 2:25; Rev 2:5,16).[370] It is "repentance" to which they cannot be restored, not salvation.

Two participial clauses follow the statement "to renew them to repentance," expressing the cause or reason why there can be no renewal to repentance: "crucifying" and "exposing."[371] Some debate exists over the meaning of "crucifying." The compound verb bears the prefix *ana-*, which would normally be interpreted "again." A few, however, take it to mean "up" with the focus on Jesus being crucified "up on" the cross.[372] Others see no significance to the prefix and take the meaning to be simply "crucify." The best sense is that of "to crucify again." This is followed by the dative of reference meaning: "with reference to themselves."[373] The sense of the whole would be: "it is impossible to renew to repentance those who had been once enlightened . . . and who fell away." The switch to the present tense in these two participles from the aorist tense of the preceding verses may or may not be significant.[374] Some believe that a state of continuous sin accompanied by a hard heart makes it impossible

---

368 Nicole, "Some Comments," 361. "Neither of these explanations appears entirely free of difficulty, although one may prefer to have recourse to them rather than to be forced to the conclusion that regenerate individuals can be lost."

369 As Sauer, "A Critical and Exegetical Reexamination," 250.

370 See this argument in J. Dillow, *The Reign of the Servant Kings* (Hayesville, NC: Schoettle, 1992), 445. Those who interpret the falling away as apostasy understand "repentance" to have the meaning of "conversion."

371 Lane, *Hebrews 1–8*, 133. The two participles can be taken in a temporal sense. On this reading, the falling away is only irreversible as long as one continues to "crucify" and "expose." P. Proulx and L. A. Schökel, "Heb 6,4–6," *Bib* 56 (1975): 201–4, and Sabourin, "Crucifying," 267, argued the participle "crucifying again" should be interpreted to mean no one can be restored by means of attempting to repeat Christ's sacrifice. Both readings are contextually inferior to the causal sense, which is affirmed by the overwhelming majority of commentators. Windisch, *Der Hebräerbrief*, 2nd ed., HNT 14 (Tübingen: Mohr, 1931), 51, takes the two participles to be a hendiadys.

372 So Dods, "Hebrews," 298; and Bruce, *Hebrews*, 149.

373 More specifically, the dative of reference is a dative of disadvantage, as Lane, *Hebrews 1–8*, 133, and Ellingworth, *Hebrews*, 325, point out, and in the NIV rendering "to their own loss." Koester, *Hebrews*, 315, thinks the meaning is more likely the termination of the relationship to Christ, since crucifixion brings death, and death would end a relationship with Christ. This reading is based on the interpretation of the participle παραπεσόντας in Heb 6:6 as apostasy.

374 Lane, *Hebrews 1–8*, 142, thinks it is significant.

for them to be renewed. While this is a possible interpretation, actually v. 3 explains why they cannot be renewed in v. 6: because God will not permit it.

The author's statement about "crucifying the Son of God all over again and subjecting him to public disgrace" may not be a reference to repudiating Christ and his sacrifice at all. Given what is said about the readers throughout the epistle, this does not seem to be the issue. The author makes much of the finished work of Christ, not necessarily because the readers are near to repudiating that work. The phrase "to their loss" translates a dative pronoun that is literally "to themselves" or "with reference to themselves." When the author says they recrucify and disgrace the Son of God "to themselves," his focus is not on what happens publicly, though that is a dimension of Christian disobedience, but on the internal contradiction between the confession and commitment a believer has made to Christ and the illogic of failing to honor that confession and commitment by choosing sin. All sin dishonors Jesus, and persistent sin, metaphorically speaking, carries the ironic stigma of having a Christian act like a non-Christian, hence "crucifying" to themselves the Son of God.

The next step in our analysis of this passage is a consideration of the question whether there are any general or specific Old Testament allusions behind Heb 6:4–6 that will aid in determining the correct interpretation. Here we will build on the work of those who have attempted to show that behind this passage is the specific Old Testament event at Kadesh-Barnea, as well as general themes taken from the wilderness wanderings.[375] There are five warning passages in Hebrews. Leaving aside Hebrews 6 for the moment, each of the other four passages contains an Old Testament example to illustrate the warning at hand. On two occasions, the reference is to disobedience to the Mosaic law (Heb 2:1–4; 10:26–39). In Heb 3:7–4:11 the reference is to the failure of Israel at Kadesh-Barnea during the wilderness warnings. In Heb 12:14–29, the reference is to the failure of Esau coupled with the failure of the people to obey God's voice at Sinai. It seems at first that there is no Old Testament reference to go with Hebrews 6. E. Grässer and P. Ellingworth both draw the conclusion that the author was appealing here to his readers in his own words without reference to the Old Testament.[376]

However, Gleason and Mathewson have argued that the Kadesh-Barnea incident of Numbers 13–14 and Psalm 95, which were the key Old Testament

---

[375] E.g,, G. H. Lang, *Hebrews* (London: Paternoster, 1951), 98–107; N. Weeks, "Admonition and Error in Hebrews," *WTJ* 39 (1976): 7–80; J. D. Pentecost, "Kadesh Barnea in the Book of Hebrews," in *Basic Theology Applied: A Practical Application of Basic Theology in Honor of Charles C. Ryrie and His Work*, ed. W. Willis and E. Willis and John and Janet Master (Wheaton: Victor, 1995), 127–35; G. Cockerill, *Hebrews*, 138–39; M. Emmrich, "Hebrews 6:4–6—Again!," 83–95; R. Gleason, "A Moderate Reformed View," in *Four Views on the Warning Passages in Hebrews*, ed. H. Bateman (Grand Rapids: Kregel, 2007), 343–60; and his "The Old Testament Background of the Warning in Hebrews 6:4–8," *BSac* 155 (1998): 62–91; D. Mathewson, "Reading Heb 6:4–6," 209–25; Oberholtzer, "The Thorn-Infested Ground," 319–27.

[376] Grässer, *An Die Hebräer*, 1:347; P. Ellingworth, *Hebrews*, 42.

references in Hebrews 3–4, continue to inform the author's statements in Hebrews 6. This is done via allusion and "echo," not direct quotation. Likewise, Bruce stated, in reference to Heb 6:4–6:

> Just as the Hebrew spies who returned from their expedition carrying visible tokens of the good land of Canaan nevertheless failed to enter the land because of their unbelief, so those who had come to know the blessings of the new covenant might nevertheless in a spiritual sense turn back in heart to Egypt and so forfeit the saints' everlasting rest.[377]

Evidence for this claim begins with the parallels that can be found in the descriptive phrases of Heb 6:4–6 as compared with the wilderness generation. These associations, according to Mathewson, "bleed over" from Heb 3:7–4:11 into Heb 6:4–6. Most of the parallels and allusions are to statements in Exodus, Numbers, Nehemiah 9, and Psalms 78 and 95.[378] Hebrews 6:4 speaks of those who have been "enlightened." Exodus 13:21 and Neh 9:12 speaks of the "pillar of fire" that gave light to the people at night on their journey. The second phrase, they "tasted the heavenly gift," may recall the incident of the manna according to Exod 16:4,15; Num 9:15; and Ps 78:24. Exodus 16:15 and Ps 78:24 speak of the manna as that which the Lord "gave" (LXX *edōken*) to the people. Nehemiah 9:20 speaks of the gift of God's Spirit to the wilderness generation for the purpose of instructing them and probably harks back to Num 11:16–29.[379] Hebrews 6:5 speaks of those who "have tasted the goodness of the word of God and the powers of the coming age." A common Old Testament metaphor is God's word as sweet to the taste. This is another possible allusion to the provision of manna in the wilderness. The term *rhēma*, "word," is used again in Heb 12:19 of the word of God given to Moses at Sinai. Nehemiah 9:13 states, "You came down on Mount Sinai; you spoke to them from heaven. You gave them regulations and laws that are just and right, and decrees and commands that are *good*." As many commentators have pointed out, there may be an allusion here to Josh 21:45: "Not one of all the LORD's *good* promises to the house of Israel failed; every one was fulfilled.."[380] The "powers of the coming age" reminds us of Heb 2:3–4 where "signs, wonders, and various miracles" accompanied the gift of salvation to the first generation of believers. As was

---

[377] Bruce, *Hebrews*, 145. Bruce goes on to reference Heb 3:7ff. and state, "It may be that the wilderness narrative is still in our author's mind." Cf. S. Kistemaker, *Hebrews*, 158; and L. T. Johnson, *Hebrews: A Commentary* (Louisville: Westminster John Knox, 2006), 161, who noted the use of the verb παραπίπτω in Heb 6:6 "indirectly suggests the pilgrimage motif."

[378] Mathewson, "Reading Heb 6:4–6," 214–15. Ellingworth, *Hebrews*, 326, also suggested a possible allusion to Hos 10:8, a passage also alluded to in Luke 23:30 and Rev 6:16.

[379] Emmrich, "Hebrews 6:4–6—Again!" 85, citing N. Weeks, "Admonition and Error in Hebrews," *WTJ* 39 (1976): 72–80.

[380] E.g., E. Grässer, *An die Hebräer*, 1:352–53, who suggested Heb 6:5*a* may be derived from the two statements in Josh 21:45: "all the good words, which the Lord spoke to the children of Israel," and Josh 23:15: "all the good words."

shown in the comments on Heb 2:4, "signs and wonders" are frequently associated with events of the exodus (e.g., Exod 7:3). "It is this reference to the 'signs and wonders' which accompanied God's activity in Egypt and beyond which grounds the writer's articulation of the experience of the powers of the age to come in the new covenant community in Heb 6:5b."[381]

Mathewson rightly indicated that none of the proposed allusions are convincing individually, but the cumulative weight of the evidence confirms "the momentum from the use of this illustration in 3:7–4:13 has carried over into the author's statements in 6:4–6."[382] The danger of falling away that the readers of Hebrews faced is parallel to the dangers that the exodus generation faced and this is the point the author of Hebrews has been at pains to show since Heb 3:7. The wilderness generation experienced the same things the readers of Hebrews experienced, yet they "fell away" in rebellion and incurred God's wrath: they lost their opportunity to enter the Promised Land. The recipients of Hebrews were facing a similar danger.[383]

At this point, Mathewson made the same strategic error we saw in Grudem and Nicole above. Although he correctly identified the Old Testament allusions undergirding Heb 6:4–6, he concluded that "in analogy to the old covenant community the people depicted in 6:4–6 are *not genuine believers* or true members of the new covenant community."[384] For him, like so many others, the falling away is "a failure to exercise saving faith in light of the blessings to which the readers have been exposed."[385] But this misreads the evidence that Heb 6:4–6a describes those who are genuinely saved. Furthermore, it fails to carry through the analogy with the Old Testament generation, for nothing is more clear than that the rebellious and sinful wilderness generation *experienced God's forgiveness according to Num 14:20–23* where in answer to Moses' intercessory prayer, the Lord said: "*I have pardoned them* according to your word. . . . *Surely all the men who have seen My glory and My signs . . . yet have put me to the test these ten times and have not listened to My voice, shall by no means see the land which I swore to their fathers, nor shall any of those who spurned Me see it*." What else could "I have pardoned them" mean unless it means God forgave them of their rebellion? The wilderness generation did not lose their salvation because of apostasy, nor did they fail to gain salvation because they were not genuine believers (members of the covenant community). What they lost, due to their rebellion, was the right to enter the Promised Land. If the land of Canaan is by analogy taken to refer to heaven, it is problematic to assume that *all* the Israelites who died in the wilderness were excluded from heaven.

---

381 Mathewson, "Reading Heb 6:4–6," 220; cf. Buchanan, *Hebrews*, 107.
382 Mathewson, "Reading Heb 6:4–6," 222.
383 Spicq, *L'Épître aux Hebreux*, 71–72; Mathewson, "Reading Heb 6:4–6," 220.
384 Mathewson, "Reading Heb 6:4–6," 224.
385 Ibid.

If we take Num 14:39–40 at face value, it would seem two alternatives present themselves. Either God refused to accept their change of heart, or their repentance was not genuine. Compare this with what is stated about Esau in Heb 12:17. Both Esau and the wilderness generation mourned and showed at least outward expressions of repentance. In the final analysis, it does not matter which is the case since the consequence was the same in both cases: denial of the birthright/Promised Land.

In addition to the strategic role Numbers 14 and Psalm 95 play as background for Heb 6:4–6, we must also consider Psalm 78. When we compare it with Psalm 95 and Numbers 14, we find a number of similarities that help to clarify the meaning of Heb 6:4–6. Consider the following:

78:8 "stubborn and rebellious generation"; "whose hearts were not loyal to God"; "whose spirits were not faithful to him"

78:9 "[they] turned back"

78:17 "they continued to sin against him"; "rebelling"

78:21 "[God] was very angry; his *fire* broke out against Jacob, and his wrath rose against Israel" (cf. Heb 12:29)

78:22 "for they did not believe in God or trust in his deliverance"

78:28 "He made them *fall* in His camp, all around His tent" (HCSB)

78:31 "God's anger rose against them; he put to death the sturdiest among them"

78:32–33 "In spite of all this, they kept on sinning; in spite of his wonders, they did not believe. *So he ended their days in futility and their years in terror.*"

78:34–38 "Whenever God slew them, they would seek him; they eagerly turned to him again. They remembered *that God was their Rock*, that God Most High was their Redeemer. But then they would flatter him with their mouths, lying to him with their tongues; their hearts were not loyal to him, they were not faithful to his covenant. Yet he was merciful; he *forgave their iniquities and did not destroy them. Time after time he restrained his anger and did not stir up his full wrath.*"

78:63 "*Fire* consumed their young men." Compare this with Num 11:1b: "His anger was aroused. Then *fire* from the Lord burned among them and consumed some of the outskirts of the camp." (Cf. with Heb 12:29.)

Psalm 78, Numbers 14, and Psalm 95 use similar terminology to describe what the sinful people did and what God did to them as a result. Numbers 14 and Psalm 78 both refer to God's forgiveness for their willful sin.

These verses underscore that although God forgave them of their sin, yet he refused to allow them to enter the Promised Land. It was impossible to renew them to repentance because God had sworn in his wrath that they would not enter the Promised Land. He did not disinherit them or remove them from his covenant people. He did not send them back to Egypt. In fact, after the

Kadesh-Barnea incident, for the next 38 years God continued to feed them with manna, provide water, protect them from enemies, and even kept their shoes from wearing out. Yet over that period of time, one by one their bodies "fell" in the wilderness until all of that rebellious generation died.

We are now in a position to draw some conclusions concerning the meaning of *parapiptō*, "falling away," based upon our analysis of the passage in context and the biblical and extra-biblical usage of the term. We have seen that the word did not mean "apostasy" in the technical theological sense in any Old Testament context, nor in any extra-biblical example.[386] The reference to falling away in Heb 6:6 does not mean apostasy in the sense of willful rejection of Christ by those who are believers or by those who are unbelievers. Given the usage of the word in the LXX combined with the author's dependence upon the Kadesh-Barnea incident here and elsewhere in the epistle, the word means to transgress against the Lord in a way that parallels what happened in Numbers 14 when Israel rebelled against God. Israel in the wilderness had become hardened in their hearts against the Lord, and this hardness culminated in their disobedience recorded in Numbers 14. The original readers of Hebrews were in danger of something similar. If they do not hold fast their confession of faith in Christ (Heb 3:6; 4:14; Heb 10:23), if they disobey and rebel against the Lord and remain in such an unrepentant state, if they refuse to press on to maturity, God himself will not permit them to repent because of the high-handed and blatant sin that they have committed. Contextually, the key to the warning is actually Heb 6:3. Verse 4 begins with *gar*, a subordinating conjunction. God may make the decision that it is not possible for them to press on to maturity because of their disobedience, just as he did not permit Israel to enter the Promised Land for the same reason. Contextually, the meaning of "fall away" in v. 6 should be understood as the opposite of "go on to maturity" in v. 1. As Gleason said,

> Hence the sin of "falling away" [*parapiptō*] is more than merely "sluggishness of hearing"; it is coming to a decisive point when one refused "once for all" [*hapax*] to press on to maturity. The sin of "falling away" in Hebrews echoes the experience of the Israelites "who fell [*epesen*] in the wilderness" (3:17; cf. 4:11).[387]

[386] Kistemaker, *Hebrews*, 160, correctly distinguished between apostasy and falling into sin (backsliding). Heb 6:6 is a reference to apostasy according to Kistemaker, and he cites J. Owen's statement that a "total renunciation" of the Christian faith is intended. He then stated: "The author, using the example of the Israelites, has shown the process that results in apostasy (3:18; 4:6, 11)." Kistemaker, like so many, presents no word study of παραπίπτω to support this claim beyond stating that the word is used twice in Ezekiel and is synonymous with the verb ἀποστῆναι in Heb 3:12.

[387] Gleason, "A Moderate Reformed View," 355.

Five Major Views Described and Examined. There are five major interpretations of Heb 6:4–6:[388] (1) the Loss of Salvation view;[389] (2) the Hypothetical view;[390] (3) the Tests of Genuineness view;[391] (4) the Means of Salvation view[392] (which is a variation of the Tests of Genuineness view); and (5) the Loss of Rewards view.[393]

---

388 Cf. the excellent summary in H. Bateman, ed., *Four Views on the Warning Passages in Hebrews* (Grand Rapids: Kregel, 2007), with positions represented by G. Cockerill, B. Fanning, R. Gleason, and G. Osborne. T. Schreiner and A. B. Caneday, *The Race Set Before Us* (Downers Grove: InterVarsity, 2001), 19–45, also offer a balanced overview of the various approaches.

389 See J. Wesley, *Notes on the Bible: New Testament* (n.p., 1754), 741–42; R. Shank, *Life in the Son* (Springfield, MO: Westcott Publishers, 1961); id., *Elect in the Son* (Springfield, MO: Westcott Publishers, 1970); I. H. Marshall, *Kept by the Power of God*, 137–57; id., "The Problem of Apostasy in New Testament Theology," *PRSt* 14.4 (1987): 65–80; G. Osborne, "Soteriology in the Epistle to the Hebrews," in *Grace Unlimited*, ed. C. Pinnock (Minneapolis: Bethany Fellowship, 1975), 144–66. D. Moody, *The Word of Truth: A Summary of Christian Doctrine Based on Biblical Revelation* (Grand Rapids: Eerdmans, 1981), 337–65; id., *Apostasy: A Study in the Epistle to the Hebrews and in Baptist History* (Greenville, SC: Smyth and Helwys, 1991); S. McKnight, "The Warning Passages of Hebrews," 21–59; I. Salevao, *Legitimation in the Letter to the Hebrews: The Construction and Maintenance of a Symbolic Universe,* JSNTSup 219 (New York: Sheffield Academic Press, 2002), 259–338; and W. Bauder, "Fall Away," *NIDNTT* 1:610–11. Marshall, McKnight, Osborne, and Cockerill are the ablest contemporary spokesmen for the Arminian interpretation of Heb 6:4–6.

390 E.g., A. Barnes, *Barnes' Notes on the Bible*, ed. R. Flew (London: Blackie, 1885; repr., Grand Rapids: Baker, 1998), 13:130–31; G. H. Lang, *Hebrews* (London: Paternoster, 1951), 196; W. Manson, *Hebrews* (London: Hodder and Stoughton, 1951); Spicq, *L'Épître aux Hebreux*, 2:156; T. Hewitt, *Hebrews* (London: Tyndale, 1960), 111; J. Boyer, "Other Conditional Elements in New Testament Greek," *GTJ* 4 (1983): 173–88; and L. T. Johnson, *Hebrews*, 161.

391 E.g., Calvin, *Hebrews*, 71–78; J. Owen, *An Exposition of the Epistle to the Hebrews* (Edinburgh: Ritchie, 1812), 5:3–142; Robertson, *WP* 5:375; Nicole, "Some Comments"; Grudem, "Perseverance of the Saints"; Carson, "Reflections," 19; Peterson, "Apostasy," 22–23; P. W. Barnett, "Apostasy," *DLNT* 73–74; D. Mathewson, "Reading Hebrews 6:4–6 in Light of the Old Testament" *WTJ* 61 (1999): 209–25; Fanning, "A Classical Reformed View," in *Four Views*, 172–219; and R. D. Phillips, *Hebrews*, REC (Phillipsburg, NJ: P&R, 2006), 191.

392 Cf. the eighteenth century Southern Baptist theologian J. L. Dagg, *Manual of Theology* (Charleston, SC: Southern Baptist Publication Society, 1859), 287–300; C. H. Spurgeon's sermon "Final Perseverance" on Heb 6:4–6 in *The New Park Street Pulpit* (London: Passmore and Alabaster, 1856), 2:169–76; W. G. T. Shedd, *Dogmatic Theology* (New York: Charles Scribner's Sons 1899; repr., Minneapolis: K&K, 1979), 2:557; G. C. Berkouwer, *Faith and Perseverance* (Grand Rapids: Eerdmans, 1958), 118–21; Erickson, *Christian Theology*, 1005; Schreiner and Caneday, *The Race Set Before Us*, esp. 38–45; 142–213.

393 E.g., W. T. Conner, *The Gospel of Redemption* (Nashville: Broadman, 1945), 255–58; M. Eaton, "'Falling Away' in the Epistle to the Hebrews," in *No Condemnation: A Theology of Assurance*, 208–17; Oberholtzer, "The Thorn-Infested Ground"; Gleason, "The Old Testament Background," 62–91; id., "A Moderate Reformed View," in *Four Views on the Warning Passages in Hebrews*, 336–77; H. Harless, "Fallen Away or Fallen Down," 2–17; Z. Hodges, *Gospel Under Siege* (Dallas: Redención Viva, 1981), 75–77; id., *Hebrews* (Wheaton: Victor, 1983), 794; R. T. Kendall, *Once Saved, Always Saved* (London: Hodder and Stoughton, 1983), 131–34; H. Kent, *The Epistle to the Hebrews: A Commentary* (Grand Rapids: Baker, 1972), 113; N. Geisler, "A Moderate Calvinist View," in *Four Views on Eternal Security*, ed. J. M. Pinson (Grand Rapids: Zondervan, 2002), 98–100; R. Gromacki, *Stand Bold in Grace* (Woodlands, TX: Kress Christian, 2002), 110–13; 173–76. R. Govett, *Reward According to Works* (Norwich, CT: Fletcher & Son,

The Loss of Salvation view has been most ably defended in recent times by Scot McKnight.[394] This interpretation identifies the people described in Heb 6:4–6 as genuine believers who forfeit their eternal salvation due to the sin of apostasy. This is the classical Arminian position, though it should be noted that the early followers of Arminius did not at first completely affirm that genuine believers could commit apostasy and thus lose their salvation.[395] Most modern day Arminians affirm the possibility of repentance and regaining salvation, though Heb 6:6 would appear to make repentance and salvation impossible for those who have committed apostasy.[396] Adherents to this view appeal to the conditional statements made in Heb 3:6 and 3:14 as indicating if one commits apostasy, loss of salvation results. However, if the intent of these conditional statements is less a matter of cause and effect and more a matter of evidence and inference, where the "if" clause gives the evidence, then support for the Loss of Salvation view is significantly eroded. B. Fanning, in reference to the conditional statements in Heb 3:6 and 3:14, argued: "these lines do not cite what *will* be true if they hold on, but what is *already* true of them, and which is to be evidenced by their endurance through temptation."[397] The same logic applies to the Hypothetical view as discussed below.

The key weakness of this view from within the context of Heb 6:4–6 is that, as demonstrated above, the participle (lit.) "falling away" is not an adverbial conditional participle[398] and does not refer to the act of apostasy. The key weakness from the standpoint of the New Testament is the difficulty of explaining the plethora of passages that affirm the eternal security of the believer.[399]

1870–95; repr. Miami Springs, FL: Conley & Schoettle, 1989), argued for the position that the loss of rewards included not only what occurs in this life for the believer, but also loss affecting the believer's participation in the millennial reign of Christ.

394 S. McKnight, "The Warning Passages of Hebrews," 21–59.

395 Schreiner and Caneday, *The Race Set Before Us*, 23.

396 G. Osborne, "Soteriology," 150, 153, first stated that the author of Hebrews says nothing regarding whether the apostate can ever cease his apostate state, but then two pages later affirmed the impossibility of repentance for those who commit apostasy. Marshall, *Kept by the Power*, 146–47, affirmed the irredeemable nature of the apostasy in Heb 6:4–6. Most contemporary Arminians are inconsistent in their treatment of Heb 6:6 where renewal to repentance is said to be "impossible."

397 B. Fanning, "A Theology of Hebrews," in *A Biblical Theology of the New Testament*, ed. R. Zuck (Chicago: Moody, 1994), 410.

398 Although semantically, a conditional element may be a part of the meaning conveyed by the participle, even if taken adjectivally as argued above.

399 Grudem, "Perseverance of the Saints," 180, speaking about the "substantial weight" of biblical evidence supporting eternal security, correctly stated that those who believe one can lose their salvation "have an obligation not only to give a reasonable explanation of 6:4–6, but also of those other passages which repeatedly teach that true Christians will certainly persevere (for example, John 8:38–40; 10:27–29; Rom 8:1,30; Eph 1:13–14; 4:30; Phil 1:6; 1 Pet 1:5; and passages on eternal life: John 3:36; 5:24; 6:4–7; 10:28; 1 John 5:13)." Cf. the catalogue of passages in Hebrews affirming perseverance presented by Nicole, "Some Comments," 358–59. See the conclusions on this matter by J. Gundry-Volf, *Paul and Perseverance: Staying in and Falling Away* (Louisville: John Knox, 1991), 80–82, where she demonstrated that the NT indicates God's initial action in

The key weaknesses of this interpretation from the standpoint of the context of Hebrews as a whole is threefold. First, the book repeatedly affirms the "once-for-all" character of the salvation procured by Christ on the cross and speaks of believers' salvation in covenant language using the aorist and perfect tenses in Greek. Second, crucial for the author's argument throughout the epistle is the solidarity between Jesus and his redeemed people. The permanent identity of believers with Christ in 2:10–18 makes the Loss of Salvation view untenable theologically. When the author of Hebrews warns his readers to "hold on to" their confidence (3:6) or their confession (4:14; 10:24), there is no hint that any genuine believer has failed to do so.[400] Third, McKnight inconsistently excludes the pastoral encouragement statements that follow immediately upon the heels of the warning passages, especially Heb 6:9 and 10:39.[401] We conclude that this view does not adequately interpret the meaning of Heb 6:4–6.

The Hypothetical view is predicated upon interpreting the first participle in Heb 6:6 conditionally: "if they fall away." This perspective argues that the writer is presenting a hypothetical case for illustrative purposes to show what would happen if it were possible for someone to fall away from salvation through committing apostasy. The intent of the passage is still a warning, but the writer does not intend for his words to be understood other than hypothetically.[402] From the immediate context of Heb 6:4–6, the greatest weakness of this position is taking the participle *parapesontas* in v. 6 adverbially rather than adjectivally (substantivally) and then giving it a conditional translation. We have seen that exegetically it is best to take this participle in a substantival fashion as with the previous four participles in vv. 4–5. If the participle cannot be taken adverbially, as the majority of Greek scholars and commentators suggest, the Hypothetical view cannot be correct. It likewise incorrectly interprets *parapesontas* in v. 6 as "apostasy."

---

salvation will ultimately be completed in every believer's life, producing both security and assurance.

[400] Perceptively noted by J. L. Garrett, *Systematic Theology*, 2:422.

[401] See R. Peterson, "Apostasy," 29.

[402] Thiselton, "Hebrews," 1463, attempts to provide some philosophical impetus to the hypothetical view: "In philosophical logic the kind of confusions often associated with these verses [Heb 6:4–6] may be unraveled by distinguishing between *logical* possibility and possibility in life (*contingent* possibility). The writer is unpacking the logical entailments of the finished work of Christ in terms of 'progress or nothing.' Addressees who oscillate between retreat to Judaism and 'trying out' Christian faith during favorable periods have misunderstood what Christian faith consists in. To conceive of the matter in this way is like getting married to the same person over again: either a person is married or a person is not." Thiselton's analysis assumes the danger to the readers was a "retreat" to Judaism, a questionable assumption at best, as we have seen. Since the author is making a "pastoral point" rather than expounding a doctrine, as Thiselton rightly suggested, is it conceivable that at the place in his epistle where he pens his most serious warning yet, he would resort to the use of such philosophical niceties as logical and contingent possibility, asserting that while something is logically true, it is contingently impossible?

The Tests of Genuineness view harks back to Calvin and especially the Puritan John Owen. Its ablest contemporary defender is Wayne Grudem.[403] The essence of this view is that those in Heb 6:4–6 may profess faith in Christ, but they are not genuine believers. These false believers come to a point where they abandon Christ and the church, thus committing apostasy. When they fall away, they give evidence that they were not genuine believers.[404] First John 2:19 is often used to support this position.

A variation of this is the Means of Salvation view, which has been recently popularized by Schreiner and Caneday, who develop it primarily from C. H. Spurgeon, W. G. T. Shedd, and G. C. Berkouwer.[405] The essence of the view declares that the warnings of Heb 6:4–6 and other like passages, coupled with the promises given by God concerning salvation, are the means God uses to preserve his saints. The warning of Heb 6:4–6 is future oriented. Warnings as well as promises in Hebrews (and in all Scripture) should not be seen as opposites. God preserves Christians by means of warnings and conditional promises.

The Tests of Genuineness view has several weaknesses. First, those described in Heb 6:4–6a are said to be false believers, yet we have seen it is most likely they were believers. Second, the participle *parapesontas* is wrongly taken to mean "apostasy." Third, by questioning whether those in Heb 6:4–6 were genuinely converted, the orientation of the passage is redirected from a prospective focus, which the author intended, to a retrospective focus, which is forced upon the text by a preconceived theology. The conclusion is that apostasy reveals they were never genuine Christians in the first place. As Schreiner and Caneday correctly remarked, this is a case of the right theology from the wrong text.[406] In the final analysis, the warning passages end up being applied to unbelievers rather than to believers. Fourth, past good works of believer are understood as evidence of faith in a retrospective manner. Such a retrospective focus is at odds with the author's own soteriological focus, which is "fundamentally future oriented."[407] Thus, advocates of the Tests of Genuineness view, like Grudem, read the consequences of the warnings retrospectively such that they become "little more than an indicative description of the apostate."[408]

---

[403] Grudem, "Perseverance of the Saints," 133–81.

[404] So J. MacArthur, *Faith Works: The Gospel According to the Apostles* (Dallas: Word Books, 1993), 79–80; Grudem, "Perseverance of the Saints," 173. Although the majority of Calvinists affirms the Tests of Genuineness view, there are Calvinists who support the Loss of Rewards view as well as the hypothetical/ironic viewpoint.

[405] Schreiner and Caneday, *The Race Set Before Us*, esp. 38–45 and 142–213. Cf. C. H. Spurgeon's sermon "Final Perseverance," 2:169–76; W. G. T. Shedd, *Dogmatic Theology*, 2:557; and G. C. Berkouwer, *Faith and Perseverance*, 118–19. This was the position held by Augustine as well (N. R. Needham, *The Triumph of Grace: Augustine's Writings on Salvation* [London: Grace Publication Trust, 2000], 273).

[406] Schreiner and Caneday, *The Race Set Before Us*, 198.

[407] Ibid. McKnight, "The Warning Passages of Hebrews," 55–58, correctly identified this future orientation.

[408] Schreiner and Caneday, *The Race Set Before Us*, 199.

The Means of Salvation approach has also been subject to criticism.[409] B. Oropeza asks is it not conceivable that authors who used warnings in the New Testament assumed that some of their recipients were genuine believers.[410] It is clear the author of Hebrews considered his readers to be Christians, as shown above. These believers were in danger of falling away. First, this view assumes the meaning of *parapesontas* as "apostasy" in the technical theological sense of that term. As we have seen, the word itself does not mean this. Second, the forensic nature of justification is correctly affirmed in this view, but it appears that final justification awaits the completion of a life of perseverance. This is, of course, contrary to the Reformed theology of Schreiner and Caneday, but more importantly, contrary to Scripture.[411] Third, Schreiner and Caneday assert that warnings like Hebrews 6 have the objective of causing us to think what is conceivable or imaginable, not of things likely to happen.

> They appeal to our minds to conceive of cause-and-effect relationships or of the relationship between God's appointed means and end. They warn us on the basis of God's inviolable promise and threat proclaimed in the gospel: salvation is only for those who believe to the end. Thus, all the warnings caution us concerning conceivable consequences. They do not confront us with an uncertain future. They do not say that we may perish. Rather, they caution us lest we perish. They warn us that we will surely perish if we fail to heed God's call in the gospel.[412]

And again, "*God warns of conceivable consequences, not probable consequences.*"[413] Such language is at best confusing and at worst contradictory.

Fourth, Schreiner and Caneday identify the rewards spoken of in the New Testament as referring to the gift of eschatological salvation.[414] The denial of future rewards for the Christian in the face of 1 Cor 3:12–15 and other New Testament passages is difficult to sustain. William Lane Craig lodged another criticism of this view, arguing that it implicitly employs a Molinist

---

409 See R. Wilkin, "Striving for the Prize of Eternal Salvation," *Journal of the Grace Evangelical Theological Society* (2002): 3–24. This critique occasionally misreads what Schreiner and Caneday appear to be saying and sometimes presses their comments beyond their intent, yet it does point out the problems with the view, particularly in relationship to the Loss of Rewards view, which Wilkin advocates. Another substantive critique is K. Keathley, *Salvation and Sovereignty: A Molinist Approach* (Nashville: B&H, 2010), 179–90.

410 B. Oropeza, *Paul and Apostasy: Eschatology, Perseverance, and Falling Away in the Corinthian Congregation*, WUNT 2:115 (Tübingen: J. C. B. Mohr, 2000), 22–23.

411 To what extent this is commensurate with Augustine's view that the non-elect can have a real but temporary faith is unclear.

412 Schreiner and Caneday, *The Race Set Before Us*, 207–8.

413 Ibid., 212. This is a very similar appeal to Thiselton's "logical vs. contingent possibilities" as seen above.

414 Ibid., 276–305.

perspective of "middle knowledge," thus abandoning the classical Reformed doctrine of perseverance.[415] Schreiner and Caneday respond to this criticism in an appendix to their book, arguing that Craig misunderstood the difference between his own view and that of Reformed theology.[416] At issue here is the difference between the traditional Reformed view and the Molinist view of God's use of means. If, as Schreiner and Caneday advocate, God uses warnings like Heb 6:4–6 as the means to insure the perseverance of the saints, then one of two things must be true. Either Christians could or would fall away from Christ without the warnings (a departure from Reformed theology), or Christians could or would persevere without the warnings, which makes them unnecessary.[417] Erickson, who defends the Means of Salvation view, stated in reference to Heb 6:4–6,

> the writer has in view genuine believers who could fall away, but will not. . . . While Hebrews 6 indicates that genuine believers *can* fall away, John 10 teaches that they *will not.* There is a logical possibility of apostasy, but it will not come to pass in the case of believers. Although they could abandon their faith and consequently come to the fate described in Hebrews 6, the grace of God prevents them from apostasizing. God does this, not by making it impossible for believers to fall away, but by making it certain that they will not. Our emphasis on *can* and *will* not is not inconsequential. It preserves the freedom of the individual. Believers are capable of repudiating their faith, but will freely choose not to.[418]

Here again, as illustrated above, what can possibly be gained by saying genuine believers can fall away but will not fall away? The philosophical problem to be overcome in this proposal is the fact that it is logically possible for a genuine believer to commit apostasy and experience eternal damnation, but it is not actually (ontologically) possible for genuine believers to do so.[419] Put another way, how can something be subjectively possible for someone who knows it to be objectively impossible?[420] In the Means of Salvation view, apostasy becomes the impossible possibility.

Joseph Dillow subjects the Tests of Genuineness and Means of Salvation views to five criticisms. First, if one knows he is unconditionally secure, the warnings lose their force if they are interpreted to mean warning against loss

[415] W. L. Craig, "'Lest Anyone Should Fall": A Middle Knowledge Perspective on Perseverance and Apostolic Warnings," in *Philosophy of Religion* (1991), 29:65–74.

[416] Schreiner and Caneday, *The Race Set Before Us,* 332–37.

[417] Keathley, *Salvation and Sovereignty*, 181–85.

[418] M. Erickson, *Christian Theology*, 1005.

[419] See discussion in Schreiner and Caneday, *The Race Set Before Us*, 193–98. This point is well made by Keathley, *Salvation and Sovereignty*, 181–85.

[420] J. Dillow, *Reign*, 219. Dillow's critique of the Tests of Genuineness and Means of Salvation views are found on pp. 218–43.

of salvation. Second, for the reason previously stated, the warnings become logically contradictory. Third, they fail the test of human experience. "Is it not ridiculous to say that men can be alarmed by warnings if they have already been consoled by the promise that they are secure? How can they be alarmed about something which could never happen to them?"[421] Fourth, it subtly redefines the basis of salvation by making perseverance almost a condition of salvation rather than an evidence of salvation. Fifth, it makes God to be a liar.

> If God has decreed that His elect will finally persevere in holiness and if warnings are a means He uses to secure that perseverance, then God is threatening His elect with a destiny He knows will never befall them. He is telling them they might lose their salvation in order to motivate them by fear (read 'healthy tension' or 'wholesome fear') to persevere. How can a God of truth use lies to accomplish His purpose of holiness in His elect?[422]

This final criticism is overstated, but nevertheless makes a valid point. There is something logically incoherent here. These criticisms, cumulatively considered, illustrate the problems with the Tests of Genuineness and Means of Salvation views.

Before considering the Loss of Rewards view, a comparison of the four views discussed is in order. There is one key point that the Loss of Salvation (LoS), Hypothetical (H), Tests of Genuineness (ToG), and Means of Salvation (MoS) views all have in common. They understand that "fall away" in v. 6 means "to commit apostasy." The latter three all interpret Heb 6:4–6 to refer to unbelievers (with the exception of some Calvinists who interpret Heb 6:4–5 to refer to believers[423]), and they deny that genuine believers can commit apostasy and thus lose their salvation. The following chart summarizes the positions and their theological conclusions.

Loss of Salvation / Hypothetical / Tests of Genuineness / Means of Salvation

	LoS	H	ToG	MoS
Falling Away	apostasy	apostasy	apostasy	apostasy
6:4–6 Unbelievers	no	yes	yes	yes
Do true Believers Apostatize?	yes	no	no	no

[421] Ibid., 226.

[422] Ibid., 238.

[423] E.g., A. Mugridge, "Warnings in the Epistle to the Hebrews," 74–82; R. Peterson, "Apostasy," 17–31.

I contend that there are two biblically correct theological conclusions among the four positions charted above. First, those who advocate the Loss of Salvation view and the minority within the Hypothetical and Tests of Genuineness views are correct in their understanding that Heb 6:4–6 refers to genuine believers. Second, the Hypothetical and Tests of Genuineness/Means of Salvation views are correct in affirming the impossibility of genuine believers apostatizing.

We now consider the Loss of Rewards view concerning Heb 6:4–6.[424] Essentially, this view interprets the group in Heb 6:4–6 as genuine believers who "fall away" in the sense of willful disobedience to God. They do not commit apostasy in the traditional theological sense of the term. They do not finally deny Christ. They do fail to press on to spiritual maturity by virtue of direct disobedience to God's will and word. The judgment that these believers incur does not involve loss of salvation. Their judgment is more accurately designated "discipline," which involves both a temporal and an eschatological aspect. It is not final judgment in the sense of eternal loss. Temporally, this discipline involves loss of opportunity to go on to maturity in the Christian life, loss of effective service for Christ in this life, loss of the blessings of God that come from an obedient life, and in some cases perhaps premature physical death. Eschatologically, it involves loss of rewards at the Judgment Seat of Christ (Rom 14:10–12; 1 Cor 3:10–15; 2 Cor 5:10) and perhaps loss of position of leadership/service in the coming millennial kingdom (from a premillennial perspective). These are genuine believers who are in danger of forfeiting some new covenant blessings in this life as well as rewards at the Judgment Seat of Christ.

6:7–8 This interpretation incorporates several contextual factors within Hebrews. First, in the immediate context of Heb 5:11–6:8, the author is addressing genuine Christians who were failing to press on to maturity (6:1). The context of the passage is not salvation but sanctification. Second, ascribing genuine believer status to the people described in Heb 6:4–6 favors this interpretation as well. Third, the immediately following verses, Heb 6:7–8, support this interpretation. The author follows the warning with an illustration introduced by *gar*, connecting it with the previous context and showing that the previous audience continues in view. This agricultural illustration speaks of a single plot of land, not two different lands as is implied in the NIV translation.[425]

[424] Advocates for this view include G. H. Lang, *Hebrews*, esp. 93–110; Oberholtzer, "The Thorn-Infested Ground"; Dillow, *Reign;* and M. Eaton's *No Condemnation*, 208–17. The most comprehensive argument for this view is R. Gleason's "The Old Testament Background of the Warning in Hebrews 6:4–8," 62–91; and his "A Moderate Reformed View," 336–77 in *Four Views on the Warning Passages in Hebrews*. G. Guthrie, *Hebrews*, 227, calls this "the true believer under judgment view."

[425] Likewise Bruce, *Hebrews*, 149–50, mistakenly infers from the passage that two fields are being spoken of, not one, when he connects "the ground which drinks in the rain often falling on

The word "land" occurs only once in the Greek text—v. 7. It is not two kinds of land being described, but rather two possible outcomes from the same land. The ground has received the rain necessary for cultivation and growth.[426] Verse 7 speaks of the positive result of fruitfulness when the rain falls on the land and the result is vegetation.[427] Verse 8 speaks of the same land, which received the same rain, but "thorns and thistles" are the result, not fruit.

It is often argued that the group in Heb 6:4–6 is contrasted with the genuine believers in Heb 6:9. But the contrast is not between two different groups of people but rather two possibilities that may affect one group of people. This is shown by the illustration of two different results occurring to the same land in Heb 6:7–8. The author is using this illustration to depict typologically the two possible outcomes for Christians: those who press on to maturity through obedience, and those who willfully continue in disobedience. Verse 8 describes the threefold result of the land that brings forth "thorns and thistles"; it is "worthless and in danger of being cursed," and "in the end it will be burned."

Those who see in Heb 6:4–6 a reference to non-Christians interpret Heb 6:7–8 as descriptive of eternal loss.[428] This is possible given the harsh statements of v. 6 and now the use of "cursed" and "burned." But several factors make this interpretation unlikely. We have already seen that the context is more conducive to believers, not unbelievers. When the author calls the land "worthless," he uses the Greek *adokimos*, which means "not standing the test; to be disqualified or unapproved." The Pauline usage of this word indicates a dual focus. On the one hand, in 2 Cor 13:5, it seems clear Paul is using

---

it" only with the immediately following participle "producing fruit," and not with both following participles "producing fruit," and "bearing thorns." Cf. Hewitt, *Hebrews*, 109.

426 In at least two places, Montefiore, *Hebrews*, 110, and the *REB* translation, "When the soil drinks in the rain . . . ," the aorist participial clause translated "drinks in the rain that often comes on it" in the NIV is given a temporal translation, "when it has drunk." However, as Greenlee, *Exegetical Summary*, 200, correctly noted, "The definite article with the participle does not permit this interpretation; perhaps the temporal clauses are intended only as a means of showing that both refer to the same field."

427 ἐκείνοις, "those," most likely governs εὔθετον, "useful," and not τίκτουσα, "to produce," or βοτάνην, "crop." The last verb in v. 7, μεταλαμβάνει, "receives," can mean "to share in," and is so taken by Bruce, *Hebrews*, 138, and Lane, *Hebrews 1–8*, 130. Most commentators and translations take it to mean "receive."

428 See Grudem, *Systematic Theology*, 796: "In this agricultural metaphor, those who receive final judgment are compared to land that bears no vegetation or useful fruit, but rather bears thorns and thistles. When we recall the other metaphors in Scripture where good fruit is a sign of true spiritual life and fruitlessness is a sign of false believers (for example, Matt 3:8–10; 7:15–20; 12:33–35), we already have an indication that the author is speaking of people whose most trustworthy evidence of their spiritual condition (the fruit they bear) is negative, suggesting that the author is talking about people who are not genuinely Christians." Examples of allegorizing this text include Aquinas's notion that the "thorns" are small sins and "thistles" are greater sins; and Luther's notion, following Chrysostom and Augustine, that the "rain" here and in other parts of Scripture means "doctrine." Aquinas, *Commentary on the Epistle to the Hebrews,* 14.300; Luther, *Hebrews*, in *LW*, 57:182–83.

the word to mean "rejected with regard to salvation in an unconverted state." In other words, it does not mean a Christian has been rejected after conversion.[429] Rather, it refers to someone who was associated with the church, but who was not genuinely converted. On the other hand, Paul used this word in 1 Cor 9:27 to speak of disciplining himself to compete in the athletic games, lest he be *adokimos*, "disqualified." Paul is not referring to his eternal salvation by the use of this word. It is more likely, in view of the immediately preceding context of athletic games, that Paul feared the possibility of jeopardizing his rewards.[430] A careful study of this word makes it clear it is not a technical term descriptive of unbelievers.

One might assume by the use of the word "cursed" that eternal loss is in view in Heb 6:8. But the text does not say the ground is "cursed" but in *danger* of being cursed. If the reference is to apostasy, then it is not to those who are near to being cursed, but to those who would be cursed with eternal loss.[431] It would be possible to interpret (lit.) "whose end is for burning" in Heb 6:8 as a reference to eternal loss in hell. In Scripture, "fire" can be used in context of the unregenerate in hell, and it can also be used to speak of God's judgment of Christians. The latter is the case in 1 Cor 3:10–15 where the focus is on the nature of the believer's works at the Judgment Seat of Christ. The quality of the work is tested by fire, but the result for those who do not pass the test is not eternal damnation. It is works of "wood, hay or straw" that are burned up, not the individual, who entered heaven "with fire." The context of Heb 6:10, where the author mentions the "works" of his readers, make the comparison to 1 Cor 3:10–15 all the more appropriate. The "burning" of land that did not produce vegetation was a common act in the first century AD. The purpose was to cleanse the land of the "thorns and thistles" so it would bring forth fruit. The land was not destroyed in the process. By analogy, the author of Hebrews is not suggesting that those who had "fallen away" were eternally destroyed.[432] The better interpretation is to take Heb 6:7–8 as referring to loss of rewards.

DeSilva leveled three criticisms at Oberholtzer's understanding of Heb 6:7–8. First, Oberholtzer superimposed a dispensational eschatology on the author of Hebrews. While Oberholtzer's argument for a millennial kingdom reference is debatable, DeSilva's comment shows he has confused dispensational theology with millennial theology.[433] The two are not by any means equivalent. Not all millennialists are dispensationalists. The criticism fails to read Oberholtzer

---

[429] Gundry-Volf, *Paul and Perseverance*, 219.

[430] Ibid., 220: "The use of ἀδόκιμος in 1 Cor 9:27 refers not to loss of salvation but to failing the test of faithful service."

[431] ἐγγύς, "near," is taken to mean "not yet, but certain to occur" by Dods, "Hebrews," 300; Moffatt, *Hebrews*, 82; Hughes, *Hebrews*, 223–24; and Ellingworth, *Hebrews*, 328.

[432] Oberholtzer, "The Thorn-Infested Ground," 324–26; Gleason, "The Old Testament Background," 86–90.

[433] DeSilva, *Hebrews*, 233–34. This mistake is also made by S. McKnight, "The Warning Passages of Hebrews," 56; and B. Nongbri, "A Touch of Condemnation in a Word of Exhortation:

closely enough, however, in that the millennial aspect to his interpretation is a secondary issue and not critical to his overall thesis. Second, DeSilva questions a distinction between "temporal discipline" and "judgment" in a Pentateuchal setting, calling it a "false dichotomy," since only in later Judaism was the notion of eternal rewards and punishment developed. This does not overthrow Oberholtzer's point, however, since Deuteronomy does envision temporal rewards and curses, and by analogy Oberholtzer is comparing this to Hebrews. DeSilva's third criticism has a measure of validity to it. Oberholtzer partially misread Heb 12:5–11 by taking it only as a reference to punishment for sin[434] when it is better to take it primarily as an example of "educative" suffering, with a secondary application to punishment for sin.

Another contextual clue aiding in the proper interpretation of this passage is the Old Testament background of the events at Kadesh-Barnea, as we have already seen. Paul warned the Corinthian church that the events of the Old Testament, including those involving the exodus generation, were written for our learning: "So, if you think you are standing firm, be careful that you don't *fall* [*piptō*]!" (1 Cor 10:12).

There is an interesting correspondence between Paul's description of the wilderness generation's privileges in 1 Cor 10:1–4 and Heb 6:4–5. Five positive things are stated about the wilderness generation, followed by a negative statement, just as we find in Heb 6:4–6: (1) all were under the cloud; (2) all passed through the sea; (3) all were baptized into Moses; (4) all ate the same spiritual food; and (5) all drank from the same rock that followed them, which was Christ. Then follows the negative statement in v. 5: "but God was not pleased with most of them and they were scattered in the wilderness."[435] Paul does not state they were "apostates" or that they were "cursed" by God and removed from their covenant status. Other parallels occur between 1 Cor 10:1–13 and Heb 6:1–8. Hebrews 6:5 speaks of the "coming age" and 1 Cor 10:11 says, "the fulfillment of the ages has come." First Corinthians 10:3 speaks of eating and Heb 6:4–5 speaks of tasting.

Israel fell away from the right path at Kadesh-barnea. Their rebellion against God (Num 14:10) caused them to consider rejecting Moses and selecting a new leader who would lead them back to Egypt. As a result, God swore an oath in his anger that that generation would not enter the Promised Land. Through the intercession of Moses, God forgave them their sin and did not reject them as his covenant people. However, he did not grant them the blessing of the inheritance. They wandered in the wilderness until they all died. God did not permit them to return to Egypt. Though they had forfeited the Promised Land, for the next 38 years they still were the beneficiaries of God's miraculous manna and

---

Apocalyptic Language and Graeco-Roman Rhetoric in Hebrews 6:4–12," *NovT* 45, no. 3 (2003): 269.

[434] Oberholtzer, "The Thorn-Infested Ground," 325–26.

[435] L. T. Johnson, *Hebrews*, 161–62.

water. They received his divine leadership and protection. Yet they were under his "oath," his "curse" that they could not enter the land. Though they wept tears of repentance and attempted to go up into the land, God did not permit them to do so. By analogy, Heb 6:3 says: "and God permitting, we will do so." The Kadesh-Barnea episode furnishes the backdrop for Heb 6:1–8 just as it did for Hebrews 3–4.[436] The readers of Hebrews did not face the danger of apostasy from the faith through total rejection of Christ. Their danger was "falling into a permanent state of immaturity through a willful 'once for all' (*hapax*) refusal to trust God to deliver them from their present troubles."[437]

The language and imagery of Heb 6:6 are paralleled in the other warning passages of the epistle with such verbs as *aphistēmi* in 3:12; *piptō*, "fall," in 4:11; *parapiptō*, "to fall away," in 6:6; and *apostrephō*, "to turn away," in 12:25. In 4:11, *piptō*, "to fall," is translated "to perish" by Zerwick and Grosvenor.[438] Ellingworth takes it to mean "destruction," as in 3:17. Some think the writer has in mind the Israelites whose bodies fell in the wilderness.[439] Hebrews 6:6 is often interpreted against the backdrop of 3:12 where the readers are warned lest they "turn away from the living God." The Greek word used there, *aphistēmi*, also occurs in the LXX of Num 14:9, describing the rebellion at Kadesh-Barnea. In Num 14:9 the basic meaning of the Hebrew word is "to rebel," but the Greek noun *aphistēmi* has two possible contextual meanings: (1) rebel, and (2) apostate, and only context can determine which is intended. Wevers gives the translation "do not rebel against YHWH," noting that the LXX rendering best fits the Hebrew verb.[440] Gleason stated, "Later in the passage the same word is used for those who 'rejected' (*apestēte*) the land (14:31). Elsewhere in the Old Testament *aphistēmi* is associated with failing to obey God's voice (Jer 3:13–14; Dan 9:9) and trusting in man rather than God (Jer 17:5). These uses of the term suggest that *aphistēmi* is not a technical term denoting absolute apostasy."[441] Gleason goes on to give three reasons why the exodus generation did not commit apostasy. First, they were forgiven in response to Moses' prayer (Num 14:20); second, the people "mourned greatly" (14:39) and confessed they had sinned (14:40) when Moses pronounced judgment on them; and third, they were not permitted to return to Egypt. In fact, for the next 38 years, they experienced God's hand of protection, provision and guidance.

---

[436] G. H. Lang, *Hebrews*, 102–7; and esp. Gleason, "Old Testament Background," 78–80. R. D. Phillips concurs, but he does not even list or discuss the Loss of Rewards view in his commentary (*Hebrews*, Reformed Expository Commentary: New Testament (Phillipsburg, NJ: P&R, 2006).

[437] Gleason "Old Testament Background," 79.

[438] *GAGNT* 661.

[439] Kistemaker, *Hebrews*, 163; Ellingworth and Nida, *Handbook*, 82; Wray, *Rest as a Theological Metaphor*, 86–87, makes this connection between 3:17 and 4:11 as well.

[440] J. Wevers, *Notes on the Greek Text of Numbers* (Atlanta: Scholars Press, 1998), 214.

[441] Gleason, "Old Testament Background," 79.

Hebrews 6:4–8 has other Old Testament connections seen by many as its background. These include the blessings and curses of Deuteronomy. Several verbal and conceptual connections are evident.[442] Deuteronomy 11:11 (LXX) speaks of the Promised Land as a land that "drinks water from the rain of heaven." Deuteronomy 28:15 speaks of the "curses" that will come upon the exodus generation if they do not obey the Lord. The LXX uses the same Greek word for "curse" found in Heb 6:7–8. This "cursing" does not result in eternal damnation.[443] Deuteronomy 11:26–28 speaks of the "blessing" and the "curse" that the Lord will bring upon the nation depending upon whether they "listen" or not to the Lord's commands. Hebrews 6:7–8 contains the same blessing/curse motif. Deuteronomy 28–29 present a long list of blessings for obedience and curses for disobedience, with the final curse being the destruction of the land leaving it "a burning waste, unsown, and unproductive" (Deut 29:23). Given this Old Testament background, there is little warrant for viewing "cursed" in Heb 6:8 as a technical term for the eternal loss of those who are unregenerate.

Verbrugge has made the case for considering Isaiah's song of the vineyard in 5:1–7 as the background for Heb 6:7–8.[444] The LXX of Isa 5:2b, translates the Hebrew *bā'uš*, "wild grapes," as *akanthas*, "thorns," the same word as in Heb 6:8. In Heb 6:7 the field is cultivated and well-watered, while in Isa 5:6 the field receives no more "rain," both references using the same Greek word *hueton*. According to Heb 6:8, the field is good only for burning, while in Isaiah 5 the field ends up "full of thorns." Isaiah 5:7 identifies the vineyard as the "house" of Israel, and in Heb 3:1–6 the house motif of the Old Testament covenant people is used by the author for the new covenant people, the church.

This leads Verbrugge to propose Heb 6:7–8 as the hermeneutical basis for 6:4–6, with the covenant community as the primary concept in the author's mind rather than individual believers. "Thus, when we read of the falling away and of God's subsequent rejection, it is rejection of a community that is in focus. Such a rejection does not necessarily include every individual member of that community; in both Old Testament and New Testament parallel passages, this same theme can be found." By community, Verbrugge does not mean the church universal as the new covenant community, but a limited corporate body

---

442 E.g., Attridge, *Hebrews*, 173; DeSilva, *Hebrews*, 231–34; Nongbri, "Condemnation and Consolation," 271. Nongbri remarked: "The whole of LXX Deut. 11 presents vocabulary similar to Hebrews: the repetition of 'today' (σήμερον, 11:2,4,13, etc.), the 'discipline of the Lord' (παιδείαν κυρίου 11:2), God's gift of 'rain' (ὑετὸν, 11:11,14), and warnings against 'disobedience' (παραβῆτε, 11:16). That Deut. 11:26–28 stands in the background of Heb. 6:4–8 becomes all the more clear when we recognize its resonances with LXX Ps. 94:9–11, which plays a central part in the early chapters of Hebrews and which the author quotes at length in 3:7–11."

443 Some find a parallel to Gen 3:17–18, where the ground is "cursed" because of Adam's sin and will bring forth "thorns and thistles."

444 V. Verbrugge, "Towards a New Interpretation of Hebrews 6:4–6," *CTJ* 15 (1980): 61–73. F. F. Bruce, *Hebrews*, 149, makes passing reference to Isaiah 5 in his discussion of Heb 6:7–8, but does not develop the connection.

of a local church. He cites Rev 2:5; 3:3,16 as examples of "the possibility of corporate rejection of a church as a unit."[445] Such rejection does not include every single member in the local church, as is made clear in Rev 3:4.

Verbrugge is not unmindful of the warnings that have an individual flavor to them in Hebrews 3 and specifically Heb 10:26–39. He anticipates this criticism by noting that the primary focus of the section beginning with Heb 10:19 is on the community as a group. He also suggested that the quotation in Heb 10:30, "The Lord will judge his people," is from Moses final song before his death (Deut 32:35–36), and this reference is corporate in nature.[446] Whether Verbrugge's proposal is valid or not, he has at least succeeded in pointing out that at least sometimes the author of Hebrews is thinking of his readers in a corporate fashion similar to the Jewish notion of corporate solidarity.[447]

The deaths of the rebels in the exodus generation do not in themselves mean they were unconverted, since both Moses and Aaron also died in the wilderness as a result of God's discipline for their disobedience. The same Hebrew words in Deut 9:23–24 and Num 20:12,23 are used to describe their sin as are used to describe the sin of the exodus generation. They forfeited the blessing of the Promised Land, but this had nothing to do with their eternal spiritual condition.[448]

The author appears to affirm the redeemed status of the wilderness generation in Heb 11:29 when he says, "By faith the people passed through the Red Sea as on dry land." Hebrews 6:9 also points in this direction. The author does not say "we are persuaded of better things concerning you, namely, your salvation." Rather he refers to "things that accompany salvation," contextually a reference to fruitfulness that accompanies salvation.

We are thus left with three interpretative options for Heb 6:7–8. First, the author made a contrast between a genuine believer and an unbeliever. Second, he contrasted a Christian who perseveres with someone who, as a result of their apostasy, lost their salvation. Third the best option contextually seems to be that the author is contrasting a fruitful believer who endures with an unfruitful believer who is unfruitful because of willful disobedience resulting in a state of arrested development spiritually, a state confirmed by God himself.

Concluding Discussion of Loss of Rewards View. Having analyzed the meaning of Heb 6:7–8, our attention returns to the Loss of Rewards view.

---

[445] Verbrugge, "Towards a New Interpretation of Hebrews 6:4–6," 68. Ellingworth, *Hebrews*, 323, believes that the "main difference" between Heb 3:12 and 6:4–6 is the individual focus of the former and the "fate of the community as a whole in the latter."

[446] Ibid., 71. McKnight, "The Warning Passages of Hebrews," 53–54 critiques Verbrugge's proposal along these same lines, but does not take sufficient notice of Verbrugge's recognition of individual references as well.

[447] It is interesting to note how the author consistently uses plurals when speaking of Christians' access to God (4:3,11; 6:19; 10:19,22; 12:1; 13:13), and singulars when speaking of the possibility of falling away (3:12; 4:1,11b; 10:29; 12:15). This may undercut Verbrugge's hypothesis.

[448] Gleason, "Old Testament Background," 88.

Schreiner and Caneday subjected this view to critical scrutiny. It is curious that their critique fails to interact with key advocates of this position such as Lang, Oberholtzer, Gleason, and Dillow. Rather, they tend to focus on the more popular authors who have taken this position, highlighting their occasional glaring inadequacies.[449] Nevertheless, their criticism retains a measure of validity in that some advocates of this position often poorly articulated it, used Scripture imprecisely and incorrectly at times and sometimes understated the severity of the punishment and loss involved.

Schreiner and Caneday state that the Loss of Rewards adherents "radicalize eternal security by insisting that security in Jesus Christ guarantees that even those who fail to persevere in faithfulness to Christ and his gospel will never perish but are saved and will remain saved forever."[450] Though some have pressed the Loss of Rewards view to unbiblical extremes through unguarded and naïve theological assertions, most proponents of this position do not advocate that everyone who fails to persevere is indeed genuinely saved. They too recognize the import of 1 John 2:19. Not everyone who professes salvation actually possesses it, and those who fail to persevere do so because they were never genuinely converted. Persistent sin may indicate lack of salvation, though one is a part of a local church. Second, Schreiner and Caneday refer to Hodges' treatment of 1 Cor 6:9–10 and his distinction between entering the kingdom and inheriting the kingdom. They introduce this criticism with the words: "Consider how this view interprets one biblical passage."[451] Actually, it is Hodges' aberrant interpretation of the Corinthians passage, an element not inherent to the Loss of Rewards position, which Schreiner and Caneday rightly criticize. Third, Schreiner and Caneday acknowledge that Loss of Rewards proponents believe the Bible teaches eternal security, but they criticize this position for its rejection of the classical Reformed view of the warnings, including Heb 6, as a novel reading of the text. This is a case of begging the question. The question is whether the text of Heb 6:4–6 in its context best comports with a classical Calvinistic reading or can be better explained in another way.

Critics of the Loss of Rewards view argue that the harshness of Heb 6:6, with such expressions as "fall away," "crucifying the Son of God all over again," and "subjecting him to public disgrace," make it very unlikely the author is speaking of something as "benign" as disobedience and loss of rewards. Guthrie sought to verify this by four arguments against the Loss of Rewards view. First, Heb 3:6,14 and 4:1–2 describe falling short of entering God's rest because they did not respond to the gospel message with faith. Second, Heb

[449] Schreiner and Caneday, *The Race Set Before Us*, 24–29. E.g., they focus on R. Wilkin and the Grace Evangelical Society; three popular works of Z. Hodges; C. Stanley's *Eternal Security: Can You Be Sure?* and others, with Hodges, Stanley, and Wilkin receiving most of the attention.

[450] Schreiner and Caneday, *The Race Set Before Us*, 25.

[451] Ibid., 27.

10:26–31 speaks of the ones not accepting his warnings as "enemies of God" (10:27). Third, according to Heb 10:26–27, the result of their stubbornness will be that "no sacrifice for sin is left, but only a fearful expectation of judgment and of raging fire that will consume" them, and v. 39 contrasts "those who shrink back and are destroyed" with "those who believe and are saved." Fourth, Heb 6:9 contrasts with 6:4–6 by the change in pronoun, leaving us to infer that the group described in Heb 6:4–6 is unregenerate.[452] Guthrie, whose position is identical with the Tests of Genuineness view, calls his view the "phenomenological unbeliever view."[453] He is forced to give the novel interpretation "by which one is sanctified" to the phrase in Heb 10:29 (lit.) "by which he was sanctified." Guthrie says we must understand the statement as impersonal. This is grammatically feasible (though he offers no evidence) and avoids conflict with Heb 10:14. But such a reading is swimming upstream against the context and the majority of interpreters who take it in the traditional sense.

Those who affirm that Heb 6:6 refers to apostates who were not genuine believers cannot conceive of such language being applied to believers. However, if the falling away does not refer to apostasy as has been argued based on the meaning and usage of the word, there is no reason to think it cannot refer to willful disobedience on the part of Christians. It is clear that the word was so used in the LXX for sin among God's covenant people. Jesus used harsh language at times even when speaking to his own disciples. In Revelation 2–3, Jesus has some harsh words to say to some of his seven churches. The Pauline Letters are filled with serious warnings to deter Christians from sinning. First Corinthians 3:10–15 is a serious warning to Christian leaders who build on the Lord's foundation for his church using "wood, hay or straw," and the extended context applies the warning to all believers. This passage is sometimes cited by critics of the Loss of Rewards view as being misinterpreted by the view's adherents. Appeal is made to D. A. Carson's treatment of the passage as evidence against the view.[454] A careful reading of Carson's interpretation reveals that it actually does not contradict the Loss of Rewards view, nor its use of 1 Cor 3:10–15. Carson correctly argued that contextually, it is the quality of the *builder's* work that will be tested by fire at the last day, and not that of every single Christian. But the builder either receives a reward or suffers loss. He continues: "It is slightly misfocused to conclude, with Hans Conzelmann and many other commentators, that 'unsatisfactory works performed by the Christian *as a Christian* do not cause his damnation.'"[455] It is his next sentence that is telling: "Doubtless there is some sense in which that is true."[456] This

---

[452] G. Guthrie, *Hebrews*, 228.

[453] Ibid., 230.

[454] Carson, "Reflections," 390–93.

[455] Ibid. 392; quotation from H. Conzelmann, *1 Corinthians*, Her (Philadelphia: Fortress, 1975), 77.

[456] Ibid.

is exactly what the Loss of Rewards view advocates. Carson's interpretation of the passage is correct; those who use his interpretation against the Loss of Rewards view miss the point, even if some who affirm the view contextually misinterpret 1 Corinthians 3 as having immediate reference to all Christians. Carson goes on to note: "Only in vv. 16–17 is there a hint of a broader application, and it is no more than a hint."[457] But a hint it is, and one further supported by such statements found in 2 Cor 5:10. Finally, Carson concludes:

> Nevertheless, because Paul now speaks of "anyone" and not simply the builders, it suggests, in the context of the first four chapters, that those given to division, jealousy, and quarreling in the church are also in danger of doing damage to the church, God's temple. Since they are that temple, they are simultaneously doing damage to themselves and courting God's judgment.[458]

This conclusion does not vitiate the Loss of Rewards view. In commenting on this passage, Fee rightly stated, "Thus, as surely as there is final judgment, there is also 'reward' and 'loss.' What is *not* known, either from this passage or elsewhere, is the nature of the reward. This text only affirms its certainty."[459] Fee pointed out that this passage both warns and encourages, and "in the final analysis, of course, this includes all believers . . . but it has particular relevance . . . to those with teaching/leadership responsibilities."[460]

According to Heb 6:6, Christians, by their willful disobedience of the word of God, are certainly conducting themselves in such a way as to "crucify" again the Son of God. The language is metaphorical regardless of the interpretation. The key to understanding the statement in Heb 6:6 concerning the impossibility of renewing to repentance is found in Numbers 14. There, it was impossible for the people to be renewed to repentance because God had determined against permitting their entrance into the Promised Land. The same point is made in the Esau reference in Heb 12:17. Esau lost the blessing, but there is no indication he lost standing in God's covenant people. He repudiated the blessing, not God. Analogously, repudiation of Christ in the technical sense of apostasy need not be the meaning of Heb 6:6.[461]

---

[457] Ibid., 393.

[458] Ibid.

[459] G. Fee, *The First Epistle to the Corinthians,* NICNT (Grand Rapids: Eerdmans, 1987), 143. Fee thinks their behavior is so "seriously aberrant" that Paul warns in serious tones that those who persist in such conduct are in "eternal danger." If by "eternal danger" Fee intends loss of salvation, this is an example of eisegesis, imposing an Arminian theology on a text that is not referring to loss of salvation but loss of rewards.

[460] Ibid., 145.

[461] Koester, *Hebrews*, 322, exemplifies all those who wrongly analogize the death of the exodus generation in the wilderness with those who commit apostasy in Heb 6:6: "By refusing to restore apostates, God permits their decision to stand; he allows them to terminate the relationship. This corresponds to the way that God accepted the wilderness generation's refusal to enter the

THEOLOGICAL IMPLICATIONS. The history of interpretation of Hebrews 6 has often been marred by failure to avoid manipulation and superimposing a preconceived theology on this text. This has been a problem especially with Calvinistic exegesis, which in more recent times some Calvinists admit. Mugridge said that Calvinists, in their attempts to alleviate the difficulties posed to their position by Heb 6:4–6, have supported interpretations that "often depend on ingenious but forced exegesis."[462] R. Peterson remarked, "I frankly admit that some Calvinist treatments of the Hebrews warning passages leave much to be desired."[463] The theological schizophrenia of some Reformed treatments of Heb 6:4–6 leaves one scratching his head. Consider D. Hagner's explanation:

> Can Christians, then, fall away and lose their salvation? The answer again consists of a yes and a no. Certainly those described in verses 4 and 5 are Christians. . . . Christians can apostatize. . . . Yet paradoxically, if they become true apostates, they show that they were not authentic Christians (cf. 3:14). . . . Concerning the readers of Hebrews, as of all Christians, it must be said that they are Christians thus far.[464]

What can it possibly mean to say that someone is a Christian "thus far"? This could only be true from the perspective of another human being, for God knows those who are and who are not genuine Christians. No doubt, this is what Hagner intends to convey. To ask the question if Christians, not "true" Christians, but "Christians," can lose their salvation and then answer both yes and no invites misunderstanding. To say that "Christians can apostatize," and then in the next sentence say that if they do, they are not genuine Christians, is confusing language at best. If they apostatize, they were never Christians, and it is confusing to call them "Christians" when one does not mean by the word "Christian" the sense of "truly regenerated." Would it not be better to say that people who apostatize are not genuine believers? Hagner finally gets to the point where he affirms this. In the next paragraph he stated: "True Christians do not (i.e., cannot) apostatize,"[465] a statement with which I am in wholehearted agreement. Why then muddy the waters? Of course, Calvinists are not the only guilty party when it comes to this text and its treatment.

The first thing to be noted is that there are elements of truth in each of the five positions discussed above. There is a key difference, however, between

---

land, allowing them to die in the wilderness." The problem here is not concerning the analogy; the analogy is made by the author. The problem lies in equating the death of those in the exodus generation with apostasy and making the similar equation with Heb 6:6.

[462] Mugridge, "Warnings in the Epistle to the Hebrews," 74.

[463] Peterson, "Apostasy," 27.

[464] Hagner, *Hebrews*, 73.

[465] Ibid.

the Loss of Rewards view and all the others: the meaning of the participle *parapesontas* in Heb 6:6. I have argued that the word does not mean apostasy in the usual theological sense of loss of salvation by genuine believers or with reference to false believers who were not genuinely converted. It is the preconceived notion that the reference in Heb 6:6 is to apostasy in one of these two ways that is wrongheaded.

One of the difficulties that interpreters of Heb 6:6 face is the actual definition of apostasy. Many commentators identify the sin of Heb 6:4–6 as apostasy, but do not define what the word means.[466] Carson offered this working definition of apostasy: "a decisive turning away from a religious position once firmly held. It differs from ordinary unbelief in that it involves turning away from a position of belief. It differs from backsliding in that it is calculating and irrevocable."[467] Thus, with respect to the question of apostasy considered from the traditional meaning of the term and its application to Heb 6:6, one of three possibilities exists. Either apostasy is possible, in which case believers can lose their salvation (as in the Arminian position), or apostasy is not possible for genuine believers and thus those who apostatize are not genuine believers (as in the Hypothetical and Tests of Genuineness views), or apostasy is threatened but in the final analysis is not possible (as in the Means of Salvation view). We have tried to show that only the second position is theologically correct with respect to apostasy traditionally defined, *yet this is not what is taught in Heb 6:4–6*.

Some have equated apostasy with the unpardonable sin and made this correlation in Heb 6:6. Jesus revealed that the one unpardonable sin is the sin of blasphemy against the Holy Spirit (Matt 12:32; Mark 3:28–30; Luke 16:10). This sin can never be committed by a genuine believer, but only by unbelievers. The unpardonable sin is committed by those who have never been associated with the church or Christianity. The people described in Heb 6:4–6 are at the

---

[466] E.g., Attridge, *Hebrews*, 171, identifies the falling away of Heb 6:6 as apostasy, but nowhere defines what he means by the term. He assumes the technical definition of the term and implies that Heb 6:4–6 refers to genuine believers who then renounced Christ. Likewise, Lane, *Hebrews1–8*, 142, affirms the description of Heb 6:4–6 of believers and comes closest to defining apostasy when he said: "What is visualized by the expression in v. 6 is every form of departure from faith in the crucified Son of God." In Lane's more popular commentary on Hebrews (*Hebrews: A Call to Commitment* [Vancouver, BC: Regents College Publishing, 2004], 94) he is much more specific about the meaning of apostasy: "*Apostasy consists in a deliberate, planned, intelligent decision to renounce publicly association with Jesus Christ.*" He says it is a sin only a Christian can commit. Ellingworth, *Hebrews*, 322–23, does not define apostasy, but appears to understand the technical sense of denying Christ once and for all. Ellingworth seems to believe the group described in Heb 6:4–6 were genuine believers. Koester, *Hebrews*, 315, is also unclear of the meaning of apostasy in the passage, at one point stating: "Falling away from God means falling into sin." He indicates that the group described in Heb 6:4–6 are believers. F. F. Bruce, *Hebrews,* 148–49, likewise is unclear whether the group in Heb 6:4–6 are believers, but it appears he believes they are. He also appears to use the term "apostasy" in its assumed technical meaning to describe the sin in Heb 6:6.

[467] Carson, "Reflections," 396.

very least associated with the church, even if they are not genuine believers. Since, however, the context seems to support the position that they were genuine believers, it is incorrect to take the meaning of Heb 6:4–6 as a reference to the unpardonable sin.[468]

Three things seem clear in the New Testament. First, genuine believers are eternally secure in their salvation. The sheer weight of evidence in Hebrews and the entire New Testament supporting this doctrine is unavoidable. A key text is 1 John 2:19: "they went out from us because they were never of us." Speaking about this verse, D. A. Carson correctly stated, "genuine faith, by definition, perseveres; where there is no perseverance, by definition the faith cannot be genuine."[469] Second, there is no question that apparent believers who are not yet genuine believers can commit apostasy. This too is taught in the New Testament. It is just not taught in Heb 6:6. True apostasy is reserved for the unsaved. However, believers can "fall away." It is unhelpful and confusing to use the word "apostasy" to describe what genuine believers do when they rebel against the Lord and commit sin due to the technical meaning the term has developed.[470] Third, Christians can commit serious sin without being disqualified from eternal life. Part of the problem with some interpretations of Hebrews 6 is a failure to distinguish between totally renouncing Jesus and/or faith in Jesus by those who were never genuinely converted and failing Jesus on the part of those who are genuinely saved. People who call themselves Christians and yet sin without regret or desire to change show that they have never been genuinely converted. Christians sometimes do commit serious sins without being disqualified from eternal life. Examples include David, Peter, and some of the Corinthian Christians at the Lord's Supper (1 Cor 11:17–22). First Corinthians 3:1–3 affirms that carnal believers exist. Such immaturity and carnality is challenged by Paul with stern language. However, Paul does not question their salvation. He rather addresses them throughout as genuine believers. Carnal Christians are poor examples of Christians, but they are Christians. Likewise, the author of Hebrews addresses his readers as genuine believers, but they were immature spiritually (Heb 6:1). He warns them to press on to maturity, but even in the harsh words of Heb 6:4–6, he does not indicate they

---

[468] Calvin, *Institutes* 3.3.21, connected Heb 6:4–6 with the unpardonable sin. For a good discussion of why this is not the best interpretation to take concerning Heb 6:4–6, consult the excursus on this issue in Attridge, *Hebrews,* 168–69; and DeSilva, *Hebrews*, 234–36; as well as Koester, *Hebrews*, 319, who noted: "Hebrews probably does not allude to the unforgivable sin . . . since these gospel passages refer to those who persistently reject Jesus, whereas Hebrews focuses on those who come to faith, but then apostatize." For the position that the sin in Heb 6:4–6 is the same as blasphemy against the Holy Spirit, consult Delitzsch, *Hebrews*, 1: 291–93; and Hohenstein, "A Study of Hebrews 6:4–8," 543–44.

[469] Carson, "Reflections," 400. Carson thinks the issue in Heb 6:6 is apostasy of those who did not possess genuine faith.

[470] Against Dillow, *Reign*, 444, who uses "apostasy" to refer to loss of inheritance and rewards, not loss of salvation.

are not genuine believers. Hebrews 6:4–6 does not teach apostasy, in the technical theological sense of ultimately denying Christ, on the part of believers (the Arminian position) or apostasy on the part of those who are not genuine believers (the Calvinist position). Hebrews 6:1–8 is not a soteriological passage; it is a sanctification passage, as is made clear from the context.

We have observed the significance of the exodus generation in the thought of the author and how it is a context for Hebrews 6. If apostasy in the technical sense of the term was the problem the author of Hebrews feared among his readers, there was ample opportunity for him, to point to such failures as the golden calf incident (Exodus 32) in Heb 6:9 and 12:29, the people's desire to return to Egypt in Numbers 14, and the idolatry at Baal of Peor in Num 25:3. Instead, he chides his readers for failure to press on, not for any perceived desire to reject their Christian faith by a return to Judaism. One should strive not to make too much of the typological analogy between the exodus generation and the readers of Hebrews, but on the other hand, it is important not to make too little of it either. The parallels that the author attempted to show from Hebrews 3 onward furnish a key clue to the author's meaning in Hebrews 6 when he speaks of "falling away." It is not apostasy that the author of Hebrews is warning against, but persistent rebelliousness comparable to the wilderness generation in the exodus.

The concept of falling/turning away was first introduced in Heb 3:12 then referred to again in 4:11 and 6:6. Our author uses the verb *aphistēmi* only once (Heb 3:12) and not in any of the other warning passages. This speaks against understanding his meaning as "apostasy" in the traditional sense of that term. If the author intended for his readers to understand "apostasy" in Heb 6:6, why not use *aphistēmi* as in Heb 3:12? Even there we have seen that the word does not mean "apostasy" in the technical sense of the term. Carson was partially correct when he suggested little help on the nature of apostasy is to be gained by simple word studies. The word *apostasia* occurs only twice in the NT. It refers to the turning away of the Jews from Moses (Acts 21:21), and to the turning away of many after the man of lawlessness is revealed (2 Thess 2:3).[471] But Carson was partially incorrect as well. Part of the problem with the history of interpretation of Hebrews 6 is the failure to engage in a careful word study of the participle *parapesontas* in Heb 6:6. Words mean what they mean in context, and the immediate, book, canon, and wider extra-biblical contexts are not in favor of the meaning "apostasy."

Lindars, in his work on the theology of Hebrews, assumes that "apostasy" is the danger the readers face, and this apostasy lies in a return to the Jewish purificatory rites of Judaism and the synagogue that the readers had left when they entered the church. Based on Heb 13:8–16, Lindars conjectures that the readers were struggling with what to do about post-baptismal sin. They had

---

[471] Carson, "Reflections," 396.

expected the parousia to occur, and its delay caused some of the readers to begin to be oppressed by renewed consciousness of sin. The gospel, as they had received it, did not specify how Christians were to deal with post-baptismal sin. Since the Jewish rituals of purification accomplished this, the readers were leaving the fellowship of the church and returning to the Jewish synagogue for this ritual cleansing. This action created an intolerable situation for the church leadership. They appealed to the author for help in solving the problem and he responded with this epistle, arguing for the sufficiency of the atonement to cover not only past sins, but all future sins as well.[472] In the introduction, it has already been shown that this reconstruction is very unlikely. According to this interpretation, the readers of the epistle were not in danger of a complete rejection of Christ themselves. Lindars's point seems to be that the author's argument is an attempt to show that the logical progression towards such repudiation of Christ's sacrifice that attends such a move on the part of the readers risks apostasy. In explaining what the author of Hebrews would say if his readers did take the step of apostasy and then later sought reconciliation, Lindars oddly stated, "we cannot say. But I suspect that, in spite of what he says here, he would welcome them with open arms! It is unsound to assume that in a work of such marked rhetorical character the writer should never allow himself some element of exaggeration."[473] Thus Lindars inexplicably takes the harsh warning of Heb 6:4–6 in rhetorical stride and indicates that the author was engaging in "exaggeration" and really does not mean what he says.

Gundry-Volf demonstrated in both Old Testament and Intertestamental writings the clear distinction between the disciplining of the covenant community and the condemnation experienced by those who are outside that community. God disciplined his people for their sins throughout the Old Testament. What is also evident is that the covenant community, though corrected, belongs to God and remains his people. Likewise, the author of Hebrews in 12:7 views discipline of the new covenant people in a positive way.[474] The New Testament warns against sin in the lives of believers, but never threatens them with possible loss of salvation. Regression is possible, inviting divine chastisement even in the form of physical death (1 Cor 11:27–34). Yet this is temporal and not eternal loss, "and marks out even sinful Christians as God's children."[475] This is the situation with the readers in Hebrews 6. The author considered them genuine believers, although they had sinned willfully by failing to press on to maturity through obedience to the word of God. The absence of eternal

[472] Lindars, *Theology of Hebrews*, 8–15.

[473] Ibid., 70.

[474] Gundry-Volf, *Paul and Perseverance*, 107–13. In addition to Gundry-Volf, consult Oropeza, *Paul and Apostasy*, 1–34. Oropeza provides probably the best survey of the history of the doctrine of perseverance.

[475] Ibid., 285.

damnation terminology in Hebrews 6 militates against interpreting the passage as referring to eternal loss.

The New Testament teaches eternal security of the believer along with perseverance of the saints. It also warns of the danger of a spurious faith as well as the danger of sin in the life of a believer. God is sovereign and humans are responsible. Both these concepts are taught in the New Testament and must be held in tension in a compatibilist fashion. Carson is correct when he pointed out that all the Biblical authors are compatibilists when they speak of divine sovereignty and human responsibility.[476] Failure to recognize this point tends to generate interpretations that collapse one into the other.

The ground for every Christian's assurance and perseverance is the high priesthood of Christ, which the author develops throughout the epistle. The warning passage of Heb 5:11–6:20 is flanked immediately on both sides by the development of the high priesthood of Christ. Because of what Christ has done in his atoning work, the new covenant is eternal (Heb 10:18). He is a priest forever. An eternal inheritance is every Christian's promised blessing. Were it possible for a Christian to remove himself from the covenant of salvation by apostasy, then Christ's death is not eternally saving. However, the author of Hebrews affirms Christ's death as eternally saving. It is the sufficiency of Christ's death, his eternal high priesthood, and our solidarity with him as laid out in Hebrews 2 that makes these warnings so severe, but also that makes believers chafe under either an apostasy or loss of salvation interpretation. Perseverance is not the basis of assurance. The basis of assurance is Christ and his work.[477]

If assurance and perseverance ultimately rest with God, then there can be no problem with the Loss of Rewards view because it recognizes that Christians can and do sin; they can and do persist in sin; and they can have their works burned up at the judgment seat of Christ as 1 Cor 3:10–15 indicates. This view also affirms that genuine believer's persevere, not based on what they do, but on what Christ has done. If someone rejects their faith, then this is evidence they were never saved, as 1 John 2:19 makes clear. The Loss of Rewards view does not preclude cases where tests of genuineness are in play. It is difficult if not impossible to separate the wheat from the tares. Only God can do that. Christians who died prematurely for their sin as recorded in Scripture (Acts 5, 1 Corinthians 11, 1 John 5—the "sin unto death") cannot be said to have persevered to the end from the perspective of their own initiative, can they? But did they lose their salvation? There is no direct statement that they did. They experienced temporal discipline, as the Loss of Rewards view affirms.

---

[476] Carson, "Reflections," 405.

[477] As correctly noted by Carson, "Reflections," 412. Hughes, "Hebrews 6:4–6 and the Peril of Apostasy," 154, stated, "Finally, when the redeeming blood of Christ is applied by the Holy Spirit to the very heart of a man's being, it is a work of God that cannot fail. This means that those who are genuinely Christ's do not fall away into apostasy."

If this view is correct, the question arises as to how much fruit in one's life is enough to show evidence of salvation? This question is virtually impossible to answer. If there is no evidence of fruit, genuine salvation is at the very least questionable, and such a fruitless state probably indicates lack of conversion. The author follows his warning of Heb 6:4–8 with a paragraph affirming that God had not forgotten the "works" of the readers nor their "love" shown to the saints. These are examples of some fruit in the lives of his readers, showing that the author considered them genuine believers, yet immature and in need of the severe warning of Heb 6:4–6.

Finally, we note the Loss of Rewards view may be misnamed. Loss of rewards does occur to those guilty of this sin, but it is their persistent rebelliousness that, if unconfessed, opens the door for God's judgment. Such decisive refusal to press on to maturity through obedience places them in jeopardy of having God refuse to permit them to press on to maturity, with a consequent loss of blessing, growth, and usefulness in this life, and loss of rewards in the eternal state.

The Loss of Rewards view best explains the immediate context of failure to press on to spiritual maturity, the description of those in Heb 6:4–6 as believers, the Old Testament background of the events surrounding Kadesh-Barnea in Numbers 14, the meaning of *parapiptō*, the nature of the judgment in Heb 6:7–8, and the broader context of the other four warning passages in Hebrews, all of which warn genuine believers of the same danger. In one sense, the author of Hebrews is urging his readers to complete what the exodus generation failed to complete due to their sin at Kadesh-Barnea. This comes into focus thematically in Heb 12:1–2 where the readers are exhorted not to fall back, but to press forward to run the race set before them, looking unto Jesus.

(3) Persevering Strength Based on God's Faithfulness (6:9–20)

**9Even though we speak like this, dear friends, we are confident of better things
in your case—things that accompany salvation. 10God is not unjust; he will not
forget your work and the love you have shown him as you have helped his people
and continue to help them. 11We want each of you to show this same diligence to
the very end, in order to make your hope sure. 12We do not want you to become
lazy, but to imitate those who through faith and patience inherit what has been
promised.**

**13When God made his promise to Abraham, since there was no one greater for
him to swear by, he swore by himself, 14saying, "I will surely bless you and give
you many descendants." 15And so after waiting patiently, Abraham received what
was promised.**

**16Men swear by someone greater than themselves, and the oath confirms what
is said and puts an end to all argument. 17Because God wanted to make the unchanging nature of his purpose very clear to the heirs of what was promised, he
confirmed it with an oath. 18God did this so that, by two unchangeable things in
which it is impossible for God to lie, we who have fled to take hold of the hope**

offered to us may be greatly encouraged. [19]We have this hope as an anchor for the soul, firm and secure. It enters the inner sanctuary behind the curtain, [20]where Jesus, who went before us, has entered on our behalf. He has become a high priest forever, in the order of Melchizedek.

6:9 As a new paragraph, Heb 6:9–12 is introduced by *de*, "but," which indicates a contrast with the preceding paragraph. The author now moves from warning to encouragement. He calls his audience *agapētoi,* "dear friends," in v. 9, the only place in the epistle where this term occurs. This word underscores the author's deep love and concern for his readers and his attempt to reassure them. The author does not identify any specifics concerning the "better things" he is persuaded of concerning his readers. Several possibilities have been suggested: (1) a better outcome than described in v. 6; (2) a fruitful life as described in v. 7; (3) God's blessings and promises about to be mentioned by the author; (4) a better course of action; and (5) confidence in their salvation.[478] The only explanation of "better things" is the following statement connected by explanatory *kai*: "things that accompany salvation." The author does not say the "better things" refer to entrance into salvation, but to that which "accompanies" salvation. The author assumes, and thus implies by his language, that the readers are believers. This is also brought out by the final statement in the Greek text of v. 9, which is placed first in the NIV: "even though we speak like this." In spite of the author's previous warning, he affirms the condition of his hearers as that of genuine converts. Semantically, this is a concessive idea: "although," or "notwithstanding." But the author is "confident" of the "better things" concerning them, where the perfect tense verb translated "we are confident" is emphatic by its position in the sentence. Though the author uses the first person plural "we," he actually means "I."[479]

6:10 Verse 10 is introduced with *gar*, "for," giving a twofold reason for the author's confidence expressed in v. 9: God's righteous character and the reader's previous love and good works. The use of "unjust" followed by the infinitive translated "to forget" could be taken in the sense of degree: "God is not so unjust as to forget," or in the sense of result, "God is not unjust resulting in his forgetting," but it is probably better taken in an explanatory sense: "he is not unjust so that he would forget."[480] The author does not specify exactly what he means by the "work and love" of the readers. Many commentators think this

---

[478] See Ellingworth and Nida, *Handbook*, 120, for the many options.

[479] So the vast majority of commentators, against Lenski, *Hebrews*, 189–90, who thinks others are included with the writer. Wallace considers this a "debatable" example of the editorial "we." He notes the difficulty of determining when the author uses the editorial "we," made worse by the author not using the first person singular until 11:32 (and then only three more times in the epistle: 13:19,22,23). Wallace thinks this "suggests the possibility that Hebrews was actually written by at least *two* persons with one being better known to the audience" (*GGBB* 396). Wallace later suggested the two authors might be Barnabas and Apollos.

[480] So Miller, *Hebrews*, 179; Moffatt, *Hebrews*, 83, (the infinitive of conceived result); and Ellingworth, *Hebrews*, 330, ("the infinitive is epexegetic"), respectively.

refers to what is stated in Heb 10:32–34 where the readers at one point sympathized with those in prison and suffered for it. The NIV translates "the love you have shown him," that is, God, where the Greek reads (lit.) "for his name." This can be taken in two ways. It could mean the object of love is God's name in the sense of "for his sake" or in the sense of God himself. It could also be taken as indicating reference: "with reference to his name," but in the sense of meaning "to him," or simply as the equivalent of "him," as in the NIV.[481] The final two participles in v. 10 translated "as you have helped his people and continue to help" express the means[482] by which the love and good works are shown, with the use of the aorist followed by the present tense referring to past service and present service respectively.

The juxtaposition of v. 10 with v. 9 further indicates the previous warning passage was not referring to loss of salvation, but rather was a passage dealing with sanctification. The author speaks of love shown to God by means of good works shown to the saints. As Bruce pointed out, the point of the passage "is that deeds of kindness done to the people of God are reckoned by God as done to himself, and will surely receive their reward from him."[483]

6:11–12 The next two verses are one sentence in the Greek text, introduced by *de* (left untranslated by the NIV). Many commentators find a note of contrast in the use of *de*, taking it in the sense of "but."[484] The author places individual emphasis on each of his readers when he says he desires, "each of you," to be diligent. The sense of the Greek text is "we desire each one of you to demonstrate the same diligence." The noun translated "diligent" indicates diligent action and connotes the concepts of earnestness, eagerness, and devotion to the task. "To show" in the NIV translates an infinitive meaning "to demonstrate; to display." The readers are to demonstrate by their actions in the present time the same diligence described and illustrated previously in v. 10. This diligence is to be shown by the readers "with regard to the full conviction and confidence of hope to the end."

The noun *plērophoria*, translated "sure" in the NIV, probably refers both to the notion of assurance and development.[485] What the author desires his readers to possess is "hope," which in this context is virtually equivalent to the promises about to be mentioned in the next verse. The final phrase "to the very end" is emphatic by its position and has been variously connected with "showing the same diligence," "hope," and with the overall thought of v. 11 as

---

[481] Greenlee, *Exegetical Summary*, 206–7.

[482] The NIV translates the two participles as attendant circumstances of their love shown. "as you have helped."

[483] Bruce, *Hebrews*, 151. This supports the Loss of Rewards view for Heb 6:4–8 as articulated above.

[484] Among older commentators, see Dods, "Hebrews," 301, and among more recent ones, Lane, *Hebrews 1–8*, 130.

[485] See discussion in Ellingworth, *Hebrews*, 332.

a whole. The meaning of "end" has also been variously interpreted. Some take it to mean the end of the believer's life. Others think it refers to the parousia. Either interpretation is possible though the former appears more likely.

The NIV begins a new sentence at v. 12, but the Greek text continues the sentence begun in v. 11 with a subordinate *hina* clause that expresses either purpose or result.[486] The author desires his readers to be diligent in their Christian life and growth so they will not become *nōthroi*, "lazy." The author contrasts diligence with laziness, using the same word *nōthroi* with which he began the discourse section back in 5:11. This *inclusio* has the effect of bracketing off this entire section as a semantic unit. The NLT expresses the sense of the *nōthroi* well: "spiritually dull and indifferent." Some have noticed an apparent contradiction in the use of this word in 5:11 and 6:12. In 5:11 the author stated "you are slow to learn." Here he states: "We do not want you to become lazy." In 5:11, the focus is on the ability to discern spiritual truth; here the focus is on behavior. In 5:11 the readers had become lazy in their thinking; here the author challenges them not to become lazy in their actions. The noun in the Greek text, "imitator," is translated by the infinitive "to imitate," a valid translation since semantically the noun conveys an active rather than a static sense. Those who are to be imitated are the ones "who through faith and patience inherit what has been promised."

The "promises," plural in Greek, will be further defined in the next paragraph from the illustration of the life of Abraham. To "inherit" the promises means to receive them for oneself. This is done by means of "faith and patience." Faith embraces the unseen as though it were visible and the future as though it were present. Patience, better translated "steadfast endurance,"[487] waits with longsuffering for the fulfillment of the promise. The reward of faith and patient endurance is the receiving of what was promised.

With this encouragement found in Heb 6:9–12, the author concludes the unit he began at 5:11. This section comprises four paragraphs, alternating negative and positive, which creates a sense of balance in this warning passage. Hebrews 5:11–14 is negative, followed by the positive counterpart in 6:1–3. Hebrews 6:4–8 is the heart of the warning passage, followed by the encouragement of 6:9–12. All this is bracketed by the use of *nōthroi* in 5:11 and 6:12, marking off the section as a semantic unit. With the reference to the "promises," the author makes his transition to the life of Abraham in v. 13 as an illustration of God's faithfulness.

6:13 Hebrews 6:13–20[488] is introduced by the subordinating conjunction *gar*, which indicates the grounds for the preceding statement about "blessings."

[486] Ellingworth, *Hebrews*, 333, takes it as result, while Lane, *Hebrews 1–8*, 144, takes it as expressing purpose.

[487] Lane, *Hebrews 1–8*, 130.

[488] This entire pericope is characterized by forensic language (Lane, *Hebrews 1–8*, 149), is less dependent upon the LXX, and contains numerous Hellenistic parallels and non-biblical terms

The ground for the statement is in the form of an illustration about Abraham and Isaac, which the author then connects to his readers in vv. 18–20. Verses 13–15 make up a paragraph unit summarizing the experience of Abraham and Isaac recorded in Genesis 22. God's first encounter with Abraham was in Genesis 12, and there he made specific promises to him, which were reiterated in several places in the early chapters of Genesis, including 13,15,17,18, and 21. But our author does not refer to any of these passages; rather, he quotes from the Aqedah ("the offering of Isaac") in Genesis 22, where God commands Abraham to sacrifice his son Isaac. This was the supreme test of Abraham's faith since the fulfillment of God's covenant depended upon Isaac's progeny. Genesis 22:1 indicates that this incident was a "test" for Abraham, but Abraham did not know it was a test. So confident was Abraham in God's faithfulness that the author of Hebrews said in 11:19 that Abraham reckoned God would raise Isaac from the dead in order to fulfill his promise. At the last moment, God intervened and stopped Abraham from killing his son. After Abraham sacrificed the ram that was caught in the thicket nearby, the Lord not only reiterated his promises to Abraham, but swore an oath to fulfill them that our author refers to in Heb 6:14. The participle translated "made his promise" is temporally related to the main verb "he swore," and probably indicates concurrent time.[489] It is possible that the author uses the aorist participle to indicate time preceding the event of swearing the oath in Genesis 22, since the promises were originally given in Genesis 12 and reiterated several times afterward before Genesis 22.[490]

The use of *epei*, translated "since," gives the reason God swore by himself: there is no one greater than God for him to swear by. The interesting thing about this is God's promise itself is inviolable. He did not need to take an oath on top of his promise. But in the case with Abraham, he did so to bolster Abraham's faith and as the author stated in v. 17, God did so to show to all the heirs of the promise his own fidelity in keeping those promises. As Dods pointed out, God could as soon cease to exist as fail to fulfill what he has vowed.[491] The author places the noun *theos*, "God," at the end of the phrase in the first half of v. 13 for emphasis,[492] and concludes the second phrase with "he swore by himself," a quote portion taken directly from Gen 22:16, meaning, "he swore by his own name." The author does not elaborate at all on the "blessing" or on the "multiplying"; rather, he comments only on the portion of the Old Testament quotation that says "he swore by himself."

6:14 Verse 14 is a direct quote from Gen 22:17. The combination of *ei* followed by *mēn* in Greek is not found anywhere else in the New Testament, but is common in the LXX. It conveys the notion of "solemn affirmation or

(Ellingworth, *Hebrews*, 334).

[489] So Lane, *Hebrews 1–8*, 147; and Ellingworth, *Hebrews*, 336.

[490] So Lünemann, *Hebrews*, 542.

[491] Dods, "Hebrews," 302.

[492] Lit. in Greek: "for to Abraham God having promised . . ."

corroboration of an oath."[493] The NIV translates "I will surely bless you," which reflects the LXX's translation of the Hebrew infinitive absolute with cognate participle and noun. The LXX (lit.) reads "blessing I will bless you and multiplying I will multiply you." Both the Hebrew and LXX construction convey assurance and certainty. The NIV translates the meaning of the second half of the quotation as "give you many descendents." The two participles function semantically to indicate the means by which God blesses and multiplies: "by blessing I will bless, by multiplying I will multiply."[494] This statement is the content of the oath itself.

6:15 Verse 15 begins with the conjunction *houtōs*, "so," which may be connected either with the aorist participle translated "waiting patiently," or as is more likely, with the main verb "received." The participle can be taken to indicate the reason for the main verb "received," or as is more likely, it functions in a temporal sense of antecedent attitude and action to the main verb: "After waiting patiently, Abraham received what was promised." Against the causal reading of the participle is the important observation by Swetnam that v. 12 indicates both faith and endurance were the circumstances of receiving the promises, not the *cause* of the promises.[495] The "promise" refers to Abraham's many descendents and begins with its fulfillment at Isaac's birth, continues with Abraham and Isaac's experience in Genesis 22, and is further reinforced by God's oath concerning the promise in Genesis 22.[496] Less likely is Lane's view that what Abraham received was a confirmation of the promise when God swore the oath in Genesis 22, since the fulfillment of the promise depended upon Isaac.[497] Yet it is certainly true that God's oath served as confirmation to

---

[493] Lane, *Hebrews 1–8*, 148.

[494] Miller, *Hebrews*, 183. On the author's alteration of the quotation from the LXX and its differences with the MT, see Lane, *Hebrews 1–8*, 151.

[495] Swetnam, *Jesus and Isaac*, 184–85. He noted regarding v. 12: "The use of the genitive with διά implies that the faith and patience were the circumstances for the reception of the promises, not the cause (which would have been expressed by the use of διὰ with the accusative). Thus, the participle μακροθυμήσας in v. 15 is to be understood as being circumstantial, not causative." See also Lane, *Hebrews 1–8*, 148, who follows Swetnam here in taking the participle in the temporal rather than the causative sense. Ellingworth and Nida, *Handbook*, 126, suggested the conjunction οὕτως coupled with the participle suggests "not merely the manner in which Abraham received the promises, but the means by which he received them." Interestingly, later in his commentary, Ellingworth (*Hebrews*, 338) said the οὕτως "cannot be an adverb of manner . . . since Abraham's patience has not been mentioned before."

[496] So Bruce, *Hebrews*, 153. Swetnam, *Jesus and Isaac*, 185, commented on the focus of the author of Hebrews on God's promise concerning progeny. In Heb 6:12, the author speaks of "promises" (plural), referring at least to God's promises concerning offspring and land. Both promises are mentioned in the oath in Genesis 22, but the author of Hebrews only cites the promise having to do with offspring in 6:13–15. Compare this with Heb 11:17–19 where the author's focus is again only on the promise of offspring through Isaac. Swetnam concluded from this that the "many sons" spoken of in Heb 2:10 should be interpreted as an allusion to Abraham's offspring.

[497] Lane, *Hebrews 1–8*, 151. Cf. Koester, *Hebrews*, 326, who presented both options but preferred the former.

Abraham. Hebrews 6:15 does not contradict 11:13 because there the reference is to the "full realization of the promise of which the birth and, later, the restoration of Isaac were initial pledges."[498]

6:16–20 Hebrews 6:16–20 is one sentence in the Greek text introduced by *gar*, "for," which gives the grounds or reason (1) for the oath in v. 14, or (2) for the comment in v. 13, or, as is most likely, (3) for the entire thought of vv. 13–15 generally. The anarthrous use of *anthrōpos*, "man," may be interpreted as generic, stressing people by nature, and its position in v. 16 is emphatic. The author is contrasting the inviolability of oaths by men and God by using an argument from the lesser to the greater. The words translated "end" and "all" are emphatic by their position in the clause. The point is that the use of a vow settles the argument. The articular use of *orkos*, "oath," is an example of the generic use of the article, indicating what is generally true about oaths. There is some question about what the Greek nominal phrase "for confirmation," translated by the finite verb "confirms," is connected with. It can be connected with "end" with a purposeful meaning, with "the oath" in the sense of "given for confirmation," or with the entire clause.[499] Bruce is most likely correct in taking it as referring to the entire clause.[500] The meaning of the Greek noun rendered "confirmation," has been interpreted as a technical expression for a legal guarantee.[501]

The use of the preposition *en* with the dative object, (lit.) "in which" in Greek, is not made explicit in the NIV. It is variously translated "in the case of," "because," "in this matter," "so" and similar expressions. The various versions and commentaries take it in one of four ways: (1) a conclusion, (2) a reason, (3) a related circumstance, and (4) manner ("in the same way").[502] The last fits best in this context. The phrase is connected with "he confirmed it with an oath."[503] The NIV translates the Greek emphatic neuter adjective used as an adverb by "very clear." This adjective modifies the infinitive "to show." The Greek adjective for "unchanging" is sometimes translated as a noun, as in the NASB. What God wills to accomplish is unchangeable. God "confirmed" the promise by means of his oath, making himself the guarantor of the promise.[504]

---

[498] Bruce, *Hebrews*, 153. Cf. the discussion in Ellingworth, *Hebrews*, 338–39.

[499] Greenlee, *Exegetical Summary*, 216.

[500] Bruce, *Hebrews*, 154.

[501] G. A. Deissmann, *Bible Studies: Contributions Chiefly from Papyri and Inscriptions to the History of the Language, the Literature, and the Religion of Hellenistic Judaism and Primitive Christianity*, 2nd ed., trans. A. Grieve (Edinburgh: T&T Clark, 1903), 107, and since by most commentators. See Hughes, *Hebrews*, 232, and examples from Greek literature in Koester, *Hebrews*, 327.

[502] See Greenlee, *Exegetical Summary*, 218, for the respective versions and commentators.

[503] Attridge, *Hebrews*, 180, sees the antecedent as the previous verse, with v. 17 providing the reason for the oath.

[504] On the use of the *hapax legomenon* ἐμεσίτευσεν in the sense of "to mediate between," or in the technical sense of "guarantee," see A. Oepke, "μεσίτης," *TDNT* 4:598–624.

This notion of "guarantor" becomes vital for the author in Hebrews 8–9 when the author develops the theme of Jesus as the guarantor of the new covenant. The reference to God's "oath" may allude to Ps 110:4 where Christ is proclaimed by God as the high priest with an oath. It is leading up to this connection that is made explicit in Heb 7:21.

One key question in this verse is the referent of the "heirs." It is unlikely, given the overall context, that the word applies only to the Christians of the author's time.[505] More likely it refers to all Christians of all times,[506] or to all Old Testament saints as well as Christians of all times.[507] All Christians are heirs of the Abrahamic promise according to Gal 3:29: "If you belong to Christ, then you are Abraham's seed, and heirs according to the promise."

The thought is continued in v. 18 by a *hina* clause in the sense of "in order that," stating the purpose of God's oath. This purpose is for the readers to be "greatly encouraged." The means by which they are to be encouraged are "two unchangeable things,"[508] a reference in context most likely to God's promise and his oath. These things are "unchangeable" because it is impossible for God[509] to lie. The author fronted the phrase "greatly encouraged" in the Greek clause structure for emphasis. The attributive participle translated as "we who have fled" carries with it the implication of fleeing for refuge.[510] The infinitive "to take hold" is either an infinitive of purpose connected with the participle "we who have fled," or an explanatory infinitive connected with the noun *paraklēsin*, "encouragement," stating what is taken hold of.[511] The former

---

[505] As suggested by Ellingworth, *Hebrews*, 341.

[506] So Lane, *Hebrews 1–8*, 152.

[507] So Hughes, *Hebrews*, 233. Ellingworth and Nida, *Handbook*, 128, concurred: "This is confirmed by the use of 'we' in the next verse."

[508] D. R. Worley, "Fleeing to Two Immutable Things: God's Oath Taking," *ResQ* 36 (1994): 222–36.

[509] On the text critical question of whether the noun θεόν is articular or anarthrous, see the discussions in G. Zuntz, *The Text of the Epistles: A Disquisition upon the Corpus Paulinum* (London: Oxford, 1953), 130; Lane, *Hebrews 1–8*, 148; and Ellingworth, *Hebrews*, 343. If anarthrous, the character and nature of God may be what the author is emphasizing.

[510] It is possible the author has in mind the cities of refuge in Joshua 20. So Spicq, *l'Épître aux Hebreux*, 2:163, who takes καταφυγόντες as a reference to the cities of refuge (Num 35:6–28). R. Gordon, "Better Promises: Two Passages in Hebrews against the Background of the Old Testament Cultus," in *Templum Amicitiae: Essays on the Second Temple Presented to Ernst Bammel*, ed. W. Horbury, JSOTSup 48 (Sheffield: JSOT, 1991), 438–39, takes the same view and develops it. The terms "fleeing" and "laying hold" suggest the author had in mind the seeking of sanctuary at the altar as illustrated by Adonijah in 1 Kgs 1:50 and Joab in 1 Kgs 2:28. Braun, *An Die Hebräer*, HNT 14 (Tübingen: Mohr Siebeck, 1984), 190, suggested the occurrences of κατέχειν in the present tense in the LXX of the Adonijah and Joab accounts indicate the kind of clinging that may be suggested in the use of κρατῆσαι in Heb 6:18. Buchanan, *Hebrews*, 115, takes the meaning to be "have recourse" in the sense that "the people who flee to an oath are the ones who can gain support from it." Thus, as Gordon put it: "Christian hope reaches right into the most holy place and enjoys a sacrosanctity that the old Jewish system could not provide" ("Better Promises," 441).

[511] See the options in Attridge, *Hebrews*, 183.

seems more likely since that which is taken hold of is "hope."[512] Koester noted this encouragement "motivates people to 'strive' faithfully (6:11), resist sin (3:13), perform good works (10:24), and accept divine instruction (12:5)."[513] Hope is taken to refer to salvation through Christ or to Christ himself. The word is never used in Hebrews to denote a subjective attitude as is common in English usage. Rather *elpis* consistently speaks of the objective content of hope: present and future salvation.[514] The word describes a settled certainty combined with a confident expectation based upon the promises of God.

This hope is described in v. 19 as an """ of the soul that Christians presently possess.[515] The anchor became a popular symbol among early Christians. Several pictures of anchors can be found in the Roman catacombs. The use of *psuchē*, "soul," here refers to life as a whole. The entire phrase is metaphorical since an anchor connotes stability and security, hence the use of the adjectives "firm" and "secure." The anchor is "firm" because it won't bend, twist, or break when placed under strain, and it is "secure" because it won't drag or slip in the storm. The two adjectives are virtually synonymous, are placed last in the clause for emphasis, and modify "hope."[516] The author's reference to the anchor recalls Heb 2:1 where another nautical metaphor, the drifting ship, was used.

This hope anchor "enters the inner sanctuary behind the curtain." The use of the present participle may imply continuous action. The "curtain" refers to the veil that separated the holy place from the holies of holies in the tabernacle and temple. The "inner sanctuary" refers to the holy of holies itself, which was the dwelling place of the glory of God, housed the ark of the covenant in the days of the tabernacle, and into which only the high priest could enter once a year on the Day of Atonement (Exod 26:31–35; Lev 16:2,12,15). This theme will be picked up in Hebrews 9 in reference to the atoning work of Christ and his entrance into the heavenly sanctuary following his resurrection and ascension.

In the LXX, *katapetasma*,[517] "curtain," can be used to refer to any of three veils in the tabernacle: the court veil (Exod 38:18; Num 3:26), the veil at the

---

[512] The infinitive "take hold of" may be better translated as "hold fast," given the previous exhortation to "hold firmly to" in 4:14 and the coming exhortation to do the same in 10:23 (Koester, *Hebrews*, 329).

[513] Koester, *Hebrews*, 328–29.

[514] As noted by Lane, *Hebrews 1–8*, 153. Koester, *Hebrews*, 329: "The objective reality of hope . . . gives rise to the subjective act of hope." Both objective and subjective aspects are included in the meaning of the word. Calvin, *Hebrews*, 86: "The word *hope* is used by metonymy, the effect being taken for the cause. I understand it as referring to the promise on which our hope relies, and I do not agree with those who take hope as meaning the thing hoped for." See Bultmann, "ἐλπίς," *TDNTa* 229–32.

[515] Note the present tense ἔχομεν "we have."

[516] Lane, *Hebrews 1–8*, 148, 153. It can also be construed as modifying "anchor" (Moffatt, *Hebrews*, 89; Hughes, *Hebrews*, 235; and Bruce, *Hebrews*, 155.

[517] The classic study on the subject is O. Hofius, *Der Vorhang vor dem thron Gottes: Eine exegetisch-religionsgeschichtliche Untersuchung zu Hebräer 6,19 f. und 10,19 f.*, WUNT 14

entrance to the holy place in the sanctuary (Exod 26:36–37), and the inner veil between the holy place and the most holy place (Exod 26:31,33,34,35).[518] Commentators past and present have almost universally agreed that the reference in Heb 6:19 is to the inner veil.[519] G. Rice argued that Heb 6:19 does not refer to the inner veil but rather the heavenly sanctuary as a whole.[520] But his argument is difficult to sustain since the Greek phrase translated "behind the curtain" appears four times in the LXX (Exod 26:33; Lev 16:2,12,15), always referring to the inner veil.[521] Each time the LXX is translating the same Hebrew phrase (*mibbêt lāppārōket*) meaning "within the inner veil." The context of Leviticus 16 is the Day of Atonement, when the high priest would pass behind the inner veil into the most holy place. However, R. Davidson attempted to make the case that the reference to Christ entering "behind the veil" is a reference to the inauguration of the sanctuary by Moses, the only other time when there was an "entrance" behind the inner veil (Exod 40:1–9; Lev 8:10–12; Num 7:1). Davidson draws this conclusion based on the three occasions in Hebrews where Christ is described as entering into the sanctuary (Heb 9:12,24; 10:19–20).

> In each of these three parallel passages, as in Heb 6:19–20, the author's use of crucial LXX terminology—and especially the conjunction of the three key LXX terms *enkainizō*, *tragos*, and *moschos* in a single chapter dealing with inauguration (Num 7)—proves to be a key to interpretation. The immediate context of each passage is consistent with the LXX terminology pointing to inauguration.[522]

N. Young offered eight reasons Davidson's position is "flawed," concluding that the evidence points towards a reference to the Day of Atonement. Davidson's rejoinder to Young appeared in the same journal volume.[523] Davidson

(Tübingen: Mohr Siebeck, 1972).

[518] C. Schneider, "καταπέτασμα" *TDNT* 3:629. G. Rice, "Hebrews 6:19: Analysis of Some Assumptions Concerning *Katapetasma*," *AUSS* 25 (1987): 65–71.

[519] See, for example, Braun, *An die Hebräer*, 191; Grässer, *An die Hebräer*, 1:383–85; Attridge, *Hebrews*, 184; Lane, *Hebrews 1–8*, 154; Ellingworth, *Hebrews*, 347; and Gordon, "Better Promises," 441.

[520] Rice, "Hebrews 6:19," 70–71.

[521] As noted by R. Gane, "Re-opening KATAPETASMA ("Veil") in Hebrews 6:19," *AUSS* 38.1 (2000): 6; and argued more in depth by N. Young, "'Where Jesus Has Gone as a Forerunner on our Behalf' (Hebrews 6:20)," *AUSS* 39.2 (2001): 165–73.

[522] Davidson, "Christ's Entry 'Within the Veil' in Hebrews 6:19–20: The Old Testament Background," *AUSS* 39.2 (2001): 188. Cf. E. E. Andross, *A More Excellent Ministry* (Mountain View, CA: Pacific Press, 1912), 42–54.

[523] N. Young, "The Day of Dedication or the Day of Atonement? The Old Testament Background to Hebrews 6:19–20 Revisited," *AUSS* 40.1 (2002): 61–68. Six of Young's eight reasons follow: (1) Moses is not referred to as a high priest in any of the chapters related to the dedication of the tabernacle. (2) Nowhere in these chapters is the phrase "within the veil" used. (3) The differences in wording and syntax of the phrase "within the veil" between Heb 6:19–20 and the LXX do not outweigh the similarities to Lev 16. (4) Moses' dedication of the tabernacle was a singular

is correct that the author of Hebrews alludes to the dedication ritual, at least in Hebrews 9, but this is within the context of an amalgam of sacrificial ideas found in Heb 8–10, with the Day of Atonement as the focal point for the author of Hebrews in this section.[524]

Like the high priest of old on the Day of Atonement, this sacred place is where Jesus himself has entered "on our behalf" as our "forerunner," *prodromos*, translated as "who went before us." The Greek clause structure indicates that "Jesus" is the subject of the verb "has entered" and "forerunner" is the predicate, thus giving the sense "Jesus has entered as forerunner."[525] The author has placed the name "Jesus" in the emphatic position in the clause. In fact, one might say the climax of the single sentence in Greek that begins in v. 15 and ends in v. 20 is the name "Jesus."[526] A few commentators connect "on our behalf" with "forerunner," but most likely it connects to "has entered."

The author abruptly shifts from a nautical metaphor to that of the tabernacle's inner sanctuary in heaven where Jesus, after his ascension, dwells. Is it the anchor or the hope that enters behind the veil? Since the antecedent of the participle is the relative pronoun *hēn*, which is connected with "hope," it is better to understand that hope enters behind the veil. This interpretation is supported by v. 20—it is Jesus (our hope) who has entered on our behalf. In Heb 7:19 the author referred to "a better hope by which we draw near to God."[527]

The concept of Jesus as "forerunner" has engendered several interpretations.[528] The word occurs only here in the New Testament with the meaning "running before," and is used of messengers, athletes, advance military scouts, and sailing. "The idea is not so much that of an onrushing warrior or an advance ship as of the one who has run the same course and whose successful running makes that of believers possible."[529] Regardless of the specific metaphor the author may have had in mind, the enthroned Christ in the heavenly sanctuary as our forerunner is the guarantee that we shall one day enter heaven as well. As our anchor of hope, he secures our entrance. Our author has invested this term with significant Christological freight, and along with *archēgos* ("author") in

---

unrepeated event. This precludes inauguration as being the background for the repetitious nature of the sacrifices. (5) Heb 6:19–20 is the key to interpreting Heb 10:19–20, not vice versa. (6) Although τὰ ἅγια in the LXX refers to the sanctuary as a whole, Davidson fails to deal with the sentence in which the word appears. Contextually, the Day of Atonement is in view. R. Davidson's rejoinder can be found in, "Inauguration or Day of Atonement? A Response to Norman Young's 'Old Testament Background to Hebrews 6:19–20 Revisited,'" *AUSS* 40.1 (2002): 69–88.

[524] N. Young, "The Gospel According to Hebrews 9," *NTS* 27 (1981): 205–6.

[525] Greenlee, *Exegetical Summary*, 223.

[526] The KJV attempts to render the emphatic position of "Jesus": " "whither the forerunner is for us entered, even Jesus."

[527] Lane, *Hebrews 1–8*, 153–54.

[528] See O. Bauernfeind, "πρόδρομος," *TDNTa* 1189–91; BDAG 867; Lane, *Hebrews 1–8*, 154; Ellingworth, *Hebrews*, 348; and Attridge, *Hebrews*, 185.

[529] Bauernfeind, "πρόδρομος," 1191. Ellingworth, *Hebrews*, 346, views the word as a synonym for ἀρχηγός in Heb 2:10.

Heb 2:10, it identifies a crucial theme in the letter: Jesus leads his people and goes before them, preparing the way for them to follow.

The final clause of v. 20 speaks of Jesus' high priesthood as "in the order of Melchizedek," a repetition of the identical phrase used in Heb 5:10 at the conclusion of Heb 5:1–10. This clause also serves as an introduction to the theme of Hebrews 7 where Jesus and Melchizedek are compared. Thus far, the author's theological argument has unfolded in the following manner: Jesus is identified as the Son in Hebrews 1, and as high priest in Heb 2:17 and 3:1. In Heb 5:5–10, Jesus is identified as both Son and high priest. In Heb 5:10 and again in 6:20, his high priesthood is not that of the Levitical line of Aaron, but rather that of the mysterious character Melchizedek. The repetition of the phrase "in the order of Melchizedek" at 5:10 and 6:20 serves as an *inclusio* to bracket the semantic unit of 5:11–6:20.[530] As at 5:10, the author is using Ps 110:4, but with the significant addition of "forever," strategically placed at the end of the clause for marked prominence. The entire phrase "in the order of Melchizedek" is fronted in the clause for emphasis where the literal rendering of the Greek would be "according to the order of Melchizedek a high priest having become unto the ages." This participial phrase is rendered as a sentence in the NIV: "He has become a high priest forever, in the order of Melchizedek." The participle "having become" has been taken adverbially as indicating reason: "Jesus entered on our behalf because he became a high priest,"[531] or adjectivally in an attributive sense describing Jesus: "who has become a high priest."[532] The aorist participle "having become" sums up the work of Jesus begun at the incarnation, accomplished at the cross, and consummated with his resurrection, ascension and exaltation.

The singular feature of the Melchizedekian priesthood contrasted with the Levitical priesthood is the fact that it is "eternal" or "forever," and this eternality is developed extensively by the author in Hebrews 7. The reference to Ps 110:4 resumes the theological argument that the author interrupted at Heb 5:10 with the lengthy warning passage. Structurally speaking, Moffatt's suggestion that 6:20 begins the next section of the epistle[533] fails to recognize the tail-head style of linkage that the author is fond of and that was described by Vanhoye and later by G. Guthrie.

THEOLOGICAL IMPLICATIONS. The theological implications of Heb 6:13–20 at first appear to stand in stark contrast to what has been stated previously in vv. 4–6. In reality, rather than affirming the possibility of loss of salvation if one apostatizes, the entire sixth chapter of Hebrews serves to provide one of the strongest arguments for the eternal security of the believer. Hebrews

---

530 Vanhoye, *A Structured Translation of the Epistle to the Hebrews*, 16; G. Guthrie, *Hebrews*, 185–86.

531 So Dods, "Hebrews," 305–6.

532 A possibility as noted by Greenlee, *Exegetical Summary*, 224.

533 Moffatt, *Hebrews*, 90.

6:13–20 highlight two implications that all Christians must recognize. First, God has made promises to believers that by their nature demand patient endurance to receive. Second, these promises provide us a secure ground of hope because of God's fidelity to his promise and his oath. The author's purpose in using the Abraham and Isaac illustration is to demonstrate God's fidelity to his promises. Jesus as high priest has secured and guaranteed our promised salvation. His death on the cross, resurrection, ascension and enthronement at the right hand of God as both high priest and king open the door of access for us to the throne of grace. This access along with its implications has already been broached by the author in Heb 4:14–16, and are more fully developed in 10:19–25.[534]

Three important functions for Heb 6:13–20 are summarized by Attridge:

> It rounds out the hortatory introduction to the central exposition on a positive, encouraging note. It explicitly recalls the key text of Ps 110(109):4, which announced the theme of the following chapters, and it calls attention to an aspect of that verse, the divine oath, which will play a prominent part in the exegetical discussion of chap. 7.[535]

Taking Heb 6:9–20 as a whole, Ellingworth and Nida noted that from its viewpoint, the essentials of the remainder of the epistle can be summed up as follows:

> God made a firm promise to his people which was the foundation of the covenant generally (chapter 9) and of all its forms of worship and sacrifice (chapter 10). None of the Old Testament heroes, despite their faith, received what God promised (chapter 11); but Jesus, a High Priest of a different kind (chapter 8), like Melchizedek (chapter 7), has made it possible for us to receive it. So we must hold on to our faith in him (chapter 12) and put it into practice (chapter 13).[536]

Hebrews 6:20 concludes the major discourse section begun at 5:11 and resumes the topic of Christ's high priesthood compared to Melchizedek in 5:10. This section is marked by "a formalized closure" with the exact repetition of the phrase "in the order of Melchizedek" at 5:10 and 6:20.[537]

---

[534] G. Guthrie, *Hebrews*, 245; Lane, *Hebrews 1–8,* 155.

[535] Attridge, *Hebrews*, 178.

[536] Ellingworth and Nida, *Handbook*, 119.

[537] Neeley, "Discourse Analysis of Hebrews," 13. Neeley posits a special linguistic device that she calls "participial foreshadowing" used by the author of Hebrews to mark prominence in the discourse. Clauses with verbals are generally less prominent than independent clauses. "Yet when a participial phrase appears as the last phrase in a discourse unit, it often contains information that states or foreshadows the theme of the following section" (p. 29). Though Neeley does not specifically reference Heb 6:20 as an example of this phenomenon, it appears that the author's use of the aorist participle γενόμενος "having become," followed by the direct object "high priest," functions in this way. G. Guthrie, *Structure*, 71, noted the shift back to an expository genre from

2. Christ's Melchizedekian Priesthood (7:1–28)

[1]This Melchizedek was king of Salem and priest of God Most High. He met Abraham returning from the defeat of the kings and blessed him, [2]and Abraham gave him a tenth of everything. First, his name means "king of righteousness"; then also, "king of Salem" means "king of peace." [3]Without father or mother, without genealogy, without beginning of days or end of life, like the Son of God he remains a priest forever.

[4]Just think how great he was: Even the patriarch Abraham gave him a tenth of the plunder! [5]Now the law requires the descendants of Levi who become priests to collect a tenth from the people—that is, their brothers—even though their brothers are descended from Abraham. [6]This man, however, did not trace his descent from Levi, yet he collected a tenth from Abraham and blessed him who had the promises. [7]And without doubt the lesser person is blessed by the greater. [8]In the one case, the tenth is collected by men who die; but in the other case, by him who is declared to be living. [9]One might even say that Levi, who collects the tenth, paid the tenth through Abraham, [10]because when Melchizedek met Abraham, Levi was still in the body of his ancestor.

[11]If perfection could have been attained through the Levitical priesthood (for on the basis of it the law was given to the people), why was there still need for another priest to come—one in the order of Melchizedek, not in the order of Aaron? [12]For when there is a change of the priesthood, there must also be a change of the law. [13]He of whom these things are said belonged to a different tribe, and no one from that tribe has ever served at the altar. [14]For it is clear that our Lord descended from Judah, and in regard to that tribe Moses said nothing about priests. [15]And what we have said is even more clear if another priest like Melchizedek appears, [16]one who has become a priest not on the basis of a regulation as to his ancestry but on the basis of the power of an indestructible life. [17]For it is declared:

> **"You are a priest forever,**
> **in the order of Melchizedek."**

[18]The former regulation is set aside because it was weak and useless [19](for the law made nothing perfect), and a better hope is introduced, by which we draw near to God.

[20]And it was not without an oath! Others became priests without any oath, [21]but he became a priest with an oath when God said to him:

> **"The Lord has sworn**
> **and will not change his mind:**
> **'You are a priest forever.'"**

---

the hortatory genre of the previous warning passage. There is a topic shift from Jesus in 6:20 to Melchizedek in 7:1, and a tense shift from aorist to present tense as well. S. Levinsohn, *Discourse Features of New Testament Greek* (Dallas: Summer Institute of Linguistics, 1992), 281, likewise posits a paragraph break at 7:1 given the strong reference to Melchizedek. However, Westfall, *Discourse Analysis*, 153, 159, sees the unit ending at 7:3 and not 6:20 based on the indicative mood after 6:1 being broken at 7:4 with the use of an imperative. The cohesive and grammatical ties between 6:17–20 and 7:1–3 "indicate continuity rather than a shift to a new unit." Whether the shift in mood from indicative to imperative alone is enough to determine this boundary is at least problematic in light of the foregoing linguistic evidence.

[22]**Because of this oath, Jesus has become the guarantee of a better covenant.**

[23]**Now there have been many of those priests, since death prevented them from continuing in office; [24]but because Jesus lives forever, he has a permanent priesthood. [25]Therefore he is able to save completely those who come to God through him, because he always lives to intercede for them.**

[26]**Such a high priest meets our need—one who is holy, blameless, pure, set apart from sinners, exalted above the heavens. [27]Unlike the other high priests, he does not need to offer sacrifices day after day, first for his own sins, and then for the sins of the people. He sacrificed for their sins once for all when he offered himself. [28]For the law appoints as high priests men who are weak; but the oath, which came after the law, appointed the Son, who has been made perfect forever.**

The longest doctrinal section of the epistle begins with Hebrews 7 and concludes at 10:18.[538] In 7:1–28, the author carefully explains the relationship between Jesus and Melchizedek, which was introduced in 5:10 just before the lengthy warning passage of 5:11–6:8, and which was reintroduced in 6:20. Hebrews 7 is composed of three major discourse sections: vv. 1–10, vv. 11–22, and vv. 23–28. Section one contains two paragraphs: vv. 1–3[539] and vv. 4–10. The section is demarcated by *inclusio* with the repetition of the statement that Melchizedek met Abraham (vv. 1,10). These 10 verses are also given cohesion by the use of chiasm where "meeting," "blessing," and "tenth" (all in vv. 1–2) are mentioned in inverted order in vv. 4,6,10. The final section is divided into two sub units: vv. 23–25,26–28. The UBS[4] text begins a new paragraph at vv. 4,11,20,26.

Hebrews 7 falls within the larger discourse section of Heb 4:11–10:25, according to Westfall, who suggested that the most semantically dominant theme is found in the hortatory subjunctive of 6:1: "Let us press on to maturity." While her evidence for such a division is questionable, she is correct in her assertion that this theme paraphrases the commands of Heb 4:1,11 where the readers are told to seek to "enter the rest." "The paraphrasing and expansion of the goal-oriented language fleshes out what entering the rest involves."[540] The author's purpose is practical and his theological argument supports his

---

[538] For a study of this section see K. Backhaus, *Der Neue Bund und das Werden der Kirche: Die Diatheke-Deutung des Hebräerbriefs im Rahmen der Frühchristlichen Theologiegeschichte*, NTAbh 29 (Münster: Aschendorff, 1996), 73–282.

[539] Structurally, C. Westfall, *A Discourse Analysis of the Letter to the Hebrews: The Relationship Between Form and Meaning*, LNTS 297 (London: T&T Clark, 2006), 159–60, 170, argued that 7:1–3 was the conclusion of the previous discourse section and not the beginning of a new discourse section as most interpret it. She bases this primarily on four grounds: (1) 7:1 begins with the subordinating conjunction γάρ and 7:4 begins with δὲ; (2) both cohesive and grammatical ties with what precedes suggests continuity; (3) the imperative in 7:4 introduces a "conversational style" that characterizes the writing until 10:18; and (4) the use of the imperative in 7:4 is a common way the author effects a discourse shift. More likely is the traditional understanding of beginning a new unit with 7:1 since the author uses the lexical chiasm with "meeting," "blessing," and "tenth" in 7:1–10.

[540] Westfall, *Discourse Analysis*, 186.

hortatory purpose. Once again, the lengthy theological argument of the author primarily serves to provide the grounds for the hortatory sections where he tells his readers what he wants them to do. The structure is basically something like "on the grounds of x, do y" or "do x on the grounds of y," depending upon whether the hortatory passage precedes or follows the doctrinal argument.

The author's goal in Hebrews 7 is to establish the nature of Jesus' priesthood and prove biblically and theologically that it is superior to the Levitical order. In this chapter, the author uses "synkrisis," a rhetorical device of comparison of two subjects of similar quality. Jesus is compared to Melchizedek and the Levitical priesthood in order to demonstrate his superiority.[541] The author's reasoning is based on a key biblical text, Ps 110, which was understood messianically in Jesus' day.[542] He begins historically in 7:1–3 with a reference to the Abraham and Melchizedek episode (Gen 14:17–20). Upon Abraham's return from his victory over the four kings from the east who had taken his nephew Lot captive, he is met outside Salem (Jerusalem) by a mysterious figure named Melchizedek. Melchizedek blessed Abraham and in return, Abraham gave him a tenth of all the spoils from the victory. Within the confines of these three verses, we are told eight facts about the identity of Melchizedek. He was (1) king of Salem, (2) priest of God most high, (3) his name means "king of righteousness," (4) he is also "king of Salem," which means "king of peace," (5) he is "without father or mother," (6) he is "without genealogy," (7) he is "without beginning of days or end of life," and (8) like the Son of God he remains a priest forever.

The identity of Melchizedek has been the source of considerable discussion and debate.[543] At least seven major views can be delineated. He has been iden-

---

541 The rhetorical device of synkrisis in Hebrews 7 is ably demonstrated by T. Seid, "Synkrisis in Hebrews 7: The Rhetorical Structure and Strategy," *The Rhetorical Interpretation of Scripture: Essays from the 1996 Malibu Conference*, JSNTSup 180 (Sheffield: Sheffield Academic Press, 1999), 322–47.

542 S. Kistemaker, *The Psalm Citations in the Epistle to the Hebrews* (Amsterdam: G. van Soest, 1961), 118, says Heb 7 is an exegesis of Ps 110:4: "The author takes hold of the last 'Melchizedek' and places it in a historical setting (7:1–3); in the next passage he discusses the word 'priest' (7:4–11) and priestly 'order' (7:11–13); two verses are devoted to the personal pronoun 'thou' (7:13–14); and the remainder (7:15–25) elaborates the epithet 'for ever.'"

543 The literature is immense. For surveys, consult M. Astour, "Melchizedek," *ABD* 4:684–86; D. C. Allison, "Melchizedek," *DLNT* 729–31; and K. Mathews, *Genesis 11:27–50:26*, NAC (Nashville: B&H, 2005), 151–56, which provides an excellent excursus on Melchizedek. Among the more significant treatments, excluding commentaries, see J. A. Fitzmyer, "'Now This Melchizedek . . .' (Heb. 7:1)," in *Essays on the Semitic Background of the New Testament* (London: Geoffrey Chapman, 1971), 221–43; F. L. Horton Jr., *The Melchizedek Tradition: A Critical Examination of the Sources to the Fifth Century A.D. and in the Epistle to the Hebrews* (SNTSMS 30; Cambridge, England: 1976), esp. 152–93, for a survey of the church fathers concerning Melchizedek; G. Cockerill, *The Melchizedek Christology in Heb 7:1–28* (Ann Arbor: University Microfilms International, 1979), 355–483, which in my judgment is still the best overall survey and evaluation of all the options, including one of the best exegetical treatments of Heb 7; D. W. Rooke, "Jesus as Royal Priest: Reflections on the Interpretation of the Melchizedek Tradition in Heb 7," *Bib* 81

tified by some as a divine being. There are four variations of this view that developed during the Patristic era. A second century Gnostic text identified him as Jesus himself.[544] A sect known as the Melchizedekians arose early in the third century AD. Composed mainly of Jewish converts, it affirmed Melchizedek was a heavenly being superior to Jesus since Jesus was a mediator of men, but Melchizedek was considered a mediator of angels.[545] In the third century, according to Epiphanius (fourth century bishop of Salamis), Melchizedek was identified as the Holy Spirit by the Coptic heresiarch Hieracas.[546] Others understood Melchizedek to be a pre-incarnate appearance of Jesus.[547]

A second interpretation suggests Melchizedek is an angelic being, perhaps Michael the archangel.[548] A third view, suggested by some Jewish rabbis in the

---

(2000): 81–94; M. McNamara, "Melchizedek Gen 14, 17–20 in the Targums, in Rabbinic and Early Christian Literature," *Bib* 81 (2000): 1–31; J. R. Davila, "Melchizedek, Michael, and War in Heaven," *SBLSP* (Atlanta: Scholars Press, 1996), 259–72; id., "Melchizedek: King, Priest, and God," in *The Seductiveness of Jewish Myth: Challenge or Response?*, ed. S. D. Breslauer (Albany: SUNY, 1997), 217–34; and P. Kobelski, *Melchizedek and Melchirea,* CBQMS 10, ed. B. Vawter (Washington, DC: Catholic Biblical Association of America, 1981), 115–29. For Melchizedek in Gnostic literature, see B. A. Pearson, "The Figure Melchizedek in Gnostic Literature," in *Gnosticism, Judaism, and Egyptian Christianity*, Studies in Antiquity and Christianity 5 (Minneapolis: 1990), 108–23. On literature in the twentieth century prior to 1960, see D. M. Hay, *Glory at the Right Hand: Psalm 110 in Early Christianity*, SBLMS 18 (Nashville: Abingdon, 1973), 134, n. 20. On Melchizedek in Qumran literature and the question of whether a Qumran background provides the basis for interpreting Hebrews, see A. van der Woude, "11Q Melchizedek and the New Testament," *NTS* 12 (1966): 301–26; Y, Yadin, "Aspects of the Dead Sea Scrolls," *Scripta Hierosolymitana* 4 (1965): 36–55; and R. Longenecker, *Biblical Exegesis in the Apostolic Period* (Grand Rapids: Eerdmans, 1975), 172, who argued the affirmative. G. Cockerill, "Melchizedek or 'King of Righteousness'," *EvQ* 63, no. 4 (October 1991): 305–12; and W. L. Lane, *Hebrews 1–8*, WBC (Dallas: Word Books, 1991), 161, see no direct connection. J. A. Fitzmyer, "Further Light on Melchizedek from Qumran Cave 11," JBL 86 (1967): 25–41; and J. Carmignac, "Le document de Qumrân sur Melkisédeq," *Revue de Qumran 7* (1970): 343–78.

544 Melchizedek Tractate (NHC IX, 1).

545 J. M'Clintock and J. Strong, "Melchizedek," in *Cyclopaedia of Biblical, Theological and Ecclesiastical Literature* (Grand Rapids: Baker, 1981 reprint), 6:59.

546 *Panarion 4, Against Melchizedekians* 5.1–4, in Heen and Krey, eds., *Hebrews*, 99.

547 Ibid., 100.

548 A. S. Van der Woude, "11Q Melchizedek and the New Testament," 305. Astour, "Melchizedek," ABD 4:685, noted Michael and Melchizedek are not explicitly identified in the Qumran texts. This identification is not found until medieval Jewish interpretation. Astour's statement that the author of Hebrews considered Melchizedek an immortal being, coeternal with the Son of God, is wide of the mark (p. 686). J. D. G. Dunn, *Christology in the Making*, 2nd ed. (Grand Rapids: Eerdmans, 1996), 20, conjectured of 11QMelchizedek that Melchizedek had become an angelic figure because the short nature of the visit described in Gen 14 with Abraham invited this sort of interpretation. For the view that 11QMelch is not referring to the Biblical Melchizedek of Gen 14, see Cockerill, "Melchizedek or 'King of Righteousness'," *EvQ* 63, no. 4 (October 1991): 305–12, who argued that the connection between Gen 14 and 11QMelch is best explained by the supposition that the connection arose from rather than contributed to the composition of 11QMelch. A. Aschim, "Melchizedek the Liberator: An Early Interpretation of Genesis 14?" *SBLSP* (Atlanta: Scholars Press, 1996), 254, takes the opposite view.

time of Jerome, was that Melchizedek was Shem, the son of Noah.[549] Philo took Melchizedek to be an actual human high priest who represented *nous* (mind) in an allegorical fashion.[550] Carmignac suggested Melchizedek is a symbolic name for the human Davidic Messiah.[551] Kobelski regarded Melchizedek as a historical and a heavenly figure, but not an angel. He was superior to angels but inferior to the Son.[552] Davila suggested he was a tutelary deity of the Davidic house along the lines of ancestral deification in West Semitic royal cults.[553] A seventh view takes Melchizedek to be a Canaanite king-priest of Salem (Jerusalem) who was a worshipper of the true God.

Several of these proposals can be speedily ruled out of hand as nothing more than Gnostic, Jewish,[554] or Christian speculation that has no basis in Scripture. There is no biblical support for the notion that Melchizedek was an angelic being, the Holy Spirit, Shem (son of Noah), a heavenly being serving as mediator for the angels, or as a human being allegorically representing *nous*. The only two views that can be reasonably defended from Scripture are that Melchizedek was the pre-incarnate Christ or that he was a Canaanite king-priest. I offer my views about Melchizedek's identity after looking carefully at what is said about him in Hebrews and Psalm 110, since these are the only two places in Scripture where he is mentioned.[555]

7:1–10 In this passage, the author couches his writing in the form of a homiletical midrash on Gen 14:17–20. However, as Michel and Lane correctly noted, Genesis 14 is not the focal text of Hebrews 7 but rather is subordinated to

---

[549] Some rabbis identified Melchizedek with Shem who was thought to have survived Abraham by 25 years based on one reading of the chronology of Genesis (Astour, "Melchizedek," 686). This was the prevailing view of the Jews in the time of Jerome (McClintock & Strong, *Cyclopaedia,* 6:58).

[550] Philo discussed Melchizedek in *Allegorical Interpretations,* 3.79–82; *On the Preliminary Studies,* 99; and *On Abraham,* 235, the latter of which makes it clear Philo believed Melchizedek to be a human being, not an angelic or divine being. See Horton, *Melchizedek,* 89; and R. Williamson, *Philo* (Leiden: Brill, 1970), 434–37. G. Cockerill, "Melchizedek: A Test Case for the Hermeneutics of Hebrews," ETS unpublished paper, (November 17, 2001), 1–19, against Longenecker ("Melchizedek Argument," 177), noted Philo did not view Melchizedek primarily as a manifestation of the eternal logos. See his *Melchizedek Christology*, 388–411, for a critique of the Philonic interpretation.

[551] J. Carmignac, "Le document de Qumrân sur Melkisédeq," *Revue de Qumran* 7 (1970): 343–78.

[552] Kobelski, *Melchizedek and Melchirea,* 127.

[553] Davila, "Melchizedek: King, Priest, and God?," 217–34.

[554] For attitudes toward Melchizedek in late Judaism, see R. Longenecker, "The Melchizedek Argument of Hebrews: A Study in the Development and Circumstantial Expression of New Testament Thought," 162–71. In Longenecker's summary of late Judaism's treatment of Melchizedek, he noted two assumptions that must be relinquished: (1) Ps 110:1 describes a heavenly monarch, and (2) Melchizedek was an insignificant figure in the first century AD (p. 171). That Hebrews is not influenced by the Dead Sea Scrolls, see L. D. Hurst, *Background,* 52–60; and Kobelski, *Melchizedek,* 127–29.

[555] Hebrews is the only Christian work before Justin Martyr that mentions Melchizedek.

Ps 110:4 by the author.[556] The author briefly summarizes the historical account of Gen 14:17–20[557] and focuses on two significant actions: the blessing given by Melchizedek to Abraham, and the tithe of the spoils given by Abraham to Melchizedek. The blessing is mentioned again in vv. 6,7 and the giving of the tithe (or the collecting of the tithe in Levitical law) is mentioned in vv. 4, 5, 6, 8 (twice, once unexpressed), and 9 (twice). This would indicate that the author's focus is not so much on the blessing[558] as on the giving of the tithe by Abraham. In this way the author establishes the superiority of Melchizedek to Abraham and prepares the way to argue for the superiority of the priestly order of Melchizedek (which according to Ps 110:4 is a type of Christ), over against the Levitical order.

7:1 The author begins by stating two facts about Melchizedek: he is "king of Salem," and he is "priest of God Most High." Salem is probably best identified with Jerusalem.[559] Melchizedek functioned as both king and priest. What is startling in the Genesis account is that a Canaanite is apparently functioning as a priest for Yahweh. As Balaam was a prophet of non-Jewish origin, so Melchizedek was a priest of Canaanite descent. Melchizedek is said to be a priest of "God Most High," a designation that our author understood, based on its usage in Judaism and early Christianity, to be a reference to God with emphasis on his transcendence.

7:2 The author then moves to an examination of the etymology and meaning of the name "Melchizedek." At this point, he leaves the actual statements in the Genesis 14 account aside and begins his own reflection on the text. He

---

556 O. Michel, *Der Brief an die Hebräer*, KEK 13 (Göttingen, Vandenhoeck und Ruprecht, 1936), 256; Lane, *Hebrews 1–8*, 158–59.

557 Gianotto's supposition that Gen 14:17–20 was inserted into Genesis early in the postexilic period is without any support (C. Gianotto, "Melchisedek e la sua tipologia: Tradizioni giudaiche, cristiane e gnostiche," Section II a.C.–III d.C, *Supplementi Alla Rivista Biblica* 12 [Brescia: Paidei, 1984]: 748).

558 G. Cockerill, "Melchizedek: A Test Case," 13, saw the importance of the "blessing" concept in Gen 14 where Abraham refuses to receive the blessing of the king of Sodom, but accepts the blessing of Melchizedek. In his judgment, Melchizedek appears "for no other purpose than to mediate God's blessing." The root *brk,* "bless," appears three times in Gen 14:19. This harks back to Gen 12 where Abram was promised that he would be a blessing and that all families would find blessing in him (G. J. Wenham, *Genesis 1–15*, WBC [Waco: Word Books, 1987], 317). See B. K. Waltke, *Genesis: A Commentary* (Grand Rapids: Zondervan, 2001), 234; and J. Sailhamer, *The Pentateuch as Narrative: A Biblical-Theological Commentary* (Grand Rapids: Zondervan, 1992), 147–48. However when Ps 110:4 is brought into the picture by the author of Hebrews, much more is at stake. The author interpreted Gen 14:17–20 in the light of Ps 110:4 as well as in the light of Jesus as Messiah, and his argument in the whole of Heb 7:1–28 is not focused on the "blessing" by Melchizedek, but on the paying of a tithe to him by Abraham, which establishes Melchizedek's superiority over the Levitical priesthood.

559 On the various views of the location of Salem, see McClintock and Strong, *Cyclopaedia,* 6:59. The equation of Salem with Jerusalem is found in Ps 76:2. Josephus also makes the equation (*Antiquities* 1.10.2). Longenecker ("Melchizedek Argument," 183) stated, "The Ebla texts speak of a Palestinian 'Salem' as being in existence in the third millennium BC."

states in v. 2 "first" that Melchizedek's name means "king of righteousness,"[560] from the two Hebrew words meaning "king" and "righteousness," "then also" his name "king of Salem" means "king of peace," based on the Hebrew word for "peace." In certain Old Testament texts, righteousness and peace have Messianic associations (Isa 9:6), and the author earlier identified Jesus as the righteous king in Heb 1:8–9 and in his benediction he referred to the God of "peace" (Heb 13:20). The two phrases are best understood as further descriptions of Melchizedek, but Miller interpreted the phrase as semantically expressing the reason for the giving of the tithe and Dods took the phrase as semantically indicating the reason for Melchizedek's abiding forever as stated in v. 3.[561]

7:3 The author continues his description of Melchizedek in v. 3, which is the *crux interpretum* of the entire chapter and sets the stage for the remainder of the argument in Hebrews 7.[562] The NIV "without father or mother, without genealogy" translates three words in the Greek text. It is possible to take the words literally as implying supernatural origin.[563] However, the better interpretation is that his parents are not recorded in Scripture and the Scripture is silent concerning his genealogy.[564] Lane translates the words: "His father, mother, and line of descent are unknown."[565] Lane is correct when he suggested the key to the interpretation of the three words in Greek is found in the final word translated "without genealogy," a word that may have been coined by the author. This word amplifies the meaning of the previous two and places the focus on priestly qualification and not a miraculous birth. The words do not mean that he literally had no father or mother. In the LXX of Esth 2:7, Esther is described as having no father or mother. Scripture's silence concerning Melchizedek's origin "is stressed by the writer to amplify the concept of the uniqueness of his priesthood, and not as proof of that uniqueness."[566]

---

[560] The actual name in the Hebrew of Gen 14 and Ps 110 means "King of Righteousness" and is written in two parts connected by a *maqqēp* as if it were a title rather than a personal name (Astour, "Melchizedek," *ABD* 4:684).

[561] N. Miller, *The Epistle to the Hebrews: An Analytical and Exegetical Handbook* (Dallas: Summer Institute of Linguistics, 1988), 193; M. Dods, "Epistle to the Hebrews," in *The Expositor's Greek Testament*, ed. W. R. Nicoll (Grand Rapids: Eerdmans, 1974), 308.

[562] On the significance of the interpretation of this verse historically, consult B. Demarest, "Hebrews 7:3: A *Crux Interpretum* Historically Considered," *EvQ* 49 (1977): 141–62. Cf. Kobelski, *Melchizedek*, 119–27; and W. H. Attridge, *The Epistle to the Hebrews*, (Philadelphia: Fortress, 1989), 189–95.

[563] J. W. Thompson, "The Conceptual Background and Purpose of the Midrash in Heb VII," *NovT* 19 (1977): 209–23.

[564] M. Barker, *The Older Testament: The Survival of Themes from the Ancient Royal Cult in Sectarian Judaism and Early Christianity* (London: S.P.C.K., 1987), 260, makes the point that the silence of the Pentateuch about Melchizedek's background "may be *due to* Melchizedek's exalted role, and not the cause of it."

[565] Lane, *Hebrews 1–8*, 157.

[566] Ibid., 166; cf. Horton, *Melchizedek Tradition,* 160; and Cockerill, *Melchizedek*, 149–50. Kobelski, *Melchizedek and Melchiresa*, 123, thinks the argument from silence on Melchizedek's

The phrase "without beginning of days or end of life" in v. 3 has been taken literally by some to suggest that Melchizedek was a divine being. If this is the author's intention, the problem of a dual eternal priesthood develops.[567] It is hermeneutically, contextually and theologically more likely that the author is not attempting to "establish a factual point but to exhibit the radical difference that existed between the priesthood of Melchizedek and the more familiar Levitical line of priests."[568] The silence of Scripture regarding Melchizedek's parentage and genealogy is now extended by the author with a phrase that evokes the notion of eternity; an eternity that is only typified in Melchizedek but is realized in Christ.[569] The use of the perfect passive participle in v. 3 could be literally translated "having been made to resemble [by God]," an example of the so-called "divine passive" where the author's construction indicates God's appointment of Melchizedek as a type of Jesus that subordinates Melchizedek to Christ.[570] It is this phrase, "like the Son of God," that the author uses to indicate two important truths: the greatness of Melchizedek; yet he only resembles someone greater.[571]

Several times the author refers to Jesus as "Son" but only three times is Jesus designated as "Son of God" (6:6; 7:3; 10:29). Mason correctly pointed out that the use of the phrase "is far from random in these passages, however, as in each case use of this term heightens the rhetoric of the author or subtly expresses Jesus' superiority over an inferior entity."[572]

The final phrase of v. 3, "he remains a priest forever," is the author's paraphrase of Ps 110:4. The phrase is dependent upon the preceding participial clause

---

lack of genealogy is insufficient for three reasons: (1) evidence from the Qumran texts, (2) the statement in Heb 7:8, and (3) Ps 110:4 led to the tradition of Melchizedek himself as "living." He viewed Melchizedek as a "historical/heavenly being" (p. 126). However, Kobelski is incorrect when he asserted that the author of Hebrews is recounting a tradition in Heb 7:3 "that cannot be traced to biblical sources and that presents Melchizedek as an eternal figure with an eternal priesthood" (p. 125).

[567] Demarest, *History of Interpretation*, 9. Cf. Neyrey, "'Without Beginning of Days or End of Life,' (Hebrews 7:3): Topos for a True Deity," *CBQ* 53 (1991): 439–55.

[568] Lane, *Hebrews 1–8*, 165.

[569] Ibid., 166. F. F. Bruce, *The Epistle to the Hebrews*, NICNT (Grand Rapids: Eerdmans, 1964), 160: "In the only record which Scripture provides of Melchizedek—Gen. 14:18–20—nothing is said of his parentage, nothing is said of his ancestry or progeny, nothing is said of his birth, nothing is said of his death. He appears as a living man, king of Salem and priest of God Most High; and as such he disappears. In all this—in the silences as well as in the statements—he is a fitting type of Christ." C. Gieschen, *Angelomorphic Christology: Antecedents and Early Evidence*, AGJU (Leiden: Brill, 1998), 309–10, took the opposite position and argued that the testimony of Ps 110 "silences" this argument from silence since Ps 110 shows a highly developed understanding of Melchizedek that greatly influenced the author of Hebrews.

[570] So Lane, *Hebrews 1–8*, 166; and Horton, *Melchizedek Tradition*, 156.

[571] Kobelski, *Melchizedek and Melchiresa*, 124–25.

[572] E. Mason, *You are a Priest Forever: Second Temple Jewish Messianism and Priestly Christology of the Epistle to the Hebrews*, in Studies on the Texts of the Desert of Judah 74 (Leiden: Brill, 2008), 12–13.

and functions to relate the eternal priesthood of Melchizedek, typologically presented, to his resemblance to Jesus, the Son of God.[573] The Greek phrase *eis to diēnekes* occurs four times in Hebrews (7:3; 10:1,12,14) and nowhere else in the New Testament. It denotes that which continues uninterruptedly or perpetually. The phrase is not to be interpreted literally, but typologically. The relationship between Melchizedek and Jesus is best described in terms of typology.[574] C. Bird's statement regarding the author's methodology is apropos: he is "harvesting exegetical fruit from the typological trees" already planted in the Old Testament.[575] The purpose of the comparison of Jesus with Melchizedek now becomes clear. By grounding Christ's priesthood in the biblical source of Ps 110:4[576] and connecting it with the historical source of Gen 14:17–20,[577] the author establishes the eternality of Christ's priesthood.[578] In the remainder of Hebrews 7, the author will demonstrate the implications of this fact with respect to the Levitical priesthood, and lay the groundwork for the next step in the theological argument to be taken in Hebrews 8. Mathews rightly reminds us, "Typologically, it is not

---

[573] Ibid., 125.

[574] Gieschen, *Angelomorphic Christology*, 311. On the issue of typology in the OT, see M. Fishbane, *Biblical Interpretation in Ancient Israel* (Oxford: Clarendon Press, 1985), 350–79; and L. Goppelt, *Typos: The Typological Interpretation of the Old Testament in the New* (Grand Rapids: Eerdmans, 1982), 163–70, although Goppelt does not see a Melchizedek-Christ typology in Hebrews.

[575] C. Bird, "Typological Interpretation within the Old Testament: Melchizedekian Typology," *Concordia Journal* 26 (2000): 48.

[576] Mathews, *Genesis 11:27–50:26*, 156, noted the prophetic oracles addressed to "my Lord" in Ps 110:1,4 must be taken as referencing David's "Lord," not David himself by a court prophet as is often assumed by many commentators. The reason for this is twofold. First, Psalm 110 is oriented toward a future king who will be priest as well. Such a role could not be fulfilled by David's lineage until the coming of the Messiah since it is the Messiah who unites the two functions of king and priest. It is clear from Matt 22:41–46 that Jesus understood David's 'Lord" to be the Messiah, and the apostles followed suit as evidenced by Acts 2:34–35; 5:31; Rom 8:34; Heb 1:13; 10:12–13. Second, if David is the recipient of the prophecy, rather than the author of the psalm, then the argument of Jesus and his apostles founders. See also D. Bock, *Luke 9:51–24:53*, BECNT (Grand Rapids: Baker, 1996), 1635–36, on this matter.

[577] W. Brueggemann, *Genesis*, in *Interpretation: A Bible Commentary for Teaching and Preaching* (Atlanta: John Knox, 1982), 139, is incorrect in his assertion that Gen 14:17–20 "contributes nothing substantive to Hebrews." The passage is vital to the author in connecting it with Ps 110:4 to make his theological argument. Fitzmyer, "Now this Melchizedek," 241, pointed out how the author illustrates the superiority of Christ's priesthood over the Levitical priesthood from three elements in Genesis alone: "the lack of genealogy, the reception of tithes, and the blessing bestowed."

[578] Kobelski, *Melchizedek and Melchiresa*, 125. Fitzmyer, "Further Light on Melchizedek from Qumran Cave 11," 267, believed the author of Hebrews developed his exegesis in Hebrews 7 "almost exclusively" in terms of Genesis 14 and Psalm 110. Cockerill, "Melchizedek: A Test Case," 1–19, concurred with this view. Demarest, "*Crux Interpretum*", 161, concluded, "The statements in vs. 3 were stimulated by the Messianic prophecy of Psalm 110:4." Others believe this position to be problematic, but on balance, the evidence better supports Fitzmyer, Cockerill, and Demarest.

necessary for Jesus and Melchizedek to share in all traits; thus the ancient interpretation that Melchizedek was the pre-incarnate Christ is not required."[579]

7:4 Hebrews 7:4–10 is a self-contained paragraph unit in which the author further theologizes about Melchizedek.[580] Louw and Nida wrongly take the verb *theōreite*, translated "just think," as an indicative.[581] It is better taken as an imperative as do virtually all commentators and all translations with the exception of the TEV. The word translated "how great" is used by the author as a term of exclamation, and coupled with the imperative verb is an attention getter: "see (just think, consider, notice) how great he is (was)!" The demonstrative pronoun "this one," translated "he," must have an equative verb supplied to finish out the meaning in English. Translators and commentators are about evenly divided in favor of the present or past tense of the verb to be supplied. Contextually, either is permissible.

The greatness of Melchizedek is defined by the author in the next statement: "Even the patriarch Abraham gave him a tenth of the plunder!" Two words in this clause are emphatic by their position: "tenth," which is fronted in the clause before the subject and verb, and "the patriarch," which is placed last in the clause to emphasize further the greatness of Melchizedek. The use of the definite article further suggests Melchizedek's greatness.[582] The word translated "plunder" may signal that Abraham gave not only a tenth of the spoils taken in his victory over the kings, but the choicest or best of the spoils.[583]

7:5 The *men . . . de* construction in Greek at the beginning of vv. 5,6 ties them together in the sense of "on the one hand [v. 5] . . . on the other hand [v. 6]." Verse 5 functions as an explanatory statement giving the ground or reason for the collection of the tithe by the Levites. The ground for such an action is the Mosaic law, specifically given in Num 18:21–24. Those decedents of Levi who have "received" the priestly office (the Greek implies they received this office from God) are responsible for the collection of the tithe. This "commandment" that the priests have received concerning the tithe is "according to the law."[584] Lane caught the important nuance from the author's identification

---

[579] Mathews, *Genesis 11:27–50:26*, 156. The view that Melchizedek was a pre-incarnate appearance of Jesus was more recently argued by A. Hanson, *Jesus Christ in the Old Testament* (London: S.P.C.K., 1965), 70–71. B. Joslin, "The Theology of the Mosaic Law in Hebrews 7:1–10:18" (Ph.D. dissertation, Southern Baptist Theological Seminary, 2005), 171, perceived Hanson's suggestion that Melchizedek was Christ pre-incarnate to be "speculative and doubtful." Cf. the critique in J. Borland, *Christ in the Old Testament* (Chicago: Moody, 1978), 164–74.

[580] Westfall, *Discourse Analysis*, 182, views Heb 7:4–28 as "the deferred answer to the questions that are raised by 2:5–18 and 5:1–10."

[581] L&N 32.11. They correctly note that the semantic domain of this verb is "come to understand" and that semantically the dominant meaning of such verbs has to do with the process by which one arrives at understanding.

[582] Hughes, *Hebrews*, 251.

[583] Lane, *Hebrews 1–8*, 168.

[584] The phrase κατὰ τὸν νόμον, "according to the Law," can be connected with "to collect a tenth from the people," but it is better to connect it with ἐντολὴν ἔχουσιν, "they have a

of the "people" as "brothers," namely, those who received the tithes (sons of Levi) and those who gave them (the people of Israel) are all Abraham's descendants and are treated by the author as equals. It was Abraham from whom both groups, Levitical priests and all the people, sprang; and it was Abraham, great as he was, who recognized the claim of Melchizedek, one even greater than Abraham, to receive a tithe. From this the author concludes in vv. 9–10 that Melchizedek is superior to the Levitical priests, hence his priesthood is superior to that of the Levitical line.[585]

7:6 Friberg and Friberg give the introductory *de* of v. 6 a hyperordinating tag, which semantically signals the information in v. 6 is more prominent than v. 5.[586] The present tense participle with the negative ("did not trace his descent") indicates customary action[587] in the sense that Melchizedek regularly does not have his genealogy traced from Levi. The participle is attributive by virtue of the definite article, but it functions concessively, as expressed with "however . . . yet," where the two verbs "collected" and "blessed" express contraexpectation. Melchizedek did two things that Levitical priests do: he collected a tithe, and he blessed Abraham. Yet the author's point is that Melchizedek himself was not descended from Levi. Not only that, he was not descended from Abraham either, but was Abraham's contemporary in time and superior in rank. As the recipient of the blessing, Abraham is in an inferior position to the one who gave the blessing. The use of the perfect tense "blessed him" indicates the superiority of Melchizedek, the ongoing relevance of the action from the author's perspective, and the permanent status of Melchizedek as superior to Abraham.[588] Abraham is described as "him who had the promises," harking back to the discussion in Heb 6:13–20. Nothing else is said about the "promises," indicating the meaning would be clear to the readers. We have seen how important the concept of "promise" is to the author; God is the author of the promises to Abraham, through whom Christ would come and fulfill them all. This is the theological trajectory of the author in Heb 7:1–10:18

7:7 In v. 7, the author parenthetically draws the lesser-greater distinction by pointing out that "without doubt"[589] the lesser person, Abraham, is blessed by the greater, Melchizedek. The "lesser person" indicates a person with less-

commandment." The NIV conflates the specific word ἐντολὴν into the more general word νόμος in keeping with the Hebrew notion that the latter is the sum of all the commandments. The word used in this verse for collecting tithes is used in the same manner in the LXX in 1 Sam 8:15,17 and Neh 10:37.

585 Lane, *Hebrews 1–8*, 168–69.

586 D. Friberg and B. Friberg, *Analytical Greek New Testament* (Grand Rapids: Baker, 1981), 671.

587 Alford, "Prolegomena and Hebrews," *Alford's Greek Testament*, 4:133.

588 See Bruce, *Hebrews*, 162–63; Lane, *Hebrews 1–8*, 169; and Ellingworth, *Hebrews*, 365–66.

589 The phrase in Greek means "without contradiction, question, doubt." The author's statement is one with which everyone would agree.

er status; the "greater" indicates a person of greater status, prominence, or rank. The inferior is blessed by the superior. Abraham is only "inferior" to Melchizedek in terms of rank or status. Both words "lesser" and "greater" are articular and in the neuter gender in Greek, where the article focuses on the qualities indicated by the words,[590] and the neuter gender serves to generalize the reference.[591]

7:8 New information is added to the argument in v. 8 with the assertion that the collection of the tithe under Mosaic law was made by Levitical priests who die. However, in the case of Melchizedek, the tithe is collected by one "who is declared to be living." This contrast is made all the more emphatic by the Greek construction. Levites are mortals, but it is said of Melchizedek that he is "declared" to be living. The Levites are dying men (the participle[592] precedes the noun in Greek to emphasize mortality) who receive tithes; Melchizedek is one who, typologically declared to be living, received a tithe from Abraham. The obvious result of the death of the Levitical priests is that the priesthood is left to another person. This harks back to 7:3 and to the argument from silence made there concerning any lack of information historically about Melchizedek's death. The text does not say that Melchizedek is living, but is "declared"[593] to be living. It is Scripture that bears this testimony, specifically the author's juxtaposition of Gen 14:17–20 with Ps 110:4. The author is still moving in a typological milieu. Bruce captures the intent well: "The tithe which Abraham gave to Melchizedek was received by one who, as far as the record goes, has no 'end of life.'"[594]

7:9–10 The section is concluded in vv. 9–10, a single sentence in Greek. The idiomatic expression translated "one might even say" in v. 9 leads to the author's concluding point in the comparison of Melchizedek and Levi with respect to the tithe. "One might even say" implies a certain "conscious literary license" on the part of the author indicating he was not speaking "literally" of Levi being in Abraham's loins. This provides another indication that the overall tenor of Heb 7:1–10 is typological in nature, and not an attempt by the author to affirm any divine status on Melchizedek. The author deftly makes the point by playing on the noun translated "tenth" and the verb translated "collect," the

---

[590] Greenlee, *Exegetical Summary*, 238; Lane, *Hebrews 1–8*, 158.

[591] Attridge, *Hebrews*, 196.

[592] The participle functions attributively describing "men" and can be so without the article since the noun it modifies, ἄνθρωποι, is anarthrous as well (Greenlee, *Exegetical Summary,* 239). The present tense is "frequentative," describing action that recurs from time to time (Lane, *Hebrews 1–8,* 158). Some translators (NASB) and commentators (Bruce, *Hebrews*, 161; and Lane, *Hebrews 1–8*, 158–59) give it an adjectival translation: "mortal men."

[593] The use of the Greek present passive participle of μαρτυρέω, "to be testified" or "to have witness borne," indicates it is Scripture that is bearing this ongoing testimony. Gieschen's assessment (*Angelomorphic Christology,* 310) may be correct that the testimony is not that of the silence of Gen 14, but the testimony of Ps 110:4 as it was interpreted by the author.

[594] Bruce, *Hebrews*, 163.

same root word in Greek used first as an active participle ("who collects the tenth") then as a perfect passive verb. The meaning could be rendered "One might even say that Levi, who collects the tithe, was through Abraham 'tithed' or 'collected from' by Melchizedek."[595] Abraham, as a representative of all his descendents, including Levi, by means of the concept of corporate solidarity, contained in his body the seed of all his offspring. Levi, who centuries later would receive tithes from the people, paid tithes to Melchizedek through Abraham, since he was considered by the author to be "still in the body of his ancestor." For the author of Hebrews, since Levi was reckoned as still in the body of his ancestor, actions taken by Abraham were actions taken by Levi as well.

The author has now completed his purpose in Heb 7:4–10 by showing why the Melchizedekian priesthood is superior to the Levitical priesthood. From his own exegetical treatment of Gen 14:17–20, the author has made his case for the superiority of the Melchizedekian priesthood over the Levitical priesthood because the Levites paid tithes to Melchizedek while still in the "loins" of Abraham. In one fell theological swoop, the author subordinates the entire Levitical priesthood to Melchizedek. Building on this point, the author shifts the focus of the argument from Melchizedek to the Levitical priests in Heb 7:11–19, and from there he makes the shift to Christ in Heb 7:20–28.[596]

Melchizedek has become for the author a "type" of Christ in the sense of the timeless nature of his priestly office without successor. The author builds on the historical account of Melchizedek in Genesis 14, but his argument is "thoroughly Christological."[597] Lane concluded: "Accordingly, christology, and not speculation, is the determining factor in the portrayal of Melchizedek in 7:1–10."[598]

7:11–19 In this section, the author develops the topic of Jesus as the high priest after the order of Melchizedek. This is accomplished primarily by the semantic feature of contrast where the Levitical priesthood is contrasted with that of Melchizedek and Christ. The author builds the case for the inferiority of the Levitical priesthood based on its temporality and consequent inability to bring perfection.[599] Perfection language is replete in Hebrews and indicates

---

[595] See C. Moll (*The Epistle to the Hebrews*, in *Lange's Commentary on the Holy Scriptures*, trans. A. C. Kendrick [New York: Charles Scribner, 1868], 125), where the translator A. C. Kendrick (in an additional note) indicated Levi stands before us "tithed." English versions that translate "paid" or "was tithed" lose the accuracy, play on words, and picturesqueness of the perfect tense δεδεκάτωται.

[596] Joslin, "Theology of the Mosaic Law in Hebrews 7:1–10:18," 178.

[597] Lane, *Hebrews 1–8*, 171. Melchizedek has "no independent significance in Hebrews; he is introduced only for the sake of the Son (7:3c)."

[598] Ibid., 172.

[599] On "perfection" in Hebrews, see D. Peterson, *Hebrews and Perfection: An Examination of the Concept of Perfection in the "Epistle to the Hebrews,"* in SNTSMS 47 (Cambridge: Cambridge University Press, 1982), 108–12, 128–30. Cf. Lane, *Hebrews 1–8,* 181; and Koester, *Hebrews*, 122–25.

the concept of completion defined as the removal of sins that provides access to God via the new covenant in Christ. This "perfection" involves both present and future aspects, which the author will develop in Heb 8:1–10:18. It was a common notion in rabbinic thought that the priesthood was "perfect" and thus never-ending, probably deriving from such statements as Exod 40:15 and Num 25:13, where the Levitical priesthood is described as "a permanent/lasting priesthood" (HCSB; cf. Jer 33:18), although nowhere is any individual priest described as an everlasting priest.[600] The author's primary text in this section and the remainder of Hebrews 7 is Ps 110:4.[601]

7:11 Verse 11 introduces the topic of the Levitical priesthood contrasted with the Melchizedekian priesthood, as both are mentioned specifically. The NIV does not make explicit the conjunction *oun*, which could be translated "therefore," "consequently," or "so then," and concludes the preceding argument[602] and introduces a new discourse section.[603] Verse 11 begins an interrogative sentence with a conditional "if" introducing a contrary to fact condition. It seems best to relate the condition to past or present time rather than future as do Hughes and the NIV.[604] The author makes a parenthetical statement that the people were given the law based on the Levitical priesthood.[605] Some take the "law" here to refer only to regulations within the Mosaic law applying to the priesthood, but it is better to view the usage here as referencing the entire Mosaic law.[606] The phrase "on the basis of it" can be interpreted as the grounds for the giving of the law, such that they were given the law based upon the priesthood.[607] Another possibility is they were given the law in association with the Levitical priesthood.[608] Either construal is possible. Less likely is the suggestion that the people were given the law by means of the priesthood.

---

[600] Bruce, *Hebrews*, 169.

[601] Fitzmyer, "Now This Melchizedek," 305–6, asserted that Heb 7 is a midrash on Gen 14:18–20 with Ps 110:4 being secondary in the author's mind. Two facts contravene Fitzmyer's judgment on this: (1) Gen 14:18–20 is not in view at all in 7:11–28; and (2) Ps 110:4, already introduced by the author at two significant points in 5:6 and 6:20, is quoted in vv. 17,21 and is the dominant text in Heb 11–28. (See Lane, *Hebrews 1–8*, 177; Attridge, *Hebrews*, 199; Joslin, "Theology of the Mosaic Law in Hebrews 7:1–10:18," 179).

[602] Lane, *Hebrews 1–8,* 180.

[603] Bruce, *Hebrews*,164; and Ellingworth, *Hebrews*, 370–71.

[604] Hughes, *Hebrews,* 255. Better is "if perfection had (has) occurred" than "if perfection could have been."

[605] This prepositional phrase can be translated "on the basis of" as in the NIV, "under" as in the RSV, or "in association with" as Hughes, *Hebrews*, 256. Both H. F. Weiss, *Der Brief an die Hebräer*, KEK 13 (Göttingen: Vandenhoeck & Ruprecht, 1991), 395; and Lane, *Hebrews 1–8*, 174, rightly argued in favor of construing the entire phrase "for the people received regulations concerning the Levitical priesthood."

[606] Lane, *Hebrews 1–8*, 181.

[607] Ellingworth, *Hebrews*, 372.

[608] Lane, *Hebrews 1–8*, 174.

The use of the perfect tense in "the law was given" does not mean that the law is still in force, as this would defeat the point of the author's argument. The point is that the law has a permanent place in God's overall plan as an essential part of the development of God's purpose for salvation.[609]

The consequent of the conditional statement asks why it was necessary for another priest to arise other than from the Levitical order. Ellingworth said the Greek structure indicates a strong negative statement, implying that this is the result that did occur because the preceding condition was unfulfilled.[610] There would not have been a need for a different priest if perfection had come through the Levitical priesthood. The use of *heteros,* "another," to describe "priest" stresses the idea of "another of a different kind" rather than its synonym *allos* which means "another of the same kind." The priestly order of Melchizedek, and that of Christ, is altogether different from the Levitical line. The negative particle translated "not" can be connected with the infinitive "to be called" (which is left unexpressed in the NIV),[611] or better, it can be connected to the immediately following prepositional phrase "according to the order of Aaron." The infinitive itself connects to the second *kata* phrase: "to be called according to the order of Aaron."[612] Lane takes the infinitive to be parallel in sense with the preceding infinitive "to arise."[613]

The author's use of *teleiōsis*, "the act of perfecting," rather than the word *teleiōtes*, "perfection," is worthy of scrutiny. If the use of this term parallels its usage in the LXX of Leviticus and Exodus where it occurs seven times and five times respectively in the context of the consecration of the high priest, as Vanhoye argues, then the author is referring to Israel's consecration sacrifice of the high priest. The external ceremonies of animal sacrifice and the placing of blood upon the priest for consecration (Lev 8:22–28) merely symbolized transformation, but was in fact powerless to bring it about. They did not "make perfect" the priest. For this reason, a new priest is needed. Referring to Heb 5:7–9, where perfection language is used of Christ in his humanity, and comparing this with Heb 7:28, Vanhoye thinks the author of Hebrews asserts a twofold implication of Christ's priesthood: relationship with God and relationship with humanity.[614]

7:12 Verse 12 is introduced by the subordinating conjunction *gar* and continues the line of argument concerning the change in priesthood begun in v. 11. The author's statement that a change in the law has occurred will not be further explained until vv. 16–28. The point of this verse is that a change in the

---

609 G. Milligan, *Theology of the Epistle to the Hebrews* (Edinburgh: T&T Clark, 1899), 120.

610 Ellingworth, *Hebrews*, 370.

611 So Moffatt, *Hebrews*, 96; and Lane, *Hebrews 1–8,* 174.

612 So Bruce, *Hebrews*, 164.

613 Lane, *Hebrews 1–8*, 174.

614 A. Vanhoye, *Old Testament Priests and the New Priest According to the New Testament,* trans. J. B. Orchard (Petersham: St. Bede's Publications, 1986), 167–68.

priesthood causes a change "of the law."[615] The key terms in this verse are the participle translated "when there is a change" and its cognate noun "a change." This is a change that has already taken place[616] rather than one that is presently taking place from the perspective of the author.[617] How is the participle to be interpreted? It can be taken temporally: "when it is changed";[618] conditionally: "if it is changed,"[619] as an accompanying action: "with the change";[620] or as expressing the reason for the change: "since it is changed."[621] The latter option suits the context best.

In what sense exactly has the law been "changed"? Joslin answered this question well:

> It is argued here that what the writer of Hebrews means in 7:12 is that the Law has been "transformed" in light of the Christ event. What is meant by "transformation" is simply this: the "transformed Law" is the result of what occurs when Christ intersects the Law. There are radical changes that occur in both the priesthood and the Law that involve both discontinuity and continuity, and the best term that encompasses such changes is "transformation" (*metathesis*). This involves the cessation of the Levitical priesthood due to its fulfillment in Christ. In Hebrews 7, it becomes evident that *nomou metathesis* involves cancellation of the priestly lineage requirement since a new priesthood has been declared by God in the oracle of Psalm 110:4. This cancellation necessitates the cessation of the Levitical priesthood and its cultus due to Christ's fulfillment of what it foreshadowed (which anticipates Heb 9 and 10).[622]

The author of Hebrews does not assert that the Law has been deleted or abrogated. Both law and priesthood abide. The law has become, in Joslin's terms, "internalized" as "Christological Law."[623] Joslin's analysis takes into account the broader context of Heb 7:1–10:18 as well as the entire epistle. As we have seen, the key to the author's hermeneutical method is to read the Old Testament, including the Law and cultus, through a Christological lens.

---

[615] "Law" here probably refers to the entire Mosaic law (Ellingworth, *Hebrews*, 374) and not the specific laws regulating the Levitical priesthood (Hughes, *Hebrews*, 257–58).

[616] Ellingworth, *Hebrews,* 374.

[617] Dods, "Hebrews," 311.

[618] So Hughes, *Hebrews,* 256; Lane, *Hebrews 1–8,* 173; and the NIV.

[619] So Alford, "Hebrews," 136; and Dods, "Hebrews," 311.

[620] So Bruce, *Hebrews*, 164.

[621] Not overtly stated by Ellingworth, *Hebrews*, 373–75, but implied in his discussion, as noted by Greenlee, *Exegetical Summary,* 247.

[622] Joslin, "Theology of the Mosaic Law in Hebrews 7:1–10:18," 168–69.

[623] Ibid., 182. "The Law has been radically altered in the coming of Christ the high priest, and this transformation involves both its fulfillment and internalization in the NC [new covenant]. Since the category of priesthood has been 'Christologically transposed,' so has the Law."

Verses 13–14 further explain why there must be a change in the law. The law prescribed that all priests must be from the tribe of Levi. If there is another priesthood, which supersedes the Levitical, then there must be a change in the law, otherwise the new priesthood would be in violation of the law. Jesus belonged to the tribe of Judah, not Levi. Furthermore, as Koester noted, Jewish theology does not permit multiple priesthoods to operate at the same time.[624]

7:13 This verse is introduced by *gar*, which functions to state the grounds for the comment in v. 11 that a new and different kind of priest is needed. The phrase "he of whom these things are said" in v. 13 refers to Christ. Two things are stated in this verse: Jesus belonged to a different tribe than Levi, namely, the tribe of Judah; and no one from the tribe of Judah has served as a priest. "Belonged" translates a perfect tense verb implying the voluntary nature[625] of Christ's humanity as well as its permanence—he took on human nature for all time.[626] "These things" refers to the promise in Ps 110:4. "Served at the altar" means to hold the priestly office and/or to perform priestly functions. Since only priests performed priestly functions, the phrase includes both concepts.

Lane brings out nicely how v. 13 is one among many examples of the author's use of rhetorical features, which reflect that the epistle is a sermon meant to be heard. Two examples of paronomasia occur in the Greek here: similar sounding prepositional phrases and similar sounding perfect tense main verbs translated "belonged" and "has served."[627] Such rhetorical features are difficult to bring out in translation.

7:14–15 Verse 14 continues the sentence begun in v. 13 and is semantically parallel to it. Whereas in the first clause in v. 13, reference is made to "he" and "tribe," now these slots are filled with "our Lord" and "Judah" in v. 14. In the second clause of v. 13, "tribe" and "served at the altar" are balanced by "tribe" and "priests" in the second clause of v. 14. The word in Greek translated "clear" is an emphatic word meaning "perfectly clear" or "crystal clear." The prepositional phrase "from Judah" is fronted in the clause for emphasis: "it is clear *from Judah* that our Lord descended." The perfect tense verb translated "descended" again emphasizes the permanent status of Jesus' human nature.[628] Although the verb may be translated "descended," it (lit.) means "to arise" and probably has Messianic overtones.[629] The author may have had in mind a specific event such as the blessing of Levi in Deut 33:7–11 with the words "Moses said nothing about priests."[630]

---

624 Koester, *Hebrews*, 359.

625 So Hughes, *Hebrews*, 259; and Ellingworth, *Hebrews*, 375.

626 Alford, "Hebrews," 137.

627 Lane, *Hebrews 1–8*, 174–75. ἐφ' ὅν. . . ἀφ' ἧς and μετέσχηκεν...προσέσχηκεν.

628 Ellingworth, *Hebrews*, 376.

629 The verb is used in the LXX in Messianic contexts for the rising of a star or the sprouting of a branch. So Bruce, *Hebrews,* 165; Hughes, *Hebrews*, 259; and Lane, *Hebrews 1–8*, 182.

630 So noted by Ellingworth, *Hebrews*, 377, who gives three reasons for this possibility, including the use of the aorist tense with a personal subject: "Moses said."

In vv. 13–14, the author makes a negative contrast: Jesus is not from the tribe of Levi. Now in vv. 15–16 the author proceeds to compare Jesus positively to Melchizedek. The obvious nature of what the author states is made evident by the use of an adjective translated "even more." It is used adverbially and to modify *katadēlos*, which means "very clear" or "easily understood." The prefix *kata* intensifies the word and the entire phrase is literally "all the more very clear," which is rendered "even more clear." The author argues "from an obvious fact in v. 14 to an irresistible conclusion in v. 15."[631] What is "even more clear" is itself not clear and must be discerned contextually since the author does not overtly state it. The author probably is referencing the entire argument, which includes the temporary nature of the Levitical priesthood coupled with the change that has occurred in the new covenant.[632] The NIV adds the words "and what we have said" to the beginning of v. 15 to fill in the ellipsis.

The second half of v. 15 is introduced with the conditional "if," which can function in one of three ways here: (1) as a factual condition with the meaning of "since";[633] (2) as a temporal condition indicating "when" in the sense of "when a different priest arises";[634] and (3) as a reason statement indicating why the change is clearer.[635] Options one and three are closely related and probably express the author's intent. The time factor of the conditional statement can be past[636] or indefinite.

Jesus is a different (*heteros*) priest arising from the "likeness" of Melchizedek rather than the usual "order" of Melchizedek. The author has mentioned the "order" of Melchizedek several times. Now in v. 15 he semantically substitutes "likeness" for "order." This further defines the meaning the author intends by "order" of Melchizedek and brings out the typology inherent in the comparison. What Melchizedek was symbolically, Jesus is in reality.[637] The phrase is further emphasized by being placed first in the clause in Greek. The author also emphasizes the subject phrase "different priest" by placing it after the main verb "arises." The Greek word order appears as "since according to the likeness of Melchizedek [there] arises another priest."

---

[631] Ellingworth, *Hebrews*, 377.

[632] Greenlee, *Exegetical Summary,* 251, surveys the commentaries and translations and comes away with six options: (1) the superiority of Christ's priesthood or the ineffectiveness of the Levitical priesthood; (2) the change of the law; (3) both the superiority of Christ's priesthood and the change of the law; (4) both the temporary character of the Levitical priesthood and the change of the law; (5) the argument of vv. 11–13; and (6) Christ's fulfillment of what Melchizedek was symbolically.

[633] So Lane, *Hebrews 1–8*, 175.

[634] As in the NRSV.

[635] So Hughes, *Hebrews*, 263–64; Ellingworth, *Hebrews*, 378.

[636] Hughes, *Hebrews*, 263.

[637] Lane, *Hebrews 1–8*, 183. "The writer thus understands the term τάξις in its derived meaning of 'character' or 'quality.'"

7:16 Verse 16 continues the sentence begun in v. 15 with a relative clause having the phrase "different priest" as its antecedent. Again, as in v. 15, the verse is descriptive of Jesus without naming him. Here we are informed that Jesus has become a priest not based on any legal requirement concerning his ancestry, but rather based on the "power of an indestructible life." By the use of the Greek phrase "fleshly commandment," the author refers to the commandments in the Mosaic law that concern the Levitical priesthood. "Fleshly" does not mean "carnal" in the usual Pauline sense of the term; rather it means "according to the flesh" in the sense of relating to human ancestry.[638] It is contrasted in the following statement concerning the "power of an indestructible life." The adjective "indestructible" is found only here in the Greek New Testament and is placed at the end of the clause in Greek for emphasis: "according to the power of life indestructible." Lane correctly pointed out "power" as used in Hebrews connotes "effectiveness," and the entire phrase "designates the eternity of the new priest from the perspective of his post-resurrection existence."[639] By virtue of the resurrection, Jesus inherently possesses eternal life, indestructible life, in a way that no human priest could possibly possess. This is what qualifies Jesus to be a priest.

The question arises as to when in Christ's life does "indestructible" apply? Commentators are divided on this issue. Some assert it should be applied to Jesus as the eternal Son,[640] while others take it to apply to his ascension and exaltation.[641] The former best suits the overall tenor of Hebrews.

7:17 The author now supports his argument with a direct quotation of Ps 110:4 in v. 17, the key Old Testament text in the entire chapter. The use of witness terminology in the quote formula "indicates that the biblical text has been read in the light of its eschatological fulfillment."[642] The "forever" terminology is the focal point in the quotation, which the author is using to support his statement about Jesus' indestructible life. Psalm 110:4 designates the new priesthood as eternal and independent of Aaron. The Levitical priesthood was governed by hereditary descent where genealogy was paramount. But as human beings, all priests who served in the Levitical line were limited by their mortal existence. All Aaronic priests eventually died. After noting that Jesus, as the eternal Son of God, qualifies for this new priestly order, Hay asks the salient question: *must* he belong to this order? He concluded the answer is "yes" because Ps 110:4 is, in the view of the author, meant specifically for Jesus

---

[638] Against Attridge, *Hebrews*, 202.

[639] Ibid., 184.

[640] So G. Lünemann, *The Epistle to the Hebrews,* trans. from the 4th German edition by M. Evans, *Critical and Exegetical Handbook to the New Testament*, ed. H. A. W. Meyer (NY: Funk & Wagnalls, 1885), 568; and B. F. Westcott, *The Epistle to the Hebrews* (London: MacMillan, 1892; repr., Grand Rapids: Eerdmans, 1955), 185.

[641] So Alford, "Hebrews," 138.

[642] Lane, *Hebrews 1–8*, 184.

(7:13). The author's application of Ps 110:4 to Jesus is one of the foundation blocks of the argument of Hebrews 7, and it was set in place, according to Hay, back in Heb 5:6–10.[643] The new priesthood was according to the likeness of Melchizedek (the author now dropping the use of "order" and substituting the word "likeness") to indicate the typology involved since there was no genealogical relationship between Melchizedek and Christ.

7:18–19 Verses 18–19 comprise the final sentence of Heb 7:11–19, the second section of Hebrews 7. It is introduced by *gar*, left untranslated in the NIV, but signaling a continuation of the argument by providing the grounds for the change in the priesthood and law. Here we learn that the former regulation from the Mosaic law, concerning priestly descent, has been completely cancelled or annulled, as is the meaning of the noun in Greek. It is rendered verbally as "is set aside." The word used here, *athetēsis*, is stronger than the word used in v. 12. It is used in the papyri as a juristic metaphor in a technical legal sense of the annulment of a decree or cancellation of a debt.[644] What has been set aside is not the entire law itself, but the part of the law regulating priesthood.[645] This was done because the commandment was "weak" and "useless." The adjective "weak" is used to indicate that the law itself concerning the Levitical priesthood could not bring about final atonement and the spiritual reality of access to God. In context, both the law itself and the Levitical priests were incapable of bringing this about. "Useless" conveys a similar notion to "weakness" and describes the ineffectiveness of the law. This is brought out in Hebrews 9 where the law only brought external cleansing and could not deal with matters of the heart.[646]

Verse 19 begins with a parenthetical statement concerning the inability of the law to solve the sin problem: to provide redemption and a right relationship with God, including access to God. The law simply could not accomplish what was necessary for redemption. Although the "former regulation" is set aside, a "better hope is introduced, by which we draw near to God." The old commandment is replaced by something far "better," a word emphasizing quality and signaling superiority. The NIV follows the parenthetical statement "(for the

---

[643] Hay, *Glory*, 147.

[644] Lane, *Hebrews 1–8*, 185.

[645] Peterson, *Hebrews and Perfection*, 111; and Attridge, *Hebrews,* 202–5, are among those who take the position that the Law in its entirety had been declared invalid. Following H. Windisch, *Der Hebräerbrief*, HNT (Tübingen: Mohr [Siebeck], 1931), 66, they interpret the author of Hebrews to be equating law with the temple cultus; hence a change in the priesthood necessitates an abrogation of the Mosaic law. The author does not have the entire Mosaic law in mind in this context. See the excellent discussion on this point in Joslin, "Theology of the Mosaic Law in Hebrews 7:1–10:18," 187–90.

[646] H. Montefiore, *A Commentary on the Epistle to the Hebrews* (New York: Harper; London: Black, 1964), 125; Bruce, *Hebrews*, 169; Lane, *Hebrews 1–8*, 183–84; and Ellingworth, *Hebrews*, 379. For an excellent discussion of this concept of the law's weakness, see J. Bayes, *The Weakness of the Law: God's Law and the Christian in New Testament Perspective* (Carlisle, England: Paternoster, 2000), esp. 177–89.

law made nothing perfect)" with "and," which would better be rendered "but" to reflect the adversative use of *de* in the Greek text. The author's point is contrast: not a former commandment but a better hope. This hope has already been mentioned in Heb 6:19 and is brought in again here by the author to emphasize that both salvation and the one who brings that salvation, namely Jesus, are the referents of this "better hope." This hope is the means by which we draw near (present tense implying continued access) to God.[647] By the use of "we" the author includes himself with his readers.

The author has now completed his main purpose in Heb 7:11–19, which is to "substantiate the insufficiency of the Levitical priesthood and the system based on it."[648]

The entire system of law, temple, and priesthood could not, in the final analysis, bring people into the presence of God. In fact, everything about the structure of the temple, its priesthood and regulations, prohibited people from coming anywhere near the holy place or the holy of holies, where the presence of God dwelled. Jesus, our "better hope," removes the barriers of sin and allows us entrance into God's presence—something that the law and the temple cultus could never accomplish.

7:20–28 In this third sub-section, the author continues his argument from Ps 110:4, but from here forward the focus is no longer on Melchizedek but Christ; thus the author drops the name Melchizedek when he cites Ps 110:4.

7:20 The *kai* ("and") in v. 20 signals a new sentence and also the beginning of a new sub-unit. The Greek phrase that begins this verse could be literally translated "in accordance with as much as," but smoothed out in English would read "to the degree that," or "to the same degree." The word translated "oath" places emphasis on the act of taking the oath.[649] The entire phrase is an example of litotes, a literary device used to imply strong affirmation. The clause refers to Jesus and his becoming a priest, which includes his being the mediator of the better covenant.

Many see this clause at the beginning of v. 20 as being connected with 7:22 and the intervening material as a parenthesis.[650] The *gar,* "for," introduces an explanation of the superiority of Christ's priesthood, a confirmation that it was confirmed by an oath, and a contrast with the Levitical priesthood, which did not involve such an oath.[651] Cockerill correctly noted that the author's intent to compare and contrast the Levitical priesthood with Jesus is not meant to

---

[647] Lane, *Hebrews 1–8*, 186, takes note of the use of this phrase "to draw near to God" in the LXX in Exodus, Leviticus, and Ezekiel. The phrase is used particularly of a priest who enters the sanctuary for sacrificial duty, and more generally in other places in the LXX for a worshipper who approaches God in prayer. See BDAG 270; L&N 15.75.

[648] Lane, *Hebrews 1–8*, 180.

[649] Ellingworth, *Hebrews*, 383.

[650] Cockerill, *Melchizedek*, 127; and Lane, *Hebrews 1–8*, 187.

[651] Lane, *Hebrews 1–8*, 186–87.

be a comparison between lesser and greater but of kind. Jesus is not said to become a priest by a "better oath" than the Levites. Using the argument from silence exegetically, the author observes that nowhere are any of the Levitical priests said to be priests by any oath from God. The distinction that he draws is thus not of degree, but of kind: between priests with no oath and Jesus, a priest by means of God's oath recorded in Ps 110:4.[652] The use of the periphrastic perfect tense translated "became" in v. 21 may be merely stylistic[653] or it may imply focus on the beginning of the state of being priests,[654] or it may focus on both the initial act of becoming a priest coupled with possessing the office.[655] The latter two options are the most likely. The referent of "he" in v. 21 is Christ and functions as the subject of an unexpressed phrase "became a priest." The present tense participle ("the one saying") is rendered "God said" to express the subject of the saying. It is likely that the present tense implies the timelessness of Scripture.[656] The last part of the verse is another quotation of Ps 110:4.

7:22 Here "the discussion reaches a climax, marked by a rare and emphatic use of the name Jesus, and a turning point, marked by the first occurrence of the key term *diathēkē*, which will be developed from 8:6 onwards."[657] The term "covenant" is a crucial theological term for the author. Ellingworth's table of the uses of this term in the epistle and its direct and indirect associations with other Greek words is extremely useful in identifying the meaning of the term as the author conceived it.[658] Since this is the author's theme in Hebrews 8, I have treated the term more in depth at that point. Suffice it to say here that a good "working definition" of "covenant" is given by Ellingworth, quoting Spicq in English translation. Covenant is

> a free manifestation of divine love, institutionalized in an 'economy' whose stability and consummation are guaranteed by a cultic ratification, the sacrificial death of Christ, and whose aim is to make men live in communion with God, to impart to them the treasure of grace and the heavenly inheritance.[659]

The thought continues in v. 22 with a similar structure as at the beginning of v. 20. The NIV has lost the comparative nature of this in the Greek text with the

---

[652] Cockerill, *Melchizedek*, 127–28.

[653] Moffatt, *Hebrews*, 98–99.

[654] Ellingworth, *Hebrews*, 384.

[655] Dods, "Hebrews," 314.

[656] Ellingworth, *Hebrews*, 384.

[657] Ellingworth, *Hebrews*, 385. See S. Lehne, *The New Covenant in Hebrews* (Sheffield, England: JSOT, 1990); G. E. Mendenhall and G. A. Herion, "Covenant," in *ABD* 1:1179–1202; G. von Rad, *Old Testament Theology*, trans. D. M. G. Stalker (New York: Harper & Row, 1962), 1:311; Behm, "διαθήκη," *TDNT* 2:132; and J. G. McConville, "*diathēkē*" *NIDOTTE* 1:746–54.

[658] Ibid., 386–88.

[659] Ellingworth, *Hebrews*, 388.

rendering "because of this oath." It would be better to express the meaning with something like "in accordance with" or "to that extent." In its similarity to the beginning of v. 20, the phrase points out "the same proportion as the difference between the oath and no oath."[660] The perfect tense is rendered "has become," where the implication of accomplished fact with abiding results is clear.[661] As is common for the author of Hebrews, he places the name of Jesus last in the Greek clause for emphasis. The key word in this verse is "guarantee," which conveys both meanings of guarantor and mediator.[662]

7:23 The next two verses are structured along the lines of "on the one hand . . . on the other hand." for the purpose of contrast between the Levitical priesthood, whose priests served for a limited period of time and then died, and the eternal priesthood of Christ. The Greek verbal structure here is (lit.) "are having become" (periphrastic perfect). These two words together refer to a state or condition of there having been many priests. Some think this particular structure in Greek implies the ongoing activity of Levitical priests at the time the author wrote the epistle.[663] If so, this would have implications for dating the epistle and would become evidence for a pre-AD 70 date. The Greek text does not state what it is they were not able to continue in. Most likely the supplied predicate should be "their priesthood" or "their office." A few commentators take it to mean "to continue to live."[664]

7:24 Verse 24 is straightforward in its meaning, asserting Jesus has a permanent, perpetual, unchanging priesthood because he "lives forever."[665] When the adjective *aparabaton,* "permanent," is translated attributively, as in the NIV, KJV, and a few other translations, it is a violation of Greek grammar.[666] The adverbial rendering as in the NASB is also problematic. It is better to take the adjective in a predicate relationship to the noun,[667] as "Jesus has the priesthood (and it is) permanent," or as a relative clause, "a priesthood which is permanent."[668] The nuance of the phrase probably indicates that the priesthood that Jesus possesses can never be passed on to others.[669]

7:25 In v. 25 the author draws a conclusion from the preceding two verses concerning Jesus' ability to save totally, completely, and forever those who

---

660 Greenlee, *Exegetical Summary*, 263.

661 Dods, "Hebrews," 315–16.

662 Ibid. A. B. Bruce, "The Epistle to the Hebrews," *The Expositor*, 3rd series, 10 (1899), 200, there may be an allusion to v. 19 where the cognate verb appears. He renders ἔγγυος "the one who ensures permanently near relations with God."

663 So Hughes, *Hebrews*, 268; and Ellingworth, *Hebrews*, 389–90.

664 So Lünemann, *Hebrews,* 572; and Moll, *Hebrews,* 137.

665 The Greek lit. reads "he abides to the ages."

666 Greenlee, *Exegetical Summary,* 265.

667 So Alford, "Hebrews," 142; and Lünemann, *Hebrews*, 573.

668 Bruce, *Hebrews*, 171.

669 So Moffatt, *Hebrews,* 99; Bruce, *Hebrews*, 173. Hughes thinks both notions of "unchangeableness" and the impossibility of passing it on to others are present (*Hebrews*, 268–69).

approach God through the priestly ministry of the Son. The salvation to which the author refers indicates salvation from sin and salvation resulting in a right relationship with God. A crucial question surrounds the meaning of *eis to panteles*, which is rendered as "completely." Three possibilities exist: (1) degree, in the sense of to "the utmost degree," "completely"; (2) temporally, in the sense of "forever";[670] or (3) both degree and time: "completely and forever."[671] The third option best captures the meaning.

The final participial clause indicates the reason why Jesus is able to save completely: "because he always lives to intercede on their behalf." One of the main functions of the high priest was to intercede on behalf of the people, especially on the Day of Atonement (Leviticus 16). This was symbolically expressed in the garments worn by the high priest. The ephod had two onyx stones attached to the shoulder piece, one on each side. Upon each stone were engraved the names of six of the twelve tribes of Israel (Exod 28:9–10). In addition, there were twelve stones on the breastplate the high priest wore, each containing the name of one of the twelve tribes of Israel. This notion of Jesus' intercessory ministry is closely paralleled in Rom 8:34.

The infinitive "to intercede" should not be restricted in meaning only to intercessory prayer, since the verb means "to meet or transact with one person in reference to another."[672] The word indicates "every act by which the Son, in dependence on the Father, in the Father's name, and with the perfect concurrence of the Father, takes His own with Him into the Father's presence, in order that whatever He Himself enjoys in the communications of His Father's love may become theirs also."[673]

7:26 The final sub-paragraph of Hebrews 7 begins with v. 26 and is introduced by *gar*, "for," which is left untranslated in the NIV. Some take it as introducing an additional reason why Jesus is the kind of high priest the author describes.[674] Others take it as a summary of the preceding discussion.[675] The use of *gar* connected with the use of "such" to describe the high priest we have in Jesus likely refers both to what has been said in the immediately preceding verses and to what follows here and in v. 27.[676] The author adds a *kai* in the

---

[670] Either in the sense of Jesus is able to save forever (so Moffatt, *Hebrews*, 110), or the salvation that he provided is forever (so Ellingworth, *Hebrews*, 391).

[671] So Bruce, *Hebrews*, 173–74; Cockerill, *Melchizedek*, 135–36; and Lane, *Hebrews 1–8*, 176. This particular phrase occurs in only one other place in the Greek NT: Luke 13:11.

[672] So Milligan, *Theology of Hebrews*, 125; following Westcott, *Hebrews*, 192.

[673] W. Milligan, *Ascension and Heavenly Priesthood of our Lord* (London: Macmillan, 1892), 152.

[674] Bruce, *Hebrews*, 175–76.

[675] Lane, *Hebrews 1–8*, 191.

[676] Those who lean toward the former construal include F. Delitzsch, *Commentary on the Epistle to the Hebrews,* trans. T. L. Kingsbury (Edinburgh: T&T Clark, 1872; repr., Grand Rapids: Eerdmans, 1952), 2:2; Alford, "Hebrews," 143; Hughes, *Hebrews*, 271; and Ellingworth, *Hebrews*, 393. Those who prefer the latter include Dods, "Hebrews," 317; Bruce, *Hebrews*, 175; Cockerill, *Melchizedek*, 149–50; and Lane, *Hebrews 1–8*, 191.

Greek text preceding the verb, which serves to emphasize the verb further. The dative use of *hēmin*, (lit.) "to us," is fronted in the clause before the verb, thus giving it emphasis by the author.

The author now says five things about Jesus the high priest in the form of three predicate adjectives and two adjectival participles in the Greek text. The first three adjectives are very close in meaning in terms of how the author is using them. Jesus is one who is "holy," a word describing his inner character and in the immediate context suggests sinlessness. The word in Greek connotes the idea of piety and inner purity.[677] This high priest Jesus is also "blameless," that is, "free from evil or guile." He is also "pure," that is, untainted by sin. The word indicates the absence of any legal or moral pollution.[678] The point is that Jesus is free from anything that would in any way defile, prohibit, or disqualify him from priestly service. He is also "set apart from sinners," a phrase that has been interpreted in at least three ways. First, most scholars take the phrase in a local or spatial sense in conjunction with the following words "exalted above the heavens." According to this view, Jesus is spatially separated from "sinners" in that he is not on the earth but is in heaven.[679] Second, some take the reference in conjunction with the preceding statements and construe the meaning as moral separation.[680] Third, some combine both views above.[681] The first seems best given the context and the use of the perfect participle, which suggests an historical event such as the ascension.[682] The definite article before "sinners" in the Greek text points to the whole group or race of sinners, which would be all of humanity.[683] The fifth descriptive clause, "exalted above the heavens," affirms the exalted dignity that Jesus now enjoys in heaven. These five clauses have been divided into groups of three and two,[684] but it may be better to take the first four describing Christ's nature and the fifth describing his state. Among the group of four, another division may be made where the first two speak of relation to God and the last two of relation to humanity.[685]

7:27 The preceding verse has led to the main point, which the author now drives home to his readers in v. 27. The statement has been taken to mean several closely related things. Some take it to mean Jesus had no need to offer

---

[677] See L&N 88.24 and BDAG 728.

[678] Alford, "Hebrews," 144.

[679] Delitzsch, *Hebrews*, 2:4; Westcott, *Hebrews*, 195; Moffatt, *Hebrews*, 101; Lane, *Hebrews 1–8*, 192; and Ellingworth, *Hebrews*, 394.

[680] So Calvin, *The Epistle of Paul the Apostle to the Hebrews*, 102; T. Hewitt, *The Epistle to the Hebrews: An Introduction and Commentary* (London: Tyndale, 1960), 126; and Hughes, *Hebrews*, 274–75.

[681] So Bruce, *Hebrews*, 176; and Koester, *Hebrews*, 367.

[682] See D. MacLeod, "Christ, The Believer's High Priest: An Exposition of Hebrews 7:26–28," *BS* 162 (2005): 337–39, for summary discussion of the issue.

[683] Alford, "Hebrews," 144.

[684] Westcott, *Hebrews*, 193.

[685] So noted by Milligan, *Theology of Hebrews*, 125.

daily the sin offerings that the high priest was required to make annually.[686] Others take it to mean that Jesus did not need to offer daily sacrifices for his own sins,[687] and/or to offer sacrifices for the people following his own sacrifice.[688] Some take the verse to combine references to the daily sacrifices and to the sacrifice offered on the Day of Atonement.[689] This last option makes the most sense of the context.

The author's use of "daily" poses a dilemma for interpreters since the sacrifices offered on the Day of Atonement were not offered daily, but annually, a point well known to the author. Attempted solutions to this problem are many and intricate.[690] Riggenbach's suggestion has the most promise. He argued the author has joined two offering concepts here in the same way he conjoined the covenant offering and the Day of Atonement offering in Heb 9:18–21.[691] The phrase "day after day" can be construed with "he does not need,"[692] but it is better to relate it to the phrase "to offer sacrifices."[693] The final phrase of the Greek text begins with the near demonstrative pronoun "this," but the antecedent of "this" is not expressed in the Greek text. Obviously, context demands that the antecedent be Jesus' offering of himself for the sins of the people. This is made explicit in the NIV translation. The author's use of "once for all," a statement he will make twice again in this major section (9:7; 10:10), "connects Christ's sacrifice *once* in history to the Yom Kippur ritual performed *once* a year."[694]

The participle *anenenkos* at the end of v. 27 can be taken temporally as in the NIV "when he offered," or as expressing means, "by means of offering himself [he sacrificed for their sins]." Greenlee is likely correct when he suggested both are implied in the participle.[695]

7:28 Verse 28 serves two purposes: to explain why there is a difference between Christ and the Levitical priests in terms of their priestly work of

---

[686] Alford, "Hebrews," 144–45; and Dods, "Hebrews," 318.

[687] Hughes, *Hebrews*, 275–76.

[688] Hewitt, *Hebrews*, 127.

[689] So Lünemann, *Hebrews*, 574–75; Moffatt, *Hebrews*, 102; and Ellingworth, *Hebrews*, 395.

[690] A good survey is found in Cockerill, *Melchizedek*, 175–77; and D. MacLeod, "Christ, The Believer's High Priest," 339–40. Some have taken "daily" to refer to each Day of Atonement, but this is problematic as the author used "yearly" to refer to the Day of Atonement in 9:25. Attridge, *Hebrews*, 214, suggested the reference is to the daily meal offerings in Lev 6:12–18. However, these offerings were not offered by the high priest and they were not sin offerings. Westcott, *Hebrews*, 196, interpreted "daily" to refer to Christ's regular intercession in heaven for his children, but this misses the sense of the passage where the focus is on sacrifice not intercession.

[691] E. Riggenbach, *Der Brief an die Hebräer* (Wuppertal: R. Brockhaus, 1987), 212.

[692] Moffatt, *Hebrews*, 102–3.

[693] Bruce, *Hebrews*, 177; and Lane, *Hebrews 1–8*, 193–94.

[694] D. S. Ben Ezra, *The Impact of Yom Kippur on Early Christianity: The Day of Atonement from the Second Temple to the Fifth Century,* WUNT 163 (Tübingen: Mohr-Siebeck, 2003), 181.

[695] Greenlee, *Exegetical Summary,* 272.

sacrifice and to summarize the preceding argument.[696] The direct object of the verb "appoints" is "men," and is fronted in the clause for emphasis and to drive home the contrast with "Son" in the final clause of the verse.[697] The participle *echontes*, "having," is usually translated attributively as describing men "who are weak."[698] This phrase probably should be construed with "men," although connecting it with "priests," as in the NRSV, is possible.

The author is making an important chronological point with his final statement concerning the timing of the oath in relationship to the law. His words "the word of the oath" (lit.) refers to the key Old Testament passage, Ps 110:4. This psalm was written well after the giving of the law, and it "appoints" the Son (Jesus) as high priest. Greenlee noted that commentators do not deal with the Greek construction. He suggested four possibilities: (1) "oath" is in apposition to "word": "the word, which consisted of oath-taking"; (2) "oath" is the content of the "word": "the word that expresses [the content of] the oath"; (3) the "oath" is a part of the "word": "the oath-taking included in the word"; and (4) "oath" describes the "word": "the oath-taking word."[699] The first two possibilities are the most likely options. The attributive prepositional phrase "which came after the law" is connected to "oath" and identifies it as coming after the law in time. The author is using a chronological argument to show that the law respecting priesthood has been superseded. The anarthrous use of "Son" here, as in the prologue, emphasizes the quality and characteristic of the Son in contrast to "men" above. The Son has been "made perfect forever," emphasizing the permanent effectiveness of his high priestly service.[700]

Verse 28 teaches us something about the author's view of the Old Testament Scriptures. The oath in 7:28 refers back to 7:20–22 where Jesus, unlike the Levitical high priests, was appointed by God as high priest according to Ps 110:4 ("The LORD has sworn and will not change his mind: 'You are a priest forever, in the order of Melchizedek.' "). Psalm 110:4 is the content of the oath for the author. God is the implied agent behind the oath in 7:20–22. Back in 5:10, the agent declaring Jesus as high priest is God. In 7:21, Ps 110:4 is presented by the author as words spoken by God. Finally, in 7:28, Ps 110:4 itself is the agent that appoints Jesus the Son as high priest. Kurianal tied all of this together and pointed out "a certain identification of the words of God and God himself."[701]

The author returns in v. 28 to one of his key terms, "made perfect." He used this same word in Heb 5:9 to terminate the doctrinal section of Heb 5:1–10. In Heb 7:20–28 the author introduced two important concepts are developed in 8:1–10:18: Jesus as the guarantee of a better covenant (7:22) is the theme of

---

[696] Cockerill, *Melchizedek*, 28.
[697] Alford, "Hebrews," 145.
[698] Miller, *Hebrews,* 219, takes it as concessive: "although they have weakness."
[699] Greenlee, *Exegetical Summary,* 274.
[700] Lane, *Hebrews 1–8*, 195.
[701] Kurianal, *Jesus our High Priest*, 158.

Hebrews 8, and Jesus offering himself once and for all (7:27) is developed in Heb 9:1–10:18.[702]

In conclusion, the question of whether the author makes reference to extra-biblical traditions concerning Melchizedek as a supra-being, angelic or divine, continues to be debated with no consensus on the horizon. Some are convinced the author uses Melchizedek in a polemical way, such as Jewett who argued the author historicized Melchizedek by inserting the Genesis 14 account into his argument.[703] Others, like Hughes, contest this interpretation and believe Melchizedek is presented in an "entirely favorable light. . . . There is no hint here of a polemic against a speculative image of Melchizedek."[704] Weiss argued that the statements of Heb 7:3 are intended to be applied to Jesus and not Melchizedek.[705] However, this approach creates a logical problem by means of reversal since the use of "this" in v. 4 undoubtedly refers to Melchizedek,[706] and thus Jesus' qualifications would be used to demonstrate the divine character of Melchizedek. As Balla correctly noted: "The theme of Heb 7 is clearly to say something about Jesus with a reference to Melchizedek, and not the other way round."[707]

If the descriptive terms of Heb 7:3 are an attempt to refer to Melchizedek as an angelic being, it is at least awkward since the author has already shown Jesus to be superior to the angels in Hebrews 1. To solve this problem, Balla suggested Melchizedek is not one angel among many, but that "he is in some way outstanding." The phrase "like the Son of God" in v. 3 may be a reference to earlier traditions that regard Melchizedek as a divine being.[708] Balla posited the possibility that Ps 110 may have been understood in the first century AD as implying the divine character of Melchizedek.[709] Balla concluded that the author of Hebrews wrote at a time when living traditions circulated that Melchizedek was a heavenly being.[710] He based this judgment on his study of post first century findings among Gnostic and rabbinic literature. These he believed reflected similar traditions he had found in earlier sources. Although he may be correct in his opinion, the overall evidence is tenuous. Balla and others believe Hebrews 7 reflects not only the biblical tradition concerning Melchizedek, but also the non-biblical speculation as well.[711]

---

[702] Westfall, *Discourse Analysis*, 183.

[703] R. Jewett, *Letters to Pilgrims: A Commentary on the Epistle to the Hebrews* (New York: Pilgrim, 1981), 119.

[704] Hughes, *Hebrews*, 250.

[705] Weiss, *Hebräer*, 378.

[706] Moffatt, *Hebrews*, 90.

[707] P. Balla, *The Melchizedekian Priesthood* (Budapest: Karoli Gaspar University, 1995), 65.

[708] Ibid.

[709] Ibid., 66.

[710] Ibid., 67–68.

[711] Ibid.

Whether the author of Hebrews viewed Melchizedek as only a historical figure, or a divine figure, or both, remains an open question. Likewise, the question of whether he used only the Old Testament tradition about Melchizedek or perhaps incorporated some extra-biblical tradition concerning Melchizedek cannot be settled with certainty.[712] Based on Hebrews 7, one can at least make the point that there is nothing in the author's theological argument that cannot be explained if he only used the biblical tradition concerning Melchizedek. With respect to Melchizedek's identity, it would seem that everything said about him in Hebrews 7 can be explained on the supposition that he is a historical figure being used typologically by the author to point to Christ.

THEOLOGICAL IMPLICATIONS. One might ask why the author chose to use Melchizedek in his discussion in Hebrews 7. D. Guthrie cited at least four options. (1) Psalm 110 was a favorite with the author. (2) His interest in Abraham, evidenced throughout Hebrews (2:16; 6:13,14; 7:1–19; 11:8–12), drew him toward Melchizedek. (3) He was aware of Jewish speculation concerning Melchizedek. (4) The recipients were in need of fitting a Messiah from the tribe of Judah into the cultus.[713] Options two and three are the weakest. It appears, given the author's interest in Ps 110:4 as the key text in the epistle, this text was the driving force more than anything else.

Concerning the Levitical priesthood and the law, it is unwise to say both failed in any sense that would make the coming of Christ something of a divine "plan B." Joslin is correct when he observed the failure of the law and the Levitical priesthood was a divine failure in the sense that God never intended for either to bring about salvation. With respect to the law, it has not been totally abrogated and rejected; rather it has been transformed in Christ, a transformation involving both its fulfillment in the new covenant and its internalization in the life of believers.[714] With respect to the Levitical priesthood, it has been cancelled because it was ultimately incapable of providing redemption. This was by divine design. The Levitical priesthood was intended by God all along to be temporary. The author draws this theological conclusion based on his interpretation of Ps 110:4. Melchizedek is not only a priest after a different order than Aaron; his priesthood was also a royal priesthood, something that could never be true of the Levitical priesthood. Since Christ is not from the tribe of Levi, since he is eternal, since he is a royal priest, and since there can only be

---

[712] E.g., P. Ellingworth, "'Like the Son of God': Form and Content in Hebrews 7, 1–10," *Bib* 64 (1983): 255–62, may be correct when he states: "The author appears to be addressing readers acquainted with biblically-based, non-Christian speculation about Melchizedek, and what he is saying to them may be paraphrased as follows: 'You find Melchizedek a great and fascinating figure, and you are right. He reminds us Christians of the Son of God himself'" (262).

[713] Guthrie, *New Testament Introduction*, 484–85.

[714] Joslin, "Theology of the Mosaic Law in Hebrews 7:1–10:18," 170. See also F. Thielman, *The Law and the New Testament: The Question of Continuity* (New York: Crossroad, 1999), 125; and Koester, *Hebrews*, 359, who said God did not "complete" his purposes in the Levitical priesthood.

one priesthood, it is obvious that the Levitical priesthood has come to an end with the fulfillment of Ps 110:4 in Christ.[715] The author considers Melchizedek Christologically as can be seen in the strategically placed references to Christ's enthronement in the epistle at 1:3; 8:1; and 10:12. For our author, not only is the Levitical priesthood inadequate; ultimately the same is true for Melchizedek, since the author is careful to point out it is Melchizedek who is made like Christ, not the other way around. As Isaacs correctly pointed out, "The logic of our author's argument is that there is no longer any role for an on-going priesthood, Aaronic or otherwise."[716]

The author proves the inadequacy of the Levitical priesthood by stressing the mortality of the priests that it comprised. In an interesting turn, the author argues the point of Christ's eternal nature as the grounds for his eternal priesthood. Yet, like Israel's priests, Jesus did die, but his death did not terminate his priesthood as it did with all those in the Levitical line. In one sense his death, resurrection, ascension, and seating at the right hand of God inaugurated his priesthood.[717]

Joslin cogently argued that the terms "law" and "covenant" in Hebrews 7 should not be taken as synonymous as is sometimes suggested by commentators.[718] He summarized his findings on the relationship of law and covenant in Hebrews 7 in six points. First, Heb 7:12 indicates the Law has been transformed in the new covenant age. The intersection of Christ with the law results in radical changes, including the cessation of the Levitical priesthood. These changes should not be interpreted to "abrogation" but "transformation." Second, the author is dissatisfied with the external nature of the law that renders it weak and ineffective. Third, the Levitical priesthood has been fulfilled in the new high priest, Christ. Fourth, the author's perspective on the law is not totally negative, since he considers it a gift from God that has now been transformed and internalized in the life of believers. Fifth, this new "Christologized law" will continue to play an important role in the cleansed consciences of all believers. Finally, this internalized law can now bring about obedience and knowledge of God, as the author made clear in Heb 8–10:18.[719]

---

[715] M. Isaacs, "Priesthood and the Epistle to the Hebrews," *HeyJ* 38 (1997): 57, correctly perceived the "subversive" nature of this argument to the temple cultus. "This is no mere argument as to which branch of the Levitical tribe should occupy that office. It does away with the notion of a priestly caste altogether."

[716] Isaacs, *Sacred Space,* 57.

[717] Perceptively noted by Koester, *Hebrews*, 371.

[718] See Joslin, "Theology of the Mosaic Law in Hebrews 7:1–10:18," 203; J. Guhrt, "Covenant," *NIDNTT* 1:365–66 (and editor's note that two things are true of the new covenant: the law is not abolished, and "covenant" is not synonymous with the law). Cf. J. R. Lundbom, "New Covenant," *ABD* 4:1088–94; Mendenhall and Herion, "Covenant," *ABD* 1:1179–1202; and S. Greengus, "Law: Biblical and ANE Law," *ABD* 1:242–54.

[719] Joslin, "Theology of the Mosaic Law in Hebrews 7:1–10:18," 213–14. Vanhoye, *Old Testament Priests and New Testament Priest*, 165: "In the Bible, the Law is presented as the Law of the Covenant, which regulates the life of the people of God." Cf. B. S. Childs, *Biblical Theology of the*

The question of when Christ became priest is not discussed in Hebrews 7. However, since the author stresses the chronological priority of the law to the oath, Cockerill believed Hebrews 7 implies that the priesthood of the Son had a beginning.[720] Spicq indicated the author's discussion of the tribe from which Jesus came (7:12–14) implies he did not become priest before the incarnation.[721] When Christ's priesthood is described as everlasting, the meaning is final in nature and not so much that Christ has always been a priest.[722] Yet Cockerill is careful to say the Son's everlasting priesthood is based on his eternal nature, not just on his eternal existence post-resurrection. The new priesthood of Jesus not only lasts forever, it is a priesthood of a new quality. "The new priest is effective because he shares the life of God, because he is the eternal Son."[723]

Cockerill also argued that the statements that Jesus "lives forever" (7:24) and "always lives" (7:25) make clear that the eternity of Jesus is related to the eternity of Melchizedek. Cockerill thinks the relationship between the eternity of Melchizedek and his priesthood and the eternity of Jesus and his priesthood are the same. He believes that 7:3 should be interpreted to mean Melchizedek's eternity is the basis of his priesthood *eis to diēnekes* "forever" and in 7:23–25 the Son's eternity is the basis of his *aparabatos* "permanent" priesthood. "Thus, Heb. 7:4–25 uses all of Heb. 7:3. The recognition of this usage is, in my judgment, one of the most important insights of this dissertation."[724]

But we are still left without a clear cut answer as to when Jesus became high priest. The statement in Hebrews 7:16 certainly seems to point to the resurrection and ascension as the inauguration of his heavenly intercessory ministry.[725] Peterson makes a salient point when he remarked, "If the enthronement marks also the proclamation of his eternal high-priesthood at the Father's right hand, this new representation of Christ cannot be divorced from his previous work as high priest but must be viewed as its consummation."[726] Even though the author does not explicitly state when Christ became high priest, it seems at least clear that he envisages the death, resurrection, ascension, and enthronement of Christ all as one major event, and together they serve to inaugurate Christ into his high-priestly role.[727]

Old and New Testaments: Theological Reflection on the Christian Bible (Minneapolis: Fortress: 1992), 133–34, who likewise denies that the law and the covenant are identical, but are closely united.

720 Cockerill, *Melchizedek*, 143–44.

721 C. Spicq, *L'Épître Aux Hébreux* (Paris: Librairie Lecoffre, 1952–53), 2:211.

722 Cockerill, *Melchizedek*, 143–44.

723 Ibid., 144–45.

724 Ibid., 186.

725 Peterson, *Hebrews and Perfection*, 110–12, 191. The majority Catholic view is that Christ became priest at the incarnation (see Cody, *Heavenly Sanctuary*, 96–102).

726 Ibid., 193.

727 Heb 10:5–10 makes clear that the author somehow included the crucifixion as a priestly act (G. Schrenk, "ἀρχιερεύς," *TDNT* 3:276; Peterson, *Hebrews and Perfection*, 194).

We are now in a position to offer an answer to the question as to the identity of Melchizedek in Genesis 14 and Ps 110:4. Cockerill's evidence above provides one of the best attempts to establish the possibility of taking Melchizedek to be a pre-incarnate appearance of Jesus, otherwise known as a Christophany (though it is unclear if Cockerill himself accepts this view). Nevertheless, this position seems highly unlikely. The author refers to Melchizedek's priesthood in 7:3 as remaining *eis to diēnekes*, "for all time," but Christ's priesthood is said to be "forever" in Heb 6:20 where the author quotes Ps 110:4. Both statements occur at the very end of their respective sentences in the Greek text. These two attributions are not identical. The phrase *eis to diēnekes* applied to Melchizedek is weaker; "it does not express eternity, but only the absence of interruption."[728] Vanhoye's next statement is pivotal for this question concerning the identity of Melchizedek.

> The difference reveals that in the eyes of the author, Melchizedek was only a prefiguration of the eternal priest, a sketch which represented him in a suggestive, but imperfect, fashion. Another expression that immediately precedes this clearly demonstrates this point of view: Melchizedek 'has been *made like to* the Son of God.' He was not the Son of God, but the text of Genesis has described him in such a way that his figure suggests the person of the Son of God.[729]

Vanhoye goes on to argue that the qualifications of "without father" and "without genealogy" eliminate the application of this passage to Christ in his preexistence as well as his earthly life, for Jesus has God for his Father, and while he was on the earth, it could not be said of him that he was "without mother" and "without genealogy," for the Gospels of Matthew and Luke indicate he had both, and later on in Heb 7:14 the author will speak to the genealogy of Jesus as one who "sprang from the tribe of Judah." For the author of Hebrews, Jesus has always been "Son"; but he had to *become* high priest.[730]

The best summation of the evidence as to why Melchizedek is not a Christophany can be found in Borland's *Christ in the Old Testament*, whose appendix on the subject I have summarized here. (1) The view ignores the historical details of Genesis 14, where he is described as a king of a local city. (2) The view contradictions several points made in Hebrews, including the fact that if Melchizedek is Christ, how could Christ be "better" than Melchizedek? Also, what would be the point in saying Melchizedek was like Christ if he were

[728] Vanhoye, *Old Testament Priests and the New Priests*, 153.

[729] Ibid.

[730] See the discussion in Vanhoye, ibid., 155–56. Vanhoye's own view that Heb 7:3 applies to the glorified Christ after his suffering likewise does not seem likely: "One can say of the risen Christ that he is a man 'without father, without mother, without genealogy,' for his resurrection was a new begetting of his human nature, in which neither human father nor human mother intervened, and which made of him a 'firstborn' (Heb 1:6) without genealogy" (156–57).

Christ? To say that Christ is a priest after the "order" of Melchizedek serves to *differentiate* the two individuals. (3) The Scriptural nomenclature of "the Lord appeared," or "the Angel of the Lord appeared," which always accompanies Old Testament Christophanies, is absent here. (4) The linguistic evidence can be read in such a way where the name "Melchizedek" is not so much a personal name, but as a title for ancient Jebusite rulers of "Salem."[731]

From Genesis 14, Ps 110:4, and Hebrews 7, Melchizedek was a Canaanite king who had somehow retained knowledge of the true God, possibly going back to the days following the flood. He held the dual offices of priest and king. That his genealogy, birth, and death are not mentioned in Scripture is not sufficient alone to justify making Melchizedek a Christophany. These are rather taken up by the author in typological fashion to compare Melchizedek to Christ.

3. Jesus the Mediator of a New Covenant (8:1–10:18)

1. Jesus' Inauguration of the New Covenant (8:1–13)

**1The point of what we are saying is this: We do have such a high priest, who sat
down at the right hand of the throne of the Majesty in heaven, 2and who serves in
the sanctuary, the true tabernacle set up by the Lord, not by man.**

**3Every high priest is appointed to offer both gifts and sacrifices, and so it was
necessary for this one also to have something to offer. 4If he were on earth, he would
not be a priest, for there are already men who offer the gifts prescribed by the law.
5They serve at a sanctuary that is a copy and shadow of what is in heaven. This is
why Moses was warned when he was about to build the tabernacle: "See to it that
you make everything according to the pattern shown you on the mountain." 6But
the ministry Jesus has received is as superior to theirs as the covenant of which he
is mediator is superior to the old one, and it is founded on better promises.**

**7For if there had been nothing wrong with that first covenant, no place would
have been sought for another. 8But God found fault with the people and said:**

"The time is coming, declares the Lord,
when I will make a new covenant
with the house of Israel
and with the house of Judah.
9It will not be like the covenant
I made with their forefathers
when I took them by the hand
to lead them out of Egypt,
because they did not remain faithful to my covenant,
and I turned away from them,
declares the Lord.
10This is the covenant I will make with the house of Israel

731 J. Borland, *Christ in the Old Testament*, 164–74; cf. his discussion at 139–47.

after that time, declares the Lord.
I will put my laws in their minds
and write them on their hearts.
I will be their God,
and they will be my people.
[11]No longer will a man teach his neighbor,
or a man his brother, saying, 'Know the Lord,'
because they will all know me,
from the least of them to the greatest.
[12]For I will forgive their wickedness
and will remember their sins no more."

[13]By calling this covenant "new," he has made the first one obsolete; and what is obsolete and aging will soon disappear.

8:1–2 Hebrews 8:1–2 serves as a prominent transition in the overall discourse of Hebrews. There is an immediate connection with the previous paragraph in 7:26–28, and a thematic connection with what follows through 10:18 Christ's high priestly work is developed.[732] There is a major shift in 8:1 indicated by the author's mentioning his point in writing[733] and a semantic shift,[734] where Melchizedek drops from the scene and the priesthood of Jesus in relation to the old covenant, sanctuary, cultus and law become the focus of 8:1–10:18.[735] Westfall correctly noted that this entire section (8:1–10:18) contains no imperatives or hortatory subjunctives and is characterized by third person indicative finite verbs.[736] 8:1–10:18 is the longest section of sustained exposition in the epistle. Hebrews 8 contains two major discourse units: 8:1–6 and 8:7–13, the latter being a lengthy quotation (the longest in the New Testament) of Jer 31:31–34 which ends at v. 12, followed by a short explanatory comment by the author in v. 13. Heb 8:1–6 is marked by lexical *inclusio* with the repetition of *leitourgos* (one who serves) in v. 2 and *leitourgias* (ministry) in v. 6.[737] The author marks prominence in vv. 1,6 by the use of the first person plural in v. 1 and the use of *nuni de* ("but now") plus the reference to

---

[732] See G. Guthrie, *The Structure of Hebrews*, 105–8. Westfall, *Discourse Structure*, 194, said that there is considerable back reference to 5:1–10, 6:13–18 and 7:11–25 which this verse highlights.

[733] This is an example of "deixis," a linguistic term that refers to the function of pointing or specifying from the perspective of a participant in an act of speech or writing.

[734] Westfall, *Discourse Analysis*, 188.

[735] A. Vanhoye, *Structure and Message of the Epistle to the Hebrews,* 40, saw a major division between 9:28 and 10:1, but the expanded comparisons and contrasts the author draws from 9:1–10:18 mitigates against this. Lane's critique of Vanhoye sufficiently answers the latter's contention that there is no significant break between 8:13 and 9:1 (Lane, *Hebrews 1–8*, 203). Hay, *Glory*, 151, observed Heb 7:28 joins the themes of Jesus' priesthood and sonship, while Heb 8.1 joins his priesthood with his heavenly session. It is only here and at Heb 10:12–13 that Jesus' heavenly session is linked explicitly with his priestly office.

[736] Westfall, *Discourse Structure*, 188.

[737] Vanhoye, *Structure and Message*, 92; G. Guthrie, *Structure*, 117.

Jesus in v. 6. There is also a concentration of emphatic particles in this short paragraph.[738] Ellingworth outlines the "broad logical structure" of the passage in syllogistic fashion:

> major premise: Jesus as a high priest (v. 1)
> minor premise: Jesus cannot be a priest on earth (v. 4)
> conclusion: he must be a priest in heaven (v. 6)[739]

The Jeremiah quotation is introduced by the subordinating conjunction *gar,* "for," and provides the grounds for the previous paragraph, especially for the statement in v. 6. The prominence the author gives to v. 6 and the introduction of the quotation by a subordinating conjunction combine to furnish the theme of Heb 8:1–13 which is the superiority of the new covenant inaugurated by Jesus and the obsolescence of the old covenant as a result.

Lane surveys the three options for the metaphorical use of *kephalaion* ("point) in v. 1. It can denote (1) the "main point" in an argument, the "gist" of something; (2) the summary or "recapitulation" of the main points of a subject; or (3) the "crowning affirmation" in a discussion. Lane rightly rejected the second view, and while aware that most commentators and translators opt for the first view, he argued for the third view.[740] Option one appears to be the better approach contextually. Koester correctly commented that the "point" here refers to the point of this discourse section, not that of the entire sermon, as the high priesthood of Christ is not the only point in the epistle.[741]

The posture of sitting at the right hand of the throne of God connotes both royal and priestly aspects. Here the author is bringing together Psalm 110:1,4 at a critical juncture in his theological development. Similar statements have already been made in Heb 1:3,13. That Christ, as the priest/king, is "seated"[742] further separates the person and work of Christ from the Levitical priesthood in that no high priest ever performed priestly duties while seated. There was no chair in the holy of holies. Furthermore, Heb 10:11–14 stresses that every priest "stands" daily making the required sacrifices "which can never take away sins." Jesus, however, "having offered one sacrifice for sins for all time, *sat down at the right hand of God.*" The finality of Jesus' sacrifice is observed

---

[738] Westfall, *Discourse Analysis*, 193. Friberg and Friberg, *Analytical Greek New Testament*, 673, take the δε in v. 6 as hyperordinating, signaling that semantically it conveys the more prominent information. Koester, *Hebrews*, 379, quoting Longinus, comments on the author's rhetorical strategy in this section as to how he turns the ear into an eye and puts the hearer in the presence of the action in the text. This is an important strategy for all preachers and teachers.

[739] Ellingworth, *Hebrews*, 399.

[740] Lane, *Hebrews 1–8*, 200.

[741] Koester, *Hebrews*, 375.

[742] The NIV translates the aorist verb as "sat"; Hughes translated it "is seated" (*Hebrews*, 280). The latter is better in light of the discourse structure and the use of this kind of phrasing in other Greek literature (Porter, "The Date of the Composition," 308–9).

in his seated posture at the right hand. Zechariah 6:11–13 speaks of a high priest who "sits" and "rules" on his throne:

> Take the silver and gold and make a crown, and set it on the head of the high priest, Joshua son of Jehozadak. Tell him this is what the LORD Almighty says: "Here is the man whose name is the Branch, and he will branch out from his place and build the temple of the LORD. It is he who will build the temple of the LORD, and he will be clothed with majesty and will sit and rule on his throne. And he will be a priest on his throne. And there will be harmony between the two."

The phrase "the right hand of the throne" in Heb 8:1 is left indefinite by most commentators with the implication that Christ is seated on a separate throne to the right of God's throne.[743] Ellingworth argued the throne here is figurative, implying God's presence,[744] but there seems little reason to take it this way. The phrase "in heaven" could be connected with "who sat down" but most likely is connected with "majesty" which is "in heaven."[745] In Heb 8:1 the author alludes to Ps 110:1 for the purpose of establishing that Christ as the high priest is not on the earth but in heaven. This point is a crucial linchpin for the author's argument in 8:1–10:18.[746]

Leitourgos, "who serves," in the LXX describes one who functions in the office of a priest in the tabernacle/temple.[747] That this meaning is intended by the author is further confirmed by the description of the nature of ministry performed in vv. 2–3. The phrase "of the majesty" refers to God and is functioning as a surrogate for the divine name as was the case in Heb 1:3. The noun *leitourgos* is translated verbally as "who serves" in v. 2 and refers to a priest who serves in the tabernacle/temple. The term is virtually synonymous with "high priest" with an emphasis on the activity of worship and priestly ministry.[748] The "true tabernacle" is in parallel construction with "sanctuary."[749] Some interpret the "sanctuary" as a reference to the holy of holies,[750] and "the true tabernacle"[751] as a reference to the heavenly temple in its totality. Others take the phrase *tōn hagiōn*, "the sanctuary," to refer to the sanctuary as a whole.[752]

---

743 Greenlee, *Exegetical Summary*, 277.

744 Ellingworth, *Hebrews*, 400.

745 So Hughes, *Hebrews*, 281; and Bruce, *Hebrews*, 180.

746 See Hay, *Glory at the Right Hand*, 87, 151.

747 See *BDAG* 471; and the excellent discussion in *TLNT* 2:378–84.

748 See Lane, *Hebrews 1–8*, 205.

749 Hughes, *Hebrews*, 282. The καί connecting the two words is epexegetic. See the detailed discussion in Hughes, *Hebrews*, 283–90.

750 So Attridge, *Hebrews*, 218; O. Hofius, *Vorhang*, 59–60; KJV; NASB: "the sanctuary and [in] the true tabernacle."

751 For an overview of interpretations of the "true tabernacle," consult D. MacLeod, "The Cleansing of the True Tabernacle," *BSac* 152 (1995): 60–71.

752 Spicq, *L'Épître Aux Hébreux*, 2:234; Hughes, *Hebrews*, 281; Lane, *Hebrews 1–8*, 201; Peterson, *Perfection*, 130–31; and Ellingworth, *Hebrews*, 401.

Other uses of the term in Hebrews are in 9:2,3,12,24,25; 10:19; and 13:11. The comma after "sanctuary" signals an explanatory statement connecting two descriptions of one item. That only one sanctuary is in view is bolstered by the author's frequent pairing of synonyms (as in Heb 2:2,9; 4:16; 5:1,2,7; 6:12; 8:3,5) and his contrasting the heavenly and earthly sanctuaries, not the different parts of the heavenly sanctuary.[753]

The adjective "true" modifies both "sanctuary" and "tabernacle,"[754] and is emphatic by word order, speaking of reality in contrast to a copy.[755] The "true tabernacle" refers to the heavenly sanctuary where God dwells.[756] There is no textual warrant for allegorizing the "true tabernacle" and making it refer to the church or to the body of Christ as did Aquinas and Calvin.[757] Verse 2 is in apposition with and identifies "high priest" in v. 1, indicating the capacity in which Christ took his seat at God's right hand.[758] The theme introduced here in 8:1–2 awaits development in Heb 9:11–28.

8:3 The author subordinates v. 3 to vv. 1–2 by the use of *gar,* which is untranslated in the NIV. The author is explaining that God appoints high priests to offer (present tense in Greek) gifts and sacrifices. The use of the present tense here and elsewhere in Hebrews to describe the activity of the Levitical priests offering sacrifices has iterative force and is contrasted with the aorist tense when the author is speaking about the final once-for-all sacrifice of Christ on the cross. However, although this can be construed as evidence for a pre-AD 70 date for the epistle, semantically this should not be pressed too far.

8:4 Since Jesus is also a high priest appointed by God, he too must have a sacrifice to offer. The author does not develop this thought further, but rather echoes his comment in vv. 1–2 that Jesus is not practicing his priesthood on the earth but in heaven. Semantically, that Jesus is not on the earth is encoded by the author in the contrary to fact conditional phrase "if he were on earth, he would not be a priest." Koester captures the meaning exactly: "if he were on earth (but he is not), he would not be a priest (which he is)."[759] On earth there are already those who function as priests by offering "gifts" which the law prescribes. Jesus is not on the earth but in heaven, and there his priestly ministry is conducted. The use of the present tense participles expressed in the phrase "there are already men who offer" is "frequentative," expressing repeated ac-

---

[753] As noted by Koester, *Hebrews*, 376.

[754] Dods, "Hebrews," 321; Lünemann, *Hebrews,* 587.

[755] Bruce, *Hebrews*, 182; Ellingworth, *Hebrews*, 401.

[756] See the thorough discussion on this including the translational options for 8:2 in Hughes, *Hebrews*, 283–90.

[757] Aquinas, *Commentary on the Epistle to the Hebrews* (South Bend: St. Augustine's, 2006), Book 14, Section 300, 382; Calvin, *Hebrews*, 105, 120. Westcott, *Hebrews*, 214, combined the two ideas.

[758] Lünemann, *Hebrews,* 587.

[759] Koester, *Hebrews*, 377.

tion.[760] Joslin correctly pointed out that *kata nomon*, "prescribed by the law," is used here in the sense of "the collection of Mosaic commandments that were to be obeyed by the covenant people. Here the writer has in view the specific commands that detail the priestly duties. Verse 4 could easily be read as 'according to the *commands* of the Law.'"[761] The author's thought begins with the truth of Christ's heavenly priesthood and proceeds on that basis to the logical consequences that *ipso facto* must be true.[762]

8:5 Verse 5 continues the contrast between the ministry of the earthly high priests and that of Jesus in heaven. Those earthly priests perform their ministries in a sanctuary that is a "copy and shadow" of the heavenly sanctuary. This phrase, "copy and shadow," would appear to be best taken as a hendiadys rather than as connoting two separate meanings.[763] As proof of the claim that the earthly sanctuary is a "copy," the author quotes God's warning[764] to Moses in Exod 25:40[765] to build the tabernacle according to the "pattern," *tupos*, which had been shown to him on the mount. Lane pointed out how the author has revised the meaning of *tupos* "by pairing it with [*antitupos*] 'copy' (9:24), so that [*tupos*] is to be understood as analogous to the pattern in the seal, and *antitupos* to the impression made by the seal."[766]

The argument in vv. 3–5 proceeds along the line of a comparison between the Levitical priestly ministry on earth to that of Jesus' priestly ministry in heaven (v. 3). Verses 4–5 contrast the differences between the two ministries by highlighting the superiority of Jesus' heavenly ministry on the grounds that the Levitical ministry takes place in an earthly sanctuary that is a "copy" of the heavenly. Although not overtly stated by the author, the heavenly sanctuary, unlike the earthly sanctuary, was built by God himself.[767] It is very possible

---

[760] Lane, *Hebrews 1–8*, 201.

[761] Joslin, "Theology," 224.

[762] Attridge, *Hebrews*, 218; Joslin, "Theology," 224.

[763] Moffatt, *Hebrews*, 105; Lane, *Hebrews 1–8*, 201; and Ellingworth, *Hebrews*, 406.

[764] The translation "was warned" reflects the divine passive in the Greek text where God is the understood subject.

[765] The changes in the author's quotation from the LXX are twofold. First, he adds πάντα. Speculation as to why revolves around two possibilities: (1) the author desires to incorporate the entire context of Exod 25–31, as argued by M. R. D'Angelo, *Moses in the Letter to the Hebrews*, 205–22, or (2) the author may have taken the word from Exod 15:9, as argued by Ellingworth, *Hebrews*, 407. Second, the perfect participle in the LXX, δεδειγμένον is changed to an aorist, possibly because of a shift in temporal perspective according to Ellingworth, *Hebrews*, 407.

[766] Lane, *Hebrews 1–8*, 201. For a full discussion of τύπος, see L. Goppelt, "τύπος," *TDNT* 8:246–59. There is no Platonic dualism here as C. K. Barrett, "Eschatology," in *Background of the New Testament and its Eschatology*, 389, remarked: "The heavenly Tabernacle in Hebrews is not the product of Platonic idealism, but the eschatological temple of apocalyptic Judaism, the temple which is in heaven primarily in order that it may be manifested on earth." As already shown in the introduction, the author is not dependent upon Philo's thought of Platonic dualism.

[767] Koester, *Hebrews*, 383.

that the author is making an allusion to Num 24:6 in Heb 8:1–5.[768] If this is the case, Gheorghita observed "this could have happened only as a result of the Author's reading the Greek text and not the Hebrew."[769]

8:6 Verse 6 shifts the topic back to Jesus. The contrast is continued by the use of *de*, "but," followed by a direct statement concerning the superiority of Jesus' priestly ministry. A new topic is introduced with the words "as the covenant of which he is mediator is superior to the old one." This topic will be developed by the quotation of Jer 31:31–34. The two concepts of "covenant" and "mediator" play significant roles from this point through Heb 10:18. The combination of "mediator" with "covenant" harks back to what was said in 7:22 and again comes into play in 9:15 and 12:24. The author never uses the term "mediator" in Hebrews apart from "covenant." A "mediator" connotes both one who is an intermediary for the purpose of settling a dispute and/or one who is a guarantor in a commercial sense who stands as surety for a debt or who ensures that a contract would be fulfilled.[770] The use of the perfect tense for the ministry which Jesus "has received" highlights its abiding nature, a point well established in Hebrews 7. The "covenant" is "better" because it was "founded on[771] better promises." To this point in Hebrews, the author used "promises" to refer to God's promises to Abraham. Koester rightly said the author does not use the term "covenant" in Hebrews to speak of God's promises to Abraham, but reserves his use of the term for both the Mosaic covenant and the new covenant.[772]

8:7 A new paragraph begins with v. 7, signaled by the use of the subordinate *gar*, "for." The author lexically frames Heb 8:7–13 with the use of *protos*, "first," in vv. 7,13. Two propositions are stated in v. 7: the first covenant was faulty, and as a result, a new covenant was initiated by God.[773] This first proposition is encoded by the author in a conditional clause: "if there had

---

[768] See Nestle-Aland, *Greek-English New Testament*, 7th ed. (Stuttgart: Deutsche Bibelgesellschaft/United Bible Societies, 1993), 573; R. Gheorghita, *The Role of the Septuagint in Hebrews*, WUNT (Tübingen: Mohr/Siebeck, 2003), 82–84.

[769] Ibid., 82. "It is difficult to establish with certainty whether the ideas in Heb 8:2–5 about the heavenly tabernacle and its relation to the earthly one are the result of the Author's dependency on contemporary traditions or of his direct engagement with the Greek Scriptures, which themselves may have either mirrored or generated those traditions. The fact that Heb 8:2 is imbedded in a paragraph that opens with a clear allusion to Ps 109 [110 MT], and ends with a quotation from Exod 25:40, increases the probability that 8:2 was also intended as a scriptural allusion" (p. 84).

[770] See the discussion in Oepke, "μεσίτης," *TDNT* 4:600; L&N 31.22; 40.6; and D. DeSilva, *Perseverance in Gratitude*, 230, who noted the word can refer to a broker in a patron-client relationship, but such is hardly the meaning here.

[771] ἐπί with the dative can be translated "on the basis of," "in accordance with," or "concerning." Lane, *Hebrews 1–8,* 202, thinks the details of Heb 8:8–12 would favor the translation "on the basis of."

[772] Koester, *Hebrews*, 384.

[773] Ellingworth, *Hebrews*, 412, remarked that the use of the passive "be sought" implies God is the one who sought to create a new covenant.

been nothing wrong with the first covenant." Some take the position that the problem with the Mosaic covenant was not something so much endemic to the covenant itself, but that people failed to obey it. From this perspective, the problem was more with the people than with the covenant. One must admit that there is a measure of truth in this approach; people disobeyed the Mosaic covenant. However, that God has replaced the Mosaic covenant with the new covenant suggests that the problem with the first covenant was more than just that people did not obey it. The creation of the new covenant shows that God never intended the old covenant to be permanent.[774] The similarities between the Mosaic covenant and the new covenant are patent, but there is one crucial difference: the way each covenant deals with the sin problem.

This raises the question of why God would create an ineffective covenant in the first place. This question cannot be satisfactorily answered for the simple reason that Scripture does not speak to this issue here or anywhere else. Some resolve the problem by suggesting the new covenant is a "renewal" of the Mosaic covenant, as did Calvin and many since his time.[775] This position is attractive because it highlights the many similarities that do exist between the two covenants. Kaiser concluded in favor of this view based on context, content, and Jeremiah's use of the Hebrew *ḥādās* (new) and Greek *kainos* (new), which frequently carry the meaning of "renewal" or "restoration."[776]

Yet for all this, *kainos* points to the fundamentally new character and nature of the new covenant. The Mosaic covenant was ineffective in solving the sin problem; the new covenant brought about a permanent solution to the sin problem. Thus, it would appear one cannot describe the new covenant as merely a "renewal" or "restoration" of the old covenant.

A better interpretation of the dilemma is provided by Joslin who suggested that God initiated the Mosaic covenant knowing full well it would be ineffective in dealing with the sin problem. The Mosaic covenant was "anticipatory" of the new covenant in the sense that God had always planned for the new covenant. The first covenant did not "fail" but was rather insufficient by design. In this sense the old covenant fulfilled its God-given purpose.[777] This position

[774] Koester, *Hebrews*, 389, correctly pointed out if disobedience had been the only problem, "God might have renewed people's willingness to obey the Sinai covenant." The new covenant was not established because people broke the old covenant.

[775] Calvin, *Hebrews,* 108, identified the superiority of the new covenant more in terms of its form than its actual content. Commenting on Ezek 16:61, he said: "The new covenant so flowed from the old, that it was almost the same in substance while distinguished in form." Cf. M. Woudstra, "The Everlasting Covenant in Ezekiel 16:59–63," CTJ 6 (1971): 22–48. J. Fischer, "Covenant, Fulfillment and Judaism in Hebrews," *EvRTh* 13 (1989): 176, argued that Jeremiah intended the new covenant to be viewed as a *renewed* covenant. He suggested that Ezekiel 16:60–63 and Jeremiah 33:19–26 indicate the new covenant is a ratification of the previous covenants with Abraham, Moses and David. Cf. G. Peters, *The Theocratic Kingdom* (Grand Rapids: Kregel, 1957), 1:322.

[776] Kaiser, "The Old Promise and the New Covenant," 17.

[777] Joslin, "Theology," 229.

was also articulated by Harrisville who demonstrated that the new covenant was "qualitatively" different from the old covenant in that "faithfulness to the person of Jesus determines whether or not one shares in the heavenly blessings, whereas under the old covenant the divine blessing was conditional upon faithfulness to the covenant construed as fulfillment of its demands."[778] Both covenants originated in the will of God and serve to express the single divine will. According to Harrisville and Joslin, it is this fact which provides the continuity between the two, as well as the provisional nature of the Mosaic covenant.[779]

At this point, we need to study the word *diathēkē*, "covenant," as it is used in Hebrews and the rest of the New Testament. Of the 33 uses of the term in the New Testament, 17 occur in Hebrews. Ten of these occurrences refer to the Mosaic covenant. The new covenant is mentioned in Hebrews explicitly three times: Heb 8:8–9:15; 12:24. It is also referred to in 7:22; 8:6,10; 10:16,29; 13:20. Implicitly the new covenant is referred to in 8:7 and 10:9. Only twice (Heb 9:16,17) is the word given the translation "will" or "testament."[780] The first two occurrences of *diathēkē* (7:22 and 8:6) both identify Jesus as the *enguos* ("guarantee") and the *mesitēs* ("mediator") of a "better covenant." Whatever the new covenant is, it is "better," that is, superior, to the old covenant.

8:8 Hebrews 8:8–12 contains the quotation of Jer 31:31–34 (LXX, Jer 38:31–34).[781] Jeremiah 31:31–34 plays a crucial role in the New Testament. In addition to Heb 9:15; 10:13; and 12:24, it is referenced by all three Synoptic Gospel writers as well as Paul concerning the Lord's Supper (Luke 22:20; Matt 26:28; Mark 14:24; 1 Cor 11:25). Paul makes two additional references to it (Rom 11:27; 2 Cor 3:6).[782] In v. 8, "the time is coming" is (lit.) "days are com-

---

[778] R. Harrisville, *The Concept of Newness in the New Testament* (Minneapolis: Augsburg, 1960), 47.

[779] Joslin, "Theology," 229; Harrisville, *Concept of Newness*, 49.

[780] V. Gordon, "Studies in the Covenantal Theology of the Epistle to the Hebrews in Light of its Setting," (Ph.D. dissertation, Fuller Seminary, 1979), 121–22.

[781] See J. McCullough, "Hebrews and the Old Testament," 48–68, for a detailed comparison of the quotation in the Masoretic and LXX texts. Westcott, *Hebrews*, 240–41; and Lane, *Hebrews 1–8*, 199–202, provide an accessible summary of the issues. The quotation is in substantial agreement with the LXX. Variations are probably best explained by stylistic choices of the author, although it is certainly possible a different LXX text is being used. One key text critical issue is whether the personal pronoun in the author's opening introductory phrase is to be taken as accusative or dative. Lane, *Hebrews 1–8*, 202, opts for the dative as the most primitive reading and construes it with λέγει, "he says," rather than with μεμφόμενος "finding fault." In this sense, God found fault both with the covenant and the people; cf. Hughes, *Hebrews*, 298–99. Some (G. Guthrie, *Hebrews*, 281) take the dative as the object of λέγει with the meaning: "God finds fault with the covenant and says to the people." Koester rightly noted this conflicts with the author's style elsewhere of introducing biblical quotations with some form of λέγειν without an indirect object (Koester, *Hebrews*, 385). It is unlikely that the subject of λέγειν is Jesus. Interestingly, in 10:15 the author attributes the quotation to the Holy Spirit. Koester, *Hebrews*, 389, commented on the rhetorical strategy of the author at this point: "The author now recedes into the background, allowing God to be the speaker through the quotation of Jer 31:31–34."

[782] Kaiser, "The Old Promise," 13.

ing," a favorite expression of Jeremiah occurring no where else in the prophets. The text indicates God is the initiator of the new covenant. In fact, throughout Scripture, all covenants between God and man are initiated by God and never by any man. The word "covenant," *diathēkē*, is the usual translation of the Hebrew *berith* (270 of 286 occurrences in the Hebrew text).[783] The word never occurs in the LXX with the meaning of "will" or "testament,"[784] although this is the predominate meaning of the word in Hellenistic Greek. This covenant is a "new" covenant—the only time in the Old Testament where the new covenant is specifically mentioned. The Synoptic Gospels refer to this new covenant in the last supper narratives, but it is only in Luke's account (Luke 22:20) that the adjective "new" is used. Jesus' use of this terminology references Jer 31:31–34. Furthermore, Jesus identifies the promised blessings of the new covenant in Jeremiah 31 as being inaugurated by his death on the cross.

8:9–10 In v. 9, the author identifies the Mosaic covenant as being displaced by the new covenant since it was after Israel's exodus from Egypt that the Mosaic covenant was instituted by God (Exod 20:2). The reference to God's writing his "laws" on the hearts of his people has been taken in one of two ways: (1) internalization, and (2) completeness. Contextually, both meanings seem to be in play. A problem that plagues interpreters in v. 10 is the LXX's use of the plural *nomous* "laws" where the Masoretic text has the singular. Most likely Malone is correct when he says the plural emphasizes the specific laws of the Mosaic covenant.[785]

Joslin's recent study of the use of *nomos* and its relationship to the new covenant in Hebrews is the best treatment of the subject to date. As he correctly pointed out, "law" and "covenant" should not be equated in Jeremiah 31, and the author of Hebrews did not equate them since he never refers to a "new law," "first law," "second law," or "better law," yet all of these adjectives are used to modify "covenant."[786]

As Joslin correctly argued concerning *nomos* in v. 10, the reference surely must be to the Mosaic law and not some generic sense of God's "will" since the author would need some explanation if a different meaning was intended.

---

783 BDAG 228. For the Hebrew בְּרִית, consult *HALOT* 1:157; E. B. Smick, "בְּרִית," *TWOT* 1:128–130.

784 Westcott, *Hebrews*, 299.

785 F. Malone, "A Critical Evaluation of the Use of Jeremiah 31:31–34 in the Letter to the Hebrews," (Ph.D. diss., Southwestern Baptist Theological Seminary, 1989), 186. According to Malone, νόμους refers specifically here to the Decalogue since in Jer 31:33, the Hebrew verb is only used with God as its subject in connection with the Ten Commandments in the OT (Malone, "Critical Evaluation," 79). Cf. S. Blank, "LXX Renderings of Old Testament Terms for Law," *HUCA* 7 (1930): 259–83.

786 Joslin, "Theology," 233. See his full discussion on the meaning and use of νόμους in Heb 8:10 on pp. 255–71.

Additionally, the law "written on the heart" is a common concept in the Old Testament always connected with the Mosaic law.[787]

8:11 In Heb 8:11, the new covenant carries with it such knowledge of the Lord that it will no longer be necessary (emphatic negation in the Greek text)[788] for one to teach his fellow citizen[789] of the necessity to "know the Lord" because they will all know him. Hebrews 8:11 exemplifies the contrast between the Mosaic covenant and the new covenant. Under the Mosaic covenant, teaching was a vital part of communicating the conditions and consequences of the covenant. Moses taught the people who in turn taught their children. It is unlikely this verse means there will no longer be any need for teachers, at least not until the eschaton. Certainly this is not the case at the present time, even though the new covenant is already in vogue. Furthermore, the author already stated the necessity for his readers to be taught (5:11–14). It may be that this "knowledge of the Lord" refers to God's instruction for entrance into the covenant itself.[790] Dods took it to mean understanding the details of the law.[791] Huey argued that what was rendered "superfluous" by the new covenant was "exhortation rather than instruction."[792] A better option is to recognize that the new covenant has eschatological dimensions to it. Although the new covenant has been inaugurated by Christ, this aspect of universal knowledge of the Lord awaits future fulfillment. From a premillennial perspective, perhaps the reference is to the status of knowledge of the Lord during the millennial reign of Christ. Another option is the reference could be to the eternal heavenly state. Koester identified the two aspects of the meaning of "know the Lord:" recognition and obedience.[793]

8:12 The quotation concludes in 8:12 with a final sentence introduced by *hoti*, "for," expressing the grounds for the preceding statements concerning universal knowledge of the Lord: God's promise to "forgive their wickedness" and "remember their sins no more." "I will forgive" is the translation of the Greek "I will be merciful." The result of God's mercy is his forgiveness. "Wickedness" is the translation of the plural noun *adikia*, which may in this context refer to individual acts of sin.[794] The final clause is coordinated with

---

[787] Ibid., 253. See T. E. McComiskey, *The Covenants of Promise: A Theology of the Old Testament Covenants* (Grand Rapids: Baker, 1985), 84, who notes "law" is used to refer to the Mosaic law.

[788] Οὐ μή is rendered as "by no means" by L&N 69.5; and Greenlee, *Exegetical Summary*, 296.

[789] The Greek πολίτην is best rendered as "fellow citizen" as in Lane, *Hebrews 1–8*, 200; and the NASB, although the translation "neighbor" is opted for by Bruce, *Hebrews*, 187; and the NIV is also permissible.

[790] Ellingworth, *Hebrews*, 414; Malone, "Critical Evaluation," 189.

[791] Dods, "Hebrews," 325.

[792] F. B. Huey, *Jeremiah,* NAC (Nashville: B&H, 1993), 285.

[793] Koester, *Hebrews*, 387.

[794] Lünemann, *Hebrews,* 594.

the preceding clause by *kai* and contains the emphatic negation *ou mē*. It reads according to the Greek word order: "their sins by no means I shall remember yet (or 'still')." The notion of not remembering sins is semantically equivalent to God's forgiveness of their sins.

8:13 The author's first comment in v. 13 following the quotation is vital and foundational to his argument in chapters 9–10. The quotation began with the statement, "I will make a new covenant." Now in 8:13 the author references that statement and draws a conclusion: Since God has called this covenant "new,"[795] he has declared the Mosaic covenant to be "obsolete." The infinitival phrase *en tō legein* is given an instrumental translation:[796] "by calling this covenant 'new,' he has made." It has also been taken temporally, as in the NASB, "when he said." The antecedent of "he" is God. The use of the perfect tense of *palaioō*, "make obsolete," highlights the permanent antiquated status of the old covenant. Both participles in the final clause, literally, "what is growing old" and "what is aging," are governed by a single article, which indicates a single action is in view. The first participle is passive and the second is active: the Mosaic covenant has been declared old by God and is aging in the sense of being outdated. These two participles function as the compound subject of an understood equative verb "is" followed by the adverb "soon" and a noun meaning (lit.) "in the condition of being no longer visible." Louw and Nida take the meaning to be "will soon cease to exist."[797] Whether this indicates that the Levitical cultus was still in existence at the time of writing cannot be determined with any certainty,[798] though many have drawn such a conclusion.[799]

The author determined in 7:18 that the Mosaic law has been abrogated because of its weakness. He now couples this with the Jeremiah quotation to conclude that the Mosaic covenant is obsolete.[800] As Jesus is greater than angels, Moses, the Levitical priesthood and sacrificial system, so the new covenant which he inaugurates supersedes and surpasses the old Mosaic covenant. But one must ask, what is the relationship of the law to the new covenant? How can the author of Hebrews conclude that the Mosaic law is incapable of

---

[795] On the three possible meanings of καινός, temporal newness, new as to kind or nature, and new in the sense of previously unknown or novel, see L&N 28.34, 58.71, 67.115. Most likely the meaning here is new as to kind or nature.

[796] Harrisville, *Concept of Newness,* 49, remarked that the Greek construction ἐν τῷ λέγειν describes the manner in which the old covenant is laid aside in v. 13. Ellingworth, *Hebrews*, 418, also takes ἐν τῷ λέγειν as instrumental.

[797] L&N 13.98.

[798] Bruce, *Hebrews*, 195.

[799] Hughes, *Hebrews*, 302; Hewitt, *Hebrews*, 138.

[800] Koester, *Hebrews*, 388. The Mosaic covenant had a "built-in obsolescence" (Longenecker, *Biblical Exegesis*, 184). Kaiser refers to the Mosaic covenant's "planned obsolescence" (Kaiser, "The Old Promise and the New Covenant," 19).

bringing about perfection for the new covenant believer, as he states in Heb 7:19, and yet quote Jeremiah in an affirming fashion concerning the Law being written on the hearts of new covenant believers? This has proven to be a thorny issue for interpreters. Are we to conclude, as does Lehne, that the author of Hebrews is "perhaps not altogether consistent" in what he says concerning the Law?[801]

Recently, the question has been most ably treated by Joslin, who sought to demonstrate the compatibility of a transformed law with the inward writing of the law on the hearts of new covenant believers. Joslin suggested a connection between the law of Heb 7:12 and the new covenant of Heb 8:10.[802] After noting that many commentators remain silent or ambiguous on the question (such as Ellingworth and Koester), Joslin surveyed the two main views: the No-Correspondence View and the Direct Correspondence View. Those who see no correspondence between the Mosaic law and Heb 8:10 generally interpret "law" in Heb 8:10 to refer generically to "God's will" or "instruction."[803] Regarding this approach, Joslin noted this view is "simply a way of saying that God is going to do an inward work that brings about obedience with no real connection to the laws of the [old covenant]. Thus, the promise is expressed in figurative language."[804] Joslin offered three critiques: (1) How can *nomos* be reinterpreted by the author without giving indication as to the change in meaning? The law was central to the covenant. "To empty it of its meaning without explanation or rationale is problematic." (2) There is a certain inconsistency and ambiguity in the interpretation of *nomos*. (3) Proponents of the view offer no discussion of the use of the plural form *nomous* in Heb 8:10.[805]

By contrast, the Direct Correspondence View suggests that the promises of the new covenant provide for the internalization of the Mosaic Law in the hearts of believers.[806] Joslin modified and expanded "in a more Christological direction" this view by suggesting the transformation of the Law involves "both

---

[801] Lehne, *New Covenant*, 26. Lehne believes the author of Hebrews uses cultic categories out of deference to his reader's mental frame of reference. Such categories don't have a divine teaching purpose, are mere metaphors, and are the writer's "creative reinterpretation" (p. 119). Lehne is incorrect in her assessment that the Hebrews' author has usurped Jeremiah's original intent (p. 31). See Joslin's salient critique of Lehne on this point: "The writer of Hebrews utilizes Jeremiah in a way that is sensitive to and not contrary to the original author's intent, and is imminently Christological" ("Theology," 253).

[802] Joslin, "Theology," 217.

[803] E.g., Attridge, *Hebrews*, 227.

[804] Joslin, "Theology," 259.

[805] Ibid., 261.

[806] Among those who have opted for this approach, see M. Weinfeld, "Jeremiah and the Spiritual Metamorphosis of Israel," *ZAW* 88 (1976): 28; R. P. Carroll, *Jeremiah: A Commentary* (Philadelphia: Westminster, 1986), 611; Hughes, *Hebrews*, 300; Vanhoye, *Old Testament Priests and New Testament Priest*, 183; Kistemaker, *Hebrews*, 226; B. Ware, "The New Covenant and the People(s) of God," in *Dispensationalism, Israel and the Church: the Search for Definition*, ed. C.

the *fulfillment* and *internalization* of the Law."[807] Laws concerning priesthood and sacrifice have been fulfilled in Christ and are thus non-binding on new covenant believers.[808] At no point in the Old Testament or in Hebrews do we find any suggestion that the law itself must be replaced by a new law.

THEOLOGICAL IMPLICATIONS. We are now prepared to examine the Old Testament's teaching concerning the new covenant. Gordon offered the following summary:

1. God will establish in the future a new covenant which will differ from the old covenant in significant ways.
2. The new covenant is necessary because God's people failed to obey the old covenant.
3. All members of the new covenant community will know God personally.
4. The law will be internalized; each member of the new covenant community will receive a "new heart."
5. Sin will be dealt with once and for all.
6. In some way, the new covenant will reunite Israel and Judah.
7. The new covenant will be eternally effective.
8. An individual will be involved with the establishing of this new covenant.[809]

Of these eight, only six are contained in the Jeremiah passage itself.

Ware finds four "new" elements in the covenant in Jer 31:31–34:

1. a new mode of implementation—internalization of the Law[810]
2. a new result—a "full and lasting" faithfulness to God[811]

Blaising and D. Bock (Grand Rapids: Zondervan, 1992), 75; DeSilva, *Perseverance in Gratitude*, 285–86; and Lane, *Hebrews 1–8*, 209.

[807] Joslin, "Theology," 265. When the law is viewed through Christological lenses, it is "Christologized" and "it is in this transformation that it is internalized in the NC people by God the covenant-maker" (Joslin, "Theology," 218). Whereas under the Mosaic law, disobedience was often the norm for God's people, under the new covenant this internalization of the law makes it possible for believers to obey from the heart. Cf. Peterson, *Hebrews and Perfection*, 132–40, on the significance of the internalization of the law in 8:10 which brings about the inward cleansing of the heart and conscience. S. Stanley, "A New Covenant Hermeneutic: The Use of Scripture in Hebrews 8–10," *TynBul* 46 (1995), 204–6, arrived at a similar conclusion as Joslin: Jeremiah 31 is fulfilled in the new covenant inaugurated by Christ. God's Old Testament revelation still has "meaning, significance and authority for the readers of Hebrews as New Covenant believers" (p. 206).

[808] Ibid., 269.

[809] Gordon, "Studies in the Covenantal Theology of the Epistle to the Hebrews in Light of its Setting," 115–16.

[810] Ware develops Weinfeld's treatment of the complementarity of the visions of Jeremiah and Ezek 36:24–32 and draws the conclusion that "the new covenant feature of the internalization of the law through the Spirit's permanent indwelling presence in all of God's people constitutes a central element of the newness of the new covenant" ("The New Covenant," 79).

[811] This feature of the new covenant awaits future fulfillment.

3. a new basis—full and final forgiveness
4. a new scope of inclusion—"from the least to the greatest"[812]

Koester identified four main elements of the new covenant:

1. God will write his laws on the hearts of the people.
2. The promise "I will be their God and they shall be my people" is at the heart of the new covenant.
3. All the people will know God fully to such a degree that further teaching will become unnecessary.
4. God will remember sins no more.[813]

Paul Williamson offered the following summary of the new covenant. (1) It will be both national and international—this is born out in Isa 42:6; 49:6; 55:3–5; 56:4–8; 66:18–24. "Thus the new covenant projects the ultimate fulfilment [*sic*] of the divine promises on to an ideal Israel . . . located in a rejuvenated universe (Isa 65:17; 66:22)."[814] Such a notion is not foreign to the intent of God's original promise in that from the very beginning God made it "clear that ethnic descent from Abraham was neither sufficient (Gen 17:14) nor essential (Gen 17:12) for inclusion among the people of God."[815] (2) The new covenant will involve both continuity and discontinuity. The discontinuity consists in complete removal of sin, an inner transformation of heart, and an intimate relationship with God. All three underline the new covenant's most important aspect of discontinuity with the old: its indestructibility.[816] (3) The new covenant will be both climactic and eternal.

> In some sense previous divine covenants find their culmination in this new covenant, for this future covenant encapsulates the key promises made throughout the Old Testament era (e. g., a physical inheritance, a divine-human relationship; an everlasting dynasty; blessing on a national and international scale), while at the same time transcending them. Thus, the new covenant is the climactic fulfillment of the covenants that God established with the patriarchs, the nation of Israel, and the dynasty of David.[817]

We are now prepared to consider the theological implications of Heb 8:1–13. First, one is immediately struck by the use of first person language in Jer

[812] Ware, "The New Covenant," 79–80.

[813] Koester, *Hebrews*, 391–92. Joslin, "Theology," 252, lists ten parallels between Jeremiah and Hebrews. The point of comparison between the old and new covenants in Hebrews is not Platonic, but temporal, as correctly noted by Harrisville, *Concept of Newness*, 50–51.

[814] P. Williamson, *Sealed with an Oath: Covenant in God's Unfolding Purpose*, NSBT 23 (Downers Grove: InterVarsity/Apollos, 2007), 179–80.

[815] Ibid., 180.

[816] Ibid., 181.

[817] Ibid., 181–82.

31:31–34. No less than four times God says "I will." By such language, God is establishing that the covenant originates with him alone and he in a sense obligated himself to bring about its fulfillment.

Second, that this covenant is made with "the house of Israel and the house of Judah" makes it clear that God intends a reunification of the divided nation. In addition, Isa 55:3–5 is usually interpreted as referring to the new covenant and here Isaiah speaks of the inclusion of Gentiles, although they are not addressed directly as specific recipients of God's covenant.[818] What is referenced by Isaiah concerning the Gentiles becomes specific in the New Testament, especially in Hebrews 8. Here all Christians, Jews and Gentiles, are part of the new covenant.

The greatest emphasis of Jeremiah and of the author of Hebrews is on the forgiveness of sins brought about by the new covenant. When the shorter version of Jeremiah 31 is quoted by the author again in 10:3, the same words concerning the forgiveness of sins are used. The author concludes the extensive doctrinal section of 8:1–10:18 with a twofold reference in 10:14 and 10:18 to the forgiveness of sins having come under the new covenant. Such a final forgiveness is based upon the final sacrifice of Christ which inaugurated the new covenant. Jesus' statement at the last supper (Luke 22:20) as well as Heb 8:1–10:18 both establish that Jesus' sacrifice for sin accomplished precisely what the new covenant required and that his death on the cross was, in fact, the inauguration of the new covenant.

While it is clear that many of the specific aspects of the new covenant were also a part of the old covenant, it is highly unlikely that Jeremiah was somehow using "new" in an ironic sense for the purpose of shocking his readers out of complacency.[819] Fischer argued that what was "new" in the new covenant was its internal nature and that the power of God through Christ enabled believers to obey it. He took "obsolete" to refer to "outdated" rather than to carry the sense of "annulled," and he interpreted the phrase "ready to disappear" as not actually equivalent to having disappeared. In this way Fisher argued that the new covenant was somehow a renewal of the old covenant. He was joined by Kaiser.

> We conclude that the new covenant is a continuation of the Abrahamic and Davidic covenants with the same single, promise doctrine sustained in them all. No features have been deleted except the ceremonies and ordinances of the "old" Mosaic covenant whose phasing out was planned for long ago.[820]

Kaiser continued:

---

[818] Ware, "The New Covenant," 73.

[819] So argued by I. Wallis, *The Faith of Jesus Christ in Early Christian Traditions,* 151; and J. Fischer, "Irony in Jeremiah's Prophecy of a New Covenant," *JETS* 12 (1969): 109.

[820] Kaiser, "The Old Promise and the New Covenant," 21.

> The key to understanding the 'better covenant' of Hebrews 8:6 is to observe the equation made between the Abrahamic promise (Heb. 6:13; 7:19, 22) and the new covenant (Heb. 8:6–13) . . . The Mosaic covenant did have its faults (Heb. 8:7), not because of a fault in the Covenant-making God, but because many of its provisions were deliberately built with a planned obsolescence.[821]

Against this notion of renewal stands the issue of the ineffectiveness of the old covenant's treatment of sin. F. B. Huey argued against the "renewal" viewpoint as did Keown, Scalise, and Smothers.[822] McComiskey noted that the context of Hebrews 8 mitigates against the "renewal" proposition: in 8:13 "the meaning of the word *new* (*kainos*) is determined by the linear relationship with the word *obsolete*. It is 'new' in relationship to an obsolete covenant, not in relationship to the promise."[823] The direct statement in Jer 31:32 that this new covenant will not be "like the covenant I made with their forefathers" is discontinuous with the old covenant in terms of both scope and power.[824]

Perhaps there is a sense in which we can speak of the new covenant as new and yet also in some sense as renewed. The new covenant is new in terms of the internalization of the law and the ultimate forgiveness of sins which it effects. It is renewed in the sense that the law itself is not abrogated but has continuing validity.[825] But what is indisputable is that, for the author of Hebrews, the new covenant replaces the old.

Ware spoke of the new basis for the new covenant as being that forgiveness reaches a new level. The sacrificial system in the Old Testament was a mechanism to deal with the sinfulness of God's covenant people. The new covenant has no such mechanism. In answer to the question of how this can be, Ware responded, "God will base his new covenant not simply on the forgiveness of past sin and its guilt but rather on the removal of all sin in all its respects, ensuring then, by his Spirit, that there will be no further need for forgiveness once sin is fully and finally abolished."[826] This, of course, awaits future fulfillment in the eschaton.

The author's use of the new covenant theme from Jeremiah 31 in Hebrews further stresses the continuity of salvation history of the church with Israel. The Abrahamic covenant stresses the future of Israel in a literal fulfillment. The new covenant is now in effect; its blessings are experienced by the Church, but in a future time all of the new covenant promises will be realized by Israel

---

[821] Ibid.

[822] Huey, *Jeremiah*, 280–86; G. Keown, P. Scalise, T. Smothers, *Jeremiah 26–52*, WBC 26 (Dallas: Word Books, 1995), 130–31. Note the use of the Hebrew adverbs translated "not like" in Jer 31:31 and "not anymore" in 31:34.

[823] McComiskey, *The Covenants of Promise*, 168; see the full discussion on pp. 164–70.

[824] Harrisville, *Concept of Newness*, 49.

[825] This was the position argued by W. Lemke, "Jeremiah 31:31–34," *Int* 37 (1983): 184.

[826] Ware, "The New Covenant," 81.

(Romans 11) together with Gentiles who are also a part of the new covenant through Christ.[827]

Some have taken the position that the new covenant is applicable to Israel, with the Church being only the "beneficiary of the new covenant."[828] Such a view has been effectively refuted by McComiskey in his *The Covenants of Promise*.[829] Others have espoused the view that there are actually two "new covenants," one for Israel and one for the church.[830] McComiskey's critique is again potent on this point:

> If something as monumental as a new covenant for the church—distinct from Israel's new covenant—had been instituted in the economy of God, one wonders why there is no record of its initiation, and why it is cited with no clear distinction from the new covenant of Jeremiah 31. When reading a context like Hebrews 8:6–13, one goes immediately from a reference to the better covenant, ascribed to the church in this view, to the covenant of Jeremiah 31, ascribed to Israel. The absence of any definitive contextual delineation of the allegedly different covenants is, to say the least, confusing and suspicious. The most natural reaction of the reader is to identify the two covenants as one.[831]

Here is the crux of the issue: the author of Hebrews applies Jeremiah's new covenant to the Church and yet the Old Testament connects the new covenant with the house of Israel and Judah in a future fulfillment. As Ware says, these two seemingly disparate views are reconciled "when we permit the fulfillment of such eschatological promises to take both a preliminary and partial ('already') fulfillment as well as a later full and complete ('not yet') realization."[832] Hermeneutically, one cannot spiritualize the many Old Testament promises concerning God's intention to restore Israel to the land by applying those promises somehow to the Church. There is no New Testament warrant for doing so.

---

[827] E.g., R. L. Saucy, "Israel and Church: A Case for Discontinuity," in *Continuity and Discontinuity: Perspectives on the Relationship Between the Old and New Testaments*, ed. J. S. Feinberg (Westchester, IL: Crossway, 1988), 239–59; and J. L. Burns, "The Future of Ethnic Israel in Romans 11," in *Dispensationalism, Israel and the Church*, 188–229.

[828] E.g., E. S. English, *Studies in the Epistle to the Hebrews* (Traveler's Rest, SC: Southern Bible House, 1955), 227.

[829] McComiskey, *Covenants of Promise*, 153–61.

[830] So J. D. Pentecost, *Things to Come: A Study in Biblical Eschatology* (Grand Rapids: Zondervan, 1965), 124.

[831] McComiskey, *Covenants of Promise*, 159. As an example that contemporary dispensationalists reject the two covenant idea, consult H. Kent, "The New Covenant and the Church," *GTJ* 6 (1985): 297–98.

[832] Ware, "The New Covenant," 84. Ware stated that when God brings to fulfillment the new covenant, the promised physical, national and geographic blessings would be applied to Israel (Isa 11:1–16; 32:9–20; 42:1–9; 44:1–8; 61:1–11; Jer 23:5–6; 30:4–11; 33:14–18; Ezek 34:25–31; 36:24–38; 37:24–28).

Only a literal fulfillment of these promises makes hermeneutical sense when comparing the Old Testament to the New Testament on this issue. Spiritual aspects of the new covenant are presently in vogue. However, geographical and political aspects of the promises made to Israel await fulfillment in the future. This "already/not yet" eschatological outlook best describes the author of Hebrews' perspective, and as Ware perceptively observed, parallels the same two-stage manner of messianic prophetic fulfillment.[833]

Finally, Dunnill pointed out the author of Hebrews' respect and appreciation for the old covenant and that the new covenant is superior to the old not only in degree but in kind. However, Dunnill failed to catch the author's clear meaning as to the status of the old covenant once the new covenant is in place. When he said that the author does not promote the new covenant by "setting aside the old" and that the criticism of the old covenant "does not amount to a dismissal," he has missed the point that the old covenant is no longer in effect, period.[834] Following in its train is the entire sacrificial system. A point often lost on some is that the author of Hebrews uses the Old Testament Scripture to prove that the old covenant with its sacrificial system was never intended to be permanent.[835] The author of Hebrews considers the Old Testament cultus to constitute "the human imitation of a pre-existent divine model" according to Vanhoye. In addition, the author's use of *hupodeigma*, which is better translated as "outline" or "model" rather than "copy," illustrates that for the author, the cultus has a prophetic function because it prefigures the realization of God's plan.[836]

Thus, the old covenant with its sacrificial system has been superseded by the new covenant, but such is not some clever invention of a New Testament author; rather, it is by the very design of God himself. Furthermore, in spite of this fact, the author never devalues the Old Testament; he rather uses it to prove his point.[837]

---

[833] Ibid., 95. Cf. C. Ryrie, "Covenant, New," in *WBE* 1:392, who appeals to Rom 11:26–27 in arguing that, while Christians experience the new covenant blessings brought about by Christ on the cross, "the New Testament also reveals that the blessings promised to Israel will be experienced by her at the second coming of Christ (Rom 11:26–27)."

[834] J. Dunnill, *Covenant and Sacrifice in the Letter to the Hebrews*, SNTSMS 75 (Cambridge: Cambridge University Press, 1992), 229.

[835] Concerning the logic of Heb 8:7–13, A. Thiselton, ("Hebrews," in *Eerdmans Commentary on the Bible*, ed. J. D. G. Dunn and J. W. Rogerson [Grand Rapids: Eerdmans, 2003], 1467), remarked, "[T]o speak of inadequacy or 'fault' in the old covenant (v. 8) is to do no more than heed its own self-testimony."

[836] Vanhoye, *Old Testament Priests and the New Priest*, 181, noted the term ὑπόδειγμα lit. means "a mark placed underneath," in the sense of a provisional sketch which prepares for the definitive design.

[837] W. Klassen, "To the Hebrews or Against the Hebrews? Anti-Judaism and the Epistle to the Hebrews," in *Anti-Judaism in Early Christianity*, ed. S. Wilson (Waterloo, Ontario: Wilfrid Laurier University Press, 1986), 2:9, noted that C. Wolff (*Jeremia im Frühjudentum und Urchristentum*, TU 118 [Berlin: Akadamie-Verlag, 1976]) had shown Jewish sources ignored Jer 31:31–33 until

(2) *Limitations of the First Covenant (9:1–14)*

[1]Now the first covenant had regulations for worship and also an earthly sanctuary. [2]A tabernacle was set up. In its first room were the lampstand, the table and the consecrated bread; this was called the Holy Place. [3]Behind the second curtain was a room called the Most Holy Place, [4]which had the golden altar of incense and the gold-covered ark of the covenant. This ark contained the gold jar of manna, Aaron's staff that had budded, and the stone tablets of the covenant. [5]Above the ark were the cherubim of the Glory, overshadowing the atonement cover. But we cannot discuss these things in detail now.

[6]When everything had been arranged like this, the priests entered regularly into the outer room to carry on their ministry. [7]But only the high priest entered the inner room, and that only once a year, and never without blood, which he offered for himself and for the sins the people had committed in ignorance. [8]The Holy Spirit was showing by this that the way into the Most Holy Place had not yet been disclosed as long as the first tabernacle was still standing. [9]This is an illustration for the present time, indicating that the gifts and sacrifices being offered were not able to clear the conscience of the worshiper. [10]They are only a matter of food and drink and various ceremonial washings—external regulations applying until the time of the new order.

[11]When Christ came as high priest of the good things that are already here, he went through the greater and more perfect tabernacle that is not man-made, that is to say, not a part of this creation. [12]He did not enter by means of the blood of goats and calves; but he entered the Most Holy Place once for all by his own blood, having obtained eternal redemption. [13]The blood of goats and bulls and the ashes of a heifer sprinkled on those who are ceremonially unclean sanctify them so that they are outwardly clean. [14]How much more, then, will the blood of Christ, who through the eternal Spirit offered himself unblemished to God, cleanse our consciences from acts that lead to death, so that we may serve the living God!

In Hebrews 8 the author emphasized the discontinuity between the old and new covenants. In Hebrews 9 the author moves to show that there yet remains some continuity between the two covenants, albeit in a typological fashion. The chapter contains two discourse sections: 9:1–14 and 9:15–28 with the following paragraphs: 9:1–5,6–10,11–14,15–22, vv. 23–28. Lincoln suggested an overall chiastic structure for 9:1–28.[838]

Hebrews 9:1–5 is a paragraph unit describing the tabernacle and its contents. Verse 1 announces two topics: the earthly sanctuary (9:2–5), and regulations concerning the offering of sacrifices by the high priest (9:6–10).[839] Hebrews 9:1–5 is notorious for its divergence from the Hebrew Old Testament

---

after the destruction of the temple in 70 AD. He queried: "Does this suggest that Jewish sources began to use it in response to the way it emerges in Hebrews? Or does it suggest that Hebrews itself was not written before the fall of Jerusalem?" Of course, it may not suggest either, but the former seems more likely than the latter.

[838] L. Lincoln, "Translating Hebrews 9:15–22 in its Hebraic Context," *JOTT* 12 (1999): 3–4.

[839] Attridge, Hebrews, 231; W. L. Lane, *Hebrews 9–13*, WBC (Dallas: Word Books, 1991), 217.

and its number of textual variants. Space prohibits an in-depth analysis of the intricacies of this issue, but several general statements can be made which will hopefully clarify matters for the interpreter. The three primary issues are the textual variants within the text of Hebrews itself,[840] the differences in Exodus of the account of the tabernacle in the Hebrew and LXX versions,[841] and the question of whether and how much the author's dependence upon the LXX might explain the anomalies of the passage.[842]

9:1 In v. 1, *kai* is omitted by Lane and not translated by the NIV.[843] Dods noted that the *kai* refers to both old and new covenants and emphasizes that the old covenant had such regulations concerning worship.[844] *Oun* is translated "now" by both Bruce and Lane. It has resumptive force and may reach back to 8:5[845] or 8:7. *Men oun* can be balanced by the *de* in vv. 6,[846] 7, or 11.[847] The use of the imperfect indicative of *eimi*, "had," may imply that the first covenant was no longer in effect at the time of the author's writing.[848] The author's use of "regulation" implies the "rightness" which stands behind the regulation.[849] The phrase "regulations for worship" may indicate that which was regulated, namely, worship,[850] or may indicate regulations governing or related to worship. The author probably includes not only the worship having to do with the tabernacle, but also later in the temple as well.[851] The author's reference to the

---

840 Discussions of textual variants can be found in *TCGNT* 598. Attridge, *Hebrews*, 233–38; among others.

841 Exodus contains two large pericopes on the tabernacle: Exod 25–31 and Exod 36–40. The first section in the LXX follows closely the Hebrew text, but the second section diverges considerably with respect to sequential and textual issues. The two major positions on this issue can be found in D. W. Gooding, *The Account of the Tabernacle: Translations and Textual Problems of the Greek Exodus* (Cambridge: Cambridge University Press, 1959), 99ff.; and A. Aejmelaeus, "Septuagintal Translation Techniques—A Solution to the Problem of the Tabernacle Account," in *Septuagint, Scrolls and Cognate Writings,* ed. G. J. Brooke and B. Lindars, SBLSCS 33 (Atlanta: Scholars Press, 1992), 381–402. Gooding argues that the differences between the two accounts in the LXX of Exodus are the result of a single translator and the liberties he has taken in translation. Aejmelaeus suggests the possibility that a different Hebrew source stands behind the two tabernacle accounts.

842 The most helpful summary treatment of the issues is Gheorghita, *Role of the Septuagint in Hebrews*, 84–91; cf. Attridge, *Hebrews*, 236–38.

843 The UBS[4] Greek Text gives it a "C" decision.

844 Dods, "Hebrews," 326.

845 Alford, "Hebrews," 156, takes it as going back to 8:5; Ellingworth, *Hebrews*, 420, views it as reaching back to v. 7, which is more likely.

846 Spicq, *L'Épître aux Hebreux,* 2:247. Ellingworth, *Hebrews,* 421, however, sees no relationship with any following *de*.

847 See the discussion in Westfall, *Discourse Analysis*, 197, who shows why the connection with v. 11 is best, given all the linguistic factors.

848 Alford, "Hebrews," 156; Moffatt, *Hebrews*, 112.

849 Alford, "Hebrews," 156.

850 In which case it is being construed as an objective genitive.

851 So Lane, *Hebrews 9–13*, 219.

"sanctuary" indicates the entire tabernacle and not just the inner sanctuary.[852] The sanctuary is "earthly," that is, it belongs to this world, in contrast with the new covenant and the new sanctuary in heaven.[853] "Sanctuary" is emphatic by its position at the end of the sentence.

9:2 "Was set up" refers to the construction and furnishing of the tabernacle. The "first room" refers to the "Holy Place" in the tabernacle. "First" can be construed with the preceding words[854] or with the following words.[855] It is emphatic by word order. The author's meaning in using "first" indicates one would have to enter this room first before entering the holy of holies. This verse further explains v. 1. The anarthrous use of the noun "tabernacle" has been explained in one of four ways: (1) the following use of "first" makes it definite; (2) Dods takes it as indefinite;[856] (3) it is equivalent to a proper name and thus does not need the article; (4) the absence of the article implies the author is introducing new information and that "tabernacle" in v. 2 "does not have the same meaning as in verse 1."[857] Either option one or three is most likely.

The translation "lampstand" is better than KJV's "candlestick," which is anachronistic. The "consecrated bread" is (lit.) in Greek "the presentation [setting-forth] of the loaves of bread." This entire phrase can be taken to be the third item listed, following "lampstand" and "table."[858] It can be construed as a hendiadys with "table," indicating that it was bread which was on the table.[859] The repetition of the article with "lampstand," "table," and "consecrated bread" probably indicates the uniqueness of these items and that they were well known to the readers.

The "Holy Place" is the room in the tabernacle anterior to the holy of holies. *Hētis*, translated "this," is taken in a qualitative way by Dods, emphasizing the nature of the tabernacle.[860] Ellingworth rightly viewed it as synonymous with the simple relative pronoun in its function here.[861]

9:3 The author continues his description in v. 3 with his reference to a curtain or veil separating the holy place from the "Most Holy Place." "Second" distinguishes this curtain from that which hung at the entrance to the outside court. In Exod 26:31–37, two different Hebrew words are used to describe the curtain separating the holy place from the holy of holies and the curtain

---

[852] Moffatt, *Hebrews*, 112; Ellingworth, *Hebrews*, 421. The definite article signifies the sanctuary referenced was known and understood by the readers (Ellingworth).

[853] Lane, *Hebrews 9–13*, 219; Ellingworth, *Hebrews*, 421.

[854] So Alford, "Hebrews," 157; Dods, "Hebrews," 327.

[855] So Lane, *Hebrews 9–13*, 219; Ellingworth, *Hebrews*, 422.

[856] Dods, "Hebrews," 327.

[857] Ellingworth, *Hebrews*, 422.

[858] Alford, "Hebrews," 157–58; Ellingworth, *Hebrews*, 422.

[859] So Moffatt, *Hebrews*, 113; Lane, *Hebrews 9–13*, 215. See Exod 25:23–30; 26:35; Lev 24:5–9; Num 4:7; 1 Kgs 7:48.

[860] Dods, "Hebrews," 327.

[861] Ellingworth, *Hebrews*, 423.

or screen which functioned as the door of the tabernacle. The mention of a "second" curtain implies the existence of a first curtain. The same terminology can be found in rabbinic literature,[862] Philo[863] and Josephus.[864] "Most Holy Place" can be translated as "the holy of holies" where the repetition of the noun is the Hebrew idiom for expressing the superlative. The NIV does not translate the conjunction *de* at the beginning of this verse. Alford took *de* to be indicative of a contrast, but Ellingworth is probably correct in taking it as continuing the previous thought by introducing additional information.[865]

9:4 Hebrews 9:4 raises two key questions which must be addressed. The first question concerns the identification of the "golden altar of incense." The Greek word used by the author of Hebrews, *thumiatērion*, occurs twice in the LXX (2 Chr 26:19; Ezek 8:11), and there refers not to the altar of incense but to a "censer," an instrument where incense was placed. However, as Bruce rightly explained, this fact alone is not decisive for meaning since the word also carried the general meaning of "incense altar" in both Philo and Josephus.[866] Since the entire pericope of Exod 25–40 does not mention a "censer," since there was only one "golden altar of incense" but there were many "censers" used by the priests, and since even if this "censer" referenced the one used by Aaron on the Day of Atonement it would not likely be stored in the holy of holies, it is best not to translate *thumiatērion* as "censer."[867] The reference is better taken to be to the "altar of incense" made of gold.[868]

The second difficult question in Heb 9:4 which has plagued interpreters is the author's description of the location of the "golden altar of incense." Upon first reading, the writer appears to locate the altar of incense inside the holy of holies, contrary to Exod 30:6. Several solutions to this supposed contradiction have been offered which are amply summarized by Ellingworth. (1) The author is not interested in detail and is speaking "imprecisely." Several possible reasons for this are presented by Ellingworth.[869] (2) The participle *echousa*, "had," does not refer to location, but rather to use and thus should be given the translation "associated with it." The strength of this view is that the altar of incense was closely associated with the holy of holies by virtue of its location

---

[862] As noted by Bruce, *Hebrews*, 199, fn. 14.

[863] Philo, *Vit. Mos.* [Lives of Moses] 2.101.

[864] Josephus, *Antiquities*, 3.125–27.

[865] Alford, "Hebrews," 158; Ellingworth, *Hebrews*, 424.

[866] Bruce, *Hebrews*, 200.

[867] Ibid. Riggenbach's theory that the author forgot about the incense altar and referred instead to the incense pan (θυμιατήριον) is a groundless notion (*Hebräer*, 245–46). Attridge suggests the differences can best be accounted for by the supposition that the author's statements reflect the distinction between the priests and Levites in the book of Numbers. This viewpoint is rightly rejected by Ellingworth. Hughes offers a good presentation and refutation of option three (*Hebrews*, 311–12).

[868] Χρυσοῦν is emphatic by its word order in the Greek text, appearing before the verbal and the noun.

[869] Ellingworth, *Hebrews*, 424.

immediately in front of the veil[870] and because on the Day of Atonement the high priest brought incense from that altar into the holy of holies.[871] (3) The possibility that the reference is not to the altar of incense but to a "censer" has already been addressed above. Ellingworth takes the first option, noting that the author's concern was not the details of the location of the furniture but with the distinction between the holy place and the holy of holies.[872] Gheorghita favors the view "that the placement of the altar is at least a partial result of reading the LXX passage regarding the incense altar."[873] Whatever the case, two things are apparent: (1) Exod 30:6 and Lev 16:12,18 locate the altar of incense in the holy place in front of the curtain that separates the holy place from the holy of holies; and (2) the author is less concerned about the physical location of the altar and more concerned with its functional correlation to the holy of holies. There are simply no grounds to charge the author with an error on this point.

The "ark of the covenant"[874] is described in the Greek text with a perfect tense participle "covered around," an adverb meaning "on (from) all sides"[875] and the dative "with gold." Lane and the NIV both translate this Greek phrase as "gold-covered," a descriptive phrase that gets at the meaning, but as Greenlee noted, such an attributive rendering violates Greek grammar.[876] Inside the ark are said to be three items: the gold jar of manna,[877] Aaron's staff that budded, and the stone tablets of the covenant[878] (the Ten Commandments). The location of the jar of manna and the staff "in" the ark is problematic when compared to both the Hebrew and LXX texts of Exod 16:33 and Num 17:25 [Eng. 17:10]. In the Hebrew text, the same preposition *lipnê*, "in front of" or "before" is used to describe the location of the jar as before "the Lord" and the rod as in front of "the testimony." The question is whether the jar of manna and Aaron's rod were placed *inside* the ark or *in front of* the ark. The linguistic ambiguity of

---

[870] Hughes, *Hebrews*, 309–13, argues this viewpoint well; cf. A. Nairne, *The Epistle of Paul the Apostle to the Hebrews*, CGTSC (Cambridge: Cambridge University Press, 1984). However, Bruce, *Hebrews*, 201, calls this explanation "special pleading." Moffatt's overly negative criticism of the author on this point, calling it "another one of his inaccuracies in describing what he only knew from the text of the LXX," is unfounded (*Hebrews*, 114–15).

[871] Bruce, *Hebrews,* 200–1.

[872] Ellingworth, *Hebrews,* 422–23.

[873] Gheorghita, *Role of the Septuagint in Hebrews*, 89.

[874] Διαθήκης is a genitive of content: the ark contained the covenant, as specified later in the verse.

[875] Probably indicating the ark's interior as well as its exterior was overlaid with gold (Lünemann, *Hebrews*, 605; Lane, *Hebrews 9–13*, 221).

[876] Greenlee, *Exegetical Summary,* 308.

[877] The Hebrew text does not say anything about the pot being made of gold, yet this feature is found in all the Greek manuscripts. It is therefore likely the author of Hebrews is here following the LXX.

[878] Moffatt correctly noted that the Decalogue was a summary of God's covenant with the people.

the preposition *lipnê* in the Old Testament texts above can be interpreted either way. Bruce is quite clear: "It is not to be doubted that our author represents the jar of manna and the rod as having been inside the ark along with the tables of the law."[879]

9:5 The reference in v. 5 to the "cherubim of the Glory" refers to the two golden images of cherubim, one at each end of the ark, which overshadowed the "atonement cover," otherwise known as the "mercy seat." On the Day of Atonement, the high priest would sprinkle blood on this cover over the ark. It was thus the place where sins were forgiven by God because of the atoning blood. Cherubim represent God's presence and the manifestation of God's glory. Although there is no article before "cherubim" or "glory," the NIV's insertion of the article likely is an attempt to define the glory as belonging to God. The participle "overshadowing" is in a predicate relationship to "cherubim," with the present tense signaling a continuing state: "the cherubim, overshadowing the mercy-seat."[880]

The author concludes v. 5 with the observation that he does not have the time to go into further detail concerning these things. The meaning is something akin to "this is not the time to go into detail about this." Semantically, this statement functions to highlight the following paragraph beginning with v. 6. Aquinas's treatment of Heb 9:1–5 highlights the extent to which he was willing to go to allegorize the Scripture. He likens the first tabernacle as a "figure" of the Old Testament and the second tabernacle as a figure of the New Testament. He then suggests "in another way" that the first tabernacle is the present church and the second is heavenly glory. Christ is compared to the table of the presence, the 12 loaves to the doctrine of the 12 apostles, and the two cherubim of the ark of the covenant as the Old and New testaments "looking upon Christ."[881] The reformers Luther and Calvin were at pains to correct such hermeneutical nonsense, though they occasionally fell into similar traps themselves.

---

[879] Bruce, *Hebrews*, 203. Gheorghita assumes the Hebrew text and LXX in Exod 16 and Num 17 indicate the pot of manna and Aaron's rod were *not* located inside the ark, but solves the problem by appeal to the use of the singular τοῦ μαρτυρίου in Num 17:19 and the plural τῶν μαρτυρίων in Num 17:25: "If the preposition is construed in its normal sense, the Hebrews account indeed goes beyond the Exodus and Numbers accounts by placing the pot and the rod into the Ark of the Covenant, τὴν κιβωτὸν τῆς διαθήκης, contrary to what the Hebrew and the Greek text suggest. The particular placement of the rod and pot can be explained, however, by observing the inconsistency of the Greek translation of the singular הָעֵדוּת; translated as a singular τοῦ μαρτυρίου in v. 19 [Num 17:19] and as a plural τῶν μαρτυρίων in v. 25 [Num 17:25]. While the noun in its singular form unambiguously refers to the Ark of the Covenant, the plural refers to the tablets of the law, τὰ μαρτυρία." (*Role of the Septuagint*, 91. See also Ellingworth, *Hebrews*, 429.

[880] So Greenlee, *Exegetical Summary,* 311.

[881] Aquinas, *Commentary on the Epistle to the Hebrews*, trans. C. Baer (South Bend, IN: St. Augustine's, 2006), 178–83.

9:6 Verse 6 begins a new discourse paragraph that concludes with v. 10.[882] The paragraph is divided into two sub-paragraphs, each introduced by a genitive absolute at the beginning of vv. 6,8 in the Greek text. The topic shifts from the rooms and furniture in the tabernacle to the daily activity of the priests in the holy place contrasted with that of the high priest who entered only once a year into the holy of holies. This shift is introduced by the phrase "when everything had been arranged[883] like this," which is the rendering of the Greek "now these things thus furnished."

As do some other translations, including the KJV, the NIV translates the Greek present tense with a past tense "entered regularly." No conclusion as to whether the temple worship was operative or not can be adduced from the present tense here. The "ministry" which the priests perform daily in the holy place includes attending to the lampstand and the altar of incense. The bread of the Presence on the table was replaced weekly and was a part of the regular priestly duties. The author uses a present tense participle to speak of the priests "carrying on" their ministry.[884]

9:7 Verse 7 contrasts the daily and weekly ministry of the priests with the annual work of the high priest on the Day of Atonement as outlined in Leviticus 16.[885] The NIV translates the Greek "second" with "inner" to designate the holy of holies as distinct from the holy place (the outer room). Only the high priest entered the holy of holies, and then he only entered "once a year."[886] There is no verb in this clause in the Greek text, so a verb parallel to "entered" in v. 6 must be supplied. Commentators and translators are about evenly divided in supplying a present ("enters") or a past tense verb ("entered").[887] Hughes considers the use of the present tense here to indicate a pre-AD 70 date for the

[882] The periodic nature of this paragraph has been frequently observed. See E. Grässer, *Der Glaube im Hebräerbrief* (Marburg: N. G. Elwert Verlag, 1965), 2:130–31; Lane, *Hebrews 9–13,* 216; cf. Koester, "Hebrews, Rhetoric, and the Future of Humanity," *CBQ* 64 (2002): 105; and F. Cortez, "From the Holy to the Most Holy Place: The Period of Hebrews 9:6–10 and the Day of Atonement as a Metaphor of Transition," *JBL* 125, no. 3 (2006): 527–47, for a complete discussion of this passage and its periodic nature.

[883] The same Greek word is translated as "set up" in v. 2. The present tense participle κατεσκευασμένων may be viewed as temporal (Lane, *Hebrews 9–13*, 222) or circumstantial (Alford, "Hebrews," 163): "these things thus arranged, the priests enter."

[884] The present tense participle may be construed as temporal (Lane, *Hebrews 9–13*, 222), or as telic, as in the NIV: "to carry on their ministry."

[885] For a thorough analysis of the Day of Atonement and its impact on apostolic and patristic Christianity, see D. S. Ben Ezra, *The Impact of Yom Kippur on Early Christianity: The Day of Atonement from Second Temple Judaism to the Fifth Century*.

[886] According to Lev 16:12,15, the high priest entered the holy of holies only once a year, but on the Day of Atonement he entered at least twice to perform all his duties on that occasion. Rabbinic tradition mentions four entries (*Yoma* 5.1, 3, 4).

[887] Those who use the past tense to translate the present tense here are viewing the verbs as historical presents.

epistle.[888] The use of the Greek double negative translated "never without" semantically expresses a strongly emphasized positive statement.

The high priest offers the sacrifice for himself first (Lev 16:11) and afterward for the people (Lev 16:15). It is stated that the high priest entered "never without blood." The UBS[4] and the NA[27] Greek text both place a comma before this phrase, indicating the phrase modifies the verb "offered." Cortez suggested the phrase modifies the implied verb "entered" in v. 7, which was overtly stated in v. 6.[889] By this construal, the meaning would be the high priest cannot enter the holy of holies "without blood." Both meanings are possible grammatically and both are true with respect to the Day of Atonement. The issue turns on whether one views the author's focus here as the offering or the entrance. The author makes clear the necessity of "blood" in the sacrificial offering made by the high priest on the Day of Atonement.[890] Sin is, among other things, defilement that creates ritual impurity which must be cleansed by blood.

The author includes the fact that the high priest offers the sacrifice for "the sins the people had committed in ignorance." The word used here means "unintentional, inadvertent sin," and is emphatic by its final position in the clause at the end of v. 7. This, however, poses a problem in that the Day of Atonement ritual in Leviticus 16 nowhere specifies the atoning work was only for such unintentional sins. In fact, the terminology in Leviticus 16 emphatically states that the sacrifice that day is for all sins. In Leviticus 4, deliberate high handed sin is distinguished from inadvertent sin in the case of the high priest and the people. Ellingworth concluded concerning this apparent contradiction that "the author is concentrating in the Day of Atonement, as the lesser counterpart of Christ's sacrifice, all his thinking about sin and forgiveness under the old covenant."[891] While this is no doubt true, more may be involved here. Here the author is capitalizing on the Old Testament categorization of sins as "sins of ignorance" and "high-handed sin" (see Num 15:22–31). This is not the first time the author alluded to this categorization, since in Heb 5:2 the author refers to the Jewish high priests as being able to bear gently "with those who are ignorant and going astray." Yet in Lev 16:16, the Day of Atonement ritual makes atonement for all the sins of the people. Gordon posited that the author, in his desire to show the limitations of the Levitical sacrificial system, emphasized in 9:15 that the death of Jesus atones for deliberate sins as well. In this fashion, the author of Hebrews highlights the superiority of Christ's sacrifice to that of the old covenant's sacrificial system.[892] This construal assumes, however, that

[888] Hughes, *Hebrews*, 321.

[889] Cortez, "From the Holy to the Most Holy Place," 535.

[890] On the importance of "blood" in Lev 16 and in all the sacrificial system in the OT, see W. G. Johnsson, "Defilement and Purgation" (Th.D. diss., Vanderbilt University, 1973), esp. 152–61.

[891] Ellingworth, *Hebrews*, 435–36.

[892] R. Gordon, "Better Promises: Two Passages in Hebrews Against the Background of the Old Testament Cultus," in *Temple Amicitiae: Essays on the Second Temple Presented by Ernst Bammel*

"high-handed sins" were not atoned for on the Day of Atonement, an assumption that cannot be made with any certainty based on the Old Testament text.

9:8 Verse 8 is chock full of interpretive difficulties. Does the reference to the "Holy Place" refer to the earthly or heavenly sanctuary; and does it refer to the sanctuary as a whole, only the outer part, or only the inner part? Does the "first tabernacle" refer to the outer part of the earthly sanctuary, or the sanctuary as a whole in contrast to the "greater" in v. 11? Finally, does the verb "was [still] standing" connote existence or status?[893]

The author's use of "had not yet been disclosed" is viewed by Ellingworth as a stylistic variant for "was showing." "The Most Holy Place" (1) refers to the presence of God in heaven;[894] or, as is more likely, (2) refers to the earthly holy of holies with the implication that access to God was not yet available.[895] Two possible meanings can be attributed to the phrase "was [still] standing": (1) continues to exist,[896] or (2) retaining its status.[897] The latter appears to be the most likely. The phrase "by this" can refer to what follows[898] or to what precedes.[899] It seems best to understand it to refer to what precedes. The phrase "was showing" can be taken to indicate the purpose of the pattern stated in 9:7,[900] or as expressing the Holy Spirit's interpretation of what was just mentioned.[901] Again, the latter view is probably best. The "first tabernacle" can be taken as the tabernacle as a whole with "first" being temporal in nature[902] or it can be construed as the holy place, the first room before the holy of holies.[903] Ellingworth and Nida suggest the "most probable" translation of v. 8: "The Holy Spirit shows us by this means that the way into the real tent had not yet been opened as long as the old tent still remained in use."[904]

9:9 The author sees all this as an "illustration" (Gk. *parabolē*) which is best interpreted here to mean "symbolic." Bruce's translation "parable" is too specific for the intended meaning, and "illustration"[905] is too generic, although

(Sheffield: JSOT Press, 1991), 446–47.

[893] See the excellent lengthy discussion of the possible options paired with those who argue for them in Cortez, "From the Holy Place to the Most Holy Place," 538.

[894] So Lane, *Hebrews 9–13*, 223; Hewitt, *Hebrews*, 143–44.

[895] So Bruce, *Hebrews*, 209; Hughes, *Hebrews*, 321–22.

[896] Moffatt, *Hebrews*, 118; Ellingworth, *Hebrews,* 439.

[897] Hughes, *Hebrews*, 322; Lane, *Hebrews 9–13*, 216.

[898] Alford, "Hebrews," 164; Lünemann, *Hebrews*, 608, who says it is emphatic by its position.

[899] Bruce, *Hebrews*, 206; Lane, *Hebrews 9–13*, 223; and the NIV.

[900] Lünemann, *Hebrews*, 608; Dods, "Hebrews," 331.

[901] Alford, "Hebrews," 164; and most translations with the exceptions of KJV and NASB.

[902] Hughes, *Hebrews*, 322; Bruce, *Hebrews*, 208.

[903] Michel, *Hebräer,* 307; Lane, *Hebrews 9–13,* 216, 223–24. Lane believed the spatial reference back in v. 6 is "incontestable," and a shift to a temporal idea within the span of two verses is "unnecessarily harsh and abrupt."

[904] P. Ellingworth and E. A. Nida, *Translator's Handbook on the Letter to the Hebrews* (London/New York: United Bible Societies, 1983), 186.

[905] NIV; Lane, *Hebrews 9–13*, 223.

not inaccurate. The author appears to intend to show some comparison, hence "symbolic" is better than "illustration."[906] This "illustration" is "for the present time," a phrase capable of referring to the time when Hebrews was written[907] or to the time of the tabernacle.[908] The former interpretation appears most likely contextually. Those who construe the meaning in the former manner offer varying suggestions as to the symbolism. Bruce thought the temple veil emphasized the contrast between the limited access to God under the old covenant and the full access now available through Christ.[909] In a similar fashion, Alford supposed the outer tabernacle, as a symbol of the old covenant, represented an obstruction to entrance into the most holy place, which could be viewed as a figure of heavenly things to which access is now available through Christ's work.[910] Kistemaker took the earthly sanctuary to be a symbol of the situation under the old covenant which still existed when the epistle was written.[911] Some who construe the phrase "for the present time" as referring to the time of the tabernacle take the outer tent as a parable of the Old Testament dispensation, showing that access to God had not yet been opened.[912] Hewitt considered the earthly tabernacle, as a symbol of the heavenly tabernacle, to be a symbol for the people under the old covenant in the Old Testament.[913]

The relative pronoun translated "this" in v. 9 has several possible antecedents. It has been taken by some to refer to the outer tabernacle[914] and by others to refer to the earthly tabernacle as a whole as a type of the heavenly tabernacle.[915] It may refer to "illustration" in the preceding clause,[916] to the tabernacle,[917] or to the outer tent of the tabernacle.[918] The phrase "indicating that the gifts" explains how the outer tabernacle is the symbol mentioned in the preceding clause.[919]

The NIV's "to clear the conscience" may be too mild for the Greek which uses the verb "perfect." Ellingworth found a negative and a positive aspect: "the fulfillment of the purpose of worship; negatively, the forgiveness of our purification from sin(s), and positively, the opening of access to God."[920]

---

[906] See L&N 58.63.

[907] So Alford, "Hebrews," 165; Kistemaker, *Hebrews*, 244.

[908] Dods, "Hebrews," 331; Hewitt, *Hebrews*, 144.

[909] Bruce, *Hebrews*, 209.

[910] Alford, "Hebrews," 164.

[911] Kistemaker, *Hebrews*, 244.

[912] Dods, "Hebrews," 331.

[913] Hewitt, *Hebrews*, 144.

[914] Alford, "Hebrews," 165; Dods, "Hebrews," 331.

[915] Ellingworth, *Hebrews*, 439.

[916] Alford, "Hebrews," 165; Dods, "Hebrews," 331.

[917] Hughes, *Hebrews*, 323.

[918] Lane, *Hebrews 9–13*, 224.

[919] R. C. H. Lenski, *The Interpretation of the Epistle to the Hebrews and of the Epistle of James* (Columbus, OH: Wartburg, 1946), 285.

[920] Ellingworth, *Hebrews,* 442; cf. Lane, *Hebrews 9–13,* 216.

Lane took the notion of perfection here as involving purgation. The parallel to this statement in v. 9 is v. 14, the conscience must be cleansed to serve God effectively.[921] The author does not necessarily view "conscience" as only a distinct aspect of human nature as he does in Heb 9:9,14, but he also can use "conscience" to refer to the whole person as he does in Heb 10:1,14.[922] Hughes views the author's concept of conscience as "man's inner knowledge of himself, especially in the sense of his *answerability* for his motives and actions in view of the fact that he . . . stands before and must give an account of himself to his Creator."[923]

9:10 Verse 10 makes clear that the symbolic value of the Old Testament sacrifices is negative, not positive. "What the Old Testament says about worship under the old covenant is proof that something more effective was needed."[924] In what way is the first part of v. 10 related to the latter part of v. 9? Four options have been suggested, the first three of which are related. Hughes and Ellingworth considered v. 10 to state what the offering of the gifts and sacrifices in 9:9 relate to, namely, matters of food, drink, and washings.[925] Dods and Lane thought it stated the area in which the offerings mentioned in 9:9 are effective.[926] Alford and Moffatt took it as appositional, telling what the gifts and sacrifices consist of: food, drink, and washings.[927] Lünemann and Lenski considered the items to be in addition to the gifts and sacrifices of v. 9.[928] The "external regulations" may be regulations governing the physical area of life,[929] or they may describe the ordinances (NIV) dealing with physical rather than spiritual matters. Both views are virtually semantic equivalents.

We are now in a position to understand why the author interjects 9:1–5 into the discussion. He concluded in 8:13 that the new covenant renders the old covenant obsolete. The question could be asked: if the old covenant is rendered obsolete, why mention the description of the old covenant's sanctuary furniture placement. There is a certain "logical suspense" in all this, as Cortez put it, which is not solved until one reads 9:6–10. "It is there that it becomes clear that this description is necessary to describe the two-phased ministry of the Israelite sanctuary, which in turn illustrates the transition between two ages represented by the old and new covenants."[930] What appears to be a digression (9:1–5) is actually "the preparation of the elements that will illustrate the 'passing away'

[921] Lane, *Hebrews 9–13,* 224; cf. Peterson, *Hebrews and Perfection,* 234–35.

[922] Ellingworth, *Hebrews,* 442.

[923] Hughes, *Hebrews,* 324.

[924] Ellingworth and Nida, *Translator's Handbook*, 186.

[925] Hughes, *Hebrews*, 324–25; Ellingworth, *Hebrews*, 442–43.

[926] Dods, "Hebrews," 331; Lane, *Hebrews 9–13*, 225.

[927] Alford, "Hebrews," 166; Moffatt, *Hebrews*, 118–19.

[928] Lünemann, *Hebrews*, 610–11; Lenski, *Hebrews*, 286. Lane considers the "external regulations" to describe only the offerings mentioned in the first part of v. 10.

[929] So Moll, *Hebrews*, 153; Lenski, *Hebrews*, 286.

[930] F. Cortez, "From the Holy to the Most Holy Place," 541.

of the first covenant asserted in vv. 6–10."[931] The same semantic theme is asserted in 8:13 and 9:10: the passing away of the old covenant. The participle translated "applying" is placed at the very end of v. 10 in the Greek text. Thus "the author is using a hyperbaton to close the period; however, and more important, by placing the fundamental idea at the end, the author not only gives a circular structure to the logical flow of the whole sentence but reserves the rhetorical punch for the end."[932]

Thus, Cortez argued, correctly in my view, that the periodic paragraph Heb 9:6–10 serves as a "microcosm foreshadowing the argument that follows in chs. 9 and 10." He concluded that the author presents the Day of Atonement more as a parable of transition from the present to the future age and from the old covenant to the new covenant and not so much as a typology for Jesus' sacrifice.[933] The key elements which will be developed by the author in Heb 9:11–10:18 include the change from many priests in the old covenant to one high priest in the new covenant; from many sacrifices to one sacrifice by Christ; and from external cleansing of the flesh to internal cleansing of the conscience.[934] The Old Testament sacrificial system actually erected a barrier between the people and God (9:8), and mandated gifts and sacrifices on the part of the worshipper, which although commanded by God, were incapable of inward cleansing from sin. All of this was, of course, by God's design in preparation for the new covenant.

9:11–12 A new sub-paragraph begins in v. 11 with the use of *de*, which is untranslated, contrasting the ineffectiveness of the Levitical system with the finished atoning work of Christ our high priest. Two sentences comprise the paragraph in the Greek text: 9:11–12 speaks of Christ's entry into the heavenly sanctuary, and 9:13–14 shows the superiority of Christ's sacrifice over the Levitical sacrifices. Many have asserted that 9:11 is the keystone or heart of the entire epistle,[935] however, Westfall has shown semantically why this is

---

931 Ibid.

932 Ibid., 542.

933 Ibid., 529. Here Cortez is building on Loader's point (*Sohn und Hoherpriester. Eine traditionsgeschichtliche Untersuchung zur Christologie des Hebräerbriefes,* WMANT 53 [Neukirchen-Vluyn: Neukirchener Verlag, 1981], 172) that although the Day of Atonement typology plays an important role in the author's thought in 9:1–10:18, yet this should not be overemphasized to the point that one designates it as the prevailing thought of this section. Cortez asks: "How do we explain on the one hand the pervasive nature of the imagery of the Day of Atonement but on the other hand account for the inconsistencies in the Day of Atonement typology for Jesus' death on the cross?" The differences between the Pentateuchal account and Hebrews are illustrated by Cortez on pp. 528–29. The differences do not amount to real inconsistencies given the flexible nature with which the author of Hebrews uses the OT in his argument.

934 Cortez, "From the Holy to the Most Holy Place," 547.

935 E.g., Vanhoye, *Structure of Hebrews*, 46; L. Dussaut, *Synopse Structurelle De L'Épître Aux Hébreux* (Paris: Editions du Cerf, 1981), 73; Ellingworth, *Hebrews,* 445; and Koester, *Hebrews,* 411.

not the case. Verse 14 is more prominent than v. 11 in the discourse.[936] The use of "Christ" is emphatic by word order and is used by the author as a title. The aorist participle translated "came" can be construed temporally[937] or as indicating a separate action in the sense "Christ came and he went through the . . . tabernacle."[938] This particular participle, when used with the conjunction *de* at the beginning of a sentence as here, often indicates arrival at a destination.[939] The participial phrase "high priest of the good things already here" indicates what it was the high priest accomplished, namely, "the good things." These "good things" consist of cleansing and access to God according to Lane[940] and are all-inclusive of the blessings Christ has gained for believers according to Ellingworth.[941] Hughes summarizes the meaning as the fulfillment of the new covenant promises here and hereafter.[942]

The comparative adjective in Greek translated "more perfect" does not imply the possibility of another still more perfect tabernacle, but continues the author's theme that the new covenant is "better" than the old covenant.[943] The use of "not man-made" intends to indicate semantically it was made by God. The phrase "not a part of this creation" refers to the present material created order.[944] Grammatically, it is in apposition to "not hand-made" and serves to further describe it.

Most commentators connect the entire phrase "through the greater and more perfect tabernacle" with the main verb "enter" in v. 12. Interpretations of *skēnē*, "tabernacle" in v. 11 vary considerably.[945] Some take the meaning to refer to Christ's incarnate body while others take it to mean Christ's resurrected body.[946] A third view is that *skēnē* refers to the church.[947] Swetnam takes the phrase "greater and more perfect tabernacle" to refer to the eucharistic body

---

[936] Westfall, *Discourse Analysis*, 202–3.

[937] Lane, *Hebrews 9–13*, 236; NIV.

[938] Bruce, *Hebrews*, 211–12; Kistemaker, *Hebrews*, 248–49.

[939] This construction is also found in Luke 7:20; Acts 9:26; 14:27; 15:14.

[940] Lane, *Hebrews 9–13*, 236.

[941] Ellingworth, *Hebrews*, 449–50.

[942] Hughes, *Hebrews*, 327.

[943] Greenlee, *Exegetical Summary*, 324.

[944] Moffatt, *Hebrews*, 120–21; Lane, *Hebrews 9–13*, 230.

[945] A. Vanhoye, "Par la tente plus grande et plus parfait . . . (Heb 9,11)," *Bib* 46 (1965): 1–28; Hughes, *Hebrews*, 283–90; J. Swetnam, "Greater and More Perfect Tent: A Contribution to the Discussion of Hebrews 9:11," *Bib* 47 (1966): 91–106.

[946] Several of the church fathers, including Chrysostom, held this view. F. Laub, *Bekenntnis und Auslegung: Die paränetische Funktion der Christologie im Hebräerbrief*, in *Biblische Untersuchungen* 15 (Regensburg: Pustet, 1980), 186–200, argued the passage must be interpreted in connection with Heb 10:20 where the veil is identified as the flesh of Jesus. Laub viewed the phrase "through the greater and more perfect tabernacle" in 9:11 and "through his own blood" in 9:12 as parallel. Vanhoye, "Par la tente," 22, took the reference to be to the resurrected body of Christ. See D. Peterson's critique in *Hebrews and Perfection*, 142.

[947] Argued by Westcott, *Hebrews*, 258. Hughes, *Hebrews*, 287, offers a salient critique: "There is no way in which one can speak of his having entered into the heavenly sanctuary through the

of Christ, with the reference in Heb 9:10 to "food and drink and various ceremonial washings" as "OT foreshadowings of the NT Eucharistic elements and baptism."[948] Some who see in Hebrews a Gnostic background take the reference to be to a cosmic passageway. Some see the reference to heaven itself.[949] Delitzsch is an example of those who take the approach that a distinction must be made between "the greater and more perfect tabernacle" in v. 11 and the "Most Holy Place" of v. 12.[950] Although this view has many supporters, S. Kubo has raised serious objections to it, noting "it goes against the leading motif of the theology of the epistle by proposing that the heavenly counterpart of the earthly sanctuary includes the holy place."[951] Others take the *dia* in v. 11 in a local sense but take *ta hagia* in v. 12 to refer to the "greater and more perfect tabernacle" in v. 11.[952]

The key to the passage concerns the interpretation of *dia* as either local or instrumental in vv. 11–12. If it is taken as instrumental in v. 11, the meaning would be "Christ is the high priest by means of."[953] The best approach is to take *dia* as local in 9:11 and as instrumental in 9:12.[954] Jesus "passed through" in order to enter into the heavenly Most Holy Place. Lane concluded the way was through "the heavenly counterpart to the front compartment of the earthly tabernacle."[955] See the parallel passage in Heb 9:24–25. The Day of Atonement imagery from

---

church: the church is not the means of his entry . . . but, to the contrary, he is the means of the church's entry."

[948] J. Swetnam, "On the Imagery and Significance of Hebrews 9, 9–10," *CBQ* 28 (1966): 171. See the critique of this position in R. Williamson, "The Eucharist and the Epistle to the Hebrews," *NTS* 21 (1974–75), 300–10.

[949] Alford, "Hebrews," 168; Bruce, *Hebrews*, 212.

[950] Delitzsch, *Hebrews*, 2:80–81.

[951] S. Kubo, "Hebrews 9:11–12: Christ's Body, Heavenly Region, or . . . ?" in *Scribes, Scrolls and Scripture* (Grand Rapids: Eerdmans, 1985), 102–3.

[952] Hughes, *Hebrews*, 290, argued this position. Cf. Lenski, *Hebrews*, 290–91; R. Jewett, *Letter to Pilgrims: A Commentary on the Epistle to the Hebrews* (New York: Pilgrim, 1981), 150; D. Hagner, *Hebrews*. NIBC (Peabody, MA.: Hendrickson Publishers, 1990), 116; Kubo, "Hebrews 9:11–12," 103–7; and Koester, *Hebrews*, 409. Kubo (106–7) attempts to solve the problem by suggesting we should recognize there is "syntactical dissonance" in the author's text and that there is no way to solve this without creating theological and contextual dissonance. Kubo suggest the following emendation: "we supply a different verb to the first part of this sentence as the original intention of the author and begin a new sentence with οὐδὲ changed to οὐ . . . .This emendation would then be in harmony with the immediate context, and the interpretation of 'the greater and more perfect tent' would harmonize with the predominant theological motif of the book. Thus the sentence would read χριστὸς δὲ παραγενόμενος ἀρχιερεὺς τῶν γενομένων ἀγαθῶν διὰ τῆς μείζονος καὶ τελειοτέρας σκηνῆς οὐ χειροποιήτου, τοῦτ᾽ ἔστιν οὐ ταύτης τῆς κτίσεως, ἐπιτελέι τὰς λατρείας: 'But when Christ appeared as a high priest of the good things that have come, through the greater and more perfect tent he performs his religious service.' The preposition διὰ then must be understood instrumentally." This approach to the problem seems much to contrived to be plausible.

[953] Dods, "Hebrews," 332.

[954] As seen in Bruce, *Hebrews*, 211; Lane, *Hebrews 9–13*, 236–38; and Ellingworth, *Hebrews*, 450–51.

[955] Lane, *Hebrews 9–13,* 238.

Leviticus 16 undergirds the passage and should be seen as the backdrop for interpretation.

The "goats and calves" of v. 12 are considered to be generic plurals.[956] Dods noted the repeated annual offering on the Day of Atonement consisted of one of each animal. Strong contrast is introduced by *de*; it is not animal blood but Christ's own blood. The high priest entered the holy of holies annually on the Day of Atonement. However, in stark contrast, Christ entered "once for all." No repetition of this act is now necessary as a result of Christ's finished work. In addition, Lane said no repetition is even possible.[957] In a figurative way, by his death on the cross, Christ entered the holy of holies in the temple and procured atonement once and for all. The rash of theories concerning how Christ entered heaven with his blood is ably treated by Hughes in his commentary and is not treated in detail here.[958] It should also be observed that 9:12 is a *crux interpretum* for Seventh-Day Adventism and their theology concerning the Day of Atonement.[959]

The result of this act is Christ's "having obtained" our redemption (aorist middle participle, implying Christ's full involvement in the action).[960] The participle can be construed as indicating the results of Christ's entering,[961] the grounds of his entering (based on his death on the cross, he entered),[962] or

[956] Alford, "Hebrews," 169; Bruce, *Hebrews*, 213.

[957] Lane, *Hebrews 9–13*, 239.

[958] Hughes, *Hebrews*, 329–54. Aquinas speculated that Jesus' resurrected body contained his blood which had somehow been replaced into his body; Bengel speculated that Jesus' resurrection body contained no blood; and Delitzsch believed that Jesus presented himself to God in a body that somehow contained the blood he had shed on the cross. All such theories founder on two problems: the silence of Scripture on such matters and the attempt to pour language that conveys figurative truth into too literal a mold.

[959] Hebrews is a crucial book for Seventh-Day Adventist theologians, who rely on Heb 9:12 for their view concerning a literal heavenly sanctuary. See W. Johnsson, "The Significance of the Day of Atonement Allusions in the Epistle to the Hebrews," in *The Sanctuary and the Atonement: Biblical, Historical and Theological Studies*, ed. A. V. Wallenkampf & W. R. Lesher (Washington, DC: Review and Herald Publishing Association, 1981), 380–93. Seventh-Day Adventism believes that Jesus began the final phase of his ministry in 1844, preparing to return for the Second Advent. With regard to the Seventh-Day Adventist theory that 1844 is the commencement of the Day of Atonement, Johnsson, a Seventh-Day Adventist, writes candidly: "If Calvary is set forth as the NT day of atonement, what becomes of our emphasis upon 1844 as the commencement of the day of atonement. Then the book of Hebrews . . . would prove to be our theological Waterloo" (Johnsson, "Significance," 380). Johnsson freely admits if the heavenly temple and sacrifice are meant to be merely figurative, their traditional teaching would need to be reordered (380). Cf. W. G. Johnsson, "The Cultus of Hebrews in Twentieth-Century Scholarship," *ExpTim* 89/4: 104–8; and W. G. Johnsson, "The Heavenly Cultus in the Book of Hebrews—Figurative or Real?" *The Sanctuary and the Atonement*, 362–79. For references from E. G. White quoting Hebrews in support of an actual heavenly sanctuary and an actual heavenly work by Jesus, see pp. 363–64 in Johnsson's "The Heavenly Cultus."

[960] Alford, "Hebrews," 169; Dods, "Hebrews," 333. Ellingworth (*Hebrews*, 452–53) suggested Christ obtained deliverance for himself and for his people.

[961] Dods, "Hebrews," 333; Lane, *Hebrews 9–13*, 239.

[962] Kistemaker, *Hebrews*, 248–49.

temporally (he entered after he obtained redemption).[963] Contextually, it is difficult to determine which of these three construals was intended by the author. This redemption is qualified as "eternal," indicating its complete and unrepeatable nature, and also indicating an eschatological meaning.[964] The use of the word "redemption" semantically incorporates the price paid for it as well.

9:13–14 The sub-paragraph concludes with vv. 13–14. It is introduced with *gar* and gives the grounds for the statement in the previous verse that the blood of Christ has obtained eternal redemption. The conditional "if" in v. 13 expresses the grounds for the conclusion in 9:14—the first part of an argument from the lesser to the greater.[965] Some take "blood of bulls and goats" to refer only to the Day of Atonement offering.[966] Others take it to refer to other sacrifices.[967] It is difficult to say whether the "sprinkling" connects with only the ashes of the red heifer, or with all the preceding items.[968] The participle can be attributive (ashes which sprinkle) or expressing means (by sprinkling).[969] There is also some ambiguity as to what "those who are ceremonially unclean" refers to. It can be construed with "sprinkling" or with "sanctify."[970] The result of this sprinkling is outward cleansing, which probably includes cleansing from ritual defilement. The reference to the "ashes of a heifer" recalls the ritual of cleansing in Numbers 19. Bruce explained the ceremony well:

> A perfect red heifer, which had never borne the yoke, was to be slaughtered outside the camp of Israel in the presence of Eleazar the priest . . . who was then to sprinkle its blood seven times in front of the tabernacle. The body of the heifer was then to be completely incinerated; Eleazar was to throw cedar wood, hyssop (marjoram), and scarlet thread into the burning fire. When all was consumed, the ashes were to be gathered up and stored out-side the camp to be used as occasion required for the preparation of *mι niddᵃh* "water for (the removal of) impurity." Anyone who contracted ceremonial defilement through touching or approaching a dead body was to be cleansed by being sprinkled with water containing some of the ashes of the heifer.

[963] Bruce, *Hebrews*, 213–14; Hughes, *Hebrews*, 347. Regarding 9:13, Porter remarks: "Temporal deixis gives past implicature, while the structure and use of emphatic negation reinforces the emphasis of the marked Perfect" (*Verbal Aspect*, 264).

[964] Lane, *Hebrews 9–13*, 239.

[965] Moffatt, *Hebrews*, 121; Lane, *Hebrews 9–13*, 230.

[966] So Alford, "Hebrews," 170; and Hughes, *Hebrews*, 354–55 who take the plural to refer to the annual offering of one of each animal.

[967] Bruce, *Hebrews*, 214; and Ellingworth, *Hebrews*, 454.

[968] Moffatt, *Hebrews*, 122; and Bruce, *Hebrews*, 214–15 take it in the former sense while Ellingworth, *Hebrews*, 455 and the NIV take it in the latter sense.

[969] Lane, *Hebrews 9–13*, 228 takes it in the former sense.

[970] Bruce, *Hebrews*, 215; and Hughes, *Hebrews*, 363 take it in the former sense; Lane, *Hebrews 9–13*, 239 in the latter.

> Hence the allusion here to "the ashes of a heifer sprinkled on those who have been defiled" so as to "sanctify" them in respect of "bodily cleansing." . . . The ritual of the red heifer is appropriately mentioned by our author at this point because, like the sacrifices on the Day of Atonement, "it is a sin offering" (Num 19:9).[971]

Bruce understood the "how much more" in v. 14 as introducing a rhetorical question,[972] but it seems better to see it as introducing an exclamation.[973] The use of the phrase "the blood of Christ" connotes a death that was sacrificial. The author's use of the definite article with "Christ" may indicate a titular reference,[974] or, as less likely, a personal name.[975] An introductory relative pronoun has a causal sense giving the reason for the effectiveness of the sacrifice.[976]

The "eternal Spirit" in v. 14 may be a reference to the Holy Spirit, though many disagree. For those who take it other than as a reference to the Holy Spirit, possible options include Christ's eternal nature or the spiritual nature of the sacrifice.[977] In the Greek text, the pronoun precedes the verb in the phrase "offered himself" and is emphatic. The phrase *nekrōn ergōn,* (lit.) "dead works," has been taken to refer to works that cannot give eternal life, works that lead to death,[978] or works that are dead because the person who does them is dead spiritually.[979] The latter meaning is the least likely. The first option is perhaps the best. The phrase translated "the living God" has no definite article in Greek. Most commentators and translations consider it definite. Greenlee considers the qualitative possibility with a focus on God's nature as deity: "God as a living God."[980]

The author concludes this entire section, 9:1–14, with an application to his hearers in his reference to cleansing "our" consciences so that "we" may serve God. Luther commented: "This means that a man is not bitten by the recollection of his sins and is not disquieted by the fear of future punishment."[981] The use of *latreuein*, "to serve," recalls this same word or cognate used in Heb 8:2,5,6. There the reference is to priestly service, and the author's statement in this verse "unexpectedly places the readers in the priestly role in the heav-

---

[971] Bruce, *Hebrews*, 214–15. For the connection between the red heifer and Yom Kippur, see W. Horbury, "The Aaronic Priesthood in the Epistle to the Hebrews," *JSNT* 19 (1983): 51–52.

[972] Ibid., 216.

[973] Lane, *Hebrews 9–13*, 239; Ellingworth, *Hebrews*, 456; NIV.

[974] So Dods, "Hebrews," 334.

[975] So Hughes, *Hebrews*, 257.

[976] Lane, *Hebrews 9–13*, 240.

[977] Hewitt, (*Hebrews*, 148) takes it in the former sense, Moffatt (*Hebrews*, 124) in the latter.

[978] Lane, *Hebrews 9–13*, 240; NIV.

[979] As argued by Hughes. Luther, *Lectures on Titus, Philemon, and Hebrews, LW* 29:209, takes the "dead works" to refer to sins. See the discussion at Heb 6:2 on "dead works."

[980] Greenlee, *Exegetical Summary,* 333.

[981] Luther, *Lectures on Titus, Philemon, and Hebrews, LW* 29:208.

enly tabernacle."[982] The author is linking the Old Testament priestly service to his readers. However, the term as it is used here may carry its broader, more general sense of one's entire life lived out in service to God.[983] Nothing in the text or the entire epistle prohibits our understanding the word "to serve" here in this way. Luther correctly noted that without Christ one does not serve the living God.[984]

The Pentateuch speaks of two categories of sin: inadvertent and high-handed (Num 15:22–31). This distinction was noted in Heb 5:2 and occurs again in 10:26. This is why the translation "sins of ignorance" in 9:6 is preferred.[985] Gordon rightly compares "acts that lead to death" in 9:14 with what the author of Hebrews previously said in 6:1,3. There we have already seen that some take the reference to indicate the works of the Jewish law, as did Westcott,[986] and others see the reference to moral offences, such as Moffatt: "works that lead to death." But the point the author of Hebrews is making is well stated by Gordon: "The distinction [between inadvertent and high-handed sins] is there just so that it can be shown to have been dissolved through Christ's high priestly ministrations."[987]

In summary, Heb 9:1–14 makes clear that the way to God was not open to people under the old covenant (9:1–11), but now Jesus, the eternal high priest, has made atonement, cleansed the inner conscience of believers, and fitted them to serve God as spiritual priests themselves (9:11–14).

(3) Christ the Mediator of the New Covenant (9:15–28)

15For this reason Christ is the mediator of a new covenant, that those who are called may receive the promised eternal inheritance—now that he has died as a ransom to set them free from the sins committed under the first covenant.

16In the case of a will, it is necessary to prove the death of the one who made it, 17because a will is in force only when somebody has died; it never takes effect while the one who made it is living. 18This is why even the first covenant was not put into effect without blood. 19When Moses had proclaimed every commandment of the law to all the people, he took the blood of calves, together with water, scarlet wool and branches of hyssop, and sprinkled the scroll and all the people. 20He said, "This is the blood of the covenant, which God has commanded you

---

982 Westfall, *Discourse Analysis*, 203. Given the priestly imagery that is often invoked concerning the readers and their relationship to God in this epistle, I think it likely that this proposed focus by Westfall and others is valid.

983 See H. Strathmann, "λατρεύω," *TDNT* 4:63–65.

984 Luther, *Lectures on Titus, Philemon, and Hebrews, LW* 29:211.

985 Gordon, "Better Promises", 443, states: "The view that it is to be interpreted broadly as an equivalent of *hamartia* because Lev 16:34 may be taken to mean that the Day of Atonement covers *all* the sins of Israel . . . , or because of the claimed equivalence of *hamartia* and *agnōma* in the Septuagint and in some extra-biblical texts seriously weakens the contrast which the author of Hebrews is seeking to establish."

986 Westcott, 144. See the critique of this by Peterson, *Hebrews and Perfection*, 139.

987 Gordon, "Better Promises", 445. See his entire discussion on pp. 442–49.

**to keep." 21In the same way, he sprinkled with the blood both the tabernacle
and everything used in its ceremonies. 22In fact, the law requires that nearly everything be cleansed with blood, and without the shedding of blood there is no
forgiveness.**

**23It was necessary, then, for the copies of the heavenly things to be purified
with these sacrifices, but the heavenly things themselves with better sacrifices than
these. 24For Christ did not enter a man-made sanctuary that was only a copy of the
true one; he entered heaven itself, now to appear for us in God's presence. 25Nor
did he enter heaven to offer himself again and again, the way the high priest enters the Most Holy Place every year with blood that is not his own. 26Then Christ
would have had to suffer many times since the creation of the world. But now he
has appeared once for all at the end of the ages to do away with sin by the sacrifice
of himself. 27Just as man is destined to die once, and after that to face judgment,
28so Christ was sacrificed once to take away the sins of many people; and he will
appear a second time, not to bear sin, but to bring salvation to those who are waiting for him.**

9:15 The author begins a new paragraph in Heb 9:15 with the use of *oun*, untranslated in the NIV. The rhetorical question in 9:14 and the use of *kai* and *dia touto* in 9:15 further serve to mark the beginning of a new paragraph at 9:15. The conclusion of this paragraph at v. 22 is signaled by the use of *oun*, "then," again at 9:23 which marks the inception of the final paragraph of Hebrews 9.[988] Some consider 9:16–22 to be a parenthesis in the argument. If so, 9:23–28 would be a restatement or development of 9:11–14.[989] It is best not to take 9:16–22 as a parenthesis, as Westfall has shown.[990]

Hebrews 9:15 is the hinge verse in the entire chapter. It begins the second major paragraph (9:15–28) and is marked by the use of a compound conjunction in Greek. It draws a conclusion based on the preceding paragraph: the superiority of the shed blood of Christ with its atoning and cleansing effects. It is also semantically the theme of chap. 9. It has semantic parallels to Heb 8:6, which is the most prominent verse in chap. 8: Christ as mediator of the new covenant and the reference to "promise." The NIV translators treat v. 15 as a single paragraph, which further serves to denote its prominence. The internal structure of 9:15 contains three major propositions. The first is the statement "Christ is the mediator of a new covenant." This statement functions as a conclusion to 9:1–14. The second proposition provides the result of Christ's mediation of the new covenant: "those who are called may receive the promised eternal inheritance." The condition upon which this result is founded is stated in the third proposition: the necessity of Christ's death to provide atonement.[991]

---

988 L. L. Neeley, "A Discourse Analysis of Hebrews," *OPTAT* 3–4 (1987): 75, 93, 108–9.

989 This is argued by Attridge, *Hebrews,* 260; and Lane, *Hebrews 9–13,* 234. Moll, *Hebrews,* 161–63, considers 9:16–22 to be a discourse unit.

990 Westfall, *Hebrews,* 206–10.

991 See Neeley, "Discourse Analysis," 75, 93, 108; Miller, *Hebrews,* 257–58; J. Courter, "Semantic Structural Analysis of Hebrews 1–10," M. A. Thesis, University of Texas at Arlington

As Westfall said: "The central sentence in 9:15 aptly summarizes the message of Hebrews 9:15–28."[992] She identified three concepts stated in 9:15 which are then elaborated in vv. 16–28: Jesus is the mediator of a new covenant, the covenant is established through death, and the death of Jesus brings about the forgiveness of sins. Hebrews 9:16–18 elaborates on the necessity of death for ratifying the covenant; 9:19–22 elaborates on the necessity of death, sprinkling of blood, and the forgiveness of sins; and 9:23–28 elaborates on how the death of Jesus inaugurates the new covenant and provides forgiveness of sins.[993]

Ellingworth is probably incorrect in his suggestion that *dia touto*, "for this reason," in v. 15 points forward to *labōsin*, "may receive," rather than backward, as do most commentators.[994] Jesus is the "mediator of a new covenant." Though the absence of the definite article with "mediator" stresses the noun's qualitative aspects, it is still considered to be definite by many commentators and is so rendered in most translations. The phrase *diathēkēs kainēs* is fronted in the clause for prominence. The point of v. 15 is to stress Christ's mediation as essentially soteriological in nature. This is brought out by the author's use of *apolutrōsis*, wrongly translated "ransom" in the NIV, a compound form of *lutrōsis*, the standard word for "redemption" in the New Testament. There is little difference in meaning between the two forms of the word. The word does not necessarily imply a debt payment, as the NIV's "ransom" might suggest, but does convey deliverance or liberation and forgiveness. That from which[995] believers are delivered is their *tōn . . . parabaseōn*, "sins." The entire clause translated "now that he has died as a ransom" indicates how Jesus' death frees us from the consequences of sin. The participial phrase rendered as "that he has died" is a reference back to the previous verses where Christ's death is spoken of. It can be taken as expressing (1) reason—"because a death has occurred"; (2) means—by means of death having occurred; (3) temporality—"now that a death has occurred."[996] The use of *parabaseōn*, "sins," rather than the more

(1983), 135; Westfall, *Discourse Analysis*, 206–7, 213–14, 216, 218; Lane, *Hebrews 9–13*, 231; and the excellent semantic structural analysis of this text based on the Beekman-Callow model in an unpublished paper at the Criswell College by D. Streett, "An Exegesis of Hebrews 9:15–22," (2000), 9–10.

[992] Westfall, *Discourse Structure*, 218. Porter, *Verbal Aspect*, 83–84 suggested there is a hierarchy of prominence among tense forms with the subjunctive more naturally prominent than the indicative. In Heb 9:15–22, the subjunctive λάβωσιν in v. 15 is followed by a string of indicatives in vv. 16–22, thus serving as another linguistic indicator that v. 15 is the semantically dominant sentence in the unit.

[993] Westfall, *Discourse Analysis*, 216.

[994] Ellingworth and Nida, *Translator's Handbook*, 197. See Attridge, *Hebrews*, 254; and Bere'nyi, "La Port'ee de διαθήκη en He'9,15," *Bib* 69 (1988): 111.

[995] Dods, "Hebrews," 335; and Ellingworth, *Hebrews*, 460, both see it as a genitive of separation in Greek.

[996] Hughes, *Hebrews*, 366; Ellingworth, *Hebrews*, 460, take it as a reason; KJV and Miller, *Hebrews*, 258 view it as means; and Bruce, *Hebrews*, 218, and the NIV are examples of those who take it temporally.

common term for sin (*hamartia*) connotes "sin in its most aggravated form, as conscious transgression of that [God's] revealed will."[997] The sins were committed "under" the first covenant, where the Greek preposition could be taken temporally in the sense of "while the first covenant was in effect," but it is better to translate it as "under."[998] "Those who are called" likely refers in the context of this verse both to the author's recipients and those who lived under the old covenant.[999] *Epangelia*, "promise," has reference to the content of the promise,[1000] and the singular form distinguishes the promise of eternal life from the promise made to Abraham of innumerable offspring.[1001] *Klēronomia* is better translated here as "possession" and not "inheritance."[1002] This "possession" is said to be "eternal" here and in 13:20. Hurst suggested the possibility that *aionios*, "eternal," could refer to heaven as the source of the inheritance and he suggested "everlasting" as a better translation.[1003] "The promised eternal inheritance" is literally "the promise of the everlasting inheritance," where "promise" can be viewed as that which is received and "inheritance" identifies the content of the promise. Better, however, is to view the "inheritance" as identifying both the "promise" and as that which is "received."[1004]

9:16–17 Verses 16–17 contain one of the thorniest interpretative issues in the epistle. Considerable debate exists over whether the translation of *diathēkē* in 9:16–17 should be rendered as "will/testament" or "covenant."[1005] Like Heb 6:4–6, there remains no consensus on this issue. Here is the lineup. Those who opt for the translation of "testament" include Vos, Vanhoye, Swetnam, Bruce, Hughes, Dunnill, Attridge, Ellingworth, Lindars, Stanley, DeSilva, and Koester.[1006] On the other side of the fence are Westcott, Nairne, Kilpatrick,

---

[997] Delitzsch, *Hebrews*, 2:105.

[998] For the temporal translation, see Alford, "Hebrews," 173; and Dods, "Hebrews," 335.

[999] See Dods, "Hebrews," 335; and Moffatt, *Hebrews*, 127.

[1000] Lane, *Hebrews 9–13,* 231.

[1001] As correctly noted by J. Swetnam, *Jesus and Isaac: A Study of the Epistle to the Hebrews in the Light of the Aqedah*, AnBib 94, (Rome: Biblical Institute, 1981), 185.

[1002] So BDAG 548, against DeSilva, *Perseverance in Gratitude*, 292, and many others. Cf. Acts 7:5 for the same usage.

[1003] L. D. Hurst, *The Glory of Christ in the New Testament* (Oxford: Clarendon Press, 1987), 34–35. Hurst also pointed out the possibility of temporal origin as the meaning here. E. Ellis argued for the meaning of "everlasting effect" ("New Testament Teaching on Hell," *Eschatology in Bible and Theology: Evangelical Essays at the Dawn of a New Millennium*, ed. K. E. Brower and M. W. Elliott [Downers Grove: InterVarsity, 1997], 215).

[1004] So Moffatt, *Hebrews*, 127; Lane, *Hebrews 9–13*, 242.

[1005] See BDAG 228; L&N 57.124.

[1006] J. Behm and G. Quell, "διατίθημι, διαθήκη," *TDNT* 2:131–32; Delitzsch, *Hebrews,* 105ff.; G. Vos, *The Teaching of the Epistle to the Hebrews* (Grand Rapids: Eerdmans, 1956), 27–45; Vanhoye, *Old Testament Priests and New Testament Priest*, 203; J. Swetnam, "A Suggested Interpretation of Hebrews 9:15–18," *CBQ* 27 (1965): 374; Bruce, *Hebrews*, 221–22; Hughes, *Hebrews*, 368; Dunnill, *Covenant and Sacrifice*, 250–51; Ellingworth, *Hebrews*, 462–64; B. Lindars, *The Theology of the Letter to the Hebrews* (Cambridge: Cambridge University Press, 1991), 95–96; S. Stanley, "A New Covenant in Hebrews: The Use of Scripture in Hebrews 8–10," Ph.D. Dis-

Johnsson, J. J. Hughes, Lane, G. Guthrie, S. Hahn, and B. Joslin.[1007] Space does not permit a detailed discussion of this issue.

The primary use of the term *diathēkē*, "will," in first century AD Hellenistic Greek is that of "testament" in the sense of a last will or testament wherein one passed on possessions or property to another upon death. This fact is one of the strong arguments in favor of the translation "testament." Furthermore, the author's use of "inheritance" in v. 15 and the significance he gives to the term in Heb 1:2 set the stage for a transition of meaning from "covenant" in v. 15 to "will" in v. 16. It is argued that in a will, the testator must die before the will is valid, but this is not the case with a covenant. In addition, Wiid argued there is a "universal quality" in 9:16–17 which supports the background of the Greek courts and not the temple cultus.[1008] In addition, Attridge noted the common legal technical terms found in this section.[1009] Campbell spoke of the unilateral nature of the new covenant and the contractual nature of a "will" stipulating a gift that is received by another as further evidence in favor of the translation "will" or "testament."[1010] The author's penchant for wordplay and rhetorical devices makes such a subtle meaning shift possible as well. Ellingworth stated the author's anarthrous use of *diathēkē* in 9:16 indicates a shift in meaning.[1011] More problematic is the suggestion that the second century AD Gnostic text Gospel of Truth relies upon Hebrews and speaks of Christ's death on the cross as a testament that bequeaths salvation to others.[1012] Nevertheless, Swetnam argued that the translation "testament" is "essential" for a proper understanding of the new covenant in Hebrews.[1013]

sertation, University of Sheffield (1994), 141–44; DeSilva, *Perseverance in Gratitude*, 308–9; and Koester, *Hebrews*, 417–18, 424–26; 255–56. Chrysostom took this approach as well. Speaking of 9:17, he said: "For a testament is made when the day of death is near. Moreover, such a testament regards some as heirs but disinherits others. Again, a testament contains certain provisions on the part of the one who makes it and certain requirements to be met by the heirs, so that they receive certain things and do certain things. Again, a testament must have witnesses" ("Homilies on the Epistle to the Hebrews," *NPNF*[1] 14:443).

[1007] Westcott, *Hebrews*, 265–68; A. Nairne, *The Epistle of Priesthood* (Edinburgh: T&T Clark, 1913), 140, 364–66; G. D. Kilpatrick, "*Diathēkē* in Hebrews," *ZNW* 68 (1977): 263–65; Johnsson, "Defilement and Purgation," 308–18; J. J. Hughes, "Hebrews 9:15ff and Galatians 3:15ff: A Study in Covenant Practice and Procedure," *NTS* 21 (1979): 27–96; Lane, *Hebrews 9–13*, 231, 242–43; G. Guthrie, *Hebrews*, 313; S. Hahn, "A Broken Covenant and the Curse of Death: A Study of Hebrews 9:15–22," *CBQ* 66 (2004): 416–36; and Joslin, "Theology of the Mosaic Law," 284.

[1008] J. S. Wiid, "The Testamental Significance of διαθήκη in Hebrews 9:15–22," *Neot* 26 (1992): 154.

[1009] Attridge, *Hebrews*, 253.

[1010] Campbell, "Covenant or Testament? Hebrews 9:16–17 Reconsidered," *EvQ* 44 (1972): 108.

[1011] Ellingworth, *Hebrews*, 462–64.

[1012] Ibid., 464.

[1013] Swetnam, "A Suggested Interpretation," 374.

In favor of the translation "covenant" is the evidence from the LXX itself, where *diathēkē* is used to translate the Hebrew *berith* some 270 plus times.[1014] Furthermore, the word is used 33 times in the Greek New Testament, and this would be the only place it could be translated "will" or "testament." The syntactical evidence mitigates against the translation of "will." The author's use of conjunctions (*gar*, *epei*, *hothen*) in this context shows the tight connections within vv. 15–18. That *klēronomia* probably should be translated as "possession" and not "inheritance" suggests the covenant view as well.[1015] That the articular participle *ho diathemenos* can be translated as "covenant-sacrifice" or "covenant-ratifier" rather than as "one who makes a will/covenant" would open the door for the meaning of a covenant being inaugurated by means of a sacrificial death.[1016] Behm and Quell said the Hebrew idiom "to cut a covenant" is translated in the LXX as *diatithesthai diathēkēn*,[1017] and thus *ho diathemenos* in v. 17 can be translated as "covenant maker" as well as "testator." In fact, Acts 3:25 is precisely an example of this meaning.[1018] Although some of the terms can be construed as having a Greek legal provenance, they fit better in the context of covenant and the temple cultus found in the paragraph immediately following: Heb 9:18–22.[1019] Lane observed that *pherein* is never used in any extra-biblical context in connection to a "will" or "testament."[1020] In addition, the use of the plural *nekrois*, translated with the singular in the NIV as "somebody has died," is very difficult to explain with the translation of "will" since there can be only one testator who dies to bring the will into effect. One possible explanation is *nekroi* could refer to a plurality of sacrificial animals on the covenant view.[1021] Less effective are the arguments contending that Greek testamentary practice would be little known to the Jews and thus the audience would most likely miss the play on words,[1022] and the suggestion that Biblical covenants do not always involve sacrifice. The first is based on mere supposition and the latter is an argument from silence.

Those who argue for "covenant" and view the death of the one who makes the covenant as being symbolized in the use of *pherō*, "to prove," in the sense of animal sacrifices (plural use of *nekroi*) which usually accompanied the

[1014] Gheorghita, *Role of the Septuagint*, 119, outlined two contrasting positions as to why the LXX uses διαθήκη to translate the Hebrew *berith*: (1) Translators selected and used διαθήκη instead of συνθήκη because the former "consistently bore the legal nuance needed for a correct rendering of *berith*." (2) A diachronic change (semantic evolution during the intertestamental period and early first century) was taking place in the meaning of *berith*. The translation "testament" reflects the meaning of the term at the time the LXX was translated.

[1015] See Lincoln, "Translating Hebrews 9:15–22 in its Hebraic Context," 14.

[1016] G. D. Kilpatrick, "Διαθήκη in Hebrews," *ZNW* 68 (1977): 265.

[1017] Behm and Quell, "διαθήκη," *TDNT* 2:105.

[1018] Note also the use of this word twice in Luke 22:29.

[1019] Lincoln, "Translating Hebrews 9:15–22 in its Hebraic Context," 25.

[1020] Lane, *Hebrews 9–13*, 231.

[1021] See F. Gardiner, "On διαθηκη in Hebrews 9;16, 17," *JBL* 5 (1885): 16.

[1022] G. Milligan, *Theology of Hebrews*, 167.

inauguration of a covenant,[1023] may be straining the author's language beyond the breaking point. It is questionable whether the author intended this much symbolism behind his words.

Recently, Hahn proffered a variation on this view that strengthens the case for translating *diathēkē* as "covenant." Hahn's thesis is contextually grounded in the broken first covenant in that 9:15 and 9:18–22 deal with the old covenant which has been broken. If *hopou*, "where," at the beginning of v. 16 is taken causally, then in light of v. 15 where Christ the mediator of the covenant "died," v. 16 could be translated: "Since there is a covenant, it is necessary for the death of the covenant-maker to be borne," meaning it is necessary for someone (unspecified according to Hahn since the name "Jesus" or "Christ" is not used overtly by the author in v. 15 and since "death" is used without the article) to bear the curse of death as the covenant-maker. Verse 16 would then be semantically rephrasing v. 15. Hahn compares *pherō*, "to prove," in 9:16 and 9:28 with Isaiah 53. Hebrews 9:28 is a reference to Isa 53:12 LXX. Given this, perhaps the use of *pherō* in the sense of "bear on another's behalf" in Isa 53:3–4 "elucidates the use of *pherō* in Heb 9:16."[1024] This is a reasonable supposition. Less reasonable is his argument that the plural *nekrois*, "somebody has died," refers to covenant-makers who have become covenant-breakers who fall under the curse of death (Deut 28:26 LXX). He argued the covenant curse of death is only finally visited upon Israel when Christ dies as their representative (Heb 9:15).

> In sum, it may be that the author of Hebrews regards the divine oath to Abraham at the Aqedah as a foundational act for Israel, which is renewed in Christ. The divine oath of the Aqedah is an expression of God's providential mercy, inasmuch as it prevents the full enforcement of the curses of the first covenant (Exod 32:13–14) until the coming of the Christ, who can bear the curse-of-death on behalf of all (Heb 2:9; 9:15) and restore for Israel the Abrahamic blessing (Heb 6:13–20; Gen 2:15–18). Christ's death is simultaneously the legal execution of the curses of the old covenant and the liturgical ritual of sacrifice which establishes the new.[1025]

Thus, there are three possible interpretations concerning the translation of *diathēkē* in Heb 9:16–17 and throughout the epistle: (1) the word should be translated "covenant" throughout Hebrews; (2) the word should be translated

[1023] So Kilpatrick, "Διαθήκη in Hebrews," 265; Lane, *Hebrews 9–13*, 242–43.

[1024] S. Hahn, "Covenant, Cult, and the Curse-of-Death: διαθήκη in Heb 9:15–22," in *Hebrews: Contemporary Methods—New Insights*, ed. G. Gelardini, *Biblical Interpretation Series* 75 (Leiden/Boston: Brill, 2005), 83.

[1025] Ibid., 87–88. Compare this with Gal 3:6–25.

"testament" throughout Hebrews;[1026] and (3) the author uses a double meaning for *diathēkē* in 9:16–17 as "testament."[1027]

When all the evidence is sifted and weighed, the following conclusions can be drawn. First, the translation "will" or "testament" is possible and the author may be engaging in word play. Second, it is certain that *diathēkē* means "covenant" in v. 15 and again in vv. 18–19. Third, the use of conjunctions tends to preclude the translation of "testament." Therefore, linguistically and contextually, it seems preferable to opt for "covenant" over against "will/testament" for *diathēkē* in Heb 9:16–17.

Hebrews 9:16–17 is one sentence in the Greek text. The introductory particle *hopou* functions temporally or circumstantially to the event idea encoded in the noun "covenant."[1028] "Death" is fronted in the clause. The meaning of the infinitive *pheresthai*, "to prove," can be interpreted in three different senses: (1) in the sense of "offering" within a sacrificial context;[1029] (2) "to be represented,"[1030] or (3) in the sense of "bringing something forward." The word is never found extra biblically in relation to "will" or "testament."[1031]

Verse 17 provides the grounds for what was stated in v. 16 as evidenced by the use of *gar*, "for." The Greek phrase *epi nekrois*, "when somebody has died," is difficult to interpret. Literally the entire clause reads: "for a covenant/testament is confirmed upon dead [bodies]." The phrase *epi nekrois* should not be translated "at death" as is often the case, since there is no evidence for this, according to Lane.[1032] The preposition means "on the basis of" regardless of the meaning of *nekrois*. The translation "in force" renders the Greek word *bebaia*, an objective certainty that guarantees an effect. The temporal particle *hote*, "while," expresses a durative focus and is the condition for the previous clause.

Whether one chooses the translation of "covenant" or "testament" for *diathēkē,* the point of Heb 9:16–17 is to show the necessity of the death of the covenant-maker/testator for the covenant/testament to be ratified. Verse 15 stated Christ, the mediator of the new covenant, died to provide redemption from sins so that sinners would be set free. The covenant/testament is put in force because of his death.

Hebrews 9:18–22 is a sub-paragraph functioning to provide an example from Exodus to illustrate the necessity of the death of a sacrifice argued in

---

[1026] As argued by Swetnam, "A Suggested Interpretation," 374.

[1027] Commenting on the use of διαθήκη in 9:16–17, Westfall, *Discourse Analysis*, 207–8, stated the author of Hebrews treats both concepts of "covenant" and "will" as one concept: "what applies to wills also applies to covenants."

[1028] Wiid, "The Testamental Significance of διαθήκη in Hebrews 9:15–22," 154, translates ὅπου as "whenever" in an attempt to capture the universality of the thought.

[1029] Lincoln, "Translating Hebrews 9:15–22," 25.

[1030] Westcott, *Hebrews*, 267.

[1031] Lane, *Hebrews 9–13,* 231.

[1032] Ibid., 232. Nor is there support for Attridge's "for the dead" (*Hebrews*, 256).

vv. 16–17 which is summarized in v. 22: "without the shedding of blood there is no forgiveness." The unit is straightforward: v. 18 states the old covenant was inaugurated with blood; vv. 19–21summarize the ratification of the covenant according to the ceremony by Moses in Exod 24:1–8; and v. 22 draws two conclusions: the law demands cleansing with blood, and without the shedding of blood there is no forgiveness of sins. "All/every" is used five times in vv. 19–22, which stresses the necessity of cleansing by blood for the scroll, the tabernacle, the utensils of the tabernacle, and the people. "Blood" is also used five times, one of which is in the word *haimatekchusia*, "shedding of blood," which occurs only here in the New Testament.

9:18 The conjunction *hothen*, "this is why," functions to signal a shift to a new but related subject. Friberg and Friberg give this conjunction a "hyperordinating" tag which identifies the shift from the generic principle of 9:16–17 to the specific example from the Exodus account and identifies what follows as semantically more important information.[1033] The use of *hothen*, "this is why," signals the author is making a deduction from the preceding material.[1034]

The author does not repeat but assumes the noun *diathēkē* in v. 18, using only *hē prōtē*, "the first," referring to the "first covenant." This provides another reason why "covenant" and not "will" is the meaning of the term in vv. 16–17. The use of the perfect tense emphasizes the perfective idea of "inauguration" ("was put into effect" in the NIV) for the Mosaic covenant.[1035]

9:19 Verse 19 begins with *gar,* untranslated in the NIV, which introduces the grounds for v. 18. The reference is to Exod 24. After reading the terms of the covenant, "every commandment of the Law," to the people, Moses took blood from the sacrificial animals (calves) and sprinkled the altar and the people with it. The sprinkling of the blood was for the purpose of consecration and purification. The author's description of this event differs from the Exodus account in the following ways: (1) goats as well as bulls were sacrificed; (2) the blood was mixed with water; (3) the instruments of sprinkling are named: scarlet wool and a hyssop branch; and (4) the scroll on which was written the law was sprinkled as well.

Bruce listed two options as explanations for the differences. (1) It is possible the author made use of a midrashic source no longer extant. (2) Another possibility is the author could be making use of a "triennial synagogue lectionary, in which Exod 24 and Num 19 would have been read around the same

---

[1033] Friberg and Friberg, *Analytical Greek Testament*, 677. Semantically, in a generic-specific communication relation, the "specific" side of the equation receives the dominant focus. See Beekman, Callow, Kopesec, *Semantic Structure*, 96–97.

[1034] Lane, *Hebrews 9–13,* 119, translates the conjunction as "this is why," as does the NIV; cf. Ellingworth, *Hebrews*, 465.

[1035] Ellingworth, *Hebrews*, 466, following Riggenbach and Michel, noted the perfect tense "suggests a reference to the inauguration of the first covenant, not as a past event, but as permanently recorded in scripture."

season."[1036] A better option was suggested by Aquinas, who thought the problem could be solved by recognizing that all future consecrations, which did include these items, can be contained in the first as far as our author is concerned.[1037]

9:20–21 The speech orienter *legōn*, "saying," in v. 20 is not functioning here as an introduction to a quotation, but rather indicates the speaking of a character in the Old Testament narrative, namely, Moses. Although many suggest it, there is no reference here to the words of Jesus at the Last Supper.[1038] In v. 21 the genitive *tēs leitourgias*, "in its ceremonies," is descriptive and encodes a means-purpose relationship.[1039] *Tō haimati*, "with the blood," is instrumental in sense. The same event as described in v. 19 is in view here as well, and the parallel aorist form of *erantisen*, "he sprinkled," is used as in v. 19.

9:22 The paragraph concludes with a twofold statement in v. 22. The first statement, "nearly[1040] everything [must] be cleansed with blood," uses the present tense verb form *katharizetai*, "to cleanse." This present tense form is, according to Westfall, "a marked past-referring present tense form" that functions to summarize "what the author was highlighting in the repetition of *pas* in the inauguration scenario."[1041] The second statement is "without the shedding of blood, there is no forgiveness."

In this latter phrase, two words in Greek deserve consideration: "shedding of blood" and "forgiveness." Regarding *haimatekchusia*, "shedding of blood," some view the author as having coined this word, while others disagree.[1042] It is routinely translated "shedding of blood." Lane argued in a cultic setting such as this passage the added nuance of the application of blood to an object or person is also present.[1043] The use of *aphesis* in Leviticus 16 describes the scapegoat ritual from the LXX. Because of this it probably is to be read with *hamartiōn*, "sins," implied.[1044] Forgiveness involves both concepts of "release," as from

---

[1036] Bruce, *Hebrews*, 215–16.

[1037] Aquinas, *Hebrews*, 193.

[1038] See Bruce, *Hebrews*, 208; and Lane, *Hebrews 9–13*, 245. Bruce is probably right that there is not a single reference in Hebrews to the Lord's Supper (Bruce, *Hebrews*, 401). It is interesting to note in the Synoptic accounts of the words of Jesus, only Luke elides the verb ἔστιν (Luke 22:20) while all other accounts, including Paul's reference to the accounts in 1 Cor 11:25, use the verb. The author of Hebrews, like Luke, elides the verb as well. Such examples in Hebrews support the contention that Luke may have been the author of Hebrews.

[1039] Miller, *Hebrews*, 266.

[1040] The Greek σχεδόν is an adverbial modifier of the substantival adjective πάντα. Interestingly, there are only three occurrences of this adverb in the NT, here and in Acts 13:44 and 19:26. In all three places it is used to modify a form of πᾶς.

[1041] Westfall, *Discourse Analysis*, 209. Ellingworth understands the present tense as applying to the totality of the event of inauguration of the Mosaic law as recorded in Exodus.

[1042] Bruce, *Hebrews*, 217, represents the former; Hughes, *Hebrews*, 378, the latter. It is very unlikely that the word was coined by the author.

[1043] Lane, *Hebrews 9–13*, 246.

[1044] Against Lane, *Hebrews 9–13*, 232; and Ellingworth, *Hebrews*, 474. The uses of ἄφεσις in Luke, Acts, and Heb 10:18 are especially instructive of this point.

debt, prison, slavery, and "cleansing." In 9:22, "cleanse" and "forgiveness" are virtually synonymous.[1045] The position of *aphesis* at the end of the sentence in the Greek text makes it emphatic, and its use in v. 22 harks back to the statement of redemption from sins at the beginning of the paragraph in v. 15. Ellingworth suggested that the verb *ginetai*, "is," "indicates, not merely a state of affairs: 'there is no forgiveness,' but an event: 'forgiveness does not take place,' implying 'God does not forgive.'"[1046] This is an important semantic point to make in that the author's overall argument is to say that this entire matter of a sacrificial death and the shedding of blood for atonement is God's way of dealing with the sin problem. Under the new covenant, without the cross of Christ, God does not forgive sins. Atonement is the basis of forgiveness and both are based on the work of Christ on the cross.

Given these linguistic factors, it is incorrect to suggest as some do that v. 22 is parenthetical.[1047] In fact, it is the "destination" of the paragraph in that it semantically rephrases what was stated in v. 15 and it provides a concluding summary.[1048]

One final question remains to be considered. How is the last part of v. 22 to be construed with the first part of the verse? Lane argued that an adversative relationship exists with the statement "without the shedding of blood there is no forgiveness" as adversative to "nearly everything [must] be cleansed with blood."[1049] Such a view contrasts "cleansing" with "forgiveness." However, this would seem to be ruled out by v. 23. It is better to take 9:22b as the second half of an example of antithetical parallelism. Hebrews 9:22b restates 9:22a in a negative fashion. Thus, the semantic relationship is one of condition-consequence.[1050]

Haber pointed out the author's treatment of the LXX account in Exod 24:4–8 in Heb 9:18–22 reveals he introduced two new elements not found in the Exodus account. First, the author "assumes a strong association between the covenant and the cult . . . by merging the covenant ceremony with the consecration of the tent found in Num 7:1, so that the initiation of covenant and cult take place together on the altar."[1051] Second, the author associates the blood of the covenant with purification and atonement, "a connection that is entirely absent from the Exodus account."[1052] The author is conflating separate ceremonies with an eye toward a Christological interpretation to show that the covenant inaugurated by Jesus is *new* and not *old* and it is *second* and not *first*

[1045] Koester, *Hebrews*, 420.

[1046] Ellingworth, *Hebrews*, 474.

[1047] As do Moffatt, *Hebrews*, 131; and Hughes, *Hebrews*, 380.

[1048] Westfall, *Discourse Analysis*, 209.

[1049] Lane, *Hebrews 9–13*, 246.

[1050] So argued by Miller, *Hebrews,* 267.

[1051] S. Haber, "From Priestly Torah to Christ Cultus: The Re-Vision of Covenant and Cult in Hebrews," *JSNT* 28.1 (2005): 109.

[1052] Ibid.

(in the sense that it is superior to the first. In Heb 8:13 the "new" covenant is contrasted with the "first" covenant).

9:23 Hebrews 9:23–28 is the final paragraph of the chapter. The paragraph begins a new topic and is built around three sentences in the Greek New Testament (vv. 23,24–26,27–28) with a pair of contrasting clauses in each sentence. Verse 23 is introduced with the discourse marker of prominence, *oun*, "then," which could also be translated "consequently" to bring out the conclusion to 9:22. It is possible this connector reaches back to 9:11–12, but it certainly connects to 9:15–22. "It was necessary" is emphatic by word order, being placed at the front of the clause. The notion here is the necessity is grounded in God's purpose.

Three questions arise regarding the first half of the verse. What is the meaning of "copies," "heavenly things," and "these sacrifices"? The Greek word *hupodeigma*, "copies," by context must refer to the earthly tabernacle.[1053] I treat the meaning of "heavenly things" when considering the second half of this verse. "These sacrifices" can refer to the Old Testament tabernacle and its vessels,[1054] or to the purification rites of the tabernacle.[1055] The following contrastive clause does not contain an overt verb and thus "to be purified" must be supplied or at least understood. Ellingworth thinks the sense of the verb here is that of consecration and inauguration rather than removing impurity.[1056] The sacrifices which cleanse the heavenly things are "better," which can connote either "superior" or "greater."[1057]

Much disagreement centers over the meaning of "the heavenly things themselves." Nine different interpretations have been offered.[1058] Some assert this should not be taken literally, but see the reference to spiritual reality as the realm where atonement is accomplished.[1059] Others view the reference to people who are the temple of God and who need cleansing of conscience. A third option is that the reference is to the heavenly sanctuary itself as the pattern for the earthly sanctuary.[1060] A similar view takes the meaning to be to heaven itself and the things within which need cleansing because even believers can somehow bring defilement as they approach heaven to worship.[1061] Some who take this view mitigate it by suggesting the language here should not be taken

---

[1053] So Lünemann, *Hebrews*, 623; Dods, "Hebrews," 338.

[1054] Ellingworth, *Hebrews*, 476.

[1055] Lünemann, *Hebrews*, 622–23; Alford, "Hebrews," 179.

[1056] Ellingworth, *Hebrews*, 475–76.

[1057] See L&N 65.21; 87.28.

[1058] For a listing and discussion, see MacLeod, "Cleansing," 60–71.

[1059] Bruce, *Hebrews*, 228; Hewitt, *Hebrews*, 152.

[1060] So Lünemann, *Hebrews*, 622–23; and Lane, *Hebrews 9–13*, 247.

[1061] So Alford, "Hebrews," 179; Moffatt, *Hebrews*, 131–32. This view parallels the necessity of cleansing referred to in 9:19–22. MacLeod writes: "The implication of 9:23 is that the 'heavenly things' are defiled by this constant process of forgiving believers who sin" ("Cleansing," 70). Since Christians have not yet reached a state of glorification, even their worship is tainted with sin.

literally such that heaven itself is somehow defiled, but that the author is speaking "relationally" in the sense that the "sphere and all means of their relations to God . . . must be sanctified by the blood of the New Covenant."[1062] Another view takes the meaning to be the approach to heaven rather than heaven itself.[1063] Michel's view that the heavenly things refer to demonic forces of evil is highly unlikely.[1064]

Bruce cautions against failure to recognize the analogical use of language in this passage. "By the removal of the defilement of sin from the hearts and consciences of the worshippers, the heavenly sphere in which they approach God to worship him is itself cleansed from this defilement."[1065] The views with the least problems are option one and the mitigated version of option four. The phrase "better sacrifices" refers to the blood of Christ. The reason for the plural "sacrifices" is its connection to the plural *toutois* "these," which is a "generic" plural.[1066]

9:24 This verse restates Heb 9:11–12 and further states a negative reason for the necessity of better sacrifices.[1067] The adjective "man-made" is emphatic by word order in the clause. The author refers to the Old Testament sanctuary as a "copy," *antitupos*, which brings to mind the author's use of *tupos*, "copy," in Heb 8:5. The point is that the earthly corresponds to the heavenly as a copy corresponds to the copied reality.[1068] This copy of the "true" means "the true sanctuary is copied by the earthly antitype."[1069] The second clause is introduced by the strong adversative conjunction *alla*, "but," which places focus on Christ's entrance into heaven.[1070] "Now" is emphatic by word order. Coupled with the infinitive of purpose "to appear," the reference is to Christ's continuing high priestly work in heaven. The phrase "heaven itself" refers to the presence of God. "For us" is placed final in the clause for emphasis. According to 9:24, the author appears to be connecting the heavenly sanctuary with the promised land of rest and inheritance for believers (4:9–11; 9:15).

9:25 This continues the Greek sentence with a *hina* clause, which if it expresses purpose, necessitates the supplying of the verb "to be." Otherwise, the verb "to enter" would be supplied as a carryover from the preceding verse. The

---

[1062] MacLeod, "Cleansing," 70.

[1063] S. T. Bloomfield, *Critical Annotations, Additional and Supplementary, on the New Testament: Being a Supplemental Volume to the Ninth Edition of the Greek Testament, with English Notes*, 3rd ed. (London: Longman, Green, Longman, and Roberts, 1860), 2:287.

[1064] Michel, *Hebräer*, 213–14.

[1065] Bruce, *Hebrews*, 229.

[1066] Ibid., 228; Ellingworth, *Hebrews*, 478.

[1067] Westfall, *Discourse Analysis*, 211.

[1068] Bruce, *Hebrews*, 230. The only other occurrence of the word is in 1 Pet 3:21.

[1069] Greenlee, *Exegetical Summary*, 349, where the objective genitive is used.

[1070] So Westfall, *Discourse Analysis*, 211.

phrase "to offer himself" probably refers to Christ's death on the cross rather than his offering himself in heaven.[1071]

The statement that the high priest enters (present tense) is taken as timeless by Ellingworth, but is taken as referring to present action by Hughes, with the implication that the Levitical system was still in operation at the time of writing.[1072]

9:26 The argument continues from the previous verse by drawing a conclusion. It shows the absurdity of the alternative if Christ's one sacrifice were not sufficient: Christ would have had to suffer and die over and over again. "But now," expressing logical contrast rather than temporality, Jesus has appeared "once for all." This adverb modifies the verb "appeared," which is placed last in the sentence to emphasize Christ's incarnation and death on the cross. The phrase "end of the ages" can mean the end of time[1073] or Christ's appearance on earth.[1074] Actually, both are theologically correct. The means by which Jesus does away with sin is "by the sacrifice of himself," where the subjective genitive *autou*, "of himself," is emphatic and can be read as a personal pronoun, translated "of him," telling who made the sacrifice.[1075] It can also be read as a reflexive pronoun telling who was sacrificed: himself.[1076]

9:27 The final sentence of the chapter in the Greek text begins here. Both a comparison as well as the grounds for the following clause is introduced by "just as." The use of the article in Greek with "men" makes the noun generic. Men are "destined to die once," indicating finality, which is further emphasized by the statement that after death follows judgment. The purpose of the comparison of the similarity of the human situation with Jesus is to show there is one death for each person and thus Jesus would die only once. Another verb must be supplied in the phrase "after this the judgment." Possibilities include "experienced,"[1077] "to come,"[1078] "to face,"[1079] or the noun can be rendered as a verb: "to be judged."[1080]

9:28 This completes the comparison with *houtōs*, "so." Christ "was sacrificed," aorist passive participle, indicating something appointed to him with God as the implied agent.[1081] The action in this verb either describes action that is parallel to the verb "appear" or the meaning is temporal: "after he was

[1071] Moffatt, *Hebrews*, 132; and Lane, *Hebrews 9–13*, 249, take it in the former sense, while Alford, "Hebrews," 181, and the NIV take it in the latter sense.

[1072] Ellingworth, *Hebrews*, 482; Hughes, *Hebrews*, 383.

[1073] So Moffatt, *Hebrews*, 133.

[1074] So Hughes, *Hebrews*, 385; Ellingworth, *Hebrews*, 484–85.

[1075] Bruce, *Hebrews*, 231.

[1076] Hughes, *Hebrews*, 385; Ellingworth, *Hebrews*, 483, and the NIV read it this way.

[1077] Lane, *Hebrews 9–13*, 229, 250.

[1078] As in the NASB.

[1079] As in the NIV.

[1080] As in the CEV and TEV.

[1081] Ellingworth, *Hebrews*, 486.

offered."[1082] The phrase "many people" is a qualitative reference meaning "all."[1083] It contrasts the many with Christ's one sacrifice. Calvin interprets the "many" here to mean "all": "'To bear the sins' means to free those who have sinned from their guilt by his satisfaction. He says many meaning all [*Multos dicit pro Omnibus*], as in Rom 5:15. It is of course certain that not all enjoy the fruit of Christ's death . . . , but this happens because their unbelief hinders them."[1084] Here Calvin articulates universal atonement in his universalizing the term "many" to include all people, not just the elect.

The second coming of Jesus will not be for the purpose of having to atone for sin but rather will be for the purpose of bringing final salvation.[1085] "Forgiveness of sins" is mentioned three times as the purpose for the death of Christ (9:26; twice in v. 28). That Jesus is said to "bear the sins of many" is a reference to Isa 53:10–12. The same Greek verb, *anenenkein*, is found in 1 Pet 2:24, where Jesus is said to have borne the sins of many. The salvation which Jesus brings is said to be "to those who are waiting for him." The same verb is used by Paul in Phil 3:20 to describe the eager awaiting of the second coming of Christ.

The two appearances of Jesus mentioned in Heb 9:26,28 correspond to the appearances of the high priest on the Day of Atonement. His first appearance was in the outside courtyard to offer the sacrifice on the altar of burnt offering. From here, he entered the sanctuary, carrying the blood for atonement, and in so doing he passed out of sight of the people. The people anxiously awaited his return. Upon completion of his duties in the inner sanctuary, he emerged to the great joy of all the people. In a similar fashion, Jesus our high priest appeared the first time in his incarnation to make atonement for our sins on the cross (9:26). His ascension took him out of sight into the presence of God where he continually appears as our advocate (7:25). One day he will return to this earth and "appear again a second time" (9:28) to bring final salvation.

THEOLOGICAL IMPLICATIONS. The central theme of Hebrews 9 is to show how Jesus' death on the cross, as our high priest, inaugurated the new covenant and thus obtained eternal redemption for his people. What the priests of the Levitical sacrificial system could not accomplish, namely, the permanent internal cleansing from sin, Jesus has accomplished by his once for all offering of himself on the cross. Jesus is the mediator of the new covenant because his death has liberated us from our sins. According to the Mosaic law, without the shedding of blood there could be no forgiveness of sins (Heb 9:22). Jesus has appeared once for all to take away sin permanently through his own sacrifice on the cross.

[1082] Lane, *Hebrews 9–13*, 250.

[1083] Hughes, *Hebrews*, 388.

[1084] Calvin, *Hebrews*, 131.

[1085] See W. Pannenberg, *Systematic Theology,* trans. G. W. Bromiley (Grand Rapids: Eerdmans, 1991–98), 2:444.

The Old Testament tabernacle and sacrificial system was but a copy and shadow of the true reality, which is Christ and his new covenant ratified in his own blood. Hebrews 9 makes it clear why the old covenant had been rendered obsolete (see Heb 8:13). Under the old covenant, the sacrifice had to be re-enacted annually on the Day of Atonement. Under the new covenant, inaugurated by the blood of Christ, once and for all sins were atoned for and the consciences of individual worshippers were cleansed. Now we may serve the living God (Heb 9:15).

The author of Hebrews has shown that the Mosaic covenant involved a priesthood, a sanctuary, and a sacrifice. Through careful theological analysis, he has shown how Jesus is the ultimate fulfillment of each of these categories. He is a superior priest who is eternal; he serves in a heavenly sanctuary; and he has offered once for all a sacrifice which not only atones for sin but which cleanses the inward conscience of believers, something the old Levitical order could never accomplish.

The allusion to Isaiah 53 in Heb 9:28 that Christ has appeared to "bear the sins of many" affirms that the writer understands the death of Jesus on the cross to be a substitutionary atonement.[1086] Hebrews 9 also affirms the necessity of death and the shedding of blood as the means of ratifying the new covenant and effecting redemption. All theologies that downplay or denigrate the necessity of a sacrificial and substitutionary death and the shedding of blood to procure atonement for sinful people fail to come to grips with the clear teaching of Hebrews, not to mention the New Testament as a whole.

During the Reformation, based on Heb 9:16–17, Luther rejected the notion of the mass as a sacrifice offered to God and came to understand it as a testament offered by Christ to his people which is received by faith alone. He was joined in this understanding by Calvin and all other reformers. In response, the Council of Trent reaffirmed the mass as an unbloody propitiatory sacrifice offered by priests who were so designated by God.[1087]

In summary fashion, throughout Hebrews 9, and in fact, throughout Heb 7:1–10:18, the author describes Jesus as high priest who performs several acts associated with Yom Kippur, the Day of Atonement: (1) his victory over the forces of evil (9:26); (2) the atonement offering and the sprinkling of blood (9:13,14,19,21,25); (3) entrance into the heavenly holy of holies (9:24); and (4) intercession for the people (9:24).[1088] These acts are also overtly or im-

---

[1086] Against I. Willi-Plein, "Some Remarks on Hebrews from the Viewpoint of Old Testament Exegesis," in *Hebrews: Contemporary Methods—New Insights*, 25–35, who argued based on Leviticus 16 that Christ's sin-offering in Hebrews should not be viewed as a vicarious dying or as an expiatory self-sacrifice. Rather, Jesus brings his blood, the symbol of uncontaminated life, into the sanctuary to remove pollutions due to sin (33–34). Such a position falls far short of the clear teaching of Hebrews, not to mention the entire NT.

[1087] J. Laansma, "Hebrews, Book of," *DTIB* 275.

[1088] So noted by D. S. Ben Ezra, *The Impact of Yom Kippur on Early Christianity*, 185. Ben Ezra argued that "Yom Kippur lies at the *root* of Christ's high priesthood, which belongs to the

plicitly mentioned in several other places throughout the epistle. The author of Hebrews approached the person and work of Christ in typological fashion, building his theology, especially in 7:1–10:18, around the high priest and Yom Kippur.

(4) Jesus' Effectual Sacrifice for Sin (10:1–18)

**[1]The law is only a shadow of the good things that are coming—not the realities
themselves. For this reason it can never, by the same sacrifices repeated endlessly
year after year, make perfect those who draw near to worship. [2]If it could, would
they not have stopped being offered? For the worshipers would have been cleansed
once for all, and would no longer have felt guilty for their sins. [3]But those sacrifices
are an annual reminder of sins, [4]because it is impossible for the blood of bulls and
goats to take away sins.**

[5]Therefore, when Christ came into the world, he said:

"Sacrifice and offering you did not desire,
but a body you prepared for me;
[6]with burnt offerings and sin offerings
you were not pleased.
[7]Then I said, 'Here I am—it is written about me in the scroll—
I have come to do your will, O God.'"

**[8]First he said, "Sacrifices and offerings, burnt offerings and sin offerings you did
not desire, nor were you pleased with them" (although the law required them to be
made). [9]Then he said, "Here I am, I have come to do your will." He sets aside the
first to establish the second. [10]And by that will, we have been made holy through
the sacrifice of the body of Jesus Christ once for all.**

**[11]Day after day every priest stands and performs his religious duties; again and
again he offers the same sacrifices, which can never take away sins. [12]But when
this priest had offered for all time one sacrifice for sins, he sat down at the right
hand of God. [13]Since that time he waits for his enemies to be made his footstool,
[14]because by one sacrifice he has made perfect forever those who are being made
holy.**

[15]The Holy Spirit also testifies to us about this. First he says:

[16]"This is the covenant I will make with them
after that time, says the Lord.
I will put my laws in their hearts,
and I will write them on their minds."

[17]Then he adds:

"Their sins and lawless acts
I will remember no more."

[18]And where these have been forgiven, there is no longer any sacrifice for sin.

Jewish tradition of the eschatological high-priestly redeemer" (p. 197).

The author can now conclude his lengthy expositional section begun at 7:1. Lane identified four paragraphs in this division and noted that the argument progresses in chiastic fashion:[1089]

A The inadequacy of the provisions of the law for repeated sacrifices (1–4)

B The repeated sacrifices have been superseded by the one sacrifice of Christ (10:5–9)

B´ The Levitical priests superseded by the one priest enthroned at God's right hand (10:11–14)

A´ The adequacy of the provisions of the new covenant, which render a sacrifice for sins no longer necessary (10:15–18)

This literary structure is also indicated by the parallel symmetry in the concluding statements to the second, third, and fourth paragraphs:

"we have been consecrated through the offering"

"by one offering he has decisively purged those who are being consecrated"

"where there is a decisive putting away of these, an offering . . . is no longer necessary"[1090]

Westfall concurred and suggested the following outline for Heb 10:1–18:[1091]

A. The Law cannot perfect believers (10:1–4)
B. It was God's will that Christ's sacrifice sanctify us (10:5–10)
C. Jesus' sacrifice perfected the sanctified believers (10:11–14)
D. Sacrifices have been abolished (10:15–18)

This section's relationship to its context is problematic. Attridge takes it not as a recapitulation of the previous section, but as the completion of the argument of Heb 8:1–10:18.[1092] Ellingworth viewed the passage as a summary of the central teaching of the whole epistle.[1093] Westfall observed: "The contrast of the requirements of the law in contrast with perfection, sanctification and the internal law promised in Jer. 31 is developed in 10:1–18 for the first time, so the subunit is an extension rather than a recapitulation or conclusion."[1094] In addition, the repetition of the abbreviated quotation of Jer 31:31–33 in 10:16–17

[1089] Lane, *Hebrews 9–13*, 258.

[1090] Ibid., 259.

[1091] Westfall, *Hebrews*, 219. Vanhoye and Dussaut begin the second paragraph with v. 4, but this is difficult to sustain linguistically.

[1092] Attridge, *Hebrews*, 279.

[1093] Ellingworth, *Hebrews*, 489.

[1094] Westfall, *Discourse Analysis*, 229.

adds to the unity and cohesion of the entire section 8:1–10:18.[1095] A number of features provide cohesion to this unit, including references to perfection, sanctification, and forgiveness in vv. 1,10,14,18.[1096] There is a parallel between the perfect tense *teteleiōken* "he has made perfect," in v. 14 and the periphrastic perfect in v. 10 (*hēgiasmenoi esmen*), translated "we have been made holy," and both serve to form a semantic tie with v. 1, where the law and the Levitical system cannot "perfect" (aorist tense) those who draw near for worship.[1097]

A fundamental shift in perspective occurs in 10:1–18. Whereas in 9:11–28 the focus was on the objective aspects of Christ's offering, in 10:1–18 the focus shifts to the subjective effects of Christ's offering.[1098] Hebrews 10:1–18 is given lexical cohesion through the repetition of three key terms associated with the offering of sacrifice for sins: "to offer sacrifice" (10:1,2,8,11,12), "offering" (10:5,8,10,14,18), and "sins" (10:2,3,6,8,12,17,18).[1099]

In vv. 1–4, the author demonstrates the Mosaic law is incapable of bringing perfection. Most of the semantic content of these verses is either repetition or paraphrase of the previous two chapters.[1100] Hughes summarizes 10:1–4 as to how the author shows the Levitical system to be inferior to the priesthood of Christ in four respects: (1) the insubstantial character of the Mosaic system, (2) the repetitive nature of sacrifices in the Levitical system, (3) the function of the Levitical sacrifices as a repeated reminder of sin, and (4) the inability of animal blood to remove sin.[1101]

10:1 Verse 1 begins with *gar*, untranslated in the NIV and provides the grounds for 9:24–28.[1102] The "law" refers to the whole Old Testament, primarily to its cultic aspect.[1103] "Shadow" is emphatic because of its sentence initial placement. "It can never" refers to the law. The participle *echōn*, translated "is," gives the reason for the result expressed in the verb "it can never."[1104] The author refers to "the good things that are coming" as the reality of which the law is merely a shadow. There are several possible referents to "the coming good things:" (1) blessings which are still future but made certain in Christ;[1105]

[1095] Against Vanhoye, who treats 8:1–9:28 as a distinct unit from 10:1–18.

[1096] Lane, *Hebrews 9–13*, 259; Westfall, *Discourse Analysis*, 224.

[1097] Porter, *Verbal Aspect*, 264; Westfall, *Discourse Analysis*, 227.

[1098] Lane, *Hebrews 9–13,* 258: "In terms of the logical structure, 9:15–28 clarifies the character of the objective salvation summarized in 9:11–12. The function of 10:1–18 is to clarify the subjective benefits of salvation reviewed in 9:13–14."

[1099] See A. Vanhoye, *La structure littéraire de l'Épître aux Hébreux* (Paris: Desclée de Brouwer, 1976), 162–63; Lane, *Hebrews 9–13*, 258.

[1100] Westfall, *Discourse Analysis*, 220.

[1101] Hughes, *Hebrews*, 389–92.

[1102] Ellingworth, *Hebrews*, 492, takes it with 9:23–28; Lane, *Hebrews 9–13*, 259, takes it with 8:3–5 and 9:23–26; and Hughes, *Hebrews*, 389, considers it a restatement of 8:5.

[1103] Ellingworth, *Hebrews*, 492.

[1104] So Bruce, *Hebrews,* 235; Lane, *Hebrews 9–13,* 260; NIV.

[1105] Moffatt, *Hebrews*, 135.

(2) the things not fulfilled in the Mosaic covenant;[1106] (3) Christ's sacrifice, present ministry, access to God, and eternal redemption;[1107] and (4) the blessings of salvation.[1108] The phrase "realities themselves" translates the more literal "the form of the things." The author uses both "shadow" and "reality." The Greek word *eikōn,* translated "reality," does not, as noted by Hughes, "connote a copy or likeness which as such would be other than the reality. . . . Its sense, rather, is the *manifestation* of the reality itself, and this sense is found in both classical and contemporary Greek."[1109] No matter how many times the shadow is repeated, it always remains a shadow; it is never the substance.

The NIV does not make explicit that the verb "to offer" appears in the Greek text. The verb is used impersonally and its implied subject is the priests.[1110] The two adverbial phrases "year after year" and "repeated endlessly" signal repetitiveness and ineffectiveness. "Year after year" may be connected with "they offer," or it can be connected with "by the same sacrifices."[1111] The former appears more likely. "Endlessly" or "continuously" can be connected with "they offer" or with "to perfect."[1112] The former is correct according to Lane since the usage of this phrase elsewhere in Hebrews follows the verb it qualifies.[1113] The phrase "by the same sacrifices" refers to sacrifices on the Day of Atonement as the phrase "year after year" implies, but also it includes the whole system of daily sacrifices, but not the sacrificed animals.[1114] The implied subject of the offering of sacrifices is the priests. Lane translates "make perfect" as "decisively purge."[1115]

10:2 Verse 2 begins with *epei,* "since" (NIV "if"), which introduces a consequence to an implied contrary to fact condition couched in the surface structure form of a rhetorical question.[1116] The conjunction stands as a semantic surrogate for something like "if the law, by the sacrifice it prescribes, could have perfected the worshipers." The rhetorical question implies that the Old

---

[1106] Ellingworth, *Hebrews*, 492.

[1107] Bruce, *Hebrews*, 235.

[1108] Lane, *Hebrews 9–13*, 260.

[1109] Hughes, *Hebrews*, 390. Delitzsch, *Hebrews*, 2:143–44, connects the usage of εἰκόνα in Heb 10:1 with Col 3:10 and Rom 8:9. He takes the "realities" (πραγμάτων) to be themselves the εἰκόνα, where the genitive πραγμάτων is a genitive of apposition: the realities themselves state what the "form" is (so also Greenlee, *Hebrews,* 361). Hence, the NIV translates the entire phrase "the realities themselves," and not something like the NRSV's "the true form of these realities." Delitzsch continues: "The Old Testament is but a shadowy and unsubstantial sketch or outline of the good things of the future world, not the substantial image and form, which is that of the realities themselves" (144).

[1110] Lane, *Hebrews 9–13*, 255; Ellingworth, *Hebrews*, 493.

[1111] Alford, "Hebrews," 185; Dods, "Hebrews," 341; Lünemann, *Hebrews*, 639.

[1112] L. Morris, Hebrews, 95; Montefiore, *Hebrews*, 164.

[1113] Lane, *Hebrews 9–13*, 255.

[1114] Ellingworth, *Hebrews*, 255.

[1115] Lane, *Hebrews 9–13*, 253.

[1116] Ibid., 255; Miller, *Hebrews,* 278.

Testament ritual was ongoing when the epistle was written.[1117] Miller swims against the stream of interpreters and translators when she takes the question to imply the consequence of an understood: "if the OT sacrifices could have perfected."[1118] The participle *prospheromenai*, "being offered," expresses the object of the preceding verb "stopped," telling what was stopped. The combination *suneidēsin hamartiōn*, rendered "felt guilty for their sins," is best taken in the cognitive sense of "consciousness of sins,"[1119] much like the NRSV's "consciousness of sin," where the singular functions the same as the plural.

The phrase "would have been cleansed" translates the perfect passive participle *kekatharismenous*. This participle encodes the condition of a condition-consequence relationship—if they had been cleansed, they would no longer have any consciousness of sins. The perfect tense emphasizes the continuing results; the cleansing is permanent. The participle could express reason or temporality. "This complicated passage of inferred contrary-to-fact condition and consequence, rendered contrary to fact by an unfulfilled reason-result situation, adds up to a strong case for the truth of the grounds found in the closing proposition: animal blood cannot remove sin."[1120] The author makes the strong point that the sacrificial system, including the Day of Atonement ritual, was a constant reminder of sins, because it is impossible that the blood of sacrificial animals should atone for sin. Why is it that the blood of animals cannot take away sin? As Dods said, "there is no relation between the physical blood of animals and man's moral offense."[1121] Dods might well have added there is no relation between animals and human beings that would permit the former to atone somehow for the latter. Here again, as emphasized in Hebrews 2 and later in Hebrews 10, the necessity of the incarnation of Christ for atonement to be made becomes evident.

10:3 The conjunction *alla*, "but," at the beginning of v. 3 can be construed in an adversative sense or adverbially in the sense of assent: "really, in them." Lane argued "to treat v. 3 as an adversative, as is usually done (RSV, NEB, JB, NIV), disrupts the argument and makes v. 4 apply inappropriately to v. 3 instead of to v. 1.[1122] The author's point is the law did accomplish God's purpose: it was a constant reminder to the people concerning their sins and need for cleansing. The entire Old Testament sacrificial system failed to secure the actual heart purification needed for ongoing fellowship with God. In reference to Jesus' statement to the disciples at the Last Supper, "Do this in remembrance

---

1117 Bruce, *Hebrews,* 236. Ellingworth, *Hebrews*, 490, is much more cautious about this, but he considers it a possibility.

1118 Miller, *Hebrews,* 279.

1119 Lane, *Hebrews 9–13,* 255; following Michel, *Hebräer,* 332; and C. Maurer, "συνείδησις," *TDNT* 7:918.

1120 Miller, *Hebrews,* 279.

1121 Dods, "Hebrews," 342.

1122 Lane, *Hebrews 9–13*, 255.

of me," Hughes remarked: "The gospel transforms *anamnēsis* [remembrance] from a remembrance of guilt to a remembrance of grace!"[1123]

10:4 The use of *gar*, "because," gives the reason the Old Testament sacrifices were inadequate and also explains 10:1.[1124] The reference is to the blood itself, not only the death of the animals.[1125] The reference to the blood of "bulls" and "goats" includes but may not be limited to the Day of Atonement. Complete removal of sins is in view in the Greek *aphairein*. The word means "to cause a state or condition to cease"[1126] and conjures up the picture of removing a load. The present tense at least implies a continuing situation: the ongoing sacrificial system cannot remove sins.

10:5–6 Verse 5 is introduced with the conjunction *dio*, "therefore," which governs the second paragraph of this unit (10:5–10). This paragraph contains an important quotation from Ps 40:6–8. The introduction to this quotation is the statement concerning Christ coming into the world, which refers to Jesus' earthly life including his entrance into the world via incarnation. The implied subject of *legei*, "he said," is Christ, whom the Greek text does not mention until v. 10, but the NIV inserts it in the text in v. 5 for clarity. Ellingworth takes the present tense *legei* to imply the permanent record of Scripture.[1127]

This is a rather remarkable hermeneutical move on the part of the author: he places an Old Testament passage of Scripture on the lips of Jesus. How are we to account for this? Several options have been proffered. Some take the psalm to be prophetic concerning the coming of Christ.[1128] Others see the pre-existent Christ speaking through the psalm.[1129] A third approach is to understand the Old Testament as now embodied in the person of Jesus.[1130] Schröger thinks the author is interpreting the psalm according to the method of midrash-pesher.[1131] Keil and Delitzsch, along with Kraus, argue the usage is typological.[1132] K. Jobes has concluded that the author's purpose in so doing is "an expression of the dynastic continuity of Jesus with Israel's King David."[1133] Stanley concurred, noting this is the "simplest and most persuasive

---

[1123] Hughes, *Hebrews*, 394.

[1124] Lane, *Hebrews 9–13*, 261.

[1125] Ellingworth, *Hebrews*, 498.

[1126] Danker, GELNT, 154.

[1127] Ellingworth, *Hebrews,* 500.

[1128] W. Manson, *The Epistle to the Hebrews: an Historical and Theological Reconsideration* (London: Hodder & Stoughton, 1951), 144.

[1129] Westcott, *Hebrews*, 307–8.

[1130] Hughes, *Hebrews*, 394–95.

[1131] F. Schröger, *Der Verfasser des Hebräerbriefes als Schriftausleger* (Biblische Untersuchungen 4; Regensburg: Pustet, 1968), 176.

[1132] C. F. Keil and F. Delitzsch, *Psalms*, Commentary on the Old Testament 5 (Edinburgh: T&T Clark, 1871; repr., Grand Rapids: Eerdmans, 1991), 34; H. Kraus, *Psalms 1–59*, trans. H. C. Oswald (Minneapolis: Fortress, 1993), 427.

[1133] K. Jobes, "The Function of Paronomasia in Hebrews 10:5–7," *TJ* 13 NS (1992): 186.

suggestion" that provides the author of Hebrews an opportunity to capitalize on the relationship between King David and Christ.[1134]

Interpretations of Ps 40:6–8 can be categorized into two groups: (1) those who see the animal sacrifices as being replaced with obedience,[1135] and (2) those who see the point being the offense of offering a sacrifice without obedience.[1136] The point is this: if God does not desire the Levitical sacrificial system, support is given to the author's point that the old covenant is now replaced with the new covenant. Stanley observed, "Abandoning the Levitical sacrifices is not as shocking as the readers might believe, since these sacrifices never were the ultimate focus of God's will or desire anyway."[1137] "A body you prepared for me" is the LXX translation of the Hebrew "ears you have dug" or "my ears you have opened." Most think this is an interpretive paraphrase of the MT where the Greek translators probably interpreted the Hebrew "ears" with "body."[1138] Only by means of the incarnation can Jesus accomplish the will of God to do away with sin. The LXX translates the Hebrew "my ears you have opened" with this intended sense in mind. The open ear and the yielded body both signify obedience to the will of God.[1139] Is this an example of dynamic equivalence at work in translation? It is indeed if the intent is to communicate the concept of obedient service implied in the term "ear."[1140]

However, another insightful explanation has been suggested by Jobes. The author's quotation of Ps 40:6–8 contains four variations from the MT and the LXX, which is itself very close to the MT. These variations are minor and usually dismissed as exegetically inconsequential.[1141] Jobes presented evidence that these variations are actually all related phonetically. She argued that the author is engaged in a "deliberate use of a phonetically based rhetorical technique called paronomasia which was highly valued in the first century."[1142] Citing Quintilian's discussion of the function of paronomasia, Jobes argued these subtle changes by the author contribute to marking of semantic prominence, "highlighting and emphasizing those particular thoughts."[1143] In answer to the question how these variations by the author contribute to his theological argument in Hebrews 10, Jobes pointed to the author's programmatic state-

---

1134 S. Stanley, "A New Covenant Hermeneutic," 164.

1135 So Keil and Delitzsch, *Psalms*, 5:38.

1136 So S. Stanley, "A New Covenant in Hebrews," 168.

1137 Ibid., 176.

1138 So Lane, *Hebrews 9–13*, 262.

1139 So Dods, "Hebrews," 343; Alford, "Hebrews," 187–88.

1140 So argued by S. Stanley, "A New Covenant Hermeneutic," 167.

1141 For example, Calvin, *Hebrews*, 136; Moffatt, *Hebrews*, 138; and Attridge, *Hebrews*, 165, are examples of those who explain the textual variants as part of the first century Greek text of the psalm. W. C. Kaiser Jr., *The Uses of the Old Testament in the New* (Chicago: Moody, 1985), 137–38, chalks them up to the author's minor semantic changes with no appreciable significance.

1142 K. Jobes, "Function of Paronomasia," 182. Cf. id., "Rhetorical Achievement in the Hebrews 10 'Misquote' of Psalm 40," *Bib* 72 (1991): 388–96.

1143 Jobes, "Function," 185.

ment in Heb 1:1 concerning the continuity and discontinuity of God's speech through the prophets and through the Son.[1144] The minor variations are now to be viewed as variations between David's speech in Psalm 40 and Christ's speech in the Hebrews 10 quotation of Psalm 40. These variations explain why it was not possible for David to say what Christ says in the Hebrews 10 version of the quotation.[1145]

The theological upshot of these variations emphasizes that sacrifice and offering were not God's will, nor burnt offering and sin offering his good pleasure. They were *never* the means by which God would deal permanently with sin. "The past speaking of the old sacrificial system [Heb 1:1] is superseded when God's redemptive plan is revealed in Christ."[1146] It is only when Christ offers himself as the final sacrifice for sins that atonement is achieved. "The author of Hebrews 10 was expressing the line of dynastic continuity between David and Jesus by putting David's words in Christ's mouth."[1147] Finally, the placement of this quotation between the two Jeremiah quotations is not accidental and supports the author's final effort to transition from the old covenant to the new covenant context.[1148]

The general phrase "sacrifice and offering" is virtually equivalent to "sacrifice" and can refer to animal sacrifices, the peace (cereal) offering,[1149]or all sacrifices. Hughes pointed out the four designations "sacrifice," "offering," "burnt offerings," and "sin offerings" "cover in effect the whole range of the Levitical sacrificial system."[1150] This is most likely the author's meaning.

10:7 The quotation continues in v. 7 with the statement "then I said," which introduces an unusual quote within a quote and indicates Jesus regarded himself as consciously fulfilling this prophecy. *Tote*, "then," can be taken tem-

---

[1144] Ibid., 186: "I suggest that the identification of the words of Ps 40:6–8 with Christ is to be construed as an expression of the dynastic continuity of Jesus with Israel's King David."

[1145] Ibid., 188. One of the variations is the substitution of *eudokēsas* for *hētēsas* which achieves phonetic assonance and puts the ending word of both clauses into the semantic domain of "wish" ("sacrifice and offering you did not desire"; "with burnt offerings and sin offerings you were not pleased"). Three times in the NT one finds *eudokeō* conjoined with *thelō* or its cognate (Eph 1:5, 9; Phil 2:13). Jobes pointed out this association between God's will and good pleasure used three times within the same context of the redemptive work of Jesus "suggests that the verb *eudokeō* when used with God as subject had taken on a specific, almost technical, sense, referring to the outworking of God's redemptive plan in Christ."

[1146] Ibid.

[1147] Ibid., 191.

[1148] As noted by D. Buck, "Rhetorical Arrangement," 265.

[1149] Bruce, *Hebrews*, 241, thinks the underlying Hebrew refers to the cereal offering.

[1150] Hughes, *Hebrews*, 397. Chrysostom, *Discourses Against Judaizing Christians* 7.2.1–7 (in Heen and Krey, eds., *Hebrews*, 155), in his inimitable way, showed how these verses, coupled with the fact of the destruction of Jerusalem, spell the end of the levitical Priesthood: "There can be no emperor if there are no armies, no crown, no purple robe, none of the other things that weld together an empire. So, too, there can be no priesthood if sacrifice has been destroyed, if offerings are forbidden, if the sanctuary has been trampled into the dust, if everything that constituted it has disappeared. For the priesthood depended on all these things."

porally, as do most, indicating the point in time when it became apparent God himself would never be satisfied with any animal sacrifice, or any other sacrifice for that matter; *then* Jesus came to fulfill God's will in this matter. It has been construed as circumstantial[1151] with the meaning "since the Old Testament sacrifices were inadequate." The infinitive translated "to do" expresses purpose, with means as to how shown in the verb "I am here." The use of the present tense *hēkō*, "I come," actually denotes a state and has the force of a perfect to the verb *erchomai*,[1152] "I have come." "To do your will, O God" is emphatic.[1153] Westcott commented how often the notion of God's will is connected with the redemption and consummation of man: John 4:34; 5:30; 6:38–40; Eph 1:5,9,11; 1 Thess 4:3; 1 Tim 2:4.[1154] Michel suggested it was Jesus alone and no other who could make this statement. Jeremiah 31:31–34 describes the new covenant; Psalm 40:4–6 describes the new sacrifice: Jesus.[1155]

The Greek has "in the scroll of the book," which is rendered as "in the scroll." The noun *kephalis* originally denoted the tips or knobs of the rollers around which parchments were rolled and came to mean the scroll itself.[1156] It is also found in Ezek 2:9. The reference is to the Old Testament Scripture.

10:8 The word "first" in v. 8 is the interpretative rendering of the Greek "above," with the meaning "referring to what has just been said." It can be taken to refer to v. 5 or v. 6 or both. The present participle *legōn* is translated "he said." It is subordinate to the following finite verb "he said" in v. 9 and thus moves the focus to the next verse. The present tense is used because the quotation is judged to be still in effect in Scripture.[1157] The use of the plurals generalizes the sacrifices which are mentioned in v. 8, emphasizing their inadequacy by multiplicity and repetition.[1158] Ellingworth takes the plurals as semantic equivalents to the generic singulars in 10:5.[1159] The phrase "although the law[1160] required them to be made" is placed in parentheses, thus treating it as parenthetical.[1161] The indefinite relative pronoun *haitines*, "although," refers

---

[1151] Morris, "Hebrews," 98.

[1152] Miller, *Hebrews,* 281.

[1153] Ellingworth, *Hebrews,* 501.

[1154] Westcott, *Hebrews*, 311.

[1155] Michel, *Hebräer,* 337.

[1156] In the phrase "in the roll of the book" in Greek, the genitive can be taken appositionally where the roll is equivalent to the scroll, as does Hughes (*Hebrews*, 397–98) and the NIV. Another option is to interpret the phrase to mean the "roll" is in the form of a scroll, as does Bruce, *Hebrews*, 242; and Lane, *Hebrews 9–13*, 255. This latter option is best. See the detailed discussion of the possible meanings of "it is written about me in the scroll" in Hughes, *Hebrews*, 397–98.

[1157] Ellingworth, *Hebrews*, 503.

[1158] Lane, *Hebrews 9–13*, 264.

[1159] Ellingworth, *Hebrews*, 503.

[1160] "Law" is definite here with or without the article, as mentioned by Alford, "Hebrews," 189; and Ellingworth, *Hebrews*, 504.

[1161] Bruce, *Hebrews*, 239; Lane, *Hebrews 9–13*, 254–55. Ellingworth, *Hebrews*, 504, does not think it is parenthetical.

to all four types of sacrifices. It can be construed in one of three ways: (1) as a simple relative pronoun describing the sacrifices;[1162] (2) qualitatively, focusing on the kind of things they are;[1163] or (3) as a concession, "although."[1164] The latter option is probably the best.

10:9 In v. 9, the author follows up the repetition of the first part of the quotation in v. 8 with the repetition of the latter part of the quotation. He shifts from the first person aorist "I said" in v. 7 to the third person perfect "he said" here in v. 9. With the use of the perfect tense verb, the author stresses the permanence of what has been said here, whereas in v. 7 the focus was that Jesus, not David, was the speaker. The statement "He sets aside . . . second" can be viewed as (1) expressing an implication of the preceding quotation,[1165] (2) summarizing the two parts of the quotation,[1166] (3) as a parenthetical statement,[1167] or (4) as indicating the significance of the preceding quotation as it is attributed to Christ.[1168] The fourth option incorporates the first option as well and is the most likely meaning. The meaning of "first" and "second" may refer to the first and second covenants,[1169] though this is highly unlikely. More likely the reference is either to the old sacrifices and Christ's sacrifice,[1170] or "first" refers to the offering of the sacrifices and offerings, while "second" refers to doing the will of God.[1171] What is being "set aside" here is the Levitical sacrifices. Thus the word "first" is in the neuter gender in Greek. Since three of the four types of sacrifices mentioned in vv. 5–6 are feminine while one is neuter, such a mixture of genders probably caused the author to use the neuter "first."[1172] Bruce also interprets the author to mean by "first" the animal sacrifices and "second" to mean doing God's will.[1173] The meaning is expressed well by Stanley: "He takes away the first (Levitical) sacrifices that he might establish the second will of God that requires Christ's sacrifice."[1174] The author places *stēsē*, "to establish," last in the clause for emphasis. Lane's comment is helpful:

> The semantic value of *stēsē* reflects the usage of the LXX, where the verb *histanai* receives an intensification and a characteristic juridical aspect. . . . It denotes "to establish, to remain valid". . . . See especial-

---

[1162] So Bruce, *Hebrews*, 239; Lane, *Hebrews 9–13*, 255.
[1163] So Alford, "Hebrews," 189; and Miller, *Hebrews,* 283.
[1164] So NIV and Morris, *Hebrews*, 97.
[1165] Hughes, *Hebrews*, 399.
[1166] Kistemaker, *Hebrews*, 278.
[1167] Lünemann, *Hebrews,* 644.
[1168] Lane, *Hebrews 9–13*, 264–65.
[1169] Miller, *Hebrews,* 283.
[1170] So Hughes, *Hebrews*, 399; Ellingworth, *Hebrews*, 504–5.
[1171] So Bruce, *Hebrews*, 242–43; Lane, *Hebrews 9–13*, 265.
[1172] S. Stanley, "A New Covenant Hermeneutic," 175. Cf. H. Braun, *An die Hebräer,* HNT (Tübingen: Mohr, 1984), 298.
[1173] Bruce, *Hebrews*, 242–43.
[1174] S. Stanley, "A New Covenant Hermeneutic," 176.

ly Num 30:12–16, where the paired verbs "to confirm" and "to annul" offer a close semantic parallel to the formulation in Heb 10:9b.[1175]

10:10 Verse 10 concludes the second paragraph in Heb 10 and is in the Greek text the continuation of a sentence begun in v. 8. Because God willed it, and by means of Christ's sacrifice for our sins on the cross, believers have been made holy. The will of God expresses the reason for believers being made holy, and the result is shown in the construction in Greek which literally reads, "we are having been made holy." The means of our sanctification is the offering of the body of Christ in obedience to the will of God.[1176] The construction in Greek is used by the author to highlight the permanence of Christ's work and the continuing state of sanctification which believers enjoy.[1177] The placing of the Greek *ephapax*, "once for all," as the last word in the sentence also serves to focus on the notion of the permanence of Christ's work and the permanent state of believer's sanctification.[1178] Although it is possible to construe *ephapax* with the entire verse,[1179] or with "we have been made holy,"[1180] it is probably better to construe it with the semantically implied event in the noun "sacrifice."[1181] Theologically, sanctification is both an objective and a subjective matter. We have been made holy objectively by the cross of Christ and we are in the process of being made holy through ongoing sanctification by the Holy Spirit throughout our lifetime. The statement here in v. 10 points to objective sanctification. In v. 14 the author referred to subjective sanctification. Although rare in Hebrews, the combination "Jesus Christ" is used here in v. 10 with the words coming at the end of the verse, thus adding "considerable emphasis to the prominence of v. 10."[1182] The combination may be an allusion on the part of the author to the human and divine nature of Christ

---

[1175] Lane, *Hebrews 9–13*, 256.

[1176] Westcott, *Hebrews*, 312, said that the author's use of the preposition ἐν at the beginning of the verse and not διά, "through," or κατά, "according to," signifies that the will of God which Jesus performed in the giving of his body for our sanctification indicates that believers are "included in it, even in that purpose of love which Christ has realized." Alford, "Hebrews," 190, draws an unlikely distinction between the body and blood of Jesus when he remarks that the blood of Jesus reconciles to God and the offering of the body of Jesus sanctifies the believer.

[1177] Alford, "Hebrews," 190; Bruce, *Hebrews*, 243; Ellingworth, *Hebrews*, 505. Z. Hodges wrongly states, "Nowhere in Hebrews does the writer refer to the 'progressive sanctification' of a believer's life" ("Hebrews," in *Bible Knowledge Commentary: New Testament*, ed. J. Walvoord and R. Zuck (Colorado Springs, CO: David C. Cook, 1983), 804.

[1178] Westcott, *Hebrews*, 313.

[1179] M. Vincent, *Word Studies in the New Testament* (Grand Rapids: Eerdmans, 1946), 4:497–98.

[1180] So Bruce, *Hebrews*, 243; and Moll, *Hebrews*, 171.

[1181] So Alford, "Hebrews," 190; Hughes, *Hebrews*, 399. Lane, *Hebrews 9–13*, 256 said: "It is more likely that the term defines the unique and definitive offering of the body of Jesus, as in 7:27; 9:12."

[1182] Westfall, *Discourse Analysis*, 227.

together involved in believers' sanctification.[1183] Verse 10 sums up the results that are accomplished by virtue of Christ doing God's will. The application to believers of Christ's offering his body in obedience to the will of God is our sanctification.

10:11 The use of *kai*, "and," in v. 11 marks a new paragraph and the *men . . . de* construction marks out the paragraph boundary through v. 14. Verse 11 (*men*) speaks of the ongoing activity of the priests contrasted in vv. 12–14 (*de*) with Christ and his once for all sacrifice. This statement of priestly posture (standing) conveys at the very least an implication that the sacrificial work of the priests is never completed. Additionally, the use of the phrase translated "day after day" supports this notion of incompleteness. In the Greek text, the phrase can be connected with the verb "stands" or with the participle "performs," or with both.[1184] The NIV places the phrase first in the translation and thus construes the phrase with the entire clause.[1185] The perfect tense here has the force of the present tense and is correctly translated "stands." Hughes thinks this usage may imply a pre-AD 70 date for the epistle.[1186] The mention of "every priest" is inclusive of the high priest. The second *kai*, "and," (following the participle translated "performs his religious duties") connects this participle with the following one translated "he offers." The connection can be construed in one of two ways. Either the actions expressed in the two participles are coordinated or the second participle is something of an expansion of the first.[1187] The final relative clause describes the total inability of the Levitical system and its sacrifices in the sense of "any one of which and all of which [sacrifices] cannot take away sin."[1188] The clause is usually taken in a qualitative sense, although Kistemaker takes it as concessive.[1189] The use of the verb translated "take away" is emphatic and conveys the meaning of "to deliver completely."[1190]

10:12 Verse 12 begins with *de*, "but," thus balancing out the *men* (untranslated in the NIV) in v. 11. "This priest" refers of course to Jesus. The NIV adds "priest" to the lone demonstrative pronoun in the Greek text to clarify who is being spoken about. The author has fronted the word translated "one" in the clause for emphasis. The participle translated "had offered" can be taken temporally,[1191] expressing when he offered, or it can be viewed as semanti-

[1183] Westcott, *Hebrews*, 313, says the usage "characterizes the completeness of the sacrifice under the divine and human aspects of the Lord's person."

[1184] As does Bruce, *Hebrews*, 244.

[1185] Greenlee, *Exegetical Summary*, 375.

[1186] Hughes, *Hebrews*, 399.

[1187] Ellingworth, *Hebrews*, 508, takes it in the latter sense.

[1188] Miller, *Hebrews*, 286.

[1189] Kistemaker, *Hebrews*, 280–81.

[1190] So noted by Lane, *Hebrews 9–13*, 256; but Moffatt, *Hebrews*, 140, does not think the usage is emphatic.

[1191] So Hughes, *Hebrews*, 400–1; Lane *Hebrews 9–13*, 267. The NIV translates "when."

cally parallel to the following verb "sat down."[1192] The Greek prepositional phrase translated "for all time" can be connected with what precedes,[1193] or with the following "he sat down."[1194] Again the contrast is between the standing position of the priests mentioned previously with Jesus whose work is completely finished. Furthermore, theologically, his seated position also guarantees his atoning work has been completely accomplished (see the perfect tense *tetelestai* "it is finished" in John 19:30) and implies God's acceptance of his sacrifice.[1195] The Son's "seating" echoes Heb 1:3,13; 8:1; 12:2 and is a direct reference to Ps 110:4, the author's key verse in the epistle.

10:13 Here is a statement concerning the Son's waiting for his enemies "to be made his footstool." Ellingworth takes the "since that time" to mean "in this connection" and sees the author continuing his allusion to Ps 110:1, which he began in the previous verse.[1196] The participle "waiting" is translated by the finite verb "waits." There is no implication of doubt concerning the outcome of the waiting,[1197] and the participle implies eager anticipation.[1198] According to the metaphor "footstool," when enemies become such, they are completely subdued.

10:14 *Gar*, "because," introduces this verse that gives the grounds for the conclusion in vv. 12–13 that atonement is completed. The reference to "sacrifice" harks back to v. 10 where the offering of Christ's body paid the sin debt. The word "one" is again fronted in the Greek text for emphasis. The perfect tense verb here, "he has made perfect," is the last of nine such perfects in the doctrinal section of the epistle (7:1–10:18).[1199] Lane, following Johnsson, translated it "decisively purged" and stated that it "has the merit of sustaining the emphasis of 9:9 and 10:1."[1200]This verb is followed by the important prepositional phrase translated "forever," which can modify either the notion of sacrifice or Jesus' sitting at God's right hand.[1201] The verse ends with the

---

1192 Bruce, *Hebrews*, 244–45.

1193 So Bruce, *Hebrews*, 244; Lane *Hebrews 9–13*, 256, and most translations. Westcott, *Hebrews*, 314, construes the phrase with what precedes on the grounds that the other option "is contrary to the usage of the Epistle; it obscures the idea of the perpetual efficacy of Christ's one sacrifice; it weakens the contrast with ἕστηκεν; and it imports a foreign idea into the image of the assumption (ἐκάθισεν) of royal dignity by Christ."

1194 So Alford, "Hebrews," 191; Dods, "Hebrews," 344.

1195 The later point so mentioned by Bruce, *Hebrews*, 246.

1196 Ellingworth, *Hebrews*, 510 (though his text erroneously has "Ps. 110:4" rather than Psalm 110:1).

1197 Hughes, *Hebrews*, 402.

1198 Ellingworth, *Hebrews*, 510.

1199 (7:3,13,14; 8:5,6 (twice); 9:18,26; 10:14). The perfect tense is used nine times in 1:1–4:15 (1:4,13; 2:14; 3:3,14; 4:2,14,15) and five times in 11:1–12:3 (11:5,17,28; 12:2,3). Westcott, *Hebrews*, 177, lists these occurrences and stated the use of the perfect tense in Hebrews "is worthy of careful study."

1200 Lane, *Hebrews 9–13*, 256. See Johnsson, "Defilement and Purgation," 454.

1201 Ellingworth, *Hebrews*, 509–10, prefers the latter alternative, as does Attridge, *Hebrews*, 279–80; Bruce, *Hebrews*, 245–46; and Lane, *Hebrews 9–13*, 267.

present participle translated "those who are being made holy." The author is making good use of the Greek tense system to contrast the perfect finished work of Christ on the cross and its sanctifying effect on believers (note the perfective aspect of the participle in v. 10) with the ongoing work of progressive sanctification here in v. 14 (note the present tense participle). Lane argued that the perfect tense defines a finished work on its author's side (Christ), but one that is progressively realized (subjective sanctification) in the process which the present participle depicts in v. 14.[1202] The present participle may be understood progressively, iteratively, or as timeless.[1203] Bruce outlined three effects which the author ascribes to the sacrifice of Christ: (1) "by it his people have had their conscience cleansed from guilt"; (2) "by it they have been fitted to approach God as accepted worshipers"; and (3) "by it they have experienced the fulfillment of what was promised in earlier days, being brought into the perfect relation to God which is involved in the new covenant."[1204]

10:15 Verse 15 begins a new paragraph (vv. 15–18) with *de* (untranslated in the NIV) and the topic shifts where the proof that Christ's sacrifice is complete and final is given.[1205] The use of the perfect tense "to say" to introduce a quotation in the latter part of v. 15 places strong emphasis on the quotation.[1206] Miller takes the statement "the Holy Spirit testifies to us" as the main proposition of the final paragraph, with everything following it in subordination to it.[1207] The present tense "testifies" indicates the Holy Spirit is speaking now, bringing the text from the past into the present.[1208] The author placed the previous quotation from Psalm 40 on the lips of Jesus; now he appeals to the Holy Spirit himself as the one giving final confirmation through the abbreviated quote of Jer 31:31–34. The introductory formula translated "first he says" may be connected with nothing overtly in the text,[1209] or it can be connected with an understood "then he says" in v. 17, paralleling the quote formula of v. 15. Ellingworth takes it in the sense of "after the Holy Spirit had spoken in the preceding verses, he witnesses in the following words."[1210]

10:16 By the author's substitution of "with them" for "with Israel" in the LXX, he is probably universalizing the text so as to broaden the promise out to include Gentiles as well. The LXX text has "giving my laws upon their hearts." The NIV translates this as "I will put my laws in their hearts." Greenlee's sug-

---

[1202] Ibid., 256.

[1203] Alford ("Hebrews," 192) and Lane (*Hebrews 9–13*, 254, 256) take it as indicating a process of sanctification. Dods ("Hebrews," 345) and Bruce (*Hebrews*, 247) take it as timeless.

[1204] Bruce, *Hebrews*, 247.

[1205] Montefiore, *Hebrews*, 170.

[1206] So Westfall, *Discourse Analysis*, 228. Cf. Porter, *Verbal Aspect*, 388.

[1207] Miller, *Hebrews,* 291.

[1208] Lane, *Hebrews 9–13*, 268.

[1209] So Dods, "Hebrews," 345; Moffatt, *Hebrews*, 141.

[1210] Ellingworth, *Hebrews*, 513.

gestion that this may describe how the new covenant was "given: . . . by giving their laws in their hearts" is plausible.[1211]

10:17 Verse 17 continues the quotation with *kai*, (untranslated in the NIV), which is actually part of the quoted text, but is here used to introduce the second part of the quotation.[1212] This part of the quotation in v. 17 is separated from the preceding part of the quotation by an implied phrase "he also says."[1213] There is a break between this and the preceding verse, and this verse carries the point of the quotation.[1214] The double negative in the Greek text indicates an emphatic negative on the part of the author. The compound predicates "sins" and "lawless acts" are placed first in the clause for prominence: (lit.) "their sins and lawless acts no more I will remember still."

10:18 Verse 18 begins with *hopou*, "where," followed by the resumptive *de*,[1215] (untranslated in the NIV) with the meaning that these circumstances (where sins are forgiven) result in the fact stated in the following clause: that no "sacrifice for sin" is needed any longer or even possible. "No longer" can mean that an offering is no longer possible,[1216] or, as Lane takes it, no longer necessary.[1217] Verse 18 concludes the immediate discussion and may be viewed as concluding all of 10:1–18 or perhaps even the entire section 7:1–10:18.[1218]

The author's argument in the four paragraphs that make up Heb 10:1–18 can be analyzed as follows: Verses 1–4 make the point that the repetition of sacrifices proves their ineffectiveness; this is followed by a quotation of Psalm 40 placed on the lips of Jesus whereby he obeys God's will by his sacrifice on the cross; this is followed by an allusion to Ps 110:1 in vv. 11–14, the key psalm for the author in the epistle; and this is followed by a repeated but abbreviated quotation of Jer 31:31–34 in vv. 15–18 stressing the new covenant and its final disposition of the sin problem coupled with the impossibility of another sacrifice for sin being made by Jesus and certainly by anyone else. It is clear that the author considers the new covenant to be currently in force for Christians and not as beginning at some later date.

THEOLOGICAL IMPLICATIONS. In Heb 5:9–10, the author announced three thematic aspects of the high priestly work of Christ which he delays in developing until 7:1–10:18. What is stated in Heb 5:9 is developed theologically in 8:1–9:28. Only Jesus is qualified to be the high priest in the heavenly sanctuary because of the unique circumstances of his death and exaltation. What is stated in Heb 5:9 concerning Jesus being the "source of eternal salvation" is

---

[1211] Greenlee, *Exegetical Summary,* 382.

[1212] So noted by Alford, "Hebrews," 192–93; and Ellingworth, *Hebrews*, 514.

[1213] So Lane, *Hebrews 9–13*, 256–57, and most translations.

[1214] Alford, "Hebrews," 193.

[1215] Ellingworth, *Hebrews,* 515.

[1216] Hughes, *Hebrews*, 404; NIV.

[1217] Lane, *Hebrews 9–13*, 269.

[1218] Alford takes the latter option ("Hebrews," 193).

developed in 10:1–18. The author's use of Ps 110:1 in Heb 8:1 is reiterated in 10:12–13 and serves as a literary *inclusio*. Other parallels can be noted: 9:1–10 parallels 10:1–4 (ineffectiveness of the sacrifices); 9:11–14 parallels 10:5–10; and 9:15–28 parallels 10:11–18.[1219]

The summary in 10:18 makes it clear that the new covenant is currently in force for Christians.[1220] The author concludes the entire lengthy theological section of Heb 8:1–10:18 with several astonishing affirmations. First, the repeated sacrifices of the Mosaic law have been forever rendered obsolete by the final atonement of Christ on the cross. The new covenant in the blood of Christ forever abolishes the old covenant, including its sacrificial system. Not only is the old abolished by the new, but the new covenant itself *excludes* the old, which is important for contemporary Jewish-Christian dialogue. Second, Jesus' death on the cross perfectly fulfilled God's will, hence there is no further need for any sacrifice. Third, all of this was accomplished by the *incarnate* Christ, hence the use of Psalm 40. Fourth, in the new covenant, sin has been forever dealt with. The inefficiency of the old covenant sacrifices to take away sin is contrasted with the final once for all nature of the new covenant through the death of Christ on the cross. Fifth, Jesus now *sits* enthroned in heaven, signifying the completion and finality of his sacrifice on the cross. His posture attests that the benefits of his atoning sacrifice endure forever. Sixth, the future prospects of the new covenant from Jeremiah's perspective have now become a present reality in the lives of Christians as the Holy Spirit *testifies* (present tense) to us. Seventh, the old Mosaic law was external; now under the new covenant the law is inscribed on the hearts of believers and they are empowered from within to obey it. Eighth, forgiveness and cleansing of sin has been accomplished and access to God through Christ attained. In summary, the substitutionary death of Christ on the cross has purchased forever our redemption and right standing before God. In Christ, shadow has given way to substance; the temporary has been replaced with the eternal; the imperfect has become perfect; judgment has become mercy; and law has become grace.

Now we are in a position to see how and why the author has made Ps 110:1,4 the key Old Testament text for Hebrews. With only one exception (Heb 12:2), all of the quotations or allusions to Ps 110:1,4 in Hebrews occur prior to the beginning of the third major discourse section of the epistle at 10:19. As has been observed throughout, it is only the author of Hebrews who juxtaposes Ps 110:1 with Ps 110:4 in the entire New Testament. Interestingly, Ps 110:1 is actually directly quoted only once in the epistle: Heb 1:13. It is alluded to in the following five places: 1:3; 8:1; 10:12–13; 12:2. There are three direct quotes of Ps 110:4: Heb 5:6; 7:17; 7:21. There are three allusions to Ps 110:4 as well: Heb 5:10; 6:20; 7:3.

[1219] See the full discussion in Lane, *Hebrews 9–13*, 257.

[1220] R. Decker, "The Church's Relationship to the New Covenant," *BSac* 152 (1995): 301.

The primary focus of Hebrews 1–4 is on the kingship of the Son while the focus in Hebrews 5–10 is on the priesthood of the Son. The theme of cleansing, a priestly act, introduced in Heb 1:3, became the focal point of the discussion in Hebrews 5–10, but for four chapters it is subordinated to the kingly aspects of the Son which the author develops. That Ps 110:1 is used by the author to create an *inclusio* via its allusion in Heb 1:3 and its direct quotation in Heb 1:13 is the first clue that this psalm is going to be programmatic for the author throughout the epistle and that he is using it to establish the royal dignity of Jesus the Son.

Furthermore, the author's use of seven Old Testament quotations in the catena of Heb 1:5–13, all of which are connected in one way or another with a royal theme, culminating with Ps 110:1, further highlights the author's focus on the kingship of the Son in Hebrews 1. The juxtaposition of the two quotations, Ps 2:7 and 2 Sam 7:14 in Heb 1:5, has great significance. First, 2 Sam 7:14 is a Messianic text. Second, the name Jesus has inherited by virtue of his seating at the right hand (Heb 1:4) is most likely that of "Son." Third, by the use of two key texts having to do with the Davidic covenant, it is also likely that the author of Hebrews views the Son who is seated at the right hand of God as in some sense fulfilling part of the Davidic covenant. On this point, Anderson's critique of Saucy's argument for the current "passivity" of the Son seated on the throne appears salient.[1221] Thus, at least in some sense presently, the reign of Christ has begun, as illustrated in the author's clarifying argument in Heb 2:5–9 with his use of Psalm 8.

All six of the quotations and allusions to Ps 110:4 occur within the span of Hebrews 5–7. It occurs twice in Heb 5:6–10 and three times in Hebrews 7. In the occurrences in Heb 5:5–10, the author connects Ps 110:4 with Ps 2:7 here just as he connected Ps 110:1 with Ps 2:7 in chap. 1. Following the Son's exaltation, his ongoing priestly ministry is inaugurated. Thus, by his theological use of Ps 110:1,4, the author is bringing together two aspects of the ministry of the Son: his kingly and priestly roles. A very critical point the author makes is that God's oath to the Son in Ps 110:4 is what makes Jesus the guarantor of the new covenant (Heb 7:21–22). His single sacrifice for all time and for all sin forever does away with the need for the Levitical sacrificial system. His eternal priestly nature and work, a salient point of Ps 110:4, is highlighted by

[1221] See D. Anderson, *The King-Priest of Psalm 110 in Hebrews* (New York: Peter Lang, 2001), 142–45. Anderson finds three problems with Saucy's interpretation. First, he fails to take into account the structure of Heb 1 where the theme of exaltation and reign is paramount, not the atoning work on the cross. No reference to "cleansing" is found in the catena of Heb 1:5–13. Second, Saucy fails to consider Ps 110:1 in its NT context as a whole, especially its use by Paul in 1 Cor 15:25; Eph 1:21 and Col 3:1, all of which emphasize Christ's present reign as well as his future coming. Third, Saucy misses the tandem use of Ps 8:7 with Ps 110:1 in Paul, Peter and the author of Hebrews. Again, the present reign of Christ is the focus.

the author's use of five Greek phrases from 6:20–7:25, each of which stresses the eternality of his priestly work.

In the concluding doctrinal section, 8:1–10:18, the author reverts to his use of Ps 110:1 as evidenced by the *inclusio* it forms in the allusion in 8:1 and 10:12–13. The significance of Heb 8:1 structurally has already been seen. Its significance theologically is that it brings together for the first time in the epistle both Ps 110:1 and Ps 110:4, since Jesus as high priest has sat down at the right hand of the throne of God. Likewise in Heb 10:12–13, the inescapable juxtaposition of Ps 110:1 and 4 in the argument and conclusion of the author cannot be missed.[1222] The climactic hortatory paragraph of Heb 12:1–2 again alludes to Ps 110. The strongest compound conjunction in Hebrews (*toigaroun*, "consequently") occurs in 12:1. In fact, this is the only place in the entire New Testament that this conjunction occurs. This signifies the focus which the author is placing on the exhortation to "run with endurance the race" as Jesus ran and finished his race so that he "sat down" (perfect tense) at the right hand of God.

Finally, as C. H. Dodd so brilliantly demonstrated elsewhere, the author of Hebrews operated from a dualist "already/not yet" eschatological outlook with respect to the reign of Christ. The evidence in Hebrews and the rest of the New Testament for a future eschatological reign of Christ is overwhelming. According to Paul and the author of Hebrews, the enemies of Christ are *presently* subjected to him (Heb 2:5–9; 1 Cor 15:23–26). Yet in these same verses it is clear that at his second coming, Christ will subjugate all his enemies permanently. There is a world to come (*oikoumenē* in Heb 2:5), but there is also a world that has already come (a heavenly Jerusalem, Heb 12:22) to which believers have *already come* according to the author of Hebrews.

[1222] See the excellent summary in Anderson, *King Priest of Psalm 110*, 173–74, 236–39, 285–89.

DIVISION OUTLINE

III. Exhortation to Draw Near, Hold Fast, and Love One Another (10:19–13:21)
   1. Confidence to Persevere and Avoid Willful Sin (10:19–39)
      (1) Spiritual Resources, Privileges, and Requirements (10:19–25)
      (2) Dangers of Deliberate Sin (10:26–34)
      (3) Need to Persevere (10:35–39)
      Excursus: On Smuggling Presuppositions into Exegesis
   2. Conviction to Live by Faith (11:1–40)
      (1) Necessity of Faith (11:1–2)
      (2) Foresight of Faith (11:3–16)
      (3) Accomplishments of Faith (11:17–40)
   3. Encouragement to Run with Endurance and Pursue Peace (12:1–29)
      (1) Running with Endurance (12:1–3)
      (2) Enduring Discipline (12:4–13)
      (3) Pursuing Peace and Holiness (12:14–17)
      (4) Arrival at Mount Zion (12:18–24)
      (5) Dangers of Turning Away (12:25–29)
   4. Final Exhortations to Love and Humble Submission (13:1–21)
      (1) Continuing in Love (13:1–8)
      (2) Continuing Sacrifices of Praise (13:9–16)
      (3) Continuing in Submission and Prayer (13:17–21)

III. EXHORTATION TO DRAW NEAR, HOLD FAST, AND LOVE ONE ANOTHER (10:19–13:21)

1. Confidence to Persevere and Avoid Willful Sin (10:19–39)

(1) Spiritual Resources, Privileges, and Requirements (10:19–25)

The third major discourse unit of the epistle begins with the paragraph in Heb 10:19–25. Several indicators confirm this as not only the beginning of a new paragraph, but the beginning of a new major section. The parallels with Heb 4:14–16, which functions to introduce the second major discourse section, are unmistakable.[1223] Two of the three imperatives are also found in Heb 10:22–25: "draw near" and "hold unswervingly." Both 4:14 and 10:19 begin in Greek with *echontes oun*, "having therefore." These are the only two places in the epistle where this construction is found. Hebrews 10:19–21 contains a significant amount of "back-reference" to the basic content of 5:1–10:18, further indicating that 10:19 begins a new major section in the epistle.

The relationship of this paragraph to the preceding and following co-text is disputed. It can hardly be viewed only as transitional in nature, as Attridge suggested.[1224] Bruce is correct that this paragraph "might well have formed the conclusion of the homily."[1225] The summary nature[1226] of this paragraph of the preceding section (4:14–10:18) is difficult to deny. Several commentators link the paragraph with the preceding section,[1227] while others view it as the beginning of the next section.[1228] It is no doubt linked to the previous section, but it seems clear that it functions within the discourse to introduce a third major section. Guthrie is correct in his analysis of the unit as functioning in an "overlapping" fashion as both the conclusion of the preceding section and the introduction to a new section.[1229]

[19]Therefore, brothers, since we have confidence to enter the Most Holy Place by the blood of Jesus, [20]by a new and living way opened for us through the curtain, that is, his body, [21]and since we have a great priest over the house of God, [22]let us draw near to God with a sincere heart in full assurance of faith, having our hearts sprinkled to cleanse us from a guilty conscience and having our bodies washed with pure water. [23]Let us hold unswervingly to the hope we profess, for he who promised is faithful. [24]And let us consider how we may spur one another on toward love and good deeds. [25]Let us not give up meeting together, as some are in the habit of doing, but let us encourage one another—and all the more as you see the Day approaching.

[1223] See C. Westfall, *A Discourse Analysis of the Letter to the Hebrews: The Relationship Between Form and Meaning*, LNTS 297 (London: T&T Clark, 2006), 238.

[1224] W. H. Attridge, *The Epistle to the Hebrews*, (Philadelphia: Fortress, 1989), 283.

[1225] F. F. Bruce, *The Epistle to the Hebrews*, NICNT (Grand Rapids: Eerdmans, 1964), 249.

[1226] W. L. Lane, *Hebrews 9–13*, WBC (Dallas: Word Books, 1991), 282.

[1227] So A. Vanhoye, *Structure and Message of the Epistle to the Hebrews,* SubBi 12 (Rome: Pontifical Biblical Institute, 1989), 40; L. Dussaut, *Synopse Structurelle De L'Épître aux Hébreux* (Paris: Editions du Cerf, 1981), 1; Attridge, *Hebrews*, 19; and Lane, *Hebrews 9–13*, viii. Westfall, *Discourse Analysis*, 235, viewed the paragraph as "a summary of the entire preceding discourse" which she takes to include 8:1–10:25.

[1228] So B. F. Westcott, *The Epistle to the Hebrews* (London: Macmillan, 1892; repr., Grand Rapids: Eerdmans, 1955), 317; J. A. Moffatt, *A Critical and Exegetical Commentary to the Hebrews,* ICC (Edinburgh: T&T Clark, 1924), 141; Bruce, *Hebrews*, ix, 248–49; P. E. Hughes, *A Commentary on the Epistle to the Hebrews* (Grand Rapids: Eerdmans, 1977), 405; L. L. Neeley, "A Discourse Analysis of Hebrews." *OPTAT* 3–4 (1987): 10; and D. DeSilva, *Perseverance in Gratitude: A Socio-Rhetorical Commentary on the Epistle to the Hebrews* (Grand Rapids: Eerdmans, 2000), 74.

[1229] G. Guthrie, *The Structure of Hebrews: A Text-Linguistic Analysis* (Leiden: Brill, 1994), 144.

10:19 One indication that the third major unit of the epistle begins here is the proportionately higher use of the second person plural in this section as compared to the previous section. Second person plural pronouns occur a total of 12 times in Heb 1:1–10:18, but they occur 14 times in 10:19–13:25. Second person plural verbs occur 11 times in Heb 1:1–10:18, but they occur 26 times in 10:19–13:25. Second person plural imperatives occur 7 times in 1:1–10:18, but they occur 18 times in 10:19–13:25.[1] This highlights the hortatory nature of this section and serves as a cohesive device to bind the unit together as well. This heavy use of the second person plural supports Neeley's contention that the third major section of Hebrews, 10:19–13:25, is semantically the most dominant information in the discourse. She considers the preceding two sections to function in the role of grounds for the exhortation in 10:19–13:25:

1:1–4:13	grounds for 10:19–13:25
4:14–10:18	grounds for 10:19–13:25
10:19–13:25	Hortatory section with the most prominence in the discourse.[2]

Hebrews 10:19–39 is comprised of at least three paragraphs (vv. 19–25,26–31,32–39). Some divide the third paragraph into two: vv. 32–34,35–39. Lane divides the third paragraph into vv. 32–35 and vv. 36–39.[3] Lünemann observed the balance in 10:19–39 where the positive exhortation of 10:19–25 is followed by warning in 10:26–31 and encouragement in 10:32–34. In v. 35, the first exhortation of vv. 9–25 is given in negative form, followed by encouragement in vv. 36–37 and finally a warning in v. 38.[4]

The paragraph is a tightly knit logical and rhetorical unit that is actually one sentence in the Greek text. There is a lengthy introduction covering vv. 19–21 that functions to recall the argument of the preceding section in summary fashion. This is followed by three parallel hortatory subjunctives functioning as imperatives: "let us draw near," "let us hold unswervingly," and "let us consider how we may spur one another on." The NIV obscures the force and balance of these three main verbs by translating the two participles in v. 25 as hortatory subjunctives as well. Actually, the participles serve to modify the third hortatory subjunctive by telling the readers how they are to go about spurring one another on: by not giving up meeting together and by encouraging one another. The new paragraph is introduced with the conjunction *oun*, translated

[1] See Westfall, *Discourse Analysis,* 242.

[2] Neeley, "Discourse Analysis," 41.

[3] Lane, *Hebrews 9–13*, 281–82.

[4] G. Lünemann, *The Epistle to the Hebrews,* trans. from the 4th German ed., by M. Evans, *Critical and Exegetical Handbook to the New Testament*, ed. H. A. W. Meyer (NY: Funk & Wagnalls, 1885), 646–57.

"therefore."[5] It is followed by the vocative "Brothers," which oftentimes, as here, marks a paragraph onset. After a lengthy doctrinal section, the author shifts here to exhortation/application. The participle translated "since we have" is emphatic by being placed first in the clause and denotes the reason Christians have bold access to God. The present tense underscores that this bold access is currently present and ongoing. The "confidence" which we have is "to enter," (lit.) "unto the entrance," but accurately expressed by the infinitive "to enter." The focus is more on the means of access rather than the act of entering,[6] though both are true. That which we have confidence to enter is the "Most Holy Place," a reference to the sanctuary in heaven as contextually established from Heb 8:1–10:18. The means by which we have entrance is "the blood of Jesus," where the author again places the name "Jesus" last in the clause, probably for emphasis, as mentioned by Ellingworth.[7] A key word in this verse is "confidence," which denotes the objective idea of "authorization" granted by God by means of Christ's blood but also entails the subjective notion of "confidence" or "boldness."[8] Previously in Heb 4:16 the author exhorted the readers to "draw near to the throne of grace." Now they are presented with another ground for assurance: Jesus has opened the way for entrance.

10:20 Verse 20 is introduced with a relative pronoun whose antecedent could be connected with *hodon*, "way," as numerous translators do, but which is more likely connected with *eisodon* in v. 19.[9] This way has been "opened," in the sense of inaugurated or put into effect. The word can convey the notion of "consecrated" or "dedicated."[10] The author already used this word in 9:18 with reference to the inauguration of the new covenant. Here the word refers to the opening of a way that was previously unavailable. It is the "entrance" and the "way" which has been inaugurated, since "way" is in apposition to "entrance." This "way" is further qualified by "new," "living," and "through the curtain." The word "new" here in Greek etymologically means "to slaughter in advance," but by the time of the New Testament, the sacrificial metaphor was no longer primary, as indicated by the semantic range of the term with the

---

[5] This conjunction at least reaches back to 8:1, but as noted by P. Ellingworth, *The Epistle to the Hebrews*, NIGTC (Grand Rapids: Eerdmans, 1993), 517, it may reach back as far as 4:14.

[6] C. R. Koester, *Hebrews*, AB (New York: Doubleday, 2001), 442. Lane, *Hebrews 9–13*, 274, posited "[t]he expression has reference to the act of entering, and εἴσοδος carries the nuance of 'the right of entry' or 'access.'"

[7] Ellingworth, *Hebrews*, 518.

[8] See Schlier, "παρρησία," *TDNT* 5:884. L&N (307) note the word sometime implies "intimidating circumstances." Cf. Eph 3:12 for the concept expressed in a similar fashion by Paul.

[9] So H. Alford, "Prolegomena and Hebrews," *Alford's Greek Testament: An Exegetical and Critical Commentary*, part 1, 5th ed. (Boston: Lee & Shepard, 1878; repr., Grand Rapids: Guardian, 1976), 4:194; M. Dods, "Epistle to the Hebrews," in *The Expositor's Greek Testament*, ed. W. R. Nicoll (Grand Rapids: Eerdmans, 1974), 346; Moffatt, *Hebrews*, 142; Lane, *Hebrews 9–13*, 274; and Ellingworth, *Hebrews*, 518.

[10] See J. Behm, "εἴσοδος," *TDNT* 3:453–54.

meaning of "fresh" or "recent."[11] This "way" is also "living" in that it was pioneered by the ever-living high priest Jesus. Also inherent in the term may be the sense of "life-giving" in that it is our way to eternal life.[12] The third descriptive phrase, "through the curtain," can be construed with the verb "opened" or with the noun "way." Lane took it as connected with both.[13]

A difficult exegetical problem concerns the interpretation of the last phrase "through the curtain, that is, his body." The first issue concerns just what the clause "that is, his body," should be construed with. Some take it with "curtain" and others with "new and living way."[14] The latter is best argued by Westcott who suggested the meaning is "the way of his flesh."[15] With respect to the meaning of the overall clause, three options are possible. Many interpret "curtain" and "flesh" in apposition to one another. In this interpretation, the author would be using curtain as a metaphor for the flesh of Christ. A second option is best expressed in the NEB: "the new, living way which he has opened for us through the curtain, the way of his flesh."[16] A third suggestion takes "flesh" in an instrumental sense, as rendered by Lane in his translation: "through the curtain (that is to say, by means of his flesh)."[17] Lane grounds this reading on the threefold analogous structure of vv. 19–20 where "by the blood of Jesus"

---

[11] See L&N 58.73. See the discussion in Ellingworth, *Hebrews*, 518. Lane, *Hebrews 9–13*, 274, notes both the temporal and qualitative aspect of the description: it is "recent" and it is "fresh." The adverbial form occurs in Acts 18:2.

[12] See Ellingworth, *Hebrews*, 519, for the latter.

[13] Lane, *Hebrews 9–13*, 275.

[14] See Ellingworth, *Hebrews*, 251, for the various exegetical possibilities for the genitive τῆς σαρκός.

[15] Westcott, *Hebrews*, 320. Westcott takes the word "flesh" as modifying the entire clause "a fresh and living way through the veil" which he takes as a "compound noun." Cf. A. Nairne, *The Epistle of Priesthood* (Edinburgh: T&T Clark, 1913), 381.

[16] This is the view of W. G. Johnsson, "The Heavenly Cultus in the Book of Hebrews—Figurative or Real?" in *The Sanctuary and the Atonement: Biblical, Historical and Theological Studies*, ed. A. V. Wallenkampf & W. R. Lesher (Washington, DC: Review and Herald Publishing Association, 1981), 372–73. He asks the question if "veil" here means flesh, what are we to do with Heb 9:3, the "second veil?" A similar concern occurs with the use of καταπετάσματος in 6:19. He pointed out parallels between 6:19–20 and 10:19–20, 22:

Confidence "anchor of the soul"	Boldness
Christ entered	Christ inaugurated
High priest	Great Priest
Veil	Veil
Forerunner	For us . . . let us draw near

He concluded the best alternative is to see "way" as the referent, as in the NEB.

[17] Lane, *Hebrews 9–13*, 273. See his discussion of all the possible interpretations on 275. Cf. Hughes, *Hebrews*, 407–10 for patristic and medieval interpretations as well. E.g., both Chrysostom and J. Calvin, *The Epistle of Paul the Apostle to the Hebrews and the First and Second Epistles of Peter*, CNTC (Grand Rapids: Eerdmans, 1963), 141, took the clause to refer to the flesh of Jesus as the veil of his deity. Hughes correctly identified the inappropriateness of this interpretation.

in v. 19 parallels "that is, by means of his flesh" in v. 20.[18] This latter option comports best with the context. The sense is expressed by Guthrie: "As the old covenant priest had to pass through the veil, the new covenant people of God enter his presence via the sacrificial death of Christ."[19]

10:21 Verse 21 begins with *kai*, "and"; introduces the second direct object to the participle *echontes* in v. 19: "having therefore . . . boldness . . . and a great priest." This verse expresses a second ground or reason for the three command forms which immediately follow. The "great priest" is of course Jesus and is equivalent to calling him "high priest."[20] He is a great priest "over the house of God," where the preposition translated "over" connotes administration and responsibility for something. The phrase "house of God" refers to all of God's people, whether on earth or in heaven.[21]

10:22 Following these three introductory verses, the author lays down three commands[22] for the people in vv. 22–24: "draw near," "hold unswervingly," and "consider." The first command "let us draw near" has an implied indirect object that the NIV has supplied: "to God." "Draw near" occurs frequently in Hebrews and in the LXX, where it is used of the priests approaching God with a sacrifice for worship.[23] The idea is that of "approach" and the present tense[24] of the verb implies continuous or repeated approaching. There is a clear parallel here with Heb 4:16 where the identical verb form is used. There the focus is specifically on prayer, and this is included in the meaning of 10:22. However, given the overall context, it would appear the author has in mind all aspects of worship individually and corporately, with the focus here on corporate worship.[25]

---

[18] Lane, *Hebrews 9–13*, 275–76, "The structure of vv 19–20 calls for an interpretation of 'flesh' in an *instrumental* sense. The internal logic of the sentence presupposes a shift in thought from διά taken locally with τοῦ καταπετάσματος, 'the curtain,' to διά (unexpressed) taken instrumentally with τῆς σαρκὸς αὐτοῦ, 'his flesh.' The same variation in prepositional use, which is rhetorically motivated, occurs in 9:11–12. . . . Both v 19 and v 20 conclude with a reference to Jesus' sacrificial death as the means by which the way into the heavenly sanctuary was provided." In agreement are Attridge, *Hebrews*, 286–87; Ellingworth, *Hebrews*, 520–21; O. Hofius, *Der Vorhang vor dem Thron Gottes*, WUNT 14 (Tübingen: Mohr, 1972), 81; and N. H. Young, "τοῦτ' ἔστιν τῆς σαρκὸς αὐτοῦ (Hebr. X, 20): Apposition, Dependent or Explicative?", *NTS* 20 (1973): 100–4.

[19] G. Guthrie, *Structure of Hebrews*, 343.

[20] Jesus is called "great high priest" in 4:14. Some, such as Alford, "Hebrews," 195; Dods, "Hebrews," 346; and Hughes, *Hebrews*, 410, have suggested the term refers to the greatness of his priesthood without reference to his high priesthood. Bruce, *Hebrews*, 253; Lane, *Hebrews 9–13*, 285; and Ellingworth, *Hebrews*, 521–22, take it as referring to his high priesthood. Ellingworth, *Hebrews*, 522, indicated the use of "great priest" in 10:21 may indicate association with Lev 21:10, where the high priest is described in the LXX as τετελειώμενου.

[21] See 3:1–6, and Ellingworth, *Hebrews*, 522.

[22] Hortatory subjunctives in Greek: "Let us draw near," etc. Hortatory subjunctives are one step removed from a direct imperative.

[23] When this verb is used in a sacrificial context in the OT, it carries a technical sense where the priest approaches the altar to offer a sacrifice. See R. Daly, "New Testament Concept of Christian Sacrificial Activity," *BTB* 8 (1978): 106–7, and the discussion above on Heb 4:16.

[24] This conveys an iterative idea and not so much a progressive idea.

[25] Hence the first person plurals, "Let us."

The command to "draw near" is followed by four statements: two prepositional phrases which express the manner of one's drawing near, and two participial clauses expressing the basis on which we are allowed to approach God. Greenlee conveys the sense of the Greek word order: "let us approach with (a) true heart in full assurance of faith, sprinkled (with respect to) the hearts from (an) evil conscience and washed (with respect to) the body with pure water."[26] The manner by which we approach God is with a "sincere" heart, where "sincere" is the translation of a word meaning "true, genuine, sincere."[27] We are also to approach "in full assurance of faith," where the notion of "assurance" means "complete confidence, certainty" which is produced by "faith."[28] The two grounds for our drawing near in vv. 19–21 are both objective: an entrance by the blood of Jesus and a great priest over the house of God. Here in these two prepositional phrases is the subjective grounds for entrance: a sincere heart and full assurance produced by faith.[29] God has done his part so we can be enabled to do ours.

Verse 22 is rounded out with two perfect tense participles: "having our hearts sprinkled" and "having our bodies washed." Some have suggested that the first participle is governed by the verb "draw near" in v. 22 and the final participle is governed by the verb "hold unswervingly" in v. 23.[30] However, both participles should be construed together as dependent on the main verb "draw near," and the nominative case of each indicates they modify the subject of the verb, which is "us/we." They function to give the reasons why we can draw near with a sincere heart and full confidence: because we have been cleansed and washed. These are actions which have already been accomplished for us at the moment of conversion, when the atonement is applied to our hearts resulting in the objective forgiveness of sins, internal cleansing, and the concomitant deliverance from a guilty conscience.[31] This metaphorical language of sprinkling a heart emphasizes the internal nature of salvation in contrast to the external nature of the old covenant. It was precisely at this point, according to our author, where the old covenant failed. The "washing" of our bodies has usually been viewed as a reference to baptism. Calvin, however, rightly dissented from this,

---

[26] J. H. Greenlee, *An Exegetical Summary of Hebrews* (Dallas: Summer Institute of Linguistics, 1998), 389–93.

[27] See L&N 73.2.

[28] The genitive πίστεως is subjective: it is faith which precedes and produces the confidence. Some take it as a descriptive genitive: "fully assured faith." On πληροφορίᾳ, "full assurance," see BDAG 827 and L&N 31.45.

[29] Lünemann, *Hebrews*, 648, is incorrect in asserting "full inner certainty of faith" is a further description of the "sincere heart."

[30] So C. Moll, *The Epistle to the Hebrews*, in *Lange's Commentary on the Holy Scriptures*, trans. A. C. Kendrick (New York: Charles Scribner, 1868), 174–75; Lünemann, *Hebrews*, 648–49.

[31] All of these concepts were delineated as results of the final and complete atonement wrought by Christ in the preceding doctrinal section of Heb 8:1–10:18.

stating the author contextually is referring to the "old ceremonies of the law" where the priests had to wash at the laver in the tabernacle before beginning their daily duties. He also rightly connects the "washing" concept with other Old and New Testament passages which use this language to refer to cleansing by the Holy Spirit or the Word of God and not to baptism.[32] Guthrie correctly pointed out that our author "gives no overt signals that he has the Christian rite [of baptism] in mind," and that the author is continuing his use of the Old Testament imagery of purification from Hebrews 9.[33]

It has been suggested that the two participles, "sprinkling" and "washing" allude to the Lord's Supper and baptism respectively.[34] Such an interpretation is defeated by two facts. First, there is never any reference in the New Testament to the Lord's Supper being described in terms of sprinkling. Second, the use of the perfect tense precludes reference to the Lord's Supper since, unlike baptism, it is a repeatable ordinance of the local church.[35]

10:23 The second of three parallel commands occurs in v. 23: "Let us hold unswervingly."[36] That which Christians are to hold unswervingly is their "confession" or "profession," a noun in Greek which contains semantically an active idea of "profession" or "confession," hence the NIV translation "we profess."[37] This confession is the essence of the Christian faith. Its use here may be compared to Heb 4:14, but whereas there the usage probably indicates a technical term for a traditional confession of faith, here it is likely that it "refers more generally to the 'profession' of a definite, distinct belief."[38] The Greek phrase reads (lit.) "the confession of hope" and is rendered by the NIV "the hope we profess," where "hope" is seen as the object[39] of the confession rather than the

---

[32] Calvin, *Hebrews*, 142. Ezekiel 36:25–26 says, "I will sprinkle clean water upon you . . ." and "a new heart I will give you, and a new spirit I will put in you." Paul uses of this concept of "washing" in Eph 5:26 and Titus 3:5. Ellingworth, *Hebrews*, 523, also suggested the OT washings furnishes the background for the author's thought. For the case that the reference is to baptism, consult Bruce, *Hebrews*, 254–55; Hughes, *Hebrews*, 411–12 and Lane, *Hebrews 9–13*, 287.

[33] G. Guthrie, *Structure of Hebrews*, 344.

[34] So F. Delitzsch, *Commentary on the Epistle to the Hebrews,* trans. T. L. Kingsbury (Edinburgh: T&T Clark, 1872; repr., Grand Rapids: Eerdmans, 1952), *2*:178–79; and Westcott, *Hebrews*, 323.

[35] So Bruce, *Hebrews*, 255; and Hughes, *Hebrews*, 412.

[36] On the meaning of this verb and the concept of "holding fast" expressed by a different but related verb, see the discussion at 4:14 and C. Spicq, "κατέχω," *TLNT* 2:288. Ellingworth, *Hebrews*, 524–25, identified three complementary aspects involved in the meaning of "holding fast:" (1) subjective—the reader's confidence; (2) objective—God's promise to believers including the oath by which Christ was established a high priest; and (3) witnessing—as evidenced by the use of ὁμολογία in Heb 3:1. Ellingworth perceptively noted that in the latter two, both God's action and human response "are described in linguistic terms."

[37] See also L&N 33.274; and Lane's translation (*Hebrews 9–13*, 273).

[38] So Lane, *Hebrews 9–13*, 288.

[39] Objective genitive in Greek. Lane, *Hebrews 9–13*, 288, compared the first part of v. 23 to Heb 6:18 rather than 4:14, since in the former the reference is to "an objective reality related to the priestly activity of Jesus. In Hebrews, the term 'hope' always describes the objective content of

subjective act of "hoping." Another alternative is to view "hope" in apposition to the noun "confession," as did Ellingworth.[40] The use of the definite article in the Greek text may imply the possessive idea "our hope."[41] This confession is to be held "unswervingly," that is, in an unwavering manner. Some interpret the Greek adjective as describing the firmness of the confession itself.[42] It is better to take it in an adverbial sense, as does Koester.[43] Finally, the verse concludes with a declaration of the faithfulness of God who has made the promise. The final clause is introduced by *gar*, "for," and indicates the grounds for the exhortation to "hold unswervingly." The adjective "faithful" is fronted in the clause for emphasis (lit.): "Faithful is the one who promised." The word in Greek also connotes constancy. Believers can count on God standing behind his promise, hence the reason we can "hold unswervingly" to the confession of our hope.

10:24–25 The paragraph concludes with the third imperatival idea in vv. 24–25. The verb "let us consider" conveys the concept of careful consideration, thoughtful attention and deep concern. The latter is reflected in Lane's translation, following Pelser, "keep on caring for one another."[44]

The verb is followed by the direct object "one another," expressing the mutual reciprocity of members of the Christian community in the act of careful consideration. This action is for the purpose[45] of "spurring" each other on to an attitude of love that is then expressed in outward "good deeds." The noun in Greek is the picturesque *paroxusmon*,[46] "spur one another on," which denotes intense emotion, almost always with a negative connotation. It is often linked with anger or disagreement. Because of this, the noun is often translated as a verb, as in the NIV's "to spur."

Other words that can be used to render the idea are "stimulation," "incitement," "rouse," "stir up" and "provoke." The goal of this provocation is expressed in the compound "love and good deeds."[47] The author connected love

---

hope, consisting of present and future salvation." So also E. Grässer, *Der Glaube im Hebräerbrief* (Marburg: N. G. Elwert Verlag, 1965), 32–33.

[40] Thus, "the confession, which is the hope." Ellingworth, *Hebrews*, 525.

[41] So Alford, "Hebrews," 197; and Bruce, *Hebrews*, 256.

[42] E.g., Alford, "Hebrews," 197; Bruce, *Hebrews*, 256; and Attridge, *Hebrews*, 289.

[43] Koester, *Hebrews*, 445, reasoned: "Since the 'confession' has a definite article, whereas 'unwavering' does not, the adverbial sense is preferable." Lane, *Hebrews 9–13*, 289, used the words "firm," "stable," "fixed" and "steadfast" to define its meaning.

[44] Lane, *Hebrews 9–13*, 273; G. Pelser, "A Translation Problem—Heb. 10:19–25," *Neot* 8 (1974): 50–51. See Balz and Schneider, *EDNT* 2:265; L&N 30.43, and note the same word was used in Heb 3:1: "consider Jesus." Don't miss the rhetorical technique of the author here as he "stimulates thought by putting a word with negative connotations to positive use" (Koester, *Hebrews*, 445).

[45] Εἰς followed by an accusative object connotes "for the purpose of." See L&N 89.57.

[46] See L&N 90.55; BDAG 780; H. Seesemann, "παροξυσμός," *TDNT* 5:857, where he notes the word was used of an irritation or even a fever. The word in modern English is a medical term meaning a violent shaking.

[47] Possibly a hendiadys, as "good works are the direct expression of love" (Ellingworth, *Hebrews*, 527).

with good works in Heb 6:10. The connection is replete in the New Testament. The order is important: love is the internal attitude and spiritual disposition that expresses itself in outward tangible good works.

The command to consider one another to stimulate them to love and good deeds is modified in v. 25 by two contrasting present tense participles, (lit.) "not forsaking . . . but encouraging." Lane described the former word as "a singularly strong expression in Koine Gk, signifying 'to desert,' 'to abandon,' 'to leave in the lurch' (2 Tim 4:10)," but offered a rather timid translation of "not discontinuing."[48] Bruce translated it "to abandon."[49]

What they are not to abandon is *episunagōgēn heautōn,* (lit.) "the assembling of ourselves" (NIV "meeting together") referring more to the activity of assembling than the assembled group itself.[50] Some disagreement exists, however, over the nature and meaning of the Greek term *episunagōgēn*, which is the Greek term *sunagōgē*, "place of assembly, synagogue," with the prefixed preposition *epi*. Some incorrectly assert that the prefix indicates the assembling occurred at a certain place.[51] Others take it as implying the notion of "together."[52] Calvin committed the etymological fallacy of taking the preposition to indicate "an addition" and therefore the word "has the force of a congregation increased by new additions."[53] Manson suggested the prefix *epi* indicates something of a group of Jewish believers who had not yet severed the ties with the synagogue, but who were, in addition to their synagogue attendance, meeting together as a "Christian appendage to the Jewish synagogue," and were in danger of "dissolving back into the general life of the Jewish community."[54] This is a weight the preposition simply cannot bear. Most likely the author did not intend any such implications by his use of the term. However, Manson's general thesis may still have merit. It is possible, given the obvious root of the word, that the author was contrasting the Christian assembly with the Jewish assembly, or that he was stressing the actual continuity between Israel and the church as the people of God. Koester suggested there may be eschatological connotations to the term in that both the noun and its verbal form (*episunagō*, "bring together") were used in the New Testament "for the eschatological ingathering of Israel."[55]

---

[48] Lane, *Hebrews 9–13*, 276.

[49] Bruce, *Hebrews*, 249.

[50] So Bruce, *Hebrews*, 257; Hughes, *Hebrews*, 415; and Lane, *Hebrews 9–13*, 273, 289; against Moffatt, *Hebrews*, 147–48. On the word itself, consult W. Schrage, "ἐπισυναγωγή," *TDNT* 7:841–43; and *TLNT* 2.63–64.

[51] So K. Wuest, "Hebrews in the Greek New Testament," in *Word Studies in the Greek New Testament*, 2:182; Koester, *Hebrews*, 446.

[52] So T. Hewitt, *The Epistle to the Hebrews: An Introduction and Commentary* (London: Tyndale, 1960), 164.

[53] Calvin, *Hebrews*, 143.

[54] W. Manson, *The Epistle to the Hebrews: an Historical and Theological Reconsideration*, (London: Hodder & Stoughton, 1951), 69. Bruce, *Hebrews*, 258, considers Manson's thesis possible.

[55] E.g., 2 Thess 2:1. Koester, *Hebrews*, 446: "Since the context refers to the coming Day of the Lord and since the listeners understood that they already shared in the powers of the age to come

Of course, there may be none of these connotations associated with the word, and the author may be merely urging his readers not to forsake the meetings of the church, as the next phrase "as some are in the habit of doing" indicates.[56] Hughes's comment that such unconcern for fellow believers "argues unconcern for Christ himself and portends the danger of apostasy" is reading one's presupposition into the text as no such statement is made overtly or even implied by the author in this verse.[57] Alford and Lange more accurately reflect the author's meaning when they suggest the participial phrase means negligence, not apostasy.[58]

The negative participle concerning failure to meet together is followed by a participle which positively instructs the readers to "encourage one another." The word connotes both notions of encouragement and exhortation. Ellingworth takes it as indicating "urgent insistence (13:19)."[59] They are to do this "by so much more by as much as,"[60] which is the literal rendering of the Greek phrase. The meaning is they are to encourage one another and more so in comparison as they see "the day" approaching, which is smoothed out in the NIV as "and all the more as you see the Day approaching." Alford takes the phrase as modifying both preceding participles in v. 25.[61]

What does the author mean by his use of the approaching "day"? Two major possibilities exist. The "day" may refer to the impending destruction of the city of Jerusalem if the author were writing just prior to AD 70.[62] Another option is to interpret the term to refer to the eschatological "day of judgment" at the time of the second coming of Christ. This day, known in the New Testament as the "Day of the Lord" (found many times in the Gospels, as well as in Acts

---

(Heb 6:5), they may have understood their gathering to anticipate the final ingathering of God's people. The assembly is the earthly counterpart to the heavenly 'congregation' (ἐκκλησία) of God's people (12:23; cf. 2:12)." For other interpretations, see the note on the meaning of ἐπισυναγωγή in Hughes, *Hebrews*, 417–18.

[56] Hughes, *Hebrews*, 418, most likely captures the meaning of the term "as simply the regular gathering together of Christian believers for worship and exhortation in a particular place."

[57] Hughes, *Hebrews*, 415.

[58] Alford, "Hebrews," 198; Moll in Lange's *Hebrews*, 175.

[59] Ellingworth, *Hebrews*, 529.

[60] So Greenlee, *Exegetical Summary*, 398.

[61] Alford, "Hebrews," 198. Lane, *Hebrews 9–13*, 290, takes the phrase as implying the reason they are to encourage one another: because they see the day approaching.

[62] Bruce, *Hebrews*, 258–59, provides one of the best arguments for this possibility. The 40 years in the wilderness corresponds to the 40 years from crucifixion to the destruction of Jerusalem in AD 70. Numbers 14 may be the key not only to 3:7–4:13, but also to 10:25. Faith and endurance which the author emphasizes in 10:19–12:29 are the answer to the failure of Israel in the wilderness. If the author is writing after the death of Peter and Paul in the later part of the decade of the sixties, he might have heard that the Roman army is moving toward Jerusalem. Hebrews 10:25 could be a veiled warning to flee before the destruction that Jesus predicted in Luke 21:20–24. Luke 21:25–28 uses language similar to Hebrews: "men will faint," "coming on the world" [οἰκουμένη]," "shaken," "stand up and lift up your heads." Cf. Luke 10:19—"by your endurance you will gain your life."

2:20; 1 Cor 3:13; 1 Thess 5:2; 2 Thess 2:2; Jude 6; Rev 6:17; and many other places in the New Testament), is an eschatological day that comes when Christ returns to the earth and brings judgment.

With this final word, the author closes this vital summary paragraph of the epistle through Heb 10:18. He has exhorted his readers to three critical actions based on the theological teaching thus far. With the third exhortation to consider how they may spur one another on to love and good deeds, the author paves the way for the themes he developed in chaps. 11–13.

(2) Dangers of Deliberate Sin (10:26–34)

**[26]If we deliberately keep on sinning after we have received the knowledge of the
truth, no sacrifice for sins is left, [27]but only a fearful expectation of judgment and
of raging fire that will consume the enemies of God. [28]Anyone who rejected the law
of Moses died without mercy on the testimony of two or three witnesses. [29]How
much more severely do you think a man deserves to be punished who has trampled
the Son of God under foot, who has treated as an unholy thing the blood of the covenant that sanctified him, and who has insulted the Spirit of grace? [30]For we know
him who said, "It is mine to avenge; I will repay," and again, "The Lord will judge
his people." [31]It is a dreadful thing to fall into the hands of the living God.**

**[32]Remember those earlier days after you had received the light, when you stood
your ground in a great contest in the face of suffering. [33]Sometimes you were publicly exposed to insult and persecution; at other times you stood side by side with
those who were so treated. [34]You sympathized with those in prison and joyfully
accepted the confiscation of your property, because you knew that you yourselves
had better and lasting possessions.**

Hebrews 10:26–31 is the second major paragraph of this section and also constitutes the fourth warning passage in Hebrews. The paragraph addresses the consequences of "willful sin" in the most severe tones. It is introduced by the subordinating conjunction *gar*, which is left untranslated in the NIV. This conjunction functions to indicate 10:26–31 serves as the grounds for either the entire preceding paragraph or at least for the warning expressed in v. 25.[63] The adverb translated "deliberately" is placed sentence initial in the Greek text for emphasis. There is a clear semantic link with 10:18 where "sin" and the concept of "no longer any sacrifice for sin" occur.

10:26 Three propositions are encoded in v. 26: (1) reception of the knowledge of the truth; (2) in spite of this, one continues to sin willfully; and (3) consequently, no sacrifice for sin remains. The present tense participle in Greek, *hamartanontōn*, is correctly rendered conditionally as "if we keep on sinning." The author uses "we" to include himself with his readers. Such language

[63] Both Dods, "Hebrews," 348; and R. C. H. Lenski, *The Interpretation of the Epistle to the Hebrews and of the Epistle of James* (Columbus, OH: Wartburg, 1946), 356, connect it with v. 25. Ellingworth, *Hebrews*, 532, also thinks it should be connected with the completed argument in 10:18.

strongly indicates the warning is addressed to believers. Another significant matter is the author's lexical choice for the concept of sin. Unlike what we found in the warnings of Heb 3:12 and 6:4–6, the author does not use the words *apostēnai* or *parapiptō*. We have already seen how many interpret these passages to refer to apostasy, either on the part of those who were genuinely converted and lost their salvation (the Arminian view), or those who were not genuinely converted and who apostatized in the sense of repudiating Christ and forsaking the Christian community (the Reformed view). We have argued against both of these interpretations of the warning passages heretofore. One might reasonably ask: if the author had in mind the same kind of sin here as there—as seems evident since most agree, regardless of how they interpret the warning passages, that they all should be grouped together as warning against essentially the same sin)—[64] then why does he use the common word for "sin" and not something stronger in the context? The third significant point to note is the use of the present tense of the participle coupled with the adverb "deliberately,"[65] which indicates two things: ongoing sin and willful sin. This is said to occur after one has received "the knowledge of the truth," a phrase which is descriptive of the gospel and which refers to genuine conversion (see discussion on 6:4). Bruce noted this recurring phrase "knowledge of the truth" in the Pastoral Epistles and similarly in the Johannine writings.[66] A straightforward interpretation of this phrase would take it to refer to believers. Osborne correctly pointed out the strong term *epignōsis* here for "knowledge" coupled with "truth" means believers, but then errs when he concluded this "favors the view that apostasy entails true believers denying their faith."[67]

The author may have in mind Num 15:27–31 where sacrifice is available for unintentional sins, but for "high-handed" sins no sacrifice is available. Ellingworth is on target when, despite the use of "deliberately," he said, "the author does not develop a distinction between sins which can be forgiven and those which cannot."[68] The key question which must be answered is what does the author mean by the phrase "no sacrifice for sins is left"? Contextually, this statement must be compared to 10:18. The adverb translated "no" can be construed with the verb "is left," or it can be treated as an adjective modifying "sacrifice." The difference in overall meaning is negligible. One thing is clear: under the Mosaic covenant, the penalty for willful sin was physical death. In

[64] E.g., Lane compares this passage with Heb 6:4–8 where the same four-part structure is evident: (1) knowledge of the truth, (2) willful sin, (3) impossibility of renewal, and (4) the prospect of judgment (*Hebrews 9–13*, 291); and see S. McKnight, "The Warning Passages of Hebrews: A Formal Analysis and Theological Conclusions," *TJ* 13 NS, no. 1 (1992), 21–59, who conclusively showed that the warning passages all address the same sin and should be viewed together.

[65] BDAG 307. The only other occurrence of the Greek adverb ἑκουσίως is 1 Pet 5:2.

[66] Bruce, *Hebrews*, 261.

[67] G. Osborne, "A Classical Arminian View," in *Four Views on the Warning Passages in Hebrews*, ed. H. W. Bateman IV (Grand Rapids: Kregel, 2007), 120.

[68] Ellingworth, *Hebrews*, 531.

Numbers 15, soteriology is not the issue. The issue is what happens when one violated the Mosaic covenant. For example, in Num 15:32–36, a man found picking up sticks on the Sabbath day was in violation of the Mosaic law. The penalty for such was severe according to Exod 31:14–15: the person was to be "cut off," where the clear meaning is "put to death." That this scenario from the Old Testament is in the author's mind in Heb 10:26 is confirmed by his statement in 10:28 that one who has violated the law of Moses dies without mercy "on the testimony of two or three witnesses." Gleason sums up the meaning of the author of Hebrews:

> Far from a public repudiation of belief in Christ, the sin in view denotes any deliberate act of covenant unfaithfulness, including in the Old Testament context even the seemingly harmless act of picking up sticks on the Sabbath. The gravity of the sin is determined by the defiant attitude with which it is committed. However, the penalty is not eternal damnation but rather physical punishment resulting in death.[69]

In comparison, the author of Hebrews states that willful sin committed after conversion creates a situation where there is no sacrifice for sins available just as there was none available in the Old Testament for willful disobedience to God under the Mosaic covenant. The point is that new covenant believers cannot presume upon the salvation brought to them in Christ to cause God to overlook their willful disobedience. Just as in Numbers 15, so too here in Hebrews 10, judgment does not result in loss of salvation, nor does the text overtly say it does.

The question as to the referent of the willful sin has caused commentators much difficulty since the author does not define it. Contextually, we may conclude that failure to draw near, hold fast, and to stir up one another to love and good deeds because of habitual absence from the community is at least part of the willful sin.[70] The answer to the question of the meaning of the phrase "no sacrifice for sins is left" must take into account the immediate context of the following verse, which presents the opposite that can be expected—judgment—and the larger context of the meaning of the other warning passages. The usual interpretation given follows this line of reasoning: since Jesus is the only sacrifice that can deal with sin and place one in a right relationship with God, to sin willfully means in essence to apostatize, an act which cuts one off from Jesus and his sacrifice which is the only means of salvation. To accept

[69] R. C. Gleason, "A Moderate Reformed View," in *Four Views on the Warning Passages in Hebrews*, ed. H. W. Bateman IV (Grand Rapids: Kregel, 2007), 359.

[70] See T. K. Oberholtzer, "The Danger of Willful Sin in Hebrews 10:26–39," *BSac* 145 (1988): 412–13. Cf. G. Mora, *La Carta a los Hebreos como Escrito Pastoral*, (Sección de San Paciano: Facultad de Teolog'a de Barcelona,1974), 91–96, who dissents with the view that 10:26 means apostasy alone, but rather that it is inclusive of other serious sins.

the sacrifice of Jesus and then to reject it willfully is to cut oneself off from the only means of salvation. When this is done, one has no other option than to face "judgment," which is taken to mean eternal punishment.[71] Before we look at another way of interpreting this verse, we need to examine the rest of the paragraph.

10:27 Verse 27 says the only thing left or remaining (implied from the previous verse) for such willful sin is a "fearful expectation of judgment" and "a raging fire that will consume the enemies of God." The Greek text uses an indefinite pronoun which would be translated "some" but which is left untranslated by the NIV, and which is said to be a rhetorical device whereby the author heightens the terror of the coming judgment.[72] This expectation of judgment is "fearful," meaning "terrifying." The adjective is placed clause initial for emphasis. The NIV's "raging fire" is (lit.) "zeal of fire," where "fire" is in the genitive case in Greek. It can be taken descriptively or in apposition with "zeal." The entire phrase is best interpreted as explaining the preceding statement (so Ellingworth), rather than as being parallel to "judgment."[73] Most take the reference here to "fire" as eternal judgment, but many commentators are reluctant to state overtly whether this is a reference to hell or not.[74] That fire in the Old Testament can refer to God's anger towards his own people is clear from Isa 9:18–19 and 10:17. In explaining Heb 10:31, Bruce makes reference to Isa 33:14: "Who among us can dwell with the devouring fire? Who among us can dwell with everlasting burnings?"[75] Preferable to taking "fire" here as a reference to eternal judgment is to view the author's comments against the backdrop of the Old Testament, since the metaphor of fire is used there to refer to God's anger against even his covenant people. Here in v. 27 the author is alluding to Isa 26:11, whose wider context refers not to eternal punishment but to physical destruction coming upon the land and people due to their sin.[76] This judgment is said by the author "to be about to" (*mellontos*) fall upon the "adversaries," which the NIV renders as "enemies of God," where "God" is implied in the

[71] E.g., Calvin, *Hebrews*, 146: "It is clear from the context that the apostle is referring here only to apostates." Bruce, *Hebrews*, 261; Hughes, *Hebrews*, 418–21; Lane, *Hebrews 9–13*, 291–93; Ellingworth, *Hebrews*, 530–33; and Koester, *Hebrews*, 452, concurred.

[72] So Moffatt, *Hebrews*, 150; Lane, *Hebrews 9–13*, 277; and Ellingworth, *Hebrews*, 534; all of whom are following the Greek grammars.

[73] Greenlee, *Exegetical Summary*, 403, rightly observed the nominative ζῆλος, "zeal," "is erroneously translated as a genitive, and this phrase is thus mistakenly made parallel to κρίσεως 'judgment,'" as do Bruce, *Hebrews*, 260; Lane, *Hebrews 9–13*, 273; and the NIV. The author may have Isa 26:11 in mind, since he will quote from the same Isaianic chapter in Heb 10:37.

[74] One exception is H. Kent, *The Epistle to the Hebrews: A Commentary* (Grand Rapids: Baker, 1972), 205.

[75] Bruce, *Hebrews*, 265.

[76] See E. J. Young, *The Book of Isaiah* (Grand Rapids: Eerdmans, 1969), 2:217; and Gleason, "A Moderate Reformed View," 363.

text. Calvin's novel interpretation of "fire" in this verse is generally rejected.[77] Paul in 1 Cor 3:15 warns of Christians who at the time of judgment will "suffer loss . . . but only as one escaping through the flames." Here the loss is not salvation, and fire is being used metaphorically for judgment of those who are Christians and who enter heaven after the judgment.[78]

One interesting fact frequently missed by those who view the warning passages as referring to eternal judgment on apostates is the absence of the adjective "eternal" connected with the judgment mentioned in the warning passages. Given the frequency of the use of this adjective throughout the New Testament to speak of eternal judgment ("eternal fire," Matt 18:8; 25:41; "eternal punishment," Matt 25:46; "everlasting destruction," 2 Thess 1:9; "punishment of eternal fire," Jude 7), and given the frequency of the use of "eternal" in Hebrews itself, the absence of the term in the warning passages is significant.[79]

10:28 Verse 28 and v. 29 function together as a lesser to greater argument. Verse 28 illustrates the principle of judgment from the exodus generation in an allusion to Deut 17:6 and 19:15. There is an interesting shift in tense in the Greek text from the aorist participle "rejecting" (NIV "rejected") to the present indicative "dies" (NIV "died").[80] This punishment by death was "without mercy" and "on the testimony of two or three witnesses," as prescribed in the Mosaic law. The point of this verse is that the Mosaic law provided for a death penalty. What is evident from the Old Testament is the fact, however, that this penalty was applied to a variety of sins, ranging from picking up sticks on the Sabbath day to idolatry and murder.[81] It should be observed that the issue in the Old Testament was not soteriological, as is often assumed. If the penalty of death in the Old Testament always signified eternal rejection by God, then not only the idolater and murder, but the one who picked up sticks on the Sabbath day, was eternally lost as well.

10:29 Here the lesser to greater argument is completed by a rhetorical question. The Greek (lit.) reads, "by how much more do you think he will be considered worthy of severer punishment." Greenlee suggested that the dative pronoun *posō*, "by how much," should be connected with the main verb

---

[77] Calvin, *Hebrews*, 147: "a forceful impulse or a violent passion. Just as unbelievers are now inflamed by the fear of divine wrath, so they will then burn with the same feeling."

[78] See D. Garland, *1 Corinthians* (Grand Rapids: Baker, 2003), 117–18. Cf. N. Geisler, "A Moderate Calvinist View," in *Four Views on Eternal Security*, ed. J. M. Pinson (Grand Rapids: Zondervan, 2002), 99–100, who read this reference to "fiery judgment" in Hebrews in the light of 1 Cor 3:15.

[79] So noted by Gleason, "A Moderate Reformed View," 361.

[80] Lane interpreted the present tense here to be frequentive, indicating the death of individuals from time to time (Lane, *Hebrews 9–13*, 277). Ellingworth, *Hebrews*, 536–37, following MHT 1:114, viewed the present tense as signifying the "permanent record of scripture."

[81] In light of the clear teaching of the Pentateuch, Calvin's error in the following statement is remarkable: "The law did not punish any kind of transgression by death but only apostasy when a man departed completely from his religion" (Calvin, *Hebrews*, 148).

and not "erroneously translated as a genitive and connected with the genitive *cheironos timōrias*, 'worse punishment,'" as in many commentators and most translations.[82] "Do you think" serves as an appeal to the readers' "sense of appropriateness" by appearing to give them "the privilege of making the decision, but without indicating any doubt of the appropriate response."[83] The subject of the main verb "will deserve" (lit. "will be counted worthy") consists of a compound relative clause governed by a single article ("who") but with three substantival aorist participles:[84] "trampled [the Son of God under foot]," "treated [as an unholy thing the blood of the covenant that sanctified him]," and "insulted [the Spirit of grace]." To "trample under foot" means to treat with disdain and contempt. In the Greek text, the object phrase "the Son of God" is fronted in the clause for emphasis and heightens the abject revulsion of such an act.

The willful sinner also treats the precious, sacred blood of Christ, which inaugurated the new covenant and by which he was sanctified, as something common and profane, "an unholy thing." The phrase "blood of the covenant" comes directly from the LXX of Exod 24:8 and has already been cited by the author in Heb 9:20. This blood "sanctified" the individual,[85] a reference back to Heb 10:10,14. In light of this, it seems virtually impossible to interpret the author as referring here to someone who is not a Christian. In fact, Lane indicated this phrase "corroborates that 10:26–31 is descriptive of the Christian who has experienced the action of Christ upon his life."[86] Guthrie is an example of many who, forced by preconceived theological notions that apostates are referred to in this passage, are compelled to mitigate the clear meaning of this sanctification: "Based on broader contextual concerns we translate the phrase 'that sanctified him' as 'by which one is sanctified,' suggesting that those in this condition in reality have not been sanctified by Christ. Those who truly have been sanctified by the offering of the Son of God have been perfected for all time (10:14)."[87] What are these "broader contextual concerns"? With Guthrie, as with all who approach the text from a Reformed framework following Calvin and Owen, there is no alternative but to interpret the text in this way. But the author makes it clear, not only here but also in Heb 10:10,14, Christians have been, as Guthrie correctly stated, "perfected for all time." This passage illustrates once again the tension between Calvinists and Arminians when it comes to the warning passages in Hebrews. Arminians interpret the passages

---

[82] Greenlee, *Exegetical Summary*, 407.

[83] Ibid.

[84] Lane, *Hebrews 9–13*, 294, takes the aorist participles as summarizing a persistent attitude.

[85] R. Ward, *The Pattern of Our Salvation: A Study of New Testament Unity* (Waco: Word Books, 1978), 68, correctly affirmed: "If a man with faith received the knowledge of the truth, he was thereupon (note the aorist) sanctified by the blood of the covenant (10:26, 29)."

[86] Ibid.

[87] G. Guthrie, *Structure of Hebrews*, 357.

as meaning loss of eternal salvation (explaining away the myriad of verses to the contrary in the New Testament), and most Calvinists wrongly conclude that these severe warnings cannot possibly be addressed to those who are genuine Christians.[88]

It is an interesting fact, as observed by Gleason, that the only two passages in the New Testament that speak of judgment due to mistreatment of the blood of the covenant are 1 Cor 11:25–30 and Heb 10:27–29. Paul warned the Corinthian believers that some were guilty of profaning the body and the blood of the Lord due to their unworthy behavior in partaking of the Lord's Supper. This behavior resulted in some of the Corinthian believers being "judged." In fact, 1 Cor 11:30 goes on to describe this judgment: many were "weak" and "sick" and some had "fallen asleep [i.e., died]."[89] Gleason compared this to the statement in Heb 6:6 that those who had "fallen away" were "crucifying the Son of God":

> The only difference was that among the Corinthians some were held guilty of Christ's death for drinking from the cup of the new covenant "in an unworthy Manner" (1 Cor. 11:27), while the readers of Hebrews were in danger of the same guilt for their neglect of the Christian assembly (Heb. 10:25; 13:16), which is sanctified by "the blood of the covenant" (Heb. 10:29; cf. 13:20). Neither act involved a public renunciation of faith in Christ, yet in both cases the perpetrators were held guilty of his death in a way that demanded judgment.[90]

Finally, the willful sinner has insulted the Holy Spirit of grace. The reference may be an allusion to Zech 12:10 in the LXX. Contextually, as Lane suggested, this would then be the author's way of referring to the Holy Spirit being poured out at Pentecost.[91] To "insult" the Spirit is to treat him with insolence and arrogance by disregarding his work of saving grace in one's life.[92]

10:30–31 The author concludes this paragraph with an appeal again to Scripture as he has done so many times throughout the epistle. Two quotations (v. 30) and a comment (v. 31) round out the paragraph. The use of *gar* "for" indicates the grounds for the warning. In fact, the warning should be taken by

---

[88] Nor have the valiant efforts of Schreiner and Caneday, *The Race Set Before Us* (Downers Grove: InterVarsity, 2001), extricated them from the horns of this same dilemma as we have seen in the discussion of Heb 6:4–6.

[89] R. C. Gleason, "Moderate Reformed Response," in *Four Views on the Warning Passages in Hebrews*, ed. H. W. Bateman IV (Grand Rapids: Kregel, 2007), 251–52.

[90] Ibid., 252.

[91] Lane, *Hebrews 9–13*, 294.

[92] Ellingworth, *Hebrews*, 541, took the genitive χάριτος "grace" as adjectival: "the gracious Spirit." D. Guthrie, *Hebrews*, TNTC, 219, and others take it as indicating it is grace which the Spirit gives. Kistemaker takes it in both ways simultaneously. Whatever the author's intention, the phrase serves as a reference to the Holy Spirit and his involvement in the salvation event, especially from a subjective perspective (the working of grace in the life of a believer).

the readers as serious, since it is God himself who has said he will punish in this fashion. Deut 32:35 speaks of vengeance as belonging to the Lord and that he will repay; Deut 32:36 asserts "the Lord will judge his people."[93] In the first quotation, the order of the Greek text emphasizes that God is the one who will judge: "to me belongs vengeance; I (myself) will repay." The point might be expressed this way: "To me (and to no other) does vengeance belong; I (and no other) will repay."[94] Whereas Deuteronomy speaks of God judging the enemies of Israel, the author of Hebrews applies these quotations as a warning concerning God judging his own people.[95]

Verse 31 functions as a summary conclusion at least for the warning of the previous verse and probably of the entire paragraph. It speaks of how "dreadful" it is to fall into God's hands in judgment. The predicate adjective "dreadful" is placed first in the sentence for emphasis. The word connotes "fear," "dread," and "terror." The arresting expression "the living God"[96] occurs only here and in 3:12 and 9:14 in the epistle. Interestingly, in 3:12, what is to be feared is turning away from God; here it is falling into his hands which should be feared. Bruce asserted the possibility that 2 Sam 24:14, where David says "Let us fall into the hand of the LORD, for his mercy is great," might have been in the author's mind and suggested the form of the words he chose.[97] Swetnam's attempt to turn this verse upon its head and interpret it as a positive statement about the "awesome" experience of being "judged" unto salvation needs no refutation.[98]

10:32 A new paragraph begins with v. 32 and continues to the end of the chapter. The paragraph contains two sub-paragraphs: 10:32–34 and 10:35–39. Westfall observed the formal shift that takes place between vv. 26–31 and vv. 32–39 in terms of "person, tense, temporal reference and semantic shift from warning to confidence. While vv. 26–31 are characterized by the third person present indicative and temporal reference to the present, vv. 32–39 are characterized by a second person plural aorist imperative[99] and a temporal

[93] The variation from the LXX in the first quotation is identical in Paul's quotation of the same verse in Rom 12:19. On the textual issues involved in both quotations, see Ellingworth, *Hebrews*, 541–43.

[94] R. Ward, *Pattern of Salvation*, 34.

[95] Koester, *Hebrews*, 453. Bruce, *Hebrews*, 265: "These words have no doubt been used frequently as a warning to the ungodly of what lies in store for them unless they amend their ways; but their primary application is to the people of God." J. A. Thompson, *Deuteronomy*, TOTC (Downers Grove: InterVarsity, 1974), 502–3, writes concerning the use of Deut 32:35 in Heb 10:30: "But God's own people were not exempt from this law and should expect to reap judgment where they had 'profaned' the blood of the covenant by which (they were) sanctified, and outraged the Spirit of grace (Heb. 10:29)."

[96] Ellingworth, *Hebrews*, 544, interpreted "living" to refer to God as the "source of life."

[97] Bruce, *Hebrews*, 266.

[98] J. Swetnam, "Hebrews 10, 30–31: A Suggestion," *Bib* 75.3 (1994): 388–94.

[99] Lane, *Hebrews 9–13*, 277, makes the interesting point that this is the first imperative (excluding hortatory subjunctives) since 7:4.

references to the past."[100] Lane charted the parallels between the warning of 6:4–6 and 10:26–31 and the parallels between the encouragement of 6:9–12 and 10:32–36.[101] The clearest parallels are between 6:10 and 10:33, where the readers are said to have demonstrated love and service to fellow believers, and 6:12 and 10:36, where the concept of "inheriting the promise" is given. Rhee argued for a chiastic arrangement of 10:32–39:

A In the past you have endured the suffering after you have been enlightened, realizing that you have a better possession (10:32–24)
  B Therefore, do not throw away your confidence which has a great reward (10:35)
A´ In the present time you need to have endurance, in order that you may receive the promise of God, after having done the will of God (10:36–39)[102]

Verse 32 begins with *de*, "but," which also signals a shift by contrast with the previous paragraph. In contrast to the warning of the previous paragraph, the author now utters words of encouragement to his readers. He calls on them to think back to former days, meaning the time when they heard the gospel and became Christians, when their faithfulness to Christ was exhibited by their own attitude and actions in the face of persecution. The aorist participle is temporal and is translated "after you had received the light." Both the NIV and Lane connect this participle with the preceding noun phrase: the former days after you were enlightened.[103] Virtually all other translations connect it with the following verb "endured" (in the Greek text), translated as "stood your ground." This notion of endurance will surface overtly in 11:27 in reference to Moses who endured, and again in 12:1–3, where the word itself will occur three times within the span of three verses. The author connects this endurance of persecution metaphorically to an athletic contest,[104] again a reference which will resurface in 12:2.

10:33–34 Verses 33–34 highlight the readers' public exposure to insult and persecution, their solidarity with others who were so persecuted, their concern for those in prison (presumably who were there as a result of their Christian faith), and their own experience of having their property confiscated by the authorities.[105] The historical setting behind these details is not given and remains elusive. Some suggest a possible reference to the persecution suffered

[100] Westfall, *Discourse Analysis*, 247.

[101] Lane, *Hebrews 9–13*, 296–97.

[102] V. Rhee, "Christology, Chiasm, and the Concept of Faith in Hebrews 10:19–39," *FN* 16 (2003): 45.

[103] Lane, *Hebrews 9–13*, 298.

[104] Ἄθλησις and other related words are used by NT authors metaphorically for enduring difficulties and suffering.

[105] Lane, *Hebrews 9–13*, 299, identified a chiastic structure (ABBA) in vv. 33–34. He does not note that the author speaks generally in v. 33, then specifies in v. 34.

by Jewish Christians in the first ten years of the early church; others look to the Jewish expulsion from Rome in AD 49, or to AD 64 and the aftermath of the great fire in Rome when Nero persecuted and martyred many Christians; or to the days of the Jewish War in AD 66–70. Without further detail from the author, speculation is fruitless.

The author uses *theatrizomenoi*,[106] which originally meant "to be brought up on stage," but over time acquired the figurative meaning of "making a spectacle of someone." "Insult" translates a word which indicates verbal abuse, perhaps in the form of public jeering or scoffing. It was used to describe the treatment of Jesus as well as the early Christians. "Persecution" translates the Greek word *thlipsis,* which Lane thinks "appears to indicate that acts of violence had accompanied verbal abuse."[107] Luke records numerous examples of this in Acts. They accepted the confiscation of their property "joyfully," that paradox of the Christians who experience joy amid persecution and sufferings. The reason[108] the readers could endure such persecution was because they kept an eschatological eye towards God's future promises: they knew they had "better and lasting possessions." Their heavenly "possessions" are described as being "better" and "lasting." Their eschatological reward is "better," a favorite word of the author in this epistle where heavenly realities are far superior to earthly ones.[109] The author places the attributive participle translated "lasting" clause final for emphasis. The plural pronoun is given an emphatic translation "you yourselves."[110]

(3) Need to Persevere (10:35–39)

35So do not throw away your confidence; it will be richly rewarded. 36You need to persevere so that when you have done the will of God, you will receive what he has promised. 37For in just a very little while,

"He who is coming will come and will not delay.
38 But my righteous one will live by faith.
And if he shrinks back,
I will not be pleased with him."

39But we are not of those who shrink back and are destroyed, but of those who believe and are saved.

---

106 The participle expresses events which accompany the preceding verb ὑπεμείνατε, "stood your ground."

107 Lane, *Hebrews 9–13*, 299.

108 Note the causal participle γινώσκοντες, "because you knew."

109 Ellingworth, *Hebrews*, 550.

110 Both Bruce, *Hebrews*, 267, and Dods, "Hebrews," 350, viewed it as emphatic as well. Ellingworth, *Hebrews*, 550 took it as reflexive: "knowing yourselves to have." Greenlee, *Exegetical Summary*, 419, argued that the structure of the text requires the pronoun to be expressed and it is therefore not emphatic.

10:35 The final sub-paragraph of the chapter, 10:35–39, is introduced by the inferential conjunction *oun*, "therefore," signaling the author is drawing a conclusion from 10:32–34. Given all that the readers had endured in the past, the author challenges them not to "throw away"[111] their "confidence." The author uses litotes, a negative which implies a strong positive statement: "by all means hold fast your assurance no matter what comes!"[112] The verb "to throw away" can be taken in its more passive sense, as of a tree losing its leaves, or as is more likely, in the strong active sense of deliberately throwing something away, negatively in the sense of "abandoning."[113] They are to hold fast their "confidence," a word used several times already in Hebrews (Greek *parrēsia*—3:6; 4:16; 10:19) and here referring to their "courageous confession"[114] of faith. Those who hold fast to their confession will be "richly rewarded." The word in Greek, *misthapodosia*,[115] is found only in Hebrews, is emphatic by position, and connotes the eschatological reward that awaits all true believers in Christ. It occurs negatively in Heb 2:2 with the sense of "penalty" and positively here and in 11:26 with the sense "reward." A form of the word is used of God himself who is a "rewarder" of those who seek him by faith in Heb 11:6. The word "has reference to the blessing of full salvation God has promised to those who wait for Christ (cf. 9:28; 10:23, 25)."[116] Hence it is called a "great" reward." Kistemaker rightly noted the reward is not because one maintains the confidence; rather it is the retaining of confidence that enables one to receive what God has already promised.[117] The Greek text (lit.) reads "which has great reward"; the present tense has been interpreted here to imply the reward is presently available, if only in part,[118] and that it is certain.[119]

10:36 Verse 36 is subordinated to v. 35 by the use of *gar*,[120] which provides the grounds for the preceding exhortation, and does so in counterpart fashion by pitting "endurance" against "throwing away." "Endurance" connotes perseverance. Hughes interpreted it as referring to the means for doing the will of God mentioned later in the verse.[121] Hewitt understood it in the sense of "endurance is God's will for you."[122] Moffatt observed a conditional element

---

[111] Here the author speaks of the very opposite of "holding fast," which he exhorted in 3:6.

[112] Lenski, *Hebrews*, 367.

[113] See Ellingworth, *Hebrews*, 550.

[114] Bruce, *Hebrews*, 271.

[115] On the meaning and use of μισθαποδοσία, see E. Würthwein, "μισθαποδοσία," *TDNT* 4:710–12; TLNT 2.502–15; and Pesch, EDNT 2.432–33.

[116] Lane, *Hebrews 9–13*, 302.

[117] S. Kistemaker, *The Psalm Citations in the Epistle to the Hebrews* (Amsterdam: G. van Soest, 1961), 301.

[118] So Alford, "Hebrews," 205; Dods, "Hebrews," 351; and TNTC.

[119] Moffatt, *Hebrews*, 156.

[120] Γὰρ is inferential here rather than causal.

[121] Hughes, *Hebrews*, 432–33.

[122] Hewitt, *Hebrews*, 169.

reflected in the noun "endurance" in the sense that "if you endure, you will receive the promise."[123] The result[124] of having such endurance is the reception of what God has promised.[125] As Koester pointed out, "Endurance is not a precondition for God making the promise, but an expression of confidence that God will keep the promise."[126] What God has promised is eternal life (9:15); a share in God's rest (4:10); and a place in the heavenly Jerusalem (12:22–24). The phrase "the will of God" contextually and semantically indicates the notion of remaining faithful to the end.

10:37–38 In vv. 37–38, the author injects a very important quotation[127] of Hab 2:3–4,[128] the theme of which governs the rest of the epistle. The author's choice of this quotation is significant for three reasons. First, he uses this quotation to launch the lengthy discourse on faith in Hebrews 11. Second, Gheorghita has demonstrated the many thematic parallels among "a network of texts" which the author of Hebrews quotes from the Old Testament and Hab 2:3–4. "The context of Hab. 2:3–4 demonstrates a thematic overlap with the contexts of the other quotations employed in this section [the last paraenetic section] of the epistle."[129] Third, the author makes significant modifications to the LXX version which are theologically driven.[130]

Gheorghita summarized three types of modifications of the LXX text by the author of Hebrews. First, he shifts the position of words or clauses. For example, the possessive pronoun *mou* is shifted from qualifying *pisteōs* to qualifying *dikaios*. Second, he inserts the masculine article *ho* before the participle *erchomenos*. Third, he changes the aorist subjunctive *chronisē* into a future indicative *chronisei*, "will not delay." The first change shifts the emphasis from God's faithfulness in the LXX text to the faith of Christians in the Hebrews

---

[123] Moffatt, *Hebrews*, 156.

[124] Note the use of ἵνα indicating result.

[125] Hughes, *Hebrews*, 433: "In this epistle there are two expressions in the Greek for receiving the promise: (1) ἐπιτυγχάνειν τῆς ἐπαγγελίας (6:15), which means to receive the word of the promise, that is, in anticipation of its fulfillment, and (2) κομίζεσθαι τὴν ἐπαγγελίαν (here and 11:13 and 39), which means to receive the promise in the actuality of one's own experience, that is, to receive the fulfillment of the promise. In 11:33, however, the verb ἐπιτυγχάνειν probably carries both these meanings, in an ambivalent manner."

[126] Koester, *Hebrews*, 461.

[127] F. Schröger, *Der Verfasser des Hebräerbriefes als Schriftausleger* (Regensburg: Pustet, 1968), 185; and S. Stanley, "A New Covenant Hermeneutic: The Use of Scripture in Hebrews 8–10," *TynBul* 46 (1995): 230. Both think it possible the author is not quoting Hab 2:3–4, but similar to Heb 10:12,13, which alludes to Ps 110:1, perhaps the author is here alluding to Hab 2:3–4. While possible, it seems best to take it as an actual quotation.

[128] Hab 2:3–4 was frequently quoted in rabbinical literature (Str-B 4:1011). Cf. S. J. Kistemaker, *Hebrews, Expositions of the Epistle to the Hebrews* (Grand Rapids: Baker, 1984), 48.

[129] R. Gheorghita, *The Role of the Septuagint in Hebrews*, in WUNT (Tübingen: Mohr/Siebeck, 2003), 188. See esp. 180–88.

[130] For a thorough comparison between the MT and the LXX of Hab 2:3–4, see Gheorghita, *Role of the Septuagint*, 211–18. Cf. Lane, *Hebrews 9–13*, 304–5; Ellingworth, *Hebrews*, 553–56; Bruce, *Hebrews*, 272–74; and Koester, *Hebrews*, 462–63.

text. Second, the insertion of the masculine article makes it crystal clear that the author intends a Messianic reference to the Second Coming of Christ.[131] The third change emphasizes the certainty of the return of the Messiah.[132] A comparison between the MT and the LXX of Hab 2:3–4 does not answer the question as to whether the passage is Messianic in its original setting. In the MT, that which is coming is a reference to the revelation from the Lord. Whether there is a Messianic overtone here is debatable. The LXX alters the structure of the MT by using a masculine participle for "the coming [one]" which does not correspond to the feminine noun "vision" or "revelation." This has led some, like Schröger and Lane, to see a Messianic reference in the LXX text.[133] However, there can be no doubt that the author of Hebrews sees a Messianic reference in the LXX text. As Stanley well stated: "In Hab. 2:1,2 the prophet is waiting to hear what the Lord would say, while Heb 1:1 describes how God spoke in the past through the prophets. In Hab. 2:2,3 the Lord promises a vision that turns out to be a person—the writer uses a masculine pronoun and participle to describe the (feminine) vision in v. 3."[134] What Habakkuk waited to hear has now been heard: "God spoke to our forefathers through the prophets at many times and in various ways, but in these last days he has spoken to us by his Son" (Heb 1:1–2).

Verses 37–38 are introduced by *gar* which serves to provide the reason for the previous verse: Christians are to endure because they have not yet received God's promise. The actual quotation itself is introduced in a catchy way in Greek: (lit.) "yet a little, how much, how much!"[135] The phrase serves to encourage the audience that their wait for the return of Jesus will not be unrewarded: he will return. Until then, endurance by faith is the order of the day. "My righteous one" is applied by the author generically to all Christians, who must live by means of faith until the return of Jesus. Lane translated "will live by faithfulness."[136] This exhortation for the righteous one to live by faith is given in the context of the imminence of the Second Coming of Jesus and harks back to 9:28 where Christ is said to appear a second time to those who are eagerly awaiting his return.

---

[131] Ὁ ἐρχόμενος occurs 17 times in the NT; six times to refer to the first advent; eight times to refer to the second coming. The phrase is a Christological title (Rhee, "Christology, Chiasm," 47).

[132] Gheorghita, *Role of the Septuagint*, 220–21.

[133] Schröger, *Verfasser des Hebräerbriefes*, 187; Lane, *Hebrews 9–13*, 304; among others.

[134] S. Stanley, "A New Covenant Hermeneutic," 204.

[135] In Greek: ἔτι γὰρ μικρὸν ὅσον ὅσον. L&N 67.107 translates it, "very soon, in a very short while," or "just a very little while longer." The doubling of ὅσον serves to emphasize the shortness of time. The phrase, minus ἔτι, comes from the LXX of Isa 26:20. Kistemaker, *Hebrews*, 47, suggests the possibility that the combination of Isa 26:20 with Hab 2:3–4 may suggest a background of synagogue and church liturgies. What a catchy sermon title one could use from this Greek phrase: "A Little How-long How-long!"

[136] Lane, *Hebrews 9–13*, 278. On the similarities and differences between Paul's use of Hab 2:3–4 and Hebrews, see Bruce, *Hebrews*, 274–75.

What does the author mean by his choice of the word *hupostellō*, "shrinks/draws back"? Michel remarked that there is a cline of meanings ranging from failure to meet with the assembly for worship all the way to apostasy.[137] Lane took it to refer to apostasy,[138] as do most commentators. Lewis, among others, argued against the meaning of apostasy,[139] showing that contextually the word here means failure to hold fast, failure to endure, and failure to go on meeting together with the assembly. His argument is as follows. "The inner connections by which the speech progresses from v. 32 through v. 36 are important not only for a clearer perception of how the paradigm unfolds, but also for understanding the relationship of the paradigm to x. 37–38, where the contrast between *ek pisteōs . . . zēsetai* and *huposteilētai* occurs."[140] He further stated: "The notion of 'endurance' of 'continuing in' (x. 36) is suggested already in v. 35 with the mention of *parrasia*; for it has already been stressed that it is precisely the latter that the community must 'hold firm until the end' (iii. 6b)."[141] Lewis lamented the fact of insufficient attention given by commentators to the partial quotation of Isa 26:20 as it is conflated with Hab 2:3–4. Both passages contextually refer to Israel's endurance during times of persecution and peril. Isaiah 26:20 "calls for a specific mode of endurance: 'Come, my people, go into your chambers, shut your door, and hide a little while (*mikron hoson hoson*) until the wrath of the Lord pass by.' In other words, the Isaiah passage views *withdrawal* and *concealment* as the proper mode of enduring a time of 'wrath.'"[142]

Lewis argued that the author cited this passage in Isaiah "because he wishes to allude to a mode of endurance being taken up or advocated in the community, a mode which he in turn views as conflicting with the way that has been forged and disclosed by the Christ."[143] He suggested the author's comments in Heb 6:9–12 indicate "the author does not consider them apostate, but finds them manifesting 'zeal for the fullness of hope' through the works of love they perform for the saints. . . . Against this background, the explication of endurance . . . appears as a corrective measure."[144] Thus, the contrast is between faith and withdrawal, which is brought to a conclusion in 10:39: "we are not of those who shrink back and are destroyed." This is reminiscent of the failure of the exodus generation as discussed in 3:6–4:13, and connects this warning passage to that earlier warning passage.[145] Thus, Lewis concluded:

---

[137] Michel, *Hebräer*, 363–65.

[138] Lane, *Hebrews 9–13*, 305.

[139] T. W. Lewis, "' . . . And if he shrinks back' (Heb X. 38b)," *NTS* 22 (1975–76): 88–94.

[140] Ibid., 89.

[141] Ibid., 90.

[142] Ibid., 91.

[143] Ibid., 91–92.

[144] Ibid., 92.

[145] C. Spicq, *L'Épître aux Hébreux* (Paris: Librairie Lecoffre, 1952–53), 2:333, observed this connection.

> [T]he author addresses himself to a community that has begun to interpret its lifestyle, in a world in which it encounters suffering, abuse and affliction, in terms of withdrawal and concealment—scriptural basis for such an interpretation being found in Isa xxvi. 20. The author counters this situation by (1) presenting to the community a moment from its own past as a paradigm for continuing its inter-course with the world with boldness, (2) alluding to an Old Testament verse supporting withdrawal, (3) then rejecting the latter by opposition it with a significantly modified form of Habakkuk, and (4) connecting the motif of 'withdrawal' with the paradigm of Israel's turning back in fear from the call to invade Canaan.
>
> From this perspective, *huposteilētai* in Heb. x. 38b would refer not to apostasy, but to a mode of endurance which in the view of the author would result in the community's drifting 'away [from what we have heard]' (ii. 1), losing its way in the world, and forfeiting its ultimate goal.[146]

Lane argued against Lewis's interpretation, calling it a "reinterpretation." He gave three reasons: (1) it fails to take into account the strong terminology used in v. 25 for "forsaking" the meetings of the Christian assembly;[147] (2) it fails to take into account the warning against apostasy in 10:26–31; and (3) it fails to take into account the force of the negative construction in Heb 10:38 ("I myself will reject him). Not one of these reasons is valid. We have already shown there is no contextual ground for interpreting the failure of the readers to meet together with the community as a matter of "desertion" or apostasy. Reason two assumes the argument Lane is trying to prove. We have shown that these verses need not be interpreted to refer to apostasy at all. Reason three interprets the statement from the Old Testament quotation in Hab 2:4 as meaning God's rejection of the apostate, but again neither the text itself nor the context states such. Lane is reading into the text a particular meaning concerning God's rejection of the apostate.

Verse 38 ends with the conditional "if he shrinks back," followed by the consequence "I [lit. "my soul"] will not be pleased with him." Here "my soul" is a Semitism referring to God and connotes the idea of "I myself."[148]

10:39 The author concludes with a balanced contrastive comment in v. 39 concerning two classes of people. The word "we" is emphatic in that a separate pronoun is used (it is unnecessary since the verb is first-person plural) and that it is placed first in the sentence.[149] The author uses the cognate noun of the verb "to shrink back" in v. 38. The word is used only here in the Greek New

---

[146] Lewis, "' . . . And if he shrinks back' (Heb X. 38b)," 93–94.

[147] Lane, *Hebrews 9–13*, 306, uses the term "desertion."

[148] So Lane, *Hebrews 9–13*, 278.

[149] So ibid., following *GAGNT* 678–79.

Testament and does not itself refer to apostasy, but it is often so interpreted in this context. The word here refers contextually to a lack of endurance. Whether this is referring to apostasy or not is another matter altogether. Those who take it to mean apostasy point to the phrase "to destruction," where the preposition in Greek means "with the result that."[150] Here the word is often taken to refer to everlasting destruction. The active sense of the noun "destruction" is rendered verbally as "to be destroyed." Again, however, this noun does not itself mean "everlasting destruction," though such an interpretation is contextually possible.

The class of people who withdraw is contrasted with the "faith" class. The noun *pistis*[151] is usually translated in such a way as to bring out the verbal idea as in the NIV's "those who believe." The final noun phrase reads (lit.) "unto [with the result that] [the] preservation of [the] soul." The word in Greek indicates preserving something in the sense of keeping it safe. "Soul" here does not necessarily refer to "eternal life" but to one's physical life or being.[152]

THEOLOGICAL IMPLICATIONS. The history of the interpretation of this passage is interesting. Chrysostom took Heb 10:26 to mean exclusion from a second baptism for those who had lapsed.[153] Luther said in reference to 10:32–34: "from 'recall the former days'—Here he [the author of Hebrews] clearly calls them—as though they had fallen away—to repentance which they seemed to deny." Luther concluded: "Thus . . . he is describing the existing state of affairs, not declaring a change to be impossible."[154] We have already seen that Calvin interpreted the passage as referring to apostates, and he is followed by virtually all Calvinists today. Arminians take the passage as affirming that one may lose salvation through apostasy.[155]

The meaning of Heb 10:26 must be viewed in tandem with 10:18. In both places the author asserts once the forgiveness of sins is granted, there is no longer any sin offering that can be made. Lundbom commented:

---

[150] See L&N 89.48.

[151] Grässer, *Glaube*, 63–66, argued that the concept of faith in Hebrews is not soteriological, but ethical. He has been followed in this by B. Lindars, *The Theology of the Letter to the Hebrews* (Cambridge: Cambridge University Press, 1991), 108; and Attridge, *Hebrews*, 313; among others. However, Grässer's assessment has been shown to be in error, and the majority of commentators regard the author's concept to be in line with the Pauline understanding of faith in Christ. See D. Peterson, *Hebrews and Perfection: An Examination of the Concept of Perfection in the "Epistle to the Hebrews,"* in SNTSMS 47 (Cambridge: Cambridge University Press, 1982), 164; Rhee, "Christology, Chiasm," 39.

[152] So Bruce, *Hebrews*, 267; Hughes, *Hebrews*, 437.

[153] Chrysostom, *On the Epistle to the Hebrews* 20.2, in E. M. Heen and P. D. W. Krey, eds., *Hebrews*, ACCS 10 (Downers Grove: InterVarsity, 2005), 166.

[154] Luther, *Lectures on Titus, Philemon, and Hebrews, LW* 29:228.

[155] G. Osborne, "A Classical Arminian View," 118–22; G. L. Cockerill, "A Wesleyan Arminian View," in *Four Views on the Warning Passages in Hebrews*, ed. H. W. Bateman IV (Grand Rapids: Kregel, 2007), 280–83.

> The "once for all" view of Jesus' sacrifice is matched in Hebrews with a 'once for all' view of repentance, enlightenment (baptism), and sanctification of the believer. Deliberate sin nullifies a sin offering according to Num 15:30–31. But note Heb 13:20–21 in the benediction where the author speaks of the "blood of the eternal covenant" as equipping the elect to do God's will.[156]

Is this text, in comparison to the New Testament revelation concerning the eternal security of the believer, capable of being interpreted from a standpoint other than soteriological? Based on the strong language in Hebrews asserting the "once-for-all-ness" of the atonement, how can the Arminian view be sustained? Joslin's conclusions from his study of the meaning and use of the Mosaic law in Heb 7:1–10:18 are helpful on this point:

> [T]he research here perhaps can be helpful in offering a new manner of understanding the difficult warnings of Heb 6:4–6 and 10:26–31. If it is true that the main purpose of the internalization of the Law in the NC [new covenant] is the obedience of the people, and it is true that this NC blessing is a *divine* work accomplished by the covenant-maker himself, then is true apostasy and loss of salvation a viable interpretive option for the warning texts? Can human sin nullify the divine works of internalization of the Law and the assurance of forgiveness (and the "divine forgetting" that accompanies forgiveness of sin in the NC)? In Hebrews 8:8–12 (10:16–17, cf. 18) text there is a distinct emphasis on the work accomplished by God on behalf of the NC people which leads to obedience, in contrast to the OC [old covenant] people who did not continue/remain in the covenant and whom God rejected (8:9). In short, if it is a distinctly divine work, the question is raised as to whether human sinfulness can overturn it.[157]

Likewise, given the contextual considerations of passages like Heb 6:4–6 and 10:26–31, not to mention the lexical meaning of key words and phrases which can be taken to refer to genuine believers and to something other than eternal damnation, how can it be asserted unequivocally by many in the Reformed tradition that the meaning is to apostasy in the traditional theological sense of that term? That interpretation is certainly possible, but it is not at all certain, or even probable, as I have endeavored to show. Apostasy is certainly a possibility for one who is a member of the outward church, as we acknowledged in the discussion of Heb 6:4–6. Since salvation is a work of God in one's life and since Scripture teaches the eternal security of a genuine believ-

[156] J. R. Lundbom, *Jeremiah: A Study in Ancient Hebrew Rhetoric*, 2nd ed. (Winona Lake, IN: Eisenbrauns, 1997) 21–36.

[157] B. Joslin, "The Theology of the Mosaic Law in Hebrews 7:1–10:18" (Ph.D. dissertation, Southern Baptist Theological Seminary, 2005), 325–26.

er, apostasy shows that a person was never truly converted. This approach is compatible with the Reformed understanding of apostasy. The problem comes when interpreters attempt to foist this construct on the warning passages of Hebrews. When that happens, one must make a number of hermeneutical "adjustments"[158] to create a fit: posit two audiences the author is addressing, one comprised of genuine believers and the other comprised of false believers; re-interpret straight-forward language so as to make it describe mere "professors" who are not genuine believers; minimize or ignore the Old Testament background of the warning passages; and minimize or ignore the concept of spiritual maturity as the context of the warning passages. One question that arises for those who see apostasy in this passage is how can those who are righteous (10:38) be called righteous if they apostatize?

The key point and conclusion is this: the warning passages are not addressing the danger of apostasy. They address the danger of willful disobedience to God on the part of a genuine believer and the serious consequences to that disobedience.

Excursus: On Smuggling Presuppositions into Exegesis

The old saying "even a stopped clock is right twice a day" is applicable to Rudolph Bultmann's outstanding article "Is Exegesis without Presupposition Possible?" Evangelicals and Bultmann don't have much in common, but most Evangelicals would concur with Bultmann in answering "no." All who labor in exegesis must fight the urge to smuggle our presuppositions into the task. There is no more glaring example of this syndrome than in the way some Arminians and Calvinists approach the warning passages in Hebrews. By definition, an Arminian believes it is possible for a truly born again Christian to lose one's salvation. Arminian interpreters correctly recognize that the author of Hebrews addresses his readers as believers throughout the epistle. When they encounter the warning passages with such language as "falling away," "trampling under foot the Son of God," and "destruction," they are usually all too quick to presuppose the author is talking about loss of salvation and thus they describe the passages in this way before the first spade of exegetical dirt is turned. Thus, to take one example, Grant Osborne, in his chapter "A Classical Arminian View" in *Four Views on the Warning Passages* in Hebrews, 86–128, informs his readers in the second paragraph that Heb 6:4–6 speaks of genuine believers who commit apostasy which is the unpardonable sin, and thus lose their salvation forever.[159] Forty-one pages later, he draws the same conclusion. Undoubtedly, he is convinced that the

---

[158] So B. M. Fanning, after acknowledging that the specific words of Heb 6:4–5 "seem to reflect a true experience of Christian conversion," further acknowledges that his approach (the classical Reformed view) "does require an adjustment to the straight-forward reading of Hebrews 6:4–8 and 10:26–29 (and similar texts; these are the most problematic)." ("A Classical Reformed View," in *Four Views on the Warning Passages in Hebrews*, ed. H. W. Bateman IV (Grand Rapids: Kregel, 2007), 218). This is a refreshing admission; one could wish others would be so forthcoming as well in the discussion.

[159] G. Osborne, "Classical Arminian View," 87.

text warrants such a conclusion. But his chapter evidences the presupposition smuggled in at the beginning of the argument. Another example is the excellent and influential article on the subject by Scot McKnight.[160]

Calvinists are no less guilty in their approach to the warning passages. For example, Calvin himself, in commenting on Heb 10:26, in the very first sentence pronounces the passage a reference to apostasy. Two paragraphs later, he said that "it is clear from the context the apostle is referring here only to apostates."[161] Hughes, in commenting on 10:26, writes in the very first sentence: "The very real danger of apostasy . . . is now stressed once more. Persons who lapse into the irremediable state of apostasy are precisely those members of the Christian fellowship who sin deliberately after receiving the knowledge of the truth."[162]

Finally, we consider two stellar commentaries on Hebrews in English by William Lane and Paul Ellingworth. Lane's discussion of v. 26 is interesting in the way he develops the logic of what the author is saying. First, he notes that the passage is introduced by *gar* which closely connects it to the preceding paragraph 10:19–25. Lane says nothing about apostasy in 10:19–25. Second, Lane spoke of those who "deserted" the community in 10:25. The author of Hebrews said nothing about the readers "deserting" the community. Lane then stated: "the neglect of God's gifts is almost tantamount to a decisive rejection of them." Note the phrase "almost tantamount." Lane is conjecturing here. The author of Hebrews spoke of "neglect" in 2:1–4, but not of "rejection." Lane next speaks of the readers' neglect of meeting together as displaying "contemptuous disregard" for the truth. True enough, but again there is nothing here concerning apostasy. He points out that such an attitude exposes "hardened offenders" to divine judgment, and then stated the severe warning is parallel to Heb 6:4–6. Lastly, he concludes "it exposes the gravity of apostasy."[163] All of this is in the confines of the first paragraph of commentary on Heb 10:26 and precedes any exegesis or explanation of the text. Turning to Ellingworth's commentary on Hebrews, in his second sentence of commentary on Heb 10:26 we are told the author is describing "the nature and consequences of apostasy."

From these examples it ought to be evident that commentators have perhaps not always been aware of their own presuppositions which get smuggled into the argument. Even if their interpretation of Heb 6:4–6 and 10:26–31 is correct, smuggling the supposed meaning of the text into their writing before the exegetical spadework is done is problematic.

2. Conviction to Live by Faith (11:1–40)

In Heb 10:38–39, the author prepared the way for the great hall of faith in Hebrews 11 by his quotation of Hab 2:3–4 and the reference in v. 39 to "those who believe." There is a clear shift in the discourse structure from exhortation

[160] S. McKnight, "Warning Passages of Hebrews," 21–59.
[161] Calvin, *Hebrews*, 146.
[162] Hughes, *Hebrews*, 418.
[163] Lane, *Hebrews 9–13*, 291.

in 10:35–40 to exposition in 11:1–40. Although Hebrews 11 is expositional in genre, the author has something of a hortatory purpose in mind, as can be seen by its connection with 12:1–3.[164] Lane and Ellingworth both consider 11:1–12:13 one discourse unit with 11:1–40 being, according to Lane, "a celebration of the character of faith," and 12:1–13 being "a summons to steadfast endurance."[165] Westfall considers 10:19–12:2 one discourse unit, with 11:1–40 clearly marked out.[166]

The chapter is marked as a unit by the *inclusio* formed by the author's use of "faith" and "commended" in vv. 1,39. The author also made use of lexical chiasm in the order found in the Greek text: "faith" and "commended" in v. 1; "commended" and "faith" in v. 39, thus creating an ABBA pattern. The chapter is also given cohesion by the lexical repetition of the word "faith" which occurs 24 times. In vv. 1–2, the author offers a two-pronged definition of sorts for faith, followed by the statement that the "elders" or "men of old" received divine approval. Verses 3–31 proceed to give examples of these Old Testament characters who illustrate the kind faith mentioned in v. 1. This section is unified by the repetition of the dative *pistei*, "by faith," at the beginning of successive clauses. This usage of *pistei* occurs 18 times in vv. 3–31, but nowhere else in the epistle.[167] In vv. 3–31 the author selectively surveys key figures from the Old Testament from Genesis 1 through Joshua 6 who were characterized by their faith. Verses 32–38 continue in this same vein, but with the marked difference that the author employs short, staccato like clauses to contrast those who won great victories by their faith with those who suffered and were martyred for their faith. The contrast is only in the end result: some were victorious through miraculous means while others suffered and died. The point of the author, however, is that whether in life or in death, all were victorious "by faith." Their victory was not just the result of their faith, but was the result of the working of God in their lives in response to their faith in him. This section begins by mentioning four names from the period of the judges: Gideon, Barak, Samson, Jephthah, followed by David, Samuel and "the prophets." Contrary to the previous section, the author does not mention specific events from their lives that illustrate faith. The chapter concludes with a summary statement in v. 39 harking back to vv. 1–2, followed by the author's comments that these Old Testament saints, though commended for their faith, did not receive what God had promised because "God had planned something better for us so that only together with us would they be made perfect."

---

[164] Attridge, *Hebrews*, 307, noted how this chapter has both an expository and a paraenetic purpose.

[165] Lane, *Hebrews 9–13*, 312; Ellingworth, *Hebrews*, 558.

[166] Westfall, *Discourse Analysis*, 263.

[167] On the structure of Heb 11, consult A. Vanhoye, *La structure littéraire de l'Épître aux Hébreux* (Paris: Desclée de Brouwer, 1976), 46–47, 183–94; Westfall, *Discourse Analysis*, 247–51; Lane, *Hebrews 9–13*, 320–23; and Ellingworth, *Hebrews*, 558–62.

In addition to the commentaries and Grässer's work on the subject of faith in Hebrews,[168] there are two important monographs on Hebrews 11, one from a rhetorical standpoint which compares Hebrews 11 with example lists from antiquity,[169] the other which treats Hebrews 11 in its literary context.[170] Westfall divided the chapter into four major sections:

11:1–2	Faith is Described
11:3–31	Actions of Faith
11:32–38	Post-Conquest Actions of Faith
11:39–40	Conclusion: The Faithful Did Not Receive the Promises[171]

Ellingworth offers the following assessment of the structure and outline:

11:1–2	introduction
11:3–12	first *pistei* series
11:13–16	interim comment
11:17–31	second *pistei* series
11:32–38	rapid survey
11:39–40	final comment[172]

Hebrews 11 can be compared to *I Clement* 17:1–19:3, which is its closest parallel in Christian literature outside of Stephen's speech in Acts 7.[173] Both Cosby and Eisenbaum offer detailed analyses of Hebrews 11 in comparison with other Jewish and Hellenistic example lists.[174] Windisch and Michel both suggested the author used a source for Hebrews 11. This is generally rejected

168 E. Grässer, *Der Glaube Im Hebräerbrief*, Marburger Theologische Studien 2 (Marburg: N. G. Elwert Verlag, 1965); esp. pp. 13–63.

169 M. Cosby, *The Rhetorical Composition and Function of Hebrews 11: in Light of Example Lists in Antiquity* (Macon, GA: Mercer University Press, 1988), 1–91.

170 P. Eisenbaum, *The Jewish Heroes of Christian History: Hebrews 11 in Literary Context*, SBLDS 156, ed. P. Perkins (Atlanta: Scholars Press, 1997). Eisenbaum argued Hebrews 11 shares much in common with Jewish example lists and less in common with Greco-Roman lists. However, she concluded "Hebrews 11 is most influenced by the Jewish material in its form and content, but we must add to this evidence of influence from Greco-Roman methods of rhetorical communication" (79).

171 Westfall, *Discourse Analysis*, 248–51. Most commentaries posit this same overall division. Eisenbaum, *Jewish Heroes*, 228, places v. 3 with the introduction because the author references understanding of creation by his readers' faith (note "we understand" in 11:3). Rhee, "Christology, Chiasm," 181, also takes the introduction as including v. 3 based on content more so than form. Semantically, it is better to take v. 3 as beginning the second major division since it begins with the characteristic "by faith," which serves to give coherence to 11:3–31.

172 Ellingworth, *Hebrews*, 561.

173 See M. R. D'Angelo, *Moses in the Letter to the Hebrews*, SBLDS 42 (Missoula, MT: Scholars Press, 1979), 18–26; and Lane, *Hebrews 9–13*, 317–20.

174 Cosby, *Rhetorical Composition*; Eisenbaum, *Jewish Heroes*. Eisenbaum describes the primary purpose of a hero list as "to explain and legitimate the existence of the community which is being addressed, by grounding the members of that community in a significant genealogical history" (87).

by scholars. Hebrews 11 gives every evidence of having been constructed by the author and not taken from a source.[175] For example, Eisenbaum noted the symmetry of the author's grouping of names into threes: Abel, Enoch, and Noah; then a lengthy treatment of Abraham. This is followed by Isaac, Jacob, and Joseph; then a lengthy section on Moses. A final grouping of three—those who crossed the Red Sea, the walls of Jericho, and Rahab concludes the major section at v. 31. This gives a pattern of 3–1–3–1–3.[176]

(1) Necessity of Faith (11:1–2)

[1]Now faith is being sure of what we hope for and certain of what we do not see.
[2]This is what the ancients were commended for.

11:1 Hebrews 11:1 has been something of a conundrum for commentators and translators. Should it be taken as a definition of faith? Westcott and Lane are representative of those who do not see v. 1 as a formal definition of faith.[177] Cosby and Eisenbaum are most likely correct in their assertion that v. 1 should be viewed as a rhetorical definition of faith.[178] The predominant view of faith in Hebrews 11 is that the word connotes trust in God and reliance on him in the sense of fidelity and firmness.

There are three basic views regarding the nature of faith in Hebrews, especially chap. 11. Grässer argued that faith in Hebrews has no Christological or even Christian content, but is merely an ethical quality. His thesis is almost universally rejected today,[179] although Lindars and Attridge argue that it is basically ethical.[180] This approach fails to consider that in Hebrews, as in the rest of the New Testament, Jesus is depicted as the believer's object of faith as well as the exemplar of faith.[181] The second view, the eschatological view, takes the author's concept of faith in Hebrews as primarily futuristic. This perspective is represented by Käsemann and Thompson.[182] This viewpoint gives too much weight to the

---

[175] H. Windisch, *Der Hebräerbrief*, 2nd ed., HNT 14 (Tübingen: Mohr, 1931), 98–99; O. Michel, *Der Brief an die Hebräer*, KEK (Göttingen: Vandenhoeck & Ruprecht, 1975), 422–23. Ellingworth, *Hebrews*, 558–59, argues against Windisch and Michel.

[176] Eisenbaum, *Jewish Heroes*, 79–80.

[177] Westcott, *Hebrews*, 351; Lane, *Hebrews 9–13*, 328.

[178] Cosby, *Rhetorical Composition*, 25–40; Eisenbaum, *Jewish Heroes*, 143.

[179] Grässer, *Glaube*, 34–35. H. Kosmala, *Hebräer-Essener-Christen* (Leiden: Brill, 1959) 101–6 also argued that faith in Hebrews has no Christological basis and is in fact a development of Jewish messianic thought. This viewpoint is strongly refuted by D. Hamm, "Faith in the Epistle to the Hebrews: The Jesus Factor," *CBQ* 52 (1990): 270–91. See also R. Bultmann, "πίστις," *TDNT* 6:208–9, where he argues that in the NT, faith in God is essentially equivalent to faith in Christ.

[180] See Lindars, *Theology*, 108; Attridge, *Hebrews*, 311–14.

[181] See the critique of this position in V. Rhee, "Christology, Chiasm," 35–39.

[182] E. Käsemann, *The Wandering People of God: An Investigation of the Letter to the Hebrews*, trans. R. Harrisville & I. Sanders (Minneapolis: Augsburg, 1984); J. W. Thompson, *The Beginnings of Christian Philosophy*, CBQMS (Washington, DC: Catholic Biblical Association, 1982). Käsemann and Thompson should not be read as having no concept of realized eschatology; rather their focus is primarily on the future.

notion of Platonic influence in the epistle. We have already seen that the author of Hebrews is not so much influenced by Philo as he is by Jewish understanding of eschatology.[183] The third view, the Christological view, comports best with the overall context of Hebrews as well as the canonical context of the New Testament. Among those who adhere to this view are Lane and Rhee.[184]

Verse 1 begins with the sentence initial *estin,* "is," for emphasis.[185] Faith is said to be the *hupostasis* of things hoped for. The NIV renders this noun verbally with the translation "being sure of." The word carried a range of meanings during the Classical and Hellenistic periods. Danker gives the word's basic meaning as "the essential or basic structure/nature of an entity, *substantial nature, essence, actual being, reality* (underlying structure, oft. in contrast to what merely seems to be . . .)." He goes on to explain that "among the meanings that can be authenticated for Hb 11:1 a strong claim can be made for realization," as in the "realization of a plan." Here he suggests the meaning, "*in faith things hoped for become realized.*"[186] Another usage of the word according to Danker is "guarantee of ownership/entitlement," where, following Moulton and Milligan, "title deed" is given as a possible translation.[187] Based on this, Lane thinks it "imperative" that the objective sense of the term be reflected in its translation. He cites other translations given along these lines: "objective guarantee," "certainty," "reality," and "title-deed," something which legally guarantees future possession. Lane calls translations such as "confidence" and "assurance" "untenable" because they ascribe to the word a subjective connotation which does not adequately convey its objective sense.[188] Grässer is no doubt correct to note the conceptual relationship between faith, confidence and endurance, although the latter two words do not appear in Hebrews 11. Baugh, building on J. D. Smith, questioned the traditional understanding of both *hupostasis* and *elenchos* in 11:1 as having only an objective sense with

---

[183] See the critique in V. Rhee, "Christology, Chiasm," 49–52.

[184] Lane, *Hebrews 9–13*, 412; V. Rhee, "Christology, Chiasm," 52–63, 243–53. Rhee's work constitutes the best presentation of all three viewpoints as well as a defense of the Christological view based on his exegetical and theological analysis of Hebrews.

[185] So Alford, "Hebrews," 207; Lünemann, *Hebrews*, 667; A. Nairne, *The Epistle to the Hebrews*, CGTSC (London: Cambridge University Press, 1922),110; Lane, *Hebrews 9–13*, 325. Moffatt, *Hebrews*, 158–59, disagrees. Hebrews tends to omit the copula (i.e., the "be" verb in clauses like "A is B"), as Turner noted, and the presence of ἔστιν is "very exceptional" if it is functioning as a copula. Turner translated ἔστιν somewhat idiomatically as "represents" (Turner, *Grammar*, 3:307). The author of Hebrews is conveying the notion that "faith REALLY IS substance (substantial)."

[186] BDAG 1040. Cf. H. Koester, "ὑπόστασις," *TDNT* 8:572–84. Ellingworth, *Hebrews*, 564, takes the basic nuance here to be "tangible reality in contrast to mere appearance." Emphasis original.

[187] BDAG 1041.

[188] Lane, *Hebrews 9–13*, 325–26. Danker (BDAG 1041) agrees that "the sense 'confidence', 'assurance' . . . has enjoyed much favor but must be eliminated, since examples of it cannot be found."

no concept of subjective assurance, and he suggested the Old Testament heroes were "recipients of divine testimony to the coming eschatological realities, and thence by faith they became participants in and witnesses to the world to come."[189] In short, Baugh argued that the author presented these Old Testament saints as "witnesses to various aspects of this eschatological reality to which we have now come in Christ."[190]

The use of the present passive participle ("what we hope for") "connotes the objects of hope, i.e., the totality of the expected heavenly blessings viewed in their objective certainty."[191] Thus, it is best to take the clause in 11:1 to have an objective sense with the meaning "faith gives substance to what is hoped for," and not a subjective sense that faith is the assurance that what is hoped for will come to pass (although this latter perspective is certainly true).[192] The second clause of v. 1 is in apposition to the first. This would indicate the author intended *elenchos* also to have an objective meaning along the lines of "proof," "evidence," and not only the subjective sense of "conviction" or "demonstration."[193] As Lane pointed out, "faith" is objective because it bestows upon the objects of hope a present reality, enabling the believer to enjoy now the "full certainty of future realization." Faith is the objective grounds upon which subjective confidence may be based. Such faith springs from a personal encounter with God. This kind of faith enables one to venture into the future "supported only by the word of God." Such faith "has the capacity to unveil the future so that the solid reality of events as yet unseen can be grasped by the believer."[194] In secular Greek usage, *elenchos* is the "test" or "trial" which shows a thing as it really is. Consequently, Nairne prefers the translation "test" over "evidence" in this context.[195]

11:2 The *gar* in v. 2 (untranslated in the NIV) indicates the grounds for the preceding description of faith.[196] The faith described in v. 1[197] is what the

[189] S. Baugh, "The Cloud of Witnesses in Hebrews 11," *WTJ* 68 (2006): 113. Cf. J. D. Smith III, "Faith as Substance or Surety: Historical Perspectives on *Hypostasis* in Hebrews 11:1," in *The Challenge of Bible Translation*, ed. G. Scorgie, M. Strauss, and S. Voth (Grand Rapids: Zondervan, 2003), 381–92.

[190] Baugh, "The Cloud of Witnesses in Hebrews 11," 132.

[191] Lane, *Hebrews 9-13*, 326..

[192] For the subjective idea, see Moffatt, *Hebrews*, 159; Bruce, *Hebrews*, 277; and the NIV. For the objective idea, see Hughes, *Hebrews*, 440; and Lane, *Hebrews 9–13*, 325.

[193] For the subjective notion, see Bruce, *Hebrews*, 276, 277; and Buschel, "ἔλεγχος," *TDNT* 2:476. For the objective notion, see Lane, *Hebrews 9–13*, 326.

[194] Lane, *Hebrews 9–13*, 329. R. Brawley, "Discoursive Structure and the Unseen in Hebrews 2:8 and 11:1: A Neglected Aspect of the Context," *CBQ* 55 (1993): 81–98, argued that the "unseen things" in 11:1 hark back to 2:8 where the author is quoting Psalm 8. The subjection of all things under Jesus' feet awaits future fulfillment. According to Brawley (p. 85), the concept of faith in 11:1 relates to the eschatological subjection of all things to Christ which as of now is "not yet seen."

[195] Nairne, *Hebrews*, 110.

[196] L&N (89.26) translates it "by reason of; on account of."

[197] Ταύτῃ, "this," is stronger than the pronoun αὐτῇ according to Ellingworth, 567.

"ancients" were commended for. The "ancients" (Greek "elders") are men and women of the Old Testament, possibly inclusive of the intertestamental period as well. Lane said that the verb *martureō* occurs seven times in Hebrews, "and in each instance the reference is to the witness of the biblical record." It occurs four times in Hebrews 11 (vv. 2,4,5,39).[198]

(2) Foresight of Faith (11:3–16)

3By faith we understand that the universe was formed at God's command, so that what is seen was not made out of what was visible.

4By faith Abel offered God a better sacrifice than Cain did. By faith he was commended as a righteous man, when God spoke well of his offerings. And by faith he still speaks, even though he is dead.

5By faith Enoch was taken from this life, so that he did not experience death; he could not be found, because God had taken him away. For before he was taken, he was commended as one who pleased God. 6And without faith it is impossible to please God, because anyone who comes to him must believe that he exists and that he rewards those who earnestly seek him.

7By faith Noah, when warned about things not yet seen, in holy fear built an ark to save his family. By his faith he condemned the world and became heir of the righteousness that comes by faith.

8By faith Abraham, when called to go to a place he would later receive as his inheritance, obeyed and went, even though he did not know where he was going. 9By faith he made his home in the promised land like a stranger in a foreign country; he lived in tents, as did Isaac and Jacob, who were heirs with him of the same promise. 10For he was looking forward to the city with foundations, whose architect and builder is God.

11By faith Abraham, even though he was past age—and Sarah herself was barren—was enabled to become a father because he considered him faithful who had made the promise. 12And so from this one man, and he as good as dead, came descendants as numerous as the stars in the sky and as countless as the sand on the seashore.

13All these people were still living by faith when they died. They did not receive the things promised; they only saw them and welcomed them from a distance. And they admitted that they were aliens and strangers on earth. 14People who say such things show that they are looking for a country of their own. 15If they had been thinking of the country they had left, they would have had opportunity to return. 16Instead, they were longing for a better country—a heavenly one. Therefore God is not ashamed to be called their God, for he has prepared a city for them.

11:3 Cosby and Eisenbaum both place v. 3 in the introduction because of the use of *nooumen,* "we understand." The reason is that the first person plural is not used again until v. 40, thus forming an *inclusio.*[199] However, the use of *pistei*, "by faith," which will be repeated many times in the following verses

---

198 Lane, *Hebrews 9–13*, 330.

199 Cosby, *Rhetorical Composition*, 25; Eisenbaum, *Jewish Heroes*, 147.

marks the beginning of a new paragraph.[200] Verse 3 serves to illustrate and supplement the statements in vv. 1–2. The clause initial "by faith" is marked for emphasis. Its repetition through v. 31 also adds emphasis. The dative noun translated "by faith" can be read as an instrumental dative (by means of faith), a dative of manner (in accordance with the modality of faith), or as a causal dative (because of faith). Contextually, the instrumental use is best.[201] "Understand" connotes intellectual perception as opposed to sense perception, with the possible idea of spiritual perception as well. The idea of time in *aiōnas* is better translated as "ages" not "worlds" and is "extended into faith in the growing process of God's already perfect will, cf. x.10. Thus moral purpose enters creation. The troubled days of the first readers appeared disorderly. Seeing life steadily and whole, perceives the divine continuity of history."[202] The author speaks of the creation of the universe as "by [means of] the word" (*rhēmati*, dative of means). This alludes to the seven times in Genesis 1 where God's speech is connected with creation. The allusion to the biblical text of Genesis serves to indicate the medium of understanding is the written word of God. Faith in the written biblical account generates understanding.[203] This statement, when connected with what is said in Heb 1:2, makes clear that God did not have two agents in creation, the Son and the Word, but only one—the Son and the Word are identical.[204] The result is that what is seen is (lit.) "not from appearing things." This phrase is emphatic by its position and is taken as causal by Ellingworth.[205] The negative "not" can be connected with "to come into being," or with "from appearing things," as Moffatt and Ellingworth.[206] There is nothing of Philo here. In fact, Lane conjectures it may have been the writer's intention to correct the tendency in Hellenistic Judaism to read Genesis 1 in the light of Plato's doctrine of creation.[207] This verse on its face affirms a doctrine of *creation ex nihilo* "creation out of nothing," but whether this was in the mind of the author or not cannot be determined with certainty from the text alone. It is a misplaced argument to assert or deny *creation ex nihilo* from this verse.

11:4 The reference to Abel's faith in v. 4 is an allusion to Gen 4:3–5. Abel's sacrifice is said to have been better than Cain's. The phrase "than Cain did" can be connected with Abel[208] or with his "sacrifice"[209] in the sense of a

[200] So Westfall, *Discourse Analysis*, 248.

[201] Lane, *Hebrews 9–13*, 326.

[202] Nairne, *Hebrews*, 110.

[203] See Behm, "νοέω," *TDNT* 4:951; and Lane, *Hebrews 9–13*, 331.

[204] Ward, *The Pattern of Salvation*, 16.

[205] Ellingworth, *Hebrews*, 569.

[206] Bruce, *Hebrews*, 276; Lane, *Hebrews 9–13*, 327; NIV favored the former; Moffatt, *Hebrews*, 161; Ellingworth, *Hebrews*, 569 the latter.

[207] Lane, *Hebrews 9–13*, 332.

[208] Alford, "Hebrews," 210; NIV.

[209] H. Montefiore, *A Commentary on the Epistle to the Hebrews* (New York: Harper; London: Black, 1964), 188–89.

sacrifice that is better than Cain's. Why was Cain's offering rejected and Abel's accepted? The text in Genesis does not say. Jewish tradition on the subject revolves around the following suggestions. (1) Perhaps there was a deficiency in the ritual of the offering itself. (2) Perhaps the quality of the offering was the issue: Cain's offering was lifeless, or Cain did not bring the firstfruits of the harvest, but a portion of a later harvest. (3) Perhaps some moral deficiency characterized Cain.[210] Most contemporary commentators focus on either the integrity of Abel's heart or the fact that he made his offering "by faith" or both. Some note that Abel's sacrifice was accepted because it followed God's mandate that the sacrifice must be a blood sacrifice. Two things must be kept in mind if one takes this approach. First, nothing overtly in Genesis indicates that God required an animal sacrifice. Second, nothing in the Hebrews text indicates that was the reason for acceptance or rejection.

The antecedent of "which" in the phrase (lit.) "through which he was approved to be righteous" (NIV "By faith he was commended as a righteous man") can be "faith"[211] or Abel's "sacrifice."[212] The clause is then expanded by reference to God speaking well of Abel's offerings.[213] The phrase "even though he is dead" translates as concessive the Greek participle, though it could be translated temporally as well in the since of "after he died."[214] Commentators are divided over the meaning of the phrase "he still speaks." It could be taken to refer to his blood speaking as the voice of a martyr crying out for justice.[215] Another option is that he still speaks concerning his faith in the record of Scripture.[216] This statement should be compared with Heb 12:24, where we are told the blood of Jesus speaks better than the blood of Abel. Lane pointed out that it is by his faith and not his blood that Abel speaks. The allusion is not to Gen 4:10, but rather to Gen 4:4 where God approves of his sacrifice.[217] That he "still" speaks means right up to the time of writing, and by implication, to the present time.

11:5 In v. 5 the author speaks of Enoch who, according to Gen 5:22–24, did not experience death but was taken to heaven by God supernaturally. Enoch "walked with God" according to the Hebrew text, but the LXX translates Enoch "pleased God." The word in Greek translated "taken" is a Semitism for death and connotes being transferred from one realm to another or one place to another; in this passage from earth to heaven. The Greek text uses

---

[210] For discussion on these options, see Lane, *Hebrews 9–13*, 333–34.

[211] So Hughes, *Hebrews*, 455; Lane, *Hebrews 9–13*, 335; and Ellingworth, *Hebrews*, 573.

[212] So Dods, "Hebrews," 23; Hewitt, *Epistle to the Hebrews*, 172; and Bruce, *Hebrews*, 280.

[213] So noted by Lane, *Hebrews 9–13*, 335; and Ellingworth, *Hebrews*, 572.

[214] Ellingworth, *Hebrews*, 573; and Lane, *Hebrews 9–13*, 327, take it concessively.

[215] E.g., Spicq, *L'Épître aux Hebreux*, 2:342; Bruce, *Hebrews*, 283–84; and Attridge, *Hebrews*, 317.

[216] So Moffatt, *Hebrews*, 165; Lane, *Hebrews 9–13*, 335; and Eisenbaum, *Jewish Heroes*, 149.

[217] Lane, *Hebrews 9–13*, 335.

the infinitive "to see" followed by "death" as its object. Here the meaning of "see" is "experience."[218] The entire phrase can be taken as indicating result or purpose.[219] The imperfect tense in the statement "he could not be found" implies repeated searching.[220] The reason he could not be found was God had taken him away, where "God" in the text is emphatic in its being placed clause final. The phrase "he was commended" renders the Greek perfect tense, which probably implies the continuing (permanent) testimony of Scripture.[221] Verse 5 actually contains two sentences in Greek, which is reflected in the NIV translation. The phrase "before he was taken" can be connected with "as one who pleased God" or with "he was commended."[222] The author is not dependent upon Hellenistic-Jewish speculation concerning Enoch, although he may have been aware of it. As in Hebrews 7 with Melchizedek, he bases his conclusions on the biblical text.

11:6 Closely following the comments in v. 5, the author offers an interpretive comment stating a general truth in v. 6. "Without" is used in the sense of "apart from." Faith is indispensable when it comes to "pleasing" God. The reason for this is given in the remainder of the verse. The author uses *dei*, "it is necessary," a word denoting compulsion of any kind and the context usually determines the cause of the necessity. Here it is God who is the cause. Those who come to God must believe two things: he exists, and he rewards those who seek him. The rare Greek word *misthapodotēs*, "rewarder," is found only here in the Greek New Testament and signifies one who pays wages, a paymaster. God rewards those who "earnestly seek him," as the NIV correctly renders the compound Greek verb stressing that the seeking is done diligently. Lane takes it in the sense of seeking to serve God, while Ellingworth takes it to seek in order to worship.[223] Both concepts are included in the word. Our author frequently uses the words "reward" and "promise" in Hebrews. In addition to "rewarder" here in 11:6, the author uses "reward" in 2:2; 10:36; and 11:26.

Hartley made the case that the author is not actually making a statement about God's "existence," but rather that the author's focus is on God's faithfulness as the basis of his rewarding activity. He argued that contextually there is nothing that would call for an ontological discussion of God's existence. At issue is whether the *estin,* "is," should be construed existentially or predicatively. If taken in the former sense, the meaning is metaphysical and speaks of existence. If taken predicatively, a noun or adjective would need to be supplied in

---

218 L&N 90.79.

219 Moffatt, *Hebrews*, 165; Lane, *Hebrews 1–9*, 336; and the NIV take it in the former sense; Bruce in the latter, *Hebrews*, 281.

220 Kistemaker, *Hebrews*, 320.

221 So stated by Alford, "Hebrews," 212.

222 The former is argued by Bruce, *Hebrews*, 286; and Ellingworth, *Hebrews*, 576; the latter by Alford, "Hebrews," 212; Dods, "Hebrews," 354; Lane, *Hebrews 9–13*, 325; and the NIV.

223 Lane, *Hebrews 9–13*, 338; Ellingworth, *Hebrews*, 577.

the predicate position. Hartley makes the case that the immediate and broader context of Hebrews supports supplying the adjective "faithful" following the equative verb. He suggested the translation: "God is faithful and he becomes a rewarder of those who diligently seek him."[224] Hartley's case has merit.

11:7 In v. 7 the author speaks of the faith of Noah from Gen 6:9–21. Noah received an oracle concerning things "not yet seen," a reference back to 11:1. A lexical *inclusio* marks off this paragraph unit.[225] What was not yet seen was the flood. The Greek verb translated "he condemned" can be either imperfect or aorist. Alford takes it as aorist indicating a single act; Ellingworth takes it as imperfect, implying continuation.[226] See also 2 Pet 2:5 where Noah is called a "preacher of righteousness," which further explains the phrase "he condemned humanity." Noah is an "heir," which recalls Heb 1:2, where Christ is the heir of all things; Heb 1:14, where believers "inherit salvation"; and Heb 6:12,17; 9:15. What Noah inherited was righteousness. The phrase *kata pistin*, (lit.) "according to faith," can be adjectival, describing "righteousness" (NIV "that comes by faith"), or equivalent to a dative of means: "righteousness obtained by means of faith."[227]

11:8 Verse 8 begins a new paragraph which ends at v. 12 with Abraham as the topic. Eisenbaum observed that this section and the following two paragraphs are all about Abraham: (vv. 8–12, Abraham's migration towards land of promise; vv. 13–16, the author's commentary on the true homeland; vv. 17–19, offering of Isaac).[228] Even though Abraham is not mentioned by name in vv. 13–16, and the author refers in v. 13 to "all these people," Abraham is still the primary referent. The infinitive *exelthein* translated "to go" is best construed with the immediately preceding verb "he obeyed," although grammatically it can be connected with the participle translated "when called."[229] The participle translated "did not know" is best taken concessively, as the NIV "even though he did not know where he was going."

11:9 Verse 9 calls attention to the nomadic nature of Abraham's sojourning in the promised land "like a stranger in a foreign country." The phrase "like

---

[224] D. Hartley, "Heb 11:6—A Reassessment of the Translation 'God Exists,'" *TJ* 27 NS, no. 2 (2006), 289. He lists seven reasons against the existential interpretation (pp. 299–302) and eight reasons for his proposal (pp. 302–6). He provides the following idiomatic rendering of Heb 11:1, 6: "So what is faith? Faith is really the heart-felt *confidence* of coming to pass all that is rightly hoped for, the deep seated *certitude* that untranspired but promised events will eventually take place. . . . And without this type of faith, it is impossible to please God. Why? Because when approaching God, only this faith treats him as absolutely *trustworthy* to keep his promises and he must therefore be a rewarder of those who earnestly seek him" (p. 307).

[225] Eisenbaum, *Jewish Heroes*, 152.

[226] Alford, "Hebrews," 213; Ellingworth, *Hebrews*, 579.

[227] Lane, *Hebrews 9–13*, 328; and NIV opt for the former; Ellingworth, *Hebrews*, 580, the latter.

[228] Eisenbaum, *Jewish Heroes*, 154.

[229] Lane, *Hebrews 1–9*, 343, and Ellingworth, *Hebrews*, 581, connect it with the verb "he obeyed." Montefiore, *Hebrews*, 192, connected it with the participle "when called."

a stranger" can describe the manner of his sojourning with the sense of "as one sojourns in a foreign land."[230] It can also be viewed as describing Abraham's personal situation.[231] A third option is to construe the phrase adjectivally as indicating where Abraham went. In this case the adjective modifies "land" and not "Abraham."[232] The Greek participle is translated as "he lived" and provides the circumstance of how he lived: "in tents." Both Isaac and Jacob are mentioned as also living in tents and as being heirs of the same promise as Abraham. From Old Testament chronology, this mention of Isaac and Jacob can be taken to mean they lived concurrently with Abraham, since at the time of his death, both Isaac and Jacob were alive, Jacob being 15 years old at the time. No mention is made of Esau, who was alive at the time, but who of course did not inherit the promise (see Heb 12:16).

11:10 Verse 10 is introduced by the subordinating conjunction *gar*, which indicates the reason Abraham lived in tents as a foreigner: "he was looking forward to the city." The "city" here refers to the heavenly Jerusalem of Heb 12:22. This verse contrasts with the previous verse: cities have foundations; tents do not. This city has God for its "architect and builder." "God" is emphatic being placed clause final. Lane takes the clause in a causal fashion: the foundations are eternal because God is the designer and builder.[233]

11:11 Verse 11 has been something of a conundrum for commentators with its surprising use of *spermatos* with Sarah.[234] The word "Abraham" does not occur in the Greek text, which could then be most naturally translated, "By faith, even barren Sarah [*Sarra steira*] herself received power for sowing seed—though beyond the normal age—since she considered faithful the one who promised." The key question is who is the implied agent/actor of the verb

---

[230] Bruce, *Hebrews*, 292; Ellingworth, *Hebrews*, 583.

[231] Moffatt, *Hebrews*, 169; Hughes, *Hebrews*, 468; Hewitt, *Hebrews*, 174; and the NIV.

[232] Lane, *Hebrews 9–13*, 344.

[233] Ibid., 352.

[234] On the textual issues, see *TCGNT* 672–73; J. Swetnam, *Jesus and Isaac: A Study of the Epistle to the Hebrews in the Light of the Aqedah*, AnBib 94 (Rome: Pontifical Biblical Institute, 1981), 98–101; and Lane, *Hebrews 9–13*, 344–45. Windisch, *Hebräerbrief*, 101, among others, suggested καὶ αὐτὴ Σάρρα is a textual gloss. Metzger noted the UBS[4] committee understood the text "to be a Hebraic circumstantial clause allowing Abraham from v. 8 to serve as the subject of ἔλαβεν with the following meaning: "by faith, even though Sarah was barren, he [Abraham] received power to beget." Another option given by Metzger is to construe the phrase as a dative of accompaniment with the meaning "By faith he [Abraham] also, together with barren Sarah, received power to beget." Attridge, *Hebrews*, 321, 325; and Ellingworth, *Hebrews*, 586–89, among others, opt for this solution. This is problematic in that the dative form has no manuscript support nor was the view supported by the church fathers, according to Hughes, *Hebrews*, 473. S. Sowers, *The Hermeneutics of Philo and Hebrews* (Zürich: EVG-Verlag, 1965), 134–35, followed by Eisenbaum, *Jewish Heroes*, 158, suggested that Philo's comments in *Abr.* 100 might be the key. He allegorizes Sarah as Sophia (wisdom) who brings the seeds of correct instruction to Abraham. But this stretches credibility to the breaking point. Cosby, *Rhetorical Composition*, 43, points out there may be an example of paronomasia with the words Σάρρα and στεῖρα which would be roughly equivalent in English to "Sterile Cheryl."

elaben, "received"? The earliest and still the best solution is that which takes "Sarah" to be the subject of the sentence.[235] However, the tide of twentieth century scholarship shifted toward viewing Abraham as the implied subject. There is only one substantial text-critical issue in this verse: the presence or absence of *steira*. The major (but by no means only) difficulty that has caused Abraham to be proposed as the implied subject is the unnaturalness of Sarah being the one to "sow" or "deposit" seed (lit. "for laying down of seed"). The phrase *katabolē spermatos* normally describes an exclusively male activity. To solve this dilemma, three major proposals have been made.

First, some accept that Sarah is the subject of the sentence and conclude that the author has merely proffered a biological inaccuracy.[236] Such an approach need not detain us long as it reflects not only a low view of biblical authority but also of the biblical author's intelligence. Besides, there are other, much more plausible, solutions.

Second, many propose that Abraham is the understood subject of the sentence. In addition to the biological question, commentators have been concerned about supposed "historical difficulties" of reconciling this passage with what is said about Sarah in Genesis. Sarah is not specifically singled out for her faith in the Abraham narrative of Genesis. In fact, one would receive the opposite impression from Gen 18:10–15. Another problem with making Sarah the subject is the supposed interruption of the paragraph (Heb 11:8–12) since Abraham is the subject of the rest. Additionally, how could the author fail to mention Abraham's faith regarding Isaac?[237]

However, there are serious grammatical problems with making Abraham the subject of v. 11. One has to make slight emendations to the text with little or no warrant for doing so. For example, Attridge proposed converting *autē Sarra* ("Sarah herself") into the dative case rather than the nominative,[238] which would function as a dative of accompaniment: "with barren Sarah." Abraham would thus be retained as the implied subject of the sentence. Zuntz strongly argued against this construal, and others have noted its awkwardness and that there is no textual support for such an emendation.[239] Zuntz suggested, again

235 So Alford, "Hebrews," 215; Dods, "Hebrews," 356; Moffatt, *Hebrews*, 171; Hughes, *Hebrews*, 471; and Ellingworth, *Hebrews*, 586. Those who opt for "Abraham" as functioning as the subject include Bruce, *Hebrews*, 294–96; Lane, *Hebrews 9–13*, 334; and the NIV.

236 See H. J. Cadbury, "The Ancient Physiological Notions Underlying John I.13 and Hebrews XI.11," *The Expositor* 2 (1924), 439; P. W. Van der Horst, "Sarah's Seminal Emission: Hebrews 11:11 in the Light of Ancient Embryology," in *A Feminist Companion to the Hebrew Bible in the New Testament*, ed. A. Brewer (Sheffield: Sheffield Academic Press, 1996), 112–34 (first published in *Greeks, Romans, and Christians: Essays in Honor of Abraham J. Malherbe*, ed. D. L. Balch, E. Ferguson, and W. A. Meeks (Minneapolis: Fortress, 1990), 287–302).

237 Bruce, *Hebrews*, 295.

238 Attridge, *Hebrews*, 326.

239 G. Zuntz, *The Text of the Epistles: A Disquisition upon the Corpus Paulinum* (London: Oxford, 1953), 16; Koester, *Hebrews*, 488.

with no manuscript evidence, that *kai autē Sarra* ("even Sarah herself") was an early insertion and should be excised.[240] Matthew Black took the words *kai autē Sarra steira* to be original (as well as the participle *ousa*, "being," after *steira,* found only in a few manuscripts) and explained them based on an Aramaic or "Hebraized" Greek in which "the words are Greek but the vocabulary, grammar, and syntax may be Hebrew."[241] Many have followed this approach, although Ellingworth remains unconvinced.[242]

However plausible some of these solutions may be, they all are actually unnecessary. Sarah, as Isaac's mother, was as involved in the matter as was Abraham. Though at first her faith may have been weak, she believed and received the promised blessing of a son. Hughes's comment is telling:

> These proposals are not unattractive, but they come up against the considerable obstacle that there is no evidence to indicate that the verse was construed along these lines by any of the ancient authors, including, significantly, the Greek fathers. If the author had intended Abraham as the subject of verse 11 it is improbable that this would not have been reflected, at least partially, in the interpretation of the post-apostolic centuries.[243]

A third solution to the problem accepts Sarah as the subject of the verse, but attempts a reinterpretation of the Greek of the passage. At least three interpretive solutions have been proposed along this line. Some have suggested that *katabolē spermatos* should be interpreted to mean Sarah "received power for the founding of a posterity." But this interpretation is strained.[244] Another approach, reflected in some translations, takes the phrase in question to mean "conceive." This is also not without its problems, as stated by Bruce.[245] Greenlee offers a third interpretation along these lines, translating the phrase "for (the purpose of) deposition of seed." He indicated this approach "leaves the subject of *katabolēn* open, to be determined by the context and not limited to being the same as the subject of the verb *elaben* 'received.'"[246] Greenlee's translation of the verse reads as follows: "By faith Sarah herself also received ability for the deposition of seed [in her body by Abraham], even beyond (her/their) normal age, since she considered

---

240 Zuntz, *Text*, 16.

241 M. Black, *An Aramaic approach to the Gospels and Acts*, 2nd ed. (Oxford: Clarendon Press, 1954), 87–88.

242 Ellingworth, *Hebrews*, 587.

243 Hughes, *Hebrews*, 43.

244 See critiques by Delitzsch, *Hebrews*, 2:241; Attridge, *Hebrews*, 325.

245 Bruce, *Hebrews*, 296.

246 H. Greenlee, "Hebrews 11:11—'By Faith Sarah Received Ability'," *AsTJ* 54.1 (1999): 70.

the one having promised to be faithful."[247] This approach has the least problems associated with it and has significant explanatory power.[248]

The use of the pronoun *autē* with "Sarah" gives the emphatic "Sarah herself." This can be taken to indicate a contrast with Sarah's previous unbelief that she would have a child.[249] Moffatt took it as emphasizing her physical condition.[250] Those, like Lane, who take Abraham to be the subject and not Sarah usually give two reasons: (1) *eis katabolēn spermatos* is a Hellenistic idiom "for the specifically male function in procreation"; and (2) the subject of v. 12 is Abraham, "since both the pronoun *henos*, "one," and the qualifying participle *nenekrōmenou*, "already impotent," are masculine in gender. Thus, from v. 8, Abraham remains the subject.[251] To whom does the NIV's phrase "was enabled to become" refer? The phrase reads (lit.) "unto the laying down of seed" which Greenlee translated as "for deposition of seed."[252] Some argue, given the ambiguity in the Greek text, that the phrase should be translated in such a way as to leave open who is the agent/subject. Metzger suggested the verse refers to Abraham's deposition of seed together with Sarah. As stated in the footnote above, the problem with this view is there is no manuscript evidence for the dative required by this option. Bruce, Lane, and Louw-Nida translate the phrase with the sense of an infinitive, "to lay down seed." Greenlee identified the problem with this translation: "which therefore erroneously requires that the actor be the same person as the subject of the preceding verb."[253] The best approach to v. 11 is to understand "Sarah" to be the subject.

11:12 Verse 12 draws the conclusion that from the aged Abraham and Sarah have come descendents as innumerable as the stars in the sky and the sand on the seashore. The phrase "and he as good as dead" reads (lit.), "and these things [neuter plural here has the same meaning as the singular] from [understood] one [understood] dead," with the meaning that one is too old to have children. The perfect participle in Greek translated "dead" attributively modifies the understood "one" in the text. Lane, following Zerwick and Grosvenor, takes it as expressing concession and translates "and he already impotent."[254] The two similes which follow: "as numerous as" and "as countless as" express

---

[247] Ibid., 71.

[248] Part of the solution to this problem in Heb 11:11 may be provided if Luke is the author of Hebrews. The possible use of two technical medical phrases in this verse may indicate the hand of a physician. If καταβολὴν σπέρματος and καιρὸν ἡλικίας are technical phrases that express impregnation and being past the point of menstruation respectively, then this may contribute to the position that Sarah should be seen as the subject of v. 11 and that perhaps Luke is the author. Note the use of καὶ αυτός only in Luke and Hebrews.

[249] So Dods, "Hebrews," 356; and Bruce, *Hebrews*, 296.

[250] Moffatt, *Hebrews*, 171.

[251] Lane, *Hebrews 9–13*, 344.

[252] Greenlee, *Exegetical Summary*, 451.

[253] Ibid., 453.

[254] See Lane, *Hebrews 9–13*, 345; *GAGNT* 680.

comparison indicating the impossibility of counting the number of descendants which have come from Abraham and Sarah. This allusion to the stars and sand is not a direct quotation but a conflation of the content of several Old Testament texts (Gen 22:17 LXX; Exod 32:13 LXX). Given the context, it is likely that the author was thinking primarily about Gen 22:17.

11:13 Verse 13 begins a new paragraph running through v. 16 where the author comments on the nature of this faith he has been illustrating. It has often been noticed that these verses would fit more naturally after v. 22 when the author completes the mention of Abraham (vv. 17–19), Isaac (v. 20), Jacob (v. 21) and Joseph (v. 22). Bligh takes the position that the author displaced these verses from their natural position after v. 22 in order to place them in the center of a chiasm.[255] Such placement, assuming the validity of the chiastic arrangement, places semantic emphasis on vv. 13–16. The verses may be placed in this position for rhetorical effect even if Bligh's chiastic proposal is inaccurate.

Verse 13 begins with (lit.) "according to faith these all died." Lane translated this as "in accordance with the principle of faith" and commented that "according to faith" is emphatic by its clause initial position.[256] Ellingworth took this phrase to be expressing manner in contradistinction from the usage of the dative "by faith" elsewhere in the chapter.[257] Bruce, however, interpreted the phrase to be a stylistic change only.[258] The change from the characteristic "by faith" in the clause initial position may be motivated by two factors: (1) new paragraph onset, and (2) the discussion shifts from individual examples of faith to the author's comment on the group as a whole up to this point in the discourse.

Most commentators understand the phrase "all these" to refer only to the patriarchs since Enoch did not die. But the summary nature of this phrase makes it more likely the author is making a general comment on all the heroes of faith mentioned to this point.[259] These heroes did not receive "the things promised" which includes the possession of the land, the founding of a nation, and the blessing which would come through Abraham's descendants.[260] Alford takes the plural "promises" to refer to the repetition of the promises given to Abraham, Isaac, and Jacob.[261] Eisenbaum suggested the word "promise" in Hebrews "carries overlapping meanings and refers to the promise of ultimate salvation in addition to the national promises."[262] In contrast to receiving the promises, the patriarchs saw and "welcomed" them from a distance. The Greek

---

[255] J. Bligh, "The Structure of Hebrews," *HeyJ* 5 (1964): 176.

[256] Lane, *Hebrews 9–13*, 343, 345.

[257] Ellingworth, *Hebrews*, 592.

[258] Bruce, *Hebrews*, 298.

[259] So Eisenbaum, *Jewish Heroes*, 160. Lane, *Hebrews 9–13*, 356, disagrees, as did Westcott, *Hebrews,* 394; Moffatt, *Hebrews*, 173; and Spicq, *L'Épître aux Hebreux*, 2:350.

[260] Lane, *Hebrews 9–13*, 356.

[261] Alford, "Hebrews," 217.

[262] Eisenbaum, *Jewish Heroes*, 160.

verb *aspazomai* means "to anticipate with pleasure, to look forward with happiness to what was going to happen."[263] Lane proffered the interesting suggestion that the use of *patris*, "homeland, country," in v. 14 "suggests that the writer was thinking of the metaphorical salute given by the returning traveler to his homeland."[264] The use of *porrōthen*, "from a distance," can be taken to refer to time as well as distance.[265] In fact, given the nature of the context, the reference must include some time element in the sense of "the distant future." Finally, an additional fact is stated: the patriarchs openly acknowledged they were "aliens and strangers," the combination of which probably forms a hendiadys meaning "sojourning stranger."[266] The present tense "they are" in Greek is translated with the past tense "they were." Greenlee explains: "It is the indirect form of a statement whose direct form would be 'they are"; the tense of the direct form is retained in the Greek indirect form, but is rendered as a past tense in English."[267] Most commentators take "on earth" to refer to planet earth, but a few, such as Dods and Lane, take it in reference to the land of Canaan.[268] Verse 13 finds its echo in Heb 11:39 where the heroes are commended for their faith and the statement is made that they did not receive the promises.

11:14 Verse 14 is introduced with *gar* (untranslated in the NIV). It introduces either the grounds for the preceding statement or the conclusion from the preceding statement. Ellingworth understood the conjunction to introduce the conclusion drawn from the comments of the patriarchs in the previous verse, where they "admitted" they were pilgrims on earth.[269] Lane viewed the present tense "show" as an emphatic reference to a continuing attitude that "serves to bring the confession of v 13c into the current experience of the house church."[270] The NIV's "looking" is too tame a translation since the word in Greek means to seek or desire intently and is emphatic by word order. Its semantic equivalents occur in v. 10 and v. 16. The use of "country" means "homeland."

11:15 Verses 15 and the first part of 16 are bound together as one sentence in the Greek text by a *men . . . de* construction: "one the one hand . . . but on the other hand." The sentence is coordinated with the previous sentence (v. 14) by *kai*. The conditional clause "if they had been thinking of the country they had left" can be construed with its following clause in one of three ways: (1) as

---

[263] L&N 25.30.

[264] Lane, *Hebrews 9–13*, 356–57.

[265] L&N 67.46; Lane, *Hebrews 9–13*, 366; Ellingworth, *Hebrews*, 693.

[266] Lane, *Hebrews 9–13*, 357, who says the source is Gen 23:4 LXX.

[267] Greenlee, *Exegetical Summary*, 461.

[268] Dods, "Hebrews," 357; Lane, *Hebrews 9–13*, 357.

[269] Ellingworth, *Hebrews*, 595.

[270] Lane, *Hebrews 9–13*, 358.

a contrary-to-fact condition;[271] (2) the imperfect tenses indicate a constative condition in the past in the sense of "if they were continually thinking . . . , they would repeatedly have opportunity to return";[272] (3) although the manuscript evidence is weak, Bruce opts for the present tense reading over the past tense reading in the Greek text, thus taking the first clause as stating a present condition of fact but giving it a past translation.[273] The imperfect tenses are translated as if they were Greek aorists in the NIV.

11:16 Verse 16 begins with *nun*, "instead" (sometimes translated "now"), which in the Greek text indicates logic, not time.[274] The "better country" is further described as a "heavenly one." The conjunction *dio*, "therefore," introduces either a result of the preceding sentence, or a reason for why God is not ashamed: because he has prepared a city for them.[275] That God is not ashamed may be an example of litotes, implying a strong positive affirmation. The NIV, as do many translations, leaves untranslated the plural direct object "them."[276] The "city" refers to the heavenly Jerusalem which will be further explicated in Heb 12:22.

(3) Accomplishments of Faith (11:17–40)

**17By faith Abraham, when God tested him, offered Isaac as a sacrifice. He
who had received the promises was about to sacrifice his one and only son, 18even
though God had said to him, "It is through Isaac that your offspring will be reckoned." 19Abraham reasoned that God could raise the dead, and figuratively speaking, he did receive Isaac back from death.**

20By faith Isaac blessed Jacob and Esau in regard to their future.

21By faith Jacob, when he was dying, blessed each of Joseph's sons, and worshiped as he leaned on the top of his staff.

22By faith Joseph, when his end was near, spoke about the exodus of the Israelites from Egypt and gave instructions about his bones.

23By faith Moses' parents hid him for three months after he was born, because they saw he was no ordinary child, and they were not afraid of the king's edict.

**24By faith Moses, when he had grown up, refused to be known as the son of
Pharaoh's daughter. 25He chose to be mistreated along with the people of God**

---

[271] Greenlee, *Exegetical Summary*, 463: "It is actually a slightly irregular construction, since the apodosis (the second clause) would logically be 'they would return.' The imperfect tenses indicate that this is a *present* time contrary-to-fact condition, not past time . . . ; it is related to the present tense ἐμφανίζουσιν 'they make clear' in the preceding verse, and the present tense is continued in v. 16."

[272] So Dods, "Hebrews," 358; Alford, "Hebrews," 218; Moffatt, *Hebrews*, 175; and Lane, *Hebrews 9–13*, 346, with translation cited by Greenlee, *Exegetical Summary*, 463.

[273] Bruce, *Hebrews*, 297.

[274] Lane, *Hebrews*, 346; and Ellingworth, *Hebrews*, 598.

[275] Ellingworth, *Hebrews*, 598–99, opts for the latter meaning.

[276] So Ellingworth, *Hebrews*, 599, on the basis that it is redundant and anticipates the αὐτῶν of the next clause. Lünemann, *Hebrews*, 679, takes it as the predicate of "he is ashamed," with the infinitive "to be called" functioning as the second predicate which provides additional explanation.

**rather than to enjoy the pleasures of sin for a short time. 26He regarded disgrace
for the sake of Christ as of greater value than the treasures of Egypt, because he
was looking ahead to his reward. 27By faith he left Egypt, not fearing the king's
anger; he persevered because he saw him who is invisible. 28By faith he kept the
Passover and the sprinkling of blood, so that the destroyer of the firstborn would
not touch the firstborn of Israel.**

**29By faith the people passed through the Red Sea as on dry land; but when the
Egyptians tried to do so, they were drowned.**

**30By faith the walls of Jericho fell, after the people had marched around them
for seven days.**

**31By faith the prostitute Rahab, because she welcomed the spies, was not killed
with those who were disobedient.**

**32And what more shall I say? I do not have time to tell about Gideon, Barak,
Samson, Jephthah, David, Samuel and the prophets, 33who through faith conquered kingdoms, administered justice, and gained what was promised; who shut
the mouths of lions, 34quenched the fury of the flames, and escaped the edge of
the sword; whose weakness was turned to strength; and who became powerful
in battle and routed foreign armies. 35Women received back their dead, raised
to life again. Others were tortured and refused to be released, so that they might
gain a better resurrection. 36Some faced jeers and flogging, while still others were
chained and put in prison. 37They were stoned; they were sawed in two; they were
put to death by the sword. They went about in sheepskins and goatskins, destitute,
persecuted and mistreated— 38the world was not worthy of them. They wandered
in deserts and mountains, and in caves and holes in the ground.**

**39These were all commended for their faith, yet none of them received what had
been promised. 40God had planned something better for us so that only together
with us would they be made perfect.**

11:17 Verses 17–22 constitute the fourth paragraph unit of the chapter 11. It covers the patriarchs Abraham (vv. 17–19), Isaac (v. 20), Jacob (v. 21) and Joseph (v. 22). Verse 17 resumes the anaphoric use of *pistei*, describing Abraham's willingness to offer up Isaac in response to the command of God as done "by faith." The verb "offered," used twice in v. 17, has a sacrificial nuance. "The verb has been used with a precise concern for tenses in each of the complementary clauses of v 17, (perfect, then imperfect) which are arranged on the model of OT poetic sense-parallelism."[277] The perfect tense implies abiding results of the offering as permanently recorded in Scripture according to Ellingworth,[278] whereas Lane observed the offering was completed from Abraham's point of view, although he did not physically offer Isaac.[279] Dods and Moffatt take the perfect tense to refer only to a past act with no emphasis being suggested by the author.[280] The use of the present tense participle translated "when God tested him" implies action concurrent with the perfect tense

[277] Lane, *Hebrews 9–13*, 361.
[278] Ellingworth, *Hebrews*, 600.
[279] Lane, *Hebrews 9–13*, 361. So also Hughes, *Hebrews*, 482; and Bruce, *Hebrews*, 301.
[280] Dods, "Hebrews," 358; Moffatt, *Hebrews*, 176.

verb. The Greek text does not have the subject "God" which is supplied by the NIV based on the statement in Gen 22:1 that "God tested Abraham." The second use of the verb "offer" is in the imperfect tense and indicates the act was begun but not completed.[281] The substitution of *monogenēs*, "only begotten," for "beloved" in the LXX text of Gen 22:2 should not be taken to have any Christological significance in this context.[282] Ishmael is not considered because he was not the son of Sarah and because he had already been "sent away" in Genesis 21 before the testing of Abraham in Genesis 22.

11:18 The NIV gives v. 18 a concessive translation with "even though." Most commentators and translations take it as an additional comment concerning Isaac. The phrase which begins the verse is (lit.) "to whom" and can grammatically be a reference to Abraham or Isaac. The purpose of the quotation "It is through Isaac that your offspring will be reckoned" is to explain the nature of the promises mentioned in v. 17. "In Isaac" is emphatic by word order in the clause. Swetnam takes *sperma*, "seed," translated "offspring," to refer to the spiritual descendants and not the physical descendants of Abraham throughout Hebrews.[283] His argument is, however, too dependent upon Pauline arguments. Additionally, it misses the point that the first readers of Hebrews were both physical descendants of Abraham (Jews) and spiritual descendants (believers by faith in Christ).

11:19 It seemed to Abraham illogical for God to ask him to kill his only son when God had said it would be through that son that he would give Abraham numerous descendants. It could only be sorted out in Abraham's mind that God must intend to raise Isaac from the dead. Thus Abraham "reasoned," a word meaning inward conviction and not merely a considered opinion.[284] The use of the aorist tense has been taken to imply Abraham's conclusion was made once and with finality.[285] However, from an aspectual angle, this may be over-interpretation. The participle indicates the reason for the action or it may merely state an additional fact. The first *kai* which appears in the clause "Abraham reasoned that God could raise the dead" is incorrectly left untranslated in the NIV and should be given an ascensive translation of "even" since it is used emphatically to emphasize God's power in the act of raising the dead.[286] The second clause of the verse is introduced by the Greek *hothen* which is taken by the NIV as indicating source in the translation "from death."[287] However,

---

[281] So Bruce, *Hebrews*, 301; Hughes, *Hebrews*, 482.

[282] So Attridge, *Hebrews*, 334; Eisenbaum, *Jewish Heroes*, 162; and L&N 58.52.

[283] Swetnam, *Jesus and Isaac*, 90–127.

[284] Lane, *Hebrews 9–13*, 362.

[285] Westcott, *Hebrews*, 366.

[286] So Lane, *Hebrews 9–13*, 347, and Ellingworth, *Hebrews*, 602.

[287] Westcott, *Hebrews*, 366; Alford, "Hebrews," 220; and Dods, "Hebrews," 359, all take it as indicating source.

it seems better to take it as result in the sense of "as a result Abraham received him back."[288]

The prepositional phrase "in a parable" (NIV "figuratively speaking") should not be over-interpreted to refer to the resurrection of Jesus or the believer according to Eisenbaum.[289] However, Swetnam and Lane, based on the use of *parabolē* in Heb 9:8–9 and the context here, took the meaning to be foreshadowing the future resurrection from the dead. According to Lane, it is the Christian community which recognizes the foreshadowing, whether Abraham did or not.[290] Eisenbaum summed up the point of the verse nicely: "What is stressed is that from one who was almost never born, and who after being born was almost killed, the descendants of Abraham, . . . are born."[291] Likewise Lane: "[W]hen Abraham obeyed God's mandate to leave Ur, he simply gave up his past. But when he was summoned to Mount Moriah to deliver his own son to God, he was asked to surrender his future as well."[292]

11:20 The patriarchal family line continued with Isaac blessing Jacob and Esau. The reference is to Gen 27:27–40 where the future aspect of the blessing is mentioned in vv. 29,37. For the author, the act of blessing is related to the theme of the promise in Hebrews. The Greek reads (lit.), "by faith also concerning coming things Isaac blessed Jacob and Esau." The conjunction *kai* is connected with the following prepositional phrase "in regard to their future." It is left untranslated in the NIV, but it adds emphasis to the statement. Lane translated it "even with respect to their future."[293] The meaning is to future things which were unseen by virtue of their being in the future. Lünemann suggested that the order of the names, Jacob before Esau, implies that it was Jacob and not Esau through whom the promises were to be fulfilled and that this order reflects the order in which they received their blessing according to the Genesis text.[294]

11:21 The NIV adds the understood "leaned" which is not in the Greek text. Jacob supported himself in his old age by leaning on his staff. The phrase "on the top of his staff" tells where Jacob was leaning.[295] However, Lenski took it as dependent upon "worshipped."[296] Genesis 47:31 states Jacob worshipped while leaning on his staff and this is prior to the blessing of Joseph's

---

288 So Moffatt, *Hebrews*, 177; Lane, *Hebrews 9–13*, 347; and Ellingworth, *Hebrews*, 603.

289 Eisenbaum, *Jewish Heroes*, 162–63. However, Swetnam, *Jesus and Isaac*, 168, takes it to refer to the resurrection of Jesus; and Attridge, *Hebrews*, 335, takes it to refer to the resurrection of Christians.

290 Swetnam, *Jesus and Isaac*, 119–21; Lane, *Hebrews 9–13*, 363.

291 Eisenbaum, *Jewish Heroes*, 163.

292 Lane, *Hebrews 9–13*, 360.

293 Lane, *Hebrews 9–13*, 343.

294 Lünemann, *Hebrews*, 682.

295 The author of Hebrews is dependent upon the LXX of Gen 47:21 and not the MT, which reads Jacob "bowed down at the head of his bed."

296 Lenski, *Hebrews*, 405.

sons, but the entire unit of meaning is viewed together by our author.[297] The statement reflects Gen 48:21. The blessing given by Isaac and Jacob was an act of faith since neither man could give what was promised to his sons/grandsons. Both Isaac and Jacob were totally dependent upon God to fulfill the promised blessings.

11:22 Joseph did two things at the end of his life: he spoke of the coming exodus and gave instructions concerning his own burial in the promised land. The author uses a different Greek word for "dying" than in the previous verse, a word whose connotation is a figurative extension of the Greek word "to end" and is a euphemistic expression for death expressed as "when his end was near."[298] Joseph knew the promise to Abraham and his descendants concerning the land meant someday there would have to be an exodus from Egypt (see Gen 50:24–25). When the exodus took place years later, Joseph's coffin was carried from Egypt (Exod 13:19) and finally buried at Shechem (Josh 24:32).

11:23 Verses 23–28 constitute the next paragraph unit. This section concerning Moses actually begins with the faith of Moses' parents.[299] The reference is to Exod 2:2, with the background to the event in Exod 1:15–22. Two reasons are given in v. 23 for their act of hiding Moses. First, they saw he was "no ordinary child," the NIV translation for the LXX "beautiful." Commentators often suggest that the behind this word is the notion of God's favor or approval, or that God had some special purpose for Moses' life.[300] This is of course true, but it is difficult to extract this from the word itself. The second reason for their action is they were not afraid of Pharaoh's edict. Although this is not stated in the LXX of Exod 2:2, it is an implication drawn by the author of Hebrews.

11:24–26 The events narrated in 11:24–26 find no parallel in the Exodus narrative, but are the author's reflections and conclusions based on the Old Testament's overall statements about Moses and possibly on current tradition concerning Moses known to the author. The phrase "when he had grown up" in Greek is paralleled in Exod 2:11 LXX. Verse 24 is the generic statement concerning Moses' choice of refusal to be known as the son of Pharaoh's daughter, followed by the specifics of vv. 25–26.

The compound verb *sunkakoucheisthai*, "to be mistreated," is found nowhere prior to Hebrews and may have been coined by the author. The author does not

---

[297] Balz and Schneider, *EDNT* 3.206, noted Jacob's bowing over the staff suggested humility. Interpretations like that of Aquinas who viewed the staff as being Joseph's royal scepter and thus foreshadowing Christ's reign are fanciful. For this and other such interpretations during the patristic and medieval period, see Hughes, *Hebrews*, 490–91. Michel, *an die Hebräer*, 405, pointed out the staff is here a sign of pilgrimage.

[298] See L&N 23.102.

[299] The MT mentions only Moses' mother as the one hiding him, but the LXX mentions both parents.

[300] Lane, *Hebrews 9–13*, 367, following Hughes, *Hebrews,* 492, says the word "must carry the overtones of 'extraordinary.' Note the parallel use in Acts 7:20.

define the meaning of "pleasures of sin," but Michel, Weiss, and DeSilva take the sin to be refusing to live in solidarity with the people of God.[301]

Verse 26 is an authorial comment concerning Moses' motivation for his choice in v. 25. The author's phrase "reproach of Christ" (NIV "disgrace for the sake of Christ") has engendered various views as to its meaning.[302] Lane interpreted the phrase to be "an elliptical summary of Ps 88 (MT 89):51–52 LXX."[303] Westcott argued that "Christ" here should be understood generically from its etymology as "the anointed one" so that the phrase means to suffer with the people of God.[304] The immediate context and the fact that *Christos* is not used in this way anywhere else in the epistle militate against this view.[305] Koester correctly noted the primary and secondary levels of Christological meaning: (1) reproach like what was endured by Christ in his suffering and death, and (2) reproach for the sake of Christ.[306] Given the author's understanding of the role of Christ in the Old Testament, the secondary meaning is valid. Verse 26 probably should not be understood typologically such that Moses' life typifies the life of Christ.[307] However, it is certainly possible that some typological significance was in the mind of the author given the similarities of Moses' childhood and Jesus' childhood: both their lives were threatened by kings, and the baby Jesus was preserved when Joseph and Mary took him to Egypt until the time of Herod's death. The use of the Greek word translated "disgrace" in v. 26 harks back to 10:33–34, where the readers are said to have publicly endured "insult," and forward to 13:13 where they are to bear Christ's "disgrace." Lane stated concerning the phrase "looking ahead to his reward" that it "suggests concentrated attention, while the imperfect tense denotes the habitual stance of Moses."[308]

11:27 This verse seems to contradict the Exodus account of Moses' fear when he left Egypt. This in turn raises the question of whether the author is speaking of the first time Moses left Egypt in his flight to Midian (Exod 2:14–15)[309] or is it a reference to the exodus event itself under Moses' leadership (Exod 13:17–15:21).[310] D'Angelo suggested the author may have conflated

---

[301] Michel, *an die Hebräer*, 273; H. F. Weiss, *Der Brief an die Hebräer*, KEK 13 (Göttingen: Vandenhoeck & Ruprecht, 1991), 605; and DeSilva, *Perseverance in Gratitude*, 408–9.

[302] Attridge, *Hebrews*, 341–42, outlines the various views.

[303] Lane, *Hebrews 9–13*, 373; cf. D'Angelo, *Moses in Hebrews*, 48–50, for discussion of the various options.

[304] Westcott, *Hebrews*, 374.

[305] Eisenbaum, *Jewish Heroes*, 168.

[306] Koester, *Hebrews*, 502–3.

[307] As does Montefiore, *Hebrews*, 203.

[308] Lane, *Hebrews 9–13*, 373.

[309] So argued by Moffatt, *Hebrews*, 187; Bruce, *Hebrews*, 312–13; and Attridge, *Hebrews*, 342.

[310] So argued by Westcott, *Hebrews*, 373; Montefiore, *Hebrews*, 204. See Hughes, *Hebrews*, 498–99 for a good critique of this position.

the two events for his purposes in Hebrews 11.[311] Eisenbaum summed up the problem:

> If the verse refers to the departure for Midian the difficulty lies in the phrase not being afraid of the king's anger," because Exod 2:14 explicitly states that Moses left because he was afraid. If, on the other hand, the verse refers to the exodus, the problem lies with chronology. The exodus of the people happens *after* the Passover sacrifice (v. 28), and up until now the author has not deviated from following biblical chronology.[312]

In support of the first option, Hughes suggested that the author's statement concerning Moses not fearing the king's anger can be reconciled with Exod 2:14 when one understands "that it was not personal fear of Pharaoh but the awareness of his destiny as the deliverer of the covenant people that caused him to take flight."[313] Hughes continued: "In other words, the governing impulse of his flight from Egypt was faith, not fear, as is neatly suggested by the NEB translation: 'By faith he left Egypt, and not because he feared the king's anger.'"[314]

Moses "persevered" because he saw "him who is invisible." This has been applied to the burning bush experience (Exod 3:1–4:17),[315] the pillar of cloud and fire,[316] and to various visions.[317] It is probably more accurate to suggest the author was summing up all such events in the general statement he makes. The NIV translates the *hōs* causally, "because he saw." Probably better is the qualitative translation "as if he saw."[318] The translation "unseen" is preferable to "invisible." The word is used for God in many places in the New Testament (see Rom 1:20; Col 1:15; 1 Tim 1:17). Lane understood the meaning to be a reference to Moses' "fixed habit of spiritual perception. Once that is recognized, it is clear that the explanatory clause in v 27b is a parallel comment to v 26b and must be interpreted in the light of that earlier statement."[319] Finally, DeSilva rightly pointed out: "Considering how Moses left his country in a physical sense prepares for the exhortation that listeners must separate

---

[311] D'Angelo, *Moses in Hebrews*, 59–62; so also Eisenbaum, *Jewish Heroes*, 170.

[312] Eisenbaum, *Jewish Heroes*, 169.

[313] Hughes, *Hebrews*, 499. Lane, *Hebrews 9–13*, 375, takes the same approach: "Moses did express fear when he knew his violent action had become public knowledge (Exod 2:14), but by faith he overcame his fear of reprisals and left Egypt, finding in faith a substantiation of hopes as yet unrealized and events as yet unseen (v. 1)."

[314] Ibid; cf. the defense of Exod 2:11–14 as standing behind Heb 11:24–27 by Lane, *Hebrews 9–13*, 374–75.

[315] So Eisenbaum, *Jewish Heroes*, 170.

[316] So Philo, *Moses* 1.166.

[317] So Calvin, *Hebrews*, 178–79.

[318] Koester, *Hebrews*, 504; Hughes, *Hebrews*, 500, noted the phrase is ambiguous and can mean either "as in fact seeing" or "as though seeing."

[319] Lane, *Hebrews 9–13*, 376.

themselves in a social sense from their own city in order to maintain their faith."[320]

11:28 The typological significance of this verse is debated.[321] Whether typology is intended our not, either way the author does not develop the significance. The reference to the Passover and the sprinkling of blood comes from Exod 12:7,13,21–23. Moses "kept" the first Passover in direct response to the command of God. The perfect tense verb translated "kept" probably indicates the continuing annual celebration of the Passover, though Moffatt takes the tense to be equivalent to the aorist tense identifying undefined action in past time.[322] The NIV failed to retain the Greek article before "blood" in its translation "the sprinkling of blood." Bruce and Lane note that the use of the article refers to a specific sprinkling which only occurred at the first Passover, but was not continued in subsequent celebrations.[323] This act of placing the blood on the doorposts prevented "the destroyer"[324] from "touching" (an idiom for "killing") the firstborn. Rhetorically, the author employs alliteration with the use of five words beginning with the Greek letter "pi" in this verse alone. This is virtually impossible to reflect in English. From this point on in the chapter, there is a subtle transition from persons to events.[325]

11:29–31 These verses constitute a paragraph unit that contains a startling omission and a startling inclusion. The surprising omission is the absence of Joshua's name in conjunction with the fall of Jericho. The surprising inclusion is the mention of Rahab and the following three facts: she was a Gentile (in fact a Canaanite), a woman, and a prostitute. Her name is also mentioned positively in Matthew's genealogy (Matt 1:5) and in Jas 2:25.

---

[320] DeSilva, *Perseverance in Gratitude*, 509.

[321] Attridge, *Hebrews*, 343; and Koester, *Hebrews*, 504, are among those who argue it has no typological significance. On the other hand, Hughes, *Hebrews*, 500–1, sees a relation to the death of Christ.

[322] Moffatt, *Hebrews*, 182.

[323] Bruce, *Hebrews*, 314; Lane, *Hebrews 9–13*, 376–77.

[324] There is a grammatical question concerning what the noun phrase τὰ πρωτότοκα ("the firstborn ones") and the pronoun αὐτῶν should be connected with. Two options are available. If τὰ πρωτότοκα is construed as the predicate of ὁ ὀλοθρεύων, and αὐτῶν is the predicate (in the genitive case) of θίγῃ, then the meaning would be "the one destroying the firstborn ones would not touch them." This is the approach taken by Alford, "Hebrews," 266; Dods, "Hebrews," 361; Bruce, *Hebrews*, 308; and the NIV. However, Greenlee objects to this on grammatical grounds: "Grammatically, those who translate the participle ὁ ὀλοθρεύων 'the one destroying' as a noun—e.g., 'the Destroyer'—should not make it govern the accusative τὰ πρωτότοκα 'the firstborn ones', since it would have to be a genitive case" (*Exegetical Summary*, 484). The other option is to take τὰ πρωτότοκα as the predicate of θίγῃ and αὐτῶν as construed with τὰ πρωτότοκα. This would yield the translation: "the Destroyer would not touch the firstborn ones of them." This is the approach taken by Lane, *Hebrews 9–13*, 367; and Ellingworth, *Hebrews*, 618. This latter option is to be preferred.

[325] Lane, *Hebrews 9–13*, 376.

Verse 29 references the account of the crossing of the Red Sea in Exod 14:21–31.[326] The allusion is specifically to Exod 14:22 LXX. Three propositions form the verse: the people of Israel passed through the Red Sea "as on dry land"; the Egyptians attempted the same; they were drowned. Those who crossed the Red Sea are not overtly named in the text; rather they are subsumed in the third person plural ending of the verb which would be translated as (lit.) "they passed through." The Egyptians were "drowned," a compound Greek word meaning (lit.) they were "swallowed up," where the prefixed preposition intensifies the meaning of the verb. Louw-Nida note the word indicates they were "destroyed."[327]

Verse 30 references the fall of the walls of Jericho as found in Josh 6:1–21. "By faith" has no referent in the verse, but it would seem obvious that the people of Israel are being referred to here. Verse 31 speaks of Rahab from the account of Josh 2:1–21, especially vv. 10–11. She is called a "prostitute" in Josh 2:1; 6:17,22,25.[328] Rahab "was prepared to assume present peril for the sake of future preservation (Josh 2:12–16)."[329] Because of her actions which exhibited her faith, her family was spared (Josh 6:17,22–25). Mosser correctly observed Rahab's commendation is not dependent upon her relationship to any male, including husband or father.[330]

11:32 Verses 32–38 comprise the next paragraph unit. One evidence of paragraph onset at this point is the absence of the anaphoric use of *pistei* which has been prevalent to this point. In addition, the use of a rhetorical question introduces the new paragraph. At this point in the author's argument, chronology ceases to be of major importance as the author focuses less on the exploits of heroic individuals as on the summation of Israel's history during the time of the judges and the early monarchy. Eisenbaum's reference to the "disorganized chronology" combined with "mediocre names" as alluding "to what our author sees as the dissolution of biblical history" misses the mark altogether.[331] The author's method here is for rhetorical effect. The section covers a period of biblical history which extends at the very least to 2 Kings and at the most to

---

[326] F. Bovon, "Le Christ, la foi et la sagesse dans l'Épître aux Hébreux (Hébreux 11 et 1)," *RTP* 18 (1968): 129–44, argued for a literary relationship between Heb 11:29 and *Wisdom* 10:18–19, but the evidence is far too minimal to make the case.

[327] L&N 20.52.

[328] On the attempt to soften the description of Rahab as a prostitute in pre-Christian Judaism as well as in post-Christian Jewish and Christian thought, see Hughes, *Hebrews*, 503.

[329] Lane, *Hebrews 9–13*, 379.

[330] C. Mosser, "Rahab Outside the Camp," unpublished paper given at The St. Andrew Conference on Hebrews and Theology, St. Mary's College, The University of St. Andrews, Scotland, (July 18–22, 2006), 254.

[331] Eisenbaum, *Jewish Heroes*, 175.

Malachi. This section contains numerous allusions to biblical as well as intertestamental events.[332]

Verse 32 begins with a rhetorical question which reflects a common rhetorical phrase found in classical authors.[333] Thiselton takes it as functionally equivalent to the modern use of "etc."[334] The use of the participle *diēgoumenon* with its masculine ending makes clear the author was not a woman. It has become popular since Harnack's proposed theory of Priscillan authorship in AD 1900 to speculate about the possibility that Hebrews was written by a woman. If that were the case, then she has disguised her femininity here. This is of course problematic for those who hold to a high view of biblical authority. The fact remains that there is no evidence externally in the early church nor internally in the epistle itself that the author was a woman.

The names enumerated cover three historical time periods: the Judges, early Monarchy (David and Samuel) and the prophets.[335] Gideon's story is told in Judg 6:33–8:21. The remarkable reduction of his fighting force from 32000 to 300 men and their subsequent victory is one of the Old Testament's supreme example of faith. Barak was the military commander of the army of Israel who led them to a great victory over Sisera, the Canaanite commander (Judg 4:4–5:31). Samson's sordid but intriguing story of victory over the Philistines is found in Judg 13:1–16:31. Jephthah (Judg 10:6–11:32) won a great victory over the Ammonites. King David's exploits are chronicled in 1 Samuel 15–2 Samuel 24. Samuel was, of course, the last of the judges and the first of the prophets.[336] The mention of "prophets" is a general reference taking the history down through Malachi.

11:33–34 These verses are a unit and chronicle a wide range of political and military adversities overcome by faith. Westcott suggested that the nine statements in these two verses can be grouped into three triads. Hughes's comment against this on the grounds that the author's writing here is "spontaneous and unstudied" is surprising given the evidence of studied organization and rhetorical technique of the author throughout the epistle.[337] The phrase "administered justice" could allude to David in 2 Sam 8:15//1 Chr 18:14 and to Solomon in 1 Kgs 10:9. The phrase "gained what was promised" could allude to Josh 21:43–45, where the Lord gave Israel the land and it is stated, "Not one of all the LORD's good promises to the house of Israel failed; every one was

[332] See Bruce, *Hebrews*, 319–28, for references and commentary on these allusions. DeSilva, *Perseverance in Gratitude*, 416, considers the descriptions of 11:35–38 as most likely including the Maccabean martyrs.

[333] Lane, *Hebrews 9–13*, 382.

[334] Thiselton, "Hebrews," 1475.

[335] Hughes, *Hebrews*, 507.

[336] Acts 3:24.

[337] Hughes, *Hebrews*, 508.

fulfilled." The phrase "shut the mouths of lions" recalls Daniel's deliverance (Dan 6:22).

Verse 34 continues the list of faith's exploits with "quenched the fury of the flames," alluding to Shadrach, Meshach and Abednego in Nebuchadnezzar's furnace (Dan 3:17). Samson could be the one described with "whose weakness was turned to strength" (Judg 16:28). Lane takes the next two together—"powerful in battle"—and "routed," where the latter word carries the nuance of breaking a military formation.[338] These two clauses call to mind Gideon's attack against the Midianites (Judg 7:21–23) since Gideon was just mentioned.

11:35–38 This new unit is introduced with the new subject, "women" who "received back their dead." The statement most likely refers to the widow of Zarephath whose son God raised through Elijah in 1 Kgs 17:17–24 and to the son of the Shunammite woman whom Elisha raised in 2 Kgs 4:18–37. There is a sudden shift with the reference to "torture."[339] Jeremiah's experience (Jer 29:26; 37:15) would be an example of this kind of suffering, as would Isaiah if Jewish tradition can be considered accurate (*Martyrdom of Isaiah* 5:1–14). Commentators usually identify this passage with the Maccabean martyrs under the reign of Antiochus IV as recorded in 2 Macc 6:18–7:42 (Eleazar's martyrdom) and 4 Maccabees 5–18. The significance of this is the author here departs from canonical history to rely on extra-canonical sources. Considerable overlap in language suggests a reliance on the actual Maccabean texts rather than merely tradition.[340] The "better resurrection" refers to "the final defeat of death in the experience of eschatological resurrection."[341] DeSilva's identification of "those who rose to life in the realm of God rather than those who were resuscitated to the life of this world" is contextually based, comparing the women whose sons were resuscitated to life with those who were martyred and who await a future resurrection.[342]

In v. 36, "jeers" connotes verbal abuse and "flogging" indicates physical abuse. The phrase "chains and imprisonment" is rendered verbally in the NIV as "were chained and put in prison." Jeremiah was beaten and imprisoned (Jer 37:15–20). The author uses different verbs for "receiving" the promise. For example, in 10:36 the verb is *komizō*. This verb is used in Hebrews 11 only at the end in v. 39. Attridge observed that when this verb is used with "promise" in other places in the NT, the promise of eschatological salvation is in view (see 2 Cor 5:10; Eph 6:8; Col 3:25; 1 Pet 1:9; 5:4).[343]

---

[338] Lane, *Hebrews 9–13*, 381, 387.

[339] See Lane, *Hebrews 9–13*, 388, for a detailed description of the use of this word and the methods of torture that may have been employed.

[340] Gheorghita, *Role of the Septuagint*, 97.

[341] Lane, *Hebrews 9–13*, 389.

[342] DeSilva, *Perseverance in Gratitude*, 419.

[343] Attridge, *Hebrews*, 301.

The author achieves heightened rhetorical effectiveness with his use of asyndeton in v. 37. Mistreatment of the prophets of Israel is recorded in several places, including Jer 20:1–3,7–8 and Jer 37:15–18. First Kings 22:24–28 speaks of the fate of Micaiah. Zechariah son of Jehoiada was stoned according to 2 Chr 24:20–22. Jewish legends arose concerning the deaths of Isaiah, Jeremiah and Zechariah. Jeremiah was said to be stoned and Isaiah was said to be sawn in half.[344] This is probably the background of the author's statement that they were "sawed in two."[345] The phrase "put to death by the sword" is reminiscent of Jezebel who killed many of the prophets (1 Kgs 18:4,13; 19:10). The phrase "sheepskins and goatskins" immediately brings to mind the clothing of Elijah and Elisha (2 Kgs 1:8). Sometimes clothing carries associations with a specific social location, which is probably the author's point here.[346] The aorist tense shifts to the three present participles at the end of v. 37. These last three words, "destitute, persecuted and mistreated," aptly summarize the prophetic ministries of Elijah and Elisha and all the prophets who refused to compromise the word of God.

Verse 38 sums up the author's rhetorical catena by stating two final things about these persecuted heroes of faith: the world was not worthy of them and they wandered about hiding in "deserts," "mountains," "caves," and "holes in the ground." Despite the predicament of the faithful heroes, "society did not deserve to possess them."[347]

Verses 32–38 have as their goal and message that, regardless of external circumstances, what pleases God and what marks a person's worth is faith in God and in his word.[348] The staccato-like rhetorical technique in this section prepares the way for the author's final paragraph where he makes application to his readers.

11:39–40 These verses comprise the final paragraph of the chapter. It serves a twofold function: (1) to summarize the chapter in succinct fashion, and (2) to serve as a transition to 12:1–13. The author concludes his lengthy list of examples by stating two truths in v. 39: (1) all the heroes mentioned "were commended" by God for their faith, (2) "yet none of them received what had been promised." God's commendation of their faith gives warrant for the author to use these men and women as examples for his readers to emulate. Yet contrary to expectation, none of these heroes received in their lifetimes the fulfillment of the promise (singular) God had made to them. Interestingly, this is the first time in Hebrews that the word "promise" is used in the singular. The

[344] On Jeremiah, see *Lives of the Prophets* 2.1; on Isaiah, see *Lives of the Prophets* 1.1; *Ascension of Isaiah* 5:1–14; and the references in Lane, *Hebrews 9–13*, 390.

[345] On the text-critical issues surrounding ἐπρίσθησαν, see Lane, *Hebrews 9–13*, 381; *TCGNT* 674–75; and Zuntz, *Text*, 47–48.

[346] DeSilva, *Perseverance in Gratitude,* 422.

[347] Lane, *Hebrews 9–13*, 392.

[348] DeSilva, *Perseverance in Gratitude,* 417.

promise referred to is probably to salvation in Christ. Many have expressed the notion of an apparent contradiction between vv. 13,39 when compared to v. 33. The solution is that v. 33 speaks of the act of promising while vv. 13,39 refer to the fulfillment of those promises.[349]

The "something better" in v. 40 which "God had planned" for the readers is clarified by the final clause, which reads (lit.) "in order that not apart from us they should be perfected." Although the identification of "something better" is not explicitly stated in the text, contextually it involves the salvation brought to all believers in Christ.[350] The tendency to transpose the negative final clause in Greek into a positive statement in English, as in the NIV, is problematic. It is preferable to preserve the negative in the text, as does the NASB.[351] The negative particle in the Greek text can be connected with "apart from us,"[352] or with the verb "be made perfect.'[353] Greenlee noted the word order favors the former.[354] Throughout Hebrews, perfection is used in the sense of completion and fulfillment. Thus, for the author of Hebrews, Jesus has ushered in the *telos* of biblical history.[355] Perfection here has an eschatological focus, and refers to entrance into the promised eternal inheritance and "consistently has in view the totality of Christ's ministry on their behalf, in his death and heavenly exaltation."[356] Nairne's expressive translational paraphrase captures the author's words poignantly: "And yet all these, though canonized through faith in the witness of scripture, lacked fruition of the promise; inasmuch as God, with us today in view, had provided a better fulfillment than they could conceive, that the completion of their blessedness might not be achieved without our co-operation."[357] In other words, God provided something better by including us (the readers) with them (Old Testament saints) so that all his people would be made perfect in Christ.

In conclusion, what is the author's purpose in Hebrews 11? It has been argued that the author is attempting to assist his audience to understand their identity as a group of people in God's grand scheme of salvation. On this social identification theory, the author is transmitting something of a "collective memory" to aid his audience correctly to locate themselves in their world and to make some sense of their suffering.[358] While this approach has its relative

---

[349] So Eisenbaum, *Jewish Heroes,* 85.

[350] Ellingworth, *Hebrews,* 636.

[351] Lane, *Hebrews 9–13,* 382.

[352] So Ellingworth, *Hebrews,* 636.

[353] So Moffatt, *Hebrews,* 191; Bruce, *Hebrews,* 330; and Lane, *Hebrews 9–13,* 381.

[354] Greenlee, *Exegetical Summary,* 501.

[355] As noted by Eisenbaum, *Jewish Heroes,* 178. See Peterson, *Hebrews and Perfection,* for the definitive study on this word in the epistle.

[356] Lane, *Hebrews 9–13,* 393.

[357] Nairne, *Hebrews,* 118.

[358] P. Esler, "Collective Memory and Hebrews 11: Outlining a New Investigative Framework,"' in *Social Memory and Christian Origins*, ed. A. Kirk and T. Thatcher, Semeia Monographs 52 (Atlanta: Society of Biblical Literature, 2005), 151–71.

merits, the author is doing more than mere social identity. He is challenging his readers/hearers to *act* in a certain way in spite of current trials. Such action is motivated "by faith," and ensues in various things which Old Testament saints do, as narrated by the author.

Eisenbaum identified four characteristics of the heroes in Hebrews 11. First, most experience death or have a near death experience.[359] Second, they all have the ability to see beyond their own day by their faith. Not only did they accomplish great things by faith, but because of their faith they developed the capacity to look beyond their own lifetime. Third, they all experience some alteration of their status. Fourth, they all experience some form of marginalization.[360]

The point the author is driving home to his readers is summed up well by DeSilva:

> Their gratitude and loyalty should be all the greater since God has given them a special place in the fulfillment of his promise to all the people of faith. However, their responsibility is likewise greater. Will they, at the very end of the relay race, drop the baton that has been passed to them in plain sight of the many who have already run the race so well and honorably (see 12:1)?[361]

3. Encouragement to Run with Endurance and Pursue Peace (12:1–29)

The discourse unit comprising Hebrews 12 can be subdivided into two smaller units: 12:1-17 and 12:18-29.[362] Hebrews 12:1–17 contains three paragraphs: vv. 1–3,[363] vv. 4–13, and vv. 14–17. Hebrews 12:18–29 contains two paragraphs: vv. 18–24, and vv. 25–29. Lane, following Vanhoye, considers

---

[359] This fact is also affirmed and elaborated by R. Gordon, "Better Promises: Two Passages in Hebrews Against the Background of the Old Testament Cultus," *Templum Amicitiae: Essays on the Second Temple Presented to Ernst Bammel*, in JSNTSup 48, ed. D. Hill (Sheffield: JSOT Press, 1991), 434–49. Gordon sees this as a sub-theme in Heb 11—faith overcomes death in whatever form it presents itself, and in any one of a number of ways (Heb 11:4,5,12,19,21,22,28–31,33–35,35–37). This carries over into Hebrews 12 in vv. 2,9.

[360] Eisenbaum, *Jewish Heroes*, 178–85. Eisenbaum thinks the key to the author's choice and use of OT heroes is due to the author's attempt to portray each as an "outsider who is depicted as living apart from any national body or institution" (142). E.g., Eisenbaum noted the way Abraham is treated in Jewish tradition as the father of the Jewish nation and how his alien status in the land is either avoided or ignored by these traditions. In contrast, the author of Hebrews actually focuses on Abraham's lack of connection to Israel (156–57).

[361] DeSilva, *Perseverance in Gratitude*, 424.

[362] For the linguistic justification of this division, as well as the alternative divisions that have been proposed, see Westfall, *Discourse Analysis*, 263–82.

[363] G. Guthrie, *Structure of Hebrews*, 72; and Westfall, *Discourse Analysis*, 263–65, wrongly divide the paragraph between vv. 2,3, on the grounds that γὰρ normally begins a new paragraph or larger semantic unit, and the shift from the first person pronoun in 12:1–2 to the second person plural pronoun in 12:3–8. However, γάρ can be used to conclude a unit as noted by S. Porter, *Idioms of the Greek New Testament* (Sheffield: Academic Press, 1995), 288; and P. W. van der Horst, "Can a

12:14 to begin the fifth major section of the entire epistle. Lane bases this division primarily on three grounds. First, the command to endure, which is so prominent in 12:1–13, disappears afterward. Second, the "introduction of a new focus for pastoral concern" ("make every effort to live in peace") marks the transition. Third, the *inclusio* formed by the use of the noun "peace" in 12:14 and 13:20 serves to delineate the section.[364] Lane takes the general allusion to Prov 4:26 LXX, "make level paths for your feet," in Heb 12:13 to be specified in 12:14–13:21.[365] Such an approach fails to appreciate two crucial facts: (1) the semantic unity of Heb 12:1–29 as demonstrated by Westfall, and (2) that 13:1 actually begins a new sub-division that is distinct thematically from chap. 12. In addition, both the UBS[4] and NA[27] Greek New Testaments do not even begin a new paragraph with 12:14. Although 12:14 can be viewed as introducing a new sub-paragraph (14–17) within a larger paragraph unit, it does not begin a new division and certainly not a new major division. Vanhoye argued for 12:1–13 as a unit based on the lexical *inclusio* formed by *trechōmen*, "let us run," in v. 1 and the cognate *trochias*, "path," in v. 13,[366] but this alone is insufficient to serve as a unit marker. It is possible, even preferable, to consider 12:12–13 to be a sub-paragraph, followed by another sub-paragraph in 12:14–17. Some consider the first paragraph to reach to v. 4 on the basis that an *inclusio* is created by the use of *agōn*, "race," in v. 1 and *antagōnizein*, "struggle," in v. 4, and the repetition of "sin" and "sinners" in 12:1,3,4.[367]

Hebrews 12 is marked immediately by a shift in genre from expository to hortatory, and a corresponding shift in mood from the indicative to the imperative with its concomitant shift from the third person to the use of the first and second person. The author uses tail-head linkage in the final paragraph of Heb 11:39–40 and 12:1 with the repetition of "witness" and the references to "us" and "we." The chapter is framed by an *inclusio* formed by the hortatory subjunctive in 12:1, "let us run," and by two hortatory subjunctives in 12:28, "let us be thankful," and "[let us] worship God."

The repetition of "endurance" in each of the first three verses marks the theme of the section through v. 17. The author sets the stage for this section with his statement in 10:36 that the readers need endurance. The main point of 12:1–3 is the command to "run with perseverance," considering the suffering

---

Book end with Γὰρ? A Note on Mk 16:8," *JTS* 23 (1972): 121–24. Additionally, the lexical repetition of ὑπομένω in vv. 1–3 and the new theme which begins in v. 4 marks it as new paragraph.

[364] Lane, *Hebrews 9–13*, 432; cf. A. Vanhoye, "Discussions sur La Structure de l'Épître aux Hébreux," *Bib* 55 (1974): 361–63, 373–74; Kistemaker, *Hebrews*, 365; and Ellingworth, *Hebrews*, 637.

[365] Lane, *Hebrews 9–13*, 433.

[366] Vanhoye, *La Structure*, 47.

[367] So Spicq, *L'Épître aux Hebreux*, 2:386–90; and Koester, *Hebrews*, 534. G. Guthrie, *Structure of Hebrews*, 144, considers 12:3–17 as a single unit, as does Westfall, *Discourse Analysis*, 264–67.

of Jesus himself who endured the cross and completed the work of atonement. The main point of Heb 12:4–11 is to explain why the readers must endure the disciplinary/educative sufferings which God allows them to experience. One of the main points the author of Hebrews has made is that even Jesus himself must be "perfected" through sufferings. If this is true of him, how much more is it true for all believers. Hebrews 12:4–11 is followed by a short paragraph (12:12–13) introduced by the conjunction *dio,* "therefore," and a final short paragraph (12:14–17) concerning Esau's failure. Westfall correctly observed that vv. 14–17 expand the command of v. 14 and this paragraph should be taken with 12:1–17 rather than with 12:18–29.[368]

Lane viewed 12:1–13 in a chiastic framework:

A Exhortation to run with endurance (vv. 1–3)
  B Meaning of the sufferings to be endured (vv. 4–11)
A´ Exhortation to renewed commitment to complete the race (vv. 12–13)[369]

Guthrie suggests a chiasm ranging from 3:1–12:2.[370] Hebrews 12:3–11 is bound together by the lexical and semantic repetition (chain) of "endurance" and "discipline."[371]

In 12:4–11, the author is basing his comments on Prov 3:11–12. His exposition includes three propositions: (1) genuine sonship entails fatherly discipline (vv. 7–8); (2) Christians should submit to God's discipline (v. 9); and (v. 3) God's discipline is beneficial (10–11). Lane made note of the many examples of rhetoric which the author exhibits in these 13 verses: word order, paronomasia (word play), alliteration, balanced clauses, and lexical repetition.[372] This is not surprising since the author is coming to the conclusion of his sermon, since the fifth and last warning passage occurs in Hebrews 12, and since Hebrews 12 in many ways is the conclusion to the main point of the discourse: press on to maturity through endurance.

---

368 Westfall, *Discourse Analysis*, 264–67, 271. "The most misunderstood part of the unit is vv. 14–17. If an analysis fails to recognize that v. 14 belongs to the span of commands in vv. 12–13, and the analysis misses its concluding relationship with the race metaphor in vv. 1–17, the result is a lack of coherence in the middle of the unit" (p. 271). She suggests the decision to group vv. 12–17 with vv. 18–29 "probably comes from a misunderstanding of the topic of the first subunit" (p. 271). Lane, *Hebrews 9–13*, 444–45, places 14–17 with the following section and suggests that vv. 14–17 is an unrelated train of thought. Ellingworth, *Hebrews*, 661, concluded that the absence of a conjunction at the beginning of v. 14 means this verse should be related to what follows rather than what precedes. This is effectively countered by Westfall who correctly notes that asyndeton is a form of connective that is "consistent with a close semantic relationship" (*Discourse Analysis*, 266).

369 So Lane, *Hebrews 9–13*, 405.

370 G. Guthrie, *Structure of Hebrews*, 136. Although there are a number of parallels in this section, it is questionable whether the entire unit is a chiasm.

371 Westfall, *Discourse Analysis*, 272, visually identifies the chain in the Greek text.

372 Lane, *Hebrews 9–13*, 406.

(1) *Running with Endurance (12:1–3)*

[1]Therefore, since we are surrounded by such a great cloud of witnesses, let us throw off everything that hinders and the sin that so easily entangles, and let us run with perseverance the race marked out for us. [2]Let us fix our eyes on Jesus, the author and perfecter of our faith, who for the joy set before him endured the cross, scorning its shame, and sat down at the right hand of the throne of God. [3]Consider him who endured such opposition from sinful men, so that you will not grow weary and lose heart.

Hebrews 12:1–17 is closely connected with the preceding chapter by the use of the strong inferential conjunction *toigaroun*, "therefore," which occurs only one other time in the New Testament. The heroes of Hebrews 11 endured and overcame by faith. In like manner, Christians must do the same (12:1–3). However, the author does not base his exhortations to "run with perseverance" or to endure suffering on the grounds used in Hebrews 11. Rather, he appeals to the sufferings of Christ (12:3, "consider him."). According to Lane, this is because "there is a necessary and integral relationship between disciplinary sufferings and sonship."[373] This is the point the author develops throughout the epistle.

The main verb in Heb 12:1–3 is the hortatory subjunctive "let us run" in v. 2. Three participles modify this verb and provide the reason and the means/manner in which Christians are to run. This syntactical structure is obscured by the NIV's translation of the latter two participles in a hortatory fashion: "Let us throw off" and "Let us fix our eyes." Although it is not uncommon to find commentators and translators rendering the participle *apothemenoi*, "let us throw off," in a hortatory manner,[374] it is preferable to view it semantically as indicating the means by which the race is to be run: "let us run by means of throwing off."[375] In the same way, *aphorōntes,* "let us fix our eyes," can be taken to encode means/manner as well: "run the race by means of fixing our eyes." The first participle, *echontes,* "having," is usually taken in a causal way: "because we have a great cloud of witnesses . . . let us run the race." However one construes the participles, it is important to note their modification of the main verb "let us run," since linguistically the finite verb carries more semantic weight than the subordinate participles.

The author develops the metaphor of the footrace in 12:1–2.[376] He does so by the use of the main verb "let us run" which has the phrase "with perseverance (endurance)" fronted before the verb for emphasis. Hebrews 12:1–2 is one sentence in the Greek text comprised of a main clause and three subor-

---

[373] Ibid., 407.

[374] E.g. Bruce, *Hebrews*, 332; Lane, *Hebrews 9–13*, 398, 409; and Ellingworth, *Hebrews*, 638.

[375] So Lenski, *Hebrews*, 424.

[376] On the concept of "race" as a metaphor in Paul, see V. C. Pfitzner, *Paul and the Agon Motif: Traditional Athletic Imagery in the Pauline Literature* (Leiden: Brill, 1967), 1–72, 134–38.

dinate clauses, each introduced by participles. Rendered propositionally and placed in block diagram to show subordination, the clauses in the verses can be structured as follows:

having a great cloud of witnesses surrounding us
laying aside every weight and the easily ensnaring sin
let us run with endurance the race set before us
looking unto Jesus the author and finisher of the faith
who for the joy set before him endured the cross, despised the shame,
and sat down at the right hand of the throne of God.

12:1 I consider each clause in order. The first participial clause, "surrounded by such a great cloud of witnesses" (present tense) is preceded in the Greek text by the emphatic "we also" (not represented in the NIV) where the writer continues the plural reference to his readers in 11:40. The clause itself has as its referent the heroes of faith in Hebrews 11, now referred to as "a great cloud of witnesses." This cloud of witnesses is said to be "surrounding us." "Cloud" is used metaphorically to indicate a great host of people. The Greek *tosouton*, translated "such a great," is emphatic by being fronted in its clause. The qualitativeness of this word focuses on the nature of the heroes whom Hebrews 11 characterizes by faith. The identification of these heroes of faith as "witnesses" has been interpreted in two ways. Perhaps besides these heroes being faithful witnesses in the past, now they are witnessing from heaven the lives of present believers.[377] The overall context, however, favors the meaning to be that their lives have borne witness to their faith.[378] The author's focus is on the importance of current believers learning from those who have gone before, not on those who have gone before watching current believers. As Moffatt put it, "It is what we see in them, not what they see in us, that is the writer's main point."[379]

The second participial clause, "let us throw off (aorist tense) everything that hinders and the sin that so easily entangles,"[380] expresses the means of

[377] So Westcott, *Hebrews*, 393; Hughes, *Hebrews*, 519; and Lane, *Hebrews 9–13*, 408, among others.

[378] So Lenski, *Hebrews*, 424; Bruce, *Hebrews*, 333; and Hewitt, *Hebrews*, 189. Dods notes they are witnesses in the sense that their faith is witnessed to by Scripture ("Hebrews," 365). A. Trites, *The New Testament Concept of Witness*, SNTSMS 31 (Cambridge: Cambridge University Press, 1977), 220–21, argued the context rules out the heroes of Hebrews 11 as spectators "and instead speaks of God's testimony to the heroes of faith in the pages of the OT."

[379] Moffatt, *Hebrews*, 193.

[380] The adjective translated "easily entangles" precedes the verb in the text. The Greek variant εὐπερίσπαστον, "easily-distracting," does not have strong manuscript support. Only Lane, *Hebrews 9–13*, 398–99, adopts it, and he does so because of its advantage in removing difficulties associated with the more common reading and because the word in the dominant reading is not found anywhere else in Biblical or secular Greek.

running: "by means of having thrown off . . . let us run." It could also express an attendant circumstance or be taken in a hortatory manner.[381] The participle is completed with a compound direct object: "everything that hinders and the sin." Some see the *kai*, "and," as just coordinating two items: "everything that hinders" and "sin."[382] Others take it as introducing a specific kind of weight: "laying aside every weight, especially the sin."[383] The former is probably to be preferred. The noun *onkos* is emphatic by word order and refers to anything that impedes or hinders the runner's progress. It can be translated as "weight," "hindrance," or the like. In the first century AD, runners ran in the stadium virtually naked. They would enter wearing long flowing, colorful robes. At the start of the race, these would be discarded. In like manner, the author is exhorting believers to discard anything that would encumber them and hinder them from running the race. Many take the word to be inclusive of things that are sinful and things that are not. Ellingworth takes the word to mean "sin" in context.[384] The second half of the compound direct object is "sin" which is described as "easily entangles." The use of the definite article in Greek can be taken in a generic sense, referring to sin in general, or it can be taken to give definiteness to the verb.[385] The unusual adjective *euperistatos*, (lit.) "well standing around," means "to control tightly."[386] The sense is something that would wind around the body and thus "bind" or hinder movement. Although the "sin" here is left undefined, one could contextually argue that the article and the context of Hebrews 11 indicate the sin of faithlessness.

The main clause of vv. 1–2 literally reads, "through endurance let us run [present tense implying continuously] the race lying before us." The prepositional phrase is emphatic by having been fronted before the verb. The function of this prepositional phrase is to express means. "Endurance" is an active noun and semantically encodes more than the "state" by which the race is run (Alford) or an attendant circumstance (Ellingworth). The Greek word translated "perseverance" connotes an active endurance involving effort and struggle, not a passive patience.[387] The noun *agōn,* "race," may refer to any kind of athletic contest, but the context points to a footrace—not a short sprint, where speed is important, but a lengthy race where endurance is essential to passing

---

[381] Wallace *(GGBB* 644, 650) argued for a hortatory meaning.

[382] So Dods, "Hebrews," 365; Kistemaker, *Hebrews*, 366–67.

[383] So Lünemann, *Hebrews*, 701; Lenski, *Hebrews*, 424; and Ellingworth, *Hebrews*, 638.

[384] Ellingworth, *Hebrews*, 638.

[385] Moffatt, *Hebrew*, 194; and Bruce, *Hebrews*, 336, take it in the former sense. Morris, "Hebrews," in *EBC* (Grand Rapids: Zondervan, 1981), 12:134; and Kistemaker, *Hebrews*, 367, in the latter. Lane, *Hebrews 9–13*, 409, rightly disagrees with Käsemann's attempt to interpret this sin in reference to apostasy.

[386] L&N 37.6; and Moffatt, *Hebrews*, 194, take the prefix εὐ to be intensive.

[387] For a full discussion on this concept in Hebrews, see N. C. Croy, *Endurance in Suffering: Hebrews 12:1–13 in its Rhetorical, Religious, and Philosophical Context* (Cambridge: Cambridge University Press, 1998).

the finish line. Koester noted the marathon race was not a standard race in the first century and that most races were no more than three miles in length.[388] The race is "marked out for us" by God, implying that every believer's duty is to run the race.

12:2 This verse is introduced with the third participial phrase (lit.), "fixing our eyes on Jesus." The prefixed preposition in the compound word in Greek indicates focused attention in the sense of "to look away" from everything else and to focus on one object or person.[389] The present tense connotes action that is concurrent with that of the main verb "let us run." We are not to model our lives after the heroes of faith in Hebrews 11, but after Jesus who is the "author" and "perfecter" of faith.[390] The use of *archēgos* "perfecter" has the sense of "originator," "founder" or "author."[391] It can also have the meaning of "champion," as reflected in Lane's translation of the phrase "the champion in the exercise of faith and the one who brought faith to complete expression."[392] The title should be read with Heb 6:20 in mind, where Jesus is said to be our "forerunner," indicating that others would follow later on the trail he blazed. The unusual title translated "perfecter" occurs nowhere else in the New Testament. It does not occur in the LXX and likewise is unknown in contemporary first century literature. The insertion of "our" in the NIV and several other translations is misleading as it is not in the Greek text, though translators are probably interpreting the article in the possessive sense. Whether the word connotes the subjective aspect of faith or the objective aspect of faith here cannot be determined with any certainty. Lenski took "the faith" to be that which has been described in 11:1.[393] Ellingworth, noting that no particular significance should be attached to the article before "faith," took it to refer to the faith of the author along with his readers and only less directly to the faith of the heroes of Hebrews 11.[394] Koester pointed out that Jesus is the pioneer and perfecter of faith in two ways: (1) he is the source of faith; and (2) he is the model of faith. Jesus is the source of faith in that by his death and resurrection, he has become the "source of eternal salvation" (Heb 5:9); he is the model of faith in that he trusted God as evidenced by his total obedience to the Father in the work of atonement.[395] The author placed the name "Jesus" at the very end of

---

[388] Koester, *Hebrews*, 522–23.

[389] See L&N 30.31.

[390] The entire phrase is fronted before the name "Jesus" and is in apposition to it: "the author and perfecter of our faith: Jesus." The two nouns are linked by a single article in Greek and the genitive πίστεως is fronted before both nouns but placed after the article.

[391] L&N 68.2. See comments in 2:10 on this word, and note its parallel use in Acts 5:31. See M. Hengel, *Studies in Early Christology* (Edinburgh: T&T Clark, 1995), 142–43, on the connection to Acts 5:31.

[392] Lane, *Hebrews 9–13*, 411.

[393] Lenski, *Hebrews*, 427.

[394] Ellingworth, *Hebrews*, 640.

[395] Koester, *Hebrews*, 523.

the clause for emphasis. The human name "Jesus" emphasizes his humanity in the context.

The sentence concludes with a relative clause further describing "Jesus." The unusual use of the preposition *anti* in Greek introducing the phrase "for the joy set before him" can be interpreted in two ways in this context: "instead of", and "because of." Lane makes a good case for the former meaning, noting the parallel between the race "set before us" in v. 1 and the joy "set before him" in v. 2.[396] Thus, the meaning would coordinate with Heb 5:7–9 along the lines of "submitting to the cross, Jesus did not pursue his own pleasure."[397] Croy makes a good case for the latter meaning, concluding that the preposition indicates "the prospective joy of Jesus' exaltation to God's right hand, a joy for which he endured the cross."[398] Whether the author intended to refer to the joy Jesus already possessed or would possess as a result of his exaltation or whether it refers to the joy he would have experienced had he been delivered from the death of the cross cannot be determined with certainty. Although noting the sense of "instead of" is a possible meaning, Ellingworth, along with the majority of commentators, preferred the meaning "because of."[399] In this case, the sense would be the joy of what his death would accomplish, inclusive of present and future blessings.[400]

The phrase "endured the cross"[401] is the only reference overtly to the cross in Hebrews. The gruesome and painful suffering which the cross engendered illustrates for the author why it is that Jesus is both the source and the model of a faith that endures to the end. Jesus "despised" or "disdained" the shame of the cross in the sense that he willingly accepted the ignominy of his public crucifixion and did not let either its suffering or its shame deter him from his goal. The author will echo this statement in Heb 13:12–13 when he urges his readers to identify with Jesus by bearing his "shame."

The final phrase in v. 2 is significant for several reasons. First, the author places the verb "sat down" at the end of the clause (sentence) for emphasis. Second, the verb is in the perfect tense, emphasizing the permanence of the enthronement and exaltation of Jesus. Third, the author is here alluding to his key Old Testament passage for the entire epistle: Ps 110:1. The Greek reads (lit.) "at (the) right of the throne of God is seated." This can be taken to mean that he sat on the throne at God's right hand.[402] Greenlee observed "it may

---

[396] Lane, *Hebrews 9–13*, 399–400, 413; cf. Kistemaker, *Hebrews*, 368.

[397] Ibid., 414.

[398] Croy, *Endurance in Suffering*, 162ff., 216.

[399] See his discussion in *Hebrews*, 641. Space considerations prevent a detailed examination of these two possibilities. See Lane and Ellingworth for a thorough discussion.

[400] So Bruce, *Hebrews*, 339.

[401] The Greek word is anarthrous. Some take the author to be emphasizing the qualitative aspect of the suffering, others translate it as definite: "the cross." Most translators opt to use the article in translation. The same situation applies to the anarthrous use of αἰσχύνης.

[402] So Alford, "Hebrews," 239, and most commentators.

mean seated on a different seat from God's throne, located at the right side of God's throne."[403]

This paragraph is closely connected with Hebrews 11 and is the culmination of the author's argument that his readers should press on with endurance by faith, with eyes focused on Jesus as their supreme example. Unlike the heroes and heroines of faith mentioned in Hebrews 11, Jesus is able to strengthen his followers to endure because he is the one who sits at the right hand of the throne of God and awaits their cry for help. This paragraph also underscores the key theme in the epistle which the author is developing: pressing on to maturity rather than falling back through disobedience and lack of faith. From this point he will press his argument clear through to v. 29.

12:3 This verse is introduced by *gar* and gives the grounds for the exhortation in vv. 1–2. Its use here with the imperative suggests strong affirmation in the sense of "by all means consider."[404] The readers are exhorted to "consider" Jesus and his endurance, so they will likewise endure. The aorist imperative translated "consider" occurs only here in the Greek New Testament and connotes a process of serious thinking where a matter is weighed with the utmost care through comparison, reflection, and conclusion.[405] The object of their consideration is expressed by an articular perfect participle translated "him who endured," where the significance of the perfect tense serves to highlight the permanent exemplary nature of Jesus' sufferings for the readers. The phrase translated "such opposition from sinful men" serves to focus qualitatively on the intensity of the entire crucifixion event, including not only the physical suffering entailed, but also the concomitant opposition of all involved in the physical and spiritual realm. The Greek text does not have "men" but reads "by the sinners" where the article is left untranslated: "by sinners." The word translated "opposition" means "strong opposition, hostility" and includes any form of opposition verbal or otherwise. The NIV does not make explicit the phrase "against himself"[406] which appears in the Greek text. The text critical issue discussed in the footnote below has bearing upon the translation and meaning of this phrase. If the singular reading is adopted, the translation would be "against himself" and would refer to opposition against Jesus. This is the simplest way of understanding the verse. If the plural reading is adopted, the translation would be "against themselves" and would refer to the people who crucified Jesus. The problem is this latter reading of the text has the best manuscript support but its meaning is difficult to construe. How can those who op-

[403] Greenlee, *Exegetical Summary*, 509.

[404] See Lane, *Hebrews 9–13*, 400; and Ellingworth, *Hebrews*, 643.

[405] L&N 30.10.

[406] There is a text critical issue here concerning whether the text should read the plural ἑαυτούς, the singular ἑαυτόν, or the singular αὐτόν. The UBS[4] adopts the singular reading, but assigns it a "D" classification, indicating the committee had doubts about it. Lane, *Hebrews 9–13*, 400, 416–17, and Ellingworth, *Hebrews*, 643–44, argue for the plural ἑαυτούς.

posed Jesus be said to have been opposing themselves? Lane interpreted the statement to be an example of "biting irony," where the author of Hebrews is essentially saying to his readers "if they were to relinquish their commitment to Christ under the pressure of persistent opposition they would express active opposition against themselves (as in 6:6!), just as did Jesus' tormentors."[407] While such an approach is certainly possible, it is also unusually awkward. Koester pointed out examples where the notion of sinners injuring themselves was "commonplace," nevertheless, based on context, he suggested that internal evidence favors the singular reading.[408]

Verse 3 concludes with a purpose clause introduced by the conjunction *hina*. The reason the readers are to consider the endurance of Christ is twofold: "that they would not grow weary and lose heart."[409] This statement further delineates the situation of the readers that has already been mentioned by the author on previous occasions. The stress of persecution was taking its toll on the Christian community. They were in danger of growing spiritually fatigued and discouraged and needed to be braced to press on in the Christian life. The phrase in Greek, "in your souls," can be construed with the first verb, "growing weary," with the participle "fainting," or as is most likely, with both. The phrase clarifies that the fatigue was not merely physical. The lexical repetition of "endurance" in each of the three verses of this paragraph coupled with this purpose statement serves to reinforce the overall pastoral tone of Hebrews.[410]

(2) Enduring Discipline (12:4–13)

4In your struggle against sin, you have not yet resisted to the point of shedding your blood. 5And you have forgotten that word of encouragement that addresses you as sons:

"My son, do not make light of the Lord's discipline,
and do not lose heart when he rebukes you,
6because the Lord disciplines those he loves,
and he punishes everyone he accepts as a son."

7Endure hardship as discipline; God is treating you as sons. For what son is not disciplined by his father? 8If you are not disciplined (and everyone undergoes discipline), then you are illegitimate children and not true sons. 9Moreover, we

---

407 Lane, *Hebrews 9–13*, 416–17.

408 Koester, *Hebrews*, 525; cf. the discussion of the issue in *TCGNT* 675.

409 On the verb "to grow weary," see L&N 25.291. The word can refer to physical, emotional or spiritual fatigue. On the verb "to lose heart," see L&N 23.79; 25.288. This word connotes becoming faint with exhaustion; to give out. It can, as it does here, convey the notion of discouragement and losing heart. The construction in Greek is (lit.) "in order that you may not grow weary in your souls, fainting."

410 The suggestion of Peterson, *Hebrews and Perfection*, 174, and DeSilva, *Perseverance in Gratitude*, 446, that the author's intent is to shame his readers cannot be proven from the text, and seems unlikely.

have all had human fathers who disciplined us and we respected them for it. How much more should we submit to the Father of our spirits and live! [10]Our fathers disciplined us for a little while as they thought best; but God disciplines us for our good, that we may share in his holiness. [11]No discipline seems pleasant at the time, but painful. Later on, however, it produces a harvest of righteousness and peace for those who have been trained by it.

[12]Therefore, strengthen your feeble arms and weak knees. [13]"Make level paths for your feet," so that the lame may not be disabled, but rather healed.

12:4 Both the main verb translated "you have not resisted"[411] and the present participle translated "in your struggle"[412] occur only here in the New Testament. The former continues the athletic metaphor of v. 1, but with a shift from the footrace to boxing.[413] The participle can be taken temporally, as an accompanying action with the main verb, or as means.[414] Hebrews 10:32–34 is a parallel where physical abuse is mentioned, but not martyrdom. The phrase "not yet" implies a possible future danger.[415] The phrase "to the point of" coupled with "blood" suggests degree or measure. In the Greek text, the noun "blood" is correctly translated as "shedding your blood." The reference is physical and not metaphorical. If it were taken as metaphorical, the picture would be of the readers in mortal combat with sin. Ellingworth considers this to be an "unmistakable" allusion to Judas Maccabaeus in 2 Macc 13:14.[416] The word "sin" can refer to sin within the Christian community (from the context of v. 1),[417] or can be personifying those who oppose Christianity.[418]

12:5–6 In Heb 12:5–11, the author addresses the subject of how God uses suffering and adversity in the lives of Christians. We have already seen how the readers of this epistle had and were experiencing persecution and the concomitant hardship which it brings. Developing the cultural concept of *paideia*, "discipline," the author cogently shows just how it is that his readers can and should reinterpret suffering and adversity as God's education of their lives, training them for righteous living. The key Old Testament text which the author uses in this section is Prov 3:11–12. Discipline in the life of every

---

[411] BDAG 88; L&N 39.18; and Spicq, "ἀντικαθίστημι," *TLNT* 1:128–30.

[412] BDAG 86; L&N 39.31.

[413] See Spicq, "ἀντικαθίστημι," *TLNT* 1.129, and secular references.

[414] It is taken temporally by Lane, *Hebrews 9–13*, 397; as an accompanying action by Kistemaker, *Hebrews*, 372; and as means by N. Miller, *The Epistle to the Hebrews: An Analytical and Exegetical Handbook* (Dallas: Summer Institutes of Linguistics, 1988), 389.

[415] Morris, "Hebrews," 136.

[416] Ellingworth, *Hebrews*, 645.

[417] Dods wrongly takes the sin to be apostasy ("Hebrews," 367).

[418] So Hughes, *Hebrews*, 527; Croy, *Endurance in Suffering*, 98 (Cambridge: Cambridge University Press, 1998), 194; and Lane, *Hebrews 9–13*, 419, who takes "sin" as a periphrasis for ἁμαρτωλῶν in v. 3 referring objectively to any source of hostility to Christianity. Cf. Lane, "Living a Life of Faith in the Face of Death: The Witness of Hebrews," in *Life in the Face of Death: The Resurrection Message of the New Testament*, ed. R. Longenecker (Grand Rapids: Eerdmans, 1998), 250–51.

Christian is comforting evidence that one is in the family of God. Such is the promise of the written word. "Rather than allow their hard experiences to nurture seeds of doubt about their relationship to God, they are to recognize that the testimony of Scripture trumps their experience in this instance."[419]

Verse 5 is connected to v. 4 by the conjunction *kai*. Ellingworth thinks it implies result.[420] One interpretive issue in the opening clause is whether it is a statement or a question.[421] The latter seems more likely. The author continues his theme of losing heart by his quotation of Prov 3:11–12 in vv. 5–6. The perfect tense verb translated "forgotten" is intensified in Greek by the prepositional prefix as well as being in the perfect tense, implying the notion of "completely." Greenlee translated it as "have entirely forgotten" and Lane translated it as "to forget completely."[422] It would seem the readers were in danger of developing amnesia brought on by their many trials. The phrase "word of encouragement" in Greek can also be translated as "exhortation." Commentators are divided as to whether it implies exhortation or encouragement. Both notions can be semantically a part of the word and one is often dependent upon context for clues as to which sense is intended. Both meanings are often in play when the word is used, as is probably the case here. The relative pronoun *hētis* is qualitative in force, describing the nature of the following exhortation: it is such that a father might give his son. The author's use of the verb *dialegetai* "addresses," "underscores the relational dimension that the writer intends to develop, since it views the utterance of the text of Scripture as the voice of God in conversation with his child."[423] The subject of the verb "addresses" has been taken to refer either to the exhortation itself,[424] to Scripture,[425] or to God in the sense of his speaking through Scripture.[426] The phrase "as sons" does not imply they are not actually sons. There is an important divergence in the LXX from the MT: the addition of *mastigoi* ("punishes") and *panta* ("everyone"). The former brings to mind the author's focus on physical suffering, and the latter individualizes the suffering: "every son."[427] The use of synonymous parallelism in the quotation can be seen in the four propositions:

---

[419] P. Gray, *Godly Fear: The Epistle to the Hebrews and Greco-Roman Critiques of Superstition* (Dallas: Society of Biblical Literature, 2003), 179.

[420] Ellingworth, Hebrews, 646.

[421] In favor of the former are Bruce, *Hebrews*, 341; Gray, *Godly Fear*, 179, and the NIV. In favor of the latter are Moffatt, *Hebrews*, 199–200, and Lane, *Hebrews 9–13*, 420.

[422] Greenlee, *Exegetical Summary*, 514; Lane, *Hebrews 9–13*, 397.

[423] Lane, *Hebrews 9–13*, 420. Cf. G. Schrenk, "διαλέγομαι," *TDNT* 2:94; and G. D. Kilpatrick, "Διαλέγεσθαι and διαλογίζεσθαι in the New Testament," *JTS* 11 NS (1960), 338–40.

[424] So Bruce, *Hebrews*, 341; and the NIV.

[425] So Hughes, *Hebrews*, 528; and Ellingworth, *Hebrews*, 646.

[426] So Lane, *Hebrews 9–13*, 420.

[427] On the differences between the MT and LXX of Prov 3:11–12, see Gheorghita, *Role of the Septuagint*, 49–50; R. J. Clifford, *Proverbs*, OTL (Louisville: Westminster John Knox, 1999), 50; and Ellingworth, *Hebrews*, 648.

1. Do not make light of the Lord's discipline
2. Do not lose heart when he rebukes you
3. The Lord disciplines those he loves
4. He punishes everyone he accepts as a son

The key word in this quotation which the author develops is *paideia*, whose meaning ranges between training and corporal punishment. Generally speaking, it refers to education in Greek tradition and to discipline by punishment in Hebrew tradition.[428] The word combines training, instruction, guidance, reproof, correction, and punishment.[429] The use of the term "rebuke" indicates verbal correction as well.

The meaning which should be stressed behind the word "punishes" is the positive notion of corrective punishment. It can be defined as "to assist in the development of a person's ability to make appropriate choices" in the sense of "to discipline with punishment."[430] Here the word refers to divine discipline; in 12:7,10 it refers to discipline by human fathers. The word is used in Luke 23:16,22 by Pilate who tells the crowd he will release Barabbas but have Jesus "punished." The relative clause "those he loves" is emphatic by word order in the Greek text. The final word in the quotation is the verb "he accepts," which is placed clause final for emphasis. Koester asks the two crucial questions of the use of "punishes." First, is it punitive or nonpunitive? Calvin took it as punitive; Chrysostom, based on the context, took it as non-punitive.[431] Although punitive discipline is beyond question part and parcel of Christian living, the focus in this passage is on non-punitive discipline. The second question is whether the meaning is primarily instruction or correction? It would seem that both are included in the meaning of the word: instruction has the goal of education.[432] Ellingworth correctly captures the author's main point in the use of the quotation: "discipline is an essential element in a father-son relationship: as in human families, so also within the family of God."[433]

---

[428] Bertram, "παιδεύω," *TDNT* 5.621–23; BDAG 748–49: "the act of providing guidance for responsible living" which is attained mainly by discipline and correction. Two works on educative suffering in the NT are C. Talbert, *Learning Through Suffering: The Educational Value of Suffering in the New Testament and Its Milieu* (Collegeville, MN: Liturgical, 1991), and Croy, *Endurance in Suffering*. Croy's exegesis of the passage in Hebrews and his analysis of the nature and use of παιδεία are most helpful for their analysis of Talbert's work along with his survey of Greco-Roman as well as Jewish literature on athletic imagery and the question of suffering as punitive versus non-punitive.

[429] Lane, *Hebrews 9–13*, 420.

[430] BDAG 749; so also in v. 10; cf. C. Schneider, "μάστιξ," *TDNT* 4.518 and Lane, *Hebrews 9–13*, 401.

[431] Calvin, *Hebrews*, 190–91; Chrysostom, *On the Epistle to the Hebrews*, 29.2 (in Heen and Krey, eds., *Hebrews*, 214).

[432] See Koester, *Hebrews*, 527.

[433] Ellingworth, *Hebrews*, 649.

12:7 In vv. 7–11, the author gives his exposition on the Proverbs text. Three points are made: the necessity of discipline; the proper response to discipline; and the benefits of discipline. *Eis paideian* is clause initial for emphasis.[434] The exact meaning of this prepositional phrase has been disputed. The phrase can be construed as purposive ("it is for discipline that you endure") or causal ("it is because of discipline that you are enduring").[435] Either decision makes good sense in the context, and in fact either approach would be theologically true. A slight contextual edge might be given to the causal translation. "Endure" should be read as an imperative.[436] There is no overt object in the text; many translators and commentators insert something such as "trials" or "hardship" (NIV). Trials and sufferings demonstrate one's sonship in the family of God. The phrase "as sons" is clause initial for emphasis.[437] The anarthrous use of "sons" in vv. 5,7 is qualitative and indicates the author considers his readers to be genuine sons of God. The author's point is to show his readers that they ought not be surprised when they experience discipline. Their sonship makes such discipline a necessity. "To expect anything else is to betray an appalling ignorance of the implications of their sonship. To wish for anything different is tantamount to forfeiting one's status as son and heir."[438]

12:8 The word *nothoi* in v. 8 occurs only here in the Greek New Testament and should be understood in its ancient legal sense as descriptive of those who lack the privileges of family and the protection of a father.[439] Ellingworth took v. 8 to be a contrary-to-fact condition in the sense of "if you were without discipline, then you would not be genuine sons." However, Greenlee noted such an interpretation "violates the rules of Greek grammar; a contrary to fact condition would require the imperfect tense ἦν [*ēn*] 'were' here and in the following clause."[440]

12:9 A new sub-paragraph begins here, signaled by *eita*, "moreover." The imperfect tenses in the verse indicate customary action in the past.[441] The word *paideutēs* refers to one who is an instructor or teacher. "Sometimes the emphasis is on the idea of correcting or disciplining" as in "one who disciplines."[442] The result clause at the end of v. 9a provides the point of transition to the rhetorical question in v. 9b which is introduced by the negative particle in Greek. The author is again using the lesser to greater argument: from earthly fathers

---

[434] Morris, "Hebrews," 137.

[435] See the discussion in Lane, *Hebrews 9–13*, 401.

[436] See BDAG 1039; Lane, *Hebrews 9–13*, 421; and Westfall, *Discourse Analysis*, 265.

[437] So Ellingworth, *Hebrews*, 651.

[438] Gray, *Godly Fear*, 180.

[439] So H. Braun, *An die Hebräer,* HNT 14 (Tübingen: Mohr/Siebeck, 1984), 413, followed by Lane, *Hebrews 9–13*, 423; and Koester, *Hebrews*, 528.

[440] Greenlee, *Exegetical Summary*, 520.

[441] Lane, *Hebrews 9–13*, 424.

[442] BDAG 749.

whom we respect (there is no Gk. word here corresponding to NIV "all"), to respect for God our Heavenly Father.

The unusual phrase (lit.), "the father of the spirits," has attracted much attention from scholars, resulting in several interpretations. It could refer to spirits in general.[443] Some scholars (and the NIV) understand the second article as possessive in the sense of "our spirits."[444] A third view is that it refers to the spiritual life of believers.[445] The fourth possibility is to interpret the genitive adjectivally as describing "Father" in the sense of "our spiritual father."[446] This fourth view seems least likely, with the second and third views being possible. The first approach probably comes nearest to the author's intended meaning. The phrase may betray the influence of Num 16:22; 27:16. The sense would be that the heavenly world not just the earthly world is subject to God. He is the Father of that which is spiritual as well as that which is physical (earthly).

The final result clause "and live" means "so that we may live." The *kai* "and" in the first clause of the verse can be taken simply as a connective, or as result.[447] Lenski and Dods took it as contraexpectation "and yet."[448] Although the author does not use an overt imperative in the last half of this verse, semantically he is engaging in mitigated exhortation. By saying "how much more should we submit," he is exhorting his readers to do just that.

12:10 Here the author speaks of the benefits of discipline. The verse begins with a temporal description of the discipline, "for a little while," followed by the motivation behind it, "as they thought best." The reference is to childhood discipline which was temporary. Some think the notion of the brevity of the discipline should be understood in the second half of verse as well, which speaks of God's discipline of his children.[449] Earthly fathers are fallible in their discipline. They may do it for the wrong motives and in the wrong manner or with the wrong attitude such as anger. God, our heavenly Father, is a perfect disciplinarian in all his dealings with us. God disciplines us "for our good," where this Greek idiomatic expression conveys the legal notion of advantage that is relevant to the Christian throughout life.[450] God's purpose for all of his children is "that we may share in his holiness," where "holiness" in Greek occurs only here and "denotes the holiness that is the essential attribute of God's character."[451]

---

[443] Lane, *Hebrews 9–13*, 424; Ellingworth, *Hebrews*, 654.

[444] So Kistemaker, *Hebrews*, 377; Hughes, *Hebrews*, 530–31; and the NIV.

[445] So Moffatt, *Hebrews*, 203.

[446] Morris, "Hebrews," 137.

[447] Bruce, *Hebrews*, 341, takes it as a connective, Lane *Hebrews 9–13*, 398,402; and the NIV take it as result.

[448] Lenski, *Hebrews*, 438; Dods, "Hebrews," 368.

[449] Lünemann takes the fronted position of the phrase to imply this (*Hebrews*, 707).

[450] Lane, *Hebrews 9–13*, 424.

[451] See D. Procksch, "ἁγιότης," *TDNT* 1.114; Lane, *Hebrews 9–13*, 425.

12:11 The conjunction *de* beginning this verse introduces a summary of 12:4–10. When we undergo discipline, it is a painful experience. However, "latter on" it will bring forth a harvest which consists of "peace and righteousness." The genitive phrase reads (lit.) "peaceable fruit of righteousness." This phrase is capable of being interpreted in different ways. The adjective "peaceable" modifies "fruit" and the genitive "righteousness" can be taken as a genitive of apposition with the phrase "peaceable fruit": "peaceable fruit which is righteousness." Another option is to construe the adjective as a noun parallel to the noun "righteousness" in the genitive case. In this case "righteousness" would be a genitive of content stating what is contained in the fruit. There is little appreciable semantic difference between the two approaches. This harvest can be viewed as having both a present and a future eschatological aspect to it. The fruit comes in this life and is perfected in heaven. The verse closes with a return to the athletic motif of 12:1 in the phrase "for those who have been trained by it." The use of the perfect passive participle ("have been trained") specifies enduring results. The author's commentary on Prov 3:11–12 makes it clear he is using this text in a non-punitive fashion, though the text itself in its Old Testament context includes the punitive meaning.

12:12–13 A new paragraph is begun with *dio* in v. 12 that ends in v. 13 and serves as a transition to the concluding exhortation of the paragraph begun in v. 4. Many see here an allusion to Isa 35:3. Weakened hands and paralyzed knees imply physical and emotional/spiritual exhaustion. Both participles are in the perfect tense. Verse 13 contains a quotation of Prov 4:26 LXX (see the context of Prov 4:25–26). In the larger context of Heb 12:1–11, the sense is "pursue ways that are directed straight to the goal" or "move in a straight direction with your feet."[452] The phrase "but rather healed" indicates "disabled" should be taken in its medical sense of "dislocation."

This short paragraph has about it a certain Lukan flavor in that within the short confines of two verses there is a cluster of six words which are primarily Lukan,[453] three of which are unique to Luke and Hebrews.[454] Such evidence strengthens the suggestion that Luke may have written Hebrews.

THEOLOGICAL IMPLICATIONS. Several theological implications emerge from Heb 12:1–13. First, the "race" which all Christians are called upon to run is nothing less than the living out of the Christian life through faith and endurance amid hostility. This race can be completed successfully and believers are given encouragement to look to Jesus who successfully completed his race by means of faith and endurance. Second, suffering, especially if it is

---

[452] Lane, *Hebrews 9–13*, 427; see H. Preisker, "ὀρθός," *TDNT* 5:449–50.

[453] Παραλελυμένα, γόνατα, ἀνορθώσατε, ὀρθάς, χωλόν and ἰαθῇ.

[454] Παραλελυμένα, ἀνορθώσατε and ὀρθάς. This connection is strengthened by the fact that ἀνορθόω is not found in the LXX quotation of Isa 35:3 but has been added by the author of Hebrews. In a similar way, Luke, when quoting Amos 9:11 in Acts 15:16, uses ἀνορθόω which likewise does not appear in the LXX text.

brought about by persecution, is a form of divine discipline—not in a punitive sense (though there are occasions when suffering is punitive), but in the sense of education and training for holiness and righteousness. Hebrews makes clear that suffering entails positive spiritual benefits. Jesus himself, as the divine Son, had to endure suffering as one who is in solidarity with his people (Heb 2:10–18; 4:15; 5:7–9; 13:12–13). Jesus' "testing through suffering" both presupposed and confirmed his divine Sonship.[455] Third, it thus becomes evident that all suffering in the life of a Christian is not punitive in nature. This is born out not only here in Hebrews 12, but also in many other places in the New Testament, including the teaching of Jesus in Luke 13:1–5 and John 9 in the case of the man born blind. Other examples include Rom 5:3–4 and Jas 1:2–3. In both these latter examples, suffering and endurance are connected in a cause-effect relationship. Fourth, one must avoid using Heb 12:1–13 as "a facile application of the author's arguments to other kinds of suffering" since such could be "theologically risky and pastorally disastrous."[456] Fifth, as the author of Hebrews reminds us, we do not have a high priest who cannot sympathize with us in our weaknesses and sufferings, but rather we have Jesus as our high priest who, because of his own suffering, is able to identify with us and minister to us in our sufferings. Sixth, a theology of suffering must include an eschatological perspective which informs not only how Christians view suffering, but also as that which gives them strength to endure it. This is the focus of Heb 12:2–3 in speaking about Jesus' suffering and how we are to look to him in our own suffering. The future reward serves as a present incentive to endure and remain faithful whatever the cost. Only in the eschaton will suffering itself be overcome by Christ's victory. The fulfillment of God's promises to his people is independent of whatever external circumstances they may experience. Suffering and adversity cannot and will not hinder God from making good on all his promises. Discipline will last only a short time, and then God's people will receive what he has promised (10:35–36).[457]

(3) Pursuing Peace and Holiness (12:14–17)

[14]Make every effort to live in peace with all men and to be holy; without holiness no one will see the Lord. [15]See to it that no one misses the grace of God and that no bitter root grows up to cause trouble and defile many. [16]See that no one is sexually immoral, or is godless like Esau, who for a single meal sold his inheritance rights as the oldest son. [17]Afterward, as you know, when he wanted to inherit this

[455] Croy, *Endurance in Suffering*, 220.

[456] Ibid., 222. This text has sometimes been misinterpreted and misapplied. An example is M. D'Angelo, "Hebrews," *The Women's Bible Commentary*, ed. C. Newsom and S. Ringe (Louisville: Westminster/John Knox, 1992), 364–67, who noted this text "puts a divine sanction behind the abuse of women and abusive child rearing." Such an approach is a misinterpretation of the text and a misuse of the author's intended meaning of the passage.

[457] See Gray, *Godly Fear*, 184.

blessing, he was rejected. He could bring about no change of mind, though he sought the blessing with tears.

12:14 The final sub-paragraph in this section is 12:14–17. Verses 14–16 form one sentence in the Greek text. The NIV's "make every effort" renders the present imperative verb in Greek which connotes earnest, diligent, continuous pursuit of something. "Peace" is emphatic by word order. The meaning of this command is usually taken as a striving to be at peace with other people. Moffatt and Lane give the meaning something of a twist when they suggested the clause connotes seeking peace as other people should be doing. In another odd twist, Lane took the "peace" here to be a reference to "salvation." Believers are to make every effort to be at peace with "all" people, which can be taken to refer to all fellow Christians[458] or, as is more likely, to refer to all people everywhere, which would be inclusive of all Christians.[459] It seems unlikely that the author's meaning would be limited only to the local church or only to all Christians. The verbal rendering "to be holy" is the translation of the noun *hagiasmos* in Greek, which means "holiness" or "sanctification." It has been taken to refer to a state of holiness[460] or to the process of becoming holy.[461] The noun "holiness" is articular in the Greek text but oftentimes the article is left untranslated. It may be the article was used but not translated because it is a specific term following the general term "peace."[462] The word in Greek translated "without" signifies "apart from." It stresses the necessity of holiness if one is to see the Lord.

12:15 Verse 15 also begins with an imperatival use of the participle *episkopeō*,[463] translated "see to it," which governs the three following clauses, each introduced by *mē tis*, "lest any."[464] The first clause contains the verb *hustereō*[465] translated "misses." Hughes, in light of 12:1–2, took it as meaning falling behind in the race and failing to finish. He, along with Lane, wrongly interpreted it as implying apostasy.[466] The second clause warns of a "root of bitterness,"[467] which has been taken to refer to anyone within the church who

[458] So Lane, *Hebrews 9–13*, 438; and Ellingworth, *Hebrews*, 662.

[459] Hughes, *Hebrews*, 536.

[460] D. Hagner, *Hebrews.* NIBC (Peabody, MA.: Hendrickson Publishers, 1990), 207.

[461] E.g., Alford, "Hebrews," 247; and Kistemaker, *Hebrews*, 385, 388.

[462] So suggested by Alford, "Hebrews," 247.

[463] The present participle is used here with the force of an imperative because of its dependence upon "pursue" in the previous verse. The present tense implies continuing effort. The action can be construed as accompanying the main verb, or translated independently, as in Bruce and most translations (*Hebrews*, 346).

[464] So Lane, *Hebrews 9–13*, 438–39.

[465] See L&N 13.21, which identifies the meaning as "to fail to attain." Bruce, *Hebrews,* translates it "to fall short."

[466] Hughes, *Hebrews*, 538–39; and Lane, *Hebrews 9–13*, 448. With an understood ᾖ (subjunctive of εἰμὶ) "should be," it is translated as a finite verb, "lest anyone should be falling away."

[467] Syntactically, the genitive can be taken as a genitive of quality: "bitter root," as does Ellingworth, *Hebrews*, 664; and the NIV; or in the sense of a root which produces bitter fruit

introduces evil into the congregation.[468] This root of bitterness "grows up"[469] and "causes trouble"[470] in the church. The NIV translates the verb causatively without any overt object expressed. It has also been translated transitively with an implied object "you."[471] The result of this root of bitterness causing trouble is many are "defiled,"[472] an aorist passive verb translated as active in the NIV.

12:16 This verse begins with the third clause governed by the imperatival participle in v. 15 (which the NIV repeats as "see that"). The NIV translates *pornos* as "sexually immoral," which is the literal meaning of the word. However, given that it is coupled with "godless" as descriptive of Esau, the meaning is likely that of spiritual unfaithfulness.[473] *Bebēlos* connotes that which is "worldly, godless, secular," and describes one who has no appreciation for spiritual things and who treats them with contempt.[474] The phrase "like Esau" can be connected with both "immoral" and "godless," or it can be connected only with "godless," as in the NIV. The relative clause "who for a single meal" explains why Esau is called "immoral" and "godless." "Single" is emphatic in the Greek text. The reflexive pronoun "his own," translated "his," is also emphatic and serves to intensify the priceless worth of the inheritance coupled with the perverseness of his willingness to trade it all away for a single meal. The meaning conveyed by the author is along the lines of "for only one single meal he sold his own birthright; a paltry price to pay for such a precious possession." Esau's fool-hearty trade is recorded in Gen 25:29–34. The inheritance rights belong only to the firstborn son and indicate one is the heir of his father's possessions. For Esau, it specifically included the blessing of Isaac originally promised by God to Abraham. Lane goes too far when he says concerning Esau: "By descriptive analogy, he is representative of apostate persons who are ready to turn their backs on God and the divine promises, in reckless disregard of the covenant blessings secured by the sacrificial death of Jesus."[475] The

---

(Bruce, *Hebrews*, 346–47). Lane thinks both senses are present in the phrase (*Hebrews 9–13*, 439). Alford takes it as a genitive of origin: "a root whose source is bitterness" (*Hebrews*, 247), and Lenski takes it as a genitive of apposition: "a root which is bitterness" (*Hebrews*, 445).

468 So Dods, "Hebrews," 370; and Hughes, *Hebrews*, 539.

469 Present participle translated as a finite verb.

470 Present active subjunctive whose subject is the immediately preceding phrase (Moffatt, *Hebrews*, 210; Bruce, *Hebrews*, 347; and Lane, *Hebrews 9–13*, 437) or whose subject is both preceding phrases introduced by "lest": lest any root of bitterness should cause trouble (Alford, "Hebrews," 247; and Lünemann, *Hebrews*, 710). On the use of this verb, cf. Luke 6:18.

471 So Alford, "Hebrews," 247; Dods, "Hebrews," 370; and Bruce, *Hebrews*, 347.

472 On this word, see L&N 88.260.

473 So Lane, *Hebrews 9–13*, 439; and Ellingworth, *Hebrews*, 665. Lane, *Hebrews 9–13*, 439, is incorrect in suggesting the word implies apostasy. Esau is called "immoral" (πόρνος) just as the wilderness generation committed "fornication" (πορνείαν) according to Num 14:33. Contextually, Esau's unfaithfulness is being compared to the same sin of the wilderness generation. See DeSilva, *Perseverance in Gratitude*, 461.

474 BDAG 173.

475 Lane, *Hebrews 9–13*, 455. For Lane, as we have seen, his interpretation of the warning passages in Hebrews 6 and 10 constrains his understanding of the meaning of verses like these, and he

author of Hebrews is not suggesting that Esau has "lost his salvation," but as Westcott rightly noted, the warning here is not against losing one's salvation but against "falling behind . . . the movement of divine grace which meets and stirs the progress of the Christian."[476] It is the neglect of "such a great salvation" (Heb 2:1–2) which invites the discipline of God upon one who is his child such as Esau under the old covenant or a Christian under the new covenant, as the immediately preceding discussion in Heb 12:4–11 makes clear. Furthermore, we are told in Heb 11:20 that Isaac blessed *both* Jacob and Esau, which indicates that Esau forfeited the birthright with its concomitant blessings, but he did not forfeit his sonship. Esau later was reconciled with his brother Jacob and received God's blessings even without the birthright.

12:17 Verse 17 is introduced by the subordinating conjunction *gar* (untranslated by NIV), which introduces the ground or reason for the preceding warning. "Afterward" refers to the time after Isaac had given the blessing to Jacob. Ellingworth notes the beginning of a new sentence in v. 17 "indicates that this verse will contain the main point of the passage, the culmination of the author's warning. The author thus begins by appealing implicitly to the authority of scripture which both he and his readers presuppose."[477] The phrase "when he wanted" temporally identifies the time referred to by "afterwards," and has been taken by some concessively: "although he wanted."[478] The author flatly states that Esau "was rejected."[479] The text does not overtly state who rejected Esau. The implied actor for the verb has been taken to be Esau's father, Isaac,[480] or God.[481] Alford takes it to be both.[482] From this point on, the verse has been problematic for interpreters. The second *gar* in the verse indicates the reason why Esau was rejected: "he could bring about no change of mind," where the literal Greek reads "for a place of repentance he found not." This means either there was no opportunity for Esau to repent,[483]or Esau's attempts to change his father's mind were unsuccessful.[484] The NIV's interpretive translation "though he sought the blessing with tears" renders the

is not alone. Osborne, reflecting his Arminian presuppositions, takes Esau to be an example of one who once possessed salvation then lost it because he committed the unpardonable sin ("A Classical Arminian View" in *Four Views*, 123).

[476] Westcott, *Hebrews*, 408. Cf. A. Nairne, *Hebrews*, 123, who noted Esau's loss "is not represented in Gen. as eternal rejection from God."

[477] Ellingworth, *Hebrews*, 667.

[478] E.g., Dods, "Hebrews," 370.

[479] Bruce translates "disqualified" (*Hebrews*, 368).

[480] So Lünemann, *Hebrews*, 711; and Ellingworth, *Hebrews*, 667–68.

[481] So Moffatt, *Hebrews*, 212; and Lane, *Hebrews 9–13*, 457.

[482] Alford, "Hebrews," 249.

[483] Lane, *Hebrews 9–13*, 457–58; Ellingworth, *Hebrews*, 668.

[484] So Lünemann, BDAG 412. Lane thinks this unlikely because μετανοίας τόπον εὗρεν is a Jewish idiom meaning repentance in a religious sense (*Hebrews 9–13*, 440). The Genesis account makes it clear that once the blessing had been pronounced on Jacob, there was no opportunity for Esau to change his father's mind.

literal "although with tears having sought it." The participle "having sought it" coupled with the preceding *kaiper* makes the meaning concessive. The implied object is God: he sought the blessing from God with tears. The interpretive problem revolves around the antecedent of *autēn,* "it." Again, two possibilities exist. The referent may be "blessing."[485] The other alternative is to understand the referent to be "repentance."[486] Lane argued against this latter interpretation, noting the grammar is against it and it does not accord well with Gen 27:34,38.[487] On the other hand, Ellingworth said this latter interpretation is preferable on "linguistic grounds" and in "light of the purpose of Hebrews." He admitted this interpretation "involves acknowledging that the author's pastorally oriented interpretation strains the meaning of the story in Genesis."[488] As mentioned above concerning Lane, Ellingworth is basing his interpretation on his understanding of the meaning of 6:4–6 to refer to apostasy. Interestingly, both Hughes and Kistemaker take the antecedent of *autēn* to be both "blessing" and "repentance,"[489] but this seems hardly feasible. Given the overall context and linguistic data, it appears more likely the author means the referent to be "blessing" and not "repentance."

Esau's bad example is used by the author to challenge his readers to act in the opposite fashion. It should be observed that neither the Genesis account of Esau's loss of the birthright or blessing nor what is stated overtly of him here in Hebrews 12 indicates that he was somehow outside of or removed from the covenant family of God. What he lost through his disobedience was the birthright, not his "salvation," to put it in New Testament terms.

(4) Arrival at Mount Zion (12:18–24)

18You have not come to a mountain that can be touched and that is burning
with fire; to darkness, gloom and storm; 19to a trumpet blast or to such a voice
speaking words that those who heard it begged that no further word be spoken to
them, 20because they could not bear what was commanded: "If even an animal
touches the mountain, it must be stoned." 21The sight was so terrifying that Moses
said, "I am trembling with fear."

22But you have come to Mount Zion, to the heavenly Jerusalem, the city of
the living God. You have come to thousands upon thousands of angels in joyful

---

485 So Bruce, *Hebrews*, 351; Lane, *Hebrews 9–13*, 437, 440; and the NIV.

486 So Alford, "Hebrews," 249; Moffatt, *Hebrews*, 212; Hewitt, *Hebrews*, 198; and Ellingworth, *Hebrews*, 668.

487 "The gen μετανοίας in this instance is dependent upon the anarthrous masc noun τόπος, 'opportunity.' The two terms constitute a fixed idiom, to which antecedent reference would presumably be made with the masc pronoun αὐτόν, referring to τόπος. The antecedent must be the more remote independent articular noun τὴν εὐλογίαν "the blessing," in 17a. This accords with the narrative of Gen 27:34,38, to which the writer alludes. What Esau sought with tears was the blessing, which Jacob had secured from Isaac with a ruse" (Lane, *Hebrews 9–13*, 440).

488 Ellingworth, *Hebrews*, 668.

489 Hughes, *Hebrews*, 541; Kistemaker, *Hebrews*, 387.

assembly, [23]to the church of the firstborn, whose names are written in heaven. You have come to God, the judge of all men, to the spirits of righteous men made perfect, [24]to Jesus the mediator of a new covenant, and to the sprinkled blood that speaks a better word than the blood of Abel.

Verses 18–24 constitute one paragraph in the Greek text, which the NIV divides at v. 22. The unit is marked by the double use of the perfect indicative verb *proselēluthate*,[490] "you have come," in vv. 18,22. The contrast between Mount Sinai and Mount Zion is indicated by the use of the adversative conjunction *alla,* "but," in v. 22. Each description of the two mountains is elaborated with a long string of datives, and climaxes with references to speaking (vv. 19,24).[491]

12:18 The use of *gar* again signals the author is providing the ground or reason for the preceding warning in vv. 14–17. In vv. 18–21 the author is reflecting on several texts in the Pentateuch which describe in vivid detail Israel's terrifying experience in their encounter with God on the fiery mountain of Sinai.[492] The phrase "that can be touched" is probably a reflection on Exod 19:12–13, where anyone who touched the mountain would experience death.[493] The idea behind the phrase is that something is tangible in general and thus perceptible to the senses. The repeated use of *kai*, "and," coupled with the absence of the article before each noun in v. 18 emphasizes both the enumeration and the nature of the words mentioned. The latter three nouns can be taken as separate and additional items[494] following the reference to the mountain "that can be touched and that is burning with fire," or it can be taken as a further description of the preceding phrase.[495] The Greek word for "storm" implies a windstorm.[496]

12:19–21 In v. 19, the genitive noun translated "words" conveys the content of the "voice." "Word" is the subject of the infinitive "to be spoken" (in Greek the infinitive is "to be added"). It means the people, in their terror, begged that no more words be added to those already spoken. The implication is they were not rejecting God's word, only begging that nothing more be said directly to them.[497] The *gar* that introduces v. 20 provides the reason for the fear in the

---

[490] The word is used of the priests' approach to God in a cultic context.

[491] Westfall, *Discourse Analysis*, 268; cf. Guthrie, *Structure of Hebrews*, 73.

[492] Exod 19:16–22; 20:18–21; Deut 4:11–12; 5:22–27 LXX

[493] Lane's notion (*Hebrews 9–13*, 460) that the phrase comes from Exod 10:21 (LXX), where the darkness is so dark as to be "felt," seems unlikely since the reference is to the plague of darkness over Egypt, an event significantly removed from the later experience of the people at Sinai. Lane also thinks the negative particle that accompanies this phrase is emphatic in its initial position (p. 440), but Greenlee correctly notes this position is grammatically obligatory (Greenlee, *Exegetical Summary*, 545). Hence, whether it is emphatic cannot be determined with certainty.

[494] So Kistemaker, *Hebrews*, 389; Lane, *Hebrews 9–13*, 461; and the NIV.

[495] So Ellingworth, *Hebrews*, 672.

[496] See L&N 14.6.

[497] As noted by Koester, *Hebrews*, 543.

preceding clause. The presence of God on the mountain in all his holiness was such that "if even" an animal touched the mountain, it would die. In v. 21,[498] the entire experience was so terrifying that Moses himself trembled with fear. The statement "Moses said" implies a concession in the sense of "even Moses said."[499] This can be connected to the preceding verse by the initial *kai* with the intervening clause functioning parenthetically indicating the reason for Moses' statement.[500] On the other hand, it can be construed as expressing the result of the first clause.[501] The two adjectives can be viewed as stating two concepts[502] or the adjective "fearful" may state the cause of the trembling,[503] as in the NIV. The fear which Moses and the people experienced in the presence of God at Sinai was motivated by their awareness of the infinite gap between their humanity and God's divinity. Or, as Luther is reported to have said, "no fear is the worst fear of all."

12:22–23 The scene shifts here from the terror of Sinai to the joy of Mount Zion. The use of *alla,* "but," coupled with the repetition (from v. 18) of the perfect tense verb "you have come" contrasts this sub-paragraph with the preceding one. The verb occurs three times in the NIV of vv. 22–23, but the Greek word only occurs once. The NIV repeats it as a guide for the reader since its use in v. 22 provides unity to vv. 22–24, being followed by a series of datives ("to Mount Zion, to the heavenly Jerusalem, the city of the living God . . . to thousands upon thousands of angels in joyful assembly, to the church of the firstborn . . . to God, the judge of all men, to the spirits of righteous men made perfect, to Jesus the mediator of a new covenant, and to the sprinkled blood that speaks a better word than the blood of Abel"). The perfect tense of the verb implies that the readers are converted and have entered a permanent place of eternal relationship with God.[504] The locations "Mount Zion," "city of the living God," and "heavenly Jerusalem" are all in apposition to one another and refer to the same place. What exactly is meant by these references? In Judaism,

---

498 See discussion in Gray, *Godly Fear*, 206–9. Lane, *Hebrews 9–13*, 464, surveys the three proposals for the author's source of v. 21. First, Deut 9:19a LXX and the golden calf incident; second, Exod 3:6 and the burning bush incident (see also Acts 7:32 where the word is used of Moses "trembling" at the burning bush episode); third, Jewish homiletical tradition which ascribed fear and trembling to Moses at Sinai. The first two proposals are unlikely as the actual source of v. 21, though they present a parallel response to similar situations on Moses' part.

499 So Moffatt, *Hebrews*, 216; and Bruce, *Hebrews*, 354.

500 Ellingworth, *Hebrews*, 675.

501 So Bruce, *Hebrews*, 353; Hughes, *Hebrews*, 543; Lane, *Hebrews 9–13*, 438; and the NIV.

502 Bruce, *Hebrews*, 353; Lane, *Hebrews 9–13*, 438.

503 Moffatt, *Hebrews*, 216, followed by Ellingworth, *Hebrews*, 676, take the "trembling" to have been added by the author for rhetorical effect.

504 Kistemaker, *Hebrews*, 392; Dods, "Hebrews," 472. Some scholars take it to mean the readers have drawn near but have not yet arrived. Koester, *Hebrews*, 544, appeals to 13:14 and the reader's hope for the city "that is to come."

"Zion"[505] referred to the hill in Jerusalem where the temple stood. The name covers not only the temple hill, but all of Jerusalem as well. It was the place where Israel gathered for worship and where one hoped to see God manifested in his glory. Significant for Hebrews, Ps 110:1–4 speaks of Zion as the place where the Messiah, the one seated at God's right hand, would rule.

Leithart pointed out how a number of prophetic passages in the Old Testament speak of a restoration of the Davidic kingdom in a religious/political sense under the shorthand of "Zion." Amos 9:11 predicts that Yahweh will "restore David's fallen tent," which is a reference to the tent pitched at Zion. Israel's hope was for a restoration of the Davidic forms of worship. Isaiah 16:1 exhorts the people of Israel to bring sacrifices "to the mount of the daughter of Zion," followed by a promise in v. 5 that "a man . . . from the house of David" will sit on the throne seeking justice and "the cause of righteousness." Later, in Isa 66:8, Zion gives birth to sons who are taken not only from Israel but from all the nations (66:20–21). "The hope that Gentiles will be taken for priestly ministry (v. 21) has a historical root during David's reign, when Gentiles served Yahweh at his shrine (2 Sam 6:10–11)."[506] Leithart noted that Old Testament prophecy never mentions "Moriah," the specific name for the temple mount, by name. "Zion" is the name given to the mount of Yahweh's dwelling in prophecy.

> By employing 'Zion' rather than 'Moriah', these texts cart along baggage from the earlier, more restricted usage of the word: References to Zion in the prophets hearken back specifically to David's reign as the 'golden age' that will one day be re-established. That is to say, promises of a restored Zion are promises of the order of worship and life inaugurated in the new covenant, by a Son of David who has brought His people into an undivided sanctuary in a heavenly Zion.[507]

The author's use of Zion in Hebrews 12 makes perfect sense in such a context.

The "city of God" is a major theme developed under a variety of metaphors.[508] By extension, the author is using these references in a spiritual sense to refer to a heavenly state and to the spiritual place of God's presence and his people's home. They have come to "thousands upon thousands of angels," where the genitive "of angels" relates to the preceding *muriasin* "myriads" in

---

[505] The best historical overview of Zion symbolism in the OT and Second Temple Judaism is Kiwoong Son, *Zion Symbolism in Hebrews: Hebrews 12:18–24 as a Hermeneutical Key to the Epistle* (Milton Keynes, UK: Paternoster, 2005), 29–74. On "Zion," see also G. Fohrer and E. Lohse, "Σιὼν," *TDNT* 7.292–338; Koester, *Hebrews*, 544; P. Leithart, "Where was Ancient Zion?" *TynBul*, 53.2 (2002): 161–75; and B. Ollenburger, *Zion the City of the Great King: A Theological Symbol of the Jerusalem Cult*, in JSOTSup 41 (Sheffield: JSOT Press, 1987), 53–80; 145–62.

[506] Leithart, "Where was Ancient Zion?" 174.

[507] Ibid., 175.

[508] See discussion in Lane, *Hebrews 9–13*, 466.

Greek as well as the following *panēgurei*, "festival gathering."[509] This word in Greek, translated "joyful assembly," was used in the Greco-Roman world for civic festivals and athletic competitions. The term was also used in the LXX to speak of Israel's festivals.[510]

A question arises as to whether *panēgurei* should be related to the preceding phrase "to thousands upon thousands of angels," or to the following phrase, "to the church of the firstborn" in v. 23,[511] but there is little difference in overall meaning. The NIV's "church" is the translation of *ekklēsia,* "assembly, congregation," and refers to all believers, living or dead.[512] This reference harks back to Heb 2:12 where the author quoted Ps 21:23 (LXX): "I will declare your name to my brothers, in the midst of the assembly [*ekklēsia*] I will sing praises to you." The readers have also come to "God, the judge of all men."[513] They have also come to the "spirits of righteous men made perfect." The word "spirits" here probably refers to the spirit apart from the body awaiting the final resurrection. That they have been "made perfect" means they have died and reached the state of having been perfected by Christ's atonement. The reference is to both Old Testament and New Testament saints.[514] These saints have had their names "written" in heaven, where the sense of "written" is "enrolled" or "registered."[515] The use of the perfect tense implies that their names have been "inscribed permanently."[516] Koester noted this concept of "registration" has both a legal and a theological connotation. Legally, a Roman citizen was to register any legitimate child within 30 days of birth. The father received a copy of the declaration as proof of citizenship. Theologically, this concept of being registered in a heavenly book is found in both the Old and New Testaments (Exod 32:32; Dan 12:1; Luke 10:20; Phil 4:3; and numerous times in Revelation).[517]

---

[509] So Moffatt, *Hebrews*, 216; Bruce, *Hebrews*, 353; Hughes, *Hebrews*, 547; and Ellingworth, *Hebrews*, 678.

[510] See Koester, *Hebrews*, 544–45.

[511] Westcott, *Hebrews*, 413–14; Moffatt, *Hebrews*, 216; Bruce, *Hebrews*, 310; Hughes, *Hebrews*, 552–53, and the NIV take it in the former sense; most translations take it in the latter sense. Lane says the first is preferable based on the syntax of v. 22a (*Hebrews 9–13*, 441). See Hughes, *Hebrews*, 552–55 for a thorough discussion of the issue.

[512] Lünemann takes it to refer to OT saints in heaven (*Hebrews*, 717). Kistemaker, *Hebrews*, 393, following Dods, "Hebrews," 372, takes it to refer to angels in heaven.

[513] "God" is in apposition to "judge" according to Moffatt, *Hebrews*, 217–18; Hughes, *Hebrews*, 549; Bruce, *Hebrews*, 359, and Lane, *Hebrews 9–13*, 438, 442. "Judge" is in apposition to "God" according to Alford, "Hebrews," 255, the NIV, and most translations. If the former is intended, there is a rhetorical reference to "Judge God." If the genitive "of all" is related to the first option, the meaning would be "God who judges all"; if the second option is taken, then "all" tells who is ruled by God: "the judge who is God over all." The former is to be preferred.

[514] Although Bruce, *Hebrews*, 359–60, takes it as referring only to OT saints.

[515] See L&N 33.42.

[516] So Lane, *Hebrews 9–13*, 471, who notes the use of the participle rather than the adjective "perfect" "decisively favors the soteriological interpretation of the expression."

[517] Koester, *Hebrews*, 545.

If the perfect tense verb "you have come" in v. 22 indicates the readers have come now to this place of permanent relationship with God in Zion, and if the perfect tense verb in v. 23 attests to the fact that their names have been permanently enrolled in heaven, then the possibility of apostasy would seem to be ruled out for the readers. This is further evidence that the warning passages in Hebrews must mean something other than apostasy, as we have already argued.[518]

12:24 The climax of 12:18–24 is given in v. 24.[519] The absence of the definite article with the nouns in this verse indicates a focus on quality and nature.[520] As in all other places in the epistle, the human name "Jesus" is placed last in the clause for emphasis, focusing on his humanity along with his work of redemption. The phrase "sprinkled blood" refers to Jesus' atoning blood which established the new covenant and which is the means of salvation. The genitive noun "sprinkling" indicates what was done with the blood. (Heb 10:22 speaks of "having our hearts sprinkled clean"). It also tells what the blood accomplished: purification. The participle translated "that speaks" is usually taken as attributive to the dative noun "blood" in the sense of "blood that speaks."[521] Delitzsch, Hughes, Lane, DeSilva and Koester are among the many who understand the phrase metaphorically.[522] Some of these interpret it to mean that Abel's blood, unlike the blood of Christ, could not bring about redemption.[523] Although this is true, it is unlikely the author is thinking of Abel's blood as crying out for vengeance in contrast to Christ's blood which alone can bring atonement. Also unlikely is Grässer's notion that Abel's blood cried out "from the ground," whereas Christ intercedes for his people in heaven based on his shed blood.[524] Equally unlikely is Attridge's attempt to connect this with the common Jewish notion that the blood of martyrs had atoning significance, so that Abel's blood provided in some sense a limited atonement, but Christ's blood provided full atonement.[525] The writer's point is that Jesus' once-for-all blood sacrifice "has continuing significance for the worship of God's people in the heavenly Jerusalem."[526]

---

[518] See discussion on Heb 6:4–8 above.

[519] So noted by Ellingworth, *Hebrews*, 681, among others. There is a textual variant concerning whether the article modifying "Abel" is masculine or whether it is neuter modifying an understood noun "blood." The former is read by most; however Lane, *Hebrews 9–13*, 442, reads the latter.

[520] So Lenski, *Hebrews*, 459.

[521] See Bruce, *Hebrews*, 353, 361; Kistemaker, *Hebrews*, 392; and most translations.

[522] Delitzsch, *Hebrews*, 2:354; Hughes, *Hebrews*, 551–53; Lane, *Hebrews 9–13*, 473; Koester, *Hebrews*, 546; DeSilva, *Perseverance in Gratitude*, 468.

[523] So Moffatt, *Hebrews*, 218–19; Hughes, *Hebrews*, 551–52, and Lane, *Hebrews 9–13*, 473–74.

[524] Grässer, *An die Hebräer* EKKNT 17 (Zürich: Benziger, 1990), 3:323–24.

[525] Attridge, *Hebrews*, 377.

[526] Ellingworth, *Hebrews*, 682–83.

Smillie argued that the metaphorical interpretation does not fit the syntax and context of the passage or the theology of the book. It is better to take the participle *lalounti* in v. 24 as a reference to "one who speaks" better than Abel, namely God. This allows v. 24 to "glide smoothly" into v. 25: "the one who speaks better than Abel . . . see to it that you do not refuse him who speaks."[527] He discusses three indications that the speaker in both vv. 24,25 should be taken to be God. First, the following statement in v. 25 refers to a person speaking. Second, the author does not overtly use the word "blood" following "Abel," but rather says "better than Abel." Third, against construing *kreitton* with the phrase "sprinkled blood" (lit., "blood of sprinkling") is that in 10 of the 13 uses in Hebrews it modifies a noun or a participle, and in each case *kreitton* is followed by the substantive, whereas here it is followed by the participle *lalounti.* Thus, it is far more likely that "better" is functioning adverbially, modifying the participle, than as a predicate adjective modifying the preceding "sprinkled blood."[528] It is not the blood that speaks better, but God, "the one speaking" better than Abel. "Nothing in the theology of the book, or in the syntax of the verse at hand, demands that the expression *haimati rhantismou* ('sprinkled blood') be understood as the antecedent of the implied subject of the participle *lalounti* in 12:24."[529] Smillie also suggested that with the articular participle in v. 25, the author resumes use of the articular noun for the first time since v. 22 (excepting the article before the proper name "Abel" in v. 24) after a series of more than 20 anarthrous nouns and participles. The article "serves almost like a demonstrative adjective, accentuating the relationship between the participle in v. 25 and its ostensible antecedent *lalounti* in v. 24. Thus, perhaps the text should be understood to read ' . . . to one who speaks better than Abel: watch out [then] that you do not resist that one who speaks!"[530]

(5) Dangers of Turning Away (12:25–29)

25See to it that you do not refuse him who speaks. If they did not escape when they refused him who warned them on earth, how much less will we, if we turn away from him who warns us from heaven? 26At that time his voice shook the earth, but now he has promised, "Once more I will shake not only the earth but also the heavens." 27The words "once more" indicate the removing of what can be shaken—that is, created things—so that what cannot be shaken may remain.

28Therefore, since we are receiving a kingdom that cannot be shaken, let us be thankful, and so worship God acceptably with reverence and awe, 29for our "God is a consuming fire."

12:25 Several discourse features mark v. 25 as the beginning of a new paragraph. There is a shift from the indicative which has characterized the

527 Smillie, "'The One Who is Speaking' in Hebrews 12:25," *TynBul* 55.2 (2004): 279.

528 Ibid., 280–81.

529 Ibid., 282.

530 Ibid., 283.

preceding paragraph to the imperative. The absence of any introductory conjunction intensifies the force of this imperative in the discourse. The shift in topic from Sinai to Zion also indicates paragraph onset. The preceding two paragraphs, balanced by contrast, function as the grounds for the exhortation in v. 25: "See to it that you do not refuse him who speaks."[531] Because of this semantic relationship, v. 25 should not be viewed, as it often is because of the abrupt transition to an imperative, as beginning a new unit that is distinct from the preceding paragraph.[532] There are clear indications of a new paragraph, but not independent of the previous two paragraphs. Following the imperatival clause in v. 25, additional grounds are furnished by the immediately following conditional clause. The clause "if they did not escape" implies the meaning "they did not escape," and the imperfect tense implies that attempts were made to escape.[533] Contextually, the implied speaker in the two phrases, "him who speaks" and "him who warned," is God, not Moses.[534] The latter phrase, the object of the verb "refuse," is the present tense (articular) participle, *chrēmatizonta,* from a verb that means "to make a divine message known."[535] It occurs only once in the verse but is supplied a second time to make clear that the prepositional phrase *ap' ouranōn*, "from heaven," refers to "him who warns us from heaven." Bruce wrongly translates *chrēmatizonta* temporally, which would require the absence of the article.[536] The participle translated "when they refused" expresses action prior to the punishment. Ellingworth takes the participle as conditional; Bruce takes it attributively "who refused"; which is ruled out by the absence of the article.[537] The phrase "on earth" is fronted in the clause for emphasis and contrasts with the following "from heaven."

The author is employing an argument from the lesser to the greater: if judgment is certain on those who do not heed God's speaking on earth, how much more certain is judgment on those who do not heed His speaking from heaven. The author stresses the certainty of judgment, however, in terms of the impossibility of escape. The sense is this: If *those* did not escape, how much more [certain it is that] *we* will not escape. The "how much more" (NIV "how much less")[538] clause is literally, "how much more we the ones turning away from

---

[531] Westfall, *Discourse Analysis*, 268.

[532] See, for example, Bruce, *Hebrews*, 380; Attridge, *Hebrews*, 379; and G. Guthrie, *Structure*, 133.

[533] So Lane, *Hebrews 9–13*, 442.

[534] On the debate concerning the identity of the speaker from earth and the speaker from heaven, see Smillie, "'The One Who is Speaking' in Hebrews 12:25," *TynBul* 55.2 (2004): 283–87; Attridge, *Hebrews*, 379–80; and Lane, *Hebrews 9–13*, 475.

[535] See L&N 28.39. The word is never used of a human being as the speaker.

[536] Greenlee, *Exegetical Summary*, 560.

[537] Alford, "Hebrews," 257. Cf. Ellingworth, *Hebrews*, 685; Bruce, *Hebrews*, 361.

[538] Translating πολὺ μᾶλλον, "how much more," as "how much less" is made necessary by assuming or supplying the verb phrase "will we escape" or "will we be able to escape" rather than "will we *not* escape," which is what the Gk. implies: If *they* did not escape . . . how much more will *we* not escape.

the One from heaven." The present tense participle (*apostrephomenoi*), which the NIV renders "if [we] turn away," is not conditional since it is preceded by the article. Rather, it describes the emphatic "we" that contrasts with "they" (*ekeinos*) in the conditional part of the sentence.[539]

It is God who speaks both on earth and from heaven. This indicates the contrast is not between two speakers, but rather the two modes of revealing God.[540] The form of the argument here in v. 25 parallels that of Heb 2:1–3, which further serves to link all the warning passages together as expressing the same theme.

12:26–27 The first part of v. 26 makes clear that only one speaker is in view in the previous verse with the author's use of "at that time . . . but now." The same voice which "shook the earth" at Sinai now "promises" he will again shake not only the earth but the heavens. The use of the perfect tense translated "he has promised" indicates not that the promised fulfillment has occurred, but that the making of the promise has ramifications for the present.[541] The quotation is from Hag 2:6 LXX, which the author slightly alters by inserting "not only" and "but also." By this reference, the author intends to intimate a future time of eschatological judgment, as is indicated by v. 27, where the author interprets the meaning of the quotation as "indicating" the "removing" of what can be shaken. The subject of "indicates" is actually Scripture since the author makes the first part of the quotation, "the words 'once more,'" to be the subject of the verb "indicates." The author uses the Greek *metathesin*, translated "removing," which occurs only once in the LXX and twice in Hebrews (see also 7:12). Its root meaning is that of removal from one location to another. "What can be shaken" is said to be "created things," referring to the material universe. The purpose of this "removing" is stated in the following clause "so that what cannot be shaken may remain." God's kingdom is immutable and possesses eternal stability. Following this final eschatological judgment expressed by the "shaking," God will accomplish salvation's final eschatological consummation with the new heaven and earth. Such language as used by the author here in v. 27 is reminiscent of his quotation of Ps 102:26–28 in Heb 1:10–12. "Those who seek their security in 'created things' will share in the dissolution of the created order in the final shakeup, while God's pilgrim people who accept hardships in full trust in God as their security will be vindicated; theirs will be a 'kingdom that cannot be shaken.'"[542] It is possible to interpret the author's

[539] Greenlee, *Exegetical Summary*, 561.

[540] See Spicq, *L'Épître aux Hebreux* 2:410–11; Attridge, *Hebrews*, 380–81; and Hughes, *Hebrews*, 557. Lane, *Hebrews 9–13*, 476, noted the difference is between the context of the old covenant and the new covenant, yet it is the same God who speaks. Grässer, *an die Hebräer*, 3.328, likewise asserts there is one speaker, God, but two moments of time which are compared: "then" and "now."

[541] Lane, *Hebrews 9–13*, 479.

[542] A. Thiselton, "Hebrews," in *Eerdmans Commentary on the Bible*, ed. J. D. G. Dunn and J. W. Rogerson (Grand Rapids: Eerdmans, 2003), 1479.

reference to the shaking of the heavens and earth symbolically as a description of the destruction of the temple.[543] This would be possible if one supposed a post- AD 70 date, but even if the epistle were written around AD 67–69, the author could see the handwriting on the wall for Jerusalem and the temple with the approaching Roman army.

12:28–29 Verses 28–29 function as the conclusion of the entire discourse unit 12:1–29. The conclusion is signaled by the inferential conjunction *dio*, "therefore." The present participle translated "since we are receiving" depicts the reception of an unshakable kingdom as in progress and serves as the ground or reason for the following two hortatory subjunctives.[544] The shift to the present tense in v. 28 is important. It is consistent with the depiction of believers as engaged in an ongoing athletic contest (12:1–17). The use of *nun*, "now," in v. 26 also indicates that the readers are currently in the kingdom and that its reception is not totally an eschatological event.[545] The "kingdom" is emphatic by word order and indicates the kingdom of God. It "cannot be shaken," a phrase which illumines the author's previous focus in vv. 26–27 on that which can and cannot be shaken. Since this verb was used by the LXX translators metaphorically as an expression for God's judgment, Lane noted: "Familiarity with the figurative use of σαλεύειν [*saleuein*] in passages referring to eschatological judgment in the Psalms accounts sufficiently for the writer's preference for this verbal expression in his interpretation of Hab 2:6 LXX."[546]

Based on all that has been said in 12:1–27, and since we have received an unshakable kingdom, we are now commanded to "have grace/thankfulness" and to worship God. The use of this term "worship" in the context of the book indicates the author is expressing the notion of serving God as priests in a spiritual sense. This is confirmed by the author's statement in 13:15 where we are commanded to offer to God "a sacrifice of praise." The means by which we are to serve God as priests is by our attitude of "thanksgiving." The word in Greek is the normal word for "grace," but here is probably best translated "thanksgiving." The manner in which we are to serve God is expressed by the adverb translated "acceptably"; it is found only here in the New Testament, but its cognates are used in Heb 11:5,6; 13:16,21. In the Greek text, the da-

---

[543] E.g., L. D. Hurst, "Eschatology and 'Platonism' in Hebrews," *SBLSP* 23 (1984), 70–71; C. Fletcher-Louis, "The Destruction of the Temple and the Relativization of the Old Covenant," in *The Reader Must Understand: Eschatology in Bible and Theology*, ed. K. Bower and M. Elliott (Leicester, England: Apollos, 1997), 156–62; and R. Gleason, "Moderate Reformed Response," 166.

[544] As previously stated, Lane's refusal to allow the present tense to express current possession by believers is grounded in his understanding of the warning passages as referring to apostasy. Lane cites Spicq *L'Épître aux Hebreux*, 2:413; and G. Delling, "παραλαμβάνω," *TDNT* 4:13.

[545] Westfall, *Discourse Analysis*, 270.

[546] Lane, *Hebrews 9–13*, 481. Lane follows Vanhoye's proposal that the author's source for the verb "to shake," which the writer has used to interpret Hag 2:6; is Psalm 95 LXX; see esp. Ps 95:9–10 LXX (*Hebrews 9–13*, 485).

tive translated "to God" can be connected with "let us serve," with "acceptably," or with both in the sense "let us worship God in a manner acceptable to him."[547] We are to worship God with "reverence and awe," which is possibly a hendiadys meaning "reverent awe."[548] Appropriate godly fear guarantees our focus will remain on God's grace as the only way possible that we can ever be saved from our sin and serve the Lord.

Verse 29 is subordinated to 28 by the use of *gar*, "for." The conjunction *kai* (untranslated in the NIV) here is emphatic in its use with *gar*.[549] The combined expression "indicates that it is God's essential character that provides the reason for the fear and awe that are appropriate to his worship."[550] The author alludes to Deut 4:24 LXX where Moses told the exodus generation that God is "a consuming fire, a jealous God." The reference here to God as a "consuming fire" is often taken to refer to his judgment. Lane's comment is a good example: "In these texts, consignment to the flames is a metaphor for the completeness and severity of the judgment the apostate can anticipate."[551] Lane not only opted for a meaning of eternal judgment, but based on his understanding of the meaning of the warning passages in Hebrews, he specifically applies the judgment to apostates. Given the apocalyptic imagery of Heb 12:26–27, the reference probably includes the notion of judgment. However, such an application to apostates is tenuous, and especially so in the light of the context of Deut 4:24. In Deut 4:10–20 Moses reminds Israel of the terrifying experience when they stood before God at Sinai, which the author already discussed in 12:18–21. In vv. 15–20 Moses forbids idolatry among the people. This is followed in Deut 4:21–24 with Moses' account of God's anger at him for his disobedience which meant he would not be allowed to enter the Promised Land. This is followed by an admonition for the people of Israel not to forget God's covenant and not to make any idol. Then follows v. 24: "For the Lord your God is a consuming fire, a jealous God." In the final paragraph, Deut 4:25–31, Moses warns the people concerning the consequences of idolatry after they have been in the land a long time, and tells them they will "perish from the land" and they will "not live long there but will certainly be destroyed" (Deut 4:26). They will be scattered and only a few will survive among the nations "to which the Lord will drive you out" (Deut 4:27). Moses informs the people that in those foreign lands "they will worship man-made gods." Moses then makes provision for these idolaters living in exile to repent, seek the Lord, and return to him, upon

[547] Bruce, *Hebrews*, 362; Lane, *Hebrews 9–13*, 438, and the NIV connect the dative with "let us serve." Ellingworth, *Hebrews*, 690–91, connects it with the adverb "acceptably." Kistemaker, *Hebrews*, 400, 401 connect it with both.

[548] So taken by Ellingworth, *Hebrews*, 691.

[549] Ellingworth, *Hebrews*, 692. Lane, *Hebrews 9–13*, 438, 444, takes the position that it is not emphatic.

[550] Lane, *Hebrews 9–13*, 487.

[551] Ibid.

which conditions the Lord will be found by them "for the Lord your God is a merciful God: he will not abandon or destroy you or forget the covenant with your forefathers" (Deut 4:31).

Deuteronomy 4 contains Moses' speech to the people as they were on the verge of entering the Promised Land. Similarly, in Heb 3:7–4:11 the author reflects on the disobedience of the exodus generation and that they were denied entrance into the Promised Land. Moses himself was unable to enter because of his own disobedience. Presumption must be avoided by the readers. In Deut 9:3–7, Moses reminds the people that God will cross over ahead of them "as a consuming fire."[552]

From this context it can be seen that the expression "our God is a consuming fire" is in a context of the disobedience of idolatry, the disobedience of Moses, and that those scattered to foreign lands because of idolatry will be forgiven by God if they repent and return to him, for "God is a merciful God." If idolatry is tantamount to apostasy, then in the Deuteronomy context, it is a sin which can be forgiven.

Another reason for not limiting "fire" here in Heb 12:29 to mean judgment is the immediate context of priestly worship from v. 28 and in fact from the epistle as a whole. The notion of "consuming fire" evokes images of the burnt offering in Lev 6:10. It may be the author is engaging here in something of a double *entendre* where "consuming fire" speaks of judgment from the apocalyptic imagery of Heb 12:26–27 and of priestly sacrifice from the imagery of Heb 12:28. Regardless of whether this is the case or not, the context of Deuteronomy 4 and Hebrews 12 does not support an interpretation of "consuming fire" as God's eternal judgment on those who were once considered part of the covenant community, the church, but are now apostates. As noted in the discussion of Heb 6:4–8, apostasy can occur, but when it does, the apostate gives evidence he was never genuinely converted in the first place. The author of Hebrews is warning genuine believers of the danger of God's discipline in the case of severe disobedience, but his warning does not indicate a potential loss of salvation nor is it addressed specifically to those who are only "mere professors" and not truly converted.

Hebrews 12:18–29 synthesizes the significant themes and motifs of the entire epistle and can rightly be construed as "the pastoral and theological climax of the sermon."[553] Westfall's analysis of the concluding summary of this section is right on target. The description of Mount Zion forms multiple ties with all three major sections of the epistle. The important use of the verb *proserchomai* in this section connects with the beginning of the latter two major semantic sections of the epistle (4:16 and 10:22), as well as with other impor-

[552] See Gray, *Godly Fear*, 213.

[553] Lane, *Hebrews 9–13*, 448, although Lane takes the final unit as beginning in v. 14 rather than v. 18.

tant summaries or introductions (e.g, 7:25 and 10:1). The phrase "spirits of righteous men made perfect" (12:23) is an explicit reference to the fulfillment of the promises in 11:39–40. Now the people of Hebrews 11 are "perfected," a major theme in the epistle, and are in the city of Zion. The readers also have come to this city in a spiritual sense. Jesus is described in terms that evoke the second major division of the epistle with references to his role as mediator of the new covenant and to his sprinkled blood. References to God "speaking" form ties with 1:1–4:13. Hebrews 12:25 parallels 2:1–4 and restates the major theme of the first major division of the epistle. The two hortatory subjunctives of 12:28 link to the concept of access to God in the second major section with the hortatory subjunctives in 4:16 and 10:22. The priestly metaphor is "reactivated" by the author with the verb *latreuō* in v. 28 which forms links with the cultic terms used for the priesthood in 7:5 and 10:18. This verb occurs six times in Hebrews (8:4–5; 9:8–9; 9:14; 10:2; 12:28; 13:10), all referring to priestly function. The command to approach God and serve in a priestly fashion constrains the commands in Hebrews 13 that conclude with another double hortatory subjunctive: go to Jesus outside the camp (13:12) and offer sacrifices (13:15). The central themes of the discourse, approaching God as priests, pursuing spiritual maturity, holding fast the confession, and responding to the voice of God, are all evoked in this unit, but the latter three support the theme of approaching God as priests.[554] Westfall's outline of Hebrews 12 is threefold: (1) let's run the race with endurance (12:1–29); (2) the context of the race is heavenly Jerusalem (12:18–27); and (3) therefore, let's serve God as priests through grace in heavenly Jerusalem (12:28–29).[555]

There may be an *inclusio* beginning with 10:39, "we are of those who are of faith unto the preserving of the soul"; followed by mention of Abel in 11:4 who being dead, yet speaks; followed in 12:24 with "we have come to the one who speaks better than Abel." The *inclusio* is formed by the name "Abel" and the allusion to speaking.[556]

THEOLOGICAL IMPLICATIONS. The term "kingdom" in v. 28 indicates that vv. 22–24 are descriptive of the kingdom of God, a kingdom which believers are a part of presently. The author's language in vv. 22–28 illustrates the "already/not yet" tension that exists in the New Testament with respect to kingdom eschatology. There is a sense in which the kingdom is now and Christians are a part of it. Yet future dimensions remain to be unfolded such as final eschatological judgment pictured here by the reference to Hag 2:6 and the shaking of all things. A key point in this section is the author's use of the perfect tense to indicate that his readers "have come" to this kingdom and are by implication experiencing it now (v. 22). As Westfall observed, "The

---

[554] Westfall, *Discourse Analysis*, 280–81, who saw three major discourse themes. I would add a fourth: responding to the voice of God with obedience.

[555] Ibid., 282.

[556] So suggested by Smillie, "'One Who is Speaking,'" 282–83.

location where believers run their race is identified as heavenly Jerusalem." The kingdom described in vv. 22–24 is present; it is the "shaking" in vv. 26–27 that is future.[557] Yet it must be remembered that there is yet a future aspect to the kingdom of God which will only be realized in the eschaton. It is because we "have come" to this kingdom, described as a heavenly context in which Christians currently have their existence, that we are able to fulfill the mandate of worshipping God acceptably in v. 28. The exhortations found earlier in the epistle to enter the rest, to press on to maturity, and to stir each other up to love and good works all involve the pursuit of spiritual goals which are semantically parallel to the metaphor of running a race.[558]

With respect to the author's use of Zion symbolism in Heb 12:18–24, K. Son's excellent treatment of this topic led him to the following conclusions. (1) The contrast between Sinai and Zion is between the symbolic significance of the Sinai theophany where God's anger is expressed against the unfaithful wilderness generation and Zion which symbolizes the restored state of the eschatological community through Jesus.[559] (2) The background of Heb 12:18–24 is not Platonic dualism but rather Jewish apocalyptic which contains both spatial and temporal elements.[560] (3) The antithetical structure of Heb 12:18–24 is the basis of the author's rhetorical strategy throughout the book;[561] (4) The close lexical relationship between the verbs *proserchomai* in 12:18,22 and *eiserchomai* in 3:11,18; 19:4:1,3,5,6,10,11 indicate that coming to the heavenly Zion in 12:22 is equivalent to entering God's Sabbath rest in Heb 4:9.[562] (5) Sinai and Zion are theological symbols employed by the author of Hebrews which embrace all of the theological subjects discussed in the epistle especially in relation to Jesus and his fulfillment of the Old Testament cultus;[563] (6) Sinai and Zion function for the author within a framework of temporal and spatial dualism where Zion transcends both time and space. Thus, Zion was the center of God's redemptive activity in the past, it is the center of God's present redemptive activity and the reign of Christ in heaven, and it is the center of eschatological judgment and restoration in the future as well.[564]

This section serves as the closure for both the theological and hortatory part of the epistle, hence its back reference to themes which were dominant in Heb 1:1–4:13. God spoke through the Old Testament revelation. When the author used that revelation in quotation, God was still speaking through it to

[557] Westfall, *Discourse Analysis*, 267, against Lane who takes the position that the reader's relationship to Zion is future (*Hebrews 9–13*, 465).

[558] Ibid., 279.

[559] K. Son, *Zion Symbolism in Hebrews*, 74.

[560] Ibid., 74, 93, 184.

[561] Ibid., 87, 103.

[562] Ibid., 91–93, 140–45.

[563] Ibid., 200.

[564] Ibid., 201–2.

his readers. Now, in 12:25, the one who is speaking to the readers is God, but with a twist. The author apparently intends his readers to understand that God is speaking to them *through the medium of the author's own written words* as well.[565] In 13:22, the author will call his epistle a "word of exhortation," the same nomenclature Luke uses to identify Paul's synagogue sermon in Pisidian Antioch in Acts 13:15–41. If, as Smillie suggested, the author understands his work in the same way, "then his concept of the Word of God probably includes his own Christian interpretation of the Old Testament texts, ordinances and personages."[566] In Heb 9:8–9, the author prefaces his explanation of the Old Testament cultic ceremonies with the words "the Holy Spirit is indicating this." Such a statement suggests that he believes his interpretation of the Old Testament is the Word of God.[567] Of course, that is exactly what Hebrews is, and this has been further confirmed by its canonical recognition by the church. The author says he has "written" this word of exhortation to his readers. Both the Old Testament words of God and the New Testament speech of God in Hebrews are mediated in written form. By paying attention to the written words of Scripture, we "today" can "hear God's voice" (3:7,15; 4:7).[568] This does not mean that we have an open-ended concept of revelation today that is in some sense "additional" to Scripture. Hebrews aligns hermeneutically with the Old Testament; thus the author's interpretation was not severed from the original locus of revelation. His hermeneutical approach was not arbitrary or subjective, as is often the case with those who champion the notion that God speaks a direct word of revelation today in addition to the Scriptures. Likewise, God's Word is "living and active" (Heb 4:12), and God "speaks" today through Scripture. As Smillie stated, this should deter "a stale scholasticism."[569]

Finally, since Hebrews is considered to be a written sermon, it is clear, given its central Old Testament text of Ps 110:1,4 and its use of the Old Testament throughout, that it is a text-driven sermon. The author engaged in "exposition" and "exhortation" artfully woven together in sermonic form to meet the pastoral needs of his congregation. As Smillie pointed out, all of this has repercussions for homiletics today. It suggests a model for the relationship between the Word of God in Scripture and the exposition and proclamation of that Word by preachers. "It demonstrates what interpretation of the Bible can be: not only human intellectual opinion about what a text means, but also a vehicle through which the living God, 'the one who is speaking,' personally addresses those who hear it."[570]

---

[565] Cf. Koester, *Hebrews*, 552, who says as much.
[566] Smillie, "'One Who is Speaking,'" 293.
[567] Ibid.
[568] Ibid.
[569] Ibid., 294.
[570] Ibid.

4. Final Exhortations to Love and Humble Submission (13:1–21)

In Hebrews 13, the author concludes his written sermon with several exhortations[571] for the congregation to obey. The abrupt shift that occurs with Hebrews 13 and its unique content and certain stylistic differences with the rest of the epistle have caused several scholars to question its authenticity.[572] For example, Thompson considered Heb 13:1–6 to be something of a loose collection of general exhortations unrelated to the rest of the epistle.[573] However, several studies have successfully demonstrated the integrity of Hebrews 13.[574] Thus, Lane can remark:

---

[571] The "peroration," or conclusion of a speech, was a well-known and vital part of the Greek and Latin classical rhetorical tradition. Koester, *Hebrews*, 555–56, identified two main purposes of peroration: affect emotions and refresh memory. He cites how Aristotle and Cicero taught that short sentences linked by asyndeton were the appropriate style for perorations. There is no agreement as to exactly where the peroration should begin with Hebrews. K. Backhaus views the beginning at 10:19, but this is highly unlikely (*Der neue Bund und das Werden der Kirche: Die Diatheke-Deutung des Hebräerbriefs im Rahmen der Frühchristlichen Theologiegeschichte*, in *Neutestamentliche Abhandlungen* 29 (Münster: Aschendorffsche Verlagsbuchhandlung GambH & Co., 1996), 61–63. W. G. Übelacker, *Der Hebräerbrief als Appell.* Lund: Almqvist & Wiksell, 1989), 224, thinks the peroration begins at 13:1, as do most commentators. Koester, *Hebrews,* 554, and Westfall, *Discourse Analysis*, 283–91 consider 12:28 to begin the peroration. Koester rightly takes the peroration to 13:21. C. Westfall sees it as concluding at 13:16, with 13:17–25 providing personal details from the author. In light of the closing benediction at 13:20–21 and the fact that there are clear command forms after v. 16, it seems prudent to consider the peroration as extending through 13:21. The abrupt shift at 13:1 probably marks it as the best place to identify the beginning of the epistle's peroration.

[572] The theory that part or all of Hebrews 13 was written by a different author in conscious imitation of Pauline style was suggested by W. Wrede, *Das literarische Rätsel des Hebräerbriefs* (Göttingen: Vandenhoeck und Ruprecht, 1906). Others who have followed this or a similar proposal include G. W. Buchanan, *To the Hebrews*, AB (Garden City, NY: Doubleday & Company, 1972), 268, and more recently A. J. Wedderburn, "The 'Letter' to the Hebrews and Its Thirteenth Chapter," NTS 50 (2004), 390–405. Some have theorized that chap. 13 was written by Paul himself (G. A. Simcox, "Heb. xiii; 2 Tim. iv," *ExpTim* 10 (1898–99), 430ff.) or that the concluding postscript (vv. 22–25) was written by Paul. F. J. Badcock argued vv. 23–25 were Paul's postscript to the epistle mostly written by Barnabas (*The Pauline Epistles and the Epistle to the Hebrews in their Historical Setting* [London: 1939], 199ff.). Buchanan, *Hebrews*, 242, 267, suggested that vv. 22–25 were written in imitation of Pauline style by another hand. E. D. Jones, "The Authorship of Hebrews xiii," *ExpTim* 46 (1934–35), 562–67, argued that chap. 13 was actually the conclusion of Paul's so-called "severe letter" to the church at Corinth. R. V. G. Tasker, "The Integrity of the Epistle to the Hebrews," *ExpTim* 47 (1935–36), 136–38, responded to Jones and defended the genuineness of Heb 13. L. Dussaut, *Synopse Structurelle*, 134–35, correctly noted the author's statement in 13:19 ("and I urge") and 13:22 ("and I urge") links the two sections together and not only indicates that Hebrews 13 was written by one hand, but that the chapter reflects the style of the author throughout the epistle.

[573] J. W. Thompson, *The Beginnings of Christian Philosophy*, CBQMS (Washington, DC: Catholic Biblical Association, 1982), 143.

[574] See esp. F. Filson, *Yesterday: A Study of Hebrews in the Light of Chapter 13* (Naperville: Allenson, 1967), and J. Thurén, *Das lobopfer der Hebräer: Studien zum Aufbau und Anliegen von Hebräerbrief 13* (Acta Academiae Aboensis, Series A 47 (Åbo: Åbo Akademi, 1973), 49–247, along with Lane, *Hebrews 9–13*, 496.

> It is unnecessary to call into question the authenticity of chap. 13 in the light of the very evident links between this material and the preceding chapters, both in content and thrust. Attention has been called to the character of the vocabulary, to lines of argumentation, to the sustained appeal to the texts from the Pentateuch and the Psalms, to the recurrence of key concepts, and to considerations of structure, all of which tend to exhibit the basic homogeneity of chap. 13 with the rest of the document.[575]

Lane surveyed a list of stylistic considerations that link Hebrews 13 with Hebrews 1–12 and concluded that a "distinctive literary signature" characterizes both sections of the epistle. Such "conscious literary artistry" supports the authenticity of the entire chapter.[576]

As far as the chapter itself goes, most see two major sections: 13:1–21 and 13:22–25. Westfall viewed 12:28–13:16 to be the formal conclusion of the epistle, where the commands are constrained by Hebrews 12 and especially the temple language of 12:28–29. She posited cohesion between 12:28 and 13:15–16, where the latter contains double hortatory subjunctives, suggesting the author's main topic is serving God as priests, offering sacrifices of thanksgiving, good works and sharing, all of which are pleasing to God.[577] The word *euarestōs*, "acceptably," in Heb 12:28 is echoed by the verbal form of this same word in 13:16, translated "is pleased." This same adjective also occurs in 13:21 in the benediction. Consequently, 12:28 is the key exhortation and Hebrews 13 gives specificity to it.[578]

Koester has identified three movements of thought in 12:28–13:19, with the first and the third units parallel:[579]

A.	Service to God	12:28–29
	Serving others	13:1–6
	Attention to leaders	13:7–9
B.	Priestly Sacrifice	13:10–11
	Christ's death for others	13:12
	Christians follow Christ's lead	13:13–14
C.	Sacrifice to God	13:15
	Serving others	13:16
	Attention to leaders	13:17–19

575 Lane, *Hebrews 9–13*, 496.

576 Ibid., 497.

577 Westfall, *Discourse Analysis*, 283. Cf. Lane, *Hebrews 9–13*, 497–98, and his survey of others noting this connection. Koester, *Hebrews*, 554, 555, argued for 12:28–13:21 as the conclusion with its theme of worship and service pleasing to God. On the connection of 12:28 and Hebrews 13 see F. Filson, "Yesterday," 4; Swetnam, "Form and Content in Hebrews 7–13," *Bib* 55 (1974): 340–41; and Lane, *Hebrews 9–13*, 497–98.

578 Lane, *Hebrews 9–13*, 506.

579 Koester, *Hebrews*, 555.

The commands in Hebrews 13 expand the concept of service to God commanded in 12:28. Westfall considered 13:9–16 to be a paraphrase of 12:28.[580] It is within the overarching context of priestly service that Christians are to conduct their lives on earth.

Hebrews 13:1–6 can be identified as a paragraph unit by its unity and symmetry.[581] Verses 7–19 likewise exhibit structural unity and symmetry.[582] A lexical *inclusio* is formed in v. 7 and vv. 17–18 by the words *hēgoumenoi* ("leaders") and *anastrophēs* ("way of life") and by the alliteration in the commands:

13:7	*mnēmoneuete - mimeisthe*	"remember" - "imitate"
13:17–18	*peithesthe - proseuchesthe*	"obey" - "pray"

According to Lane, "The elaborate building of the frame serves to highlight 13:10–16, which is distinguished as a unit from 13:7–9 and 17–19 by its form and construction. Formally, it consists of exposition, 13:10–12, which grounds the exhortation in 13:13–16. Each constituent part consists of three members arranged chiastically." This is Lane's chiastic structure of 13:10–16:[583]

A "We have an altar from which those who serve the tabernacle do not have the right to eat" v. 10
  B "For . . . their bodies are burned outside the camp" v. 11
    C "And so Jesus also suffered death outside the city gate" v. 12
    C´ "So then let us go out to him outside the camp, bearing the shame he bore" v. 13
  B´ "for here we do not have a permanent city, but we are expecting intently the city which is to come" v. 14
A´ "Through Jesus, therefore, let us continually offer to God a sacrifice consisting in praise." vv. 15–16

In addition, Lane noted the chiastic structure found in vv. 15–16:

A "Through him, therefore, let us continually offer a sacrifice of praise to God"
  B "this is to say, the fruit of lips that praise his name"
  B´ "Do not neglect acts of kindness and generosity"
A´ "for God is pleased because of such sacrifices'[584]

---

580 Westfall, *Discourse Analysis*, 285.

581 For surveys of proposals made by Thurén, Dussaut, Michel, and Vanhoye, see Lane, *Hebrews 9–13*, 501–2. There are nine commands connected by asyndeton in 13:1–9, which serve to give this section unity and cohesion.

582 See Lane, *Hebrews 9-13*, 502.

583 Ibid., 503. Lane correctly shows the way the author tightly weaves this unit together through the skillful use of conjunctions, particles, and prepositions.

584 Ibid., 504. In the Greek text, the first and fourth clauses speak of sacrifice and both clauses end with θεός.

McCown demonstrated the sustained argument and cohesiveness of 13:10–16 which binds it together as a unit which he calls "explanatory paraenesis" or "hortatory exposition."[585] The argument begins with the statement "we have an altar" which is based on Lev 16:27. This is further expounded in vv. 10–12 and then followed by two imperatives in v. 13 ("let us go out") and v. 15 ("let us continually offer"). The author makes it a point to specify Jesus suffered "outside the city gate." The command to follow Jesus "outside the camp" is based on Lev 16:27. The reference to the "altar" in 13:10 serves as the springboard for the commands in 13:15–16 concerning offering to God the sacrifice of praise and doing acts of kindness.[586]

All of this symmetry from Heb 12:28–13:16 cannot be accidental and must be by the author's design. Two conclusions can be drawn from this literary artistry. First, the author views the content of vv. 10–16 as of crucial importance in the final chapter. Second, these exhortations are "crucial to the writer's pastoral strategy."[587]

(1) Continuing in Love (13:1–8)

**1Keep on loving each other as brothers. 2Do not forget to entertain strangers,
for by so doing some people have entertained angels without knowing it. 3Remem-
ber those in prison as if you were their fellow prisoners, and those who are mistreated as if you yourselves were suffering.**

**4Marriage should be honored by all, and the marriage bed kept pure, for God
will judge the adulterer and all the sexually immoral. 5Keep your lives free from
the love of money and be content with what you have, because God has said,**

> **"Never will I leave you;**
> **never will I forsake you."**

6So we say with confidence,

> **"The Lord is my helper; I will not be afraid.**
> **What can man do to me?"**

**7Remember your leaders, who spoke the word of God to you. Consider the out-
come of their way of life and imitate their faith. 8Jesus Christ is the same yesterday
and today and forever.**

13:1 Hebrews 13 provides specific practical instruction on fulfilling the author's command in 12:28 to worship and serve God: serve God's people. Verse 1 is a terse statement employing the present imperative followed by the

---

585 W. G. McCown, "Ο ΛΟΓΟΣ ΤΗΣ ΠΑΡΑΚΛΗΣΕΩΣ: The Nature and Function of the Hortatory Sections in the Epistle to the Hebrews," (Ph.D. dissertation, Union Theological Seminary, 1970), 128–29.

586 See Lane, *Hebrews 9–13*, 500.

587 Ibid., 504. It is, however, overstepping the boundaries of evidence to suggest that Hebrews 13 is the key to the theology of the epistle, as does Filson, *Yesterday*, 82; and Thurén, *Lobopfer*, 246–47.

direct object which reads (lit.) "the brotherly love let remain." The author uses *philadelphia*, "brotherly love," a word used by both Paul and Peter. Lane renders the imperative "Brotherly love must continue."[588] The noun in Greek is addressed to believers and concerns their filial relationship with one another, with the implication that they already have love for one another. The author commands that such love be maintained. DeSilva defined the word as "the love that characterizes siblings."[589] Christians have been brought into the family of God and are a part of his "household" (Heb 3:6).

13:2 Verse 2 begins with another imperative which reads (lit.): "hospitality do not neglect." The imperative conveys the notion of not forgetting to do something. Stated positively, the author is exhorting the readers to remember to practice hospitality. The Greek noun *philoxenia*, (lit.) "love of strangers," means hospitality to strangers,[590] and is translated verbally in the NIV. Travel was difficult in the first century and inns were not always the safest place to be. To open one's home to a travelling stranger evidenced brotherly love and was considered a high virtue by Jews and Gentiles alike.[591] Mutual support among the early Christians would have been vital for maintaining the solidarity of new believers as well as aiding in the missionary expansion of the church.[592]

As a ground or reason[593] for this hospitality, the author states that some have entertained angelic beings who appeared in human form. Abraham had such an experience in Genesis 18 when he entertained three men in Mamre, one of whom turned out to be Yahweh himself. The other two visitors (angels) went to Sodom and were shown hospitality by Lot. Two other Old Testament examples of such an occurrence are the experiences of Gideon (Judg 6:11–21) and Manoah (Judg 13:3–20).

---

[588] Ibid., 507.

[589] DeSilva, *Perseverance in Gratitude*, 485. "Fostering an ethos of kinship within the Christian group was a widespread technique grounded in the conviction that the believers have become kin by the blood of Christ, being adopted into the one household of God as the many sons and daughters."

[590] L&N 34.57. On the concept of hospitality, see J. Koenig, *ABD* 3:299–301.

[591] Bruce, *Hebrews*, 370. "In the New Testament, hospitality is incumbent on all Christians, and Christian leaders in particular are required to be hospitable (1 Tim 3:2; Tit. 1:8)." See Rom 12:13 and 1 Pet 4:9; cf. *Didache* 11:4–6, where Christians are to receive an apostle into their home, but he must not stay for more than a day or two. A three-day stay marks him as a false prophet.

[592] Koester, *Hebrews*, 563.

[593] J. Moffatt, *Hebrews*, 225; and Kistemaker, *Hebrews,* 239, take the clauses to indicate result, not reason. Ἔλαθόν ξενίσαντες is a classical idiom where the participle contains the main idea and the main verb functions adverbially. This is an example of semantic skewing that can take place between the grammatical structure and the semantic structure of a given language. On this linguistic phenomenon, which is quite important in exegesis, see J. Beekman, J. Callow, and M. Kopesec, *The Semantic Structure of Written Communication* (Dallas: Summer Institute of Linguistics, 1981), 33–34; J. Beekman and K. Callow, *Translating the Word of God* (Grand Rapids: Zondervan, 1974), 212–28; and M. Larson, *Meaning-Based Translation: A Guide to Cross-language Equivalence* (Lanham, MD: University Press of America, 1984), 224–45. Lane, *Hebrews 9–13*, 507, pointed out the striking use of paronomasia in the Greek of v. 2.

13:3 A third imperative to remember those in prison follows in v. 3. The author previously praised the recipients for their care of those in prison in 10:32–34. The present imperative is iterative in force in the sense of "continue to remember." It is complemented by the perfect participle translated "as if you were their fellow prisoners," describing the manner in which Christians are to go about remembering those who are in prison. Furthermore, they are to remember those who are "mistreated[594] as if you yourselves[595] were suffering."[596] Jesus himself expressed concern for those in need of hospitality and those in prison in Matt 25:35,36: "I was a stranger and you invited me in . . . I was in prison and you came to visit me." Prison life was deplorable in the first century.[597] The account which Lucian gives of the imprisonment of Peregrinus Proteus sheds light on this injunction in v. 3. Christians sought his release, but to no avail. "Everything else that could be done for him they most devoutly did. They thought of nothing else. Orphans and ancient widows might be seen hanging about the prison from break of day. Their officials bribed the gaolers to let them sleep inside with him. Elegant dinners were conveyed in; their sacred writings were read."[598]

13:4 With v. 4 the subject shifts to marriage and sexual purity. The main clause of v. 4 is both compound and verbless. The KJV supplies an indicative verb in the first clause and leaves it implied in the second: "Marriage is honorable in all; and the bed undefiled." However, most commentators and translators take the author's meaning to express an imperatival idea for three reasons: the following reason clause supports it; the beginning of v. 5 is a parallel verbless construction, but one which indicates the necessity of understanding an implied imperative verb; and the fronted position of the adjective translated "honored" in the clause supports the imperatival sense as well.[599]

This verse serves as a specific example of showing brotherly love (v. 1) in that, as Bruce well says, "Chastity is not opposed to charity, but is part of

---

[594] The word in Greek has a range of meanings from mistreatment to torture; see L&N 88.126.

[595] The expressed personal pronoun in Greek gives emphasis: "you yourselves."

[596] In Greek, the participial phrase ὡς...ὄντες ἐν σώματι is (lit.) "as being in the body." The NIV renders this "as if . . . were suffering" to express manner. Whether the recipients were themselves being mistreated at the time of writing cannot be established, though the NIV and some other translations imply they are not. Bruce, *Hebrews*, 368, takes the phrase as expressing reason: "because you yourselves are also in the body." The phrase "in the body" does not mean "in the body of Christ," as Westcott, *Hebrews*, 431, correctly stated.

[597] On prison conditions in the first century, see the summary in Koester, *Hebrews,* 564; and B. Rapske, *The Book of Acts and Paul in Roman Custody*, in *The Book of Acts in Its First Century Setting*, ed. B. W. Winter (Grand Rapids: Eerdmans, 1994), 3:20–35, 369–92.

[598] Lucian, *The Death of Peregrinus,* in *The Works of Lucian Samosata* (Oxford: The Clarendon Press, 1905), 4:82.

[599] Bruce, *Hebrews*, 368; Miller, *Hebrews*, 426; the NIV has a moderating translation: "Marriage should be honored by all."

it."[600] Here the author places a high priority on the sanctity and inviolability of the marriage bond. The New Testament affirms the Old Testament's revelation concerning the divine origination of marriage.[601] The first statement, "Marriage should be honored by all," places special focus on the word translated "honored" by its fronted position in the clause. The word itself means to highly esteem and respect. This general statement about honoring marriage is followed by a more narrowed focus on the sanctity of the sexual relationship in marriage: "and[602] the marriage bed[603] kept pure." This phrase refers to sexual intercourse within marriage, meaning husbands and wives should remain sexually faithful to one another and to their marriage vows. The Greek adjective translated "pure" conveys the meaning "undefiled," "unpolluted," "untainted."[604] It is in the emphatic position in its clause. One implication of this verse is that marriage should in no way be considered as spiritually inferior to celibacy.[605] In fact, Paul warns the church about those who "forbid people to marry" in 1 Tim 4:3.

The "by all" construes the dative prepositional phrase in Greek to encode agency: "by all people." Bruce and Hughes likewise take it in reference to people, but view the phrase in a locative sense: "among all people."[606] Others take the reference to be aspectual or circumstantial with the meaning "in every respect" or "in every circumstance."[607]

The compound clause is followed by a subordinating clause, introduced by *gar* "for" expressing the grounds of the preceding exhortation: "for fornicators and adulterers God will judge." The term *pornos* in Greek does have a general meaning of a sexually immoral person and can refer to those who commit sexual sins in general, homosexual or heterosexual, outside of marriage. However, used in conjunction with *moichos*, "adulterer," *pornos* is probably best translated in its more restricted sense of "fornication," with reference to anyone who violates another's marriage by engaging in sexual relations with either partner in that marriage.[608] The term *moichos*, "adulterer," refers to anyone who violates his or her own marriage vows by having sexual relations with

[600] Bruce, *Hebrews*, 372.

[601] Including the fact that in both OT and NT, marriage is understood to be between one man and one woman. See Genesis 2; Matt 19:4–5; Mark 10:6–8; and Eph 5:22–33.

[602] Dods considers the conjunction καί "and" to imply an inference being drawn from the first half of the clause: "and thus let the (marriage) bed." ("Hebrews," 375).

[603] The word in Greek is κοίτη, translated "marriage bed" and refers euphemistically to sexual relations in marriage.

[604] See L&N 53.36.

[605] L. Morris, *Hebrews*, 146.

[606] Bruce, *Hebrews*, 368; Hughes, *Hebrews*, 566.

[607] So Morris, "Hebrews," 146; and Ellingworth, *Hebrews*, 697. Paul warns the Thessalonian church to abstain from sexual immorality on the grounds that this is God's will and the Lord judges those who so conduct themselves.

[608] See L&N 88.274; BDAG 855, 657.

someone other than their own spouse.[609] The two nouns are used together by Paul in I Cor 6:9. Such sexual immorality God will judge, where *theos*, "God," is emphasized in the Greek text by being placed clause final.

13:5 Verses 5–6 form a unit and prohibit material greed on the grounds of God's perennial care for those who are his. An inordinate concern for one's possessions can supplant care for those in the Christian family and foreigners.[610] For the third time in five verses, the author employs a noun with the root *phil-*, 'love of,' thus providing "linguistic and thematic cohesiveness" to Heb 13:1–7.[611] The staccato style of these verses continues in v. 5 where the first clause in Greek (lit.) reads: "not loving money the way of life (should be)." The adjective *aphilarguros* is fronted in the clause for emphasis and is used imperatively. The root word means "love of money" which is negated by the alpha privative and its only other occurrence in the New Testament is 1 Tim 3:3. The noun *tropos* means "way of life," in the sense of one's conduct or character. The NIV renders this, "Keep your lives free from the love of money." This is followed in the Greek text by a second participial clause "being content with (your) possessions," where the participle translated "be content" is taken imperatively and translated as a finite verb.[612] This command is reminiscent of our Lord's parable of the rich man who built bigger barns (Luke 12:15) and where Paul says "godliness with contentment is great gain" (1 Tim 6:6–10).

As in v. 4, the ground or reason for the commands is introduced by *gar* and translated "because." The personal pronoun *autos* is translated as "God" and serves as the subject of the perfect tense[613] verb translated "has said," which introduces a quotation from the Old Testament. The overt use of *autos* by the author probably indicates emphasis: "he himself has said." The following quotation is not an exact quotation from a specific Old Testament passage. Sources include the following suggestions from the LXX: Gen 28:15; Deut 31:5,6,8 (or both Deut 31:6,8); Josh 1:5 or 1 Chr 28:20.[614] The NIV's translation of the quotation stresses the double negative in Greek that introduces the first half of the parallel statement: "Never will I leave you," and the triple negative in Greek ("no not never") introducing the second half, "never will I forsake you." Such use of the negatives encodes emphatic future negation. The word

---

[609] So Hughes, *Hebrews*, 566; Bruce, *Hebrews*, 373; and Lane, *Hebrews 9–13*, 517.

[610] As noted by Koester, *Hebrews*, 559, 566.

[611] DeSilva, *Perseverance in Gratitude*, 485.

[612] Ellingworth, *Hebrews*, 699, thinks this positive statement is in synonymous parallelism with the preceding statement and thus supports the notion that the participle is not subordinate to an implied imperative in v. 5a but functions as an imperative; cf. Bruce, *Hebrews*, 368; and Lane, *Hebrews 9–13*, 509.

[613] The perfect tense, used often in quote formulae in Hebrews, stresses the contemporary application of the Scripture to the readers.

[614] See Koester, *Hebrews*, 559; and Hughes, *Hebrews*, 568, for a comparison of the LXX texts with Heb 13:5.

translated "leave" means "to desert" or "to abandon."[615] The word translated "forsake" connotes abandonment or desertion. The two words are essentially synonymous in this context.

13:6 Verse 6 follows with a second quotation from Ps 118:6 (117:6 LXX). It is introduced by "so we say with confidence" where the prepositional phrase "with confidence" renders the Greek participle indicating manner in the adverbial sense of "confidently." Some take the phrase in Greek rendered as "we say" to indicate actuality,[616] but most suggest it is best to construe the Greek as indicating potentiality in the sense of "we can say."[617] The author omitted the coordinating conjunction which appears in the LXX between the first two clauses, highlighting the terseness of the citation.[618] The first proposition "The Lord is my helper" is followed by a second, "I will not be afraid," creating a reason-result semantic relationship. A further result is stated in a third proposition: "What can man do to me?" This statement can be taken as a direct question or as a rhetorical question. If the latter, the implication is one of strong negative response, although the former suggests as much as well. Additionally, the first word in the quotation in Greek is "Lord" and the last word is "man," indicating strong contrast.[619] The anarthrous use of *anthropos*, "man," is taken by most in a qualitative sense ("any human being") but it can be taken indefinitely as a reference to any person.

13:7 A new discourse paragraph begins in v. 7 with the command to "remember your leaders." Three times in this chapter the author refers to the "leaders" of the church: 13:7,17,24. Here the reference is to those former leaders who have died. The word for "leaders" here is the participle of the verb *hēgeomai* "lead," and connotes those who lead or guide in a supervisory capacity.[620] Lane explains: "The term is not reserved for a specified official position or administrative task but designates a person entrusted with responsibility for leadership, who on the ground of the official position receives authority."[621]

These leaders are described as being those "who spoke the word of God to you." This phrase can refer both to evangelistic preaching as reflected in Acts (e.g., 8:25; 11:19; 13:46) as well as preaching to the church (Acts 4:29,31; 1 Pet 4:11). The leaders of the church are described here less by their office and more by their function of preaching and teaching the Word of God. Their

[615] See L&N 35.54.

[616] So H. Alford, "Hebrews," and the NIV.

[617] So Lane, *Hebrews 9–13*, 507, 509; and Ellingworth, *Hebrews*, 700.

[618] Lane, *Hebrews 9–13*, 509.

[619] So Dods, "Hebrews," 376.

[620] BDAG 434; TLNT 3.166–70. The word is used in Matt 2:6 and Luke 22:26 in the sense of "ruler" or "leader"; in Acts 7:10 of high officials; in Acts 14:12 of Paul as the "chief speaker" and Acts 15:22 in reference to Judas and Silas who were "leading men" among the brethren. The word occurs in Heb 13:7,17,24.

[621] Lane, *Hebrews 9–13*, 526. Lane observed that subsequent to Hebrews, the use of this term for Christian leaders "appears to be confined to documents associated with the church in Rome."

leadership authority derives from the authority of the Word. Furthermore, this designation indicates the primacy of the preaching/teaching ministry of the leaders in the local church. The author does not appeal to any other ground of authority rather than the preached word. The author of Hebrews has a very pronounced theology of the word and preaching that is evident here as well as in 1:1–3; 2:1–4; 4:12–13, among other places. His use of Scripture and method of citation coupled with the constant refrain of the importance of hearing and obeying the word of God also demonstrates his theology of the word.

The aorist tense verb, "who spoke," sums up the totality of their life and ministry. "Consider" translates a Greek participle meaning to look at something closely,[622] and can be taken to have a hortatory function as in the NIV. It can be construed as being governed by the preceding imperative "remember" or by the following imperative "imitate."[623] "Outcome" is sometimes taken to refer to martyrdom,[624] but the word itself and the usage here does not demand such a meaning.[625] It is better to take the word in the sense of "the result of how one lived," which of course could include how they died as well. From what is stated in Heb 10:32–34 and 12:4, the author seems to indicate that martyrdom was not yet exampled among the community. The combination of "remember" and "consider" leads to the present imperative "imitate their faith," where the meaning is imitate the life of faith that they lived.

13:8 This verse at first appears unconnected to the context and is so taken by some.[626] However, there is indeed a connection. It can be viewed as providing the grounds for the exhortation to follow in v. 9, or the grounds or reason for the preceding statement in v. 7. It is best to see the verse as transitional, connecting to both v. 7 and v. 9, stating the object of the former leaders' faith and the grounds for the exhortation in v. 9.[627] Earthly leaders of the church come and go. They live and they die. However, Jesus lives forever, unchanging and unaffected by mortality or anything else that would hinder him from providing leadership, counsel, encouragement, strength, and whatever else might be needed by his people. There may also be a contextual connection with what has just been stated in 13:5. In fact, the author may be reflecting back on the quotation of Ps 102:27 in Heb 1:12 where the words "you remain the same, and your years will never end" is applied to Jesus the eternal Son of God. Bruce pointed

---

[622] On ἀναθεωροῦντες, see BDAG 63. Lane, *Hebrews 9–13*, 522, takes it in the sense of "look at again and again."

[623] Most take it in the latter sense; Lane, *Hebrews 9–13*, 522, interpreted it in the former sense.

[624] So Moffatt, *Hebrews*, 230–31. Moffatt translated: "look back upon the close of their career."

[625] See Hughes, *Hebrews*, 569.

[626] E.g., Ellingworth, *Hebrews*, 704.

[627] So Moffatt, *Hebrews*, 232; Hughes, *Hebrews*, 570; and Lane, *Hebrews 9–13*, 528.

out that "yesterday" Jesus suffered and died; "today" he represents Christians as their high priest; and "forever" he lives to intercede on their behalf.[628]

There is no verb in this statement and there does not have to be, for as Nairne pointed out, "this is a battle cry rather than a creed."[629] "Jesus Christ" is emphatic in the clause. The word order in Greek is striking (lit.): "Jesus Christ yesterday and today the same, and unto the ages [forever]." There is certainly a temporal sense expressed here, culminating in an eternal perspective, along the lines of "in the past, in the present, and in the future."[630] "Yesterday" has been taken to refer to the time of the leaders mentioned previously or to the time culminating in Christ's atoning work on the cross. Moffatt is probably correct in taking the reference to include both,[631] but the word should not be limited even to these two. Jesus Christ is eternally unchanging right up to the present time from the perspective of the author, and he will be eternally so in the future. "Today" is probably best taken to refer to the present in general terms rather than to Christ's present work of intercession, although such is included. "Forever" may refer specifically to Christ's eternal high priesthood, but more likely is a general designation for the unending future. The two uses of *kai*, "and," are taken in an ascensive sense by Miller to signal an increasing emphasis and contrast between time and eternity: "not only the same in all of time but in eternity as well."[632] This verse implies at least three truths: the divinity of Christ;[633] the immutability of Christ; and the constant faithfulness of Christ to his people.

(2) Continuing Sacrifices of Praise (13:9–16)

9Do not be carried away by all kinds of strange teachings. It is good for our hearts to be strengthened by grace, not by ceremonial foods, which are of no value to those who eat them. 10We have an altar from which those who minister at the tabernacle have no right to eat.

11The high priest carries the blood of animals into the Most Holy Place as a sin offering, but the bodies are burned outside the camp. 12And so Jesus also suffered outside the city gate to make the people holy through his own blood. 13Let us, then, go to him outside the camp, bearing the disgrace he bore. 14For here we do not have an enduring city, but we are looking for the city that is to come.

---

628 Bruce, *Hebrews*, 375.

629 Nairne, *Hebrews*, 130.

630 So translated by L&N 67, 87.

631 Moffatt, *Hebrews*, 232.

632 Miller, *Hebrews*, 431; she cites Matt 10:28; Mark 4:41; and 1 Thess 2:18 as examples of this use of double καὶ.

633 The church fathers of the fourth and fifth centuries AD used this verse as something of a proof text for the immutability of Christ during the Christological debates of the period. Gregory of Nazianzus took the "yesterday and today" to indicate the humanity of Christ and the "forever" to indicate his deity. See Hughes, *Hebrews*, 571, for references; cf. Heen and Krey, eds., *Hebrews*, 233–34.

[15]Through Jesus, therefore, let us continually offer to God a sacrifice of praise—the fruit of lips that confess his name. [16]And do not forget to do good and to share with others, for with such sacrifices God is pleased.

13:9 Verse 9 has troubled commentators because it seems so out of place, even in Hebrews 13. Yet there is a contextual connection to be drawn between the exhortation not to be "carried away" by strange teachings and the eternal faithfulness of Jesus mentioned in v. 8. Some begin a new paragraph here while others begin a new paragraph with v. 10. It seems best to begin a new paragraph here with v. 9. Some mark the end of this unit at v. 14 while others extend it to v. 16.

Since Jesus is himself unchanging, strange teachings that do not comport with his Word must be rejected. The present tense "do not be carried away" can be taken iteratively as Lane, "Do not be led away whenever."[634] It can also be taken as forbidding the continuance of an action already taking place, as Hughes, "stop being led away."[635] The use of the adjective translated "all kinds" "indicates the author is not giving a precise description of the teachings he opposes."[636] The translation "all kinds of strange teachings" takes the two Greek adjectives modifying "teachings" to be a hendiadys. The fronting of the phrase in the clause places it in the emphatic position. The identity of these "strange teachings" has been debated.[637] The plural form occurs only here in the New Testament and "suggests the polyvalent and polymorphous nature of human traditions, in contrast to the singular character of the word of God."[638] Suggestions include ascetic practices, pagan meals or Jewish meal practices, ceremonial or otherwise. The suggestion by Bruce that the reference "was probably some form of syncretistic gnosis, perhaps with Essene or quasi-Essene affinities"[639] is highly unlikely. Since none of these are explicitly mentioned elsewhere in Hebrews, it is impossible to posit any of them with any degree of certainty. The immediately following clause in v. 9 speaks of "foods" and is introduced by *gar* which gives the ground or reason for the preceding statement. The NIV and many others give the interpretive translation "ceremonial foods" since contextually this is most likely the meaning. The word "foods" can be taken as delimiting the meaning of "strange teachings," in which case the reference is likely to ceremonial regulations pertaining to food, most probably of a Jewish sort. Koester took the "foods" to be parallel to the "strange teachings" and suggested a metaphorical interpretation of "foods" as

---

634 Lane, *Hebrews 9–13*, 522.

635 Hughes, *Hebrews*, 569.

636 Koester, *Hebrews*, 560.

637 For a survey of alternatives, see Filson, *Yesterday*, 50–53, and the judicious survey of Attridge, *Hebrews*, 394–96. For a critique of Lindars's interpretation of these verses, see the discussion under "Recipients" in the Introduction in this volume.

638 Lane, *Hebrews 9–13*, 532.

639 Bruce, *Hebrews*, 377.

"indicating that one should avoid teachings that are not beneficial."[640] Such seems unlikely given the overall context and the fact that the use of the word "foods" previously in Heb 9:10 connotes Jewish ceremonial regulations associated with the temple service. The "strengthening" of the heart is accomplished by "grace,"[641] where "grace" is an umbrella term for the new covenant inaugurated by Christ and in which Christians rest, and not by "ceremonial foods which are of no value to those who eat them," where the reference is to Jewish food regulations associated with the old covenant and the temple service. It is likely that Ps 104:14–15 stands behind this statement concerning the strengthening of the heart by foods: "You bring forth food from the earth . . . and bread to strengthen the human heart." Every Jewish meal was begun with this very blessing. Our author is at pains to argue that God's grace is not mediated through meal regulations, whether normal everyday household meals or the ritual meals of the temple. Rather, the heart is strengthened by the grace of God extended through Christ, God's final high priest, and his final and complete atonement on the cross. This "strengthening" contrasts with the being "carried away" by strange teachings.

Finally, there is nothing in this verse or section to indicate the readers were in danger of relapsing into Judaism. If that had been the primary concern of the author, he missed a golden opportunity to address the issue. Instead, in language reminiscent of Paul (Rom 14:17; 1 Cor 8:8; Col 2:16,21–23),[642] one's spiritual life is unaffected by rules about food.[643]

13:10 Verse 10 begins with the emphatic statement "We[644] have an altar." Interpreters differ on the meaning of "altar." Some Protestant and many Roman Catholic interpreters see here a reference to the Lord's Supper/eucharist.[645] Some interpret it positively in the sense that partaking of the eucharist conveys

---

[640] Koester, *Hebrews*, 560.

[641] Nairne, *Hebrews*, 130, says the main idea of this word in context "seems to be the absolute bounty of God which can neither be disputed nor measured."

[642] The fact of Paul's reference to this in places other than Rom 14:17 makes it clear that this cannot be used as an argument in favor of a Roman destination of the epistle, as is sometimes the case.

[643] N. Young, "'Bearing His Reproach,' (Heb 13.9–14)," NTS 48 (2003), 253 agrees. R. Gordon's suggestion that the author had the issue of food regulations in mind when he wrote of Esau selling his birthright for a meal in Heb 12:16 seems unlikely ("Hebrews," in *Readings: A New Biblical Commentary*, ed. J. Jarick [Sheffield: Sheffield Academic Press, 2000], 15).

[644] Some have taken "we" to refer to "we Hebrews" and not "we Christians." However, Bruce, *Hebrews*, 379, correctly noted that "we" here must have the same force as in 8:1.

[645] See discussion in Bruce, *Hebrews*, 379–80; Ellingworth, *Hebrews*, 711; and Williamson, "The Eucharist in the Epistle to the Hebrews," NTS 21 (1975): 300–12. In favor of this interpretation are Swetnam, "Christology and the Eucharist in the Epistle to the Hebrews," *Bib* 70 (1989): 90; and P. Grelot, *Une lecture de l'épître aux Hébreux*, Lire la Bible 132 (Paris: Cerf, 2003), 134–35, who takes 13:10 to be a clear reference to the eucharist, though he acknowledges the epistle contains no explicit mention of the eucharist (p. 136).

"grace."[646] Others interpret it as a critique of the eucharist since on the Day of Atonement the bodies of the sacrifices were burned but not eaten; so likewise the death of Jesus cannot be connected with the eucharist.[647] Two major objections have been offered against this view. First, the term "altar" was never used for or in conjunction with the eucharist until the second century. Second, the author of Hebrews nowhere in the epistle speaks about the eucharist. In fact, Bruce goes so far as to say, "It is remarkable how our author avoids mentioning the Eucharist when he has every opportunity to do so."[648]

A second interpretation of "altar" in v. 10 takes it as a reference to the heavenly sanctuary, harking back to what is stated in 8:1.[649] But there is no mention in Hebrews of any sacrificial altar in the heavenly sanctuary. A third view takes the "altar" to be a reference to the cross of Christ and/or the sacrificial death of Jesus on the cross, including the atonement it procured.[650] This view is best supported by the context. By synecdoche, the author uses "altar" (the part) to stand in for the sacrificial death of Christ (the whole). The statement "we have an altar" probably indicates the readers were being accused by their Jewish friends of having no altar, thus the author takes pains to show that Christians do have an altar, and one superior to the Jewish system.[651]

Another issue this verse raises is to whom does the phrase "those who minister at the tabernacle" refer? This phrase can be taken to refer specifically to Jewish priests who officiate in the tabernacle/temple[652] or to Jewish worshippers or both.[653] Dods takes it to be a reference to Christian worshippers who serve as priests based on Christ's finished work.[654] It has been taken metaphorically as a warning to Jewish Christians who adhere to the Jewish law in an

646 A. Vanhoye, *Old Testament Priests and the New Priest According to the New Testament,* trans. J. B. Orchard (Petersham: St. Bede's Publications, 1986), 228–29.

647 Moffatt, *Hebrews*, 233–35, saw in these verses evidence of a growing sacramentarianism which interpreted the eucharist as an "eating" of the body of Christ; cf. J. Dunnill, *Covenant and Sacrifice in the Letter to the Hebrews*, in SNTSMS 75 (Cambridge: Cambridge University Press, 1992), 240–41.

648 Bruce, *Hebrews*, 379. Bruce further argued: "The most that can be said is that our author may be pointing to the truth of Christian experience which is independently attested in the Eucharist—that Christ is both the sacrifice and the sustenance of his people, and that as sacrifice and as sustenance alike he is to be appropriated by faith" (p. 380). Cf. Lane, *Hebrews 9–13*, 538–539; and Koester, *Hebrews*, 569. T. Aquinas took the position that the reference was either to the cross of Jesus or Christ himself.

649 So Moffatt, *Hebrews*, 235; Filson, *Yesterday*, 48–50; and Thompson, *Beginnings*, 146.

650 See Lane, *Hebrews 9–13*, 538; Ellingworth, *Hebrews*, 711–12; and Koester, *Hebrews*, 568–69; and the good discussion on this issue in Hughes, *Hebrews*, 574–78.

651 On the word θυσιαστήριον, see the excellent excursus in Westcott, *Hebrews*, 455–63.

652 So Koester, *Hebrews*, 569.

653 S. Lehne, *The New Covenant in Hebrews*, JSNTSup 44 (Sheffield: JSOT, 1990), 115–16; and N. Young, "'Bearing His Reproach,'" 247.

654 Dods, "Hebrews," 377. So also Laub, *Bekenntnis und Auslegung: die paränetische Funktion der Christologie im Hebräerbrief* (Regensburg : F. Pustet, 1980), 271; followed by Grässer, *An die Hebräer*, 3:384–86.

effort to seek security at the expense of their Christian identity. Koester rightly objected to this interpretation.[655] Thompson and Koester viewed the author's strategy as creating a "foil" which contrasts the heavenly work of Christ with the old Mosaic system.[656]

These Jewish priests and worshippers who are still a part of the old Mosaic system "have no right to eat" of the altar which Christians enjoy. "To eat" is fronted in the clause for emphasis. The old covenant priests physically ate portions of certain sacrifices in accordance with the law. Christians, however, eat spiritually of the sacrifice of Christ in that they enjoy the benefits of salvation provided by Christ's once for all offering of himself on the cross. Paul refers to the right of Old Testament priests to eat of the food from the altar in 1 Cor 9:13 and 10:18. Ellingworth summarized the author's point: "There is a complete break between the levitical and the Christian cultus: levitical priests have no status in the church."[657]

Young rightly sensed the connection between vv. 9–10 in the author's thought: "'Those who live by foods' (v. 9) and 'those who serve the tent' (v. 10) are identical. Both refer to Judaism, and by extension to all those whose sense (if not practice) of community and worship is overtly swayed by the Levitical system."[658]

13:11 Verse 11 is introduced by *gar* (untranslated in the NIV) which functions as grounds for v. 10 as well as an explanation for the meaning of "altar." Verse 11 is an allusion to or loose quotation of Lev 16:27. Leviticus 16 is the key chapter on the Day of Atonement protocol. The main point of the verse is found in the final statement concerning the burning of the sacrificial carcasses outside the camp. On the Day of Atonement, the high priest carried[659] the blood into the inner chamber of the tabernacle called the "Most Holy Place," otherwise referred to as the holy of holies. The phrase "as a sin offering" is an interpretive rendering of the prepositional phrase *peri hamartias*, where the preposition *peri* is used with the sense of the preposition *huper*, "for sins." Here the preposition conveys the sense of the high priest's purpose for entering: "to deal with the matter of sin."[660] The emphatic use of the demonstrative pronoun *toutōn*, which according to Lane "serves to throw the weight of the construction on the final clause,"[661] is rendered interpretatively as "but the bodies." The phrase "outside the camp" refers to an area outside the confines of the camp of Israel during the wilderness wanderings. The position of this

[655] Koester, *Hebrews*, 570.

[656] Thompson, *Beginnings*, 145; Koester, *Hebrews*, 570.

[657] Ellingworth, *Hebrews*, 709.

[658] N. Young, "'Bearing His Reproach,'" 248.

[659] The present tense "carries" is the timeless present. Hughes interpreted the present tenses in vv. 10–11 as indicating the ongoing function of the Levitical system and thus evidence the epistle was written prior to AD 70 (*Hebrews*, 575).

[660] So paraphrased by B. Atkinson, *The Theology of Prepositions* (London: Tyndale, 1944), 9.

[661] Lane, *Hebrews 9–13*, 523.

phrase at the end of the clause marks it for emphasis and is the key point the author will use to make a comparison with Jesus' death in v. 12. Leviticus 16 prescribes the Day of Atonement ritual where the high priest, after taking the blood of the sacrificial animals into the "Most Holy Place," then disposed of the carcasses "outside the camp." The carcasses were burned so as to prevent them from being eaten.[662] The author's point is to give the reason those priests who serve the tabernacle cannot eat of the Christian's offering (v. 10): because the sin offering on the Day of Atonement was not eaten (v. 11).

13:12 The inferential conjunction *dio,* "and so," that begins this verse introduces the result or conclusion to be drawn from v. 11. "Jesus" is emphatic in the word order of v. 12 (lit.): "Therefore, Jesus also, in order that he might sanctify through his own blood the people, outside the gate suffered." *Paschein,* "suffered," and its cognates in Hebrews always refer to the death of Jesus on the cross, as in 9:26. On the use of this verb for the death of Christ in the New Testament, see Luke 22:15; 24:46; Acts 1:3; 17:3; and 1 Pet 2:21. Jesus is viewed by the author as the antitype of the sin-offering on the Day of Atonement who "through his own blood" in the sense of "by means of," or "by his own blood" (in the sense of "by the agency of his death") consecrated the people. "His own" is emphatic in the Greek text. Here the author intends "blood" to refer to death. "Outside the city gate" locates the place where Jesus was crucified, namely, outside of Jerusalem. The phrase implies the rejection of Jesus by the Jews and his being condemned as a criminal.[663] The area where Israel camped during the wilderness wandering was considered holy, but the area "outside the camp" was considered unholy. When one ventured outside the camp, ceremonial cleansing was required upon return to the camp (Lev 16:26,28).

Hughes pointed out how arresting this concept of Jesus suffering outside the gate of Jerusalem to sanctify the people would have been to Jewish ears: "How extraordinary, indeed shocking, to the Hebrew mind, to be told that he did this *in order to sanctify the people through his own blood*, precisely on this unsanctified territory! The very concept must have seemed self-contradictory."[664]

13:13 The author shifts to make application of this truth to his readers in v. 13. The conjunction *toinun,* "then," occurs only three times in the New Testament. Here it marks prominence, consequential deduction, and conclusion.[665] Christians are to follow Jesus "outside the camp," bearing his disgrace. The Greek term translated "disgrace" is emphatic by position in the clause.

---

[662] On this passage, see H. Koester, "'Outside the Camp': Hebrews 13:9–14," *HTR* 55 (1962): 299–315.

[663] Lane, *Hebrews 9–13*, 542. Luke states in Acts 1:12 that Jesus' ascension occurred outside the confines of Jerusalem.

[664] Hughes, *Hebrews*, 579.

[665] Westfall, *Discourse Analysis*, 286; Lane, *Hebrews 9–13*, 523.

Ellingworth observed 13:11–13 to contain echoes of Exod 33:7–11 where Moses erected a tabernacle "outside the camp" of Israel where the Lord appeared to Moses and spoke to him face to face.[666]

There are at least four ways in which the phrase "outside the camp" has been interpreted.[667] Some have taken it as a reference to leaving behind material securities and entering the realm of pilgrim existence in the heavenly sphere.[668] While the immediate context of 13:5–7 may be appealed to for support, this view does not seem likely.[669] Others take the phrase to indicate "the realm of the sacred." Jesus died outside the camp in unclean territory, therefore the readers are exhorted to leave the "security of ritual" to enter the world for service in the secular arena.[670] This view is likewise out of step with the overall context. A third approach interprets the phrase to refer to "Jewish practices" pertaining to food regulations, etc. A fourth view, suggested by Koester, interprets the phrase to mean "outside the city," based on the statement in v. 14 "here we do not have an enduring city." This view combines elements of the other three.[671] Whether Koester's interpretation is accepted or not, it would seem that some elements from the other three views are likely a part of what the author had in mind. Most likely the author's meaning revolves around breaking ties emotionally and socially with Judaism, no longer relying on cultic ritual but only on Christ.[672]

With respect to the phrase "outside the camp," Bruce succinctly remarked: "What was formerly sacred was now unhallowed, because Jesus had been expelled from it; what was formerly unhallowed was now sacred, because Jesus was there."[673] The exhortation of this verse calls upon the readers to recognize that they can no longer depend on the old Mosaic order to bring them into a right relationship with God. Again, Bruce caught the author's meaning well: "The 'camp' stands for the established fellowship and ordinances of Judaism. To abandon them . . . was a hard thing, but it was a necessary thing."[674] The repetition of the phrase "outside the camp" in v. 11 and v. 13 and the use of "outside the city gate" in v. 12 serve to bind these verses closely together and

---

666 Ellingworth, *Hebrews*, 714.

667 Koester, *Hebrews*, 570–71; cf. Thurén, *Lobopfer*, 91–99, for a thorough discussion of the meaning of this clause.

668 So argued by Thompson, *Beginnings*, 141, and ably critiqued by N. Young, "'Bearing His Reproach,'" 256.

669 See the critique in Lane, *Hebrews 9–13*, 545.

670 Koester, "'Outside the Camp,'" 302.

671 Koester, *Hebrews*, 570–71.

672 This is the view of Westcott, *Hebrews*, 441–42; Bruce, *Hebrews*, 381–82; Hughes, *Hebrews*, 580–82; and Lane, *Hebrews 9–13*, 545–46, among many others.

673 Bruce, *Hebrews*, 380–81.

674 Ibid., 381; cf. S. G. Wilson, "The Apostate Minority," in *Mighty Minorities? Minorities in Early Christianity—Positions and Strategies: Essays in Honour of Jacob Jervell on his 70th Birthday*, ed. D. Hellholm, et al. (Oslo: Scandinavian University, 1995), 205.

to indicate that it is this comparison between the Day of Atonement ritual and Jesus' death on the cross where the author has placed his primary focus.

Ellingworth shied away from understanding this passage as an exhortation to reject Judaism, saying such is "foreign to the whole scope of the author's thought, which moves consistently within the category of God's twofold action on behalf of his one people."[675] However, he does not explain what he means by "God's two-fold action." Furthermore, such a statement misses the full import of the epistle as a whole, which makes crystal clear that a Judaism without Jesus cannot bring one into a right relationship with God.

The phrase "bearing the disgrace he bore" takes the genitive case in Greek subjectively. It is possible, though less likely, that the objective genitive may be intended in the sense of "bearing disgrace for him." Christians must share in the shame which Christ experienced in his own crucifixion through their identification with Jesus. The author makes clear that such an identification will bring the hostility of the world against Christians. The notion of "bearing" is used figuratively by the author to express enduring any and all hostility for the sake of Jesus.[676]

The author is quoting Ps 69:7 (68:8 LXX) where "his reproach" in v. 13 means Christ's reproach referred to in Psalms. Hanson noted the author of Hebrews does not attempt to connect the scapegoat in Leviticus 16 with Christ in any typological fashion, but rather chooses to focus on the burning of the sacrificial animal bodies outside the camp. His conclusion that this suggests the author "wishes to avoid a doctrine of penal substitution" is groundless.[677] Hanson noted Lev 16:27 does not specify who should burn the animal bodies outside the camp. The Targum on Leviticus says this task must be done by someone who is a priest. Since the burning is considered to be a priestly task, Hanson takes Heb 13:13 "is in its way an indication of the priestly nature of the church."[678] Synge correctly indicated how the author of Hebrews never makes a contemporary historical comparison between Jewish and Christian practices but always makes a typological comparison drawn from Scripture. The burning of the bodies outside the camp was a relatively minor aspect of the overall ritual. Our author is investing this detail with typological significance in reference to Jesus dying "outside the camp."[679]

Hanson pointed out two questions about the Day of Atonement that interested the rabbis. The first question concerned the meaning of "to make atonement" in Lev 16:16. This was answered in one of two ways. Either the sprin-

---

[675] Ellingworth, *Hebrews*, 716.

[676] On this concept of "bearing reproach," see A. T. Hanson, "The Reproach of the Messiah in the Epistle to the Hebrews," *SE* 7 (1982). Hanson takes the essence of the reproach to be the Jewish rejection of Jesus resulting in his crucifixion (p. 239).

[677] Ibid., 236.

[678] Ibid.

[679] F. C. Synge, *Hebrews and the Scriptures* (London: SPCK, 1959), 40.

kling of blood makes atonement or confession of sin on the part of the one sacrificing makes atonement. The second question concerned whether the Day of Atonement covered all sin. The Hebrews passage underlines the two alternatives which must ultimately be faced: "Either there is one all-embracing sacrifice, in which case attempts to show the significance of any minor sacrifices are irrelevant; or the sacrifices prescribed in the Torah are still valid, in which case there is bound to be endless casuistry as to the relative value of each."[680]

13:14 The use of *gar*, "for," subordinates v. 14 to v. 13. The verse is chiastically constructed in Greek: "we do not have a permanent city; the city which is to come we seek."

The shift to language about a city is "only a linguistic change, not a conceptual shift, for Jerusalem was the holy city because within it was the holy place, the temple."[681] The reference to a "city" which does not endure could be Jerusalem, but the second reference to the city "that is to come" refers to the heavenly Jerusalem in the eschaton. Ellingworth pointed out the cumulative evidence in Hebrews for the use of *mellō* (participial form in the Greek text of v. 14, lit., "the coming [city])" "refers to that which is not wholly future, but promised and anticipated."[682] "We are looking" renders the present tense verb in Greek which connotes "expecting intently."[683] The reference to the "city" that does not "endure" and the city that is to come harks back to Hebrews 11 and the language about Abraham, especially 11:10,16. The author never loses sight of his eschatological focus and desires his readers to maintain it as well.

The upshot of Heb 13:9–14 is to contrast Judaism and its adherence to the Mosaic covenant and cultus with the new covenant inaugurated by Christ. Christians have an altar where the permanent effects of the sacrifice of Christ on the cross render the temple cultus ineffective. The blood of Christ, not the blood of animals, permanently atones for sin and renders Christ's followers "holy." Whatever "disgrace" these early Christians were facing, whether from Rome or from Judaism, the readers were exhorted to continue to identify with Jesus no matter what the cost.[684] The grounds for enduring such reproach is that in this life we do not have an enduring place of rest with God, but God has promised such a place in the future and that promise is to fortify believers to endurance to the end for Christ's sake.

---

[680] Hanson, "The Reproach of the Messiah," 237.

[681] Young, "Bearing His Reproach," 257.

[682] Ellingworth, *Hebrews*, 719, following Lohse, "Σιών," *TDNT* 7:337.

[683] Lane, *Hebrews 9–13*, 522.

[684] The notion of honor/shame in a socio-rhetorical framework is a key component of the argument of the author of Hebrews according to DeSilva in his *Despising Shame*, 296, as well as his commentary on Hebrews. While this concept is present, it is not the umbrella framework under which Hebrews should be interpreted.

If, as has often been suggested, one of the problems the author is addressing concerns Jewish Christians who were adhering to synagogue practices, Heb 13:9–14, and in fact the whole epistle, would be a strong challenge to such behavior. We know that in Syrian Antioch, it was not until the seventh century that Jewish influence on Christians ended.[685] Judaism was an ancient religion and no doubt would have appealed to those who were now Jewish Christians and a part of a "new" religion. Furthermore, Judaism was a *religio licita* providing an umbrella of protection against Roman persecution, at least until the outbreak of the Jewish war in AD 66. Between AD 60 and 70 Jewish nationalism likely brought pressure to bear on Jewish Christians to identify with the homeland against the every-growing Roman threat.[686] The bottom line for the author of Hebrews is the mutual exclusivity of Judaism and Christianity centered around the person and work of Christ.[687]

13:15 Verse 15 begins with *oun*, "therefore," and serves to draw to a conclusion the argument begun in v. 9. The phrase "through Jesus" is fronted in the clause for emphasis, with the NIV substituting "Jesus" for "him" in the Greek text. Christians are to offer continually (present subjunctive) to God a "sacrifice of praise" where the "sacrifice" consists in "praise."[688] The background of this exhortation is the fellowship offering of Lev 7:11–21. A similar passage is Ps 50:14,23 (Ps 49:14,23 LXX) where God says he has no need of bulls or goats but commands the people to offer "a sacrifice of praise." This sacrifice is further defined as the "fruit of lips," an allusion to Hosea 14:3 LXX.[689] The readers still have sacrifices to offer, even if the sacrifices are not for sin. The sacrifice of thanksgiving was once accompanied by an animal sacrifice in the temple according to Lev 7:12. Now Christians offer only the sacrifice of praise.[690]

The participle *homologountōn* attributively modifies "lips" and can be translated "confess,"[691] but contextually it conveys the nuance of "praising."[692] As

---

[685] W. Meeks, *Jews and Christians in Antioch in the First Four Centuries of the Common Era*, SBLSBS 13 (Missoula, MT: *Scholars Press*, 1978), 18.

[686] See Young, "'Bearing His Reproach,'" 260–61.

[687] See R. W. Johnson, *Going Outside the Camp: The Sociological Function of the Levitical Critique in the Epistle to the Hebrews*, JSNTSup 209 (Sheffield: Sheffield University Press, 2001), 150; and W. Lane, "Living a Life of Faith in the Face of Death," 247–69.

[688] An explanatory (epexegetical) genitive.

[689] See Hughes, *Hebrews*, 584; Bruce, *Hebrews*, 383, for discussion on the LXX and Hebrew text of Hosea 14:3. The Hebrew words in the text may be divided and vocalized as either 'bullocks of our lips" or "fruit of our lips." The expression "fruit of the lips" occurs at Qumran as well.

[690] Str-B 1:246, identify rabbinical teaching that all the Mosaic sacrifices would have an end except the thank offering, and that all prayers would cease except the prayer of thanksgiving (cited by Hughes, *Hebrews,* 583). Nairne, *Hebrews*, 131, speaking of the sacrifices here as flowing from the one final sacrifice of Christ, said: "Here the idea is rather that even in the ritual of Christian worship there is a more than adequate substitute for the many sacrifices of Judaism."

[691] So O. Michel, "ὁμολογέω," *TDNT* 5:209–10.

[692] Lane, *Hebrews 9–13*, 524; and Ellingworth, *Hebrews*, 721; cf. *GAGNT* 689.

Lane rightly remarked, the nuance in this Greek term *homologein* must be determined by its usage in a clause that explains the previous clause "sacrifice of praise," and by its following object in the dative case in Greek: "praising his name."[693] Given these contextual factors, "praising" is a superior translation than "confessing."

13:16 The connection to v. 15 is marked by the particle *de*, translated "and." The verse serves as a contrastive expansion of the exhortation to offer a sacrifice of praise. "Do not forget" renders a Greek verb in this context which conveys the notion of neglect.[694] The unusual Greek noun *eupoiias* is translated verbally in the NIV as "to do good."[695] The noun *koinōnia* is rendered "to share" and is used here of giving in the financial sense.[696] The application the author makes is his readers are to assist financially those who are in need. The phrase "with such sacrifices" can be taken in the sense of "by means of such sacrifices," or as expressing reason in the sense of "because of such sacrifices."[697] Although *theos*, "God," is the subject of the last clause in v. 16, it is placed clause final by the author for emphasis. In fact, it is the last word in the sentence.

Everything commanded in 13:1–8 can be summarized as "doing good and sharing" in v. 16. Lane views vv. 15,16 as the climax of 13:1–21.[698] Furthermore, 13:1–8 elaborates on what it means to serve as priests who are pleasing to God, thus connecting with 12:28.[699] The believers' priesthood is based on their sharing in the heavenly calling with Christ (3:1). In Heb 4:14 Christians are exhorted to approach the throne of grace in priestly access to God. Hebrews 7–10 explains how Christ's sacrifice consecrates believers to enter the holy of holies as priests, culminating in 10:22. Priestly language permeates this section, even the hortatory paragraphs addressing the readers. The author's conclusion in 12:28 and 13:15–16 is also expressed in unmistakable priestly language. Jesus is our high priest, and believers have been brought into such a relationship with Christ that they too are priests with the concomitant responsibilities and privileges that adhere to the priestly calling.[700]

Thus, the conclusion of the argument can be said in one sense to occur at Heb 12:28–29, but in another sense, it occurs at 13:16. In the discourse unit of 12:28–13:16 the three discourse themes of the epistle are repeated, but only the theme of access to God is explicitly repeated with the formulaic hortatory subjunctive. Westfall concluded: "The priesthood is a vehicle that gives

[693] Lane, *Hebrews 9–13*, 524.

[694] See L&N 29.17.

[695] BDAG 110, translates "the doing of good"; see L&N 88.7. The word is a general term for all variety of acts of kindness.

[696] BDAG 552; L&N 57.98.

[697] See Lane, *Hebrews 9–13*, 522; and Ellingworth, *Hebrews*, 722.

[698] Lane, *Hebrews 9–13*, 503.

[699] Westfall, *Discourse Analysis*, 287, rightly makes the connection with 12:28.

[700] Ibid., 289.

them access to God, positions them to hear his voice and maintain the confession, and gives them a vision for spiritual and doctrinal growth and pastoral service."[701]

(3) Continuing in Submission and Prayer (13:17–21)

[17]Obey your leaders and submit to their authority. They keep watch over you as men who must give an account. Obey them so that their work will be a joy, not a burden, for that would be of no advantage to you.

[18]Pray for us. We are sure that we have a clear conscience and desire to live honorably in every way. [19]I particularly urge you to pray so that I may be restored to you soon.

[20]May the God of peace, who through the blood of the eternal covenant brought back from the dead our Lord Jesus, that great Shepherd of the sheep, [21]equip you with everything good for doing his will, and may he work in us what is pleasing to him, through Jesus Christ, to whom be glory for ever and ever. Amen.

13:17 With v. 17 there is a shift in topic to the issue of the response of the readers to their church leaders. Verse 17 is one sentence in the Greek text. The author uses a double exhortation: "obey your leaders and submit." The present imperative "obey" probably has an iterative sense of "continue to obey" or "obey on a regular basis." The second imperative, "submit," is also in the present tense. The word originally meant "to withdraw; give way to," and then figuratively came to mean "yielding to authority."[702] It is a stronger and more specific word than the preceding "obey"[703] and carries with it the implication that one is to yield when the leader's rule is at variance with the reader's wishes.[704]

The reason for the obedience is introduced by *gar* which is left untranslated in the NIV: "[for] they keep watch over you." The Greek pronoun *autoi*, "they," is overtly used by the author in its clause initial position for emphasis. The sense is "they themselves and none other." This serves to place emphasis on the authority of the leaders. The implied predicate of "submit" may be the direct object "yourselves"[705] or an indirect object "to them."[706] Lane and the NIV supply "to their authority" as the indirect object.[707] The verb translated "keep watch" implies constant vigilance, wakefulness, or sleeplessness. It is used in Mark 13:33 and Luke 21:36 meaning "to be vigilant in awareness of threatening peril." Here and in Eph 6:18 it connotes "to be alertly concerned about."[708] The shepherding aspect of pastoral duty seems to be implied in this verb, and

[701] Ibid., 291.
[702] BDAG 1030.
[703] Ellingworth, *Hebrews*, 723.
[704] Alford, "Hebrews," 269; cf. Koester, *Hebrews*, 572.
[705] L&N 36.18; KJV.
[706] Bruce, *Hebrews*, 385.
[707] Lane, *Hebrews 9–13*, 522.
[708] See L&N 35.41; BDAG 16.

this is supported by the author's reference to Jesus the great Shepherd of the sheep in the benediction in v. 20. The NIV renders the Greek "souls" as "you." Lane, following Michel, wrongly interpreted "souls" here to be a reference to the eternal life of the readers.[709] It is better to take it as referencing their "spiritual well-being,"[710] or as simply referring to them as persons.[711]

The leaders keep watch over the readers "as men who must give an account." Most commentators take this as expressing necessity, hence the translation "must." However, Lane argued that such an approach misses the subjective-voluntative force of this classical idiom. He suggested the translation "as those who *intend* to give an account."[712] This clause is introduced by *hōs*, "as," and may be taken to indicate manner, as in the NIV, or as indicating reason with the sense, "because they must give an account."[713] This is followed by a *hina* clause which most take to be expressive of purpose: "so that they can do this with joy" (HCSB). Lane interpreted the clause imperatively: "Let them do this."[714] Either way, the notion of purpose is present. The phrase (lit.) "with joy" can be taken to mean joy "over their obedience" or joy "in keeping watch," with the latter option the most likely. The NIV "not a burden" renders the negated participle *mē stenazontes*, "not sighing/groaning." The author's desire is that the leaders may do their pastoral duty with joy and not with sighing or groaning, where the participle in Greek expresses manner. The burden can be taken as what the leaders experience if the readers disobey or in the sense of if the leaders had to give a negative account. The final clause in the sentence is introduced by the subordinating *gar* which provides another reason for the readers to obey their leaders: if the leaders' work is a burden to them because of the uncooperative spirit of the readers, "that would be of no advantage to you," The Greek *alusiteles*, "of no advantage," occurs only here in the New Testament. Its interesting etymology originally meant "not worth the price"[715] or "not covering one's expenses."[716] The meaning in our context is along the lines of "unprofitable, not advantageous, not worthwhile, detrimental."[717] Since the author uses "you" here and not "we," he probably considers himself to be one of the leaders of the church.[718]

13:18 The topic shifts again in vv. 18–19 with the author's request for prayer. The present imperative signals durative action: "keep on praying." The author's use of the first person plural "we" may be the epistolary use for

[709] Lane, *Hebrews 9–13*, 524; Michel, *Hebräer*, 528–29.
[710] Ellingworth, *Hebrews*, 723.
[711] As do Bruce, *Hebrews*, 385; Hughes, *Hebrews*, 586.
[712] Lane, *Hebrews 9–13*, 525.
[713] So Bruce, *Hebrews*, 385.
[714] Lane, *Hebrews 9–13*, 525.
[715] *GAGNT* 689.
[716] BDAG 48.
[717] L&N 65.49; cf. Lane, *Hebrews 9–13*, 525.
[718] Lane, *Hebrews 9–13*, 556; Ellingworth, *Hebrews*, 703.

stylistic effect in the sense of "pray for me," or it may indicate a reference to the author and those with him at the time of writing. The ground or reason for the request for prayer is signaled by *gar*, untranslated in the NIV, followed by the rare use of the perfective present tense translated "we are sure." This verb is actually the same as in the previous verse where it means "obey," while here it conveys the meaning of being sure or certain. It is not possible to render into English the play on words in the Greek text here with *kalēn*, "clear," and *kalōs*, "honorable." These are further examples of the author's fondness for paronomasia as a rhetorical strategy.[719] The author expresses the fact of his clear conscience, "desiring to live well," where the participle in Greek is causal. The final phrase "in every way" is fronted in the clause for emphasis and was taken by many patristic writers to mean "among all people."[720] It is better to take it either to refer to events, "in everything," or to manner, as in the NIV translation "in every way." This good conscience "is probably the fruit of a sense of duty done, a responsibility well discharged."[721] The verse speaks volumes concerning the integrity of the author and the integrity required of church leadership.

13:19 The readers are urged (lit.) "all the more" (*perissoterōs*, a comparative adverb rendered "particularly" by the NIV) to pray for the author's speedy restoration to them. This verse would seem to indicate that the author not only knew the readers but had previously been in their company. The notion of being "restored" may signal the author has been detained and desires to be "released" so he can come to the location of the readers. Whether this statement indicates the author had been confined in prison or not cannot be ascertained with any certainty. Based on v. 23, which likely indicates Timothy had been imprisoned and had been recently released, it would seem the author himself was not in prison at the time of writing. The adverb in Greek translated "soon" is defined as "pertaining to a very brief extent of time, with focus on speed of action."[722] It may be understood in its comparative sense of "sooner than if you did not pray," or as is more likely, in the sense of "quickly, soon, very soon."[723] The shift from the plural in v. 18 to the singular in v. 19 may be stylistic or it may be indicative that the author is writing in company with others.[724]

13:20 The benediction of vv. 20–21 is essentially a prayer.[725] The shift to the use of participles and paraphrastic constructions "achieves a noticeable change of rhythm and the solemnity appropriate to the conclusion of the

---

[719] The significant use of alliteration with the letter π in vv. 18–19 serves to connect Hebrews 13 with the author's style in chaps. 1–12.

[720] Ellingworth, *Hebrews*, 726.

[721] Bruce, *Hebrews*, 386.

[722] BDAG 992.

[723] See Ellingworth, *Hebrews*, 727.

[724] So Koester, *Hebrews*, 573.

[725] On these verses, see C. E. B. Cranfield, "Hebrews 13:20–21" *SJT* 20 (1967): 437–41.

sermon."[726] The two verses form one sentence in the Greek text, with "God" in v. 20 the subject of the main verb "equip" in v. 21. The main point of the benediction is God's equipping the readers with everything they need in order to do God's will. It is God's "working in us" (the equipping) what is pleasing to him that enables us to do his will.

The overall structure of the benediction is symmetrical. Between an opening invocation and a closing doxology, there are two strophes of four lines each.[727] God is described as the God "of peace," where the genitive case likely indicates source: "the God who gives peace." This phrase is common in Pauline benedictions and is closely parallel to 1 Thess 5:23. Interpreters differ over whether the reference to peace has any relationship to the tension between the readers and their leadership. The remaining structure of v. 20 is (lit.) "who brought back from the dead the shepherd of the sheep the great [one] by [through] [the] blood of the eternal covenant, our Lord Jesus." Lane considered Isa 63:11–14 LXX and Zech 9:11 LXX to be in the mind of the author.[728] Jesus has been brought back from the dead "through the blood of the eternal covenant." Lane translated "who lead out from the dead" based on the parallel with Isa 63:11–14 LXX, and concluded that "the 'leading out' is the fundamental redemptive action of God under both the old and new covenant."[729] The phrase "through the blood" is taken causally by Lane based on the allusion to Zech 9:11 LXX and the construction of the strophe itself.[730] Bruce captures the meaning: "His resurrection is the demonstration that his sacrifice of himself has been accepted by God and the new covenant established on the basis of that sacrifice."[731] The genitive noun phrase "eternal covenant" indicates what the blood accomplished. The adjective "eternal" is emphatic by word order.[732] The "eternal covenant" is equivalent to the "new covenant."

Jesus is described as "the great Shepherd of the sheep," where the adjective "great" is given prominence by the repetition of the article and its position at the end of the phrase. The shepherd imagery applied to Jesus is common in the Gospels. As always in this epistle, the name "Jesus" is placed phrase or clause final for emphasis.

---

[726] Lane, *Hebrews 9–13*, 504. Westfall, *Discourse Analysis*, 294, does not find Vanhoye's and Lane's *inclusio* between 12:28 and 13:21 to be convincing.

[727] This is reflected well in Lane's translation (*Hebrews 9–13*, 558).

[728] Lane, *Hebrews 9–13*, 561.

[729] Ibid. Lane further states: "The leading forth of Jesus is, for the new and eternal covenant, the fundamental action of God that has replaced the foundational acts of salvation under the old covenant" (562).

[730] Ibid., 563; cf. Ellingworth, *Hebrews*, 727–28. The preposition ἐν can denote accompaniment ("with") or instrumentality ("by"). Ellingworth lists those on both sides of the debate, but leans towards the instrumental use.

[731] Bruce, *Hebrews*, 388.

[732] Moffatt, *Hebrews*, 242.

13:21 Verse 21 provides the predicate to the benediction. It is God who will equip the readers with everything they need to do his will. The participle "doing" is translated as a second exhortation in the NIV, but it is better to construe it either temporally, "as he brings to pass,"[733] or as expressing purpose in the sense of "for the purpose of doing." The author's rhetorical strategy is seen in his repetition of the concept of "pleasing" which he used in 12:28 and 13:16. Based on the new covenant inaugurated by Christ, the goal of the Christian life is to obey God and do that which is pleasing to him. The phrase "through Jesus Christ" is connected with the participle "doing," although it is possible to construe it with the entire clause, as does Dods.[734] The entire thought is reminiscent of Phil 2:12–13. The concluding doxology "to whom be glory" is ambiguous as to its antecedent. Some see it as a reference to "Jesus Christ" since this is the nearest referent, but it is best to take it as referring to "God" since God is the subject of the entire sentence in Greek.[735] The benediction concludes with the traditional "Amen."

---

[733] So Bruce, *Hebrews*, 387.

[734] Dods, "Hebrews," 380.

[735] So Lane, *Hebrews 9–13*, 559, 565; and Ellingworth, *Hebrews*, 731.

CONCLUSION AND FINAL GREETINGS (13:22–25)

22Brothers, I urge you to bear with my word of exhortation, for I have written you only a short letter.
23I want you to know that our brother Timothy has been released. If he arrives soon, I will come with him to see you.
24Greet all your leaders and all God's people. Those from Italy send you their greetings.

25Grace be with you all.

13:22 With five sentences in the Greek text, vv. 22–25 comprise the author's concluding personal comments. First, the author appeals to his readers to listen patiently to his word of exhortation.[736] Lane is correct when he noted the translation of *anechomai* "bear with" is crucial because it tends to color the way the following descriptive phrase is understood.[737] If the meaning is taken to be along the lines of "bear with," then the implication of submitting to something that is difficult may be discerned. Lane translated the verb "to listen willingly," following the nuance of the word in Acts 18:14 and 2 Tim 4:3.[738] Given the tenor of the epistle and its focus on listening to the word of God, Lane's approach may be valid.

The phrase "word of exhortation" occurs only one other place in the New Testament—Acts 13:15, where the synagogue leaders in Pisidian Antioch invite Paul to address the congregation with a "word of exhortation." Lane stated that the word "appears to have been an idiomatic designation for the homily or edifying discourse that followed the public reading for the designated portions of Scripture in the Hellenistic synagogues."[739] Thus, the phrase here appears to be the author's own designation for the epistle as a sermon. The early church followed a similar model as is evidenced by the book of Acts and 1 Tim 4:13. As Westfall observed, this phrase is an apt description of the entire epistle since the indicative passages are consistently marked with conjunctions as support material for the hortatory passages.[740]

The reason for the author's charge to bear with his word of exhortation is his statement that he has written to them "briefly" ("only a short letter" NIV). Trudinger, among others, has sought to show the author meant that he had used

---

[736] For the meaning and usage of ἀνέχομαι in this passage, see BDAG 78.
[737] W. L. Lane, *Hebrews 9–13*, WBC (Dallas: Word Books, 1991), 566.
[738] Ibid.
[739] Ibid., 568. Also see his introductory discussion on this issue (lxx–lxxiv).
[740] C. Westfall, *A Discourse Analysis of the Letter to the Hebrews: The Relationship Between Form and Meaning*, LNTS 297 (London: T&T Clark, 2006), 294.

brief exhortations in Hebrews 13, and thus the word of exhortation would not be a reference to the entire epistle.[741] However, such attempts are unnecessary given the conventional use of this Greek phrase in Jewish literature as well as in 1 Pet 5:12. Louw and Nida pointed out the phrase in Greek can be taken in two ways. The first option is to take the phrase literally, "by means of a few words," and they offer the translation "I have written to you a few words."[742] A second option is to take the phrase to refer either to the act of sending the letter or the amount of time required to read it.[743] The juxtaposition of "word of exhortation" with "I have written" in this verse indicates that Hebrews is a written sermon.[744]

13:23 The reference to Timothy and his "release" is most likely to the Timothy who was Paul's coworker mentioned frequently in the Pauline Letters. He is associated with Ephesus in the Pastoral Epistles (1 Tim 1:3). He is described as "our brother." In every Pauline reference to Timothy where he is referred to as "brother," Paul places the name "Timothy" first followed by the articular noun. Here, however, the author places the noun "brother" first, followed by "Timothy." This is further evidence of the overall dissimilarity of this epistle with Pauline style even in a verse that sounds very Pauline. Though the word translated "released" can be taken generally to mean Timothy had "departed" from a particular location, it is more likely the word indicates release from custody. The proximity of this statement to 13:3 would support this contention.[745] Since the New Testament does not mention any imprisonment regarding Timothy, the circumstances of this statement are obscure. Given the data of the Pastorals, it is possible that Timothy came to Rome towards the end of Paul's imprisonment and was himself imprisoned and then released perhaps after the death of Paul. If Luke is the author of Hebrews and wrote the epistle after Paul's death in AD 67, then this reference to Timothy would not be unusual.[746] Timothy's name also links this epistle with the Pauline circle and may also intimate an early date. The final clause in v. 23 reads (lit.) "with whom if soon he comes, I will see you."

---

[741] L. P. Trudinger, "ΚΑΙ ΓΑΡ ΒΡΑΧΕΩΝ ΕΠΕΣΤΕΙΛΑ ΥΜΙΝ: a Note on Hebrews xiii.22," *JTS* 23 NS (1972): 128–30. Trudinger translates, "I appeal to you, brothers, bear with my words of instruction and admonition, for my commands have been but brief!" A. Vanhoye, *La structure littéraire de l'Épître aux Hébreux* (Paris: Desclée de Brouwer, 1976), 221–22, argued that the phrase had reference only to the postscript of 13:22–25.

[742] L&N 595.

[743] Ibid., 643.

[744] J. W. Bowman, *Hebrews, James, I and II Peter* (Atlanta: John Knox, 1962), 91–92, made the unsupported and unnecessary suggestion that the oral and written nomenclature of the author in this verse indicated that a letter accompanied the sermonic epistle.

[745] See the discussion in P. Ellingworth, *The Epistle to the Hebrews*, NIGTC (Grand Rapids: Eerdmans, 1993), 733–34.

[746] See Calvin's comment on the mention of Timothy: "[I]t is very probable that either Luke or Clement was the author of this epistle" (J. Calvin, *The Epistle of Paul the Apostle to the Hebrews and the First and Second Epistles of Peter,* CNTC [Grand Rapids: Eerdmans, 1963], 216).

The key interpretive question is the usage of the comparative adverb *tachion*. The meaning is probably along the lines of "quickly, soon, without delay," and this is the approach of the majority of commentators. It is also possible to take the meaning in the traditional comparative sense: "if he comes before I leave."[1] The author would seem to be indicating his plans to travel with Timothy to visit the readers; however, if Timothy is delayed too long, the author will come alone.

Westfall perceptively observed all the commands in 13:17–25, except for the closing in v. 25, involve some aspect of the relationship between the recipients and those who are currently in authority over them. In v. 20, Jesus is the "great shepherd" over them as well. The pastoral focus of our author comes into focus in this last section of the epistle. Furthermore, the language would seem to imply that the author and Timothy were in some leadership relationship with the recipients. "Bear with this word of exhortation" also implies the author's authority. "The author's closing personal concern is for the recipients to align themselves in an appropriate and mutually supportive relationship with their leadership."[2]

13:24 The concluding two verses contain the traditional author's greeting and benediction of grace. The author requests that his readers, on his behalf, greet "all your leaders" as well as "all God's people" (lit., "all the saints"). This twofold greeting is a further indication that the author is writing to a smaller group within a local congregation. The author then sends greetings to his readers with the phrase "those from Italy send you their greetings." This statement, ambiguous in the Greek text, can be interpreted to mean the author is writing to a group somewhere in Italy, probably Rome, or he is writing from Italy, again probably Rome, to a congregation somewhere outside of Italy. Examples of the use of the preposition *apo* in the former sense occur in Acts 10:23,38; 21:27. Acts 18:2 furnishes an exact parallel to the phrase in Heb 13:24 and there the reference is to Italians living outside of Italy. This is the strongest evidence for the interpretation that understands the writer to be in the company of Italian Christians outside of Italy. Or is it? Lane used this parallel as strong evidence for his theory of a Roman destination for the letter. Mosser agreed with Lane that the two passages are verbal parallels, but Mosser went on to note that they are not *grammatical* parallels. In Acts, the prepositional phrase modifies a participle whereas in Heb 13:24 it modifies a pronominal article. In the former case, the prepositional phrase functions adverbially; in the latter case, it functions adjectivally. The adverbial use in Acts 18:2 "requires the force of separation because of the participle. . . . No such motion is implicit in the pronoun of Heb 13:24b."[3] The church fathers interpreted this phrase in 13:24 to

[1] On this possibility, see A. T. Robertson, *GGNT* 664, and the discussion in Lane, *Hebrews 9–13*, 567.

[2] Westfall, *Discourse Analysis*, 293.

[3] C. Mosser, "No Lasting City: Rome, Jerusalem and the Place of Hebrews in the History of Earliest 'Christianity'" (Ph.D. dissertation, St. Mary's College, University of St. Andrews, 2004), 147.

mean the author was writing from Italy to a destination outside Italy.[4] In fact, this would appear to be the case until the eighteenth century. Parallels to this usage occur in Matt 24:17; Luke 11:13; Col 4:16, and Acts 17:13. Taken in this sense, the preposition *apo* is given the meaning of "domiciled at."[5] Koester cited the use in John 11:1 where Lazarus is "from Bethany," and was still in Bethany. Likewise, in Acts 10:23, Christians "from Joppa" were still in Joppa.[6] Modern commentators tend to favor the viewpoint that the author is writing to Rome and sending greetings from Italian Christians. This is primarily due to the ascendency of the theory of a Roman destination rather than the actual wording of the statement here in 13:24. In fact, there is much to commend the alternative interpretation.[7]

Making use of *Thesaurus Linguae Graecae*, Mosser searched all uses of the Greek *hoi apo*, "those from," up through the seventh century AD. He discovered, with respect to letters, that "the tendency is for authors who identify themselves as 'from' a place to be *in* that place at the time of composition."[8] This has significant ramifications for Heb 13:24 and the Roman destination theory.

13:25 The final verse concludes with the statement "Grace be with all of you." This concluding benediction is identical to Titus 3:15 and illustrates the traditional apostolic and early Christian benediction given at the conclusion of letters. Alford takes the position of *pantōn*, "all," before the pronoun to be emphatic with the focus on each individual of the congregation more so than the totality of the group.[9] To each and every reader/hearer of this sermon, our author covers them with the blessing of "grace," that pregnant New Testament word that encapsulates all that God has done for us through Christ in bringing about our salvation.

---

[4] Many manuscripts, as early as the fifth century AD, carry the subscription stating the letter was written from Rome.

[5] So J. Moffatt, *A Critical and Exegetical Commentary on the Epistle to the Hebrews*, ICC (Edinburgh: T&T Clark, 1924; repr., Edinburgh: T&T Clark, 1963), 246, who also cites evidence from Oxyrhynchus Papyrus i.81 as an example.

[6] Koester, *Hebrews*, AB (New York: Doubleday, 2001), 581.

[7] See the discussion in F. Delitzsch, *Commentary on the Epistle to the Hebrews*, trans. T. L. Kingsbury (Edinburgh: T&T Clark, 1872; repr. Grand Rapids: Eerdmans, 1952), 2:406–7, and more recently Mosser, "No Lasting City," 136–58, who demonstrated the Greek prepositional phrase used similarly in other epistolary greetings locates the people at the place named, not away from the place named. He further demonstrated that manuscript subscriptions based on this phrase are consistently interpreted "to indicate the place *from which* the epistle was written. Here we see scribal intuitions about the real 'natural' way to understand the Greek idiom" (p. 157). H. Windisch, *Der Hebräerbrief*, 2nd ed., HNT 14 (Tübingen: Mohr, 1931), 127, interpreted Heb 13:24 to indicate an Italian provenance and thus furnished to his mind a sufficient reason against a Roman destination.

[8] Mosser, "No Lasting City," 146.

[9] H. Alford, "Prolegomena and Hebrews," *Alford's Greek Testament: An Exegetical and Critical Commentary*, 5th ed. (Boston: Lee & Shepard, 1878; repr. Grand Rapids: Guardian, 1976), 4:273.

Selected Bibliography

Alford, Henry. "Hebrews." *The Greek New Testament: An Exegetical and Critical Commentary*. 7th edition. Cambridge: Rivingtons & Deighton, Bell and Co., 1877.

Allen, David L. "The Authorship of Hebrews: The Case for Luke." *Faith and Mission* 17.2 (2001): 27–40.

———. *Lukan Authorship of Hebrews*. NAC Studies in Bible & Theology. Nashville: B&H Academic, 2010.

———. "The Lukan Authorship of Hebrews: A Proposal." *Journal of Translation and Textlinguistics* 8 (1996): 1–22.

Anderson, David. *The King-Priest of Psalm 110 in Hebrews*. Studies in Biblical Literature 21. New York: Peter Lang, 2001.

Anderson, C. P. "The Epistle to the Hebrews and the Pauline Letter Collection." *Harvard Theological Review* 59 (1966): 429–38.

Anderson, H. "The Jewish Antecedents of the Christology of Hebrews." In *The Messiah: Developments in Earliest Judaism and Christianity*. Edited by J. H. Charlesworth. Minneapolis: Fortress, 1992.

Aquinas, Thomas. *Commentary on the Epistle to the Hebrews*. Trans. by C. Baer. South Bend, IN: St. Augustine's, 2006.

Attridge, Harold. *The Epistle to the Hebrews*. Hermeneia. Philadelphia: Fortress, 1989.

———. "Parenesis in a Homily (πρὸς παρακλησεως): The Possible Location of, and Socialization in, the 'Epistle to the Hebrews.'" *Semeia* 50 (1990): 210–26.

Backhaus, Knut. *Der sprechende Gott: Gesammelte Studien zum Hebräerbrief*. Wissenschaftliche Untersuchungen zum Neuen Testament 240. Tübingen: Mohr Siebeck, 2009.

Barclay, John, and John Sweet, eds. "Hebrews." *Early Christian Thought in Its Jewish Context*. Cambridge: Cambridge University Press, 1996.

Barclay, William. *The Letter to the Hebrews*. Rev. ed. The Daily Study Bible Series. Philadelphia: Westminster, 1976.

Barnes, Albert. "Hebrews." *Notes on the New Testament Explanatory and Practical*. Grand Rapids: Baker, 1977.

Barrett, C. K. "The Eschatology of the Epistle to the Hebrews." In *The Background of the New Testament and Its Eschatology: C. H. Dodd Festschrift*. Edited by W. D. Davies and D. Daube. Cambridge: Cambridge University Press. 1956.

Bateman, H. W. *Early Jewish Hermeneutics and Hebrews 1:5–13: The Impact of Early Jewish Exegesis on the Interpretation of a Significant New Testament Passage*. American University Studies 7: Theology and Religion 193. New York: Peter Lang, 1997.

Bateman, Herbert W., IV, ed. *Four Views on the Warning Passages in Hebrews*. Grand Rapids: Kregel, 2007.

Bauckham, Richard, et al., eds. *The Epistle to the Hebrews in Early Christian Theology*. Grand Rapids: Eerdmans, 2009.

Black, David. "Hebrews 1:1–4: A Study in Discourse Analysis." *Westminster Theological Journal* 49 (1987): 175–94.

———. "Literary Artistry in the Epistle to the Hebrews." *Filologia Neotestamentaria* 7 (1994): 43–51.

———. "The Problem of the Literary Structure of Hebrews: An Evaluation and a Proposal." *Grace Theological Journal* 7 (1986): 163–77.

———. "On the Pauline Authorship of Hebrews (Part 1): Overlooked Affinities between Hebrews and Paul." *Faith and Mission* 16 (Spring 1999): 32–51.

———. "On the Pauline Authorship of Hebrews (Part 2): The External Evidence Reconsidered." *Faith and Mission* 16 (Summer 1999): 78–86.

Bristol, L. O. "Primitive Christian Preaching and the Epistle to the Hebrews." *Journal of Biblical Literature* 68 (1949): 89–97.

Brown, J. Vallance. "The Authorship and Circumstances of Hebrews—Again!" *Bibliotheca Sacra* 80 (1923): 505–38.

Brown, John. *An Exposition of the Epistle of the Apostle Paul to the Hebrews*. Edinburgh: Oliphant, 1862.

Brown, Raymond. *Christ Above All: The Message of Hebrews*. Downers Grove, IL: InterVarsity, 1982.

Bruce, A. B. *The Epistle to the Hebrews: The First Apology for Christianity–An Exegetical Study*. Edinburgh: T&T Clark, 1899.

Bruce, F. F. *The Epistle to the Hebrews*. The New International Commentary on the New Testament. Grand Rapids: Eerdmans, 1990.

———. "Recent Contributions to the Understanding of Hebrews." *Expository Times* 80 (1969): 260–64.

———. "To the Hebrews or to the Essenes?" *New Testament Studies* 9 (1962–63): 217–32.

Buchanan, G. W. *To the Hebrews*. The Anchor Bible 36. Garden City: Doubleday, 1972.

Buck, Daniel. "The Rhetorical Arrangement and Function of Old Testament Citations in the Book of Hebrews: Uncovering Their Role in the Paraenetic Discourse of Access." Ph.D. dissertation, Dallas Theological Seminary, 2002.

Bullinger, E. W. *Great Cloud of Witnesses in Hebrews Eleven*. Grand Rapids: Kregel, 1979.

Caird, G. B. "The Exegetical Method of the Epistle to the Hebrews." *Canadian Journal of Theology* 5 (1959): 44–51.

Calvin, John. *The Epistle of Paul the Apostle to the Hebrews and the First and Second Epistles of St. Peter*. Translated by William B. Johnston. Edited by David W. Torrance and Thomas F. Torrance. Grand Rapids: Eerdmans, 1963.

Clarkson, M. E. "The Antecedents of the High Priest Theme in Hebrews." *Anglican Theological Review* 29 (1947): 89–95.

Cockerill, Gareth. *Hebrews: A Bible Commentary in the Wesleyan Tradition*. Indianapolis: Wesleyan, 1999.

———. "'The Better Resurrection?' (Heb 11:35): A Key to the Structure and Rhetorical Purpose of Hebrews11." *Tyndale Bulletin* 51 (2000): 215–34.

Cosby, M. R. *The Rhetorical Composition and Function of Hebrews 11 in Light of Example Lists in Ancient Antiquity*. Macon: Mercer University Press, 1988.

Craddock, F. B. "The Letter to the Hebrews: Introduction, Commentary, and Reflections." Vol. 12 of *The New Interpreter's Bible*. Nashville: Abingdon, 1998.

Croy, N. C. *Endurance in Suffering: Hebrews 12:1–13 in Its Rhetorical, Religious, and Philosophical Context*. Society of New Testament Studies Monograph Series 98. Cambridge: Cambridge University Press, 1998.

Cullmann, Oscar. *The Christology of the New Testament*. Revised edition. Translated by Shirley Guthrie and Charles Hall. Philadelphia: Westminster, 1959.

Dahms, John. "The First Readers of Hebrews." *Journal of the Evangelical Theological Society* 20 (1977): 365–75.

Dale, R. W. *The Jewish Temple and the Christian Church: A Series of Discourses on the Epistle to the Hebrews*. London: Hodder & Stoughton, 1882.

D'Angelo, Mary Rose. *Moses in the Letter to the Hebrews*. Society of Biblical Literature Dissertation Series 42. Missoula: Scholars Press, 1979.

Davidson, A. B. *The Epistle to the Hebrews: With Introduction and Notes*. Edinburgh: T&T Clark, 1882.

Delitzsch, Franz. *Commentary on the Epistle to the Hebrews*. Translated by Thomas L. Kingsbury. 2 vols. Grand Rapids: Eerdmans, 1871, 1952 reprint.

Demarest, B. A. *A History of the Interpretation of Hebrews 7:1–10 from the Reformation to the Present Day*. Tübingen: Mohr (Siebeck), 1976.

DeSilva, D. A. *Despising Shame: Honor Discourse and Community Maintenance in the Epistle to the Hebrews*. Society of Biblical Studies Dissertation Series 152. Atlanta: Scholars Press, 1995.

———. *Perseverance in Gratitude: A Socio-Rhetorical Commentary on the Epistle to the Hebrews*. Grand Rapids: Eerdmans, 2000.

Dey, L. K. K. *The Intermediary World and Patterns of Perfection in Philo and Hebrews*. Missoula, MT: Scholars Press, 1975.

Dods, Marcus. "The Epistle to the Hebrews." *Expositor's Greek New Testament*. Vol. 4. Edited by Robertson Nicoll. Grand Rapids: Eerdmans, 1974 reprint.

Draper, James. *Hebrews: The Life that Pleases God*. Wheaton, IL: Tyndale House, 1976.

Dunnill, John. *Covenant and Sacrifice in the Letter to the Hebrews*. Society for New Testament Studies Monograph Series 75. Cambridge: Cambridge University Press, 1992.

Eisenbaum, P. M. *The Jewish Heroes of Christian History: Hebrews 11 in Literary Context*. Society of Biblical Literature Dissertation Series 156. Atlanta: Scholars Press, 1997.

Ellingworth, Paul. *Commentary on Hebrews*. New International Greek Testament Commentary. Grand Rapids, MI: Eerdmans, 1993.

Ellingworth, Paul, and Eugene Nida. *A Handbook on the Letter to the Hebrews*. New York: United Bible Societies, 1983.

Evans, C. F. *The Theology of Rhetoric: The Epistle to the Hebrews*. London: Dr. Williams Trust, 1988.

Evans, Louis. *Hebrews*. The Communicator's Commentary. Waco, TX: Word, 1985.

Filson, Floyd. "'Yesterday.' A Study of Hebrews in the Light of Chapter 13." Vol. 4 in *Studies in Biblical Theology*. Edited by C. F. D. Moule, Peter Ackroyd, Floyd V. Filson, and G. Ernest Wright. London: SCM, 1967.

France, R. T. "Hebrews." *The Expositor's Bible Commentary*, vol. 13. Tremper Longman III and David Garland, General Editors. Grand Rapids: Zondervan , 2006.

———. "The Writer of Hebrews as a Biblical Expositor." *Tyndale Bulletin* 47 (1996): 245–76.

Gardiner, F. "The Language of the Epistle to the Hebrews as Bearing upon Its Authorship." *Journal of Biblical Literature* 7 (1887): 1–27.

Gelardini, G., ed. *Hebrews: Contemporary Methods—New Insights*. Biblical Interpretation Series 75. Leiden/Boston: Brill, 2005.

Gheorghita, R. *The Role of the Septuagint in Hebrews*. In Wissenschaftliche Untersuchungen zum Neuen Testament, 2. Reihe 160. Tübingen: Mohr Siebeck, 2003.

Glaze, R. E. *No Easy Salvation: A Careful Examination of the Question of Apostasy in Hebrews*. New Orleans: Insight, 1966.

Gleason, Randall. "The Old Testament Background of the Warning in Hebrews 6:4–8." *Bibliotheca Sacra* 155 (1998): 62–91.

———. "The Old Testament Background of Rest in Hebrews 3:7–4:11," *Bibliotheca Sacra* 157 (2000): 281–303.

Goppelt, L. *Typos: The Typological Interpretation of the Old Testament in the New.* Translated by D. H. Madvig. Grand Rapids: Eerdmans, 1982.

Gordon, Robert. *Hebrews.* Sheffield: Sheffield Academic, 2000.

Grässer, Erich. *Der Glaube im Hebräerbrief.* Marburg: N. G. Elwert Verlag, 1965.

———. *An die Hebräer.* 3 vols. Evangelisch-katholischer Kommentar zum Neuen Testament 17. Zurich: Benziger, 1990, 1993, 1997.

Greenlee, J. Harold. *An Exegetical Summary of Hebrews.* Dallas: Summer Institute of Linguistics, 1998.

Greer, R. A. *The Captain of Our Salvation: A Study in the Patristic Exegesis of Hebrews.* Tübingen: Mohr (Siebeck), 1973.

Gromacki, Robert. *Stand Bold in Grace: An Exposition of Hebrews.* Grand Rapids: Baker Book House, 1984.

Guthrie, Donald. *The Letter to the Hebrews: An Introduction and Commentary.* The Tyndale New Testament Commentaries. Leicester: InterVarsity, 1983.

Guthrie, George. *The Structure of Hebrews: A Text-Linguistic Analysis.* Leiden: E. J. Brill, 1994.

———. *Hebrews.* The NIV Application Commentary. Grand Rapids: Zondervan Publishing House, 1998.

———. "The Case for Apollos as the Author of Hebrews." *Faith and Mission* 18 (2002): 41–56.

———. "Hebrews in Its First Century Contexts: Recent Research." In *The Face of New Testament Studies: A Survey of Recent Research.* Scot McKnight and Grant Osborne, eds. Grand Rapids: Baker Academic, 2004.

Hagner, Donald A. *Hebrews.* New International Biblical Commentary. Peabody, MA: Hendrickson Publishers, 1990.

Hatch, William. "The Position of Hebrews in the Canon of the New Testament." *Harvard Theological Review* 29 (1936): 133–51.

Hay, D. M. *Glory at the Right Hand: Psalm 110 in Early Christianity.* Society of Biblical Literature Monograph Series 18. Nashville: Abingdon, 1973.

Heen, Erik, and Philip Krey, eds. *Hebrews. Ancient Christian Commentary on Scripture.* Vol. 10. Downers Grove: InterVarsity, 2005.

Hegermann, H. *Der Brief an die Hebräer. Theologischer Handkommentar zum Neuen Testament* XVI. Berlin: Evangelische Verlaganstalt, 1988.

Héring, Jean. *The Epistle to the Hebrews.* Translated by A. W. Heathcote and P. J. Allsock. London: Epworth, 1970.

Hewitt, Thomas. *The Epistle to the Hebrews: An Introduction and Commentary.* London: Tyndale, 1960.

Hobbs, H. *Hebrews: Challenges to Bold Discipleship.* Nashville: Broadman, 1971.

Hofius, O. *Katapausis: Die Vorstellung vom endzeitlichen Ruheort in Hebräer-brief.* WUNT 11. Tübingen: Mohr (Siebeck), 1970.

Hoppin, Ruth. *Priscilla's Letter: Finding the Author of the Epistle to the Hebrews.* Fort Bragg, CA: Lost Coast, 1997.

Horbury, W. "The Aaronic Priesthood in the Epistle to the Hebrews." *Journal for the Study of the New Testament* 19 (1983): 43–71.

Horton, F. L. *Melchizedek Tradition through the First Five Centuries of the Christian Era and in the Epistle to the Hebrews.* Society for New Testament Studies Monograph Series 30. Cambridge: Cambridge University Press, 1976.

Hughes, Graham. *Hebrews and Hermeneutics.* Society for New Testament Studies Monograph Series 36. Cambridge: Cambridge University Press, 1979.

Hughes, Phillip E. *A Commentary on the Epistle to the Hebrews.* Grand Rapids: Eerdmans, 1977.

Hurst, Lincoln D. *The Epistle to the Hebrews: Its Background of Thought*. Society for New Testament Studies Monograph Series 65. New York: Cambridge University Press, 1990.

Isaacs, Marie. *Sacred Space: An Approach to the Theology of the Epistle to the Hebrews*. Journal for the Study of the New Testament Supplement Series 73. Sheffield: Sheffield Academic, 1992.

Jewett, Robert. *Letter to Pilgrims: A Commentary on the Epistle to the Hebrews*. New York: The Pilgrim, 1981.

Johnson, Luke T. *Hebrews: A Commentary.* The New Testament Library. Edited by C. C. Black and J. T. Carroll. Louisville: Westminster/John Knox, 2006.

Johnson, R. W. *Going Outside the Camp: The Sociological Function of the Levitical Critique in the Epistle to the Hebrews*. JSNTSup 209. Sheffield: Sheffield Academic, 2001.

Jones, C. P. M. "The Epistle to the Hebrews and the Lucan Writings." In *Studies in the Gospels: Essays in Memory of R. H. Lightfoot*. Edited by D. E. Nineham. Oxford: Basil Blackwell, 1955

Joslin, Barry. *Hebrews, Christ, and the Law: The Theology of the Mosaic Law in Hebrews 7:1–10:18*. Paternoster Biblical Monographs. Milton Keynes, UK: Paternoster, 2008.

Käsemann, Ernst. *The Wandering People of God: An Investigation of the Letter to the Hebrews*. Translated from the 2nd German edition by Ray Harrisville and Irving Sandberg. Minneapolis: Augsburg Publishing House, 1984.

Keathley, Kenneth. *Salvation and Sovereignty: A Molinist Approach*. Nashville: B&H Academic, 2010.

Kistemaker, Simon. *The Psalm Citations in the Epistle to the Hebrews*. Amsterdam: Wed. G. Van Soest, 1961.

———. *New Testament Commentary: Exposition of the Epistle to the Hebrews*. Grand Rapids: Baker, 1984.

Koester, C. R. *Hebrews: A New Translation with Introduction and Commentary*. Anchor Bible 36. New York: Doubleday, 2001.

Laansma, Jon. *"I Will Give You Rest": The Rest Motif in the New Testament with Special Reference to Mt 11 and Heb 3–4*. Tübingen: Mohr Siebeck, 1997.

Lane, William L. "Hebrews: A Sermon in Search of a Setting." *Southwestern Journal of Theology* 28 (1985): 13–18.

———. *Call to Commitment: Responding to the Message of Hebrews*. Nashville: Nelson, 1985.

———. *Hebrews*. 2 vols. Word Biblical Commentary. 47. Dallas: Word, 1991.

Lange, John. "Hebrews." *Lange's Commentary on the Holy Scripture*. Vol. 8. Edited by Moll. Translated from the German by Philip Schaff. Grand Rapids: Zondervan, 1868.

Lenski, R. C. H. *The Interpretation of the Epistle to the Hebrews and the Epistle of James*. Minneapolis: Augsburg Publishing House, 1966.

Leonard, W. *The Authorship of the Epistle to the Hebrews*. London: Polyglot, 1939.

Lightfoot, Neil. *Jesus Christ Today: A Commentary on the Book of Hebrews*. Grand Rapids: Baker Book House, 1976.

Lincoln, Andrew. *Hebrews: A Guide*. London: T&T Clark, 2006.

Lindars, Barnabas. *The Theology of the Letter to the Hebrews*. Cambridge: Cambridge University Press, 1991.

———. "The Rhetorical Structure of Hebrews." *New Testament Studies* 35 (1989): 382–406.

Linnemann, Eta. "A Call for a Retrial in the Case of the Epistle to the Hebrews." Translated by David Lanier. *Faith and Mission* 19/2 (2002): 19–59.

Loader, W. R. G. *Sohn und Hoherpriester: Eine traditionsgeschichtliche Untersuchung zur Christologie des Hebräerbriefes*. WMANT 53. NeukirchenVluyn: Neukirchener Verlag, 1981.

Long, T. G. *Hebrews*. Interpretation: A Bible Commentary for Teaching and Preaching. Louisville: John Knox, 1997.

Lünemann, G. *The Epistle to the Hebrews*. Translated from the 4th German edition by Maurice Evans. Meyer's Critical and Exegetical Handbook to the New Testament. Edited by H. A. W. Meyer. New York: Funk & Wagnalls, 1885.

Luther, Martin. *Die Vorlesung über den Hebräerbrief.* Edited by J. Ficker, Weimar Ausgabe 57/3 (Weimar: Böhlaus, 1939). Translated as *Lectures on Hebrews* by W. A. Hansen, Luther's Works, 29. St. Louis: Concordia, 1968.

MacArthur, John. *Hebrews*. The MacArthur New Testament Commentary. Chicago: Moody, 1983.

MacNeill, Harris Lachlan. *The Christology of the Epistle to the Hebrews: Including Its Relation to the Developing of the Primitive Church*. Chicago: University of Chicago Press, 1914.

Manson, T. W. "The Problem of the Epistle to the Hebrews." *Bulletin of the John Rylands Library* 32 (1949): 1–17.

Manson, William. *The Epistle to the Hebrews: An Historical and Theological Reconsideration*. London: Hodder & Stoughton, 1951.

Marohl, Matthew. *Faithfulness and the Purpose of Hebrews: A Social Identity Approach*. Princeton Theological Monograph Series. 82. Eugene, OR: Pickwick Publications, 2008.

McCaul, Joseph. *The Epistle to the Hebrews, in a Paraphrastic Commentary, with Illustrations from Philo, the Targums, the Mishna and Gemara, the Later Rabbinical Writers, and Christian Annotators, etc.* London: Longmans Green, 1871.

McCullough, J. C. "Some Recent Developments in Research on the Epistle to the Hebrews." *Irish Biblical Studies* 2, 3 (1980, 1981): 2.141–165; 3.28–45.

———. "Hebrews in Recent Scholarship." *Irish Biblical Studies* 16 (1994): 66–86.

———. "Hebrews in Recent Scholarship (Part 2)." *Irish Biblical Studies* 16 (1994): 108–20.

Meier, J. P. "Structure and Theology in Heb 1, 1–14." *Biblica* 66 (1985): 168–89.

———. "Symmetry and Theology in the Old Testament Citations of Heb 1, 5–14." *Biblica* 66 (1985): 504–33.

Michel, Otto. *Der Brief an die Hebräer. Kritisch-Exegetischer Kommentar uber das Neue Testament*. Edited by Heinrich Meyer. Göttingen: Vandenhoeck & Ruprecht, reprint 1975.

Miller, Neva. *The Epistle to the Hebrews: An Analytical and Exegetical Handbook*. Dallas: Summer Institute of Linguistics, 1988.

Milligan, G. *The Theology of the Epistle to the Hebrews with a Critical Introduction*. Edinburgh: T&T Clark, 1899.

Moffatt, James. *A Critical and Exegetical Commentary on the Epistle to the Hebrews*. International Critical Commentaries. Edited by A. Plummer. Edinburgh: T&T Clark. 1924.

Montefiore, H. W. *A Commentary on the Epistle to the Hebrews*. Black's New Testament Commentaries. London: Adam and Charles Black, 1964.

Morgan, G. Campbell. *God's Last Word to Man: Studies in Hebrews*. Grand Rapids: Baker, 1974.

———. *The Triumphs of Faith: Expositions of Hebrews 11*. Grand Rapids: Baker, 1976.

Mosser, Carl. "No Lasting City: Rome, Jerusalem and the Place of Hebrews in the History of Earliest 'Christianity.'" Ph.D. Dissertation, University of St. Andrews, 2005.

Moule, H. C. G. *Studies in Hebrews*. Kregel Popular Commentary Series. Grand Rapids: Kregel, 1977.

Murray, Andrew. *The Holiest of All: An Exposition of the Epistle to the Hebrews*. London: Fleming H. Revell, 1978.

Nairne, A. *The Epistle of Priesthood: Studies in the Epistle to the Hebrews*. Edinburgh: T&T Clark, 1913.

———. *The Epistle to the Hebrews*. The Cambridge Greek Testament for Schools and Colleges. Edited by R. John Parry. London: Cambridge University Press, 1922.

Neeley, Linda Lloyd. "A Discourse Analysis of Hebrews." *Occasional Papers in Translation and Textlinguistics* 3-4 (1987): 1–146.

Newell, William. *Hebrews: Verse by Verse*. Chicago: Moody, 1947.

O'Brien, Peter. *The Letter to the Hebrews*. Pillar New Testament Commentaries. Grand Rapids: Eerdmans, 2010.

Oberholtzer, T. K. "The Warning Passages in Hebrews, Part 1 (of 5 Parts): The Eschatological Salvation of Hebrews 1:5–2:4." *Bibliotheca Sacra* 145 (1988): 83–97.

Olbricht, T. H. "Hebrews as Application." In *Rhetoric and the New Testament*. Edited by S. E. Porter and T. H. Olbricht. JSNTSup 90. Sheffield: Sheffield Academic, 1993.

Peake, A. S., ed. *Hebrews*. The New Century Bible. Edinburgh: T. C. & E. C. Jack, 1906.

Peterson, David. *Hebrews and Perfection: An Examination of the Concept of Perfection in the "Epistle to the Hebrews."* Society for New Testament Studies Monograph Series 47. Cambridge: Cambridge University Press, 1982.

Pfitzner, Victor. *Hebrews*. Abingdon New Testament Commentaries. Nashville: Abingdon, 1997.

Phillips, John. *Exploring Hebrews*. Chicago: Moody, 1977.

Pink, Arthur. *An Exposition of Hebrews*. 3 vols. Grand Rapids: Baker, 1954.

Plumer, William. *Commentary on the Epistle of Paul the Apostle to the Hebrews*. Grand Rapids: Baker, 1980 reprint.

Porter, Stanley. "The Date of the Composition of Hebrews and Use of Present Tense-Form." In *Crossing the Boundaries: Essays in Biblical Interpretation in Honour of Michael D. Goulder*. Edited by Stanley Porter, P. Joyce, and D. Orton. Leiden: E. J. Brill, 1994.

Rhee, V. (Sung-Yul). *Faith in Hebrews: Analysis within the Context of Christology, Eschatology, and Ethics*. Studies in Biblical Literature 19. New York: Peter Lang, 2001.

Robinson, Theodore. *The Epistle to the Hebrews*. Moffatt New Testament Commentary. New York: Harper, 1933.

Salevao, Iutisone. *Legitimation in the Letter to the Hebrews: The Construction and Maintenance of a Symbolic Universe*. Journal for the Study of the New Testament Supplement Series 219. Edited by Stanley Porter. New York: Sheffield Academic, 2002.

Schenck, Kenneth L. *Understanding the Book of Hebrews: The Story Behind the Sermon*. Louisville: Westminster/John Knox, 2003.

Scholer, J. M. *Proleptic Priests: Priesthood in the Epistle to the Hebrews*. JSNTSup 49. Sheffield: JSOT, 1991.

Schreiner, Thomas, and Ardel Caneday. *The Race Set Before Us: A Biblical Theology of Perseverance and Assurance*. Downers Grove: InterVarsity, 2001.

Schunack, G. *Der Hebräerbrief.* Zürcher Bibelkommentar, NT 14. Zurich: Theologischer Verlag Zürich, 2002.

Smith, Robert. *Hebrews*. Augsburg Commentary on the New Testament. Minneapolis: Augsburg, 1984.

Son, Kiwoong. *Zion Symbolism in Hebrews: Hebrews 12:18–24 as a Hermeneutical Key to the Epistle*. Bletchley: Paternoster, 2005.

Sowers, S. G. *The Hermeneutics of Philo and Hebrews: A Comparison of the Interpretation of the OT in Philo Judaeus and the Epistle to the Hebrews*. Richmond: John Knox, 1965.

Spicq, C. *L'Épître aux Hebreux*. 2 vols. Paris: Librairie Lecoffre, 1952–53.

———. "L'Épître aux Hébreux: Apollos, Jean-Baptiste, les Hellénistes et Qumran." *Revue de Qumran* 1 (1959): 365–90.

Stanley, S. "The Structure of Hebrews from Three Perspectives." *Tyndale Bulletin* 45 (1994): 245–71.

Stuart, Moses. *A Commentary on the Epistle to the Hebrews*. 4th ed. Rev. by R. D. C. Robbins. Andover: Warren F. Draper, 1876.

Swetnam, James. "On the Literary Genre of the 'Epistle' to the Hebrews." *Novum Testamentum* 11 (1969): 261–69.

———. "Form and Content in Hebrews 1–6." *Biblica* 53 (1972): 368–85.

———. "Form and Content in Hebrews 7–13." *Biblica* 55 (1974): 333–48.

———. *Jesus and Isaac: A Study of the Epistle to the Hebrews in the Light of the Aqedah*. Analecta Biblica 94. Rome: Biblical Institute, 1981.

Synge, F. C. *Hebrews and the Scriptures*. London: SPCK, 1959.

Thayer, J. H. "Authorship and Canonicity of the Epistle to the Hebrews." *Bibliotheca Sacra* 24 (1867): 681–722.

Thiselton, Anthony. "Hebrews." *Eerdmans Commentary on the Bible*. James D. G. Dunn and John W. Rogersen, eds. Grand Rapids, MI: Eerdmans, 2003.

Thomas, Adrian. *A Case for Mixed-Audience with Reference to the Warning Passages in the Book of Hebrews*. New York: Peter Lang, 2008.

Thomas, W. H. Griffith. *Hebrews: A Devotional Commentary*. Grand Rapids: Wm. B. Eerdmans, 1923.

Thompson, J. W. *The Beginnings of Christian Philosophy: The Epistle to the Hebrews*. CBQMS 13. Washington, DC: Catholic Biblical Association of America, 1982.

Trotter, Andrew H. *Interpreting the Epistle to the Hebrews*. Grand Rapids: Baker, 1997.

Übelacker, Walter G. *Der Hebräerbrief als Appell*. Lund: Almqvist & Wiksell, 1989.

Vanhoye, A. *Old Testament Priests and the New Priest According to the New Testament*. Translated by J. B. Orchard. Petersham: St. Bede's Publications, 1986.

———. *Structure and Message of the Epistle to the Hebrews*. Subsidia Biblica 12. Rome: Biblical Institute, 1989.

———. *A Structured Translation of the Epistle to the Hebrews*. Rome: Pontifical Biblical Institute, 1964.

Vos, Geerhardus. *The Teaching of the Epistle to the Hebrews*. Nutley: The Presbyterian & Reformed Publishing Co., 1974.

Walker, Peter. "Jerusalem in Hebrews 13:9–14 and the Dating of the Epistle." *Tyndale Bulletin* 45 (1994): 39–71.

———. *Jesus and the Holy City: New Testament Perspectives on Jerusalem*. Grand Rapids: Eerdmans, 1996.

Watson, Duane F. "Rhetoric Criticism of Hebrews and the Catholic Epistles since 1978." *Currents in Research: Biblical Studies* 5 (1997): 175–207.

Weiss, H. F. *Der Brief an die Hebräer*. KEK 15. Göttingen: Vandenhoeck & Ruprecht, 1991.

Westcott, B. F. *The Epistle to the Hebrews*. Grand Rapids: Eerdmans, 1955 reprint.

Westfall, Cynthia. *A Discourse Analysis of the Letter to the Hebrews: The Relationship Between Form and Meaning*. London: T&T Clark, 2005.

Williamson, Ronald. *The Epistle to the Hebrews*. Epworth Preacher's Commentaries. London: Epworth, 1964.

———. *Philo and the Epistle to the Hebrews*. Leiden: E. J. Brill, 1970.

Wilson, R. *Hebrews*. New Century Bible Commentary. Grand Rapids: Eerdmans, 1987.

Witherington, Ben. *Letters and Homilies for Jewish Christians: A Socio-Rhetorical Commentary on Hebrews, James, and Jude*. Downers Grove, IL: InterVarsity, 2007.

Wray, J. H. *Rest as a Theological Metaphor in the Epistle to the Hebrews and the Gospel of Truth: Early Christian Homiletics of Rest*. SBLDS 166. Atlanta: Scholars Press, 1998.

Wuest, Kenneth. *Hebrews in the Greek New Testament*. Vol. 2 of Wuest's Word Studies from the Greek New Testament for the English Reader. Grand Rapids: Eerdmans, 1947.

Yadin, Yigael. "The Dead Sea Scrolls and the Epistle to the Hebrews." *Scripta Hierosolymitana* 4 (1958): 36–55.

Selected Subject Index

Person Index

Selected Scripture Index

Leviticus

Numbers

Deuteronomy

Proverbs

Isaiah

John

Acts

Romans

1 Corinthians

2 Corinthians

Galatians

Ephesians

Philippians

Colossians

1 Thessalonians

2 Thessalonians

1 Timothy

2 Timothy

Titus